Guitar Tab White

Volume 4

ISBN 978-1-4584-1719-0

7777 W. Bluemound Rd. P.O. Box 13819 Milwaukee, WI 53213

Visit Hal Leonard Online at
www.halleonard.com

Contents

from Iron Maiden - *Powerslave*

Aces High

Words and Music by Steven Harris

Faster ♩ = 252
Am
F
G
Play 4 times
Verse
E5 F#5 G5 A5 G5 F#5 E5 G5 F#5 D5 F#5 D5
1. There goes the si - ren that warns of the air raid,
2. Move in to fire at the main stream of bomb - ers.
Rhy. Fig. 1
Gtrs. 1 & 2
E5 F#5 G5 A5 G5 F#5 E5 G5 F#5 D5
then comes the sound of the guns send - ing flak.
Let off the sharp burst and then turn a - way.
End Rhy. Fig. 1

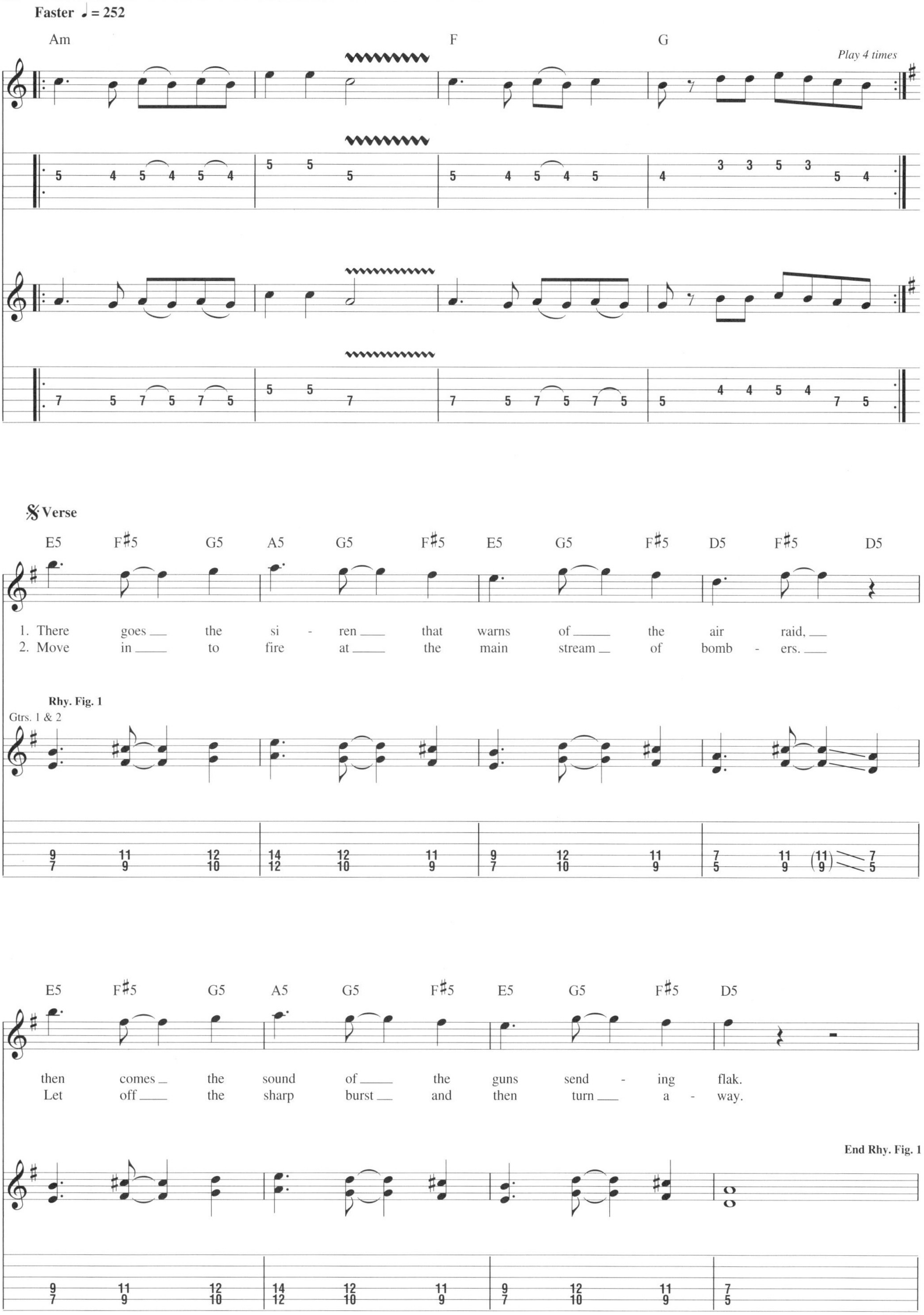

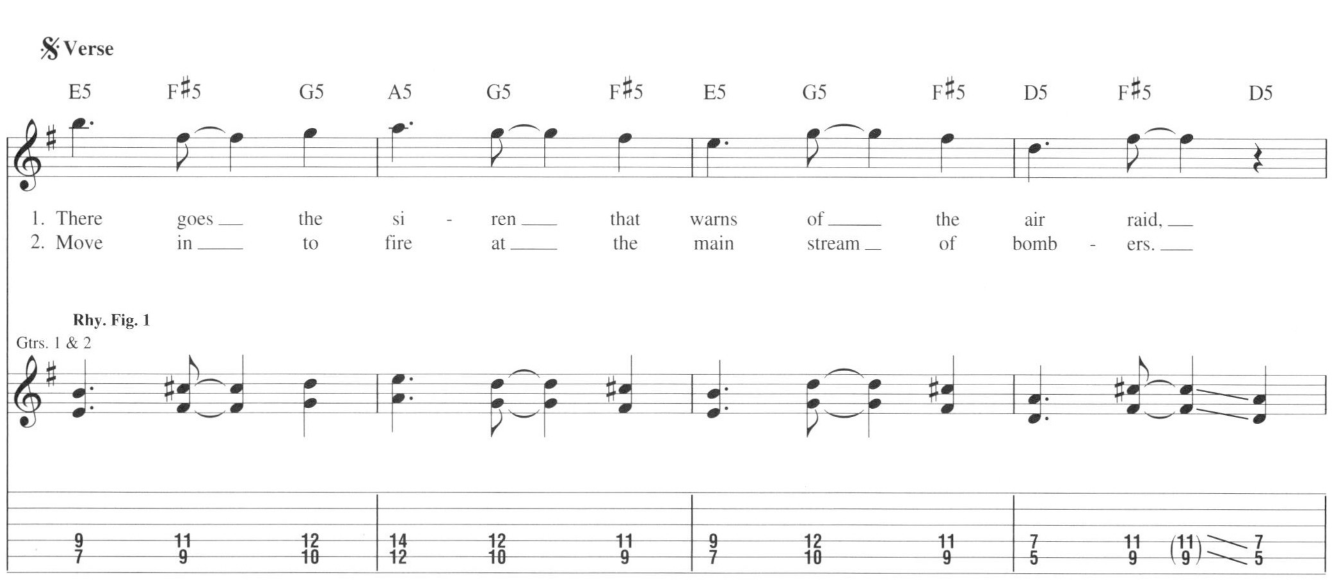

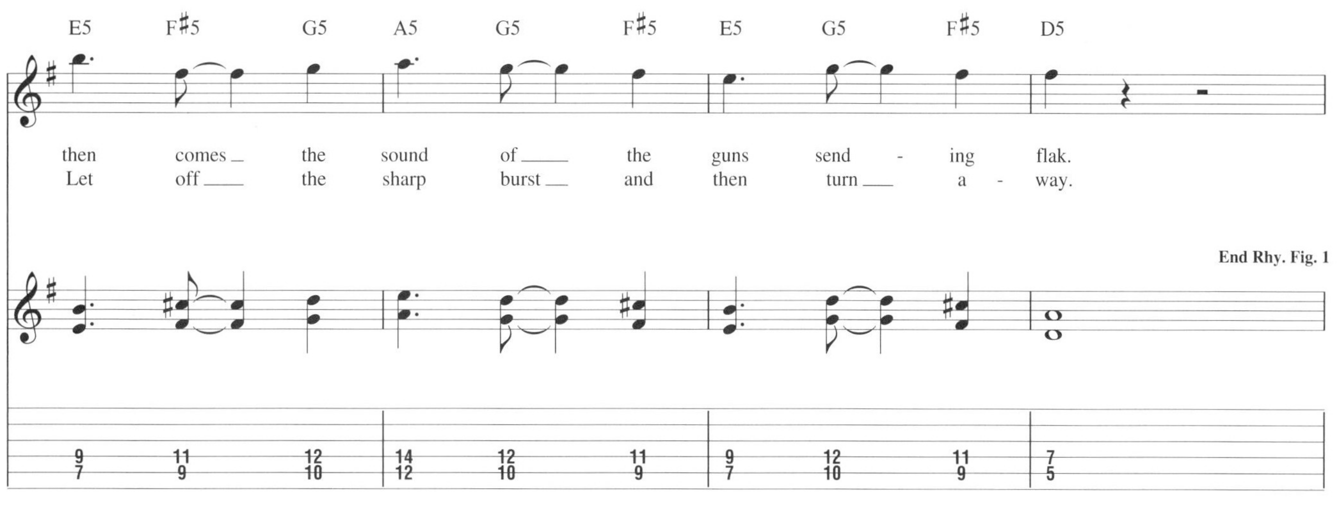

E5 F♯5 G5 A5 G5 F♯5 E5 G5 F♯5 D5 F♯5 D5
Out for the scram - ble, we've got to get air - borne.
Roll o - ver, spin 'round to come in be - hind them.
E5 F♯5 G5 A5 G5 F♯5 E5 G5 F♯5 D5
Got to get up for the com - ing at - tack.
Move to their blind - sides and fir - ing a - gain.
A5 B5 C5 D5 C5 B5 A5 C5 B5 G5 B5 G5
Jump in the cock - pit and start up the en - gines. Re -
Ban - dits at eight o' - clock move in be - hind us,
Rhy. Fig. 2
Gtrs. 1 & 2
A5 B5 C5 D5 C5 B5 A5 C5 B5 G5
move all the wheel - blocks, there's no time to waste.
ten M E one - o - nine's out of the sun. As -
End Rhy. Fig. 2
Gtrs. 1 & 2: w/ Rhy. Fig. 2
A5 B5 C5 D5 C5 B5 A5 C5 B5 G5 B5 G5
Gath - er - ing speed as we head down the run - way,
cend - ing and turn - ing our Spit - fires to face them,

A5 B5 C5 D5 C5 B5 A5 C5 B5 G5
got - ta get air - borne be - fore it's too late.
head - ing straight for them I press down my guns.
Pre-Chorus
Em
Am
1., 2. Run - nin' scramb - lin', fly - in'.
3., 4. Roll - in', turn - in', div - in'.
Gtr. 1
Gtr. 2
*w/ echo set for half-note regeneration w/ 1 repeat, next 7 meas.
1.
2.
Em
Am
Am
Roll-in', turn-in', div-in'. Go-ing in a-gain.

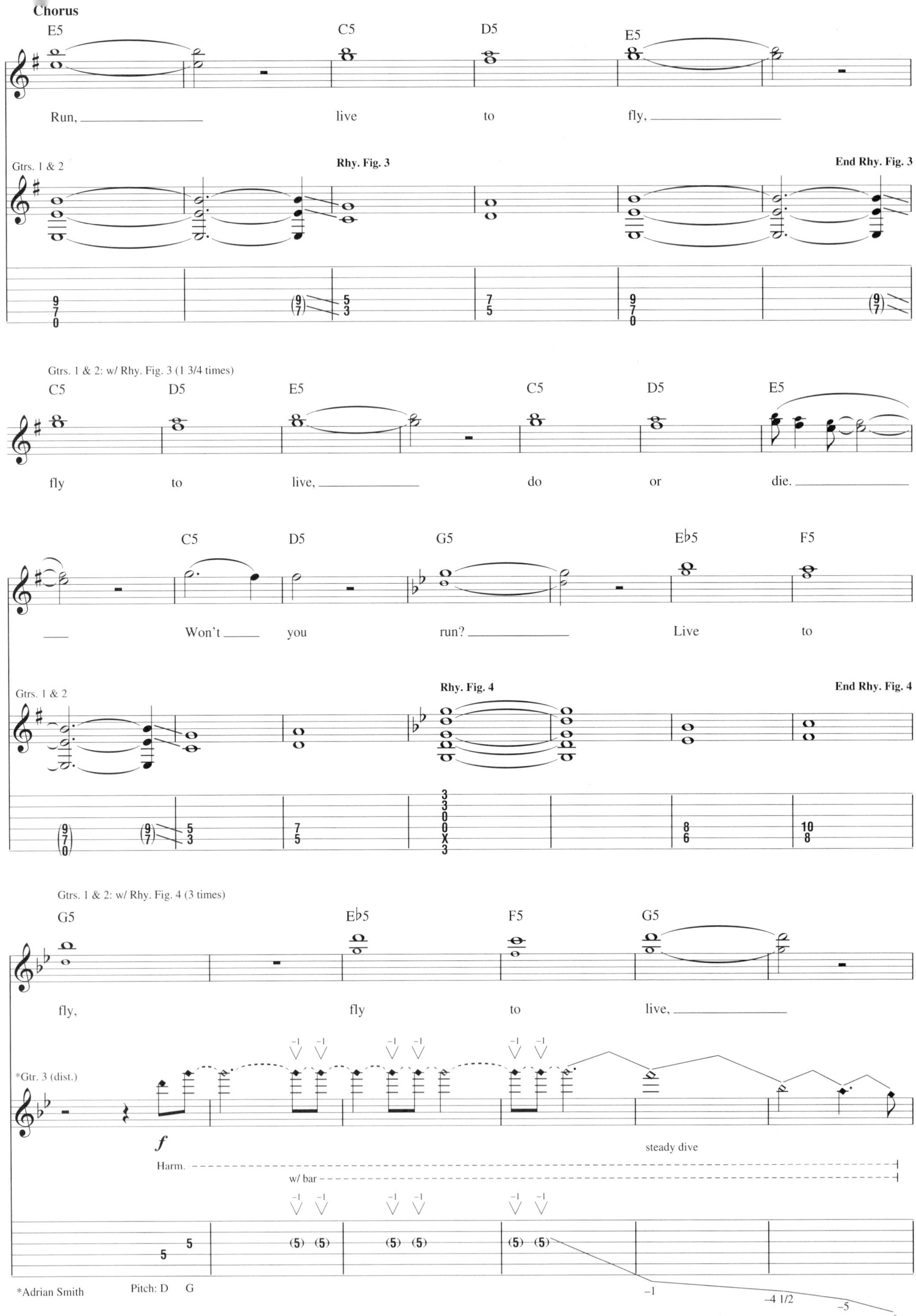
Chorus
E5
C5
D5
E5
Run, live to fly,
Gtrs. 1 & 2
Rhy. Fig. 3
End Rhy. Fig. 3
Gtrs. 1 & 2: w/ Rhy. Fig. 3 (1 3/4 times)
C5
D5
E5
C5
D5
E5
fly to live, do or die.
C5
D5
G5
E♭5
F5
Won't you run? Live to
Gtrs. 1 & 2
Rhy. Fig. 4
End Rhy. Fig. 4
Gtrs. 1 & 2: w/ Rhy. Fig. 4 (3 times)
G5
E♭5
F5
G5
fly, fly to live,
*Gtr. 3 (dist.)
f
steady dive
Harm.
w/ bar
*Adrian Smith
Pitch: D G

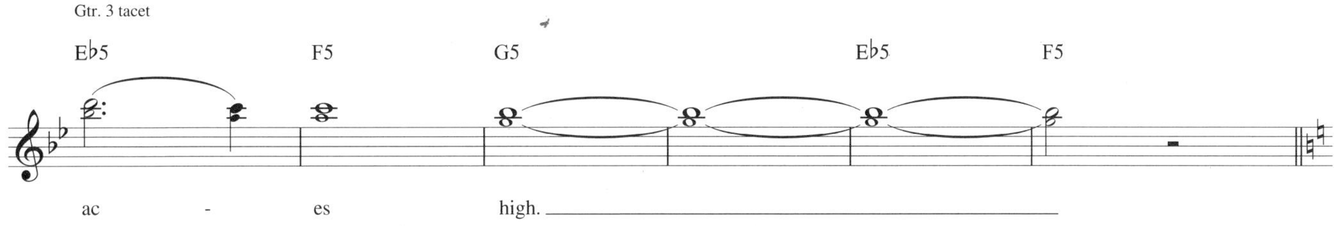

Interlude

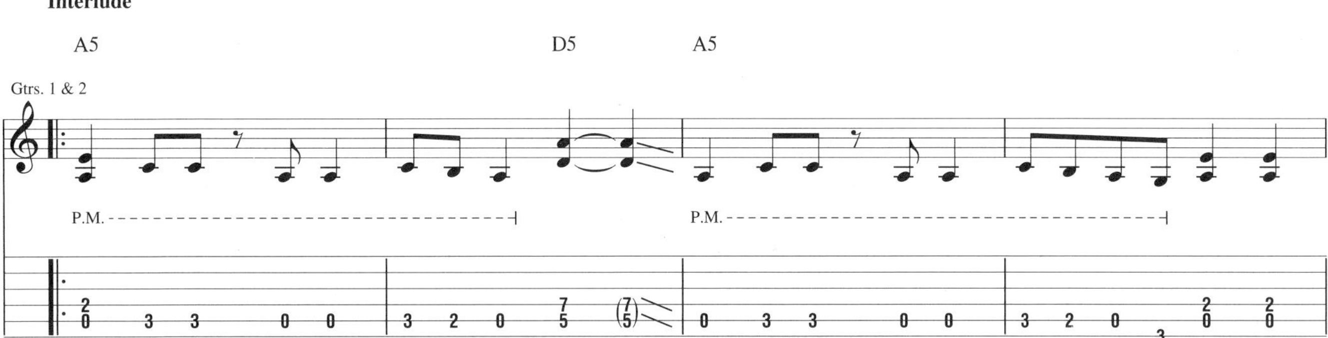

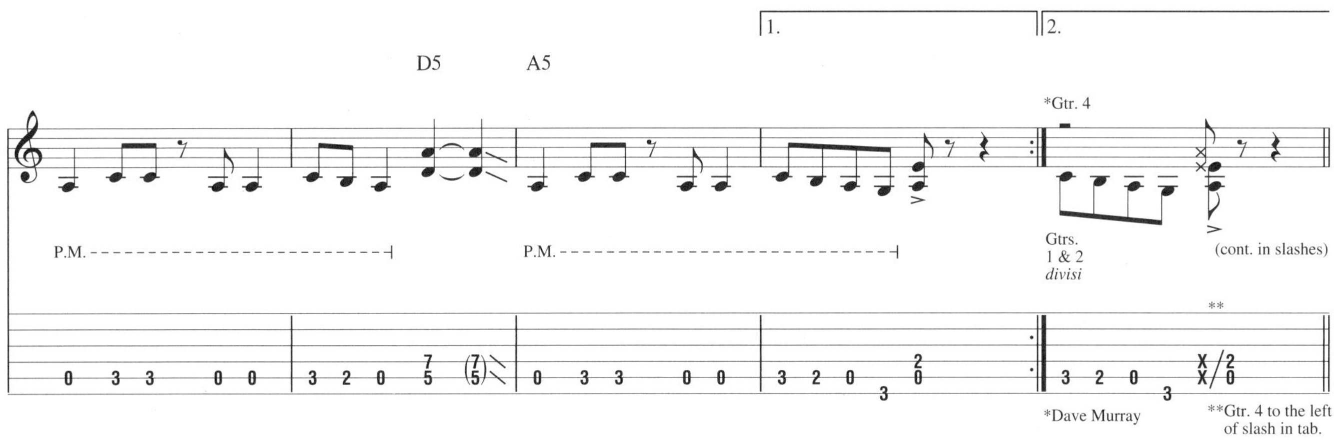

Guitar Solo

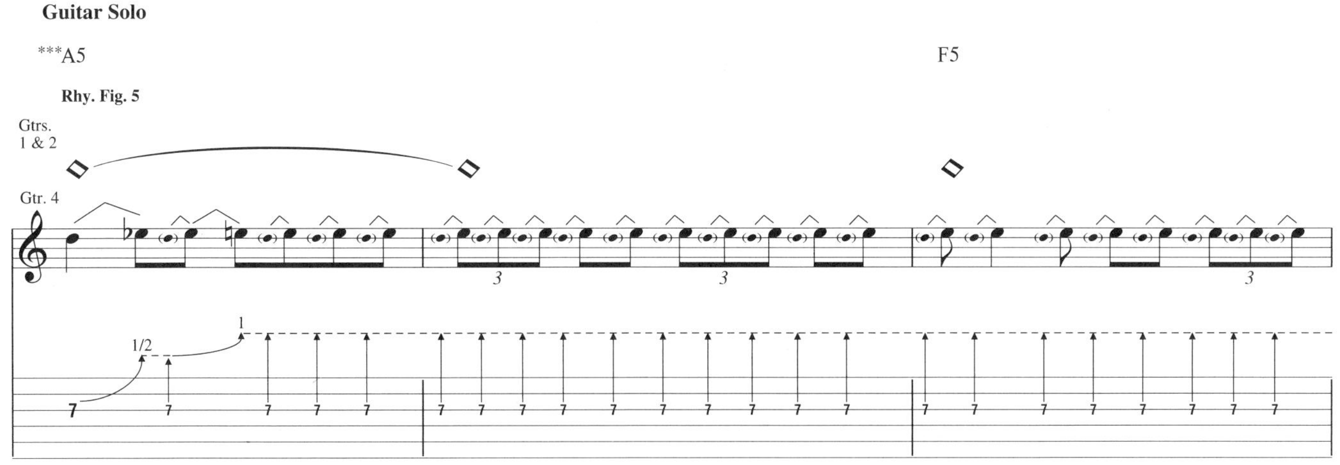

***See top of first page of song for chord diagrams pertaining to rhythm slashes.

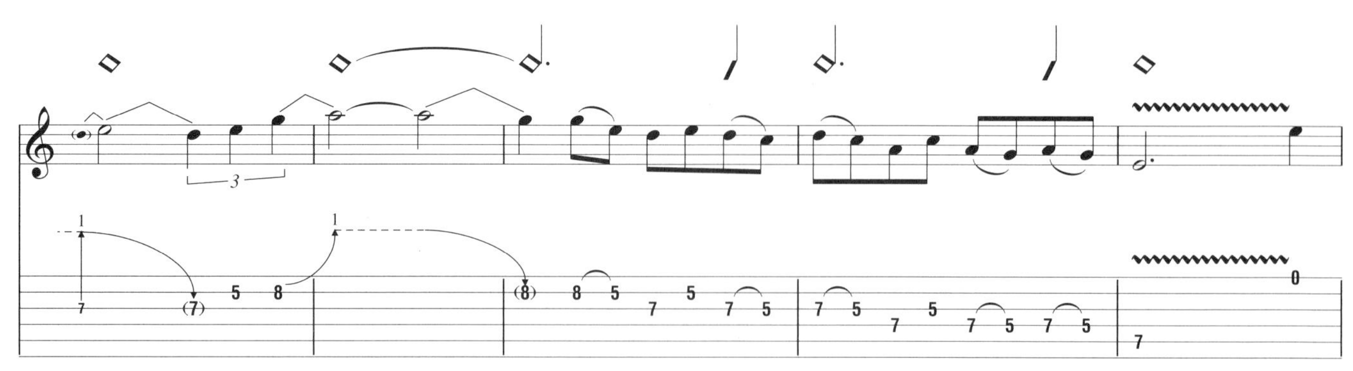

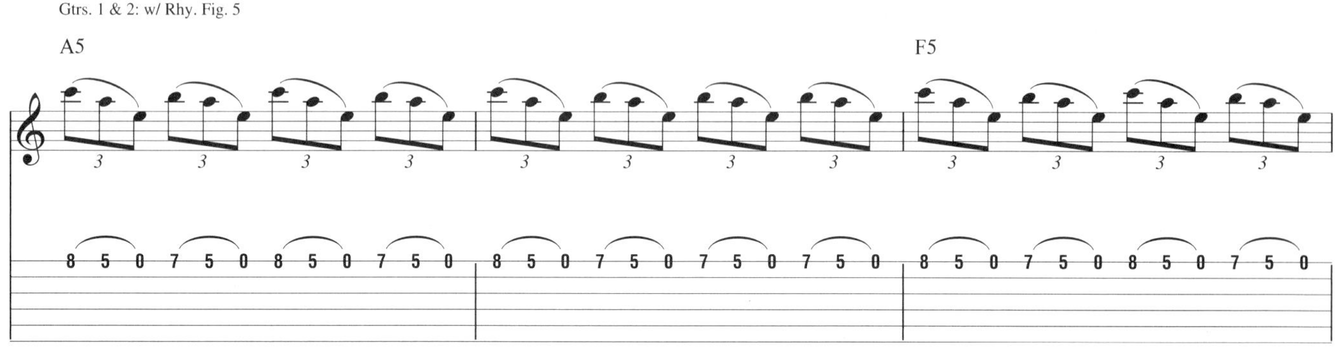

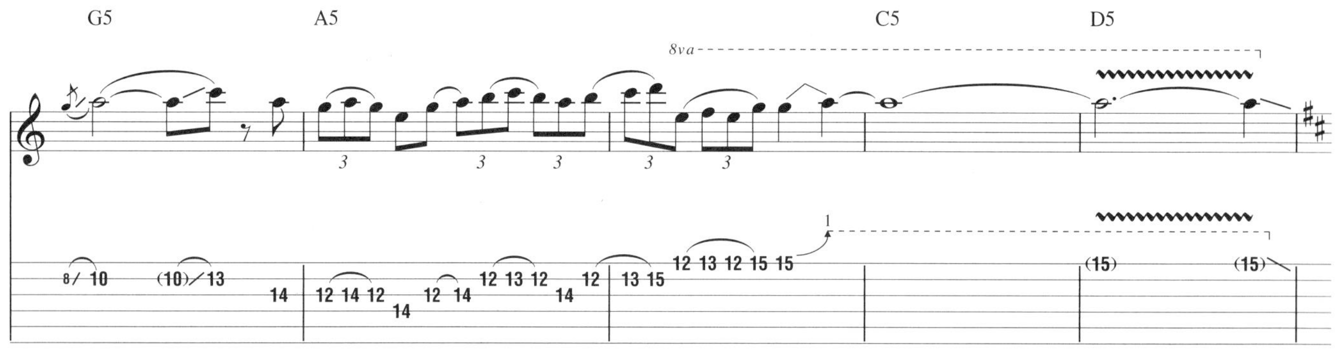

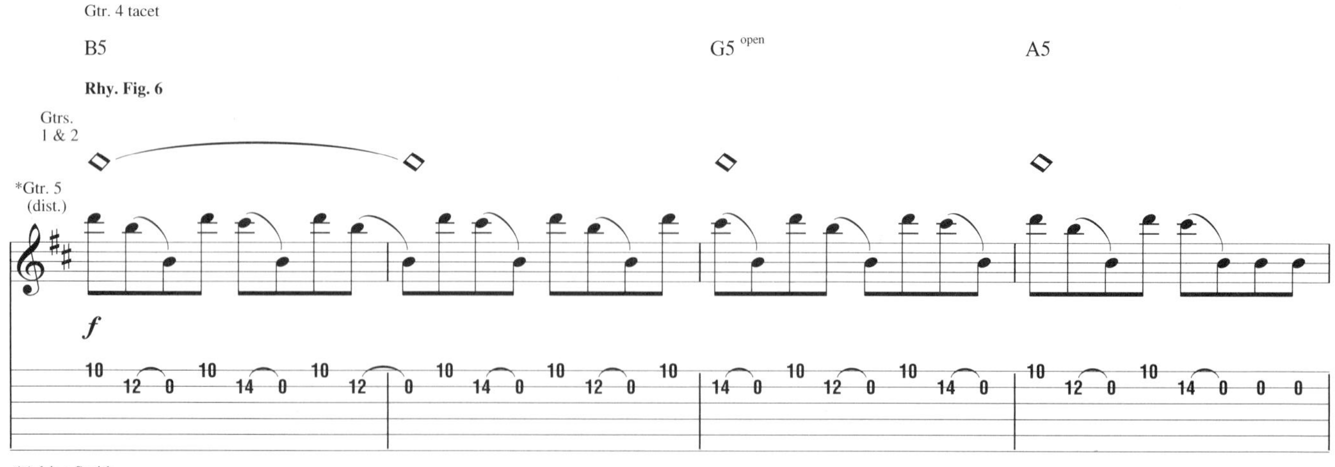

*Adrian Smith

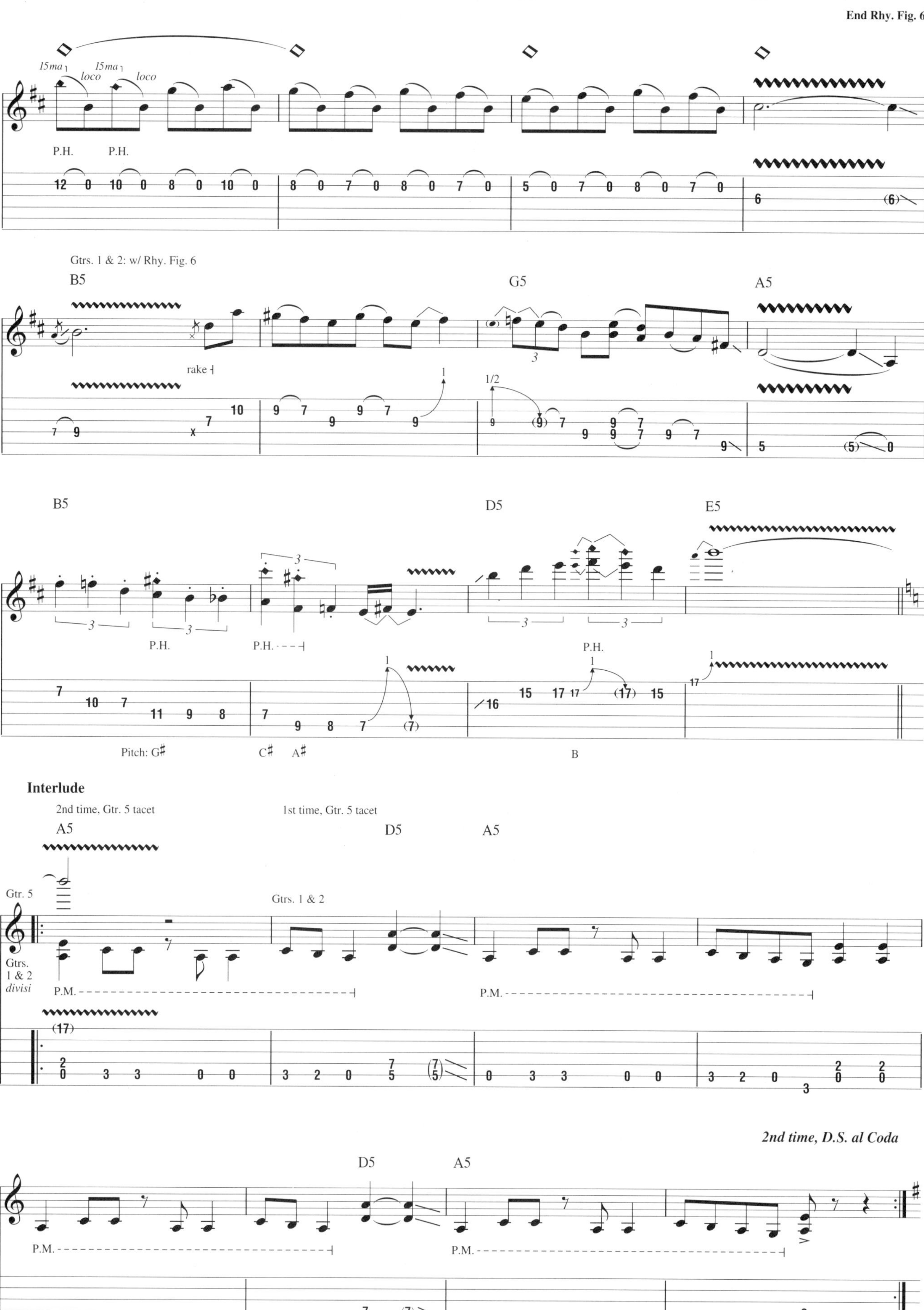

End Rhy. Fig. 6
15ma
loco
P.H.
Gtrs. 1 & 2: w/ Rhy. Fig. 6
B5
G5
A5
rake
D5
E5
Pitch: G♯
C♯
A♯
B
Interlude
2nd time, Gtr. 5 tacet
1st time, Gtr. 5 tacet
Gtr. 5
Gtrs. 1 & 2
Gtrs. 1 & 2 divisi
P.M.
2nd time, D.S. al Coda

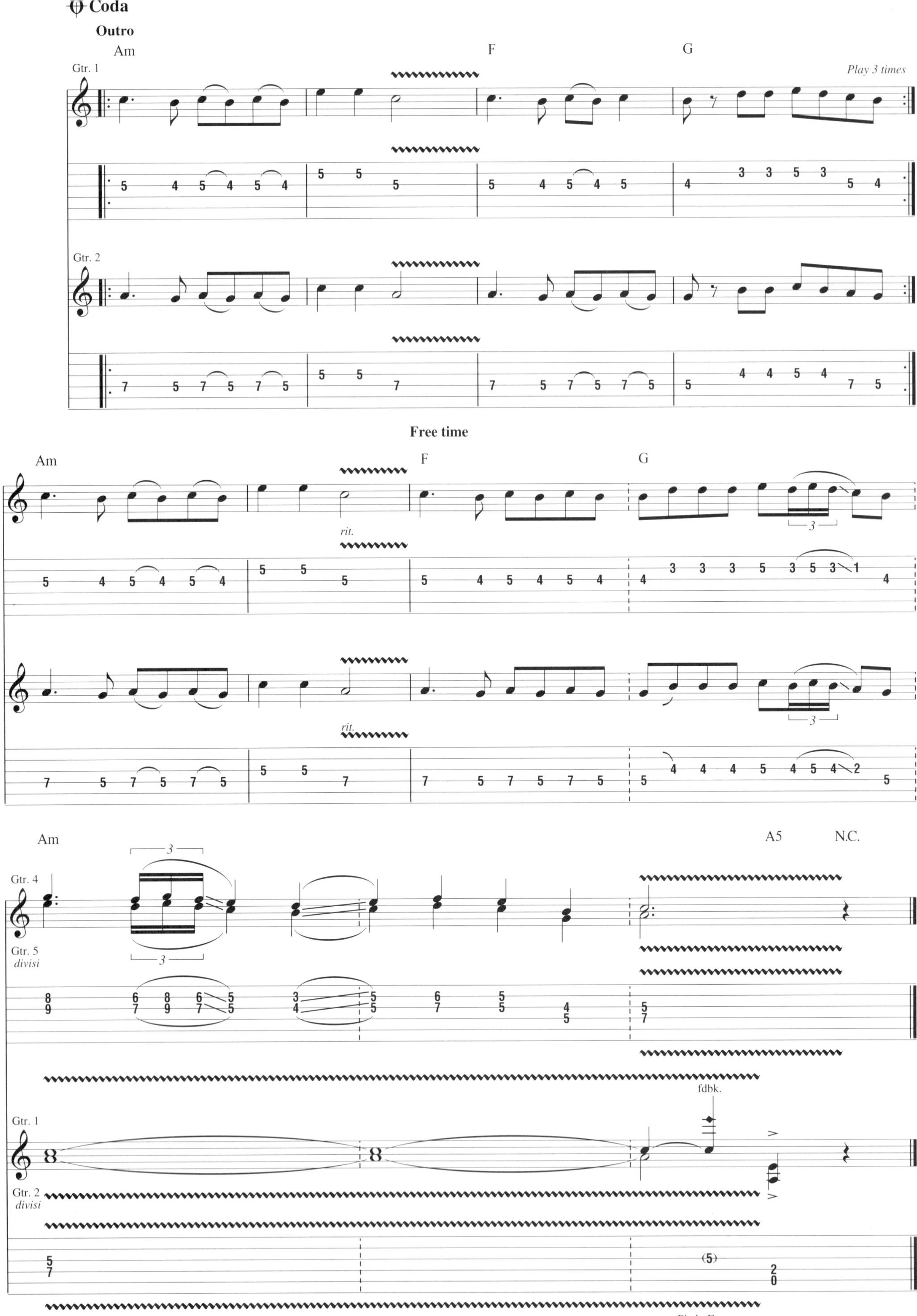
Coda
Outro
Am
F
G
Gtr. 1
Play 3 times
Gtr. 2
Free time
rit.
A5
N.C.
Gtr. 4
Gtr. 5
divisi
fdbk.
Gtr. 1
Gtr. 2
divisi
Pitch: E

from Robert Palmer - *Riptide*

Addicted to Love

Words and Music by Robert Palmer

D5
G5
own.
Your heart
sweats,
your bod - y
shakes.
An - oth - er
speed.
Your heart
beats
in dou - ble
time.
An - oth - er
P.M.
A5
Verse
A5
kiss
is what it
takes.
2. You can't
sleep,
you can't
kiss
and you'll be
mine.
4. A one
track
mind;
you can't be
5. See Additional Lyrics
(Whoa. ___)
F5
G5
C5
eat.
There's no
doubt
you're in
deep.
Your throat is
saved.
Ob - liv - i - on
is all you
crave.
If there's

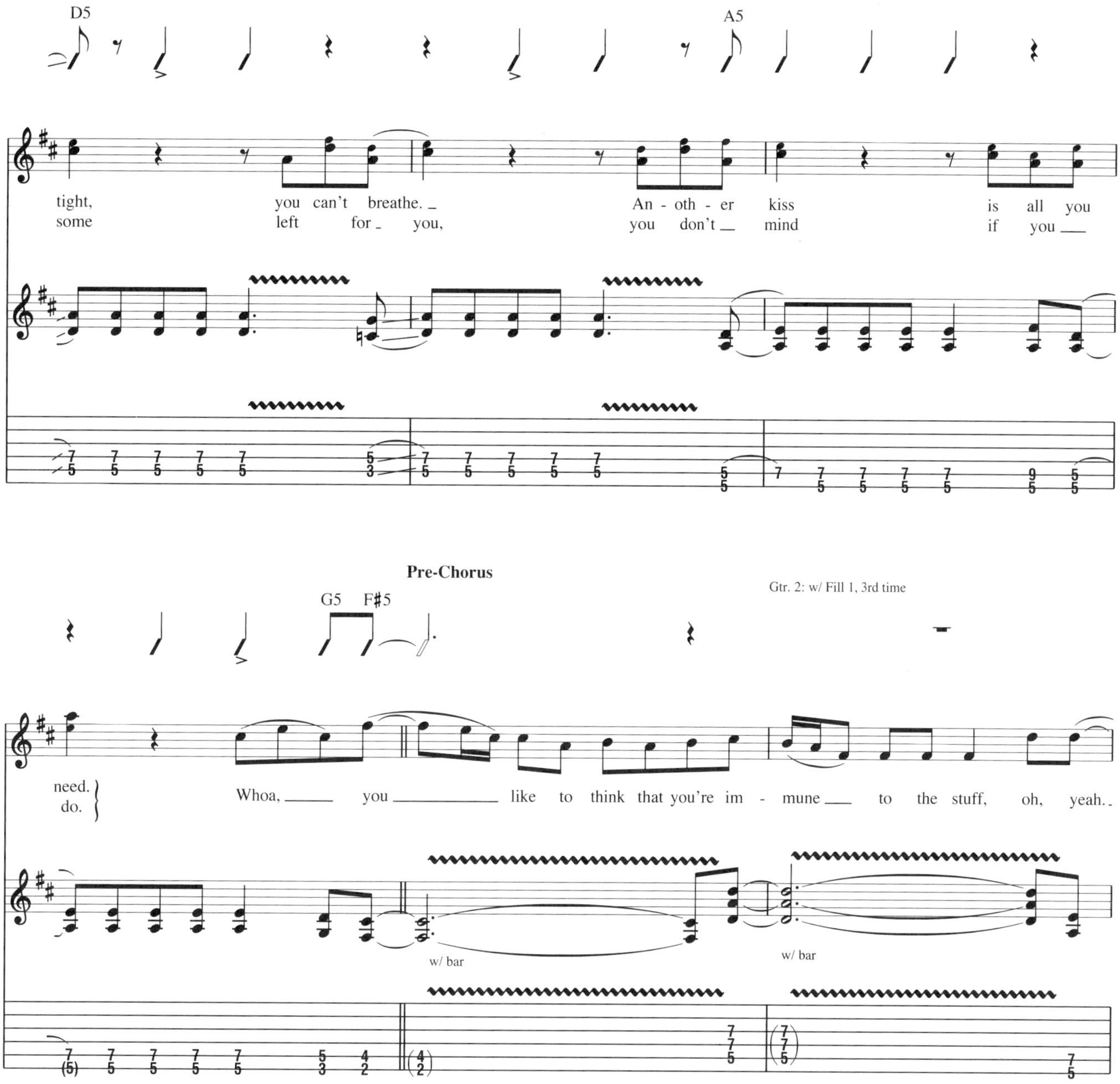

D5
A5
tight, you can't breathe. An - oth - er kiss is all you
some left for you, you don't mind if you
Pre-Chorus
G5 F#5
Gtr. 2: w/ Fill 1, 3rd time
need.
do.
Whoa, you like to think that you're im - mune to the stuff, oh, yeah.
w/ bar
w/ bar
Fill 1
Gtr. 2
P.H.
w/ bar
+1 1/2
-2 1/2
-2 1/2
pitch: F#
D
F#

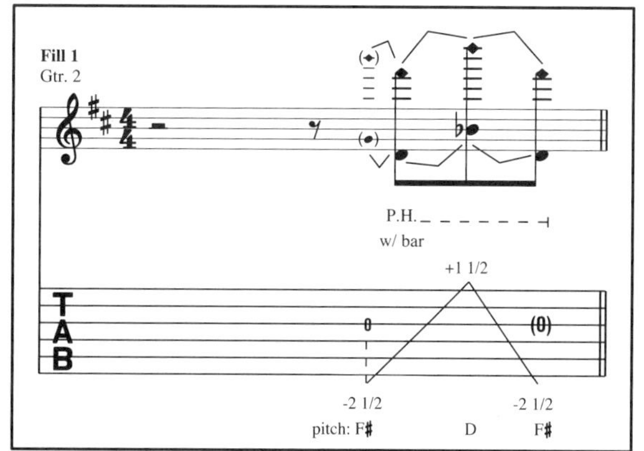

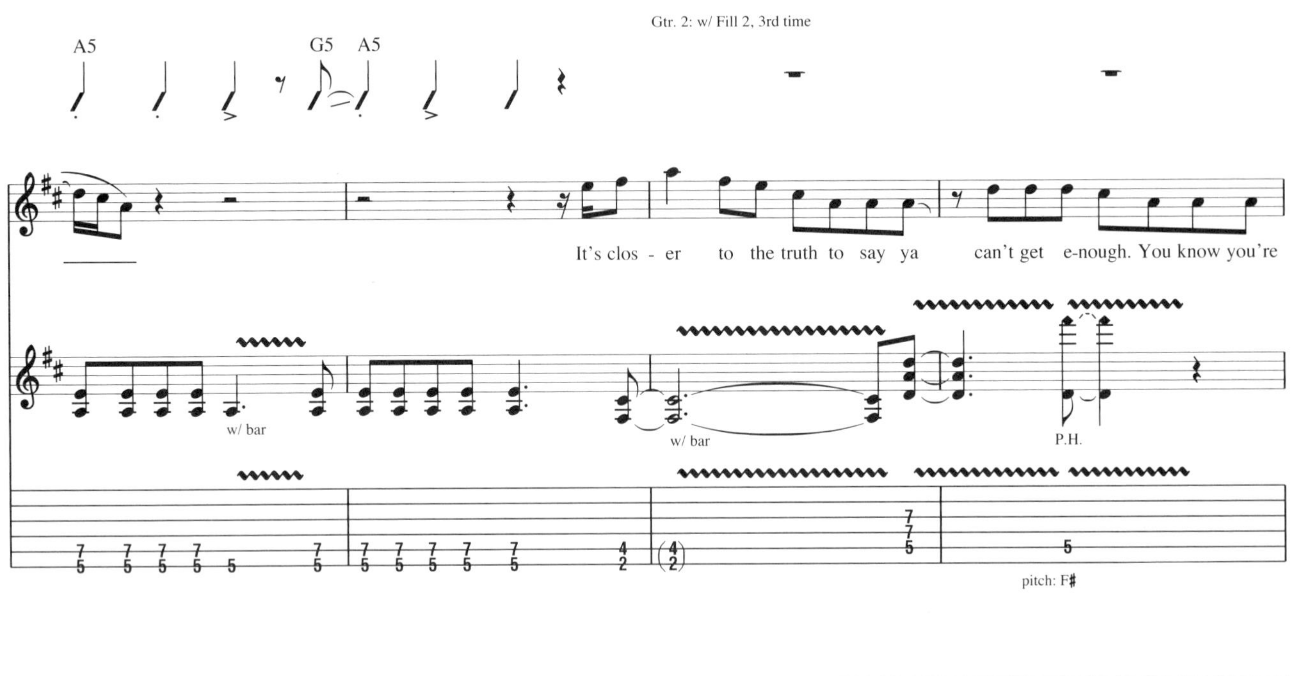
Gtr. 2: w/ Fill 2, 3rd time
A5
G5
A5
It's clos - er to the truth to say ya can't get e-nough. You know you're
w/ bar
w/ bar
P.H.
pitch: F♯

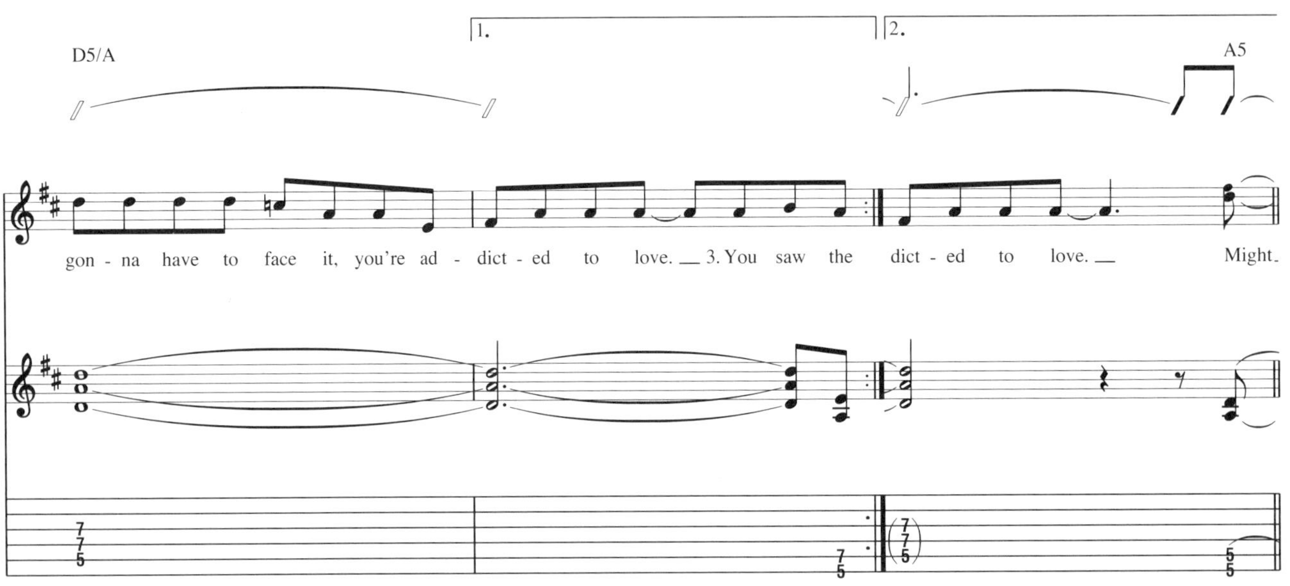
D5/A
1.
2.
A5
gon - na have to face it, you're ad - dict - ed to love. 3. You saw the dict - ed to love. Might

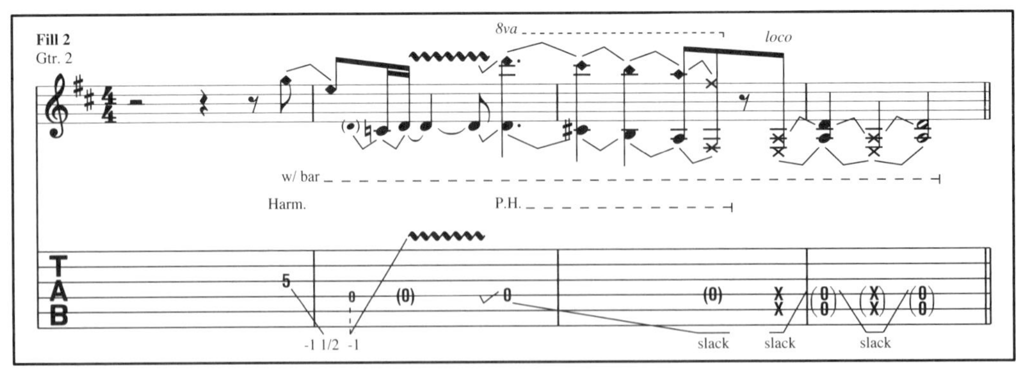
Fill 2
Gtr. 2
8va
loco
w/ bar
Harm.
P.H.
slack
slack
slack

Chorus
G5
A5
G5
as well face it, you're ad - dict - ed to love.
Might as well face it, you're ad -
(Oo, yeah.)
w/ bar
C5
D5
C5
D5
A5
G5
dict - ed to love. Might as well face it, you're ad - dict - ed to love. Might as well face it, you're ad -
To Coda
A5
C
A
G
8fr
5fr
3fr
(cont. in notation)
dict - ed to love. Might as well face it, you're ad - dict - ed to love.
(cont. in slash)

Guitar Solo

Gtr. 1: w/ Rhy. Fill 1
A5
F5
G5
F5
G5
C5
Gtr. 1
w/ bar
Hee,
yeah.
Gtr. 2
grad. bend
full
full
1/2
full

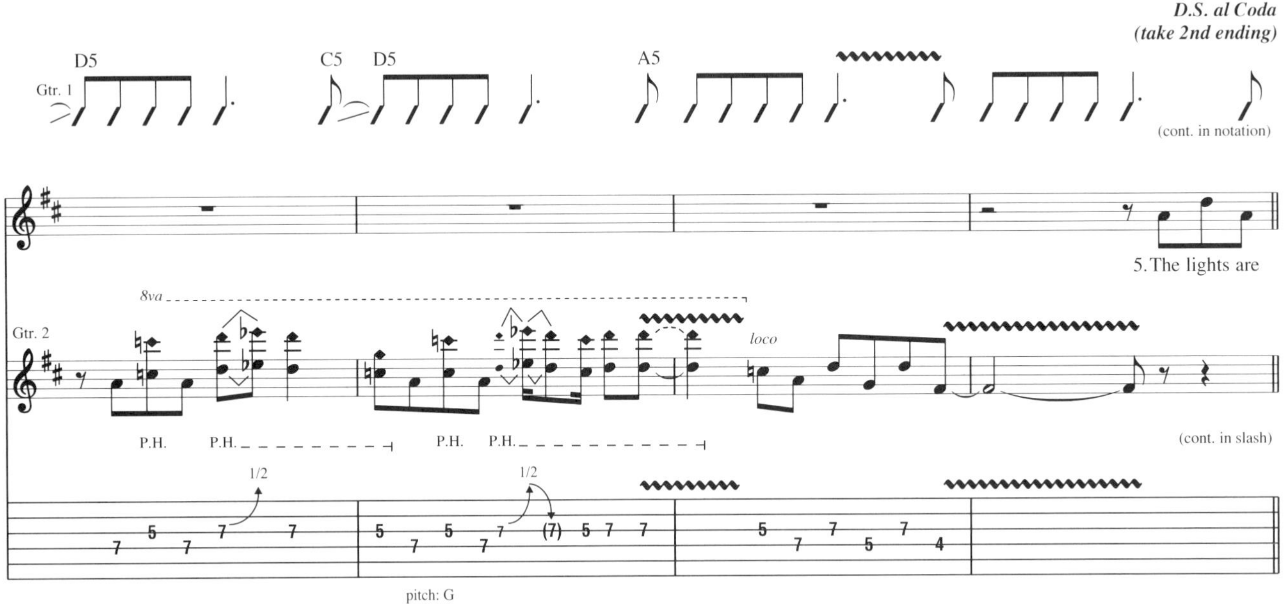
D.S. al Coda
(take 2nd ending)
D5
C5
D5
A5
Gtr. 1
(cont. in notation)
5. The lights are
8va
Gtr. 2
loco
P.H.
P.H.
P.H.
P.H.
(cont. in slash)
1/2
1/2
pitch: G

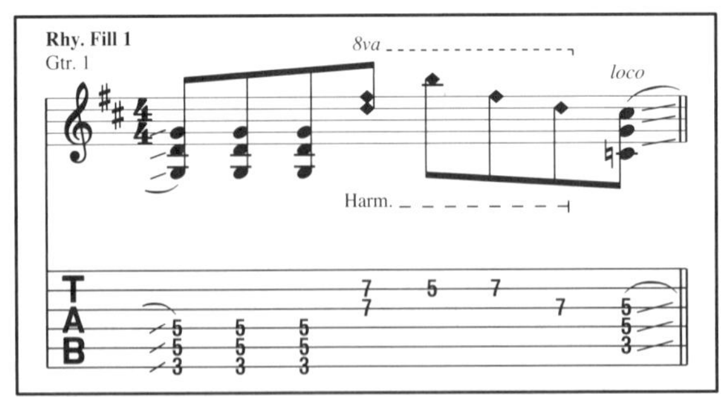
Rhy. Fill 1
Gtr. 1
8va
loco
Harm.

⊕ *Coda*

Chorus

Begin Fade

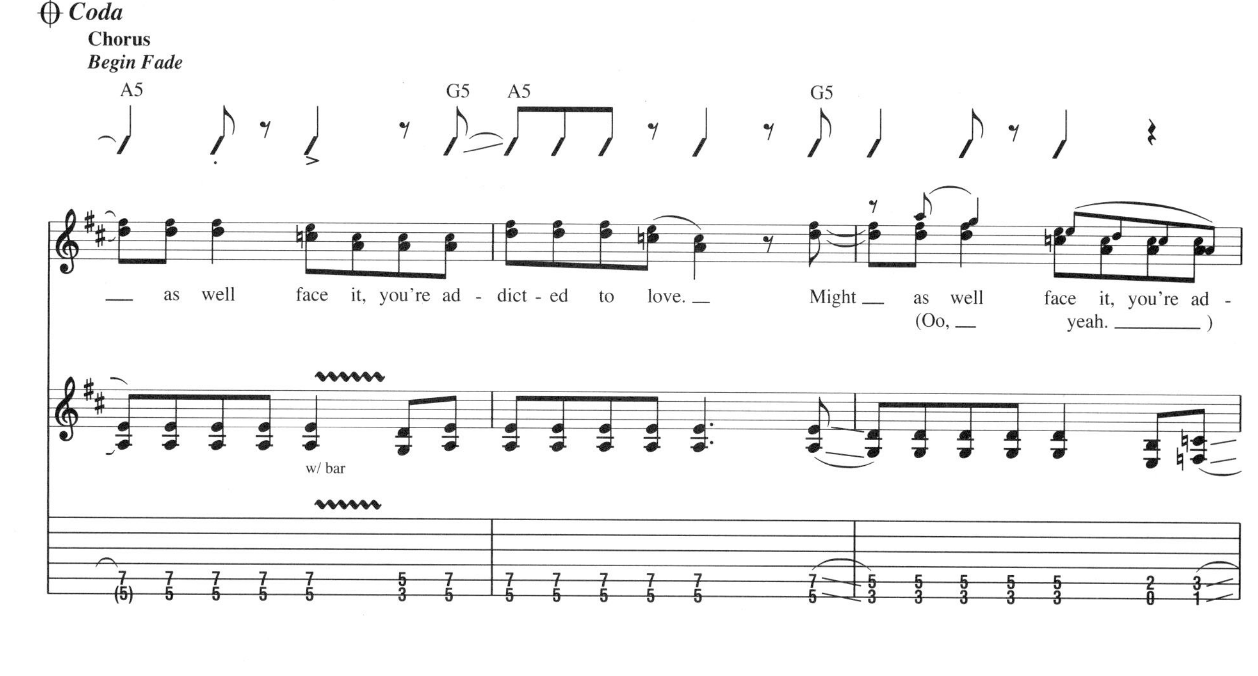

Fade Out

Additional Lyrics

5. The lights are on, but you're not home.
   Your will is not your own.
   Your heart sweats, your teeth grind.
   Another kiss and you'll be mine.

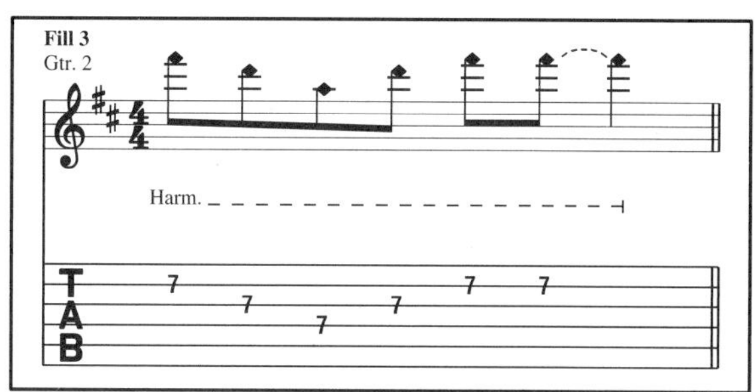

from Donnie Iris - *Back on the Streets*

Ah! Leah!

Words and Music by Mark Avsec and Dominic Ierace

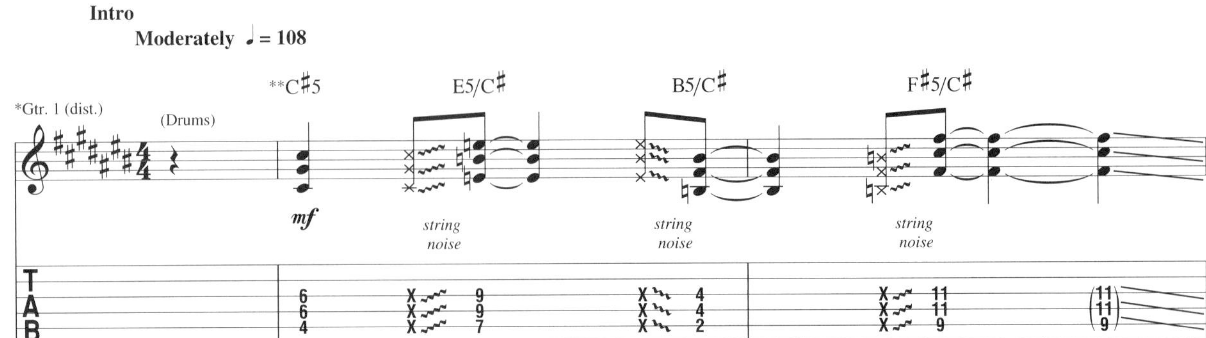

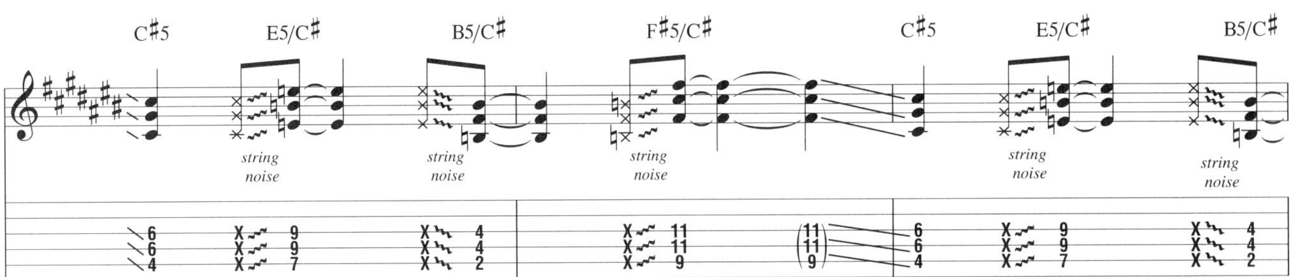

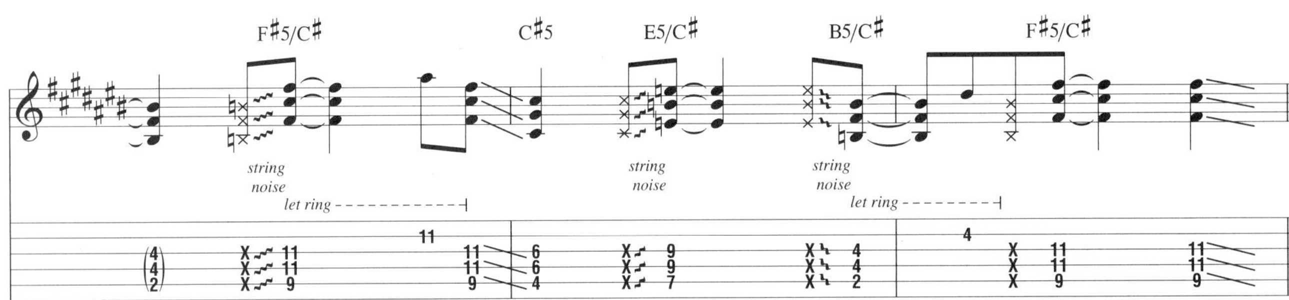

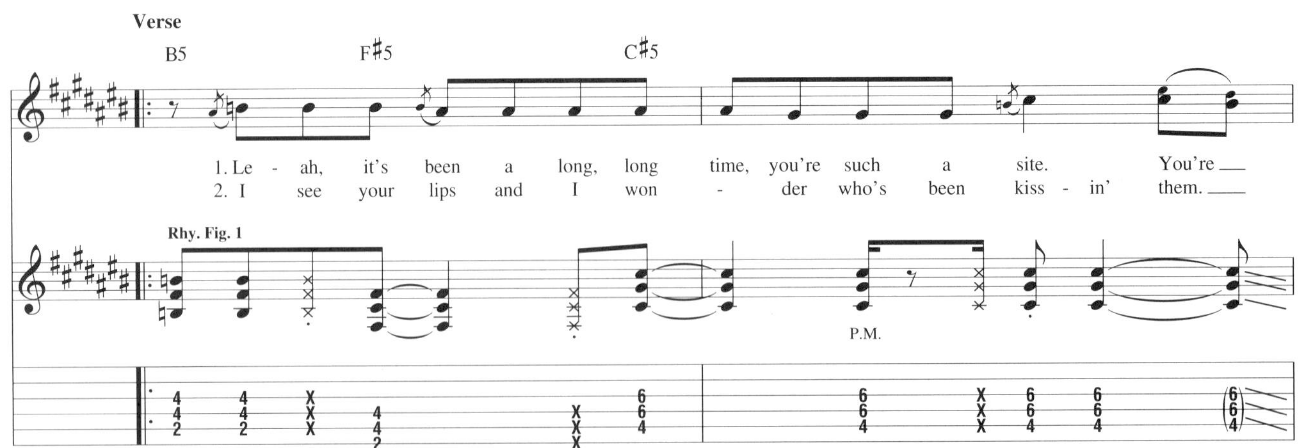

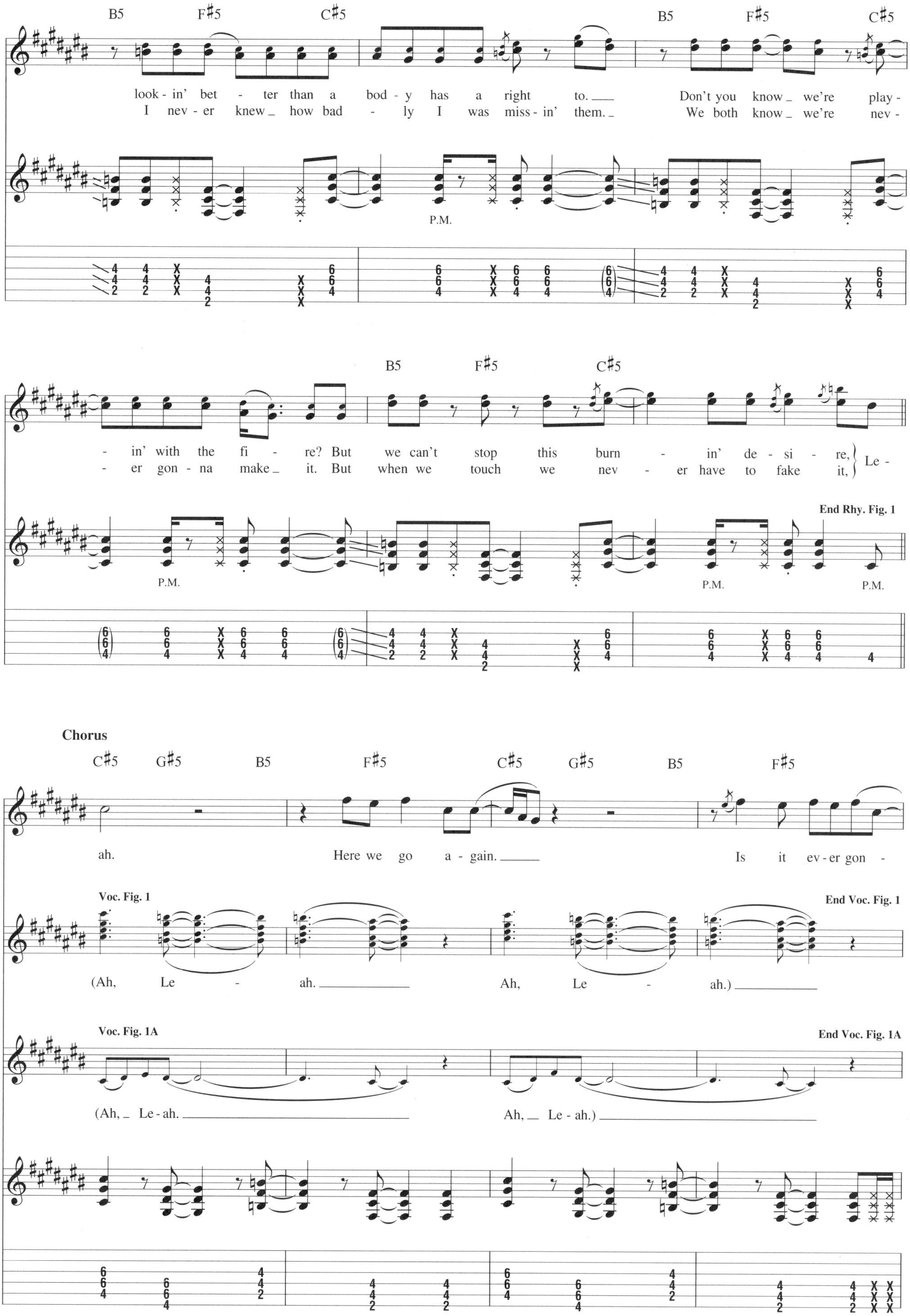

B5 F♯5 C♯5 B5 F♯5 C♯5

look - in' bet - ter than a bod - y has a right to. ___ Don't you know _ we're play -
I nev - er knew _ how bad - ly I was miss - in' them. _ We both know _ we're nev -

P.M.

B5 F♯5 C♯5

- in' with the fi - re? But we can't stop this burn - in' de - si - re, } Le -
- er gon - na make _ it. But when we touch we nev - er have to fake it, }

P.M. P.M. P.M.

End Rhy. Fig. 1

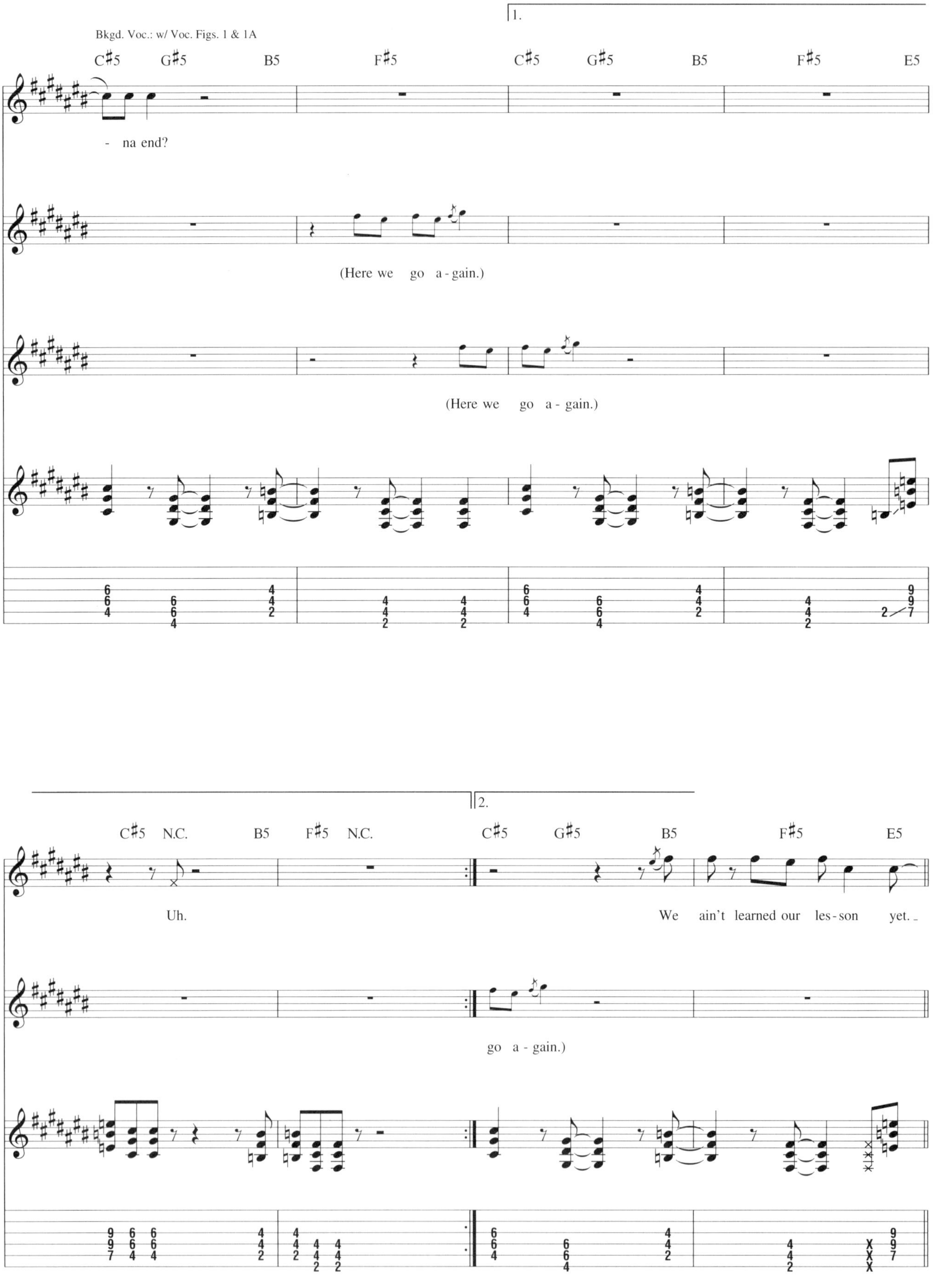

1.

Bkgd. Voc.: w/ Voc. Figs. 1 & 1A

C♯5 G♯5 B5 F♯5 C♯5 G♯5 B5 F♯5 E5

- na end?

(Here we go a - gain.)

(Here we go a - gain.)

Interlude
E5 C#5 N.C. C#5 B5 N.C. B5 F#5 N.C. F#5 C#5 N.C. E5
Ah. Oh. Oh, yeah. Ah.
(Ah, oh, ah. Ah, ah. Ah.
(Ah, ah, oh. Ah, ah. Ah.
9 6 6 6 6 4 4 4 4 4 4 4 4 6 6 9
9 6 6 6 6 4 4 4 4 4 4 4 4 6 6 9
7 4 4 4 4 2 2 2 2 4 4 2 4 4 4 7
2 2 2 2
C#5 N.C. C#5 B5 N.C. B5 F#5 N.C. F#5 C#5 N.C.
Oh. Oh. Oh.
Ah. Ah, ah. Ah.)
Ah, ah. Ah, ah. Ah.)
Gtr. 2 (dist.)
f
*w/ delay
rake
1
X 11 (11) 9
*Set for quarter-note regeneration w/ 2 repeats.
Gtr. 1
9 6 6 6 6 4 4 4 4 4 4 4 4 6 6
9 6 6 6 6 4 4 4 4 4 4 4 4 6 6
7 4 4 4 4 2 2 2 2 4 4 2 4 4 4
2 2 2 2

Guitar Solo

Verse
Gtr. 1: w/ Rhy. Fig. 1
Gtr. 2 tacet
B5
F♯5
C♯5
3. Ba - by, it's no good, we're just ask - in' for trou - ble.
Gtr. 2
(14)
(14)

B5
F♯5
C♯5
I can touch you but I don't know how to love you.
B5
F♯5
C♯5
It ain't no use, we're head -

- ed for dis - as - ter. Our
B5
F♯5
C♯5
minds said no, but our hearts were talk - in' fast - er, Le -

Chorus
Bkgd. Voc.: w/ Voc. Figs. 1 & 1A (2 times)
C♯5
G♯5
B5
F♯5
C♯5
G♯5
B5
F♯5
ah.
Here we go a - gain.
(Here we go a-gain.
(Here we
Gtr. 1

C♯5 G♯5 B5 F♯5 C♯5 G♯5 B5 F♯5
Le - ah, Le - ah, Le - ah.
Ah!
Here we go a - gain.
go a - gain.
Here we

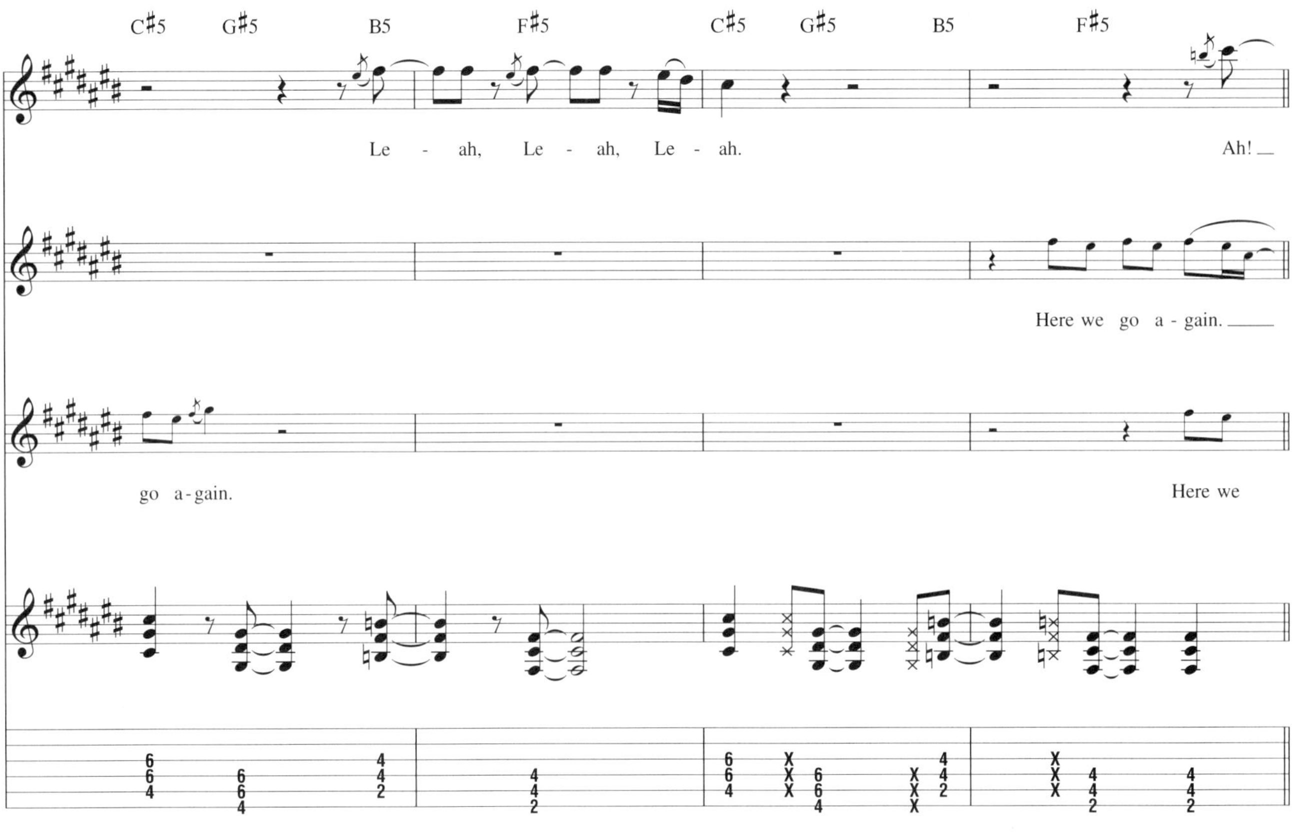

Chorus

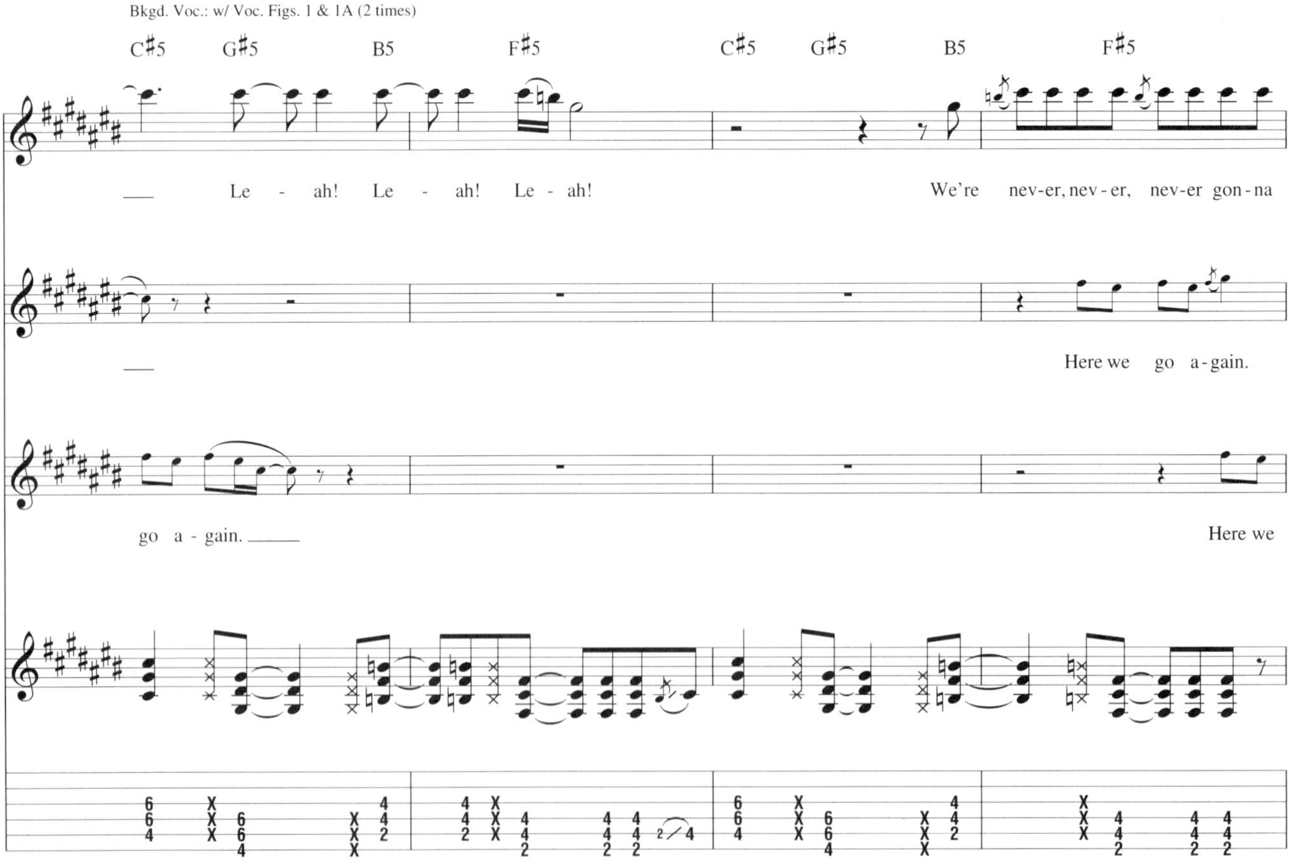

Bkgd. Voc.: w/ Voc. Figs. 1 & 1A (2 times)
C♯5 G♯5 B5 F♯5 C♯5 G♯5 B5 F♯5
Le - ah! Le - ah! Le - ah!
We're nev-er, nev-er, nev-er gon-na
Here we go a-gain.
go a - gain.
Here we

C#5 G#5 B5 F#5 C#5 G#5 B5 F#5
make it, girl! Ah! Le - ah! Yeah!
Here we go a - gain.)
go a-gain.
Here we
Interlude
C# G#m7 B5 F#5 C# G#m7 B5 F#5
go a - gain.)
Gtr. 3 (clean)
Riff A
End Riff A
mf
let ring
let ring

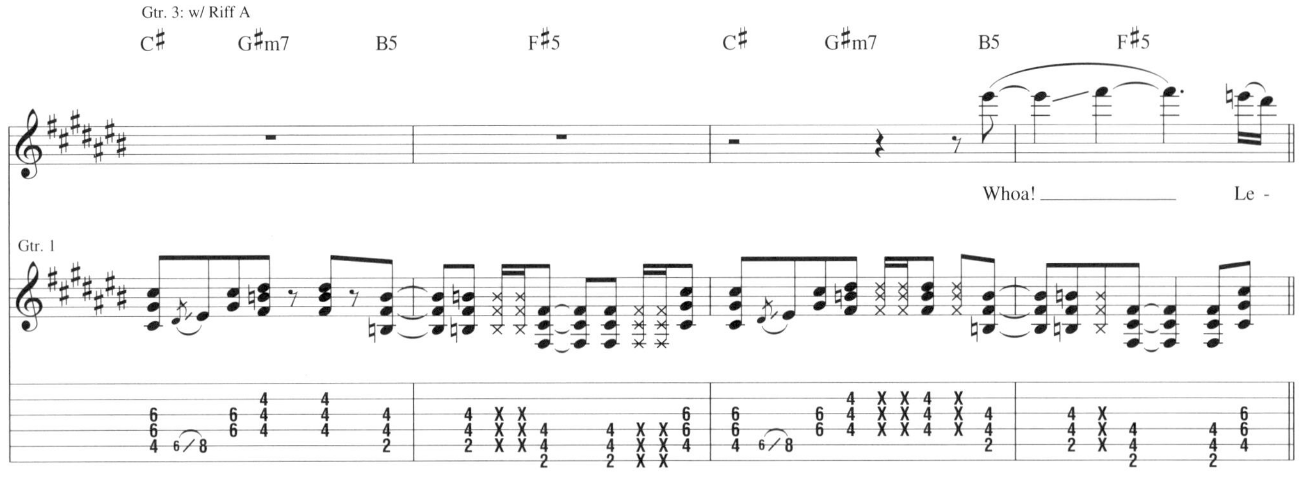
Gtr. 3: w/ Riff A
C♯
G♯m7
B5
F♯5
C♯
G♯m7
B5
F♯5
Whoa! Le -
Gtr. 1

Outro-Chorus
Begin fade
Bkgd. Voc.: w/ Voc. Figs. 1 & 1A (till fade)
Gtr. 3: w/ Riff A (till fade)
C♯
G♯m7
B5
F♯
C♯
G♯m7
B5
ah!
We're nev - er gon - na make it, girl!
let ring

Fade out
F♯5
C♯
G♯m7
B5
F♯5
Ah! Ah! Le - ah! Woo - hoo! Le - ah!
(Here we go a - gain.)
(Here we go a - gain.)

from Fleetwood Mac - *English Rose*

Albatross

Words and Music by Peter Green

B
Gtr. 1 tacet
E
Riff A
Gtr. 3 (clean)
f w/ slide
14/16 14/16 14/16 14\13 14/16 14/16 14/16 14/16 14\13 14/16 14/16 14/16
Gtr. 4 (clean)
Riff A1
mf w/ slide
11/13 11/13 11/13 11\9 11/13 11/13 11/13 11/13 11\9 11/13 11/13

F♯m
E
Gtr. 3
End Riff A
16\14 16\14 14\13 14 14\13
Gtr. 4
End Riff A1
13\11 13\11 11\9 11 11 9
Gtr. 2
16\14 17\14

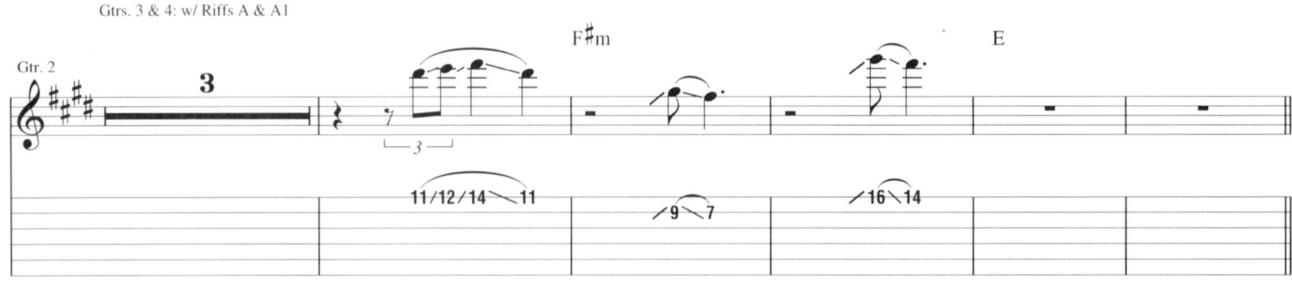
Gtrs. 3 & 4: w/ Riffs A & A1
F♯m
E
Gtr. 2
3
11/12/14\11 /9\7 /16\14

C
E
8va
Gtr. 2
Gtr. 3
Gtr. 4
F♯m
loco
Gtr. 2 tacet
E
Gtr. 1

D
Gtrs. 3 & 4 tacet
Gtr. 1
A E
A E
A E
A E

Gtr. 2
F♯m
E
Gtr. 1

F♯m
E
F♯m
E

from the Kinks - *Kinks-Size*

All Day and All of the Night

Words and Music by Ray Davies

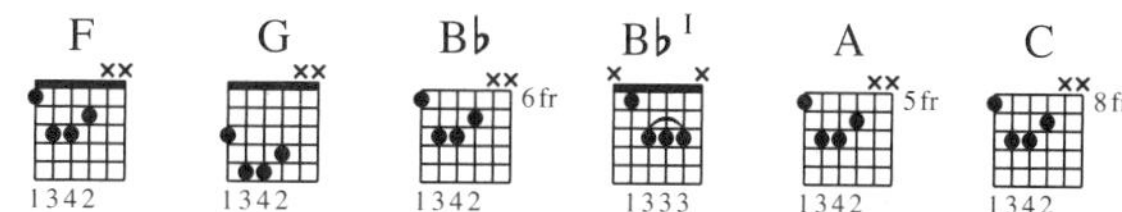

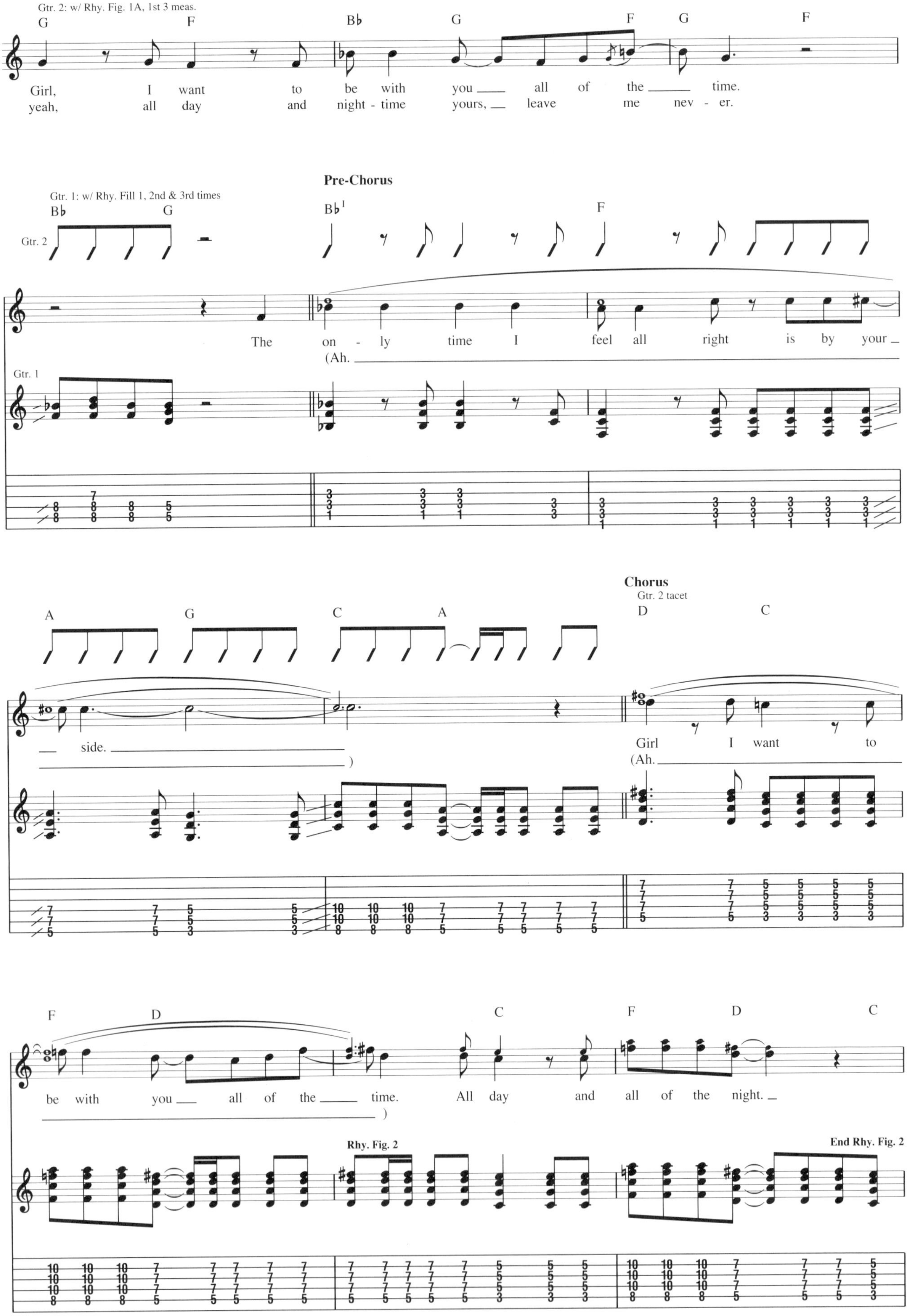

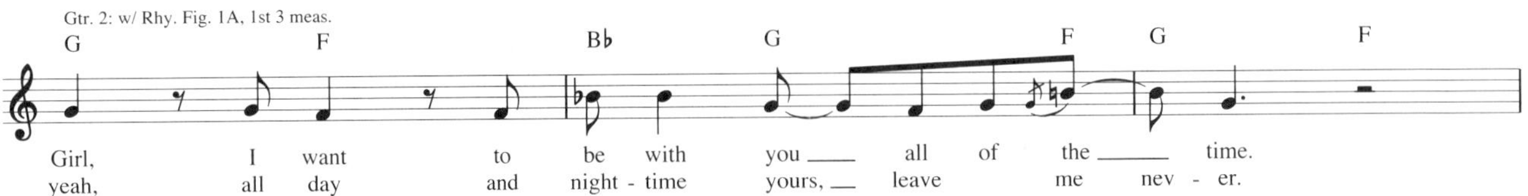

Gtr. 1: w/ Rhy. Fill 1, 2nd & 3rd times

B♭ G

Gtr. 2

Pre-Chorus

B♭1 F

The on - ly time I feel all right is by your ___
(Ah. ___

Gtr. 1

Chorus

Gtr. 2 tacet

A G C A D C

___ side. ___
___)

Girl I want to
(Ah. ___

F D C F D C

be with you ___ all of the ___ time. All day and all of the night. ___
___)

Rhy. Fig. 2

End Rhy. Fig. 2

To Coda
1.
Gtr. 1: w/ Rhy. Fig. 2, simile
D C F D C
All day and all of the night.
2.
Gtr. 1
N.C.
Oh, come on!
Guitar Solo
Gtr. 2:/w/ Rhy. Fig. 1A, 1 1/2 times, simile
G F Bb G F
let ring
D.S. al Coda
Gtr. 2
Gtr. 1
Coda
All day and all of the night.

from Dokken - *Tooth and Nail*

Alone Again

Words and Music by Don Dokken, George Lynch, Jeff Pilson and Mick Brown

Csus2
D5
Em(add9)
C5
G5
D5
morn - ing light.
turned a - way.
I like to feel you when it comes to night.
Tried to say that it was me.
Gtrs. 1 & 2
Gtr. 3 (elec.)
mf
w/ dist.
let ring
Em(add9)
Csus2
D
Gtrs. 1 & 2 tacet
C5
D5
Now I'm here and I'm all a - lone.
Now I'm here and I've lost my way.
Still I know how it
Now I know how it
mf
B5
A5/B
B5
C5
D5
Bridge
E5
Dsus4D
feels, I'm a - lone a - gain.
feels, I'm a - lone a - gain.
Tried so hard to
Gtr. 3
Rhy. Fig. 1
P.M.
P.M.

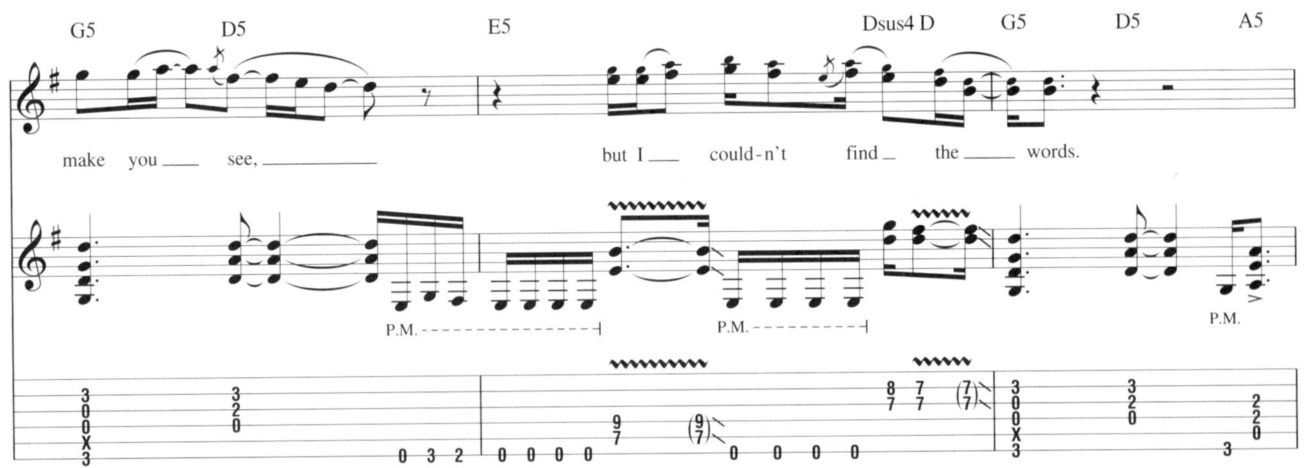
G5
D5
E5
Dsus4 D
G5
D5
A5
make you see,
but I could-n't find the words.
P.M.
P.M.
P.M.

Chorus
E5
Dsus4 D
G5
A5
C5
D5
Now the tears, they fall like rain. I'm a - lone a - gain with-out
End Rhy. Fig. 1
Rhy. Fig. 2
P.M.
P.M.

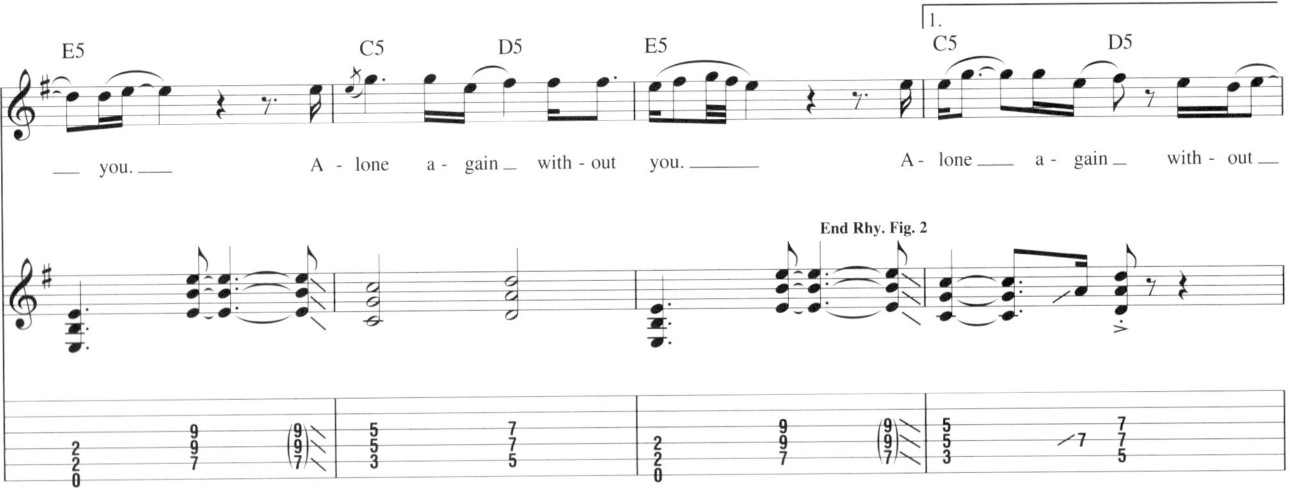
1.
E5
C5
D5
E5
C5
D5
you. A - lone a - gain with - out you. A - lone a - gain with - out
End Rhy. Fig. 2

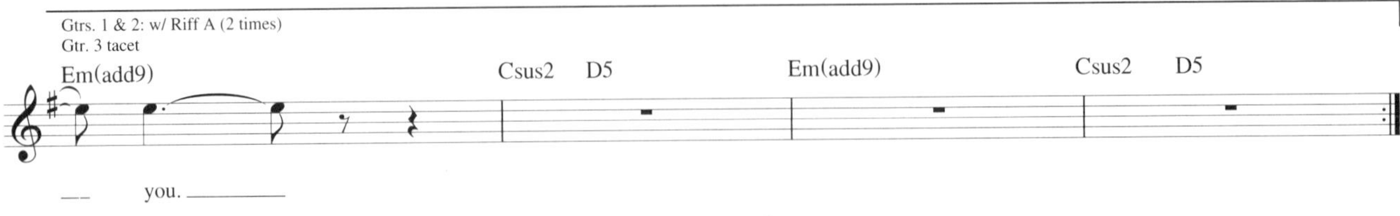
Gtrs. 1 & 2: w/ Riff A (2 times)
Gtr. 3 tacet
Em(add9)
Csus2
D5
Em(add9)
Csus2
D5
you.

2.
C5
D5
B5
A5/B
B5
C5
D5
N.C.
lone a - gain with - out you.
A - lone a - gain with - out you.
Gtr. 4 (elec.)
mf
w/ dist.
Gtr. 3
Rhy. Fig. 3
End Rhy. Fig. 3
(cont. in slashes)
Guitar Solo
E5
C5
D5
E5
Gtr. 3
Gtr. 4
P.M.
P.M.
P.M.
C5
G5
D5 open
E5
C5
D5
8va
rake
rake

C5
D5
B5
A5/B
B5
8va
loco
w/ bar
1/2
C5
D5
Bridge
Gtr. 3: w/ Rhy. Fig. 1
E5
Dsus4
D
G5
D5
I tried so hard to make you see,
Gtr. 4
P.M.
E5
Dsus4 D
G5
D5
A5
E5
Dsus4 D
but I could - n't find the words.
Now the tears, they
rake

Chorus
Gtr. 3: w/ Rhy. Fig. 2 (1 1/2 times)
G5 A5 C5 D5 E5
fall like rain. I'm a - lone a - gain with - out you. A-
8va
loco
grad. release
P.M.
C5 D5 E5 C5 D5
lone a - gain with - out you. A - lone a - gain.
P.M.
E5
Gtr. 3: w/ Rhy. Fig. 3
C5 D5 B5 A5/B B5
A - lone a - gain. A-
C5 D5 N.C.
Gtr. 4 tacet
Em(add9)
rit.
lone a - gain with - out you.
Gtrs. 1 & 2
rit.
let ring

from Lenny Kravitz - *Mama Said*

Always on the Run

Words by Lenny Kravitz
Music by Lenny Kravitz and Slash

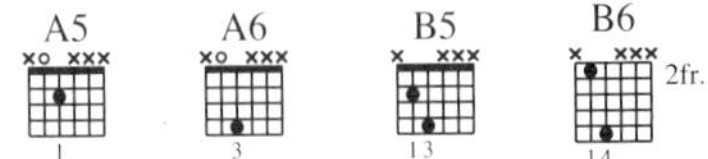

*Played by Gtr. II when recalled, throughout. Play all guitar figures w/slight variations ad lib when repeated or recalled (throughout).

Rhy. Fig. 1
(end Rhy. Fig. 1)
(Gtr. III)
sl.
H

1st Verse
w/Riff A and Rhy. Fig. 1 (both 2 times)
N.C.(E9)
1. And my ma - ma said that your life is a gift. And my ma - ma said, "There's much

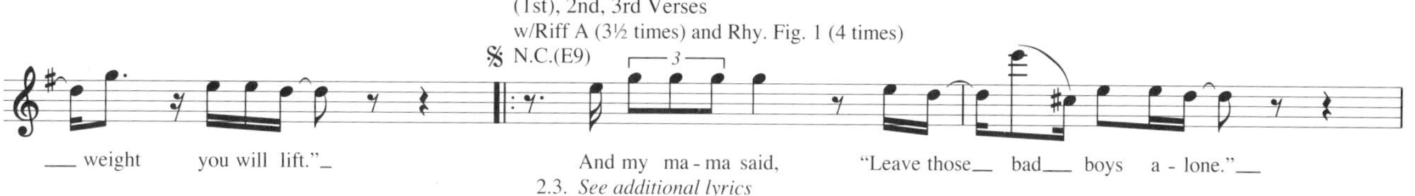
(1st), 2nd, 3rd Verses
w/Riff A (3½ times) and Rhy. Fig. 1 (4 times)
N.C.(E9)
weight you will lift." And my ma - ma said, "Leave those bad boys a - lone."
2.3. See additional lyrics

Gtr. II substitute Rhy. Fill 1
And my ma - ma said, "Be home be-fore dawn." And my ma - ma said, "You can

(resume Riff A)
3rd time Gtr. II substitute Rhy. Fill 1
3rd time Gtr. II substitute last bar of Riff A
be rich or poor." But my ma - ma said, "You can be big or small."
Gtr. II
P.M.
*Notes in parentheses are played 2nd time only.

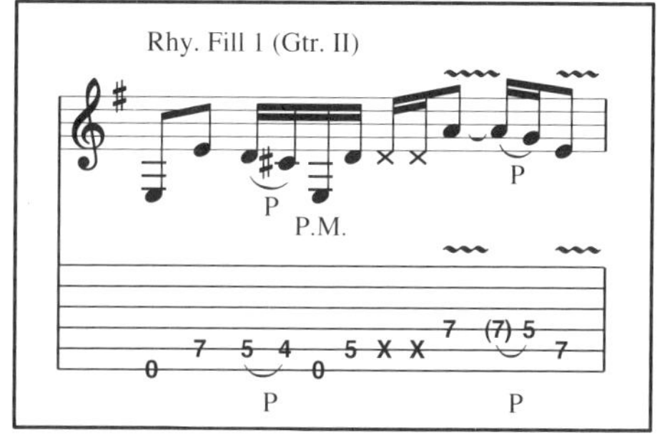
Rhy. Fill 1 (Gtr. II)
P.M.

Chorus
w/Rhy. Fig. 1
G5 A5

(But I'm al - ways on ___ the run.)

2nd time Gtr. III substitute Rhy. Fill 2
N.C.(E9)

Al - ways on ___ the run. ___

To Coda ⊕

Riff B (*Gtr. IV)

**

(end Riff B)

15
16

Rhy. Fig. 2 (Gtr. II)

1/2

P P.M. P.M. P P.M.

(end Rhy. Fig. 2)

5 5 X X X X 7 7 X X
3 3 X X X X 5 5 X X 3

0 7 5 4 0 5 0 5 0 0 7

P P

*Horns arr. for gtr.

**Vol. knob swell.

w/Riff B
2nd time Gtr. III substitute 1st bar of Rhy. Fig. 1
G5 A5

(But I'm al - ways on ___ the run.)

w/Riff A (2 times) and Rhy. Fig. 1 (1½ times)
N.C.(E9)

3

1.
w/last bar of Rhy. Fig. 1

Rhy. Fill 2 (Gtr. III)

1/2

P

X X 5 7 5 7 X X 7 (7) 5 7 5

P

3

1/2

5 5 X X X X 7 7 X X
3 3 X X X X 5 5 X X 3

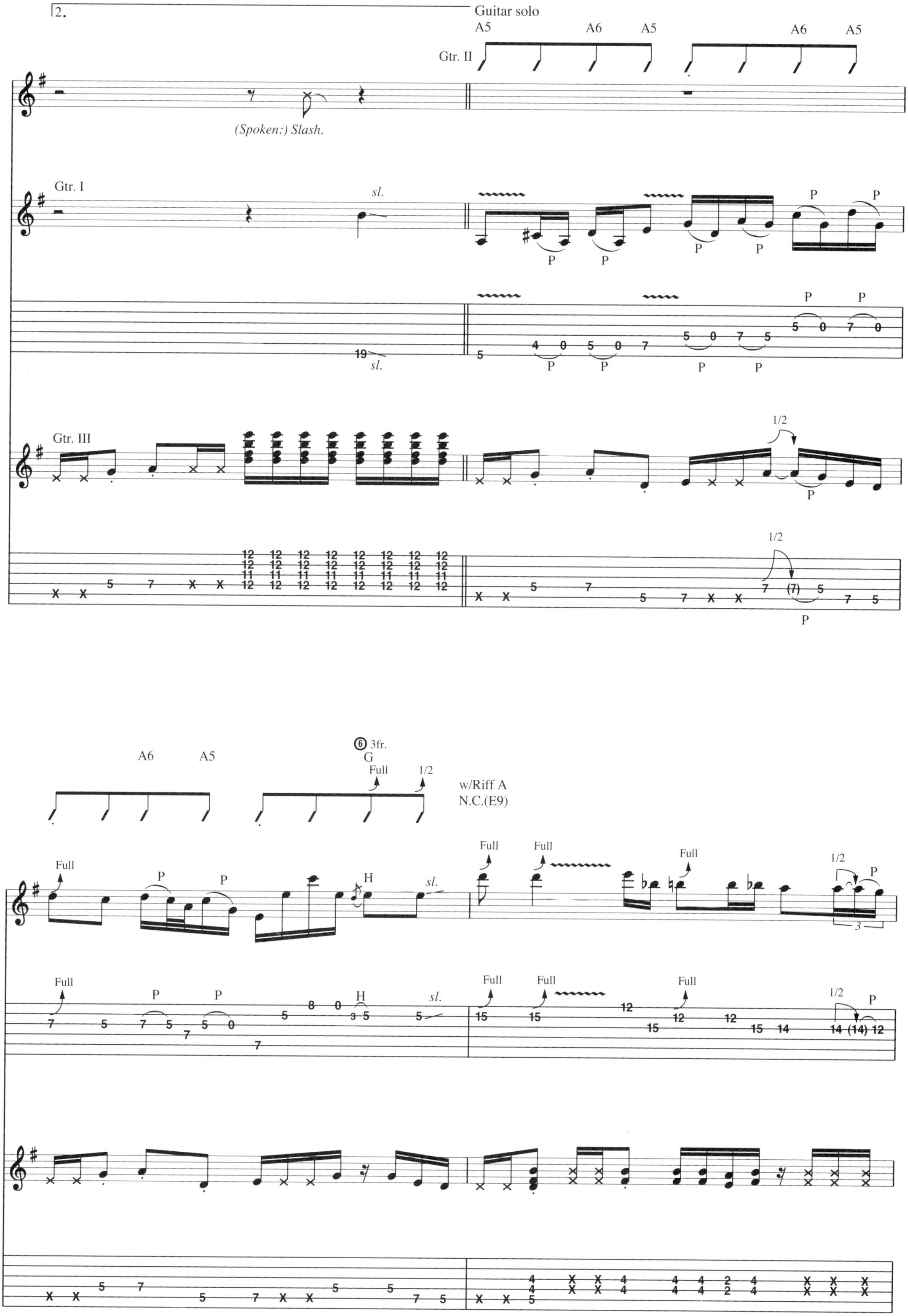

2.

Guitar solo

A5 A6 A5 A6 A5

Gtr. II

(Spoken:) Slash.

Gtr. I

Gtr. III

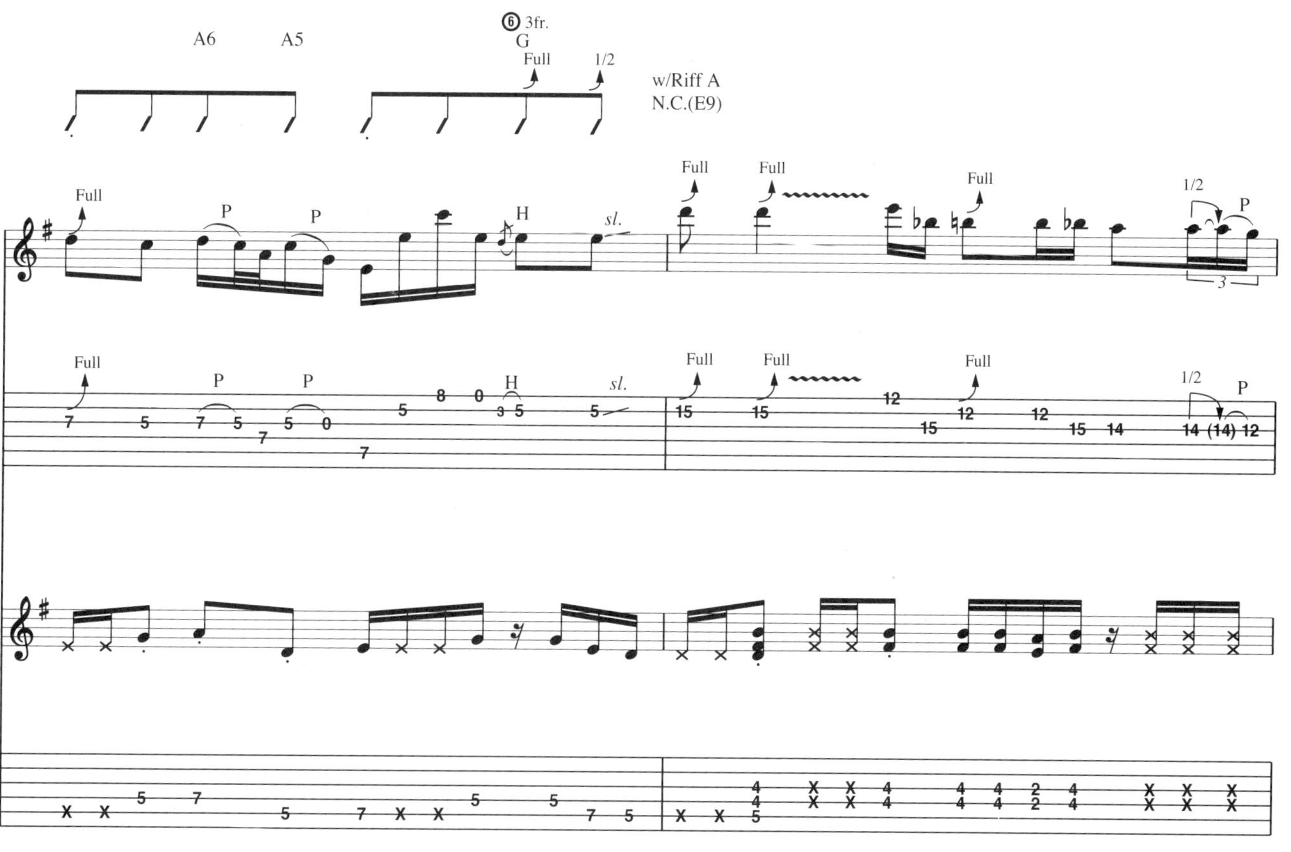

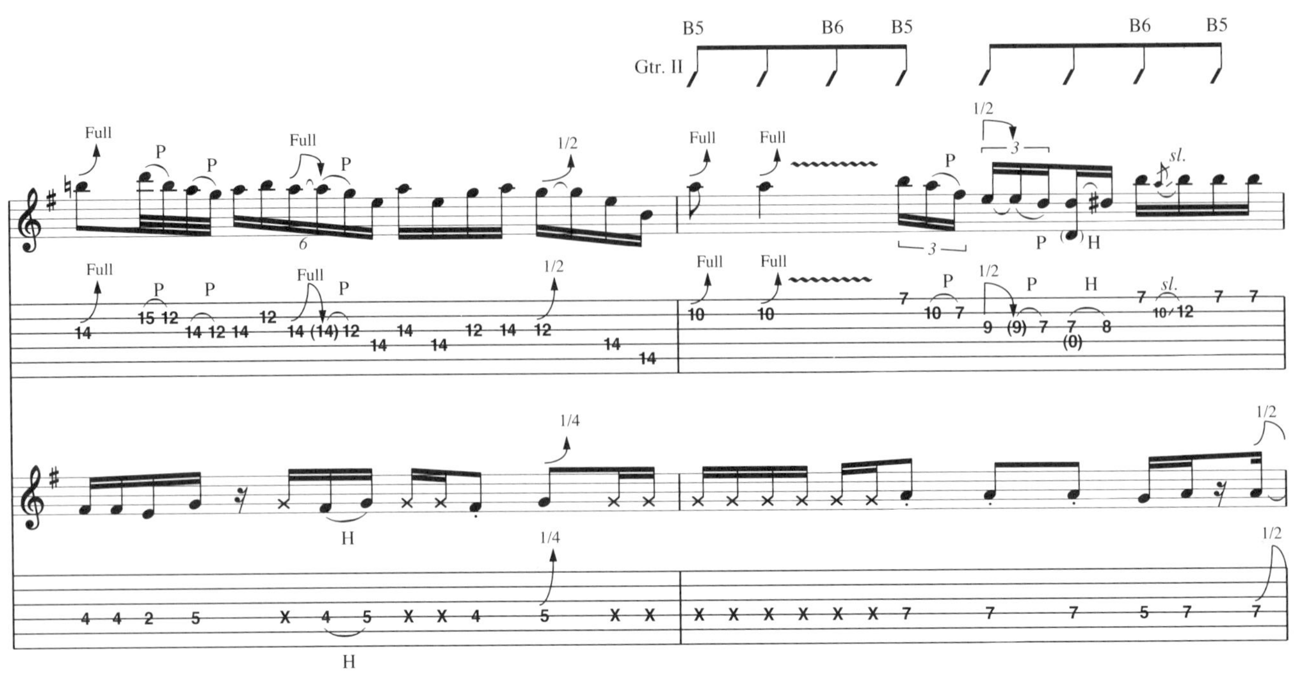
B5
B6
B5
B6
B5
Gtr. II
Full
P
P
Full
P
1/2
Full
Full
1/2
3
sl.
3
H
1/4
1/2
H
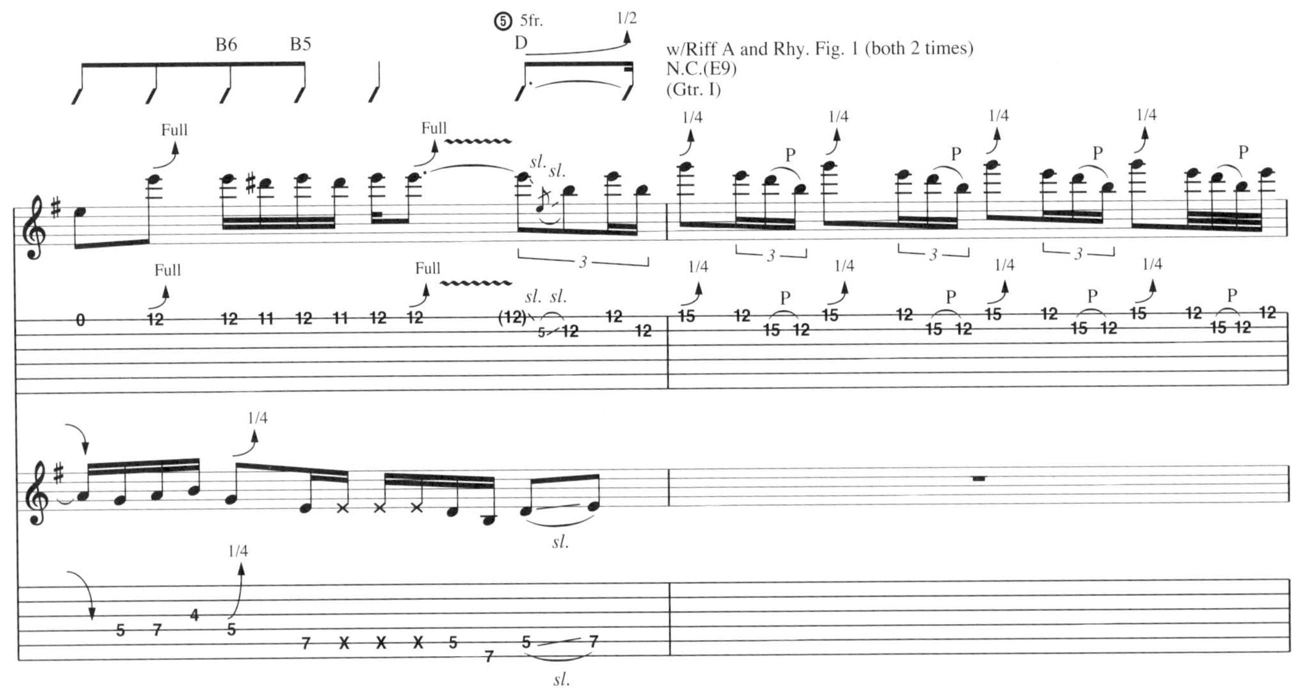
B6
B5
5 5fr.
D
1/2
w/Riff A and Rhy. Fig. 1 (both 2 times)
N.C.(E9)
(Gtr. I)
Full
Full
sl. sl.
3
1/4
P
1/4
sl.
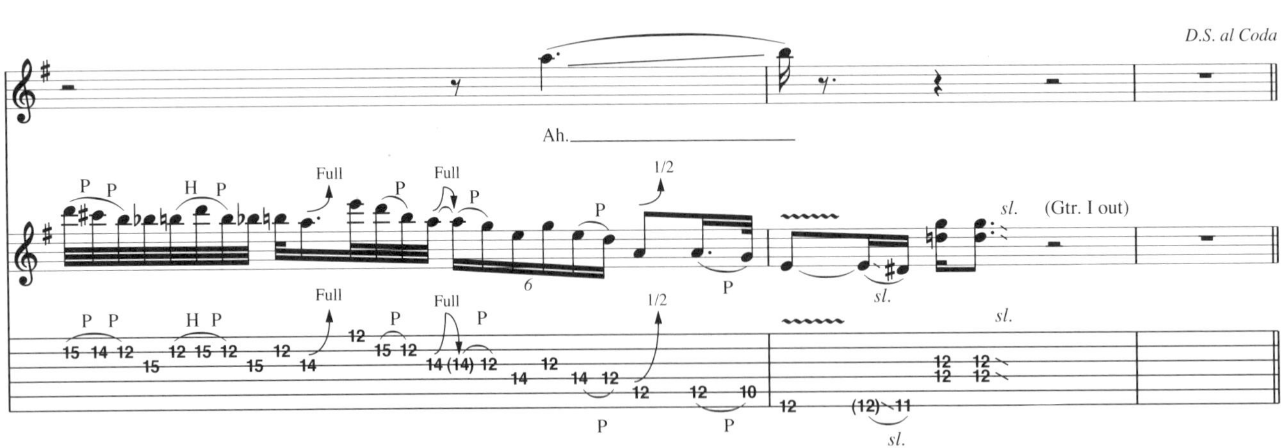
D.S. al Coda
Ah.
P P
H P
Full
P
Full
P
1/2
sl.
(Gtr. I out)
6
sl.

Coda
w/Rhy. Fig. 2 (2½ times) and Riff B (2 times)
w/Rhy. Fill 2
G5
A5
w/1st bar of Rhy. Fig. 1
N.C.(E9)
On the run.
(But I'm al - ways on the run.)

w/Rhy. Fill 2
G5
A5
w/last bar of Rhy. Fig. 1
N.C.
w/1st bar of Rhy. Fig. 1
G5
A5
(But I'm al - ways on the run.)
Al - ways on the run.
Al - ways on the run.
(But I'm al - ways on the run.

Outro
w/Riff A (2 times) and Rhy. Fig. 1 (6½ times)
N.C.(E9)
(Spoken:) Uh, what's up, ma-ma? You want it, uh, right now?

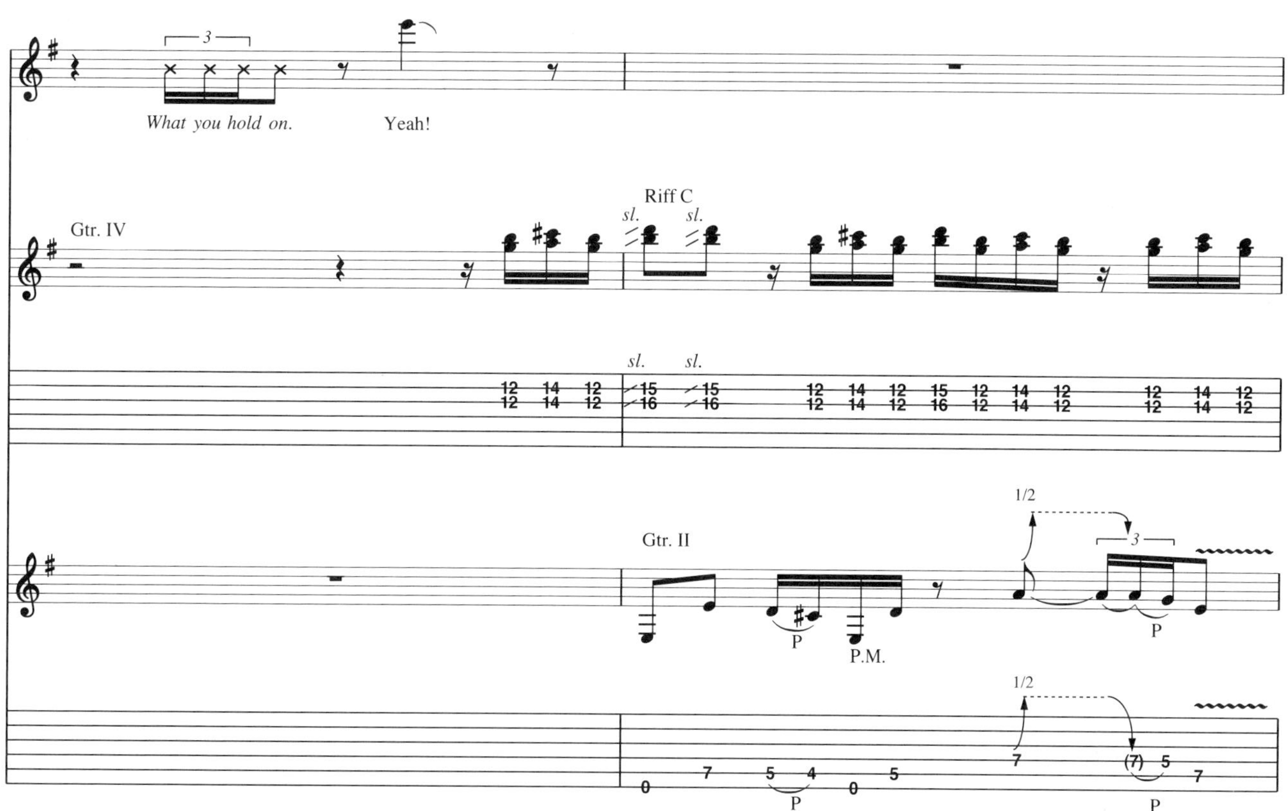
What you hold on. Yeah!
Gtr. IV
Riff C
sl.
Gtr. II
1/2
P
P.M.

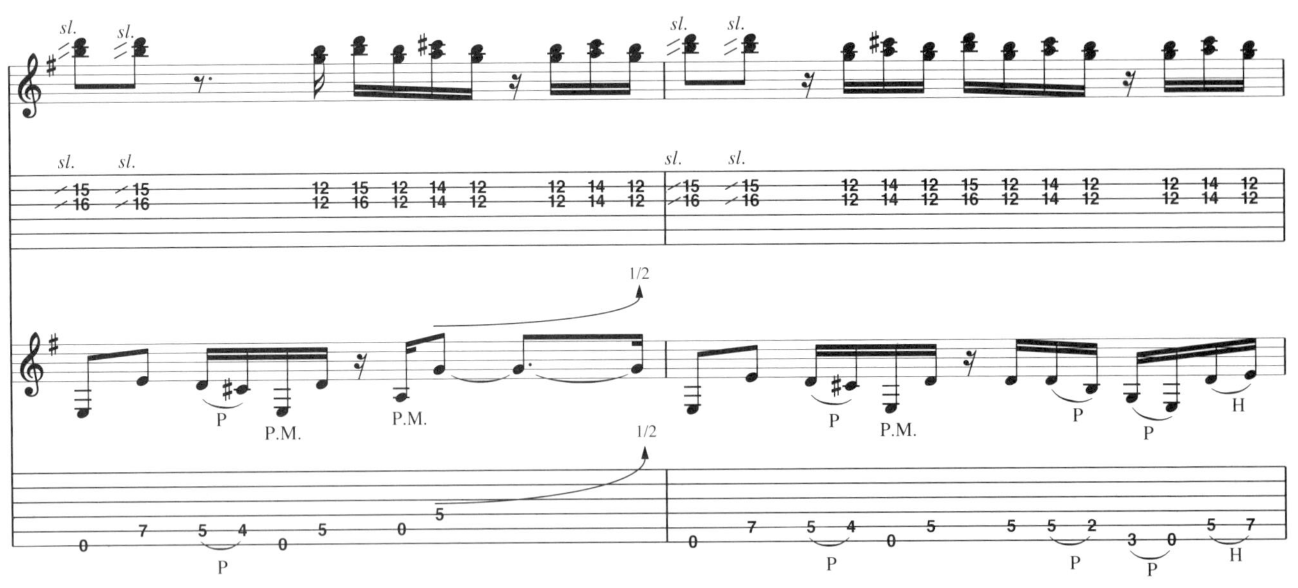
sl.
P
P.M.
H
1/2

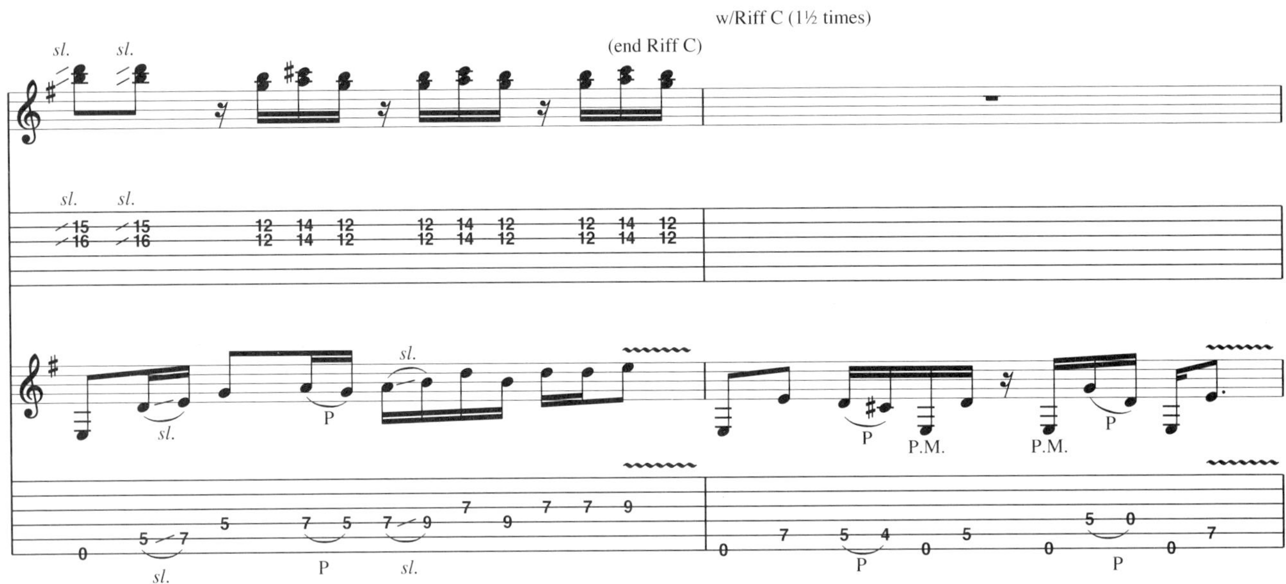
w/Riff C (1½ times)
(end Riff C)
sl.
P
P.M.

* Gtr. V
sl.
P
P.M.
H
1/4
*Horns arr. for gtr.

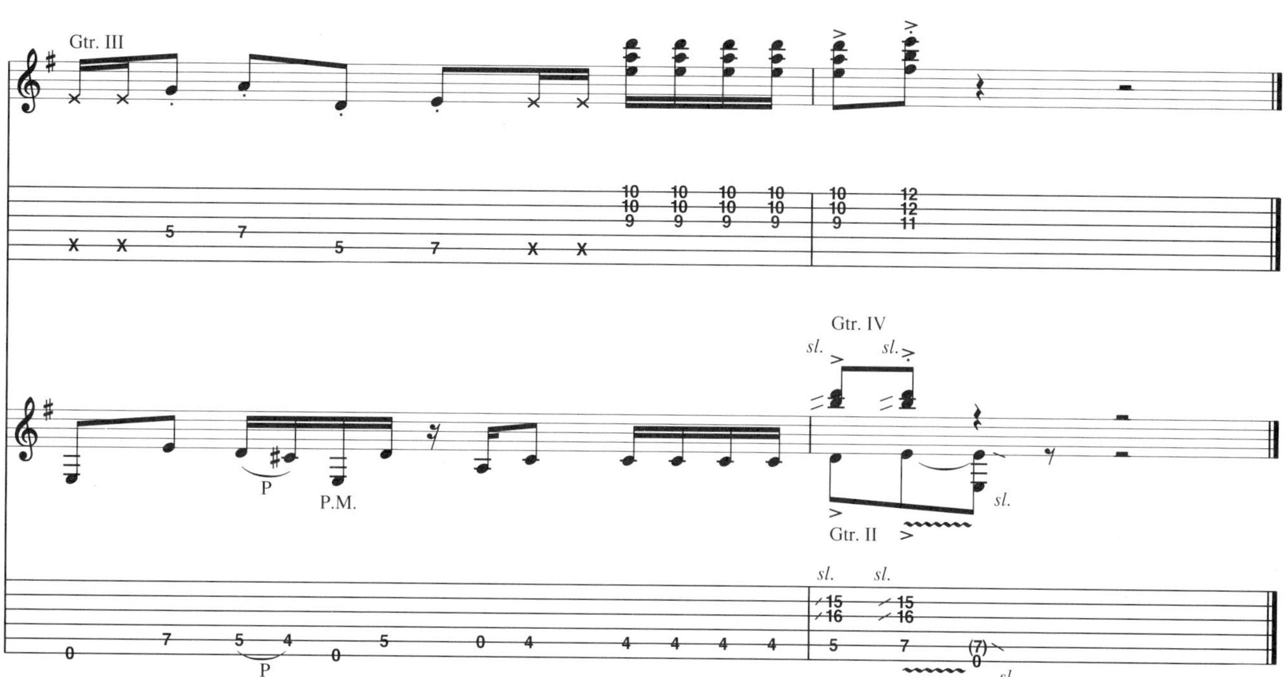

Additional Lyrics

2. And my mama said that it's good to be fruitful.
   But my mama said, "Don't take more than a mouthful."
   And my mama said that it's good to be natural.
   And my mama said that it's good to be factual. *(To Chorus)*

3. And my mama said, "Baby, don't ride that crazy horse."
   And my mama said, "You must push with much force."
   And my mama said, "Go get all that you're after."
   And my mama said that love's all that matters. *(To Chorus)*

from Journey - *Departure*

Any Way You Want It

Words and Music by Steve Perry and Neal Schon

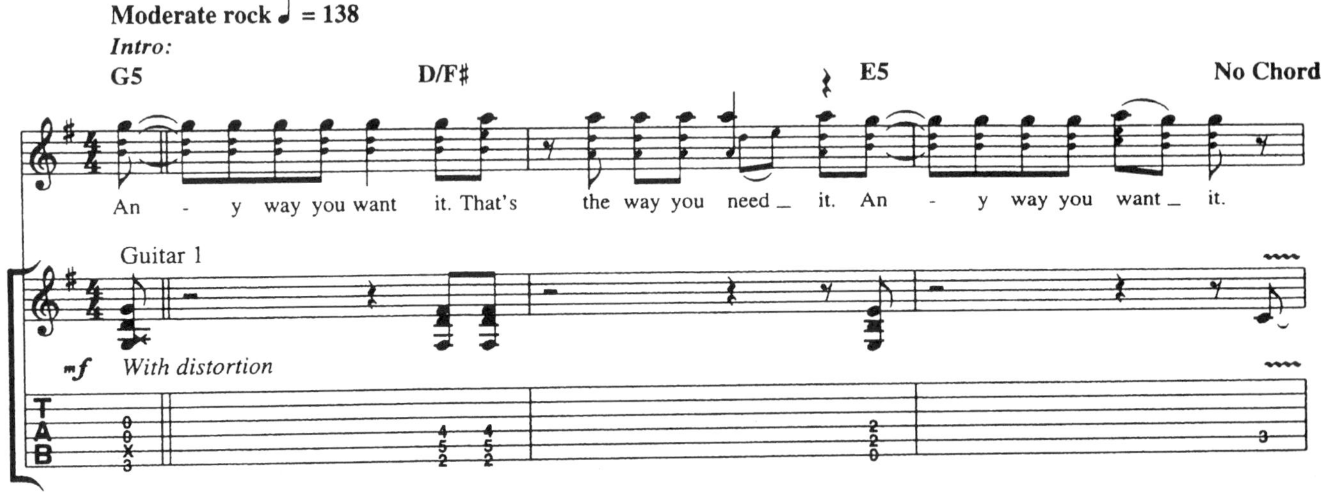

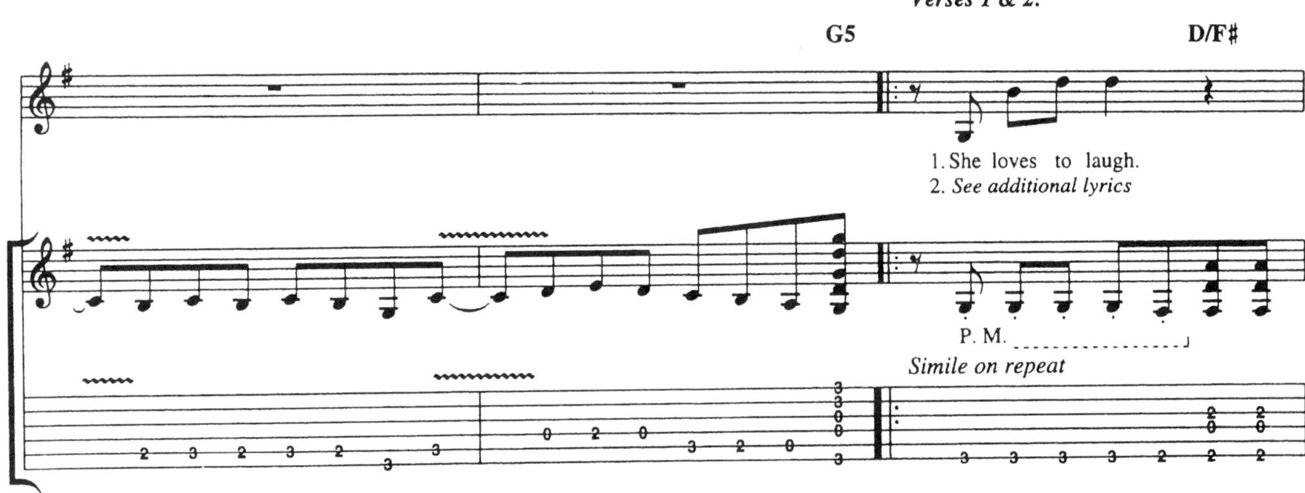

G5
D/F♯
E5
N.C.
She loves to move.
She loves to groove.
She loves the lov - in' things.
P. M.
Ooh, all night.
All night.
Oh, ev - 'ry night.
So hold tight.
Hold tight.
Ooh, ba - by, hold tight.

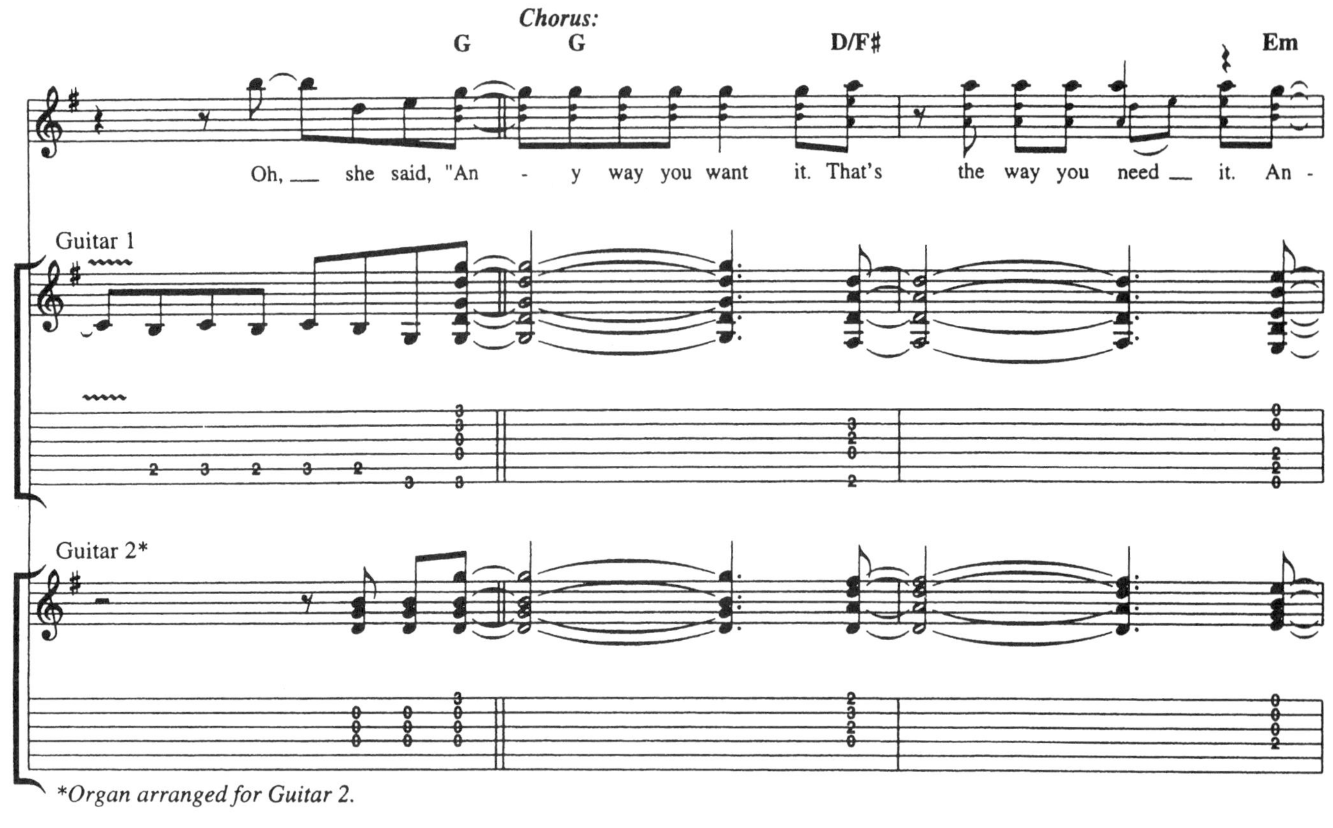

*Organ arranged for Guitar 2.

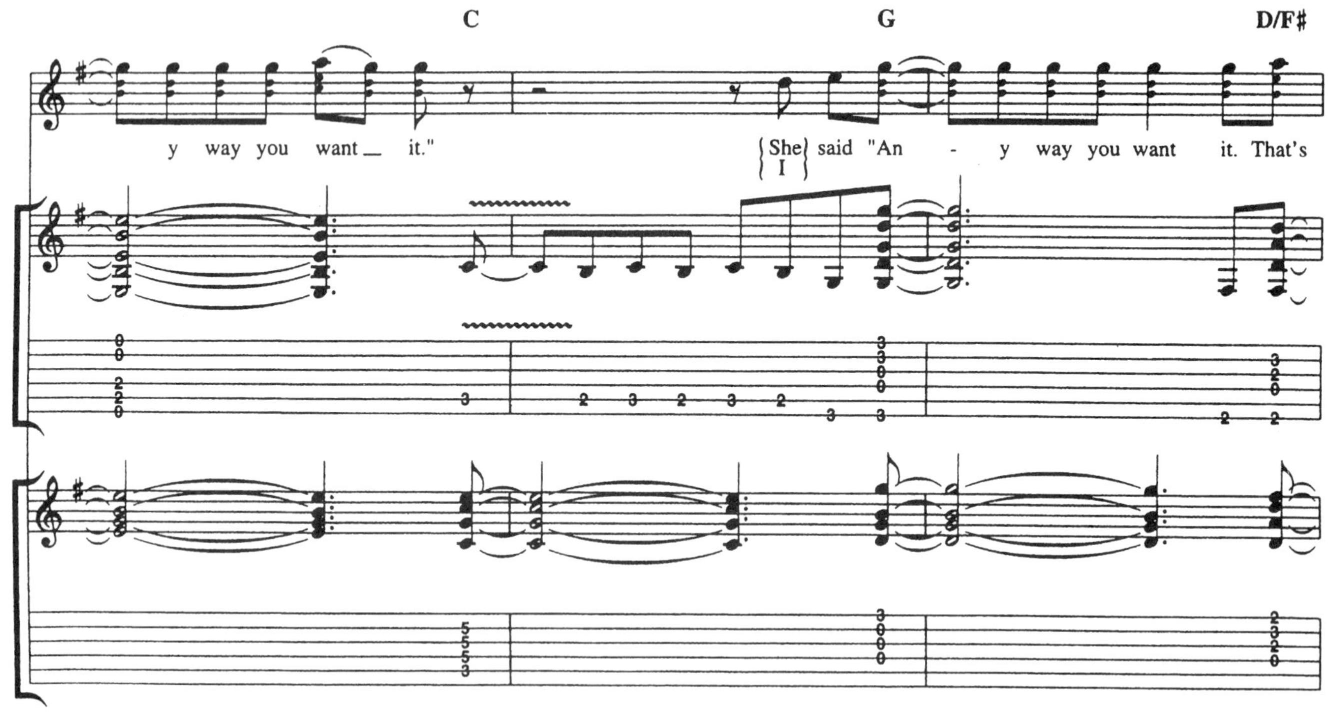

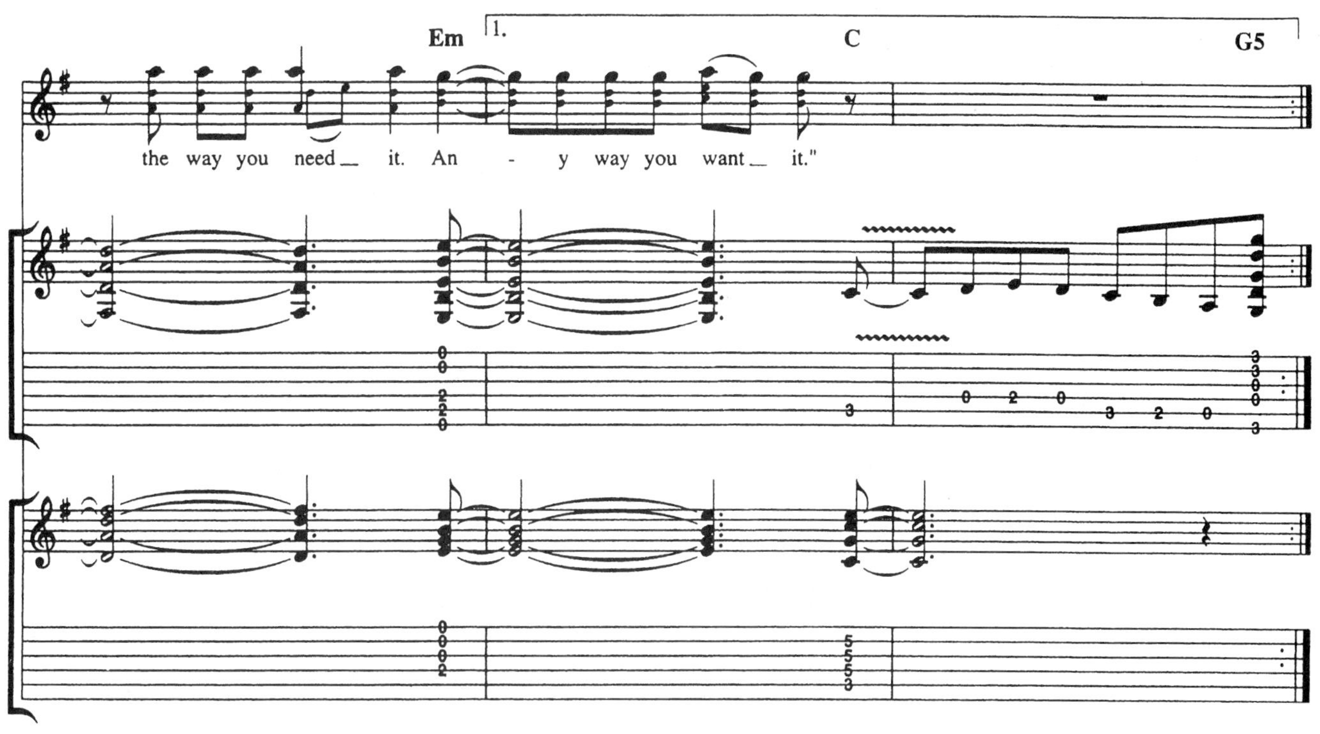
Em
1.
C
G5
the way you need_ it. An - y way you want_ it."

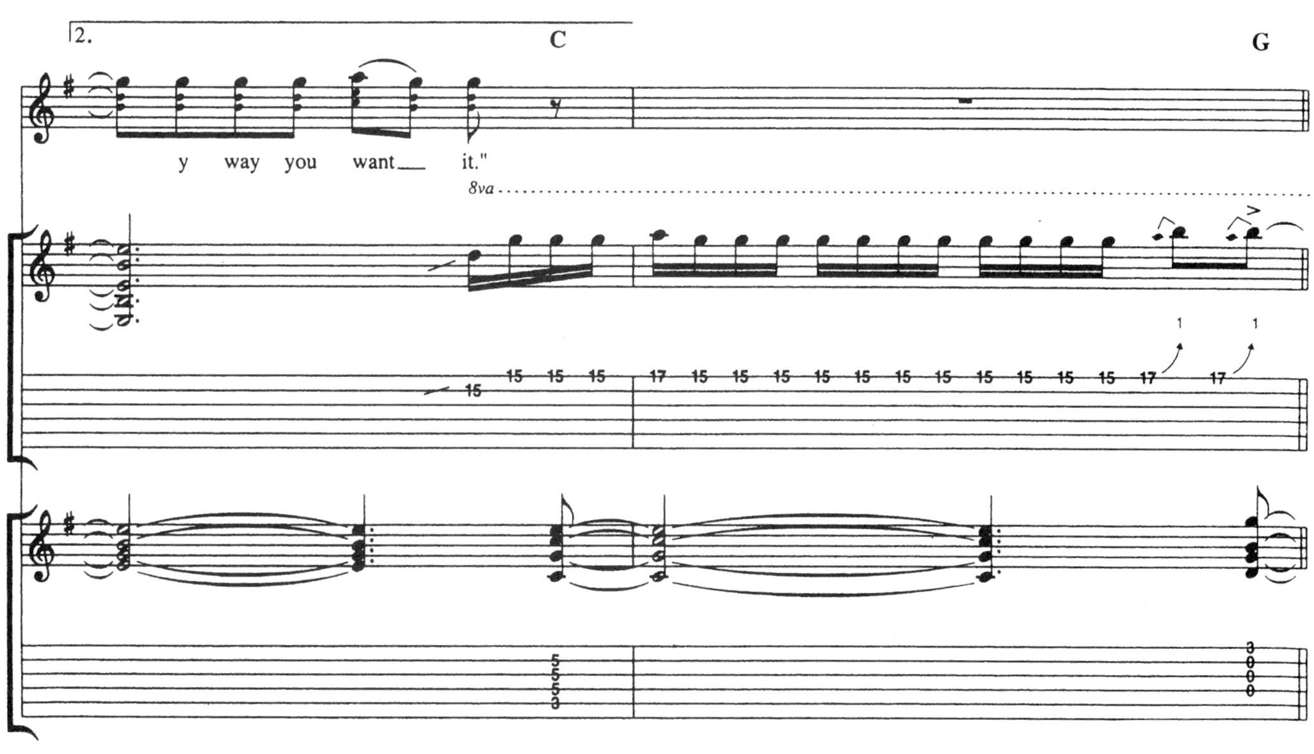
2.
C
G
y way you want_ it."
8va

Guitar Solo:
(G)
D/F#
Em
(8va)
loco
C
G
Hold bend
D/F#
Em

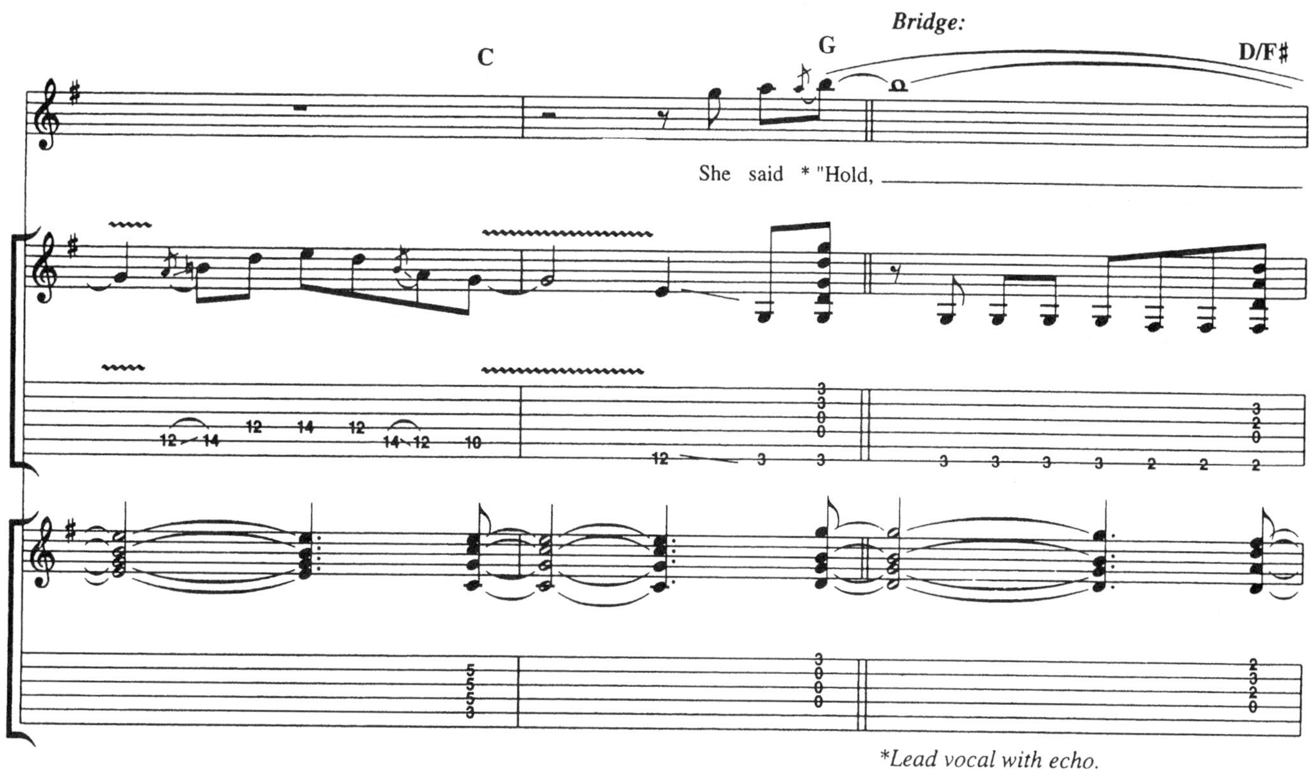

*Lead vocal with echo.

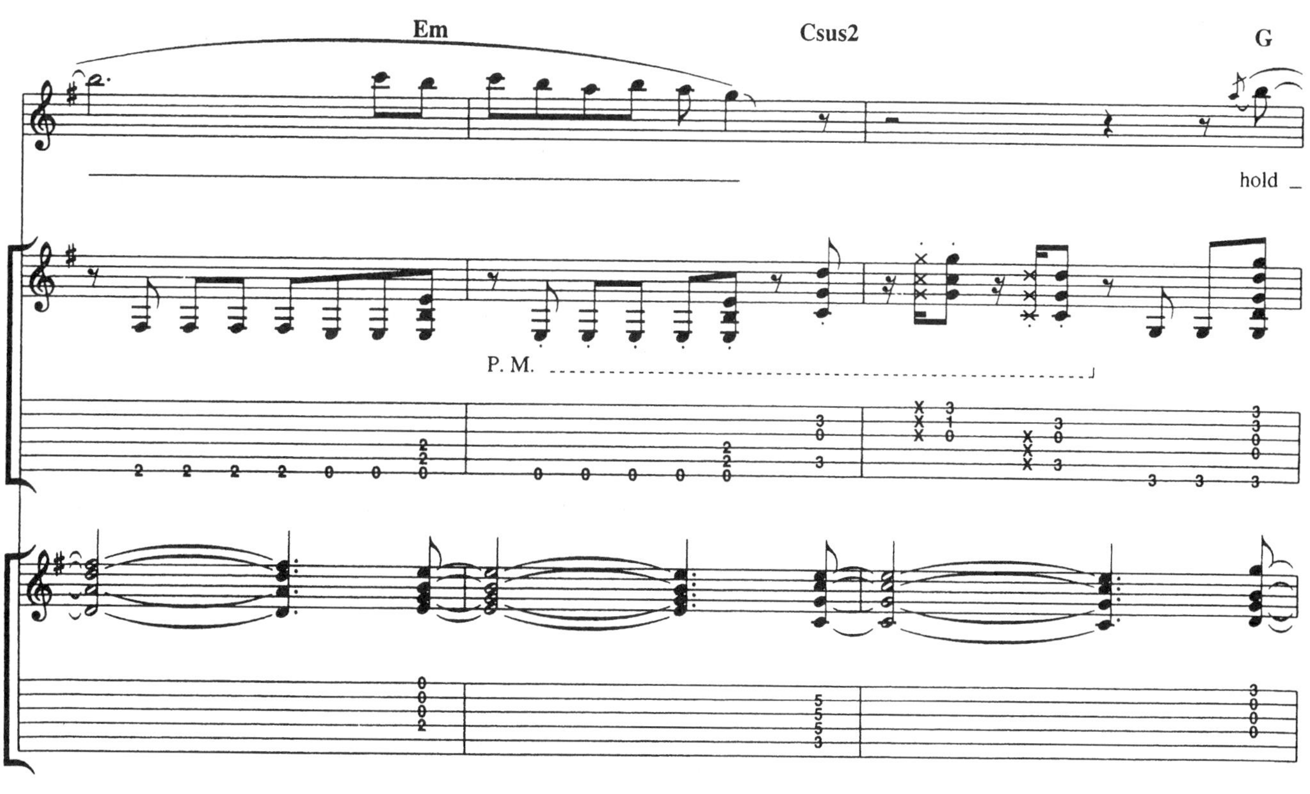

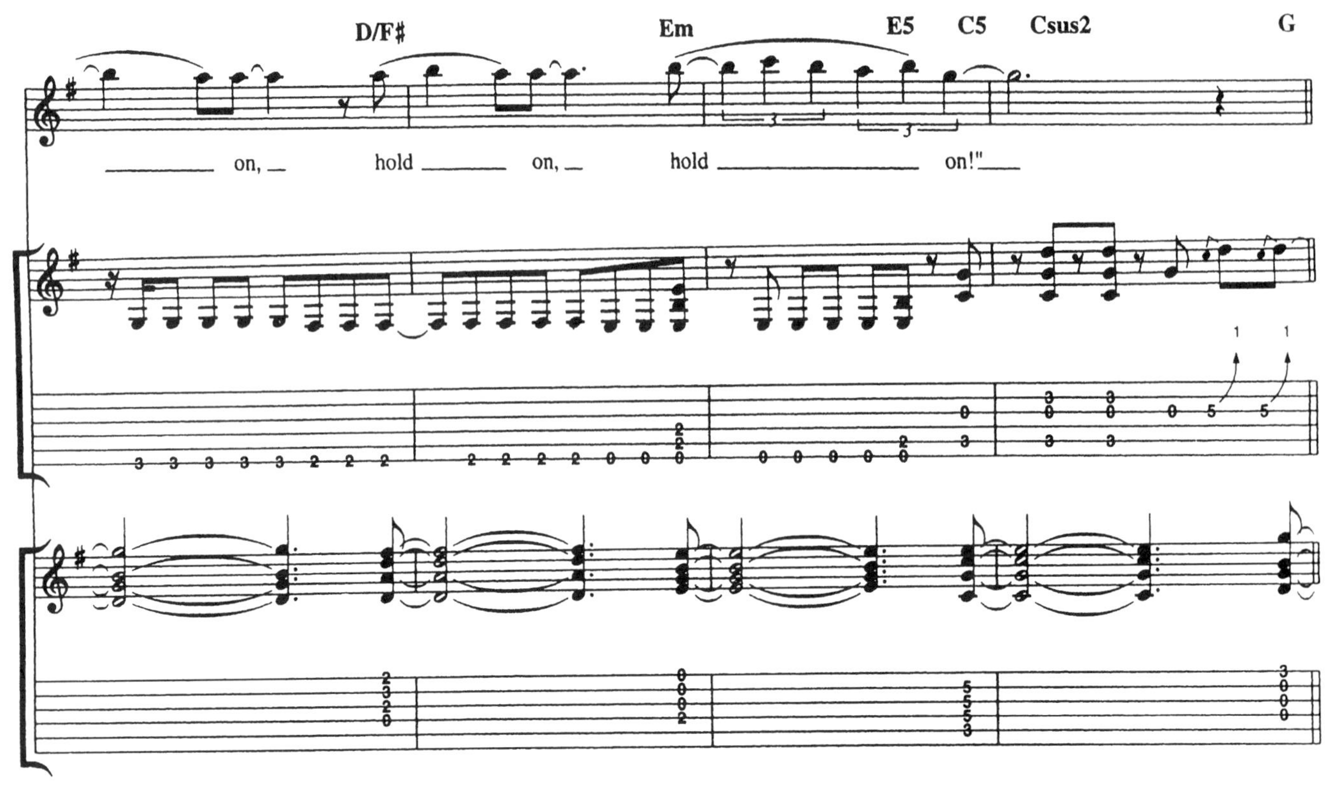

D/F♯
Em
E5
C5
Csus2
G
on,
hold
on,
hold
on!"

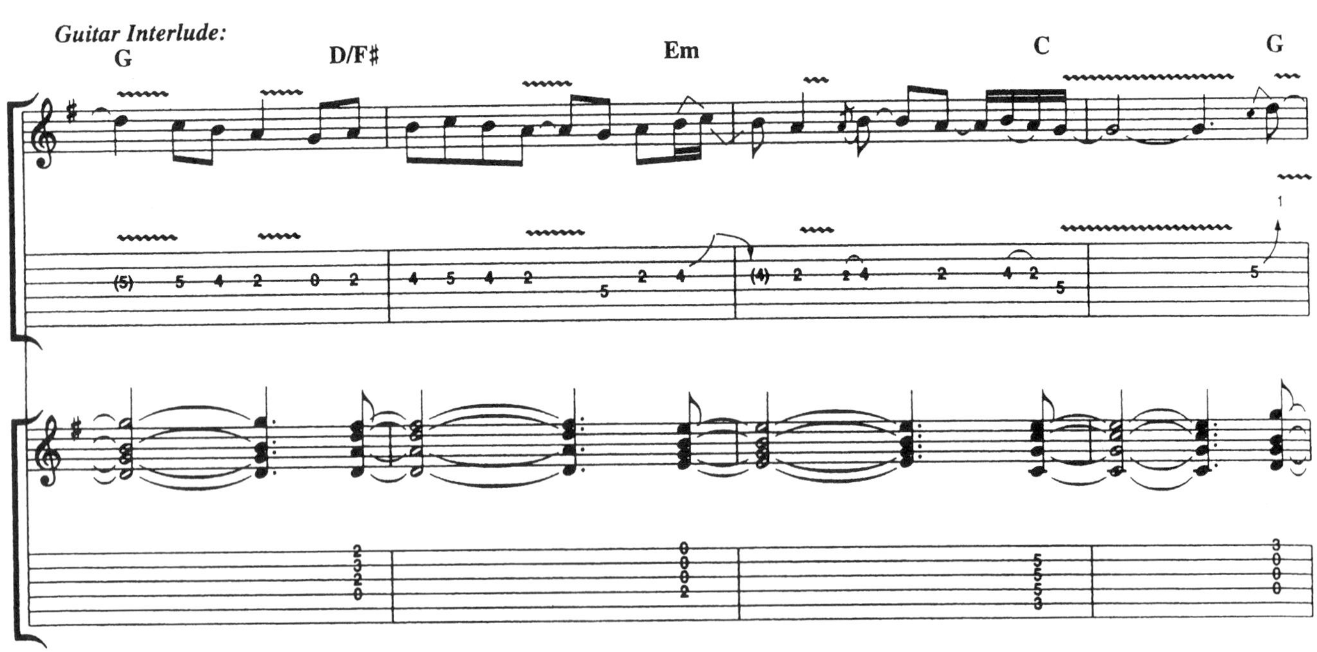

Guitar Interlude:
G
D/F♯
Em
C
G

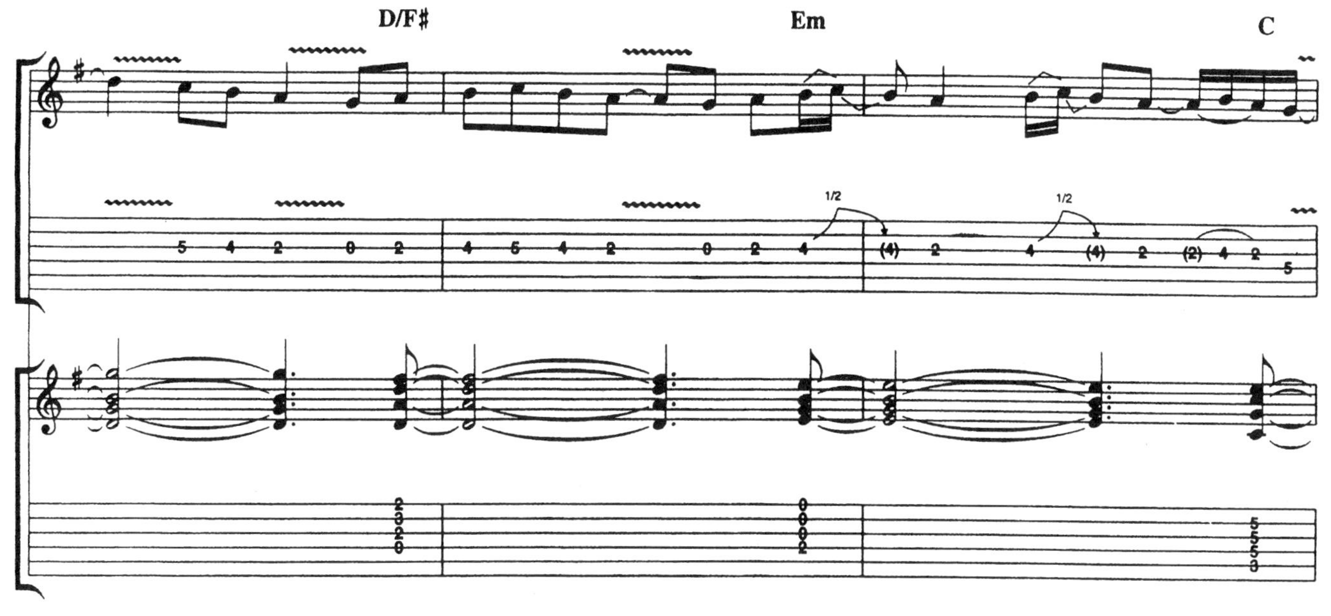
D/F♯
Em
C
1/2
1/2

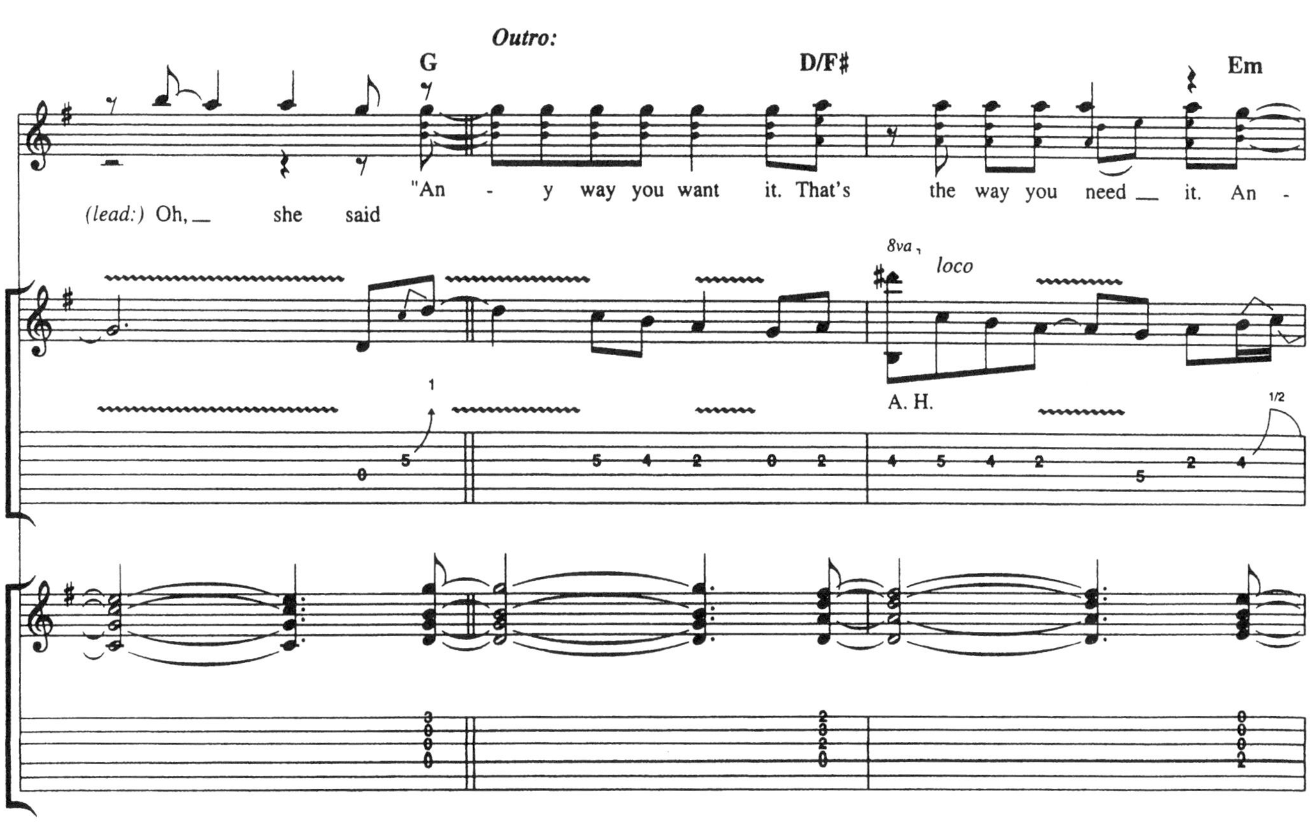
Outro:
G
D/F♯
Em
"An - y way you want it. That's the way you need it. An -
(lead:) Oh, she said
8va
loco
A. H.
1
1/2

C
G
D/F♯
y way you want it.
An - y way!
An - y way you want it. That's
Em
C
G
the way you need it. An - y way you want it."
Oh, she said
"An -
8va, loco
A. H.
1/2

G
D/F♯
Em
y way you want it. That's the way you need — it. An -
Let ring
C
G
y way you want — it.
An -

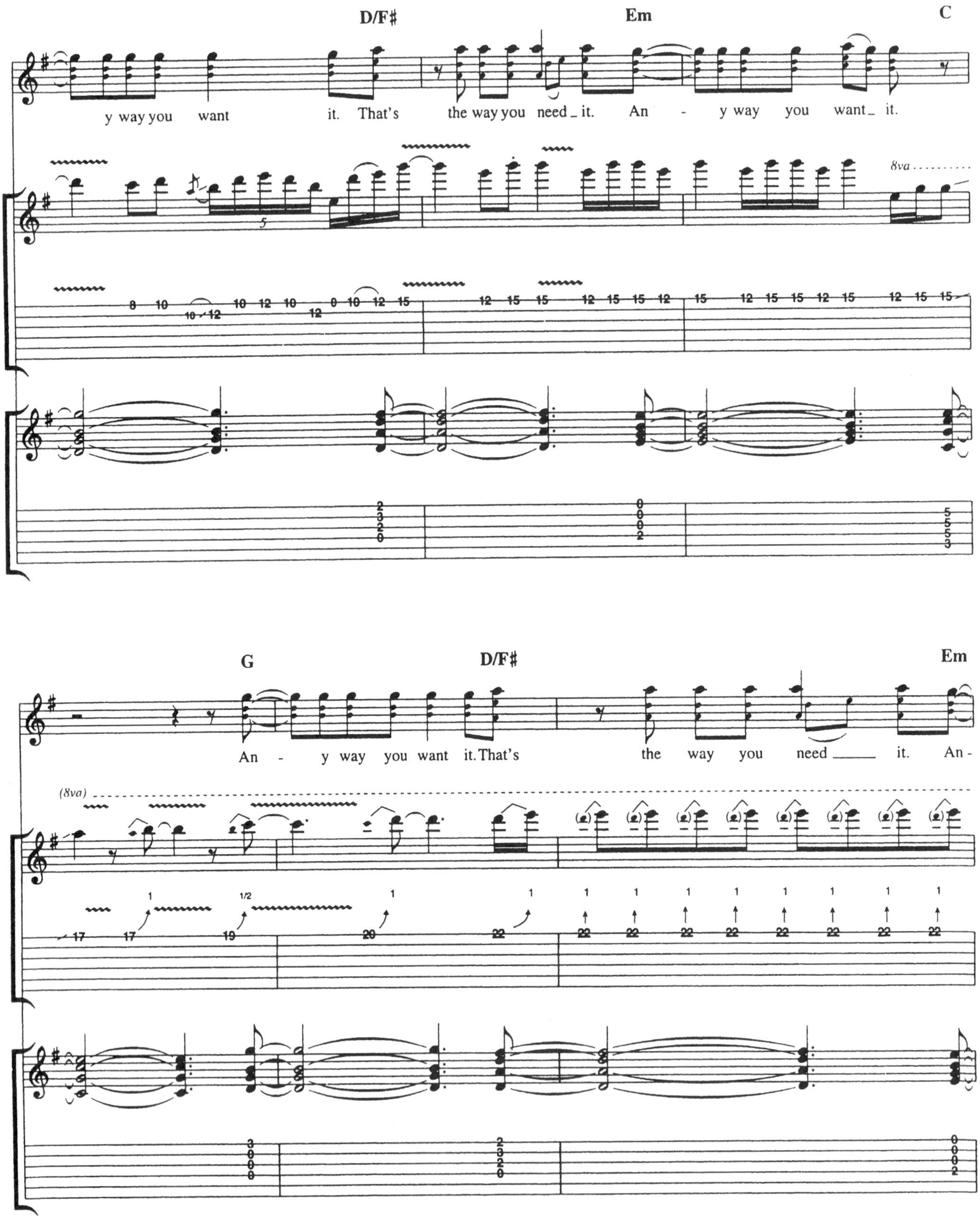

D/F♯ Em C

y way you want it. That's the way you need _ it. An - y way you want _ it.

8va

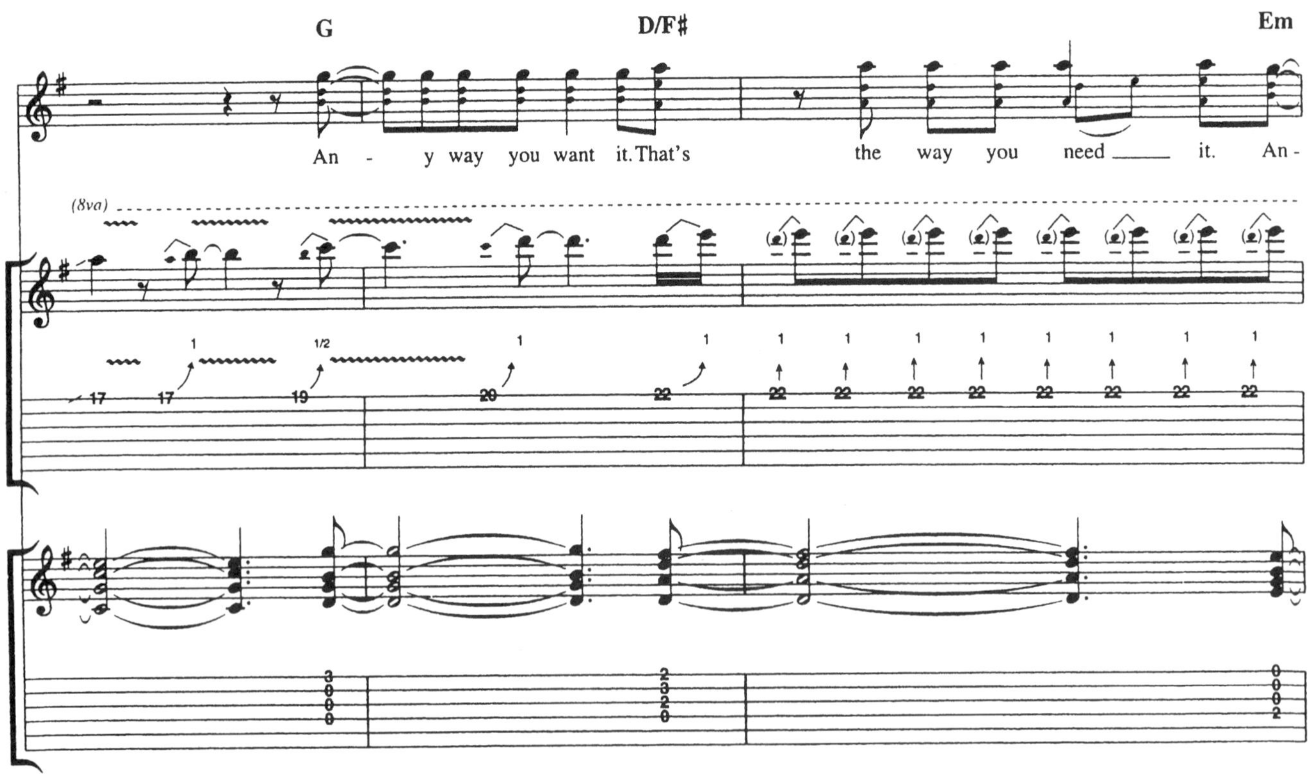

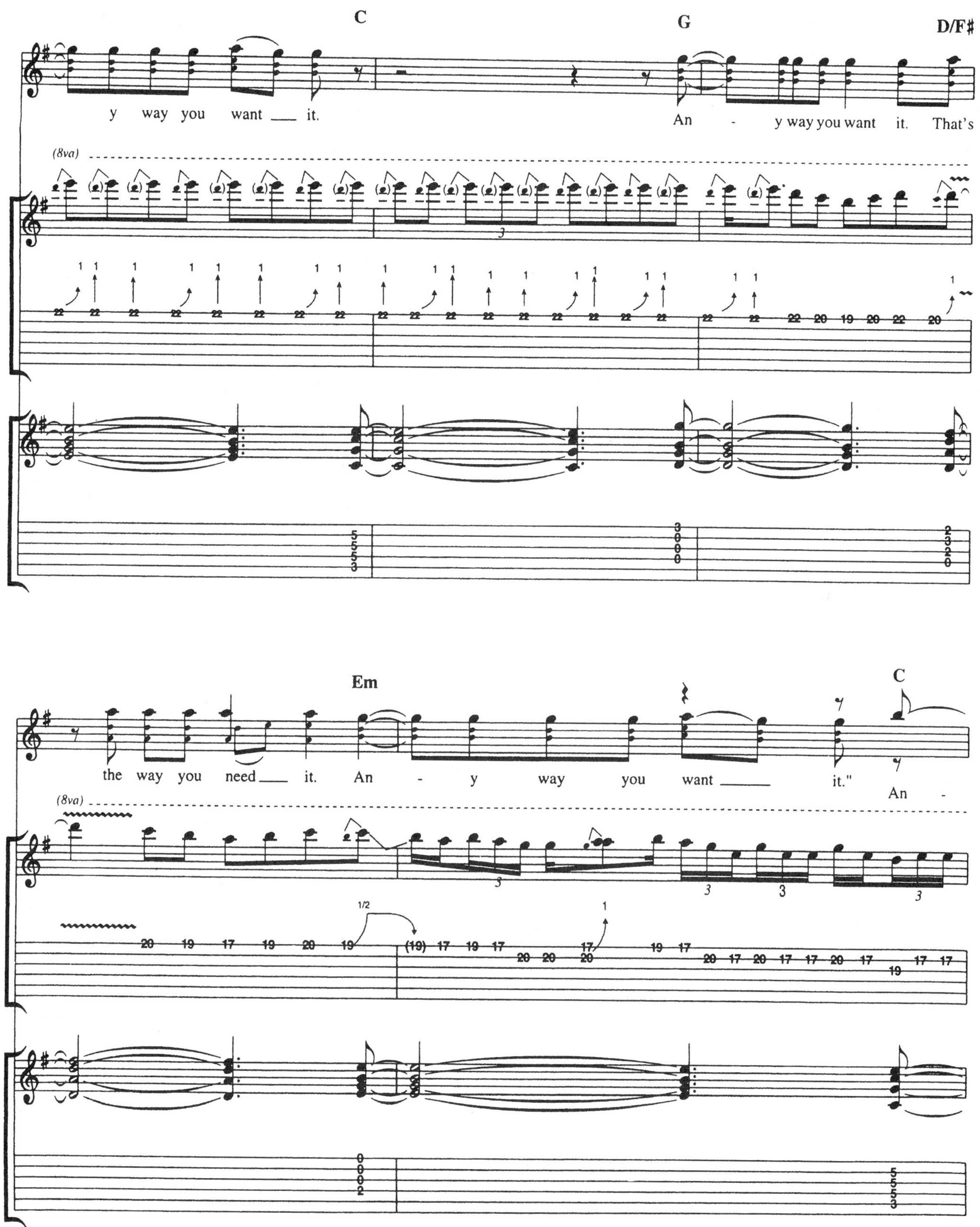
C
G
D/F♯
y way you want it.
An - y way you want it. That's
(8va)
Em
C
the way you need it. An - y way you want it."
An -
(8va)

G
D/F♯
"An - y way you want it. That's
y way!
(8va)
loco
Em
C
Start Fade
G
the way you need it. An - y way you want it."
"An-
An - y way!

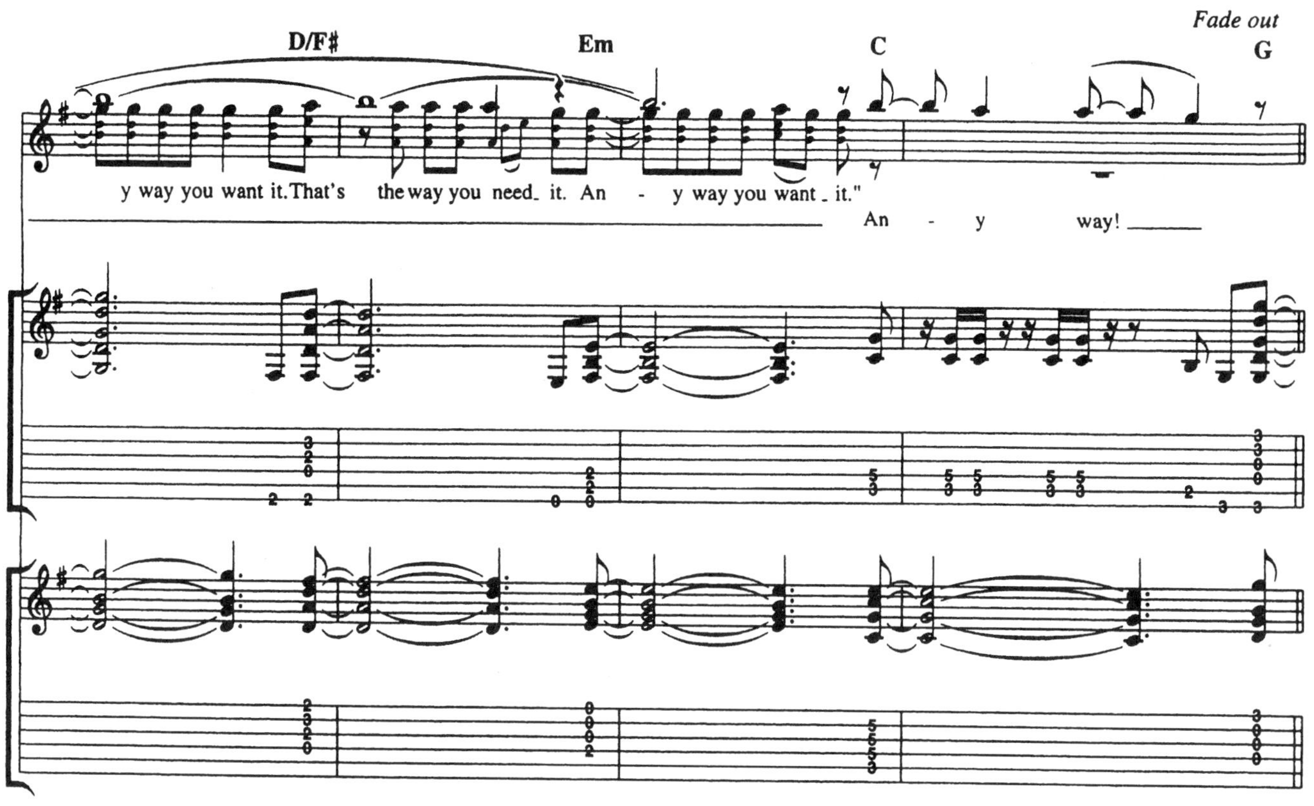

Additional Lyrics

Verse 2: I was alone,
I never knew
What good love can do.
Ooh, then we touched,
Then we sang,
About the lovin' things.

Ooh, all night, all night,
Oh, every night.
So hold tight, hold tight,
Oh, baby, hold tight.
(To chorus)

from *The Beatles (White Album)*

Back in the U.S.S.R.

Words and Music by John Lennon and Paul McCartney

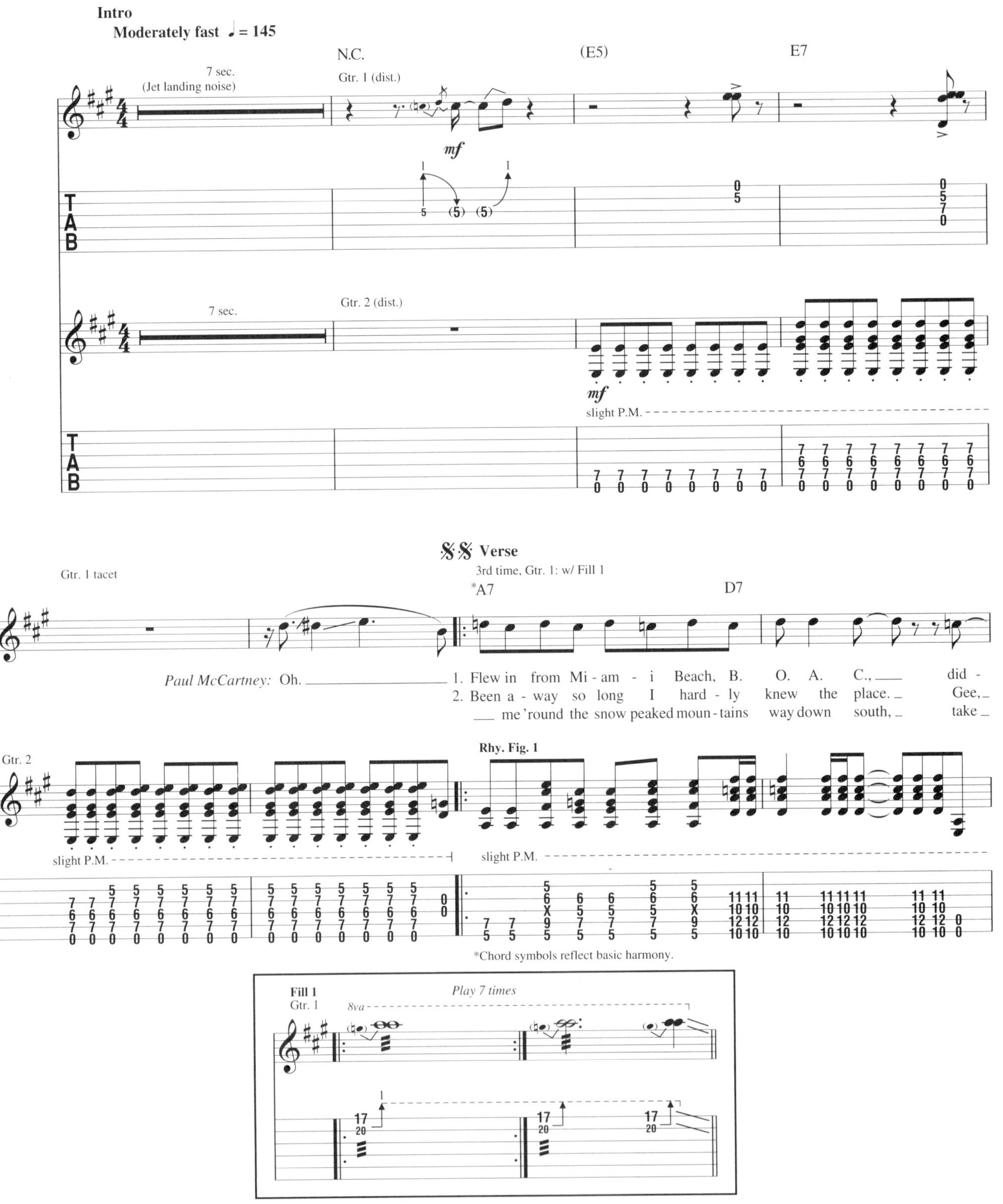

*Chord symbols reflect basic harmony.

C
D7
A7
- n't get to bed last night.
it's good to be back home.
me to your dad-dy's farm.
On the way the pa - per bag was
Leave it 'til to - mor-row to un -
Let me hear your bal - a - lai - kas
slight P.M.
D7
C
D7
on my knee, man, I had a dread-ful flight.
pack my case. Hon - ey, dis - con - nect the phone.
ring - ing out. Come and keep your com-rade warm.
I'm back in the U. S. S. R.,
End Rhy. Fig. 1
slight P.M.
1.
Chorus
A7
C7
D7
you don't know how luck - y you are, boy,
Gtr. 1
Riff A
End Riff A
Gtr. 2
Rhy. Fig. 2
End Rhy. Fig. 2
slight P.M.
Gtr. 3
Riff A1
End Riff A1
(cont. on upper staff)

To Coda 2 

N.C. Gtr. 3 tacet A7 D7 D♯7 E7

back in the U. S. S. R. Ah, let me tell you, hon - ey.

Gtr. 1

Gtr. 3 *divisi*

Gtr. 2

let ring

slight P.M.

P.M.

2.

D E7 A♭add9 Gadd9 Gtr. 3 tacet A5

boy, back in the U. S., back in the U. S., back in the U. S. S. R.

slight P.M.

slight P.M.

Bridge
A7
B5
C5
C#5
D7
Well, the U - kraine girls real-ly knock me out, they
(Da, da, da. Da, da. Da, da. Da, da.
(Oo.
Gtr. 1
Gtr. 2
slight P.M.
To Coda 1
A7
D7
C#7
C7
B7
leave the west be - hind. And Mos - cow girls make me sing and shout that
Da, da. Da, da, da, da. da, da. Da, da. Da, da.
Oo.)
slight P.M.

Gtr. 1 tacet
E7
D7
A
B
E7
Geor-gia's al-ways on my, my, my, my, my, my, my, my, my mind.
Oh, come on!
Da, da, da, da.)
Gtr. 2
slight P.M.
*Bkgd. Voc. sung ahead of the beat.
Guitar Solo
Voc.: w/ ad lib. shouts
Gtr. 2: w/ Rhy. Fig. 1
A7
D7
C
D7
A7
Gtr. 1
D7
C7
D7
Yeah, I'm back in the U. S. S. R.,
Chorus
Gtrs. 1 & 3: w/ Riffs A & A1
Gtr. 2: w/ Rhy. Fig. 2
A7
C7
D7
you don't know how luck - y you are, boys,

D.S. al Coda 1
Gtr. 3 tacet
N.C.
A
A7
back in the U. S. S. R.
Well, the
(Da, da, da.
Gtr. 1
Gtr. 1
Gtr. 3
divisi
Gtr. 2
slight P.M.
Coda 1
D.S.S. al Coda 2
(take 1st ending)
Gtr. 1 tacet
E7
D7
A
B E7
Geor-gia's al-ways on my, my, my, my, my, my, my, my, my mind.
Oh.
3. Show
Da, da, da, da, da, da, da, da.)
hoo, hoo, hoo.)
Gtr. 2
slight P.M.

Coda 2
Outro
Lead Voc.: w/ ad lib. shouts
A7
Hey, I'm _ back!
(Oo.)
Gtr. 1
p
mf
Gtr. 2
sim.
slight P.M.
Gtr. 3
(Jet noise)
4 sec.

From Creedence Clearwater Revival - *Green River*

Bad Moon Rising

Words and Music by John Fogerty

Gtrs. 1, 4 & 5: Tune down 1 step:
(low to high) D-G-C-F-A-D

*Symbols in parentheses represent chord names respective to detuned guitars. Symbols above reflect actual sounding chords.

Verse

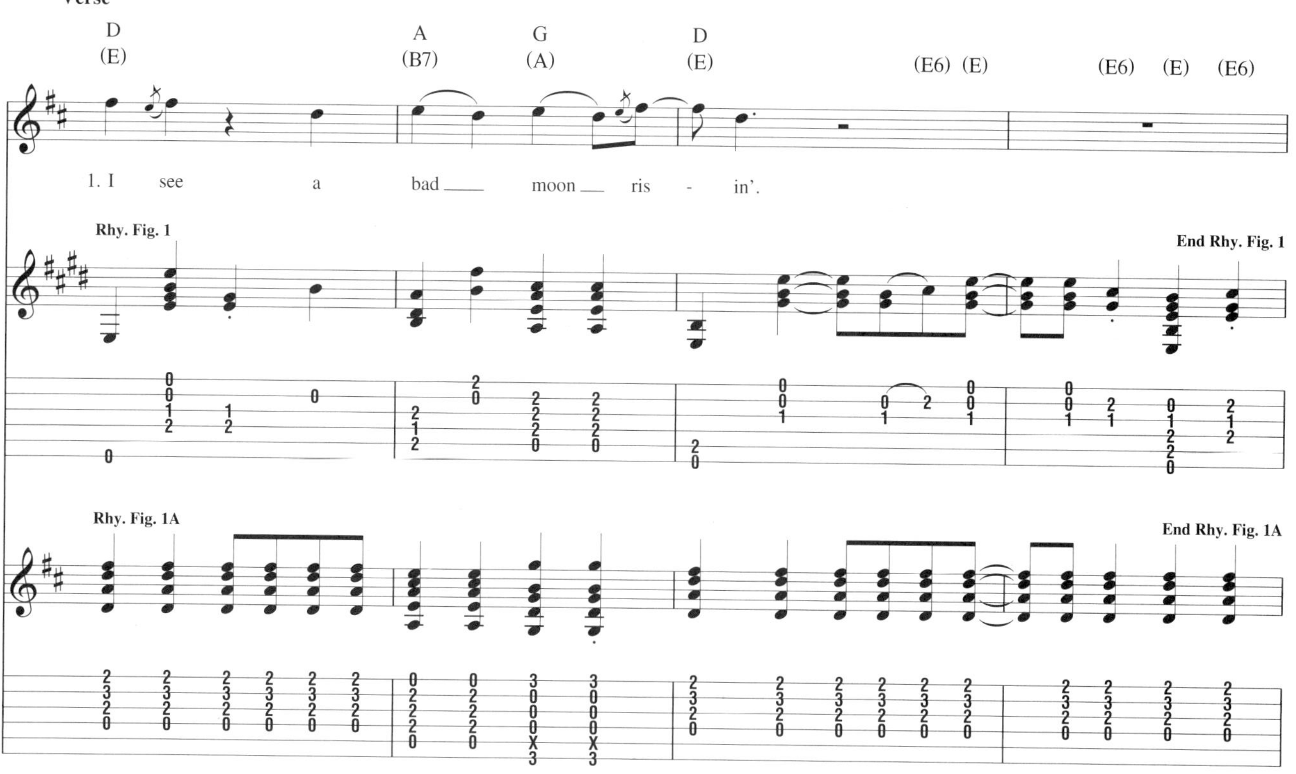

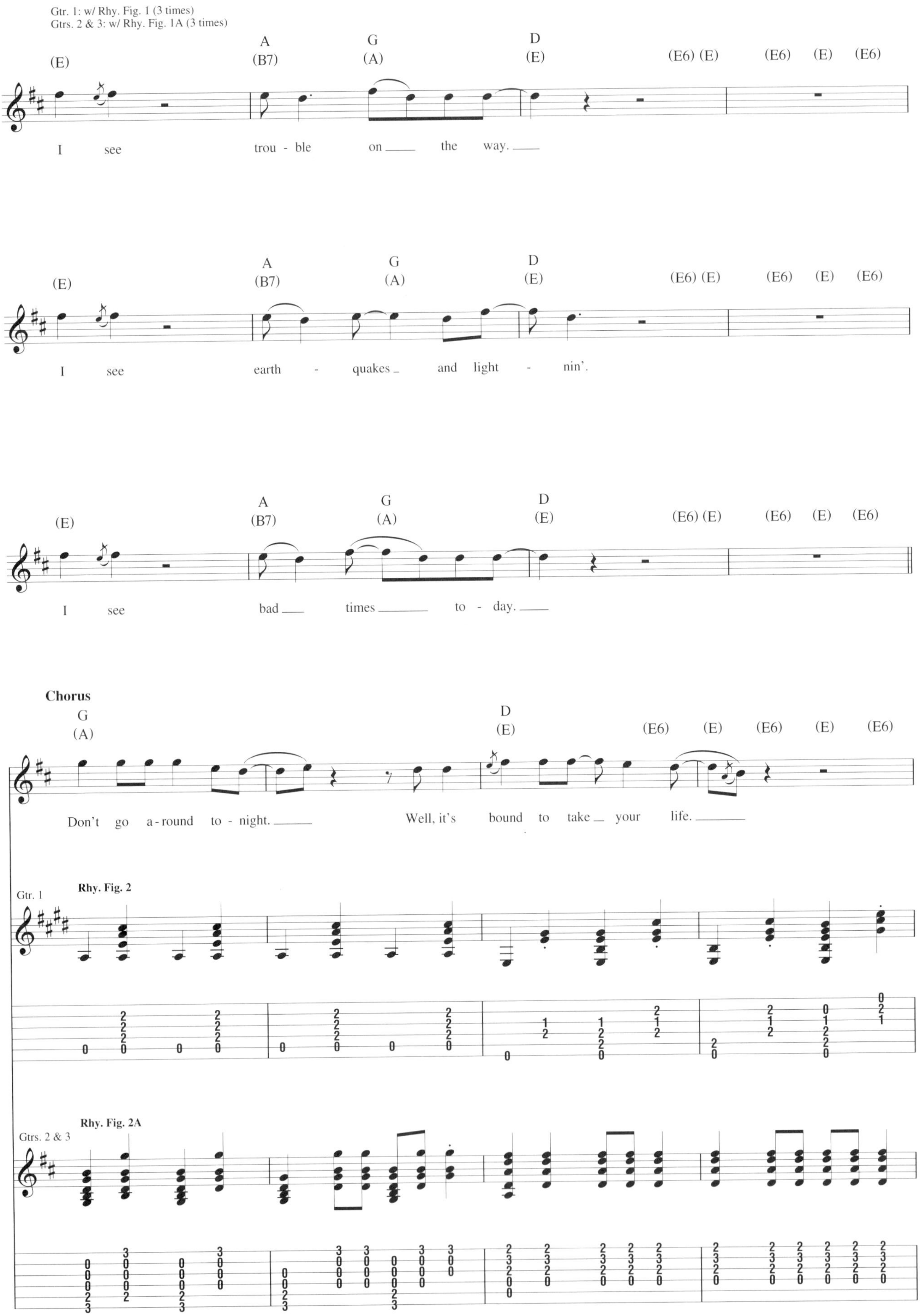

Gtr. 1: w/ Rhy. Fig. 1 (3 times)
Gtrs. 2 & 3: w/ Rhy. Fig. 1A (3 times)

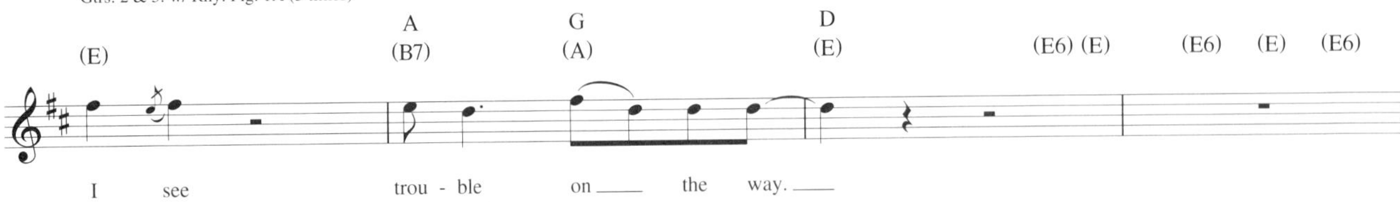

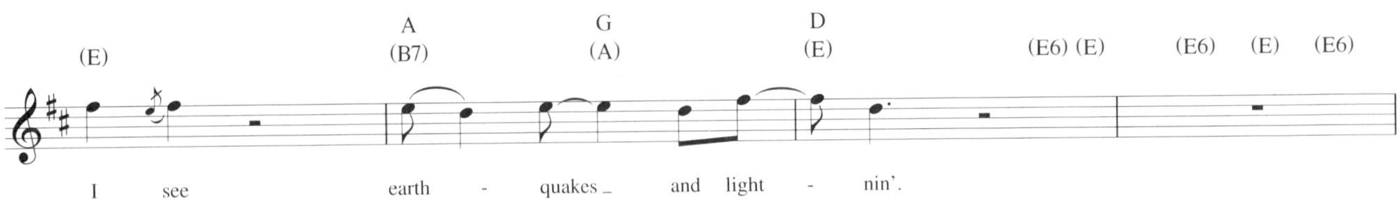

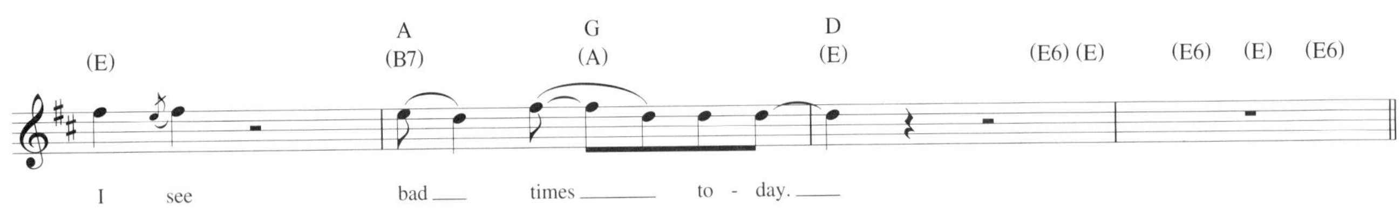

Chorus

G (A) D (E) (E6) (E) (E6) (E) (E6)

Don't go a - round to - night. Well, it's bound to take your life.

Gtr. 1 **Rhy. Fig. 2**

Gtrs. 2 & 3 **Rhy. Fig. 2A**

A
(B7)
G
(A)
D
(E)
(E6) (E)
(E6) (E) (E6)
There's a bad moon on the rise.
End Rhy. Fig. 2
End Rhy. Fig. 2A
Verse
Gtr. 1: w/ Rhy. Fig. 1 (4 times)
Gtrs. 2 & 3: w/ Rhy. Fig. 1A (4 times)
D
(E)
A
(B7)
G
(A)
D
(E)
(E6) (E)
(E6) (E) (E6)
2. I hear hur - ri - canes a blow - in'.
Gtr. 4 (elec.)
mf
w/ clean tone
(E)
A
(B7)
G
(A)
D
(E)
(E6) (E)
(E6) (E) (E6)
I know the end is com - in' soon.
Riff A
End Riff A

Gtr. 4: w/ Riff A
A G D
(E) (B7) (A) (E) (E6) (E) (E6) (E) (E6)
I fear riv - ers o - ver - flow - in'.
A G D
(E) (B7) (A) (E) (E6) (E) (E6) (E) (E6)
I hear the voice of rage and ru - in.
Gtr. 4
Chorus
Gtr. 1: w/ Rhy. Fig. 2
Gtrs. 2 & 3: w/ Rhy. Fig. 2A
Gtr. 4 tacet
G D
(A) (E) (E6) (E) (E6) (E) (E6)
Don't go a - round to - night. Well, it's bound to take your life.
A G D
(B7) (A) (E) (E6) (E) (E6) (E) (E6)
There's a bad moon on the rise. Al - right.
Gtr. 5 (elec.)
mf
w/ clean tone
Guitar Solo
Gtr. 1: w/ Rhy. Fig. 1 (2 times)
Gtrs. 2 & 3: w/ Rhy. Fig. 1A (2 times)
D A G D
Gtr. 5 (E) (B7) (A) (E) (E6) (E) (E6) (E) (E6)
Gtr. 4
mp

(E)
A
(B7)
G
(A)
D
(E)
(E6) (E)
(E6)
(E)
(E6)
Gtr. 1: w/ Rhy. Fig. 2
Gtrs. 2 & 3: w/ Rhy. Fig. 2A
Gtr. 4 tacet
G
(A)
Gtr. 5
D
(E)
(E6)
(E)
(E6)
(E)
(E6)
A
(B7)
G
(A)
D
(E)
(E6) (E)
(E6)
(E)
(E6)
Verse
Gtr. 1: w/ Rhy. Fig. 1 (4 times)
Gtrs. 2 & 3: w/ Rhy. Fig. 1A (4 times)
Gtr. 5 tacet
D
(E)
A
(B7)
G
(A)
D
(E)
(E6)(E)
(E6)
(E)
(E6)
3. Hope you got your things to - geth - er.
Gtr. 4

(E)
A
(B7)
G
(A)
D
(E)
(E6) (E)
(E6) (E) (E6)
Hope you are quite pre - pared to die.
(E)
A
(B7)
G
(A)
D
(E)
(E6) (E)
(E6) (E) (E6)
Looks like we're in for nas - ty weath - er.
(E)
A
(B7)
G
(A)
D
(E)
(E6)(E)
(E6) (E) (E6)
One eye is tak - en for an eye.
Well,
Chorus
Gtr. 1: w/ Rhy. Fig. 2 (1 6/8 times)
Gtrs. 2 & 3: w/ Rhy. Fig. 2A (1 6/8 times)
G
(A)
D
(E)
(E6) (E) (E6) (E) (E6)
don't go a-round to - night.
Well, it's bound to take your life.

A (B7) G (A) D (E) (E6) (E) (E6) (E) (E6)
There's a bad moon on the rise.
G (A) D (E) (E6) (E) (E6) (E) (E6)
Don't come a-round to-night. Well, it's bound to take your life.
mf
Gtr. 4 tacet
A (B7) G (A) D (E) (E6) (E)
There's a bad moon on the rise.
Gtr. 4
mp
Gtr. 1
Gtrs. 2 & 3

from Rory Gallagher - *Top Priority*

Bad Penny

Words and Music by Rory Gallagher

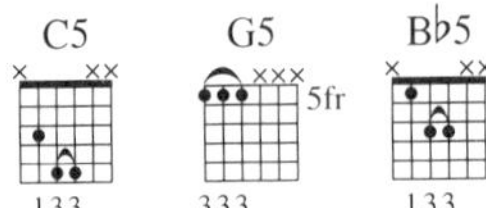

Gtr. 2: Open Dsus4 tuning:
(low to high) D-A-D-G-A-D

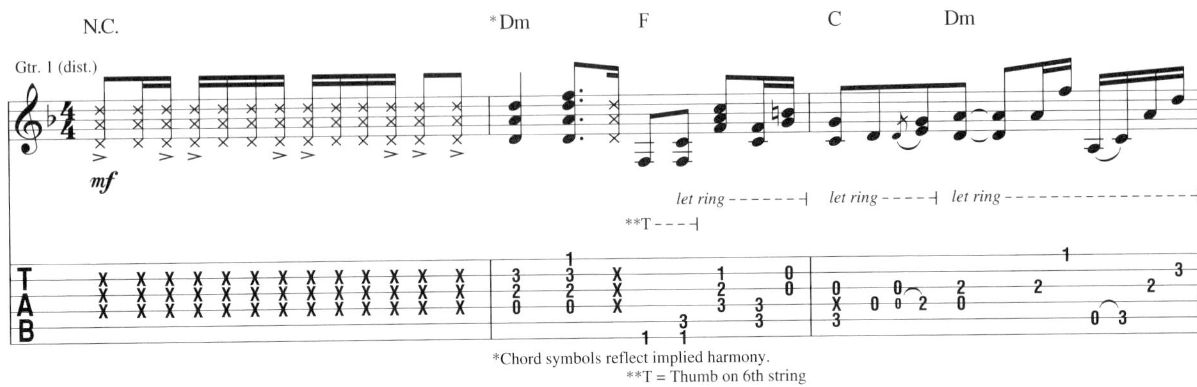

*Chord symbols reflect implied harmony.
**T = Thumb on 6th string

F C Dm F

Gtr. 3 (dist.)

f

Gtr. 1

let ring
let ring
let ring
let ring
let ring
T
T

Gtr. 2
(clean)

mf
w/ phaser
let ring throughout
Harm.

C
Dm
F
C
Dm
1. Well, like a
slight P.H.
slight P.H.
let ring
let ring
let ring
let ring
Rhy. Fig. 1
End Rhy. Fig. 1
Verse
Gtr. 2: w/ Rhy. Fig. 1 (4 times)
Dm
F
Gtr. 3 tacet
C
Dm
bad pen - ny you
turned up a - gain.
Gtr. 3
Rhy. Fig. 2
Gtr. 1
End Rhy. Fig. 2
let ring
let ring
let ring
let ring

Gtr. 1: w/ Rhy. Fig. 2 (2 1/2 times)
F
C
Dm
F
You're in my sights, there's a mist on my lens. I think you know how it was when
C
Dm
F
I tripped and fell. Well, you double-dealed me, baby, and I
Interlude
Gtr. 2: w/ Rhy. Fig. 1 (2 times)
C
Dm
Dm
F
broke like a shell. Hey.
Gtr. 3
8va
Gtr. 1
let ring
let ring
C
Dm
F
C
Dm
2. Well, like a
8va

Verse

Gtr. 1: w/ Rhy. Fig. 2 (4 times)
Gtr. 2: w/ Rhy. Fig. 1 (4 times)

Dm F C Dm F

bad pen-ny you _ sure lost the glow. _ But I'm out of reach, _ your

8va
Gtr. 3

(19) | 20 20 18 20 18 19 | 19 (19)

C Dm F C Dm

smile's sure gone cold. _ Well, it can't _ ev-er be _ like it was then. _ Well, don't you

8va

20 20 | 20 (20) X X | 20 (20) 18 20 18 19 17

F C Dm

fool _ with me, ba - by. Well, don't you mess with my plans. _ Yeah!

8va loco

P.H.

19 (19) | 8 8 8 6 8 6 7 5

C Dm F C Dm

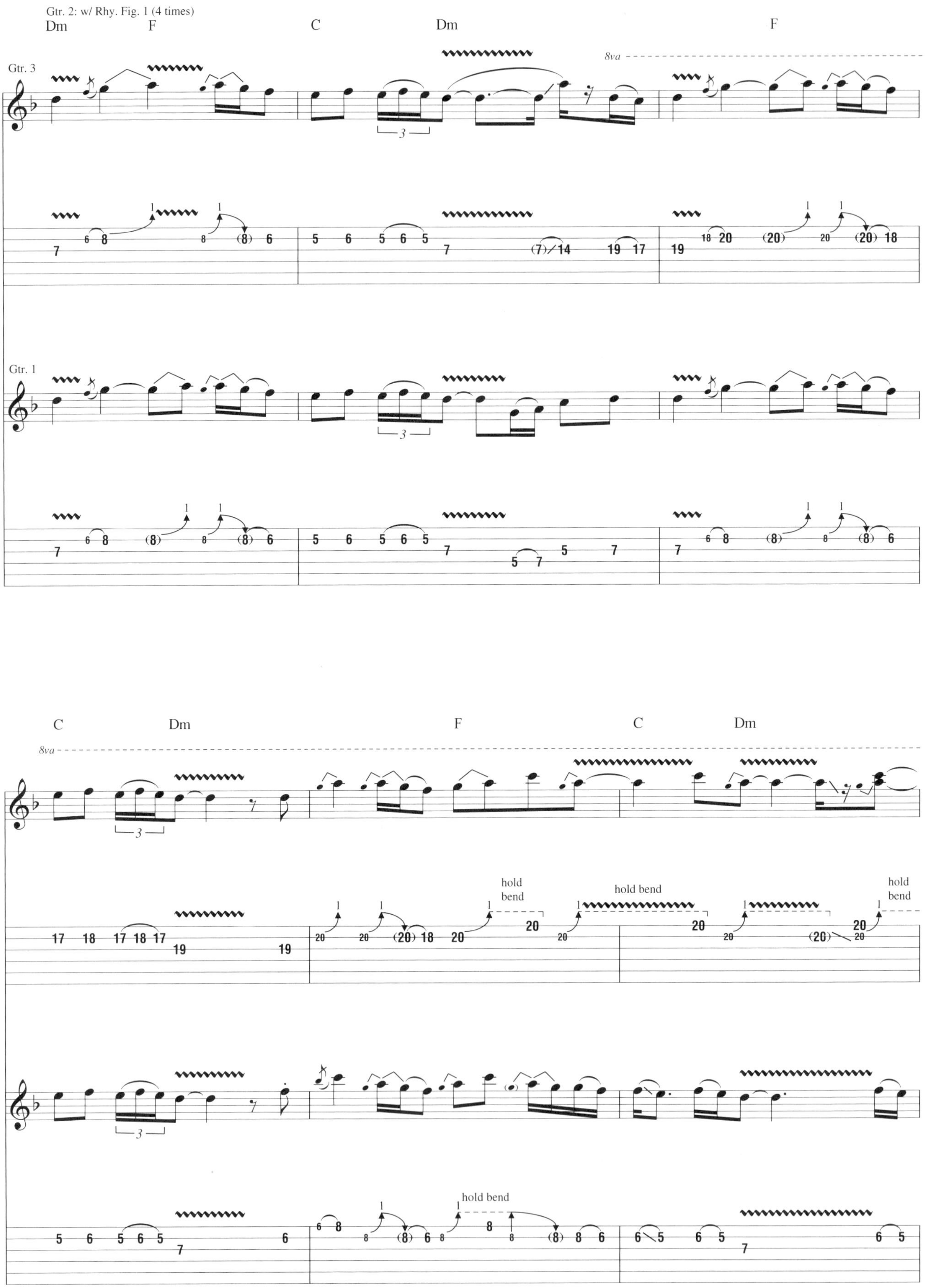

8va

hold bend

hold bend

hold bend

hold bend

𝄋 Bridge

2nd time, Gtr. 3: w/ Fill 1

F C Dm *C5 G5

Gtr. 2

Some storm - y nights
Some lone - ly nights

8va loco

*See top of first page of song for chord diagrams pertaining to rhythm slashes.

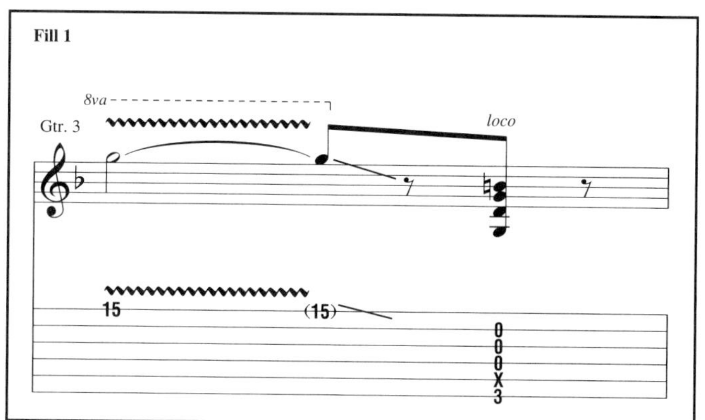

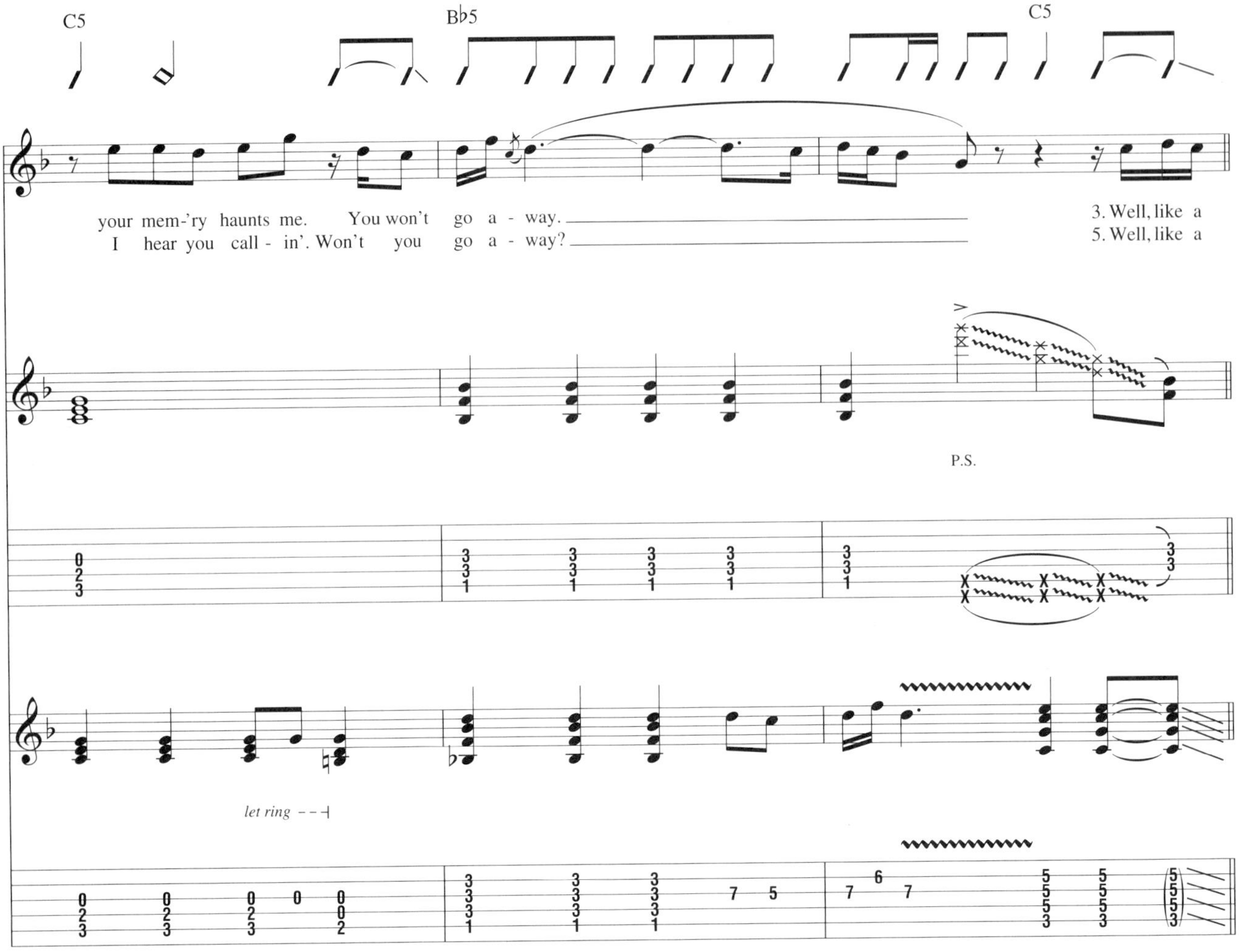

C5
B♭5
C5
your mem-'ry haunts me. You won't go a - way.
I hear you call - in'. Won't you go a - way?
3. Well, like a
5. Well, like a
P.S.
let ring

Verse

Gtr. 2: w/ Rhy. Fig. 1 (4 times)
Gtr. 3 tacet
Dm
F
C
Dm
bad pen - ny you turned up in the change. Try to
bad pen - ny you turned up a - gain.
Gtr. 1
let ring
let ring
let ring
T

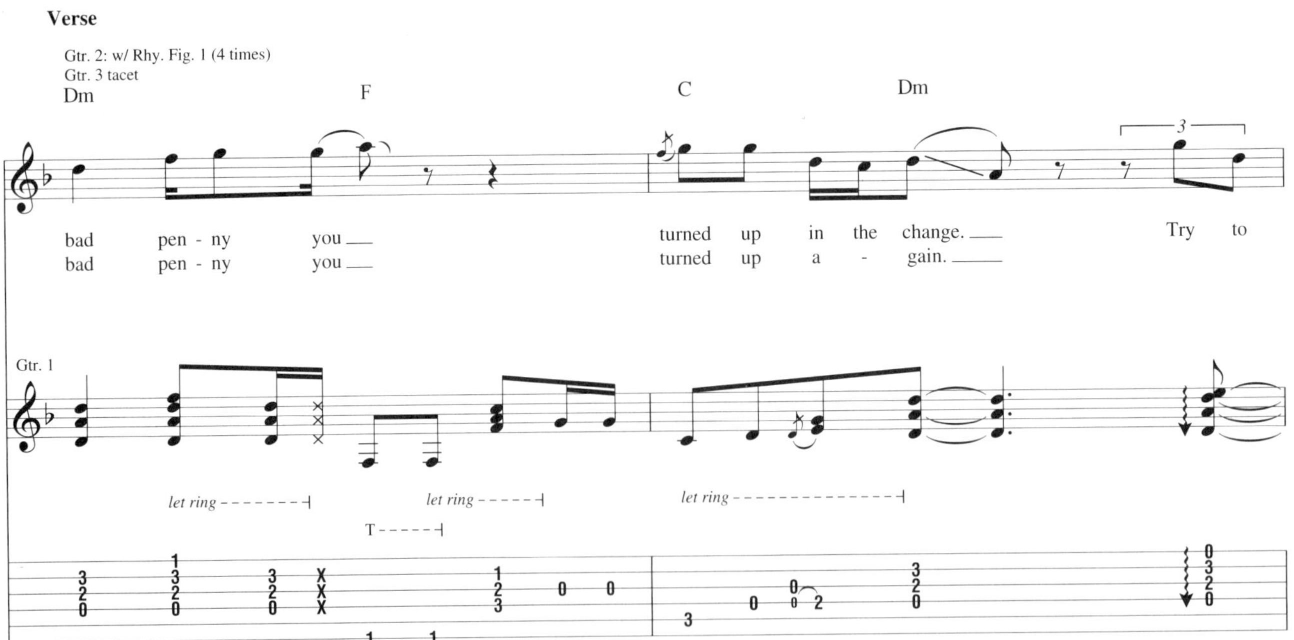

2nd time, Gtr. 3: w/ Fill 2
Gtr. 1: w/ Rhy. Fig. 2 (2 times)
F
C
Dm
F
fit in - to the pic - ture, you can't get in - side the frame. I think you know I'm still sore, but
You're in my sights, there's a mist on my lens. I think you know how it was when
Gtr. 3
Gtr. 1
let ring
To Coda
C
Dm
F
C
Dm
I'm on the mend. Times sure have changed, it won't hap - pen a - gain. 4. Well, like a
I tripped and fell. Well, you dou - ble-dealed me, ba - by, I
Gtr. 3
Fill 2
Gtr. 3
hold bend

Verse

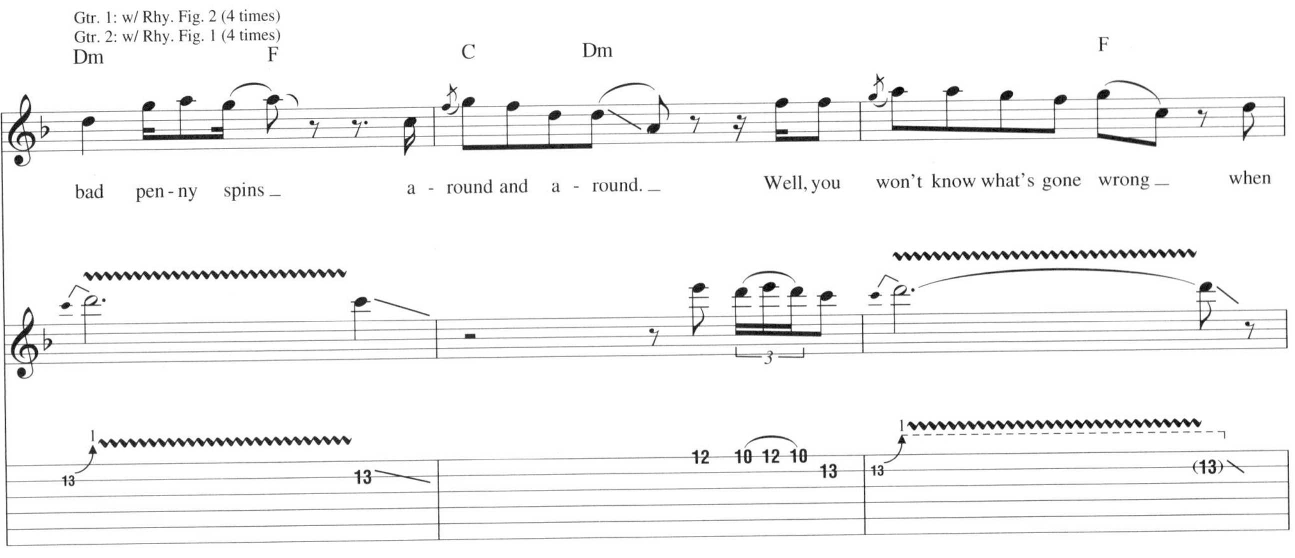
Gtr. 1: w/ Rhy. Fig. 2 (4 times)
Gtr. 2: w/ Rhy. Fig. 1 (4 times)
Dm
F
C
Dm
F
bad pen-ny spins a - round and a - round. Well, you won't know what's gone wrong when

C
Dm
F
C
Dm
it all falls down. You got to learn from now on to stop play-in' games. You
8va
loco

D.S. al Coda
F
C
Dm
ought to keep on mov - in', you got to spin on your way.
8va

Coda

Outro-Guitar Solo

*2nd string caught under bend finger.

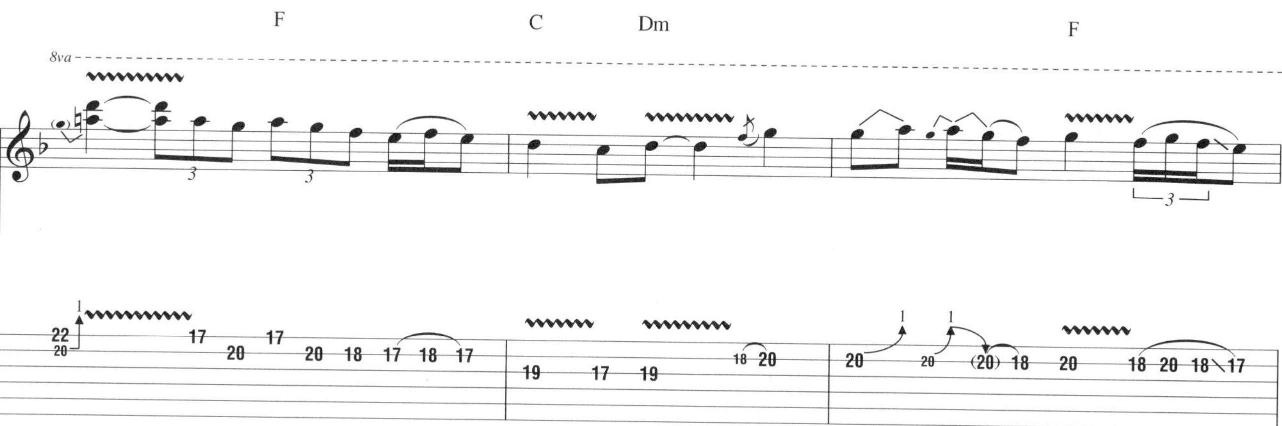

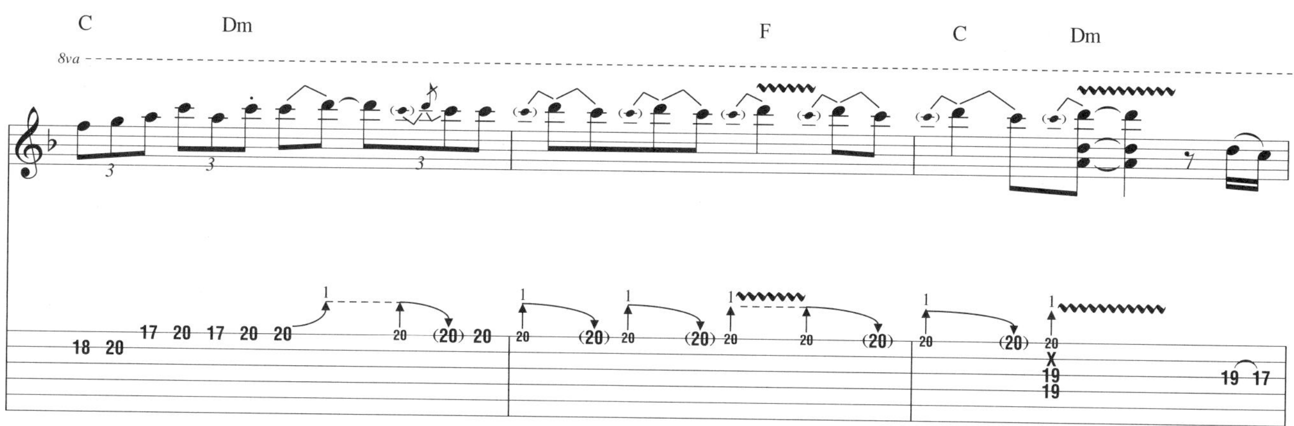

F
C
Dm
F
8va
Gtr. 3
Gtr. 1
C
Dm
F
8va
C
Dm
F
C
Dm
8va
hold bend

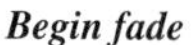
Begin fade

F
C
Dm
F
8va
loco

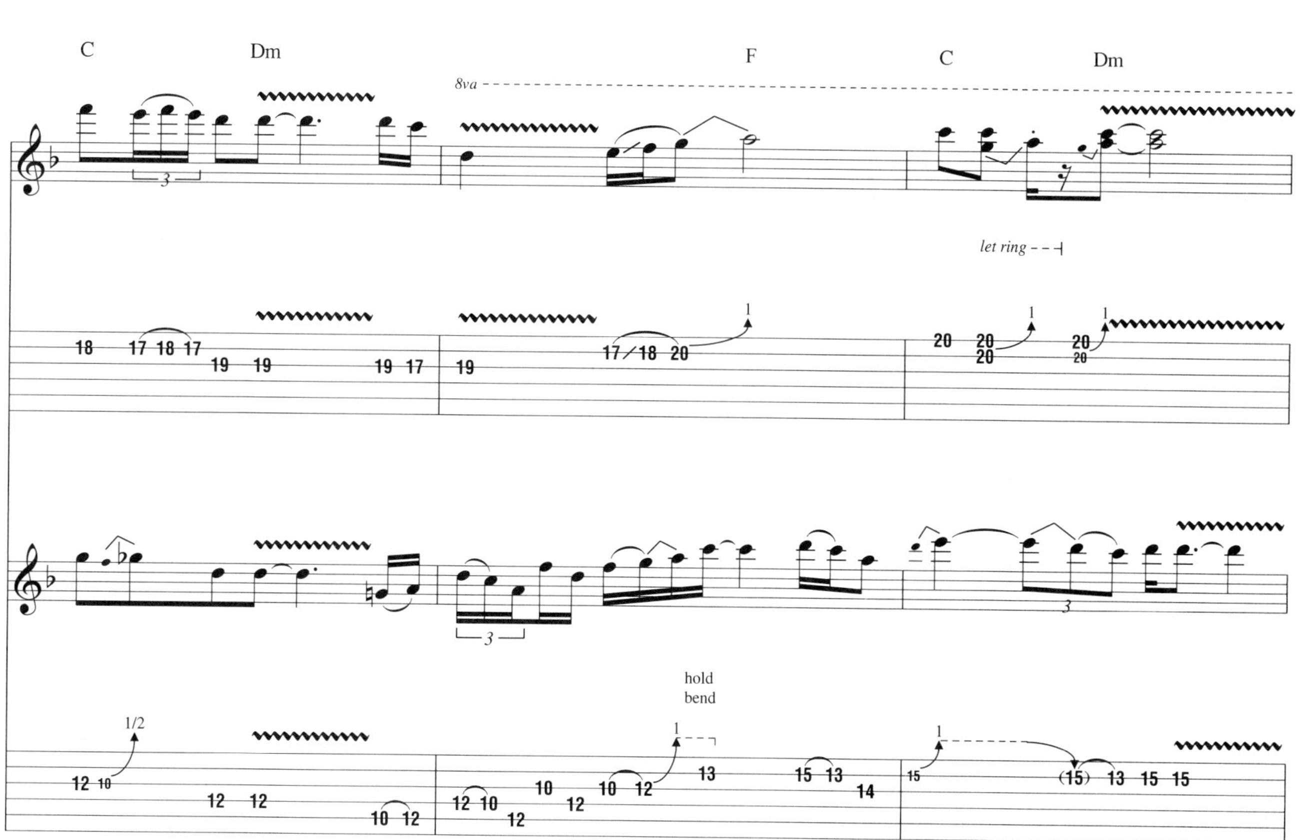
C
Dm
F
C
Dm
8va
let ring
hold
bend

F
C
Dm
8va
8va

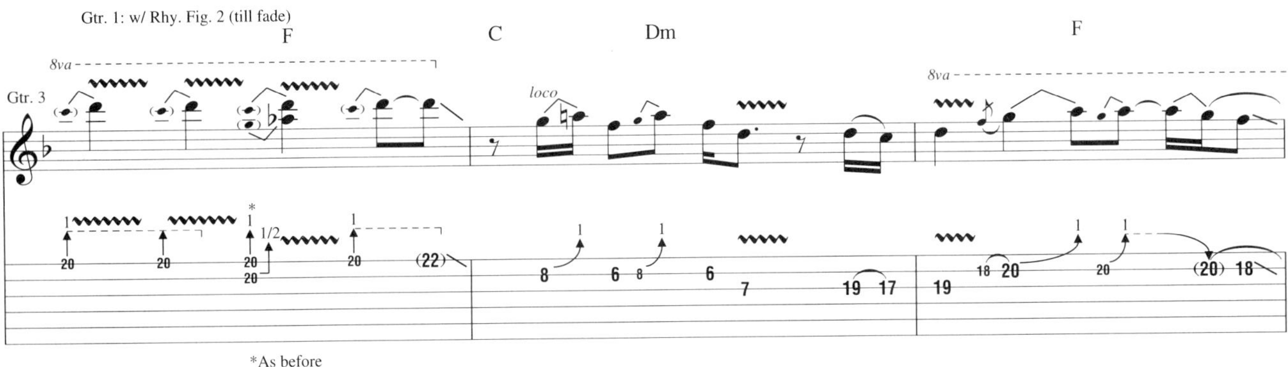

Gtr. 1: w/ Rhy. Fig. 2 (till fade)
F
C
Dm
F
8va
Gtr. 3
loco
8va
*As before

C
Dm
F
8va

Fade out
C
Dm
F
8va

from Cry of Love - *Brother*

Bad Thing

Written by Audley Freed, Kelly Holland and John Custer

Chorus

*Two gtrs. arr. for one.

Bridge
Gtrs. 1 & 2 tacet
D5
G
Just a new way you got o - ver me,
Gtr. 2
let ring
Gtr. 1
*Gtr. 3 (clean)
mf
let ring
*Elec. piano arr. for gtr.
C
F
D5
you got it all wrong.
Just a new song that
Gtr. 3
let ring
let ring
G
C
F
I got - ta sing, you got o - ver me, yeah. Just a new
Gtr. 4 (dist.)
mf
**fdbk.
Gtr. 3
**Microphonic fdbk., not caused by string vibration.
let ring

Guitar Solo

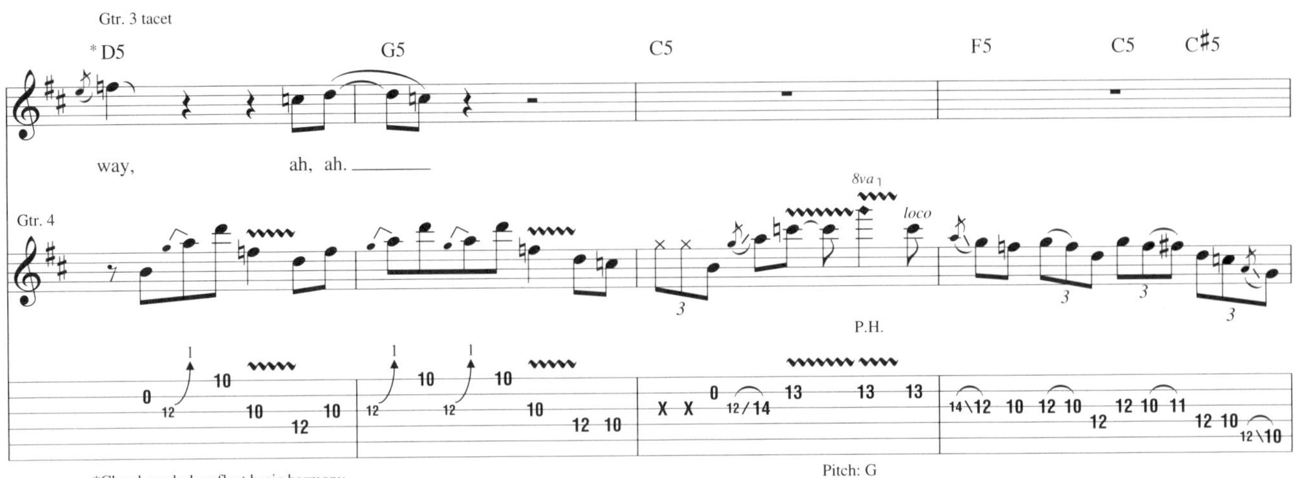
Gtr. 3 tacet
*D5
G5
C5
F5
C5
C#5
way,
ah, ah.
Gtr. 4
8va
loco
P.H.
Pitch: G
*Chord symbols reflect basic harmony.

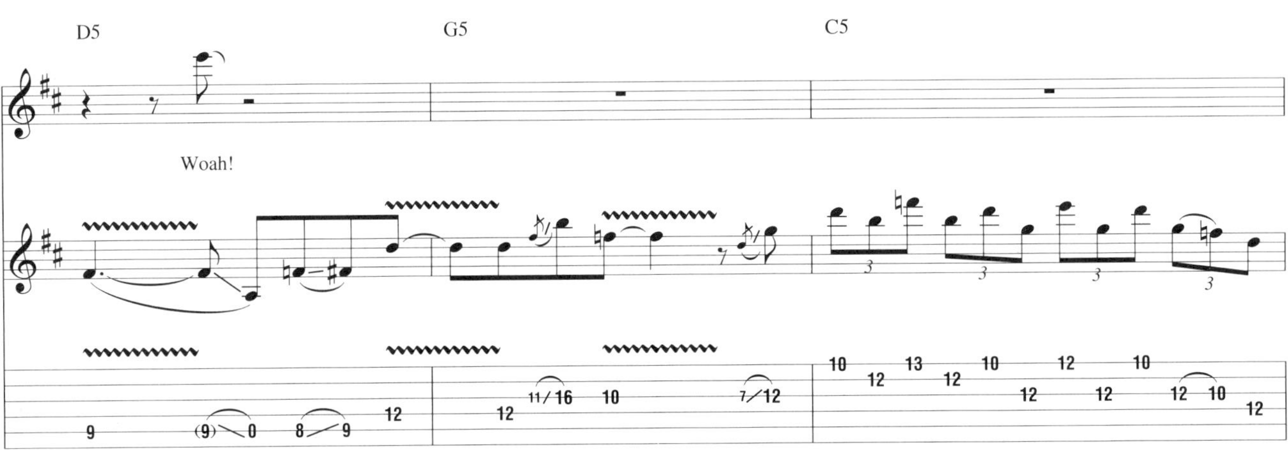
D5
G5
C5
Woah!

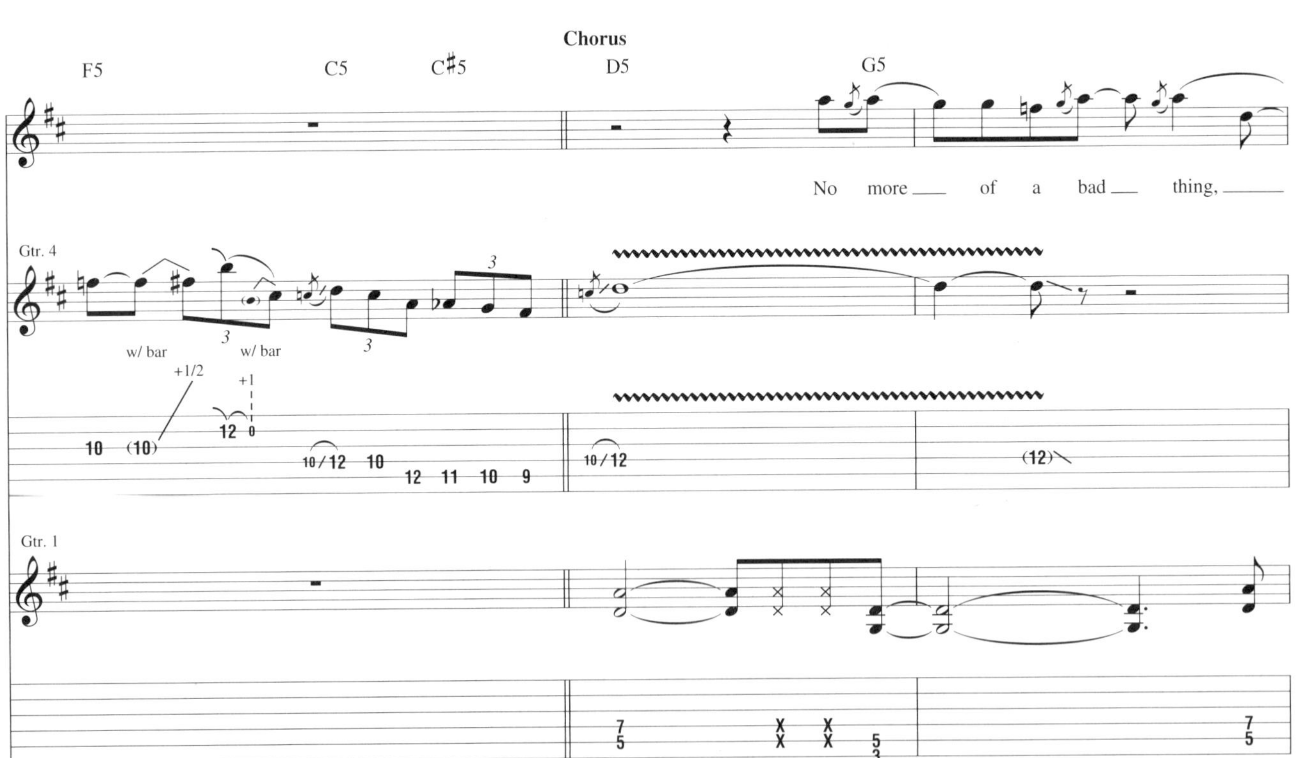
Chorus
F5
C5
C#5
D5
G5
No more of a bad thing,
Gtr. 4
w/ bar
w/ bar
+1/2
+1
Gtr. 1

Gtr. 4 tacet
D5
G5
D5
G5
no more of a bad thing,
no more of a bad thing now, ba-
Gtr. 1
Chorus
D5
G5
D5
G5
- by, no more, no more.
Hmm, no more of a bad thing,
D5
G5
D5
G5
hey! No more, no more,
no more of a bad thing,
Outro
D5
G5
D5
G5
yeah. No more, yeah, yeah.
No more,

Begin fade
D5
G5
D5
ain't got no hard feel ings now, babe, no, no, yeah. I'm just sit -
G5
D5
G5
- tin' 'round, babe. Yeah, yeah, yeah, yeah, yeah.
D5
G5
D5
G5
Well, yeah, yeah. Sing the feel - ing,
Harm.
Pitch: E
Fade out
D5
G5
D5
G5
no more, no more, ba - by. No, no more.
Harm.
Harm.
Pitch: B
B

from Jane's Addiction - *Ritual de lo Habitual*

Been Caught Stealing

Words and Music by Jane's Addiction

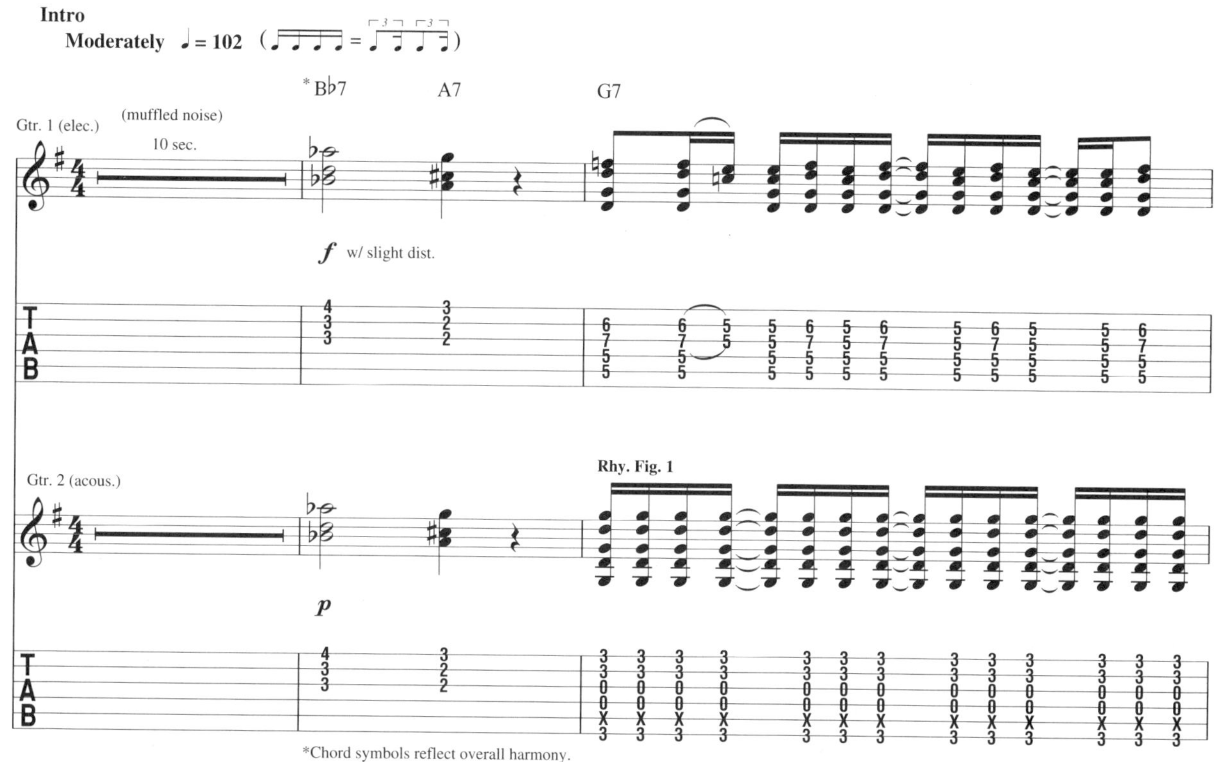

*Chord symbols reflect overall harmony.

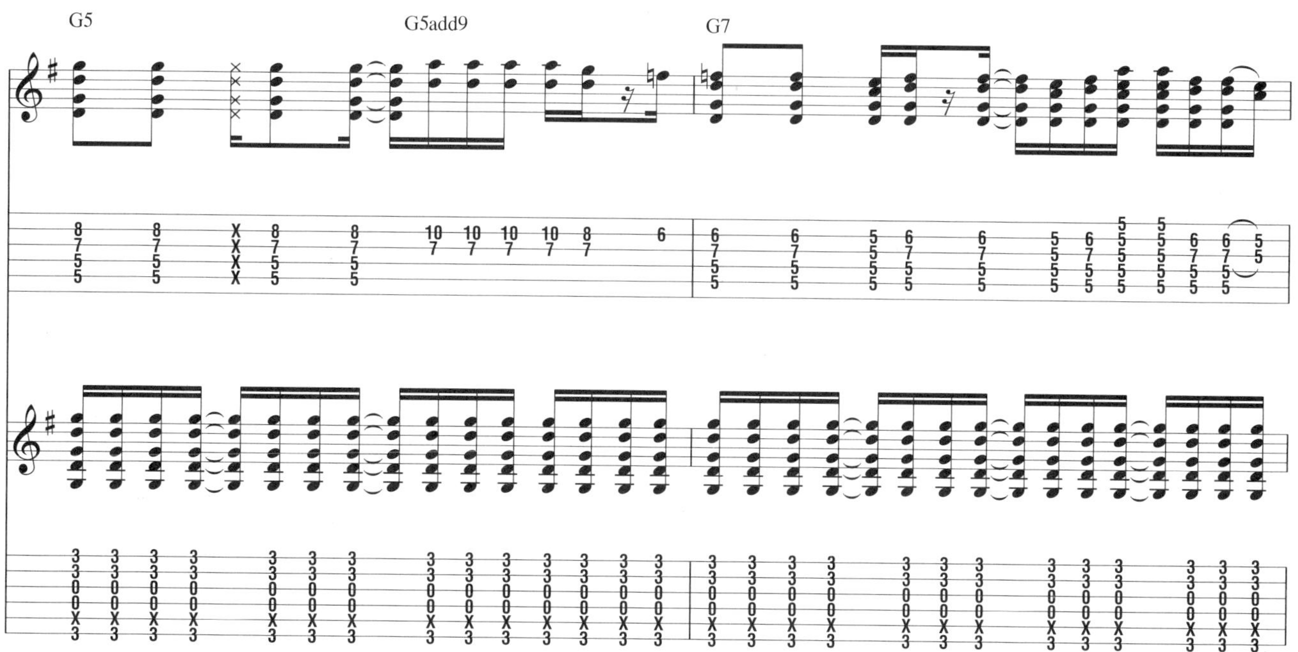

Gtr. 2: w/ Rhy. Fig. 1
G5
G7
End Rhy. Fig. 1
Gtr. 3 (elec.)
mf w/ clean tone
G5
G5add9
G7
Verse
Gtr. 2: w/ Rhy. Fig. 1
G7
1. I've been caught steal - ing once when I was five.
too. She'll go and get her a skirt.
Rhy. Fig. 2
Rhy. Fig. 2A

G5 G7

I en - joy steal - ing. It's just as sim - ple as that.
Stick it un - der her shirt. She grabbed a ra - zor for

G5 G7 G6add♯4 N.C.

Gtr. 2: w/ Rhy. Fig. 1 (last 3 meas.)

G5

A, well, it's just a simple fact. When I want some -
me. And she did it just like that. When she wants some -

Chorus

G7 G5 C

thing and I don't want to pay for it.
thing and she don't want to pay for it.

Yeah, I walk right through the
She walk right through the

End Rhy. Fig. 2 Rhy. Fig. 3

End Rhy. Fig. 2A Rhy. Fig. 3A

B♭ C B♭ F G Csus4 C

door, and I walk right through the door.
door, walk right through the door.

Csus4 C7
B♭7
A7
Hey, all right.
If I get by
it's
End Rhy. Fig. 3
End Rhy. Fig. 3A
G7
G
mine,
mine all mine.
Hey,
Let's go.
Rhy. Fig. 4
End Rhy. Fig. 4
Rhy. Fig. 4A
End Rhy. Fig. 4A
1.
Interlude
Gtrs. 1 & 3: w/ Rhy. Figs. 4 & 4A (2 times)
Gtr. 4
(elec.)
G7
8va
G
f w/ dist. & chorus

G7
G
2. Yeah, my girl, she's one
8va

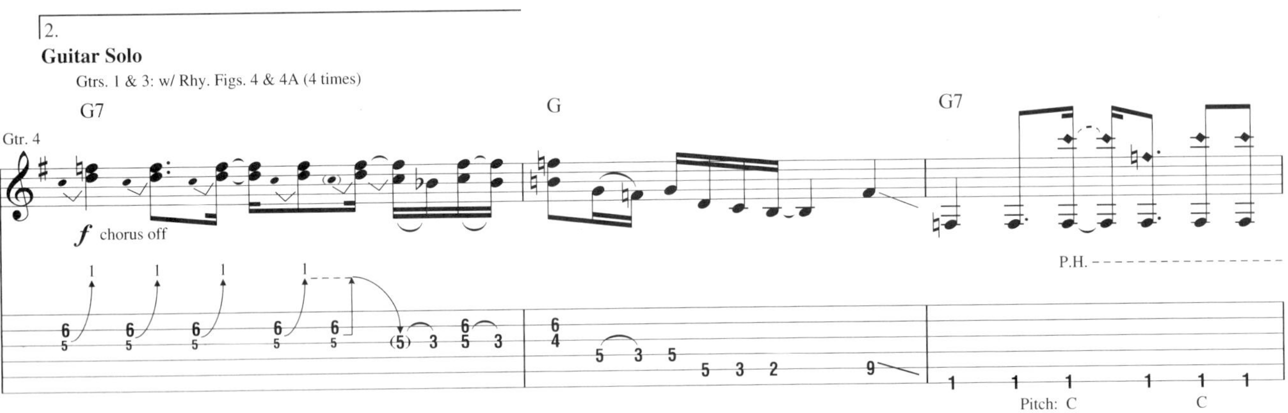
2.
Guitar Solo
Gtrs. 1 & 3: w/ Rhy. Figs. 4 & 4A (4 times)
G7
G
G7
Gtr. 4
f chorus off
P.H.
Pitch: C
C

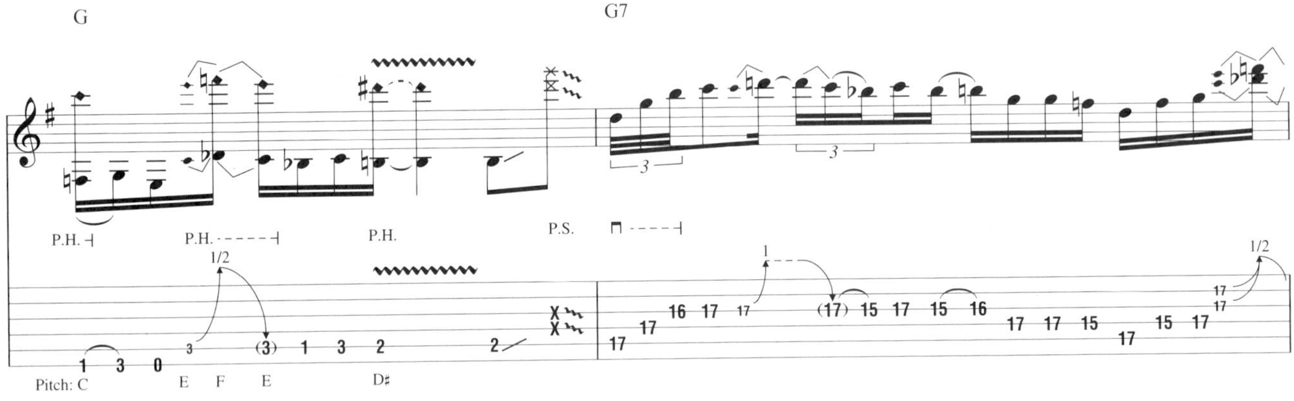
G
G7
P.H.
P.H.
P.H.
P.S.
Pitch: C
E F E
D♯

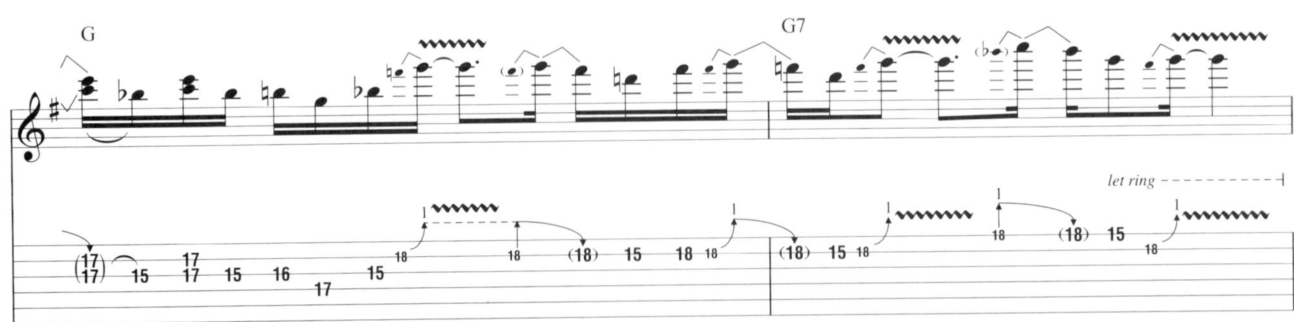
G
G7
let ring

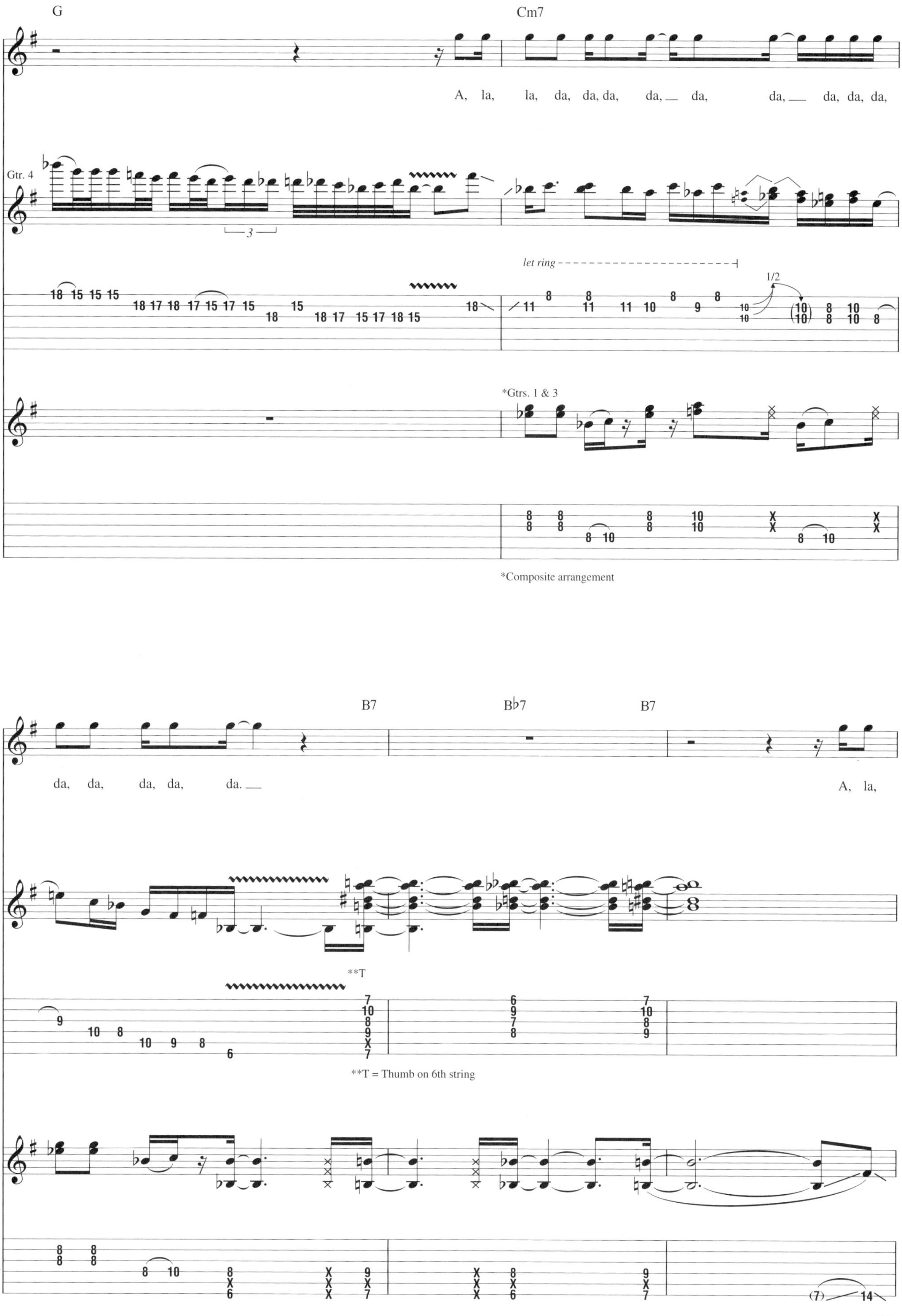

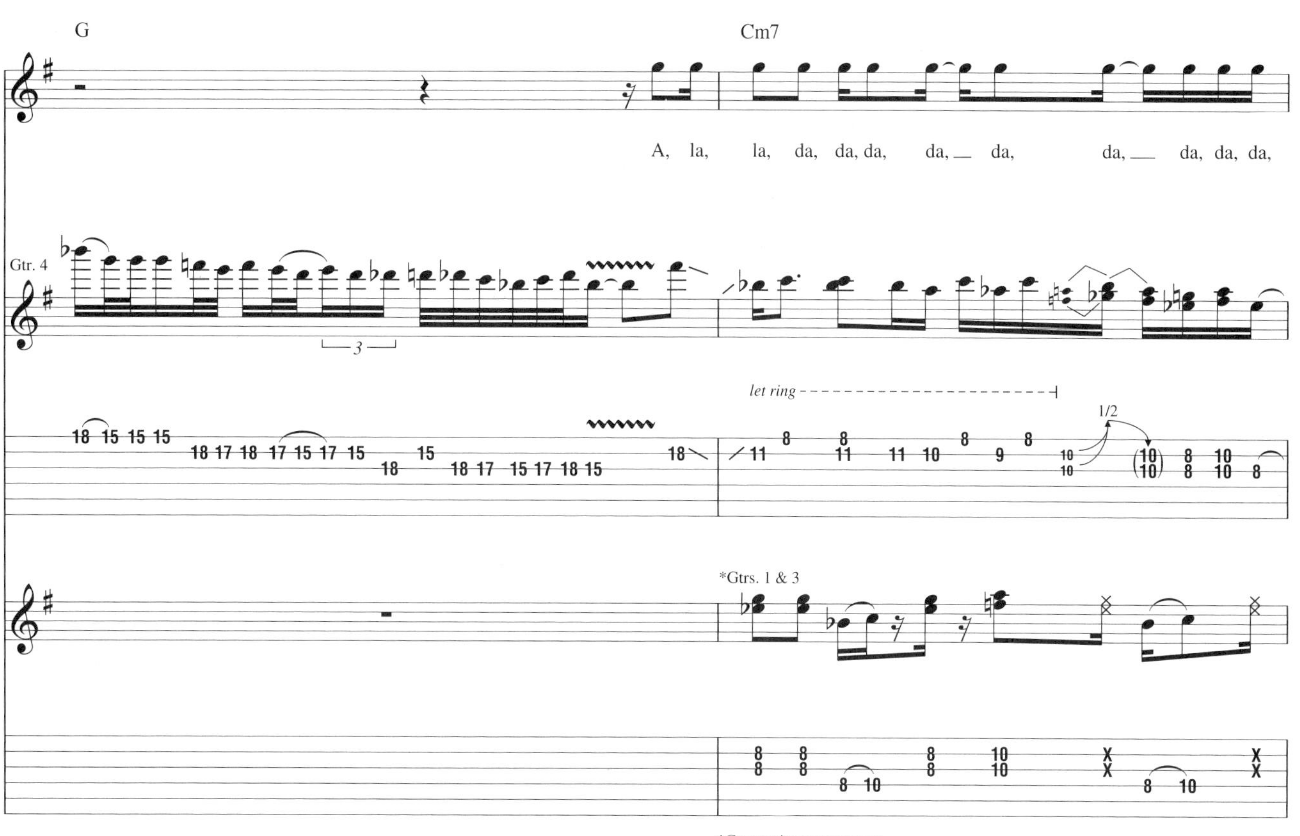

G
Cm7
A, la, la, da, da, da, da, da, da, da, da, da,
Gtr. 4
3
let ring
1/2
*Gtrs. 1 & 3
*Composite arrangement
B7
B♭7
B7
da, da, da, da, da.
A, la,
**T
**T = Thumb on 6th string

Cm7
B7
la, da, ba, da, da, da, da, da, da, da, da, da, da, da, da. Brr.
P.H.
1/2
Pitch: A B♭ A
1
B♭7
B7
Gtrs. 1 & 3 tacet
N.C.(G)
w/ bar
-6 1/2
-4
Verse
Gtrs. 1 & 3: w/ Rhy. Figs. 2 & 2A
Gtr. 2: w/ Rhy. Fig. 1 (2 times)
Gtr. 4 tacet
G7
G
3. Sat a-round the pile, sat and laughed, sat and laughed
and waved it in-to the air.
G7
G5
G7
G5
And we did it just like that when we want some-thing

Chorus
Gtrs. 1 & 3: w/ Rhy. Figs. 3 & 3A
G7
G5
C
and we don't want to pay for it.
We walk right through the
B♭
F
G
Csus4
C7
door,
walk right through the door.
Hey, all right.
B♭7
A7
If I get by
it's, a,
mine, all mine, all
mine, all mine, all
Gtr. 1
Gtr. 3
Free time
A6
mine, all mine, all mine, all mine, all mine.
It's, a, mine.

from *Korn*

Blind

Music and Lyrics by Korn

Slower ♩ = 86

Verses:

E F(♯11)

*1. This place in - side my mind, a place I like to hide.
*2. *See additional lyrics*

Gr. 1
Riff C

mf w/wah-wah

hold bend

hold bend

Gtr. 2
Rhy. Fig. 4

end Rhy. Fig. 4

mf

*Doubled by whispered vocal.

E5 F(♯11)

You don't know the chanc - es. What if I should die?

hold bend

Rhy. Fig. 5

end Rhy. Fig. 5

w/Rhy. Fig. 5 (Gtr. 2) 2 times
E5
F(♯11)
A place in - side my brain, an - oth - er kind of
Gtr. 1
harm.
E5
F(♯11)
pain. You don't know the chanc - es. I'm so blind.
end Riff C
Faster ♩ = 100
E5 F5 E5 F5 B♭5 E5 F5 E5 F5 D♯5
Blind.
Gtrs. 1 & 2
E5 F5 E5 F5 B♭5 E5 F5 E5 F5 G5/D♯5
Blind.

Slower ♩ = 94
Interlude:
w/Riff A (Gtr. 1) 4 times
w/Rhy. Fig. 2 (Gtr. 2) 4 times
C♯5 D5 C♯5 D5 N.C. C♯5 D5 C♯5 D5 N.C.
(Shouted:) Deep - er and deep - er and deep - er__ is all I'm turn - ing to. Liv - ing a life that seems_ to be a
C♯5 D5 C♯5 D5 N.C. C♯5 D5 C♯5 D5 N.C.
lost re - al - i - ty. I can nev - er find a way to reach my in - ner self. Es -
w/Riff B (Gtr. 1)
w/Rhy. Fig. 3 (Gtr. 2)
w/Riff A (Gtr. 1) 2 times
w/Rhy. Fig. 2 (Gtr. 2) 2 times
D5 C♯5 D5 N.C. C♯5 D5 C♯5 D5 N.C.
teem is low. How deep can I go? In the ground_ I lay_ if I don't_ find a way_ to
w/Riff B (Gtr. 1)
w/Rhy. Fig. 3 (Gtr. 2)
C♯5 D5 C♯5 D5 N.C. D5 C♯5 D5 N.C.
sleep. In the grave,_ I crowd_ my mind. It's time__ I looked to see when was re - al - ized.__
Slower ♩ = 90
*Pre-Chorus:
N.C.
Rhy. Fig. 6
Gtr. 1
mf
*Gtr. 2 w/misc. sound effects (next 4 bars).
w/Rhy. Fig. 6 (Gtr. 1)
(Whispered:) I can see, I can see, I'm go - ing blind. I can see, I can see, I'm go - ing blind.
Chorus:
w/Riff C (Gtr. 1) simile
*w/Rhy. Fig. 4 (Gtr. 2) 3½ times
E F(♯11)
I can see, I can see, I'm go - ing blind.___ I can see, I can see, I'm go - ing blind.
*Performed f.
E F(♯11)
I can see, I can see, I'm go - ing blind.___ I can see, I can see, I'm go - ing blind.
E F(♯11)
I can see, I can see, I'm go - ing blind.___ I can see, I can see, I'm go - ing blind.

Verse 2:
Another place I'll find,
Escape the pain inside.
You don't know the chances.
What if I should die?
A place inside my brain,
Another kind of pain.
You don't know the chances.
I'm so blind.
Blind.
Blind.
(To Interlude:)

from Ramones - *Ramones*

Blitzkrieg Bop

Words and Music by Jeffrey Hyman, John Cummings, Douglas Colvin and Thomas Erdelyi

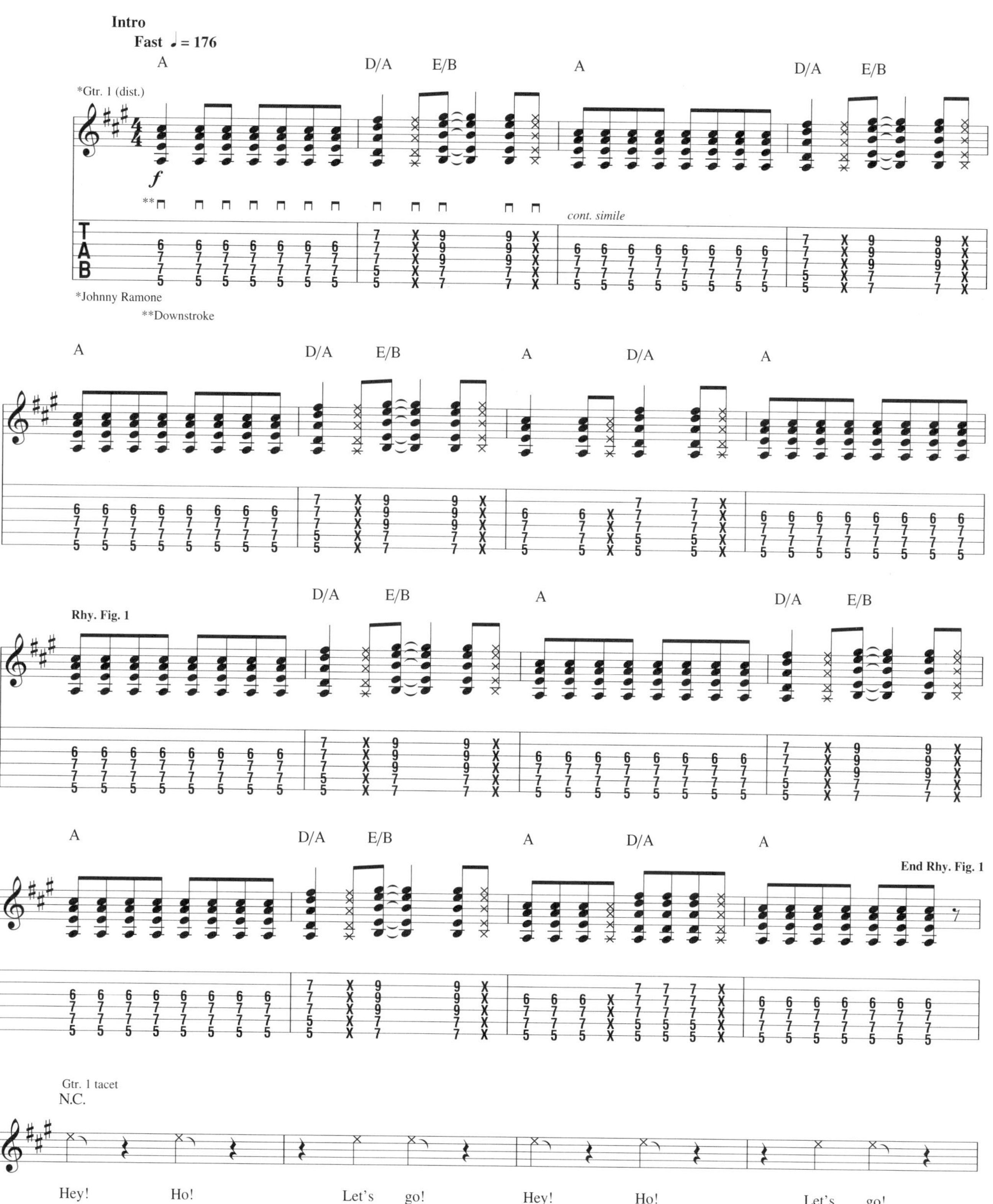

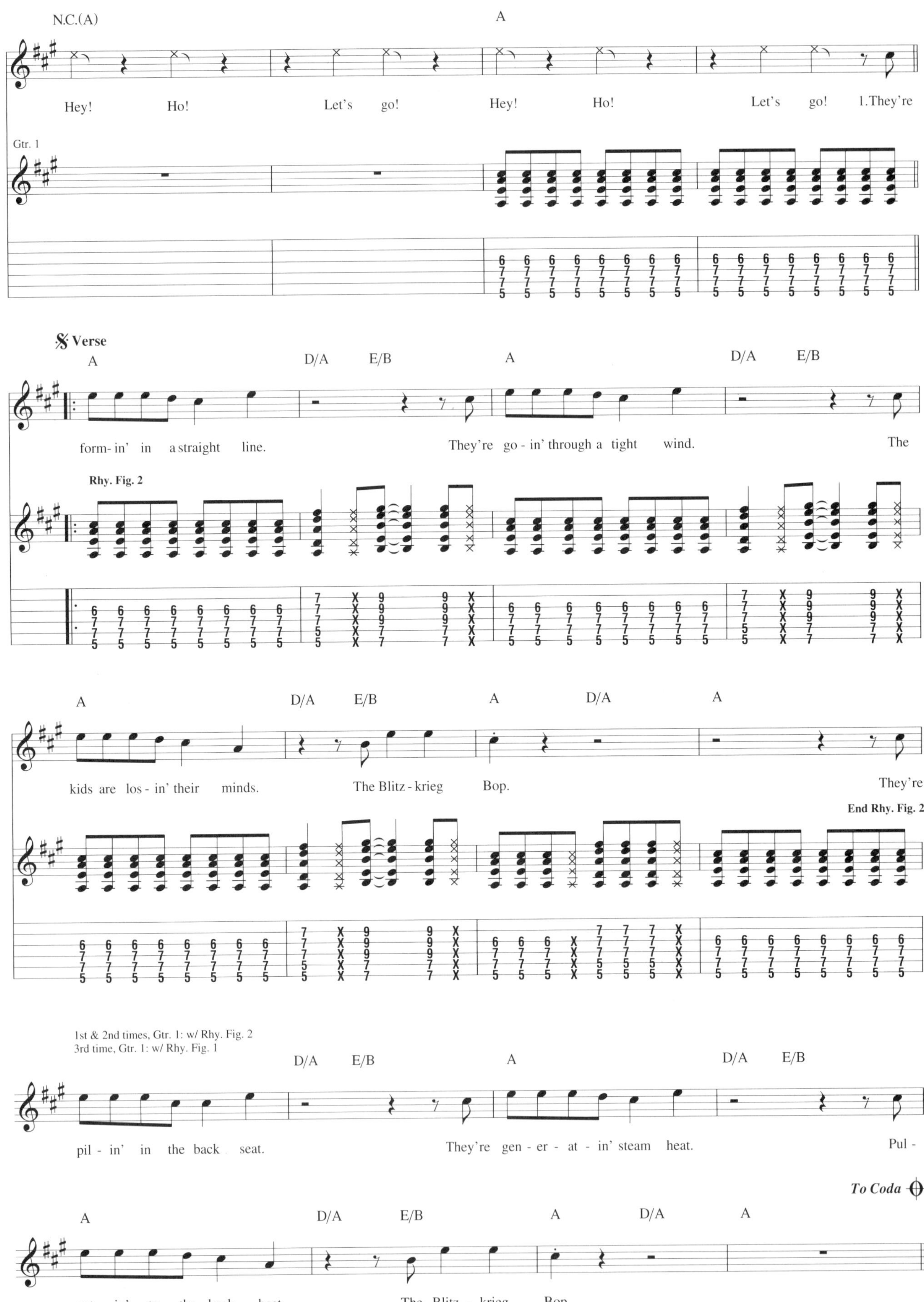
N.C.(A)
A
Hey! Ho! Let's go! Hey! Ho! Let's go! 1.They're
Gtr. 1
Verse
A D/A E/B A D/A E/B
form- in' in a straight line. They're go - in' through a tight wind. The
Rhy. Fig. 2
A D/A E/B A D/A A
kids are los - in' their minds. The Blitz - krieg Bop. They're
End Rhy. Fig. 2
1st & 2nd times, Gtr. 1: w/ Rhy. Fig. 2
3rd time, Gtr. 1: w/ Rhy. Fig. 1
D/A E/B A D/A E/B
pil - in' in the back seat. They're gen - er - at - in' steam heat. Pul -
To Coda
A D/A E/B A D/A A
sat - in' to the back beat. The Blitz - krieg Bop.

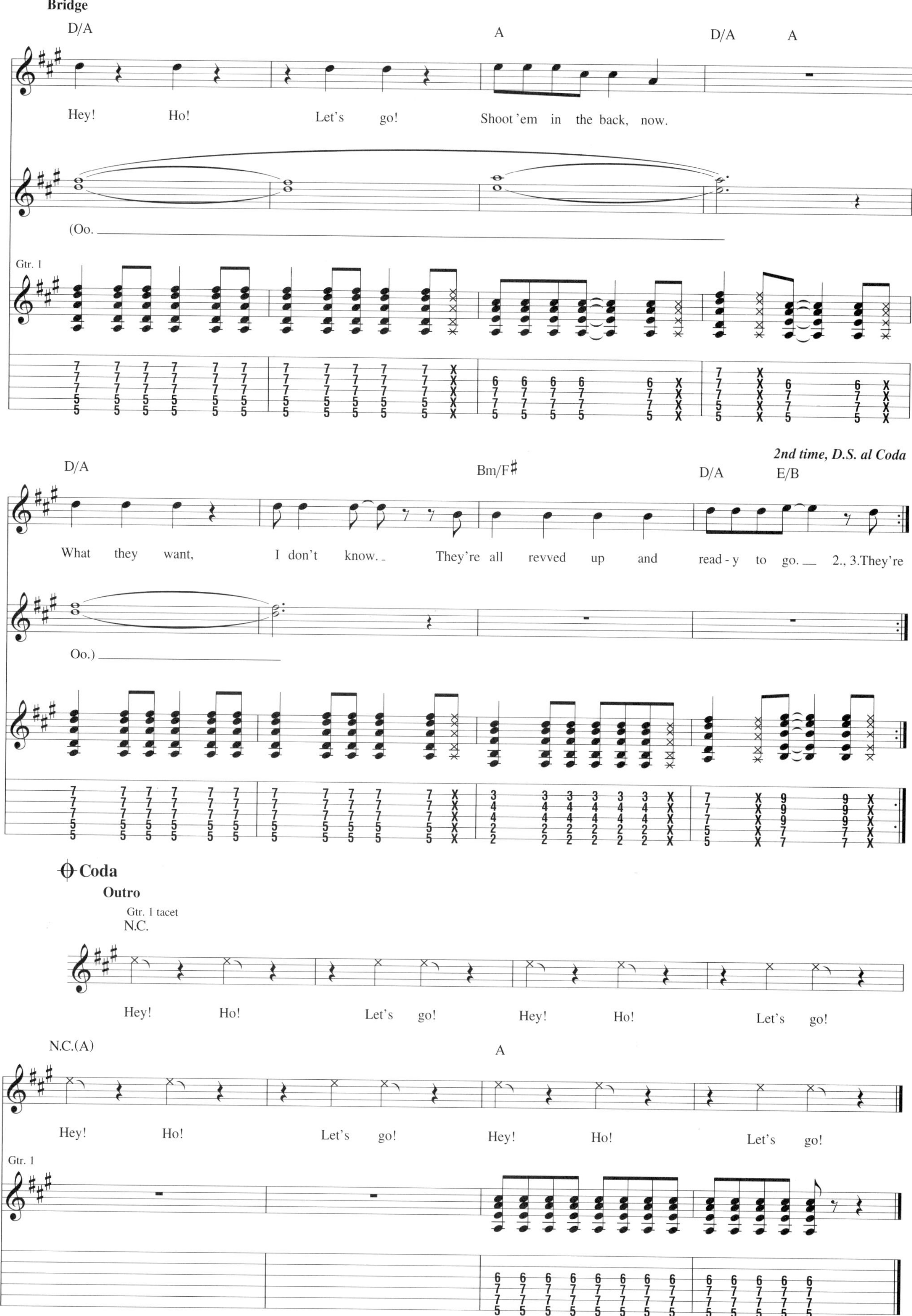

Bridge
D/A
A
D/A
A
Hey! Ho! Let's go! Shoot 'em in the back, now.
(Oo.
Gtr. 1
D/A
Bm/F♯
2nd time, D.S. al Coda
D/A
E/B
What they want, I don't know. They're all revved up and read-y to go. 2., 3.They're
Oo.)
Coda
Outro
Gtr. 1 tacet
N.C.
Hey! Ho! Let's go! Hey! Ho! Let's go!
N.C.(A)
A
Hey! Ho! Let's go! Hey! Ho! Let's go!
Gtr. 1

from Robin Trower - *Bridge of Sighs*

Bridge of Sighs

Words and Music by Robin Trower

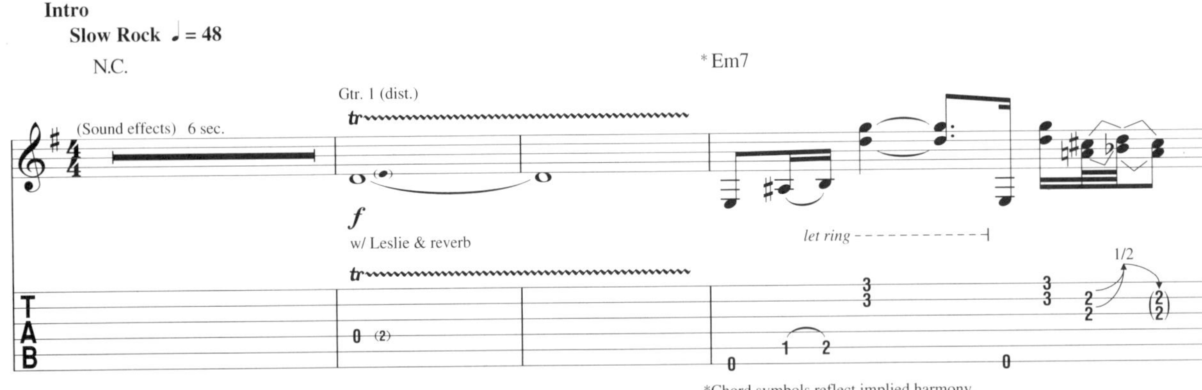

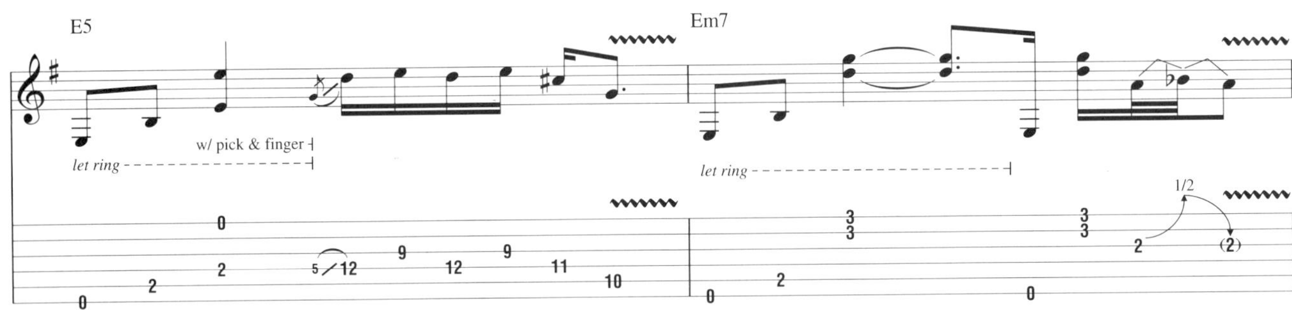

Verse

E5
Em7
1. The sun don't shine, the
let ring
* Played ahead of the beat.
moon don't move the tides to wash me clean.
The sun don't shine, the
w/ pick & finger
moon don't move the tides to wash me clean.

Chorus

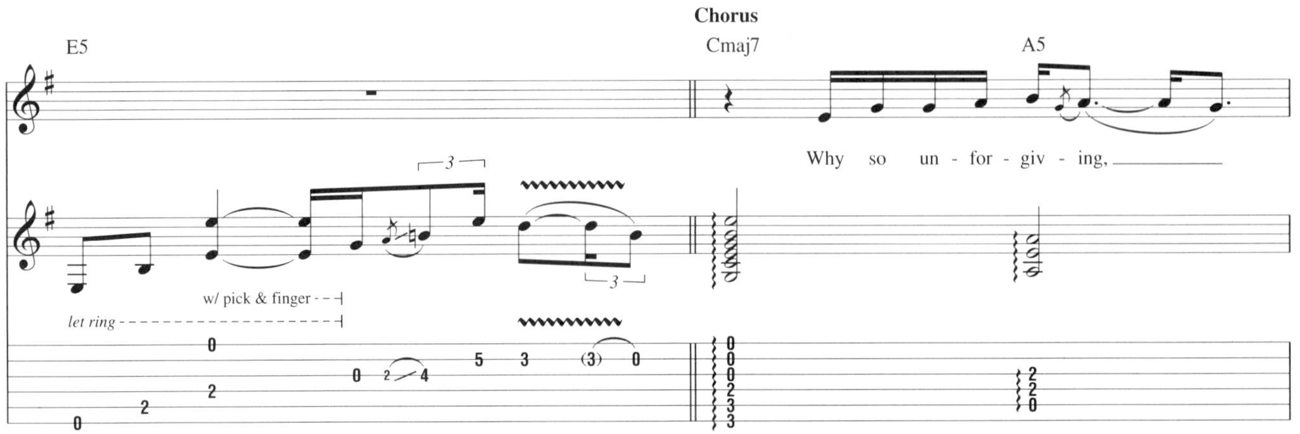

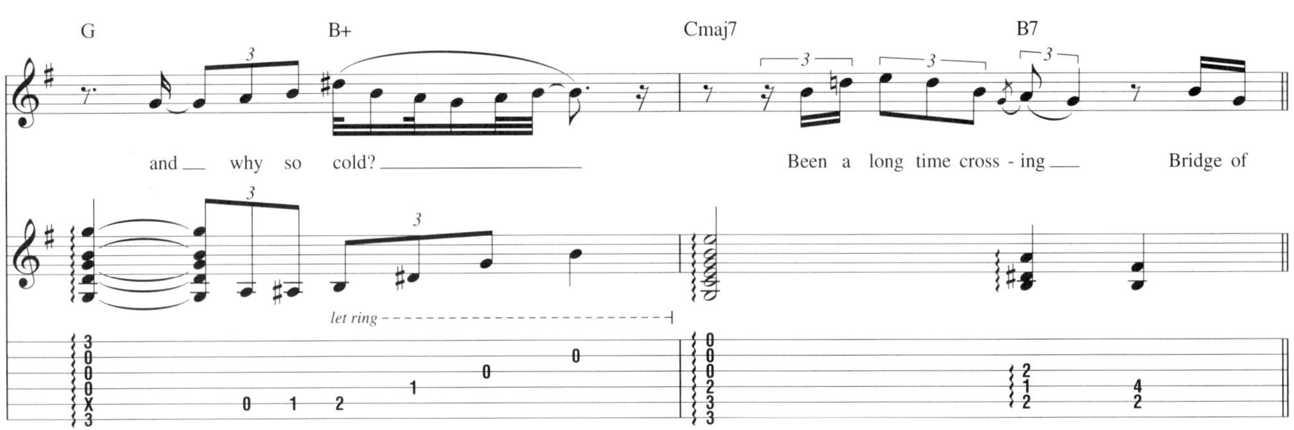

Interlude

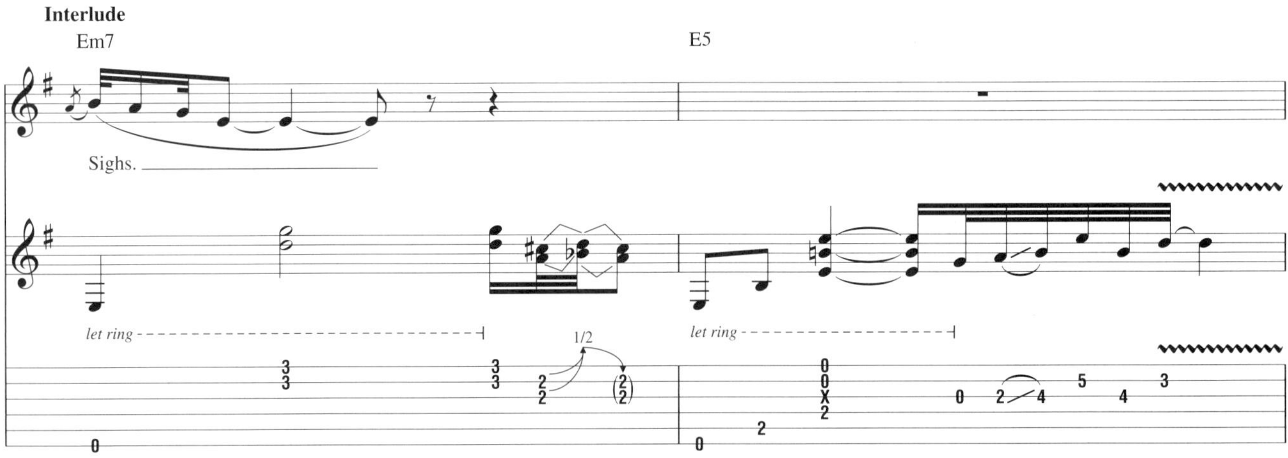

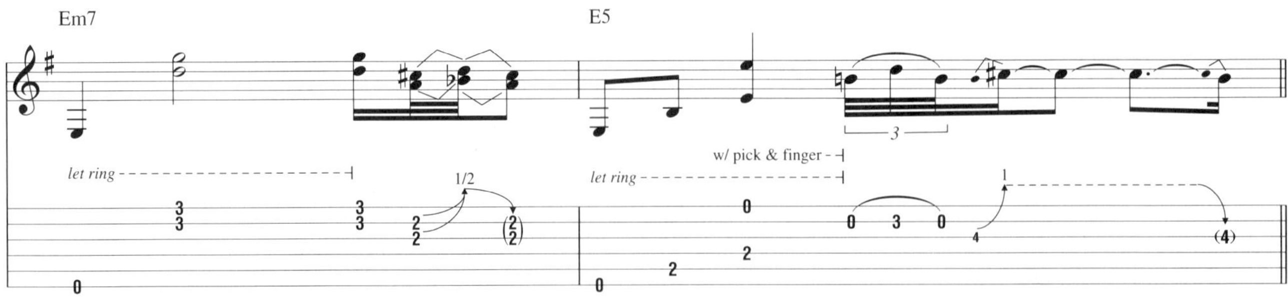

Verse

Em7
E7
2. Cold wind blows, the Gods look down in an - ger on this poor child.
let ring
1/2
Em7
E5
let ring
Em7
E5
Cold wind blows, the Gods look down in an - ger on this poor
let ring
w/ pick & finger
Em7
E5
child.
let ring
w/ pick & finger

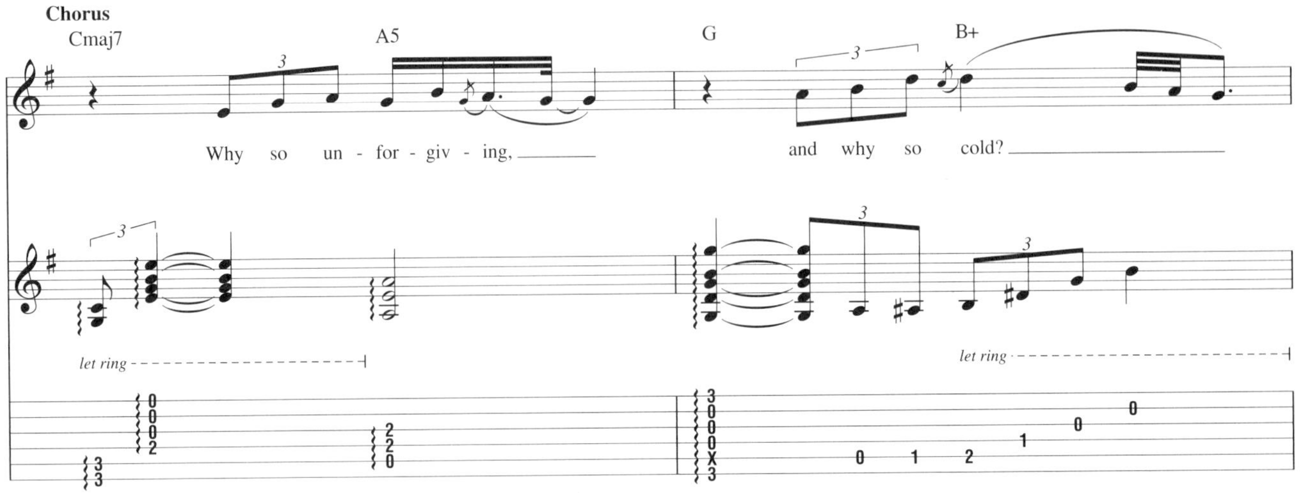
Chorus
Cmaj7
A5
G
B+
Why so un - for - giv - ing,
and why so cold?
let ring
let ring

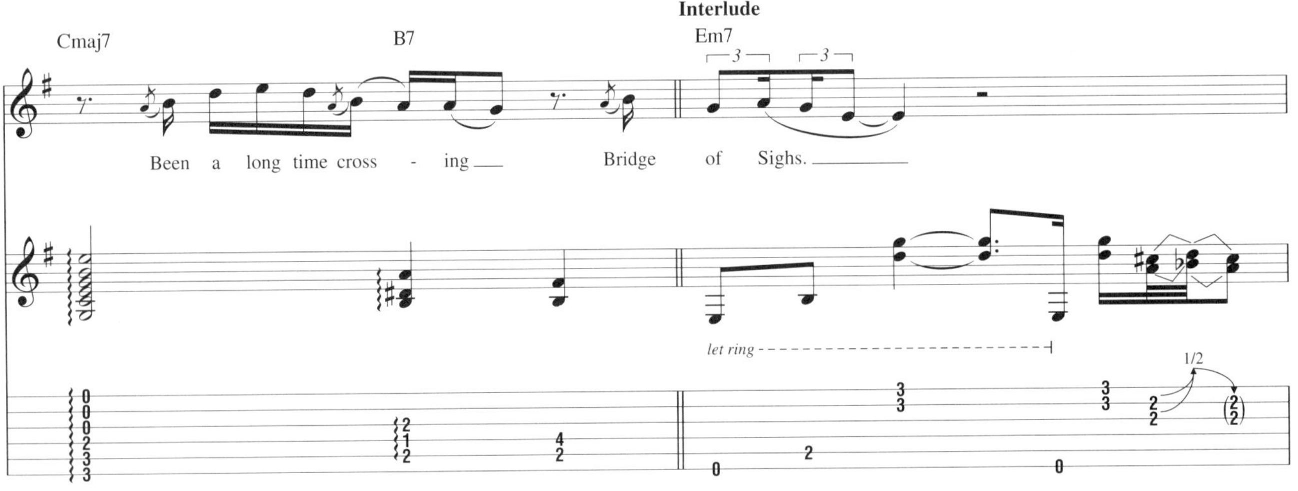
Interlude
Cmaj7
B7
Em7
Been a long time cross - ing
Bridge of Sighs.
let ring
1/2

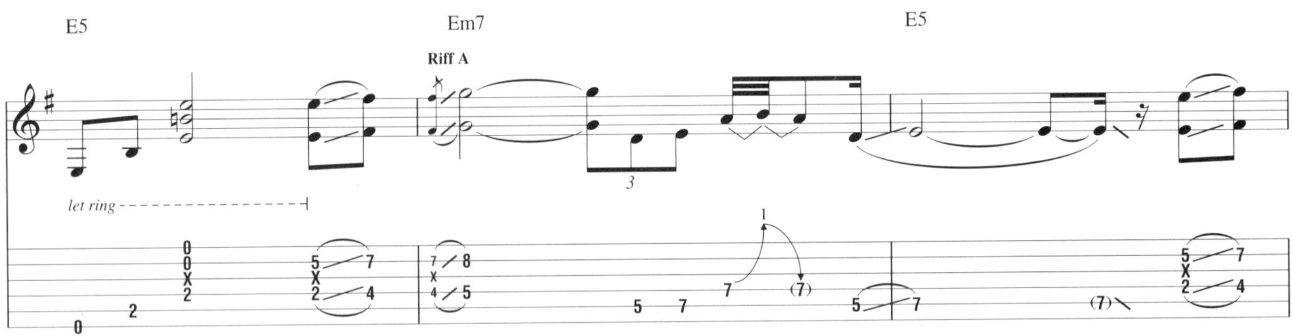
E5
Em7
E5
Riff A
let ring

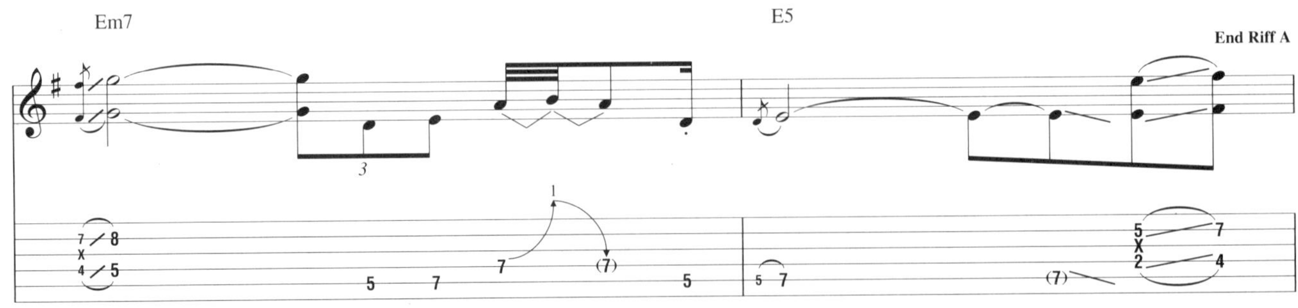
Em7
E5
End Riff A

Gtr. 1: w/ Riff A
Em7
E5
Gtr. 2 (clean)
Riff B
mf
Gtr. 3 (clean) divisi
mf
Riff B1

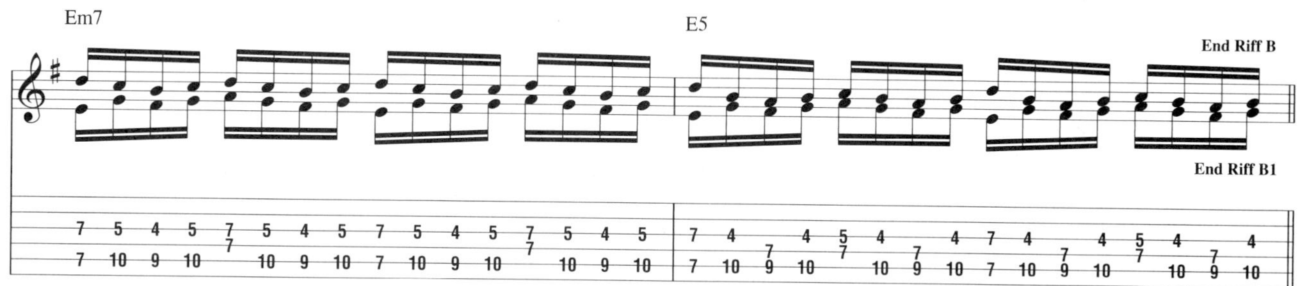
Em7
E5
End Riff B
End Riff B1

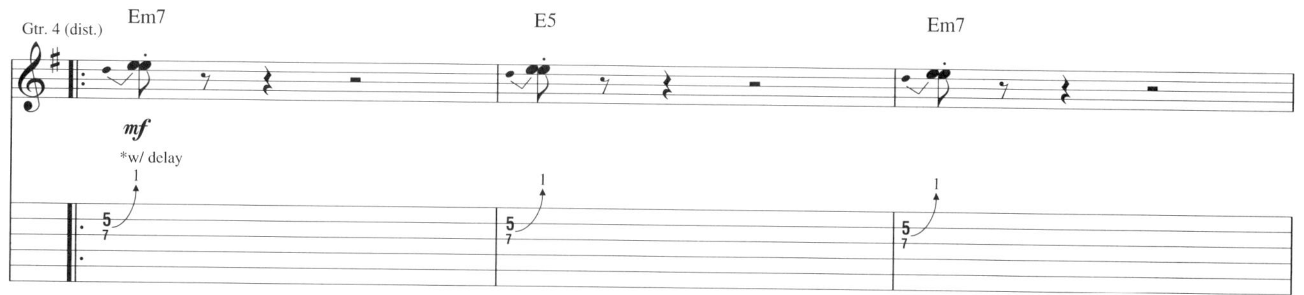
1st & 2nd times, Gtr. 1: w/ Riff A
Gtrs. 2 & 3: w/ Riffs B & B1
3rd time, Gtr. 1: w/ Riff A (1st 3 meas.)
Gtr. 4 (dist.)
Em7
E5
Em7
mf
*w/ delay
*Set delay for eighth-note regeneration w/ 7 repeats.

1., 2.
3.
Gtrs. 2 & 3: w/ Riffs B & B1 (last meas.)
Gtr. 4
E5
E5
N.C.
delay off
Gtr. 1

from Van Morrison - *Into the Music*

Bright Side of the Road

Words and Music by Van Morrison

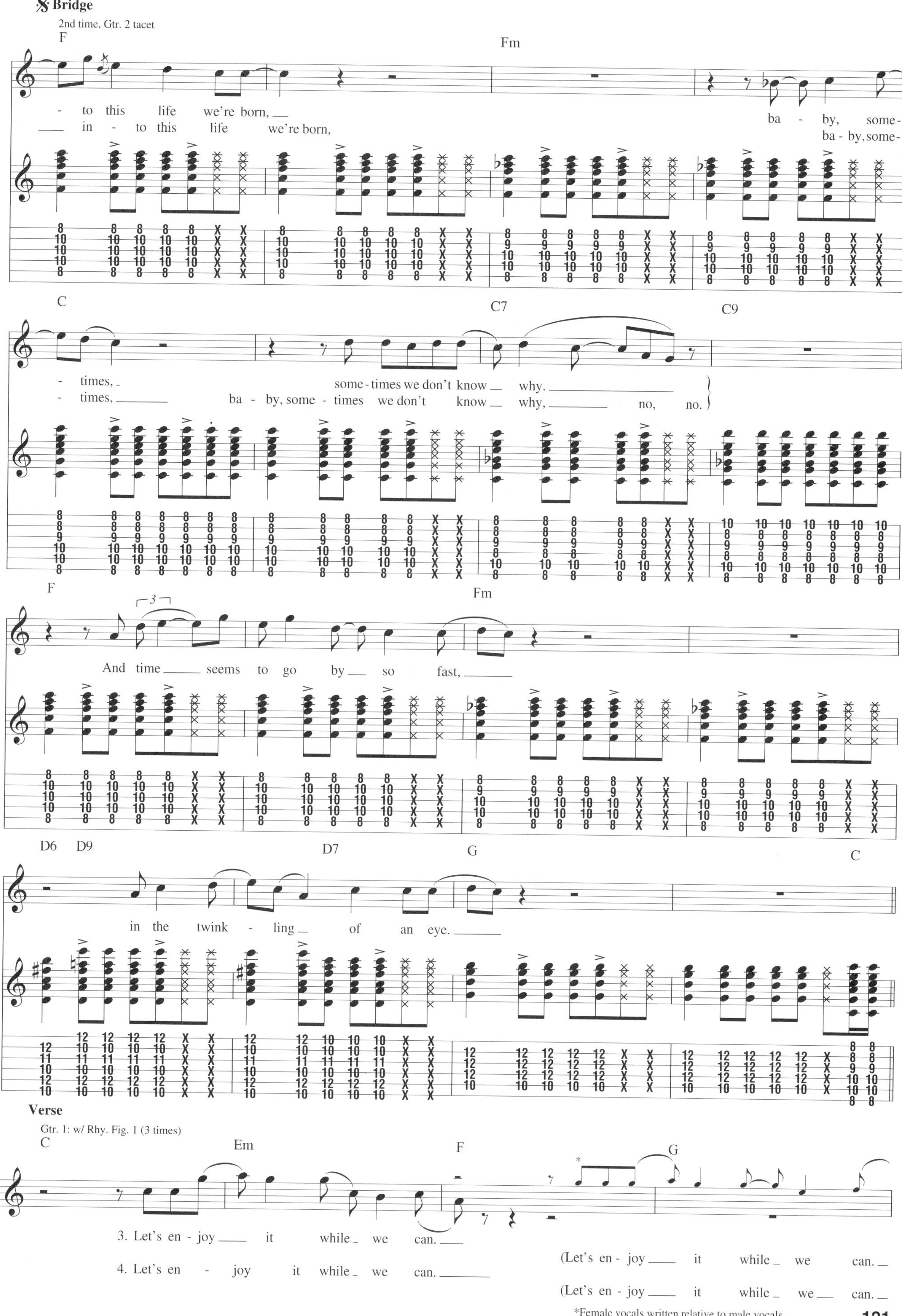
Bridge
2nd time, Gtr. 2 tacet
F
Fm
- to this life we're born,
in - to this life we're born,
ba - by, some-
ba - by, some-
C
C7
C9
- times,
- times,
some - times we don't know why.
ba - by, some - times we don't know why, no, no.
F
Fm
And time seems to go by so fast,
D6 D9
D7
G
C
in the twink - ling of an eye.
Verse
Gtr. 1: w/ Rhy. Fig. 1 (3 times)
C
Em
F
G
3. Let's en - joy it while we can.
4. Let's en - joy it while we can.
(Let's en - joy it while we can.
(Let's en - joy it while we can.
*Female vocals written relative to male vocals.

C
Em
F
G
Won't you help me share my load?
Help me share my load.)
Won't you help me sing my song?
Help me sing my song.)
To Coda
From the dark end of the street,
to
the bright side of the road.
Lit - tle dar - lin', come a - long
on
Gtr. 1: w/ Rhy. Fig. 2
Cook it!
*Gtr. 2
f
*Harmonica arr. for gtr.
Harmonica Solo
Gtr. 1: w/ Rhy. Fig. 1 (3 times)
8va
loco

Gtr. 1: w/ Rhy. Fig. 2 (1st 3 meas.)
D.S. al Coda
Gtr. 1: w/ Rhy. Fill 1
C F C C9
And
Coda
Gtr. 1: w/ Rhy. Fig. 2
C F C G
Well, uh. Oh, de, hah.
Outro-Chorus
Gtr. 1: w/ Rhy. Fig. 1 (3 times)
C Em F G
From the dark end of the street
(On the dark end of the street
to the bright side of the road.
to the bright side of the road.)
Lit-tle darl - in', come a - long,
We'll be lov - ers once a - gain,
bright side of the road.
(on the bright side of the road.
Gtr. 1: w/ Rhy. Fig. 2
One more time.
Uh, huh, ha!
Well, we be,
Gtr. 1: w/ Rhy. Fig. 1
Begin fade
we'll be lov - ers once a - gain
on the bright side of the road.
We'll be lov - ers once a - gain
Fade out

from *Led Zeppelin II*

Bring It on Home

Written by Willie Dixon

Intro

Moderately ♩ = 106 (♫ = ♩ ♪ triplet)

*E5 E6 E5 | E6 E5 | E6 E5

Gtr. 1 (clean)

Rhy. Fig. 1 — End Rhy. Fig. 1 — *Play 7 times*

mp

P.M.

*Chord symbols reflect implied harmony.

Gtr. 1: w/ Rhy. Fig. 1 (10 times)

E6 E5 | E6 E5 | E6 E5 | E6 E5

Ba - by. Mm,

E6 E5 | E6 E5 | E6 E5 | E6 E5

ba - by. Mm. Gon - na

E6 E5 | E6 E5 | E6 E5 | E6 E5

bring it on home to you. I've

E6 E5 | E6 E5 | E6 E5

got my tick - et. I got that load.

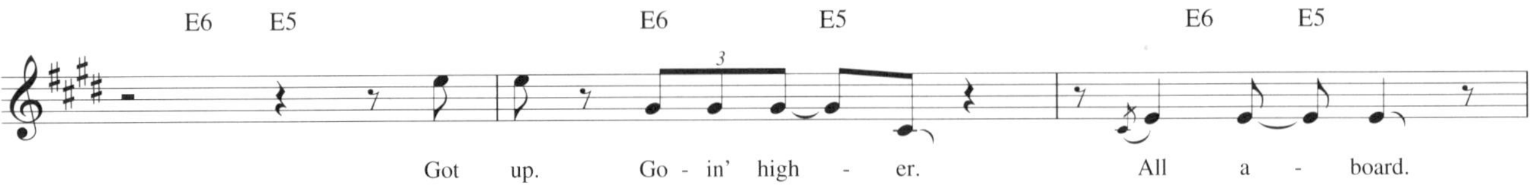

E6 E5 E6 E5 A5 A6 A5
'Ma take my seat,
Gtr. 1
P.M.
A6 A5 A6 A5 A6 A5
right way back. Oo. Yeah. I
P.M.
E6 E5 E6 E5 E6 E5
watch this train roll down the track.
P.M.
E6 E5 B5 B6 B5 B6 A5 A6 A5 A6
Gon-na bring it on home. Bring it on home to you.
P.M.

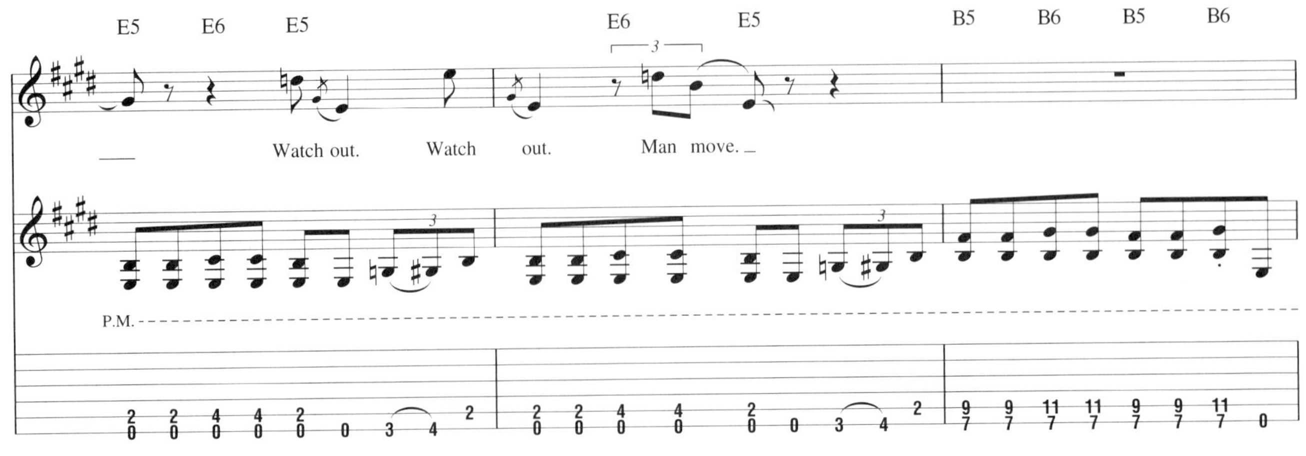

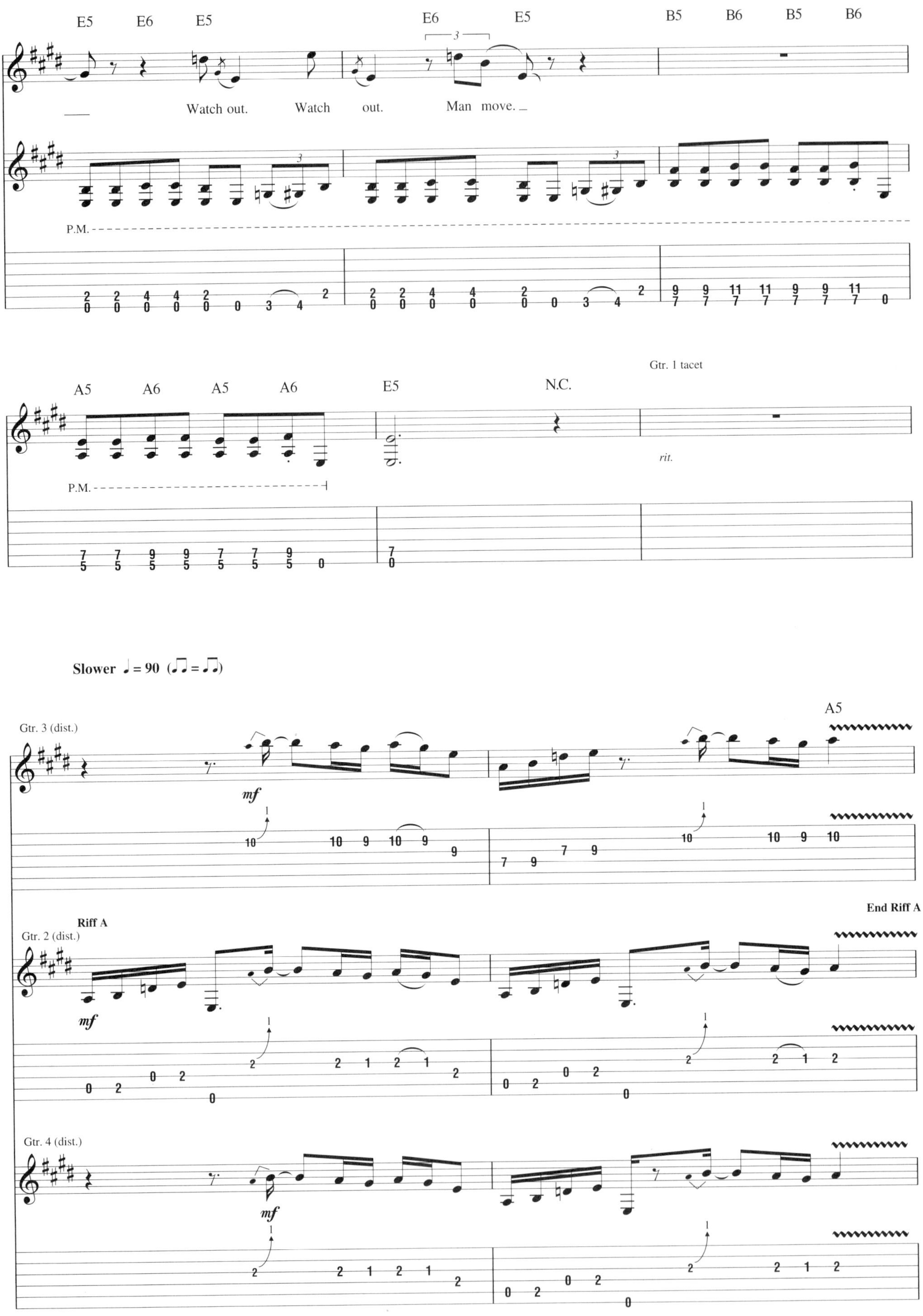

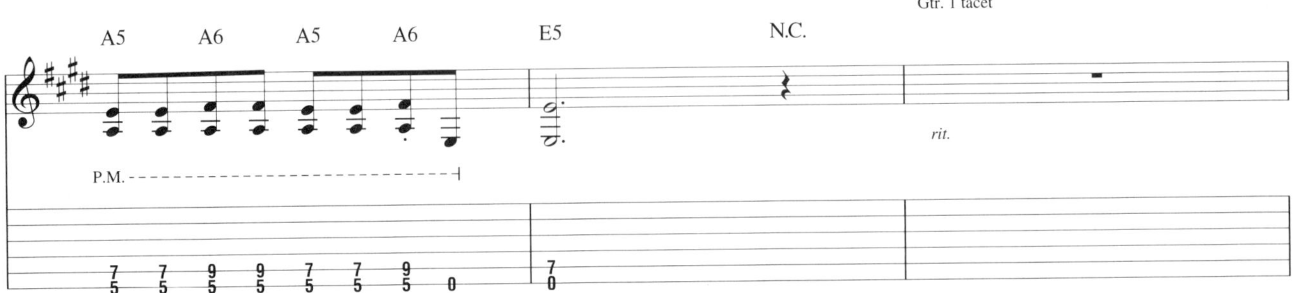

Slower ♩ = 90 (♫ = ♩♪)

Gtr. 3 (dist.)

A5

mf

Riff A

Gtr. 2 (dist.)

mf

End Riff A

Gtr. 4 (dist.)

mf

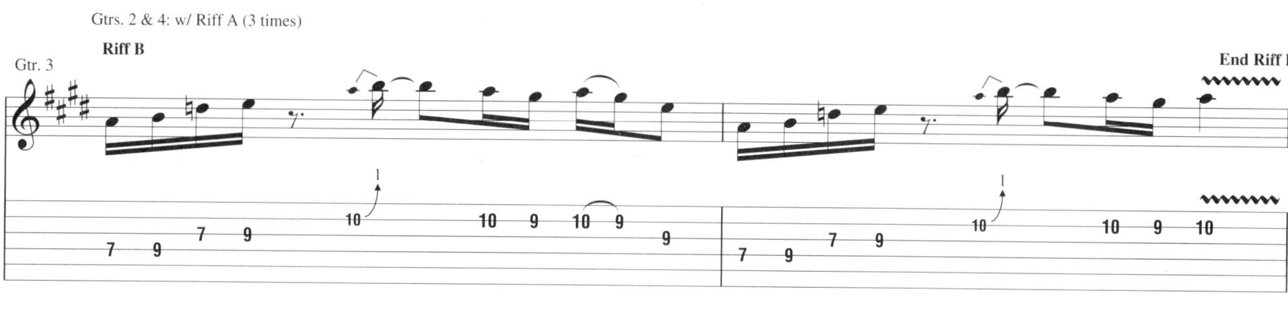
Gtrs. 2 & 4: w/ Riff A (3 times)
Riff B
Gtr. 3
End Riff B

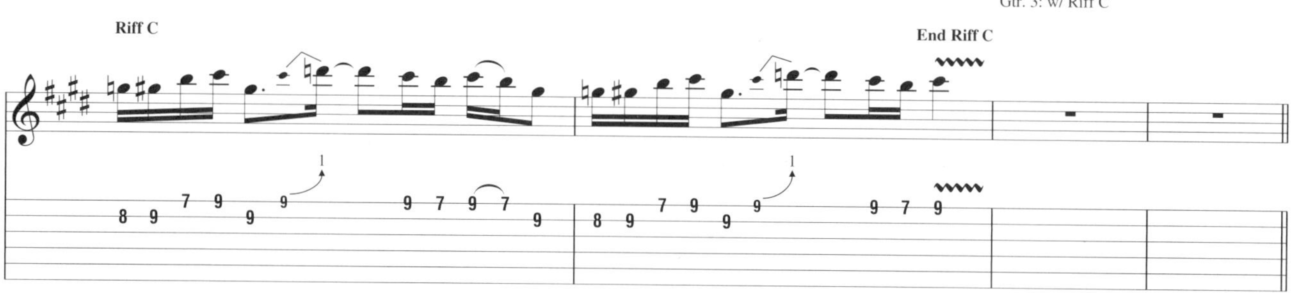
Gtr. 3: w/ Riff C
Riff C
End Riff C

Verse
E
G5 A5
E
G5 E5
1. Try to tell_ you, ba - by. What you try - in' to do.?_
2. Tell you, pret - ty ba - by. Love you mess_ me 'round._
Gtr. 2
Riff D
End Riff D
Gtr. 4
Riff D1
End Riff D1

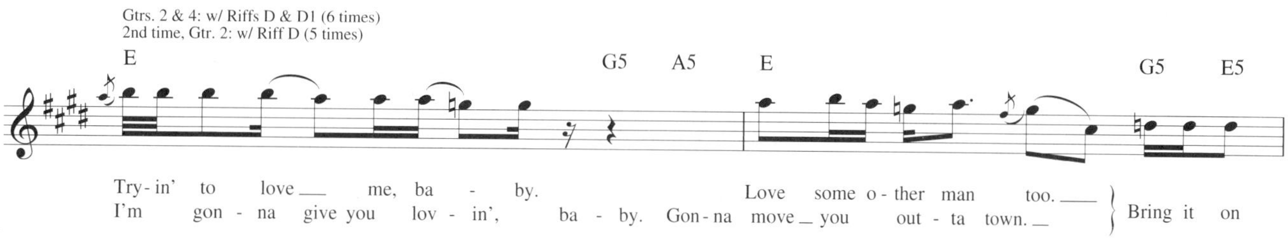
Gtrs. 2 & 4: w/ Riffs D & D1 (6 times)
2nd time, Gtr. 2: w/ Riff D (5 times)
E
G5 A5
E
G5 E5
Try - in' to love_ me, ba - by. Love some o - ther man too._
I'm gon - na give you lov - in', ba - by. Gon - na move_ you out - ta town._
Bring it on

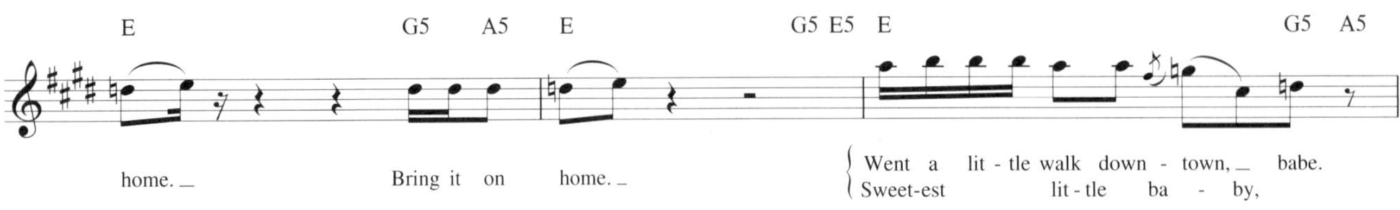
2nd time, Gtr. 3: w/ Fill 1 (8 times)
E G5 A5 E G5 E5 E G5 A5
home. Bring it on home.
Went a lit - tle walk down - town, babe.
Sweet-est lit - tle ba - by,

E G5 E5 E G5 A5
Missed and got back late.
dad - dy ev - er saw.
Found a note there wait - in'. It said
I'm gon - na give you lov - in', ba - by. I'm

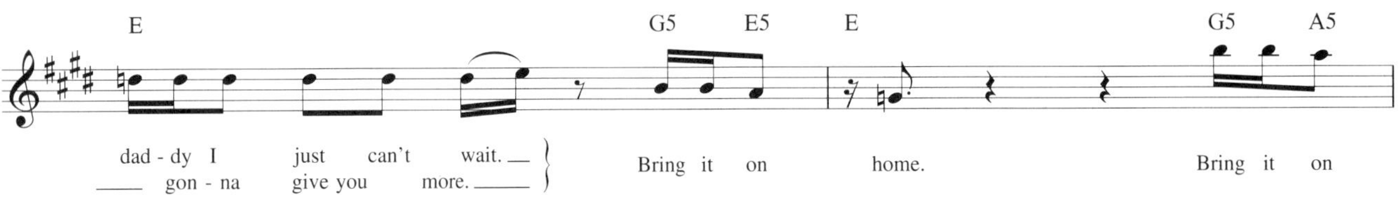
E G5 E5 E G5 A5
dad - dy I just can't wait.
gon - na give you more.
Bring it on home. Bring it on

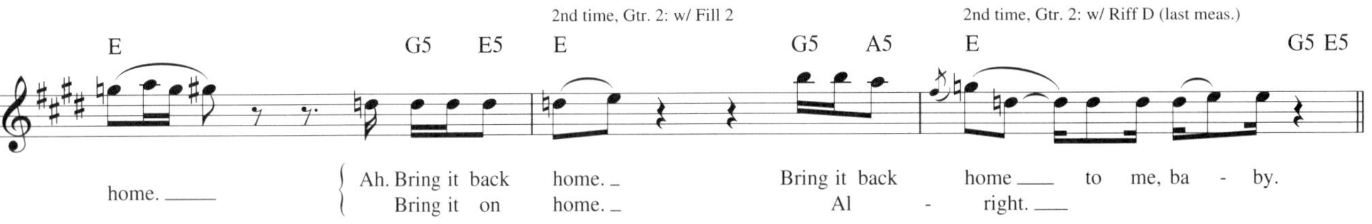
2nd time, Gtr. 2: w/ Fill 2
2nd time, Gtr. 2: w/ Riff D (last meas.)
E G5 E5 E G5 A5 E G5 E5
home.
Ah. Bring it back home. Bring it back home to me, ba - by.
Bring it on home. Al - right.

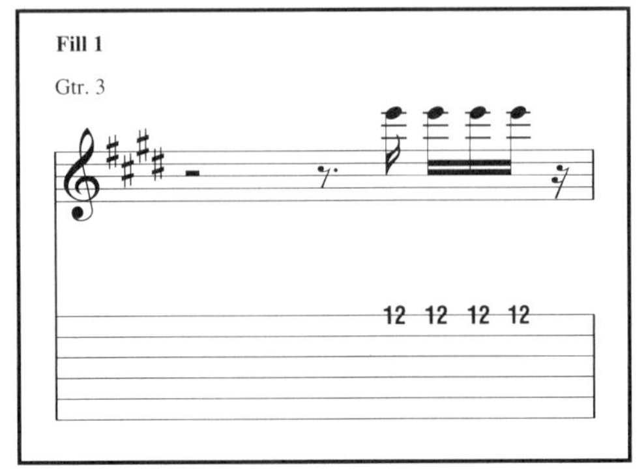
Fill 1
Gtr. 3
12 12 12 12

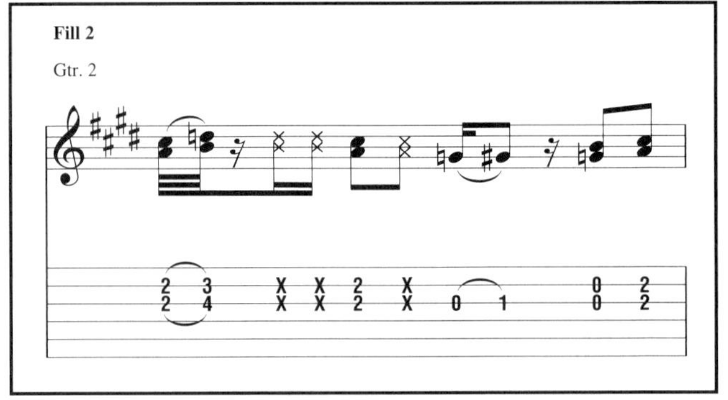
Fill 2
Gtr. 2

Interlude

1st time, Gtrs. 2 & 4: w/ Riff A (4 times)
2nd time, Gtrs. 2 & 4: w/ Riff A (3 3/4 times)

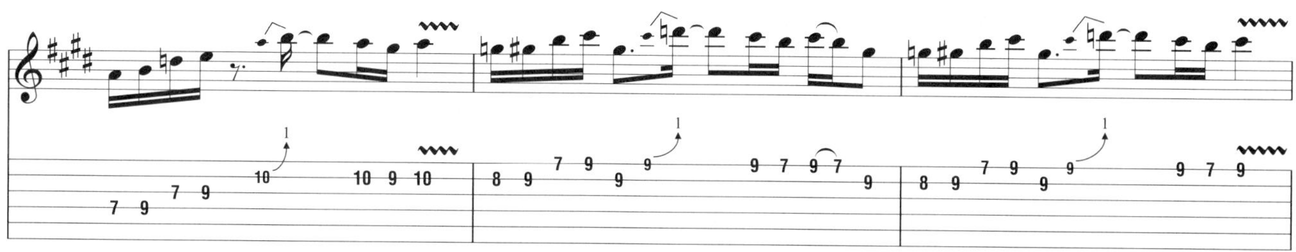

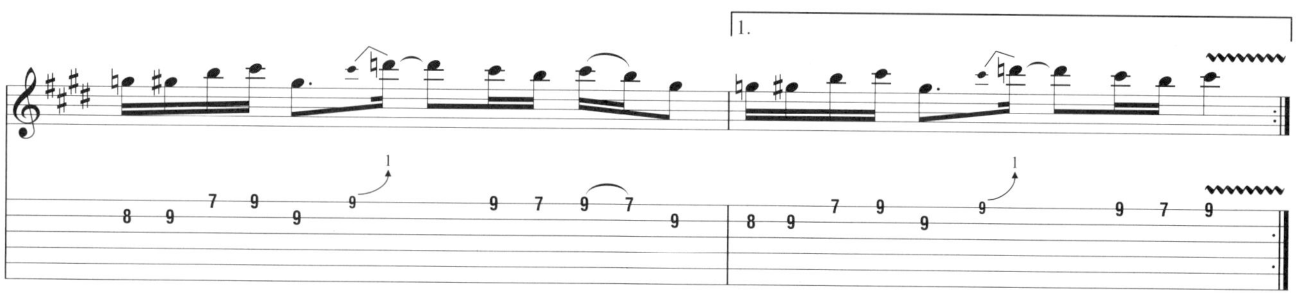

Outro
Slower ♩ = 80
Gtrs. 2, 3 & 4 tacet
B5 B6 B5 B6/9 A5 A6 A5 A6
Bring it on home.
Bring it on home to you.
Gtr. 1
P.M.
E5 E6 E5 E6 E5 E A5
B5 B6/9 B5 B6/9 A5 A6 A5 E5
rit.
let ring
E Am/E C♯m6/E E7(no3rd) E6 E7
w/ pick & fingers
mp

from Def Leppard - *High 'n' Dry*

Bringin' on the Heartbreak

Words and Music by Joe Elliott, Richard Savage, Richard Allen, Steve Clark and Peter Willis

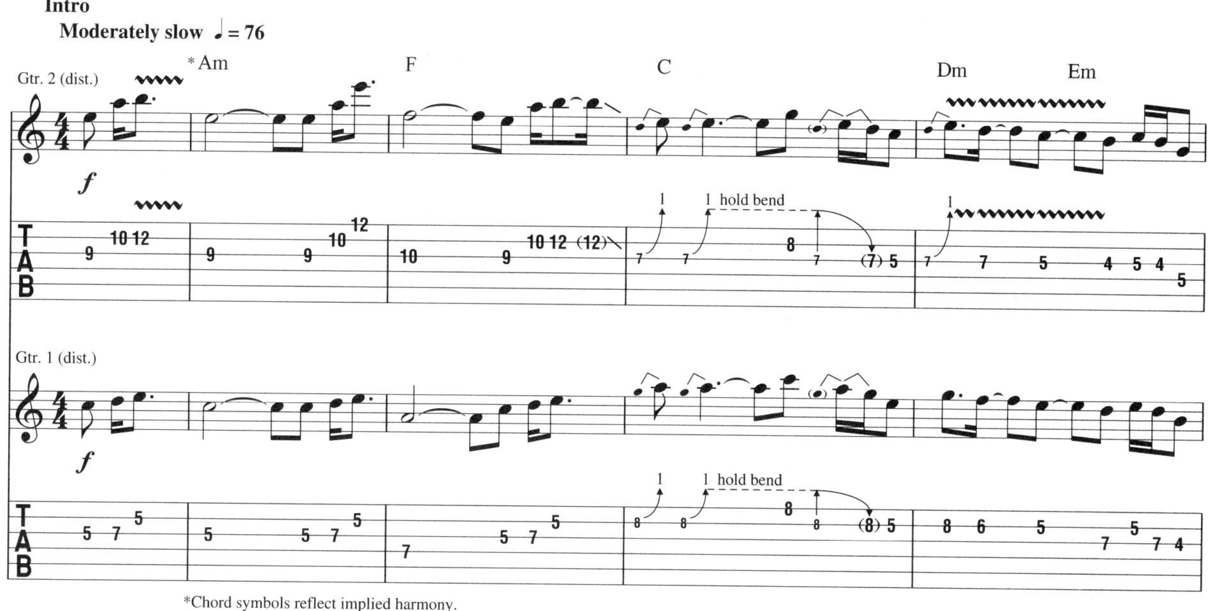

*Chord symbols reflect implied harmony.

Verse
1st time, Gtr. 3: w/ Riff A (3 times)
Am F(♯11)/A Am G6 Fmaj13
1. Gyp - sy, sit - ting look - ing pret - ty, a bro - ken rose with laugh - ing eyes.
2nd time, Gtr. 3: w/ Riff B (2 times)
Bm(maj7)♭5 E7(no3rd) Am F(♯11)/A Am G6
You're a mys - t'ry, al - ways run - ning wild like a child with -
- cret, mist - y eyed and shad - y. La - dy, how you
Fmaj13 Bm(maj7)♭5 E7(no3rd) Am F(♯11)/A
out a home. You're al - ways search - ing, search - ing for a feel -
hold the key. Oh, you're like a can - dle your flame is slow - ly fad -
Am G6 Fmaj13 Bm(maj7)♭5 E7(no3rd)
- ing, but it's eas - y come and eas - y go. Oh, I'm sor - ry, but it's
- ing, burn - ing out and burn - ing me. Can't you see? Just try'n' to say to you,
Pre-Chorus
C5 G5 D5 B5 C5 G5 C5
true, you're bring - in' on the heart - ache, tak - in' all the best of me. Oh, can't you
Riff B
*Gtr. 4 (dist.)
End Riff B
f
let ring
P.M.
*Doubled throughout
G5 C5 G5 C5 G5
see? You got the best of me. Oh, can't you see? You're bring - in' on the heart -
P.M.
slight P.M.

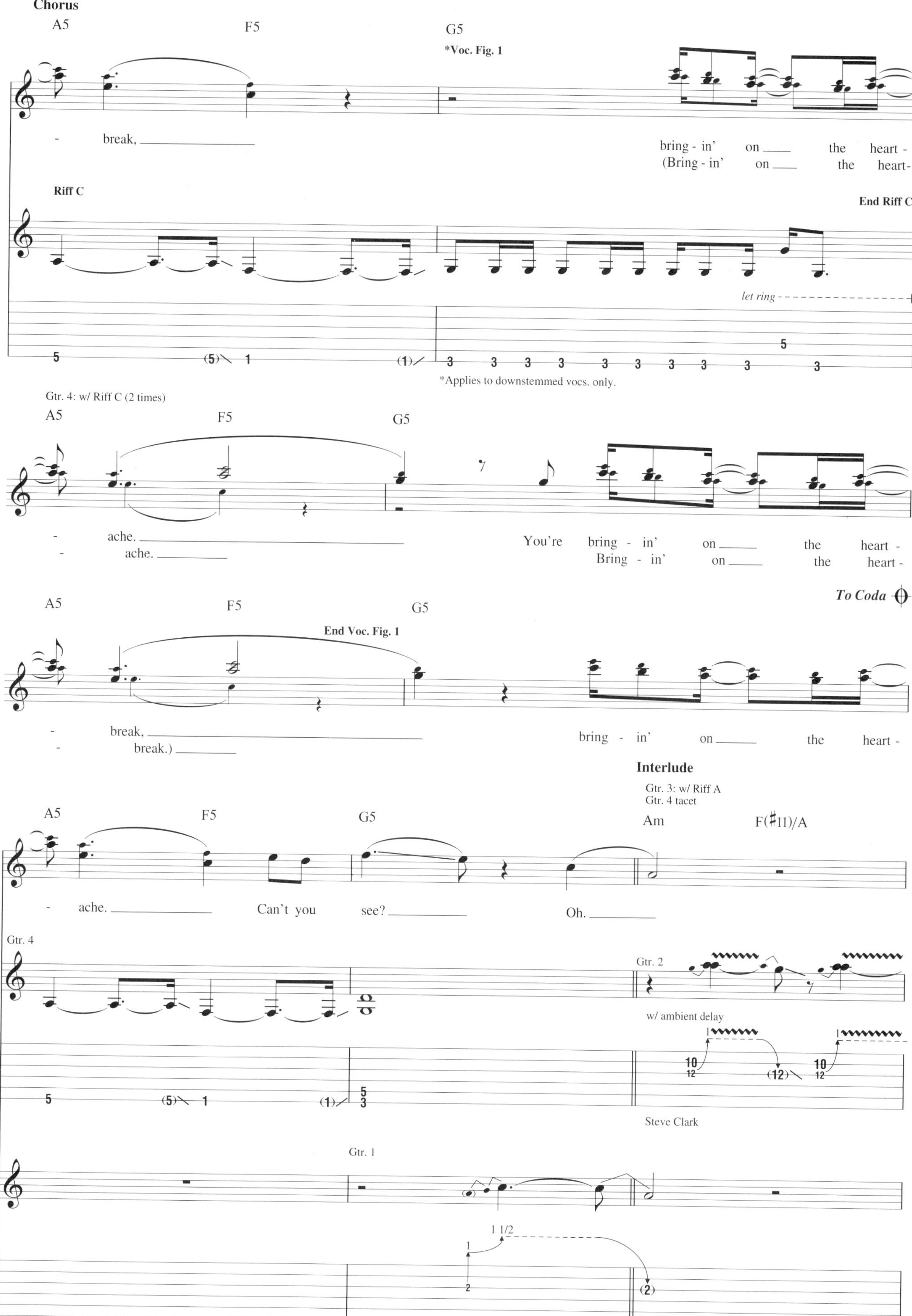

Chorus
A5
F5
G5
*Voc. Fig. 1
break,
bring - in' on the heart -
(Bring - in' on the heart-
Riff C
End Riff C
let ring
*Applies to downstemmed vocs. only.
Gtr. 4: w/ Riff C (2 times)
A5
F5
G5
ache.
ache.
You're bring - in' on the heart -
Bring - in' on the heart -
A5
F5
G5
To Coda
End Voc. Fig. 1
break,
break.)
bring - in' on the heart -
Interlude
Gtr. 3: w/ Riff A
Gtr. 4 tacet
A5
F5
G5
Am
F(♯11)/A
ache. Can't you see? Oh.
Gtr. 4
Gtr. 2
w/ ambient delay
Steve Clark
Gtr. 1

D.S. al Coda
Gtr. 1 tacet
Am
G6
Fmaj13
Bm(maj7)♭5
E7(no3rd)
2. You're such a se -
Gtr. 2
Coda
A5
F5
G5
- ache.
Can't you see?
Can't you
see?
No,
Gtr. 4
dim.
Guitar Solo
A5
F5
G5
E5
no,
no.
Gtr. 2
Gtr. 4
let ring
let ring
let ring
let ring

C5
A5
G5
F5
P.H.
let ring

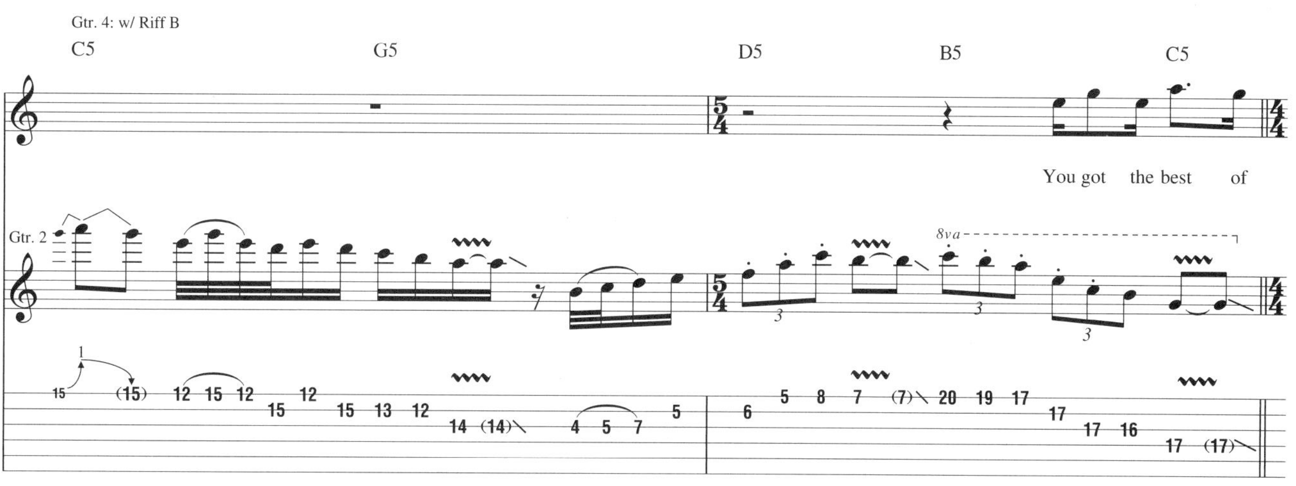
Gtr. 4: w/ Riff B
C5
G5
D5
B5
C5
You got the best of
Gtr. 2
8va

Pre-Chorus

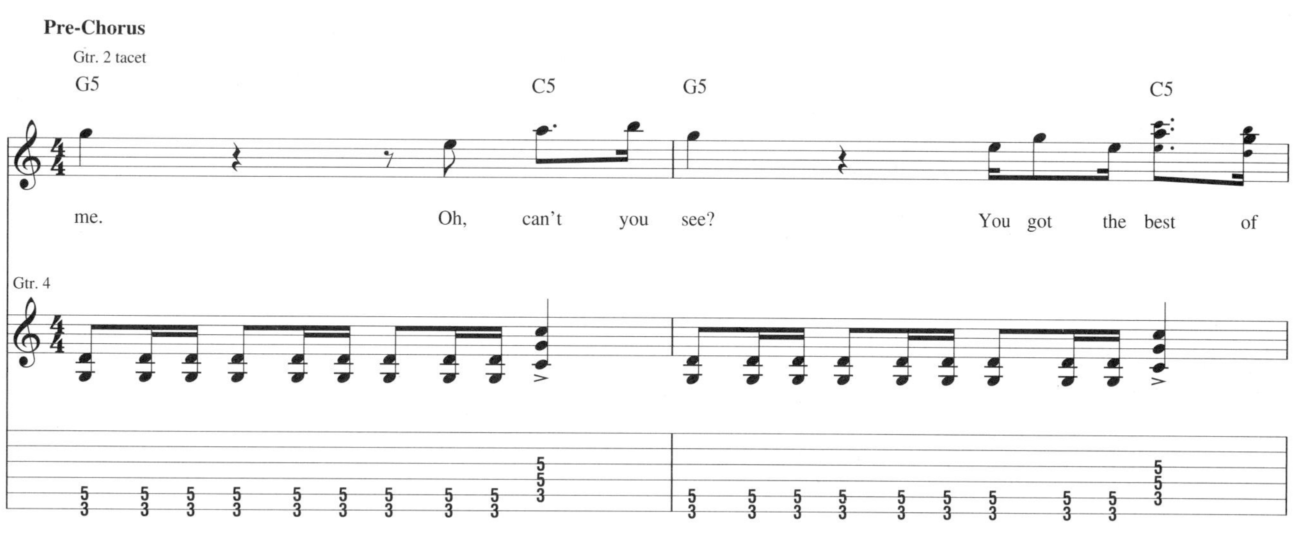
Gtr. 2 tacet
G5
C5
G5
C5
me. Oh, can't you see? You got the best of
Gtr. 4

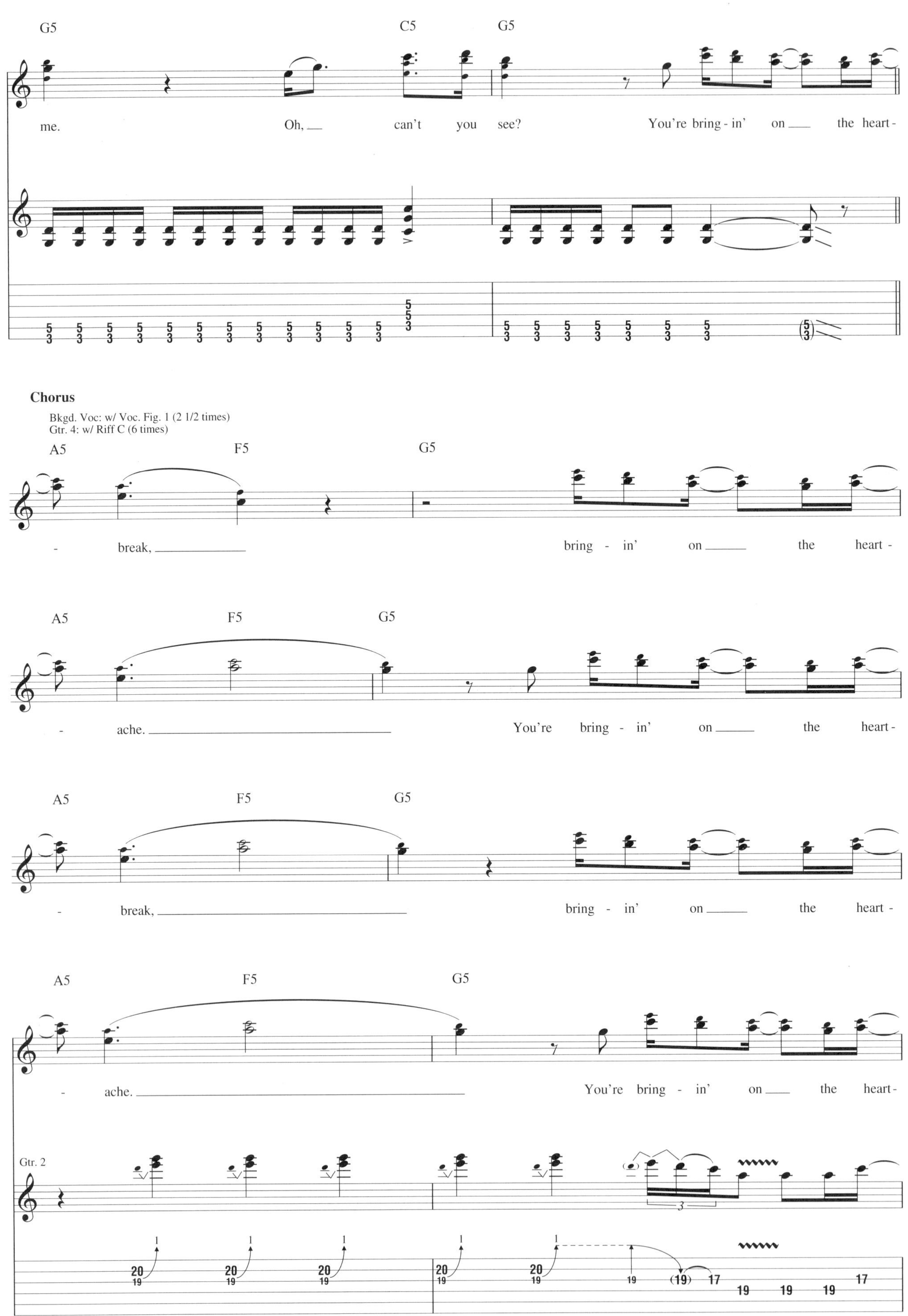
G5
C5
G5
me.
Oh, __
can't
you
see?
You're bring - in'
on __
the heart -
Chorus
Bkgd. Voc: w/ Voc. Fig. 1 (2 1/2 times)
Gtr. 4: w/ Riff C (6 times)
A5
F5
G5
- break, ______
bring - in'
on ______
the
heart -
A5
F5
G5
- ache. ______
You're
bring - in'
on ______
the
heart -
A5
F5
G5
- break, ______
bring - in'
on ______
the
heart -
A5
F5
G5
- ache. ______
You're
bring - in'
on __
the
heart -
Gtr. 2

A5
F5
G5
- break,
bring - in' on the heart -
8va
1 hold bend
A5
F5
G5
- ache.
You're bring - in' on the heart -
8va
loco
steady gliss.
Segue to "Switch 625"
Faster ♩ = 138
A5
F5
G5
rit.
- ache.
Gtr. 2
rit.
w/ bar
grad. dive
fdbk.
grad. release
Gtr. 4
rit.

from Chuck Berry - *After School Session*

Brown-Eyed Handsome Man

Words and Music by Chuck Berry

A♭
The judge-'s wife called up the dis-trict at-tor-ney. She said,
She been walk-in' thir-ty miles en route to Bom-bay to meet a
there's been a whole lot of good wom-en shed-din' tears all for a

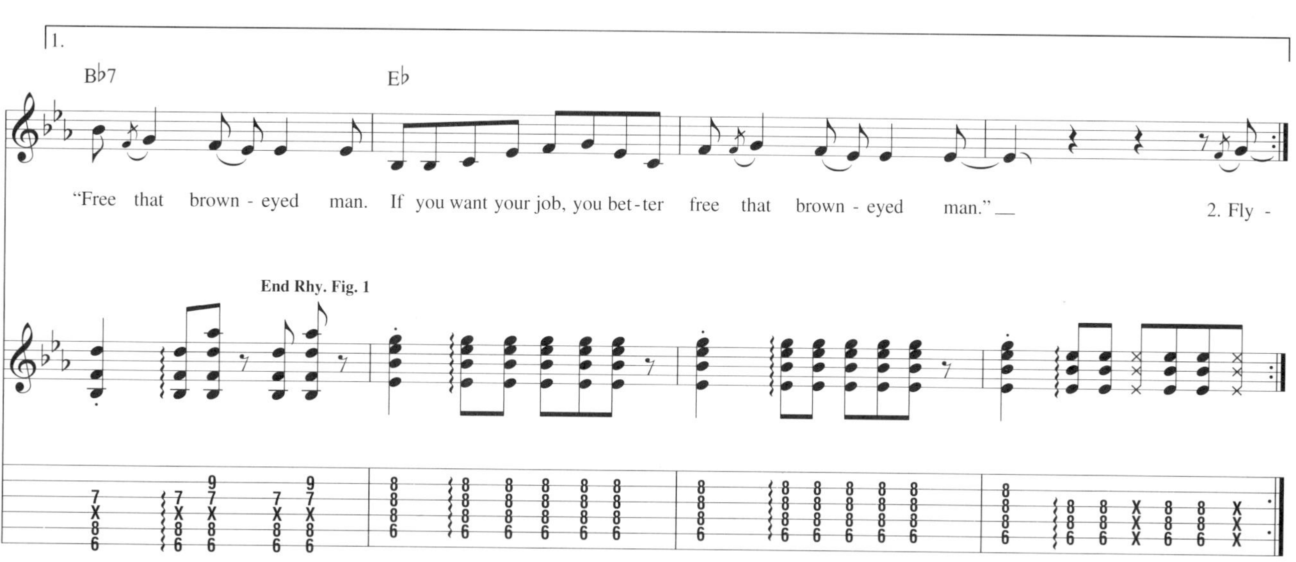
1.
B♭7
E♭
"Free that brown-eyed man. If you want your job, you bet-ter free that brown-eyed man."
2. Fly-
End Rhy. Fig. 1

2.
B♭7
E♭
brown-eyed hand-some man. Her des-ti-na-tion was a brown-eyed hand-some man.
3. Way
let ring
let ring

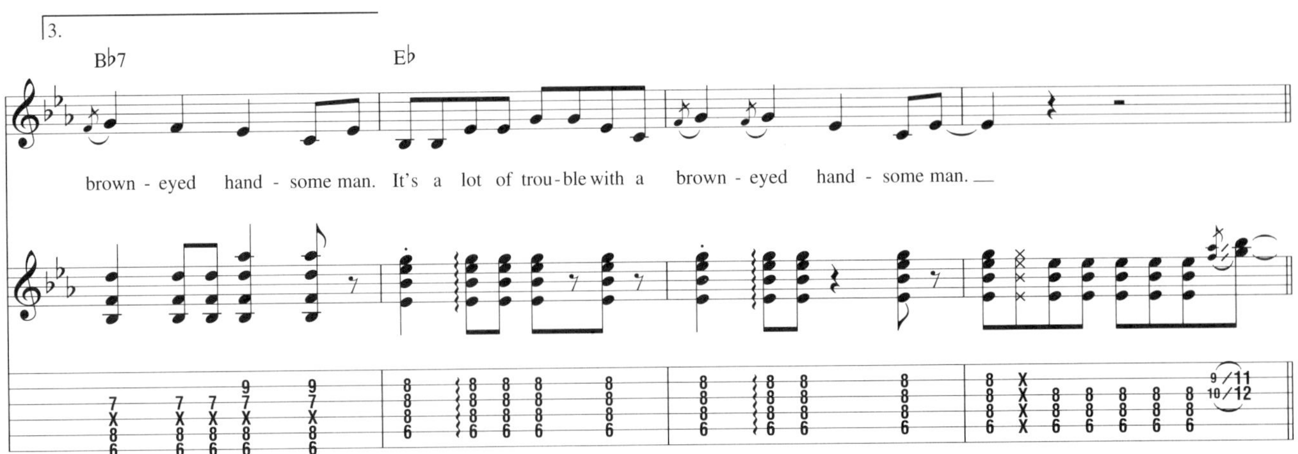

Guitar Solo

*Chord symbols reflect overall harmony.

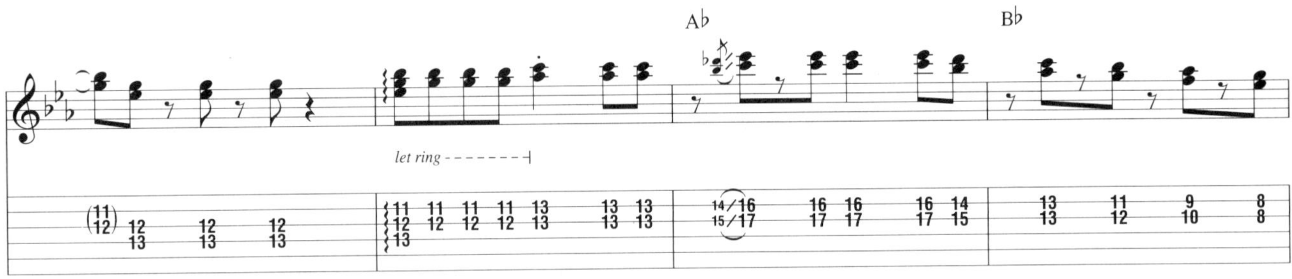

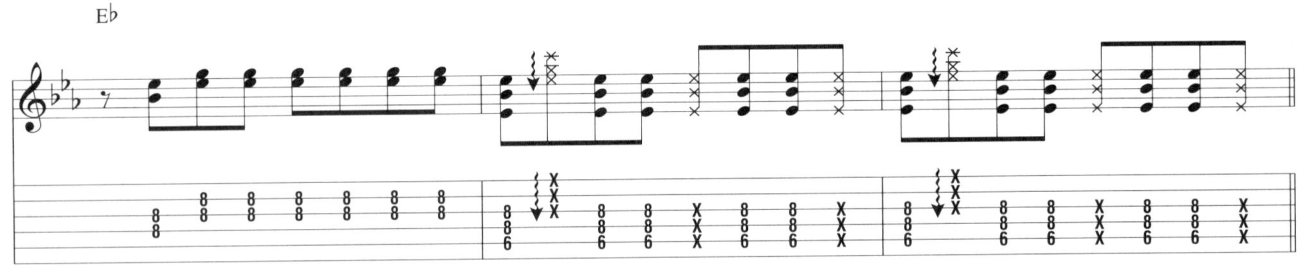

Piano Solo

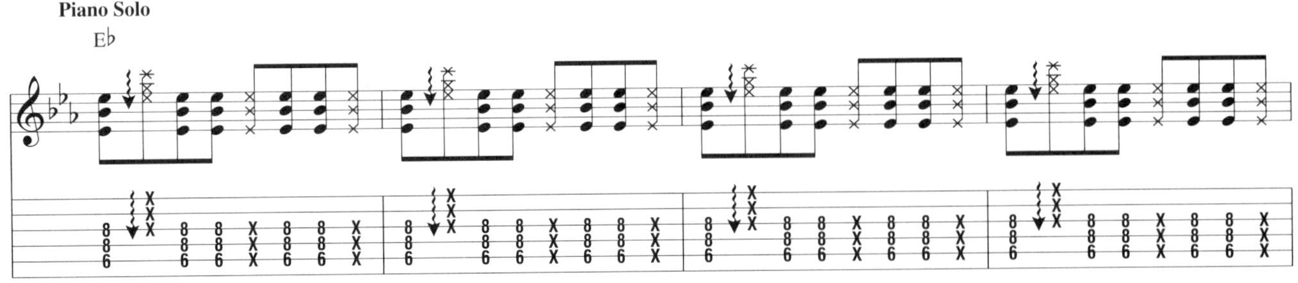

Ab
Bb7
let ring
Eb
Ab
Bb
Eb7
Guitar Solo
Eb
Ab
Bb
Eb
Verse
Gtr. 1: w/ Rhy. Fig. 1
Eb
4. Beau - ti - ful daugh - ter could - n't make up her mind _ be - tween a doc - tor and a law - yer man. _ Her
5. Mar - lo Ve - nus was a beau - ti - ful lass, _ she had the world in the palm of her hand. _ She
- three, the count with no - bod - y on, _ he hit a high fly in - to the stands. _
Ab
Bb7
moth - er told her, "Dar - ling, go _ out and find _ your - self a brown - eyed hand - some man. _
lost both her arms in a wres - tl - ing match _ to meet a brown - eyed hand - some man. _
Round - ed third, _ he was head - ed for home. _ It was a brown - eyed hand - some man _

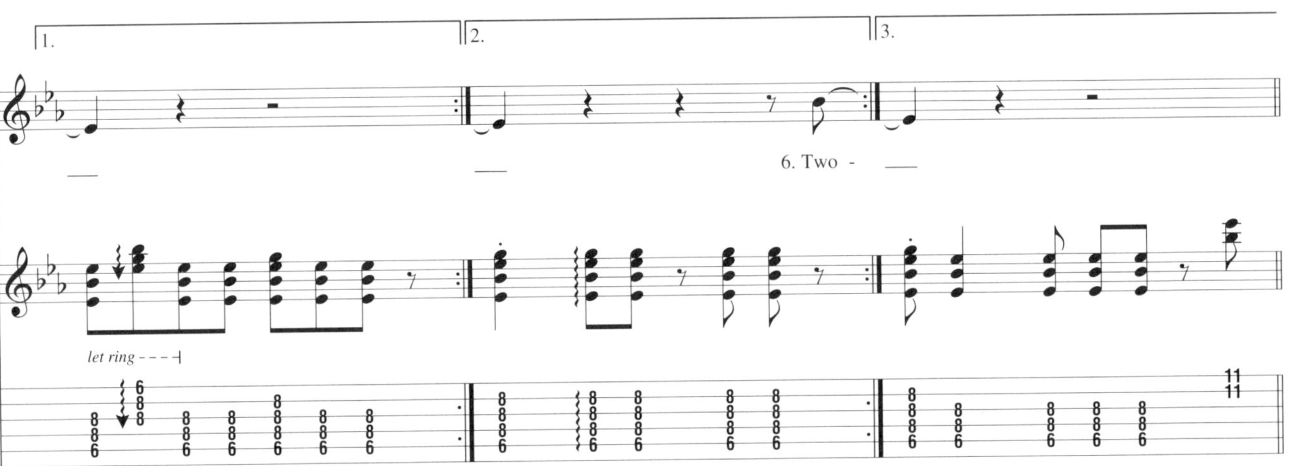

Outro-Guitar Solo

Begin fade

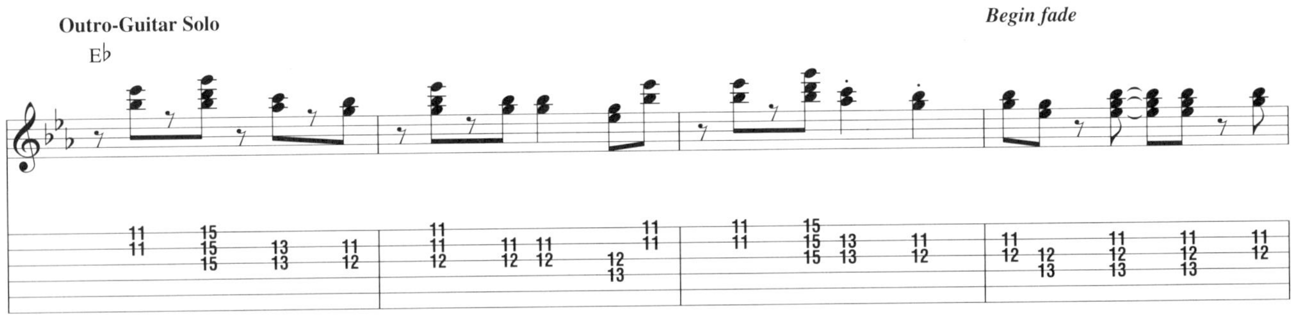

Fade out

from Bob Dylan - *Blood on the Tracks*

Buckets of Rain

Words and Music by Bob Dylan

Gtr. 1: Open E tuning:
(low to high) E-B-E-G♯-B-E

Intro

Moderately 𝅗𝅥 = 86

3rd time, Gtr. 1: w/ Rhy. Fill 1
5th time, Gtr. 1: w/ Rhy. Fill 2

*E

Gtr. 1 (acous.)

mf

w/ fingers

let ring throughout

**

*Chord symbols reflect overall harmony.

**Pull off from A (3rd str., 1st fr.) to open G♯.

E
B
A

To Coda
E/G#
F#m7
E

Verse
E
1. Buck - ets of rain, buck - ets of tears; got all them buck - ets com - in'
2.-5. See additional lyrics

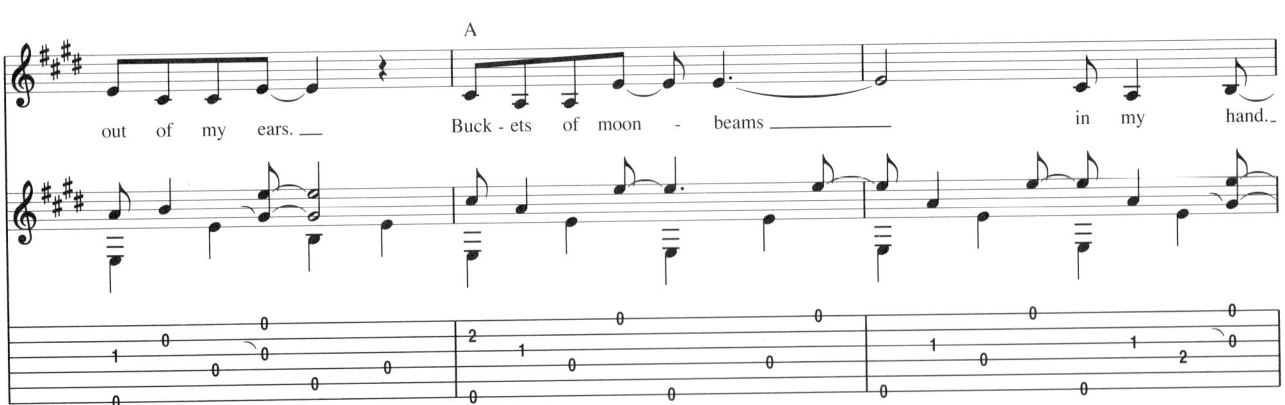
A
out of my ears. Buck - ets of moon - beams in my hand.

E
B
B/A
You got all the love, uh,

1.-4.
5.
D.C. al Coda
A/G♯
F♯m7
E
hon - ey ba - by, I can stand.

Coda
Outro
E

A

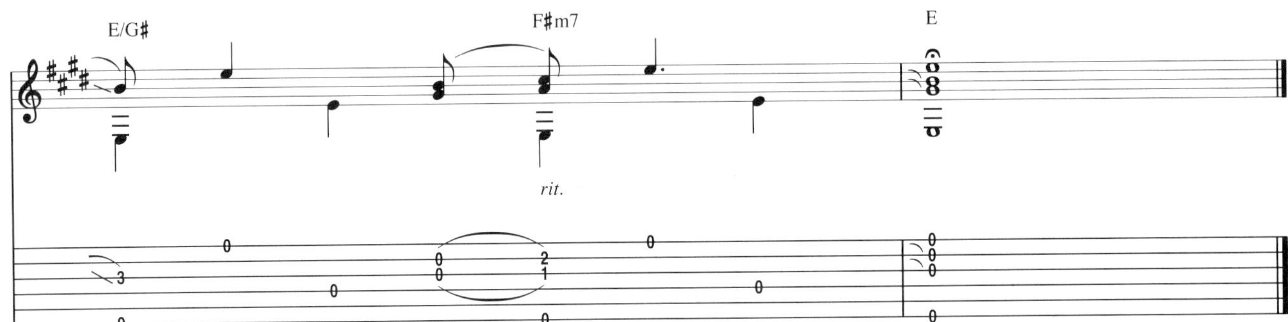

Additional Lyrics

2. I've been meek and hard like an oak.
I've seen pretty people disappear like smoke.
Friends will arrive, friends will disappear.
If you want me, honey baby, I'll be here.

3. I like your smile and your fingertips.
I like the way that you move your hips.
I like the cool way you look at me.
Everything about you is bringing me misery.

4. Little red wagon, little red bike;
I ain't no monkey but I know what I like.
I like the way you love me strong and slow.
I'm taking you with me, honey baby, when I go.

5. Life is sad, life is a bust.
All you can do is do what you must.
You do what you must do, and you do it well.
I do it for you. Honey baby, can't you tell?

from "M.U." - *The Best of Jethro Tull*

Bungle in the Jungle

Words and Music by Ian Anderson

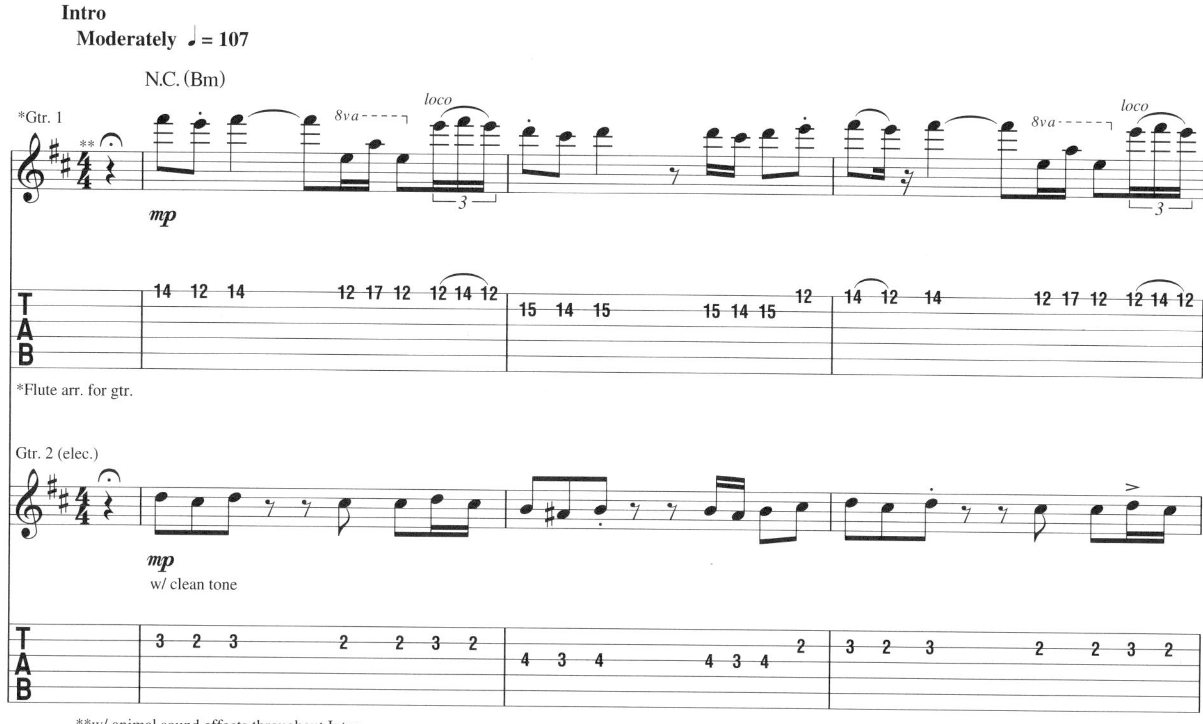

Verse
Gr. 1 tacet
Gtr. 3: w/ Fill 1
*Bm Bm/D E5 F♯ Bm Bm/D
1. Walk-ing through for - ests of palm tree a - part - ments, scoff at the mon - keys who
2. Just say a word and the boys will be right there with claws at your back to send the
riv - ers are full of croc - o - dile nas - ties and he who made kit - tens put
Gtr. 2
mf
mp
P.M.
*Chord symbols reflect overall harmony.
Pre-Chorus
E5 F♯ Bm F♯ A Bm A/C♯
live in their dark tents. Down by the wa - ter - hole, drunk ev - 'ry Fri - day,
chill through the night air. Is it so fright - 'ning to have me at your shoul - der?
snakes in the grass. He's a lov - er of life but a play - er of pawns, yes, the
w/ dist.
Gtr. 3: w/ Fill 2
F♯ A Bm A/C♯ F♯ A
eat - ing thier nuts, sav - ing their rai - sins for Sun - day. Li - ons and ti - gers who
Thun - der and light - ning could - n't be bold - er. I'll write on your tomb - stone: "I
king on his sun - set lies wait - ing for dawn to light up his jun - gle as
Gtr. 4 (acous.)
Fill 1
Gtr. 3 (elec.)
w/ dist.
Fill 2
Gtr. 3

Bm A F♯ A Bm A B

wait_ in the shad - ows,_ they're fast but they're la - zy_ and sleep in green mead - ows._
thank you for din - ner." This game that we an - i - mals play is the win - ner._
play is re - sumed.___ The mon-keys seem will - ing to strike up the tune.___

To Coda 𝄌 **Chorus**

G A D

Well, let's bun - gle_ in the jun - gle,___ well,_ that's_

Rhy. Fig. 1

Rhy. Fig. 1A

P.M.

2nd time, Gtr. 3: w/ Fill 3
G
A
B
B5
G
A
D
all right by me, yes. Well, I'm a ti - ger when I want
P.M.
2nd time, Gtr. 3: w/ Fill 4
G
A
B
love, but I'm a snake if we dis - a - gree.
End Rhy. Fig. 1
End Rhy. Fig. 1A
Fill 3
Gtr. 3
Fill 4
Gtr. 3

Interlude
Gtr. 2 tacet
Bm
A5
F♯5
Gtr. 4
Gtr. 5 (acous.)
mf
Gtr. 4
divisi
Gtr. 2
Gtrs. 4, 5 & 6 tacet
Gtr. 6 (acous.)
mf
Gtr. 5
Gtr. 4
divisi
D.S. al Coda
N.C.
3. The
Gtr. 2

Coda

Chorus

Gtrs. 2 & 4: w/ Rhy. Figs. 1 & 1A (1st 7 meas.)

G A D G A B

bun - gle in the jun - gle, well, that's all right by me,

B5 G A D

yes. I'm a ti - ger when I want love, and I'm a

Gtr. 3

Gtrs. 2 & 4: w/ Rhy. Fill 1

Gtr. 2 & 4: w/ Rhy. Figs. 1 & 1A (till fade)

G A B5 G A D

snake when we dis - a - gree, yes. Let's bun - gle in the jun -

G A B B5

- gle, well, it's all right by me, yes. Well, I'm a

grad. bend

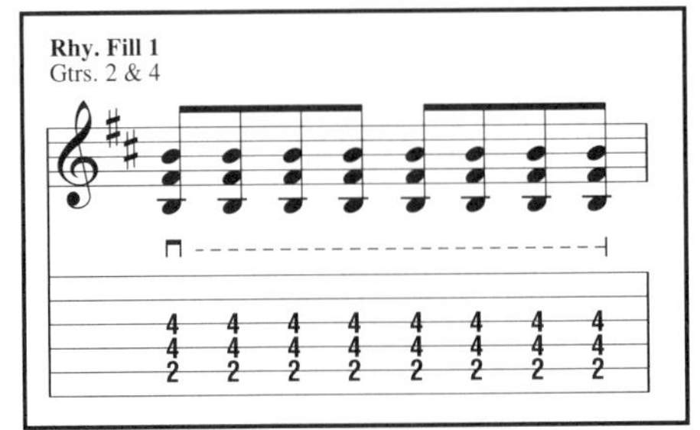

G A D G A
ti - ger when I want love, I'm a snake when we dis -
9 7

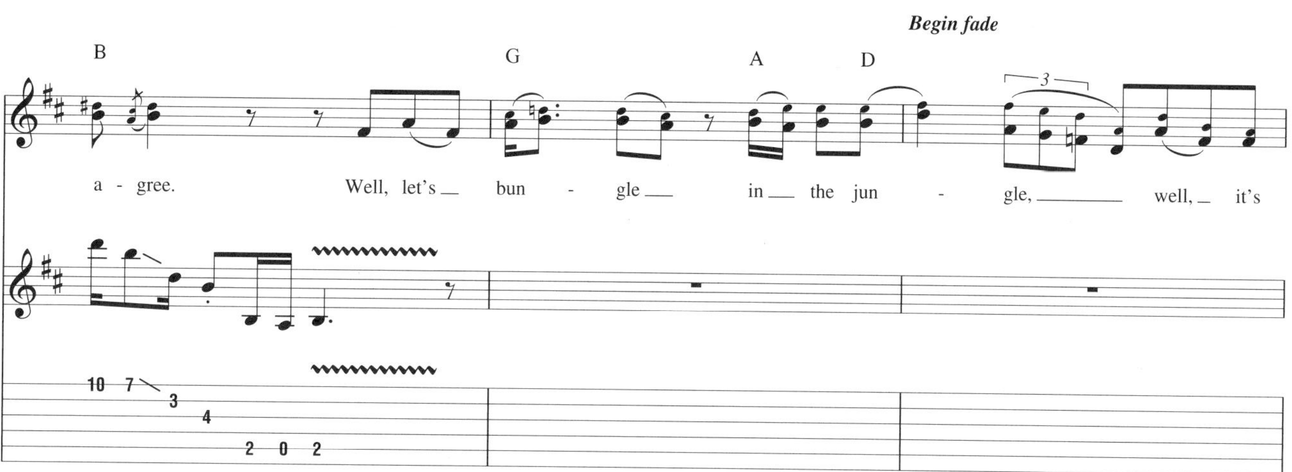
Begin fade
B G A D
a - gree. Well, let's bun - gle in the jun - gle, well, it's
10 7 3 4 2 0 2

Gtr. 7: w/ Fill 5
Fade out
G A B B5 G A D
all right by me, yes. I'm a ti - ger when I want love, I'm a...
7 10 10 7 10 10 7 10 (10) 9 7 9 5

Fill 5
Gtr. 7 (elec.)
f
w/ dist.
7 9 9 7 10 10 7 10

from The Ramones - *Leave Home*

California Sun

Words and Music by Morris Levy and Henry Glover

where the days are short and the
let ring
nights are long.
And I walk,
let ring
E
A
E
and they walk.
I twist,
and they
A
E
A
twist.
And I shim - my,
and they shim - my.
And I fly,

E
A
E
and they fly.
Well, we're out there hav - in' fun
To Coda
1.
C♯m
A
B
E
N.C.
in the warm Cal - i - for - nia sun.
2. Well, I'm
2.
Bridge
E
E
let ring
let ring
E

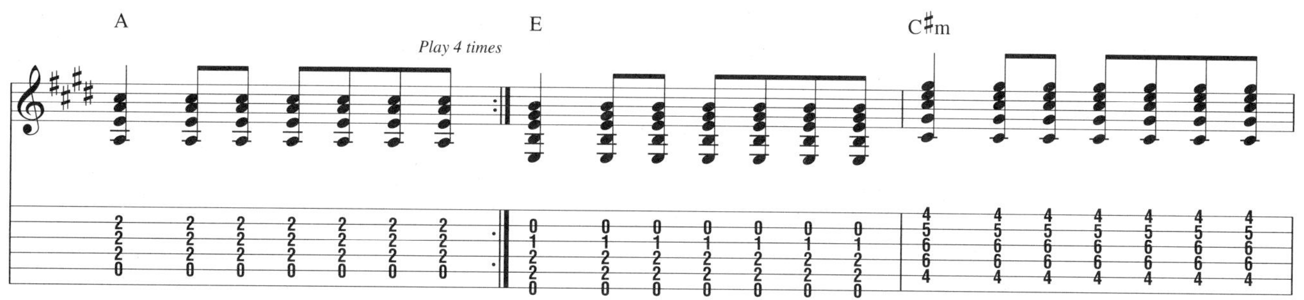

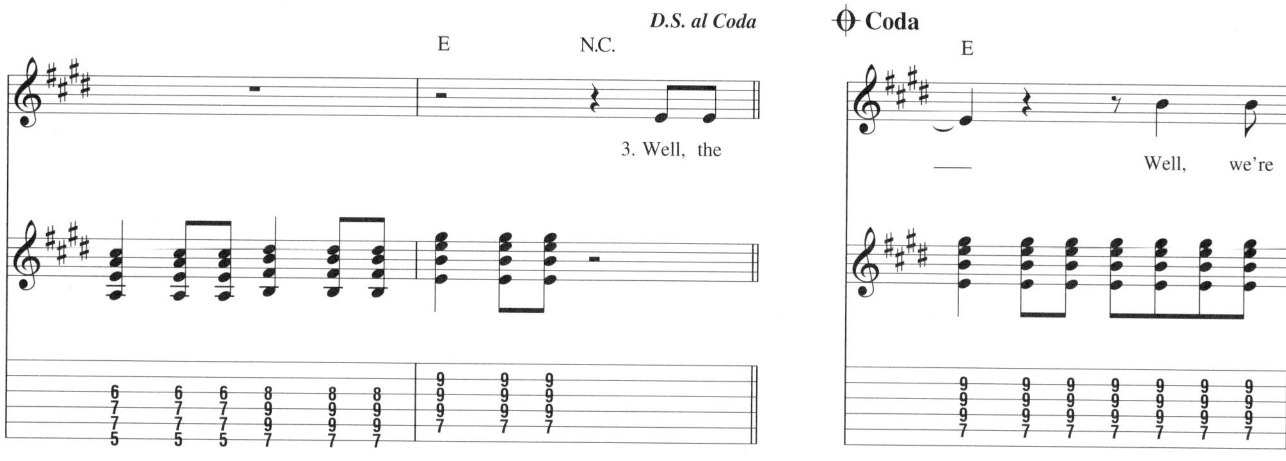

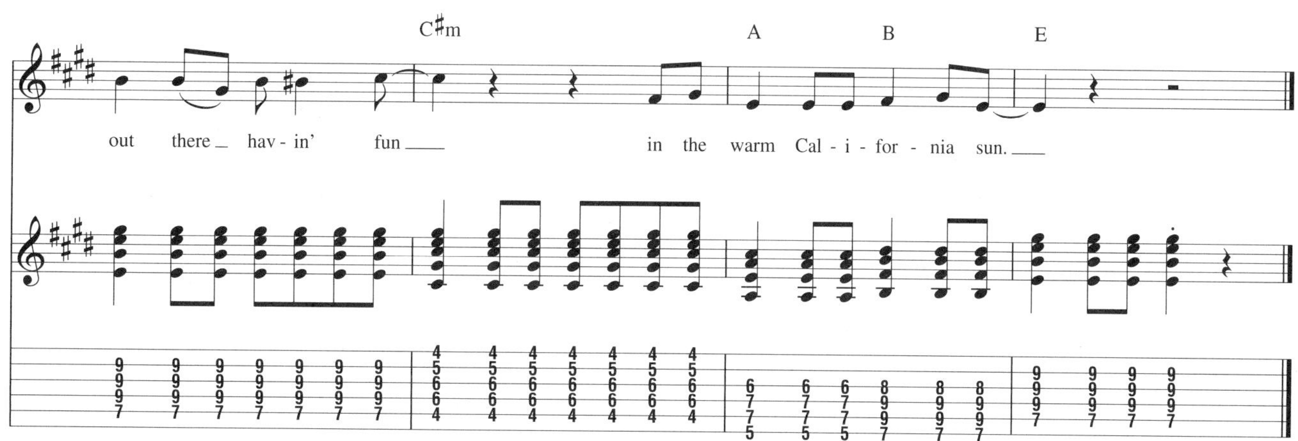

Additional Lyrics

2. Well, I'm goin' out west down on the coast
Where the California girls are really the most.
And I walk, and they walk. I twist, and they twist.
And I shimmy, and they shimmy. And I fly, and they fly.
Well, we're out there havin' fun in the warm California sun.

3. Well, the girls are frisky in old Frisco.
A pretty little chick wherever you go.
Oh, and I walk, and they walk. I twist, and they twist.
And I shimmy, and they shimmy. And I fly, and they fly.
Well, we're out there havin' fun in the warm California sun.
Well, we're out there havin' fun in the warm California sun.

from The Beatles - *A Hard Day's Night*

Can't Buy Me Love

Words and Music by John Lennon and Paul McCartney

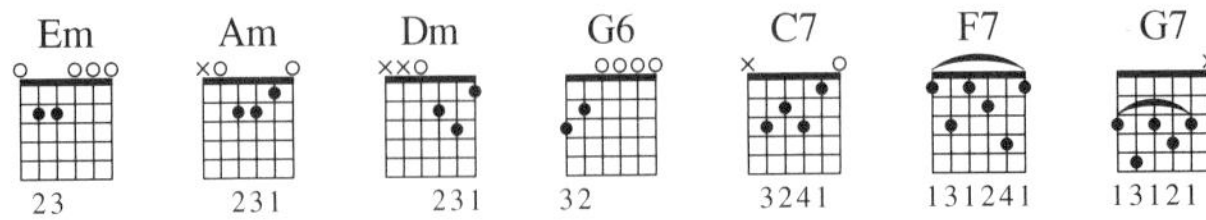

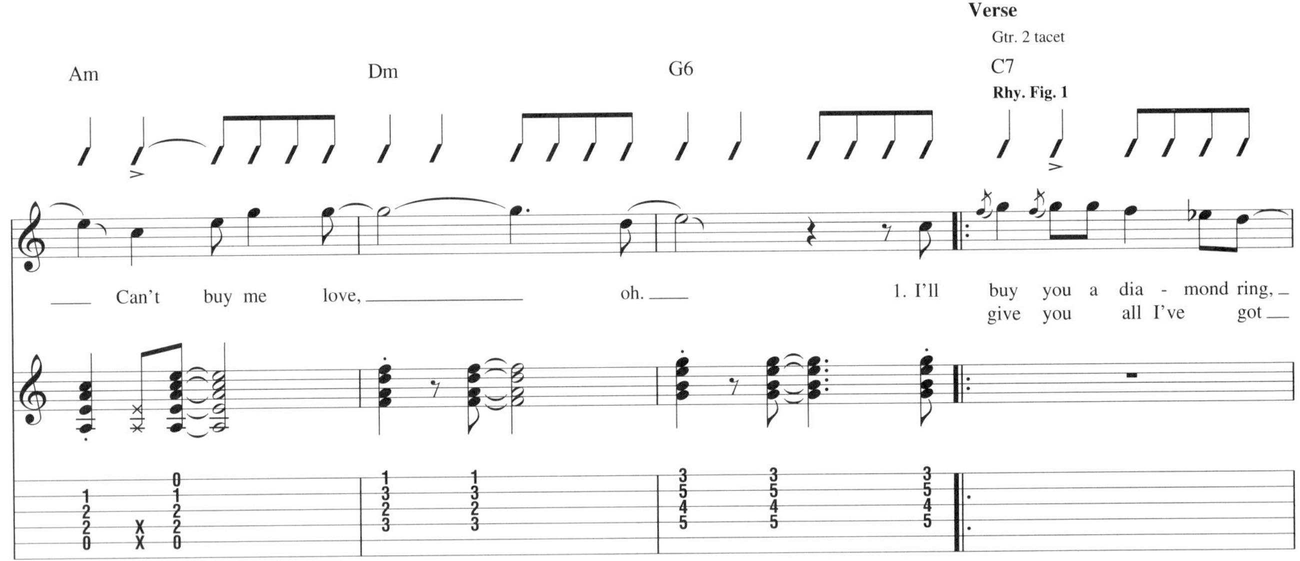

C7
G7
my friend, if it makes you feel al - right.
to give, but what I got I'll give to you.
'Cause I don't care too
F7
1.
2.
C7
End Rhy. Fig. 1
C7
much for mon-ey, 'cause mon-ey can't buy me love.
2. I'll
Can't buy me love,
Chorus
Em
Am
C7
oh.
Ev - 'ry-bod-y tells me so.
Can't buy me love,
Gtr. 2
Em
Am
Dm
G6
oh.
No, no, no, no!
3., 4. Say

Verse

Gtr. 1: w/ Rhy. Fig. 1
Gtr. 2 tacet

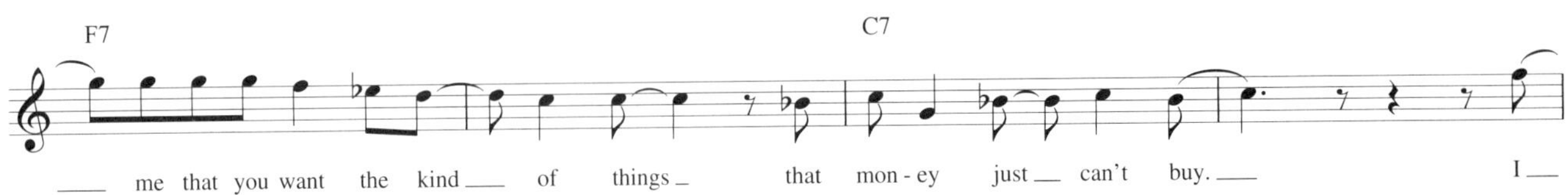

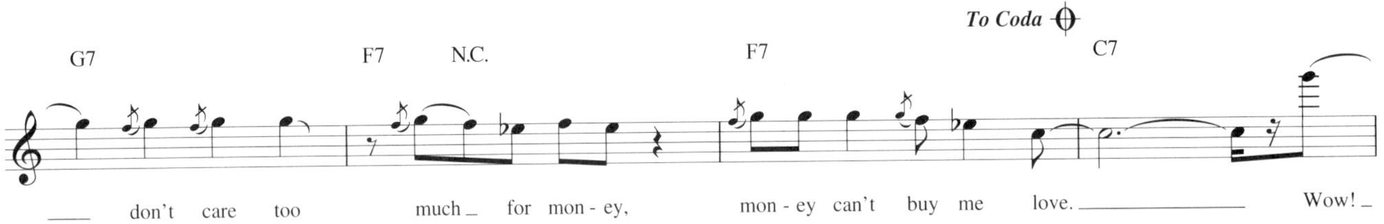

Guitar Solo

Gtr. 1: w/ Rhy. Fig. 1 (1st 9 meas.)

*Doubled throughout

G7
F7
C7
Gtr. 1
Can't buy me love,
let ring
Coda
Outro
Em
Am
Em
Can't buy me love,
oh,
love,
oh.
Gtr. 2
Am
Dm
G6
C7
Can't buy me love,
oh,
oh.

from Jeff Beck - *Blow by Blow*

Cause We've Ended as Lovers

Words and Music by Stevie Wonder

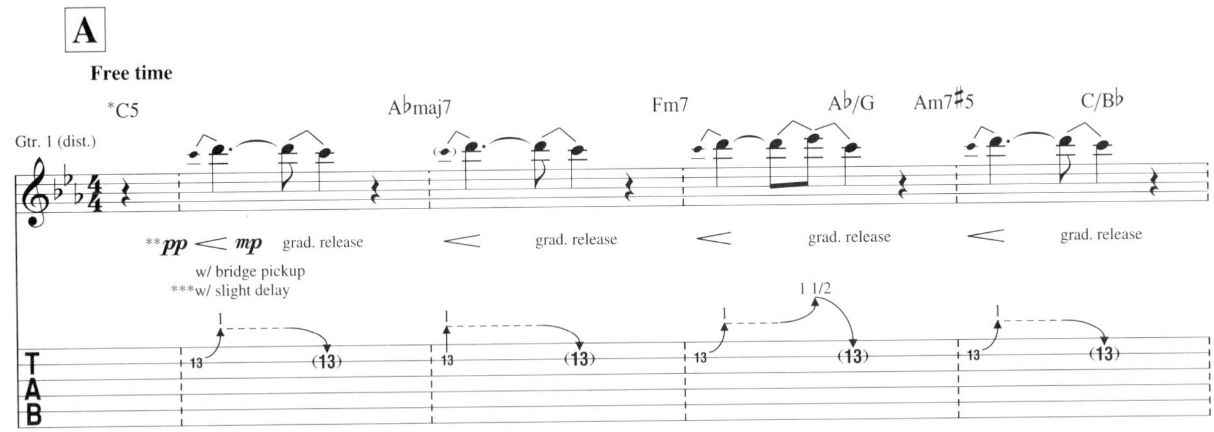

*Chord symbols reflect overall harmony.
**Vol. swell
***Set for eighth-note regeneration w/ 1 repeat.

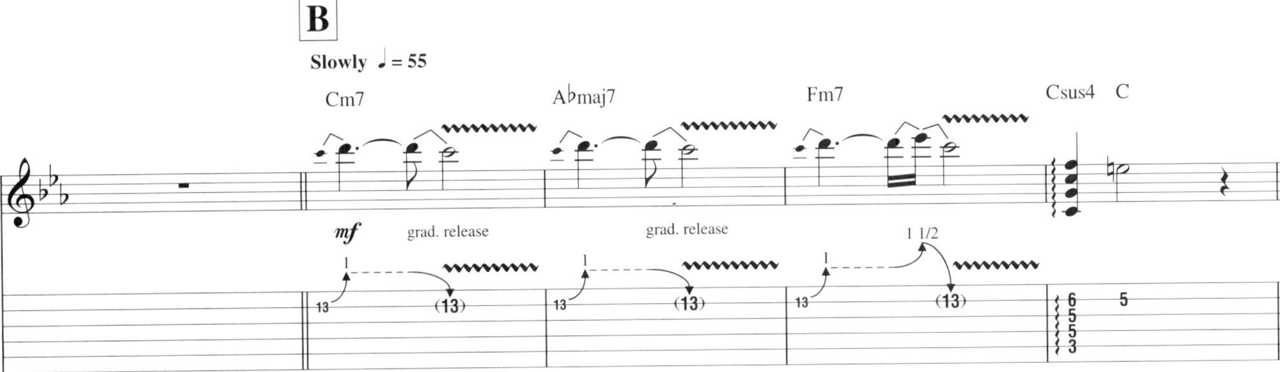

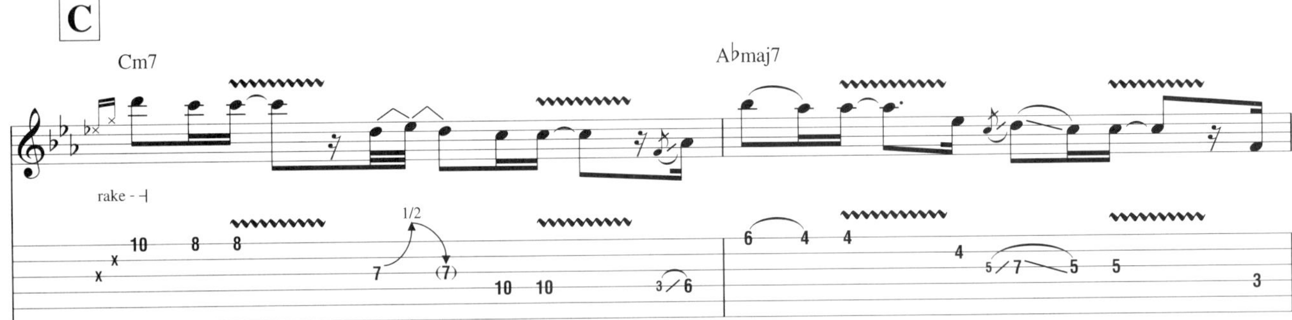

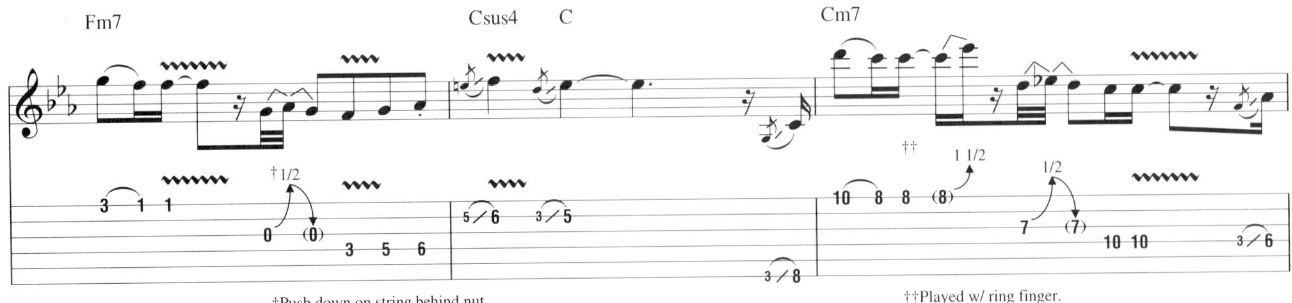

†Push down on string behind nut.

††Played w/ ring finger.

A♭maj7
Fm7
Csus4
C
semi-
P.H. 1
*1/2
*Behind nut
D
D/C
Fm7
B♭7
F°/C
C
grad. release
D/C
Fm7
B♭7
Csus4
C
grad. release
E
Cm7
A♭maj7
w/ neck
pickup
Fm7
Csus4
C
Cm7
rake
w/ bridge pickup
**1/2
**As before
A♭maj7
Fm7
Csus4
C
p
mf
***1/2
***As before

F
D/C
Fm7
B♭7
F°/C
C
grad. release
D/C
Fm7
B♭7
Csus4
C
*Hammer onto note while manipulating vol. knob.
G
Cm7
A♭maj7
Fm7
Gmaj9
Cm7
A♭maj7
Fm7
Gtr. 1
Gtr. 2 (dist.)
semi-P.H.
grad. bend

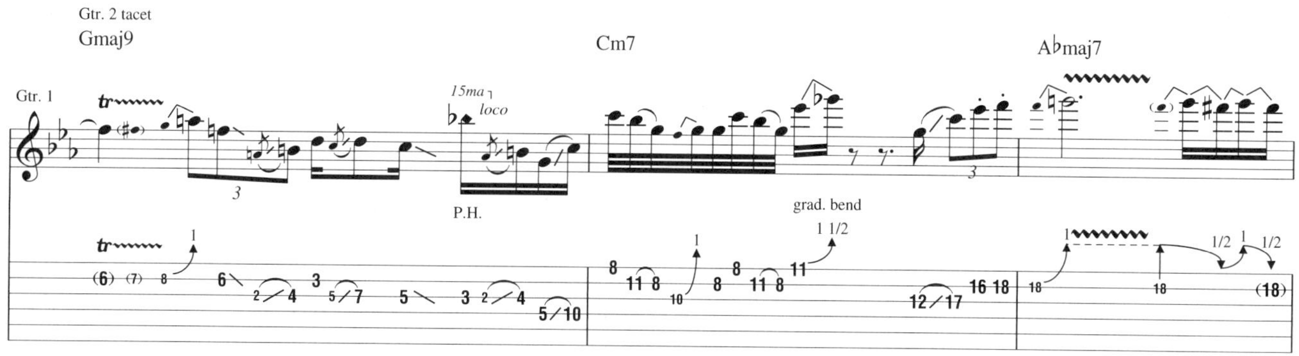

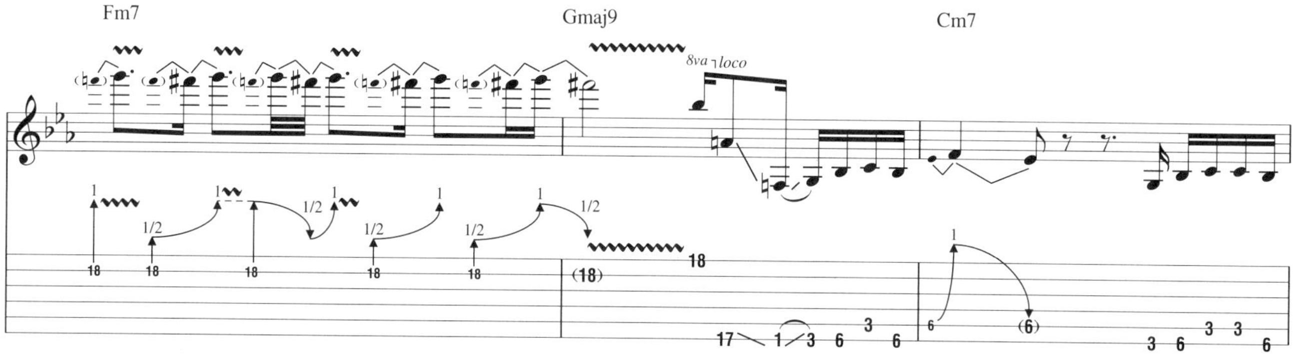

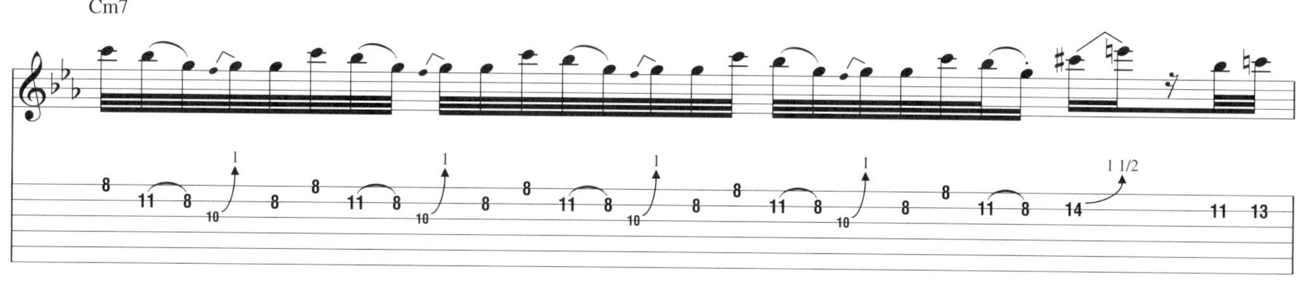

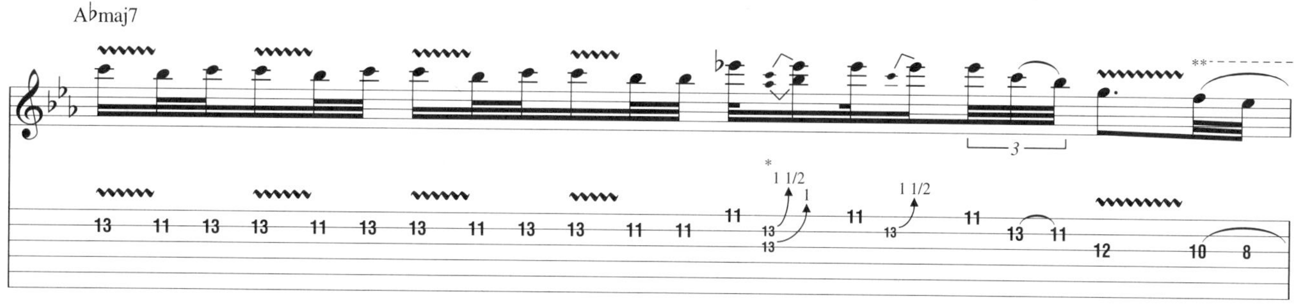

*Both strings caught and bent w/ ring finger.

**Played behind the beat.

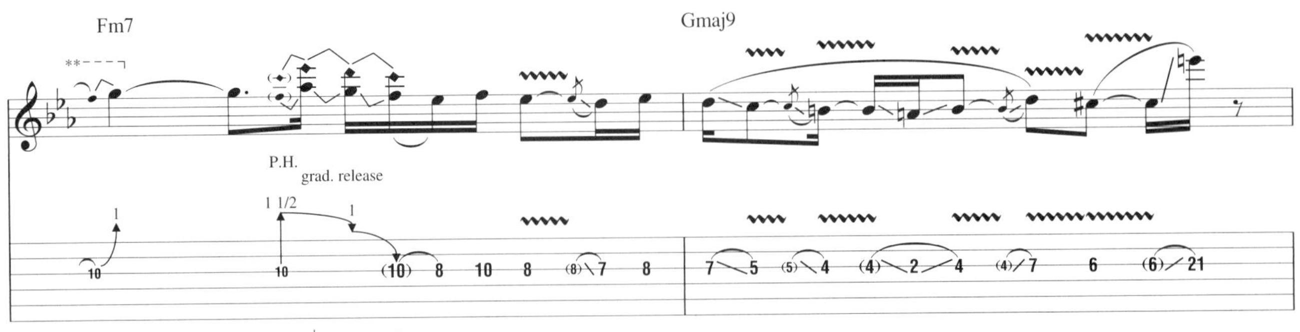
Fm7
Gmaj9
P.H.
grad. release
1 1/2
1
Pitch: C E♭ D C

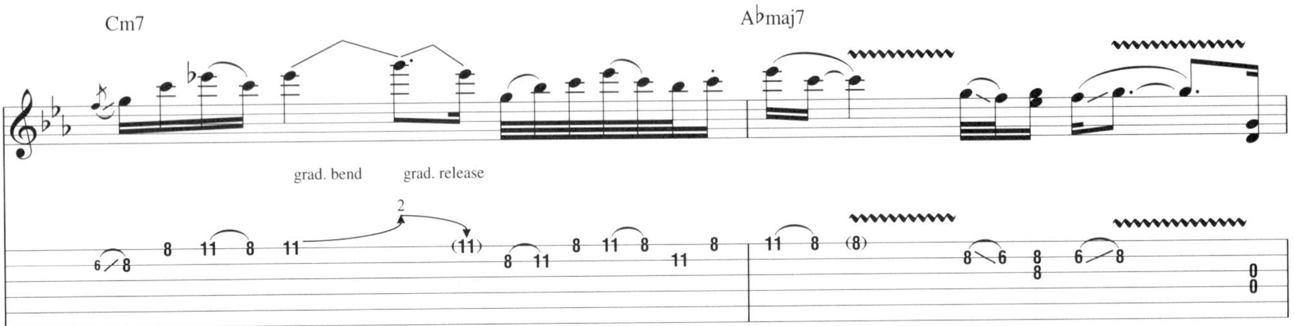
Cm7
A♭maj7
grad. bend
grad. release
2

Fm7

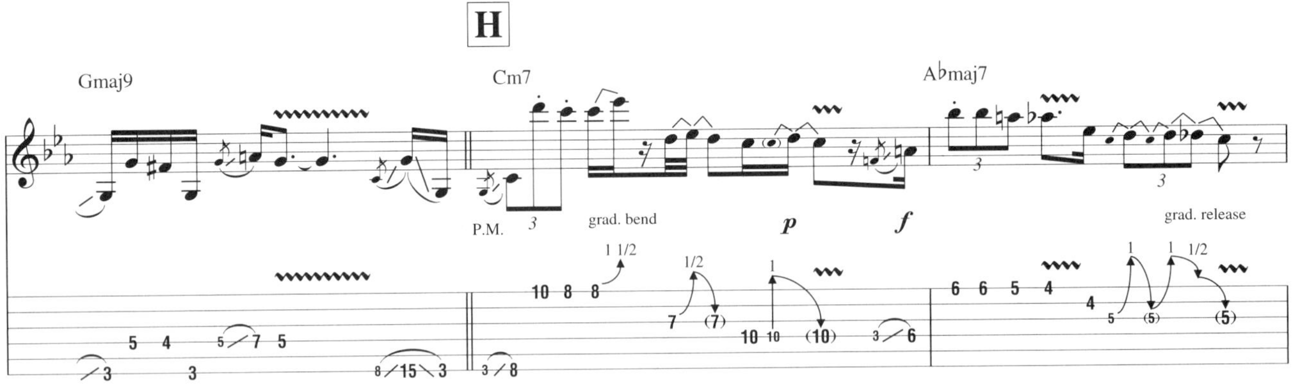
H
Gmaj9
Cm7
A♭maj7
P.M.
grad. bend
p
f
grad. release
1 1/2
1/2
1

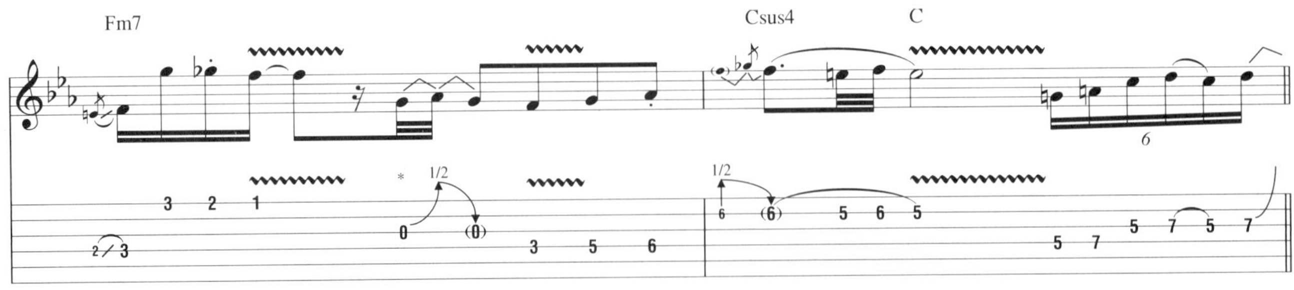
Fm7
Csus4
C
1/2
*Behind nut

I
D/C
Fm7
B♭7
F°/C
C
grad. release
D/C
Fm7
B♭7
Csus4
C
P.M.
grad. release
J
Cm7
A♭maj7
Fm7
mf
*Behind nut
K
Csus4
C
Cm7
A♭maj7
8va
loco
grad. release
Freely
Fm7
Csus4
C
**Played behind the beat.

from My Morning Jacket - *Circuital*

Circuital

Words and Music by James Olliges, Jr.

Capo III

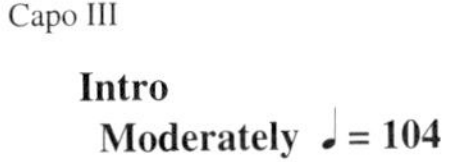

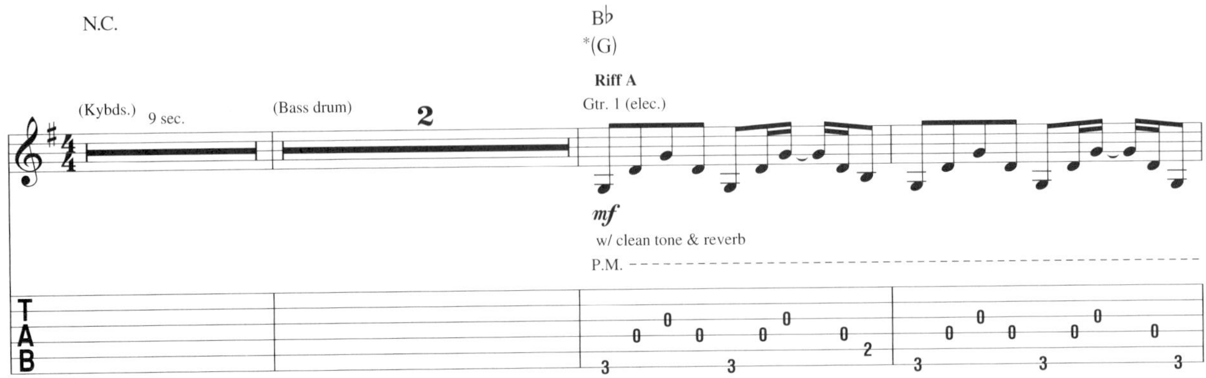

*Symbols in parentheses represent chord names respective to capoed guitars. Symbols above reflect actual sounding chords. Capoed fret is "0" in tab. Chord symbols reflect implied harmony.

Verse
E♭
(C)
D
(B)
grace - ful - ly.
Riff B
P.M.
E♭
(C)
Go - ing no - where,
P.M.
F
(D)
ah, quick - ly.
I am old -
End Riff B
P.M.
Gtr. 1: w/ Riff B
E♭
(C)
D
(B)
- er,
day by day.
Still go-ing back
E♭
(C)
F
(D)
to my child - hood way.
Woo.

Interlude
Gtr. 1 tacet
B♭
(G)
E♭/B♭
(C/G)
B♭
(G)
F
(D)
B♭
(G)
Gtr. 1
P.M.
Gtr. 2 (elec.)
w/ dist.
*Gtr. 3 (acous.)
*Two gtrs. arr. for one.
Gtr. 2 tacet
E♭/B♭
(C/G)
B♭
(G)
F
(D)
B♭
(G)
Gtr. 2
Gtr. 3

Verse
Gtr. 1: w/ Riff A
B♭
(G)
2. Cir - cu - i - tal.
Gtr. 3
3 0 0 0 X 3
Gtr. 3 tacet
D
(B)
E♭
(C)
'Round and 'round,
F
(D)
pa - tient - ly.
Gtr. 1: w/ Riff B
E♭
(C)
Get-ting lost
D
(B)
by the guide.
And I am all
E♭
(C)
F
(D)
worked up o-ver noth - ing.

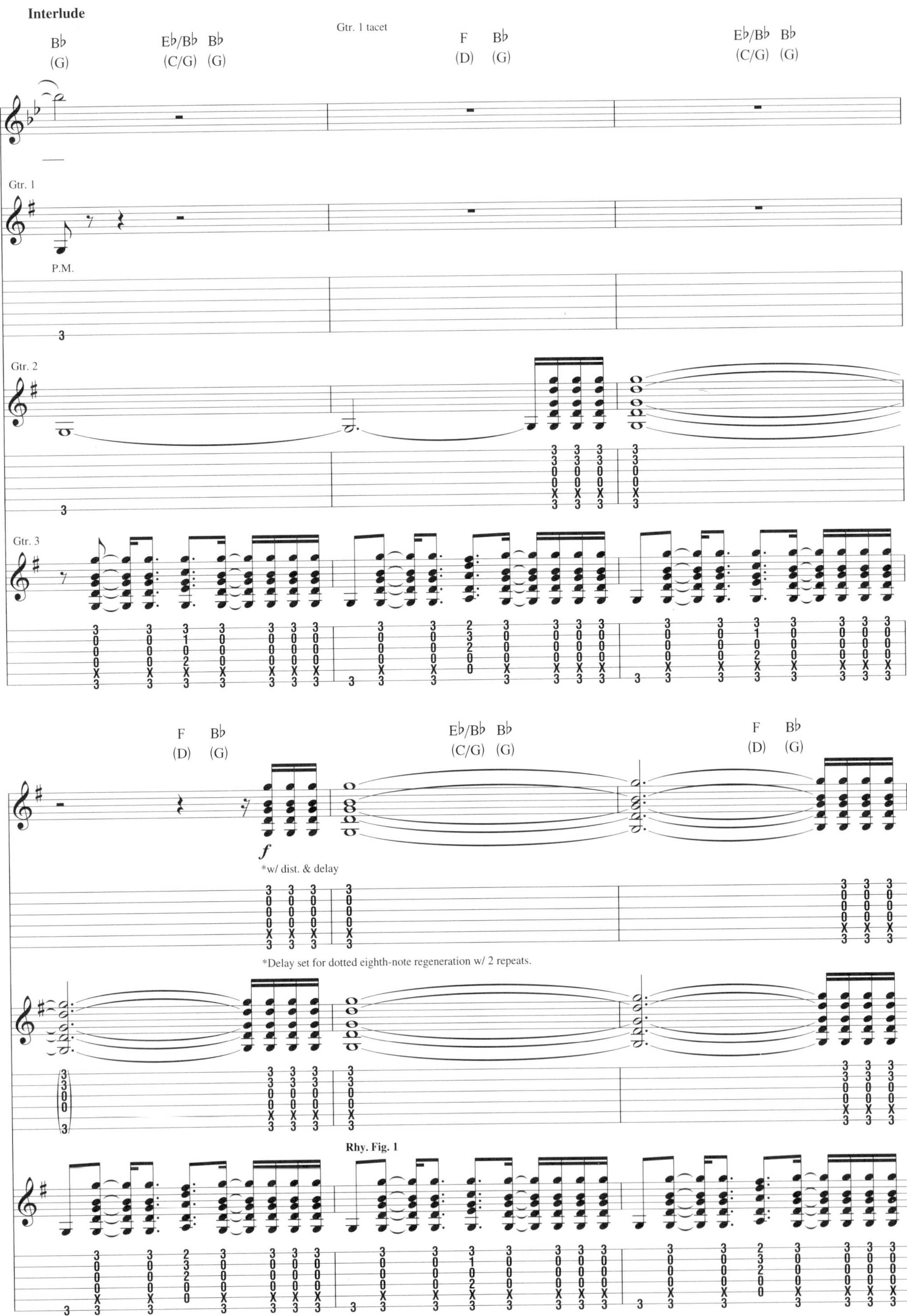
Interlude
B♭ (G)
E♭/B♭ (C/G)
B♭ (G)
Gtr. 1 tacet
F (D)
B♭ (G)
E♭/B♭ (C/G)
B♭ (G)
Gtr. 1
P.M.
Gtr. 2
Gtr. 3
F (D)
B♭ (G)
E♭/B♭ (C/G)
B♭ (G)
F (D)
B♭ (G)
*w/ dist. & delay
*Delay set for dotted eighth-note regeneration w/ 2 repeats.
Rhy. Fig. 1

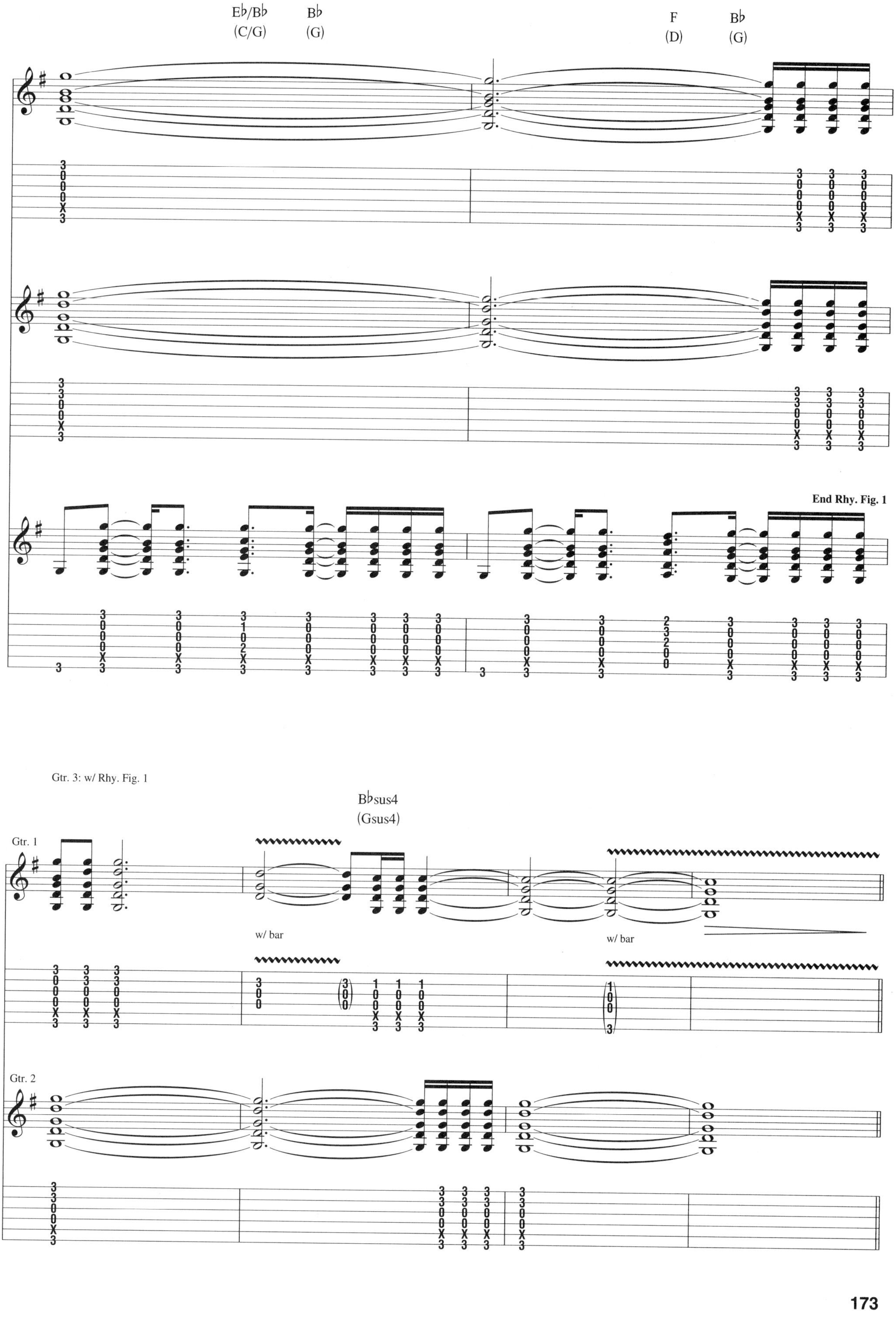

E♭/B♭ (C/G) B♭ (G) F (D) B♭ (G)

End Rhy. Fig. 1

Gtr. 3: w/ Rhy. Fig. 1

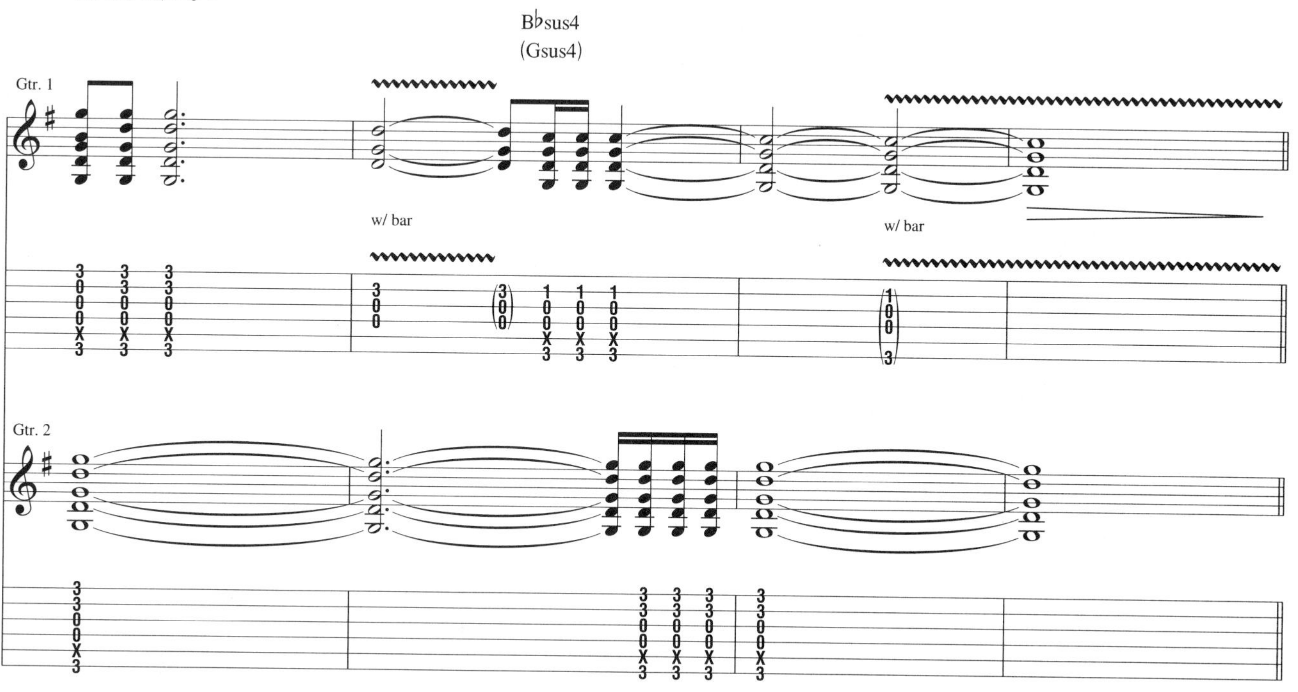

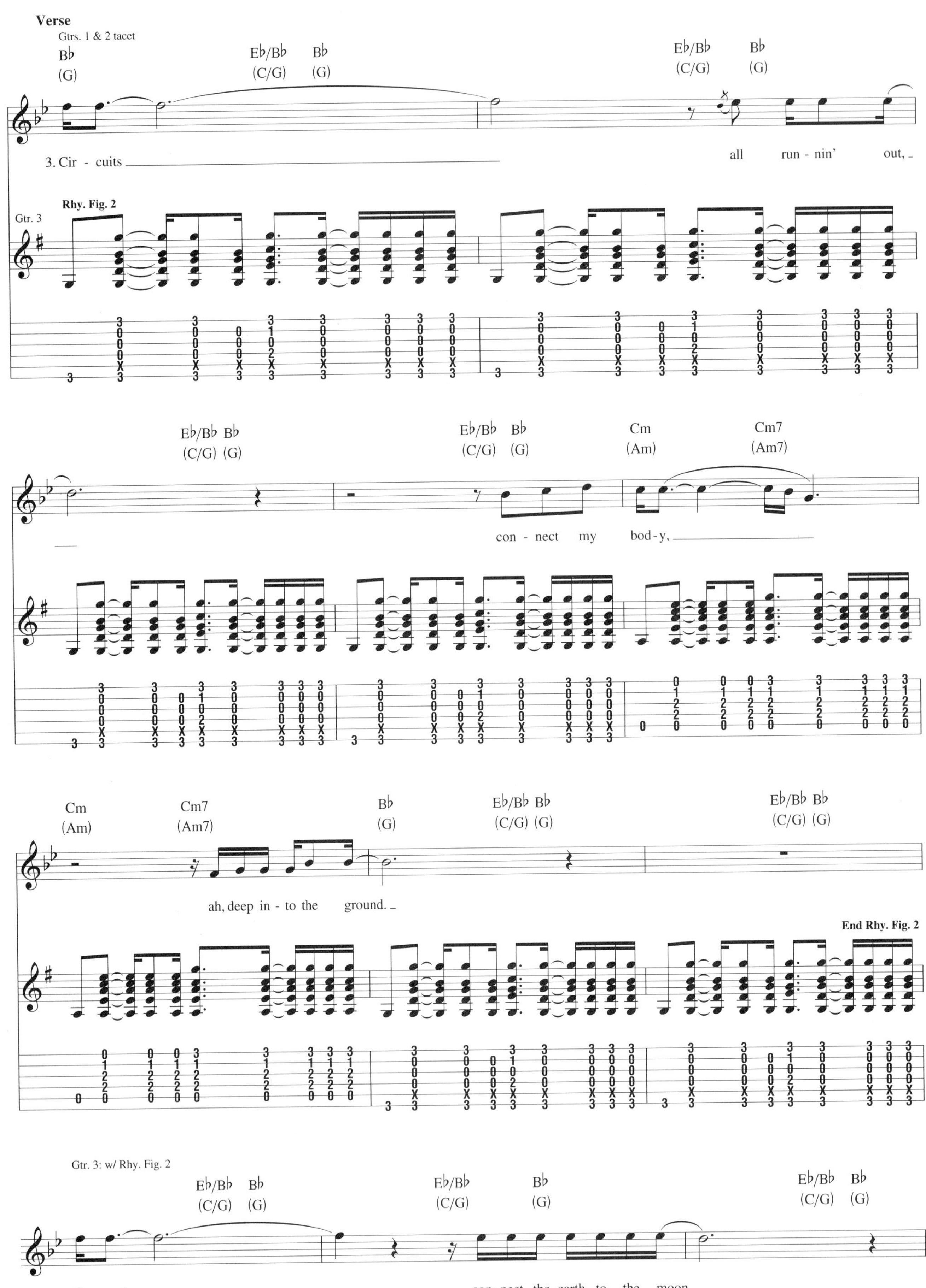
Verse
Gtrs. 1 & 2 tacet
B♭
(G)
E♭/B♭
(C/G)
3. Cir - cuits
all run - nin' out,
Rhy. Fig. 2
Gtr. 3
Cm
(Am)
Cm7
(Am7)
con - nect my bod - y,
ah, deep in - to the ground.
End Rhy. Fig. 2
Gtr. 3: w/ Rhy. Fig. 2
Cir - cuits
con - nect the earth to the moon

E♭/B♭
(C/G)
B♭
(G)
Cm
(Am)
Cm7
(Am7)
Cm
(Am)
Cm7
(Am7)
and link our heav-en-ly bod-ies,
ah, not a mo-ment too soon.
Guitar Solo
Gtr. 3: w/ Rhy. Fig. 2
B♭
(G)
E♭/B♭ B♭
(C/G) (G)
E♭/B♭ B♭
(C/G) (G)
B♭
(G)
E♭/B♭ B♭
(C/G) (G)
E♭/B♭ B♭
(C/G) (G)
Na, na.
Gtr. 1
mp
f
w/ bar
w/ bar
w/ bar
let ring
let ring
E♭/B♭ B♭
(C/G) (G)
E♭/B♭ B♭
(C/G) (G)
Cm
(Am)
Cm7
(Am7)
w/ bar
let ring
grad. bend
let ring
1/2
Cm
(Am)
Cm7
(Am7)
B♭
(G)
E♭/B♭ B♭
(C/G) (G)
E♭/B♭ B♭
(C/G) (G)
4. Well, you can
let ring
hold bend
w/ bar
w/ bar

Verse
Gtr. 3: w/ Rhy. Fig. 2 (2 times)
Gtr. 1 tacet
B♭
(G)
E♭/B♭
(C/G)
fling o - pen the win - dows
or you can board 'em up.
Sa - tan's jeweled crown
Cm
(Am)
Cm7
(Am7)
or Christ's hum-ble cup.
You think you'll
find your-self out there,
out in the li-on's den,
in some blood - y bat - tle
Gtr. 1
mp

Gtr. 1 tacet
Cm (Am) Cm7 (Am7) B♭ (G) E♭/B♭ (C/G) B♭ (G) E♭/B♭ (C/G) B♭ (G)
o - ver be - lief sys - tems?
5. Or dis - ap -
Verse
Gtr. 3: w/ Rhy. Fig. 2 (2 times)
B♭ (G) E♭/B♭ (C/G) B♭ (G) E♭/B♭ (C/G) B♭ (G)
pear in - to the vac - uum,
to - tal neu - tral - i - ty,
Gtr. 1
w/ bar
E♭/B♭ (C/G) B♭ (G) E♭/B♭ (C/G) B♭ (G) Cm (Am) Cm7 (Am7)
where you can't lose noth - ing
w/ bar
let ring
Cm (Am) Cm7 (Am7) B♭ (G) E♭/B♭ (C/G) B♭ (G) E♭/B♭ (C/G) B♭ (G)
but noth - ing can be gained.
Well, an -
let ring

E♭/B♭ (C/G) B♭ (G) E♭/B♭ (C/G) B♭ (G) E♭/B♭ (C/G) B♭ (G)
- y way you cut it,
we're just spin-nin' 'round
w/ bar
w/ bar
w/ pick & middle finger

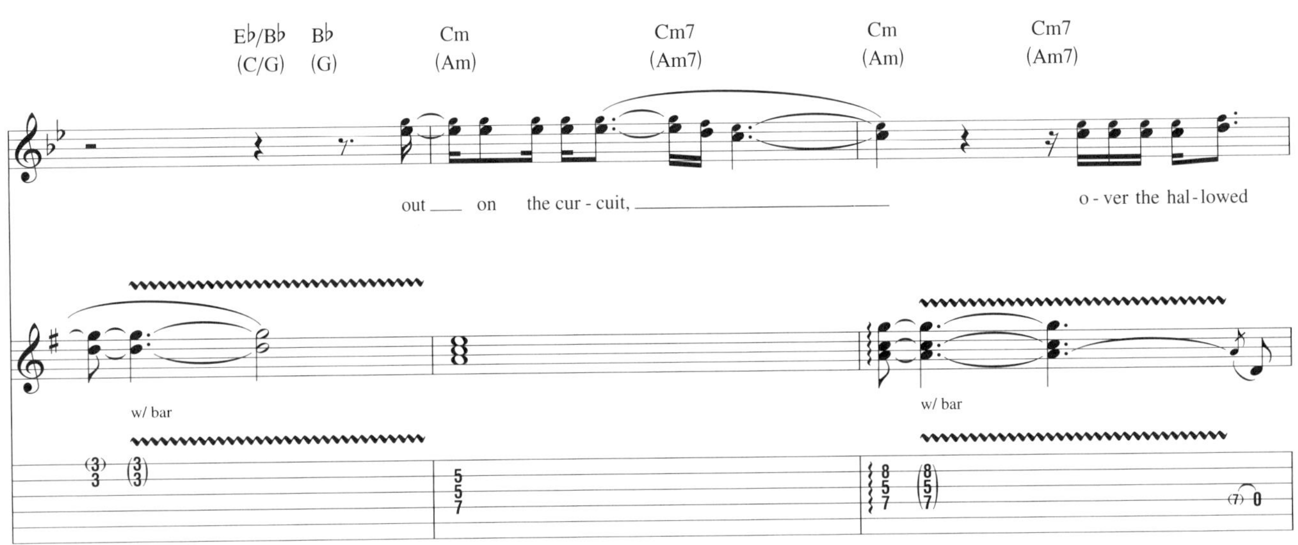
E♭/B♭ (C/G) B♭ (G) Cm (Am) Cm7 (Am7) Cm (Am) Cm7 (Am7)
out on the cur - cuit,
o - ver the hal - lowed
w/ bar
w/ bar

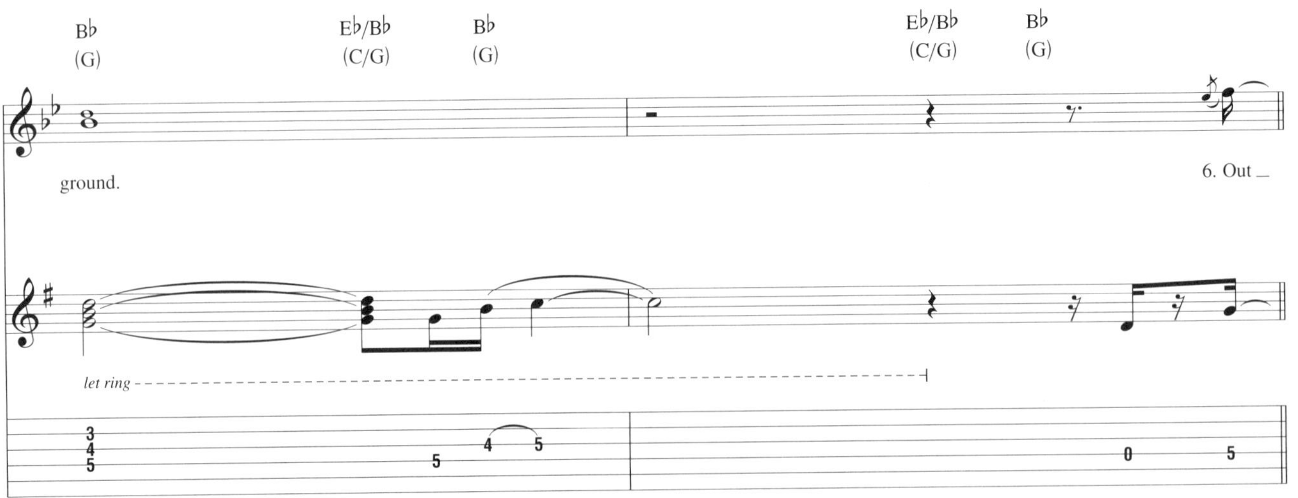
B♭ (G) E♭/B♭ (C/G) B♭ (G) E♭/B♭ (C/G) B♭ (G)
ground.
6. Out
let ring

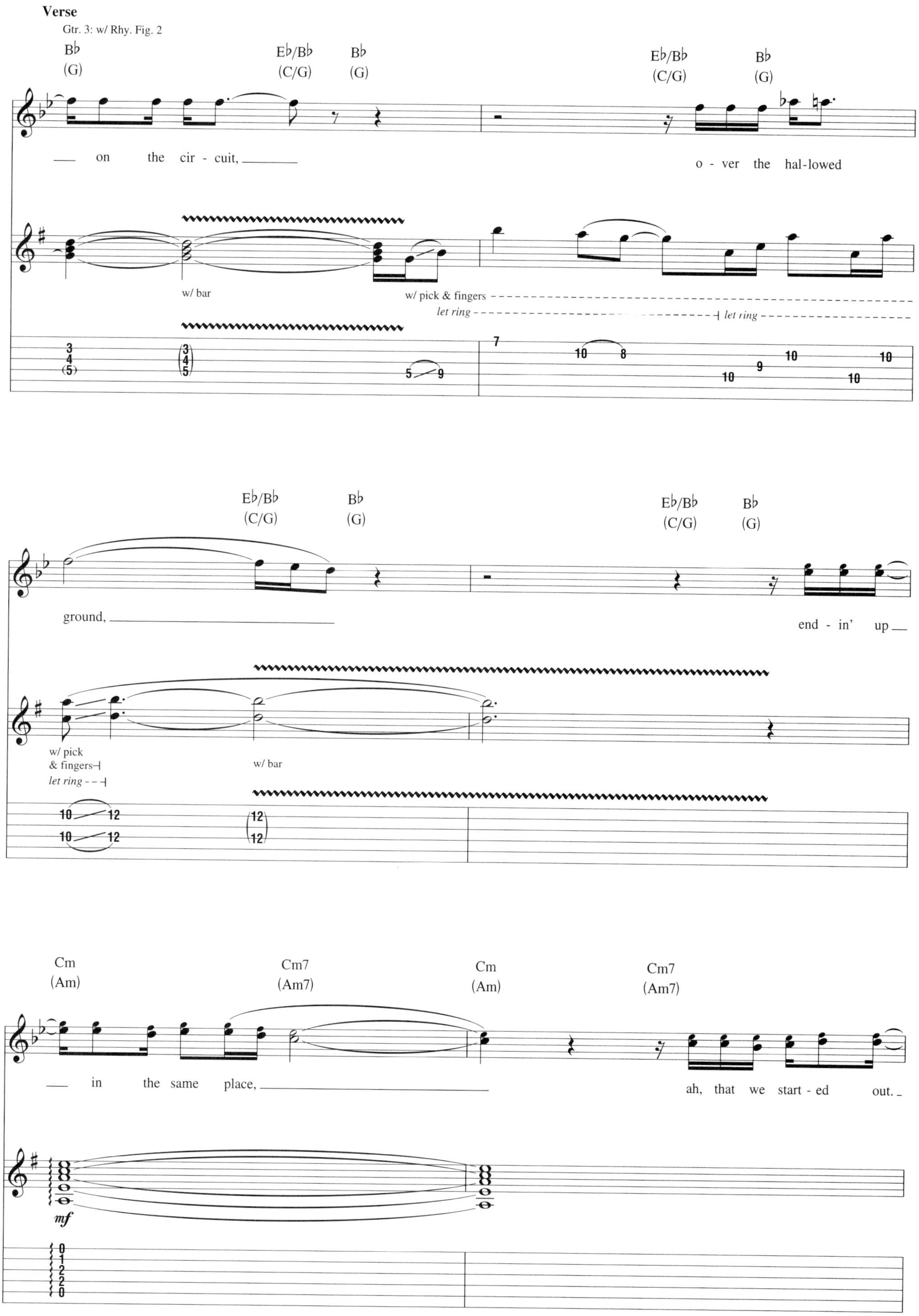

Verse
Gtr. 3: w/ Rhy. Fig. 2
B♭ (G)
E♭/B♭ (C/G)
B♭ (G)
E♭/B♭ (C/G)
B♭ (G)
on the cir - cuit,
o - ver the hal-lowed
w/ bar
w/ pick & fingers
let ring
let ring
E♭/B♭ (C/G)
B♭ (G)
E♭/B♭ (C/G)
B♭ (G)
ground,
end - in' up
w/ pick & fingers
let ring
w/ bar
Cm (Am)
Cm7 (Am7)
Cm (Am)
Cm7 (Am7)
in the same place,
ah, that we start - ed out.
mf

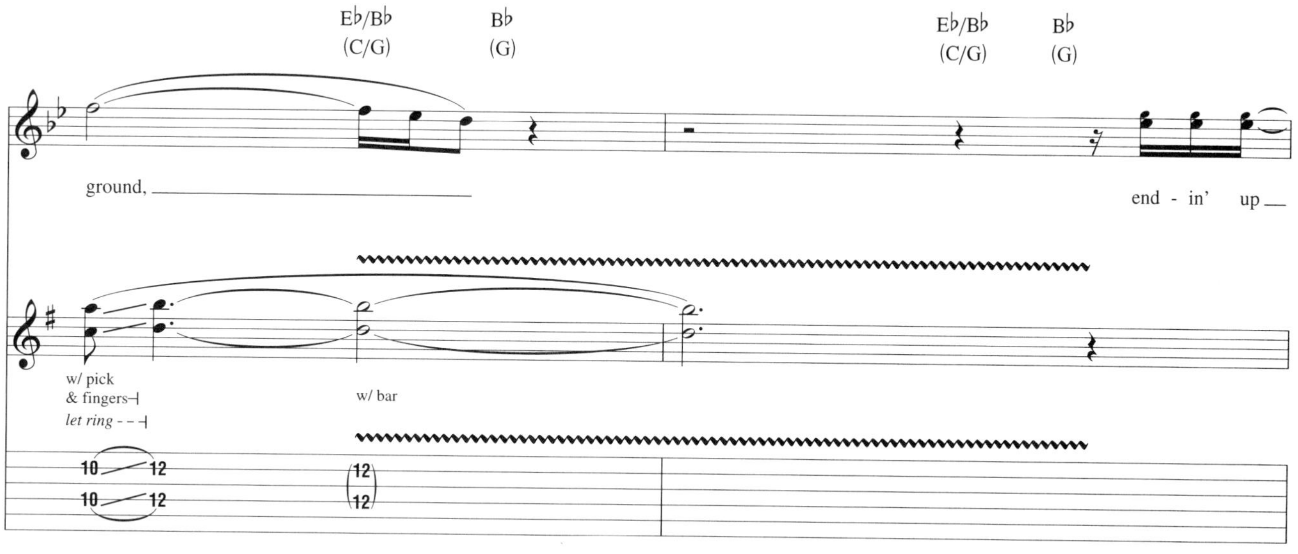

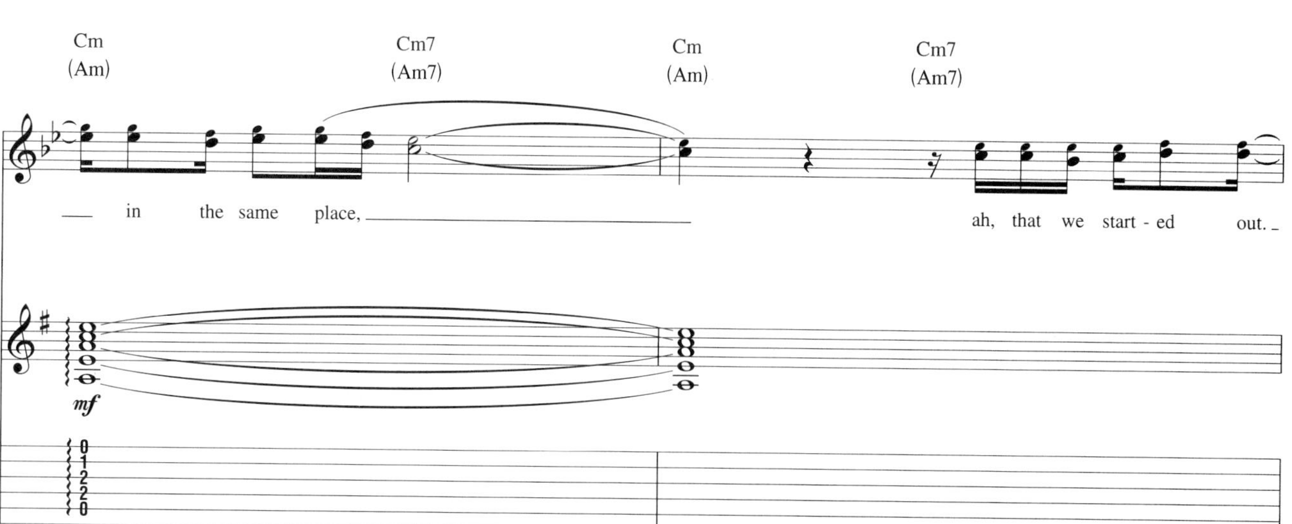

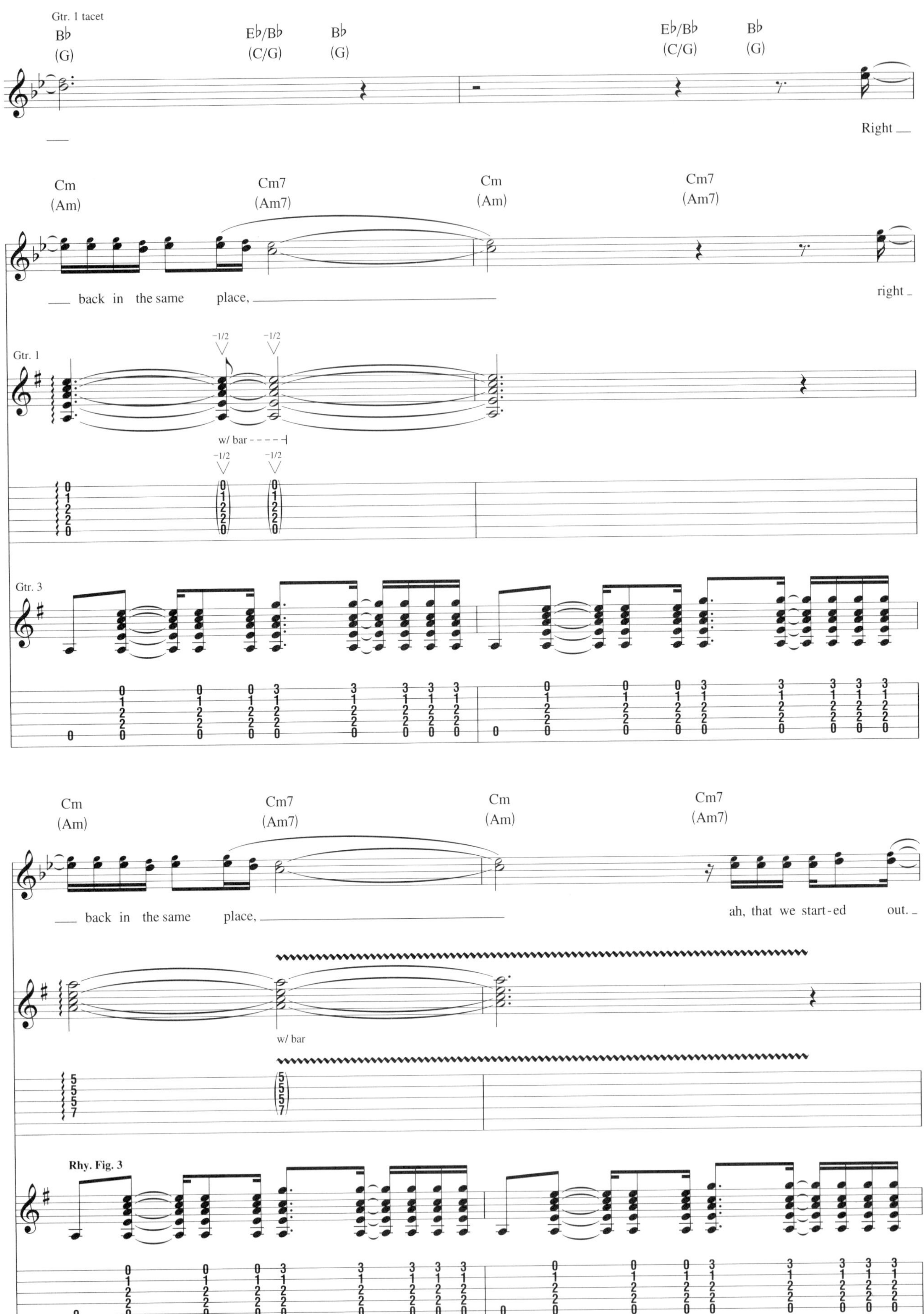
Gtr. 1 tacet
B♭
(G)
E♭/B♭
(C/G)
B♭
(G)
E♭/B♭
(C/G)
B♭
(G)
Right
Cm
(Am)
Cm7
(Am7)
Cm
(Am)
Cm7
(Am7)
back in the same place,
right
Gtr. 1
-1/2
-1/2
w/ bar
Gtr. 3
Cm
(Am)
Cm7
(Am7)
Cm
(Am)
Cm7
(Am7)
back in the same place,
ah, that we start-ed out.
w/ bar
Rhy. Fig. 3

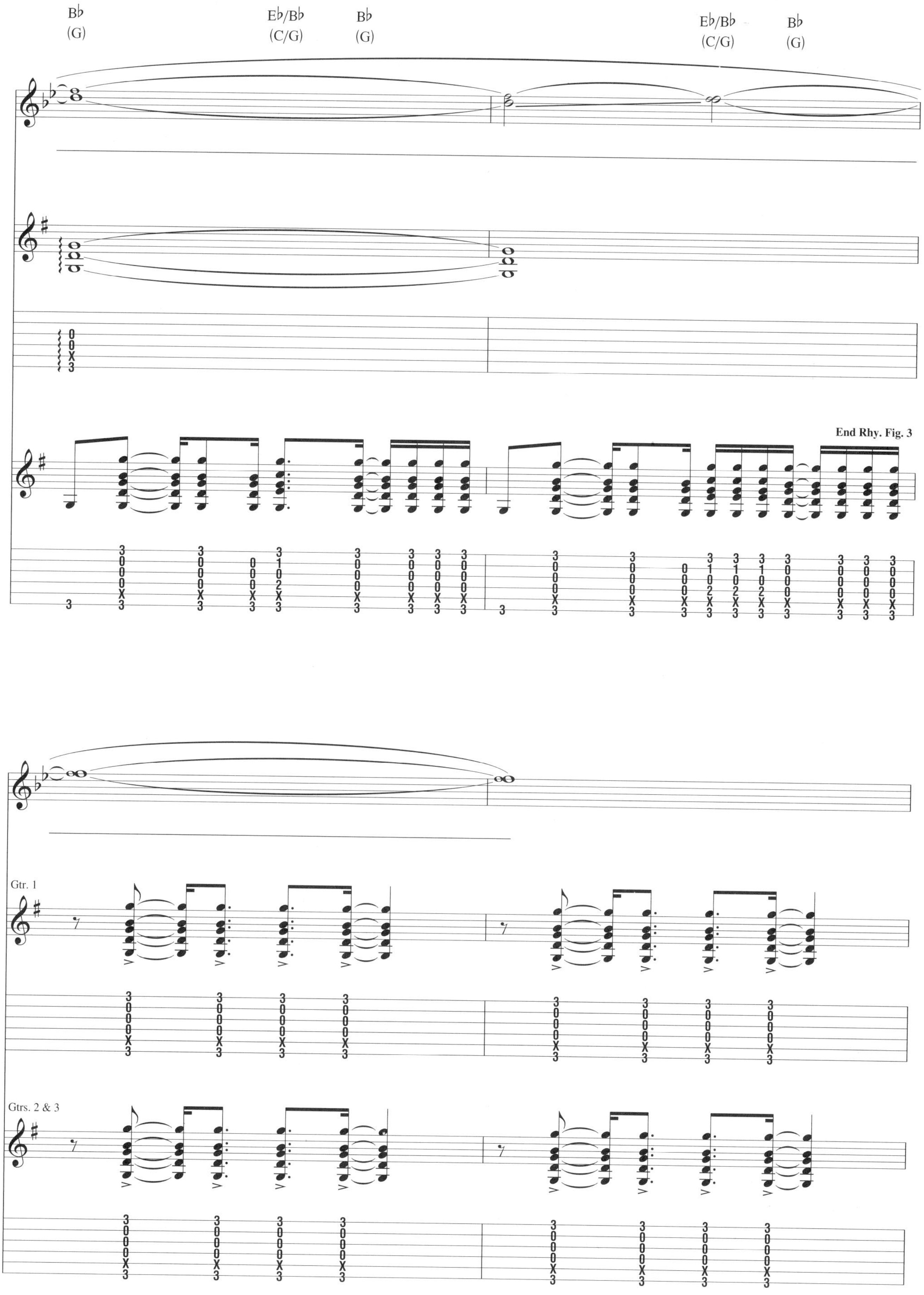

B♭
(G)

E♭/B♭
(C/G)

B♭
(G)

E♭/B♭
(C/G)

B♭
(G)

End Rhy. Fig. 3

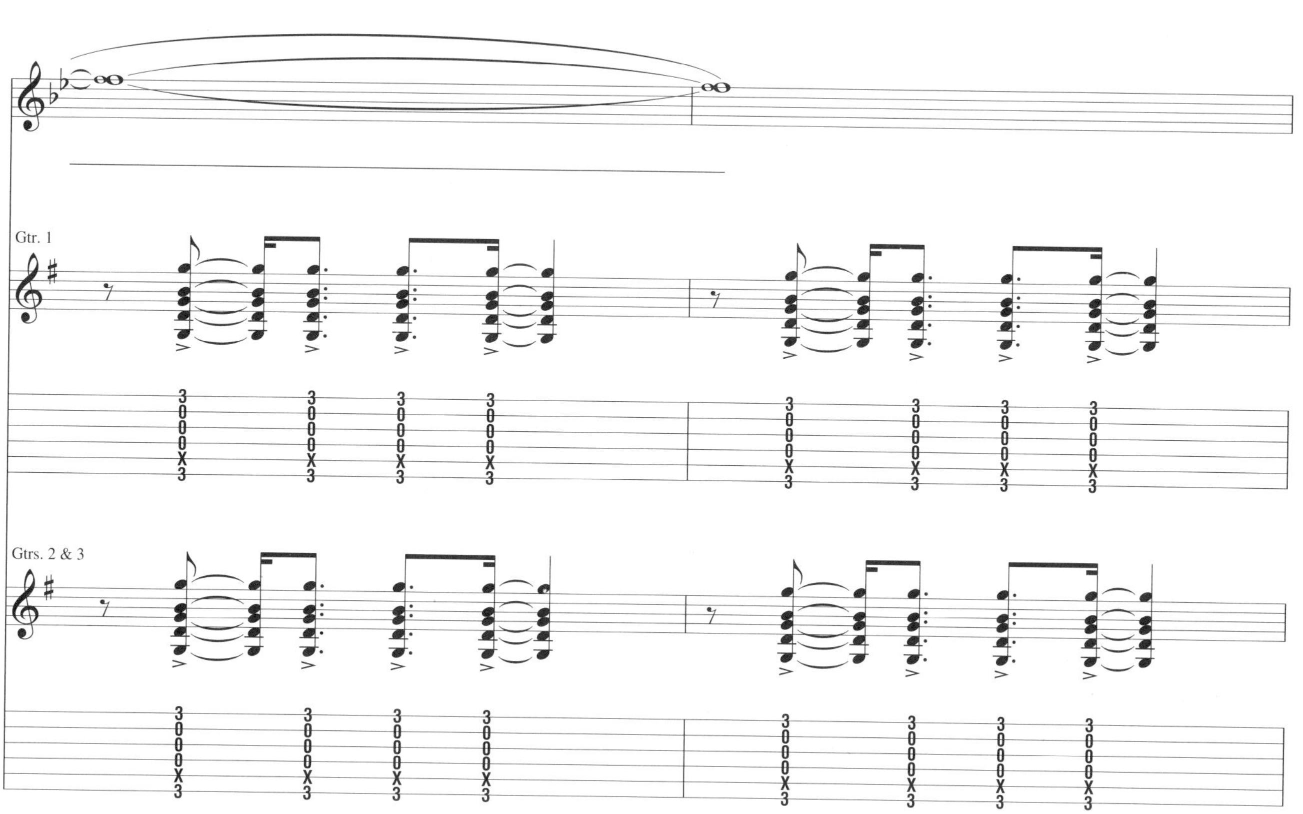

N.C.
Guitar Solo
Gtr, 2 tacet
Gtr. 3: w/ Rhy. Fig. 3 (3 times)
Cm
(Am)
Cm7
(Am7)
Bb
(G)
Eb/Bb Bb
(C/G) (G)
Gtr. 1
let ring
w/ bar

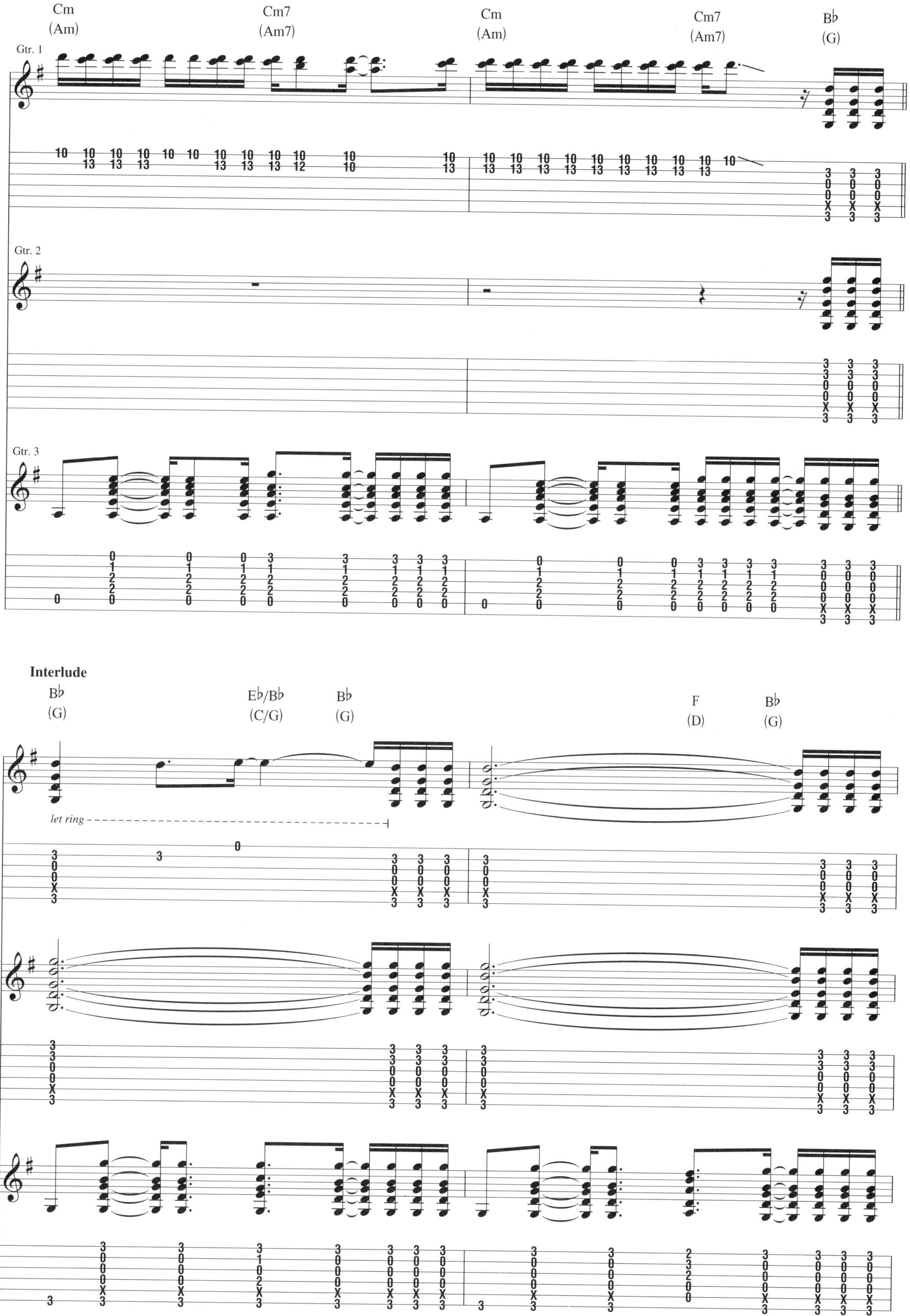

Cm
(Am)
Cm7
(Am7)
Cm
(Am)
Cm7
(Am7)
B♭
(G)
Gtr. 1
Gtr. 2
Gtr. 3
Interlude
B♭
(G)
E♭/B♭
(C/G)
B♭
(G)
F
(D)
B♭
(G)
let ring

Gtrs. 2 & 3 tacet
Eb/Bb (C/G)
Bb (G)
N.C.
dist. & delay off
Outro
Gtr. 1: w/ Riff A
F (D)
Gtr. 1: w/ Riff B
Eb (C)
Let her know.
D (B)
Eb (C)
F (D)
Woo.
Woo.
Eb (C)
D (B)
Gtr. 1
P.M.

E♭
(C)
Gtr. 4 (elec.)
mp
w/ dist. & heavy reverb
w/ bar
Gtr. 1
P.M.
F
(D)
E♭
(C)
N.C.
(Kybds.)
20 sec.
Whispered: Sha.
p
w/ bar
20 sec.
20 sec.
P.M.
*w/ echo set for eighth-note regeneration w/ 8 repeats.

from John Lennon - *Shaved Fish*

Cold Turkey

Words and Music by John Lennon

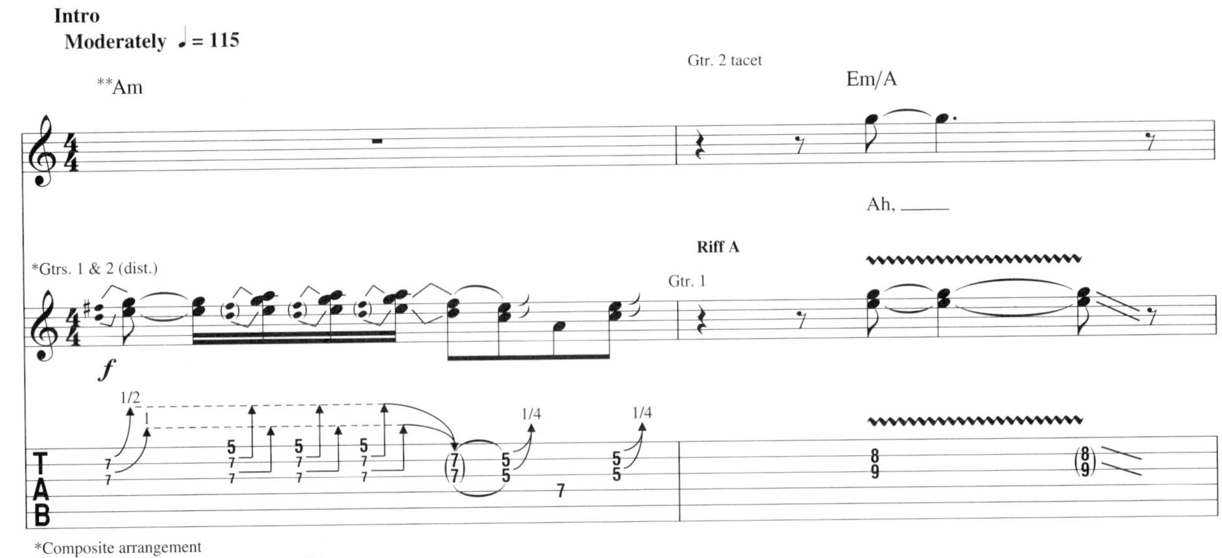

*Composite arrangement
**Chord symbols reflect overall harmony.

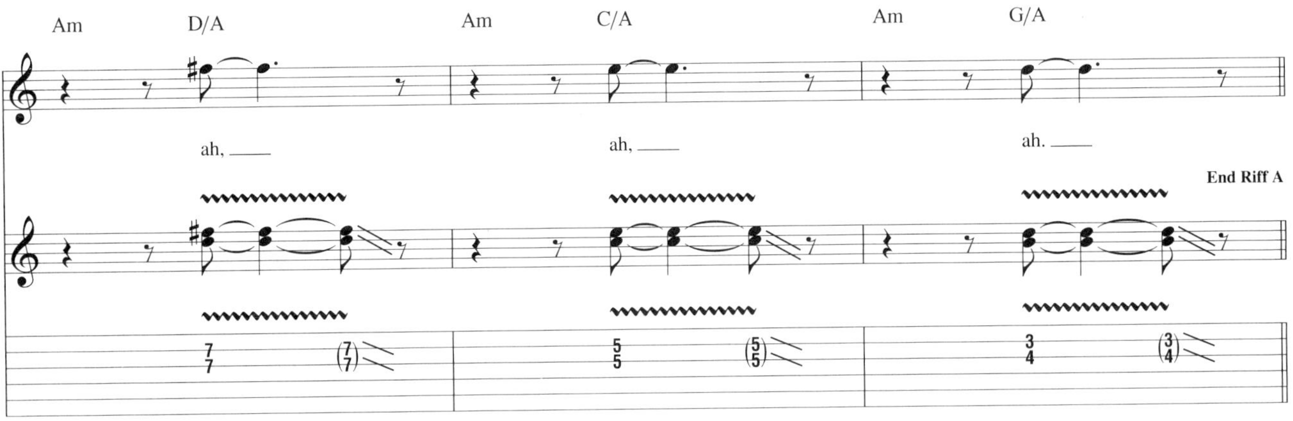

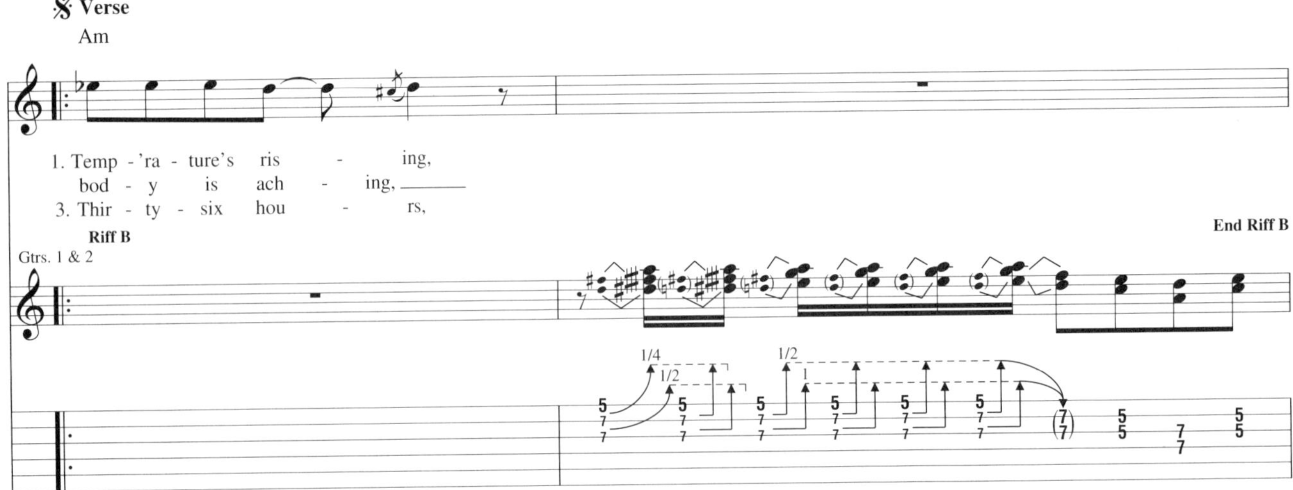

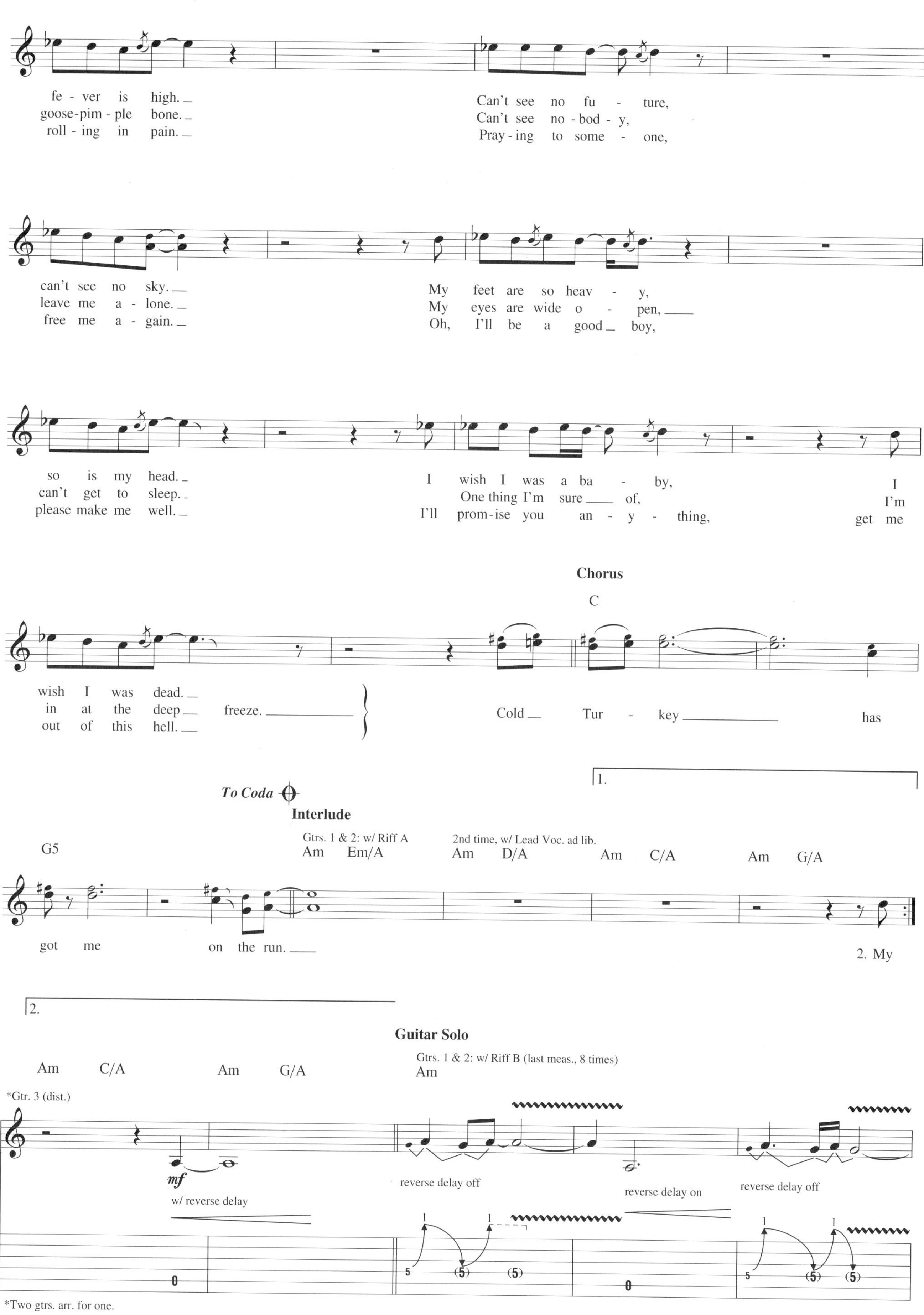

Gtrs. 1 & 2: w/ Riff B (7 times)
fe - ver is high.
goose-pim - ple bone.
roll - ing in pain.
Can't see no fu - ture,
Can't see no - bod - y,
Pray - ing to some - one,
can't see no sky.
leave me a - lone.
free me a - gain.
My feet are so heav - y,
My eyes are wide o - pen,
Oh, I'll be a good boy,
so is my head.
can't get to sleep.
please make me well.
I wish I was a ba - by,
One thing I'm sure of,
I'll prom-ise you an - y - thing,
I
I'm
get me
Chorus
C
wish I was dead.
in at the deep freeze.
out of this hell.
Cold Tur - key has
To Coda
Interlude
1.
Gtrs. 1 & 2: w/ Riff A
2nd time, w/ Lead Voc. ad lib.
G5
Am Em/A
Am D/A
Am C/A
Am G/A
got me on the run.
2. My
2.
Guitar Solo
Am C/A Am G/A
Gtrs. 1 & 2: w/ Riff B (last meas., 8 times)
Am
*Gtr. 3 (dist.)
mf
w/ reverse delay
reverse delay off
reverse delay on
reverse delay off
*Two gtrs. arr. for one.

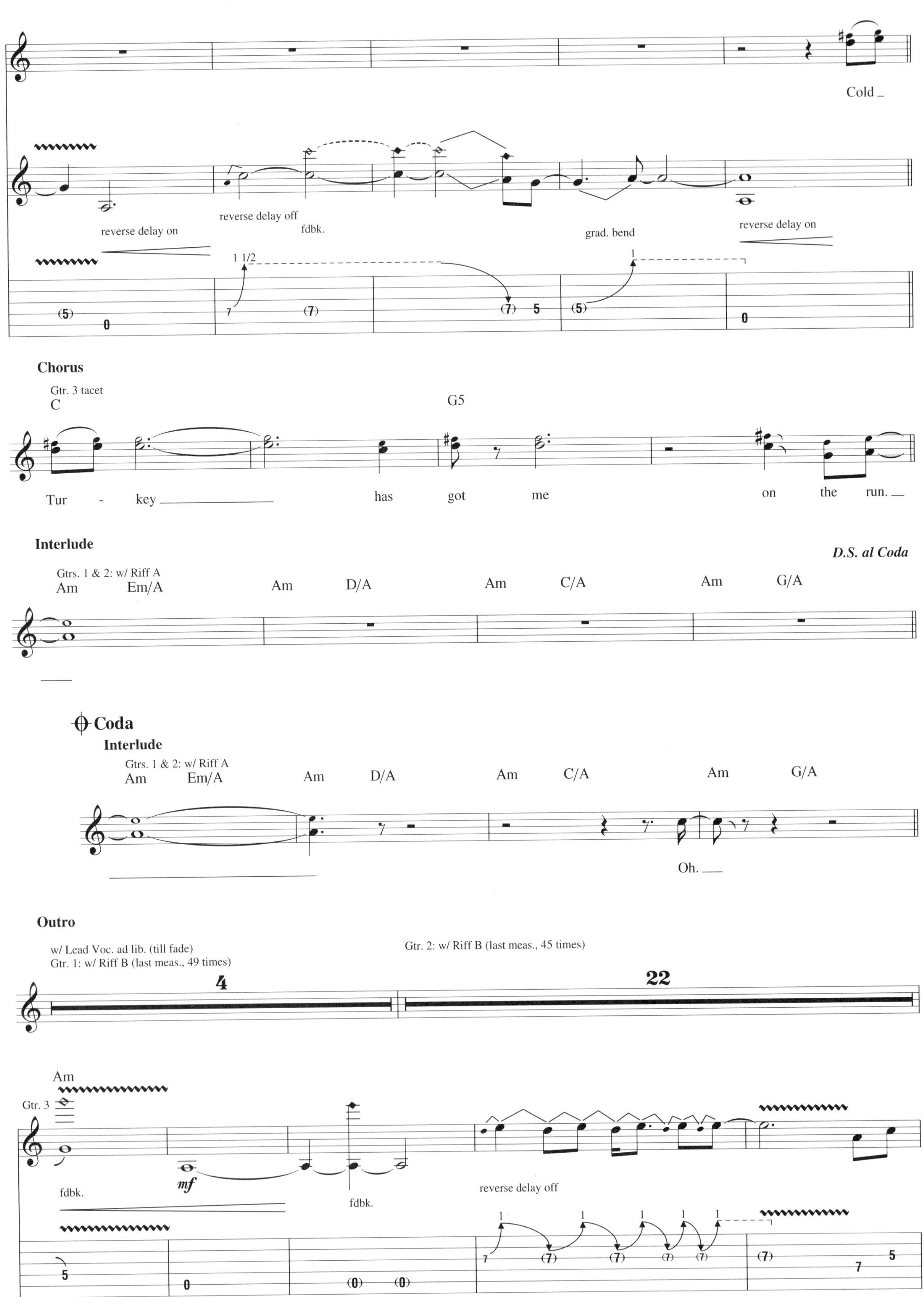

Cold
reverse delay on
reverse delay off
fdbk.
grad. bend
reverse delay on
1 1/2
1
Chorus
Gtr. 3 tacet
C
G5
Tur - key has got me on the run.
Interlude
D.S. al Coda
Gtrs. 1 & 2: w/ Riff A
Am Em/A Am D/A Am C/A Am G/A
Coda
Interlude
Gtrs. 1 & 2: w/ Riff A
Am Em/A Am D/A Am C/A Am G/A
Oh.
Outro
w/ Lead Voc. ad lib. (till fade)
Gtr. 1: w/ Riff B (last meas., 49 times)
Gtr. 2: w/ Riff B (last meas., 45 times)
4
22
Am
Gtr. 3
fdbk.
fdbk.
reverse delay off
Pitch: E

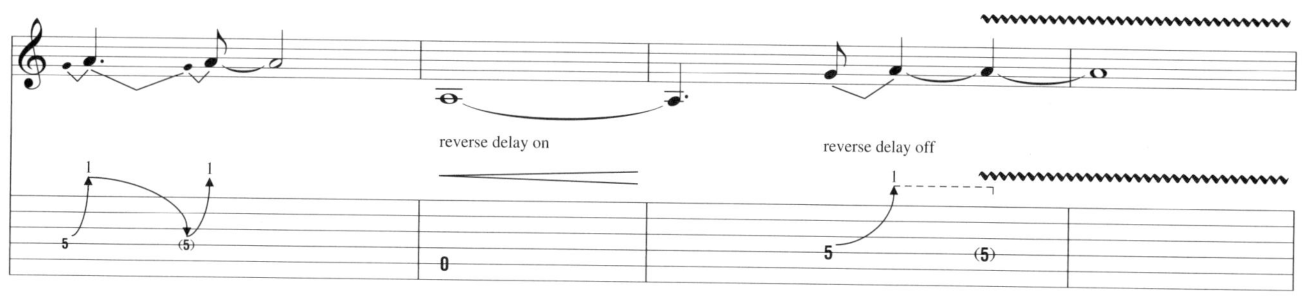
reverse delay on
reverse delay off

reverse delay on

fdbk.
reverse delay off
reverse delay on
reverse delay off
grad. release

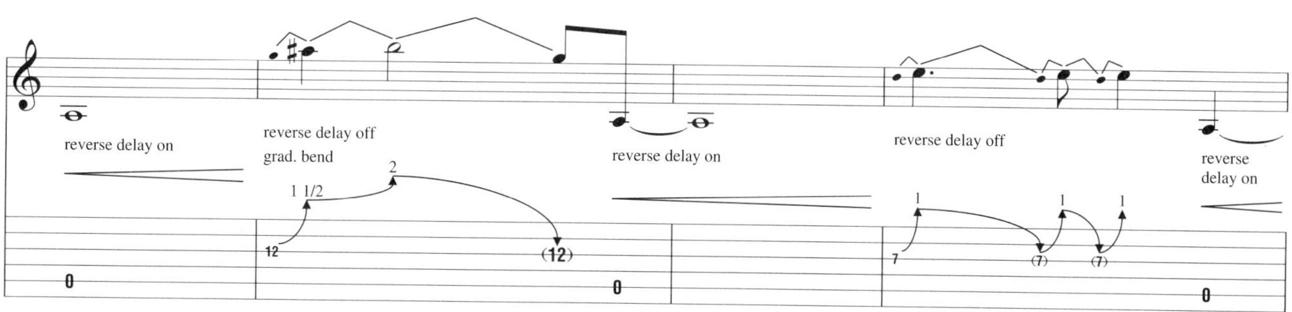
reverse delay on
reverse delay off
grad. bend
reverse delay on
reverse delay off
reverse delay on

Free time

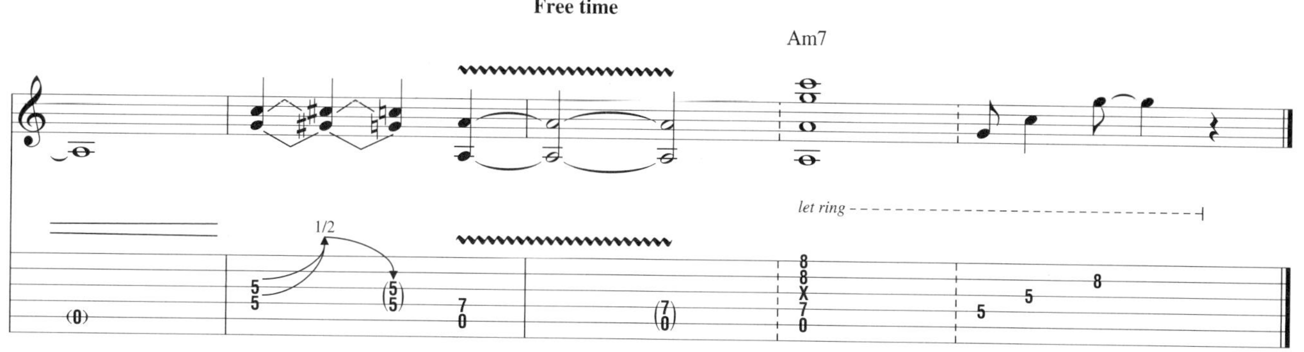
Am7
let ring

from Jimmy Buffett - *Living and Dying in 3/4 Time*

Come Monday

Words and Music by Jimmy Buffett

Gtr. 1: Capo II
Gtr. 2: Capo VII

*Symbols in single parentheses reflect chord names respective to Gtr. 1.
Symbols in double parentheses reflect chord names respective to Gtr. 2.
Symbols above reflect actual sounding chords. Capoed fret is "0" in tab.
Chord symbols reflect basic harmony.

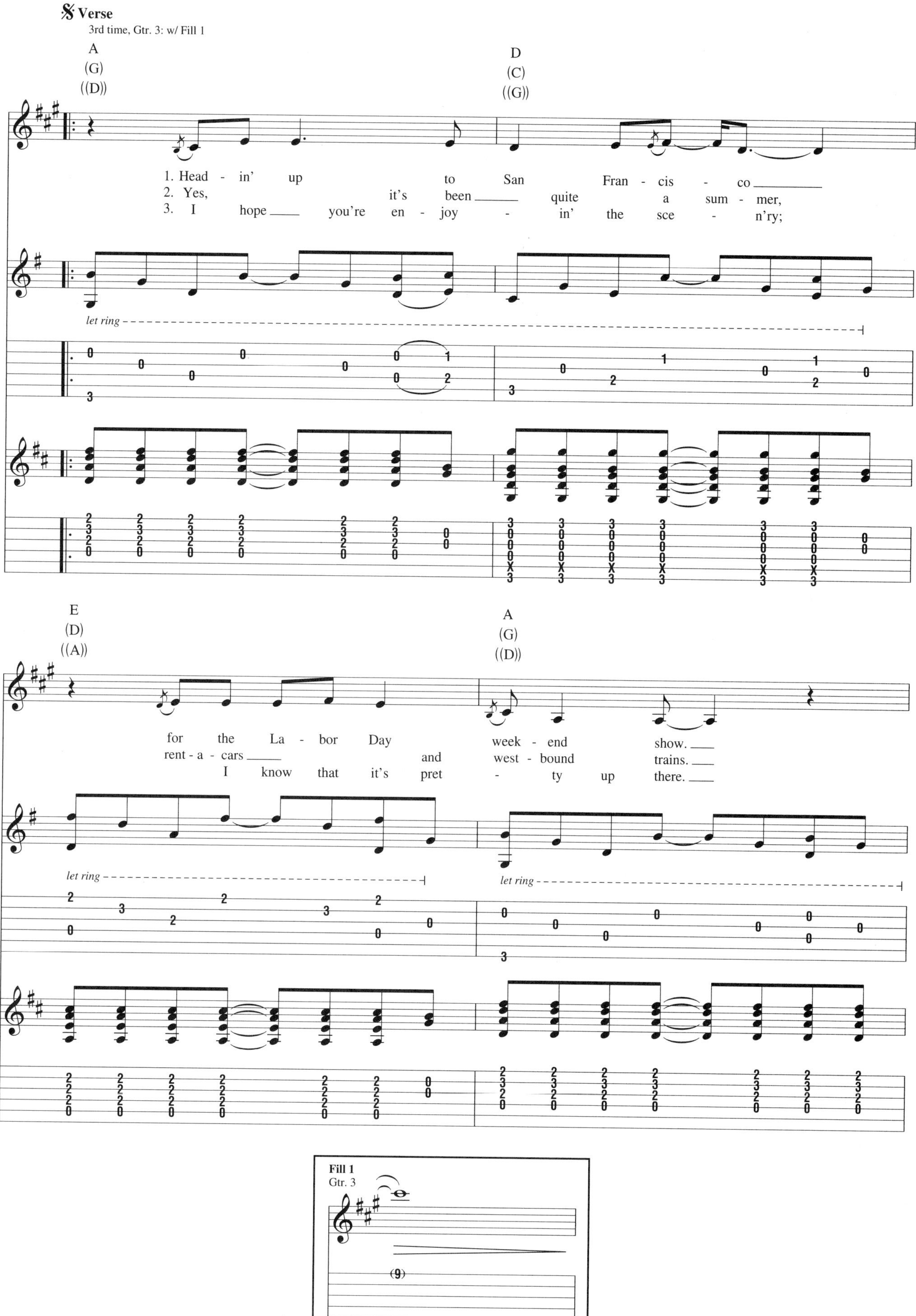

Verse
3rd time, Gtr. 3: w/ Fill 1
A
(G)
((D))
D
(C)
((G))
1. Head - in' up to San Fran - cis - co
2. Yes, it's been quite a sum - mer,
3. I hope you're en - joy - in' the sce - n'ry;
let ring
E
(D)
((A))
A
(G)
((D))
for the La - bor Day week - end show.
rent - a - cars and west - bound trains.
I know that it's pret - ty up there.
let ring
let ring
Fill 1
Gtr. 3

2nd time, Bkgd. Voc. tacet
D
(C)
((G))
E
(D)
((A))
I got my hush pup-pies on; I guess I nev-er was meant for glit-ter
And now you're off on va-ca-tion, some-thin' you tried
We can go hik-in' on Tues-day; with you I'd
(Ah.)
let ring
*Fade in
A
(G)
((D))
Bm7
(Am7)
((Em7))
D
(C)
((G))
rock-and-roll. And, hon-ey, I did-n't know
to ex-plain. And, dar-lin', since I love you so,
walk an-y-where. Cal-i-for-nia has worn me quite thin;
let ring

E7
(D7)
((A7))

that I'd be miss - in' you so.
that's the rea - son I just let you go.
I just can't wait to see you a - gain.
Come

let ring

Chorus

D (C) ((G)) — A (G) ((D)) — D (C) ((G))

Mon - day, it-'ll be all right. Come Mon - day, I'll be

strum w/ fingers

To Coda
E
(D)
((A))
A
(G)
((D))
C#m
(Bm)
((F#m))
D
(C)
((G))
E
(D)
((A))
hold - in' you tight. I spent four lone - ly days in a brown L. A. haze, and I
(Oo.)
D
(C)
((G))
E
(D)
((A))
1.
A
(G)
((D))
just want you back by my side.
w/ fingers
let ring

2.
A
(G)
((D))
side.
w/ fingers
let ring
Bridge
Bmaj7
(Amaj7)
((Emaj7))
E
(D)
((A))
Bmaj7
(Amaj7)
((Emaj7))
I can't help it, hon-ey.
You're that much a part
strum w/ fingers

E
(D)
((A))
Bmaj7
(Amaj7)
((Emaj7))
E
(D)
((A))
of me now.
Re - mem - ber that night in Mon - tan - a when we
D
(C)
((G))
E
(D)
((A))
said there'd be no room for doubt?
(Ah.)
*Gtr. 3
mf
w/ slide
*Pedal steel arr. for gtr.
Gtr. 1
w/ fingers
Gtr. 2
**Fade in

Pedal Steel Solo
D.S. al Coda
G
(F)
((C))
D
(C)
((G))
A
(G)
((D))
steady gliss.
steady gliss.
strum w/ fingers
Coda
D
(C)
((G))
E
(D)
((A))
A
(G)
((D))
just want you back by my side.
I spent

C♯m (Bm) ((F♯m))
D (C) ((G))
E (D) ((A))
D (C) ((G))
E (D) ((A))
four lone - ly days in a brown L. A. haze, and I just want you back by my
(Four lone - ly days, brown L. A. haze. Just want you back by my
G (F) ((C))
D (C) ((G))
A (G) ((D))
side.
side.)

from B.B. King - *Singin' the Blues*

Cryin' Won't Help You

Words and Music by B.B. King and Saul Bihari

way you've been treat - in' me, wom - an, it's com - in' back home to you. And your cry -
watch those seeds you scat - ter, wom - an, 'cause you're gon - na reap just what you sow. And your

Gtr. 1: w/ Fill 1, 2nd time
F7
Gtr. 1: w/ Fill 2, 3rd time
Gtr. 1: w/ Fill 3, 4th time
C7
- in' won't help you, wom-an. Oh, cry - in' won't help you babe.
cry - in' won't help you, wom-an Oh, cry - in' won't help you now.
full

Fill 1
Gtr. 1
full
full

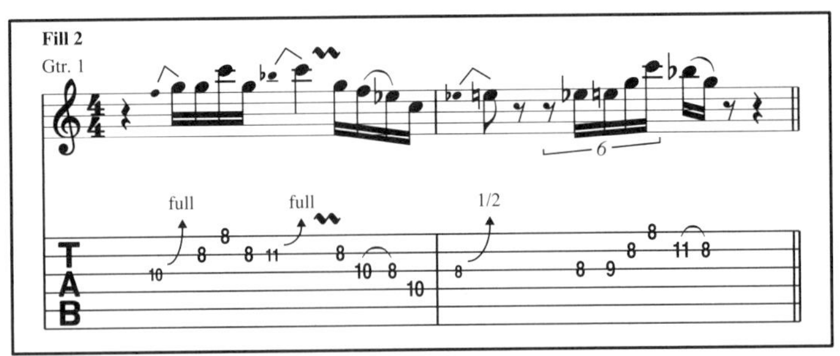
Fill 2
Gtr. 1
full
full
1/2

Fill 3
Gtr. 1
full

To Coda ⊕

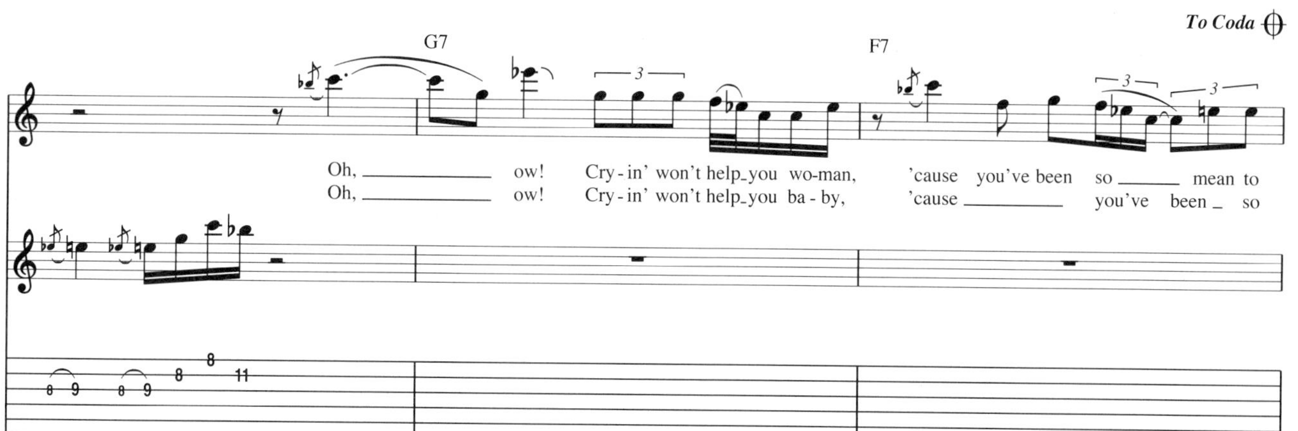
G7
F7
Oh, ow! Cry-in' won't help_you wo-man, 'cause you've been so mean to
Oh, ow! Cry-in' won't help_you ba-by, 'cause you've been so

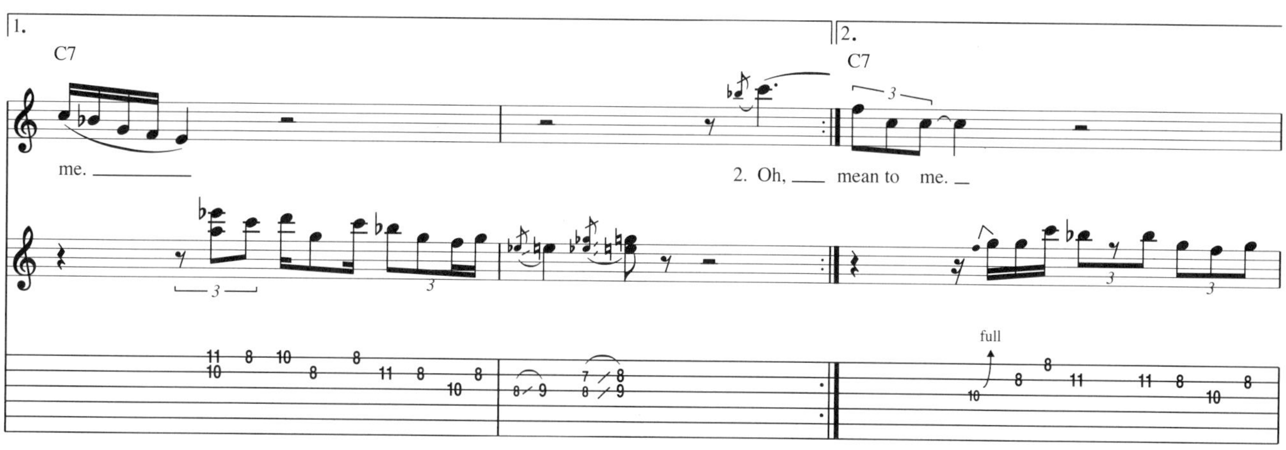
1.
C7
2.
C7
me.
2. Oh, mean to me.
full

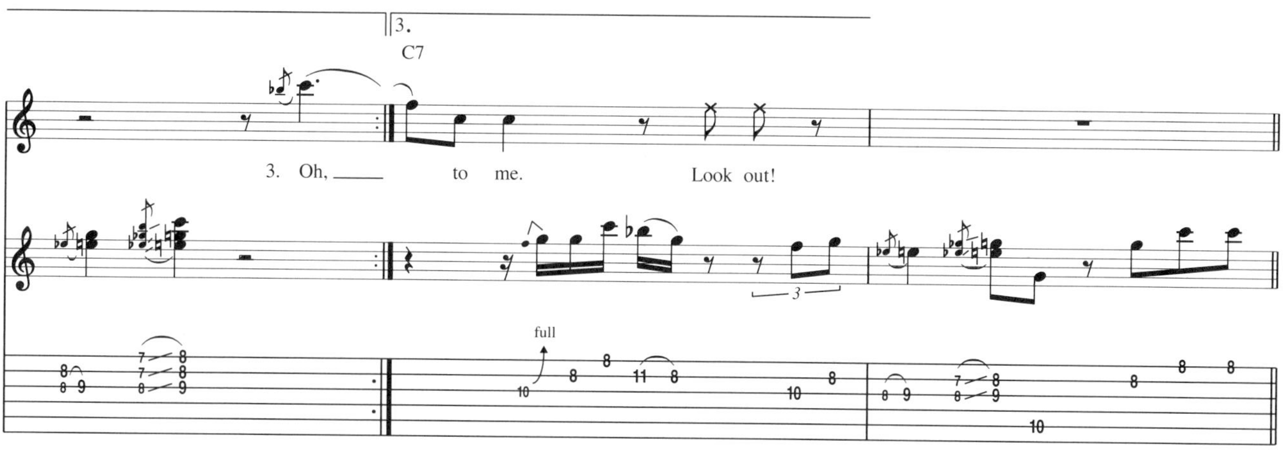
3.
C7
3. Oh, to me. Look out!
full

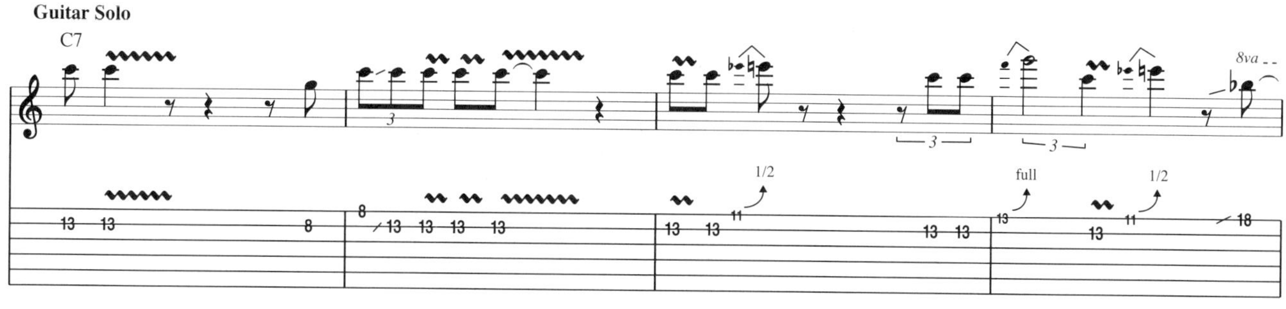
Guitar Solo
C7
1/2
full
1/2
8va

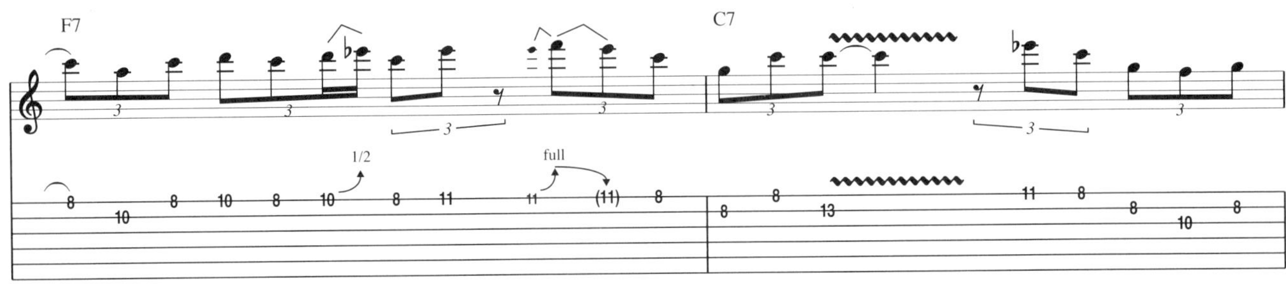

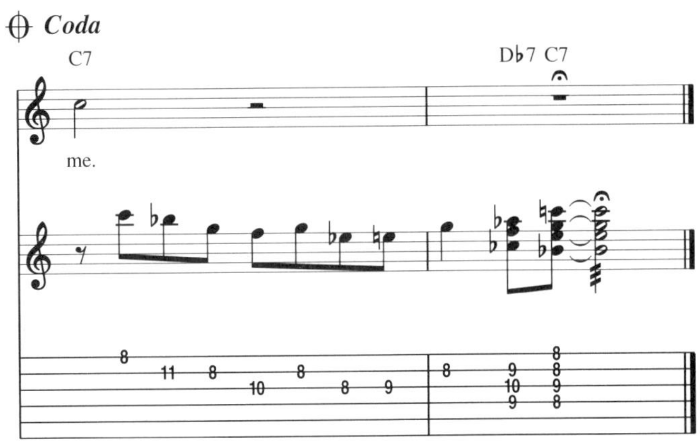

Additional Lyrics

3. Oh, the way that you treat me, woman,
   Just can't understand.
   Oh, I'm gonna leave you, woman,
   Let you do the best you can.
   And your cryin' won't help you, babe.
   Cryin' won't help you now.
   Oh, cryin' won't help you, woman,
   'Cause you've been so mean to me.

4. Oh, just before I leave you, woman,
   Just want to shake your hand.
   I'm gonna get me a woman, baby,
   Let you get you a man.
   And your cryin' won't help you, woman,
   Cryin' won't help you now.
   Oh, cryin' won't help you, baby,
   'Cause you've been so mean to me.

from *Collective Soul*

December

Words and Music by Ed Roland

Chorus
G5
F6sus2
Csus2
B♭6
G/B
Voc. Fig. 1
Don't scream a - bout. Don't think a - loud. Turn your head now, ba - by, just spit me out.
Rhy. Fig. 1
End Rhy. Fig. 1
*Gtr. 3 (acous.)
mf
*Two gtrs. arr. for one.
Riff C
End Riff C
Gtr. 4 (elec.)
mf
w/clean tone & amp tremolo
To Coda
Gtr. 3: w/ Rhy. Fig. 1 (2 times)
Gtr. 4: w/ Riff C (2 times)
G5
F6sus2
Csus2
B♭6
G/B
End Voc. Fig. 1
Don't wor - ry 'bout. Don't speak of doubt. Turn your head now, ba - by, just spit me out.
Interlude
Gtr. 3: w/ Rhy. Fig. 1 (2 times)
Gtr. 4: w/ Riff C (2 times)
G5
F6sus2
Csus2
B♭6
G/B
Voc. Fig. 2
End Voc. Fig. 2
(Oo.)
Riff D
End Riff D
Gtr. 5 (elec.)
mf
w/ slight dist.
P.M.
**Sing 1st time only.

Gtr. 1: w/ Riff A (2 times)
Gtr. 5 tacet
Gtrs. 3 & 4 tacet
G5
F6sus2
Csus2
B♭6
G/B
Rhy. Fill 1
Gtr. 3
End Rhy. Fill 1
Rhy. Fill 1A
Gtr. 4
End Rhy. Fill 1A
D.S. al Coda
Gtr. 2: w/ Riff B
Coda
Bkgd. Voc.: w/ Voc. Fig. 2 (2 times)
Gtr. 3: w/ Rhy. Fig. 1 (2 times)
Gtr. 4: w/ Riff C (2 times)
Voc. Fig. 3
Don't scream a - bout. Don't think a - loud. Turn your head now, ba - by, just spit me out.
Don't wor - ry 'bout. Don't speak of doubt. Turn your head now, ba - by, just spit me out.
End Voc. Fig. 3
Interlude
Bkgd. Voc.: w/ Voc. Fig. 2 (2 times)
Gtr. 3: w/ Rhy. Fig. 1 (2 times)
Gtr. 4: w/ Riff C (2 times)
Gtr. 5: w/ Riff D (2 times)
*Sing 1st time only.

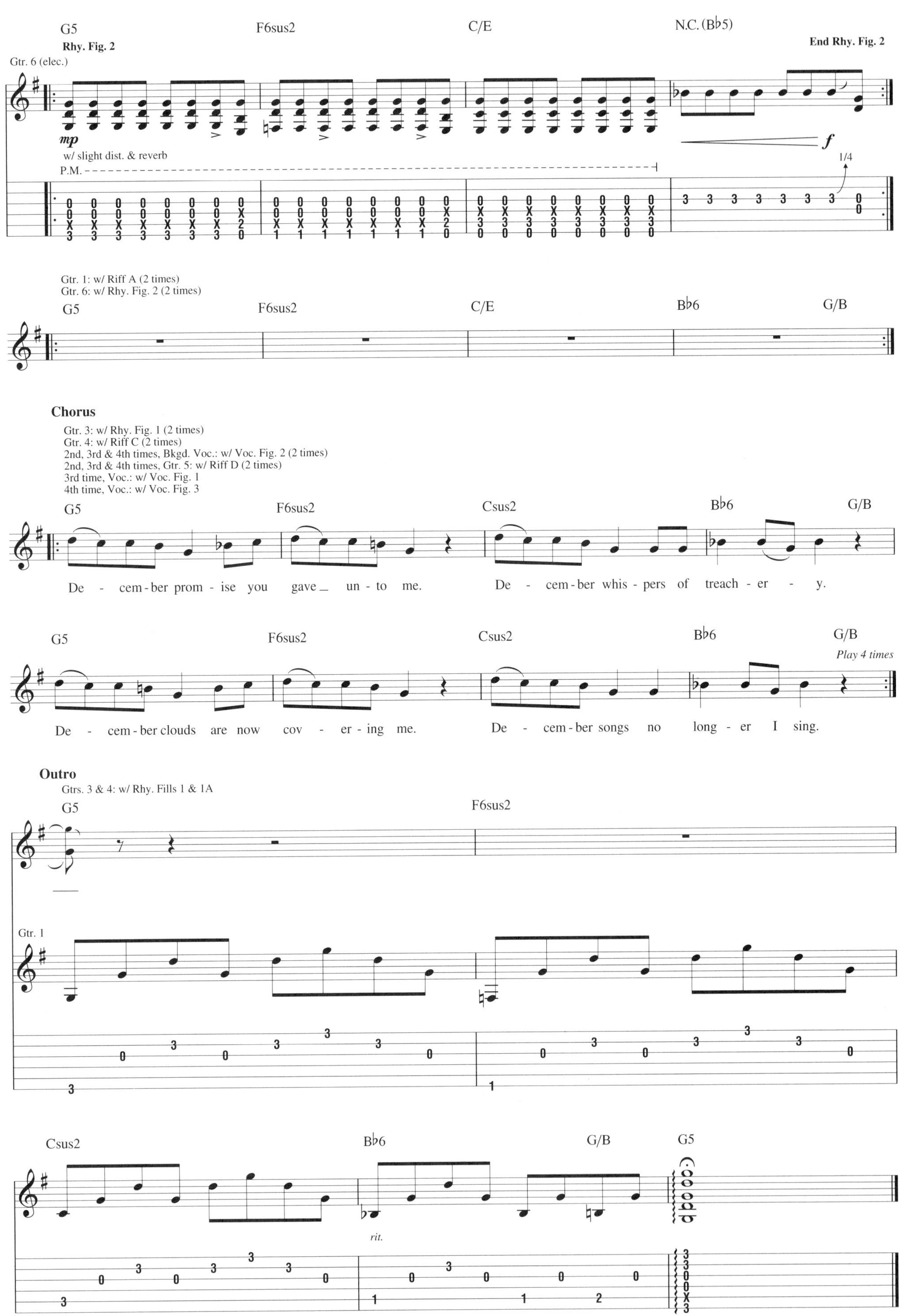

G5
F6sus2
C/E
N.C. (B♭5)
Rhy. Fig. 2
End Rhy. Fig. 2
Gtr. 6 (elec.)
mp
f
w/ slight dist. & reverb
P.M.
1/4
Gtr. 1: w/ Riff A (2 times)
Gtr. 6: w/ Rhy. Fig. 2 (2 times)
G5
F6sus2
C/E
B♭6
G/B
Chorus
Gtr. 3: w/ Rhy. Fig. 1 (2 times)
Gtr. 4: w/ Riff C (2 times)
2nd, 3rd & 4th times, Bkgd. Voc.: w/ Voc. Fig. 2 (2 times)
2nd, 3rd & 4th times, Gtr. 5: w/ Riff D (2 times)
3rd time, Voc.: w/ Voc. Fig. 1
4th time, Voc.: w/ Voc. Fig. 3
G5
F6sus2
Csus2
B♭6
G/B
De - cem-ber prom - ise you gave un - to me. De - cem-ber whis - pers of treach - er - y.
G5
F6sus2
Csus2
B♭6
G/B
Play 4 times
De - cem-ber clouds are now cov - er - ing me. De - cem-ber songs no long - er I sing.
Outro
Gtrs. 3 & 4: w/ Rhy. Fills 1 & 1A
G5
F6sus2
Gtr. 1
Csus2
B♭6
G/B
G5
rit.

from *Billy Talent II*

Devil in a Midnight Mass

Words and Music by Ian D'Sa, Ben Kowalewicz, Jon Gallant and Aaron Solowoniuk

Drop D tuning:
(low to high) D-A-D-G-B-E

Intro

Moderately fast ♩ = 178

*G5 A5 B♭5 D5 B♭5 D5 A5 D5 F5 D5 E5 D5 A5 F5 D5 G5 A5 B♭5 D5 B♭5 D5 A5 D5 F5 D5 E5

Gtr. 1 (dist.)

f

*Chord symbols reflect implied harmony.

D5 A5 F5 D5 G5 A5 B♭5 D5 B♭ D5 Asus4 D5 F D5 Em D5 A5 F5 D5 G5 A5 B♭5 D5

Screamed: Yeah!

Gtr. 1

Rhy. Fig. 1

End Rhy. Fig. 1

Gtr. 2 (dist.)

f

Gtrs. 1 & 2: w/ Rhy. Fig. 1 (2 1/2 times)

1., 2.

D5 B♭ D5 Asus4 D5 F D5 Em D5 A5 F5 D5 G5 A5 B♭5 D5

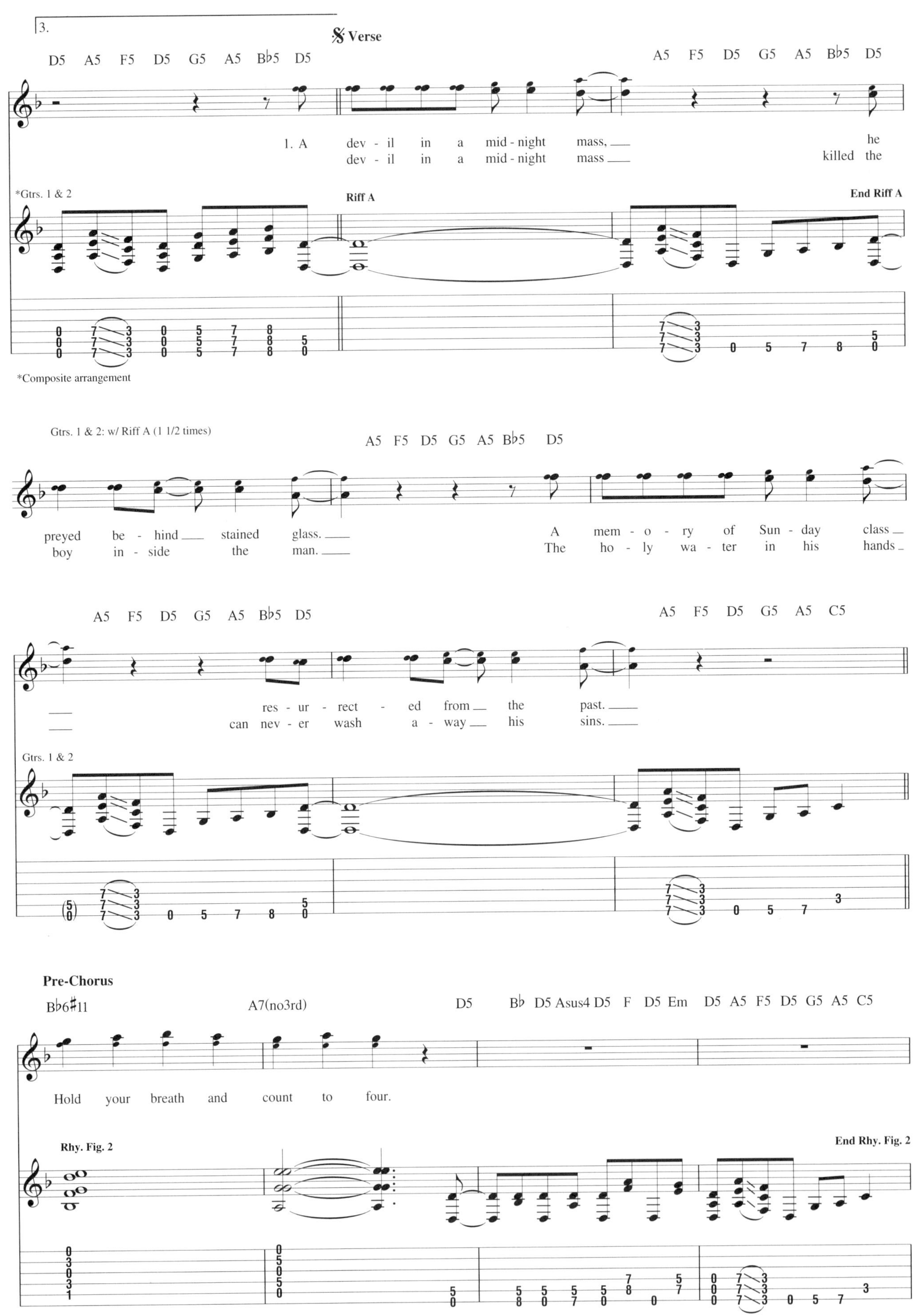
3.
Verse
D5 A5 F5 D5 G5 A5 B♭5 D5
A5 F5 D5 G5 A5 B♭5 D5
1. A dev - il in a mid - night mass, he preyed be - hind stained glass.
dev - il in a mid - night mass killed the boy in - side the man.
*Gtrs. 1 & 2
Riff A
End Riff A
*Composite arrangement
Gtrs. 1 & 2: w/ Riff A (1 1/2 times)
A memo - o - ry of Sun - day class res - ur - rect - ed from the past.
The ho - ly wa - ter in his hands can nev - er wash a - way his sins.
A5 F5 D5 G5 A5 B♭5 D5
A5 F5 D5 G5 A5 C5
Gtrs. 1 & 2
Pre-Chorus
B♭6♯11
A7(no3rd)
D5 B♭ D5 Asus4 D5 F D5 Em D5 A5 F5 D5 G5 A5 C5
Hold your breath and count to four.
Rhy. Fig. 2
End Rhy. Fig. 2

Gtrs. 1 & 2: w/ Rhy. Fig. 2
Bb6#11
A7(no3rd)
D5
Bb D5 Asus4 D5 F D5 Em D5 A5 F5 D5 G5 A5 C5
Pink - y swears don't work no more.
Bb6#11
A7 (no3rd)
Dm (add4/9)
Fmaj9
1. Foot - steps down the hall - way floor get - ting clos - er to my door.
2. Put my trust in God that day, not the man that taught His way.
I
Gtrs. 1 & 2
Bb6#11
A7 (no3rd)
A5 F5 D5 G5 A5 Bb5 Dm(add9)
was a - live, but now I'm sing - ing...
(Si -
Chorus
Fmaj9
Gm6
For the rest of my life.
For the rest of my life.
- lent Night.
Si - lent Night.
Vi -
Rhy. Fig. 3
End Rhy. Fig. 3

B♭6♯11
A7(no3rd)
F5 D5 G5 A5 B♭5 Dm(add9)
At the edge of your knife.
Won't make it right.
- o - lent knight.
"For - give me, Fa - ther."
Si -
Gtrs. 1 & 2: w/ Rhy. Fig. 3
Fmaj9
Gm6
For the rest of my life.
At the edge of your knife.
- lent Night.
Si - lent Night.
You're guilt -
To Coda
Fmaj9
E°
C
B♭6♯11
A5 F5 D5 G5 A5 B♭5 D5
- y!)
Gtrs. 1 & 2
Gtr. 1
Gtr. 2
divisi
Interlude
D.S. al Coda
D5 B♭ D5 Asus4 D5 F D5 Em
D5 A5 F5 D5 G5 A5 B♭5 D5
B♭ D5 Asus4 D5 F D5 Em
D5 A5 F5 D5 G5 A5 B♭5 D5
2. A
Gtrs. 1 & 2

Coda

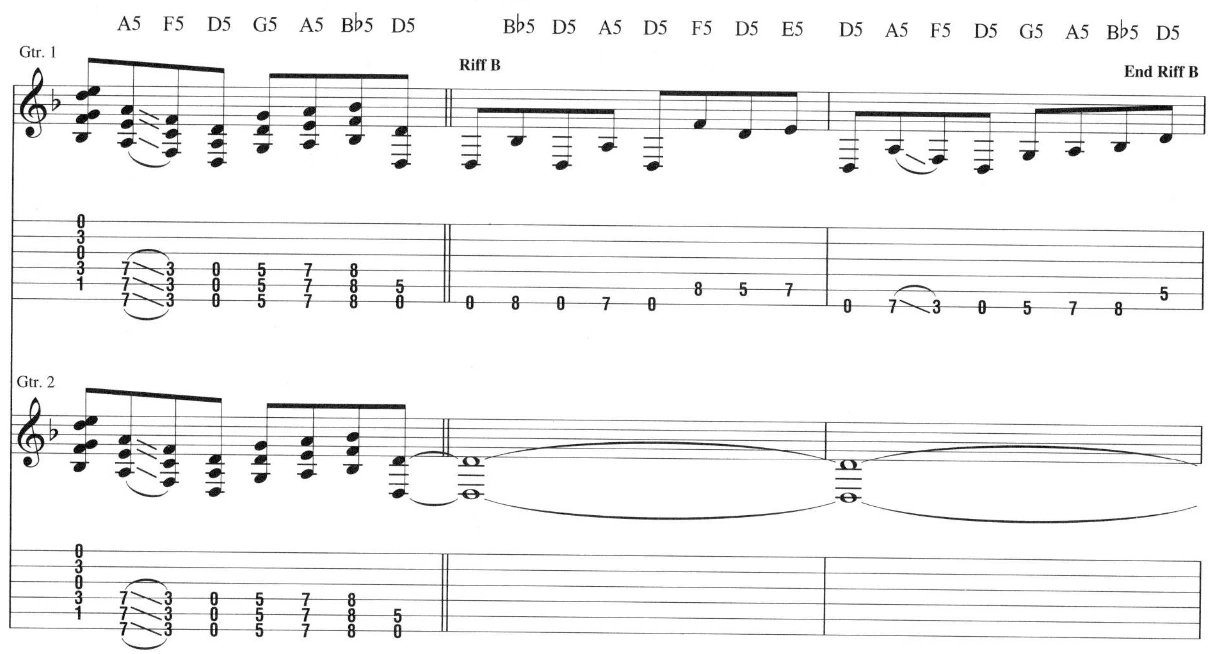

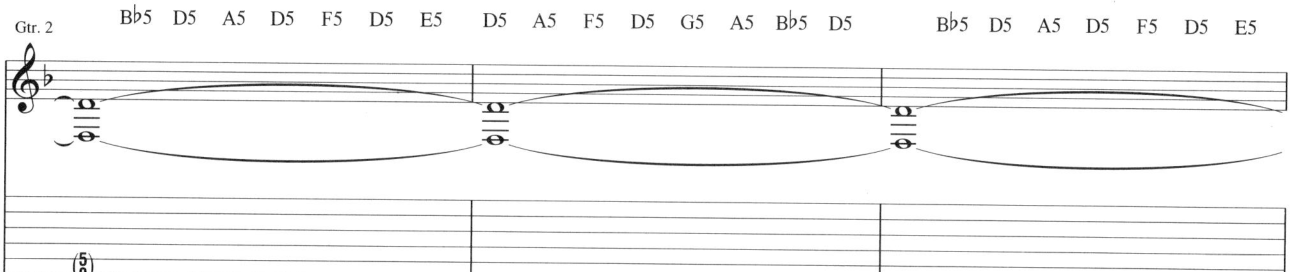

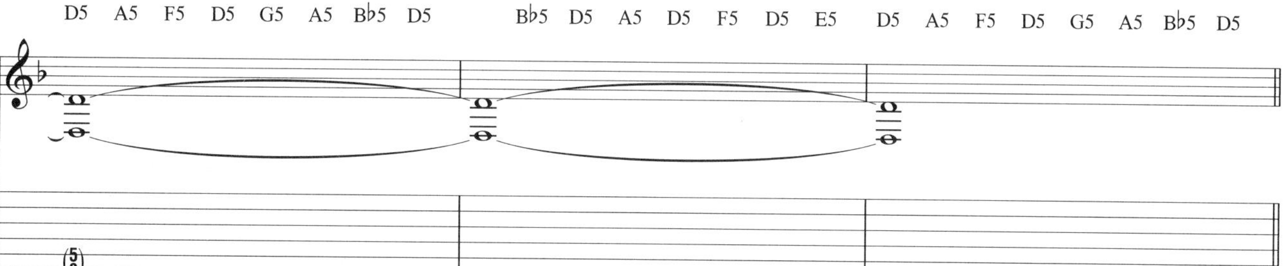

Chorus

Gtr. 1: w/ Riff B (2 times)
Gtr. 2 tacet

D5 B♭5 D5 A5 D5 F5 D5 E5 D5 A5 F5 D5 G5 A5 B♭5 D5 B♭5 D5 A5 D5 F5 D5 E5 D5 A5 F5 D5 G5 A5 B♭5 D5

Whispered:

Whis - per, whis - per, don't make a sound. Your bed is made, it's in the ground.

B♭5 D5 A5 D5 F5 D5 E5 D5 A5 F5 D5 G5 A5 B♭5 D5 B♭5 D5 A5 D5 F5 D5 E5 N.C. D5
Whis - per, whis - per, don't make a sound. Your bed is made, it's in the ground.
Gtr. 1
Gtrs. 1 & 2
Outro-Chorus
Gtrs. 1 & 2: w/ Rhy. Fig. 1 (6 times)
D5 B♭ D5 Asus4 D5 F D5 Em D5 A5 F5 D5 G5 A5 B♭5 D5 B♭ D5 Asus4 D5 F D5 Em D5 A5 F5 D5 G5 A5 B♭5 D5
*Voc. Fig. 1
End Voc. Fig. 1
Whis - per, whis - per, don't make a sound. Your bed is made, it's in the ground.
(Whis - per, whis - per.)
*Refers to downstemmed voc. only.
Bkgd. Voc.: w/ Voc. Fig. 1
B♭ D5 Asus4 D5 F D5 Em D5 A5 F5 D5 G5 A5 B♭5 D5 B♭ D5 Asus4 D5 F D5 Em D5 A5 F5 D5 G5 A5 B♭5 D5
Whis - per, whis - per, don't make a sound. Your bed is made, it's in the ground.
Bkgd. Voc.: w/ Voc. Fig. 1
B♭ D5 Asus4 D5 F D5 Em D5 A5 F5 D5 G5 A5 B♭5 D5 B♭ D5 Asus4 D5 F D5 Em D5 A5 F5 D5 G5 A5 B♭5 D5
Whis - per, whis - per, don't make a sound. Your bed is made, it's in the ground.
Bkgd. Voc.: w/ Voc. Fig. 1
B♭ D5 Asus4 D5 F D5 Em D5 A5 F5 D5 G5 A5 B♭5 D5 B♭ D5 Asus4 D5 F D5 Em D5 A5 F5 D5 G5 A5 B♭5 N.C.
Whis - per, whis - per, don't make a sound. Your bed is made and it's in the ground.
Gtrs. 1 & 2

from R.E.M. - *Automatic for the People*

Drive

Words and Music by William Berry, Peter Buck, Michael Mills, Michael Stipe

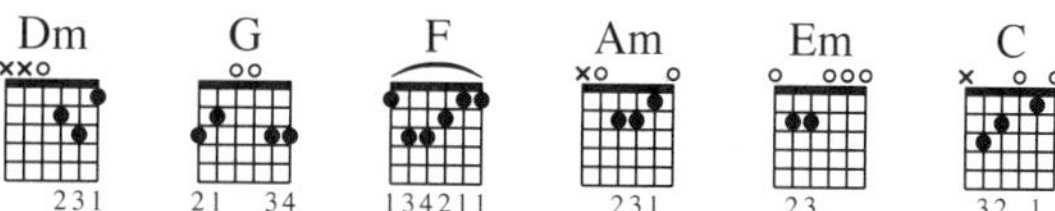

Chorus
Gtr. 1
F F A Am G G
3fr open 3fr
1. What if I ride? What if you walk? What if you rock a - round the clock? Tick, tock,
2., 3. May-be you did, may-be you walked, 2. ba - by, you rocked a - round the clock. 3. may-be you rock a - round the clock. Tick, tock,
To Coda
G G E Em E Em G
3fr open open
tick, tock. What if you did? What if you walk? What if you tried to get off, ba -
tick, tock. May-be I ride, may-be you walk, may-be I drive to get off, ba -
1. Gtr. 1: w/ Rhy. Fig. 2
Dm
- by? Oh.
2. Gtr. 1: w/ Rhy. Fig. 2
Dm
- by. Oh.
Gtr. 2 (elec.)
f w/ dist.
Bridge
Gtr. 1
C Dm
Hey kids, shake a leg. May-be you're cra - zy in the head, ba - by.
Gtr. 2

C
Ol-lie, ol-lie, ol-lie, ol-lie, ol-lie, ol-lie, ol-lie, in come free, ba -

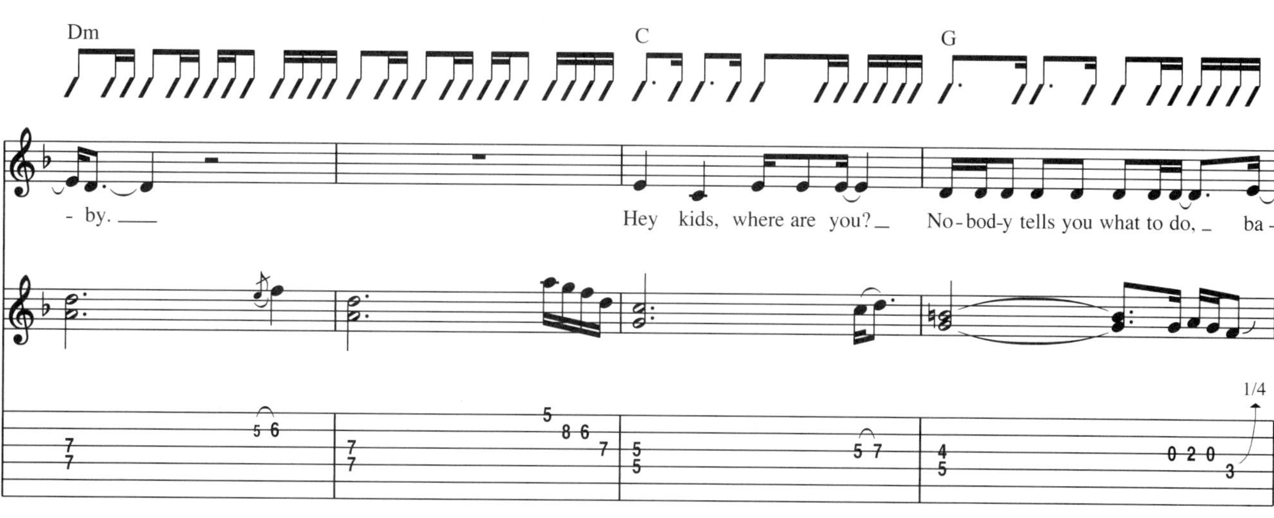
Dm
C
G
- by.
Hey kids, where are you?
No-bod-y tells you what to do, ba-
1/4

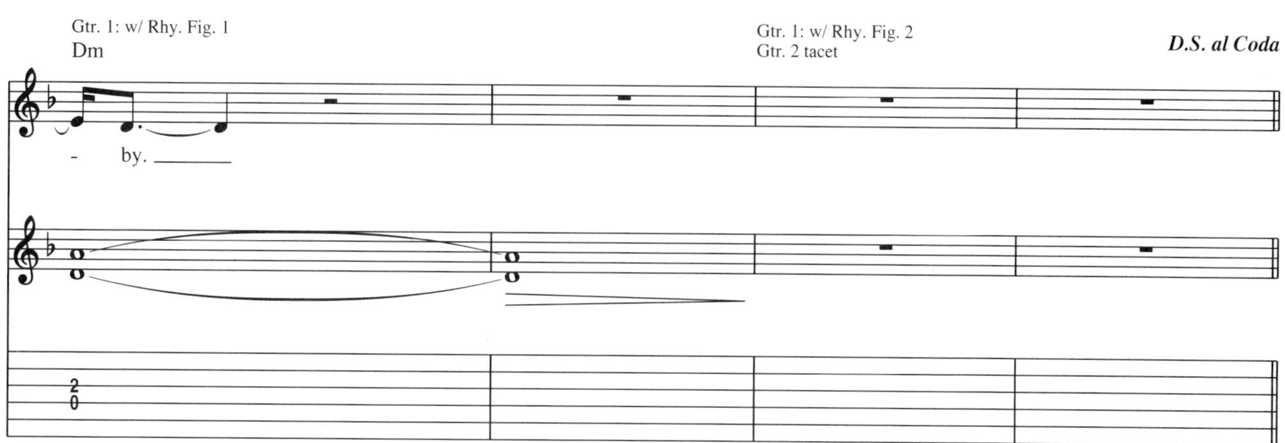
Gtr. 1: w/ Rhy. Fig. 1
Dm
Gtr. 1: w/ Rhy. Fig. 2
Gtr. 2 tacet
D.S. al Coda
- by.

Coda
Gtr. 1: w/ Rhy. Fig. 2
Dm
E
Em
open
Gtr. 1
- by.
Hey kids, where are you?
Gtr. 2
Rhy. Fig. 3
Gtr. 1: w/ Rhy. Fig. 2
G
No-bod-y tells you what to do, ba - by.
End Rhy. Fig. 3
Gtr. 2: w/ Rhy. Fig. 3
Gtr. 1: w/ Rhy. Fig. 1, 2 times, simile
Hey kids, rock and roll.
No-bod-y tells you where to go ba - by, ba -
Gtr. 2 tacet
rit.
- by, ba - by.

from Eric Johnson - *Ah Via Musicom*

East Wes

By Eric Johnson

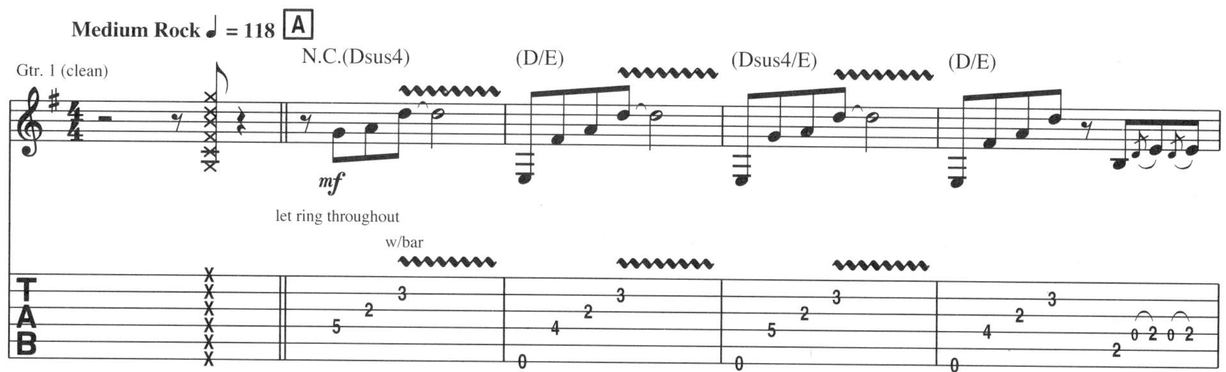

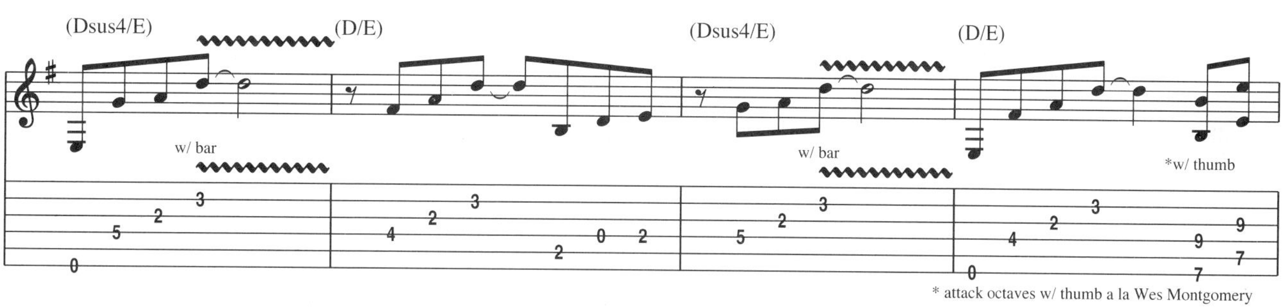

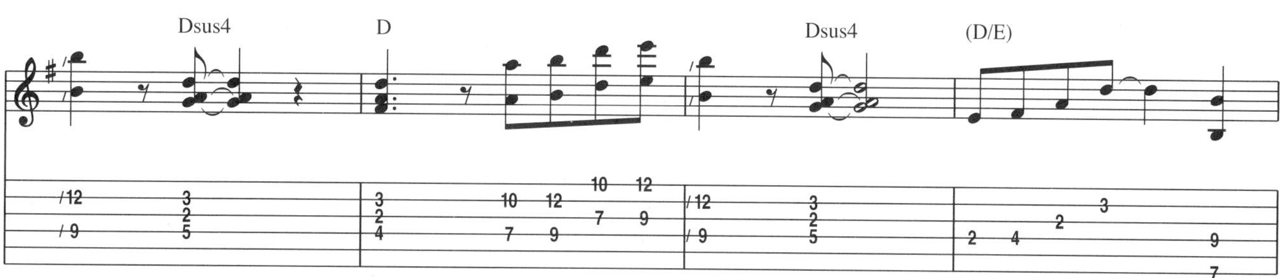

A5
Asus2
(D/E)
C6
(Dsus4)
(D/E)
let ring
w/ bar
w/ bar
(D/E)
B Guitar Solo
Dsus4
Dsus4
A5
Cmaj7/E
D6

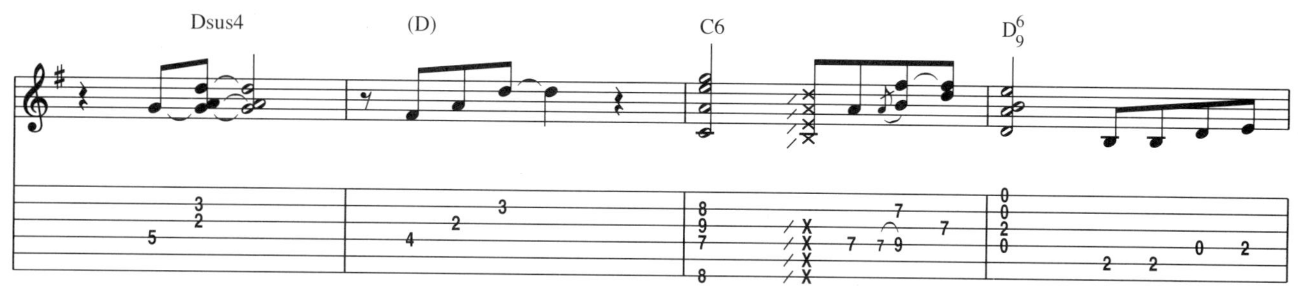
Dsus4
(D)
C6
D 6 9

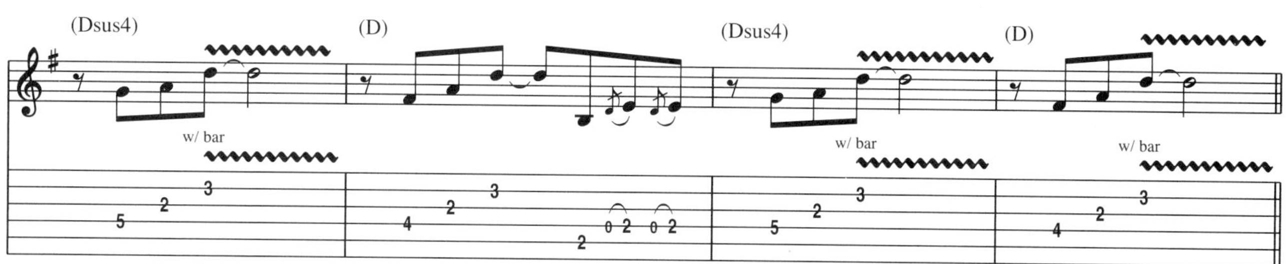
(Dsus4)
(D)
(Dsus4)
(D)
w/ bar
w/ bar
w/ bar

C
w/ dist.

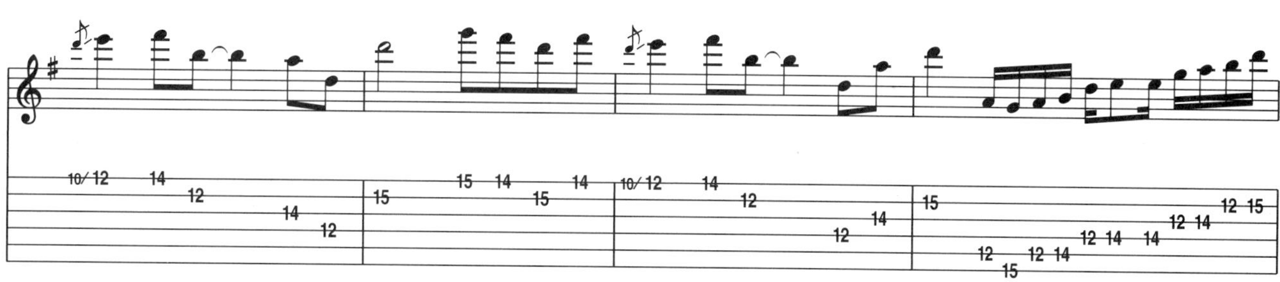

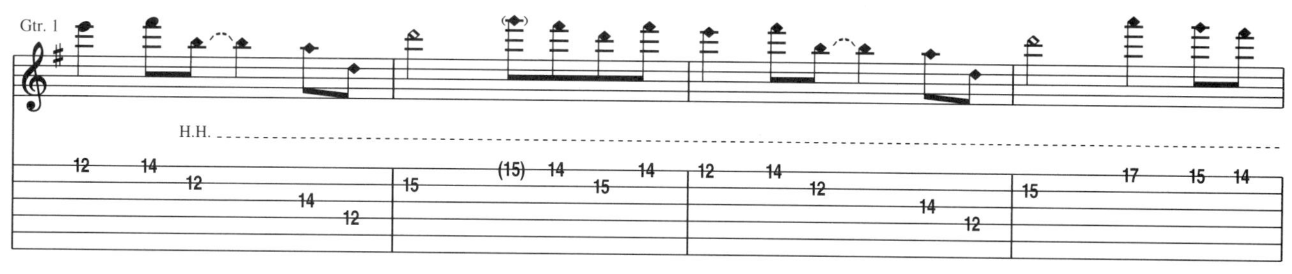
Gtr. 1
H.H.

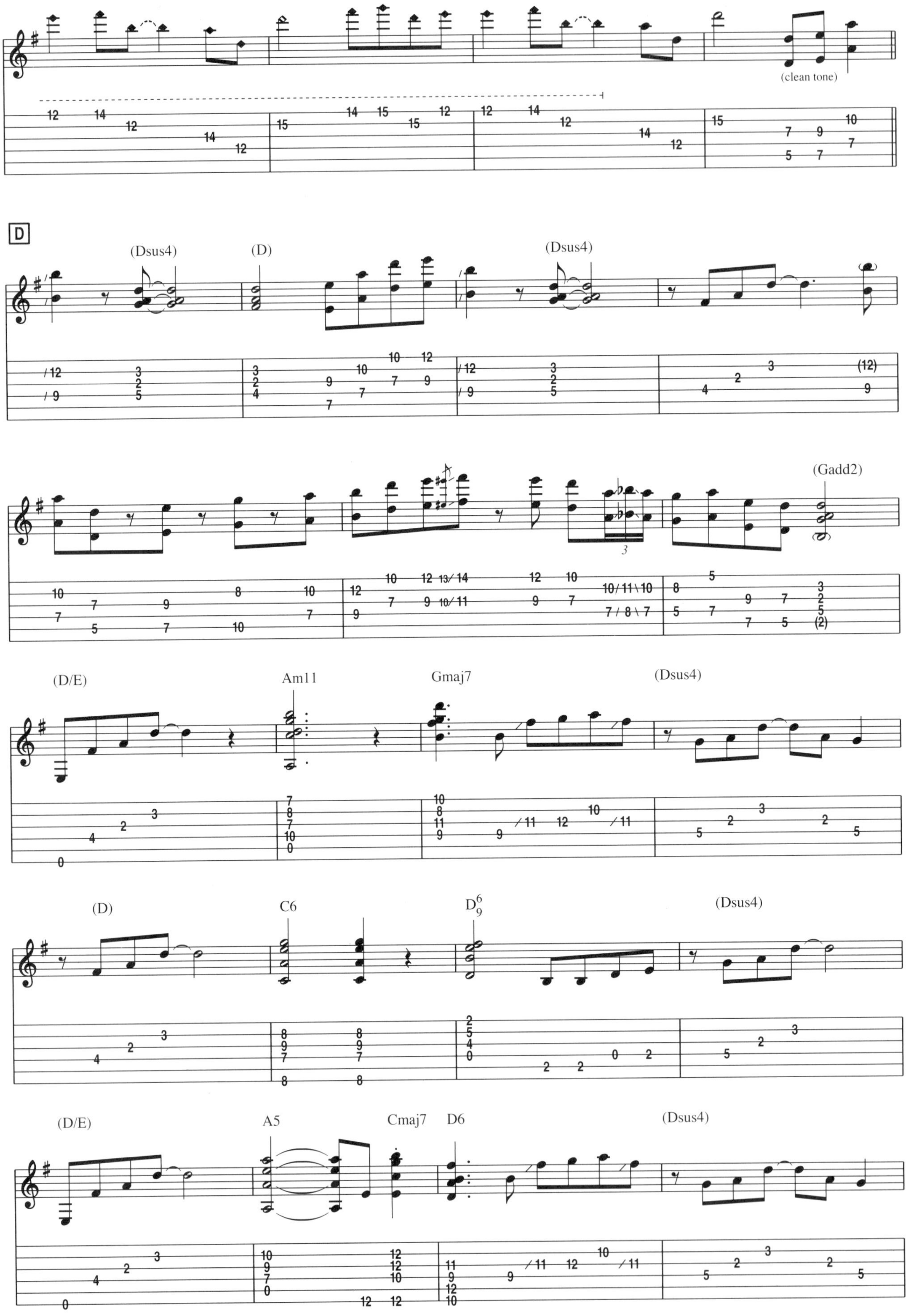

(clean tone)

D

(Dsus4) (D) (Dsus4)

(Gadd2)

(D/E) Am11 Gmaj7 (Dsus4)

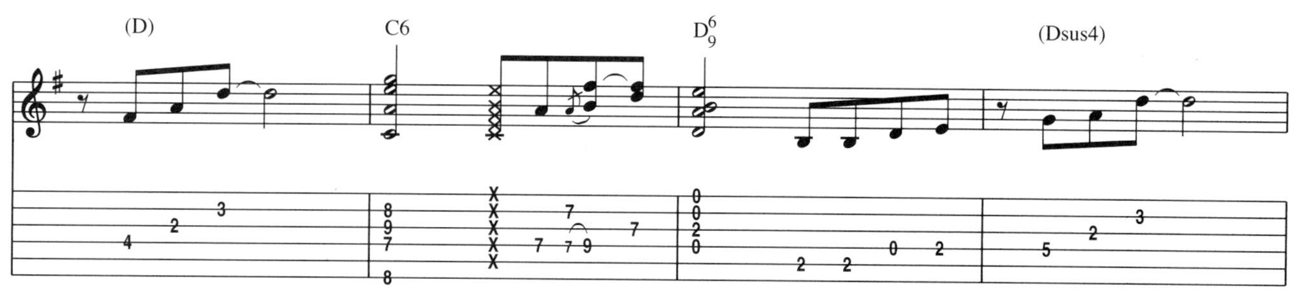

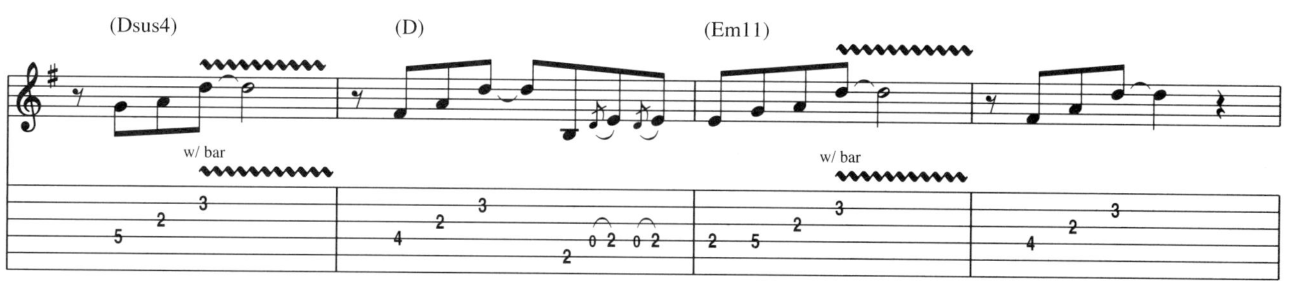

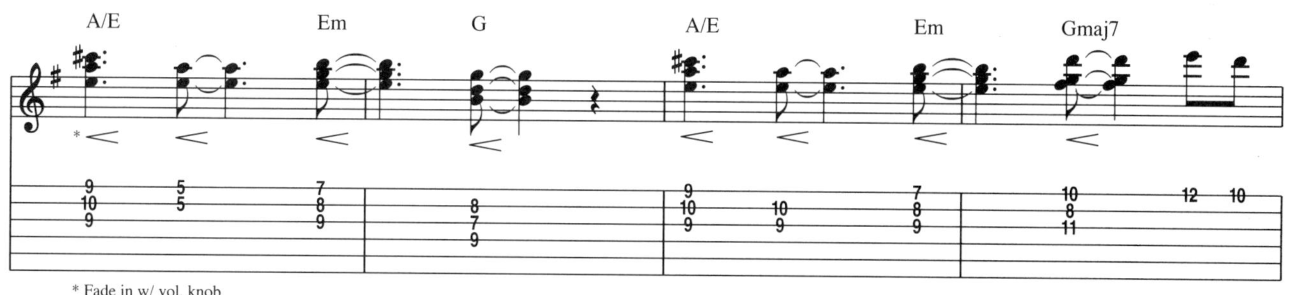

* Fade in w/ vol. knob.

from the Byrds - *Fifth Dimension*

Eight Miles High

Words and Music by Roger McGuinn, David Crosby and Gene Clark

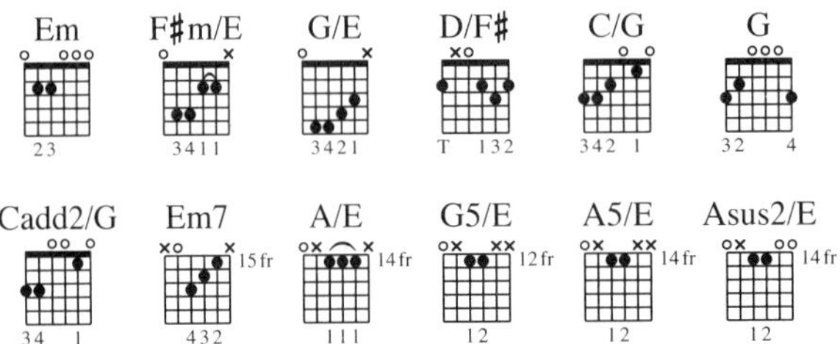

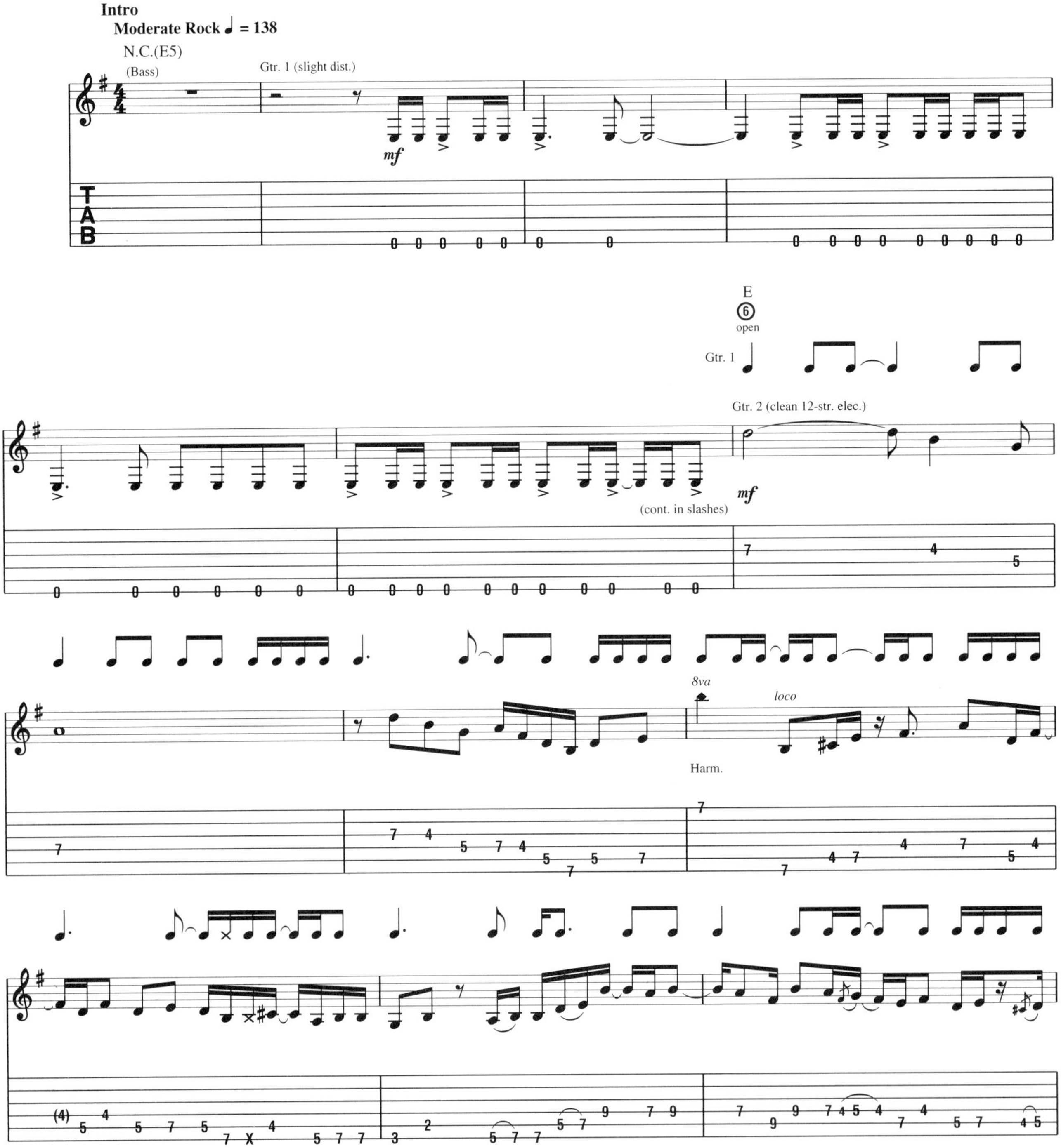

Intro
Moderate Rock ♩ = 138

N.C.(E5)
(Bass)
Gtr. 1 (slight dist.)
mf

E
⑥ open
Gtr. 1
Gtr. 2 (clean 12-str. elec.)
mf
(cont. in slashes)

8va
loco
Harm.

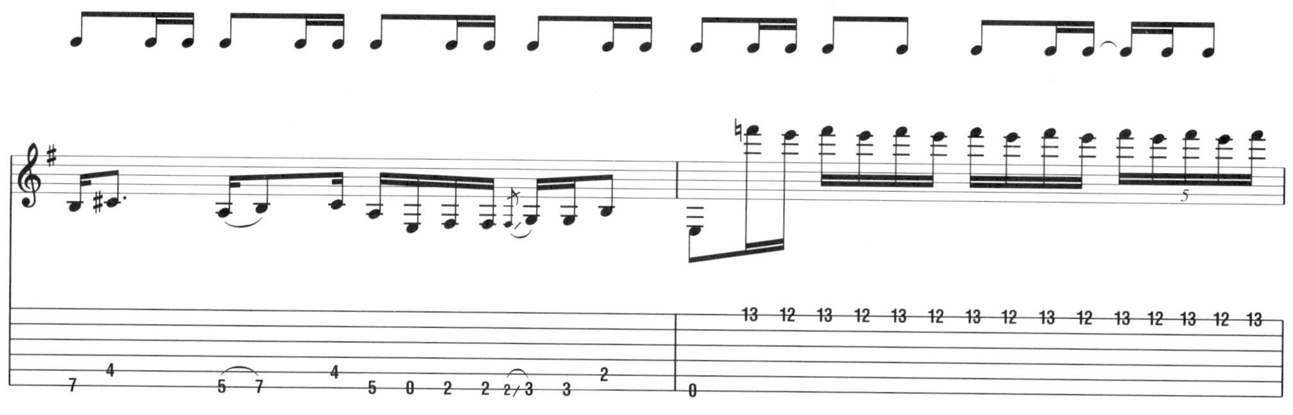
5
13 12 13 12 13 12 13 12 13 12 13 12 13 12 13
7 4 5 7 4 5 0 2 2 2/3 3 2
0

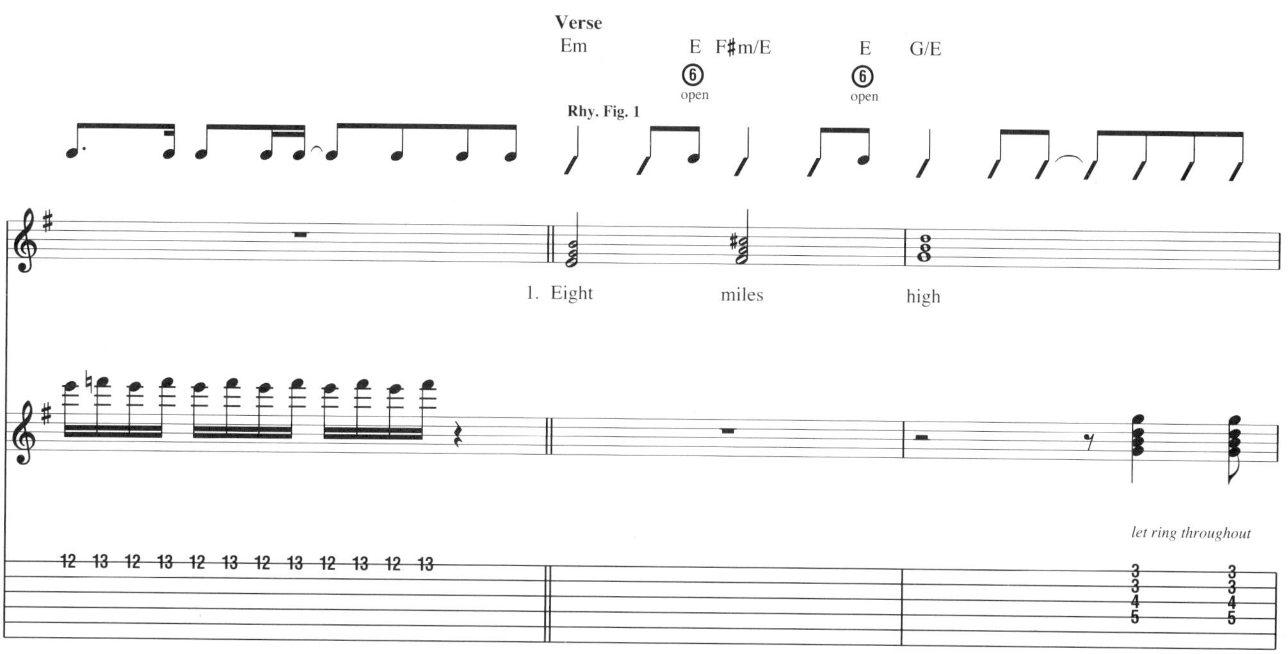
Verse
Em
E F♯m/E
⑥ open
E G/E
⑥ open
Rhy. Fig. 1
1. Eight miles high
12 13 12 13 12 13 12 13 12 13 12 13
let ring throughout

D/F♯
C/G
G
D/F♯
C/G
and light - ly touch down, you'll find that it's strang - er than

Gtr. 1: w/ Rhy. Fig. 1
Cadd2/G
C/G
Cadd2/G
Em
F♯m/E
G/E
End Rhy. Fig. 1
known.
Signs in the street
Rhy. Fig. 2

D/F♯
C/G
G
D/F♯
C/G
that say where you're going,
out somewhere just being a-

Cadd2/G
C/G
Cadd2/G
Em
F♯m/E
G/E
F♯m/E
Gtr. 1
-lone.
End Rhy. Fig. 2

Verse

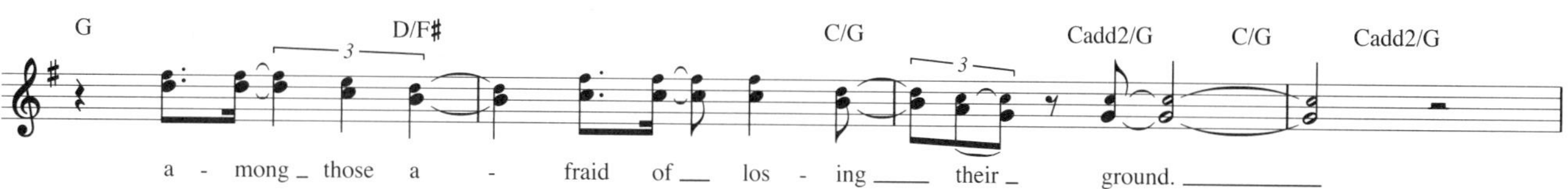

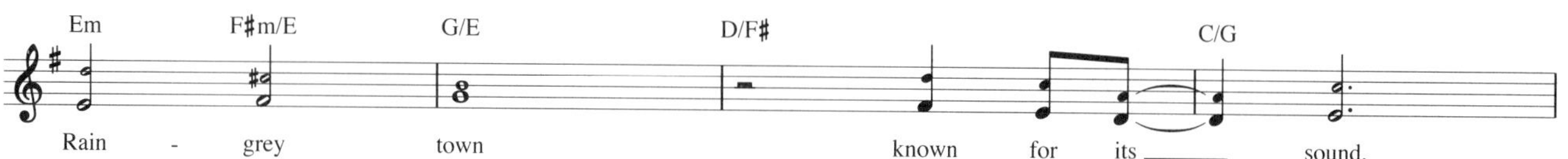

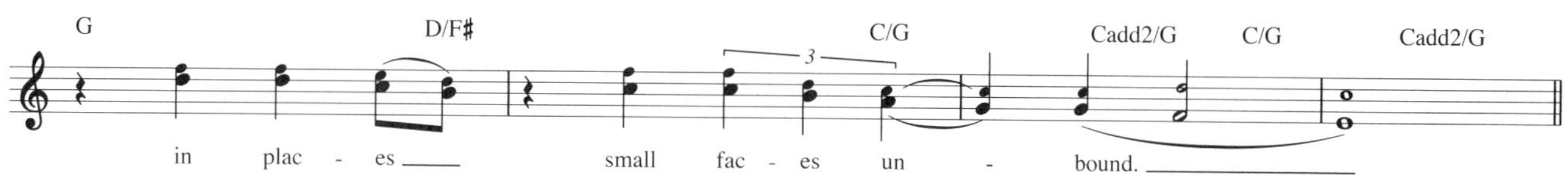

Guitar Solo

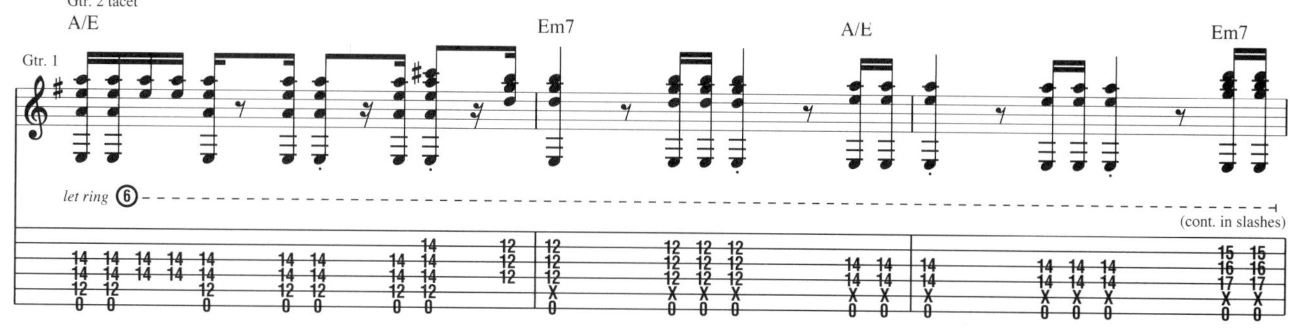

A/E
Em7
Gtr. 1
Gtr. 2
3
7 4 5 7 7
7 4 5 7 4 5 7

A/E
Em7
A/E
5 7 4 7 7 4 5 0 7 9 7 5 X 7 4
5 7 5 7 4 5 4 7 4
5 7 4 5 7 4 5 7 8 7 8 7 8 10

Em7
A/E
Em7
(10) 8 7 8 7 5 7 4 5
7 5 7 4 5 4 4 4 7 5 4 X 4
5 7 5 0 0 15 12 14 14

A/E
Em7
A/E
E
6
open
A/E
(14) 12 11 12 14 12 10 12 12 9 9 7
7 9 6 7 6 7 6 7 9 0 7 9
7 7 7 0 7 8 7 9

G5/E
A5/E
E
A5/E
Em7
open
Em7
Asus2/E
Asus2
Verse
Gtrs. 1 & 2: w/ Rhy. Figs. 1 & 2 (2 times)
Em
F#m/E
G/E
D/F#
C/G
G
Cadd2/G
3. 'Round the squares hud - dled in storms some laugh - ing, some just shape - less forms. Side - walk scenes

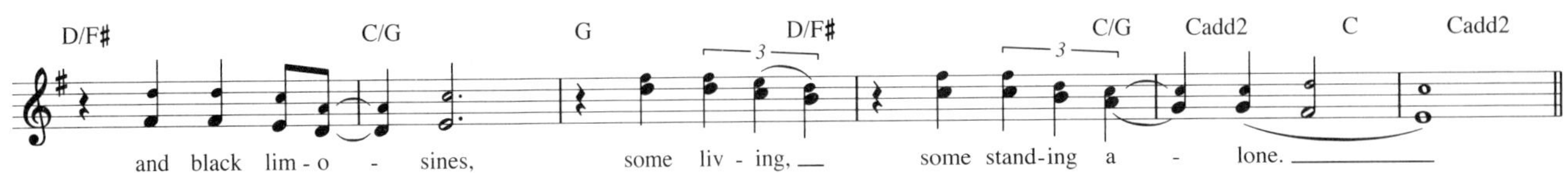
D/F♯
C/G
G
D/F♯
C/G
Cadd2
C
Cadd2
and black lim - o - sines,
some liv - ing,
some stand-ing a - lone.

Outro

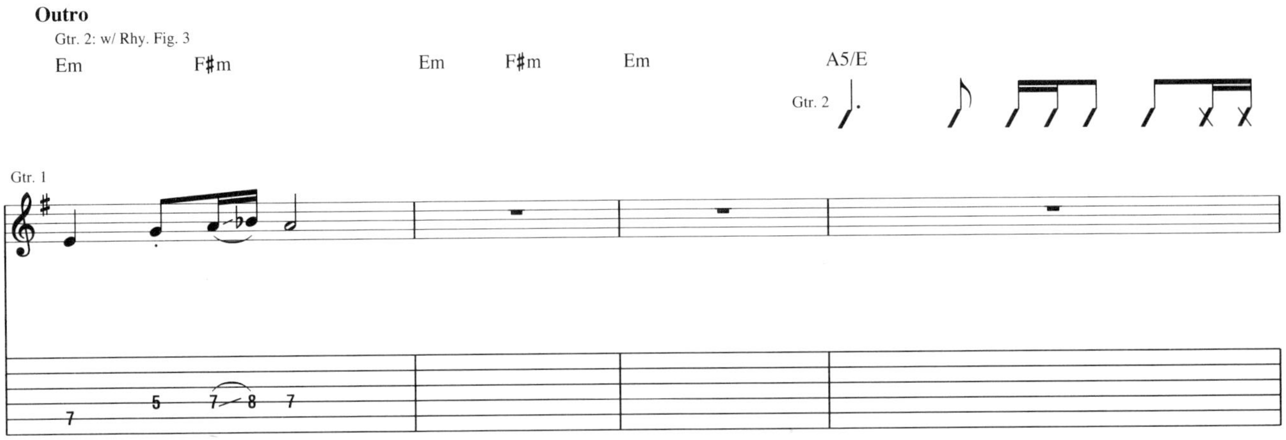
Gtr. 2: w/ Rhy. Fig. 3
Em
F♯m
Em
F♯m
Em
A5/E
Gtr. 2
Gtr. 1

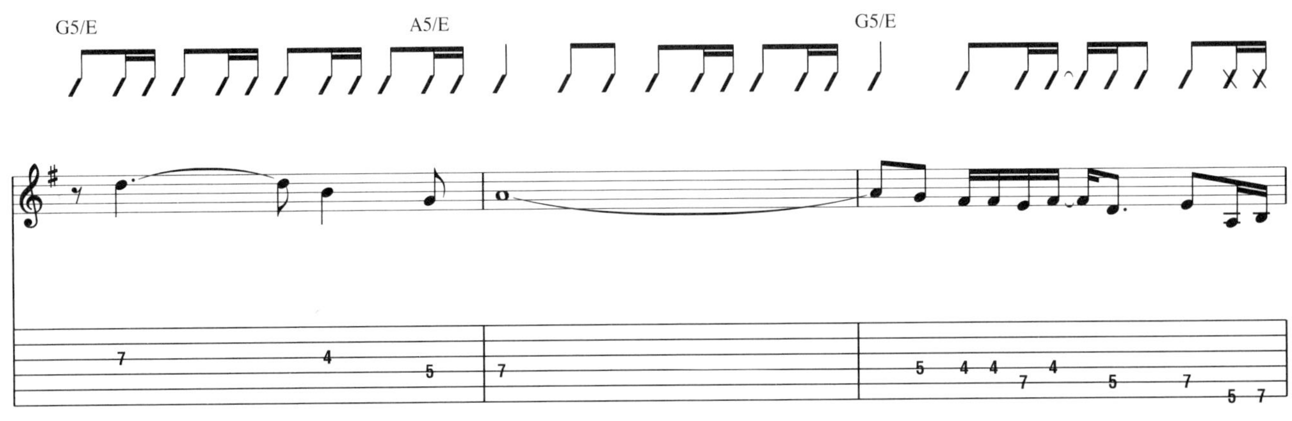
G5/E
A5/E
G5/E

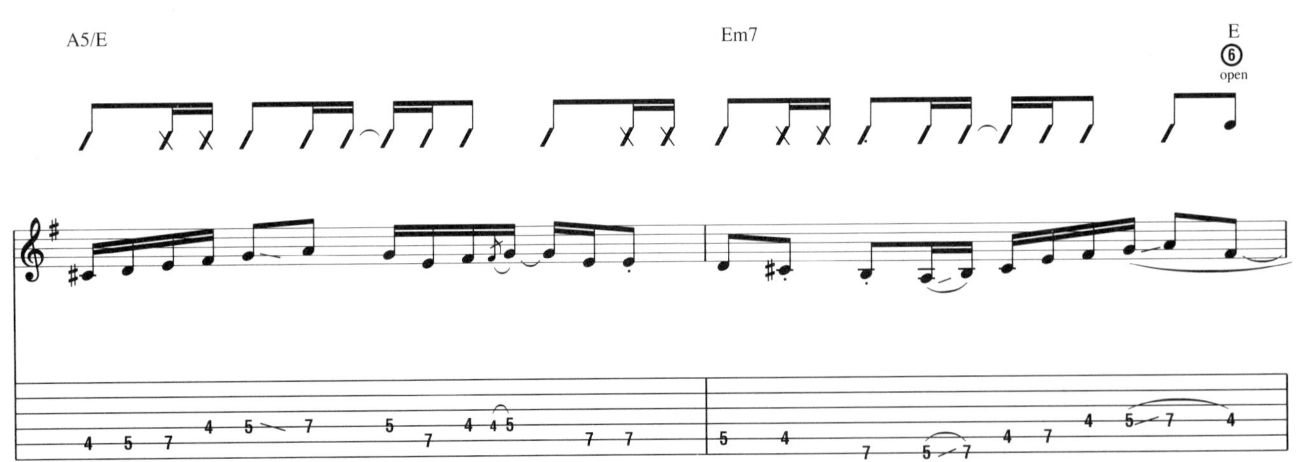
A5/E
Em7
E
6
open

Asus2/E
E
open
Em7
Asus2/E
Em7
Asus2/E
E
open
G5/E
Asus2/E
(cont. in notation)
Gtr. 2
G5/E
E
E9(no3rd)
P.S.
Gtr. 1

from Skid Row - *Skid Row*

18 and Life

Words and Music by Rachael Bolan Southworth and David Michael Sabo

C♯m
B/C♯
C♯m
B/C♯
C♯m
B/C♯
Asus2
Bsus4
Just bare - ly out of school, came from the edge of town, fought like a switch blade so no one could take him down, no!
Fill 1
End Fill 1
P.H.
w/ bar
Pre-Chorus
A5
A5/G♯
2nd time, Gtr. 4: w/ Rhy. Fill 1
F♯5
G♯5
He had no mon-ey, no, no good at home. Walked the streets a sol-dier and he
Bang, bang, shoot 'em up, the par - ty nev-er ends. You can't think of dy - in' when the
P.M.
P.H.
(cont. in slashes)
Rhy. Fill 1
Gtr. 4

*See top of first page of song for chord diagrams pertaining to rhythm slashes.

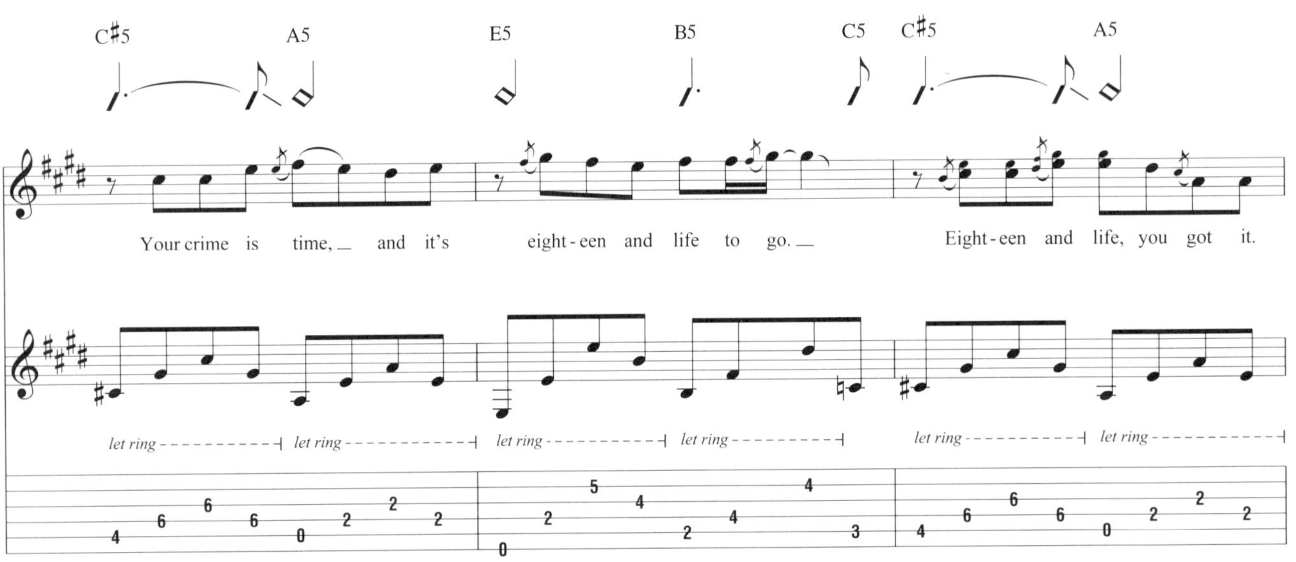

Interlude
Gtrs. 1 & 2: w/ Riff A
Gtr. 4: w/ Fill 1
C♯m B/C♯ C♯m B/C♯ C♯m B/C♯
oh, yes, ah!
Gtr. 5
Rhy. Fig. 2
End Rhy. Fig. 2
P.M.
let ring
Verse
Gtrs. 1 & 2: w/ Riff A
Asus2 Bsus4 C♯m B/C♯ C♯m B/C♯
2. Te - qui - la in his heart-beat, his veins burned gas - o - line.
*Gtr. 4
*Two gtrs. arr. for one (next 2 meas.).
**Gtr. 5
**Two gtrs. arr. for one (next 2 meas.).
Gtr. 5: w/ Rhy. Fig. 2 (last meas.)
C♯m B/C♯ Asus2 Bsus4
Gtr. 5: w/ Rhy. Fig. 2
C♯m B/C♯
It kept his mo - tor run - nin' but it nev - er kept him clean. They say he loved ad - ven - ture.
Gtr. 4
Gtrs. 4 & 5
***P.H.
Pitch: D♯
***Gtr. 4 only

D.S. al Coda
C♯m B/C♯ C♯m B/C♯ Asus2 Bsus4
Rick-y's the wi-ld one. He mar-ried trou-ble, had a court-ship, ah, with a gun.
Gtrs. 4 & 5
P.M. P.H.
Pitch: F♯
Coda
E5 B C♯m
eight-een and life to go, yeah, yeah!
Gtr. 4
Gtr. 5
8va
(cont. in slashes)
Bridge
E5VII E B5 B
7fr 2fr
"Ac-ci-dents will hap-pen," they all heard Rick-y say. He

A5
A
open
P.M.
B5
fir - ed his six - shot to the wind; that child blew a child a - way,
*Gtr. 6 (elec.)
w/ dist.
fdbk.
*Scotti Hill
Gtr. 4
Guitar Solo
Gtr. 4: w/ Rhy. Fig. 1 (1st 4 meas., 2 times)
Gtr. 5 tacet
C♯5
E5
C5
yeah, yeah.
Gtr. 6
slight
P.H.
let ring
8va
loco
rake

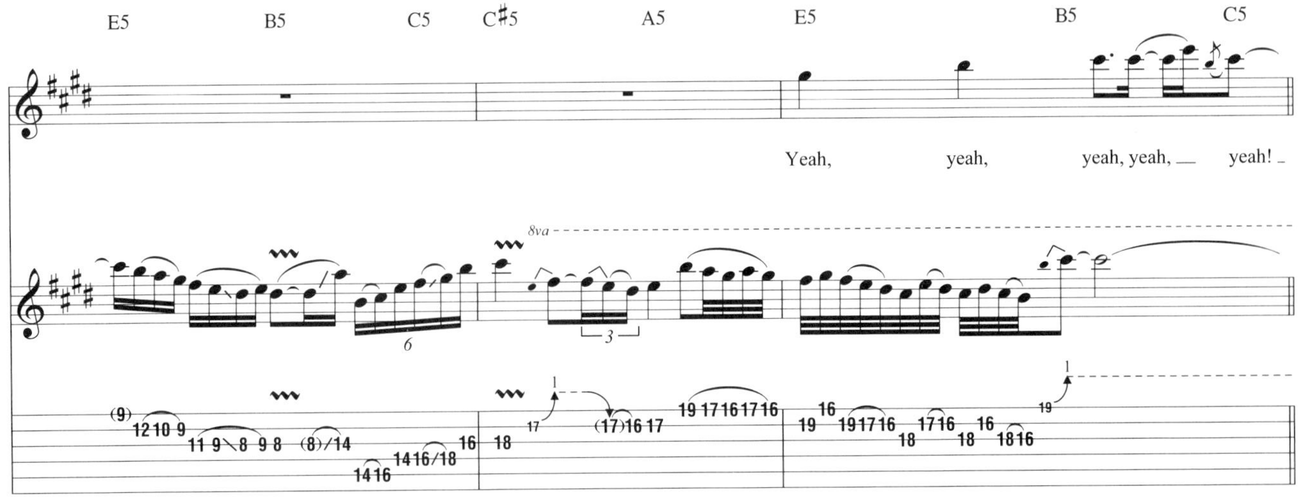
E5
B5
C5
C♯5
A5
E5
B5
C5
Yeah, yeah, yeah, yeah, yeah!
8va

Chorus

Gtr. 4: w/ Rhy. Fig. 1
Gtr. 5: w/ Riff B (1st 6 meas.)
Gtr. 6 tacet
C♯5
A5
E5
B5
C5
C♯5
A5
Eight-een and life, you got it. Eight-een and life, you know. Your crime is time, and it's
8va

E5
B5
C5
C♯5
A5
E5
B5
C5
eight-een and life to go! Eight-een and life, you got it. Eight-een and life, you know.
C♯5
A5
E5
B5
Your crime is time, and it's eight - een and life to go,
Gtr. 5
let ring
let ring

Outro

Gtr. 5: w/ Riff B
C♯5
A5
E5
B5
C5
yeah,
Gtr. 4
Gtrs. 1 & 2
Riff C
End Riff C
Gtrs. 1 & 2: w/ Riff C (2 times)
C♯5
A5
E5
B5
C5
boy!
Yeah!
Gtr. 4
C♯5
A5
E5
B5
C5
let ring

C♯5
A5
E5
B5
Gtr. 5
rit.
rit.
Whoa,
whoa,
whoa,
Gtr. 4
slight
P.H.
rit.
Gtrs. 1 & 2
rit.
C♯5
whoa.

from Foo Fighters - *The Colour and the Shape*

Everlong

Words and Music by David Grohl

sus2
Gadd♯11
sus2
B add11
End Rhy. Fig. 1B
End Rhy. Fig. 1A
Verse
Gtrs. 1, 2 & 3: w/ Rhy. Figs. 1 & 1A, 2 times, simile
Gtr. 4 tacet
Dmaj7
Bsus2
Gsus2
1. Hel - lo, I've wait - ed here for you ev - er -
2. Come down and waste a - way with me, down with
3. Breathe out so I can breathe you in, hold you
Bsus2
Dmaj7
Bsus2
- long. To - night I've thrown my - self in - to,
me slow, how you want - ed it to be.
in. And now I know you've al - ways been
Gsus2
Bsus2
and out of the red, out of her head she sang.
I'm o - ver my head, out of her head she sang.
out of your head, out of my head I sang.
Pre-Chorus
N.C.(D)
A5
N.C.(D)
And I won - der,
Gtrs. 2, 3 & 4

A5
N.C.(D)
B5
when I sing a - long with you,
Chorus
G5
D5
B5
if ev - 'ry-thing could ev - er feel this real for - ev - er,
*Sing vocal harmony 2nd & 3rd times only.
G5
D5
B5
if an - y - thing could ev - er be this good 1. a - gain. 2., 3. a - gain.
G5
D5
A5
The on - ly thing I'll ev - er ask of you; you've got to prom - ise not to

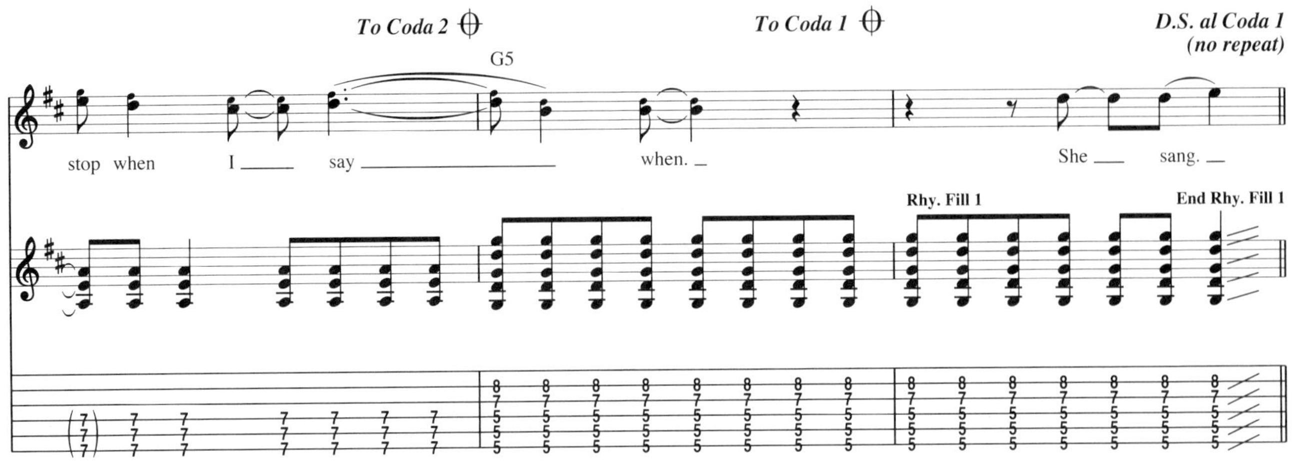
To Coda 2
To Coda 1
D.S. al Coda 1
(no repeat)
G5
stop when I say when.
She sang.
Rhy. Fill 1
End Rhy. Fill 1

Coda 1

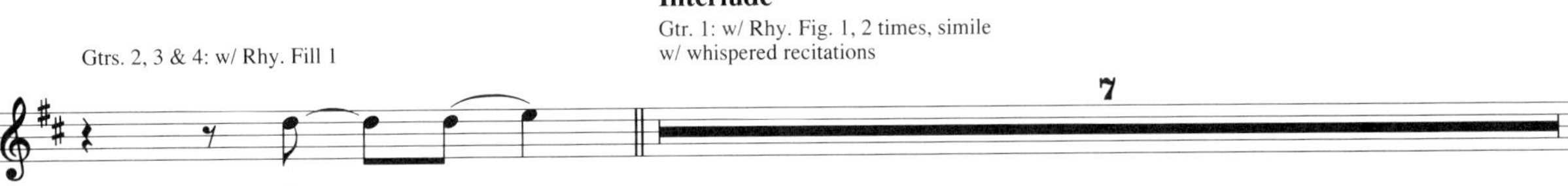
Interlude
Gtr. 1: w/ Rhy. Fig. 1, 2 times, simile
w/ whispered recitations
Gtrs. 2, 3 & 4: w/ Rhy. Fill 1
She sang.

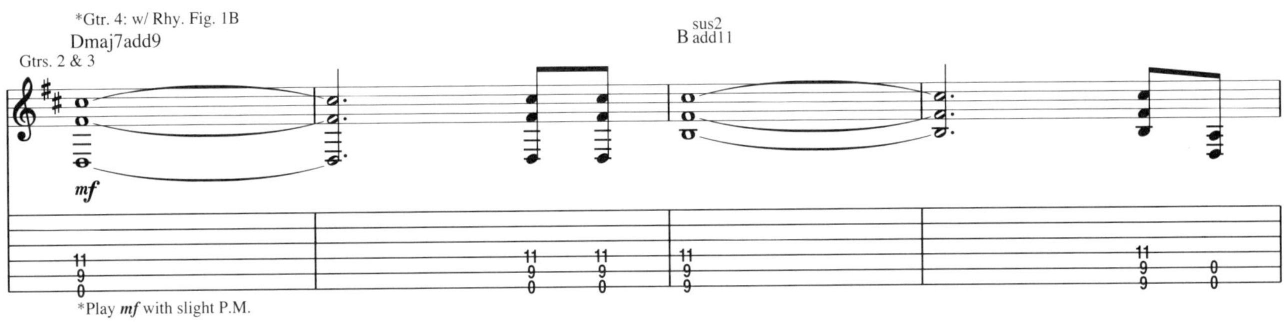
*Gtr. 4: w/ Rhy. Fig. 1B
Dmaj7add9
Gtrs. 2 & 3
mf
*Play mf with slight P.M.

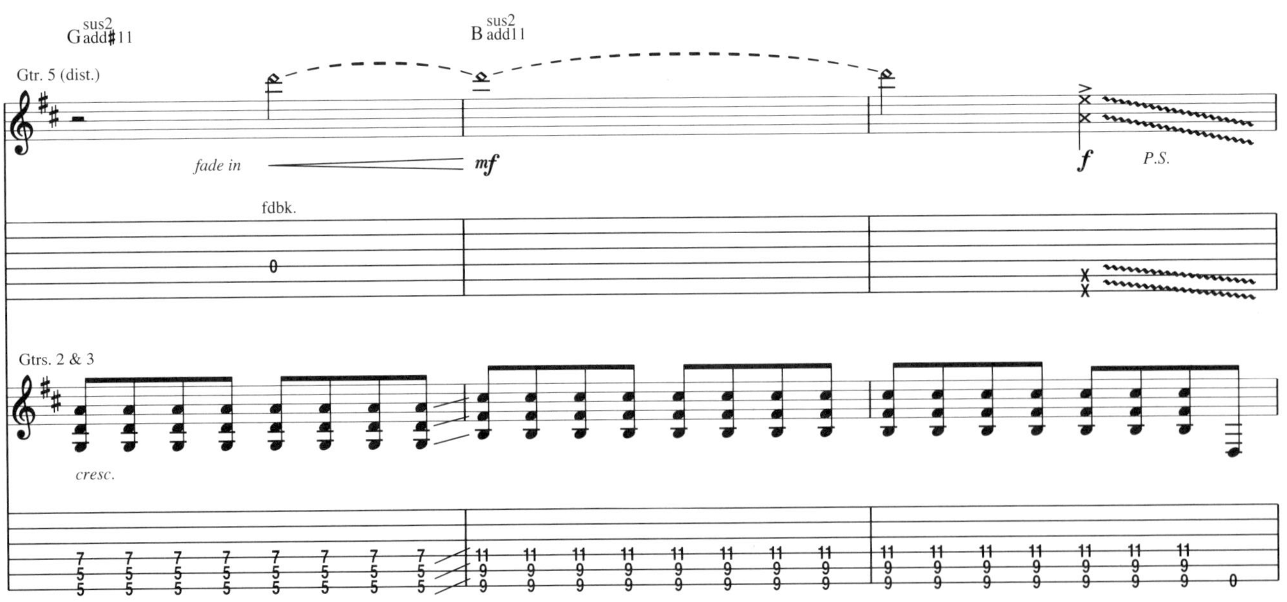
Gtr. 5 (dist.)
fade in
mf
f
P.S.
fdbk.
Gtrs. 2 & 3
cresc.

N.C.(D)
Gtrs. 5
Gtrs. 2, 3, &4
D.S.S. al Coda 2
B5
And I wonder
Coda 2
G5
when.

from Billy Squier - *Emotions in Motion*

Everybody Wants You

Words and Music by Billy Squier

*Chord symbols reflect basic harmony.

Gtr. 3 tacet
A G5 A G5 A5 C A5 G5 A G5 A G5 A G5 A5 C A5 G5 A G5
Rhy. Fig. 1
Gtr. 1
End Rhy. Fig. 1
1/4
Rhy. Fig. 1A
Gtr. 2
End Rhy. Fig. 1A
Verse
D5
3rd time, Gtr. 1: w/ Fill 2
N.C.
1. You see'em com - in' at you ev - er - y night. Strung on pre - ten - sion, they fall for you at first sight.
2. You crave at - ten - tion, you can nev - er say "no." Throw your af - fec - tions an - y way the wind blows.
3. Nights of con - fu - sion and im - pos - si - ble dreams. Days at the mir - ror, patch - in' up a - round the seams.
Rhy. Fig. 2
End Rhy. Fig. 2
let ring
1/2
1st & 2nd times, Gtr. 1: w/ Rhy. Fig. 1
Gtr. 2: w/ Rhy. Fig. 1A
3rd time, Gtr. 1: w/ Riff B
A G5 A G5 A5 C A5 G5 A G5 A G5 A G5 A5 C A5 G5 A G5
Oo.
Ah.

Gtr. 1: w/ Rhy. Fig. 2
D5
N.C.
You know their busi-ness, you think it's a bore.
You al-ways make it, you're on top of the scene.
You got your glo-ry, you paid for it all.
They make you rest-less, it's noth - in' you ain't seen be-fore.
You sell the cop-y like the cov-er of a mag - a-zine.
You take your pen-sion in lone - li-ness and al - co-hol.
Gtr. 2
Fill 2
End Fill 2
let ring
1st & 2nd times, Gtr. 1: w/ Rhy. Fig. 1 (1st 3 meas.)
Gtr. 2: w/ Rhy. Fig. 1A (1st 3 meas.)
3rd time, Gtr. 1: w/ Riff B (1st 3 meas.)
A G5 A G5 A5 C A5 G5 A G5 A G5 A G5
Oo.
Chorus
3rd time, Gtr. 1: w/ Fill 3
A5 C A5 G5 A5 G5
3rd time, Gtr. 4: w/ Fill 4 (2 times)
E5
Get a-round town, spend your time on the run.
Put-tin' on the eyes 'til there's no-bod-y else.
Say good-bye to con-ven-tion-al ways.
You
You
You
Gtr. 1
Gtr. 3
Gtr. 1 divisi
*P.M.
*Gtr. 1 only.
Gtr. 2
let ring
Fill 3
Gtr. 1
Fill 4
Gtr. 4

3rd time, Gtr. 4: w/ Fill 4 (2 times)
3rd time, Gtr. 5: w/ Fill 5 (2 times)

G5 | A5 | E5

nev - er let down, say you do it for fun. You nev - er miss a play, though you
nev - er re - al - ize what you do to your - self. The things that they see make the
can't es - cape the hours, you lose track of the days. The more you un - der - stand seems the

P.M.

1/2

let ring

1

1/4

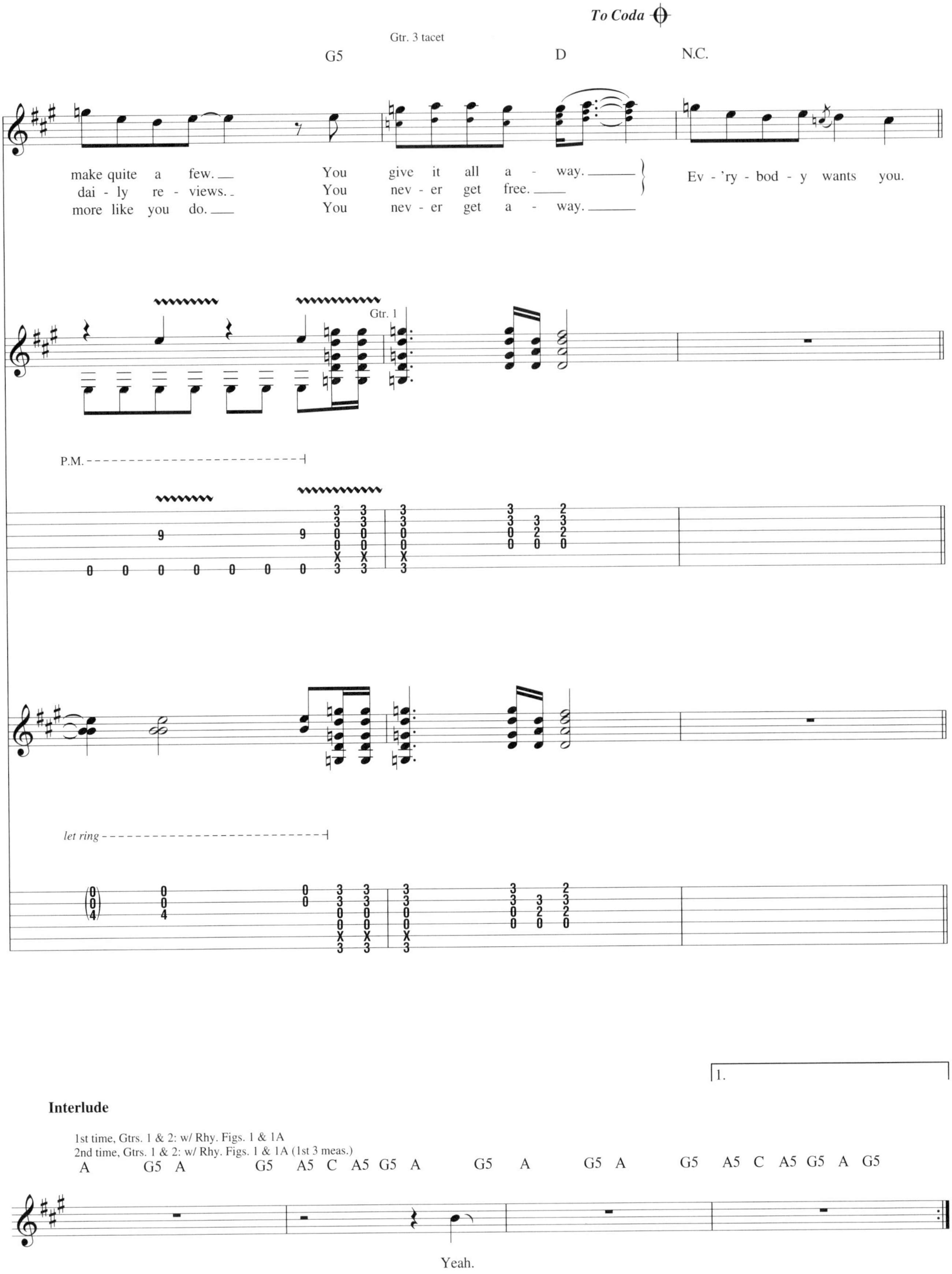

To Coda 𝄌

Gtr. 3 tacet

G5 D N.C.

make quite a few. You give it all a - way. Ev - 'ry - bod - y wants you.
dai - ly re - views. You nev - er get free.
more like you do. You nev - er get a - way.

Gtr. 1

P.M.

let ring

1.

Interlude

Yeah.

2.
Bridge
A5 C A5 G5 A N.C.
Dsus2
Csus2 G/B G
Ev - 'ry - bod - y
Riff A
End Riff A
Gtr. 1
8va
H.H.
let ring
1/4
Gtr. 2
*Gtrs. 2 & 3
Riff A1
End Riff A1
let ring
1/4
*Composite arrangement
Gtr. 1: w/ Riff A (2 times)
Gtrs. 2 & 3: w/ Riff A1 (2 times)
Dsus2 Csus2 G/B G Dsus2 Csus2 G/B G
knows you. Ev - 'ry - bod - y snows you. Ev - 'ry - bod - y
D5 E Dsus2/E
needs you, leads, a, you, bleeds you.
Gtr. 1
loco
Gtr. 2
let ring
let ring
let ring

E
N.C.
Mm.
Gtr. 3
*Gtr. 5 (dist.)
Gtr. 1
divisi
*Played mf
**Gtr. 4 (dist.)
Gtr. 2
divisi
**Played mf
Interlude
Gtrs. 1 & 2: w/ Rhy. Figs. 1 & 1A (1st 3 meas.)
Gtrs. 3, 4 & 5 tacet
A G5 A G5 A5 C A5 G5 A G5 A G5 A5 G5
A5 C A5 G5 A G5 A5 G5 A5 G5 A5 C5 A5 G5 A5 G5 A5 G5 A5 G5
Riff B
Gtr. 1
P.M.
Gtr. 2
P.M.

Coda
D.S. al Coda
A5 C5 A5 G5 A5 G5
N.C.
Ev - 'ry - bod - y wants you.
End Riff B
Gtr. 1
1/4
Gtr. 2
P.M.
1/4
Outro
Gtr. 1: w/ Rhy. Fig. 1 (1st 2 meas., till fade)
Gtr. 2: w/ Rhy. Fig. 1A (1st 3 meas.)
A G5 A G5 A5 C A5 G5 A G5 A G5 A G5
Oo.
Begin fade
Gtr. 3: w/ Fill 1
A5 C A5 G5 A G5 A G5 A5 G5 A5 C A5 G5 A G5
(Ev - 'ry - bod - y wants you.
Gtr. 2
Rhy. Fig. 3
End Rhy. Fig. 3
1/4
P.M.
Fade out
Gtr. 2: w/ Rhy. Fig. 3 (till fade)
Gtr. 3: w/ Fill 1
A G5 A G5 A5 C A5 G5 A G5 A G5 A G5 A5 C A5 G5 A G5
Ev - 'ry - bod - y wants you.)

from David Bowie - *Young Americans*

Fame

Words and Music by John Lennon, David Bowie and Carlos Alomar

F7
Rhy. Fig. 1
Gr. 3
End Rhy. Fig. 1
Gtr. 3: w/ Rhy. Fig. 1, 5 times
Gtr. 5 (elec.)
w/ clean tone
simile on repeat
Gtr. 2
w/ wah-wah
Riff B
Gtr. 4
Riff A
End Riff A
Gtr. 2: w/ Riff B, 4 times
Gtr. 4 tacet
w/ Voc. ad lib., 2nd time
*Could it be the babe, could it be?
End Riff B
Fill 1
Gtr. 6 (elec.)
8va
w/ clean tone
End Fill 1
* Sung 2nd time

Gtr. 6: w/ Fill 1, 3 times, simile
Gtr. 5
Really be, baby, really babe?
Could it be, my babe, could it be, babe?
w/ pick & finger
Could it be, babe, could it be, babe?
To Coda
Verse
Gtr. 3: w/ Rhy. Fig. 1, 4 times
Gtr. 2: w/ Riff B, 3 1/2 times
F7
1. Fame makes a man take things o - ver. Fame lets him
2. Fame, what you like is in the lim - o. Fame, what you get
(Fame. Fame.
Gtr. 5
Rhy. Fig. 2
simile on repeat
Gtr. 4
simile on repeat
1/2
loose, hard to swal-low. Fame, puts you there where things are hol-low.
is no to-mor-row. Fame, what you need you have to bor-row.
Fame.
1/2

B♭7
Rhy. Fill 1
Gtr. 3
Fame.
Fame.
Fame.
It's not your brain is
"Nein! It's mine!" is
Fame.
Gtr. 5
Riff C
Gtr. 2
Gtr. 4
1/2
1/2

End Rhy. Fill 1
Gtr. 2: w/ Riff B, 4 times
Gtr. 3: w/ Rhy. Fig. 1, 4 times
F7
just a flame that burns your change to keep you in - sane.
just his line to bind your time, it drives you to crime.
1. sane.
2. crime.
Gtr. 5
End Riff C
Gtr. 4
1/2
Fame.
Fame.
Fame.)
1/2
1/2

2nd time, D.S. al Coda

End Rhy. Fig. 2
1/2
1/2

Coda

Verse

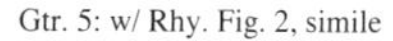
Gtr. 3: w/ Rhy. Fig. 1, 4 times
Gtr. 2: w/ Riff B, 3 1/2 times
Gtr. 5: w/ Rhy. Fig. 2, simile

F7
3. Is it an - y won - der,
I re - ject you first?
Fame, fame, fame,
Gtr. 6
mf

fame.
Is it an - y won - der,
you are too cool to fool?
full
full

Gtr. 2: w/ Riff C

Gtr. 3: w/ Rhy. Fill 1
Gtr. 6 tacet
B♭7

Fame. ___ (Fame. ___ Bul-ly for you, _ Fame. ___

Gtr. 6 P.M.

Gtr. 1 *divisi*

f

full 1/2

6 6 7 5 7 5 6 8 8 6 8 0 1 3 6 1

Gtr. 1

Gtr. 2: w/ Riff B, till fade
Gtr. 3: w/ Rhy. Fig. 1, till fade
F7

chil-ly for me, _ got to get a rain-check on ___ pain. ___ Fame. ___

0 1 3 1

Gtr. 4: w/ Riff A, 2 times

Fame. ___)

Rhy. Fill 3

End Rhy. Fill 3

1/2

(1) 1 8 6 10 8

*vol. swell

from Dinosaur Jr. - *Without a Sound*

Feel the Pain

Words and Music by Joseph Mascis, Jr.

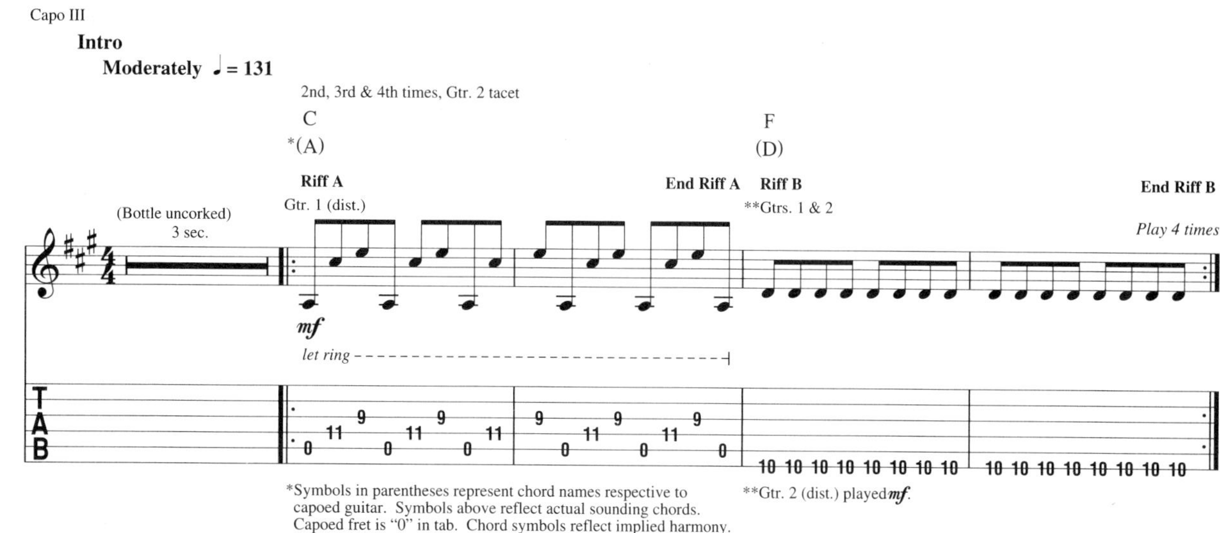

Chorus
2nd time, Tempo I

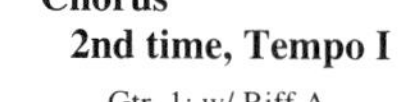

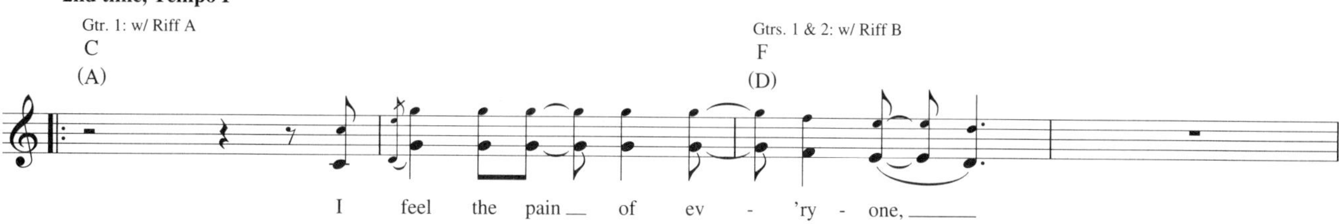

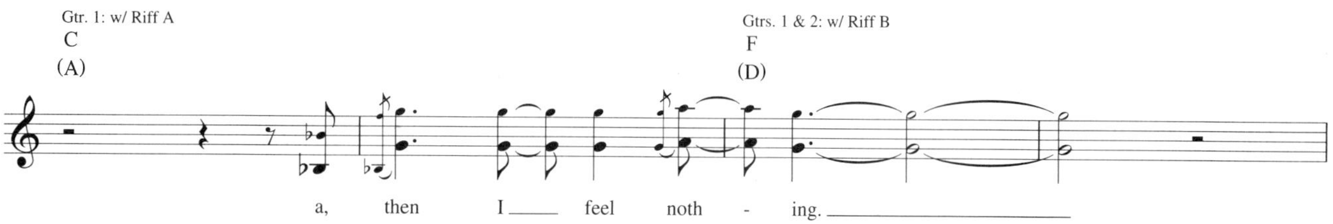

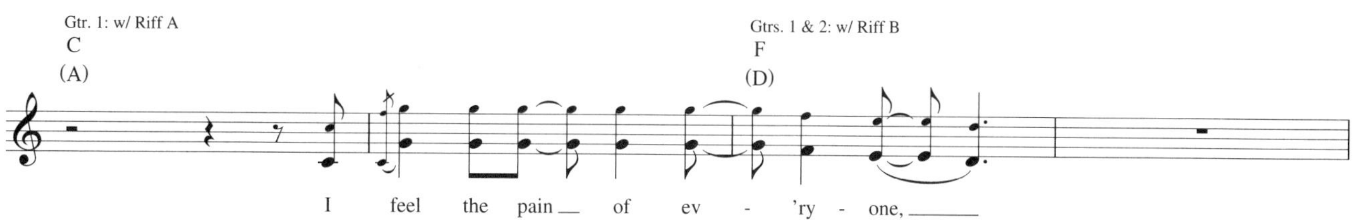

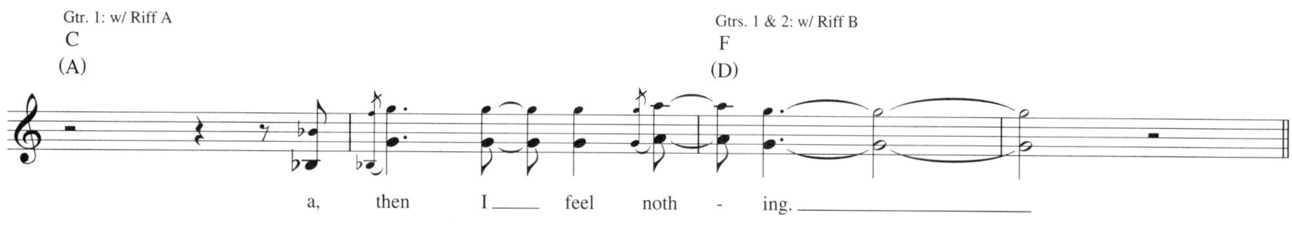

Interlude
Faster ♩ = 152
C
(A)
F
(D)
C
(A)
F
(D)
Riff C
End Riff C
*Gtrs. 1 & 2
*Composite arrangement
Gtrs. 1 & 2: w/ Riff C
C
(A)
F
(D)
C
(A)
F
(D)
Bridge
Faster ♩ = 162
Dm
(Bm)
G
(E)
Gsus4
(Esus4)
Is it up to me?
Gtrs. 1 & 2
Rhy. Fig. 1
Em/B
(C♯m/G♯)
Fmaj7/C
(Dmaj7/A)
Am
(F♯m)
G
(E)
You won't wait to see.
End Rhy. Fig. 1
Em
(C♯m)
Screwed us both / yet a - gain.
let ring
let ring

To Coda
G
(E)
Gsus4
(Esus4)
Fmaj7/C
(Dmaj7/A)
Am
(F♯m)
'Bout as close as you've been.
Rhy. Fig. 2
End Rhy. Fig. 2
let ring
Interlude
Tempo I
Gtr. 1: w/ Riff A
Gtr. 2 tacet
C
(A)
Gtrs. 1 & 2: w/ Riff B
F
(D)
Chorus
I feel the pain of ev - 'ry - one,
a, then I feel noth - ing.
I feel the pain of ev - 'ry - one,
D.S. al Coda
a, then I feel noth - ing.
Coda
Gtrs. 1 & 2: w/ Rhy. Fig. 2 (last meas.)
Gtrs. 1 & 2: w/ Rhy. Fig. 1
Dm
(Bm)
G
(E)
Gsus4
(Esus4)
Hey, now, take it back.
Gtr. 3 (dist.)

Em/B
(C♯m/G♯)
Fmaj7/C
(Dmaj7/A)
Am
(F♯m)
G
(E)
Get off the at - tack.
rake
Em
(C♯m)
Trail - ing on your scene.
Gtr. 3
*T
*T = Thumb on 6th string
Gtrs. 1 & 2
let ring
Gtrs. 1 & 2: w/ Rhy. Fig. 2
G
(E)
Gsus4
(Esus4)
Fmaj7/C
(Dmaj7/A)
Am
(F♯m)
Just try and keep it clean.
Gtr. 3
T

Outro-Guitar Solo
Gtrs. 1 & 2: w/ Riff C (3 1/4 times)
C
(A)
F
(D)
8va
loco
P.H.
Pitch: D♯
Gtr. 3
Gtrs. 1 & 2
N.C.

from Bob Seger and the Silver Bullet Band - *Against the Wind*

Fire Lake

Words and Music by Bob Seger

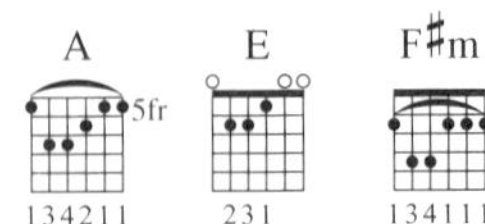

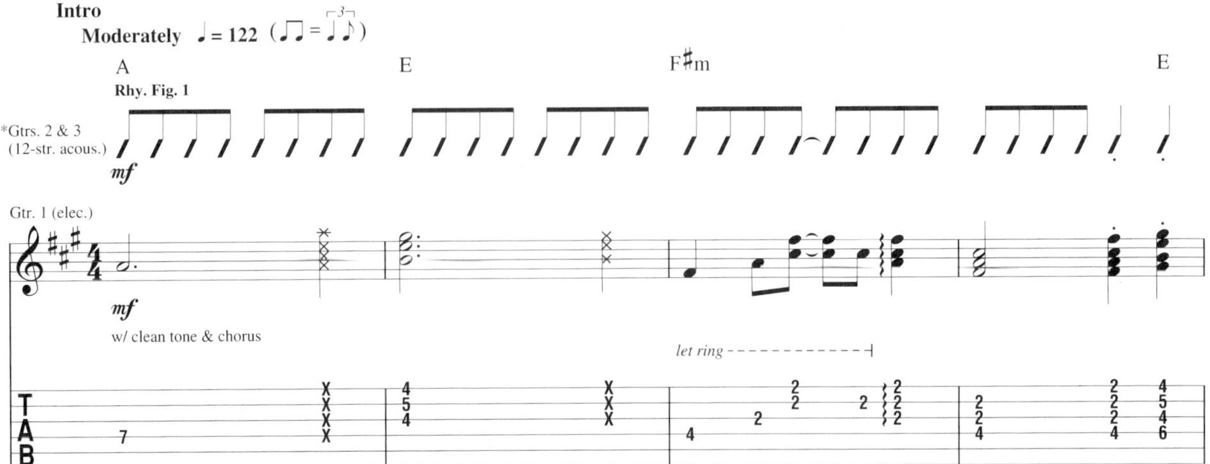

*Composite arrangement

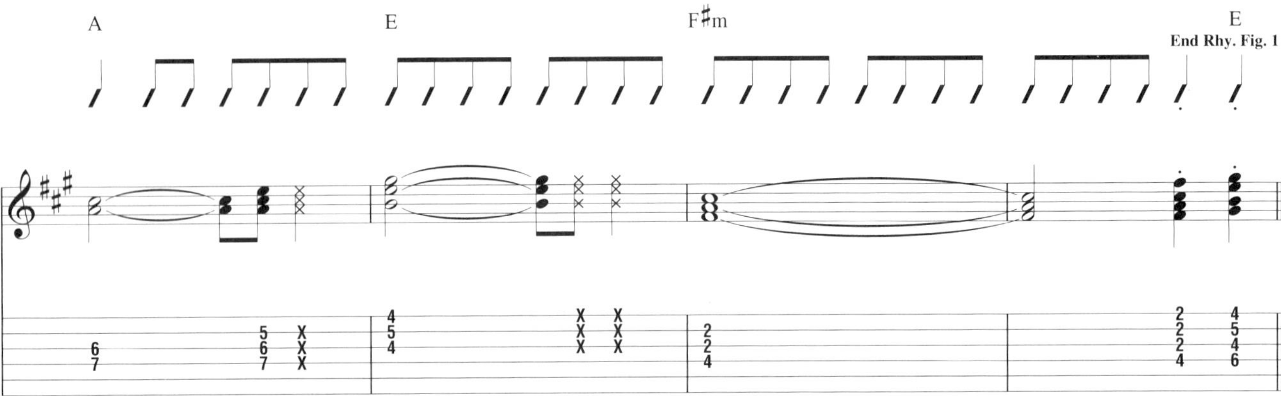

*Chord symbols reflect overall harmony.

E/G♯
A
E
Who's gon - na make that first mis - take?
let ring
let ring
F♯m
E/G♯
A
Who wants to
let ring
let ring
E
F♯m
E/G♯
wear those gyp - sy leath - ers?
let ring
let ring
A
E
F♯m
E/G♯
All the way to Fire Lake.
let ring

Verse
Gtr. 3: w/ Rhy. Fig. 1 (2 1/2 times)
A
E
F♯m
E/G♯
2. Who wants to break the news about Uncle Joe? You re-mem ber Un-
Voc. Fig. 1
End Voc. Fig. 1
(Oo.)
Gtr. 1
let ring
Gtr. 2
Rhy. Fig. 2
End Rhy. Fig. 2
let ring throughout
Bkgd. Voc.: w/ Voc. Fig. 1
Gtr. 2: w/ Rhy. Fig. 2 (3 times)
cle Joe; he was the one a - fraid to cut the cake.
Who wants to tell poor Aunt Sar - ah,
Voc. Fig. 2
End Voc. Fig. 2
(Oo,
oo.)

Bkgd. Voc.: w/ Voc. Fig. 2
A
E
F♯m
E/G♯
Joe has run off to Fire Lake?
let ring
Gtr. 2: w/ Rhy. Fig. 1 (1st 4 meas.)
A
E
F♯m
E/G♯
Joe has run off to Fire Lake.
Voc. Fig. 3
End Voc. Fig. 3
(Oo.)
let ring
let ring
let ring
Interlude
D
C♯m
F♯m
Who wants to brave those bronze beau - ties ly - ing in the sun, with their
Gtr. 1
let ring throughout
Gtr. 2
let ring throughout
Gtr. 3
let ring throughout

C♯m C♯m7 Bm Bm7

long soft hair ___ fall - ing, fly - in' as they run? ___ Oh, they

D Dmaj7 A

smile so shy and they flirt ___ so well and they lay _ you down so fast. Till you

E
Gtr. 1 tacet
look straight up and say... "Oh Lord, am I real-
Gtr. 1
Gtrs. 2 & 3
E
Gtr. 3
Verse
Bkgd. Voc.: w/ Voc. Fig. 1 (2 times)
Gtr. 2: w/ Rhy. Fig. 1 (1st 4 meas.)
Gtr. 3: w/ Rhy. Fig. 1 (2 times)
A
- ly here at last?"
3. Who wants to
Gtrs. 2 & 3
Gtrs. 1 & 2
(Gtr. 3, cont. in slashes)
Gtr. 1
E
F♯m
E/G♯
play those eights and ac - es?

Gtr. 2: w/ Rhy. Fig. 2 (3 times)
A
E
F♯m
Who wants a raise, who needs a stake?
E/G♯
Bkgd. Voc.: w/ Voc. Fig. 2
A
E
Who wants to take that long shot
F♯m
gam - ble, ha,
E/G♯
Bkgd. Voc.: w/ Voc. Fig. 3
A
and head out
E
F♯m
to Fire Lake?
E/G♯
And head out.

Outro

Gtr. 2: w/ Rhy. Fig. 2 (till end)
Gtr. 3: w/ Rhy. Fig. 1 (till end)
2nd, 3rd & 4th times, Lead. Voc., ad lib.
A
E
F♯m
(Who wants to go to Fire Lake?
E/G♯
A
And head out,
Who wants to
E
F♯m
Play 4 times & fade
E/G♯
hey.
And head out.
go to Fire Lake?)

from *Buddy Guy (Chess Masters)*

First Time I Met the Blues

Written by Eurreal "Little Brother" Montgomery

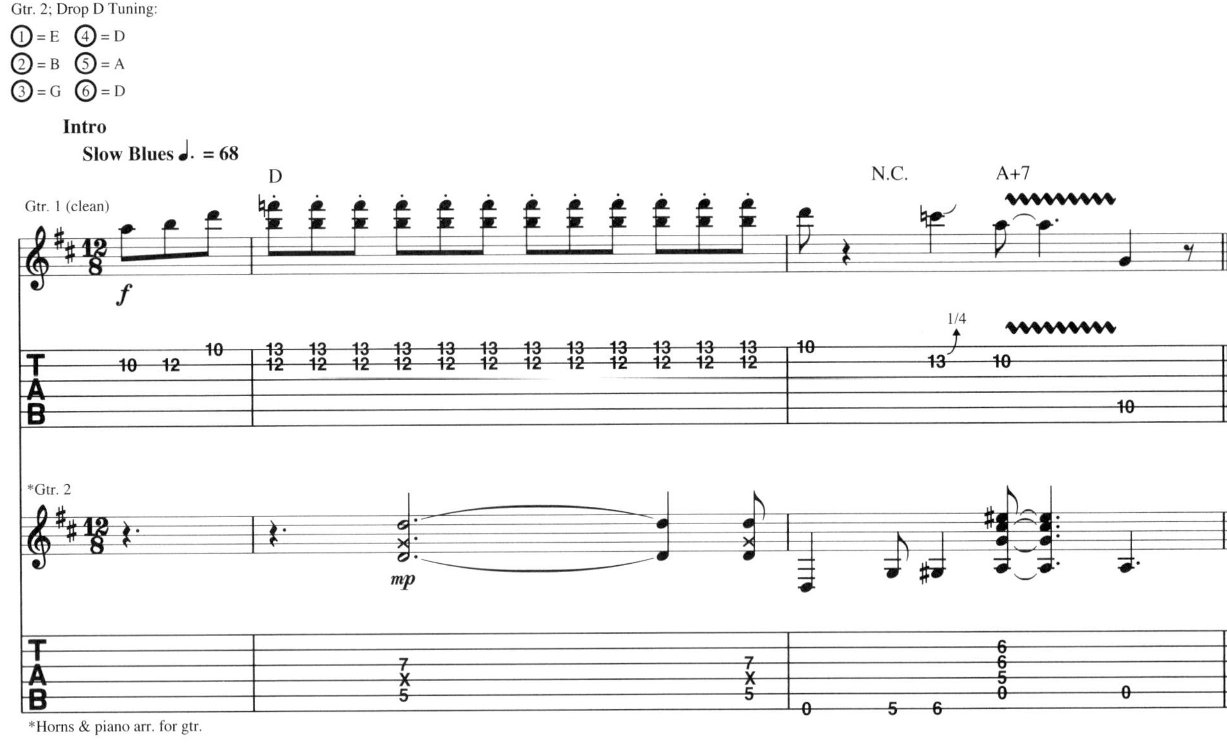

D
Yes,
mf
w/ bar
full
G
the first time, the first time I met the blues,
blues, you know, I was walk-in', I was walk-in' down through the
1/2
D
woods.
Yes,
w/ bar
full
1/4
5:3

A
A♭
G
she stop by my house, babe, blues.
Blues, you know you done me, you done me all the harm
full
let ring
T
full
D
A
that you could.
full
full
1/4
End Rhy. Fig. 1
w/ pick & fingers
full
Verse
Gtr. 2: w/ Rhy. Fig. 1, simile
D
G
2. The blues got af - ter me.
Peo - ple, you know they ran me from tree to tree.
Gtr. 1
w/ bar
full

D
Yes,
w/ bar
full
full
full
G
the blues got af - ter me.
Blues, you know you ran me, ran me from tree to tree.
4:3
w/ bar
full
D
Yes,
w/ bar
full
rake
1/4
A
Ab G
you should, a heard me beg - gin', "Blues,"
yeah,
"Blues, don't mur - der me."
3
w/ bar
full

D
A
3. Yes,
full
full
Verse
Gtr. 2: w/ Rhy. Fig. 1, 1st 8 meas., simile
D
G7
good morn - in, blues.
Blues, I won - der, I won - der what you're do - in' here so
w/ bar
full
D
soon.
Yes,
full
w/ bar
full
w/ bar
G
good morn - in', good morn-in', good morn-in', Mis-ter Blues.
Blues, I won - der, I keep won - der - in' what you're do - in' here so
full

D
soon.
Yes,
w/ bar
full
rake
A
5:3
you know you'll be with me ev-'ry morn-in', blues,
A♭ G7
ev - 'ry night and a, ev-'ry noon.
Gtr. 1
1/2
Gtr. 2
D
Dsus4
D
Whoa, yeah.
f
full
w/ pick & fingers
w/ pick

from Foghat - *Fool for the City*

Fool for the City

Words and Music by Lonesome Dave Peverett

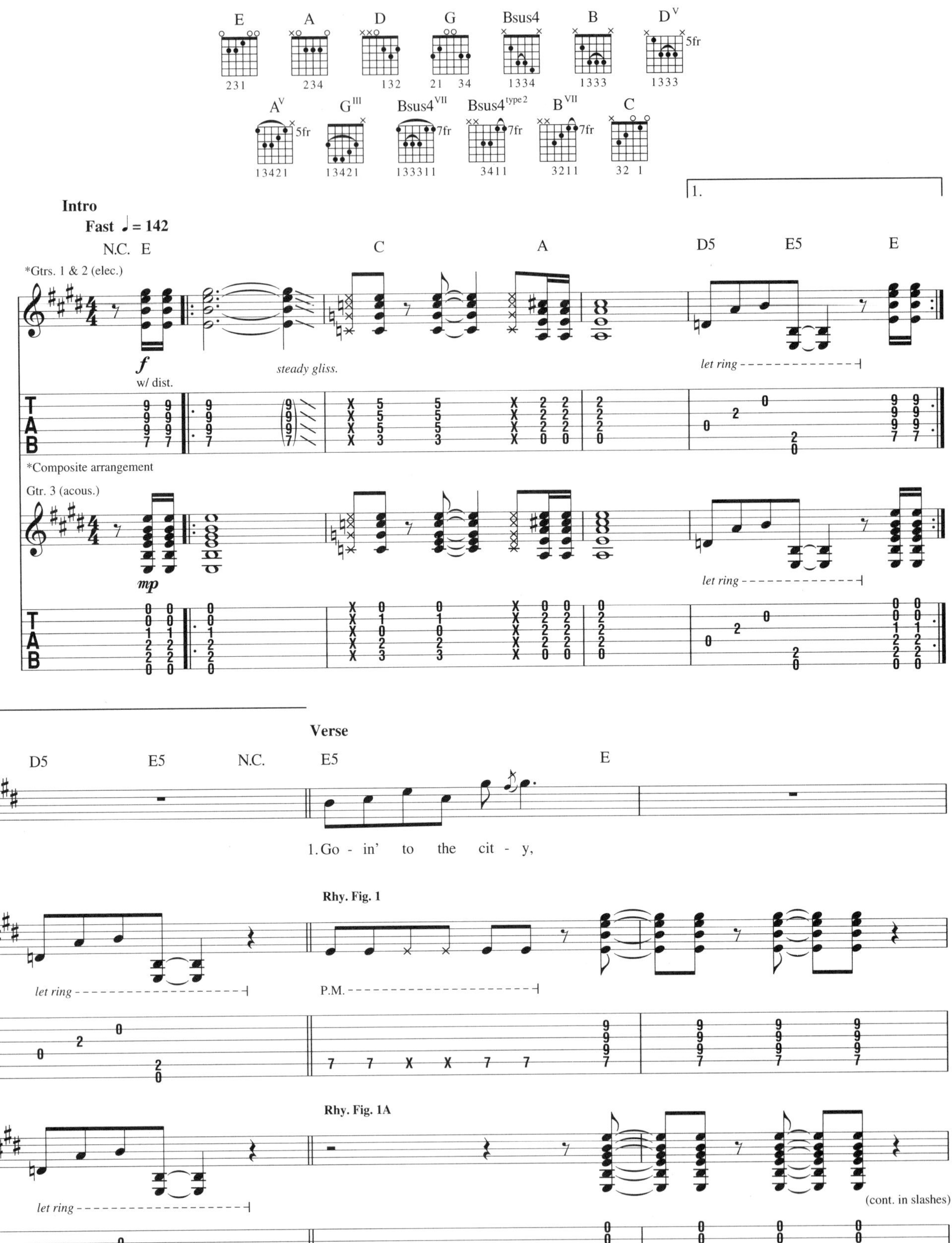

Gtr. 3
E
got you on my mind.
Coun - try sure is pret - ty,
Gtrs. 1 & 2
P.M.
A
E
End Rhy. Fig. 1A
I'd leave it all be - hind.
End Rhy. Fig. 1
Pre-Chorus
D
Rhy. Fig. 2
A
G
Bsus4
This is my de - ci - sion,
I'm com - in' home to stay this time.

Chorus
B
E
C
A
End Rhy. Fig. 2
(cont. in notation)
'Cause I'm a fool for the cit - y.
I'm a
Gtr. 1
Gtr. 2
Rhy. Fig. 3
Gtr. 3
D5
E5
E
fool for the cit - y.
Fool for the cit - y.
let ring

C
A
D5
E5
I'm a fool for the cit - y.
let ring
End Rhy. Fig. 3
(cont. in slashes)
Guitar Solo
E
Gtr. 3
Gtr. 4 (elec.)
mf
w/ dist.
Gtr. 5 (elec.)
Gtrs. 1 & 2

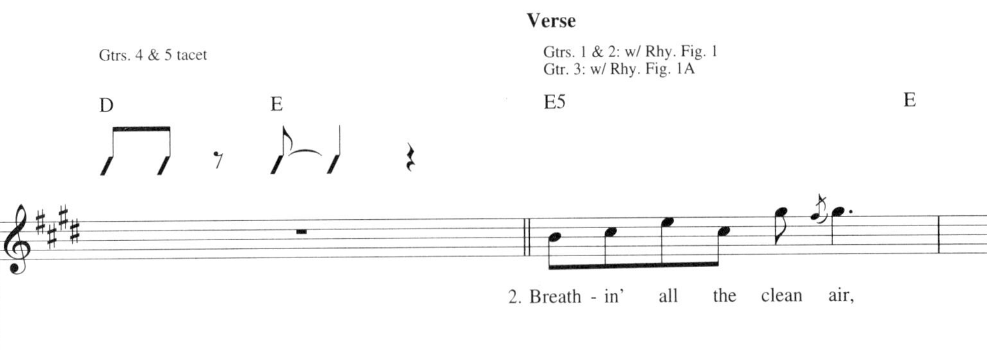
Verse
Gtrs. 4 & 5 tacet
Gtrs. 1 & 2: w/ Rhy. Fig. 1
Gtr. 3: w/ Rhy. Fig. 1A
D
E
E5
E
2. Breath - in' all the clean air,

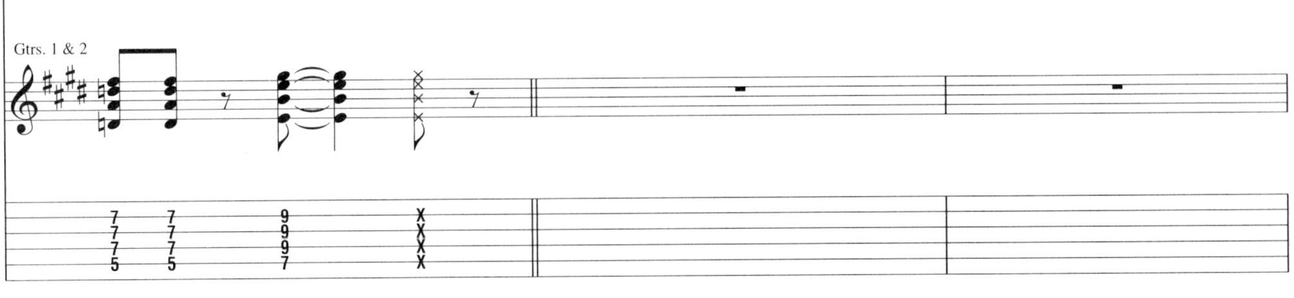
Gtrs. 1 & 2

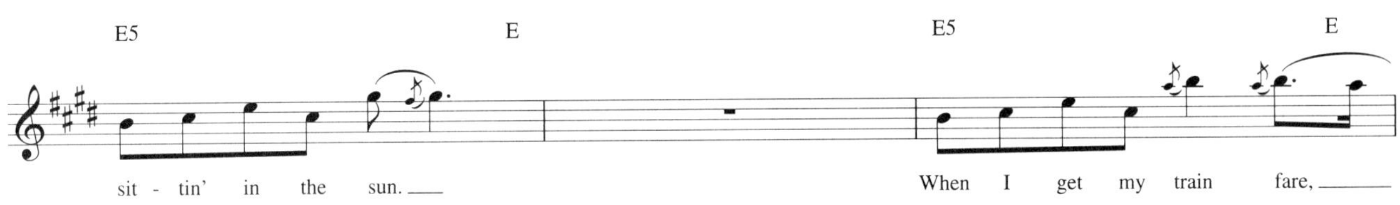
E5
E
E5
E
sit - tin' in the sun.
When I get my train fare,

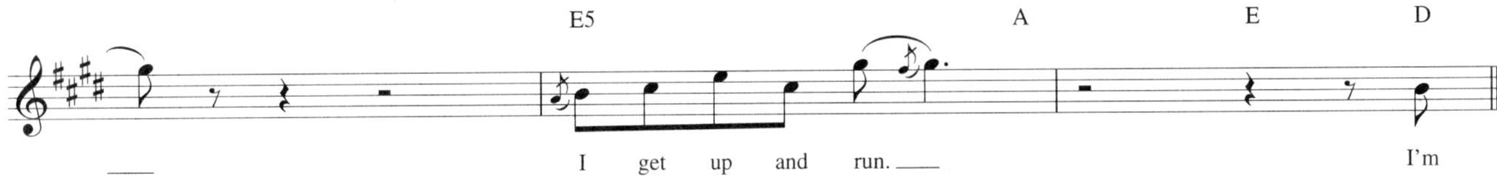
E5
A
E
D
I get up and run.
I'm

Pre-Chorus
Gtr. 3: w/ Rhy. Fig. 2
Gtr. 1
(cont. in notation)
read - y for the cit - y,
air pol - lu - tion, here I come.
Gtr. 2

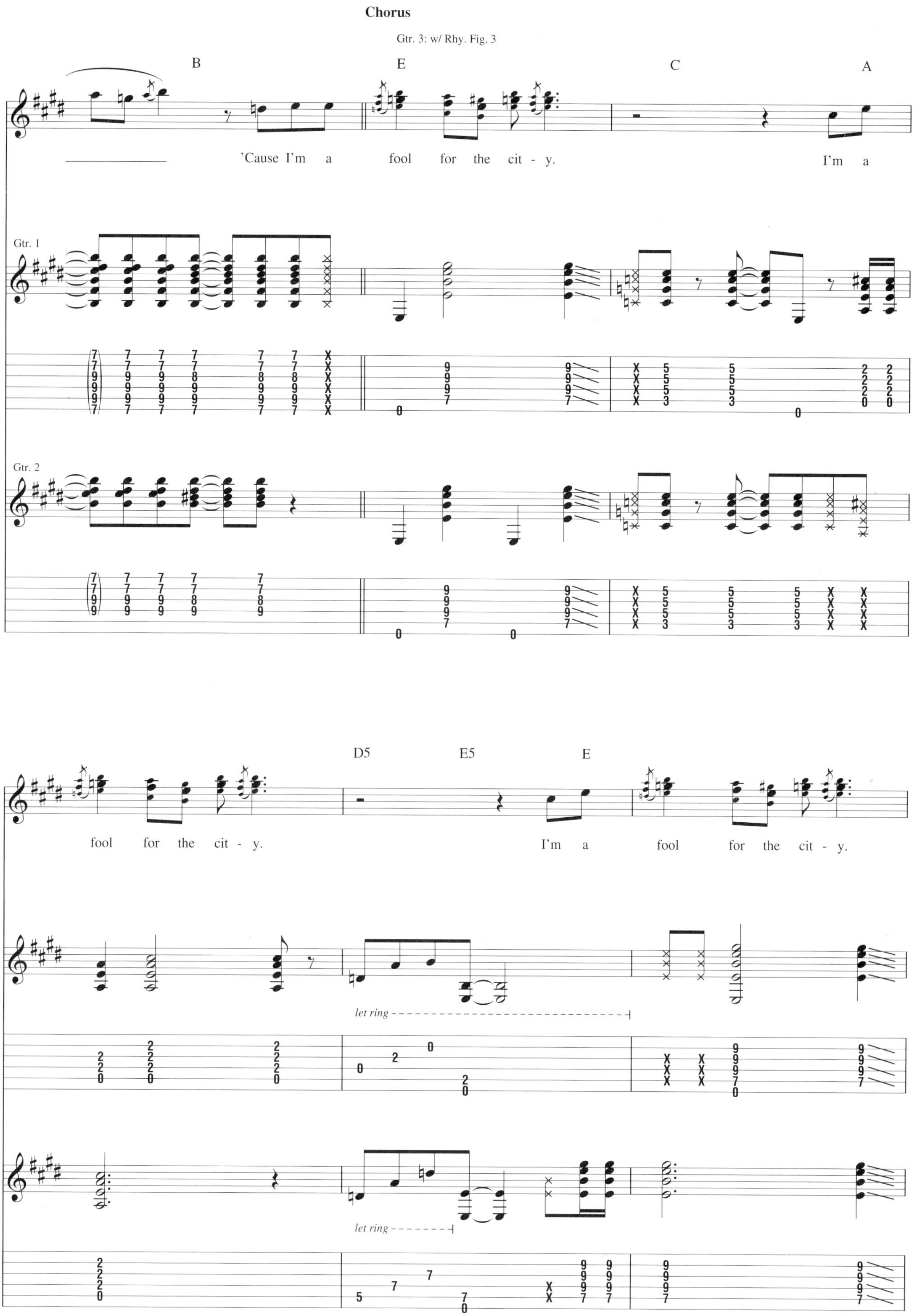

Chorus

Gtr. 3: w/ Rhy. Fig. 3

B E C A

'Cause I'm a fool for the cit - y. I'm a

Gtr. 1

Gtr. 2

Guitar Solo

Gtrs. 1 & 2: w/ Rhy. Fig. 1
Gtr. 3: w/ Rhy. Fig. 1A

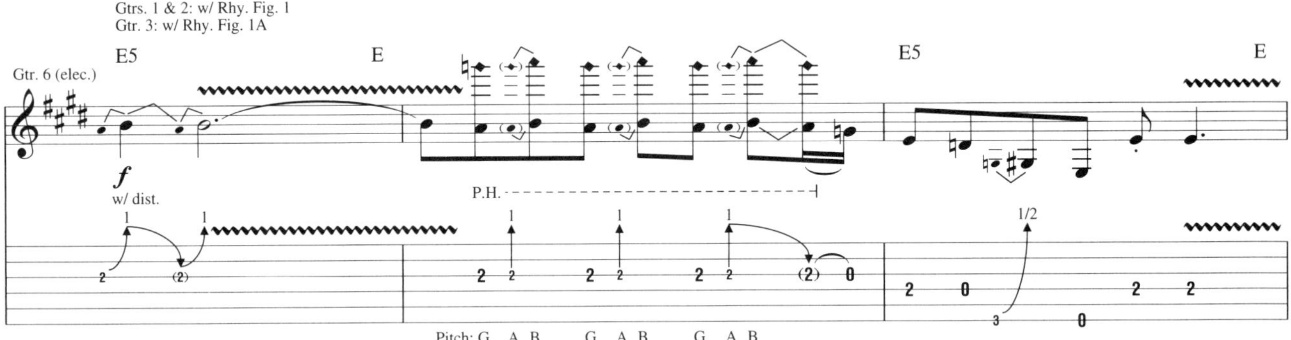

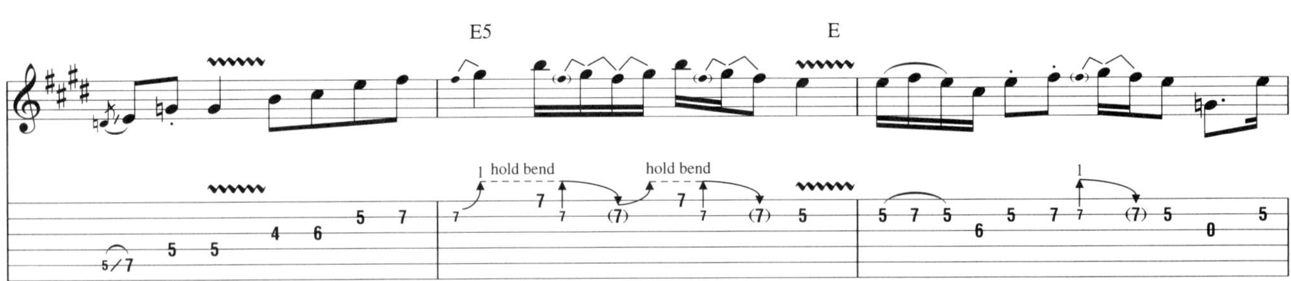

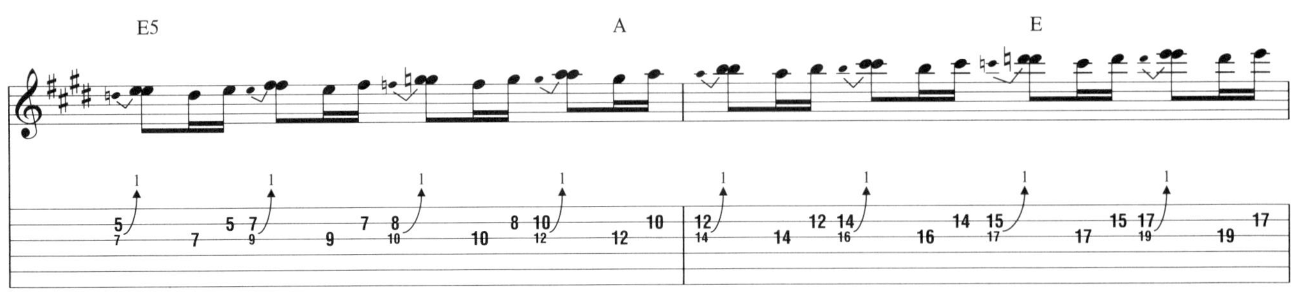

*Composite arrangement

D5
E5
E
Oo.
Oo.
8va
Gtr. 6
Harm.
Gtrs. 1 & 2
let ring
C
A
D5
E5
B
Oo.)
I
8va
let ring

Bridge

Gtr. 6 tacet
B
A
B
ain't no coun - try boy,
I'm just a home - sick man.
8va
Gtr. 6
loco
string noise
*Gtrs. 1, 2 & 3
*Composite arrangement
Gtr. 7 (elec.)
mf
w/ dist.
F5
I'm gon - na hit the grit just as fast as I can.
Gtrs. 1, 2 & 3
let ring
Gtr. 7

Verse
Half-time feel
Gtr. 7 tacet
Gtrs. 1, 2 & 3 tacet
E7
3. I get off on Main Street, step in-to the crowd,
w/ wah-wah
w/ dist.
mf
Gtr. 8 (elec.)
Gtr. 8
Gtrs. 1, 2 & 3
divisi
Gtr. 9 (elec.)
mf
w/ dist.
w/ envelope filter
1/2
Gtr. 10 (elec.)
mf
w/ dist.
w/ envelope filter
side-walk un-der my feet, yeah, traf-fic's good and loud.
1/2
1/4

Pre-Chorus
End half-time feel
Gtr. 8 tacet
Gtrs. 9 & 10 tacet
D
A
Gtr. 3
When I see my in - ner cit - y child, I'll
*Gtrs. 1 & 2
**mp
*Composite arrangement
**Volume pedal, placed before distortion in effects order.
G
Bsus4
B
be walk - in' on the ground. 'Cause I'm a
Gtrs. 1 & 2
f

Outro-Chorus

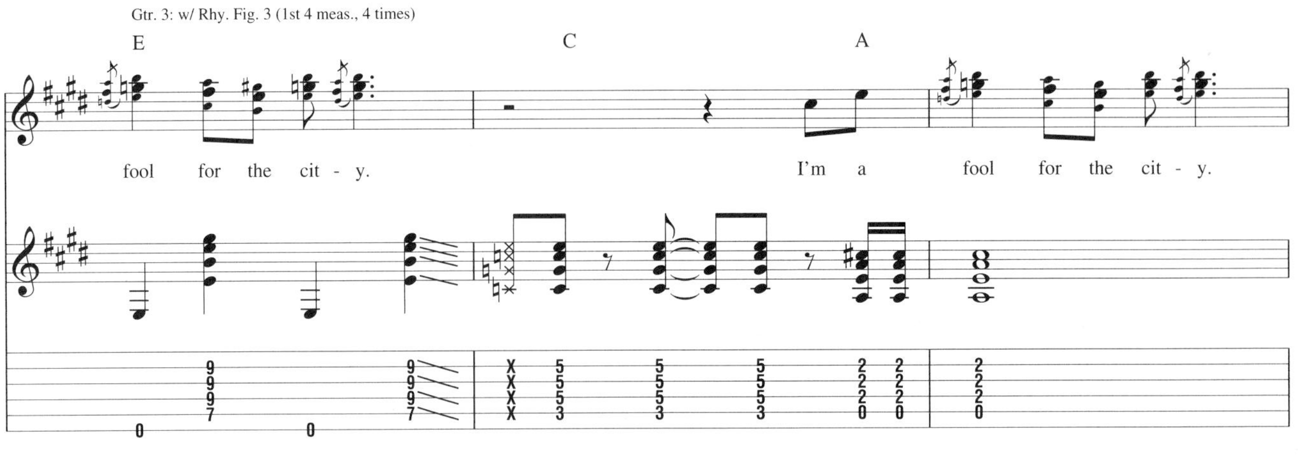

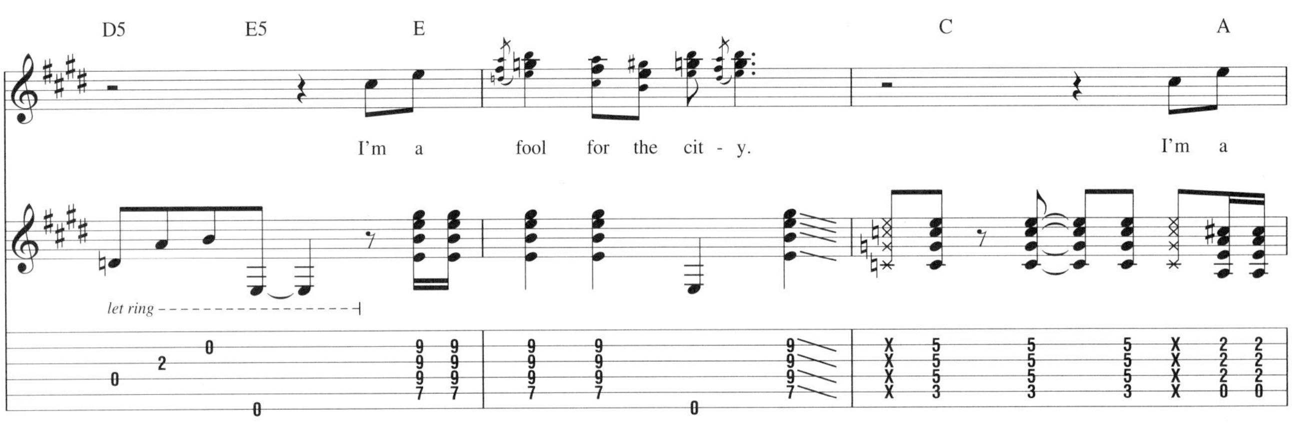

C A D5 E5 E

A cra - zy fool ______ I'm a fool, __

End Voc. Fig. 1

Fool for the cit - y.)

let ring

let ring

Bkgd. Voc.: w/ Voc. Fig. 1 (till fade)

C A

___ yeah. A fool for the cit - y. ______

D5
E5
E
E
Rhy. Fig. 4
Gtr. 3
Gtr. 6
Gtr. 1
Gtr. 2
C
A

Begin fade
Gtr. 3: w/ Rhy. Fig. 4 (till fade)
D
E
End Rhy. Fig. 4
I ain't no coun - try boy.
8va
let ring
C
A
8va

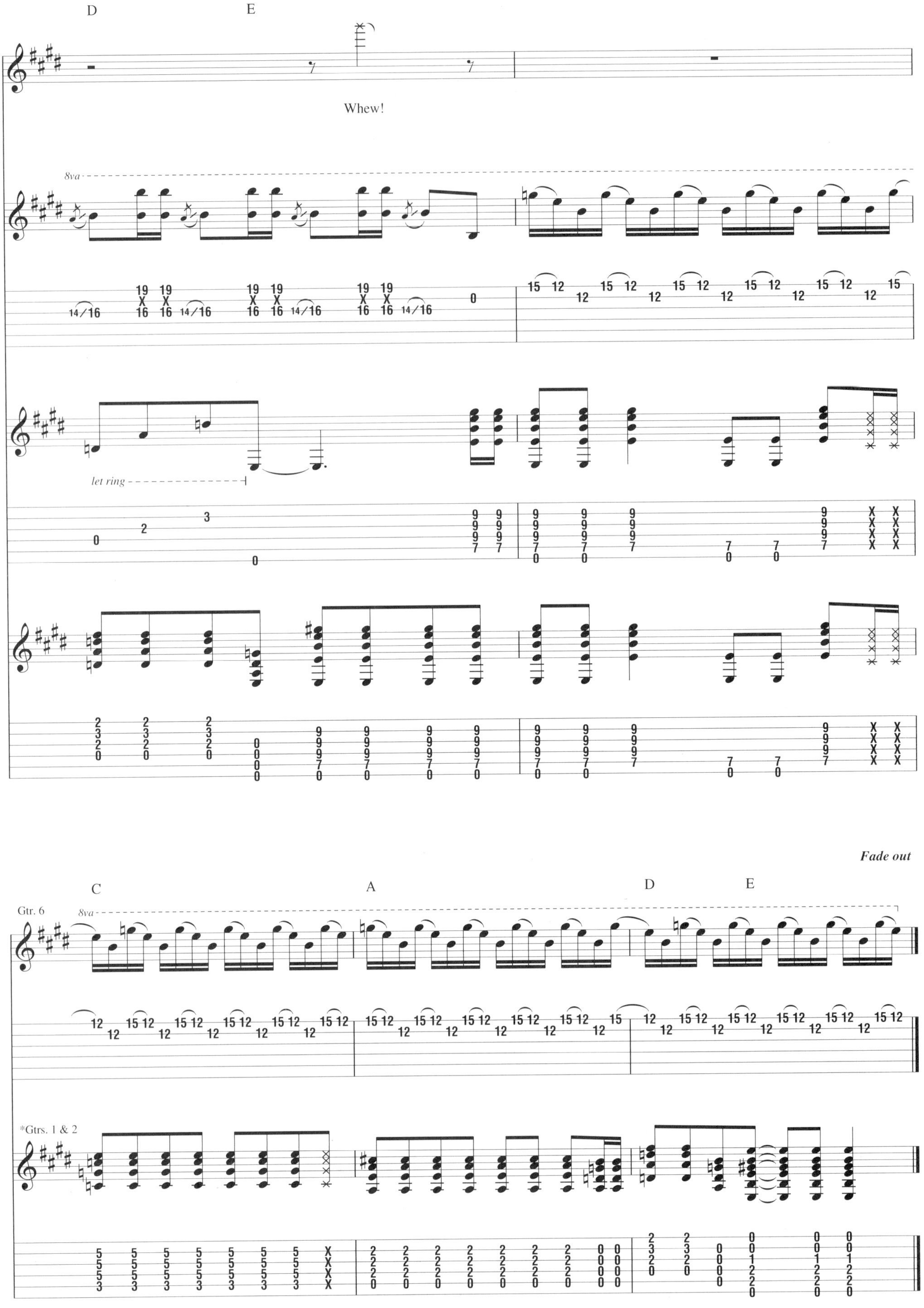

D E

Whew!

8va

let ring

Fade out

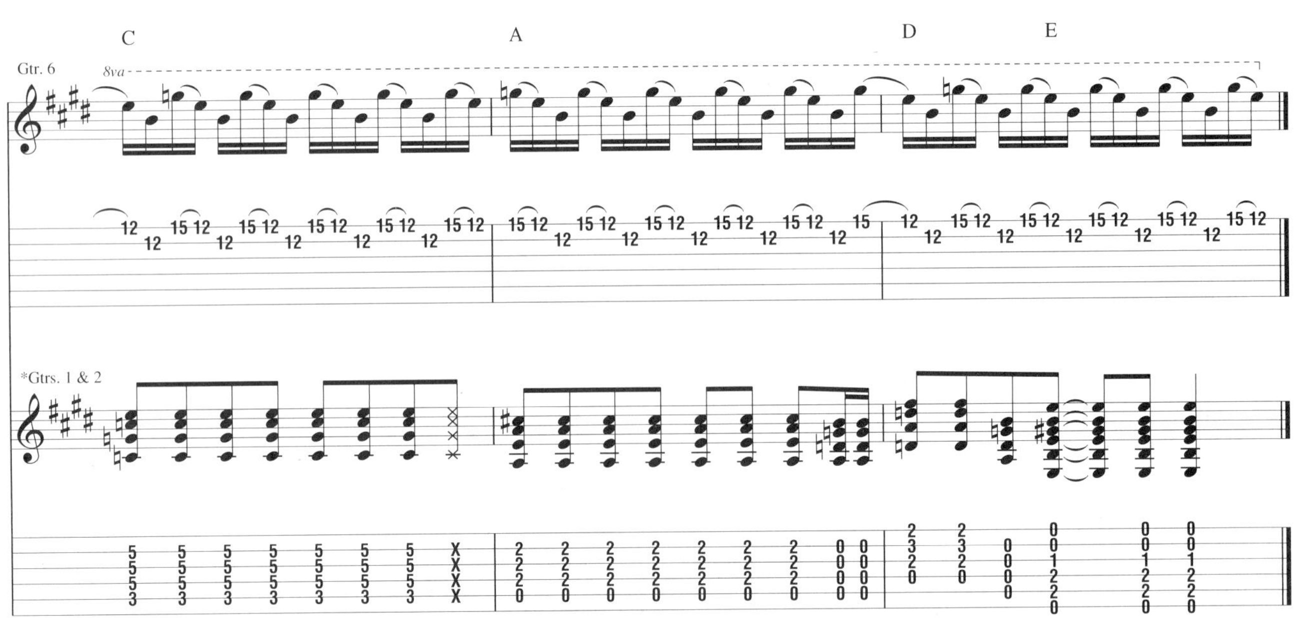

*Composite arrangement

from the Yardbirds - *For Your Love*

For Your Love

Words and Music by Graham Gouldman

To Coda
Em G A Am
There'll be days I will ex - cite to make you dream of me at night.
(For your love.
Chorus
Gtr. 1: w/ Rhy. Fig. 1, 3 times, simile
Em G A Am
For your
love.
For your
love.)
Bridge
Slower ♩ = 132
Em N.C.
(drums)
B
For your love, for your love,
Gtr. 1
*w/ slight P.M.
*Vocals doubled throughout bridge.
*next 7 meas.
A E B
I would give the stars a - bove. For your love, for your love,

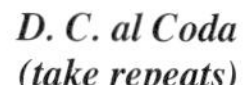
D. C. al Coda
(take repeats)

A
C#
B
I would give you all I could.

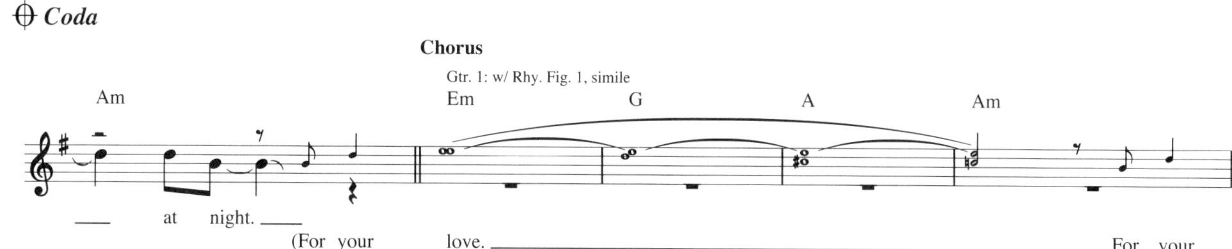
Coda
Chorus
Gtr. 1: w/ Rhy. Fig. 1, simile
Am
Em
G
A
Am
at night.
(For your love.
For your

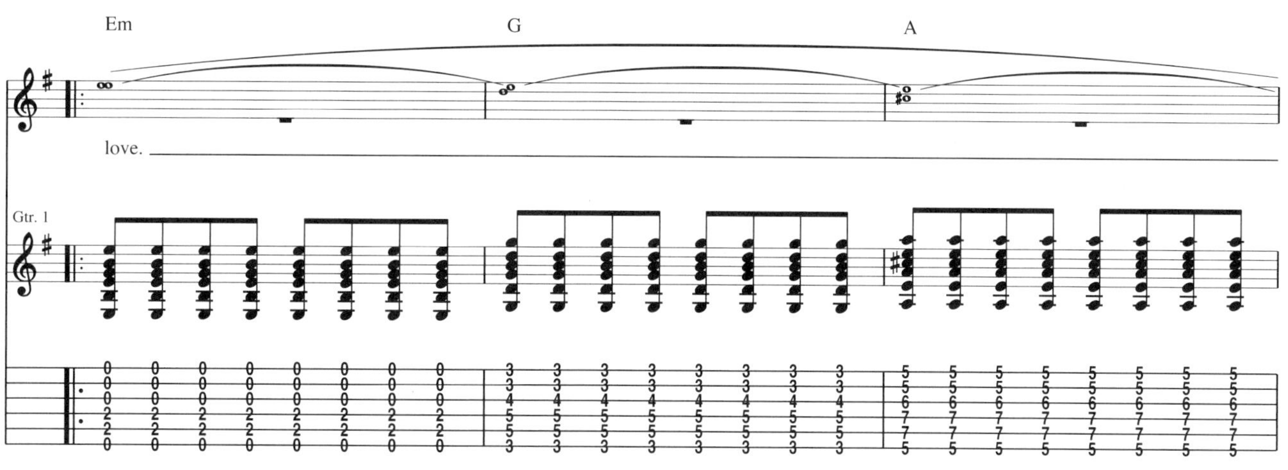
Em
G
A
love.
Gtr. 1

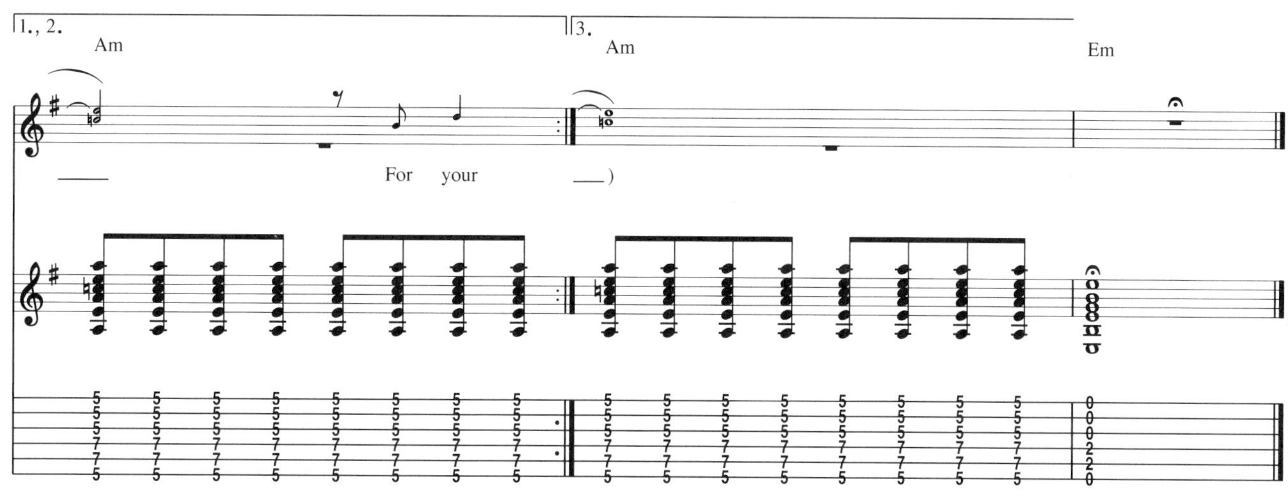
1., 2.
3.
Am
Am
Em
For your
)

from Allman Brothers Band - *Seven Turns*

Gambler's Roll

Words and Music by Warren Haynes and Johnny Neel

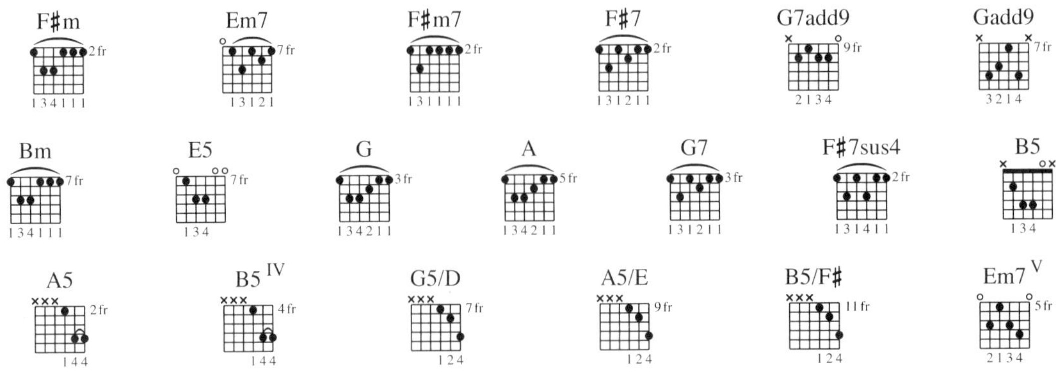

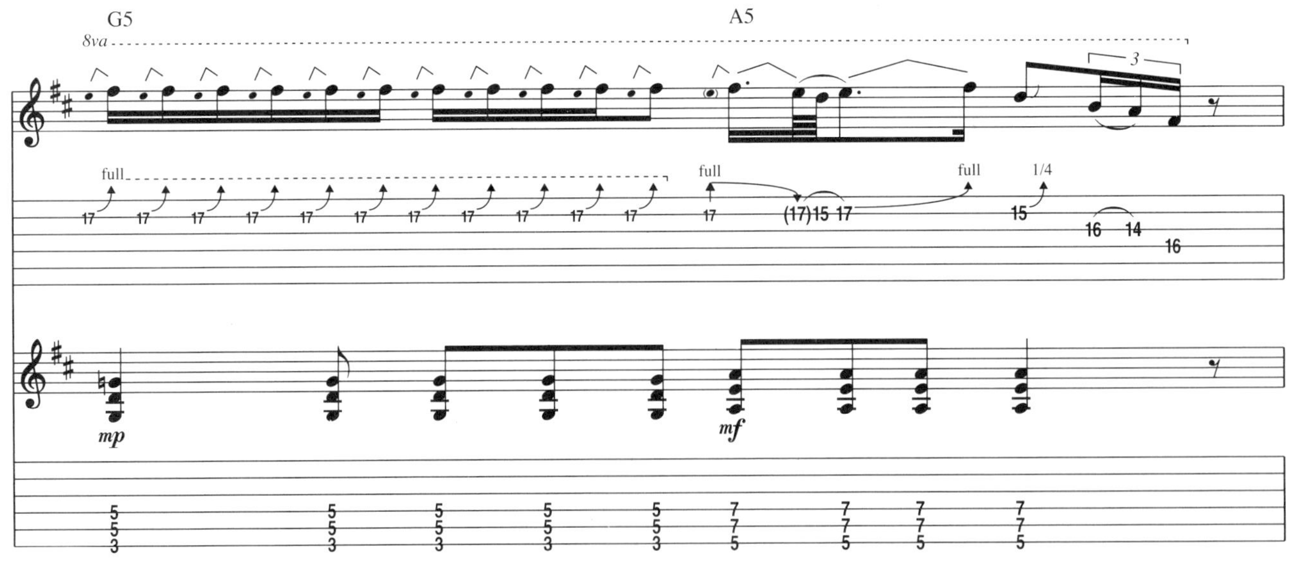

Verse
Bm
Gadd9
Bm
F♯m
Gtr. 2
mp
1. The deal - er sits ___ a - lone in the
Gtrs. 1 & 2
Gtr. 1
Rhy. Fig. 1
f
mp
w/ clean tone (let ring throughout)
Bm
F♯m
Bm
F♯m
Gtr. 2: w/ Rhy. Fill 1
Bm
dark. ___ A cig - a-rette shines ___ on his ver-y last card. _ Ev - 'ry-
Em7
F♯m
F♯m7 F♯7
Gtr. 2: w/ Fill 1
Bm
G7add9
Gtr. 2
mp
thing he had, _ he watched it come and go ___ on a gam - bler's roll. ___ Mm. ___
Rhy. Fill 1
Gtr. 2
mf
* let open B ring
* w/ fingers
Fill 1
Gtr. 2
f
mf
rake
1/2

Verse
Gtr. 1: w/ Rhy. Fig. 1, 1st 4 meas., simile
Bm
G7add9
Bm
F#m
Bm
F#m
(cont. in notation)
mp
2. (A) cold wind blows a young girl's world a - part. She bet it
knows it's just a-bout his last game. Not e-ven
End Rhy. Fig. 1
Gtr. 2
f
mp
f
mp

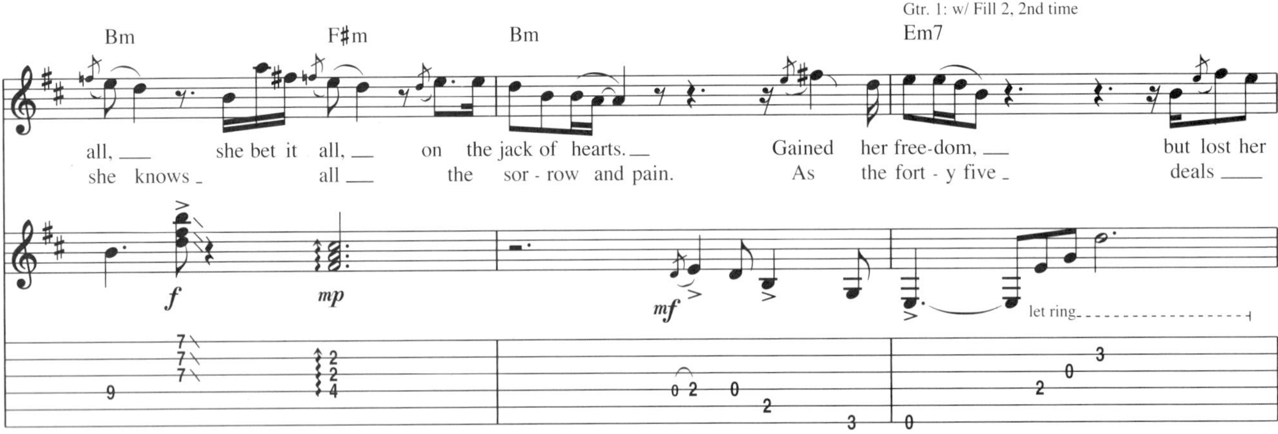
Gtr. 1: w/ Fill 2, 2nd time
Bm
F#m
Bm
Em7
all, she bet it all, on the jack of hearts. Gained her free-dom, but lost her
she knows all the sor - row and pain. As the fort - y five deals
f
mp
mf
let ring

Gtr. 1: w/ Rhy. Fig. 1, meas. 6 & 7
Gtr. 1: w/ Rhy. Fig. 1, meas. 8, 1st time, simile
Gtr. 1: w/ Rhy. Fill 3, on D.S. only
F#m
F#m7
F#7
Bm
G7add9
Bm
soul on a gam-bler's roll. On a gam - bler's roll.
the fa-tal blow on a gam-bler's roll. On a gam - bler's roll.
You know the gam-bler, he
let ring
play 1st time only

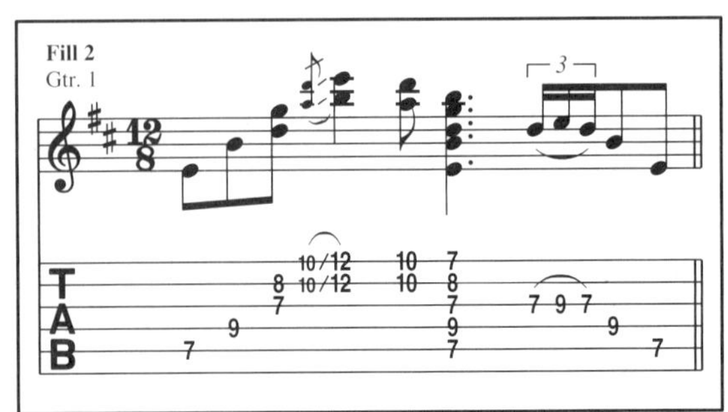
Fill 2
Gtr. 1
let ring

Rhy. Fill 3
Gtr. 1
let ring

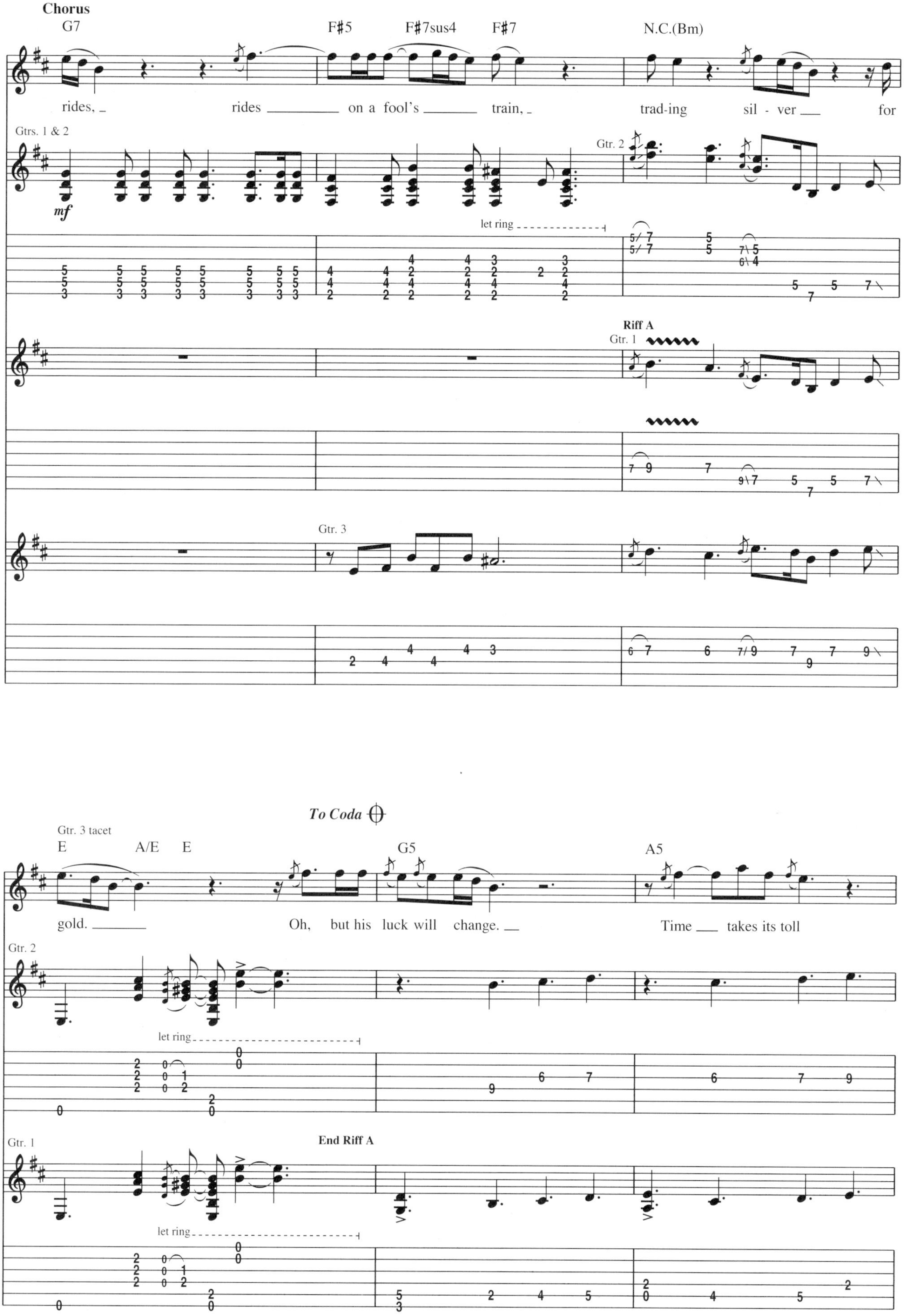

Chorus
G7
F#5
F#7sus4
F#7
N.C.(Bm)
rides, rides on a fool's train, trad-ing sil - ver for
Gtrs. 1 & 2
mf
let ring
Gtr. 2
Riff A
Gtr. 1
Gtr. 3
To Coda
Gtr. 3 tacet
E
A/E
E
G5
A5
gold. Oh, but his luck will change. Time takes its toll
Gtr. 2
let ring
Gtr. 1
End Riff A
let ring

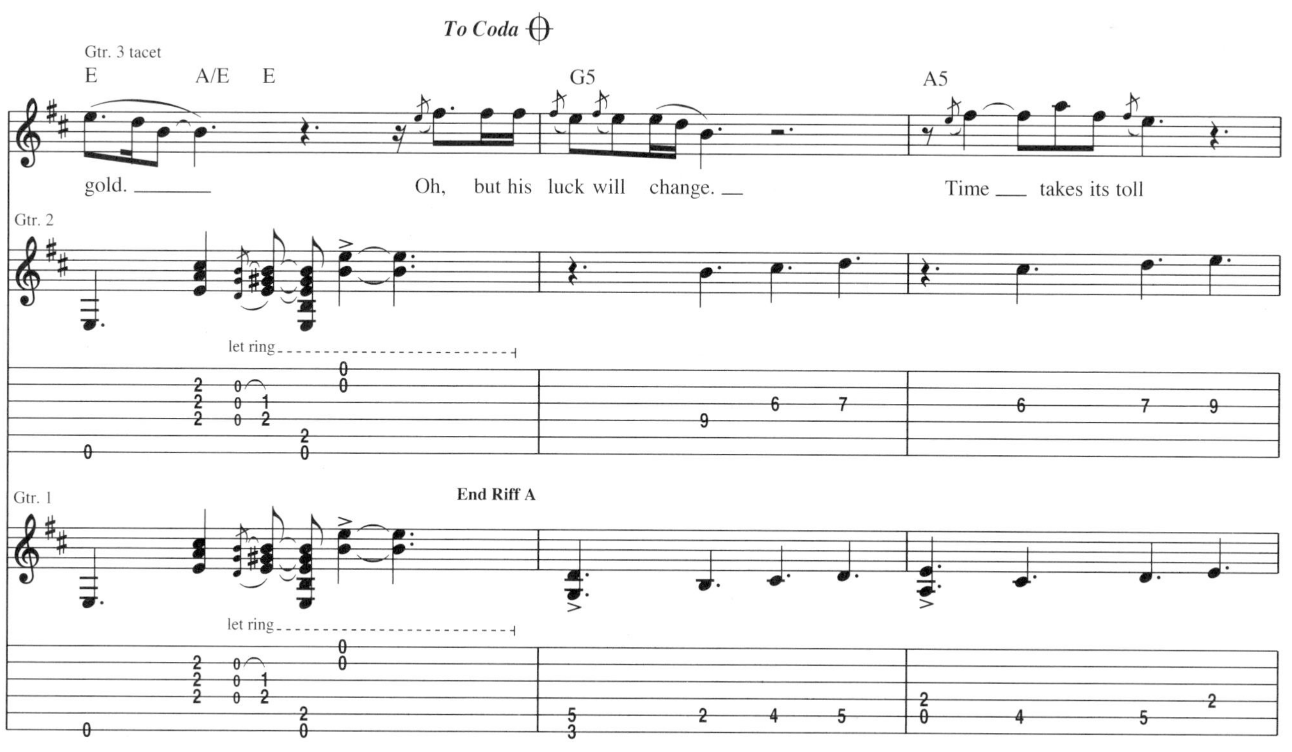

Organ Solo
Gtr. 1: w/ Rhy. Fig. 1, 1st 3 meas.
Bm
G7add9
Gadd9
F#m
on a gam - bler's roll.
Gtrs. 1 & 2
Gtr. 2
mp
Gtr. 1: w/ Rhy. Fill 2
Gtr. 1: w/ Rhy. Fig. 1, meas. 5 & 6
Bm7
Em7
F#7
let ring
Gtr. 1
(cont. in slash)
Guitar Solo
1/2
full
Rhy. Fill 2
T
A
B

Bm
E
open
E5
full
1/2
1 1/2
F#m
F#7
G
A
cont. strum simile
mf
rake
* 2nd string gets caught in bend.
Bm
G7add9
Bm
* 2nd string gets caught in bend.
G7
8va
F#7sus4
F#7
grad. bend
Gtr. 1: w/ Riff A
N.C.(Bm)
E
A/E
E
1/4
loco

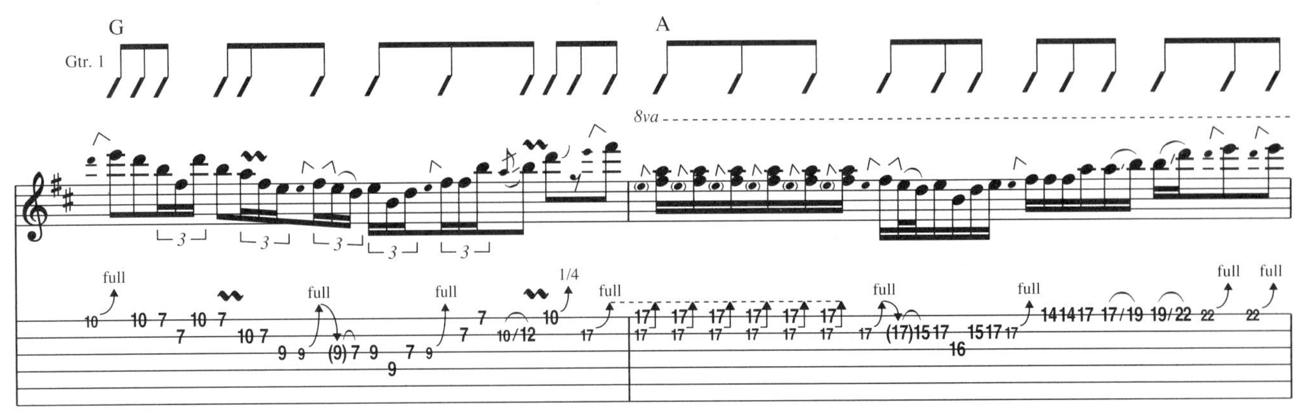
G
A
Gtr. 1
8va

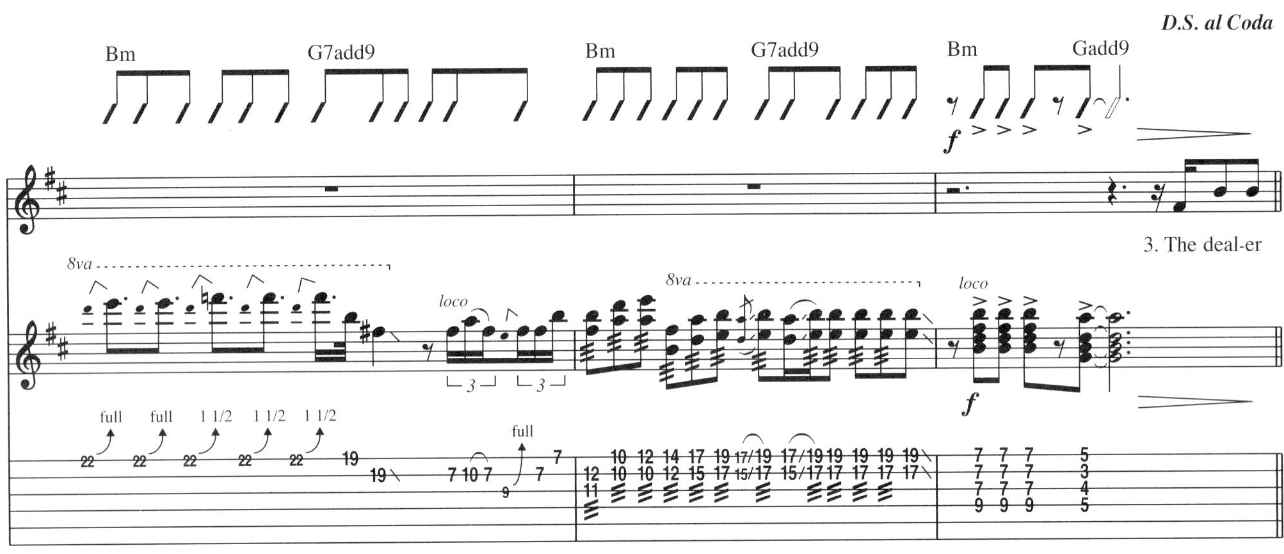
D.S. al Coda
Bm
G7add9
Bm
G7add9
Bm
Gadd9
3. The deal-er
8va
loco

Coda
G5
A5
Bm
G7add9
Gtr. 1
luck will change.
Time
takes its toll
on a gam-bler's
roll.
On the gam - bler's
Gtr. 2
(cont. in slash)

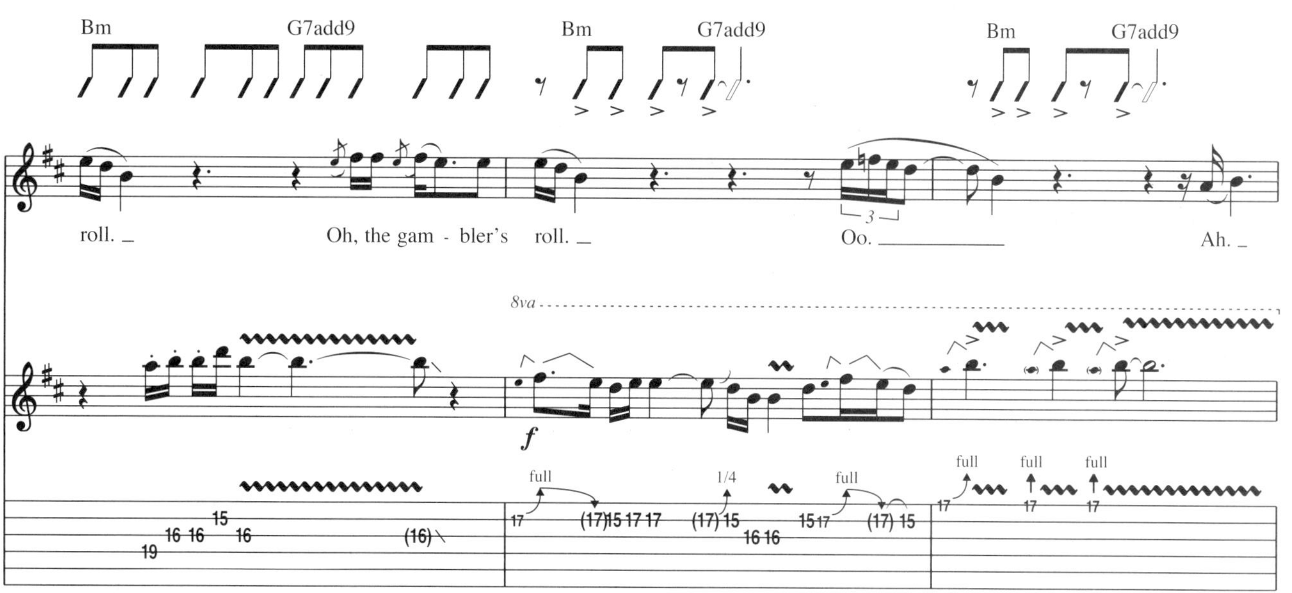
Bm
G7add9
roll. _
Oh, the gam - bler's
roll. _
Oo.
Ah. _
8va
full
1/4

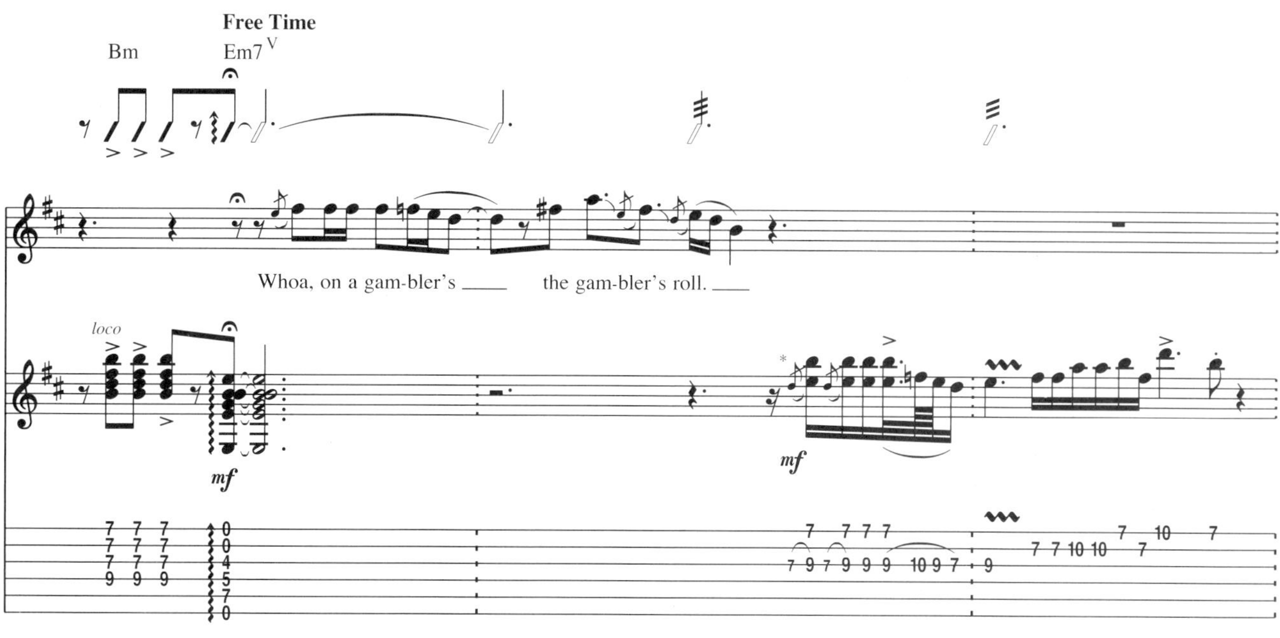
Free Time
Bm
Em7 V
Whoa, on a gam-bler's
the gam-bler's roll.
loco

B5
A5 B5 IV
G5/D A5/E
B5/F#
rake
8va

from Kiss - *Destroyer*

God of Thunder

Words and Music by Paul Stanley

Tune down 1/2 step:
(low to high) E♭-A♭-D♭-G♭-B♭-E♭

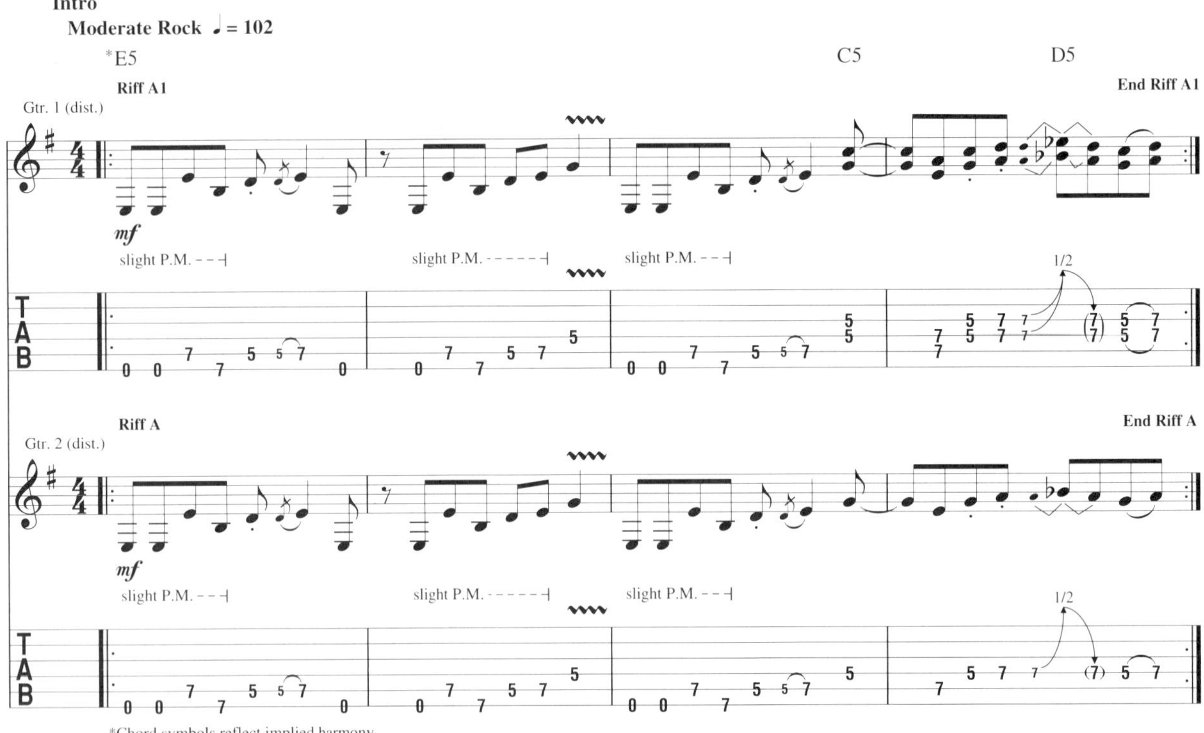

*Chord symbols reflect implied harmony.

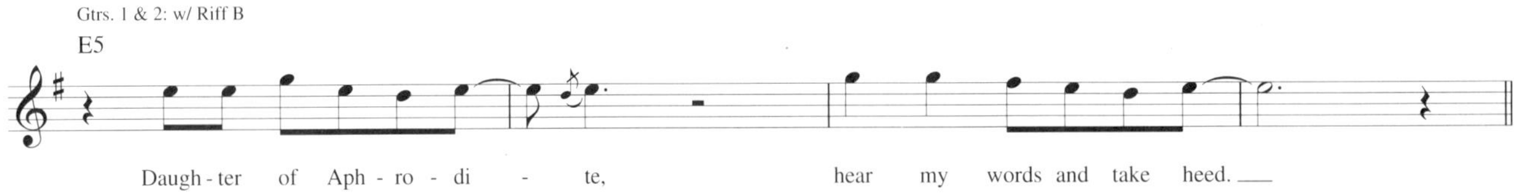

Verse

Gtrs. 1 & 2: w/ Riffs A & A1
3rd time, Gtr. 4: w/ Fill 1

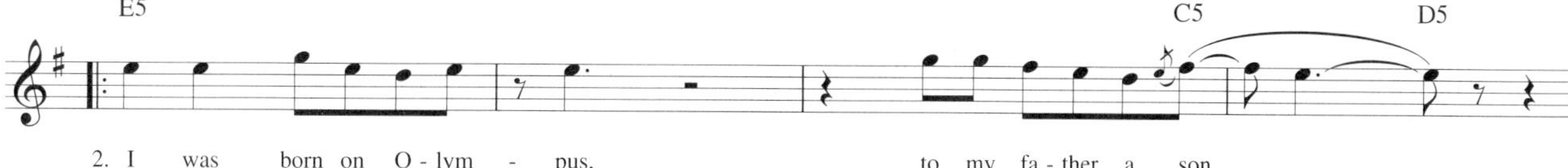

2. I was born on O - lym - pus, to my fa - ther a son.
3. I'm the lord of the waste - lands, a mod - ern day man of steel.
4. *Spoken:* I am the lord of the waste - lands, a mod - ern day man of steel.

Gtrs. 1 & 2: w/ Riff B

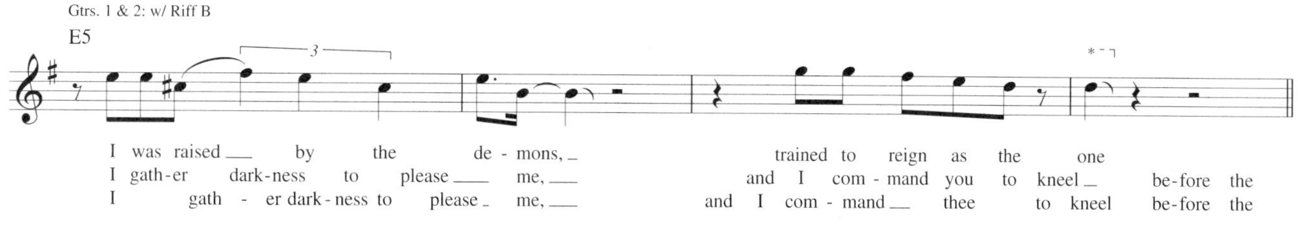

I was raised by the de - mons, trained to reign as the one
I gath - er dark - ness to please me, and I com - mand you to kneel be - fore the
I gath - er dark - ness to please me, and I com - mand thee to kneel be - fore the

*1st time, w/ echo set for approx. quarter-note regeneration w/ 3 repeats.

Chorus

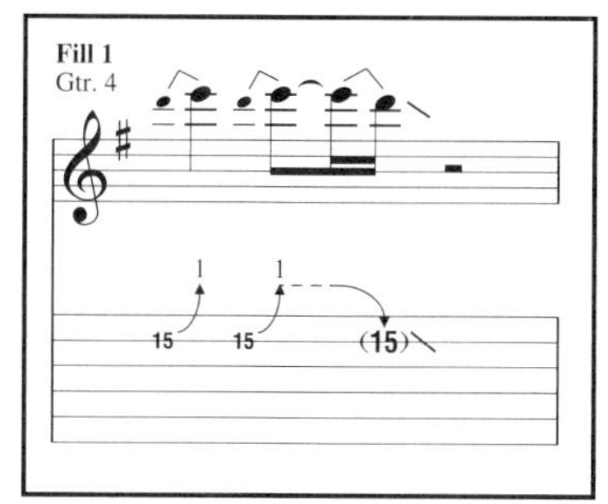

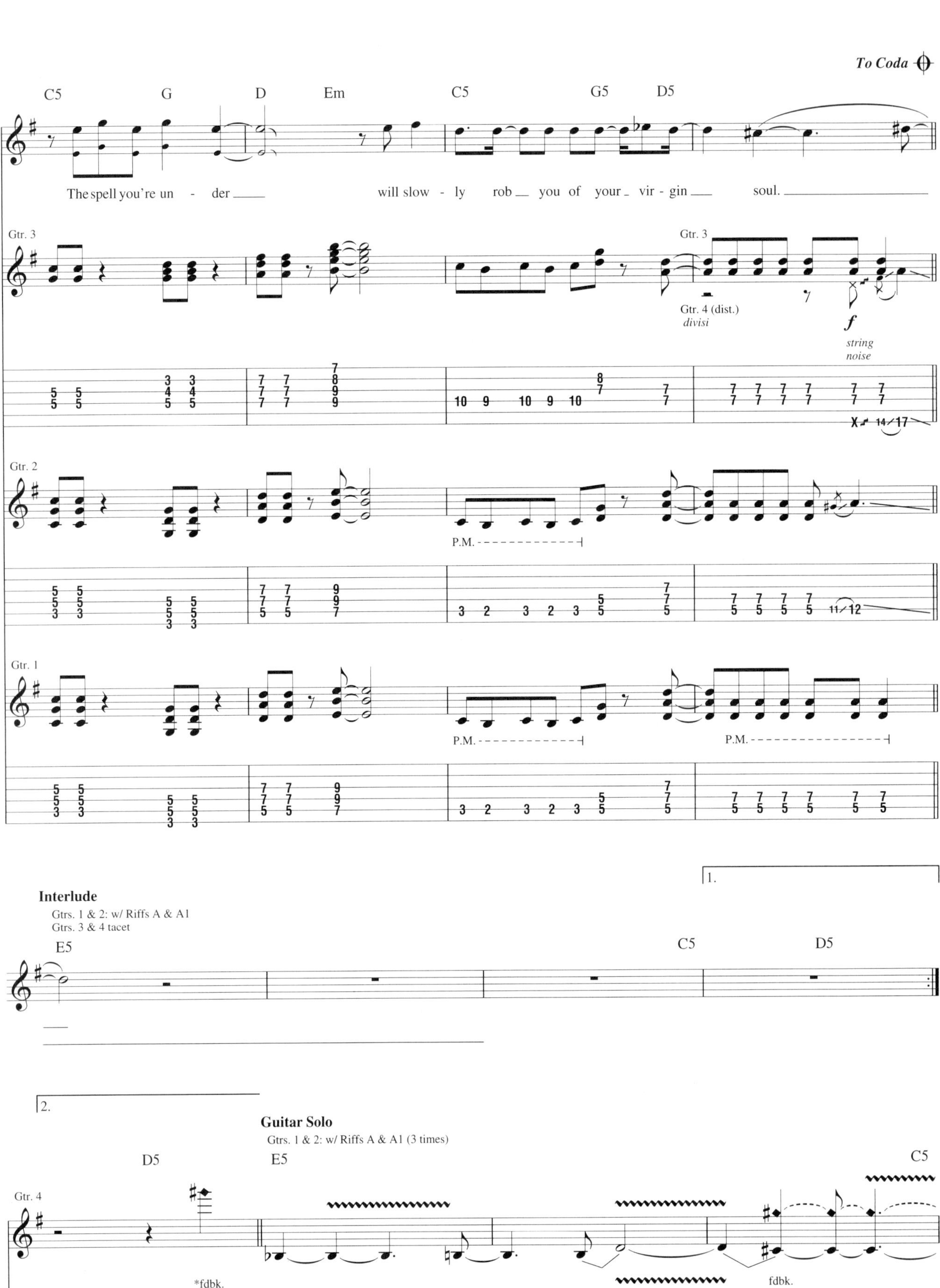
To Coda
C5
G
D
Em
G5
D5
The spell you're un - der will slow - ly rob you of your vir - gin soul.
Gtr. 3
Gtr. 4 (dist.)
divisi
string noise
Gtr. 2
P.M.
Gtr. 1
Interlude
Gtrs. 1 & 2: w/ Riffs A & A1
Gtrs. 3 & 4 tacet
E5
1.
2.
Guitar Solo
Gtrs. 1 & 2: w/ Riffs A & A1 (3 times)
*fdbk.
w/ heavy reverb
fdbk.
Pitch: G♯
*Microphonic fdbk., not caused by string vibration.

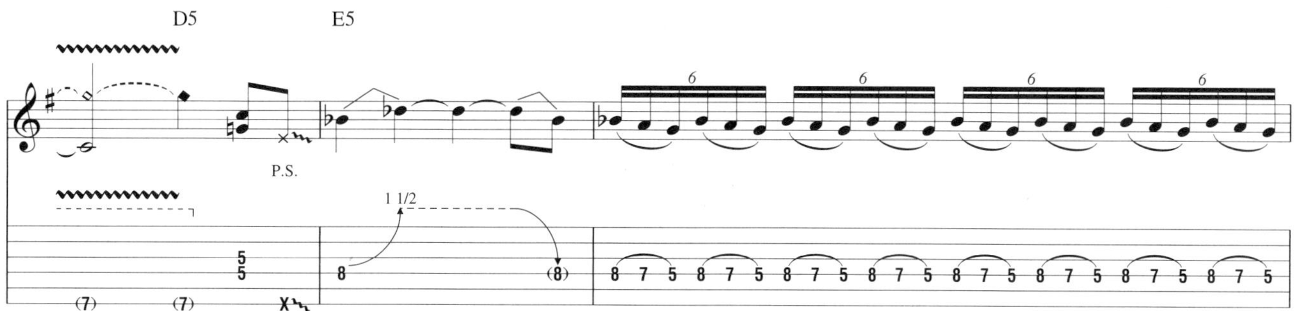
D5
E5
P.S.
1 1/2
6

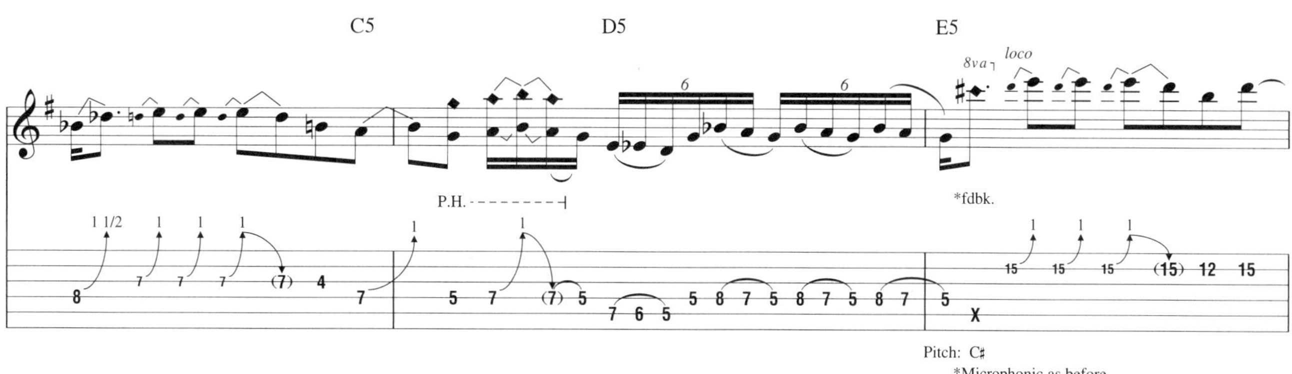
C5
D5
E5
8va
loco
P.H.
*fdbk.
hold bend
Pitch: C♯
*Microphonic as before

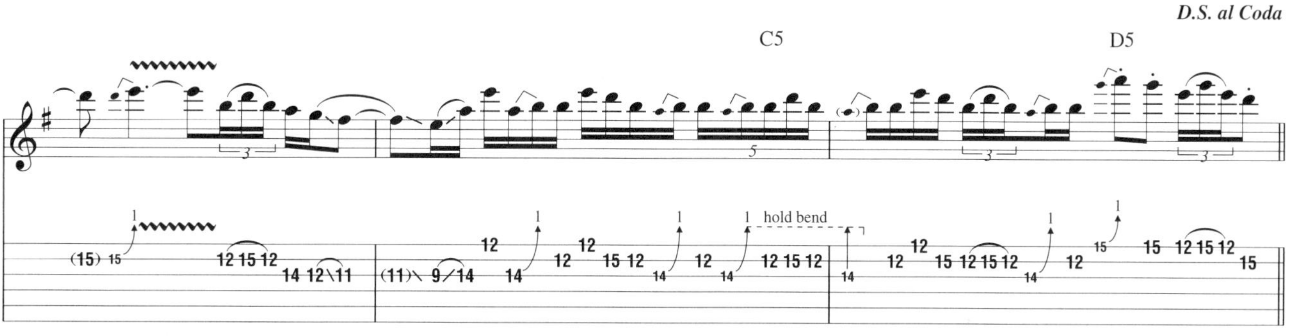
D.S. al Coda
C5
D5
hold bend

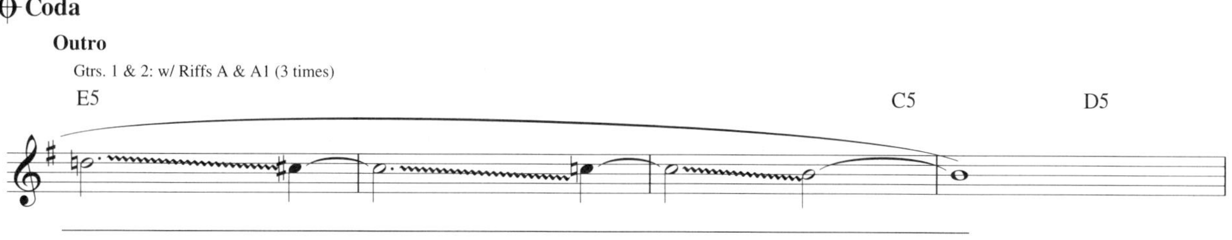
Coda
Outro
Gtrs. 1 & 2: w/ Riffs A & A1 (3 times)
E5
C5
D5

8
E5
N.C.
Gtrs. 1 & 2

from Creedence Clearwater Revival - *Chronicle*

Green River

Words and Music by John Fogerty

E
Em7
C
A
231
32 1
111

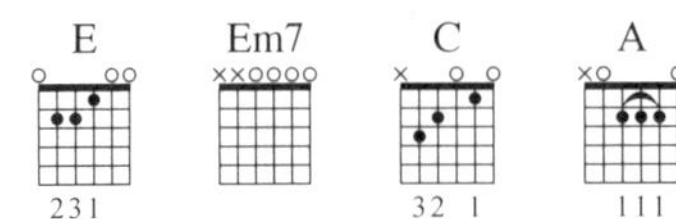

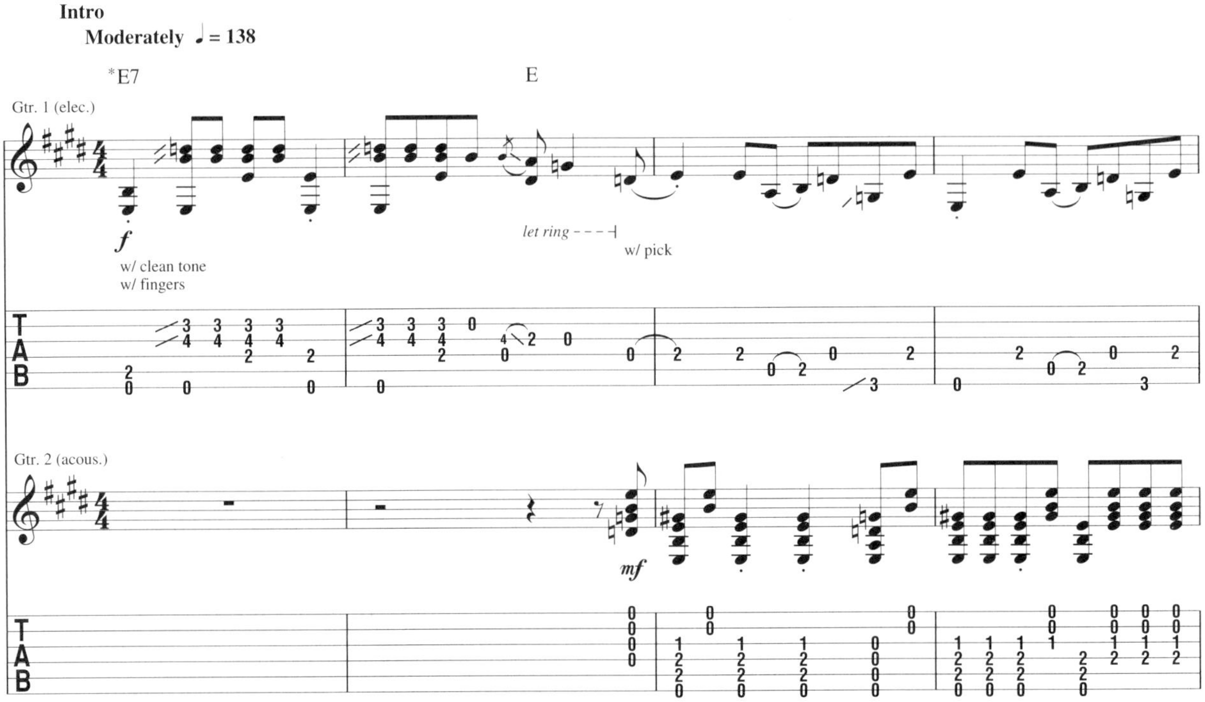

Intro
Moderately ♩ = 138
*E7
E
Gtr. 1 (elec.)
f
w/ clean tone
w/ fingers
let ring
w/ pick
Gtr. 2 (acous.)
mf

*Chord symbols reflect overall harmony.

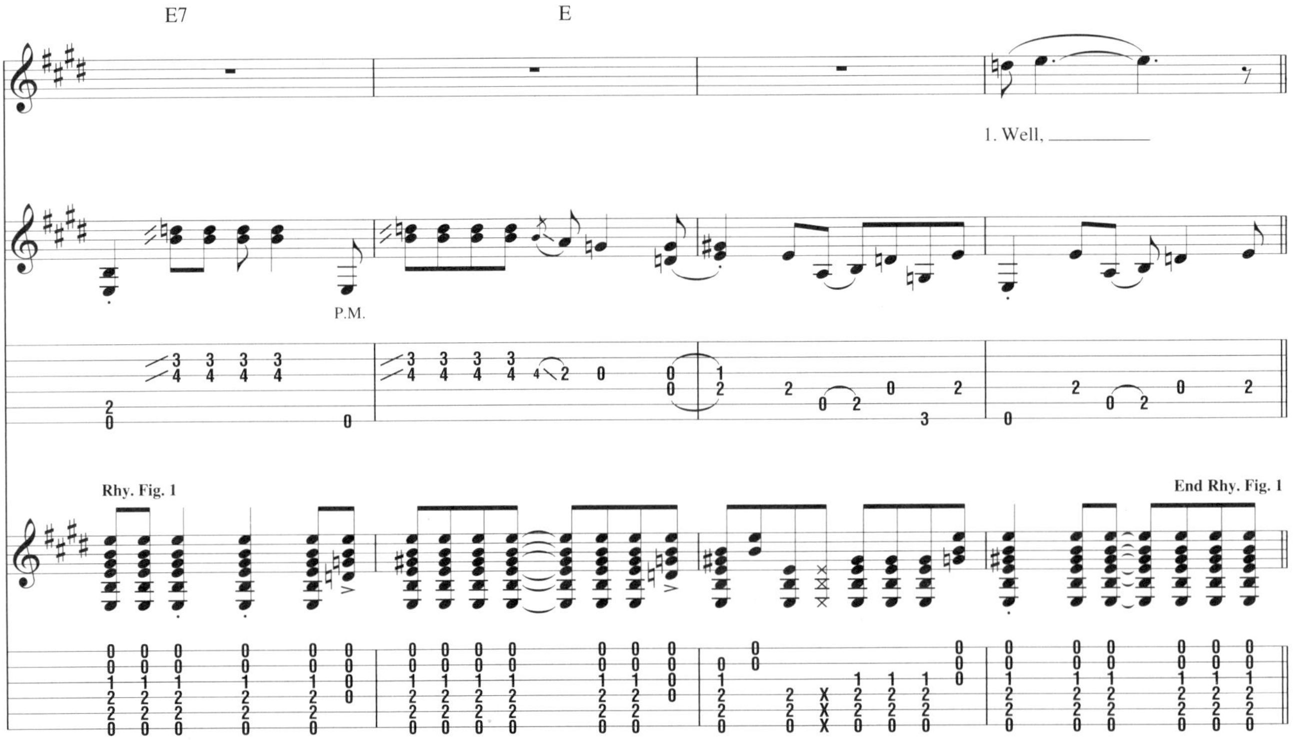

E7
E
1. Well,
P.M.
Rhy. Fig. 1
End Rhy. Fig. 1

Verse

Gtr. 2: w/ Rhy. Fig. 1 (2 times)
E
E7
E
take me back down where cool wa-ter flows, y'all.
Oh,
Gtr. 1
P.M.
P.M.
1/2
Gtr. 3 (Dobro)
tr
mp
w/ clean tone

Gtr. 3 tacet
E7
E
let me re-mem - ber things I love now.
P.M.
P.M.
1
tr

E
Em7
C
Rhy. Fig. 2
Gtr. 2
Stop-ping at the log where cat - fish bite,
walk-ing a - long the riv - er road at night,
Gtr. 1
mp
Rhy. Fig. 2A
Gtr. 4 (elec.)
p
w/ clean tone
Gtr. 5 tacet
A
E
Em7
E
End Rhy. Fig. 2
bare-foot girl dance - in' in the moon - light.
Gtr. 1
f
P.M.
Gtr. 5 (elec.)
Riff A
End Riff A
f
w/ clean tone
Gtr. 4
End Rhy. Fig. 2A

Verse
Gtr. 2: w/ Rhy. Fig. 1 (2 times)
Gtr. 4 tacet
E
E7
E
2. I can hear the bull - frog call-ing me, how!
Gtr. 1
P.M.
Gtr. 1
Gtr. 3
divisi
Gtr. 3 tacet
E7
E
Won-d'ring if the rope's still hang-ing to the tree, oh.
Gtr. 1
P.M.
Gtrs. 2 & 4: w/ Rhy. Figs. 2 & 2A
Em7 C
Love to kick my feet way down the shal-low wa-ter. Shoo, fly, drag - on-fly, get back to your moth er.
mp
A
Gtr. 5: w/ Riff A
E7
Pick up a flat rock, skip it a - cross Green Riv-er. A,
P.M.

Guitar Solo
Gtr. 2: w/ Rhy. Fig. 1 (1 1/2 times)
Gtr. 5 tacet
E
well.
Gtr. 5
Riff B
Gtr. 6 (elec.)
w/ clean tone
Gtr. 6
Gtr. 5
divisi
End Riff B
P.M.
Gtr. 1
Gtrs. 2 & 4: w/ Rhy. Figs. 2 & 2A
Em7
Gtr. 7 (elec.)
w/ dist.
Gtr. 6
let ring
Gtr. 1

C

A

grad. bend

P.M.

let ring

Gtr. 6 tacet

E E7

E

Verse

Gtr. 2: w/ Rhy. Fig. 1 (2 times)
Gtr. 7 tacet

E

3. Up at Co-dy's camp I spent my days, oh,

Gtr. 7

Gtr. 3

Gtr. 1

P.M.

let ring

Gtr. 3 tacet
with flat car rid - ers and cross tie walk - ers.
Gtr. 1
Gtrs. 2 & 4: w/ Rhy. Figs. 2 & 2A (till fade)
Gtr. 3 tacet
Em7
Old Co - dy Jun - ior took me o - ver,
Gtr. 1
Gtr. 3
divisi
C
A
said, "You're gon - na find the world is smould - 'ring, and if you get, a, lost
Gtr. 5: w/ Riff A
E
E7
come on home to Green Riv - er.
A,
P.M.

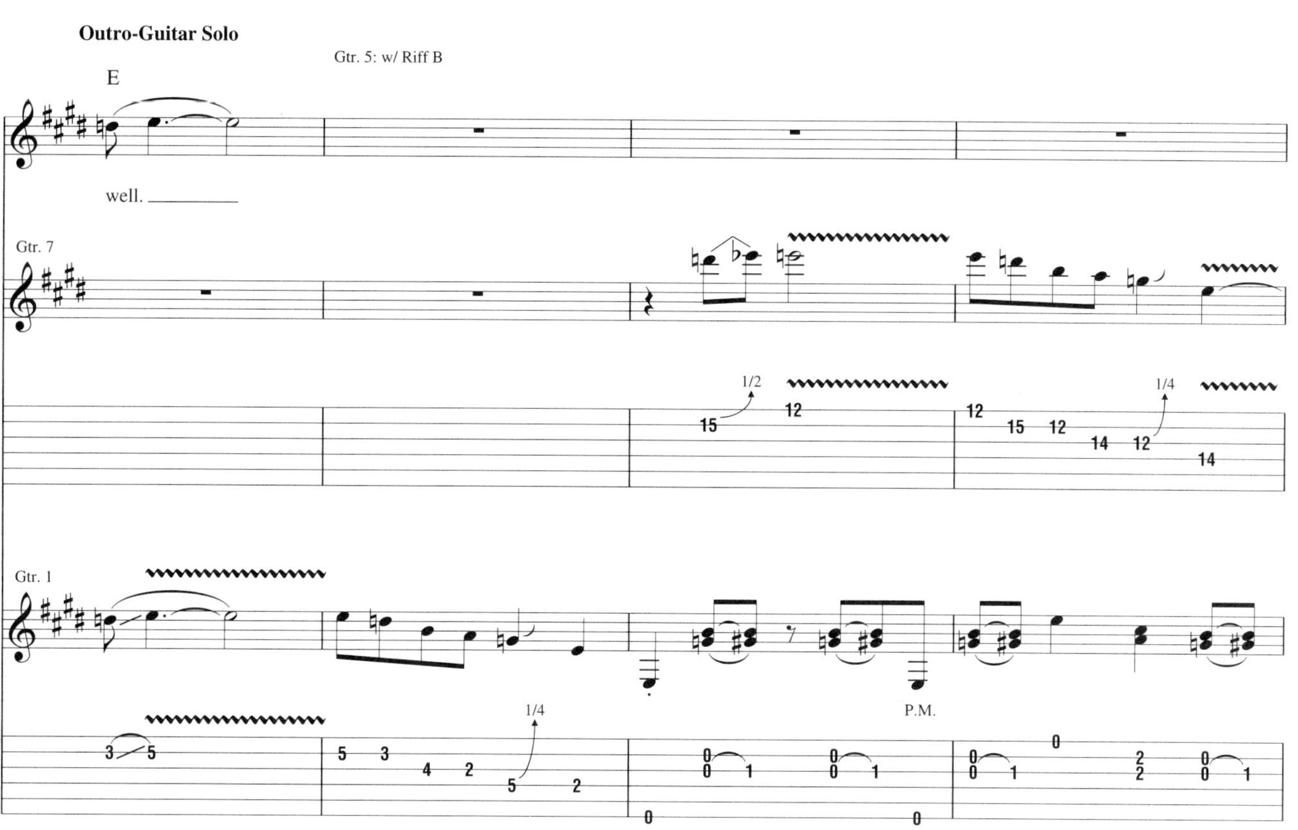

Spoken: Come on home, man.

Gtr. 7

1/2 1/4 1/2

Gtr. 5

P.M.

1/4 1/4

Gtr. 1

P.M. *let ring* P.M.

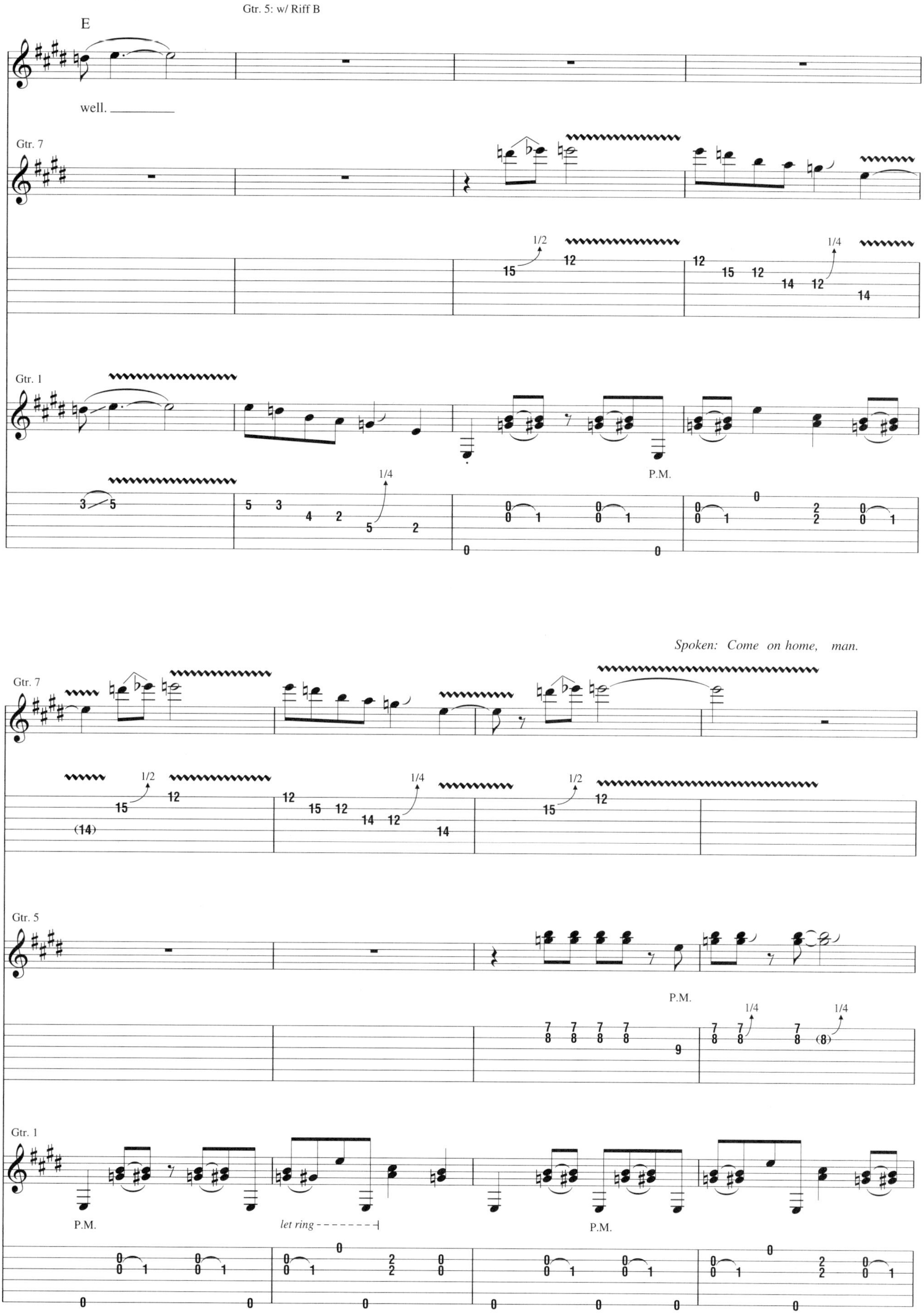

Begin fade

Gtr. 7 tacet

Gtr. 5

Gtr. 1

P.M.

Fade out

from Jeff Buckley - *Grace*

Hallelujah

Words and Music by Leonard Cohen

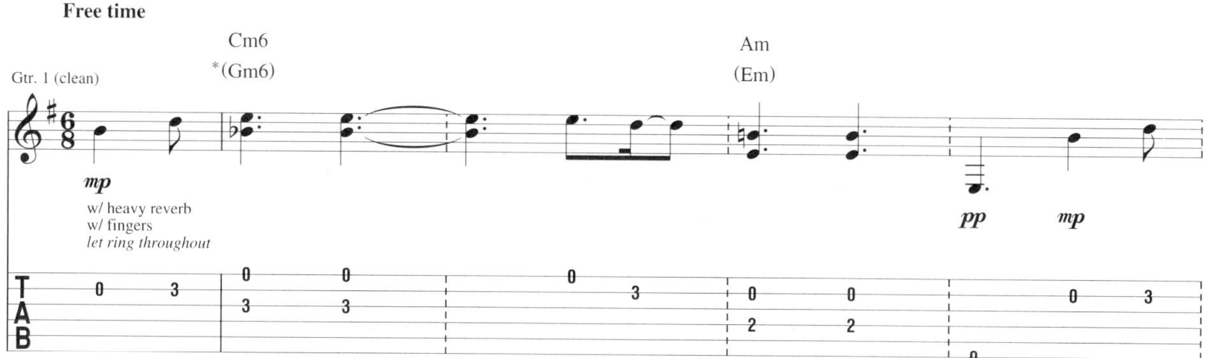

*Symbols in parentheses represent chord names respective to capoed guitar. Symbols above reflect actual sounding chords. Capoed fret is "0" in tab. Chord symbols reflect implied harmony.

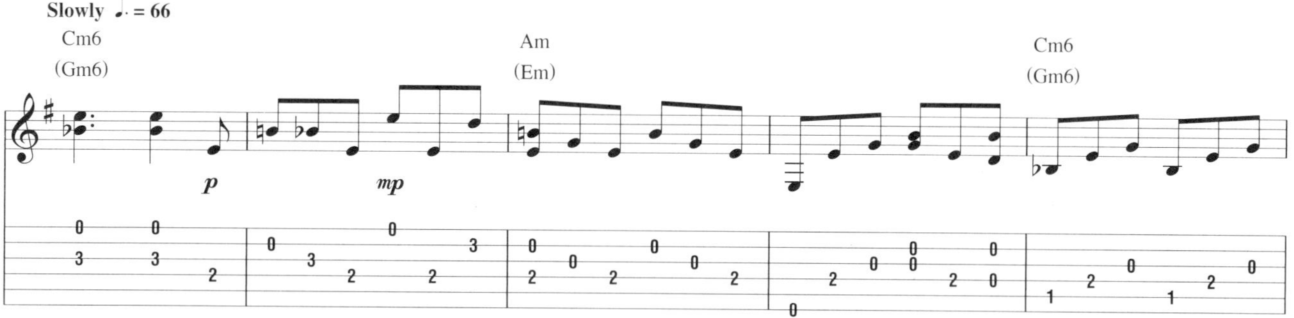

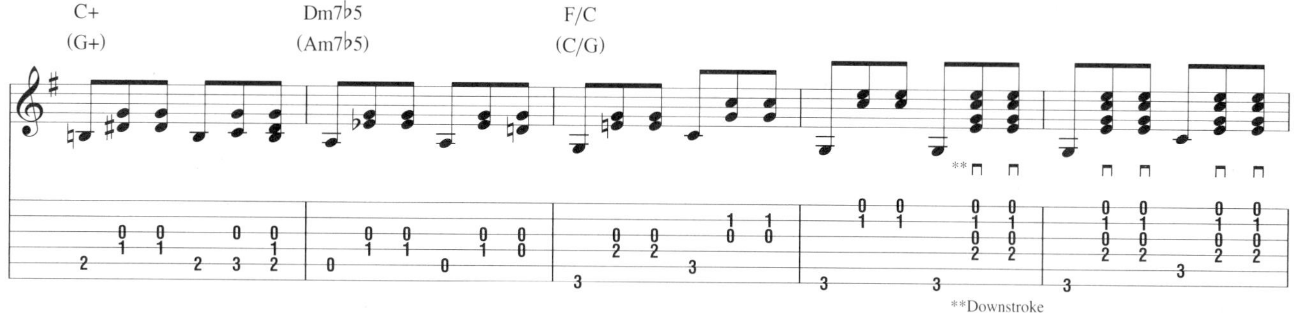

G C Am7 C Am7
(D) (G) (Em7) (G) (Em7)
pp mp
C Am7 C Am7
(G) (Em7) (G) (Em7)
1. Well, I
Verse
C Am7 C Am7
(G) (Em7) (G) (Em7)
heard there was a se - cret chord that Da-vid played, and it pleased the Lord, but
your faith was strong but you need-ed proof. You saw her bath - ing on the roof. Her
3. My ba - by, I've been here be-fore. I've seen this room and I've walked this floor. You know,
there was a time when you let me know what's real-ly go-ing on be-low, but
simile on repeats
F G C/E G
(C) (D) (G/B) (D)
you don't real-ly care for mu - sic do ya? Well, it
beau-ty and the moon-light o - ver-threw ya. As
I used to live a-lone be-fore I knew ya. And I've
now you nev-er show that to me, do ya? But,

C/E (G/B) F (C) G (D) Am (Em) F (C)
goes like this, the fourth, the fifth, the mi - nor fall and the ma - jor lift, the
she tied you to her kitch - en chair as she broke your throne and she cut your hair and
seen your flag on the mar - ble arch, and love is not a vic - t'ry march, it's a
re - mem - ber when I moved in you, and the Ho - ly Dove was mov - ing too, and
G (D) E7/G♯ (B7/D♯) Am (Em) G/B (D/A)
baf - fled king com - pos - ing, Hal - le - lu - jah.
from your lips you drew the Hal - le - lu - jah.
cold and it's a bro - ken Hal - le - lu - jah.
ev - 'ry breath we drew was Hal - le - lu - jah.
Hal - le -
Chorus
F (C) Am (Em) F (C)
lu - jah, Hal - le - lu - jah. Hal - le - lu - jah,
C (G) G/D (D/A)
1., 2., 3.
Interlude
C5 (G5) Am7 (Em7)
1., 2., 3. Hal - le - lu - jah.
4. Hal - le - lu - jah.

4.
Interlude
C
(G)
Am7
(Em7)
Fadd9
(Cadd9)
C/E
(G/B)
Am9
(Em9)
2. Well,
4. Well,
F
(C)
C/E
(G/B)
G/D
(D/A)
C5
(G5)
Am7
(Em7)
C5
(G5)
Am7
(Em7)
F
(C)
G
(D)
C
(G)
G
(D)
C
(G)
F
(C)
G
(D)
Am
(Em)
F
(C)
G
(D)
Am
(Em)
F
(C)
G
(D)

Verse
C (G) Am (Em) C (G) Am (Em)
5. May - be there is a God a - bove, but all I've ev - er learned from love was
F (C) G (D) C/E (G/B) G (D)
how to shoot some - bod - y who out - drew ya. And it's
C (G) F (C) G (D) Am (Em) F (C)
not a cry that you hear at night, and it's not some - bod - y who's seen the light, it's a
G/D (D/A) E7/G♯ (B7/D♯) Am (Em) G/D (D/A)
cold and it's a bro - ken Hal - le - lu - jah. Hal - le -

Chorus
F
(C)
Am
(Em)
F
(C)
lu - jah,
Hal - le - lu - jah.
Hal - le - lu - jah,
C/E
(G/B)
G/D
(D/A)
F
(C)
Fadd♯11
(Cadd♯11)
C6/G
(G6/D)
Hal - le - lu - jah.
Hal - le - lu - jah,
Hal - le -
Am7
(Em7)
F
(C)
C/E
(G/B)
F
(C)
Am7/E
(Em7/B)
lu - jah.
Hal - le - lu - jah,
Hal - le - lu.
G
(D)
F
(C)
Am
(Em)
Hal - le - lu - jah,
Hal - le - lu - jah.
Hal - le -

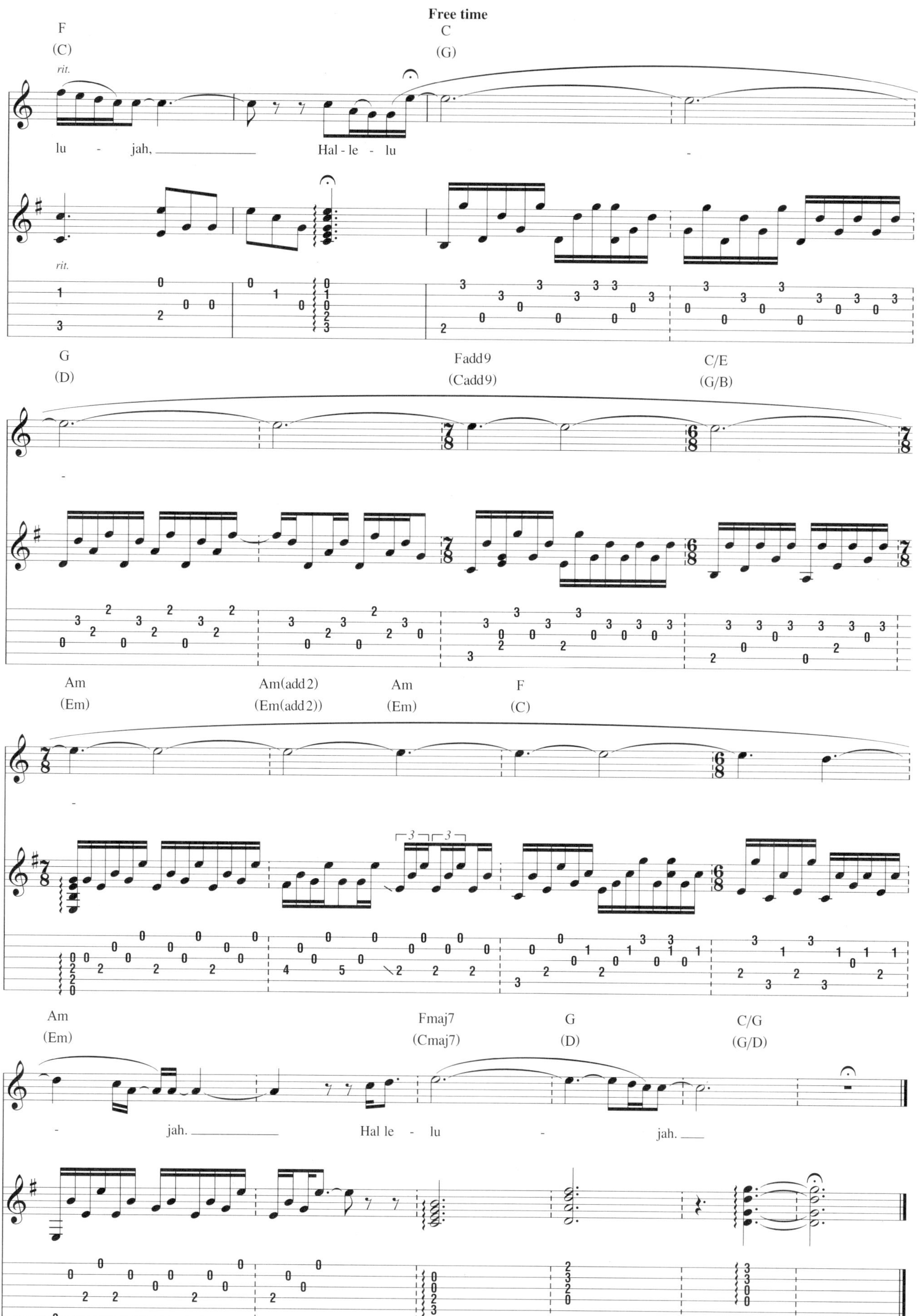
Free time
F
(C)
rit.
C
(G)
lu - jah, Hal - le - lu -
rit.
G
(D)
Fadd9
(Cadd9)
C/E
(G/B)
Am
(Em)
Am(add2)
(Em(add2))
Am
(Em)
F
(C)
Am
(Em)
Fmaj7
(Cmaj7)
G
(D)
C/G
(G/D)
- jah. Hal le - lu - jah.

from Megadeth - *Endgame*

Head Crusher

Words and Music by Dave Mustaine and Shawn Drover

*Chord symbols reflect implied harmony.

Gtrs. 2 & 3: w/ Riff A
Em
8va
Gtr. 1
loco
G5
Verse
Double-time feel
2nd time, Gtr. 1 tacet
Gtr. 1 tacet
F♯5
A5 B5 C5
1. It's time to take your last walk in this world
2. The hor - rif - ic tor - ture de - vice
Gtr. 1
Riff B
Gtrs. 2 & 3
P.M.
F♯5
E5 A5 G5
be - fore your jour - ney be - gins un - der - ground.
for those who fail in - ter - ro - ga - tion.
Gtrs. 2 & 3
P.M.

F#5
A5 B5 C5
But not be - fore we tor - ment you from your
The most pain - ful tech - nique ev - er known. Peo - ple
End Riff B
P.M.
F#5
C#5 C5 B5 G5
cell straight to hell with a short de - tour in be -
thirst for the worst: the skull's dis - in - te -
P.M.
Gtrs. 2 & 3: w/ Riff B
F#5
A5 B5 C5 F#5
tween. Beg - ging for mer - cy, you're all a - lone. Un - a - ble to
gra - tion. Beat - en, bro - ken, in blood - y rags. Add - ing in - sult to
E5 A5 G5 F#5
A5 B5 C5
han - dle the pres - sure. Be - fore it's mor - ti - fi - ca - tion...
in - ju - ry. He re - cants, but it's much too late.
End double-time feel
G5 F#5 E5 C5 B5 A5 G#5
A5
B5 G5
Now let the tor - ture be - gin!
Gtrs. 2 & 3

Chorus
E5 F#5 E5 F#5 E5 F#5 E5 F#5 E5
Death by the head crush - er.
Riff C
F#5 E5 F#5 E5 F#5 E5 G5
Head
End Riff C
Gtrs. 2 & 3: w/ Riff C
E5 F#5 E5 F#5 E5 F#5 E5 F#5 E5 F#5 E5 F#5 E5 F#5 E5 G5
1.
2.
F#5 E5 G5
crush - er!
Death by the head crush - er.
Wow.
Bridge
Half-time feel
E5 Bb5 E5 G5 E5 F5 E5 Bb5 E5 G5 E5 F5
Spoken: On your knees, pris - 'ner, and take your po - si - tion.
Gtr. 4 (dist.)
Riff D
End Riff D
mf
P.M.
let ring
Rhy. Fig. 1
Gtrs. 2 & 3
End Rhy. Fig. 1

End half-time feel
Gtrs. 2 & 3: w/ Rhy. Fig. 1
Gtr. 4: w/ Riff D
E5 B♭5 E5 G5 E5 F5 E5 B♭5 E5 G5 E5 F5
Place your chin for-ward in-to the re-straint. Your
F♯5 C5 F♯5 A F♯5 G5 F♯5 C5 F♯5 A F♯5 G5
head slow-ly caves in from the com-pres-sion. You'll
Riff E
End Riff E
Gtr. 4
P.M. let ring
Rhy. Fig. 2
End Rhy. Fig. 2
Gtrs. 2 & 3
P.M.
Gtrs. 2 & 3: w/ Rhy. Fig. 2
Gtr. 4: w/ Riff E
F♯5 C5 F♯5 A F♯5 G5 F♯5 C5 F♯5 A F♯5 G5
faint to the black-out from in-fer-nal pain.
E5
Ah!
Riff F
End Riff F
Gtrs. 2, 3 & 4
P.M.

Gtrs. 2 & 3: w/ Riff F (2 times)
Bb5 E5 G5 A5 Bb5 A5 E5
Rhy. Fig. 3
Gtr. 4
End Rhy. Fig. 3
P.M.
Gtr. 4: w/ Rhy. Fig. 3
Gtrs. 2, 3 & 4: w/ Rhy. Fig. 3 (1st 2 meas., 2 times)
Gtrs. 2, 3 & 4: w/ Rhy. Fig. 3
Bridge
E5 D#5 E5 D#5 D5
Twist - ing, turn - ing the gi - ant screw,
Rhy. Fig. 4
Gtrs. 2 & 3
E5 D5 C#5 E5 C#5 C5
your teeth are break - ing loose,

E5
C5
B5
E5
B♭5
A5
G5
crushed and splin - ter - ing in - to your mouth.
End Rhy. Fig. 4
P.M.
P.M.
Em
B♭5
Em
G5
Em
F5
Oo,
Gtr. 2
P.M.
P.M.
P.M.
Gtr. 3
P.M.
let ring
P.M.
let ring
P.M.
let ring
Gtrs. 2 & 3: w/ Rhy. Fig. 4
E5
D♯5
E5
D♯5 D5
E5
D5 C♯5
E5
C♯5 C5
wind-ing down, cut-ting through like bro-ken glass be-ing chewed, your
E5
C5 B5
E5
B♭5 A5 G5
Gtrs. 2 & 3: w/ Rhy. Fig. 3 (1st 2 meas.)
E5
B♭5
E5
G5
A5 B♭5 A5
frag-ment - ed skull and shat - ter - ing bones. There's noth - ing you can do.

Outro-Guitar Solo

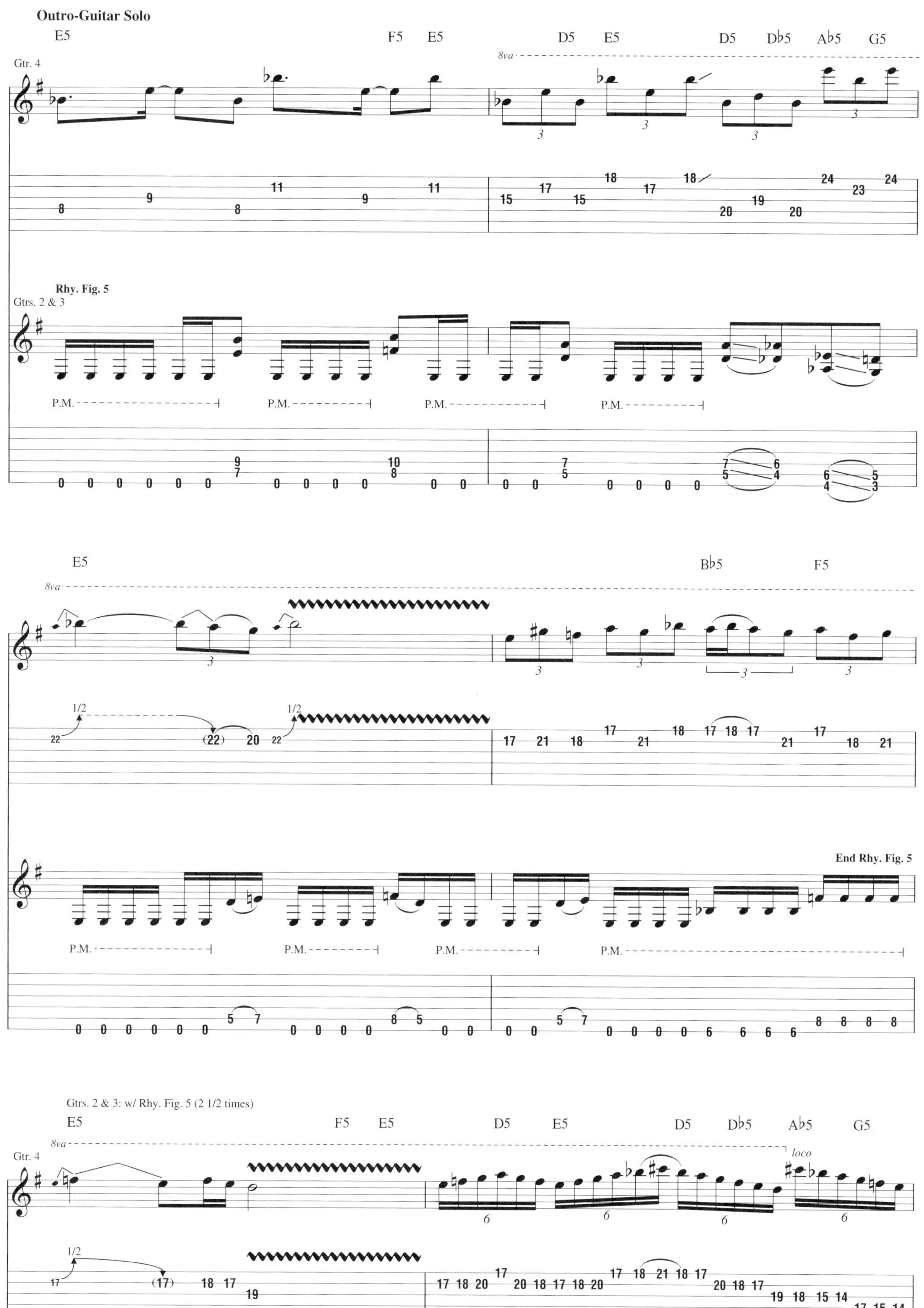

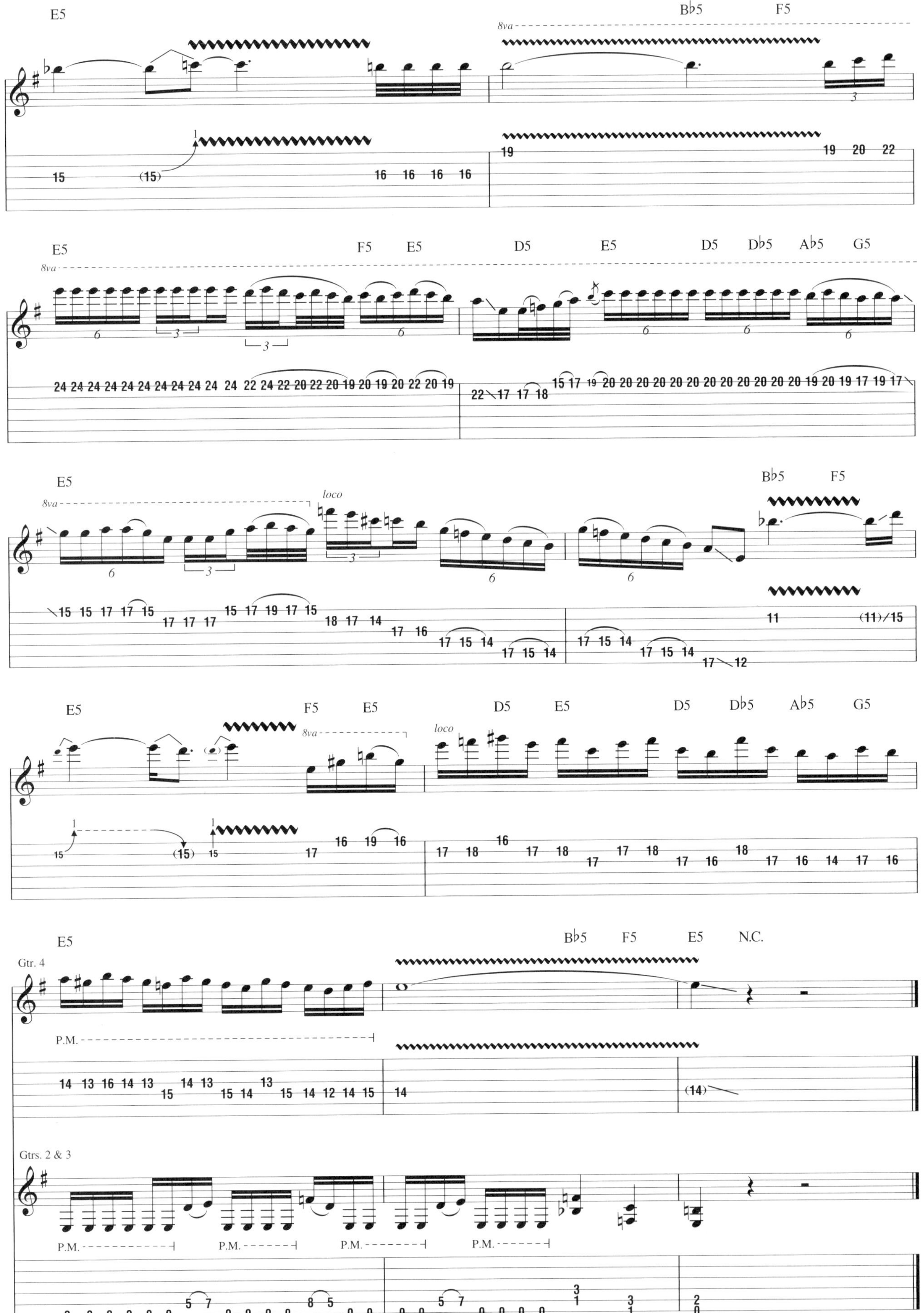
E5
B♭5
F5
8va
E5
F5
E5
D5
E5
D5
D♭5
A♭5
G5
8va
E5
8va
loco
B♭5
F5
E5
F5
E5
8va
D5
E5
D5
D♭5
A♭5
G5
loco
E5
B♭5
F5
E5
N.C.
Gtr. 4
P.M.
Gtrs. 2 & 3
P.M.
P.M.
P.M.
P.M.

from The Beatles - *Yellow Submarine*

Hey Bulldog

Words and Music by John Lennon and Paul McCartney

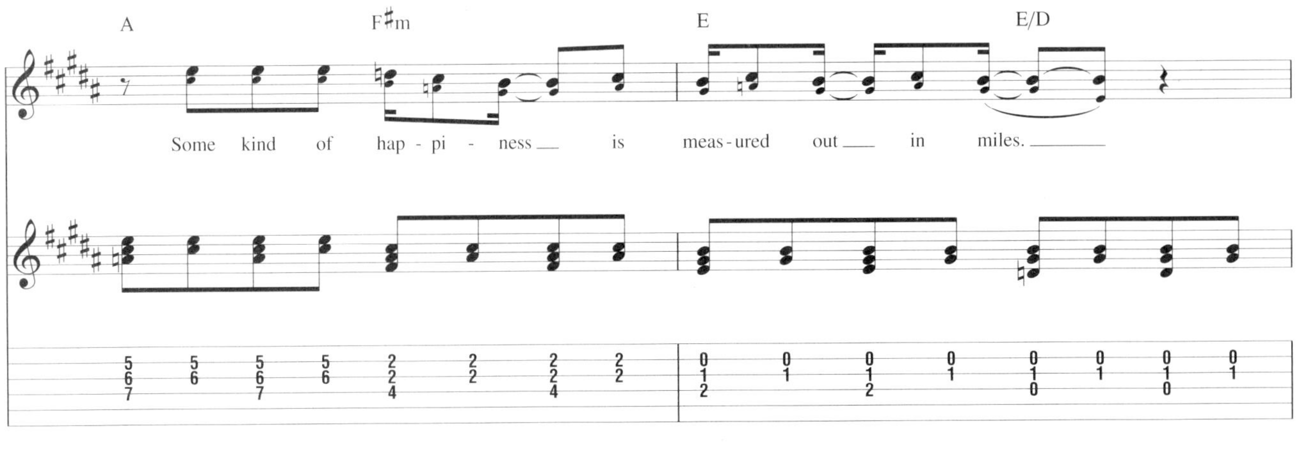
A
F♯m
E
E/D
Some kind of hap - pi - ness is meas - ured out in miles.

A
F♯m
B7
What makes you think you're some - thing spe - cial when you smile?
End Rhy. Fig. 1

Verse
Gtr. 1: w/ Rhy. Fig. 1 (1st 7 meas.)
2nd time, Gtr. 3 tacet
B7
F♯m
B7
2. Child - like, no one un - der - stands. Jack - knife
3. Big man walk - ing in the park. Wig - wam,

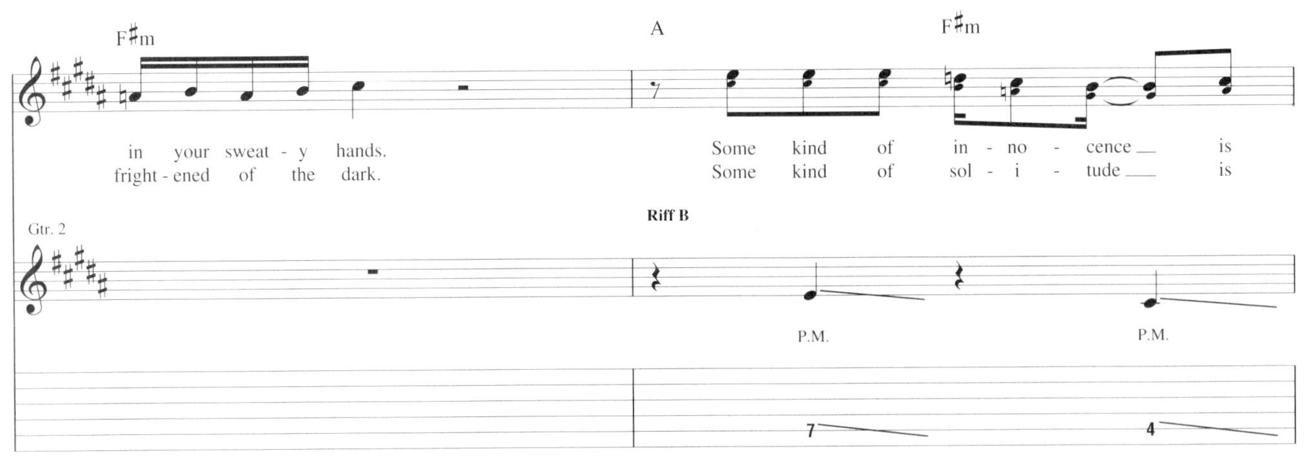
F♯m
A
F♯m
in your sweat - y hands. Some kind of in - no - cence is
fright - ened of the dark. Some kind of sol - i - tude is
Gtr. 2
Riff B
P.M.
P.M.

E
E/D
A
F♯m
meas-ured out in years.
meas-ured out in you.
You don't know what it's like to
You think you know me but you
1/2
P.M.
P.M.
Chorus
B
Bm
Bm♭6
Bm6
Bm7
lis-ten to your fears.
have-n't got a clue.
You can talk to me.
You can talk to me.
Gtr. 1
Gtr. 2
End Riff B
P.M.
P.M.
mp
Em
Em♭6
Em6
Em7
B°
Em/B
You can talk to me.
If you're lone-ly you can talk to me.
mf

Interlude

*Two gtrs. arr. for one.

Guitar Solo

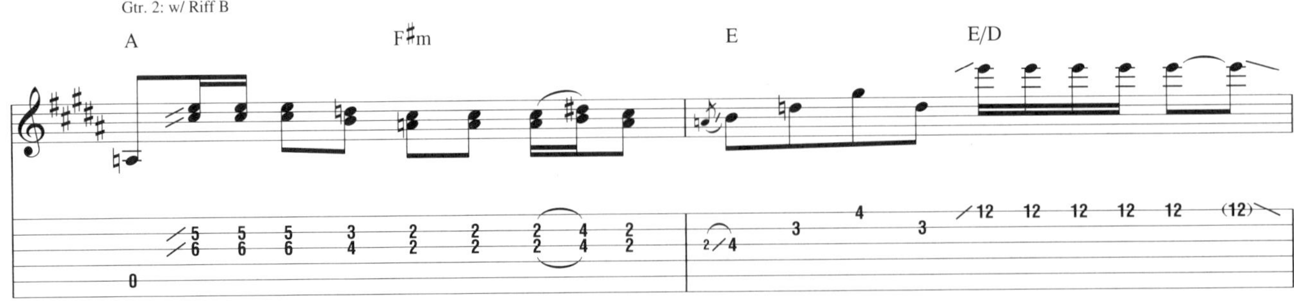

D.S. al Coda
A
F♯m
B7
Coda
Outro
Gtr. 1: w/ Rhy. Fig. 1 (1st 2 meas., till fade)
B7
F♯m
Hey, bull -
Riff C
Gtr. 2
End Riff C
Gtr. 2: w/ Riff C, till end, simile
B7
F♯m
B7
dog.
Spoken: Ruff!
Hey, bull - dog.
F♯m
B7
F♯m
Hey, bull - dog.
Spoken: Hey, man. What's that noise? Ruff!
w/ Bkgd. Voc. ad lib., till end
1., 2.
B7
F♯m
B7
F♯m
What do you say? I said, "Ruff!" You know anymore? Ruff! Ah, ha, ha.
You got it. That's right. You did it. That's it, man. Whoo! That's it. You got it. Don't look at me, man. I only had ten children.
Ah, hoo. Quiet, boy, quiet.
3.
Begin fade
Fade out
B7
F♯m
B7
F♯m
Okay, quiet!
Hey, bull - dog.
Hey, bull...

from Train - *Save Me, San Francisco*

Hey, Soul Sister

Words and Music by Pat Monahan, Espen Lind and Amund Bjorkland

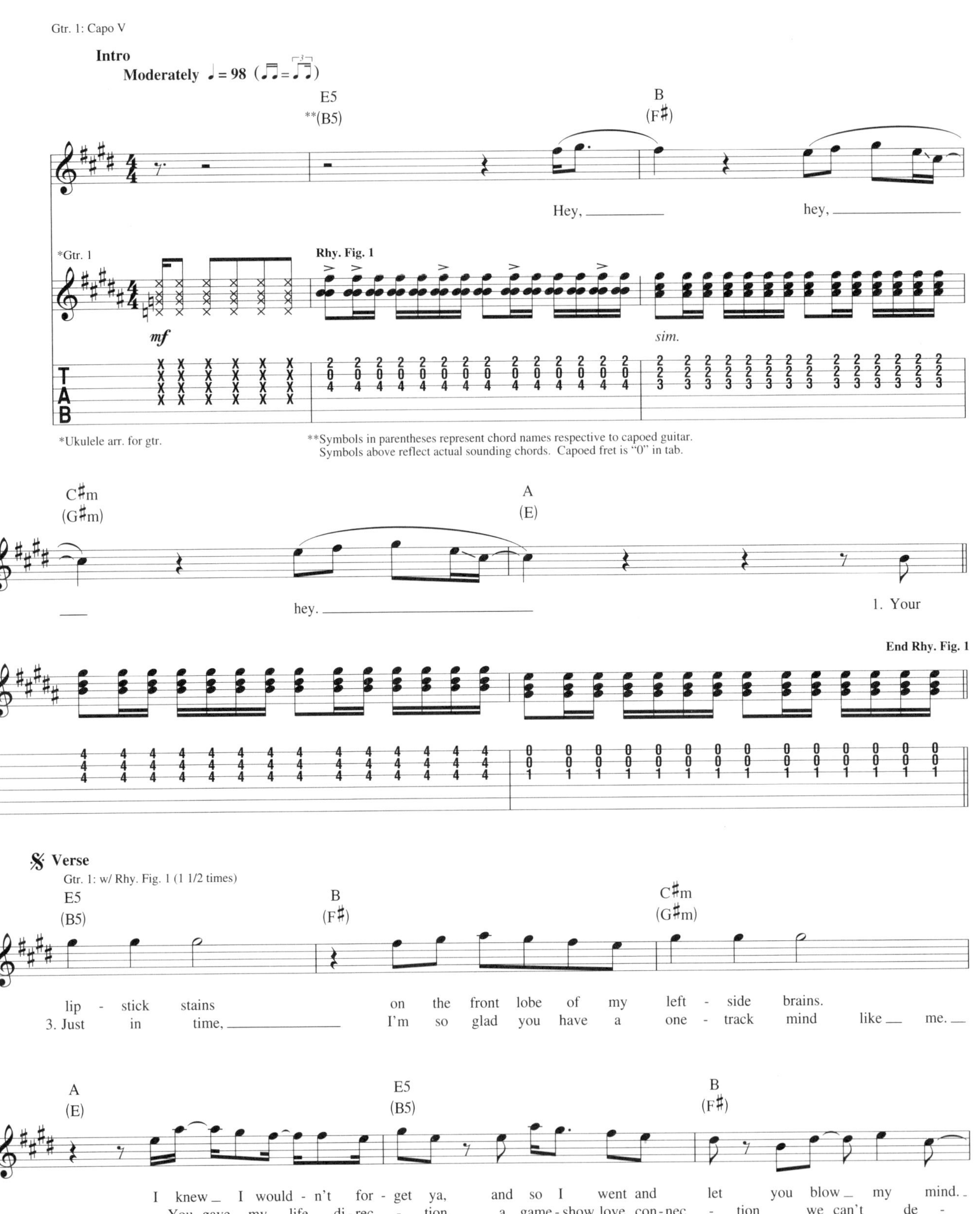

C♯m
(G♯m)
A
(E)
B
(F♯)
ny. I, I,
2. Your
4. I'm
Gtr. 1
Rhy. Fig. 2
End Rhy. Fig. 2
Verse
Gtr. 1: w/ Rhy. Fig. 1 (1 1/2 times)
E5
(B5)
B
(F♯)
C♯m
(G♯m)
sweet moon - beam, the smell of you in ev - 'ry sin - gle dream I dream.
so ob - sessed, my heart is bound to beat right out my un - trimmed chest.
A
(E)
E5
(B5)
I knew when we col - lid - ed, you're the one I have de -
I be - lieve in you. Like a vir - gin, you're Ma - don -
To Coda
Gtr. 1: w/ Rhy. Fig. 2
B
(F♯)
C♯m
(G♯m)
A
(E)
B
(F♯)
cid - ed who's one of my kind.
na and I'm al - ways gon - na wan - na blow your mind.
Chorus
A
(E)
B
(F♯)
E
(B)
B
(F♯)
Hey, soul sis - ter, ain't that Mis - ter Mis - ter on the
Gtr. 1
Rhy. Fig. 3
End Rhy. Fig. 3
Gtr. 1: w/ Rhy. Fig. 3 (1 1/2 times)
A
(E)
B
(F♯)
E
(B)
B
(F♯)
A
(E)
ra - di - o, ster - e - o? The way you move ain't fair, you know. Hey, soul sis - ter, I

B (F♯) E (B) B (F♯) A (E) B (F♯)
don't wan - na miss a sin - gle thing you do to - night.
Gtr. 1
Interlude
Gtr. 1: w/ Rhy. Fig. 1
D.S. al Coda
E5 (B5) B (F♯) C♯m (G♯m) A (E)
Hey, hey, hey.
Coda
Chorus
Gtr. 1: w/ Rhy. Fig. 3 (2 1/2 times)
Asus2 (E) Bsus4 (F♯) E5 (B) Bsus4 (F♯)
Hey, soul sis - ter, ain't that Mis - ter Mis - ter on the
Gtr. 2 (clean)
Rhy. Fig. 4
End Rhy. Fig. 4
mf
Gtr. 2: w/ Rhy. Fig. 4 (1 1/2 times)
Asus2 (E) Bsus4 (F♯) E5 (B) Bsus4 (F♯) Asus2 (E)
ra - di - o, ster - e - o? The way you move ain't fair, you know. Hey, soul sis - ter, I
Bsus4 (F♯) E5 (B) Bsus4 (F♯) Asus2 (E) Bsus4 (F♯)
don't wan - na miss a sin - gle thing you do to - night.
Gtr. 1
Rhy. Fig. 5
End Rhy. Fig. 5
Gtr. 2
Rhy. Fig. 5A
End Rhy. Fig. 5A

Verse
Gtr. 1: w/ Rhy. Fig. 1 (1 1/2 times)
E5
(B5)
B5
(F♯)
C♯m7
(G♯m)
5. The way you can cut a rug, watch-ing you's the on - ly drug I need. Some gang - sta, I'm so thug. You're the
Gtr. 2
let ring
Asus2
(E)
E5
(B5)
B5
(F♯)
on - ly one I'm dream - in' of. You see, I can be my - self now, fi - nal-ly. In fact, there's noth-in' I can't be.
let ring
Gtr. 1: w/ Rhy. Fig. 2
C♯m7
(G♯m)
Asus2
(E)
Bsus4
(F♯)
I want the world to see you'll be with me.
let ring
Chorus
Gtr. 1: w/ Rhy. Fig. 3 (5 times)
A
(E)
B
(F♯)
E
(B)
B
(F♯)
A
(E)
B
(F♯)
E5
(B)
Bsus4
(F♯)
Hey, soul - sis-ter, ain't that Mis-ter Mis-ter on the ra-di-o, ster-e-o? The way you move ain't fair, you know.

Gtr. 2: w/ Rhy. Fig. 4 (3 times)
Asus2 (E) Bsus4 (F♯) E5 (B) Bsus4 (F♯) Asus2 (E) Bsus4 (F♯) E5 (B) Bsus4 (F♯)
Hey, soul sis-ter, I don't wan-na miss a sin-gle thing you do to-night.
Gtrs. 1 & 2: w/ Rhy. Figs. 5 & 5A
Asus2 (E) Bsus4 (F♯) E5 (B) Bsus4 (F♯) Asus2 (E) Bsus4 (F♯)
Hey, soul sis-ter, I don't wan-na miss a sin-gle thing you do to-night.
1.
Outro
Gtr. 1: w/ Rhy. Fig. 1 (1 3/4 times)
E5 (B5) Bsus4 (F♯) C♯m7 (G♯m) Asus2 (E) Bsus4 (F♯)
Hey, hey, hey. to-night
Gtr. 2
2.
Asus2 (E) B (F♯) E5 (B5)
to-night.
Gtr. 1
Gtr. 2

from Orianthi - *Believe*

Highly Strung

Words and Music by Orianthi Panagaris and Steve Vai

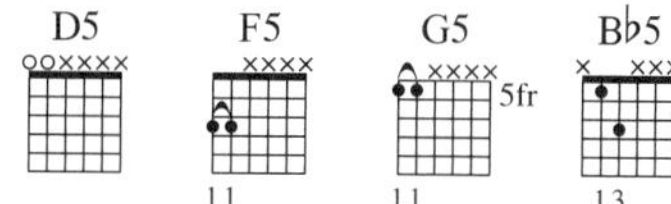

Drop D tuning:
(low to high) D-A-D-G-B-E

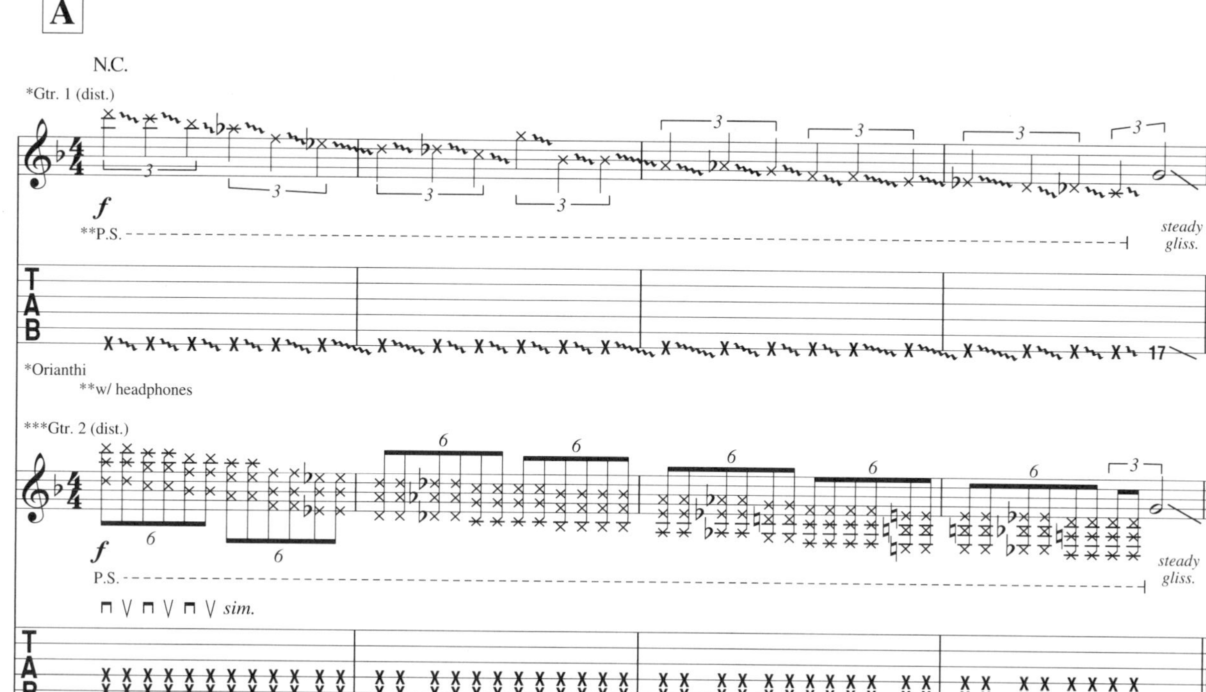

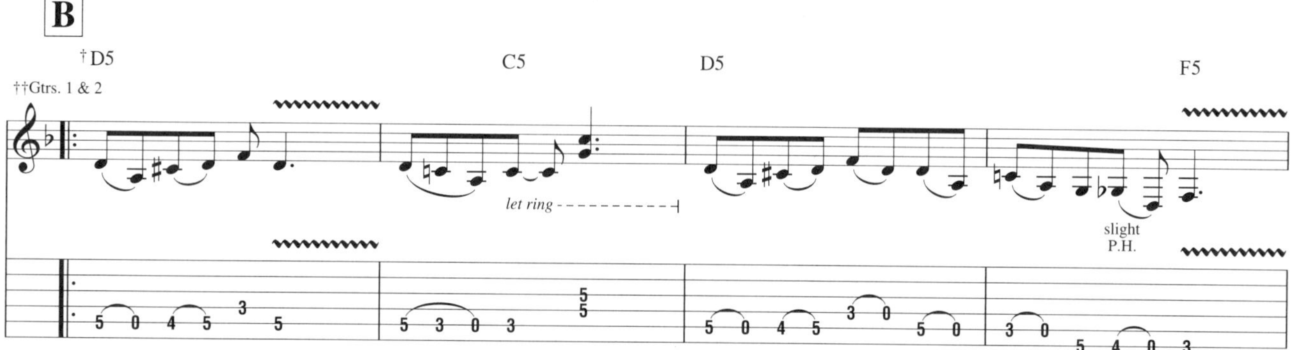

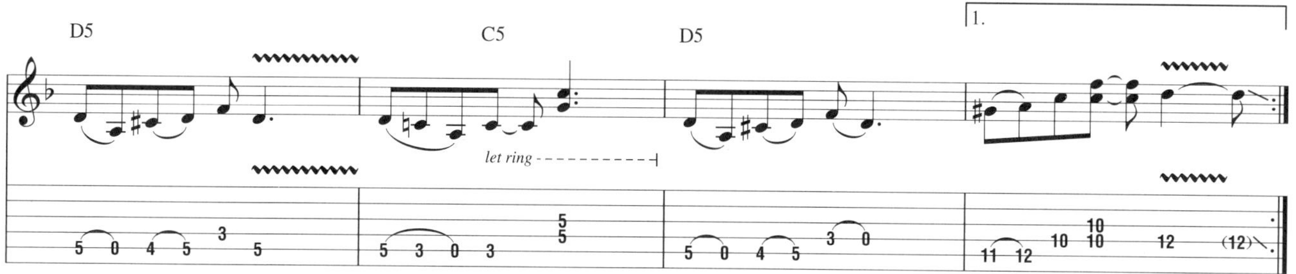

2.
G5
F5
Gtr. 1
Gtr. 2
*Gtr. 3 (dist.)
Rhy. Fig. 1
End Rhy. Fig. 1
P.M.
*Doubled throughout
C
D5
N.C.
Rhy. Fig. 2
End Rhy. Fig. 2
P.M.

*See top of first page of song for chord diagrams pertaining to rhythm slashes.

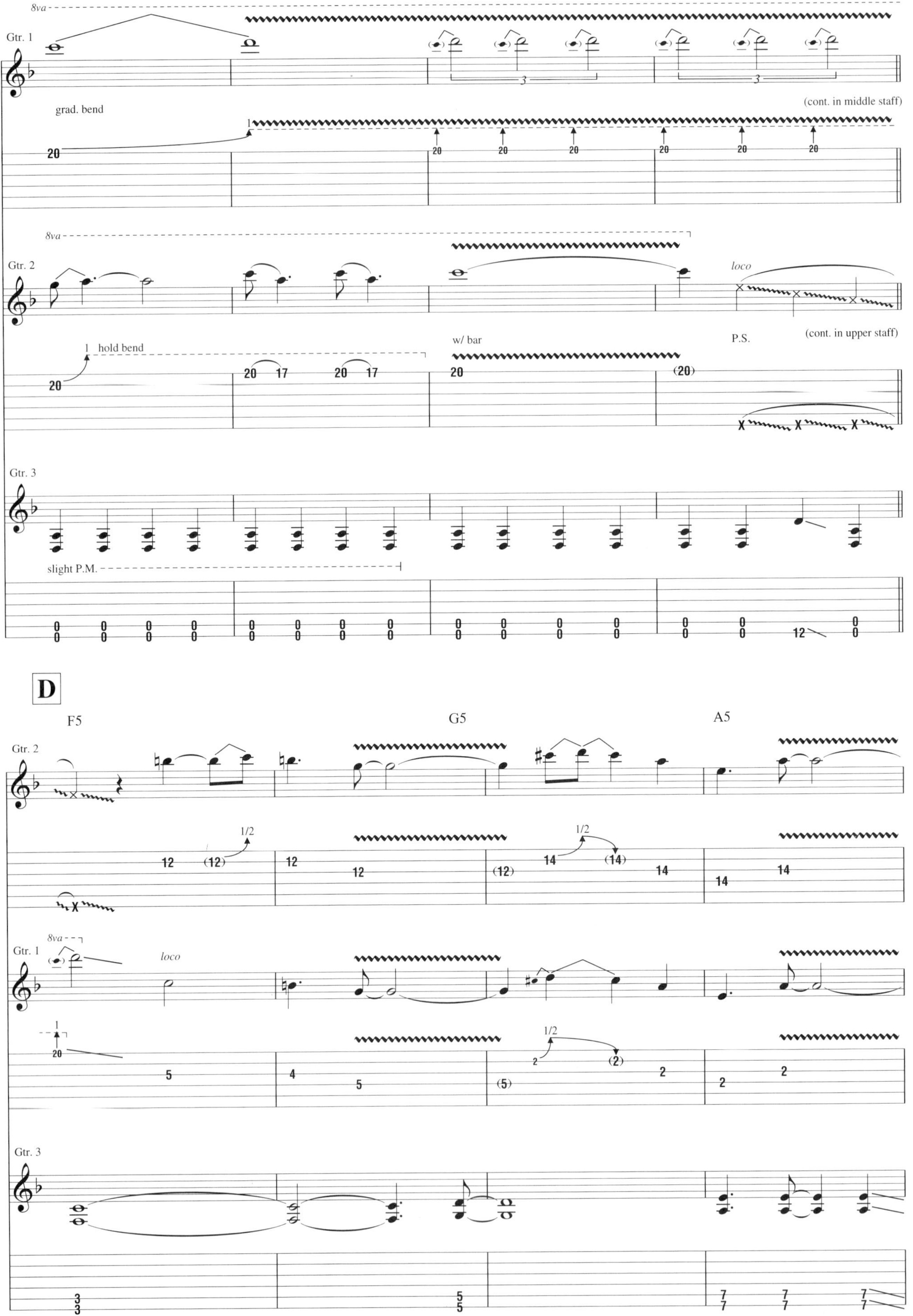
8va
Gtr. 1
grad. bend
(cont. in middle staff)
8va
Gtr. 2
loco
1 hold bend
w/ bar
P.S.
(cont. in upper staff)
Gtr. 3
slight P.M.
D
F5
G5
A5
Gtr. 2
Gtr. 1
8va
loco
Gtr. 3

2nd time, Gtr. 1: w/ Fill 1
E♭5
B♭5
C5
F5
G5
A5
B♭5
Fill 1
Gtr. 1

E
C5 D5 C5 D5 C5 D5 C5 D5 C5 D5 C5 D5
w/ wah-wah
Rhy. Fig. 3
To Coda
C5 D5 C5 D5 C5 D5 C5 D5 C5 D5
8va
Gtrs. 1 & 2
loco
wah-off
Gtr. 3
End Rhy. Fig. 3
F
Gtr. 3 tacet
D5 C5 D5 F5
Gtrs. 1 & 2
let ring

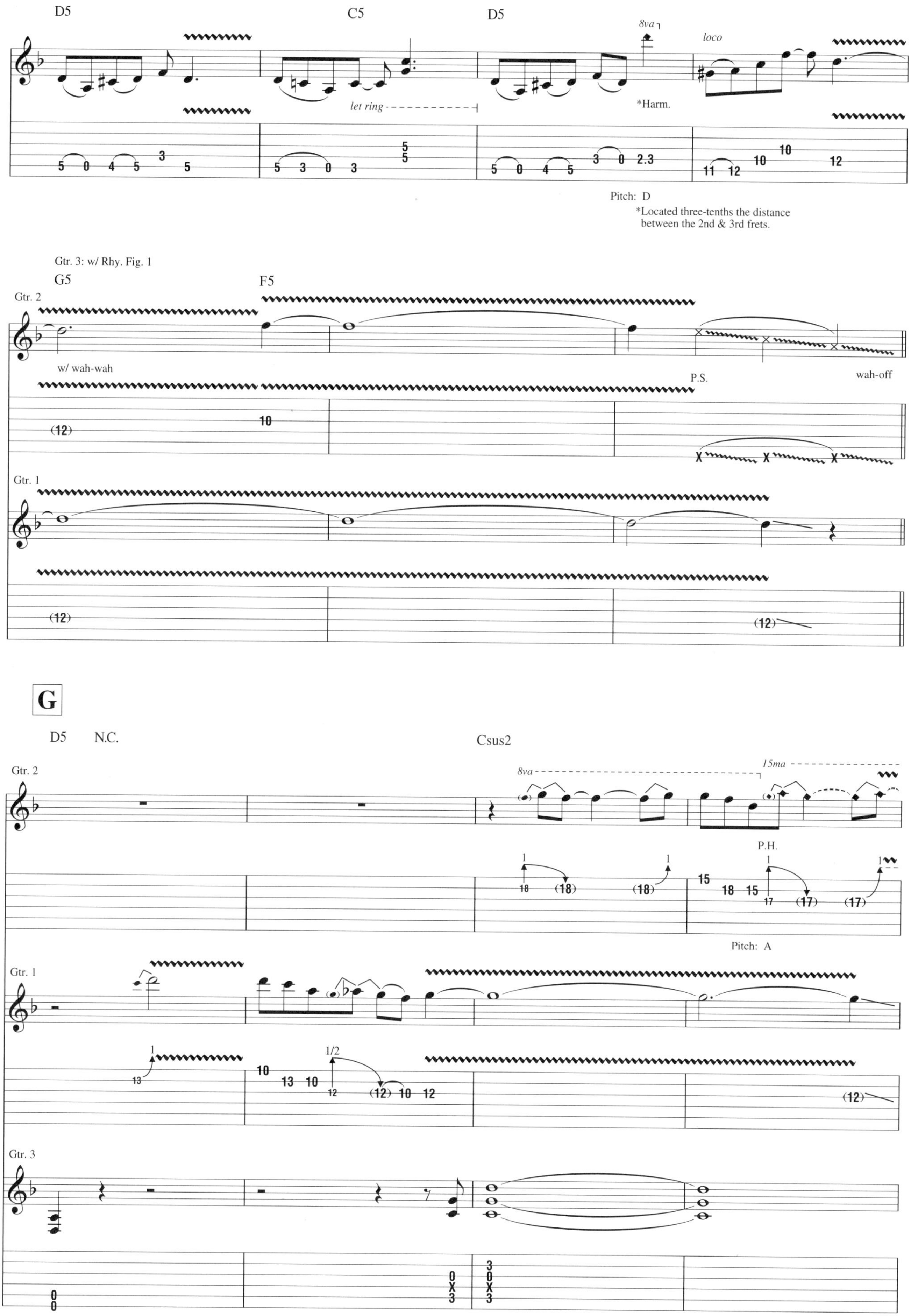

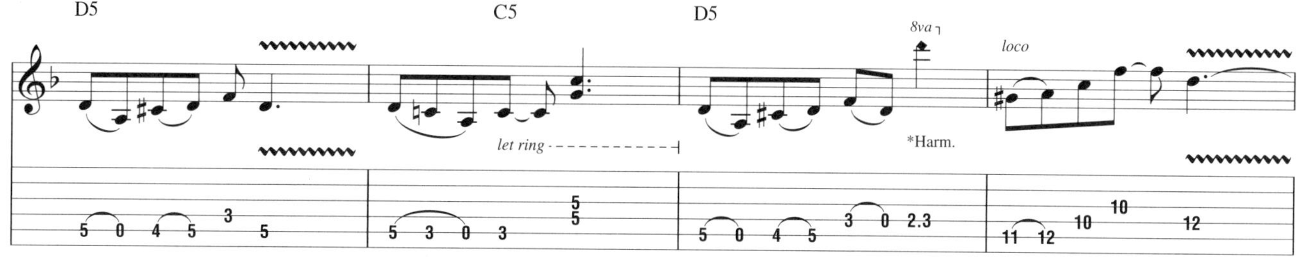

*Located three-tenths the distance between the 2nd & 3rd frets.

Gtr. 3: w/ Rhy. Fig. 1

G5 F5

Gtr. 2

w/ wah-wah

P.S.

wah-off

Gtr. 1

G

D5 N.C. Csus2

Gtr. 2

8va

15ma

P.H.

Pitch: A

Gtr. 1

Gtr. 3

D5
N.C.
Fsus2
15ma
8va
w/ bar
P.M.
let ring
let ring
grad. bend
D5
N.C.
B♭sus2
8va
loco
15ma
*Tap strings w/ edge of pick above bridge pickup, gradually descending toward nut, while muting all strings w/ fret hand.
8va
15ma
**Tap strings w/ edge of pick above fretboard, gradually ascending toward bridge, while muting all strings w/ fret-hand.

D5
loco
C5
loco
A5
C5
Am
8va
1/2
1
let ring

H
F5
G5
8va
let ring
steady gliss.
A5
E♭5
B♭5
C5
w/ bar
P.M.
(cont. in slashes)

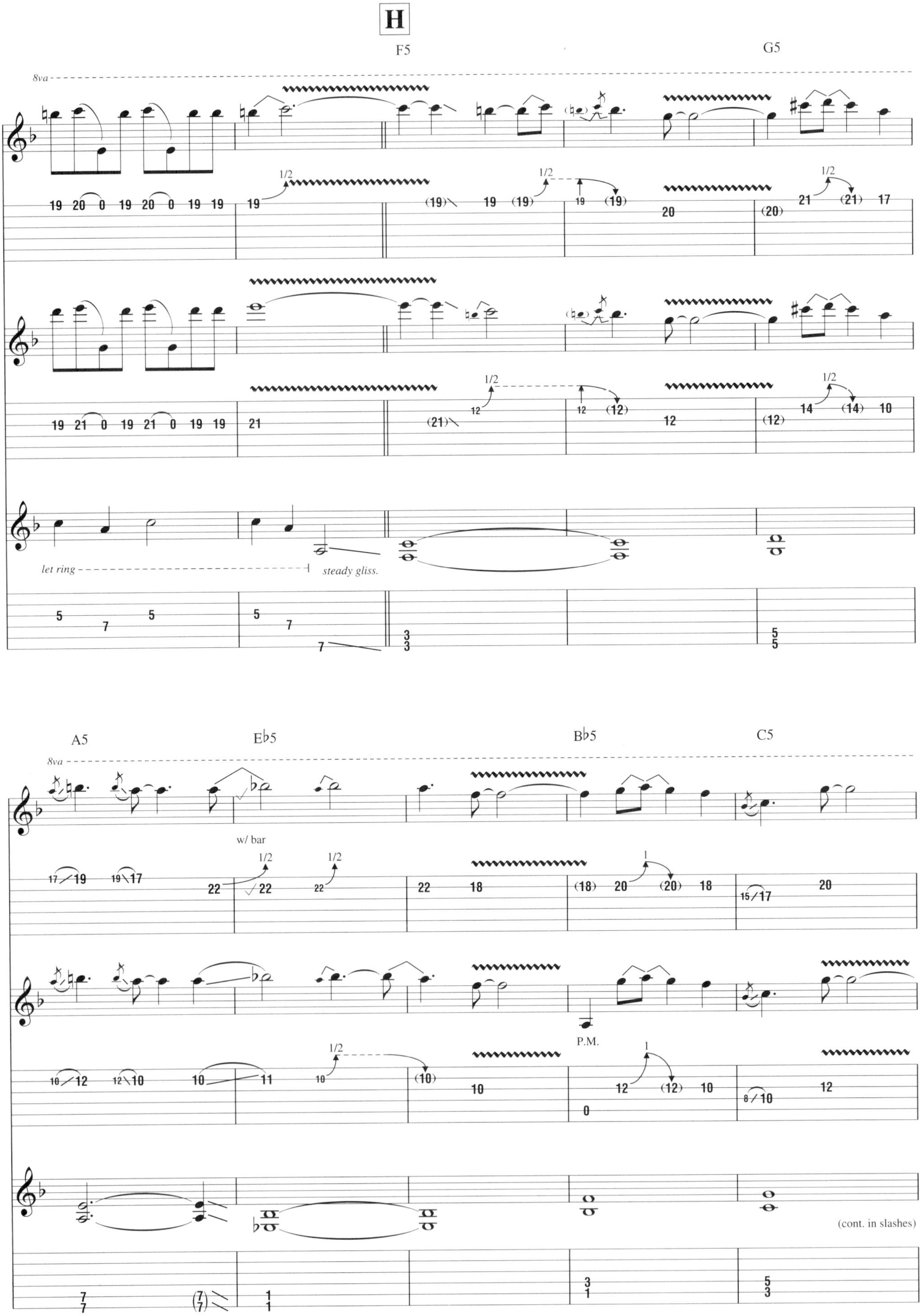

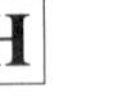

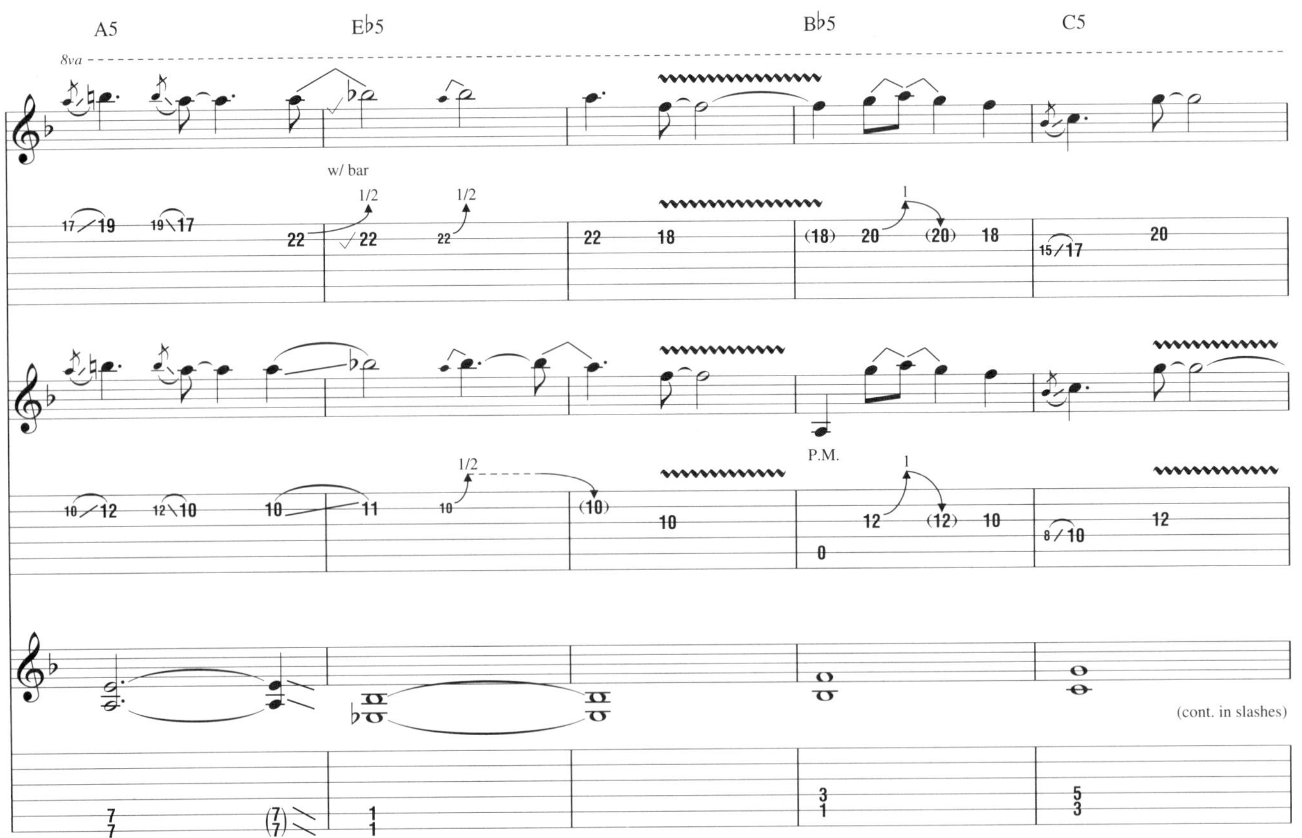

F5
G5
B♭5
Gtr. 3
8va
Gtr. 2
loco
w/ bar
1/2
Gtr. 1
1
I
Gtr. 3: w/ Rhy. Fig. 3
C5
D5
Gtrs. 1 & 2
w/ wah-wah
N.C.
P.S.
steady gliss.
wah-off
J
Gtr. 2 tacet
E5
Fmaj7(no3rd)
Rhy. Fig. 4
End Rhy. Fig. 4
let ring

Gtr. 3: w/ Rhy. Fig. 4 (2 times)
E5
D5
E5
Fmaj7(no3rd)
Gtr. 1
rake
semi P.H.
1/2
P.M.
semi P.H.
E5
D5
E5
Fmaj7(no3rd)
D5
P.M.
P.H.
P.M.
P.M.
P.M.
P.H.
P.M.
P.H.
Pitch: C♯
E5
D5
E5
Fmaj7(no3rd)
Gtr. 1
Rhy. Fig. 5
End Rhy. Fig. 5
Gtr. 3
let ring
K
Gtr. 1 tacet
G5
Fsus2
G5
Amaj7(no3rd)
Gtr. 2
w/ wah-wah
w/ bar
w/ bar
w/ bar
+1/2
-1
Rhy. Fig. 6
End Rhy. Fig. 6
Gtr. 3
let ring

Gtr. 3: w/ Rhy. Fig. 6 (2 times)
G5
Fsus2
Ab maj7(no3rd)
Gtr. 2
8va
loco
P.H.
let ring
steady gliss.
fdbk.
wah-off
Gtr. 3
L
Gtr. 2 tacet
Gtr. 3: w/ Rhy. Fig. 4 (3 times)
E5
D5
Fmaj7(no3rd)
Gtr. 1
w/ bar

E5
D5
E5
Fmaj7(no3rd)
D5
8va
grad. release
Gtr. 3: w/ Rhy. Fig. 5
loco
M
Gtr. 1 tacet
G5
G5
Gtr. 1
Gtr. 2
P.H.
w/ bar
w/ bar
Pitch: B A
Rhy. Fig. 7
End Rhy. Fig. 7
Gtr. 3
let ring
Gtr. 3: w/ Rhy. Fig. 7 (3 times)
G5
G5
Harm.
w/ bar
flutter bar

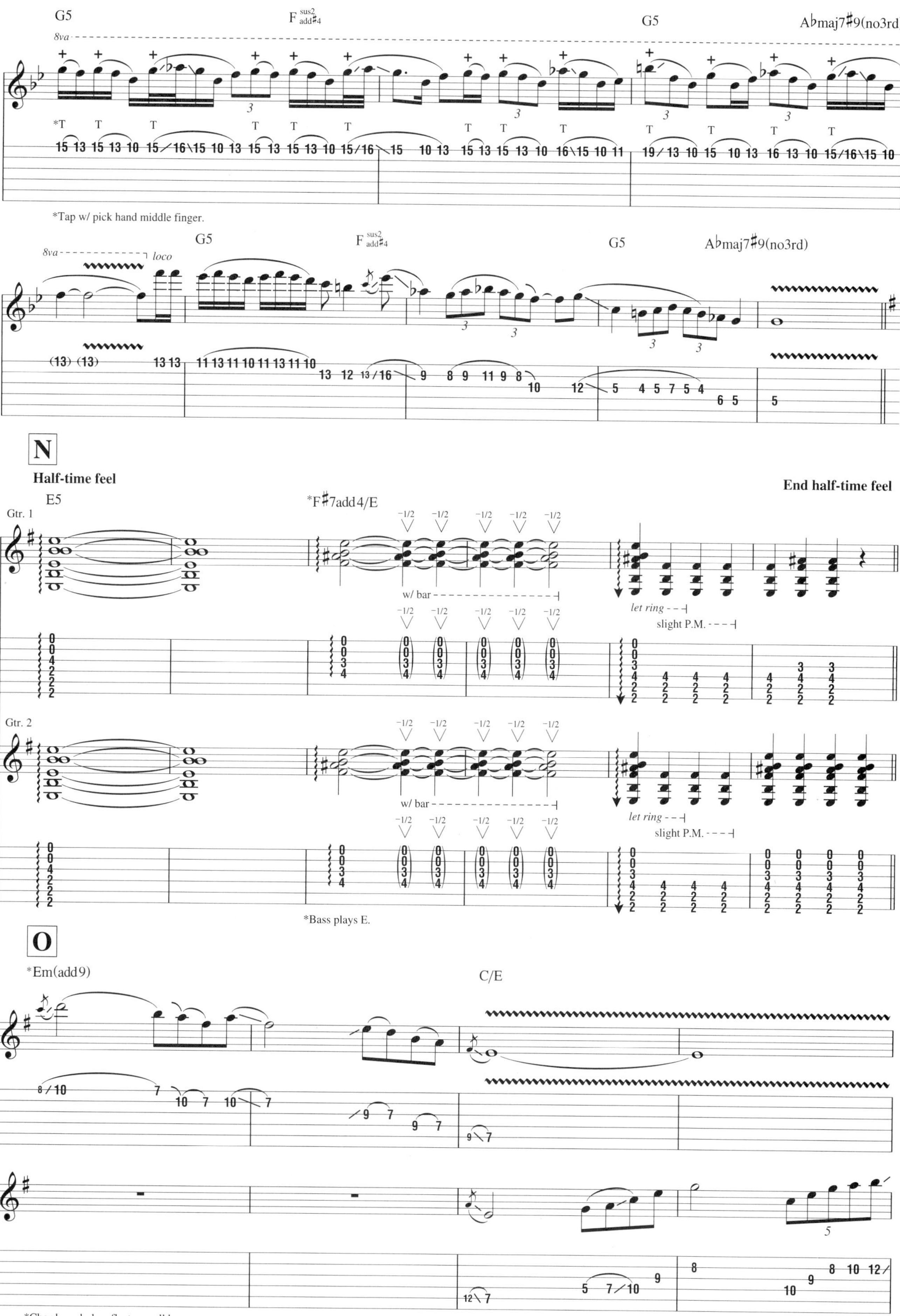
G5
F sus2 add♯4
G5
A♭maj7♯9(no3rd)
8va
*T
*Tap w/ pick hand middle finger.
loco
N
Half-time feel
End half-time feel
E5
*F♯7add4/E
Gtr. 1
w/ bar
let ring
slight P.M.
Gtr. 2
*Bass plays E.
O
*Em(add9)
C/E
*Chord symbols reflect overall harmony.

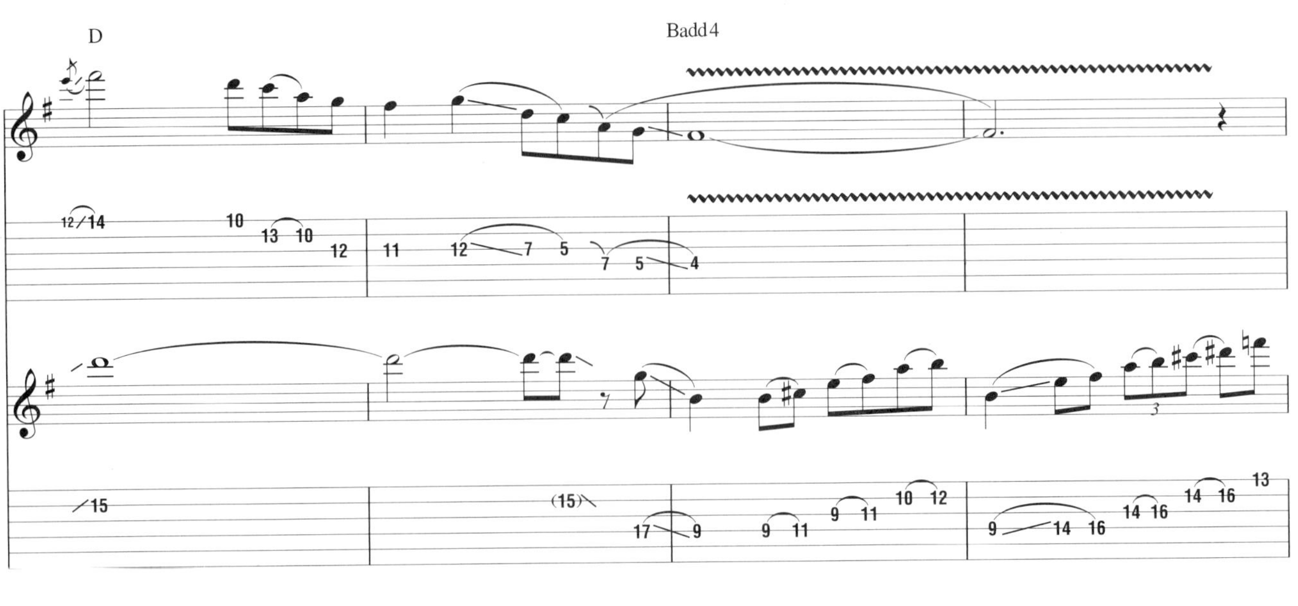

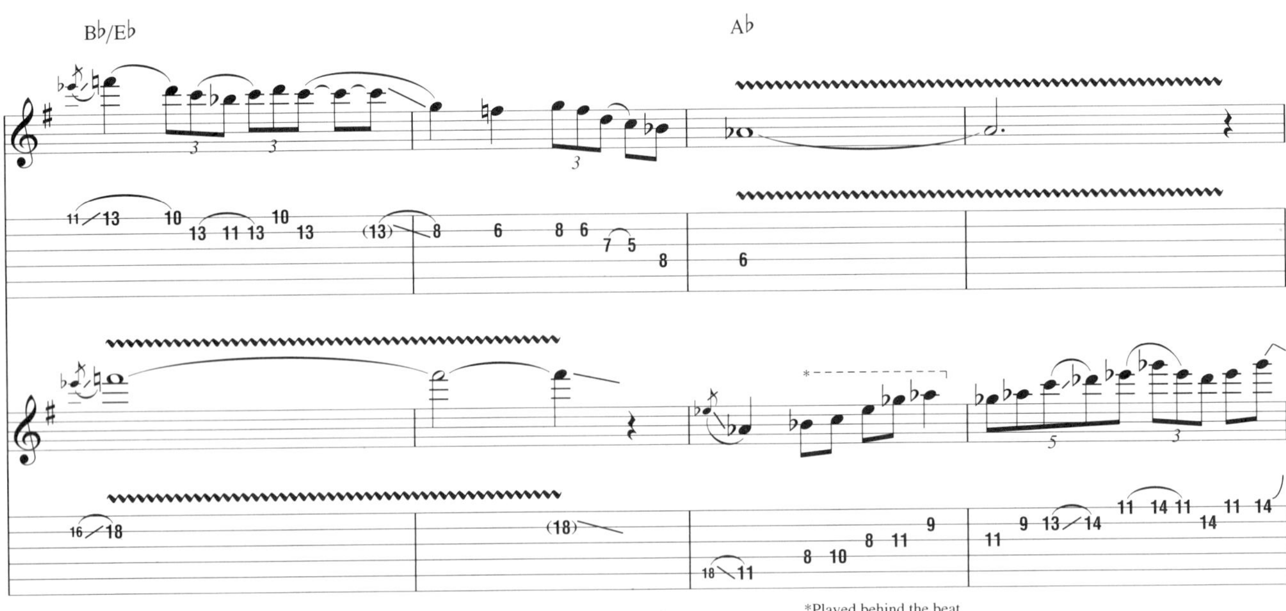

*Played behind the beat.

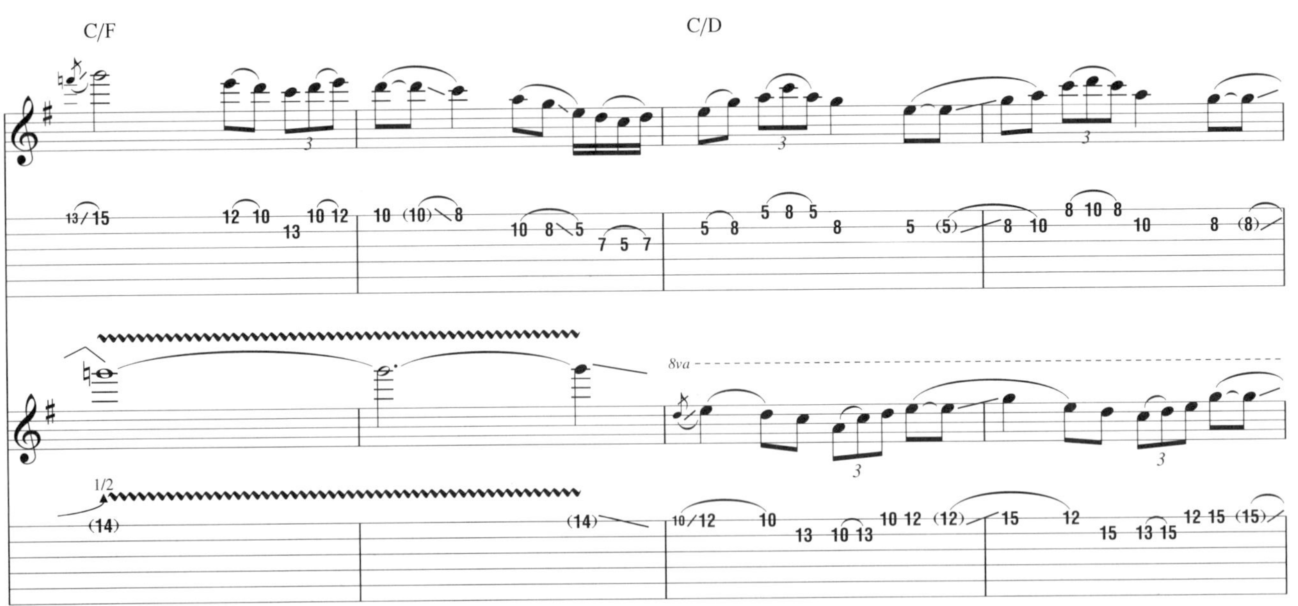

D.S. al Coda
8va
Coda
D5
C5
D5
F5
Gtrs. 1 & 2
let ring
D5
C5
D5
8va
loco
let ring
Harm.
Pitch: D
N.C.
D5
N.C.
Gtr. 2
tr
Gtr. 1
tr

from Ray LaMontagne - *Trouble*

Hold You in My Arms

Words and Music by Ray LaMontagne and Ethan Johns

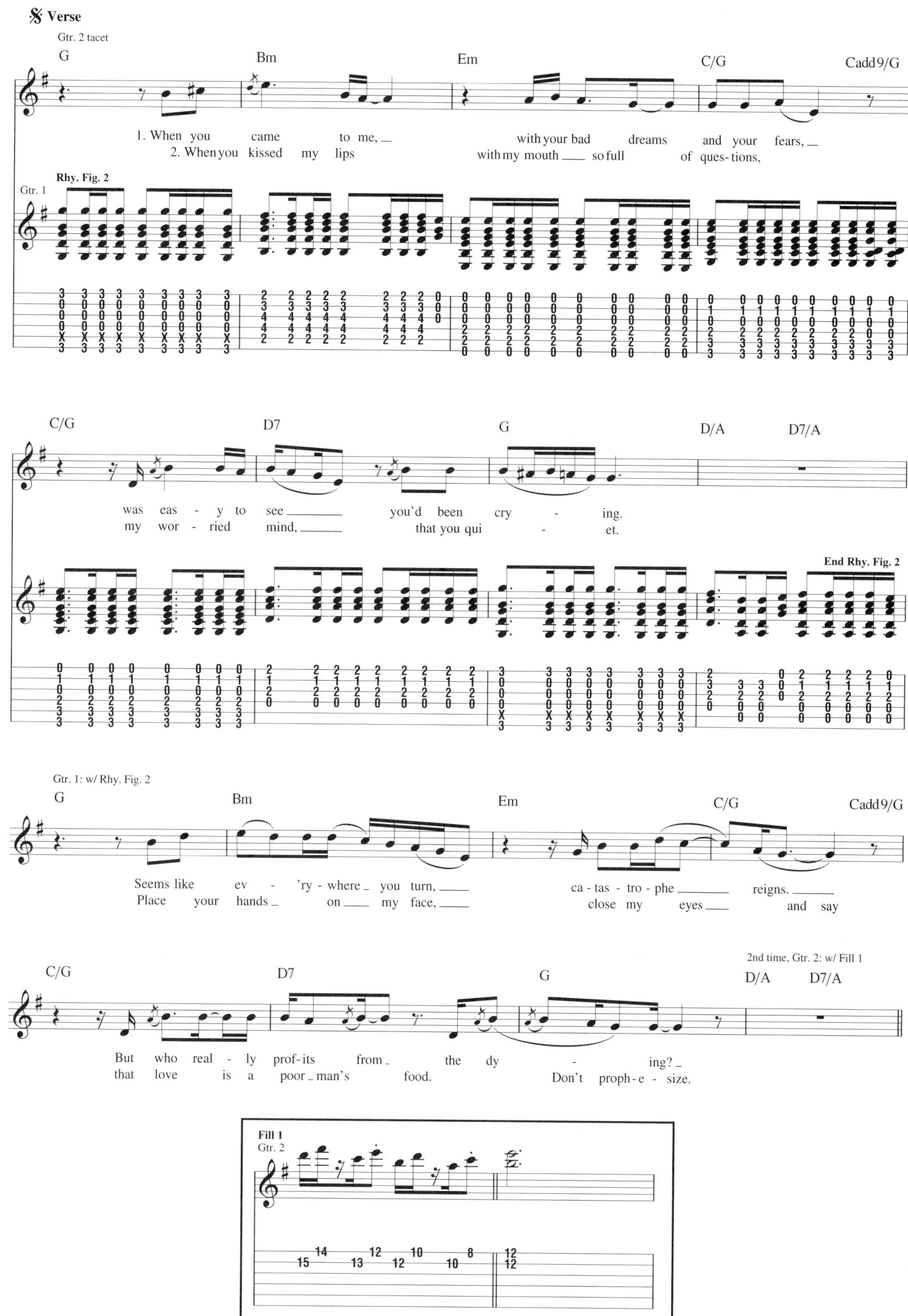

Verse
Gtr. 2 tacet
G Bm Em C/G Cadd9/G
1. When you came to me, with your bad dreams and your fears,
2. When you kissed my lips with my mouth so full of ques-tions,
Rhy. Fig. 2
Gtr. 1
C/G D7 G D/A D7/A
was eas - y to see you'd been cry - ing.
my wor - ried mind, that you qui - et.
End Rhy. Fig. 2
Gtr. 1: w/ Rhy. Fig. 2
G Bm Em C/G Cadd9/G
Seems like ev - 'ry - where you turn, ca - tas - tro - phe reigns.
Place your hands on my face, close my eyes and say
2nd time, Gtr. 2: w/ Fill 1
C/G D7 G D/A D7/A
But who real - ly prof - its from the dy - ing?
that love is a poor man's food. Don't proph - e - size.
Fill 1
Gtr. 2

𝄋𝄋 Chorus

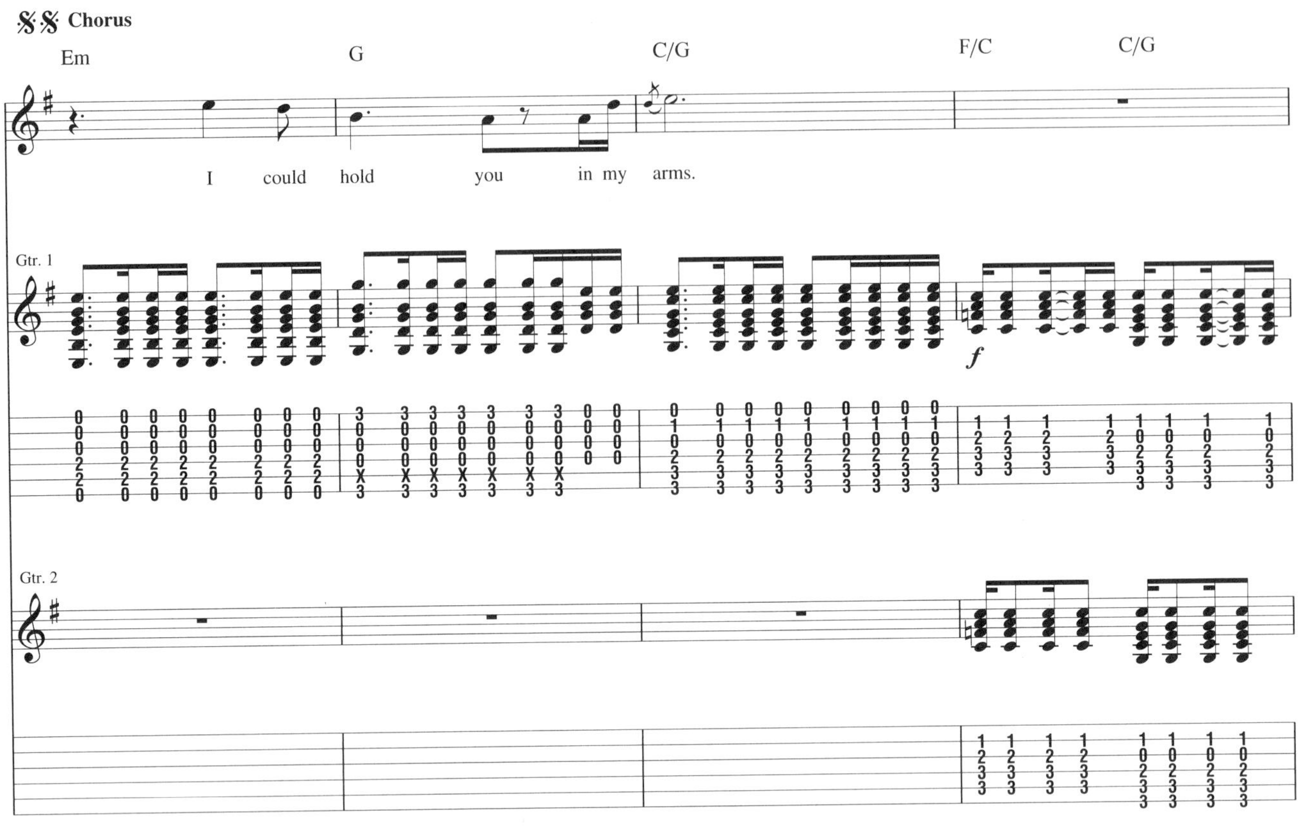

Em
G
C/G
F/C
C/G
I could hold you in my arms.
Gtr. 1
f
Gtr. 2

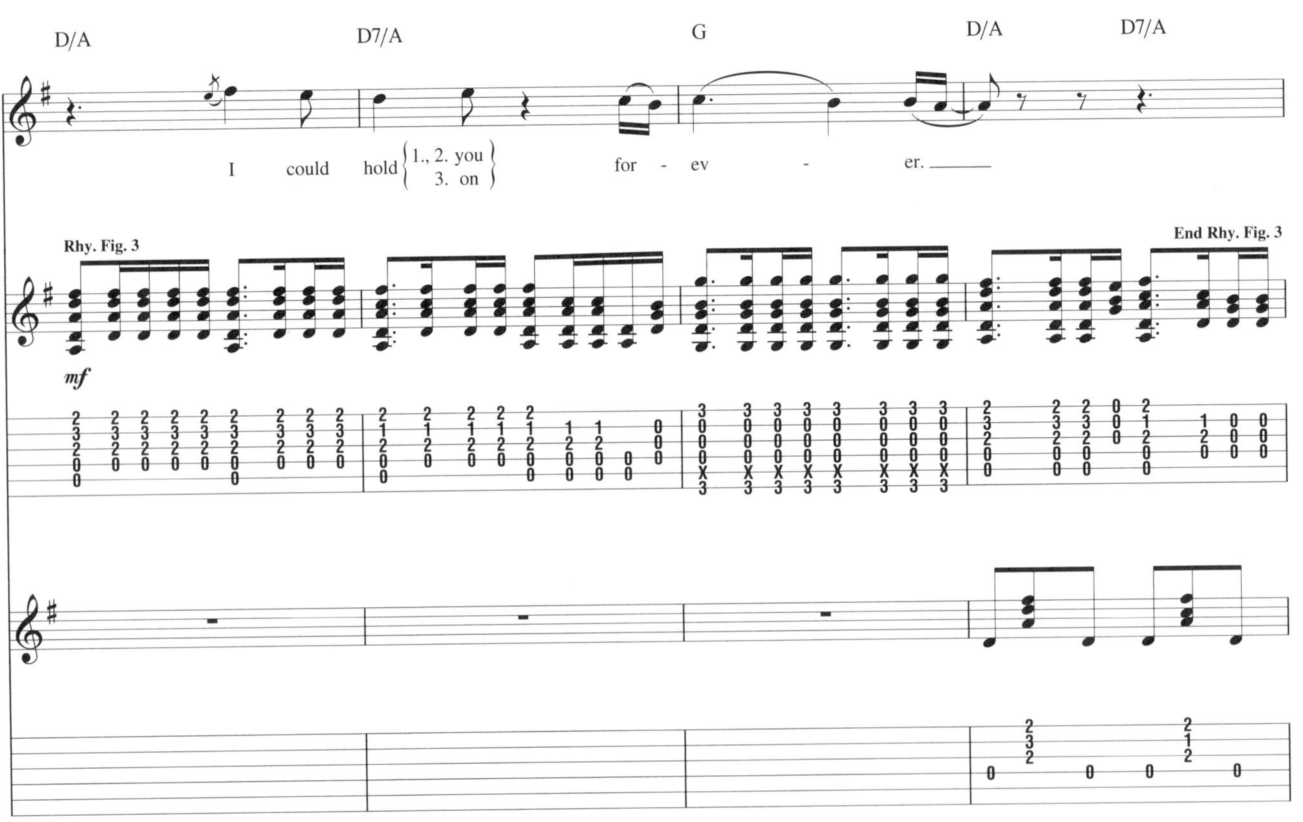

D/A
D7/A
G
D/A
D7/A
I could hold { 1., 2. you / 3. on } for - ev - er.
Rhy. Fig. 3
End Rhy. Fig. 3
mf

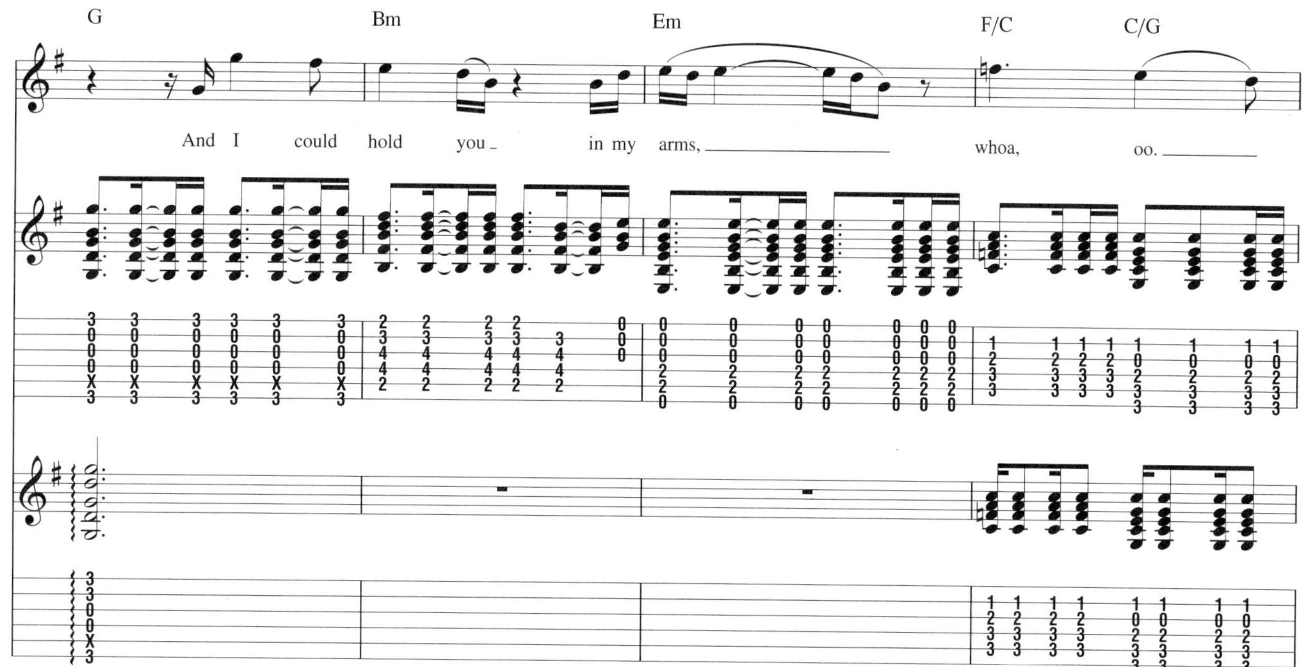

2nd time, To Coda 1

3rd time, To Coda 2

Gtr. 1: w/ Rhy. Fig. 3
2nd time, Gtr. 2: w/ Rhy. Fill 1
3rd time, Gtr. 2: w/ Rhy. Fill 2

1st time, Gtr. 2 tacet

D/A D7/A G D/A D7/A

I could hold {1., 2. you / 3. on} for - ev - er.

Gtr. 2

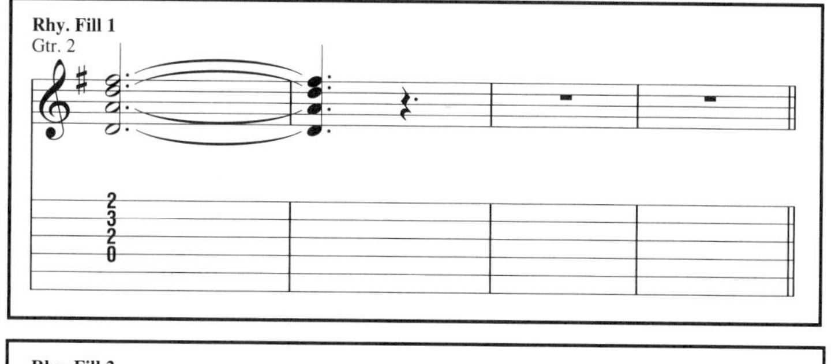

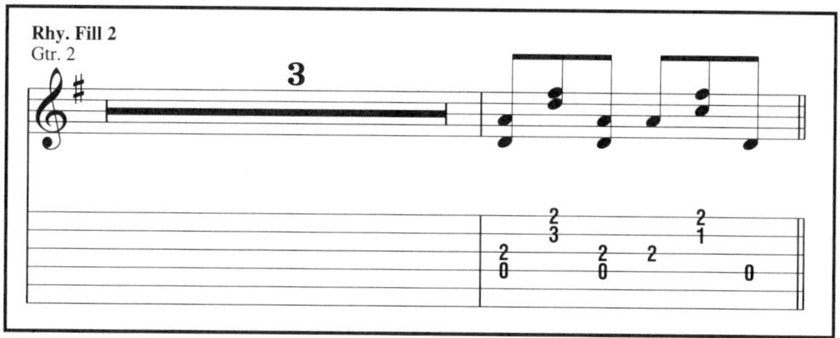

Interlude

D.S. al Coda 1

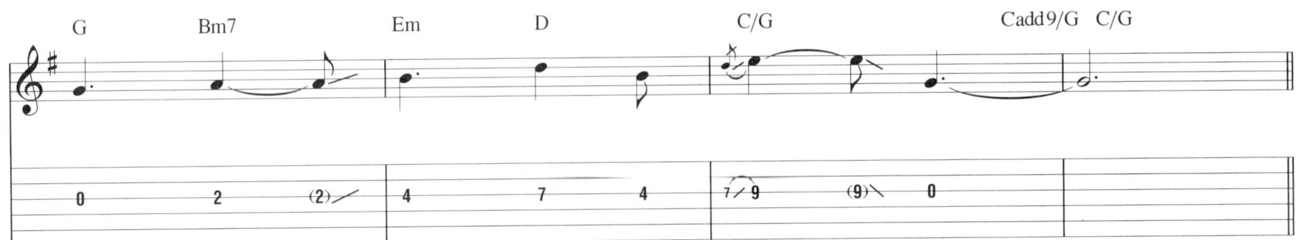

Coda 1

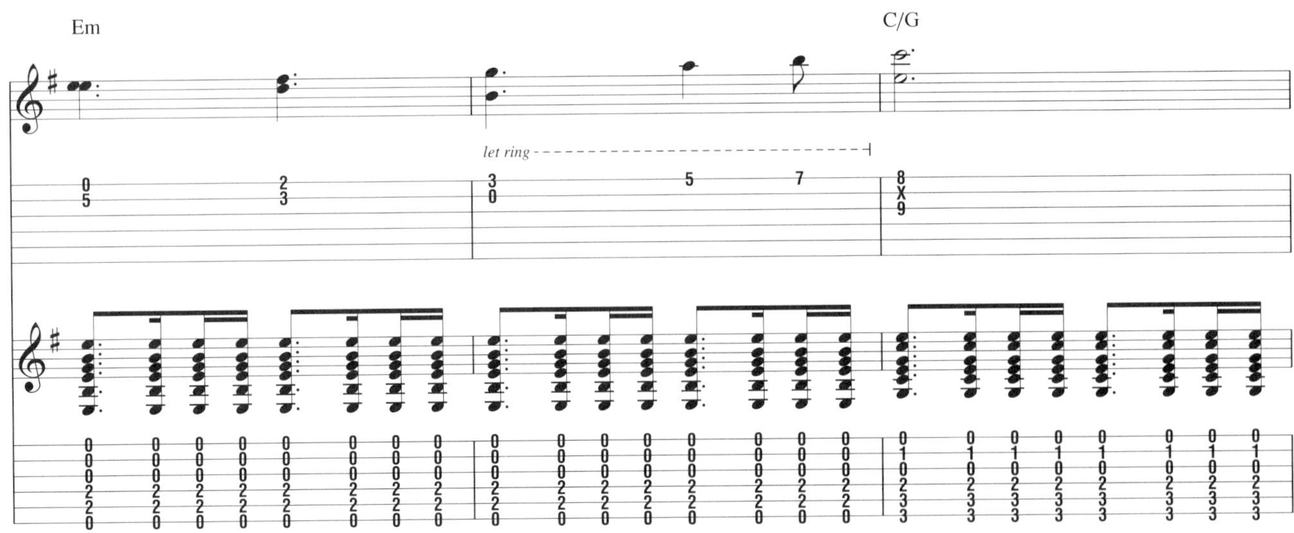

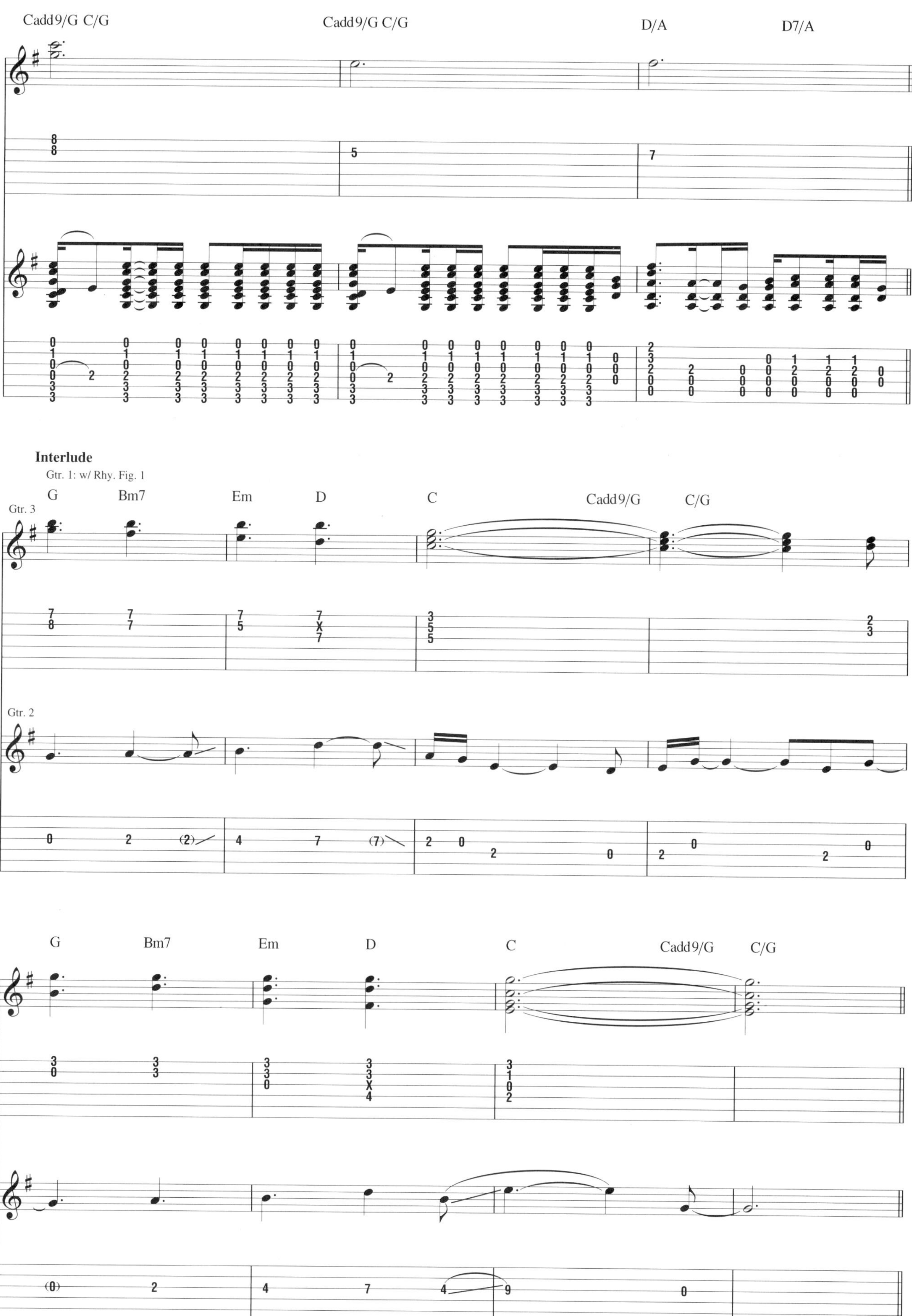
Cadd9/G C/G
Cadd9/G C/G
D/A
D7/A
Interlude
Gtr. 1: w/ Rhy. Fig. 1
G
Bm7
Em
D
C
Cadd9/G
C/G
Gtr. 3
Gtr. 2
G
Bm7
Em
D
C
Cadd9/G
C/G

Verse
Gtr. 1: w/ Rhy. Fig. 2 (2 times)
Gtr. 2 tacet
Gtr. 3 tacet
G
Bm
Em
C/G
Cadd9/G
3. So, now we see how it is as fist be - gets the spear.
Gtr. 3
C/G
D7
G
D/A
D7/A
Weap - ons of war, symp - toms of mad - ness.
Gtr. 2
G
Bm
Em
C/G
Cadd9/G
Don't let your eyes re - fuse to see.
Don't let your ears re - fuse to hear.
D.S.S. al Coda 2
C/G
D7
G
D/A
D7/A
You ain't nev - er gon - na shake this sense of sad - ness.

Coda 2

Outro

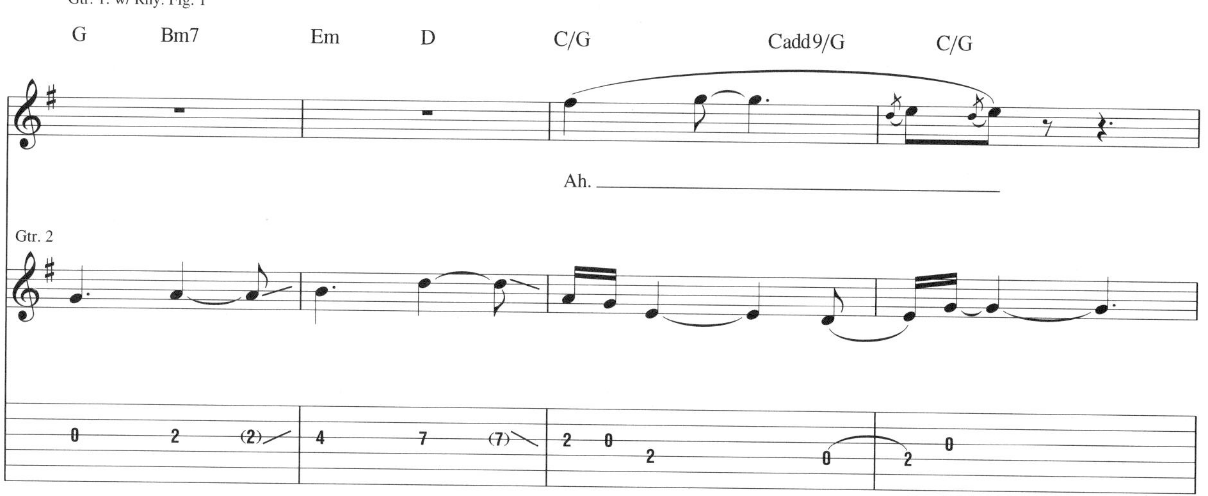

Gtr. 1: w/ Rhy. Fig. 1
G
Bm7
Em
D
C/G
Cadd9/G
C/G
Ah.
Gtr. 2

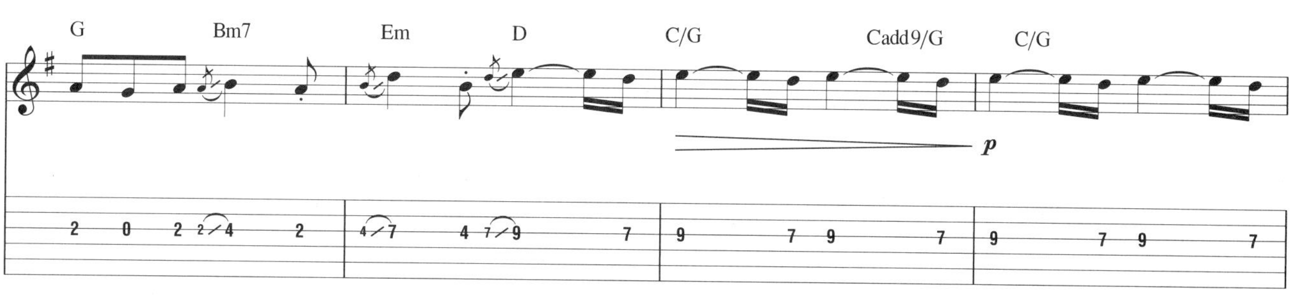

G
Bm7
Em
D
C/G
Cadd9/G
C/G
p

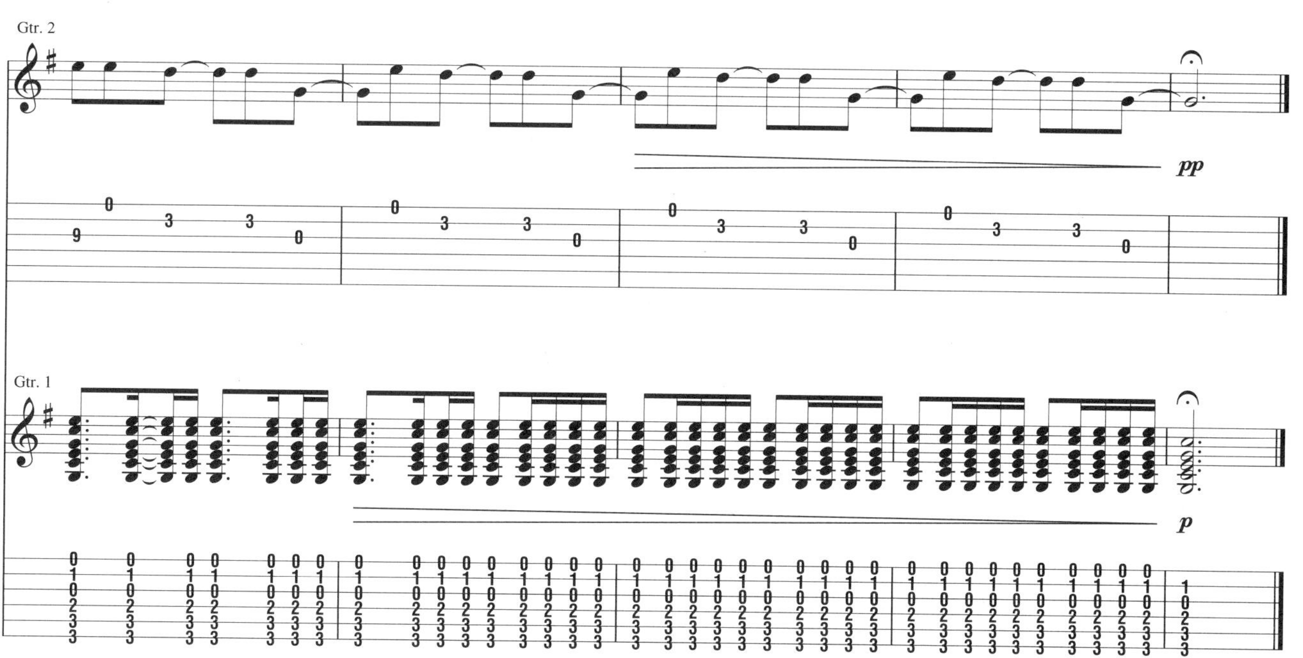

Gtr. 2
pp
Gtr. 1
p

from Stevie Ray Vaughan & Double Trouble - *Couldn't Stand the Weather*

Honey Bee

Written by Stevie Ray Vaughan

Chorus
A5 A6 A5 A6 G5 A5 A6 G5 A5 A6 G
buzz me all the time. 'Cause the way we kiss just can't miss;
real-ly groove me ba-by when you move your hips;
A5 A6 A5 A6 G5 A5 A6 A5 A6 G6 A5 A6 A5 A6 G
don't make me wait to feel your warm em-brace. Each and ev-'ry time
shake it all a-round, it takes me pound for pound. I want you all the time
A5 A6 G5 A5 (A6) G5 B5/F# N.C.
To Coda
that we get the chance, c-'mon, lit-tle ba-by, let's ah make some ro-mance.
just be-cause, you know you real-ly have give me a buzz.
Guitar Solo
E7
f

A
full
1/2
1/2

E7
B7
full
1/2
1/2
1/2
1/4

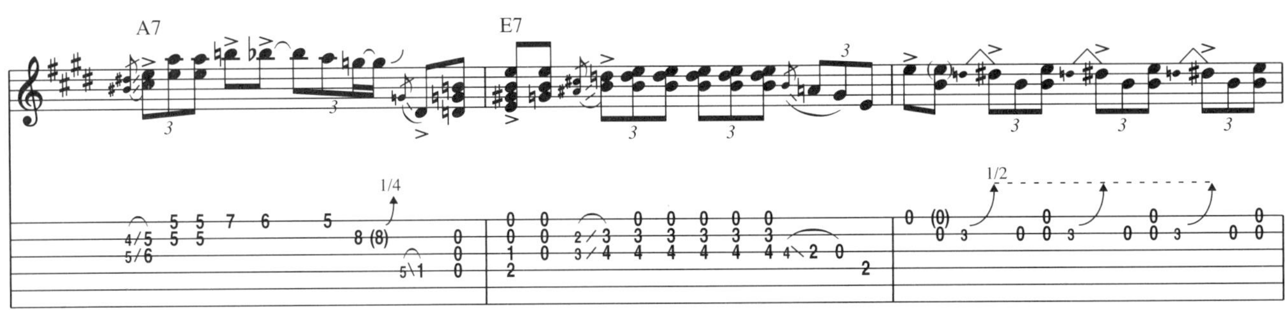
A7
E7
1/4
1/2

A7
E7
1/2
full

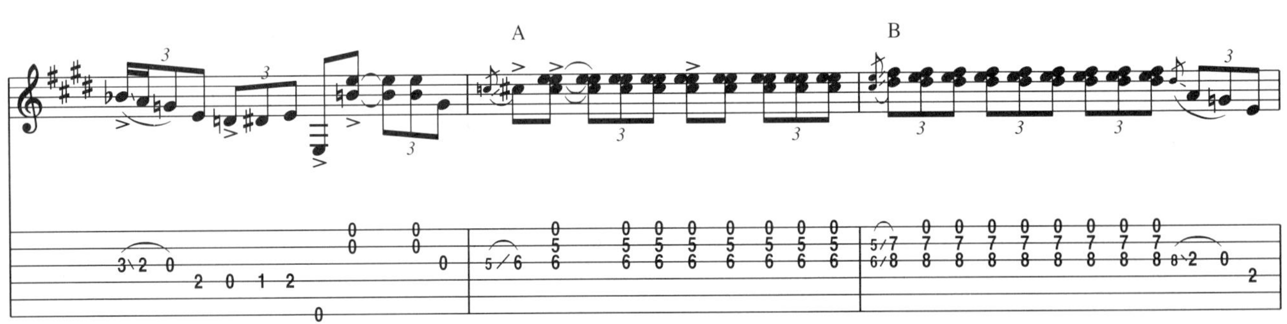
A
B

E
D.S. al Coda
Yeah, you
1/2
tr

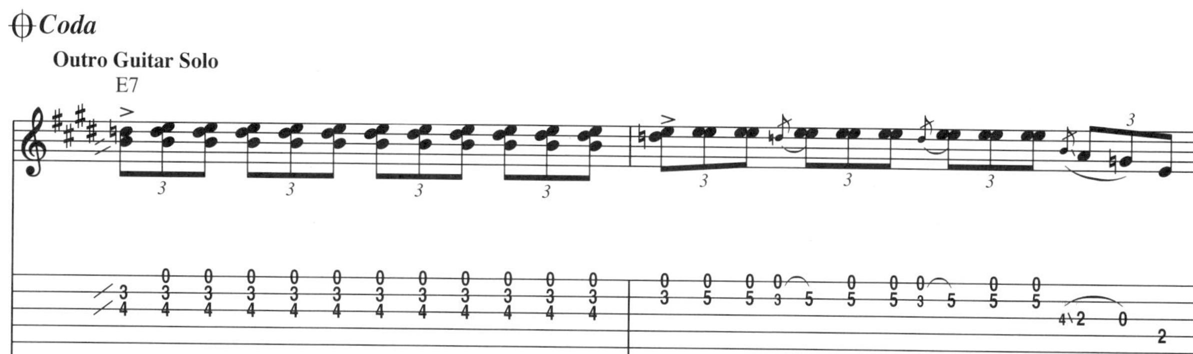
Coda
Outro Guitar Solo
E7

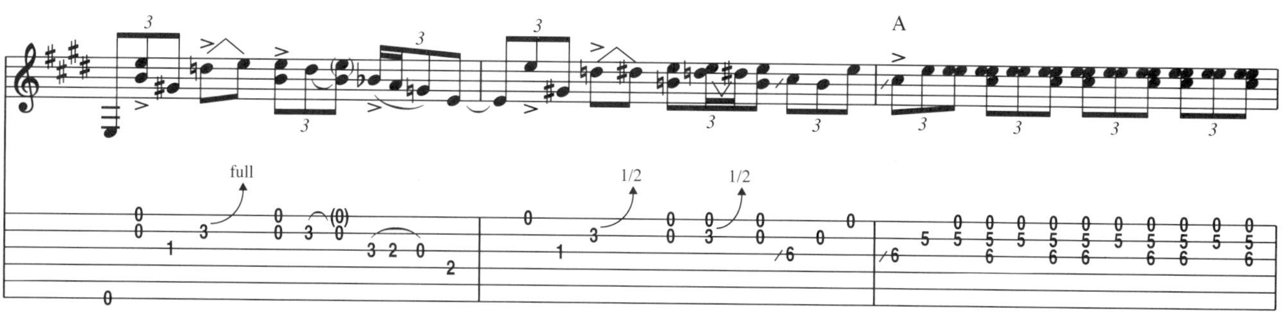
A
full
1/2
1/2

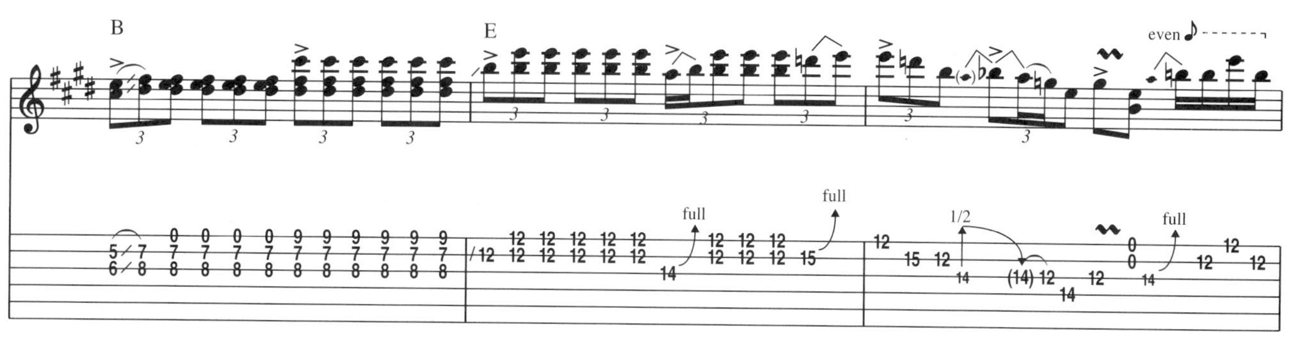
B
E
even
full
full
1/2
full

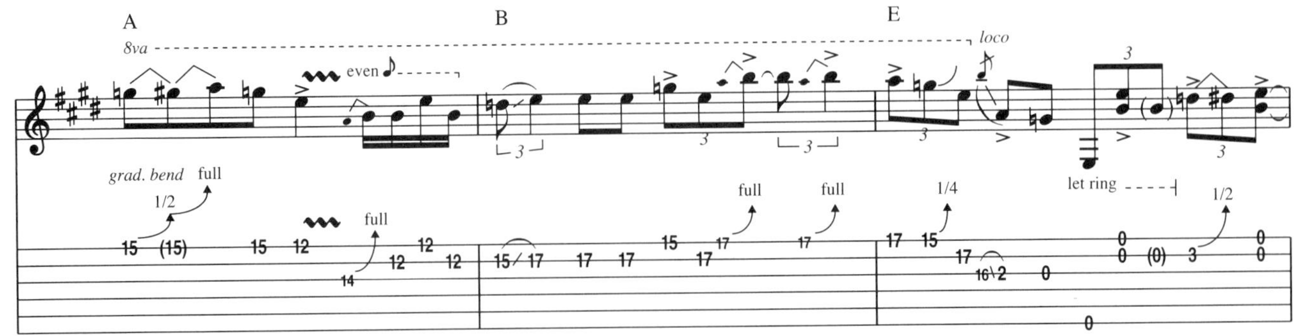
A
B
E
8va
loco
even
grad. bend
full
1/2
full
full
full
1/4
let ring
1/2

A
B
hold bend
let ring
full
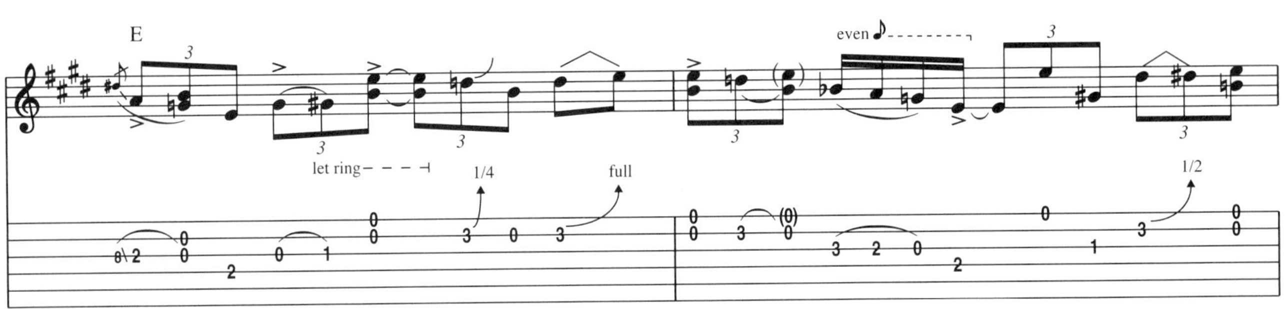
E
even
let ring
1/4
full
1/2
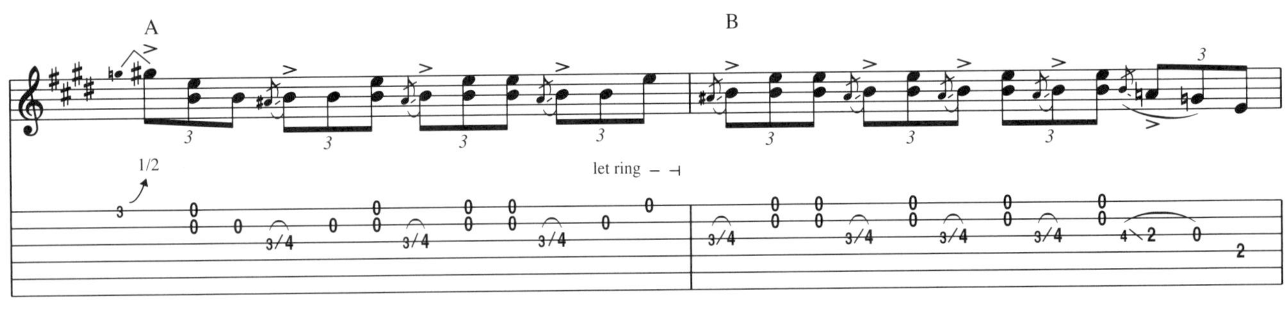
A
B
1/2
let ring
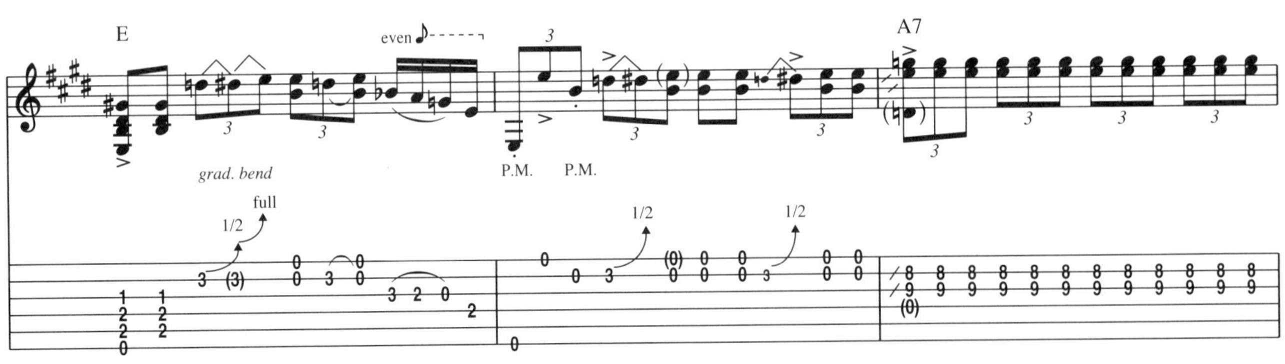
E
even
A7
grad. bend
full
1/2
P.M.
P.M.
1/2
1/2

B7
E7
A
8va
loco
B
E
even
let ring
A7
B7
E7
P.M.
F6/9
E6/9

from Carl Lee Perkins - *Best of the Best*

Honey Don't

Words and Music by Carl Lee Perkins

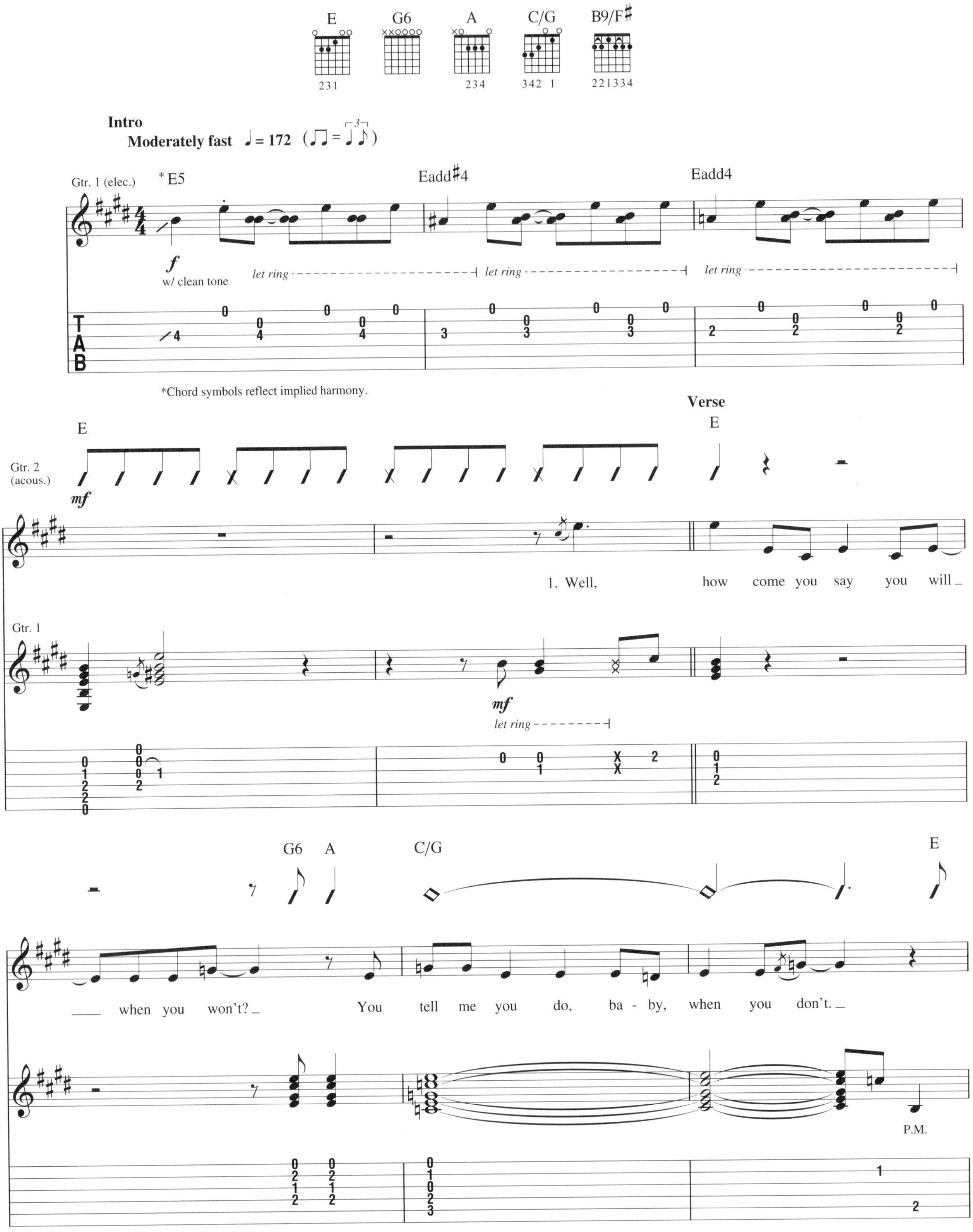

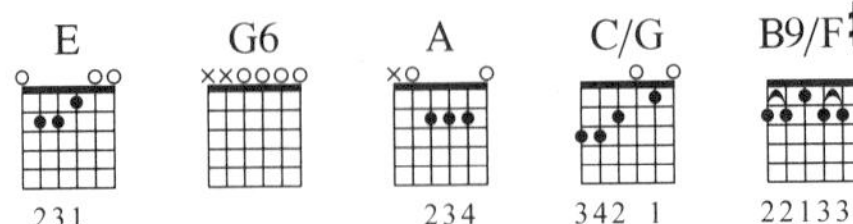

Intro

Gtr. 1 (elec.) *E5 Eadd♯4 Eadd4

f w/ clean tone let ring

*Chord symbols reflect implied harmony.

E — Gtr. 2 (acous.) *mf*

Verse

E

1. Well, how come you say you will_ _ when you won't?_ You tell me you do, ba - by, when you don't._

Gtr. 1 *mf* let ring

G6 A C/G E

P.M.

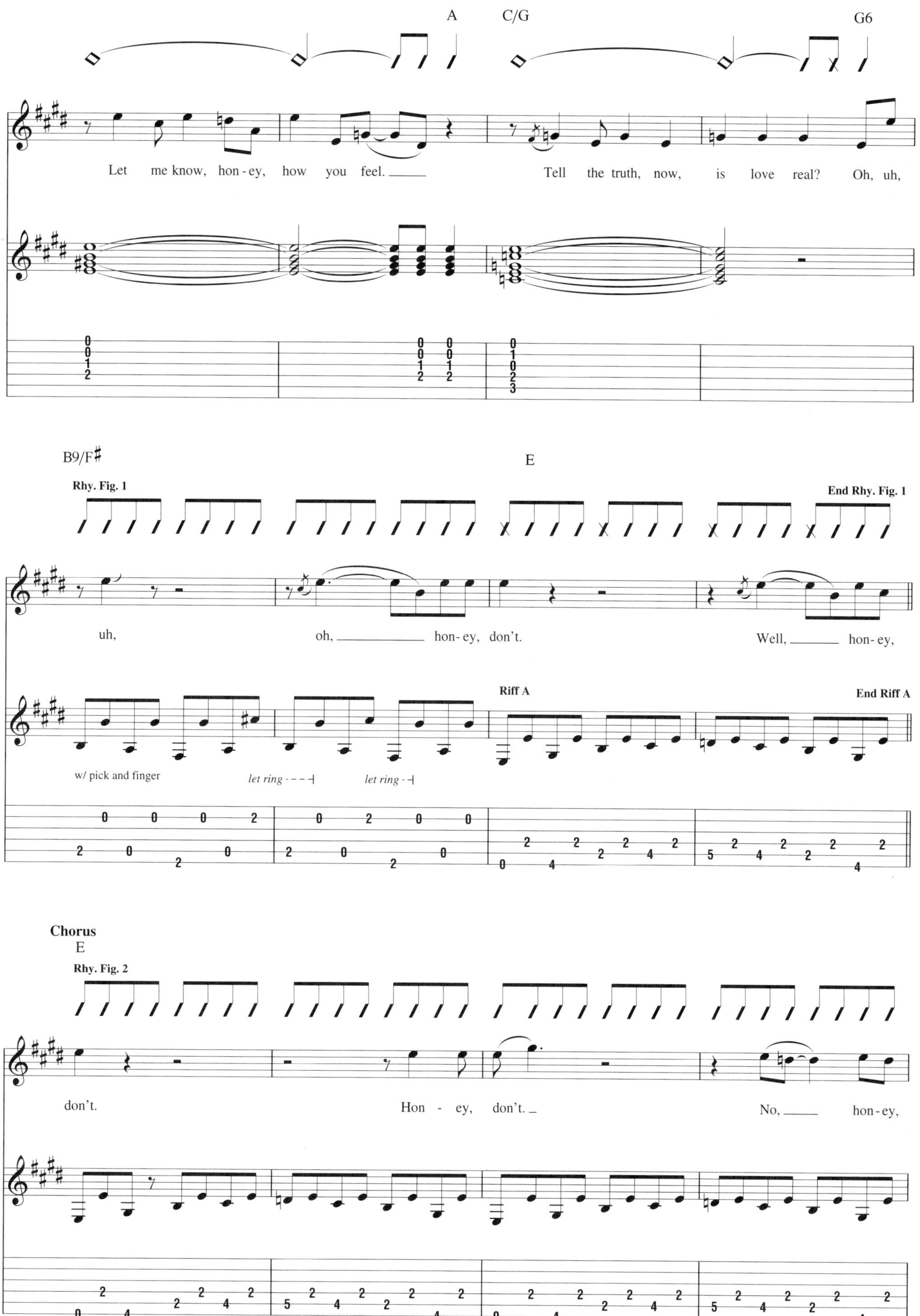

A
C/G
G6
Let me know, hon-ey, how you feel.
Tell the truth, now, is love real? Oh, uh,
B9/F♯
E
Rhy. Fig. 1
End Rhy. Fig. 1
uh,
oh,
hon-ey, don't.
Well,
hon-ey,
Riff A
End Riff A
w/ pick and finger
let ring
let ring
Chorus
E
Rhy. Fig. 2
don't.
Hon - ey, don't.
No,
hon-ey,

A
E
don't.
Hey, honey, don't
say you
Riff B
End Riff B
B9/F♯
E
End Rhy. Fig. 2
will when you won't. Huh, ah, honey, don't.
2. Well, I
Verse
E
A
Gtr. 1 tacet
C/G
G6
(cont. in notation)
love you baby, and you ought to know
I like the way that you wear your clothes.

E
G6
C/G N.C.
C/G G6
Ev-'ry-thing a-bout you is so dog - gone sweet. You got that sand all o - ver your feet, so uh,
Gtr. 2

Gtr. 2: w/ Rhy. Fig. 1
B9/F♯
E
Chorus
Gtr. 1: w/ Riff A (2 times)
Gtr. 2: w/ Rhy. Fig. 2
E
ah, hey, hon-ey don't. Hon - ey, don't.
Gtr. 1

Gtr. 1: w/ Riff B
A
Well, hon - ey, don't. Huh, ah, hon - ey, don't.

E
B9/F♯
Hon - ey, don't say you will when you won't. Huh,
Gtr. 1

E
ah, honey, don't. Hang on, children, let's rock now!

Guitar Solo

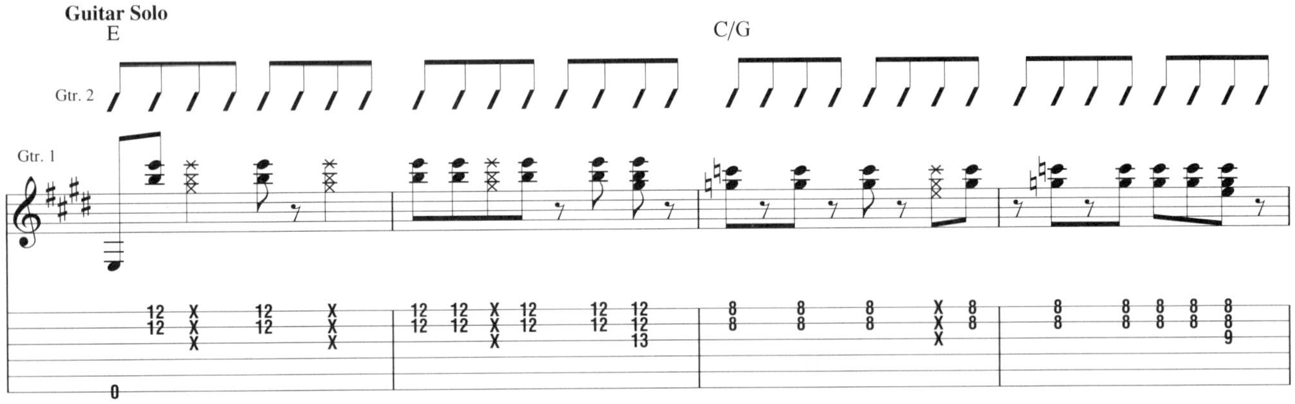
E
C/G
Gtr. 2
Gtr. 1

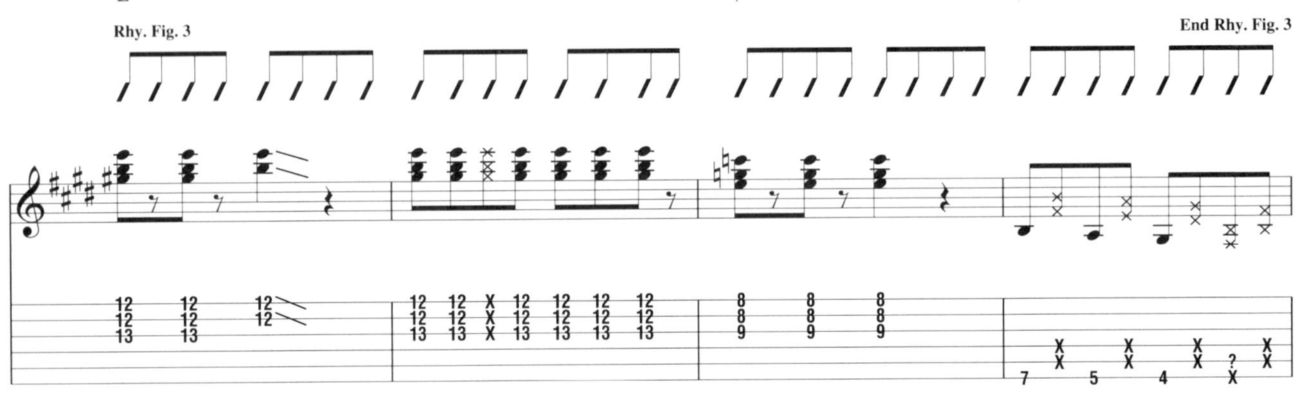
E
C/G
B9/F♯
Rhy. Fig. 3
End Rhy. Fig. 3

Gtr. 2: w/ Rhy. Fig. 2
E
Oh, honey, don't.
Gtr. 1
P.M.

A
E
B7/F♯
E
3. Well, ___
1/4
Verse
E
G6
C/G
G6
Rhy. Fig. 4
End Rhy. Fig. 4
Gtr. 2
some - times I love you on Sat - ur - day night. _ Sun - day morn - in' you don't _ look right.
Gtr. 1
Gtr. 2: w/ Rhy. Fig. 4
You been out a paint - in' the town. _ Uh, huh, babe, you been slip - pin' a - round. _ So, huh,

Gtr. 2: w/ Rhy. Fig. 1
B9/F♯
E
ah, hey, ___ hon - ey, don't. Well, hon - ey,

Chorus
Gtr. 2: w/ Rhy. Fig. 2
E
don't. Bop, bop, bop, ___ hon - ey, don't. Bop, bop, bop, bop, ___ hon - ey,

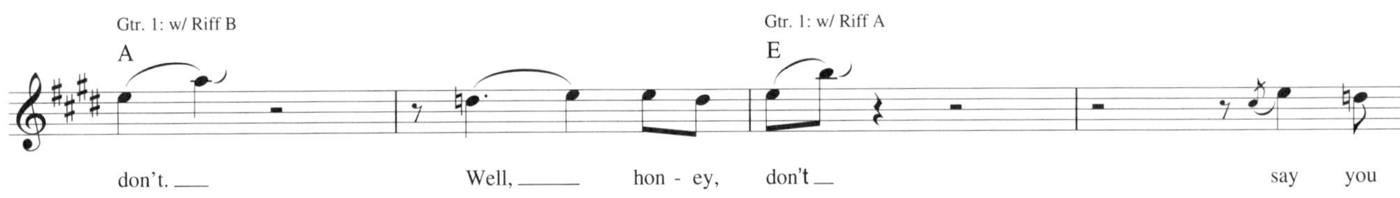
Gtr. 1: w/ Riff B
A
Gtr. 1: w/ Riff A
E
don't. ___ Well, ___ hon - ey, don't ___ say you

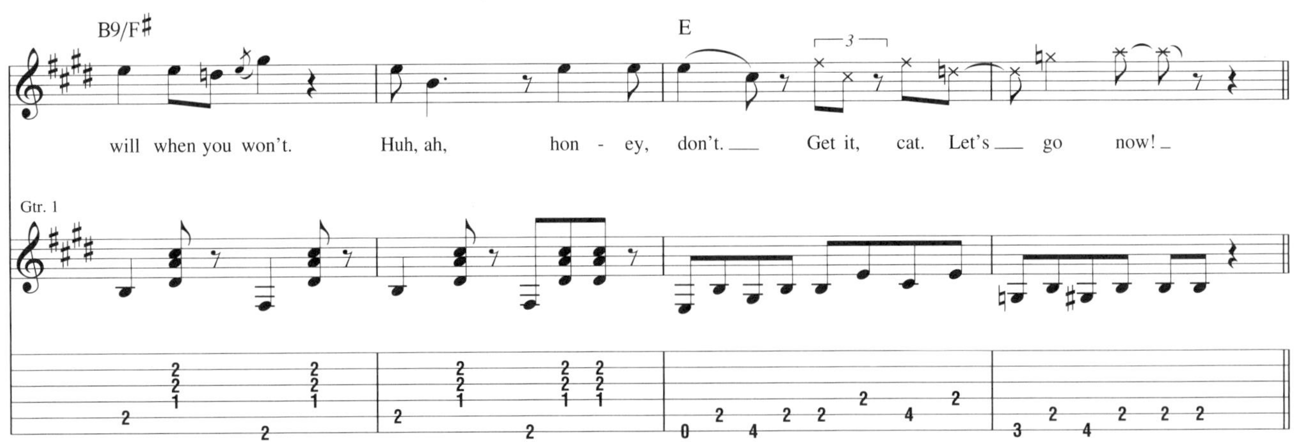
B9/F♯
E
will when you won't. Huh, ah, hon - ey, don't. ___ Get it, cat. Let's ___ go now! ___
Gtr. 1

Guitar Solo
E
C/G
Gtr. 2
Gtr. 1
Gtr. 2: w/ Rhy. Fig. 3
E
C/G
B9/F♯
E
Well, well, hon - ey,
Chorus
Gtr. 2: w/ Rhy. Fig. 2 (1st 10 meas.)
E
don't.
Ho, hon - ey, don't.

A
E
Yeah, hon-ey, don't. Bop, bop, ba, bop, ba, bop, hon-ey, don't

B9/F♯
say you will when you won't. Huh, ah, hon-ey, don't.

E
Gtr. 2
Gtr. 1

from The Smiths - *Meat Is Murder*

How Soon Is Now

Gtrs. 1 - 8: Tune up 1 whole step:
(low to high) F♯-B-E-A-C♯-F♯
Gtr. 9: Tuning:
(low to high) F♯-B-F♯-G♯-A-C♯

Words and Music by Johnny Marr and Steven Morrissey

Intro

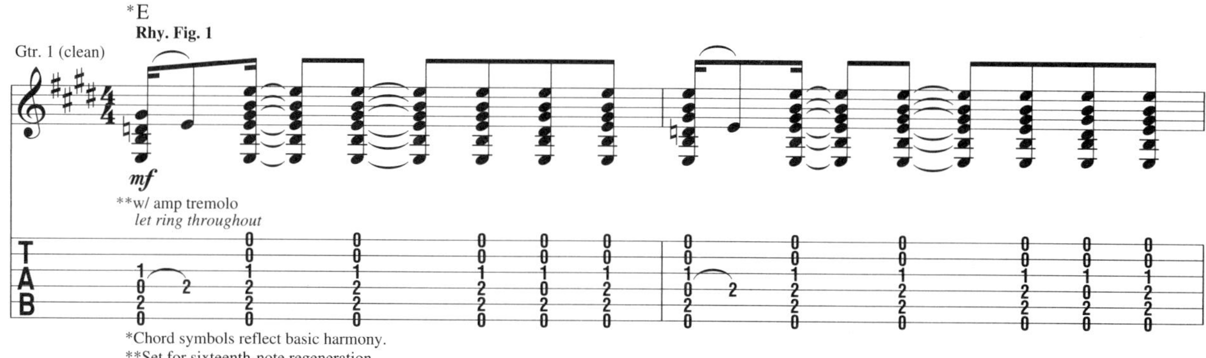

*Chord symbols reflect basic harmony.
**Set for sixteenth-note regeneration.

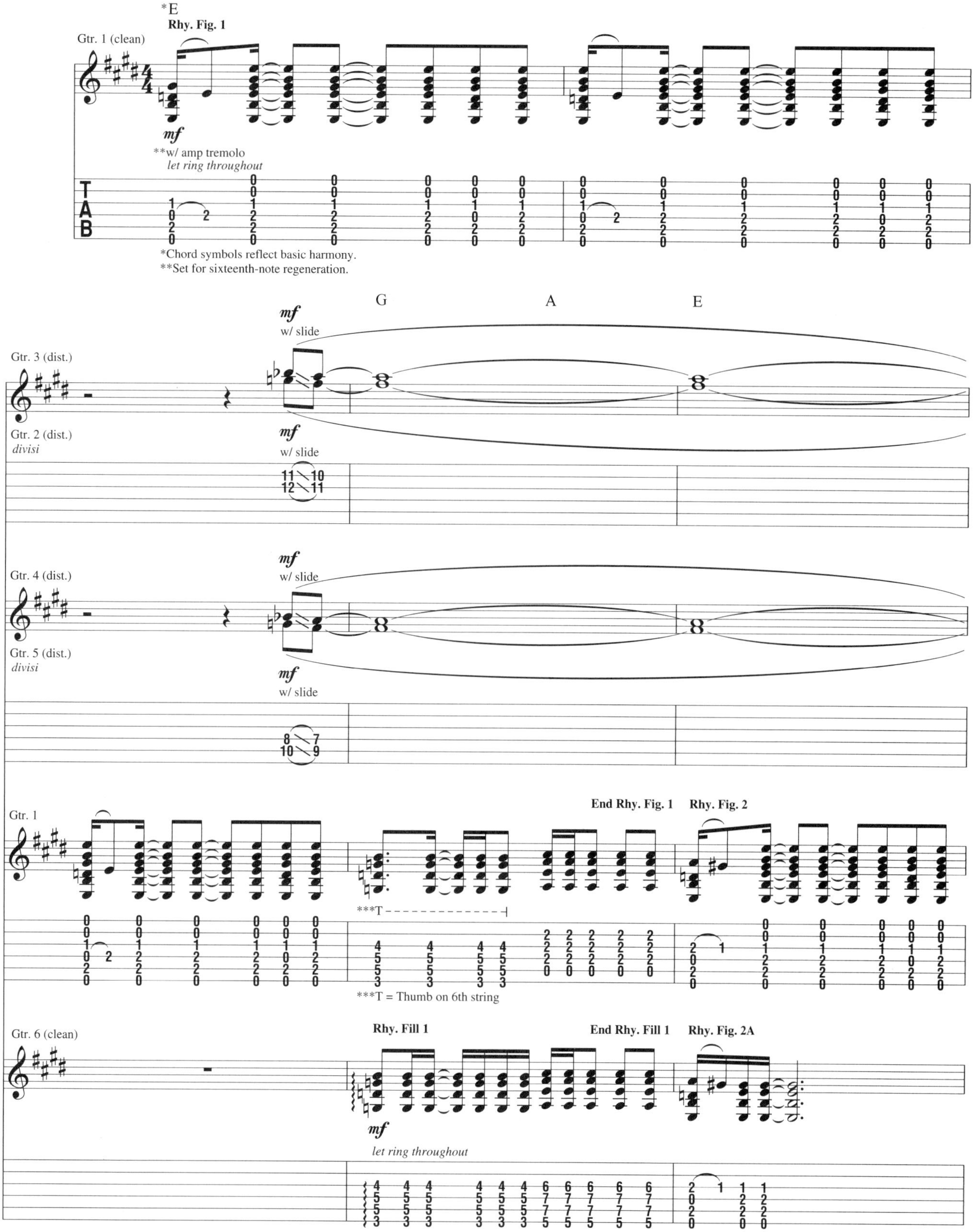

G A E

Gtr. 3 (dist.) *mf* w/ slide

Gtr. 2 (dist.) *divisi* *mf* w/ slide

Gtr. 4 (dist.) *mf* w/ slide

Gtr. 5 (dist.) *divisi* *mf* w/ slide

Gtr. 1 — End Rhy. Fig. 1 — Rhy. Fig. 2

***T = Thumb on 6th string

Gtr. 6 (clean) — Rhy. Fill 1 — End Rhy. Fill 1 — Rhy. Fig. 2A

mf *let ring throughout*

G
A
1. I am the
Riff A1
End Riff A1
Riff A
End Riff A
Riff A2
End Riff A2
Riff A3
End Riff A3
End Rhy. Fig. 2
End Rhy. Fig. 2A
Verse
Gtr. 1: w/ Rhy. Fig. 2 (1 3/4 times)
Gtr. 6: w/ Rhy. Fig. 2A
E
G
A
(1., 2.) son and the heir of a shy - ness that is crim - i - nal - ly vul -
Gtr. 3
Riff B1
Gtr. 2
Riff B
Gtr. 4
Riff B2
Gtr. 5
Riff B3

Gtrs. 2, 3, 4 & 5: w/ Riffs A, A1, A2 & A3
2nd time, Gtr. 6: w/ Rhy. Fill 2

E

gar. I am the son and heir ___ of noth - ing ___ in par - tic - u - lar.

Gtr. 3

End Riff B1

Gtr. 2

End Riff B

(10)
(11)

Gtr. 4

End Riff B2

Gtr. 5

End Riff B3

(7)
(9)

Gtr. 6

2 1 1 1
0 2 2
2 2 2
0 0 0

Chorus
G
A
Asus2
Cadd9
Gtr. 6 tacet
G
Dmaj7
You shut your mouth. How can you say
Gtr. 7 (slight dist.)
Riff C
mf
Gtr. 1
Rhy. Fig. 3
Gtr. 6
Rhy. Fill 3
End Rhy. Fill 3
Bsus4
D6add9
E
I go a - bout things the wrong way? I am hu -
End Riff C
Gtr. 7
Gtr. 1
End Rhy. Fig. 3

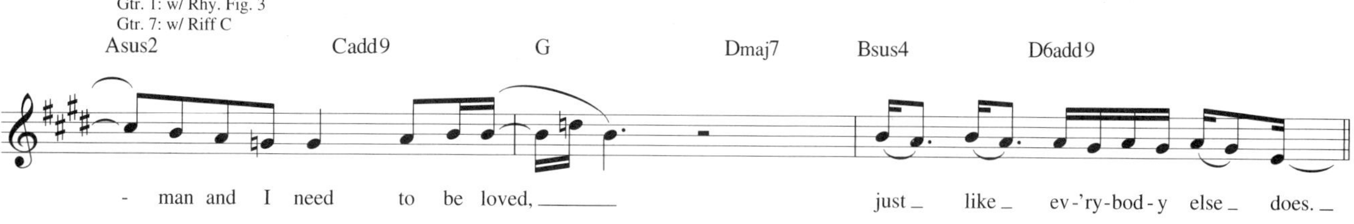
Gtr. 1: w/ Rhy. Fig. 3
Gtr. 7: w/ Riff C
Asus2
Cadd9
G
Dmaj7
Bsus4
D6add9
- man and I need to be loved,
just like ev-'ry-bod-y else does.

Interlude

2nd time, Gtr. 6: w/ Rhy. Fig. 4 (4 times)
1st time, Gtr. 1: w/ Rhy. Fig. 1
2nd time, Gtr. 1: w/ Rhy. Fill 4
E
Gtr. 8 (slight dist.)
mf

2nd time, Gtr. 1: w/ Rhy. Fig. 1 (last 3 meas.)
Gtrs. 2, 3, 4 & 5: w/ Riffs B, B1, B2 & B3
P.H.
1/2

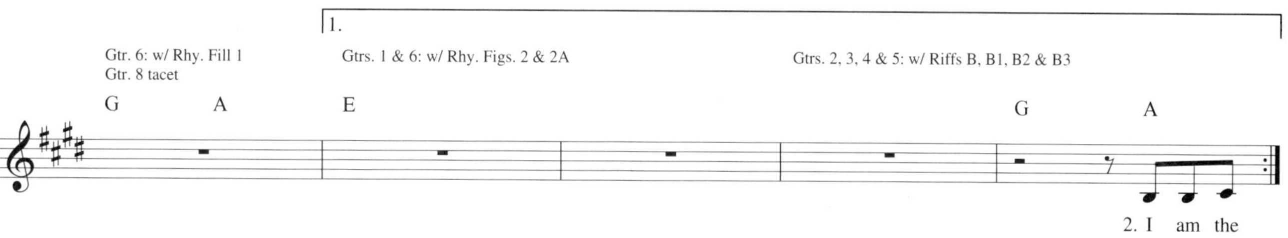
1.
Gtr. 6: w/ Rhy. Fill 1
Gtr. 8 tacet
Gtrs. 1 & 6: w/ Rhy. Figs. 2 & 2A
Gtrs. 2, 3, 4 & 5: w/ Riffs B, B1, B2 & B3
G
A
E
G
A
2. I am the

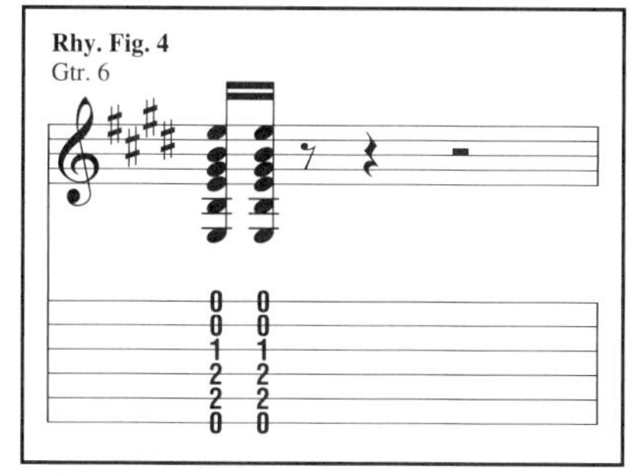
Rhy. Fig. 4
Gtr. 6

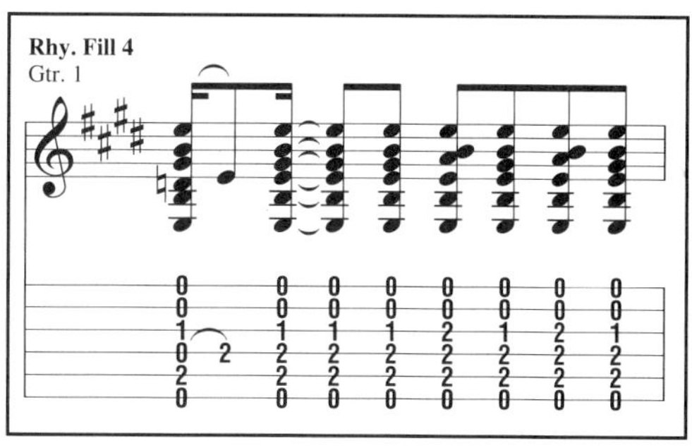
Rhy. Fill 4
Gtr. 1

2.
E
Riff D1
Gtr. 3
Gtr. 2
divisi
Riff D
Riff D2
Gtr. 4
Gtr. 5
divisi
Riff D3
Gtr. 1
Gtr. 6

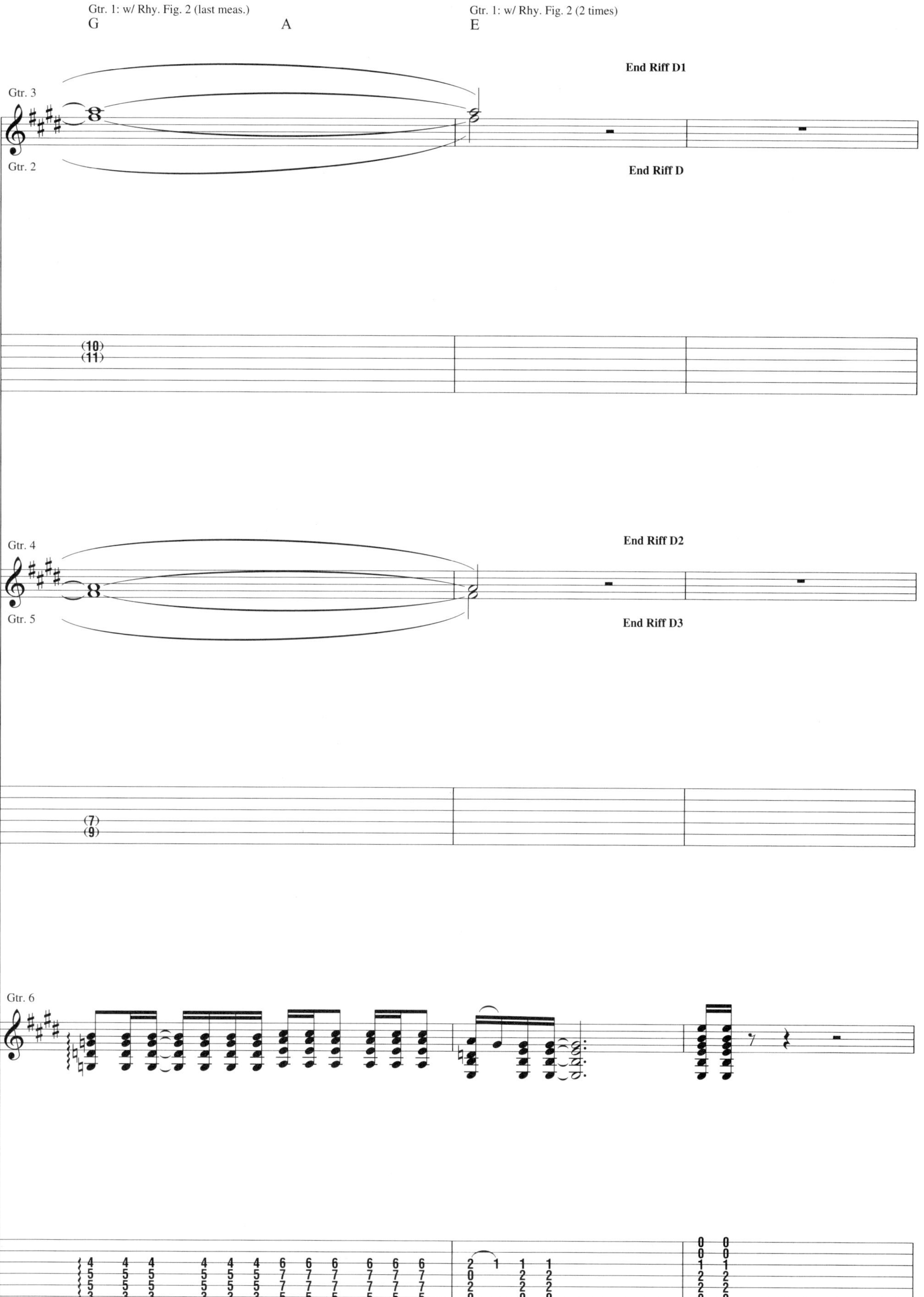
Gtr. 1: w/ Rhy. Fig. 2 (last meas.)
G
A
Gtr. 1: w/ Rhy. Fig. 2 (2 times)
E
End Riff D1
Gtr. 3
Gtr. 2
End Riff D
Gtr. 4
End Riff D2
Gtr. 5
End Riff D3
Gtr. 6

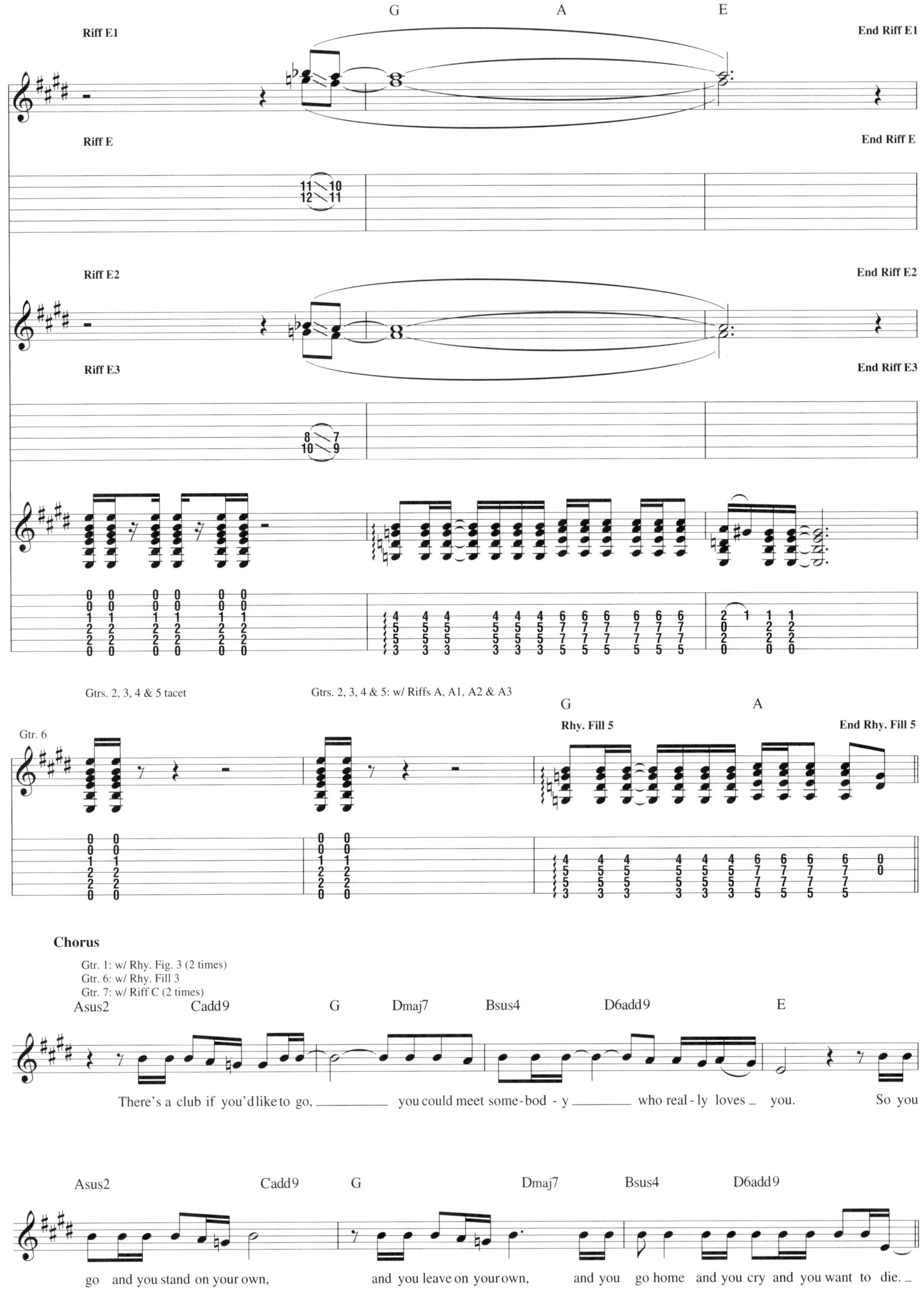

G
A
E
Riff E1
End Riff E1
Riff E
End Riff E
Riff E2
End Riff E2
Riff E3
End Riff E3
Gtrs. 2, 3, 4 & 5 tacet
Gtrs. 2, 3, 4 & 5: w/ Riffs A, A1, A2 & A3
Gtr. 6
G
A
Rhy. Fill 5
End Rhy. Fill 5
Chorus
Gtr. 1: w/ Rhy. Fig. 3 (2 times)
Gtr. 6: w/ Rhy. Fill 3
Gtr. 7: w/ Riff C (2 times)
Asus2 Cadd9 G Dmaj7 Bsus4 D6add9 E
There's a club if you'd like to go, you could meet some-bod - y who real - ly loves you. So you
Asus2 Cadd9 G Dmaj7 Bsus4 D6add9
go and you stand on your own, and you leave on your own, and you go home and you cry and you want to die.

Interlude

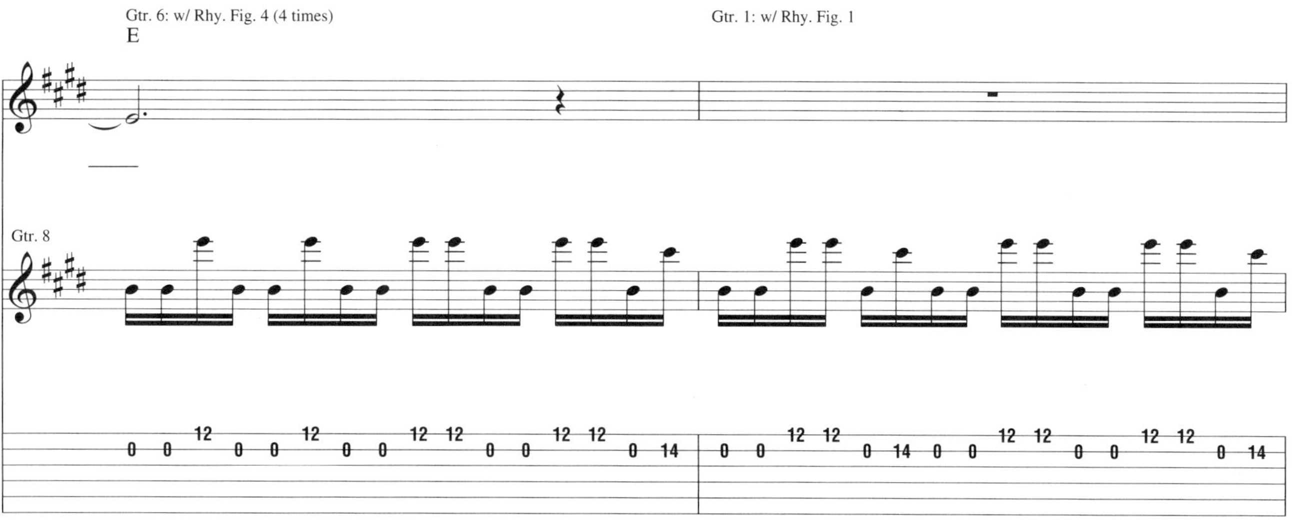
Gtr. 6: w/ Rhy. Fig. 4 (4 times)
E
Gtr. 1: w/ Rhy. Fig. 1
Gtr. 8

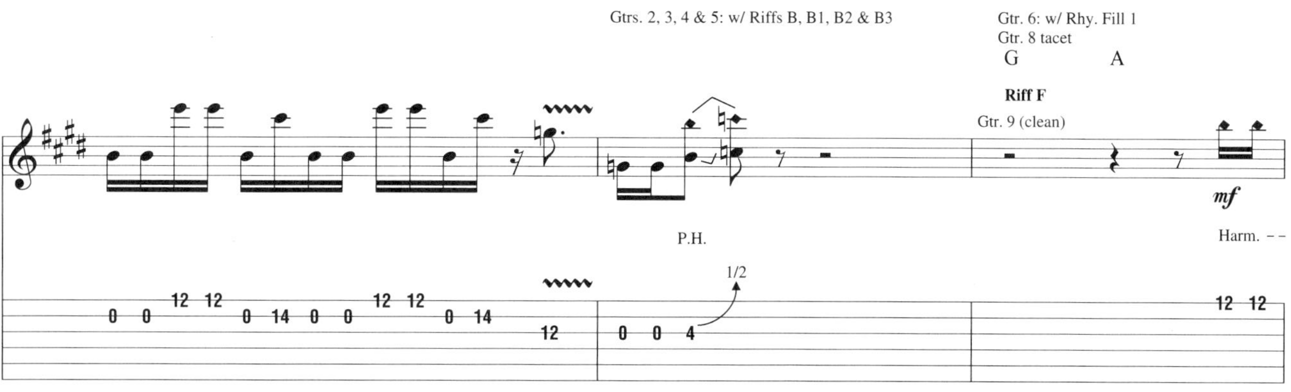
Gtrs. 2, 3, 4 & 5: w/ Riffs B, B1, B2 & B3
Gtr. 6: w/ Rhy. Fill 1
Gtr. 8 tacet
G
A
Riff F
Gtr. 9 (clean)
mf
P.H.
Harm.
1/2

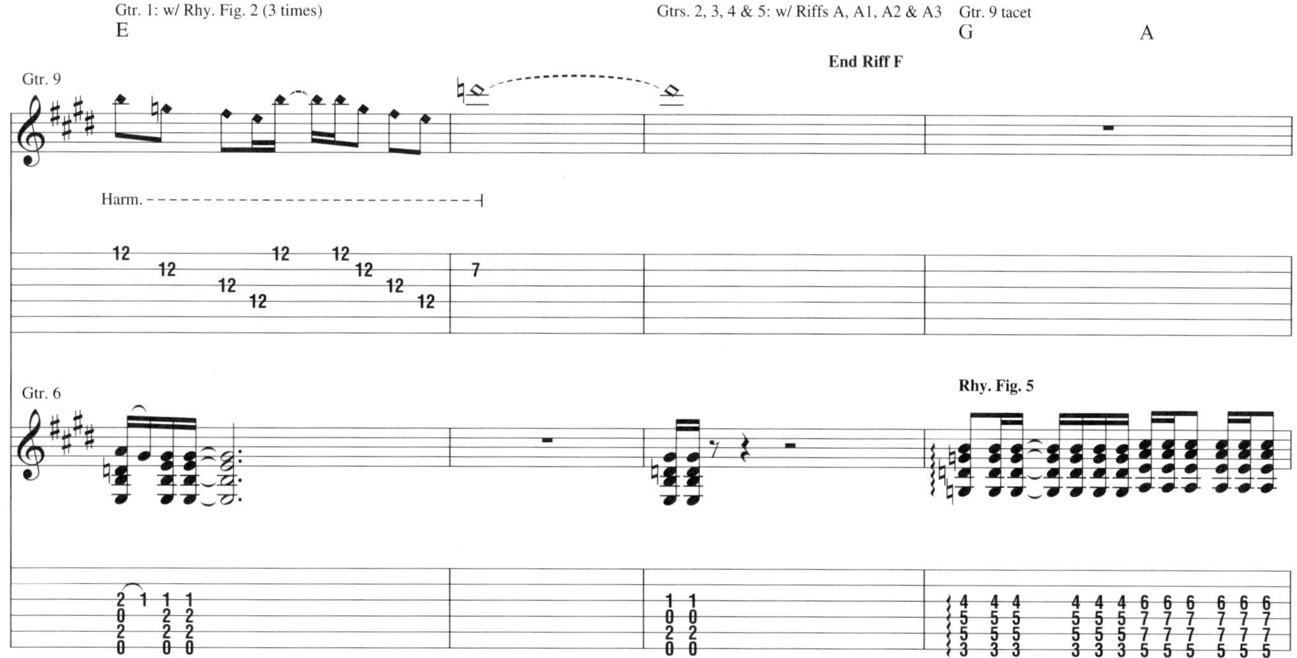
Gtr. 1: w/ Rhy. Fig. 2 (3 times)
E
Gtrs. 2, 3, 4 & 5: w/ Riffs A, A1, A2 & A3
Gtr. 9 tacet
G
A
End Riff F
Gtr. 9
Harm.
Gtr. 6
Rhy. Fig. 5

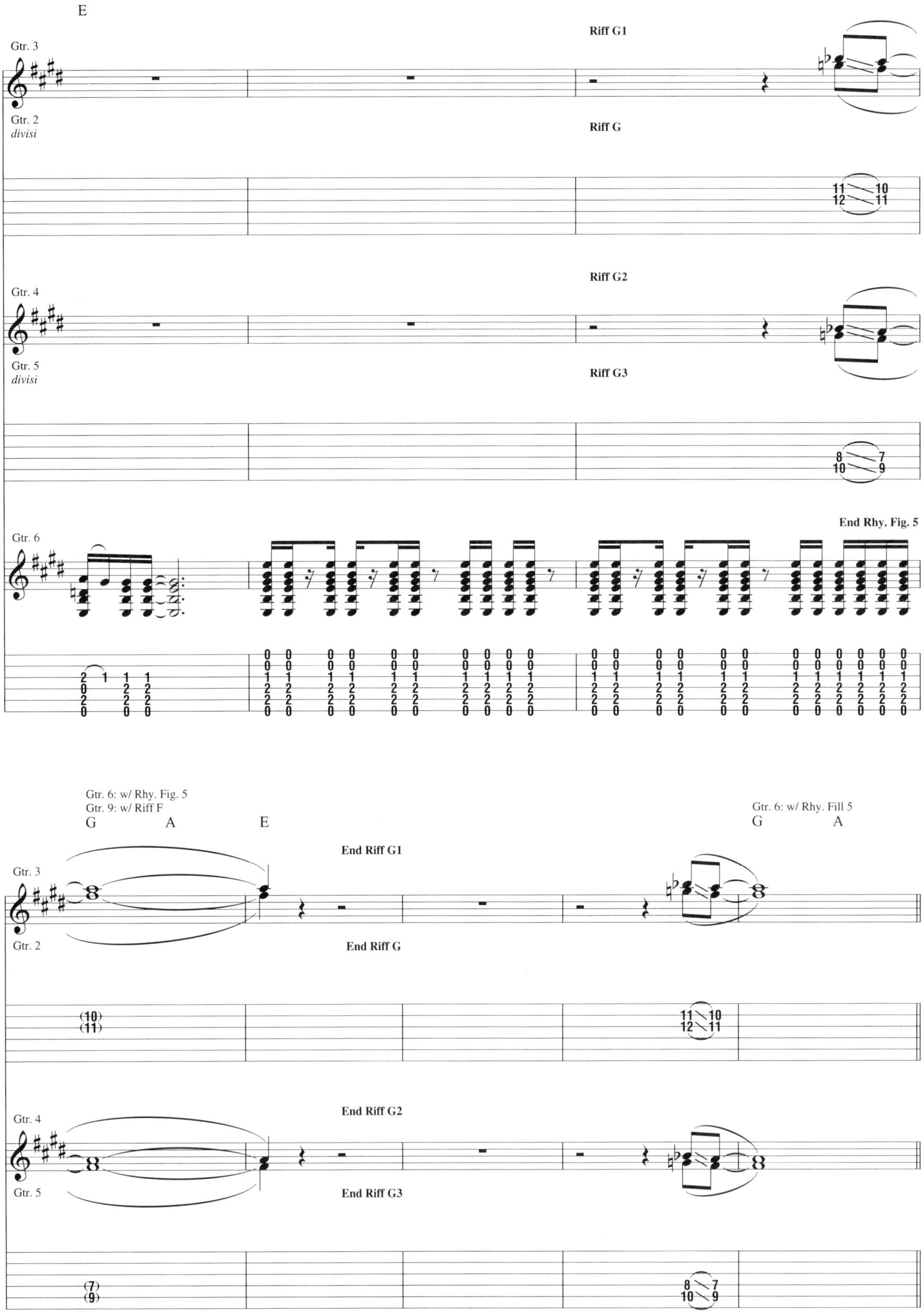

E

Riff G1

Gtr. 3

Gtr. 2
divisi

Riff G

Riff G2

Gtr. 4

Gtr. 5
divisi

Riff G3

End Rhy. Fig. 5

Gtr. 6

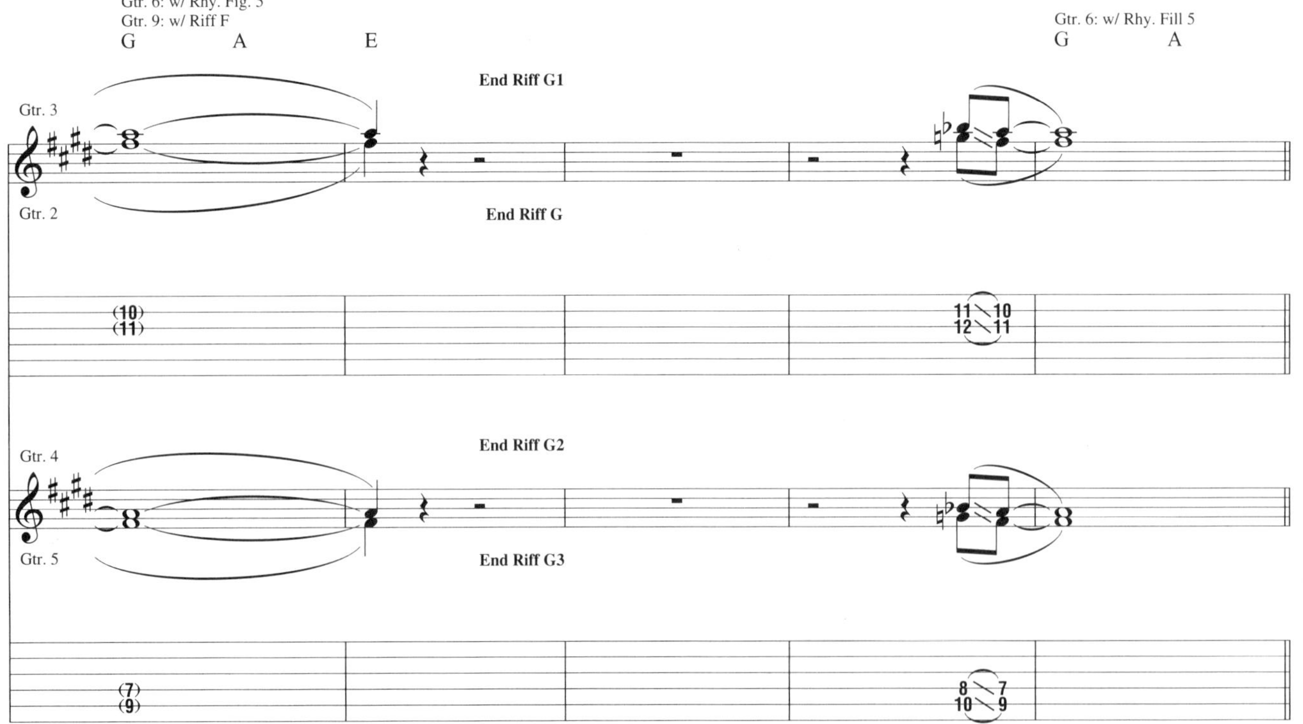

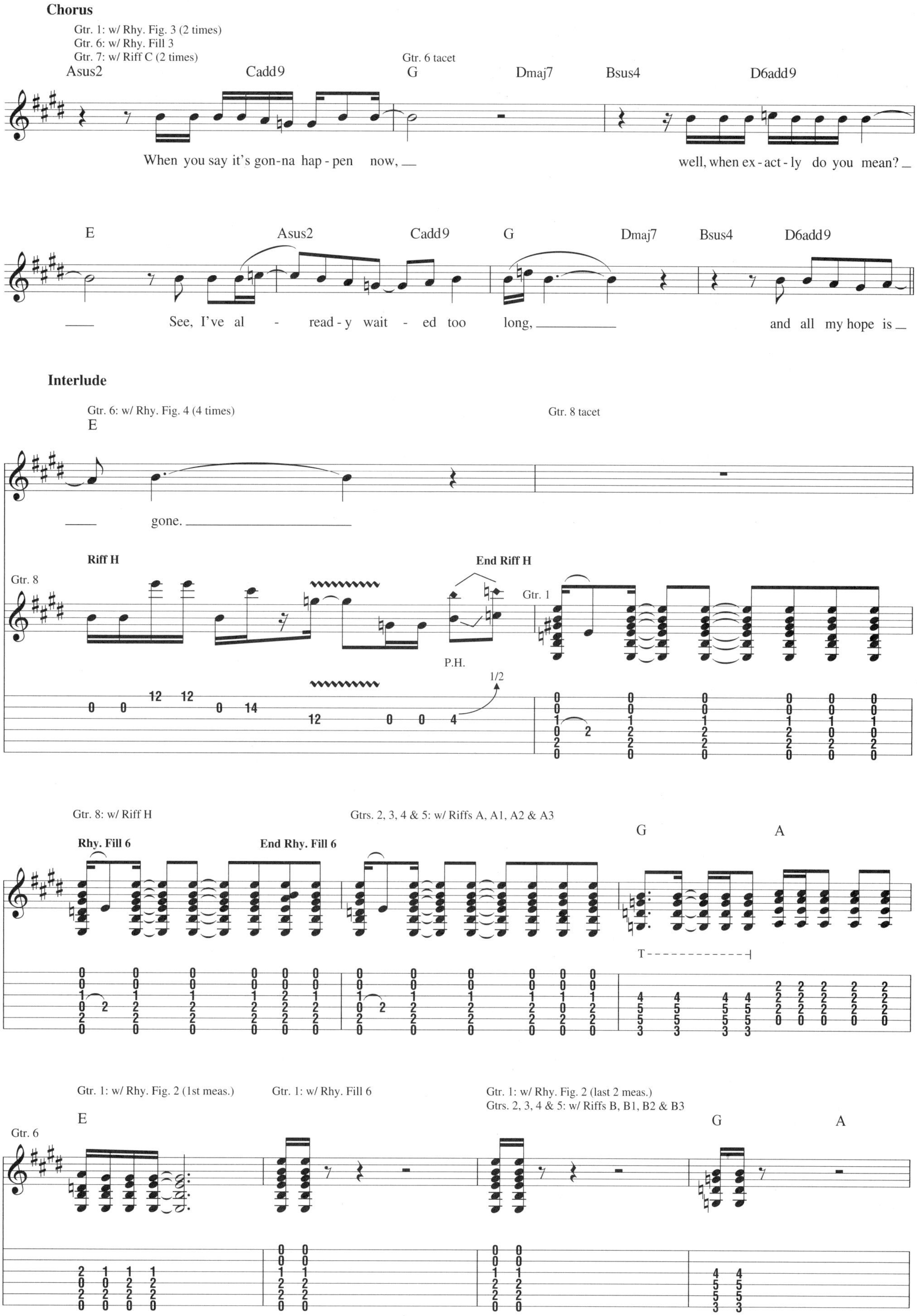

Chorus

Gtr. 1: w/ Rhy. Fig. 3 (2 times)
Gtr. 6: w/ Rhy. Fill 3
Gtr. 7: w/ Riff C (2 times)

Asus2 Cadd9 | Gtr. 6 tacet G Dmaj7 Bsus4 D6add9

When you say it's gon-na hap - pen now, __ well, when ex - act - ly do you mean? __

E Asus2 Cadd9 G Dmaj7 Bsus4 D6add9

__ See, I've al - read - y wait - ed too long, __ and all my hope is __

Interlude

Gtr. 6: w/ Rhy. Fig. 4 (4 times) | Gtr. 8 tacet

E

__ gone. __

Riff H | End Riff H

Gtr. 8 | Gtr. 1

P.H. 1/2

Gtr. 8: w/ Riff H | Gtrs. 2, 3, 4 & 5: w/ Riffs A, A1, A2 & A3

Rhy. Fill 6 | End Rhy. Fill 6

G A

T

Gtr. 1: w/ Rhy. Fig. 2 (1st meas.) | Gtr. 1: w/ Rhy. Fill 6 | Gtr. 1: w/ Rhy. Fig. 2 (last 2 meas.) Gtrs. 2, 3, 4 & 5: w/ Riffs B, B1, B2 & B3

E G A

Gtr. 6

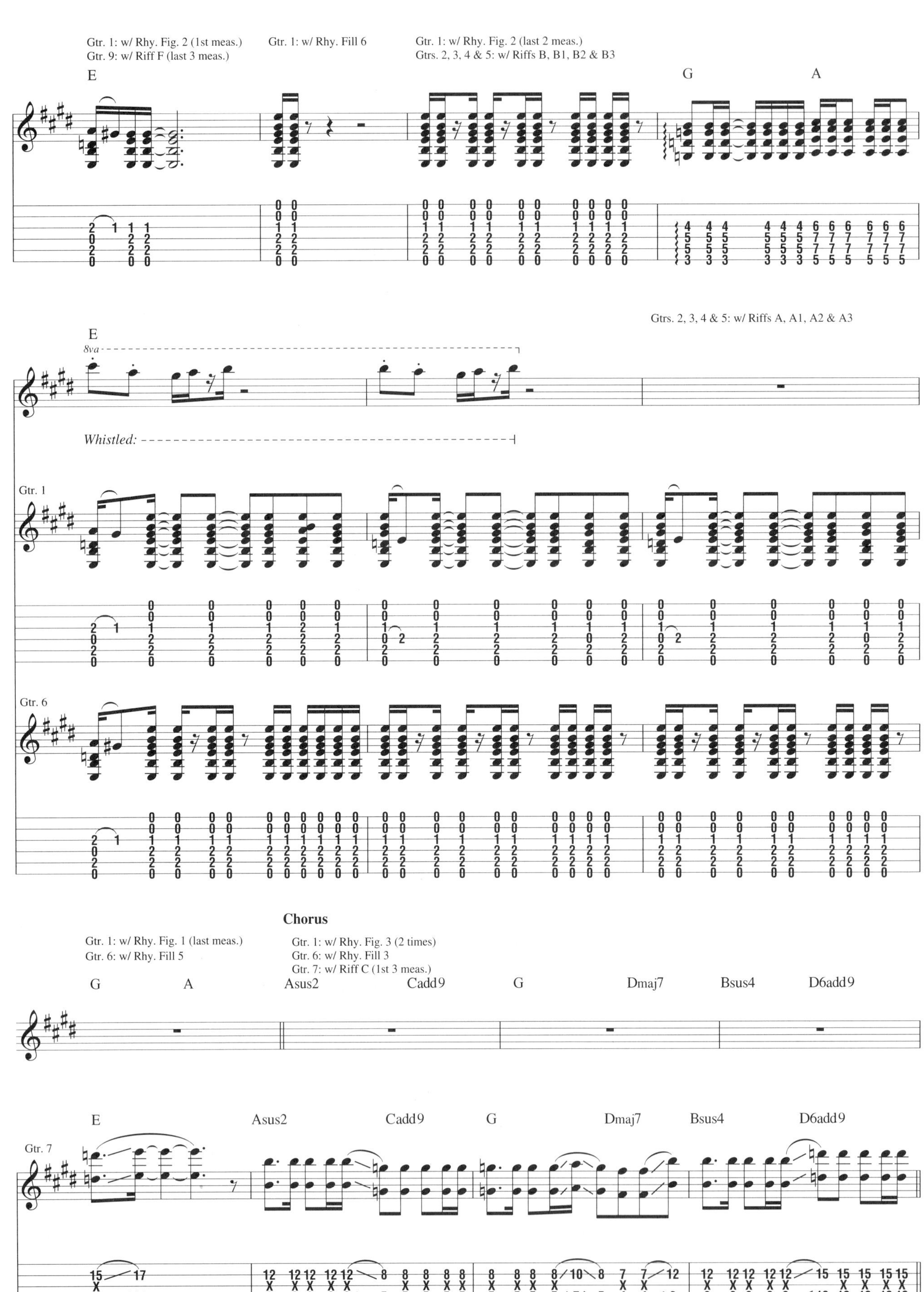
Gtr. 1: w/ Rhy. Fig. 2 (1st meas.)
Gtr. 9: w/ Riff F (last 3 meas.)
Gtr. 1: w/ Rhy. Fill 6
Gtr. 1: w/ Rhy. Fig. 2 (last 2 meas.)
Gtrs. 2, 3, 4 & 5: w/ Riffs B, B1, B2 & B3
E
G
A
Gtrs. 2, 3, 4 & 5: w/ Riffs A, A1, A2 & A3
E
8va
Whistled:
Gtr. 1
Gtr. 6
Chorus
Gtr. 1: w/ Rhy. Fig. 1 (last meas.)
Gtr. 6: w/ Rhy. Fill 5
Gtr. 1: w/ Rhy. Fig. 3 (2 times)
Gtr. 6: w/ Rhy. Fill 3
Gtr. 7: w/ Riff C (1st 3 meas.)
G
A
Asus2
Cadd9
G
Dmaj7
Bsus4
D6add9
E
Asus2
Cadd9
G
Dmaj7
Bsus4
D6add9
Gtr. 7

Interlude

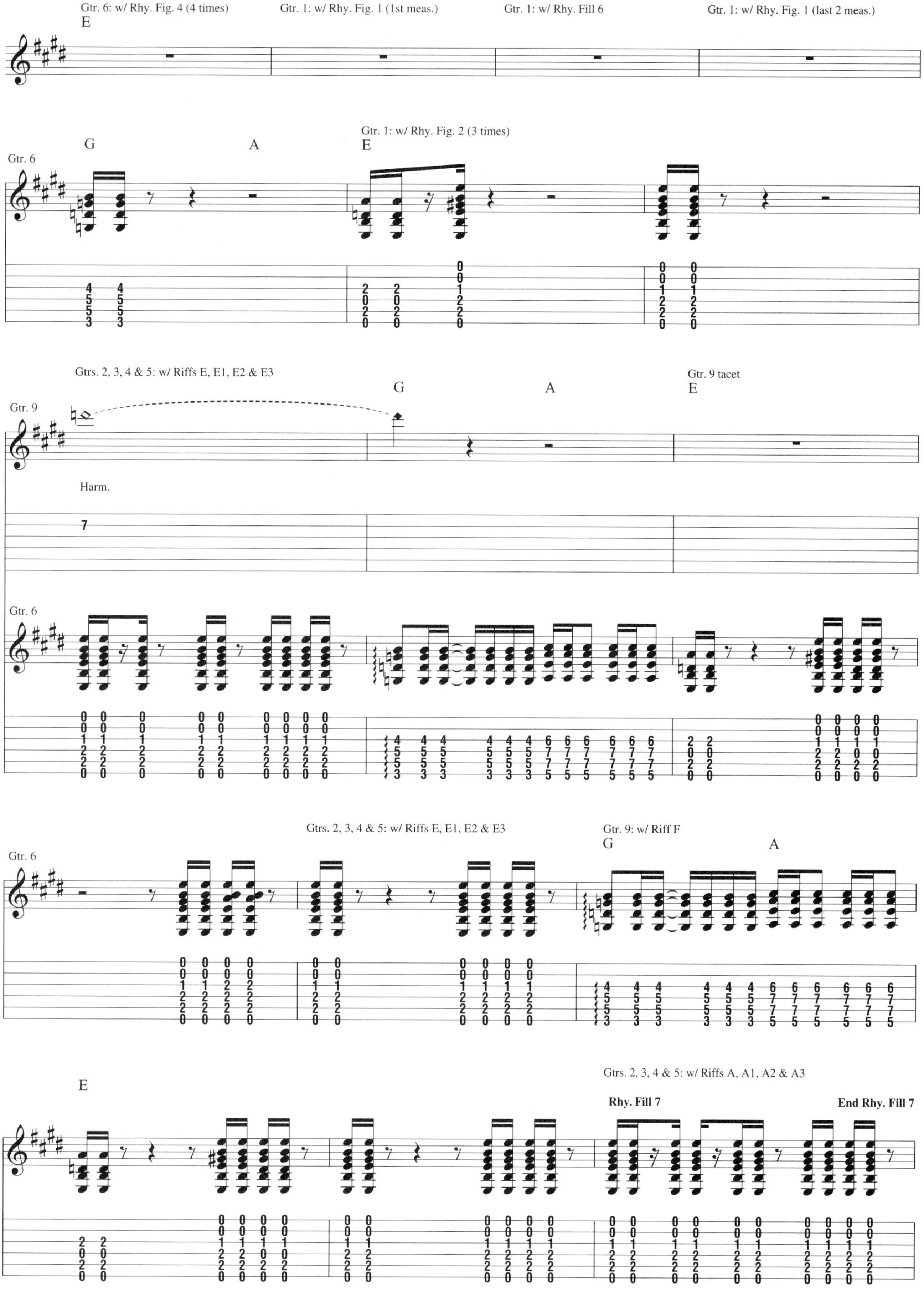

Gtr. 6: w/ Rhy. Fig. 4 (4 times)
Gtr. 1: w/ Rhy. Fig. 1 (1st meas.)
Gtr. 1: w/ Rhy. Fill 6
Gtr. 1: w/ Rhy. Fig. 1 (last 2 meas.)
E

Gtr. 1: w/ Rhy. Fig. 2 (3 times)
G A E
Gtr. 6

Gtrs. 2, 3, 4 & 5: w/ Riffs E, E1, E2 & E3
Gtr. 9 tacet
G A E
Gtr. 9
Harm.
Gtr. 6

Gtrs. 2, 3, 4 & 5: w/ Riffs E, E1, E2 & E3
Gtr. 9: w/ Riff F
G A
Gtr. 6

E
Gtrs. 2, 3, 4 & 5: w/ Riffs A, A1, A2 & A3
Rhy. Fill 7
End Rhy. Fill 7

Chorus

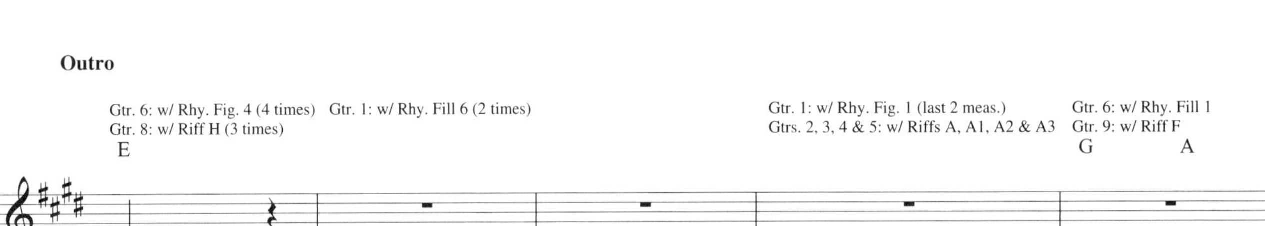

Outro

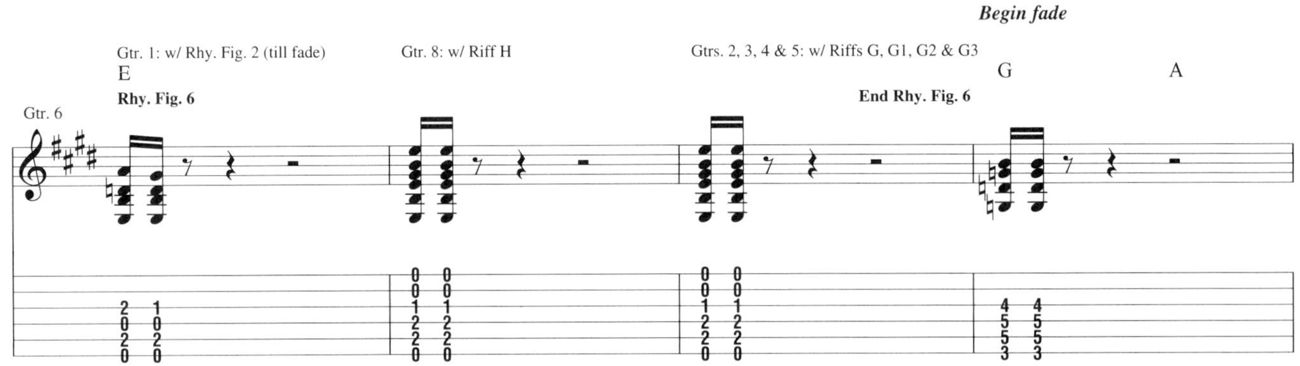

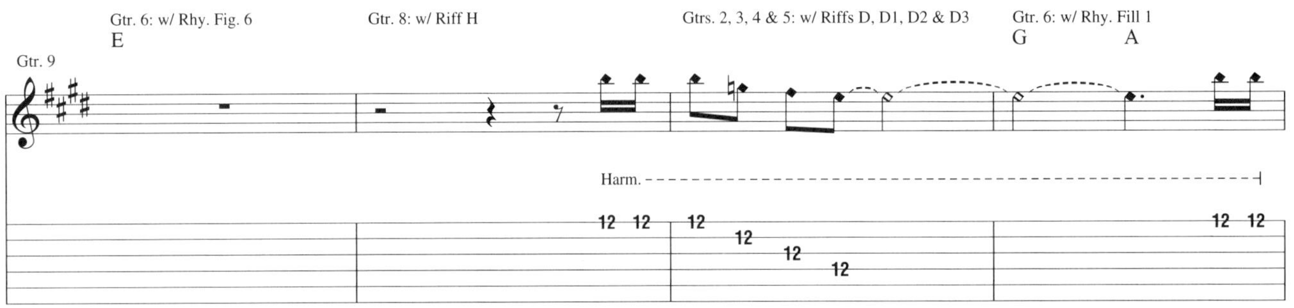

Fade out

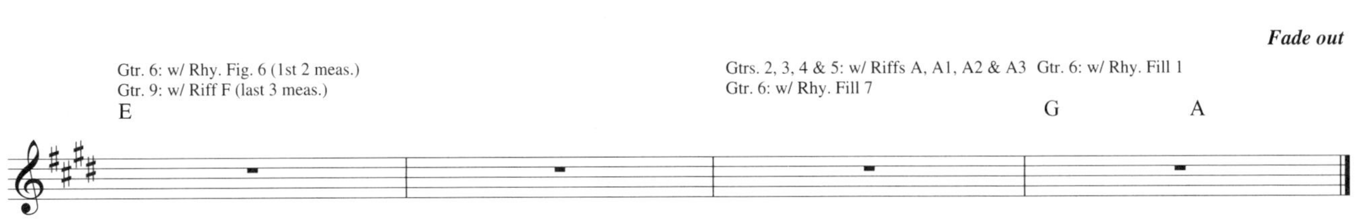

from The Stooges - *The Stooges*

I Wanna Be Your Dog

Written by Iggy Pop, David Alexander, Ronald Asheton and Scott Asheton

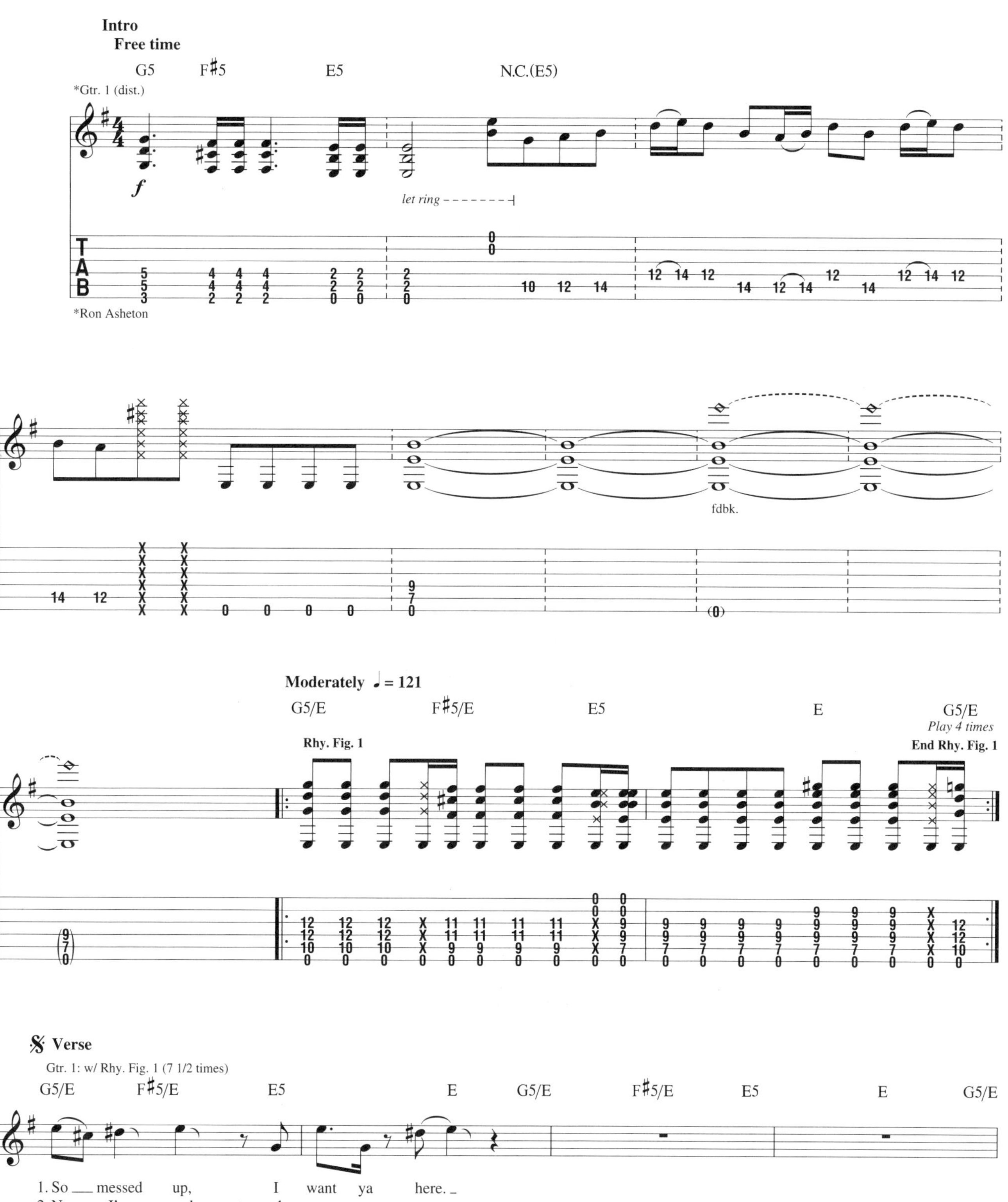

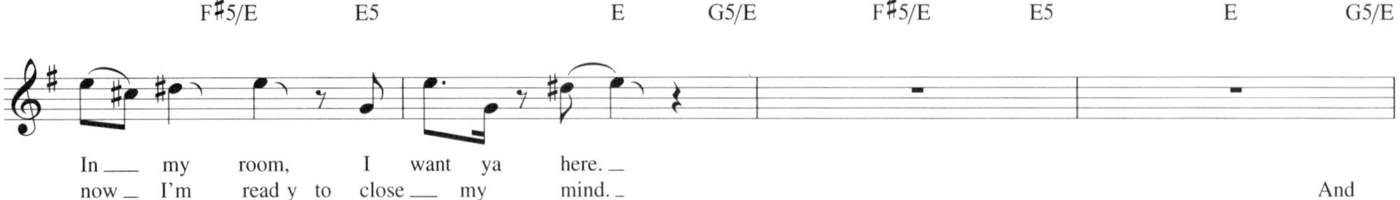
F♯5/E E5 E G5/E F♯5/E E5 E G5/E
In ___ my room, I want ya here. __
now _ I'm read y to close ___ my mind. _ And

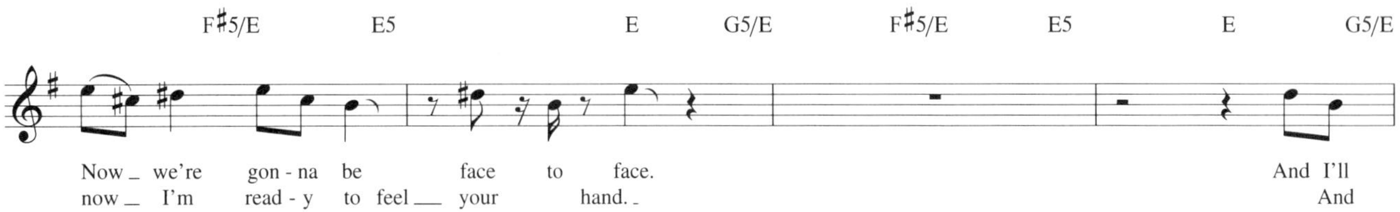
F♯5/E E5 E G5/E F♯5/E E5 E G5/E
Now _ we're gon - na be face to face. And I'll
now _ I'm read - y to feel ___ your hand. _ And

F♯5/E E5 E G5/E F♯5/E E5
lay ___ right down in my fa - vor - ite place. __
lose ___ my heart on the burn - in' sand. __

Chorus
G5/E F♯5/E E5
And now __ I wan - na be your dog. __ And
Gtr. 1
Rhy. Fig. 2
End Rhy. Fig. 2

Gtr. 1: w/ Rhy. Fig. 2 (2 times)
G5/E F♯5/E E5 G5/E F♯5/E E5
now _ I wan - na be your dog. _ And now _ I wan - na be your dog. _

Interlude

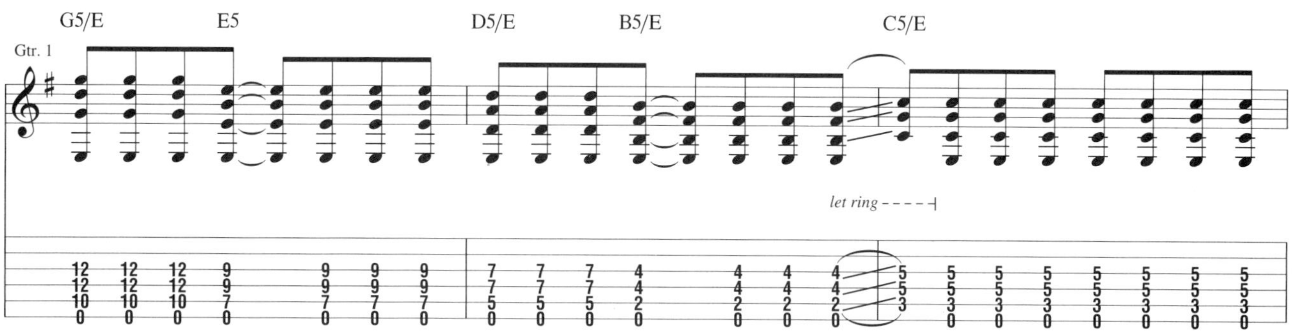

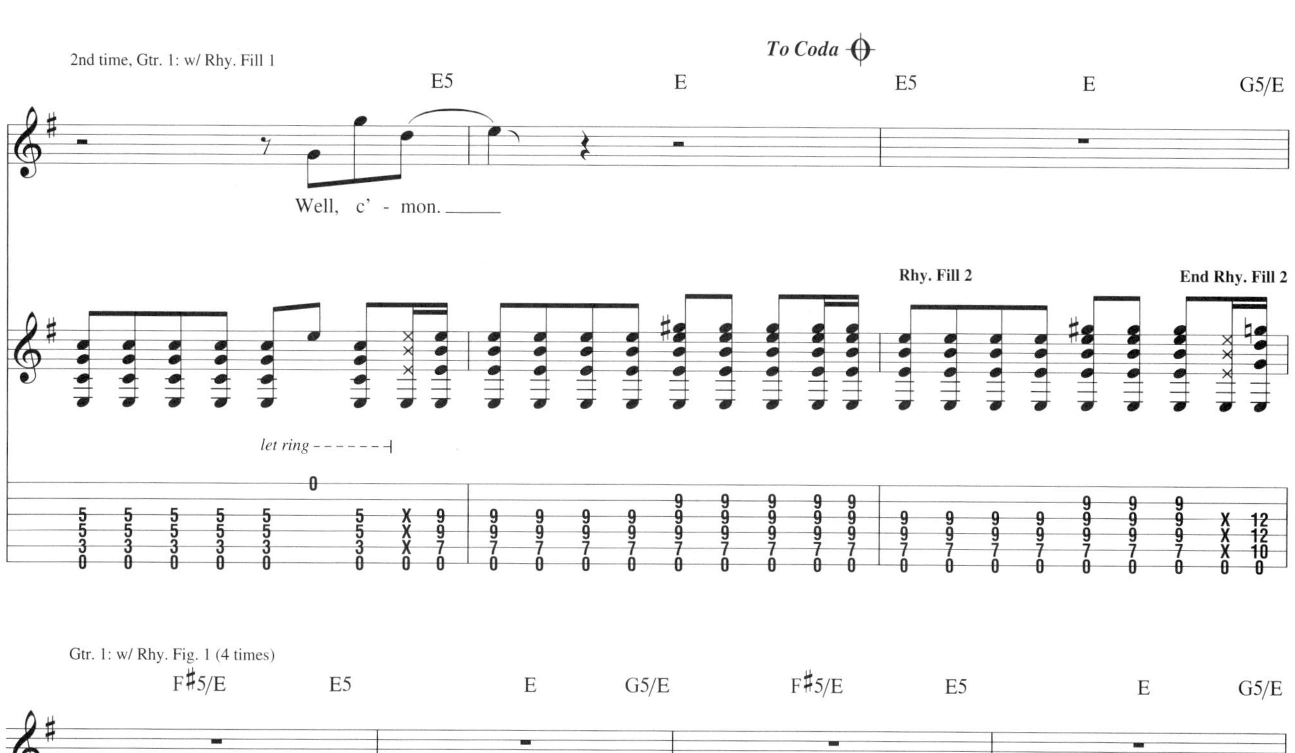

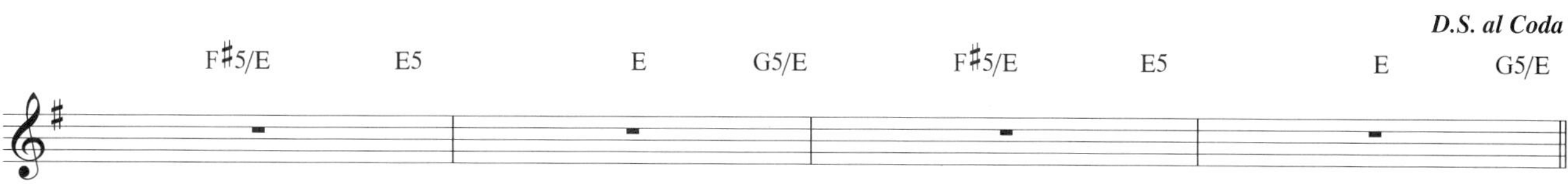

D.S. al Coda

F♯5/E E5 E G5/E F♯5/E E5 E G5/E

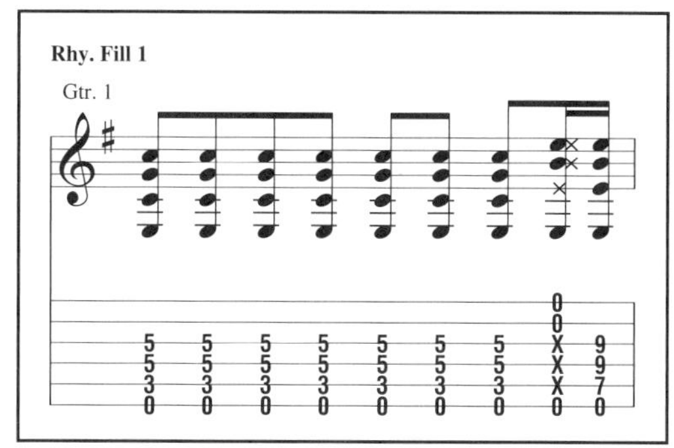

Coda

Outro-Guitar Solo

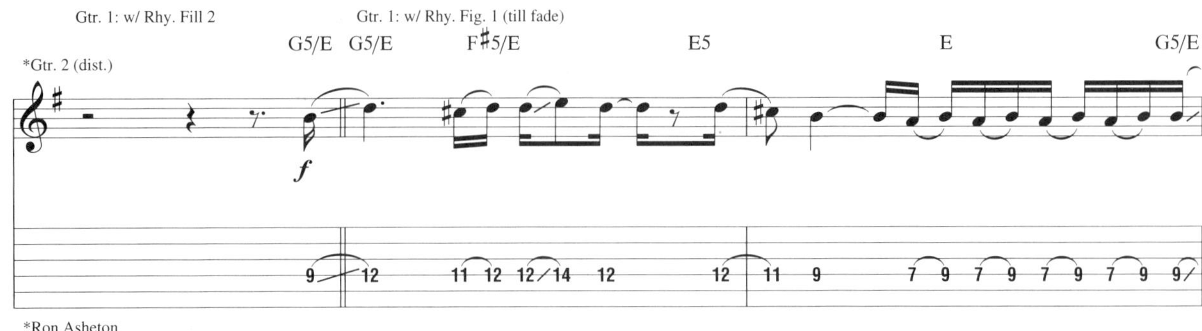

Gtr. 1: w/ Rhy. Fill 2
Gtr. 1: w/ Rhy. Fig. 1 (till fade)
G5/E G5/E F♯5/E E5 E G5/E
*Gtr. 2 (dist.)
f
*Ron Asheton

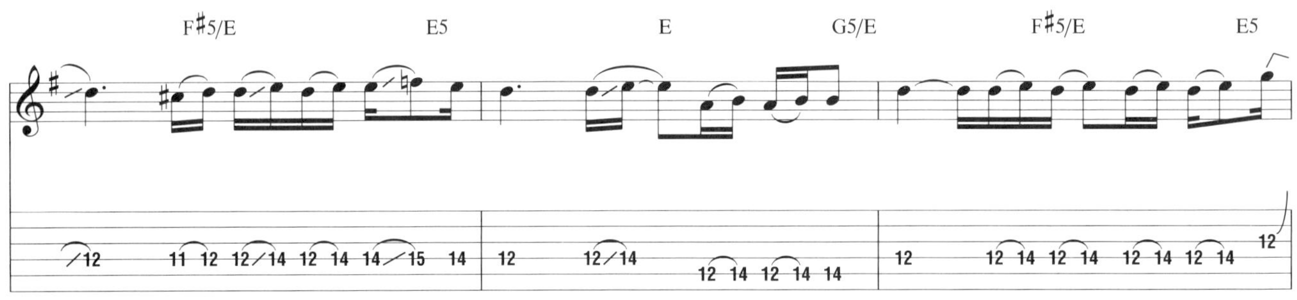

F♯5/E E5 E G5/E F♯5/E E5

E G5/E F♯5/E E5 E G5/E
1/2

Begin fade
F♯5/E E5 E G5/E F♯5/E E5
3/4

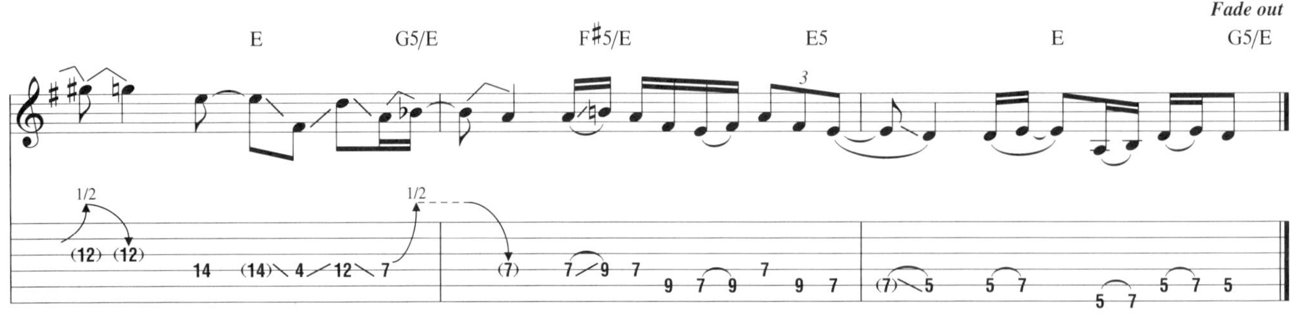

Fade out
E G5/E F♯5/E E5 E G5/E
1/2
1/2

from Twisted Sister - *Stay Hungry*

I Wanna Rock

Words and Music by D. Snider

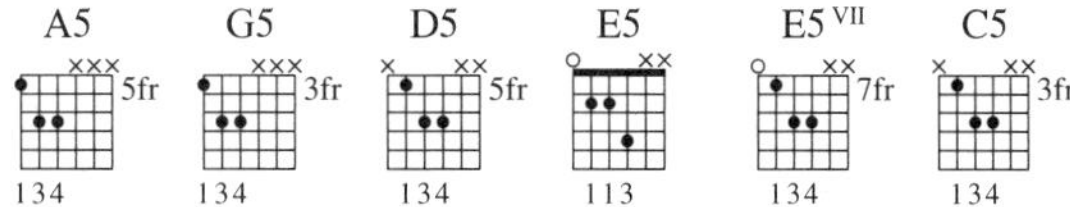

Gtr. 1: w/ Rhy. Fig. 1
Gtr. 2: w/ Rhy. Fig. 2 (2 times)
A5 G5 D5 E5 G5 A5 G5 D5 E5 C5
rock. (Rock!) I wan-na rock! (Rock!)
Verse
A5 *D5 G5
1. "Turn it down," you say. Well, all I got to say to you is time and time a - gain I say,
2. There's a feel - in' that I get from noth - in' else and there ain't noth - in' in the world that makes me
Gtr. 1
*Chord symbols reflect overall harmony.
A5 G5 D5 A5
"No!" (No!) No, no, no, no, no.
go. (Go!) Go, go, go, go, go.
Gtr. 1 tacet
D5 G5
Tell me not to play. Well, all I got to say to when you tell me not to play, I say,
Turn the pow - er up. I've wait - ed for so long so I could hear my fav - 'rite song, so let's
A5 G5 D5 A5 G5 D5
"No!" (No!) No, no, no, no, no.
go! (Go!) Go, go, go, go, go.
Gtr. 1

Pre-Chorus
G5 D5 G5 C5 G5 D5 N.C.
So if you ask me why I like the way I play it, there's on-ly one thing I can say to you.
When it's like this, I feel the mu-sic shoot-in' through me. There's noth-in' else that I would rath-er do.
I wan-na rock!
Chorus
Gtr. 1: w/ Rhy. Fig. 1 (2 times)
Gtr. 2: w/ Rhy. Fig. 2 (2 times)
A5 G5 D5 E5 G5 A5 G5 D5 E5 C5
(Rock!) I wan-na rock! (Rock!) I want to
A5 G5 D5 E5 G5
1.
A5 G5 D5 E5 C5
rock. (Rock!) I wan-na rock! (Rock!)
2.
A5 G5 D5 E5 C5
(Rock!) I wan - na rock!
Bridge
A5 E5 G5 A5 E5 C5
Voc. Fig. 1
End Voc. Fig. 1
Rock! Rock! I wan-na rock! Rock! Rock! I want to
(Rock! Rock! Rock! Rock! Rock! Rock!)
Rhy. Fig. 3
End Rhy. Fig. 3
Gtr. 1
Bkgd. Voc.: w/ Voc. Fig. 1
Gtr. 1: w/ Rhy. Fig. 3
A5 E5 G5 A5 E5 C5
rock. Rock! Rock! I wan-na rock! Rock! Rock! I wan-na rock!

Guitar Solo
*A5
G5
D5
E5
G5
Rhy. Fig. 4
Gtr. 1
Gtr. 3 (dist.)
w/ wah-wah
*See top of first page of song for chord diagrams pertaining to rhythm slashes.
A5
G5
D5
E5 VII
C5
End Rhy. Fig. 4
Gtr. 1: w/ Rhy. Fig. 4
A5
G5
D5
E5
G5
8va
A5
G5
D5
E5
C5
I wan-na rock!
8va

Chorus

Gtr. 1: w/ Rhy. Fig. 1 (2 times)
Gtr. 2: w/ Rhy. Fig. 2 (4 times)

from The Derek Trucks Band - *Songlines*

I'll Find My Way

Words and Music by Jay Joyce and Derek Trucks

Open E tuning:
(low to high) E-B-E-G♯-B-E

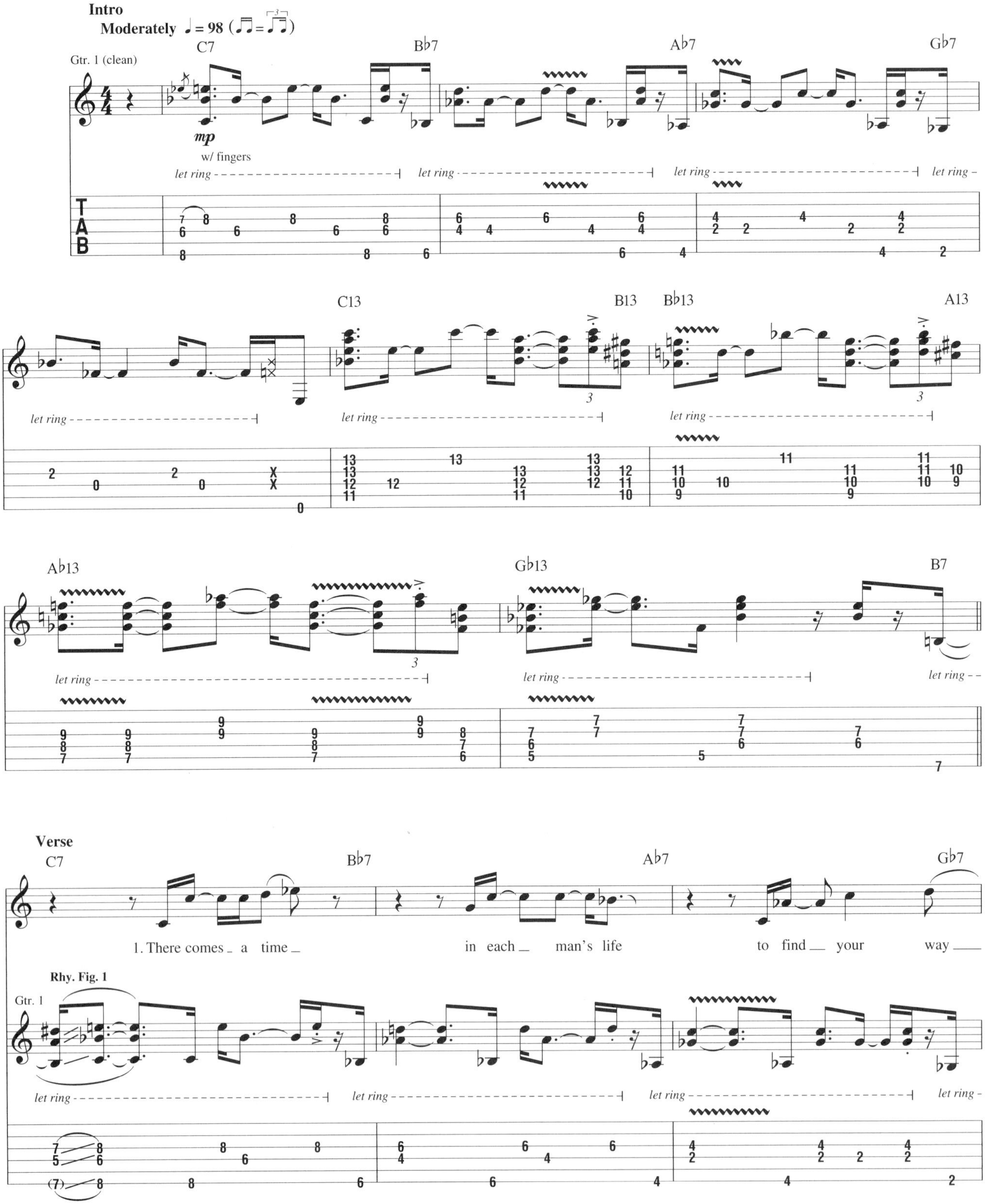

Intro
Moderately ♩ = 98 (♫ = ♪³♪)

C7 B♭7 A♭7 G♭7

Gtr. 1 (clean)

mp
w/ fingers
let ring

C13 B13 B♭13 A13

let ring

A♭13 G♭13 B7

let ring

B7 C7 B♭7 A♭7
or fall be - hind. Who you are is the path you'll take,
let ring
G♭7 B7
and I'll find my way, uh, through your mis - take.
End Rhy. Fig. 1
C7 B7 B♭7 A7 A♭7 G♭7
Some - times your tears are your bridge to the sky, but you can't trust souls
B7 C7 B7 B♭7 A7
with no truth in their eyes. Who you are is the path you'll take,

A♭7
G♭7
and I'll find my way, through your mis - take.
Rhy. Fig. 2
End Rhy. Fig. 2
let ring
let ring
Chorus
Cm7
Gm7
A♭maj7
E♭
G7
Time will heal, and all we know, if noth-ing's learned, ba - by, noth-
Gtr. 1
mf
Gtr. 2 (dist.)
mf
A♭7
Cm7
Gm7
A♭maj7
E♭
ing grows. Time will heal, and all we know, ev-'ry -
let ring

To Coda 1
To Coda 2
G7
A♭7
B♭7
thing. stays the same, noth - in' chang - es, noth - in'
let ring
Interlude
Gr.2 tacet
C7
B♭7
A♭7
G7
B7
Voc. Fig. 1
End Voc. Fig. 1
change - es.
(Oo.)
Verse
Gtr. 1: w/Rhy. Fig. 1 (1 1/4 times)
C7
B♭7
A♭7
G♭7
2. A man's not a man when he takes the low-er road, drag - gin' his tail
Rhy. Fig. 3
Gtr. 3 (clean)
mp
w/ heavy reverb
sim.

B7 C7
B♭7
A♭7
to cov - er his tracks. When you plant the seeds of doubt in my mind,
End Rhy. Fig. 3
2
2
2
2
8
8
8
8
6
6
6
6

G♭7
Gtr. 3: w/ Rhy. Fig. 3
B7 C7
B♭7
you know you run the risk of be - in' left be - hind. When I turn the mir - ror,
4
4
4
4
2
2
2
2

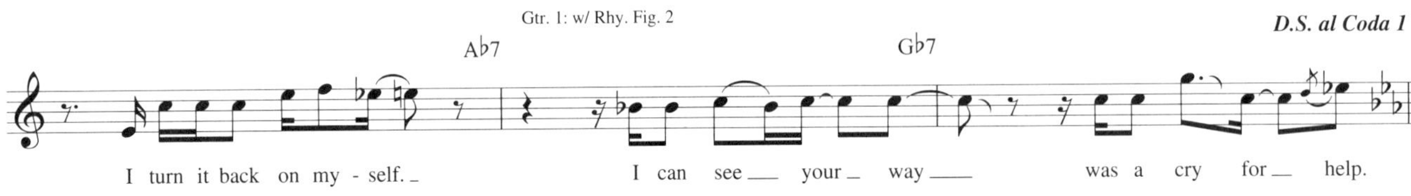
Gtr. 1: w/ Rhy. Fig. 2
A♭7
G♭7
D.S. al Coda 1
I turn it back on my - self. I can see your way was a cry for help.

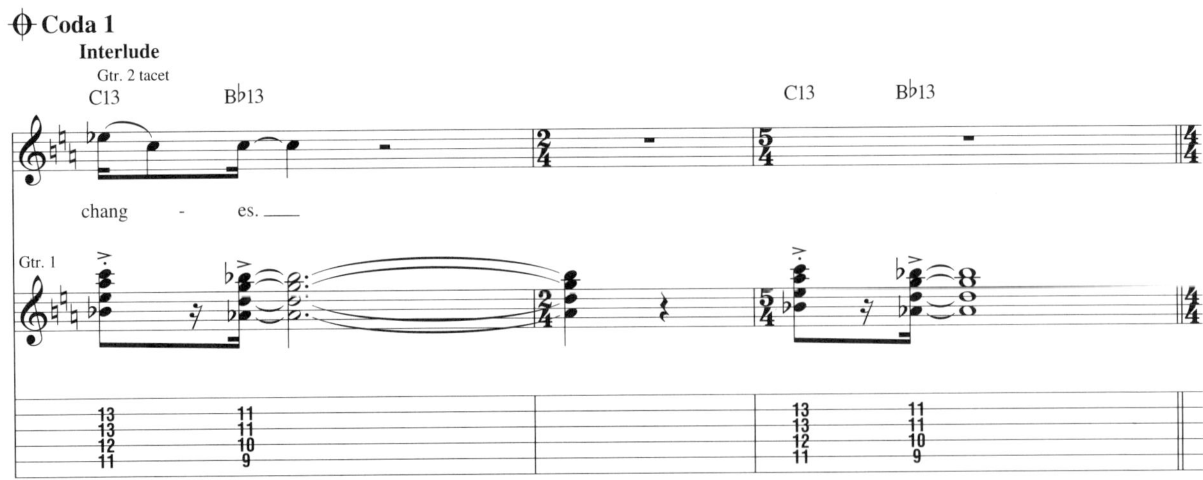
Coda 1
Interlude
Gtr. 2 tacet
C13
B♭13
C13
B♭13
chang - es.
Gtr. 1
13
13
12
11
11
11
10
9
13
13
12
11
11
11
10
9

Guitar Solo
C13
B♭13
G7♯5
C7
Gtr. 4 (slight dist.)
mf
w/ fingers
Gtr. 1
let ring
B♭7
A7
A♭7
A7
B♭7
B7
*Played behind the beat.
let ring
let ring
let ring
let ring
C7
B7
B♭7
A7
rake
let ring
let ring

A♭7
A7
B♭7
*Upstroke
**w/ delay
**Set for quarter-note regeneration w/ 4 repeats.
let ring
Interlude
Gtr. 1 tacet
C7
B♭13
E♭13
D♭9♯11
C9
B♭13
F9
E♭9
Hey,
hey,
Gtr. 4
8va
w/ ambient delay
w/ slide
**Vol. swell
***w/ echo set for quarter-note regeneration w/ multiple repeats, next 4 meas.
hey, hey.
loco
w/o slide
Verse Tag
Gtr. 4 tacet
D.S. al Coda 2
C7
B♭7
A♭7
G♭9 N.C.
There comes a chance in your life to find your way or fall be - hind.
Gtr. 3

Coda 2
Bkgd. Voc.: w/ Voc. Fig. 1 (7 times)
Gtr. 1: w/ Riff A (6 times)
C7
B♭7
A♭7
G7
changes.
Time will
Gtr. 4
Gtr. 1
Riff A
End Riff A
heal,
time will heal it.
Time,
time,
rake
*w/ echo as before, next 3 meas.

C7
B♭7
A♭7
G7
time, _
time will heal, _
time
will heal. _
8va
loco
1
1/2
F
*D9
B7
A♭
(Oo.)
Gtr. 4
mp
w/ slide
**w/ delay
don't pick
**Set for quarter-note regeneration
w/ multiple repeats.
Gtr. 1
p
*Segue into "Crow Jane."
Chords transitioning to the key of A♭.

from Sarah McLachlan - *Mirrorball*

Ice Cream

Words and Music by Sarah McLachlan

G♯m11
(Em11)
E6/9
(C6/9)
Badd9/D♯
(Gadd9/B)
C♯m11
(Am11)
F♯add4
(Dadd4)
E6/9
(C6/9)
bet - ter than ice cream. Ev - 'ry - one here knows how to cry
End Rhy. Fig. 2
Chorus
G♯m11
(Em11)
F♯add4
(Dadd4)
C♯m11
(Am11)
and fight. And it's a long way down.
Rhy. Fig. 3
G♯m11
(Em11)
F♯add4
(Dadd4)
C♯m11
(Am11)
G♯m11
(Em11)
It's a long way down. It's a long
End Rhy. Fig. 3
F♯add4
(Dadd4)
C♯m7 N.C.
(Am7)
Badd9
(Gadd9)
E6/9
(C6/9)
F♯add4
(Dadd4)
way down to the place where we start - ed from.

G♯m11
(Em11)
Badd9
(Gadd9)
C♯m11
(Am11)
F♯add4/C♯
(Dadd4/A)
Do, do, do, do, do, do, do, do, do, yeah.
F♯add4
(Dadd4)
E
(C)
Do, do, 'n', do, ah, yeah.
(Do.)
Verse
Gtr. 1: w/ Rhy. Fig. 2, simile
2. Your love is bet - ter than choc - 'late, bet - ter than an - y - thing
Eadd9
(Cadd9)
Badd9/D♯
(Gadd9/B)
else that I've tried. Oh, love is bet - ter than choc - 'late.
Ev - 'ry-one here knows how to fight.
(Fight.)
And it's a
Gtr. 1

Chorus

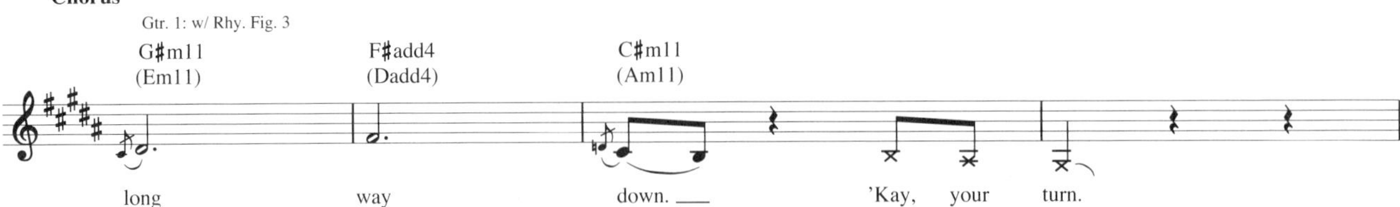

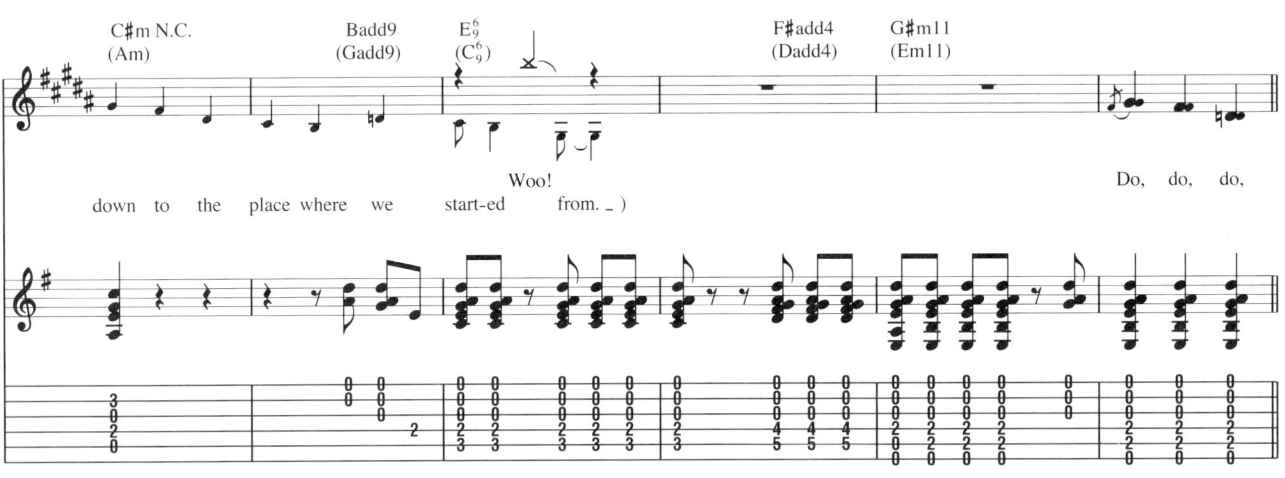

Outro

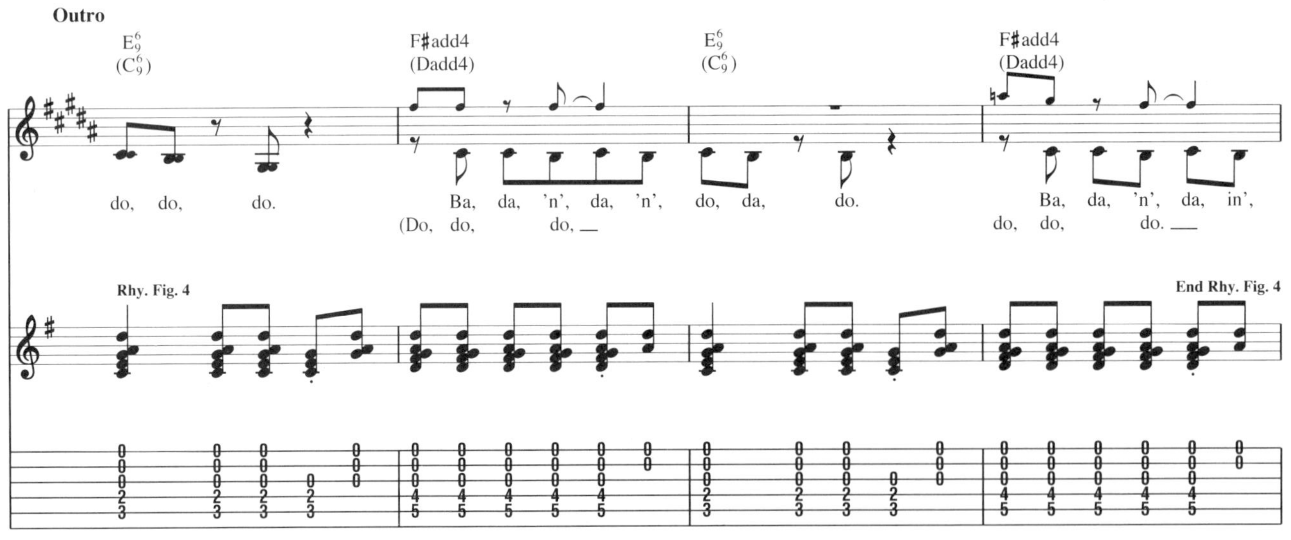

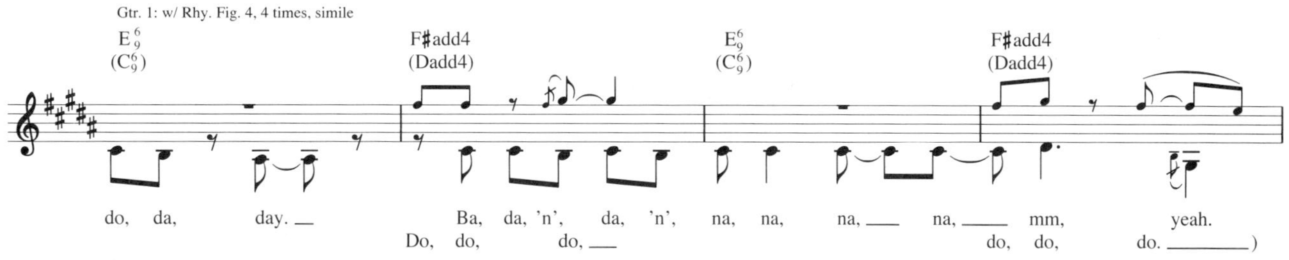
Gtr. 1: w/ Rhy. Fig. 4, 4 times, simile
E6/9
(C6/9)
F#add4
(Dadd4)
E6/9
(C6/9)
F#add4
(Dadd4)
do, da, day. Ba, da, 'n', da, 'n', na, na, na, na, mm, yeah.
Do, do, do, do, do, do.)

E6/9
(C6/9)
F#add4
(Dadd4)
E6/9
(C6/9)
F#add4
(Dadd4)
E6/9
(C6/9)
F#add4
(Dadd4)
Do, do, do, do, do, do, do, do, do, do, do, do. Do, do, do, do, do,
(Do, do, do,

E6/9
(C6/9)
F#add4
(Dadd4)
E6/9
(C6/9)
F#add4
(Dadd4)
E6/9
(C6/9)
F#add4
(Dadd4)
do, do, do, do, do. Do, do, do, do, do, do, do, do, do, do, do, do.
do, do, do.)

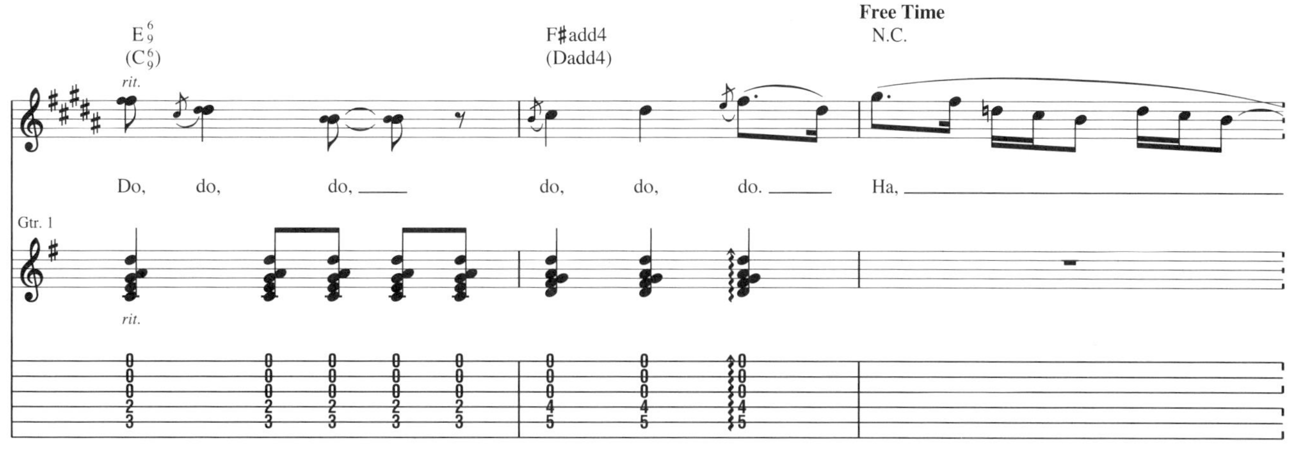
Free Time
E6/9
(C6/9)
F#add4
(Dadd4)
N.C.
rit.
Do, do, do, do, do, do. Ha,
Gtr. 1
rit.
0 0 0 0 0
0 0 0 0 0
0 0 0 0 0
2 2 2 2 2
3 3 3 3 3
0 0 0
0 0 0
0 0 0
4 4 4
5 5 5

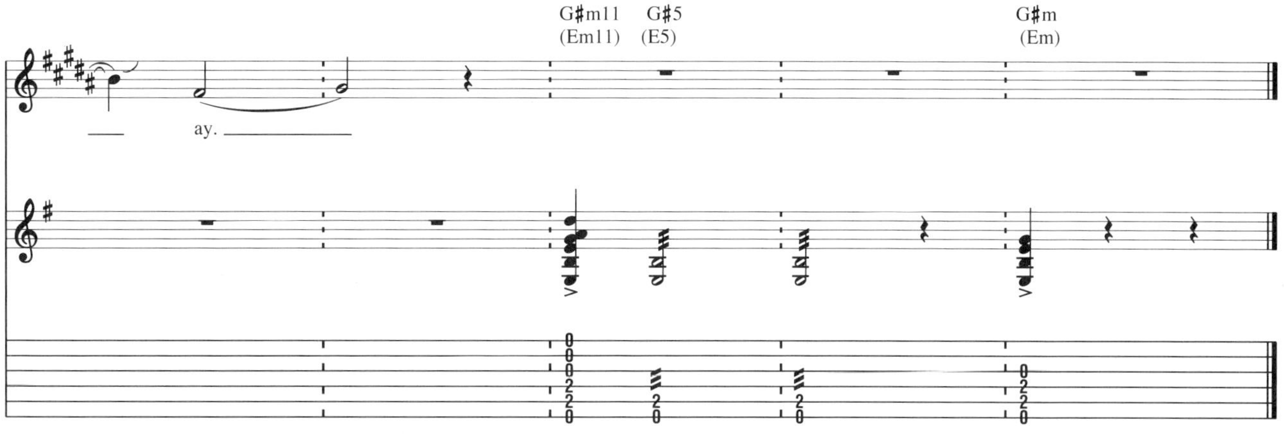
G#m11
(Em11)
G#5
(E5)
G#m
(Em)
ay.
0
0
0
2
2
0
2
0
2
0
0
2
2
0

from Nirvana - *Nevermind*

In Bloom

Words and Music by Kurt Cobain

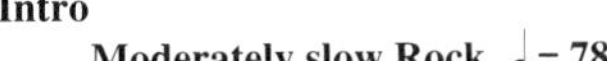

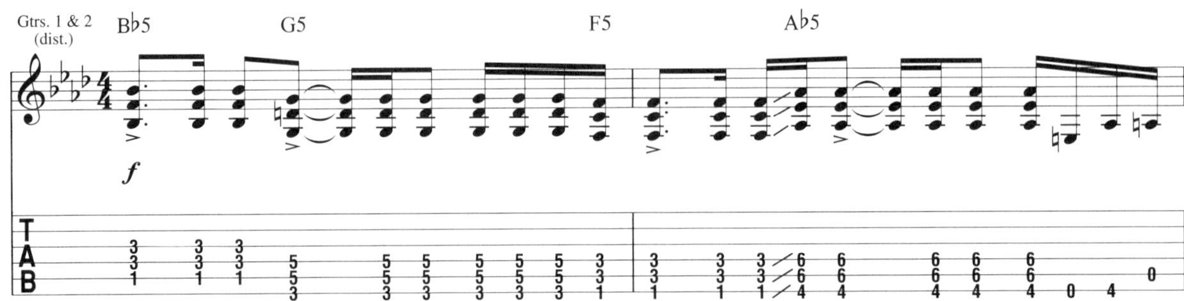

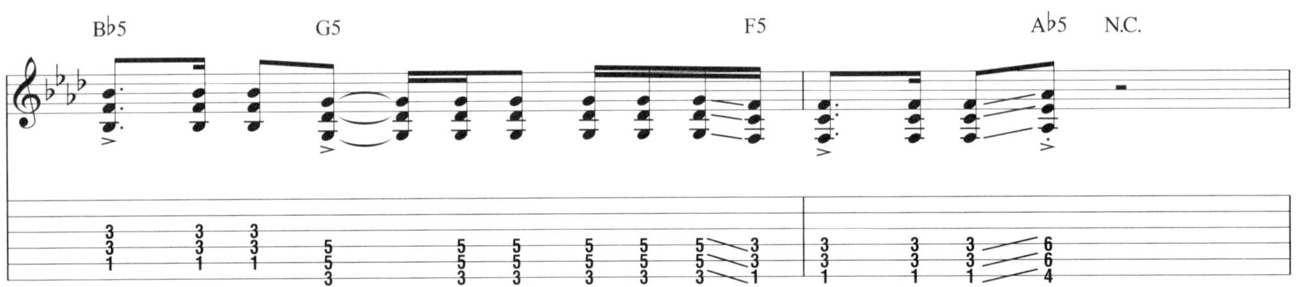

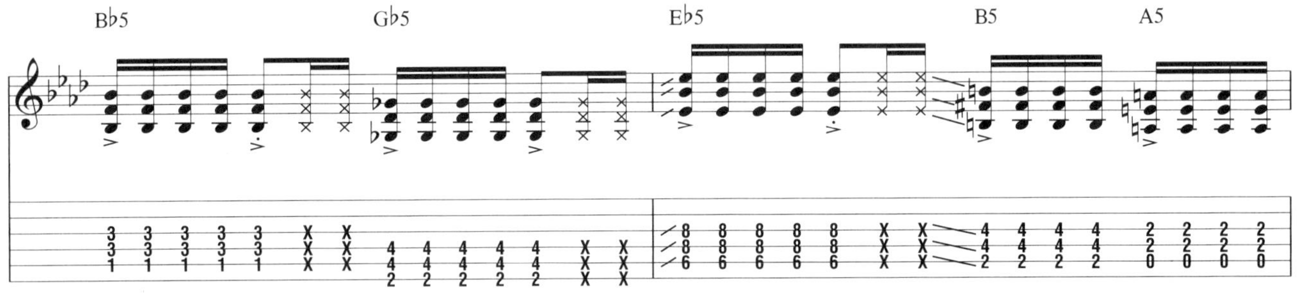

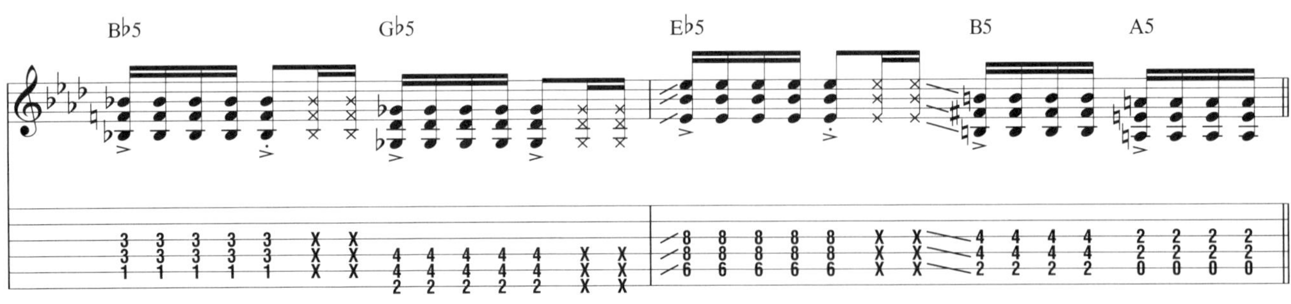

Verse
Gtrs. 1 & 2 tacet
N.C.
1. Sell the kids for food.
2. We can have some more.
*Gtr. 3
mf
*Bass arr. for gtr.
Weath - er chang - es moods.
Na - ture is a whore.
Gtr. 3 tacet
B♭ G♭ E♭ B A
Spring is here a - gain.
Bruis - es on the fruit.
Gtr. 1
mf
w/ clean tone
B♭ G♭ E♭ B5 D5
Re - pro - duc - tive glands.
Ten - der age in bloom.
He's
Gtrs. 1 & 2
f
w/ dist.

Chorus
Bb5 G5 Bb5 G5
the one who likes all our pret - ty songs and he
Rhy. Fig. 1
likes to sing a - long and he likes to shoot his gun, but he
End Rhy. Fig. 1
C Eb C Eb
don't know what it means, don't know what it means and I say,
Rhy. Fig. 2
End Rhy. Fig. 2
Gtrs. 1 & 2: w/ Rhy. Fig. 1
he's the one who likes all our pret - ty songs and he likes to sing a - long and he
To Coda
Gtrs. 1 & 2: w/ Rhy. Fig. 2
likes to shoot his gun, but he don't know what it means, don't know what it means and I say,

Bb5
G5
F5
Ab5
"Yeah."
Mm.
Gtrs. 1 & 2
Ooh.
Mm.
Guitar Solo
Gtr. 2 tacet
*Bb5
Gb5
Eb5
B5
A5
Gtr. 1
8va
loco
*Chord symbols reflect implied harmony.

D.S. al Coda
B♭5
G♭5
E♭5
B5
E♭5
D5
He's
Gtr. 1
let ring
Gtr. 2
Coda
C
E♭
Gtrs. 1 & 2: w/ Rhy. Fig. 2
don't know what it means,
don't know what it means,
B♭5
G5
F5
don't know what it means, and I say,
"Yeah.
Ooh.
Gtrs. 1 & 2
A♭5
B♭5
N.C.
Ooh."
Ooh.

from *Van Halen*

Jamie's Cryin'

Words and Music by David Lee Roth, Edward Van Halen, Alex Van Halen and Michael Anthony

Tune down 1/2 step:
(low to high) E♭-A♭-D♭-G♭-B♭-E♭

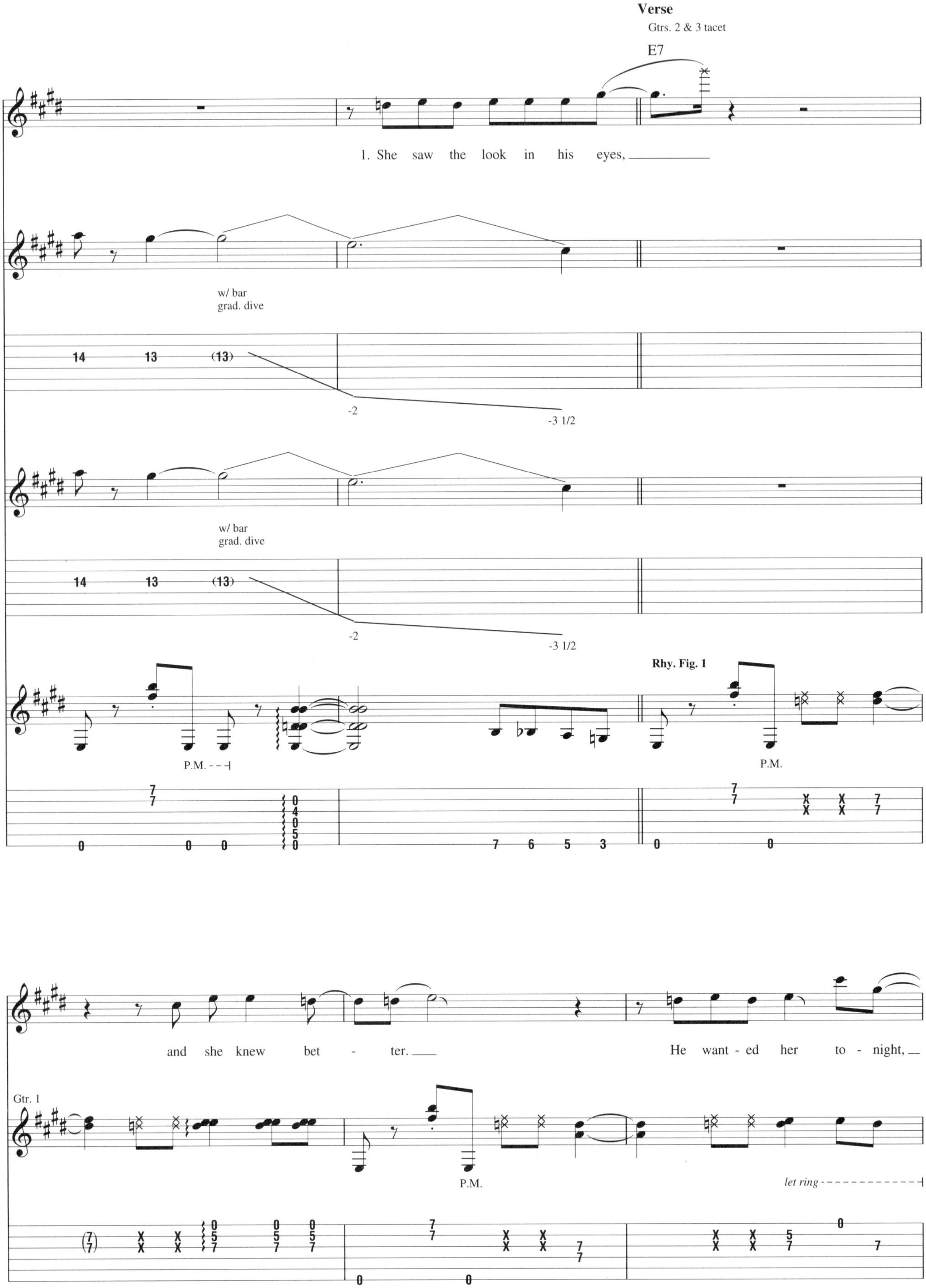

Verse

Gtrs. 2 & 3 tacet

E7

1. She saw the look in his eyes, ___

w/ bar
grad. dive

14 13 (13)

-2 -3 1/2

w/ bar
grad. dive

14 13 (13)

-2 -3 1/2

Rhy. Fig. 1

P.M. - - -┤

P.M.

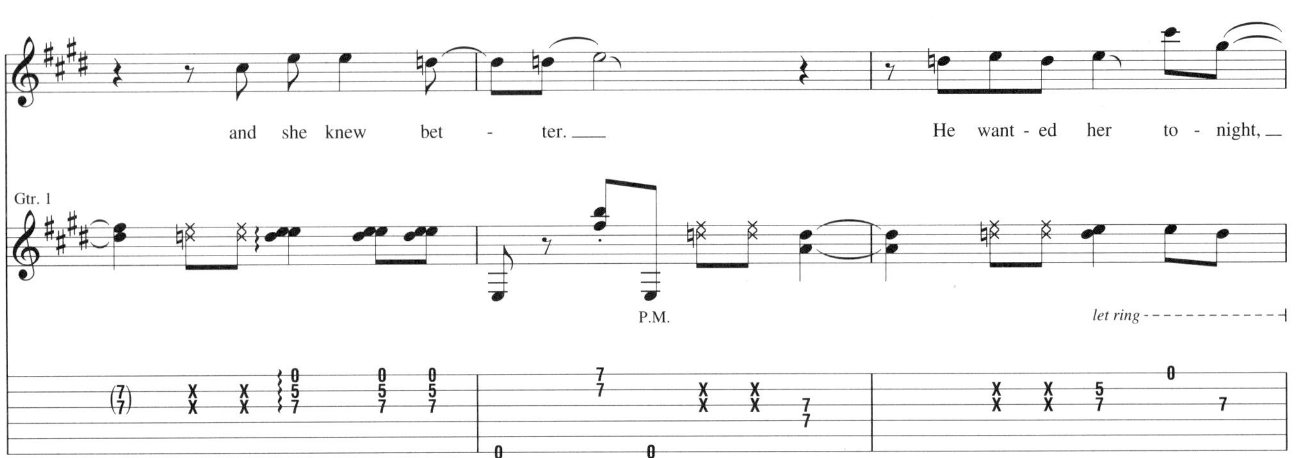

and it was now or nev - er.
End Rhy. Fig. 1
P.M.
F♯m
Bm
A5
B5
He made her feel so sad.
Chorus
E7
Oh, whoa, whoa, Ja - mie's cry - in'.
P.M.
Oh, whoa, whoa, Ja - mie's
Rhy. Fig. 2
P.M.

Verse

Gtr. 1: w/ Rhy. Fig. 1 (1st 4 meas.)

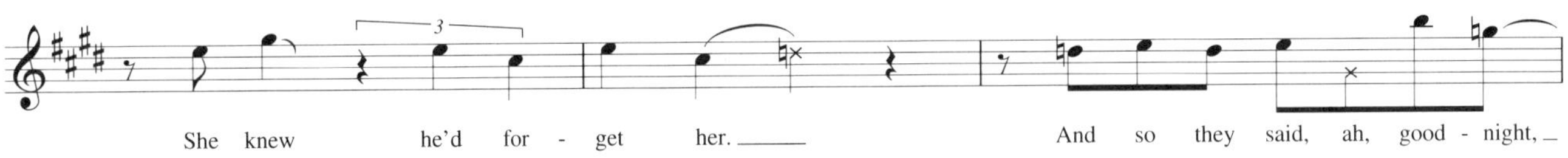

Pre-Chorus

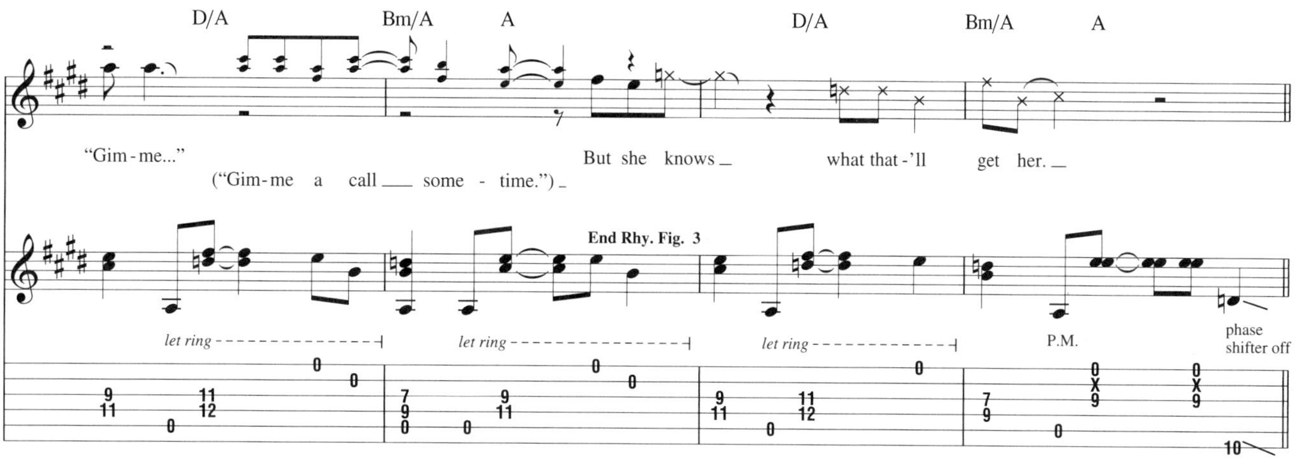
D/A Bm/A A D/A Bm/A A
"Gim-me..."
("Gim-me a call some-time.")
But she knows what that-'ll get her.
End Rhy. Fig. 3
let ring
P.M.
phase shifter off

Chorus

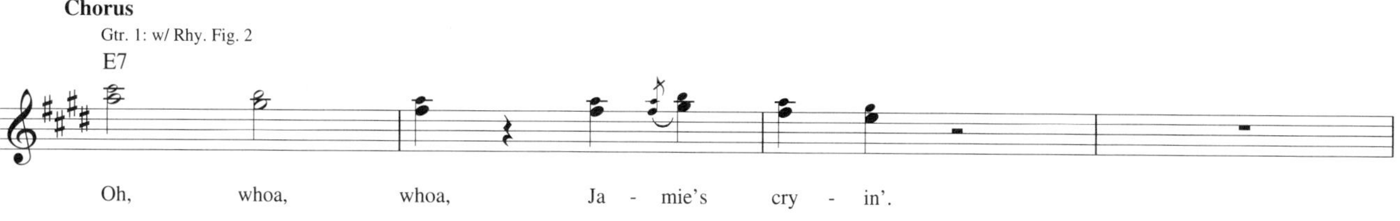
Gtr. 1: w/ Rhy. Fig. 2
E7
Oh, whoa, whoa, Ja-mie's cry-in'.

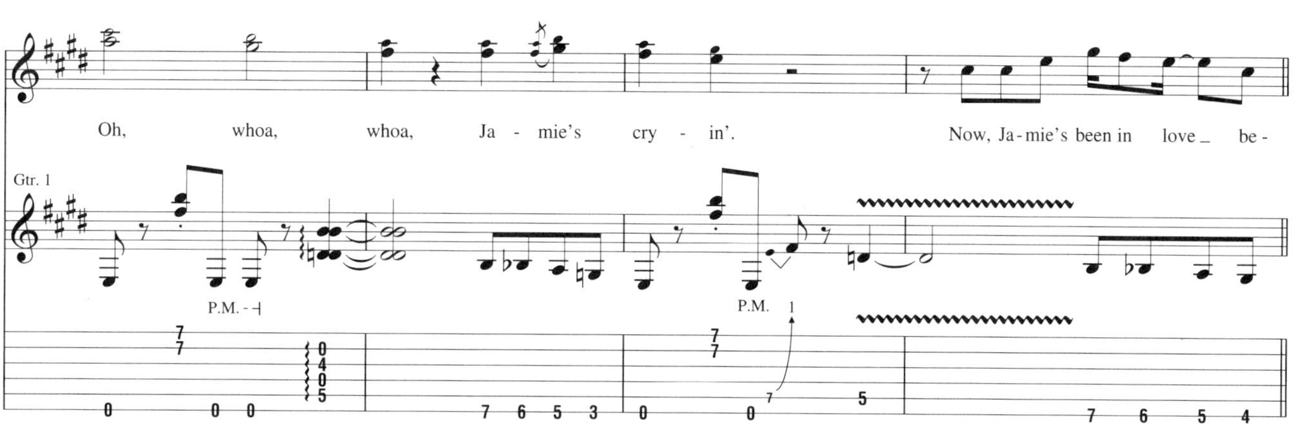
Oh, whoa, whoa, Ja-mie's cry-in'. Now, Ja-mie's been in love be-
Gtr. 1
P.M.

Bridge
C#m D C#m F#m
fore and she knows what love is for. It should mean a lit-tle, a lit-tle
(Ah, ah,
mp
let ring

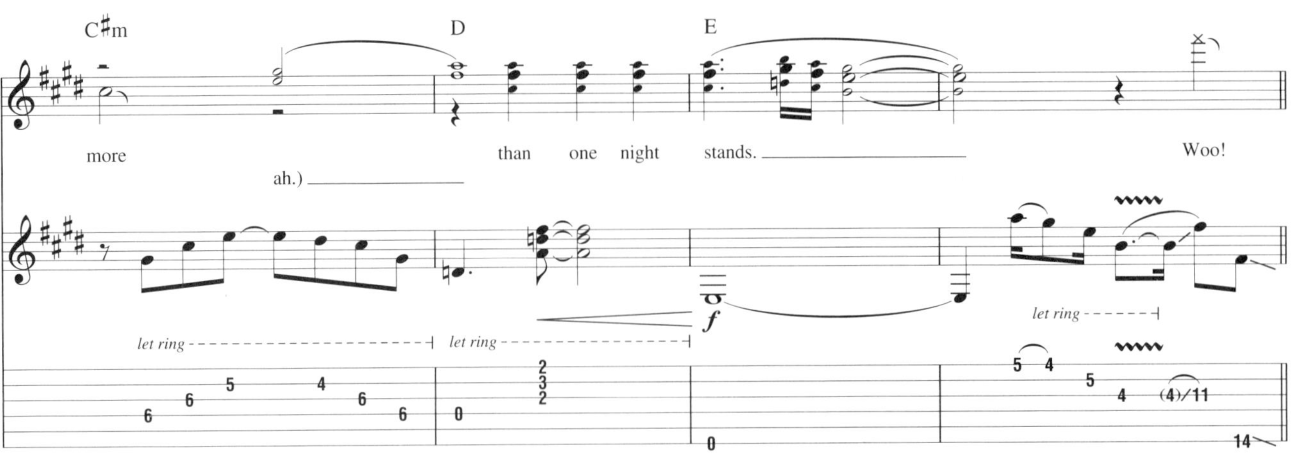

Guitar Solo

Pre-Chorus

Gtr. 1: w/ Rhy. Fig. 3

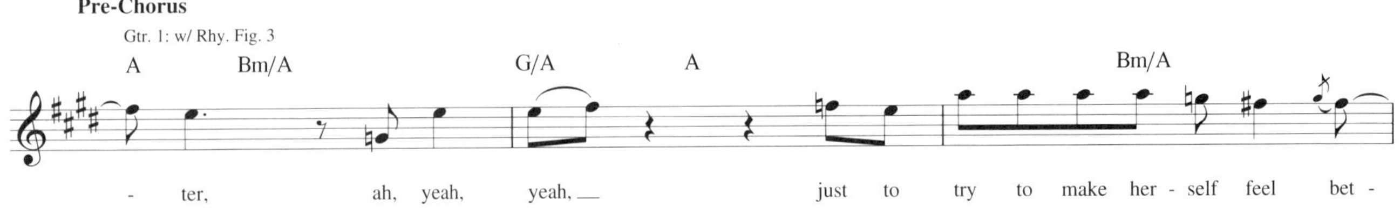

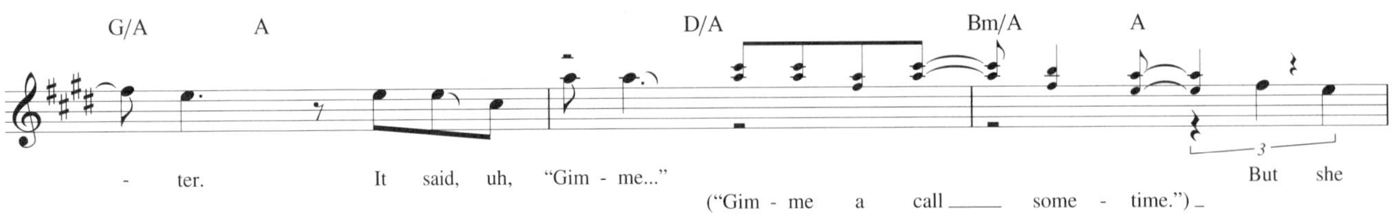

Chorus
D/A
Bm/A
A
E7
knows what that - 'll get her.
Oh, whoa, whoa, Ja - mie's
Gtr. 1
let ring
P.M.
P.M.
F♯m
Bm
A5
B5
cry - in'.
P.M.
Chorus
E7
Oh, whoa, whoa, Ja - mie's cry - in'.
Riff A
End Riff A
Gtrs. 2 & 3
Gtr. 1
P.M.
1/2

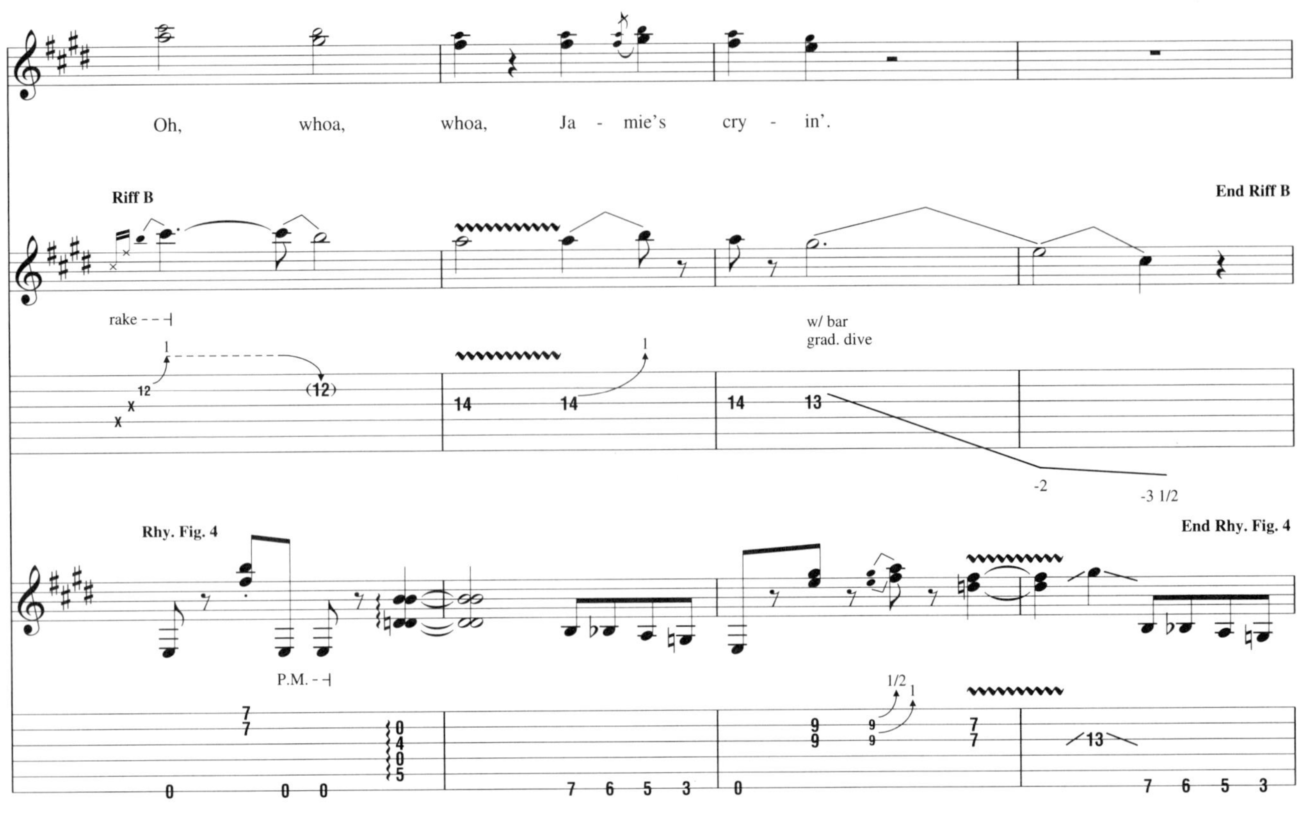

Gtr. 1: w/ Rhy. Fig. 4 (2 times)
Gtrs. 2 & 3: w/ Riff A

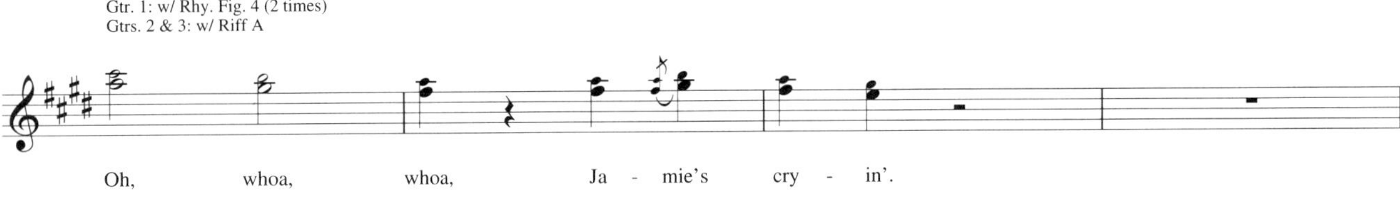

Gtr. 2: w/ Riff B

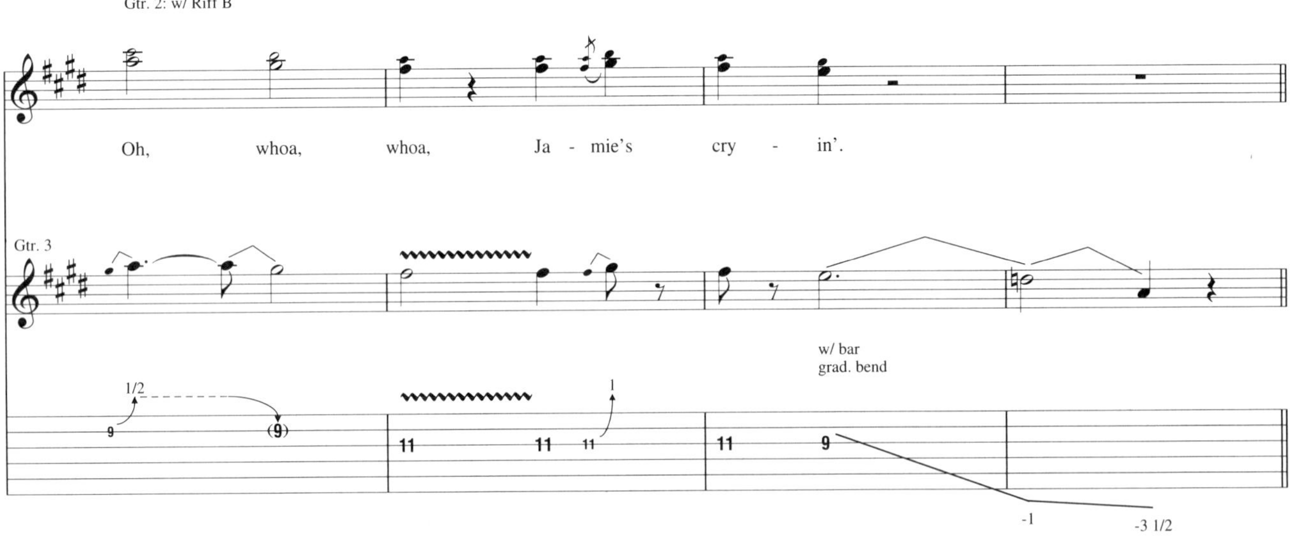

Outro

2nd time, Gtr. 1: w/ Rhy. Fill 1

E7
Gtrs. 2 & 3
Rhy. Fig. 5
Gtr. 1
End Rhy. Fig. 5
P.M.
P.M.

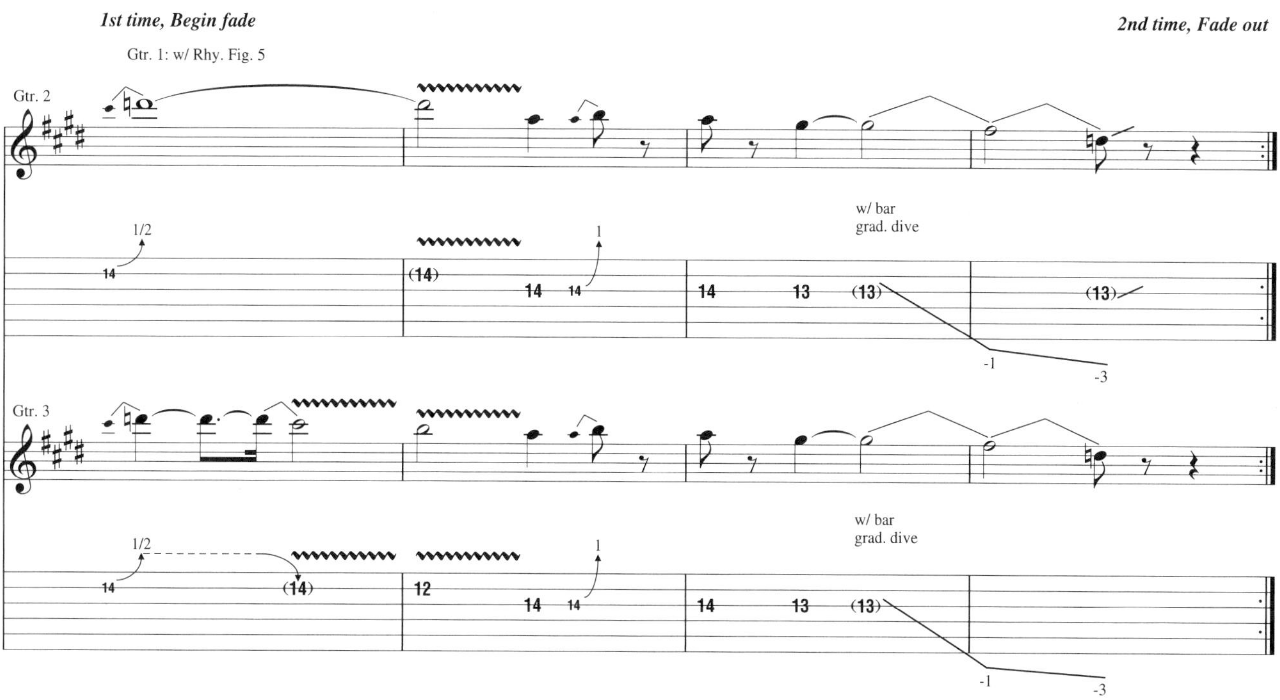
1st time, Begin fade
2nd time, Fade out
Gtr. 1: w/ Rhy. Fig. 5
Gtr. 2
w/ bar
grad. dive
Gtr. 3
w/ bar
grad. dive

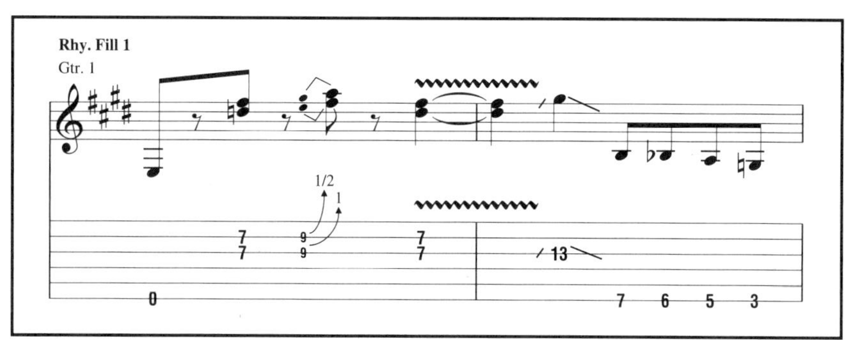
Rhy. Fill 1
Gtr. 1

from Bob Marley - *One Love: The Very Best of Bob Marley & The Wailers*

Jamming

Words and Music by Bob Marley

Bm E9(no3rd) G F#m Em

311 2 34 321 311 1342

7fr 7fr 7fr

Intro

Moderate Reggae ♩ = 124 (♫ = ♩ ♪ triplet)

Half-time feel

*Bm7 E9 G F#m

Oo, __ yeah.

Gtr. 2 (clean)

Rhy. Fig. 1 — End Rhy. Fig. 1

mf

Gtr. 1 (clean)

mp

w/ auto-wah

*Chord symbols reflect overall harmony.

Gtr. 1: w/ Rhy. Fig. 1

Bm7 E9 G F#m

Al - right. __ We're

Gtr. 1

Chorus

Gtr. 2: w/ Rhy. Fig. 1 (2 times)

Bm7 E9 G F#m

jam-min'. I wan-na jam it with you. __ We're

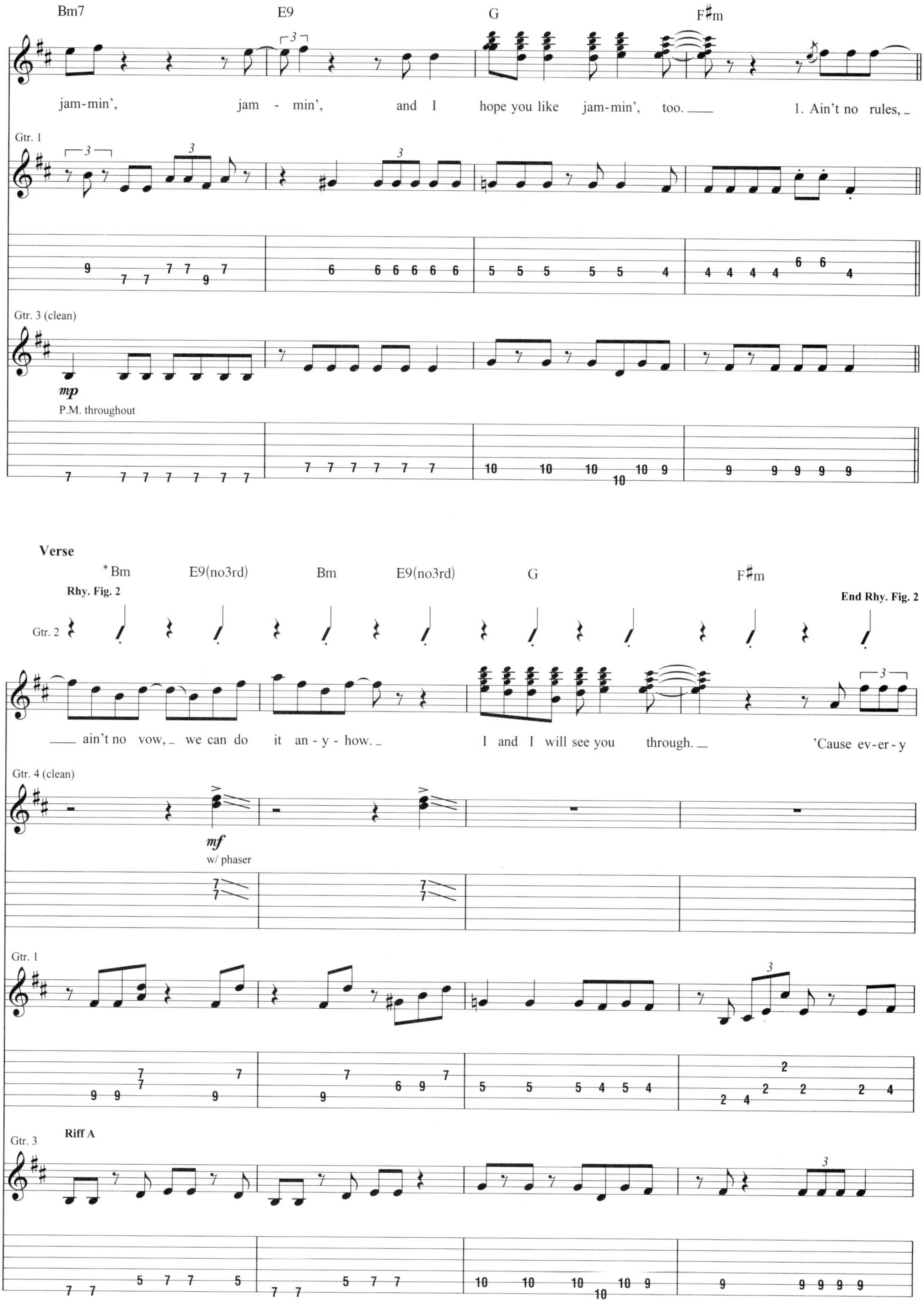

Verse

*Bm E9(no3rd) Bm E9(no3rd) G F♯m

Rhy. Fig. 2

End Rhy. Fig. 2

Gtr. 2

ain't no vow, we can do it an - y - how. I and I will see you through. 'Cause ev-er-y

Gtr. 4 (clean)

mf

w/ phaser

Gtr. 1

Gtr. 3

Riff A

*See top of first page of song for chord diagrams pertaining to rhythm slashes.

Gtr. 2: w/ Rhy. Fig. 2

Bm E9(no3rd) Bm E9(no3rd) G F♯m

day we pay the price, we're the liv - in' sac - ri - fice, jam-min' 'til the jam is through. ___ We're

P.M.

End Riff A

Chorus

Gtr. 2: w/ Rhy. Fig. 1 (2 times)
Gtr. 3 tacet

Bm7 E9 G F♯m

jam - min', to think that jam-min' was a thing of the past. ___ We're

Bm7
E9
G
F♯m
jam-min',
and I
hope this jam is gon-na
last.
2. No
Riff B
Gtr. 4
End Riff B
Gtr. 1
P.M.
Gtr. 3
Verse
Gtr. 3: w/ Riff A
Bm
E9(no3rd)
Bm
E9(no3rd)
G
F♯m
bul-let could stop us now. We nei-ther beg nor we won't bow.
Nei-ther can be bought nor
sold.
We
Gtr. 4
P.M.
P.M.
Gtr. 1

Gtr. 2: w/ Rhy. Fig. 2

Bm E9(no3rd) Bm E9(no3rd) G F#m

all de-fend the right, cha-cha - chil-dren must u-nite. Well, life is worth much more than gold. We're

P.M. P.M.

Chorus

Gtr. 2: w/ Rhy. Fig. 1 (2 times)

Bm7 E9 G F#m

jam-min', and we're jam-min' in the name of the Lord. We're
(Jam-min', jam-min', jam-min', jam-min'.)

Gtr. 4: w/ Riff B
Bm7
E9
G
F#m
* Voc. Fig. 1
End Voc. Fig. 1
jam-min', look out, we're jam-min' right straight from Jah. Sing-in',
(Jam-min', jam-min', jam-min'.)
Gtr. 1
Gtr. 3
Riff C
End Riff C
*Refers to upstemmed voc. only.
Bridge
Gtr. 1 tacet
Bm
Em
Bm
Em
Gtr. 2
ho - ly Mount Zi - on, ho - ly Mount Zi - on.
Gtr. 3
Bm
Gtr. 1 tacet
Just seat it in Mount Zi - on. And rules all cre - a - tion. Yeah, we're,
Gtrs. 1 & 4
Gtr. 3

Chorus
Gtr. 2; w/ Rhy. Fig. 1 (1st 2 meas.)
Gtr. 3: w/ Riff C (1st 2 meas.)
Gtr. 2; w/ Rhy. Fig. 1 (2 times)
Gtr. 3: w/ Riff C (2 times)
Bm7
E9
Bm7
we're jam - min'.
Wop - ju - wah - wah - wah.
We're jam - min',
(Wop - ju - wah.)
Gtr. 4
P.M.
E9
G
F♯m
see,
I wan - na jam it with you.
We're
(Wop - ju - wah.)
Gtr. 4
P.M.
Gtr. 1
Bkgd. Voc.: w/ Voc. Fig. 1
Bm7
E9
G
F♯m
jam-min',
I'm jammed. I hope you're jam-min', too.
3. Jah
P.M.

Verse
Gtr. 4 tacet
Bm E9(no3rd) Bm E9(no3rd) G F♯m
knows how much I've tried, the truth I can-not hide to keep you sat - is - fied. True
Gtr. 1 Riff D
End Riff D
Gtr. 1: w/ Riff D
Gtr. 3: w/ Riff A (last 4 meas.)
Bm E9(no3rd) Bm E9(no3rd) G F♯m
love, I know ex - ists, it's the love I can't re-sist, so jam by my side. We're
Outro-Chorus
Bkgd. Voc.: w/ Voc. Fig. 1
Gtr. 2: w/ Rhy. Fig. 1 (7 times)
Gtr. 3: w/ Riff C (7 times)
Bm7 E9 G F♯m
jam - min', yeah. I wan-na jam it with you. We're
Gtr. 1
Gtr. 4
Gtr. 4: w/ Riff B (6 times)
Bm7 E9
jam - min', we're jam - min', we're jam - min', we're jam - min', we're jam - min', we're jam - min', we're jam - min', we're jam - min'.
Gtr. 1

Bkgd. Voc.: w/ Voc. Fig. 1
G
F♯m
Bm7
Hope you like jam - min', too.
We're jam - min', we're jam - min'. We're
E9
G
* Voc. Fig. 2
jam - min', we're jam - min'.
I wan - na, I wan - na, I
(I wan - na jam it with you.)
*Refers to upstemmed voc. only.
F♯m
Bm7
E9
End Voc. Fig. 2
wan - na jam with you, now. We're jam - min', we're jam - min'.
Bkgd. Voc.: w/ Voc. Fig. 1
G
F♯m
Bm7
And I hope you like jam - min', I
(Hope you like jam - min', too.)

Bkgd. Voc.: w/ Voc. Fig. 2
E9
G
F♯m
hope you like jam - min' 'cause I wan - na jam it with you.
Bm7
E9
G
I like, I hope you, I
F♯m
Bm7
E9
hope you like, a, jam - min', too, now. I wan-na jam it,
G
F♯m
wan - na jam it.

Free time
Gtr. 2 tacet
Gtr. 3 tacet
Bm
E9
G
Gtr. 2
Oo.
Gtr. 1
Gtr. 4
P.M.
Gtr. 3
Gtr. 4 tacet
F♯m
N.C.
Gtr. 1
Gtr. 2

from Santana - *Santana*

Jingo (Jin-Go-Lo-Ba)

By Michael Olatunji

2.
To Coda
Lo ba ba, lo ba ba, lo ba ba, lo ba. Lo
ba ba, lo ba ba, lo ba ba, lo ba.
Bm7
Bm
Jin - go,
jin - go
ba.
Interlude
Bm
14
Guitar Solo
Bm
full
full
1 1/2

full
1/2
w/ bar
-1 1/2
D.S. al Coda
Coda
Outro
Bm
Play 6 Times & Fade
ba ba, lo ba ba, lo ba ba, lo ba. Lo
simile on repeats

from ZZ Top - *Rio Grande Mud*

Just Got Paid

Words and Music by Billy F Gibbons and Bill Ham

8va
loco
End Riff B
P.M.
Verse
*E
D
Em7
1. Just got paid to-day, got me a pock-et full of change.
*Chord symbols reflect overall harmony.
E
D
Said I just got paid to-day, got me a pock-et full
Riff C
tr

Em7
G5
of change.
If you be - lieve like work-in' hard all day, just
slight P.M.
End Riff C
Rhy. Fig. 1
P.M. P.M. P.M. P.M.
A5
Em7
step on my shoes and take my pay.
End Rhy. Fig. 1
Verse
Gtr. 1: w/ Riff C (2 times)
E
D
Em7
2. I was born my pa-pa's son, when I hit the ground I was on the run.
Gtr. 2
P.M.

E
D
Had one glad hand and the oth-er be-hind. You can have yours, just give me mine.
Em7
Gtr. 1: w/ Rhy. Fig. 1
G5
When the hound dog bark in the black of a night, stick my
let ring
A5
Em7
hand in my pock-et, ev-'ry-thing's all right.
Gtr. 2
A5
P.M.
Gtr. 1
P.M. P.M. P.M.
pp

Guitar Solo

A
E7
A
E7
A
E7
let ring
let ring
let ring
let ring
A
E7
A
E7
A
E7
let ring
let ring
let ring
A
E7
A
E7
let ring
let ring
let ring
let ring
let ring

A
E7
A
E7
let ring
let ring
A
E7
A
E7
A
E7
let ring
let ring
A
E7
A
E7
A
E7
let ring
let ring
let ring
let ring
let ring

A
E7
A
E7
let ring
let ring
let ring
D
A7
D
A7
D
A7
let ring
let ring
let ring
let ring
let ring
let ring
Interlude
D
A7
E
mp
don't
pick
mp
let ring
let ring
let ring

p
w/ slap back delay
let ring
let ring
let ring
delay off
pp
p
let ring
let ring
B5 N.C.
B5 N.C.
B5 N.C.
8va
loco
8va
f
P.M.
mf

B7 N.C.
Gtr. 1: w/ Riff A
Em7
8va
loco
w/ slapback delay
*Gliss. w/ slide contacting frets.
Gtr. 1: w/ Riff B
Gtr. 2
3. I
Verse
Gtr. 1: w/ Riff C (2 times)
Gtr. 2 tacet
E
D
Em7
just got paid to-day, got me a pock-et full of change.
Said,
"Black sheep, black, do you got some wool?" "Yes, I do, man, my bag is full."
It's the
**pp < p mf
**Vol. swell
Gtr. 1: w/ Rhy. Fig. 1
G5
A5
root of e - vil and you know the rest, but it's way a-head of what's sec-ond best.
let ring

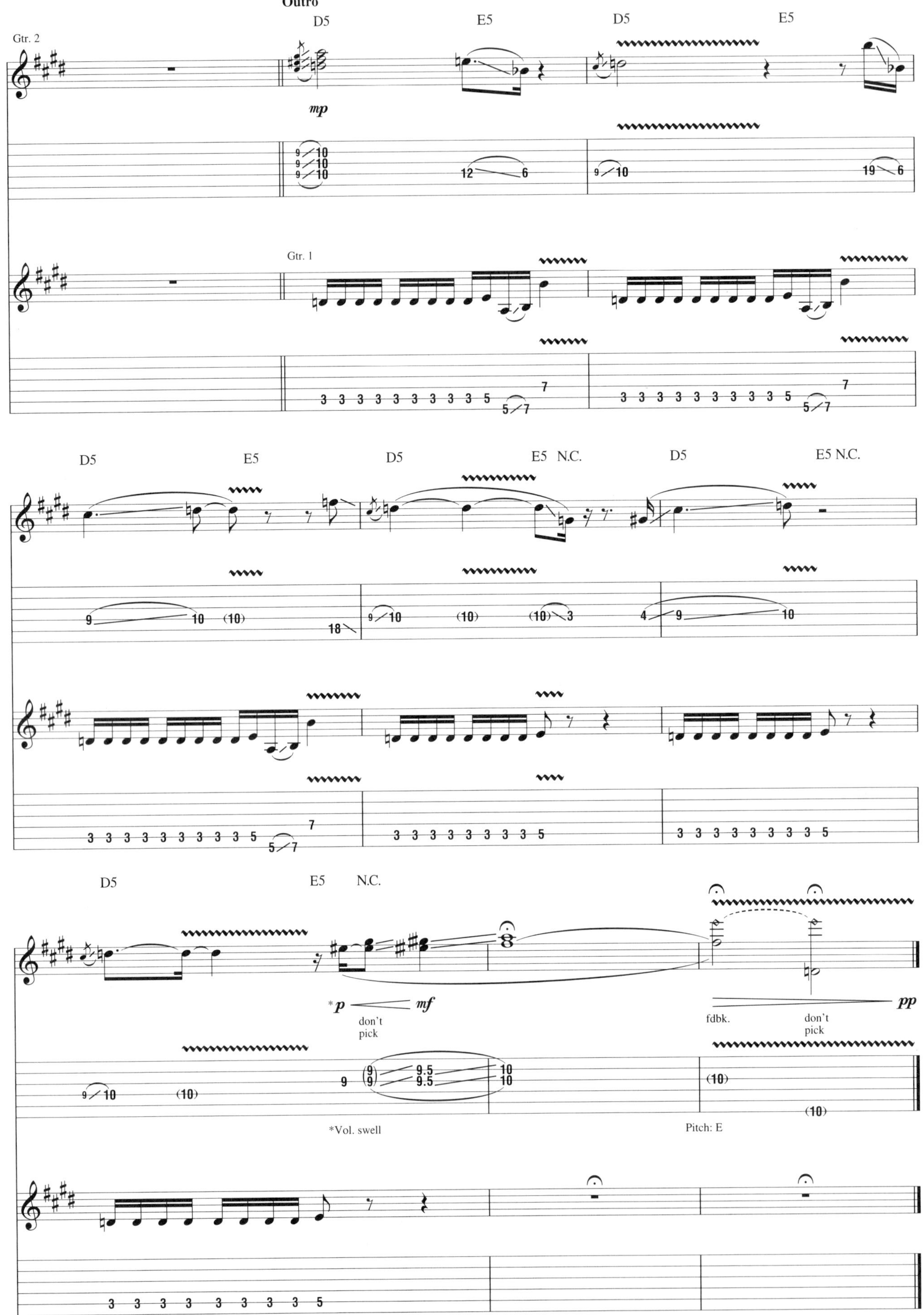
Outro
D5
E5
D5
E5
Gtr. 2
mp
Gtr. 1
D5
E5
D5
E5 N.C.
D5
E5 N.C.
D5
E5
N.C.
*p
mf
don't pick
fdbk.
don't pick
pp
*Vol. swell
Pitch: E

from *The Cars*

Just What I Needed

Words and Music by Ric Ocasek

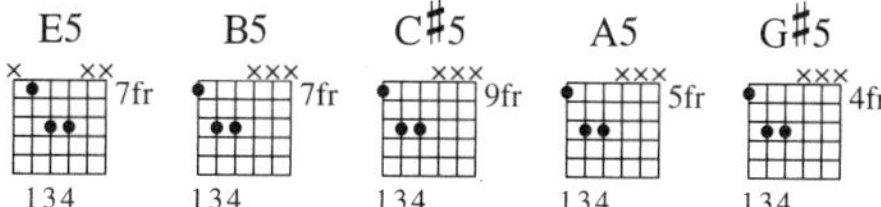

Intro

Moderately ♩ = 125

*Chord symbols reflect combined harmony.

Verse

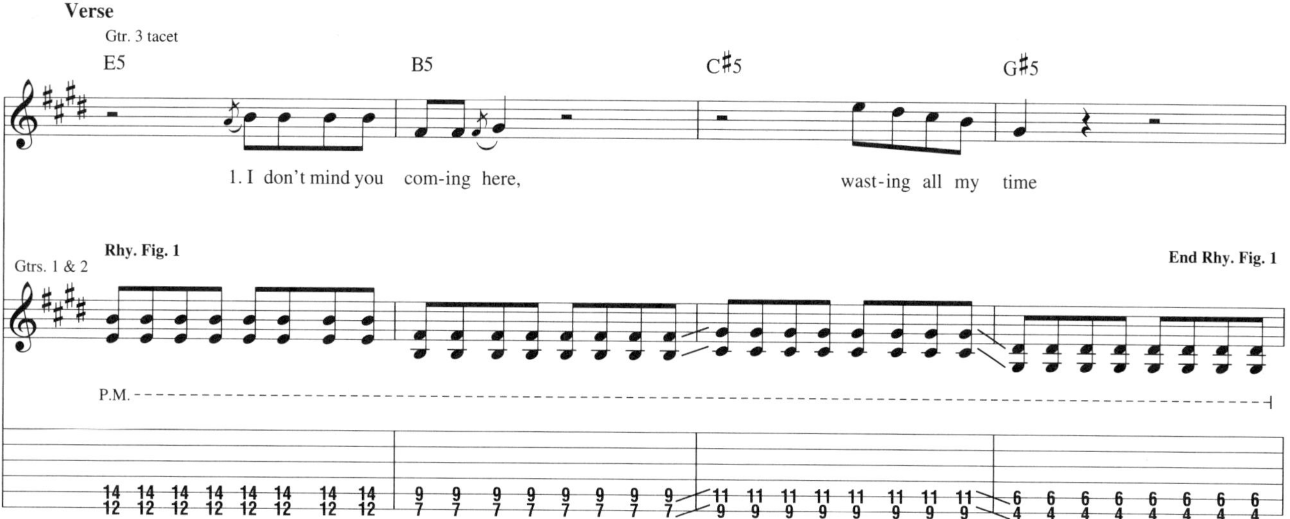

Gtrs. 1 & 2: w/ Rhy. Fig. 1 (2 times)
E5
B5
C♯5
G♯5
'cause when you're stand-ing, oh, so near I kind-a lose my mind.
Gtr. 3
P.M.
E5
B5
C♯5
G♯
It's not the per-fume that you wear. It's not the rib-bons in your hair.
Rhy. Fig. 2
End Rhy. Fig. 2
P.M.
E
B
G♯
A
And I don't mind you com-ing here and wast-ing all my time.
Gtr. 3
let ring
Gtrs. 1 & 2
Rhy. Fig. 3
End Rhy. Fig. 3
P.M.

**See top of first page of song for chord diagrams pertaining to rhythm slashes.

Verse
Gtrs. 1 & 2: w/ Rhy. Fig. 1 (3 times)
Gtr. 4 tacet
1st time, Gtr. 5 tacet
2nd time, Gtr. 5: w/ Fill 2
E5
B
C♯m
G♯
2. I don't mind you hang-ing out and talk-ing in your sleep.
3. I don't mind you com-ing here and wast-ing all my time, time,
Gtr. 3
Rhy. Fill 1
End Rhy. Fill 1
2nd time, Gtr. 3: w/ Rhy. Fill 1
E
B
C♯m
G♯
It does-n't mat-ter where you've been, as long as it was deep, yeah.
'cause when you're stand-ing, oh, so near, I kind-a lose my mind, yeah.
mf
1st time, Gtr. 3: w/ Rhy. Fig. 2
Gtr. 4: w/ Riff A
2nd time, Gtr. 3: w/ Rhy. Fill 2
2nd time, Gtr. 3: w/ Rhy. Fig. 2 (last 3 meas.)
E5
B5
C♯5
G♯
You al-ways knew to wear it well. And you look so fan-cy, I can tell.
It's not the per-fume that you wear. It's not the rib-bons in your hair.
Fill 2
Gtr. 5
w/ pick & finger
Rhy. Fill 2
Gtr. 3
P.M.
P.M.
P.M.

Gtr. 1: w/ Rhy. Fig. 3
E
B
G♯
A
And I don't mind you hang-ing out and talk-ing in your sleep.
I don't mind you com-ing here and wast-ing all my time.
Gtr. 3
P.M.
Gtr. 2
P.M.
P.M.
Chorus
E5 B5 A5 C♯5 B5 E5 B5 A5 C♯5
I guess you're just what I need - ed. I need ed some-one to feed.
Voc. Fig. 1
(Just what I need - ed.
Gtr. 6 (dist.)
mp
Rhy. Fig. 4
*Gtrs. 1, 2 & 3
*Composite arrangement

E5
B5
A5
C♯5
B5
E5
B5
A5
I guess you're just what I need - ed.
I need - ed
End Voc. Fig. 1
Just what I need - ed.)
To Coda
2nd time, Gtr. 7 tacet
C♯5
some - one to bleed.
Fill 1
Gtr. 7 (dist.)
Gtr. 7
*End Fill 1
mp
Gtr. 5
divisi
f
w/ pick
Gtr. 6
Gtrs. 1, 2 & 3
End Rhy. Fig. 4
(Gtrs. 1 & 2, cont. in slashes)
*Refers to Gtr. 7 only.

Guitar Solo

Gtrs. 6 & 7 tacet
E5 B5 C#5 G#5 E5 B5 C#5 A5
Rhy. Fig. 5
End Rhy. Fig. 5
Gtrs. 1 & 2
P.M.
Gtr. 5
Gtr. 3
Gtrs. 1 & 2: w/ Rhy. Fig. 5
E5 B5 C#5 G#5
Rhy. Fig. 6
D.S. al Coda
E5 B5 C#5 A5
hold bend
w/ pick & finger
let ring
End Rhy. Fig. 6

 Coda

Gtrs. 1, 2 & 3: w/ Rhy. Fig. 4 (last 2 meas.)

Bkgd. Voc.: w/ Voc. Fig. 1
Gtrs. 1, 2 & 3: w/ Rhy. Fig. 4

E5 B5 A5

I guess you're

Gtr. 6

steady gliss.

C♯5 B5 E5 B5 A5 C♯5

just what I need - ed. I need - ed some - one to feed.

E5 B5 A5 C♯5 B5 E5 B5 A5

I guess you're just what I need - ed. I need - ed

Gtr. 7: w/ Fill 1

C♯5

some - one to plead. *Spoken:* Yeah, yeah, so plead me.

Outro-Chorus

from Prince and the Revolution - *Parade*

Kiss

Words and Music by Prince

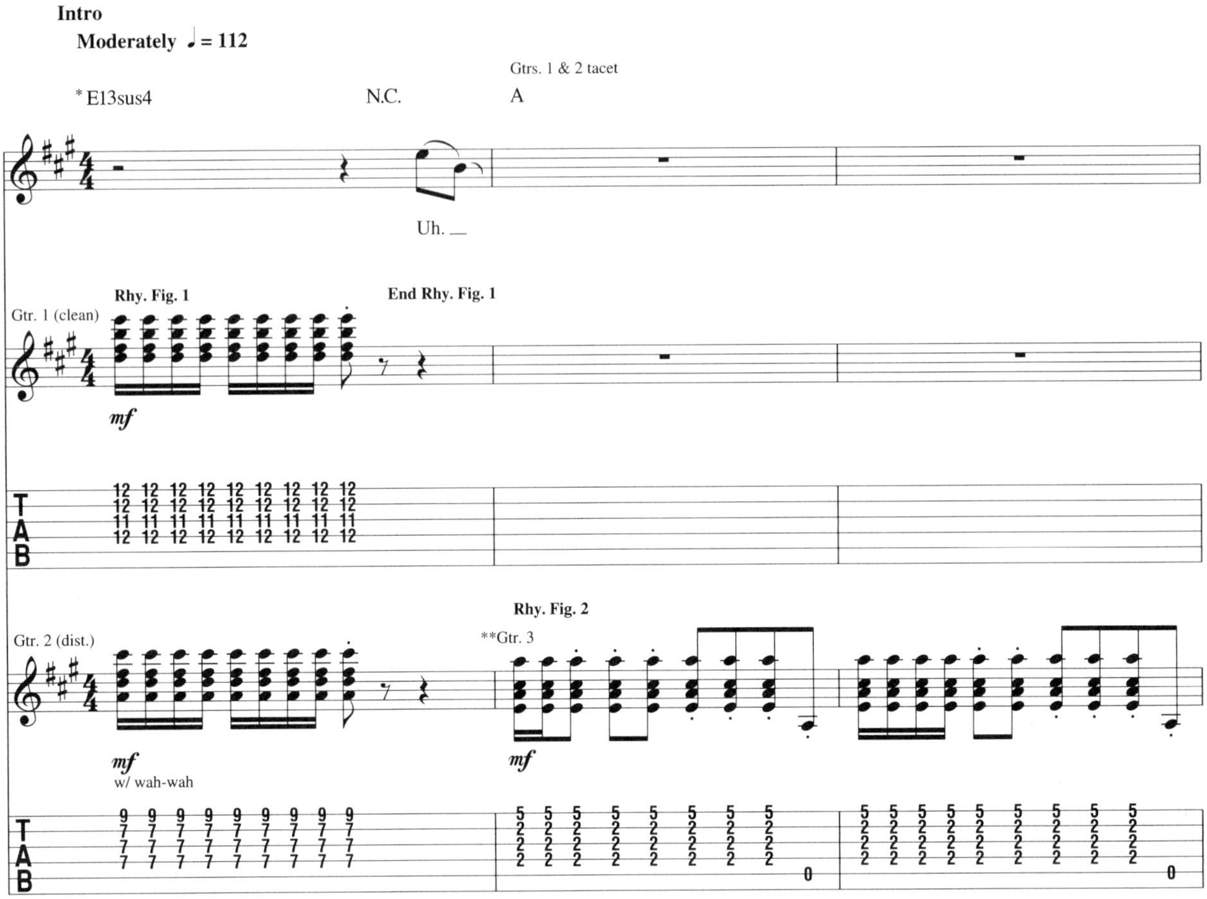

Intro
Moderately ♩ = 112
Gtrs. 1 & 2 tacet
*E13sus4
N.C.
A
Uh. __
Rhy. Fig. 1
End Rhy. Fig. 1
Gtr. 1 (clean)
mf
Rhy. Fig. 2
Gtr. 2 (dist.)
**Gtr. 3
mf
w/ wah-wah
mf

*Chord symbols reflect overall harmony.

**Synth. arr. for gtr.

Verse
N.C.
A
1. You don't have to be beau - ti - ful ______
Gtr. 3
End Rhy. Fig. 2
Rhy. Fig. 3

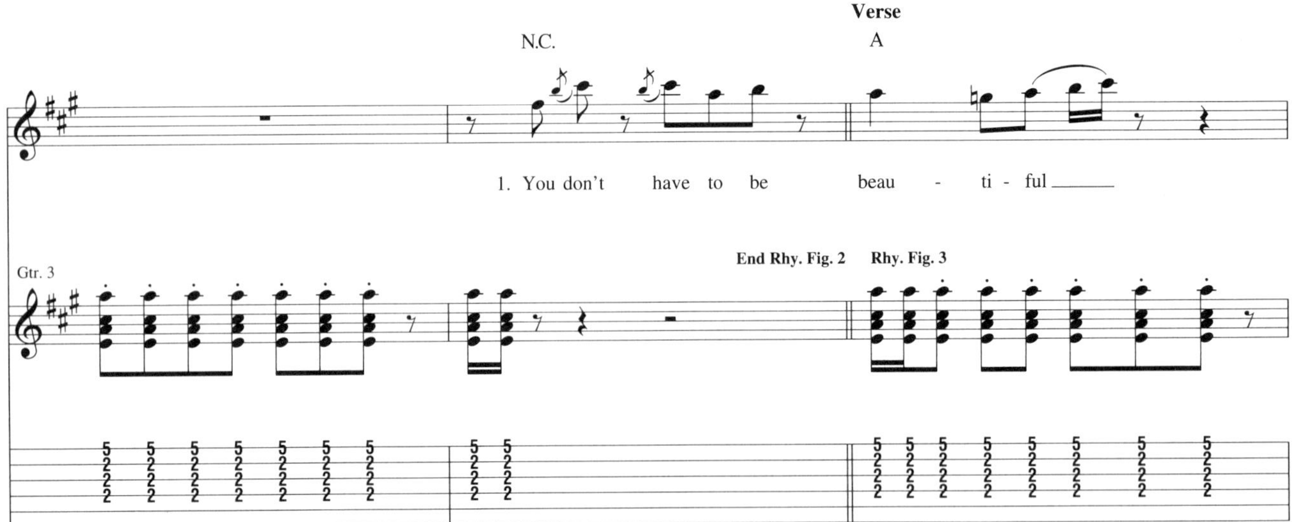

to turn me on.
I just need your
bod - y, ba - by,
from dusk 'til dawn.
D
You don't need ex - pe - ri - ence, ah,
to turn me out,
ah.
A
You just leave it all up to me, ah,

I'm gon - na show you what it's all a - bout, now.
You don't have to be
Voc. Fig. 1
Female: (Don't have to be
E
rich to be my girl. You don't have to be cool to rule my
D
world.
rich to be my girl. You don't have to be cool to rule my world.
Ain't no par - tic - u - lar sign
E
I'm more com - pat - i - ble with. I just want your
I just want your

D
Gtr. 1: w/ Rhy. Fig. 1
E13sus4
N.C.
ex - tra time and your (kissing noises) kiss.
End Voc. Fig. 1
ex - tra time and your ...)
End Rhy. Fig. 3
Interlude
Gtr. 3: w/ Rhy. Fig. 2
A
N.C.
Ah, oh, oh. 2. You got to not talk
Verse
Gtr. 3: w/ Rhy. Fig. 3
A
dirt - y, babe, uh, if you wan - na im-press me.
(Ah.)
You can't be too flirt - y, ma - ma, I know how to un - dress me,
D
yeah. I want to be your fan - ta - sy. May - be you could be mine.
(Want to be your fan - ta - sy.)
A
You just leave it all up to me,

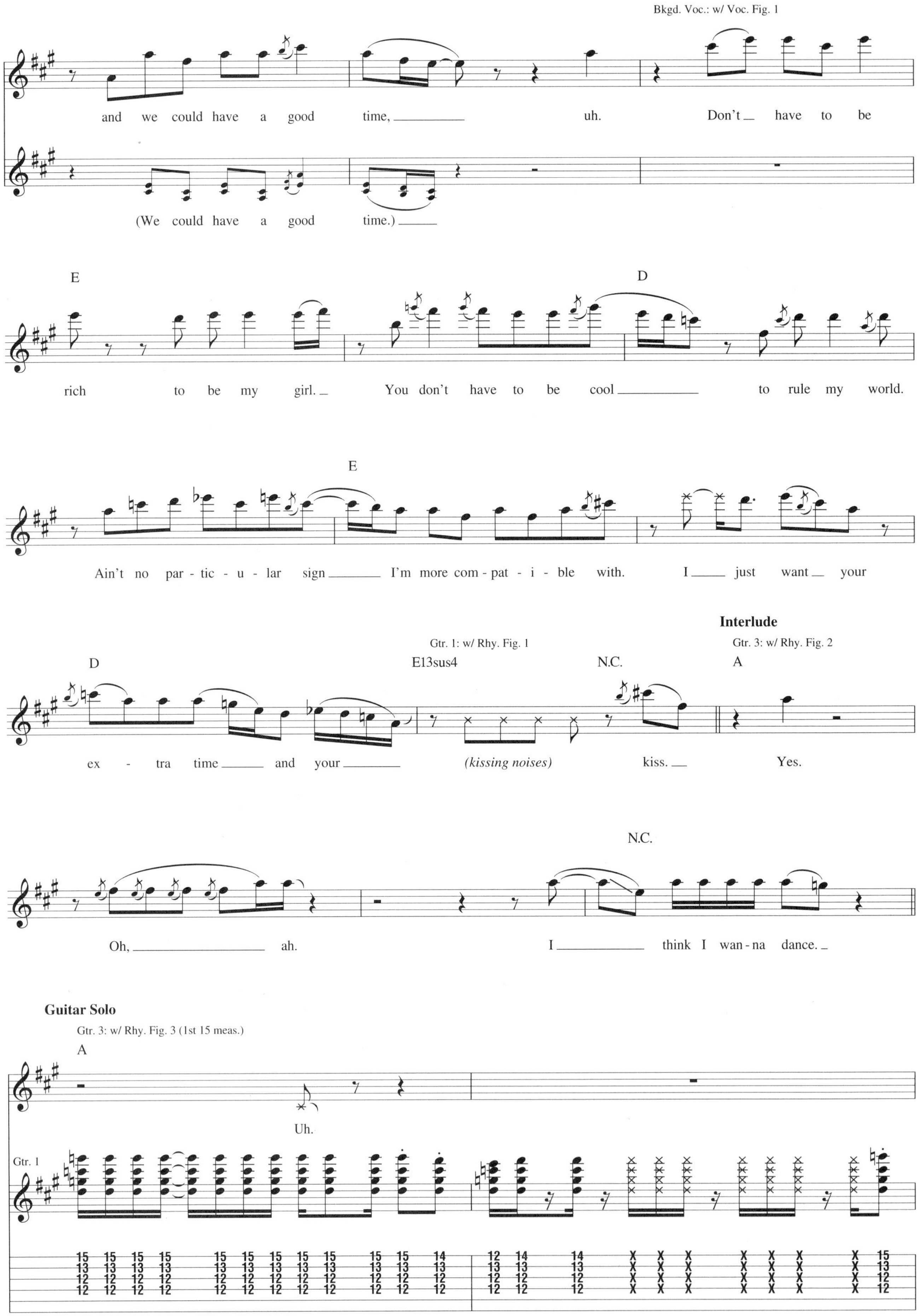

Bkgd. Voc.: w/ Voc. Fig. 1

and we could have a good time, ___ uh. Don't _ have to be

(We could have a good time.) ___

E D

rich to be my girl. _ You don't have to be cool ___ to rule my world.

E

Ain't no par - tic - u - lar sign ___ I'm more com - pat - i - ble with. I ___ just want _ your

Interlude

Gtr. 1: w/ Rhy. Fig. 1

Gtr. 3: w/ Rhy. Fig. 2

D E13sus4 N.C. A

ex - tra time ___ and your ___ *(kissing noises)* kiss. _ Yes.

Guitar Solo

Gtr. 3: w/ Rhy. Fig. 3 (1st 15 meas.)

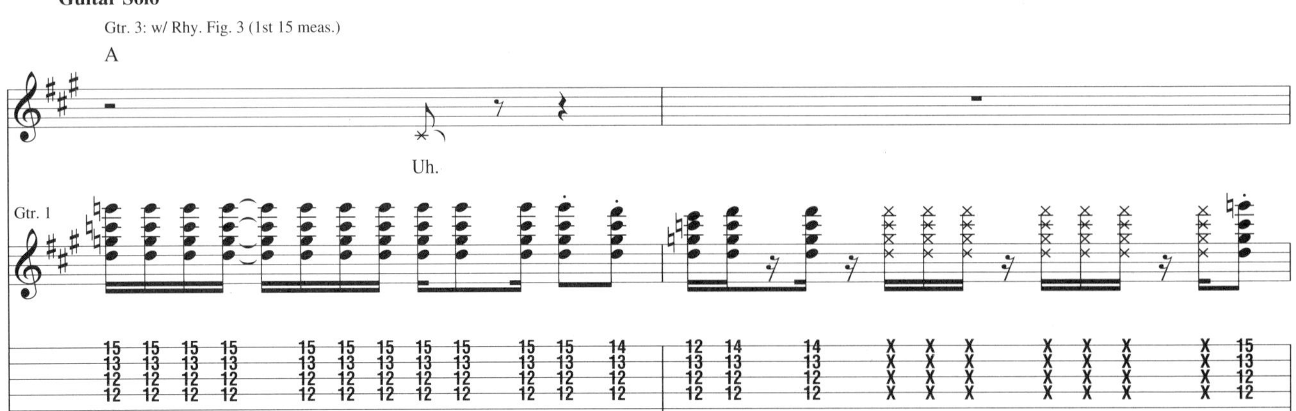

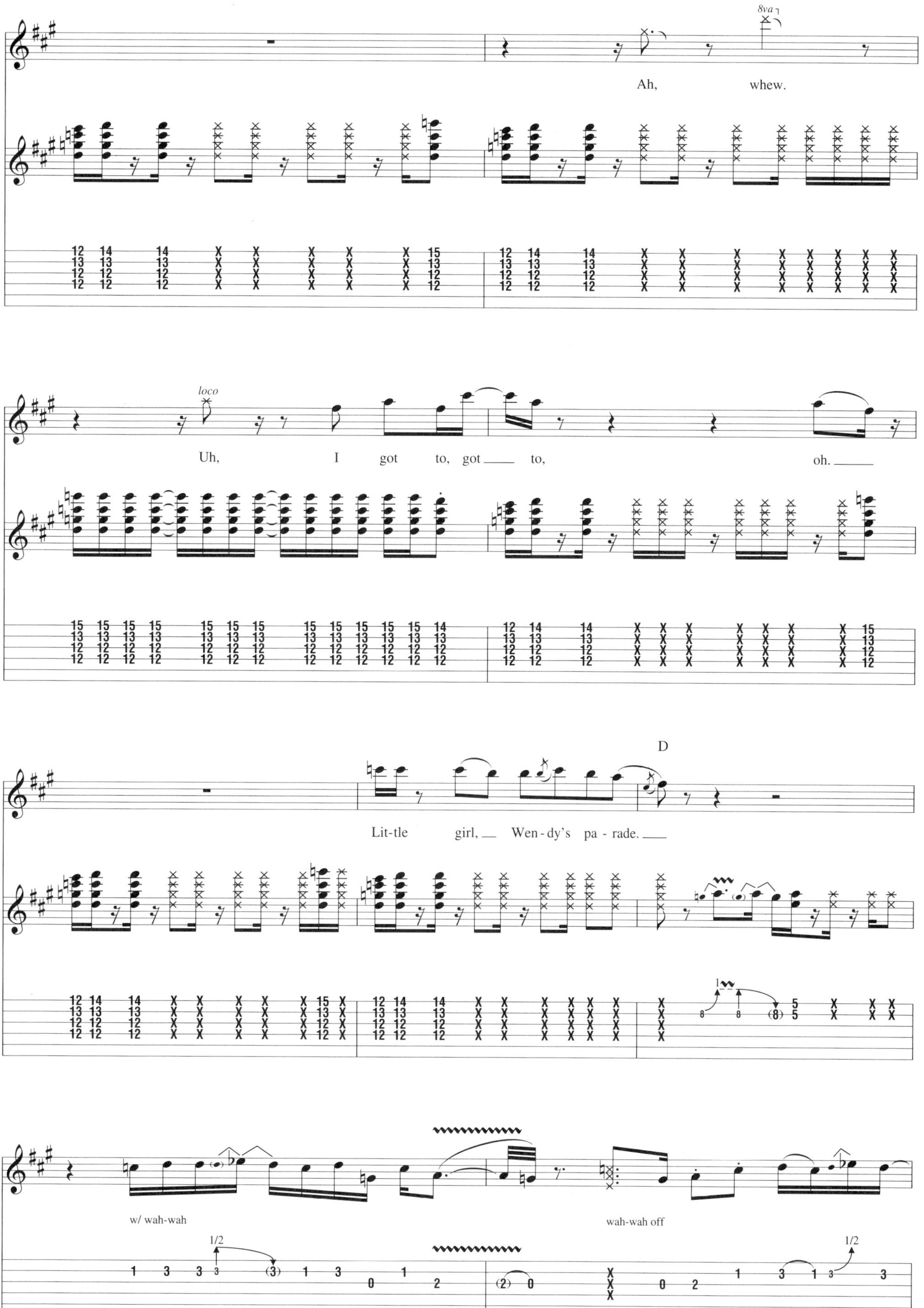
8va
Ah, whew.
loco
Uh, I got to, got to, oh.
D
Lit-tle girl, Wen-dy's pa-rade.
w/ wah-wah
wah-wah off
1/2
1/2

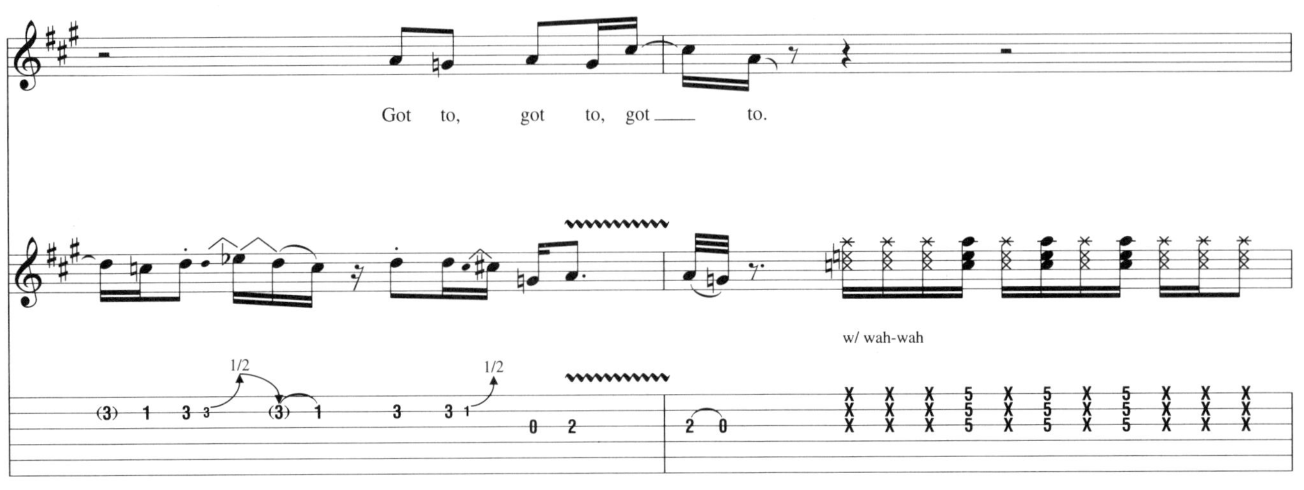
A
Got to, got to, got ___ to.
1/2
1/2
w/ wah-wah

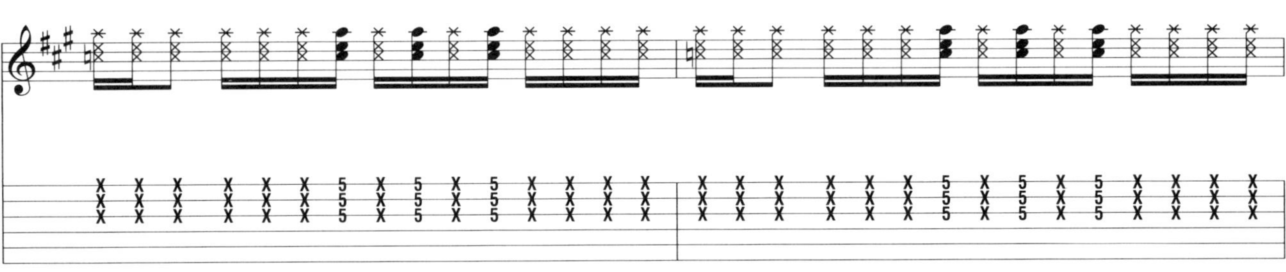

Verse
Gtr. 3: w/ Rhy. Fig. 2 (last meas.)
Gtr. 3: w/ Rhy. Fig. 3
N.C.
A
3. Wom-en, not ___ girls ___ rule my world, ___ I said they rule my
(Wom-en, not ___ girls rule my world, rule my
wah-wah off
1/2

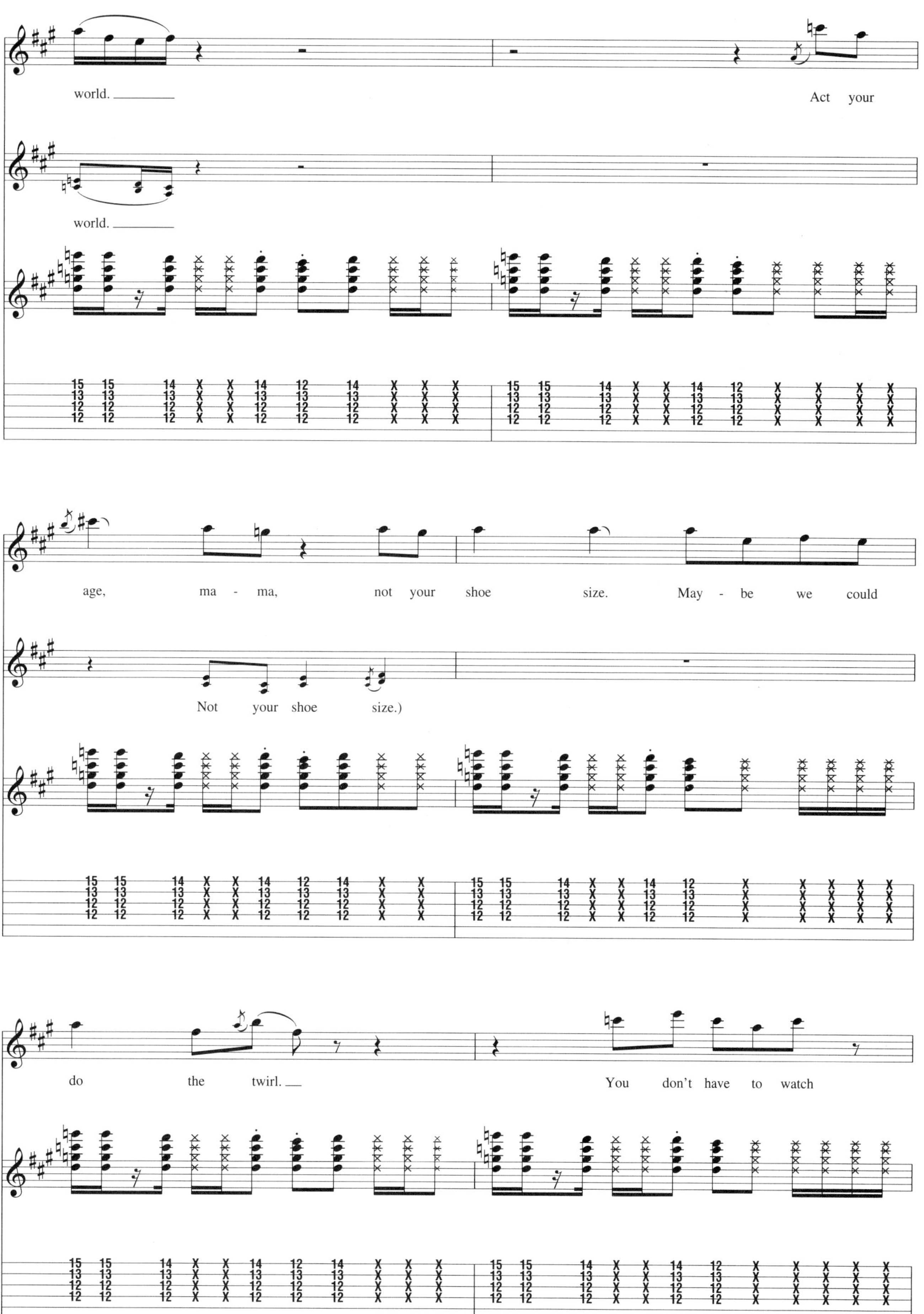
world.
Act your
world.
age, ma - ma, not your shoe size. May - be we could
Not your shoe size.)
do the twirl.
You don't have to watch

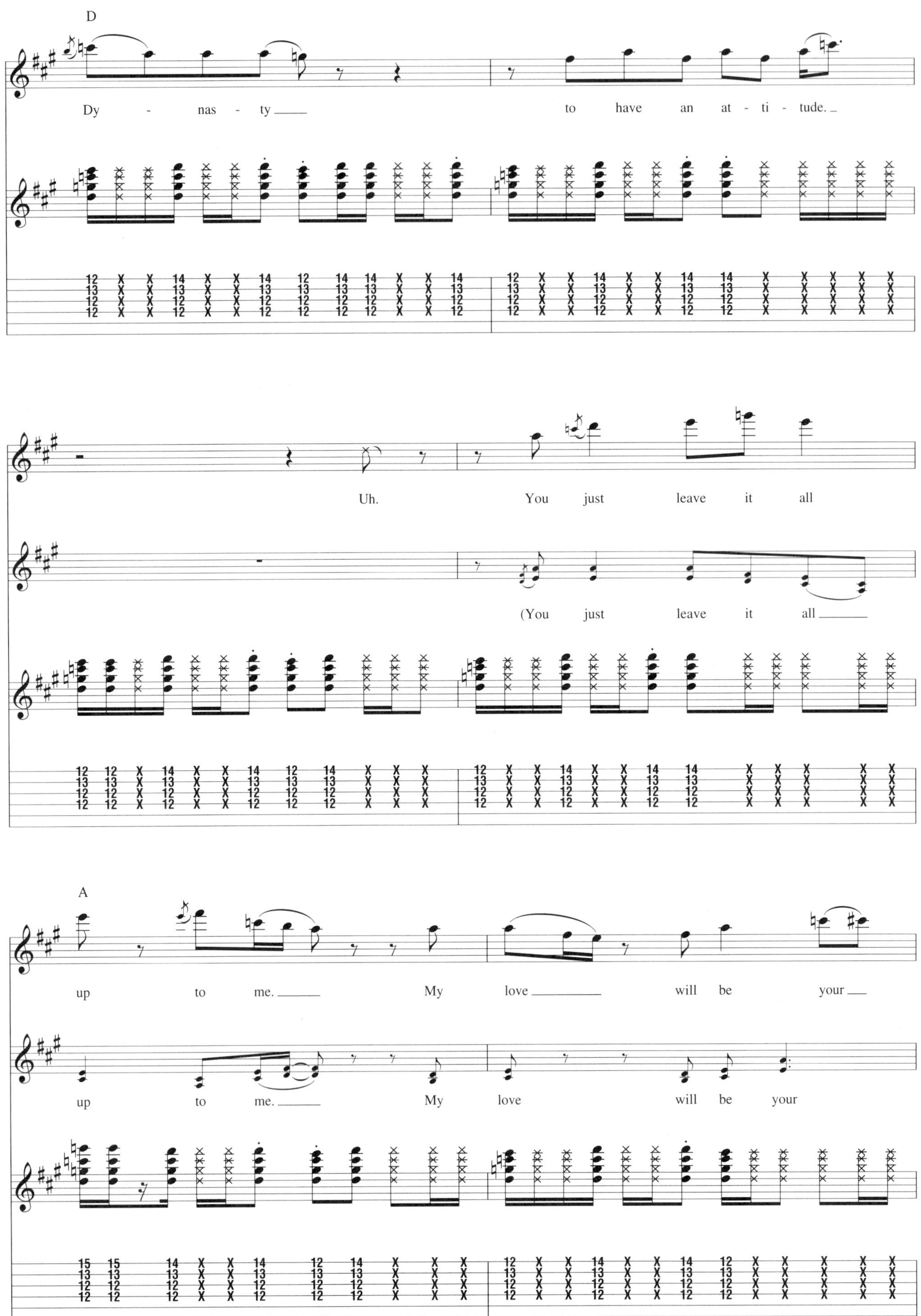
D
Dy - nas - ty
to have an at - ti - tude.
Uh.
You just leave it all
(You just leave it all
A
up to me.
My love will be your
up to me.
My love will be your

Bkgd. Voc.: w/ Voc. Fig. 1
food. Yeah. You don't have to be
food.)
E9
rich to be my girl. You don't have to be cool
D9
to rule my world. Ain't no par - tic - u - lar sign

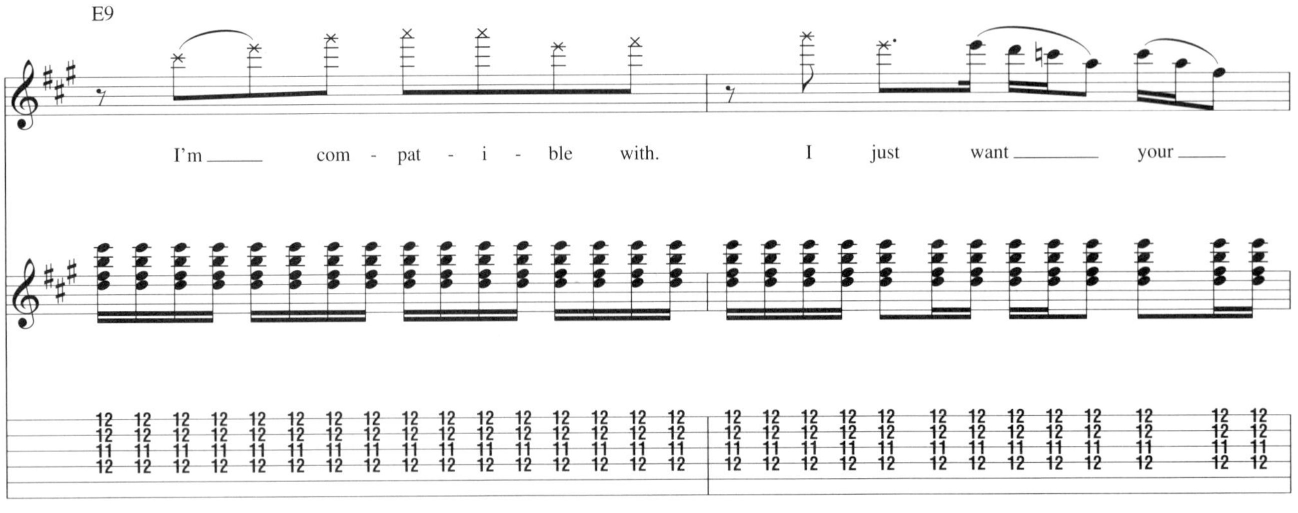
E9
I'm com - pat - i - ble with. I just want your

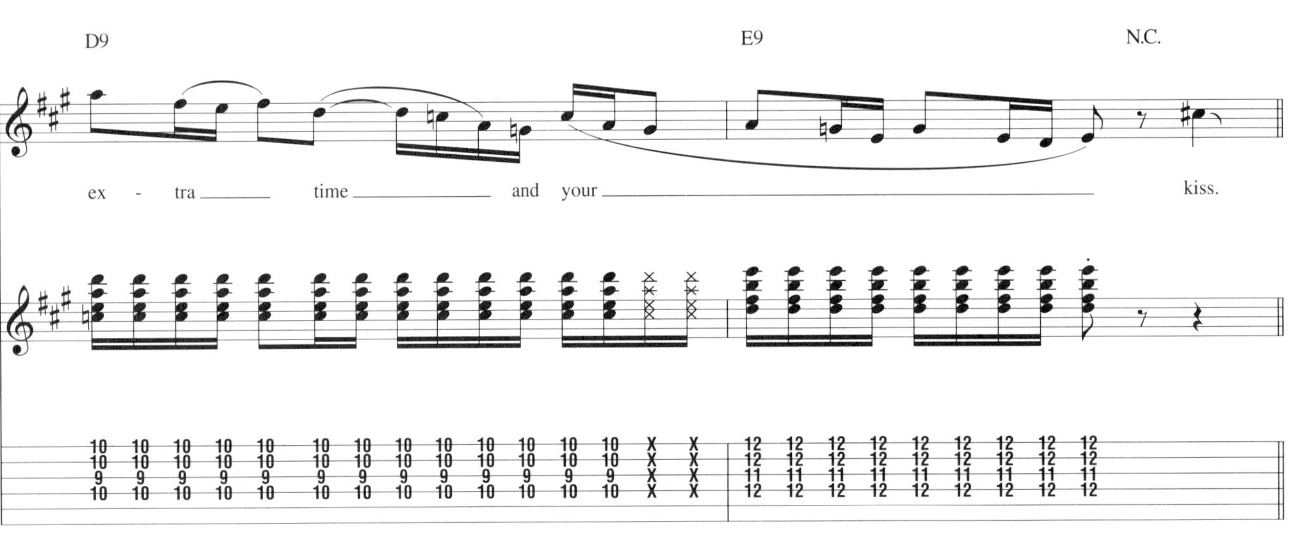
D9
E9
N.C.
ex - tra time and your kiss.

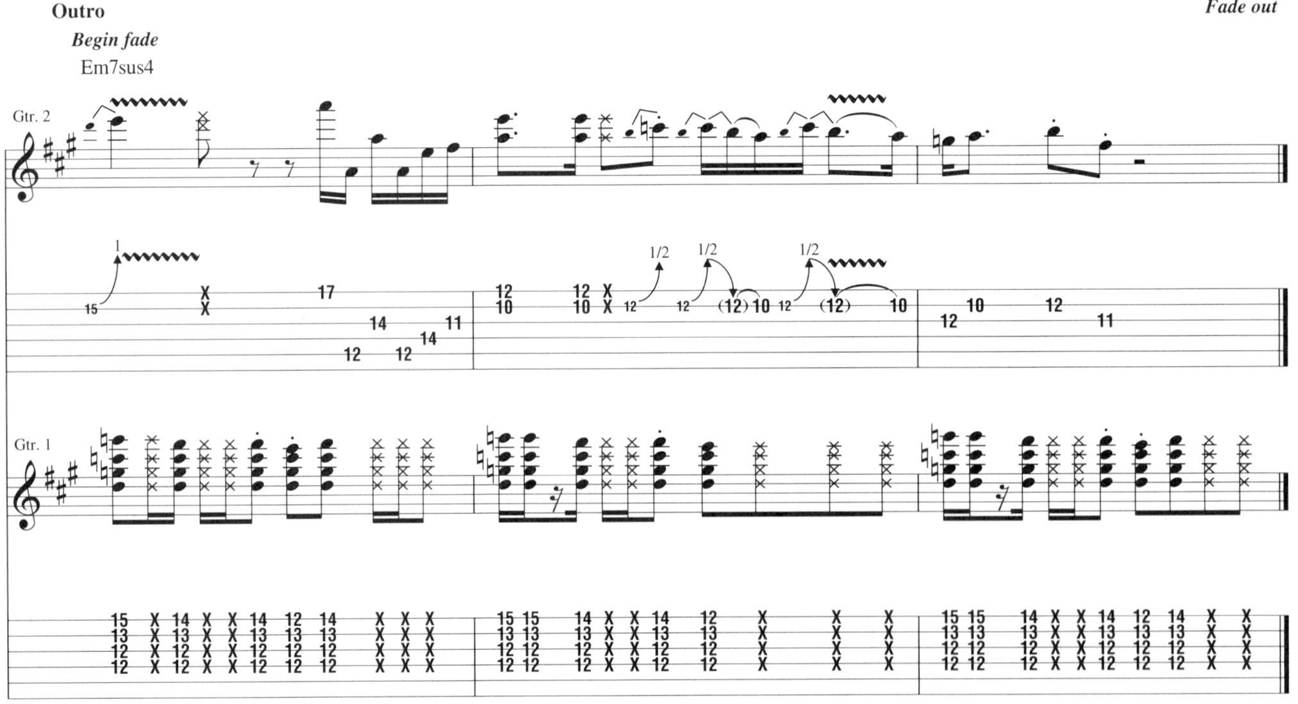
Outro
Begin fade
Fade out
Em7sus4
Gtr. 2
Gtr. 1

from Ozzy Osbourne - *Scream*

Let Me Hear You Scream

Words and Music by Ozzy Osbourne and Kevin Churko

Tune down 1 step:
(low to high) D-G-C-F-A-D

Em7
A/E
End Riff A
End Riff A1
P.M.
End Rhy. Fig. 2
Verse
Gtr. 3 tacet
2nd time, Gtr. 2: w/ Riff C
1st time, Gtr. 2 tacet
Em
Em(maj7)
1. I'm black and bruised, beat up but still,
2. I'll pull you up and push you right
Gtr. 2
Riff B
Gtr. 4 (dist.)
mp
Gtr. 1
Rhy. Fig. 3
P.M.

Em7
A/E
I take the
blows.
back in your
place.
Gtr. 4
End Riff B
Gtr. 1
End Rhy. Fig. 3
P.M.
Gtr. 1: w/ Rhy. Fig. 3 (1 1/2 times)
Gtr. 4: w/ Riff B (3 times)
Em
Em(maj7)
Em7
A/E
'Cause all I need is blood and sweat and skin and bones.
I'll take you down and wipe that smile right off your face.
Gtr. 2
Em
Em(maj7)
I'll take this rage, rat - tle your cage,
I'll watch you break, you're mine to take.
Riff C
Gtr. 2
mp
P.M.
Gtr. 5 (dist.)
mf

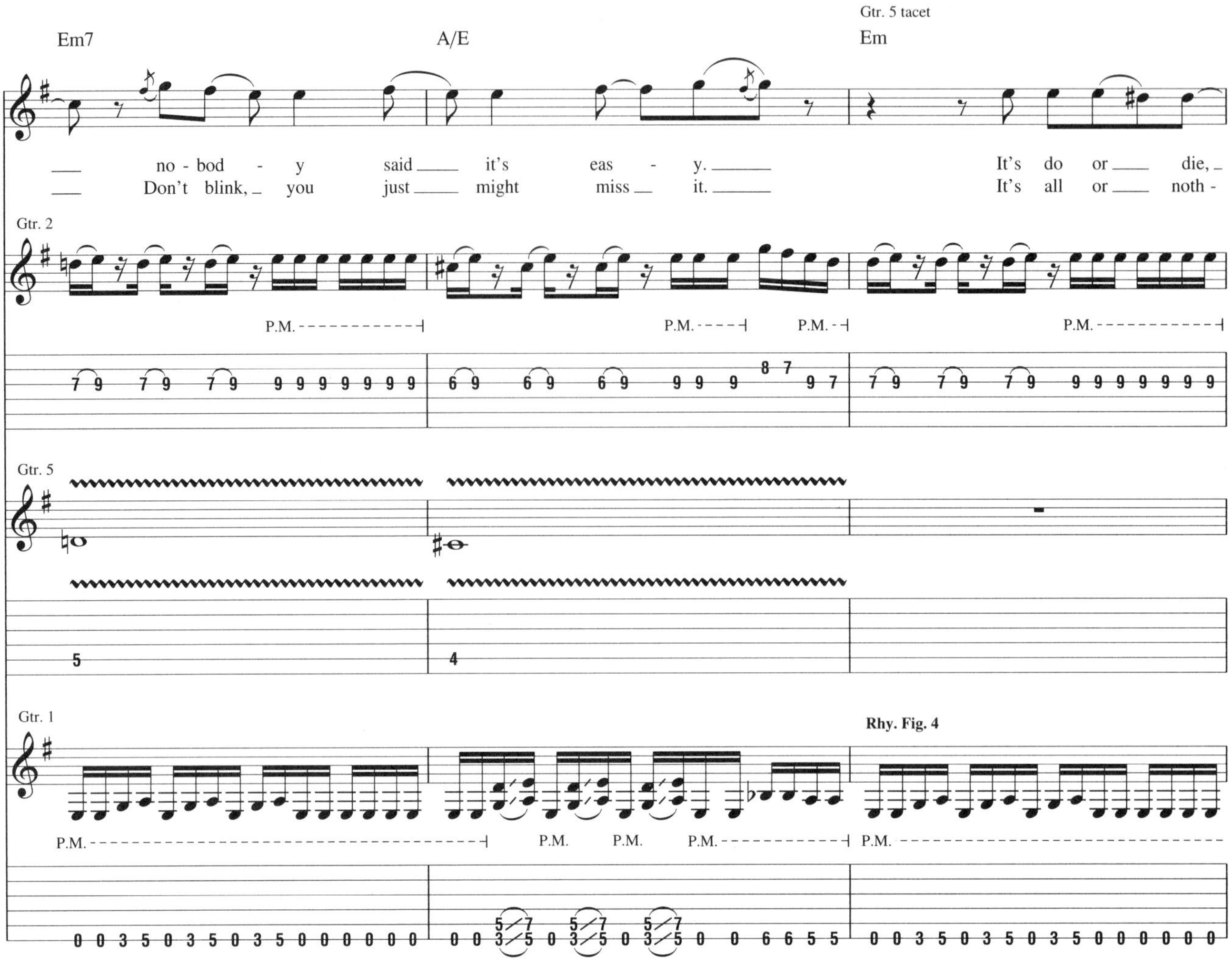

Gtr. 5 tacet

Em7 A/E Em

— no - bod - y said — it's eas - y. — It's do or — die, —
— Don't blink, — you just — might miss — it. — It's all or — noth -

Gtr. 2

P.M. P.M. P.M. P.M.

Gtr. 5

Gtr. 1

Rhy. Fig. 4

P.M. P.M. P.M. P.M. P.M.

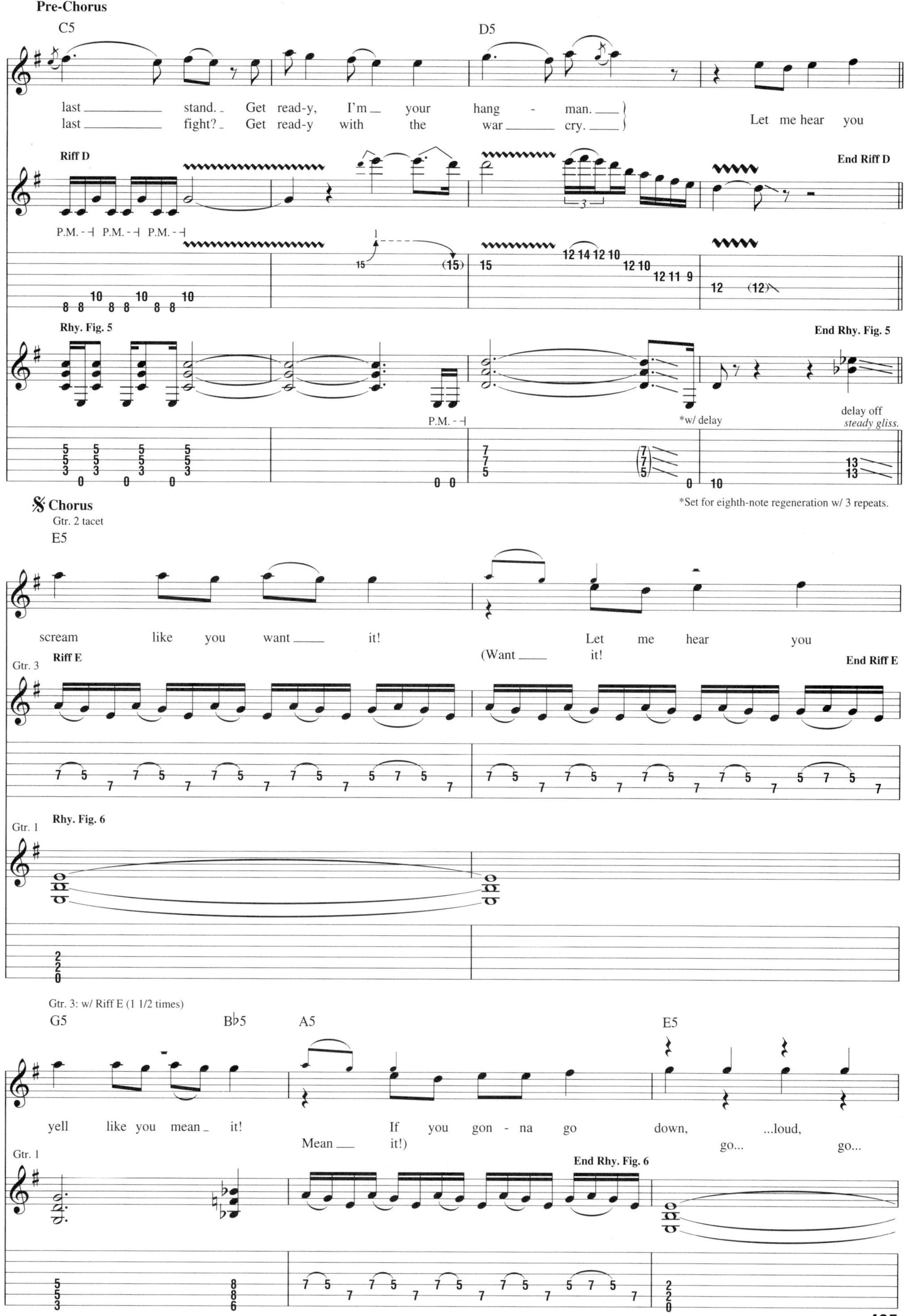
Pre-Chorus
C5
D5
last stand. Get read-y, I'm your hang - man.
last fight? Get read-y with the war cry.
Let me hear you
Riff D
End Riff D
P.M. P.M. P.M.
Rhy. Fig. 5
End Rhy. Fig. 5
P.M.
*w/ delay
delay off
steady gliss.
Chorus
Gtr. 2 tacet
E5
*Set for eighth-note regeneration w/ 3 repeats.
scream like you want it!
Let me hear you
(Want it!
Gtr. 3
Riff E
End Riff E
Gtr. 1
Rhy. Fig. 6
Gtr. 3: w/ Riff E (1 1/2 times)
G5
B♭5
A5
E5
yell like you mean - it!
If you gon - na go down, ...loud,
Mean it!)
go... go...
Gtr. 1
End Rhy. Fig. 6

G5
A5
...strong,
go...
...proud,
go...
...on,
go...
hard or go
go...
home! Let me hear you...
Gtr. 3
P.M.
Gtr. 1
P.M.
steady gliss.
*w/ echo set for half-note regeneration w/ 1 repeat.
To Coda
Gtr. 3 tacet
E5
B♭5
(Let me hear you...
Let me hear you...
Gtr. 1
P.H.
**As before.
Pitch: F
E5
A5
N.C.
Let me hear you...)
Let me hear you
P.M.
P.M.
P.M.

1.
Interlude
Gtr. 1: w/ Rhy. Fig. 2
Gtrs. 2 & 3: w/ Riffs A & A1
Em
Em(maj7)
Em7
A/E
scream!
Gtr. 5
*w/ echo set for half-note regeneration w/ multiple decaying repeats.
2.
Interlude
Gtr. 1: w/ Rhy. Fig. 1 (2 times)
G5 E5 B♭5 E5
scream!
Gtr. 6
steady gliss.
***Harm.
steady gliss.
**w/ echo as before
***While slurring notes w/ fret-hand, produce random harmonics by lightly touching 3rd string with pick-hand ring finger; beginning very close to bridge and gradually sliding toward middle pickup.
Guitar Solo
Gtr. 2: w/ Rhy. Fig. 1 (3 times)
8va
loco
P.M.
steady gliss.

G5
E5
B♭5
E5
G5 N.C.
Let me hear you
8va
Gtr. 6
loco
steady gliss.
Gtr. 1
*Gtr. 7
Gtr. 1
divisi
1/2
*Bass arr. for gtr.
**Gtr. 7 to left of slash in tab.
Chorus
Gtr. 1: w/ Rhy. Fig. 6
Gtr. 3: w/ Riff D (4 times)
Gtrs. 6 & 7 tacet
E5
G5
B♭5
A5
scream like you want it! Let me hear you yell like you mean it! If you gon-na go
(Want it! Mean it!)
E5
G5
A5
D.S. al Coda
down, ...loud, ...strong, ...proud, ...on, hard or go home! Let me hear you
go... go... go... go... go... go...
Gtr. 1
P.M.
Coda
Outro
E5
N.C.
Let me hear you scream!
Let me hear you...)
Gtr. 1
***w/ echo as before w/ multiple decaying repeats.

from The Youngbloods - *Get Together*

Let's Get Together
(Get Together)

Words and Music by Chet Powers

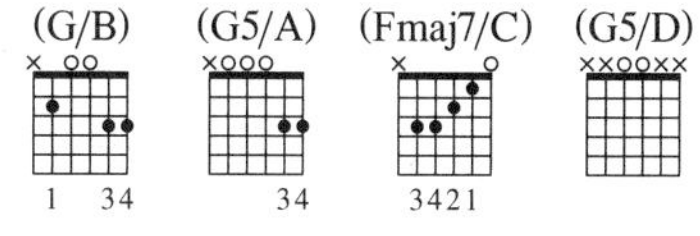

Gtr. 1: Capo II

Intro

Moderately ♩ = 102

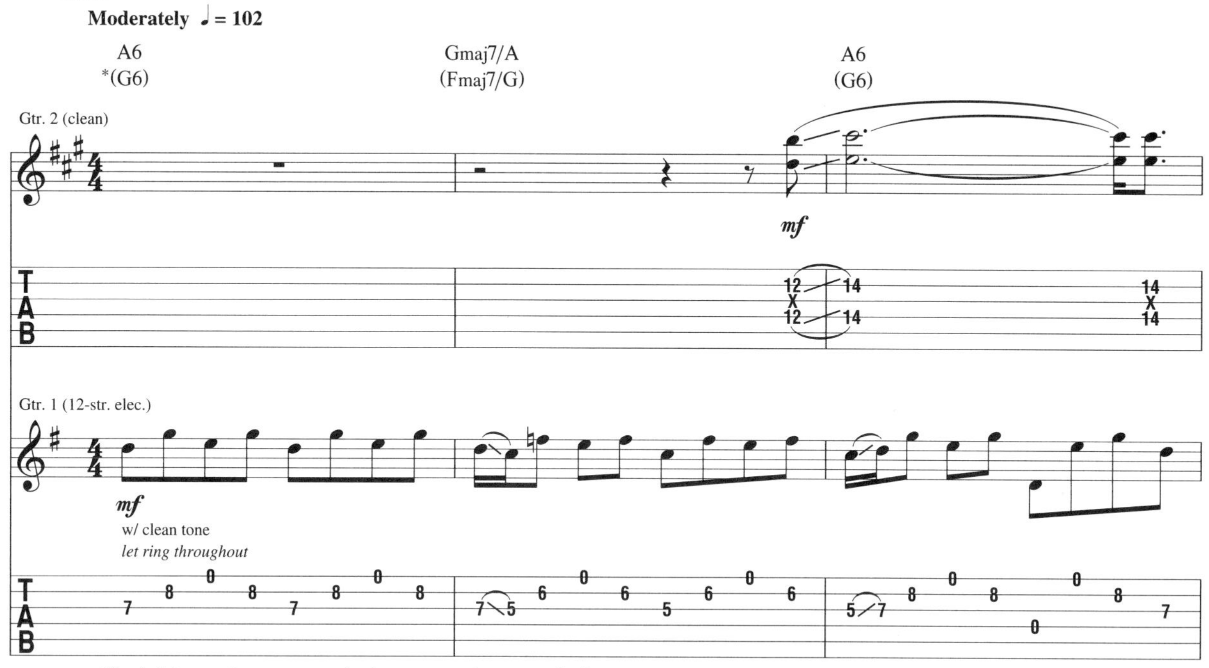

*Symbols in parentheses represent chord names respective to capoed guitar. Symbols above reflect actual sounding chords. Capoed fret is "0" in tab. Chord symbols reflect overall harmony.

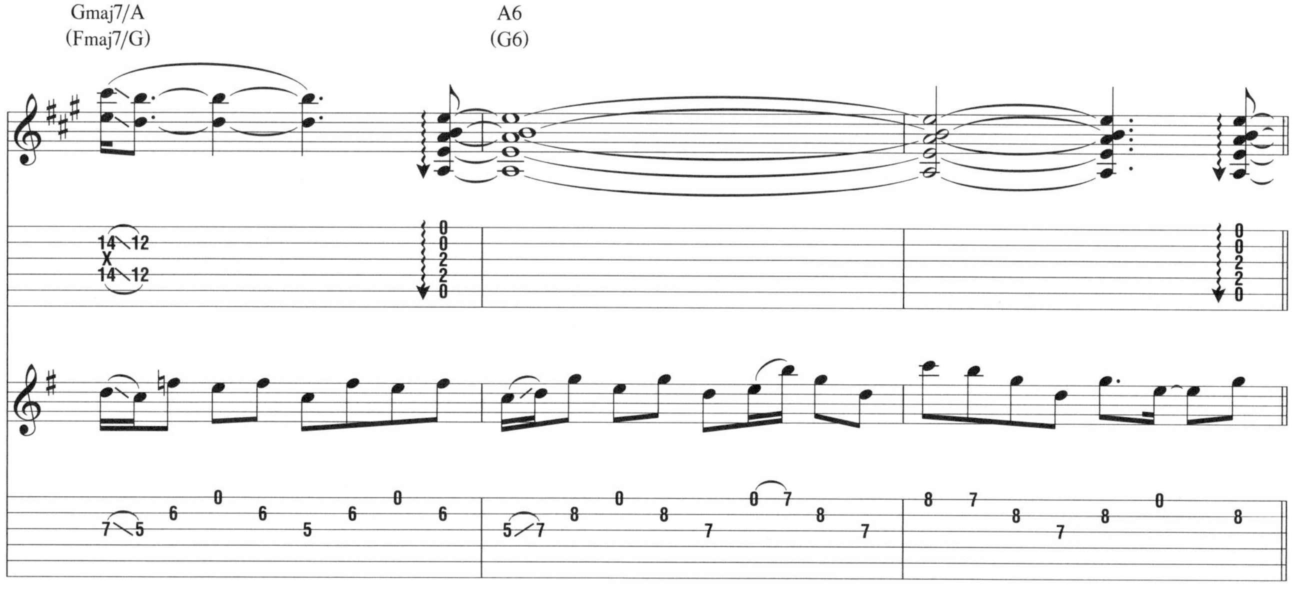

Verse

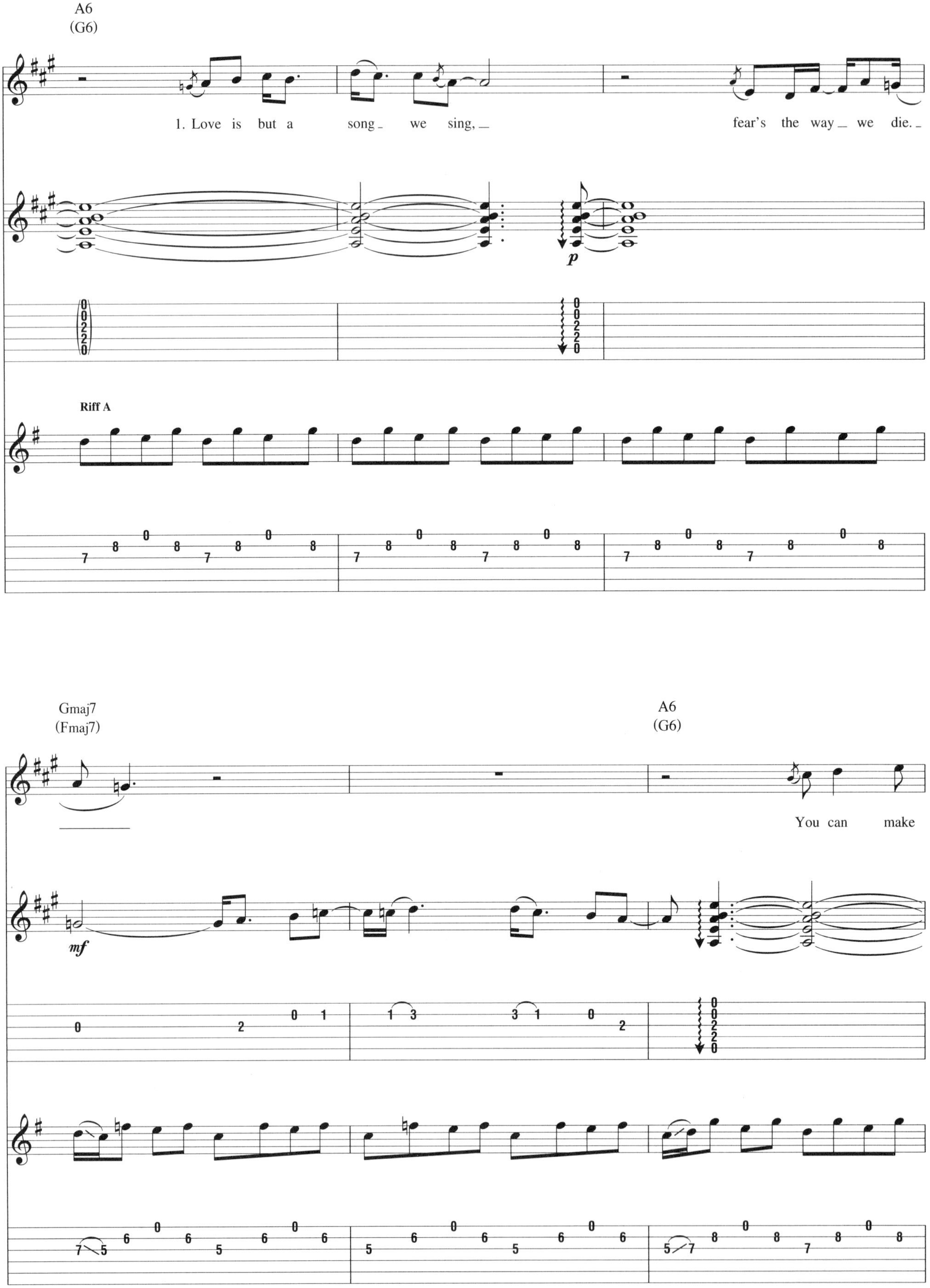

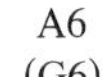

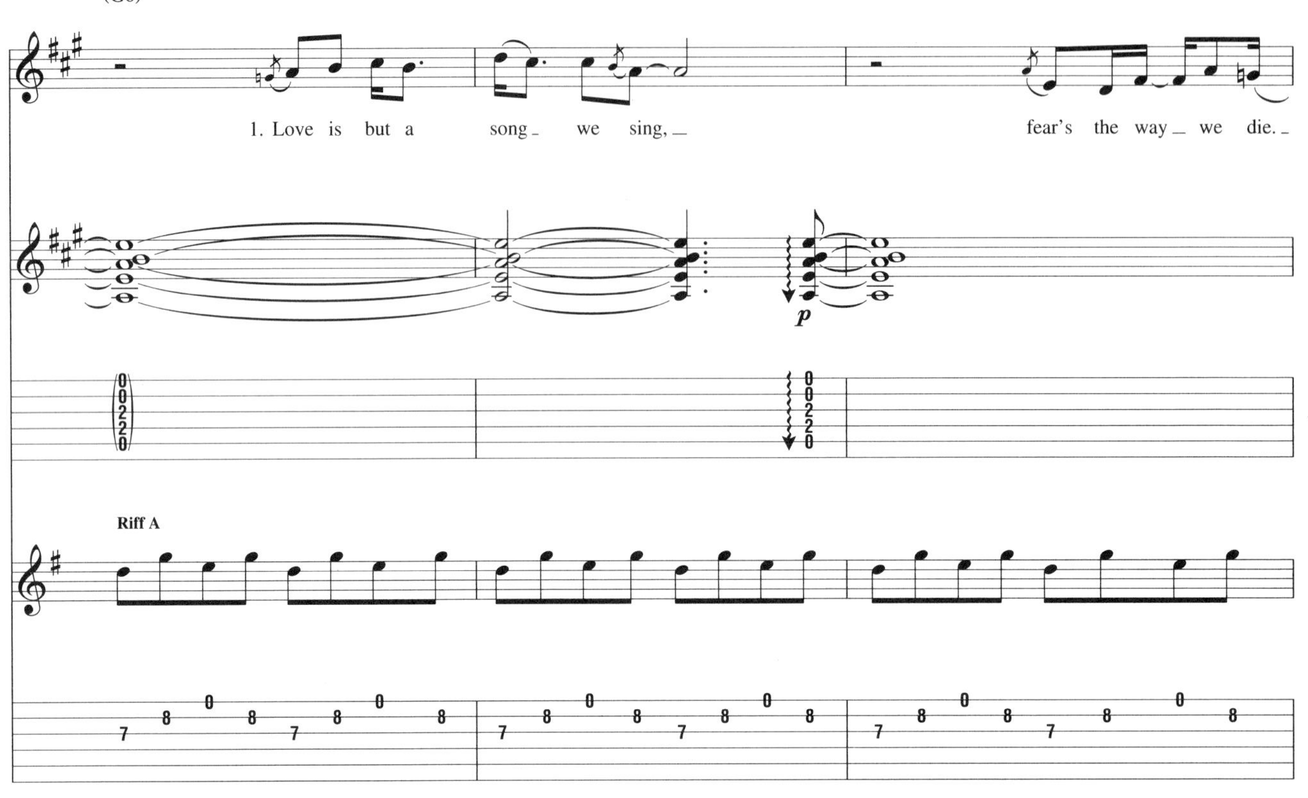

Gmaj7
(Fmaj7)

A6
(G6)

You can make

mf

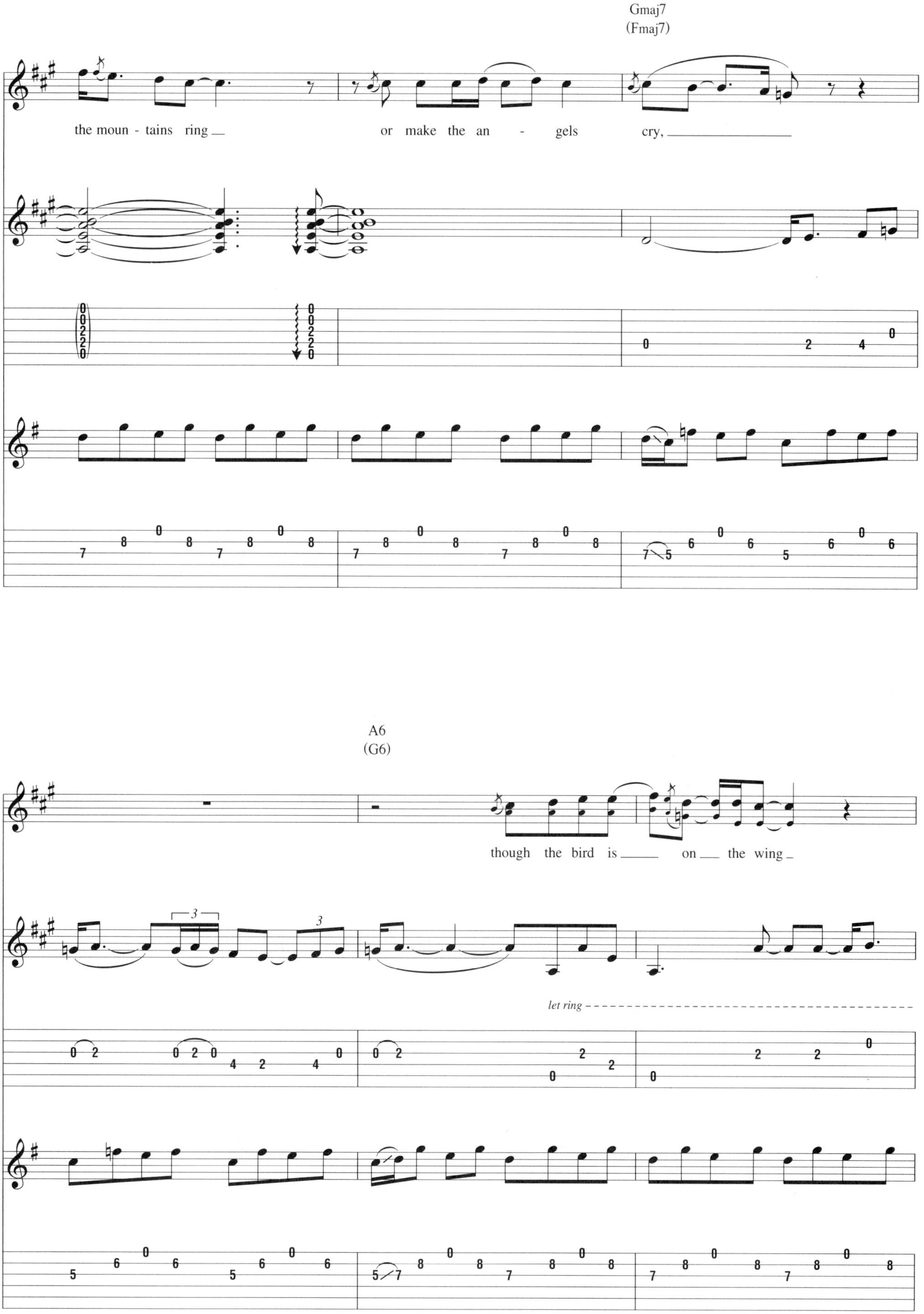

Gmaj7
(Fmaj7)

the moun - tains ring __ or make the an - gels cry, ___

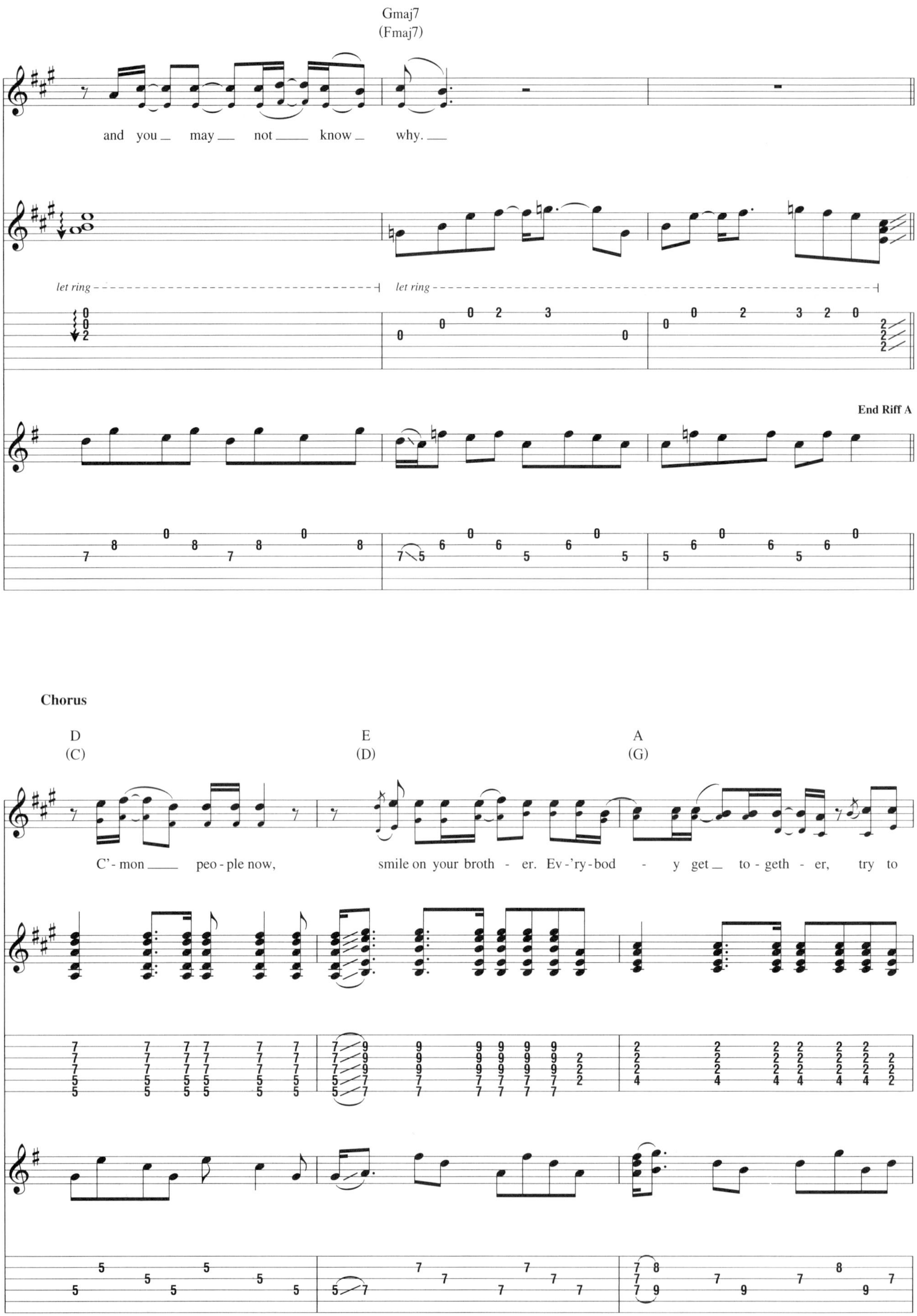

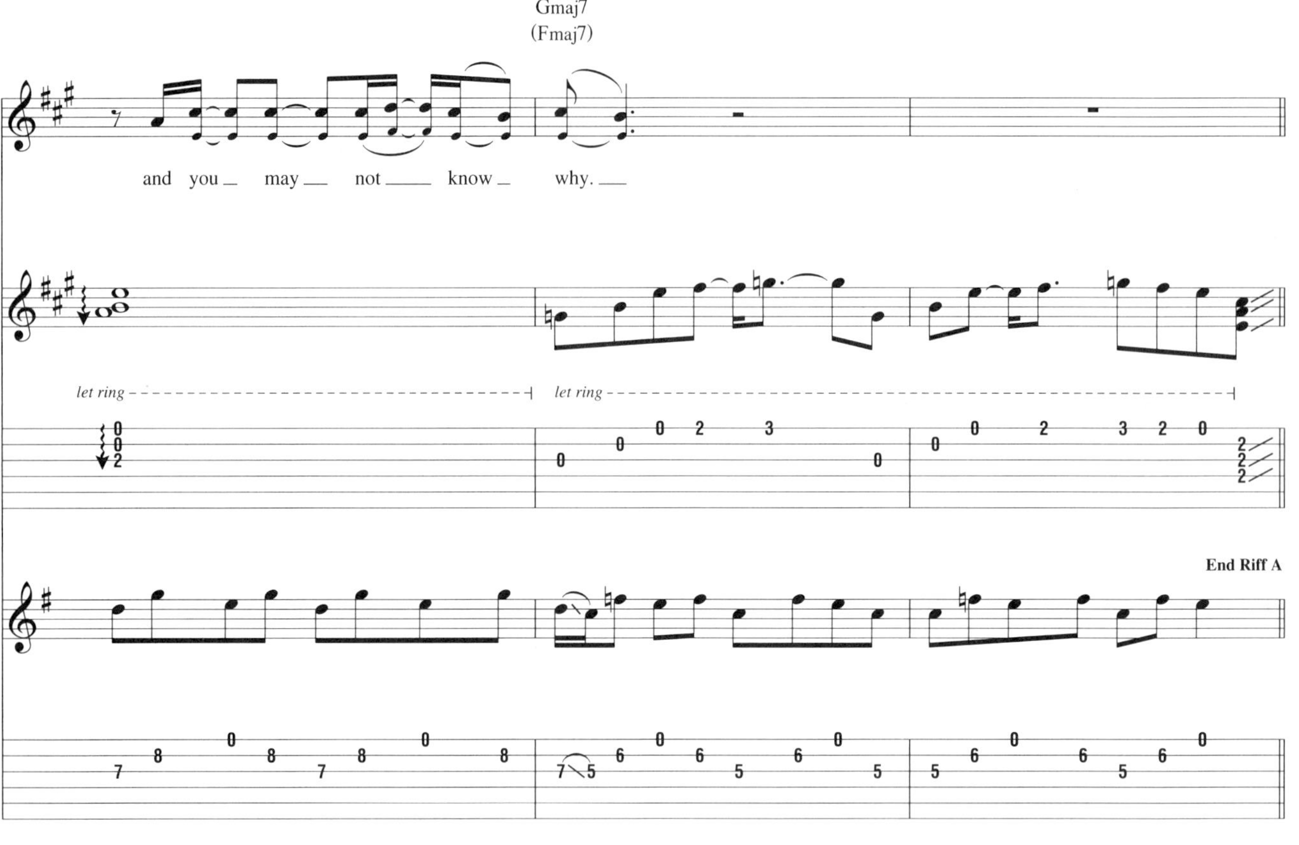

Chorus

D (C) E (D) A (G)

C'-mon people now, smile on your broth - er. Ev-'ry-bod - y get to-geth - er, try to

D
(C)
E
(D)
A
(G)
love one an - oth-er right now.
Rhy. Fill 1
End Rhy. Fill 1
let ring
Verse
Gtr. 1: w/ Riff A
A6
(G6)
2. Some may come and some may go,
he will sure - ly
Gtr. 2
let ring
let ring
let ring
Gmaj7
(Fmaj7)
A6
(G6)
pass,
when the one that
let ring
let ring

Gmaj7
(Fmaj7)
left us here re - turns for us at last.
let ring
let ring

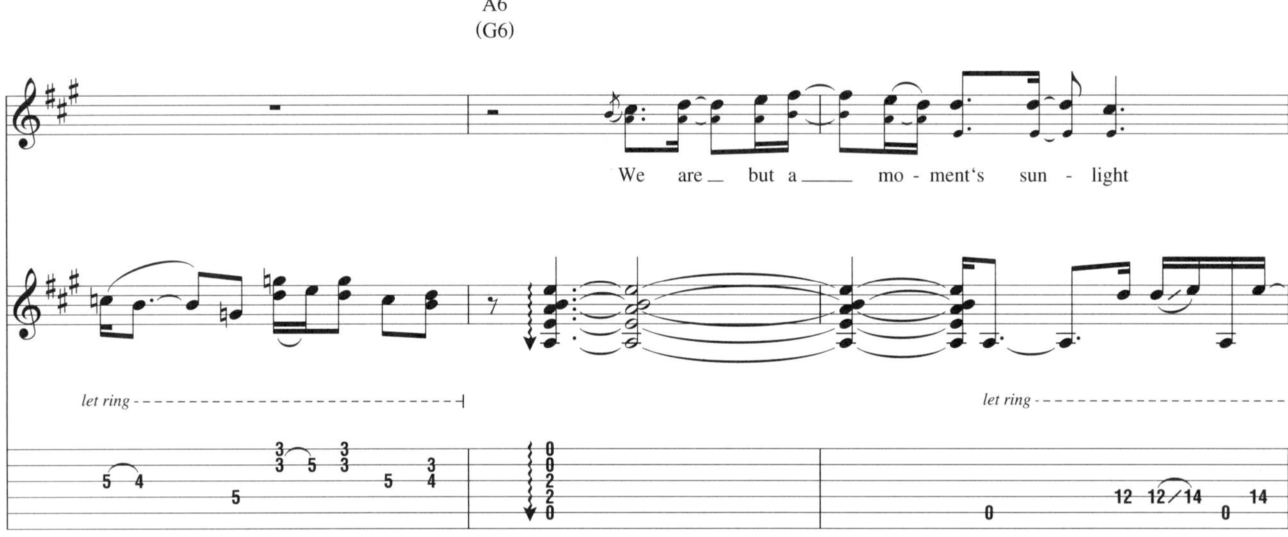
A6
(G6)
We are but a mo - ment's sun - light
let ring
let ring

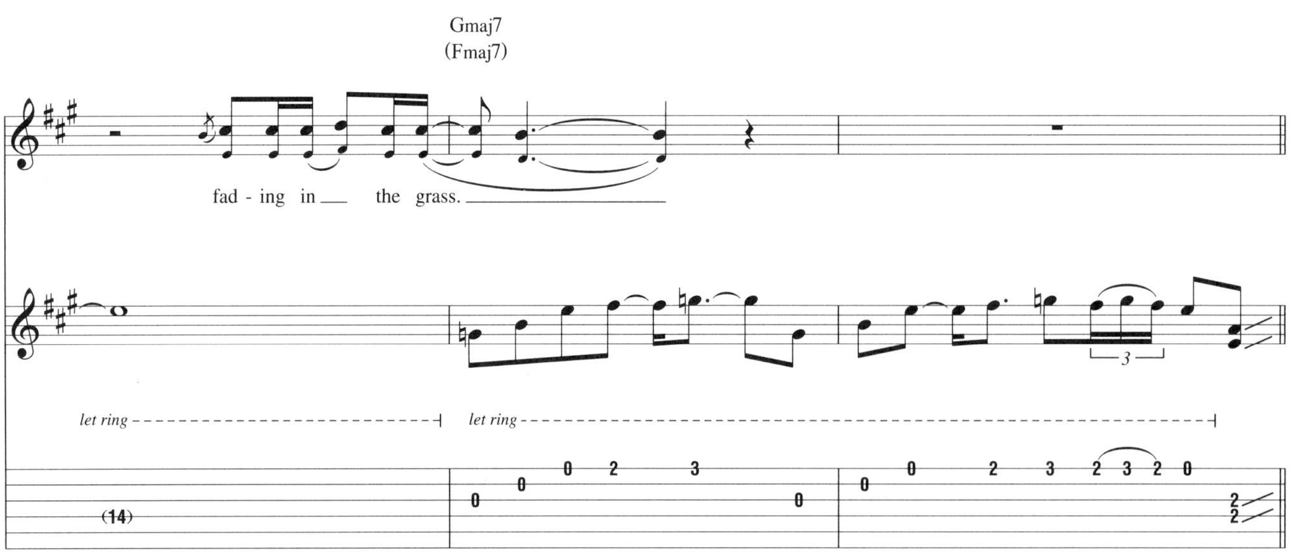
Gmaj7
(Fmaj7)
fad - ing in the grass.
let ring
let ring

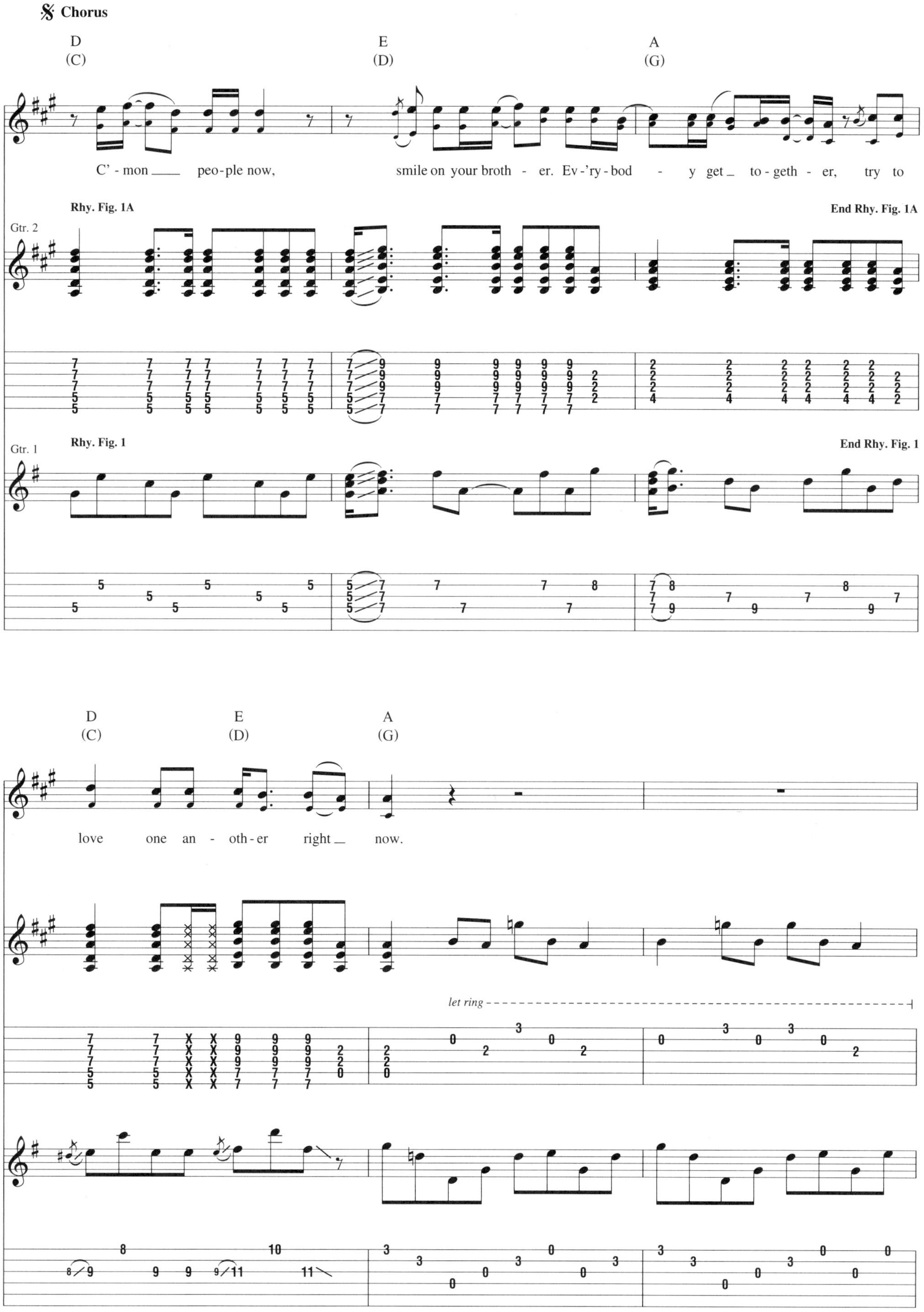

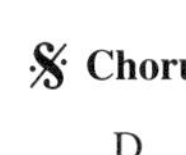 Chorus

D (C) E (D) A (G)

C'-mon ___ peo-ple now, smile on your broth - er. Ev-'ry-bod - y get _ to-geth - er, try to

Rhy. Fig. 1A

Gtr. 2

End Rhy. Fig. 1A

Gtr. 1

Rhy. Fig. 1

End Rhy. Fig. 1

D (C) E (D) A (G)

love one an - oth-er right _ now.

let ring

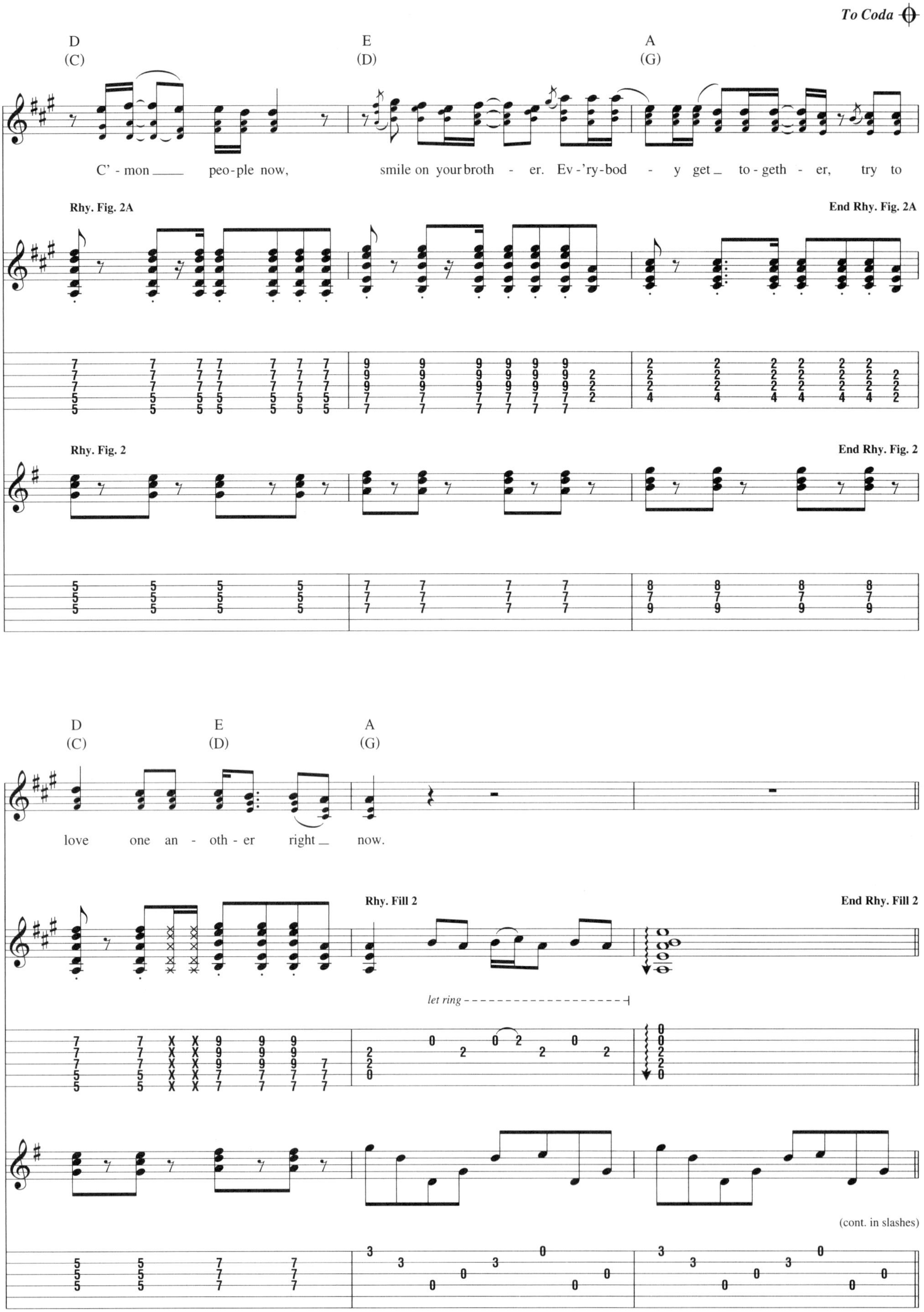

To Coda 

D (C) E (D) A (G)

C'-mon___ peo-ple now, smile on your broth - er. Ev-'ry-bod - y get_ to-geth - er, try to

Rhy. Fig. 2A

End Rhy. Fig. 2A

Rhy. Fig. 2

End Rhy. Fig. 2

D (C) E (D) A (G)

love one an - oth - er right_ now.

Rhy. Fill 2

End Rhy. Fill 2

let ring

(cont. in slashes)

Guitar Solo

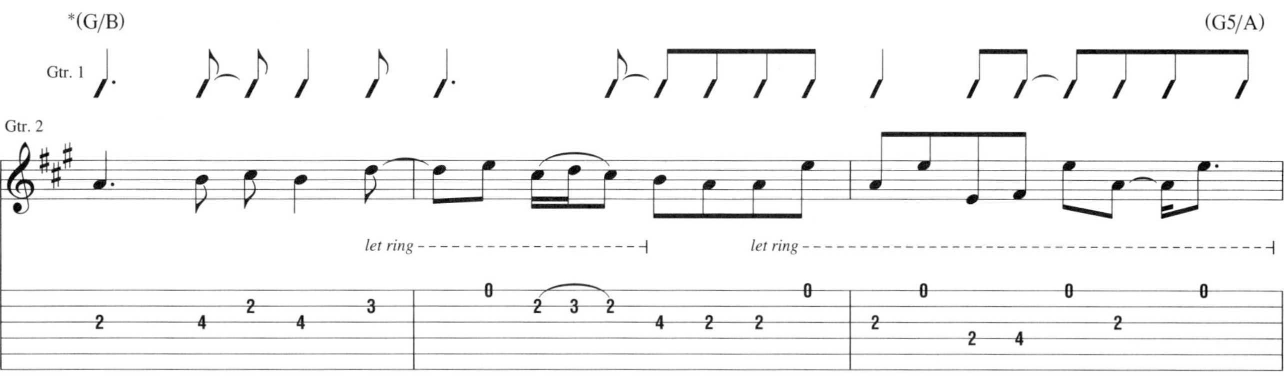

*See top of first page of song for chord diagrams pertaining to rhythm slashes.

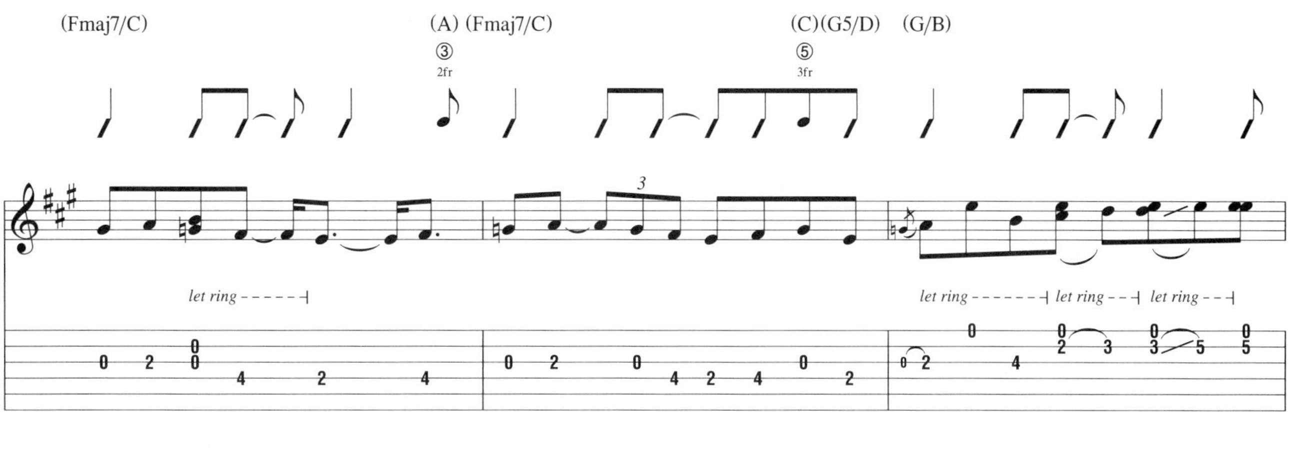

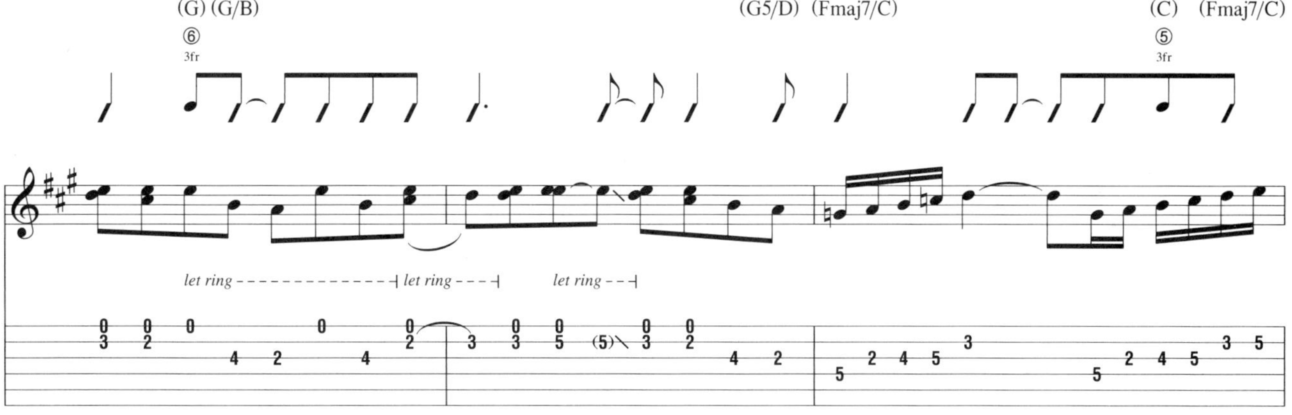

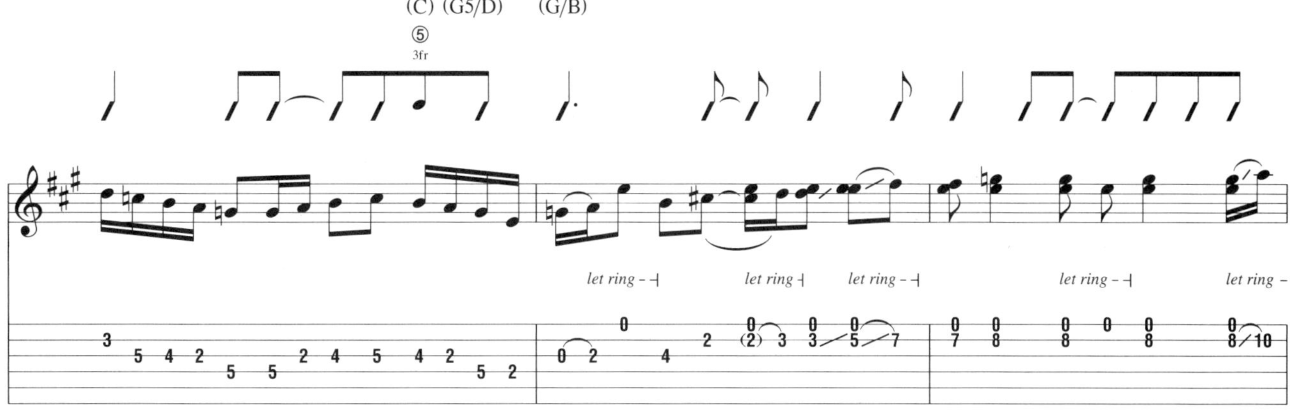

(G5/D) (Fmaj7/C)
let ring
let ring
let ring
Chorus
Gtrs. 1 & 2: w/ Rhy. Figs. 1 & 1A
D
(C)
E
(D)
A
(G)
C'-mon people now, smile on your broth - er. Ev-'ry-bod - y get to-geth - er, try to
Interlude
Gtr. 2: w/ Rhy. Fill 1
D
(C)
E
(D)
Gtr. 2: w/ Rhy. Fill 2
A
(G)
A
(G)
love one an - oth - er right now.
Gtr. 1
A6
(G6)
Gmaj7/A
(Fmaj7/G)
A6
(G6)
Gtr. 2
Gtr. 1

Gmaj7/A
(Fmaj7/G)
A6
(G6)
Verse
Gtr. 1: w/ Riff A
A6
(G6)
3. If you hear the song I sing, ___ you will un - der -
Gtr. 2
Gmaj7
(Fmaj7)
A6
(G6)
stand... ___ lis - ten. You hold the key ___ to ___

Gmaj7
(Fmaj7)
love and fear all in your trem - blin', a, hand.
mp
mf
let ring
7 7 7 9 9 11 11 12 12 11 11
0 0 0 0 0
5 4 3 5 3 5 3 5

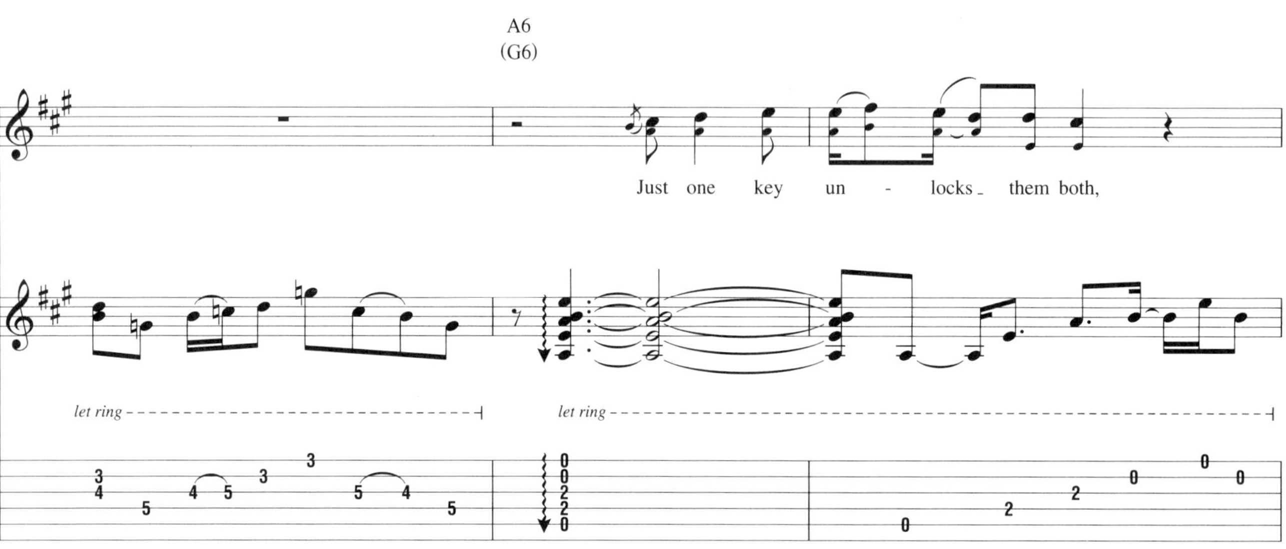
A6
(G6)
Just one key un - locks them both,
let ring
3 4 5 4 5 3 3 5 4 5
0 0 0 2 2 0
0 2 2 0 0 0

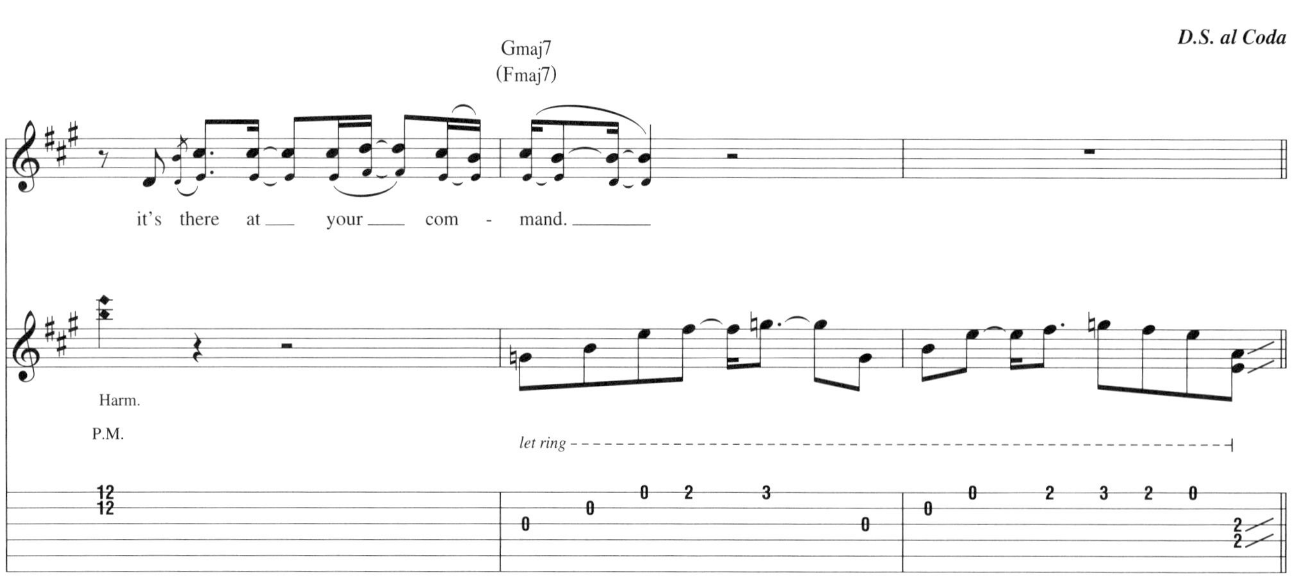
Gmaj7
(Fmaj7)
D.S. al Coda
it's there at your com - mand.
Harm.
P.M.
let ring
12
12
0 0 0 2 3 0
0 0 2 3 2 0 2 2

Coda
D (C) E (D) A (G)
love one an - oth - er right _ now.
I said,
let ring
Gtrs. 1 & 2: w/ Rhy. Figs. 2 & 2A
D (C) E (D) A (G)
c'-mon _ peo-ple now, smile on your broth - er. Ev-'ry-bod - y get _ to-geth - er, try to
D (C) E (D) A (G) A6/9 (G6/9)
rit.
love one an-oth-er right _ now, right _ now, right _ now.
Gtr. 2
let ring
rit.
Gtr. 1
rit.

from Stevie Ray Vaughan & Double Trouble - *The Sky Is Crying*

Life by the Drop

Written by Barbara Logan and Doyle Bramhall

* All notes played on 6th-3rd courses (sets of strings) are doubled 8va. Remaining courses are unisons. Unlike previous songs, this one is in standard tuning.

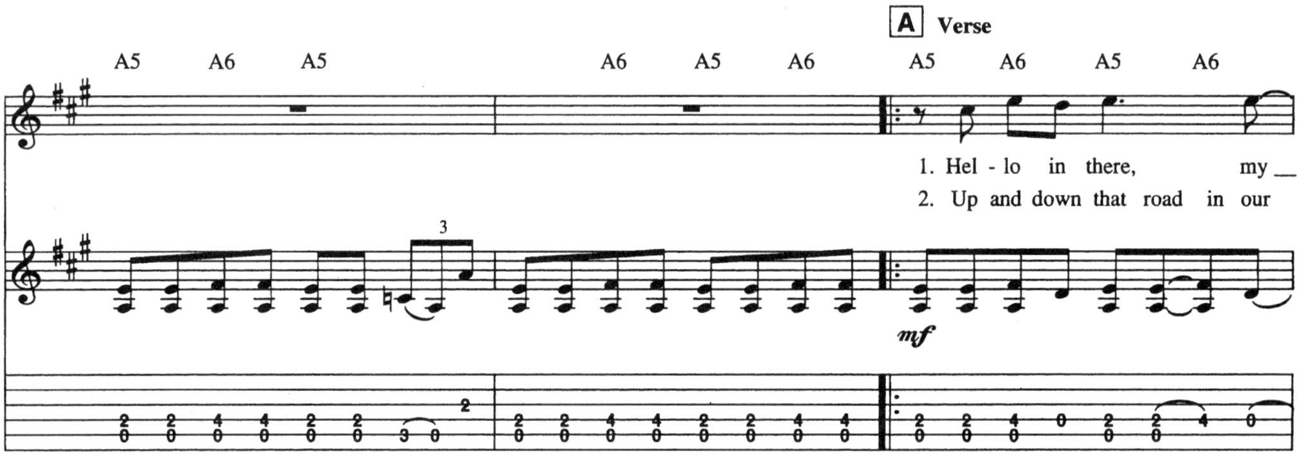

A5 A6 A5 A6 E5 E6 E5 E6 F#m
We played out - side in the pour - in' rain.
You went your way and I stayed be-hind.
On our way up the road _ we
We both knew it was just a
B Chorus
D5 D6 D5 D6 F#m D5 D6 E5 E6
start-ed o - ver a - gain.
mat - ter of time.
You're liv-in' out dreams of you on top.
2nd time play Fig. 1
F#m D5 D6 E5 E6 F#m D7 5
My mind is ach - in' and, Lord, it won't stop.
That's how it hap-pened liv - in'
Fig. 1
D7 5

E
Em7
A5
A6
1.
life by the drop.
2.
C Verse
3. No waste of time we're al - lowed to - day.
E5
E6
N.C.
(F♯m)
F♯m
D7
Churn-in' up the past, there's no eas - i - er way.
Time's been be-tween us, a means
to an end.
God, it's good to be here walk - in' to -

D Chorus
D7/5
F#m
N.C.
geth-er, my friend.
Liv-in' our dreams.
F#m
N.C.
Esus4
F#m
D7
My mind stopped ach-in'.
That's how it hap-pened liv-in'
E
A5
A6
A5
A6
A5
A6
life by the drop.
F#m
D7/5
E
A/E
That's how it hap-pened liv-in' life by the drop.

from Mumford & Sons - *Sigh No More*

Little Lion Man

Words and Music by Mumford & Sons

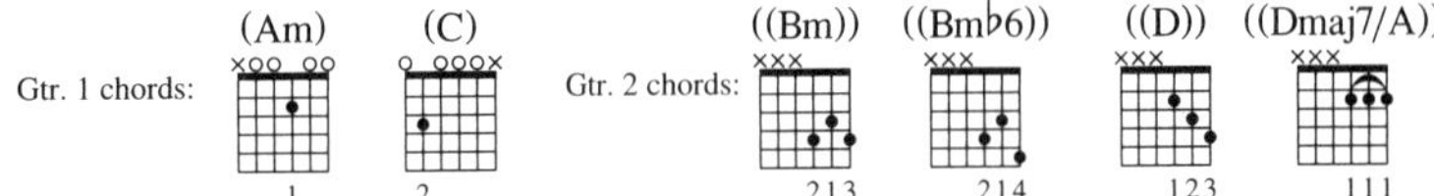

Gtr. 1: Open C6 tuning, capo V:
(low to high) C-A-C-G-C-E

Gtr. 2: Open G tuning, capo III:
(low to high) D-G-D-G-B-D

Intro

Moderately fast ♩ = 140

Dm
*(Am)

Gtr. 1 (acous.)

mf

let ring throughout

P.M. P.M. P.M. P.M. P.M.

*Symbols in parentheses represent chord names respective to Gtr. 1. Symbols above represent actual sounding chords. Capoed fret is "0" in tab. Chord symbols reflect overall harmony.

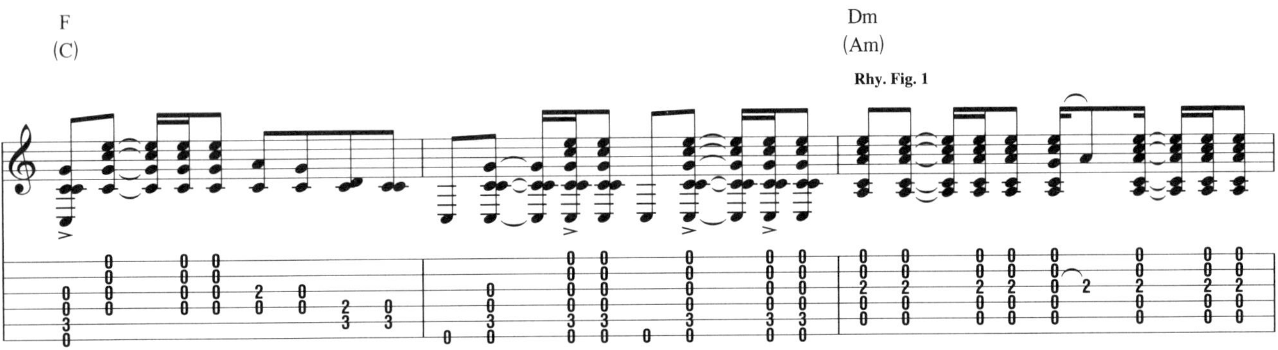

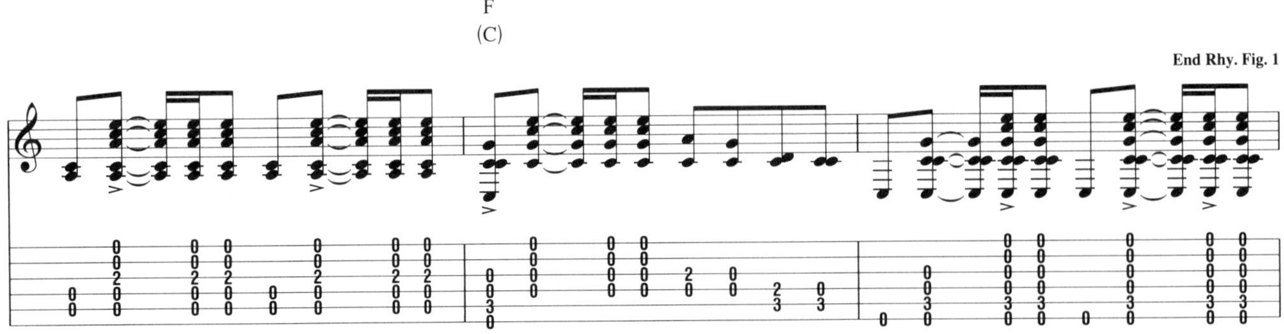

Gtr. 1: w/ Rhy. Fig. 1 (2 times)
Dm
(Am)
*((Bm))
F
(C)
((D))
Rhy. Fig. 2
**Gtr. 2 (acous.)
End Rhy. Fig. 2
mf
**Banjo arr. for gtr.
Gtr. 3 (elec.)
*** mf
w/ slight dist. & heavy reverb
w/ violin bow
*Symbols in double parentheses represent chord names respective to Gtr. 2.
***Vol. swell
Gtr. 2: w/ Rhy. Fig. 2
Dm
(Am)
((Bm))
Gtr. 3 tacet
F
(C)
((D))
Gtr. 3
Verse
Dm
(Am)
1. Weep for your - self my man, you'll nev - er be what is in your
†Gtrs. 4 & 5 (elec.)
††p
w/ slight dist., heavy reverb & ambient delay
fdbk.
†Composite arrangement
††Vol. swells throughout
Rhy. Fig. 3
Gtr. 1
P.M.

F
(C)
heart.
mp
fdbk.
(10)
End Rhy. Fig. 3
P.M.
Gtr. 1: w/ Rhy. Fig. 3
Dm
(Am)
F
(C)
Weep lit-tle li - on man, you're not as brave as you were at the start.
Gtrs. 4 & 5
p mf
fdbk.
(10)
13
Fmaj9/C
(Cmaj9/G)
Dm/B♭
(Am/F)
F/A
(C/E)
F/G
(C/D)
Rate your - self and rake your - self, take all the cour - age you have
Gtrs. 4 & 5
p mf
fdbk.
(13)
8
Gtr. 1
Rhy. Fig. 4

F
(C)
left
and
fdbk.
End Rhy. Fig. 4
P.M.
Gtr. 1: w/ Rhy. Fig. 4
Fmaj9/C
(Cmaj9/G)
Dm/B♭
(Am/F)
F/A
(C/E)
F/G
(C/D)
F
(C)
wast - ed on fix - ing all the prob - lems that you made in your own head.
But it was
Gtrs. 4 & 5
fdbk.
Chorus
Gtrs. 4 & 5 tacet
Dm
(Am)
((Bm))
B♭
(F)
((G))
F
(C)
((D))
not your fault but mine, and it was your heart on the line, I real - ly
Gtr. 2
Gtr. 1

Dm
(Am)
((Bm))
B♭
(F)
((G))
F
(C)
((D))
C6sus4
(G6sus4)
((A6sus4))
fucked it up this time, didn't I my dear?
Did-n't I my...
Gtrs. 4 & 5
p mf
fdbk.
Gtr. 2
Gtr. 1
Interlude
Dm
(Am)
((Bm))
p mf
fdbk.
p mf
Riff A
w/ fingers
let ring

F
(C)
((D))
fdbk.
End Riff A
let ring
Gtr. 2: w/ Riff A
Dm
(Am)
((Bm))
Gtrs. 4 & 5
fdbk.
p
mf
Gtr. 1
F
(C)
((D))

Verse

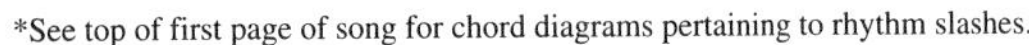
*See top of first page of song for chord diagrams pertaining to rhythm slashes.

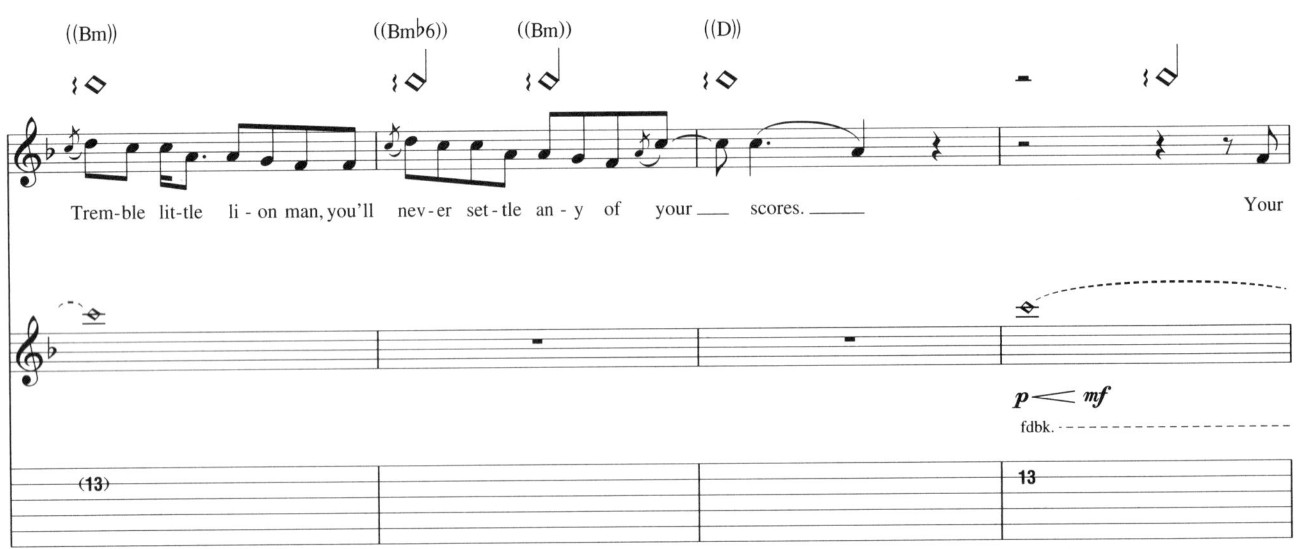

Gtr. 2: w/ Rhy. Fig. 5
Fmaj9/C
(Cmaj9/G)
((Dmaj9/A))
Dm/B♭
(Am/F)
((Bm/G))
F/A
(C/E)
((D/F♯))
F/G
(C/D)
((D/E))
F
(C)
((D))
learn from your moth-er or else spend the days bit - ing your own neck.
But it was
Gtrs. 4 & 5
fdbk.
Chorus
Gtrs. 4 & 5 tacet
Dm
(Am)
((Bm))
B♭
(F)
((G))
not your fault but mine.
And it was your heart on the line.
Riff B
Gtr. 2
let ring
Rhy. Fig. 6
Gtr. 1
I real - ly fucked it up this time,
did-n't I my

C6sus4
(G6sus4)
((A6sus4))
dear?
But it was
End Riff B
let ring
End Rhy. Fig. 6
Gtr. 1: w/ Rhy. Fig. 6
Gtr. 2: w/ Riff B
Dm (Am) ((Bm))
B♭ (F) ((G))
F (C) ((D))
not your fault but mine.
And it was your heart on the line.
I real-ly
Gtrs. 4 & 5
p
mf
fdbk.
fucked it up this time,
did-n't I my
dear?
Did-n't I my

Bridge
Gtrs. 4 & 5 tacet
Dm
(Am)
F
(C)
((D))
dear?
Gtr. 3
8va
Gtr. 2
pp
mf
p
let ring
Gtr. 1
Dm
(Am)
((Bm))
loco
F
(C)
((D))
Gtr. 3 tacet
Gtrs. 4 & 5
p
mf
fdbk.
p
pp
mp
p
let ring

Gtrs. 4 & 5 tacet
Fsus2
(Csus2)
((Dsus2))
F
(C)
((D))
B♭/F
(F/C)
((G/D))
Gtr. 2
Riff C
End Riff C
mp
cresc. poco a poco
let ring
Gtr. 1
Rhy. Fig. 7
End Rhy. Fig. 7
Gtr. 1: w/ Rhy. Fig. 7 (3 times)
*Gtr. 2: w/ Riff C (6 times)
Csus4
(Gsus4)
((Asus4))
F
(C)
((D))
B♭
(F)
((G))
Ah.
Ah.
*Played mf
Csus4
(Gsus4)
((Asus4))
F
(C)
((D))
B♭
(F)
((G))
Ah.
Cadd4
(Gadd4)
((Aadd4))
F
(C)
((D))
B♭
(F)
((G))
(Ah.
Ah.
Cadd4
(Gadd4)
((Aadd4))
F
(C)
((D))
B♭
(F)
((G))
Ah.
Ah.
Gtr. 1

Cadd4
(Gadd4)
((Aadd4))
F
(C)
((D))
B♭
(F)
((G))
Ah.
Ah.
Rhy. Fig. 8
End Rhy. Fig. 8
Gtr. 1: w/ Rhy. Fig. 8
Ah.)
But it was
Gtrs. 4 & 5
fdbk.
Chorus
Gtrs. 4 & 5 tacet
Dm
N.C.
(Am)
((Bm))
not your fault but mine.
And it was
Gtr. 2
let ring
Rhy. Fig. 9
Gtr. 1

Dm
(Am)
((Bm))
B♭
(F)
((G))
F
(C)
((D))
your heart on the line. I real - ly
let ring
End Rhy. Fig. 9
Gtr. 1: w/ Rhy. Fig. 6 (last 4 meas.)
Dm
(Am)
((Bm))
B♭
(F)
((G))
F
(C)
((D))
fucked it up this time, did-n't I my
Gtr. 2
let ring
C6sus4
(G6sus4)
((A6sus4))
dear? But it was
let ring
Gtr. 2 tacet
Gtr. 1 tacet
(Am)N.C.
Gtr. 1
not your fault but mine. And it was your heart on the line. I real-ly
(C)
Gtr. 1
fucked it up this time, did-n't I my dear? Did-n't I my dear?

from Prince - *1999*

Little Red Corvette

Words and Music by Prince

B♭m G♭

jock - eys that were there be - fore me. Be -

A♭
B♭m
lieve it or not, I start - ed to wor - ry. I won - dered if I had e - nough class.
Gtr. 2 (dist.)
steady gliss.
G♭
But it was Sat - ur - day night, I guess that
Gtr. 1
Gtr. 2
divisi
Gtr. 1 tacet
A♭
B♭m
makes it al - right. And you said, "Ba - by, have you got e-nough gas?" Oh, yeah,
Gtr. 2
Chorus
Gtr. 1: w/ Rhy. Fig. 1
Gtr. 2 tacet
G♭ A♭ D♭ G♭ A♭ B♭m
lit - tle red Cor - vette, ba - by, you're much too fast. Yes, you are.

Gb Ab Db Gb Ab
lit - tle red Cor - vette, you need to find a love that's gon - na last. Oh, oh.
Guitar Solo
Gtr. 1: w/ Rhy. Fig. 1
Gb Ab Db Gb Ab Bbm
Hoo, hoo, hoo.
Gtr. 2
Gb Ab Db Gb Ab
Hoo, hoo, hoo. 3. A
1/2
Verse
Bbm Ab
bod - y like yours ought to be in jail, it's on the
Spoken: (A body like yours oughtta be in jail,

Gtr. 2 tacet
B♭m
G♭
verge of be - in' ob - scene.
'cause it's on the verge of bein' ob - scene.
A♭
Move o - ver, ba - by, give me the keys. I'm gon - na
Move over, baby, oo, gimme the keys. I'm gonna
Gtr. 3 (dist.)
mp
P.M.

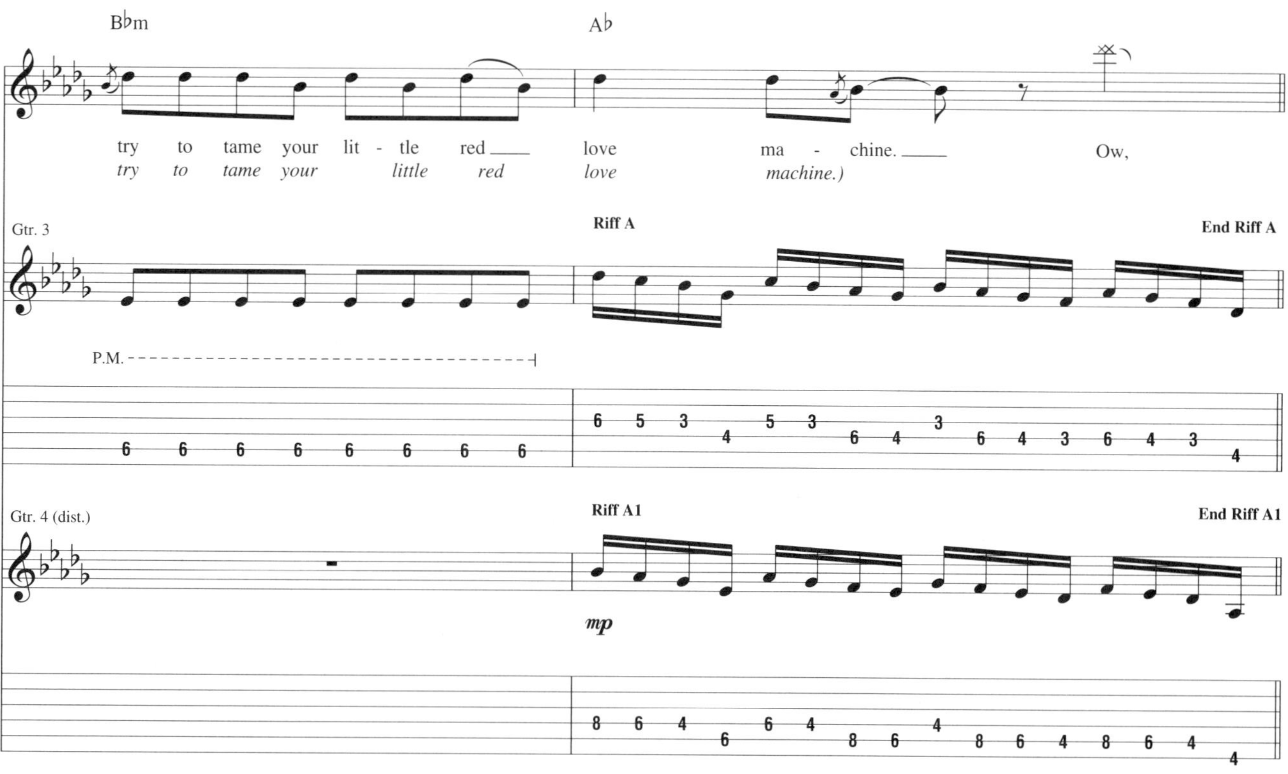
B♭m
A♭
try to tame your lit - tle red love ma - chine. Ow,
try to tame your little red love machine.)
Gtr. 3
Riff A
End Riff A
P.M.
Gtr. 4 (dist.)
Riff A1
End Riff A1
mp

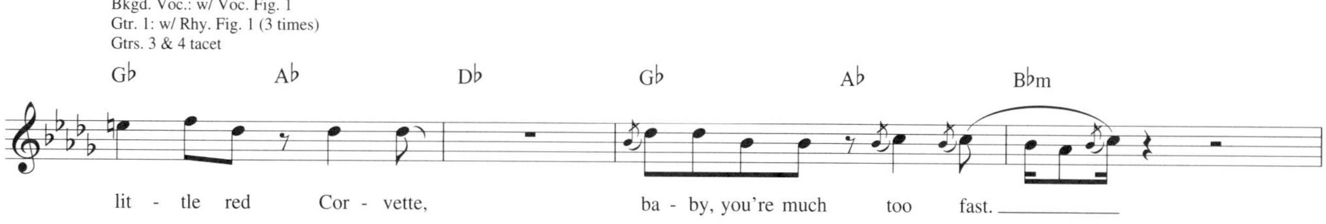
Chorus
Bkgd. Voc.: w/ Voc. Fig. 1
Gtr. 1: w/ Rhy. Fig. 1 (3 times)
Gtrs. 3 & 4 tacet
G♭ A♭ D♭ G♭ A♭ B♭m
lit - tle red Cor - vette, ba - by, you're much too fast.

Bkgd. Voc.: w/ Voc. Fig. 1
G♭
A♭
D♭
G♭
Lit - tle red Cor - vette, ah, need to find a love that's
(Ah.)
Bkgd. Voc.: w/ Voc. Fig. 1
A♭
G♭
A♭
D♭
gon - na last.
Lit - tle red Cor - vette, oo,
Gtr. 2
G♭
A♭
B♭m
Bkgd. Voc.: w/ Voc. Fig. 1
G♭
A♭
hon - ey, you got to slow down.
Oo,
lit - tle red Cor - vette,
(Got to slow down.)
w/ bar
D♭
G♭
Gtrs. 3 & 4: w/ Riffs A & A1
A♭
'cause if you don't you're gon - na run your lit - tle red Cor - vette right in the

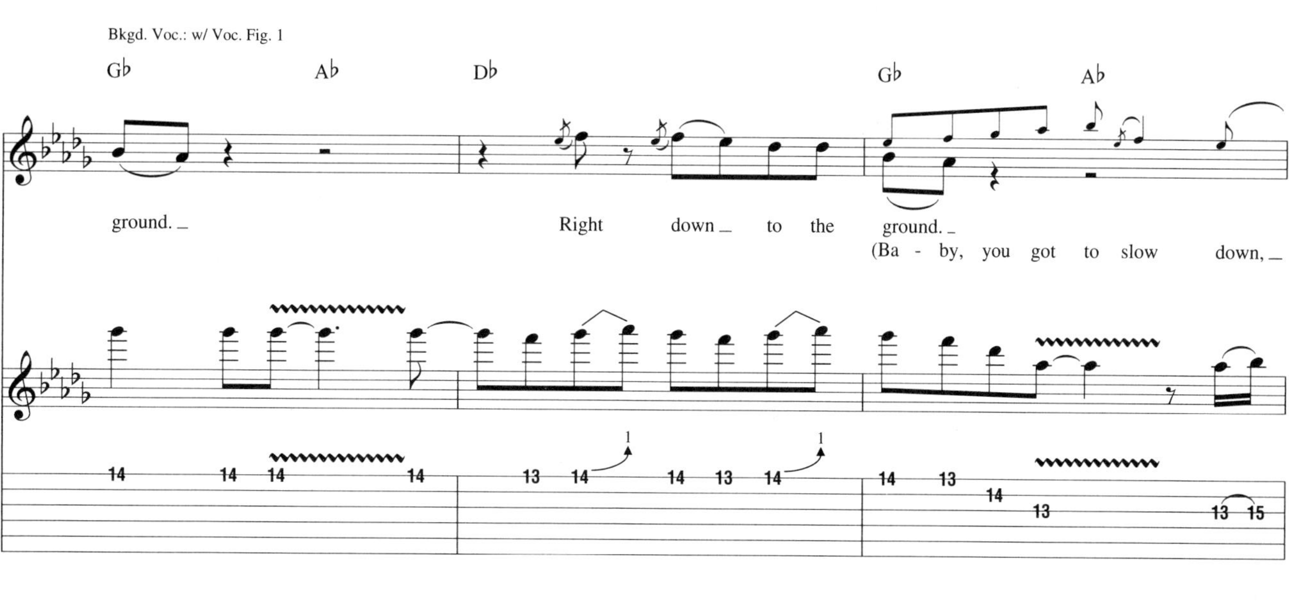
Bkgd. Voc.: w/ Voc. Fig. 1
G♭
A♭
D♭
G♭
A♭
ground.
Right down to the ground.
(Ba - by, you got to slow down,
1
1
14 14 14 14
13 14 14 13 14
14 13 14 13 13 15

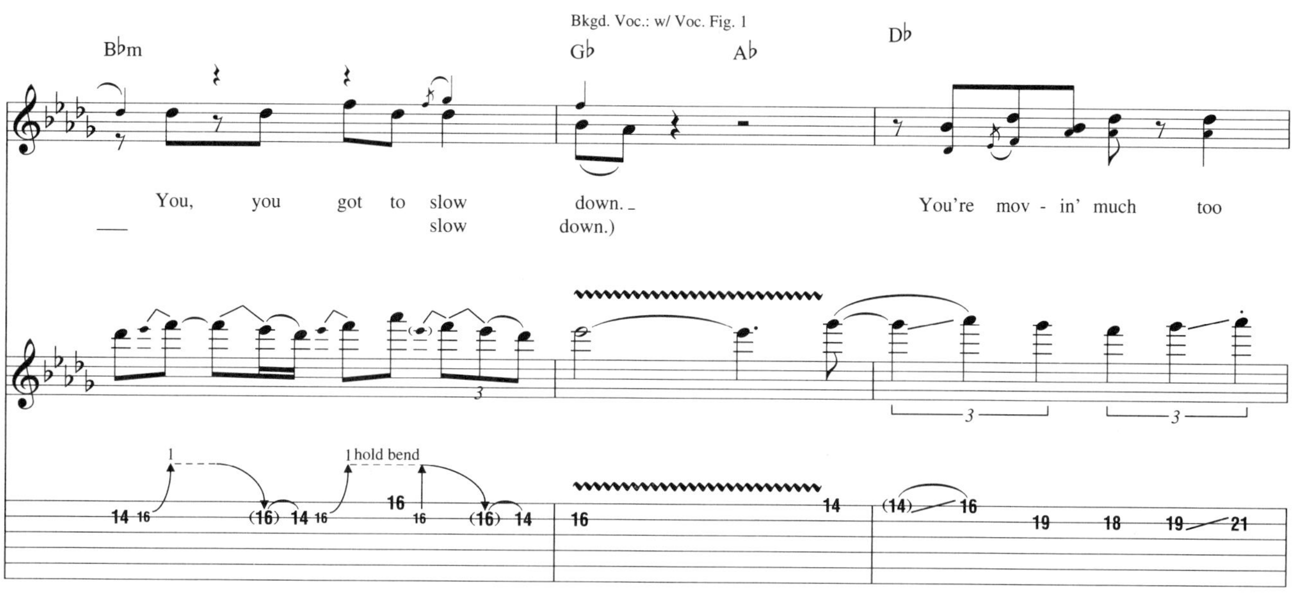
B♭m
Bkgd. Voc.: w/ Voc. Fig. 1
G♭
A♭
D♭
You, you got to slow down.
slow down.)
You're mov - in' much too
1
1 hold bend
14 16 (16) 14 16 16 16 (16) 14
16 14
(14) 16 19 18 19 21

G♭
A♭
fast.
Too fast.
(Too fast.)
Got to find a love that's
8va
21 21 21 21
21 21 21 21 21 21

Bridge

Gtr. 2 tacet
G♭
A♭
B♭m
gon - na last.
Oh, hoo, oo, oo.

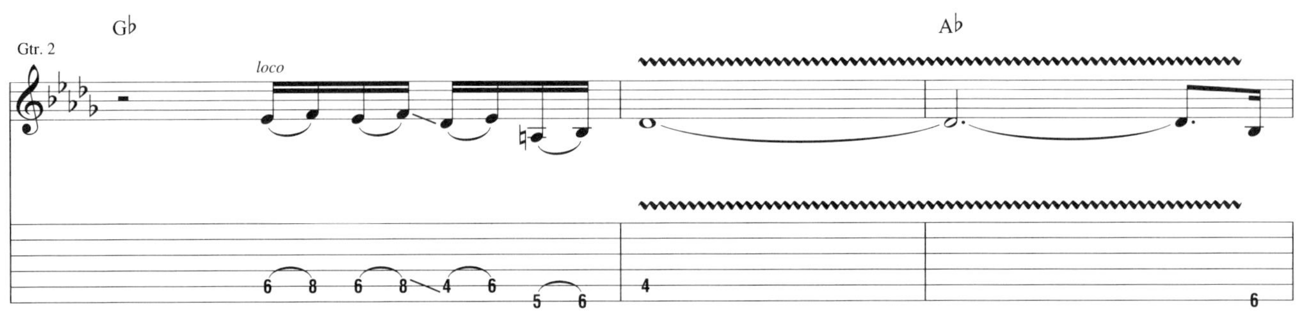
G♭
A♭
Gtr. 2
loco
6 8 6 8 4 6 5 6
4
6

B♭m
G♭
Girl, you got an ass like I nev - er
6
6 6 6

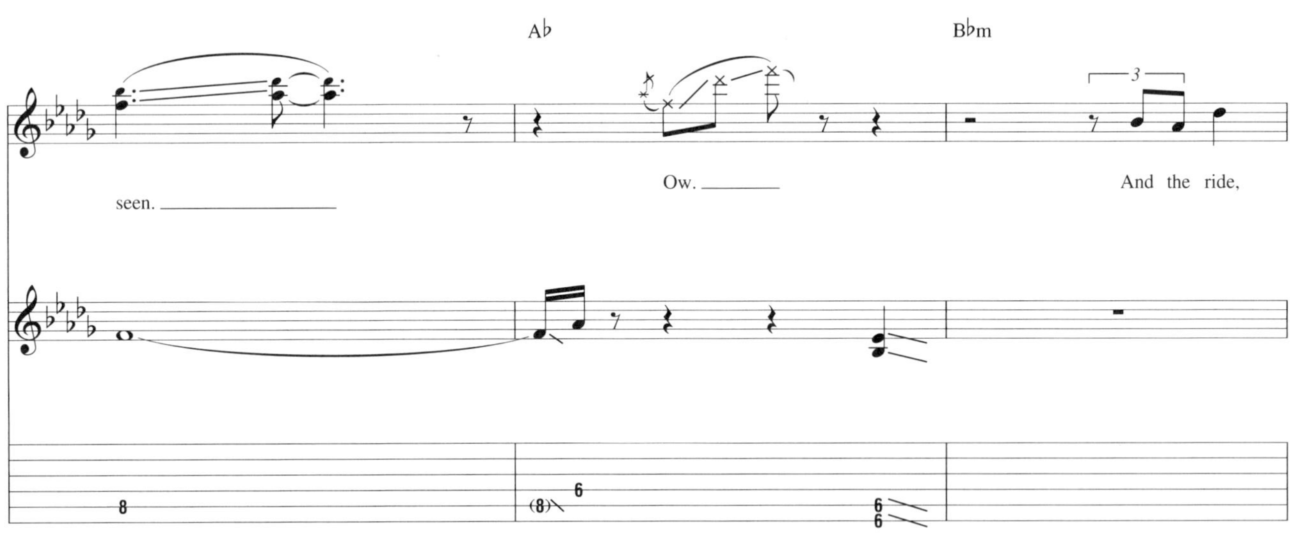
A♭
B♭m
3
seen.
Ow.
And the ride,
8
(8) 6
6
6

G♭
A♭
I say, the ride is so
*Two gtrs. arr. for one.
Outro-Chorus
Gtr. 2 tacet
Gtr. 1: w/ Rhy. Fig. 1 (till fade)
B♭m
G♭
A♭
D♭
smooth, you must be a lim - ou - sine.
Ow.
Bkgd. Voc.: w/ Voc. Fig. 1
Ba - by, you're much too fast.
Lit - tle red Cor - vette, you need a love, you
need a love, that's, uh, that's gon - na la - la - last,
oo.
Babe, you got to slow down, uh.
(You got to slow down.)
Lit - tle red Cor - vette, 'cause if you don't, 'cause if you don't you're gon - na

Ab
Gb
Ab
Db
run your bod - y right to the ground.
Right to the ground.
(Right to the ground.
Right to the
Gb
Ab
Bbm
Gb
Ab
Right to the ground.
ground.
Right to the ground.)
Gtr. 2
Db
Gb
Ab
Lit - tle red Cor- vette, oh.
Gtr. 2 tacet
Gb
Ab
Db
Gb
Ab
Oo,
oo.

Begin fade
B♭m
G♭
A♭
Oo,
oo,
D♭
G♭
A♭
oo.
G♭
A♭
D♭
Oo.
Gtr. 2
let ring
G♭
A♭
B♭m
Oo.
G♭
A♭
D♭
G♭
Fade out
Oo.
(Oo.
Oo.
Oo.
Oo,
Oo,
oo.
oo.)

from Rob Zombie - *Hellbilly Deluxe*

Living Dead Girl

Words by Scott Humphrey and Rob Zombie
Music by Rob Zombie

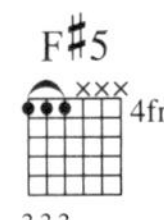

Drop D tuning:
(low to high) D-A-D-G-B-E

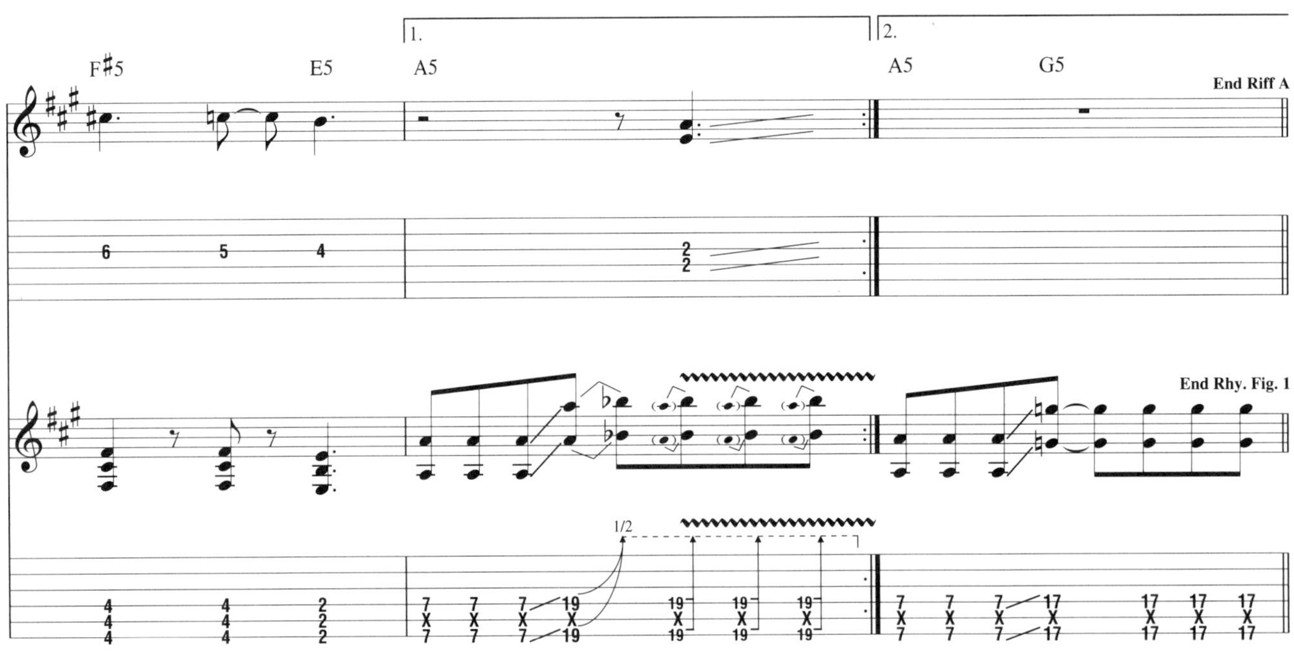

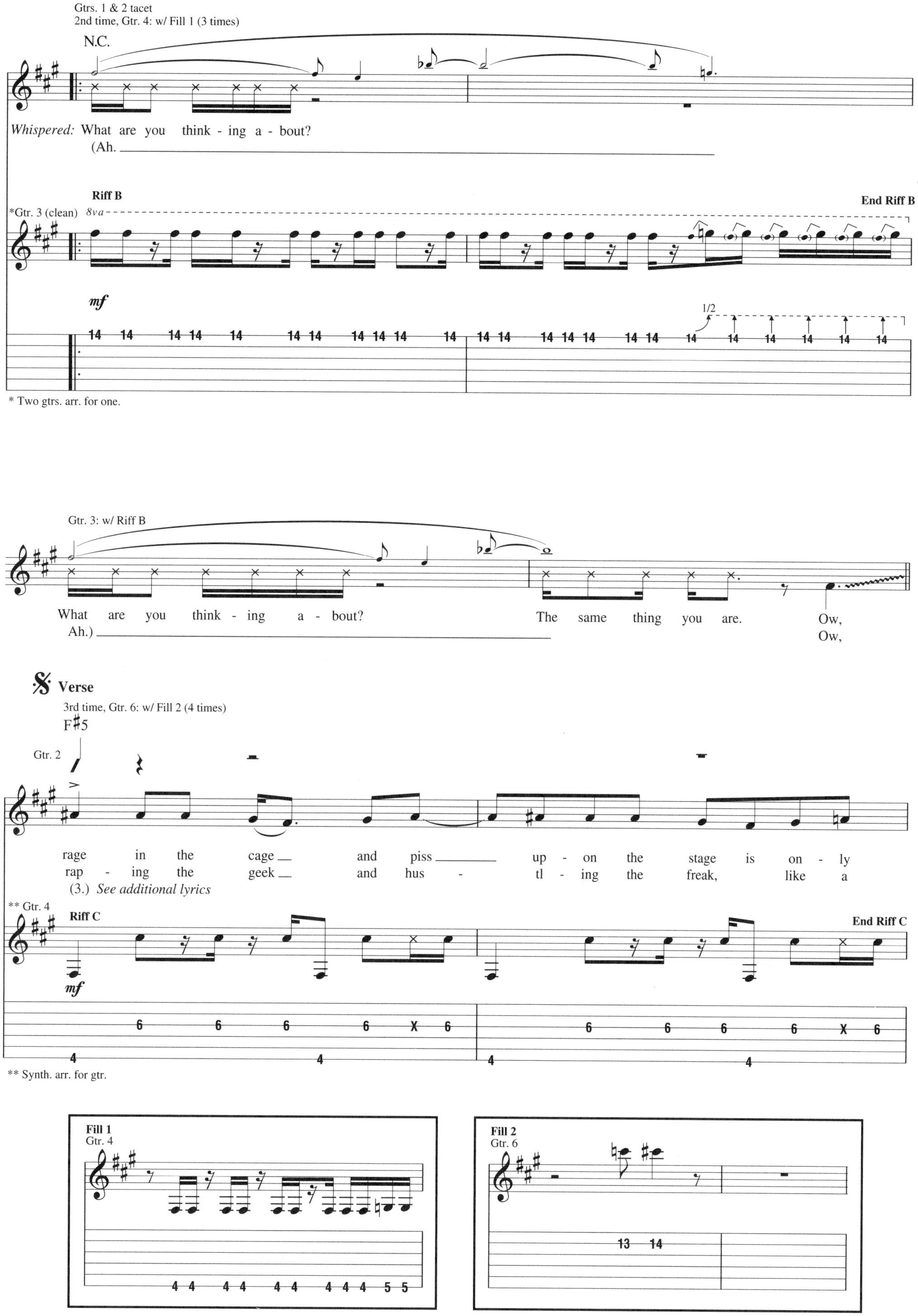

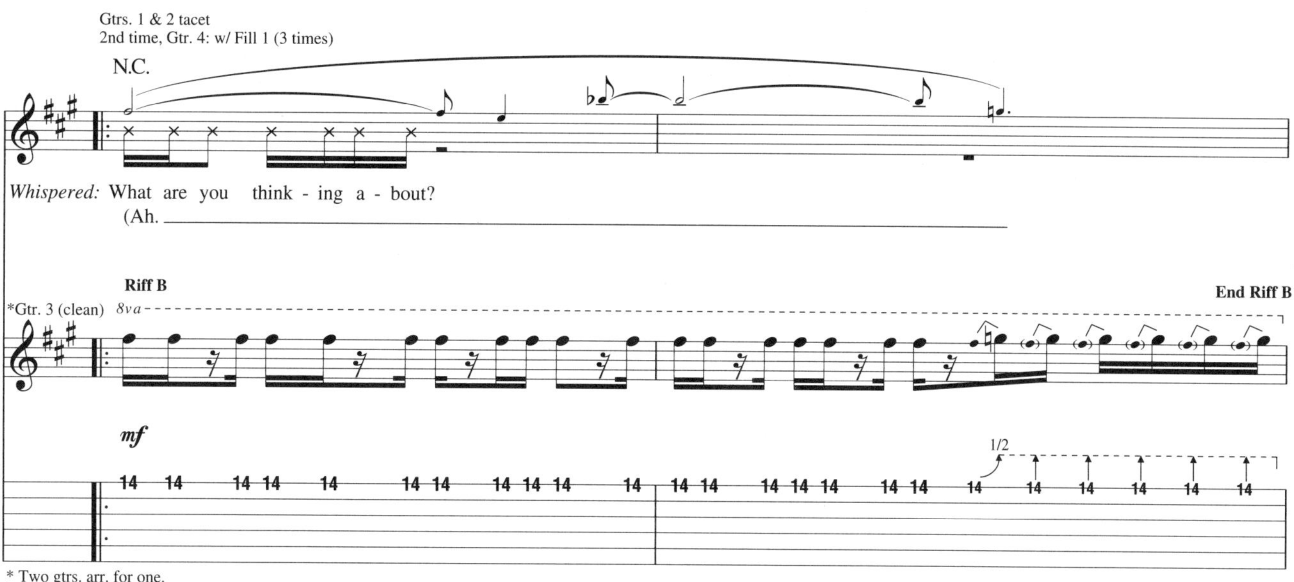

* Two gtrs. arr. for one.

Gtr. 3: w/ Riff B

What are you think - ing a - bout? The same thing you are. Ow,
Ah.) Ow,

Verse

3rd time, Gtr. 6: w/ Fill 2 (4 times)

F♯5

Gtr. 2

rage in the cage and piss up - on the stage is on - ly
rap - ing the geek and hus - tl - ing the freak, like a
(3.) *See additional lyrics*

** Gtr. 4

Riff C

mf

End Riff C

6 6 6 6 X 6 6 6 6 6 X 6
4 4 4 4

** Synth. arr. for gtr.

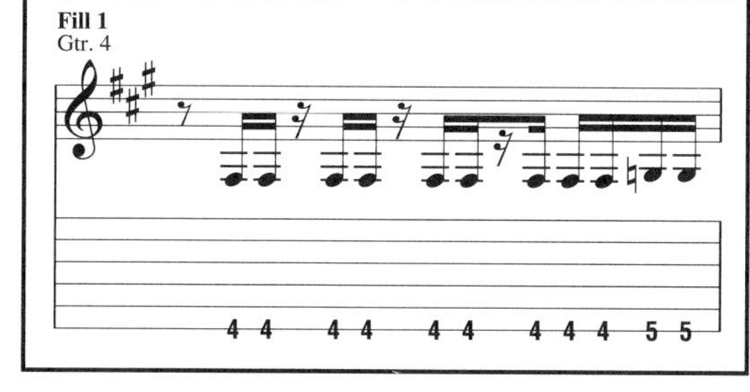

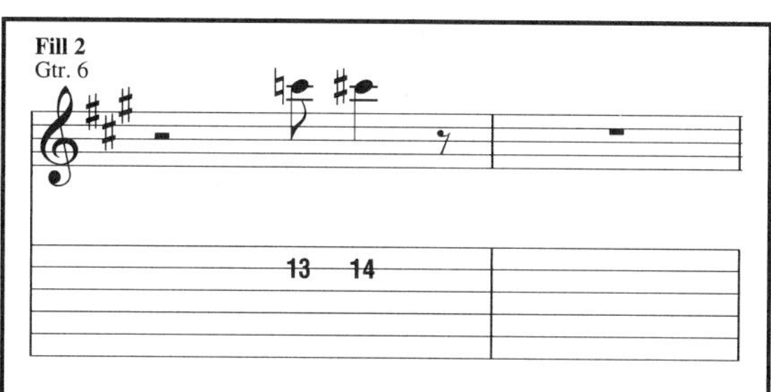

Gtr. 4: w/ Riff C (2 1/2 times)
one sure way to bring the gi - ant down. De - funct the strings of cem - e - ter - y things, with a one flat foot on the dev - il's wings.
hunch - back juice on a sen - ti - men - tal noose. Op - er - a - tion filth, they love to love the wealth of an S. S. whore mak - in' scar - y sounds.
* Gtr. 5
mf
* Bass arr. for gtr.
Gtr. 5 tacet
Gtr. 1: w/ Riff A
Chorus
1st & 2nd times, Gtr. 2: w/ Rhy. Fig. 1
3rd time, Gtr. 2: w/ Rhy. Fig. 1 (1st 3 meas.)
3rd time, Gtr. 3: w/ Fill 3
F♯5 E5 F♯5 E5 F♯5 E5 A5
Crawl on me, sink in - to me, die for me, liv - ing dead girl.
3rd time, Gtr. 2: w/ Rhy. Fig. 1 (last 4 meas.)
To Coda
F♯5 E5 F♯5 E5 F♯5 E5 A5 G5
Crawl on me, sink in - to me, die for me, liv - ing dead girl.
Fill 3
Gtr. 3
1/4 1/4 1/4

Bridge

N.C.

(Ooh, ___ ee, ___ wa. ___

* Gtr. 6

8va

mf

14 15 13 14 13 14 13 15

* Gtr. 7

mf

4 4 4 4 4 4 4 4 2 2 2 2 2 2 | 4 4 4 4 4 4 4 4 2 2 2 2 2 2 | 4 4 4 4 4 4 4 4 2 2 2 2 2 2

* Synth. arr. for gtr.

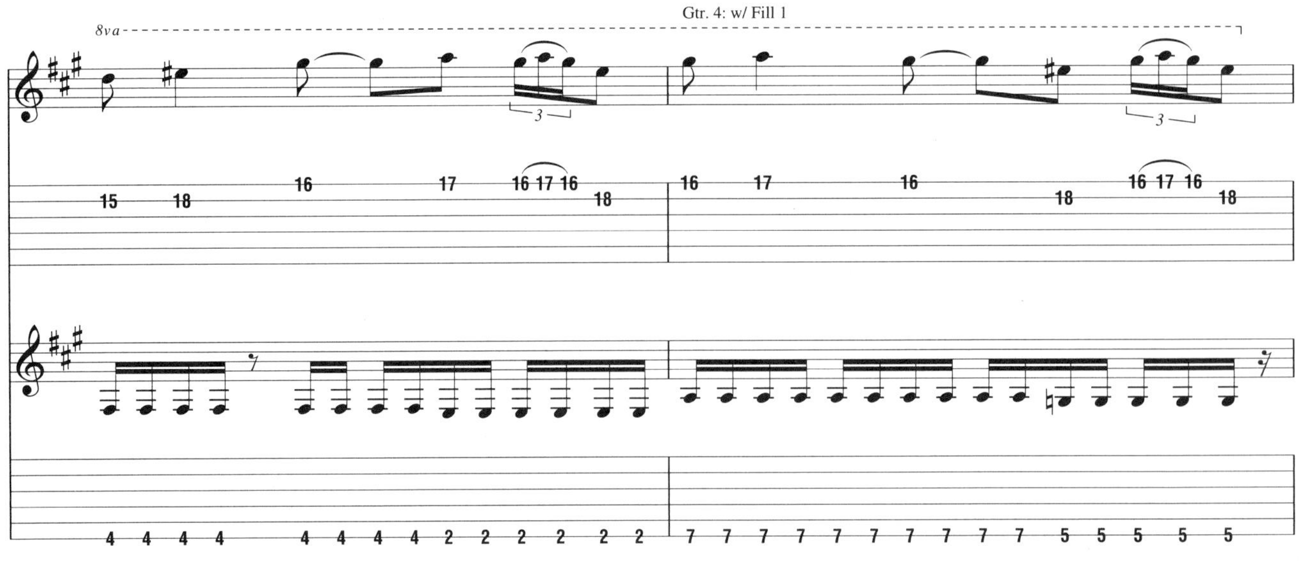

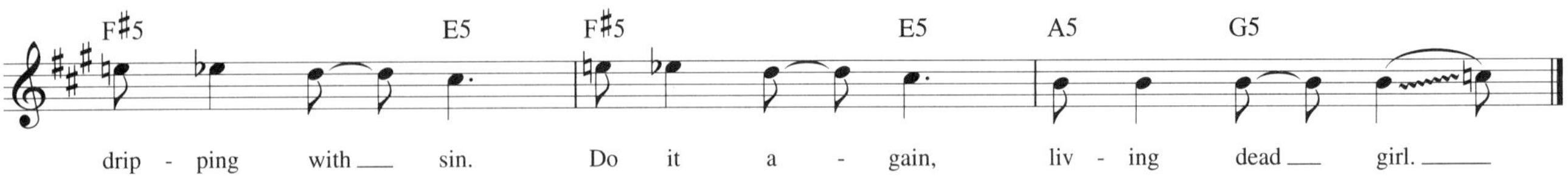

Additional Lyrics

3. Cyclone Jack, hallucinating hack,
   Thinks Donna Reed eats dollar bills.
   Goldfoot's machine creates another fiend,
   So beautiful they make you kill.

from System of a Down - *Hypnotize*

Lonely Day

Words and Music by Daron Malakian and Serj Tankian

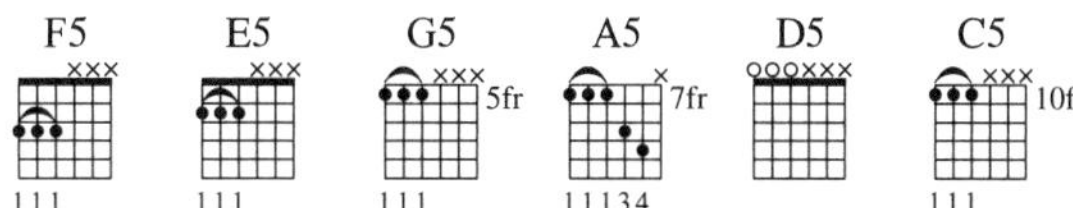

Gtrs. 1 & 3–7: Tune down 1/2 step:
(low to high) E♭-A♭-D♭-G♭-B♭-E♭

Gtr. 2: Drop D tuning, down 1/2 step:
(low to high) D♭-A♭-D♭-G♭-B♭-E♭

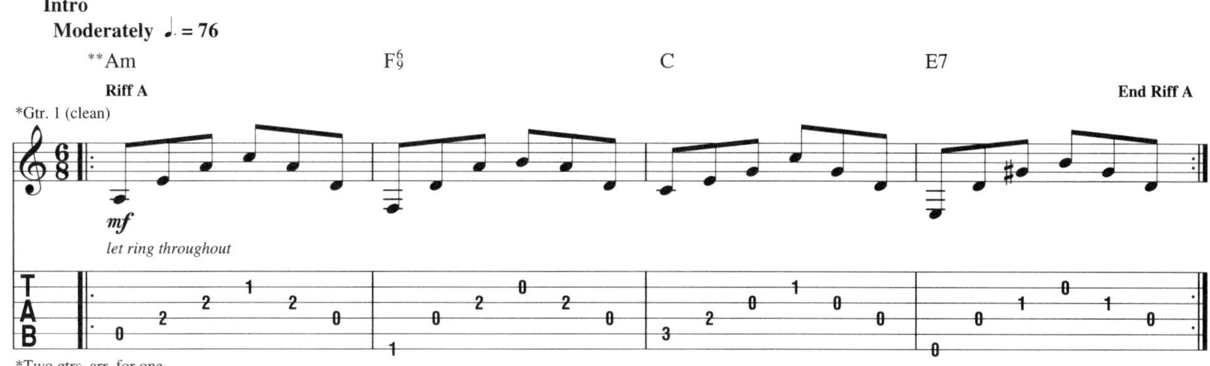

*Two gtrs. arr. for one.

**Chord symbols reflect implied harmony.

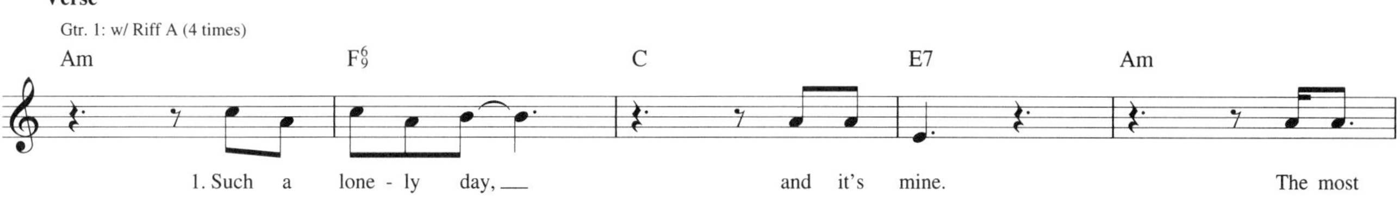

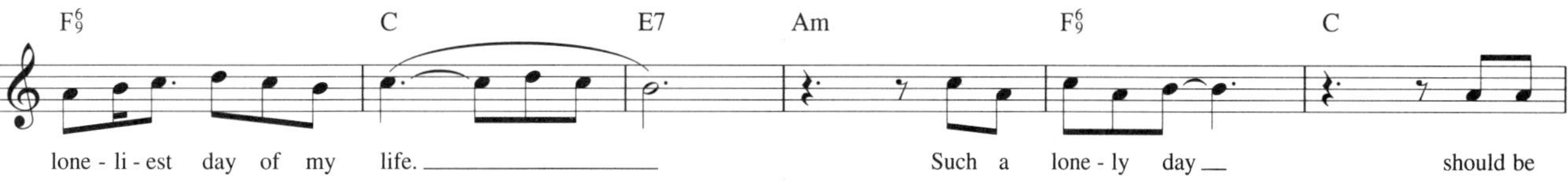

Chorus

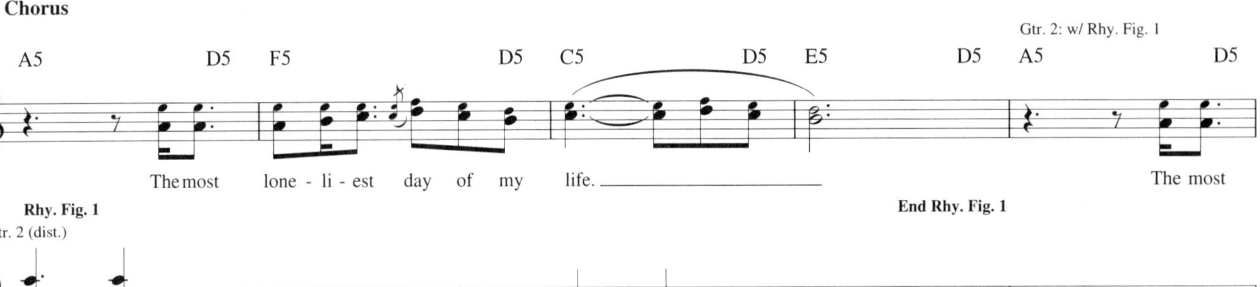

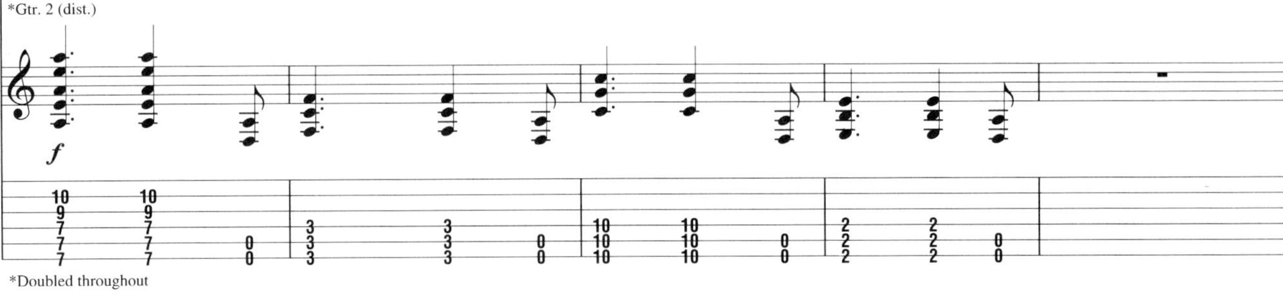

Verse

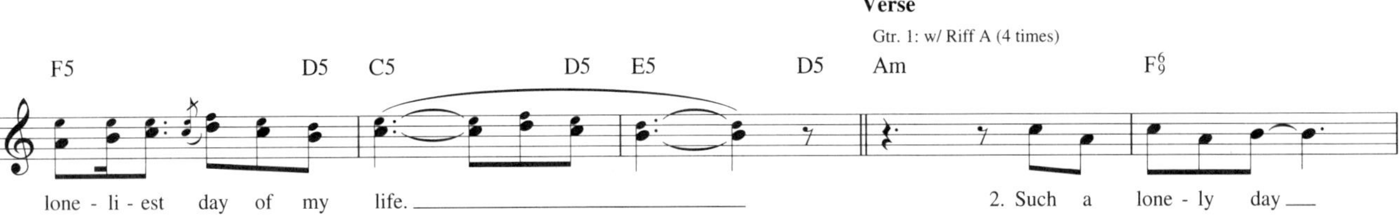

Gtrs. 3–5 tacet
Am
F6/9
C
E7
The most lone - li - est day of my life.

Bridge

F5
E5
G5
A5
D5
F5
E5
Gtr. 2
And if you go, I wan-na go with you. And if you die,
mf
Gtr. 6 (clean)
Gtr. 3
divisi
Gtr. 4
Gtr. 5
divisi

G5
A5
D5
F5
E5
D5
P.M.
I wan-na die with you. Take your hand and walk a -
Gtr. 3
Gtr. 4
Gtr. 5

Guitar Solo
Gtr. 5 tacet
A5 D5 F5 D5 C5 D5 E5 D5 A5 D5
Rhy. Fig. 2
End Rhy. Fig. 2
Gtr. 2: w/ Rhy. Fig. 2 (3 times)
way.
(way.)
Gtr. 3
Gtr. 4
F5 D5 C5 D5 E5 D5 A5 D5
Riff B
End Riff B
*8va
Gtr. 5
Gtr. 6
divisi
Riff B1
End Riff B1
*Applies to both gtrs.
8va
Gtr. 7 (clean)
mf
Gtr. 4
divisi

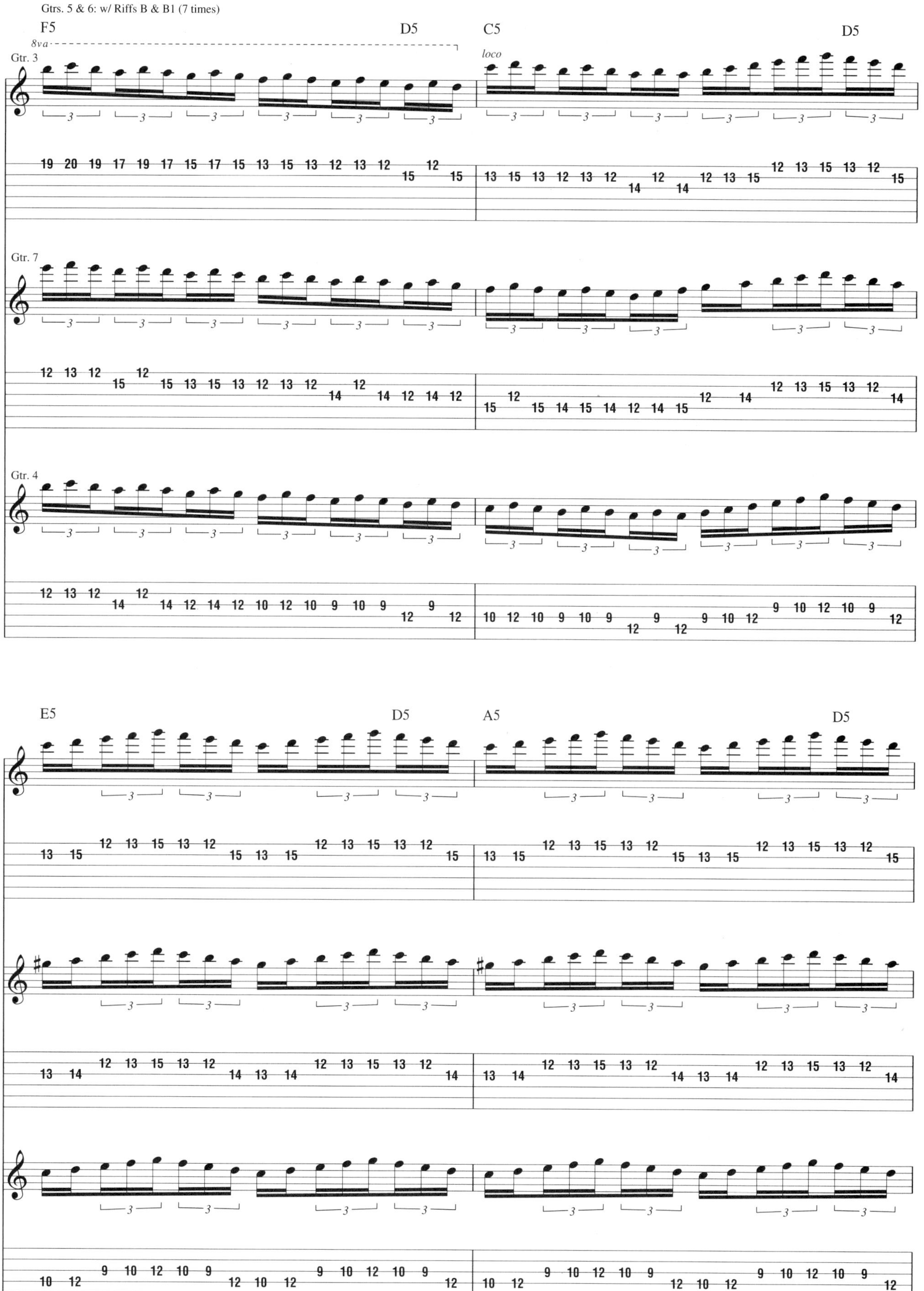
Gtrs. 5 & 6: w/ Riffs B & B1 (7 times)
F5
D5
C5
D5
8va
loco
Gtr. 3
Gtr. 7
Gtr. 4
E5
D5
A5
D5

F5
D5
C5
D5
E5
D5
Chorus
A5
D5
F5
D5
Rhy. Fig. 3
Gtr. 2
(cont. in notation)
The most lone - li - est day of my
Gtr. 5
Gtr. 6
divisi
Gtr. 3
Gtr. 7
Gtr. 4

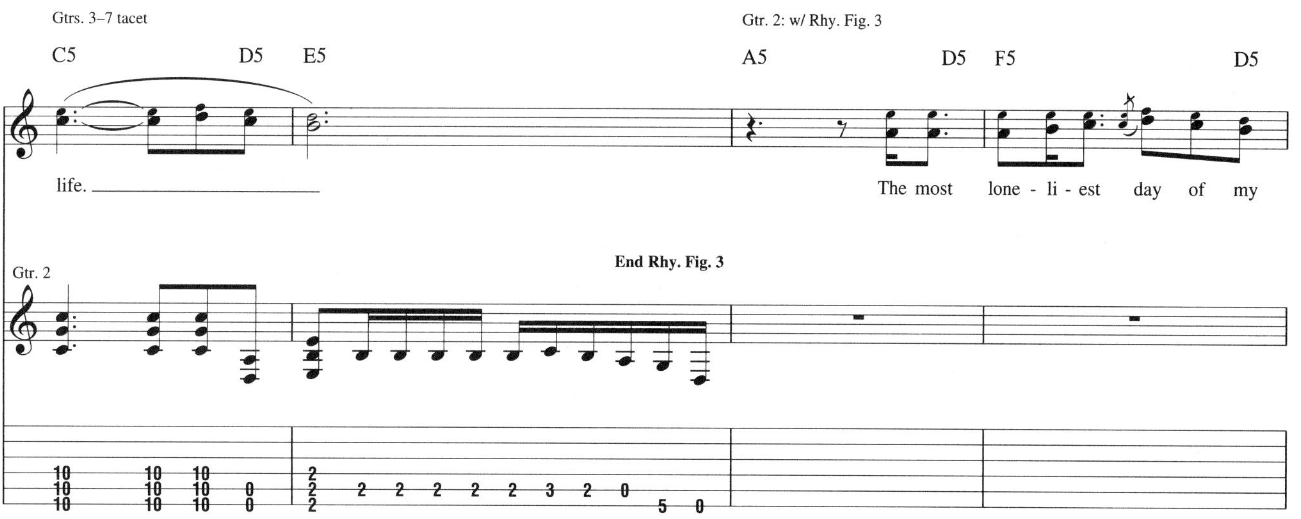
Gtrs. 3–7 tacet
Gtr. 2: w/ Rhy. Fig. 3
C5 D5 E5 A5 D5 F5 D5
life. ___
The most lone - li - est day of my
Gtr. 2
End Rhy. Fig. 3

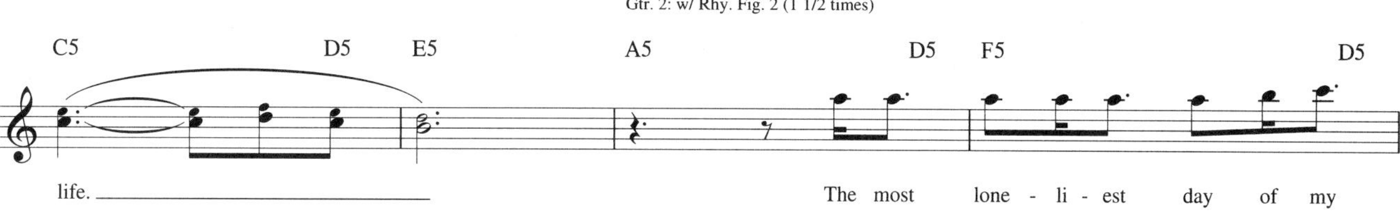
Gtr. 2: w/ Rhy. Fig. 2 (1 1/2 times)
C5 D5 E5 A5 D5 F5 D5
life. ___
The most lone - li - est day of my

C5 D5 E5 D5 A5 D5 F5 D5
life ___
(Ah.) ___

Outro-Verse

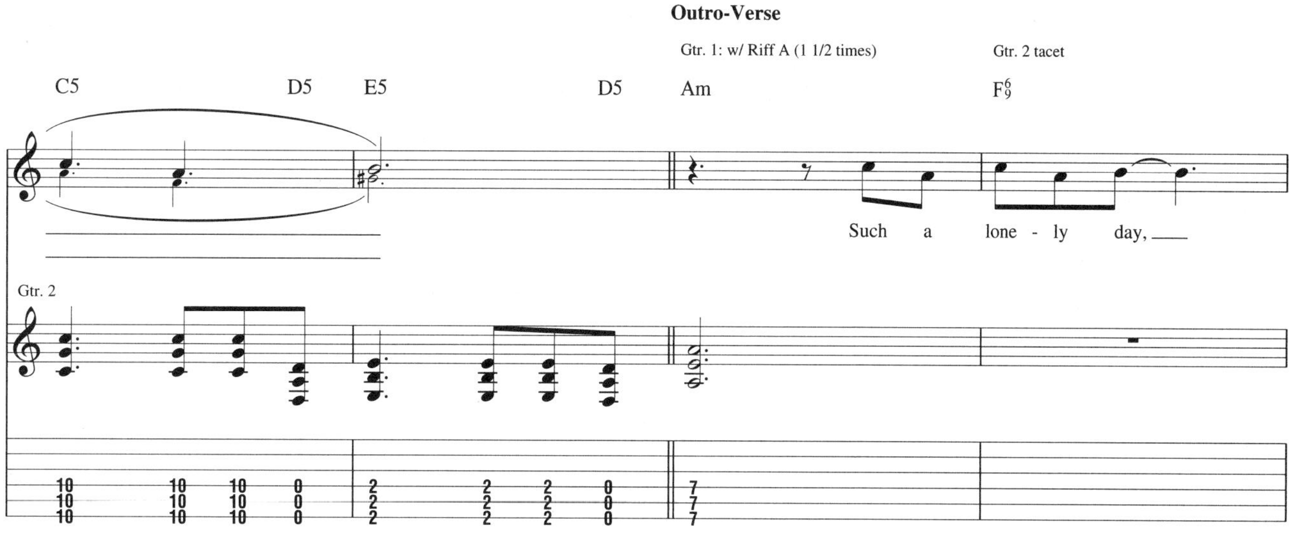
Gtr. 1: w/ Riff A (1 1/2 times)
Gtr. 2 tacet
C5 D5 E5 D5 Am F6/9
Such a lone - ly day, ___
Gtr. 2

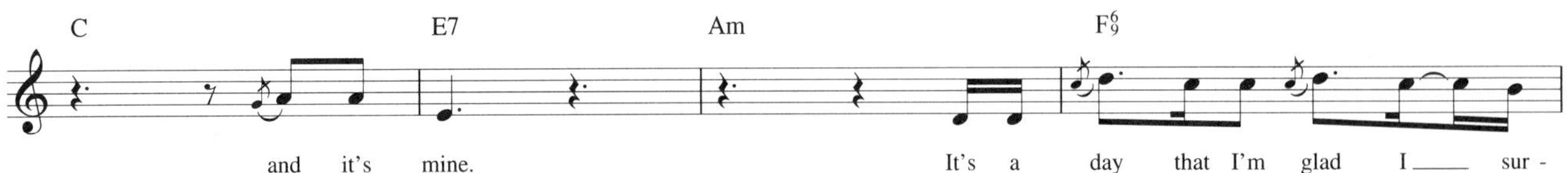

Slowly ♩ = 65

C E7 A

rit. *rit.*

vived. ___

Gtr. 3

8va

rit. *rit.*

Harm.

5

Pitch: E

Gtr. 4

* mp p

steady gliss.

rit. w/ dist. *rit.* w/ slide

20 17

*Vol. swell

Gtr. 5

** mp p

steady gliss.

rit. *rit.* w/ dist. w/ slide

16 14

**Vol. swell

Gtr. 1

rit. *rit.*

3 2 0 1 0 0 | 0 0 1 0 1 0 | 10 X 0 7 9 7 10

from Gary Moore - *Wild Frontier*

The Loner

Words and Music by Gary Moore and Max Middleton

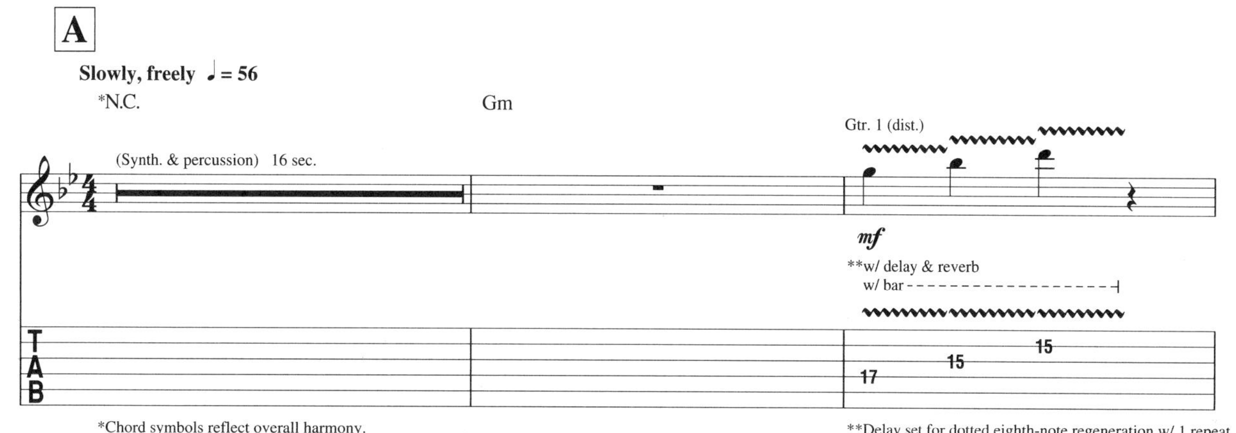

**Delay set for dotted eighth-note regeneration w/ 1 repeat.

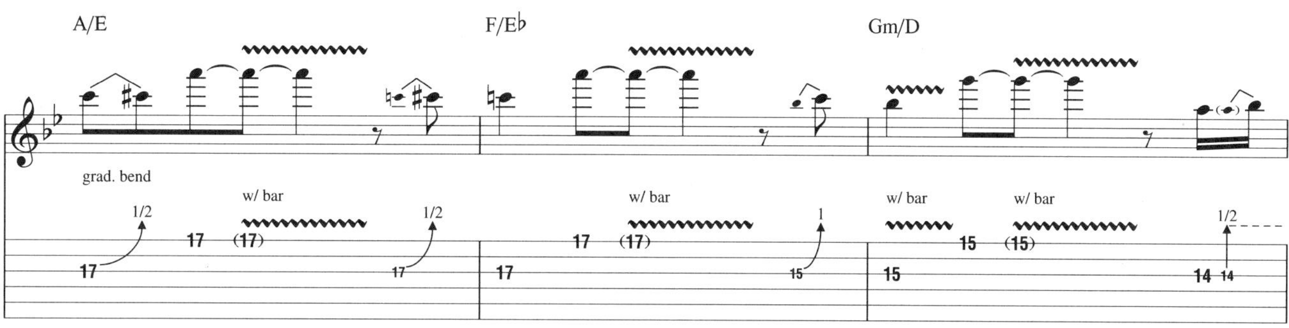

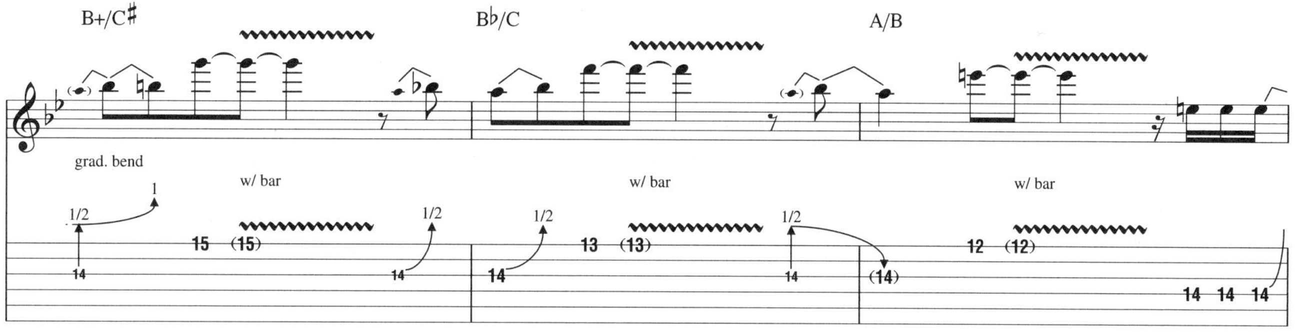

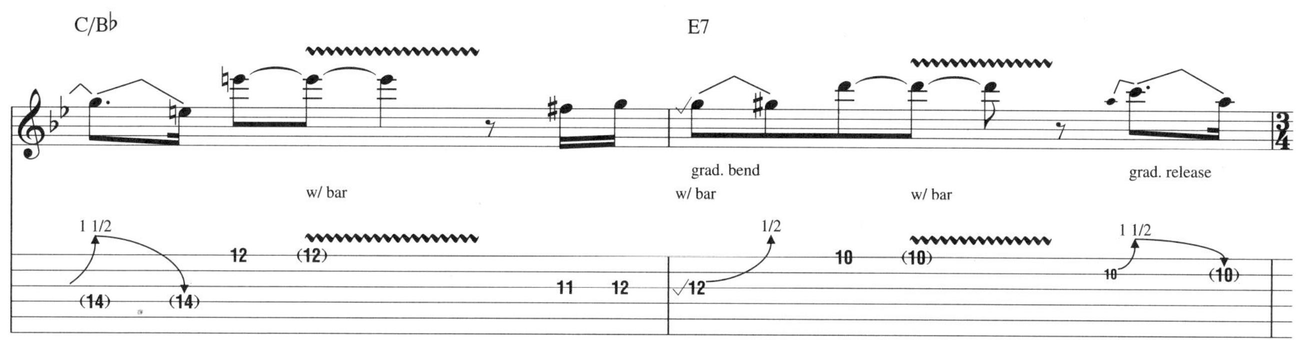

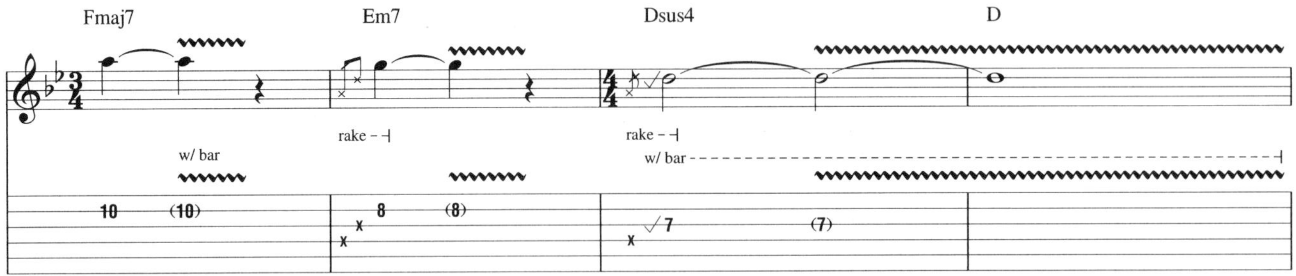
Fmaj7
Em7
Dsus4
D
rake
rake
w/ bar
w/ bar

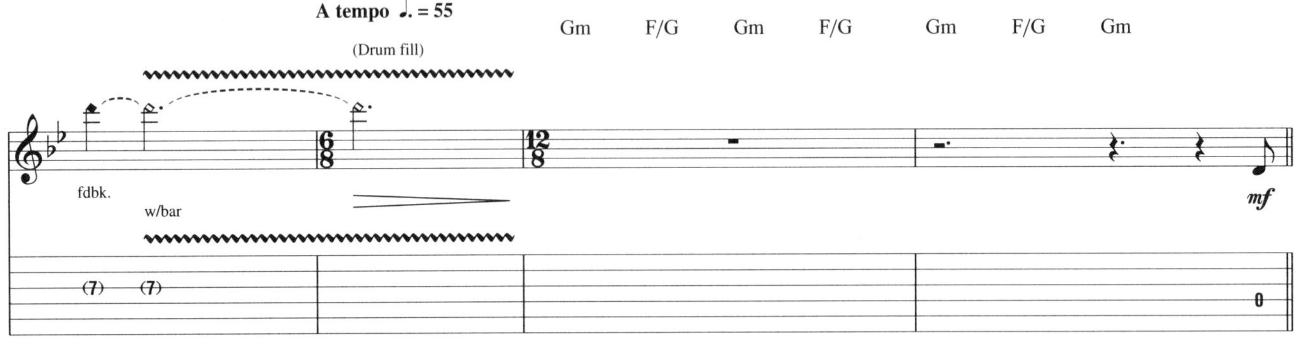
A tempo ♩. = 55
(Drum fill)
Gm F/G Gm F/G Gm F/G Gm
fdbk.
w/bar
mf

B
Gm
Cm
F
B♭maj7
1/2

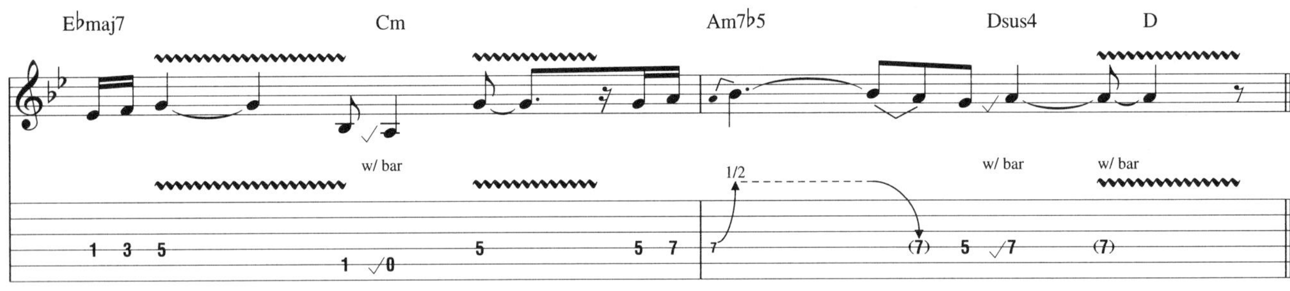
E♭maj7
Cm
Am7♭5
Dsus4
D
w/ bar
1/2
w/ bar
w/ bar

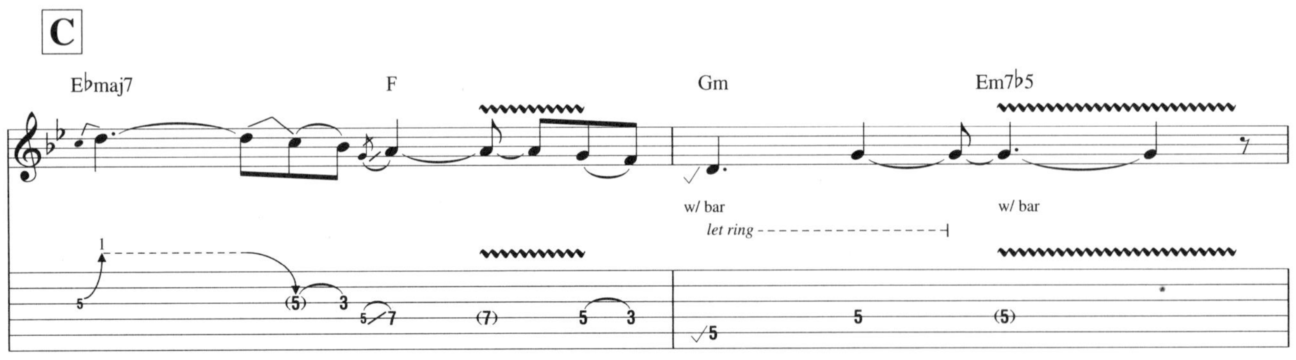
C
E♭maj7
F
Gm
Em7♭5
w/ bar
let ring
w/ bar
1

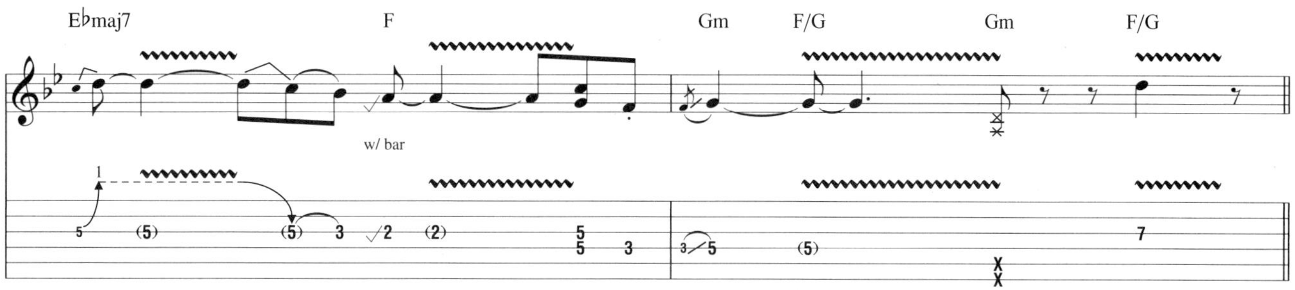

E♭maj7
F
Gm
F/G
Gm
F/G
w/ bar

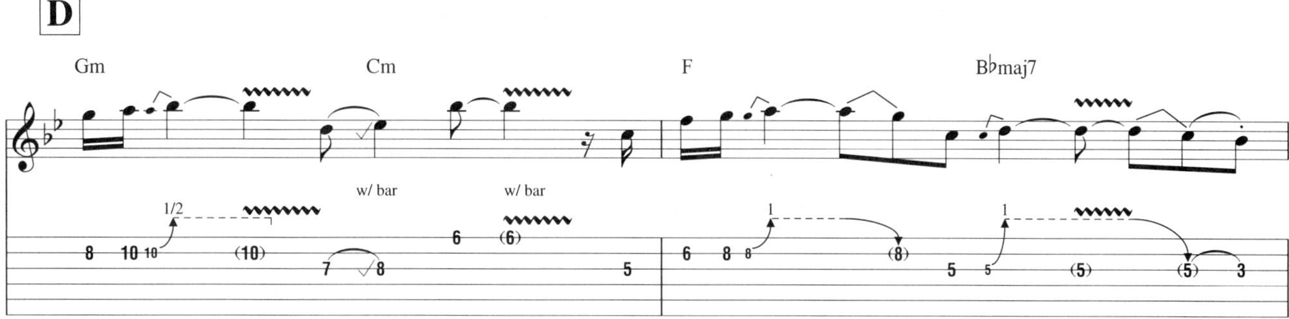

D
Gm
Cm
F
B♭maj7
w/ bar
w/ bar

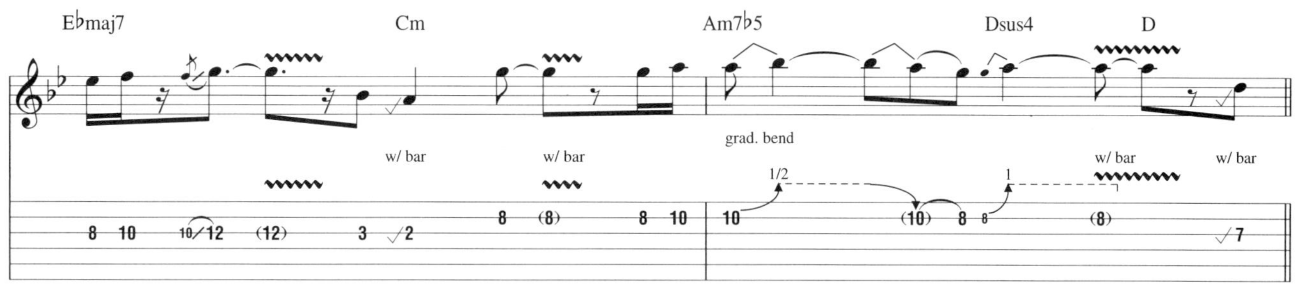

E♭maj7
Cm
Am7♭5
Dsus4
D
grad. bend
w/ bar
w/ bar
w/ bar
w/ bar

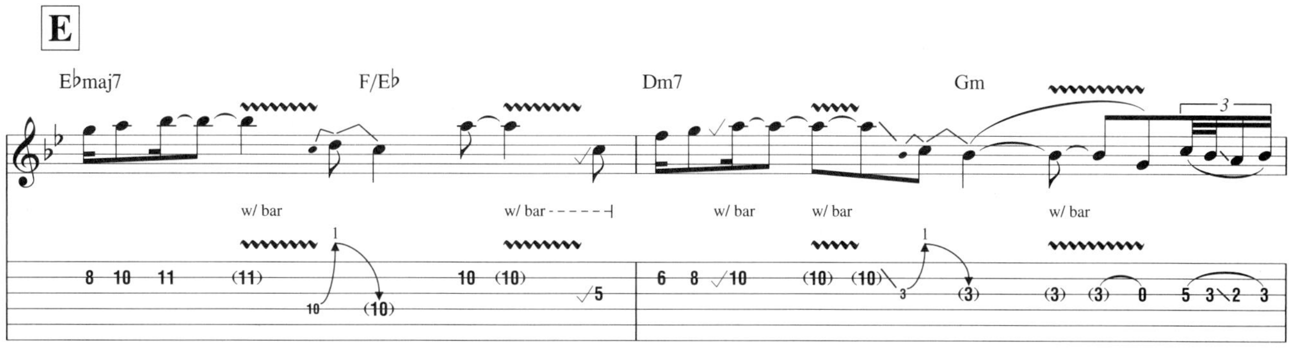

E
E♭maj7
F/E♭
Dm7
Gm
w/ bar
w/ bar
w/ bar
w/ bar
w/ bar

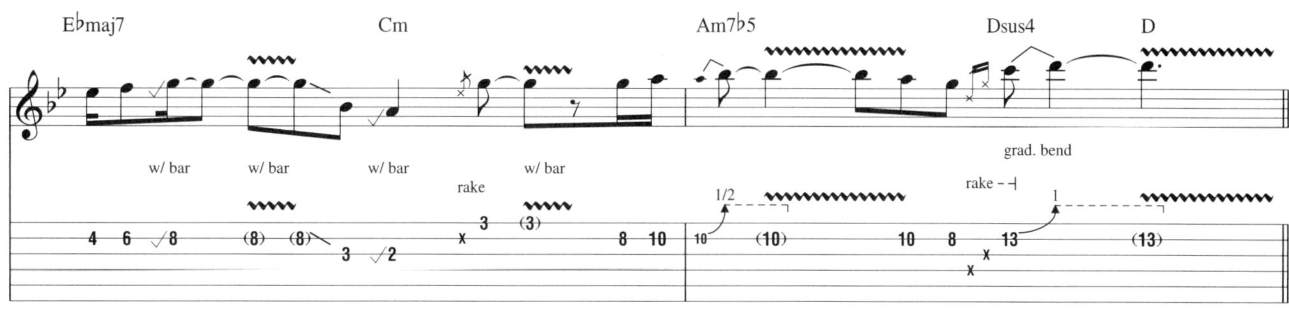

E♭maj7
Cm
Am7♭5
Dsus4
D
grad. bend
w/ bar
w/ bar
w/ bar
w/ bar
rake
rake

F

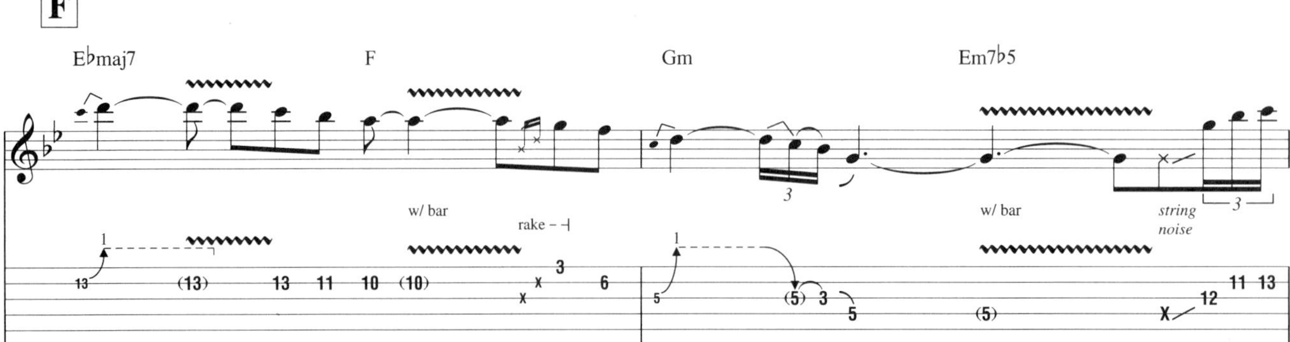

E♭maj7
F
Gm
Em7♭5
w/ bar
rake
w/ bar
string noise

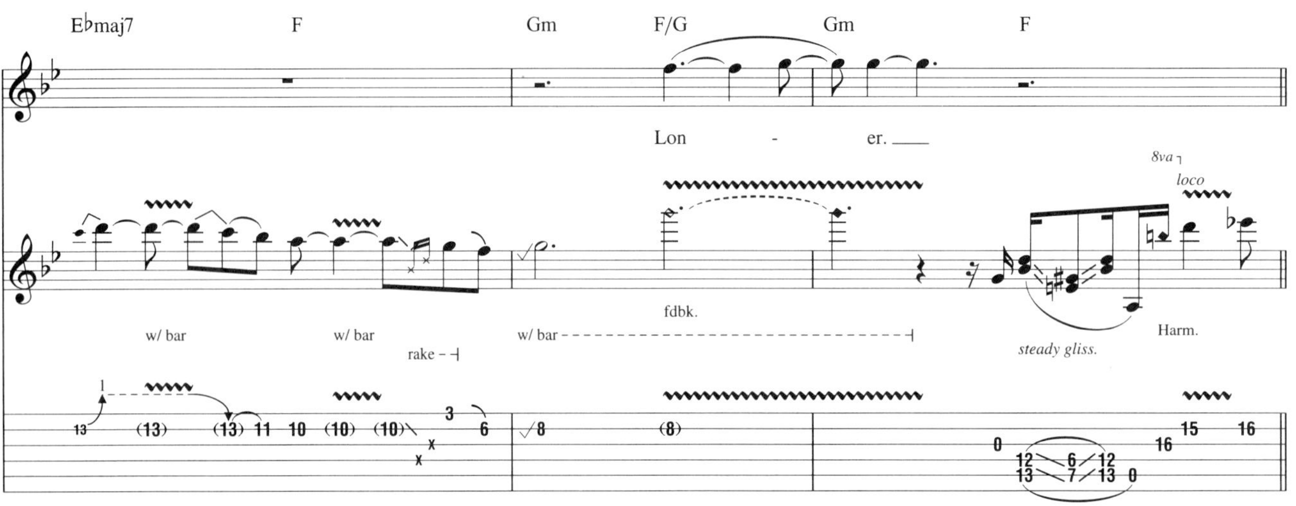

E♭maj7
F
Gm
F/G
Gm
F
Lon - er.
8va
loco
w/ bar
w/ bar
rake
w/ bar
fdbk.
steady gliss.
Harm.

G

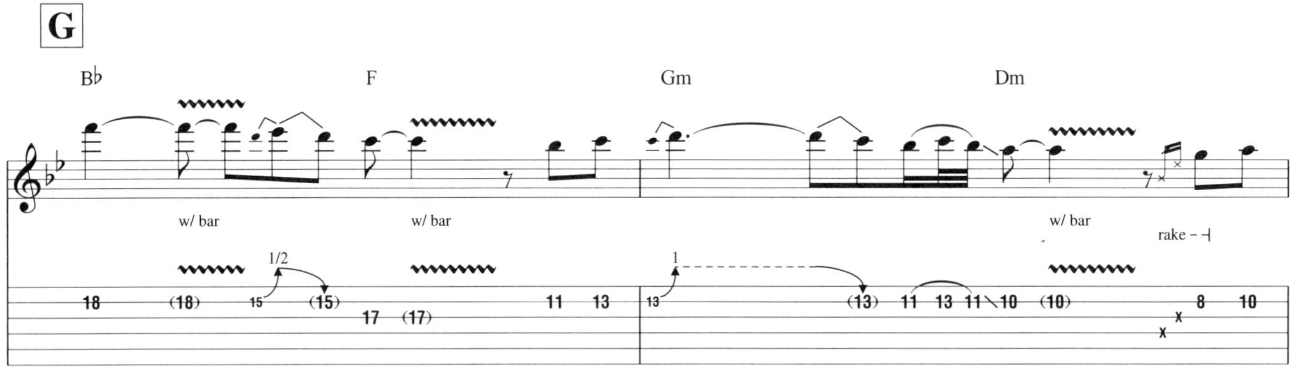

B♭
F
Gm
Dm
w/ bar
w/ bar
w/ bar
rake

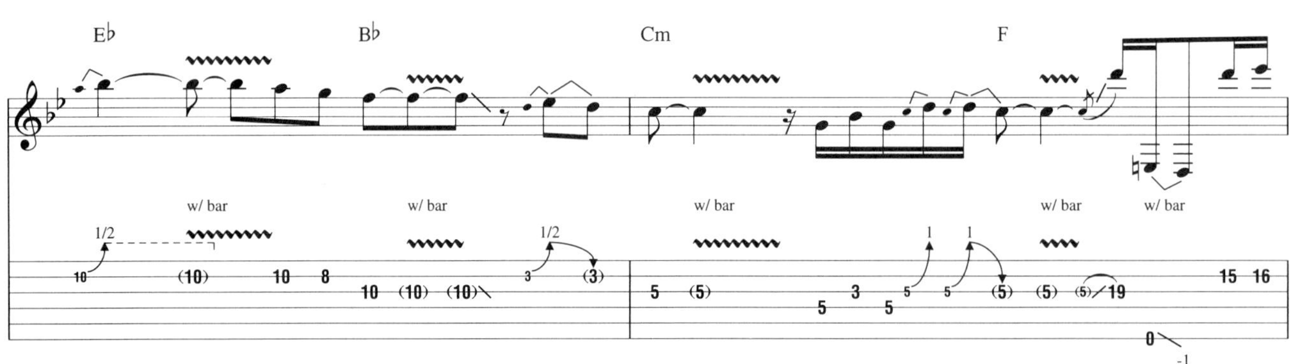

E♭
B♭
Cm
F
w/ bar
w/ bar
w/ bar
w/ bar
w/ bar

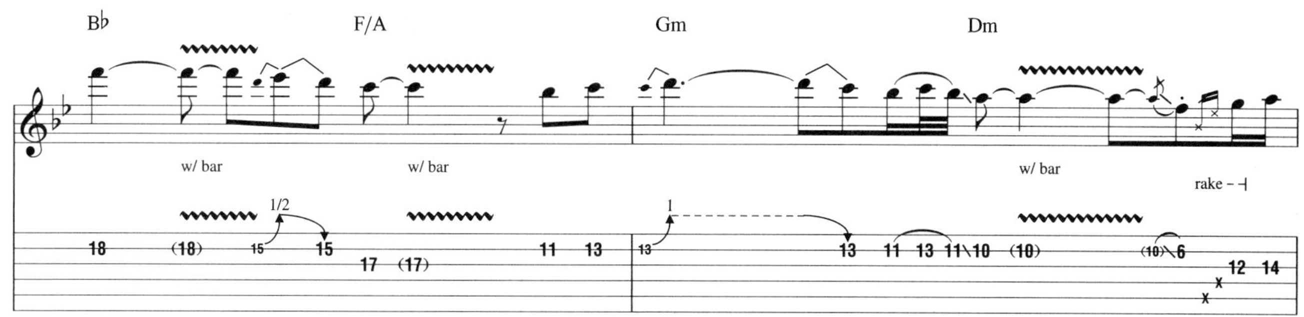

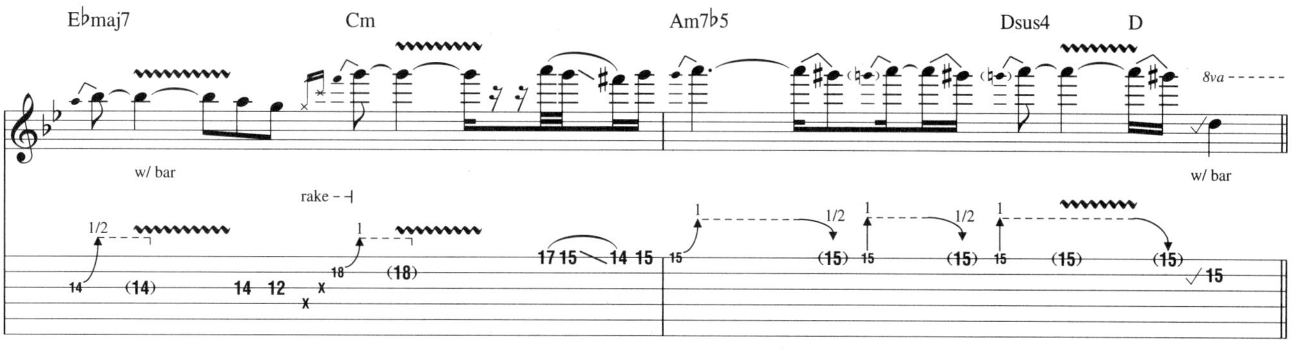

H

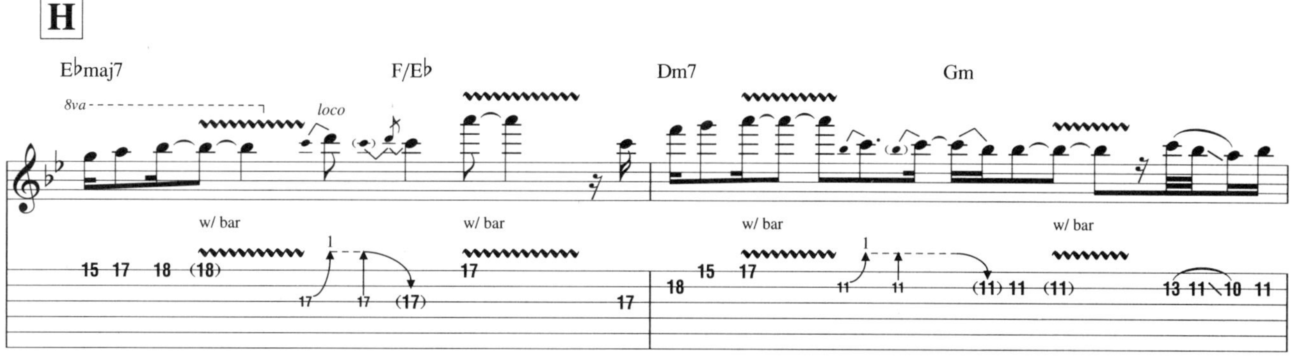

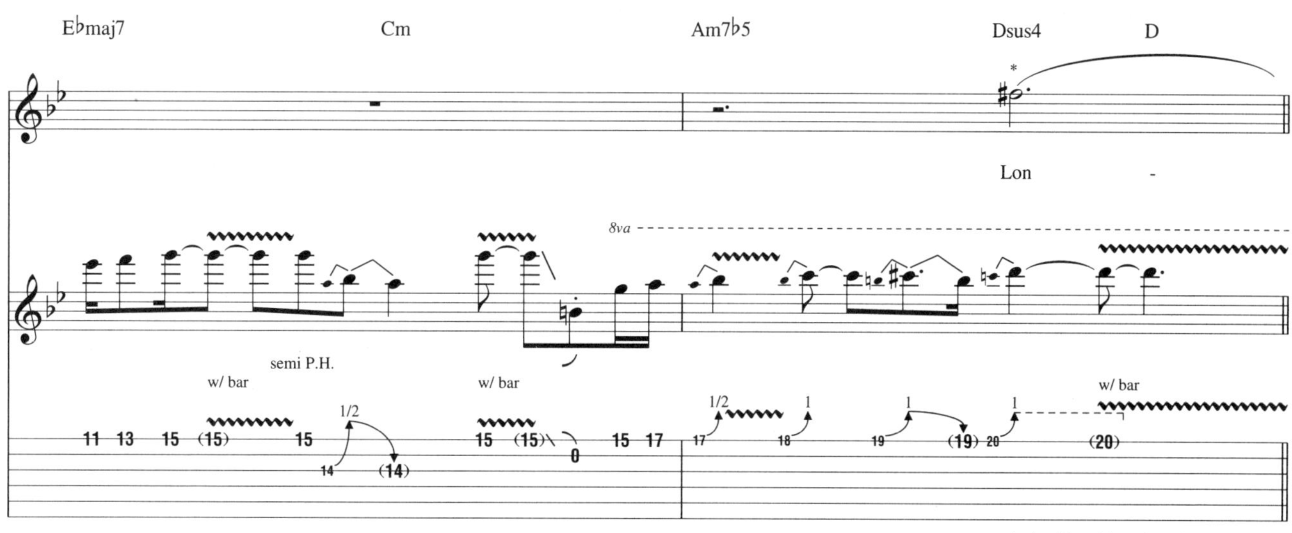

*w/ ambient delays throughout

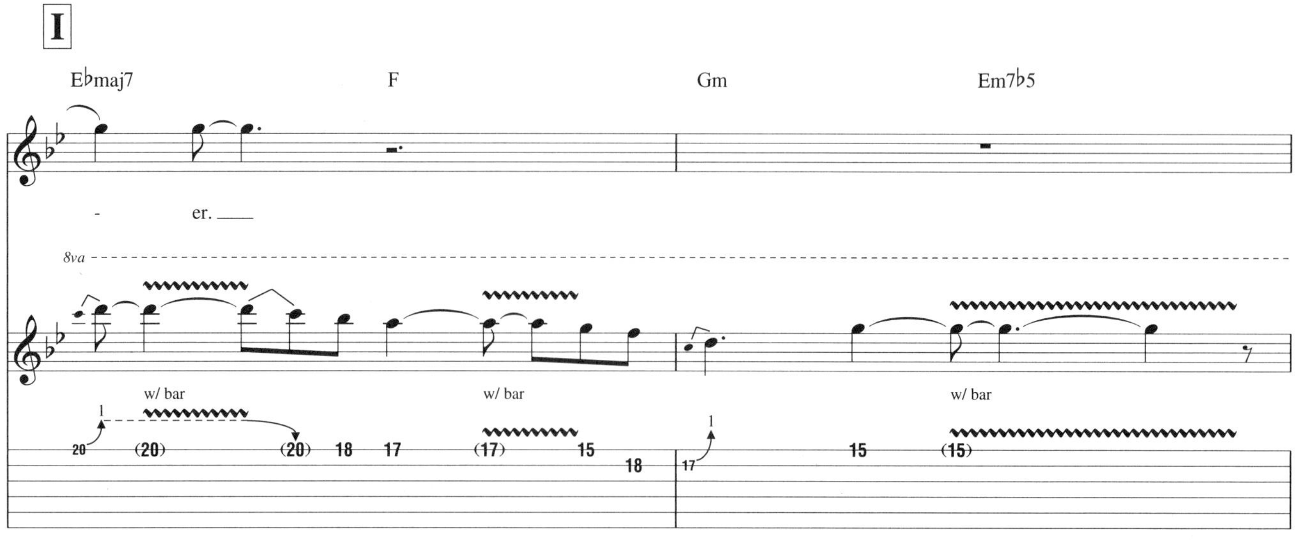
I
E♭maj7
F
Gm
Em7♭5
- er.
8va
w/ bar
w/ bar
w/ bar

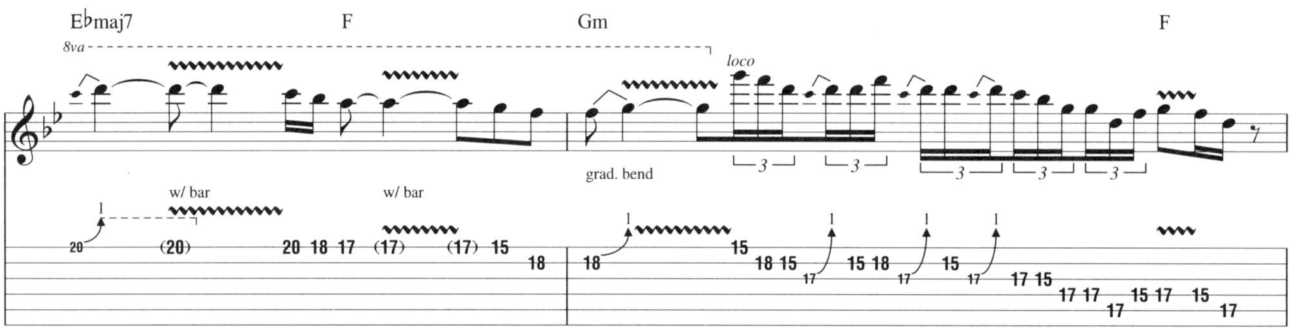
E♭maj7
F
Gm
F
8va
loco
grad. bend
w/ bar
w/ bar

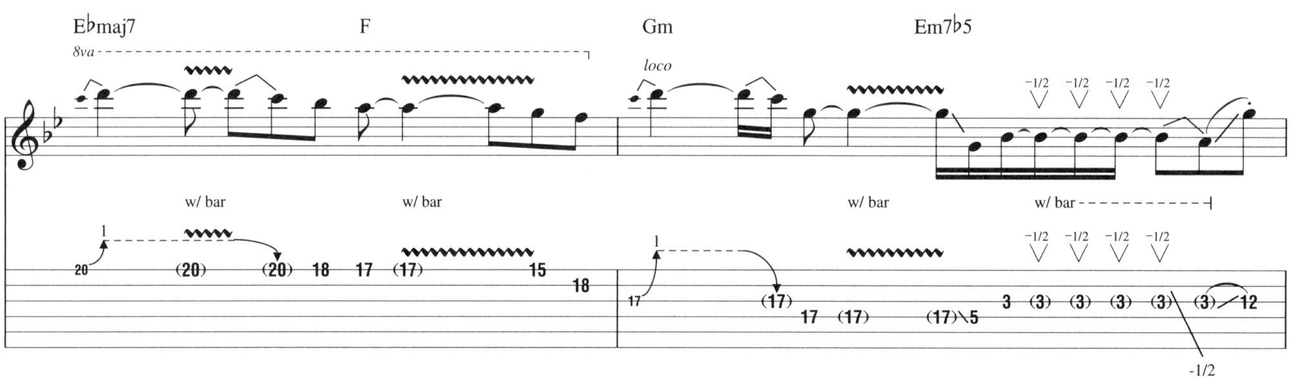
E♭maj7
F
Gm
Em7♭5
8va
loco
w/ bar
w/ bar
w/ bar
w/ bar

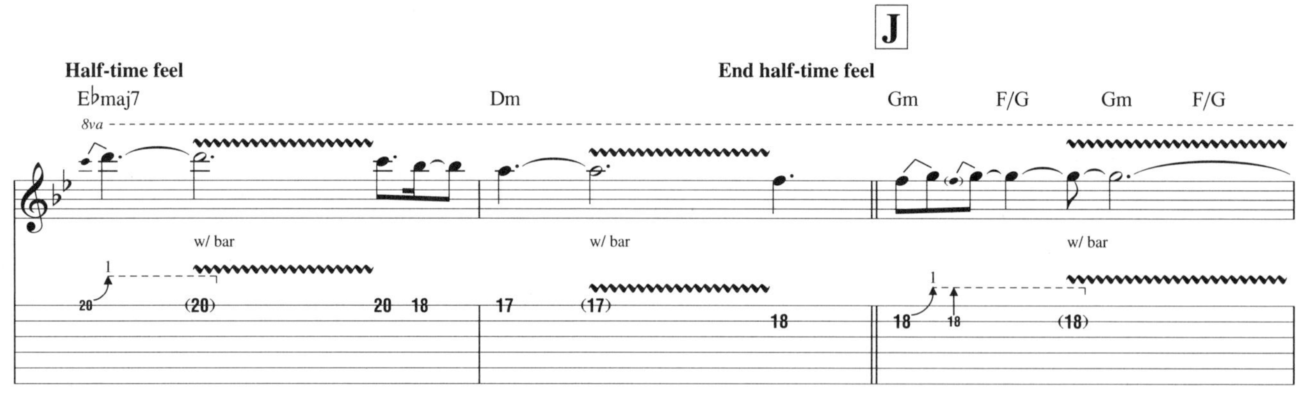
J
Half-time feel
End half-time feel
E♭maj7
Dm
Gm
F/G
Gm
F/G
8va
w/ bar
w/ bar
w/ bar

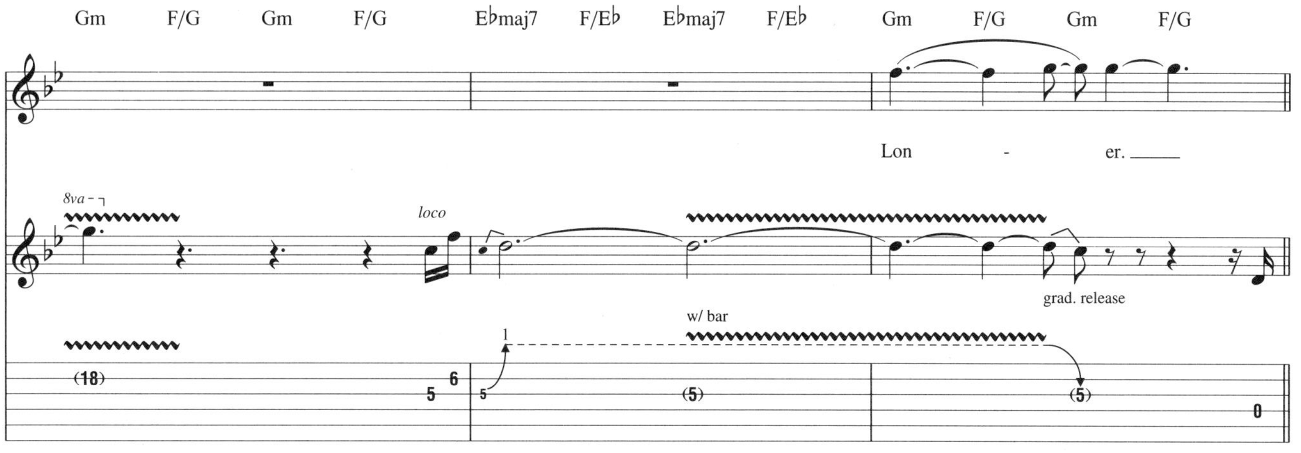
Gm
F/G
Gm
F/G
E♭maj7
F/E♭
E♭maj7
F/E♭
Gm
F/G
Gm
F/G
Lon - er.
8va
loco
grad. release
w/ bar

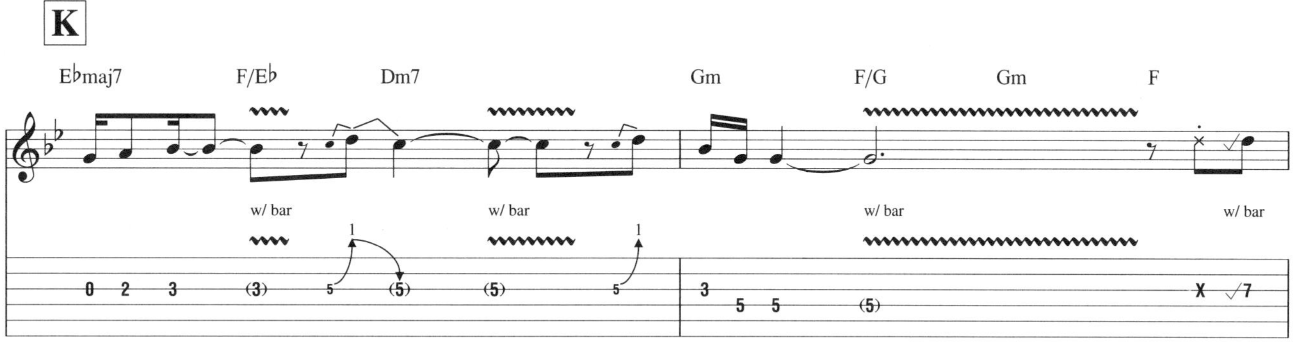
K
E♭maj7
F/E♭
Dm7
Gm
F/G
Gm
F
w/ bar

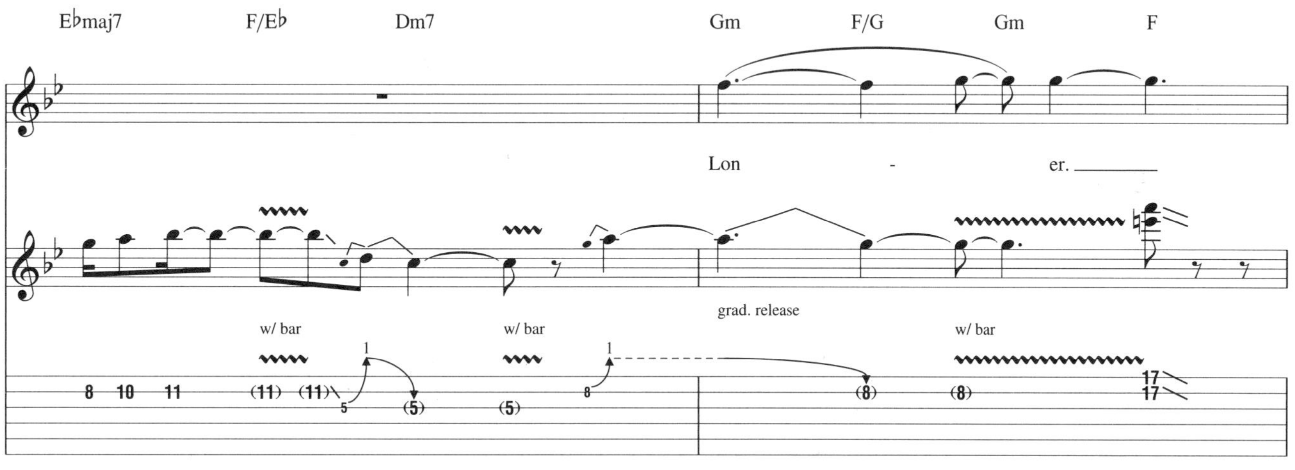
E♭maj7
F/E♭
Dm7
Gm
F/G
Gm
F
Lon - er.
w/ bar
grad. release

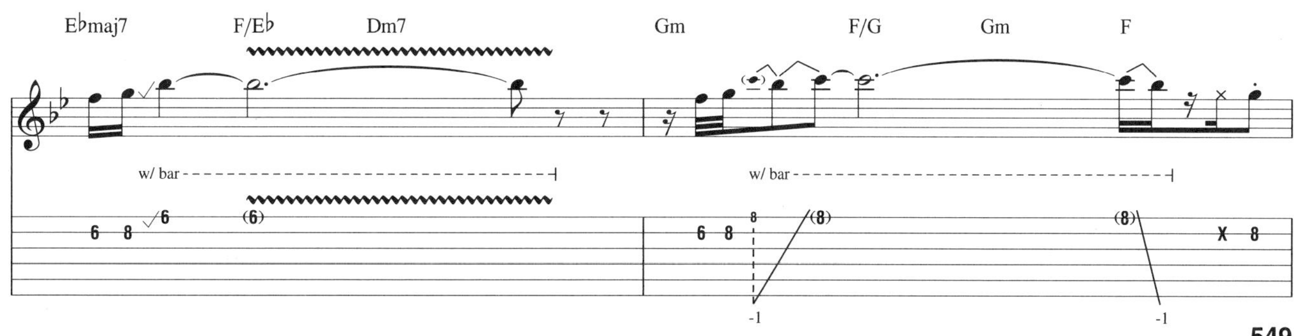
E♭maj7
F/E♭
Dm7
Gm
F/G
Gm
F
w/ bar

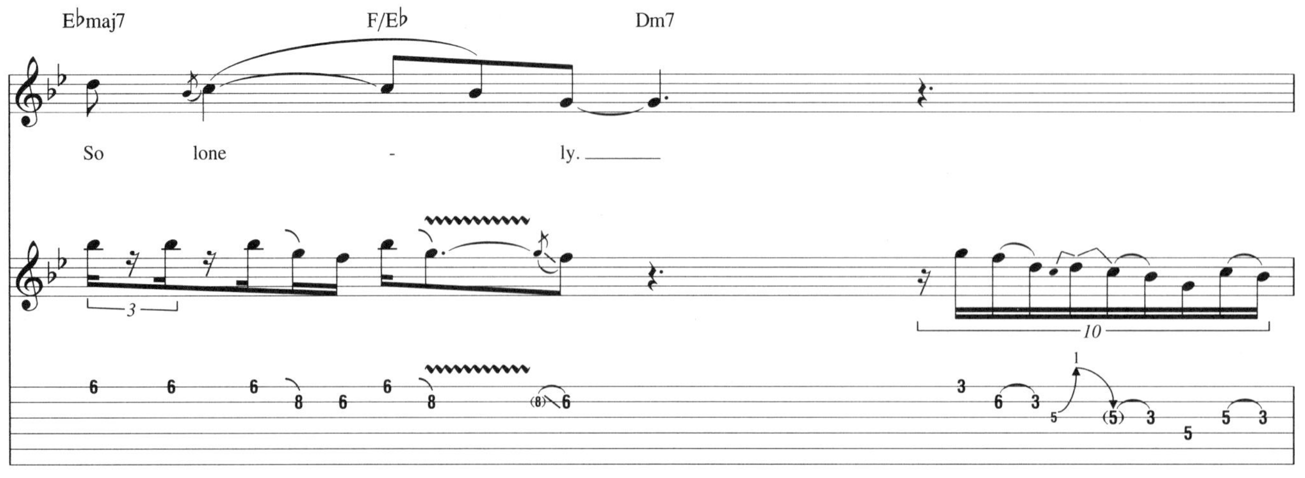
E♭maj7
F/E♭
Dm7
So lone - ly.

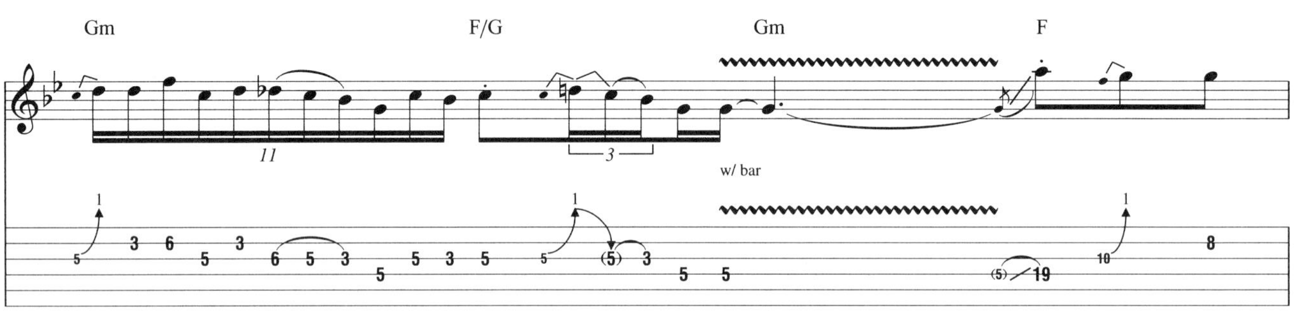
Gm
F/G
Gm
F
w/ bar

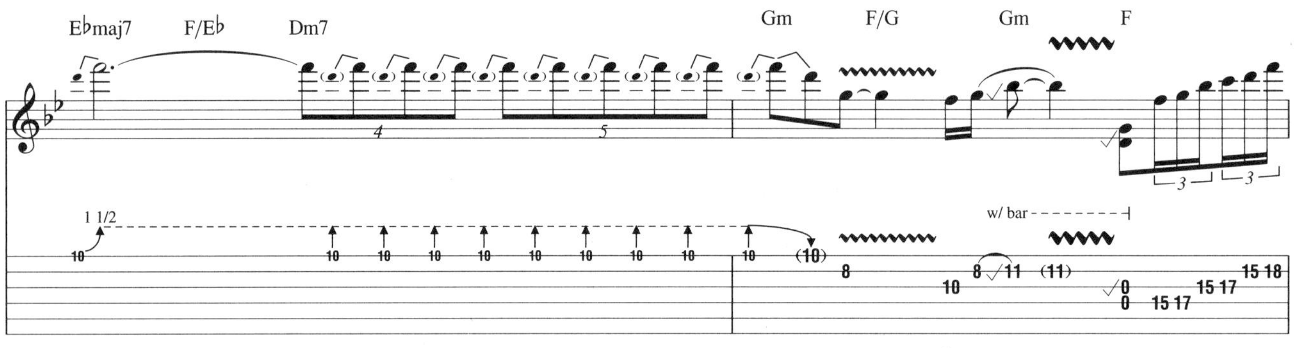
E♭maj7
F/E♭
Dm7
Gm
F/G
Gm
F
w/ bar

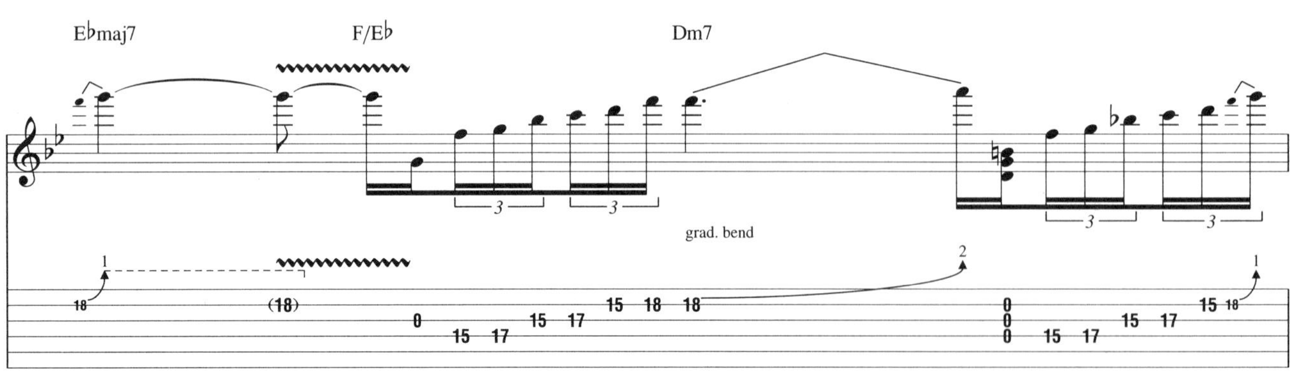
E♭maj7
F/E♭
Dm7
grad. bend

Begin fade

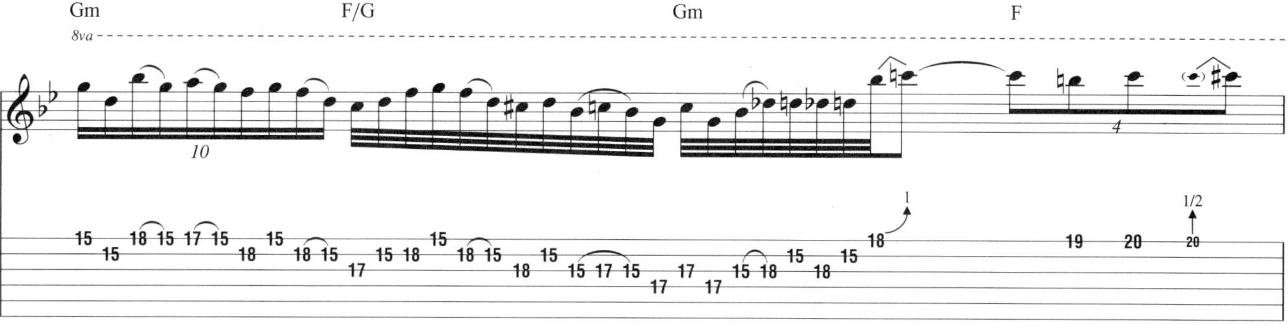
Gm
F/G
Gm
F
8va

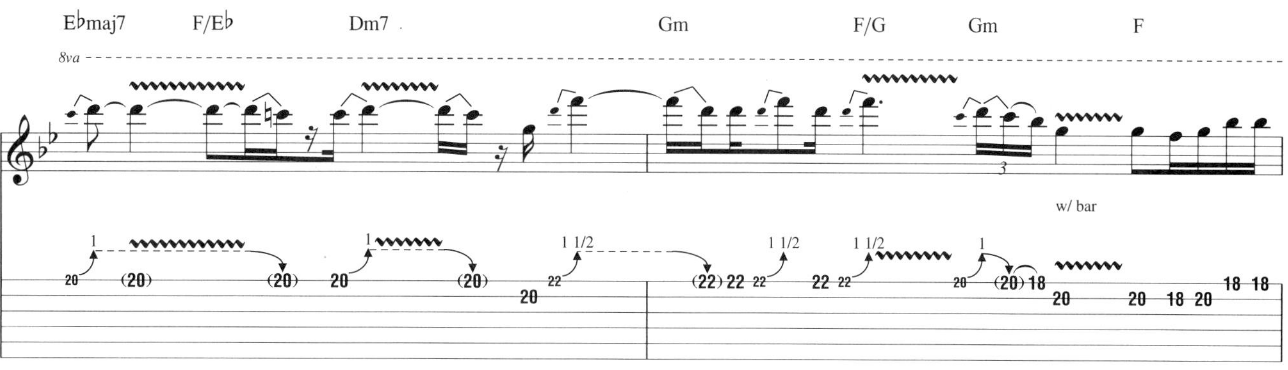
E♭maj7
F/E♭
Dm7
Gm
F/G
Gm
F
8va
w/ bar

E♭maj7
F/E♭
Dm7
8va

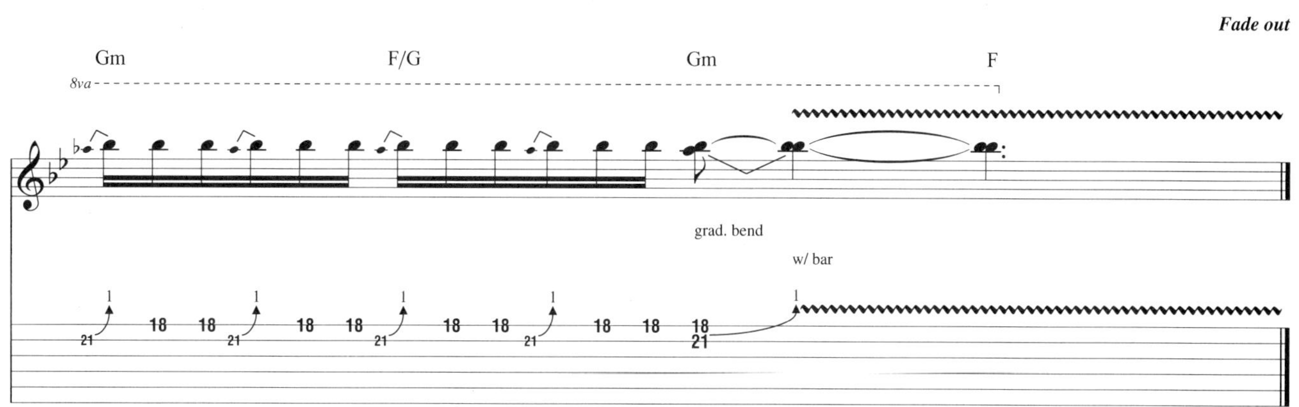
Fade out
Gm
F/G
Gm
F
8va
grad. bend
w/ bar

from The Meters - *Look-Ka Py Py*

Look-Ka-Py Py

Words and Music by Leo Nocentelli, George Porter, Arthur Neville and Joseph Modeliste

**Chord symbols reflect implied harmony.

C

2nd time, Gtr. 1: w/ Rhy. Fill 1
3rd time, Gtr. 1: w/ Rhy. Fill 2
F7
P.M.
let ring
P.M.
let ring
let ring

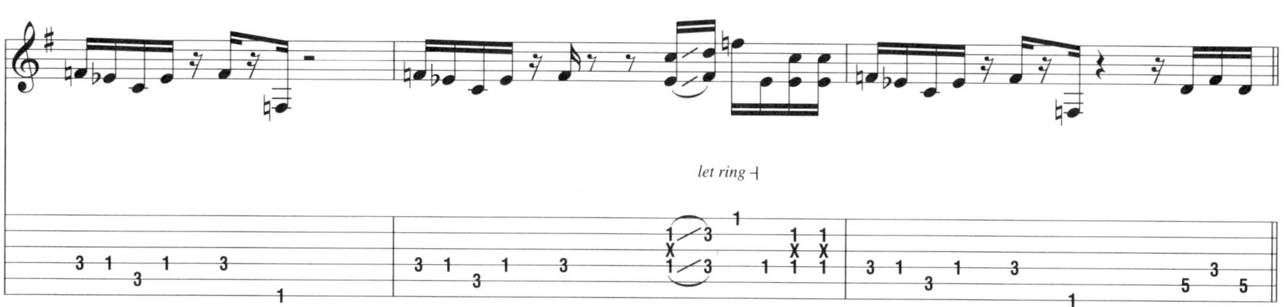
2nd & 3rd times, Gtr. 1: w/ Rhy. Fill 1
let ring

D
G7
P.M.
let ring
P.M.
let ring
P.M.

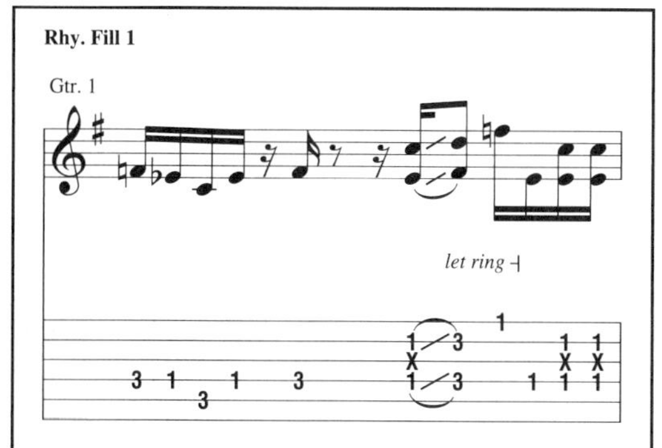
Rhy. Fill 1
Gtr. 1
let ring

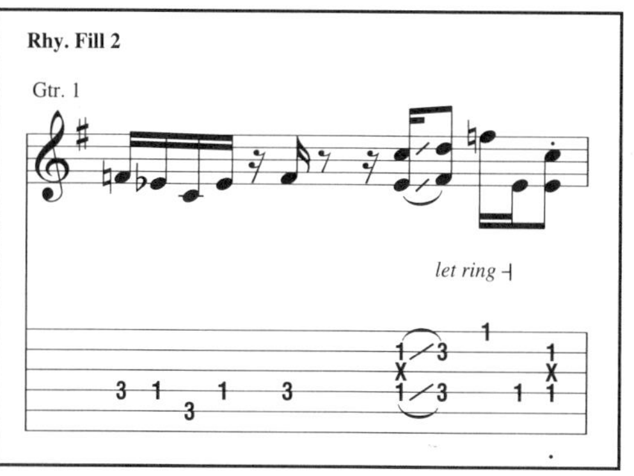
Rhy. Fill 2
Gtr. 1
let ring

To Coda 1
To Coda 2
E
G5 N.C.
P.M.
1., 2., 3.
4.
D.S. al Coda 1
G7
P.M.
P.M.
let ring
P.M.
let ring
Coda 1
F
D.S. al Coda 2
Bkgd. Voc.: w/ Voc. Fig. 1 (8 times)
Bkgd. Voc.: w/ Voc. Fig. 1A (7 times)
Gtr. 1 tacet
w/ multiple Bkgd. Voc. ad libs. (next 6 meas.)
G5 N.C.
Coda 2
G
Bkgd. Voc.: w/ Voc. Fig. 1 (till fade)
Bkgd. Voc.: w/ Voc. Fig. 1A (till fade)
G5 N.C.
F5
G5
C/E
let ring

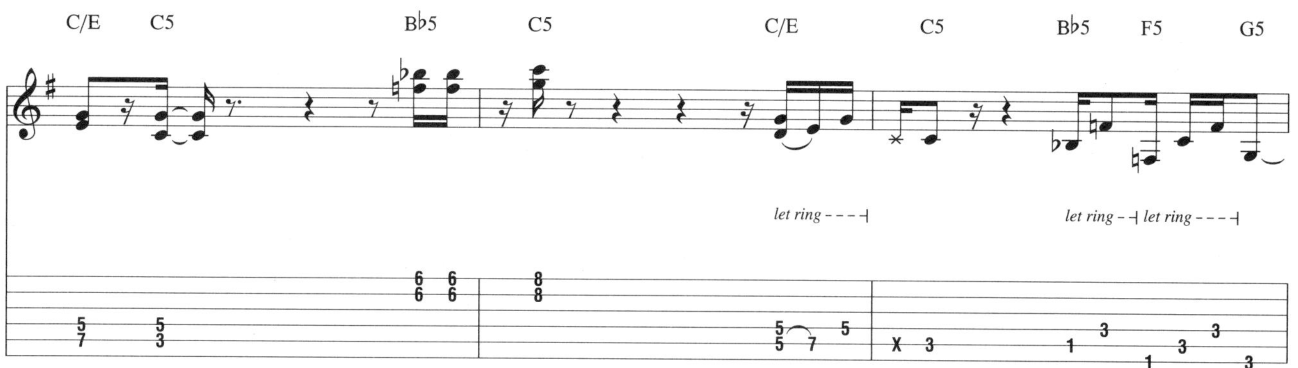

Begin fade

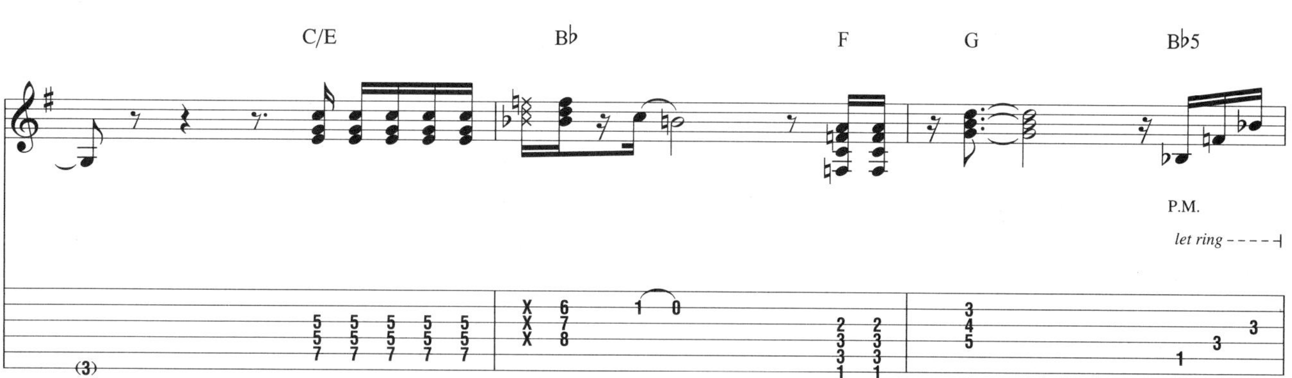

Fade out

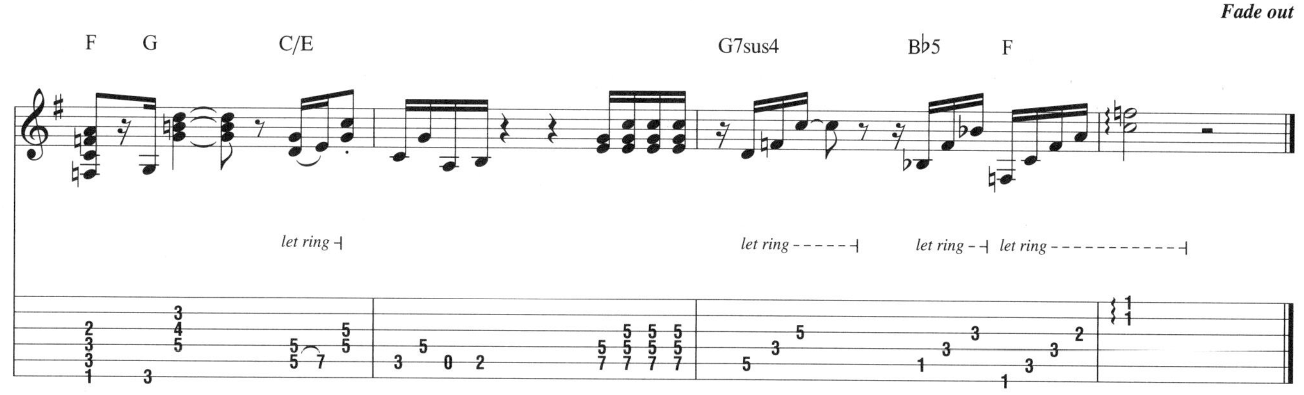

from Poison - *Look What the Cat Dragged In*

Look What the Cat Dragged In

Words and Music by Bobby Dall, Brett Michaels, Bruce Johannesson and Rikki Rockett

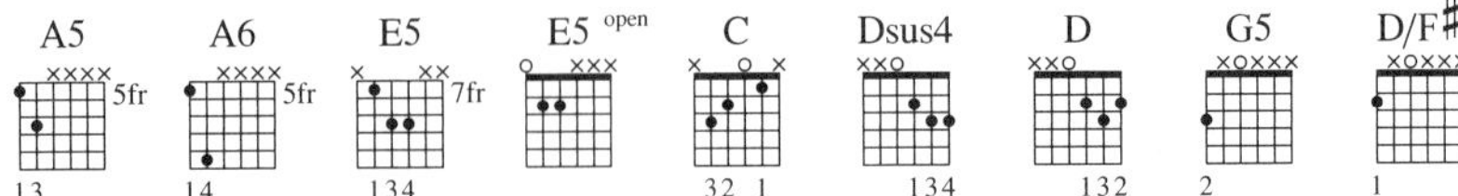

Tune down 1/2 step:
(low to high) E♭-A♭-D♭-G♭-B♭-E♭

Verse
2nd time, Gtr. 3: w/ Fill 2
G5 E5 F#5 E5 G5 E5 E5 N.C.
1. I went to bed too late and got, uh, up too soon.
2. No tell mo - tel, a ho - tel bed.
*Gtrs. 1 & 2
P.M.
steady gliss.
*Composite arrangement
Fill 1
Gtr. 3 (dist.)
End Fill 1
mf
P.S.
**Tap pick to strings.
Gtr. 3 tacet
E5 F#5 E5 G5 E5 F#5 E5 G5 D5 N.C.
My poor head's still spin - ning from, uh,
If it was - n't for the sun - light I'd
Rhy. Fig. 2
Gtrs. 1 & 2
End Rhy. Fig. 2
Gtrs. 1 & 2 tacet
1st time, Gtr. 3: w/ Fill 1
Gtrs. 1 & 2: w/ Rhy. Fig. 2
E5 F#5 E5 G5 E5 F#5 E5 G5 D5
too much booze. I got a
swear I was dead. I got a
Fill 2
Gtr. 3
steady gliss.

Pre-Chorus
C
D
foot in a gut - ter, a foot in a grave.
girl on the left of me, a girl on the right.
Ain't seen home in the
I know damn well, I slept with
Gtrs. 1 & 2
let ring
Chorus
Dsus4 G5 D/F♯ E5 C
last three days.
both last night.
Oh, my God, look what the cat dragged in! Liv -
Rhy. Fig. 3
P.M.
3rd time, Gtrs. 1 & 2: w/ Rhy. Fig. 3
D G5 D/F♯ E5
- in' my life sin af - ter sin.
And night rolls up and I
End Rhy. Fig. 3
To Coda 1
To Coda 2
C D N.C. G5 D/F♯
do it a - gain. Oh, my God, look what the cat dragged
2. (My God!)
P.M

Interlude
Gtrs. 1 & 2: w/ Rhy. Fig. 1
E5 F♯5 E5 G5 E5 F♯5 E5 F♯5 G5 E5 F♯5 E5 G5 E5 F♯5 E5 G5 D5
in! Oh, row.
Gtr. 3
P.H.
Pitch: E F♯ E
Coda 1
Interlude
Gtrs. 1 & 2: w/ Rhy. Fig. 1
E5 F♯5 E5 G5 E5 F♯5 E5 F♯5 G5 E5 F♯5 E5
in! Ah. Purr. Oh,
Guitar Solo
G5 E5 F♯5 E5 G5 D5 A5 A6 A5 A6 A5 A6 A5 A6 A5
Rhy. Fig. 4
Gtrs. 1 & 2
P.M.
sin af - ter sin.
Gtr. 3
P.M.
Gtr. 1: w/ Rhy. Fig. 4
Gtr. 2: w/ Rhy. Fig. 4 (1st 2 meas.)
E5 A5 A6 A5 A6 A5
End Rhy. Fig. 4
steady gliss.

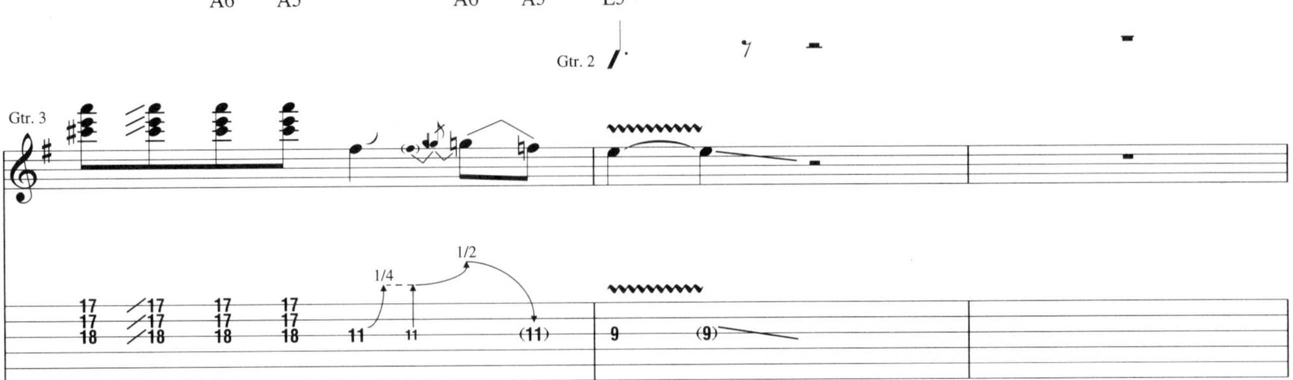
A6
A5
A6
A5
E5 open
Gtr. 2
Gtr. 3
1/4
1/2
17
17
18
11
11
(11)
9
(9)

C
Dsus4
D
Gtrs. 1 & 2
Gtr. 3
3
3
9
12
12
11
12
9
12
12
14
(14)

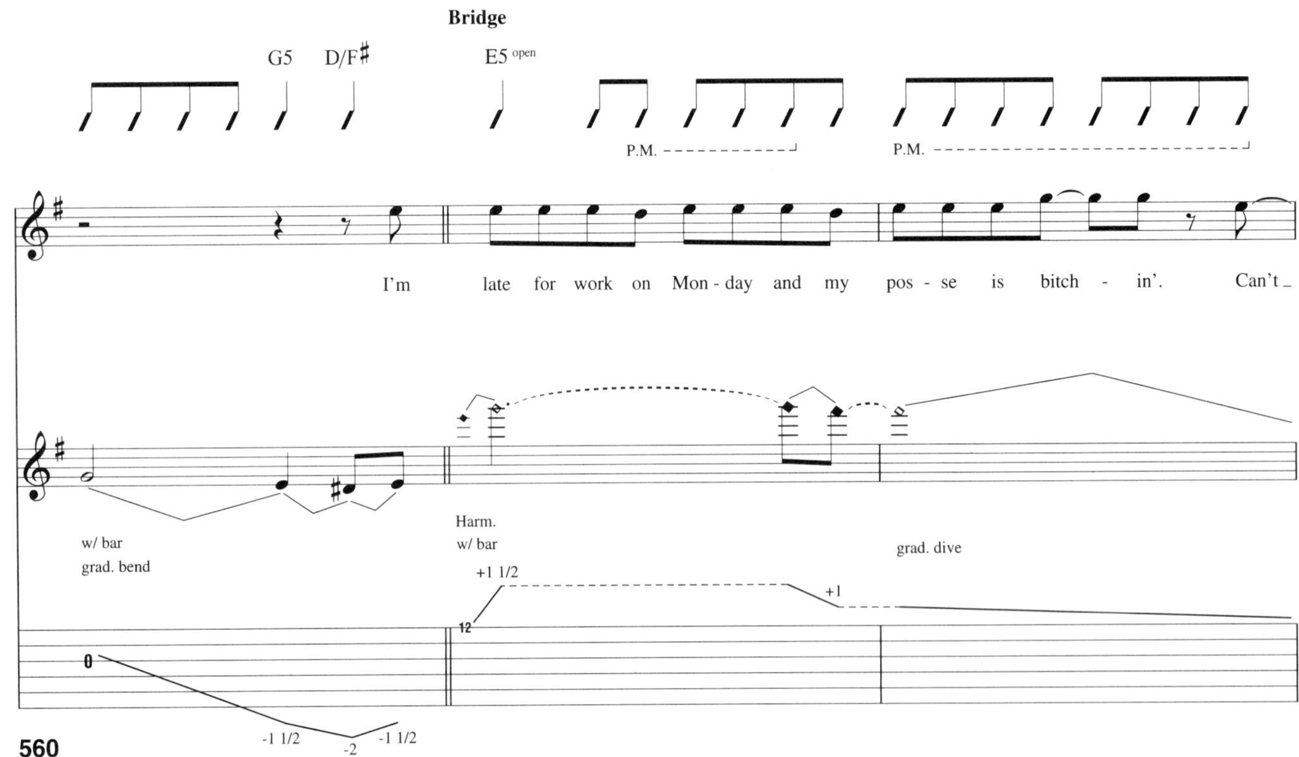
Bridge
G5
D/F#
E5 open
P.M.
P.M.
I'm late for work on Mon - day and my pos - se is bitch - in'. Can't
w/ bar
grad. bend
Harm.
w/ bar
grad. dive
+1 1/2
+1
12
0
-1 1/2
-2
-1 1/2

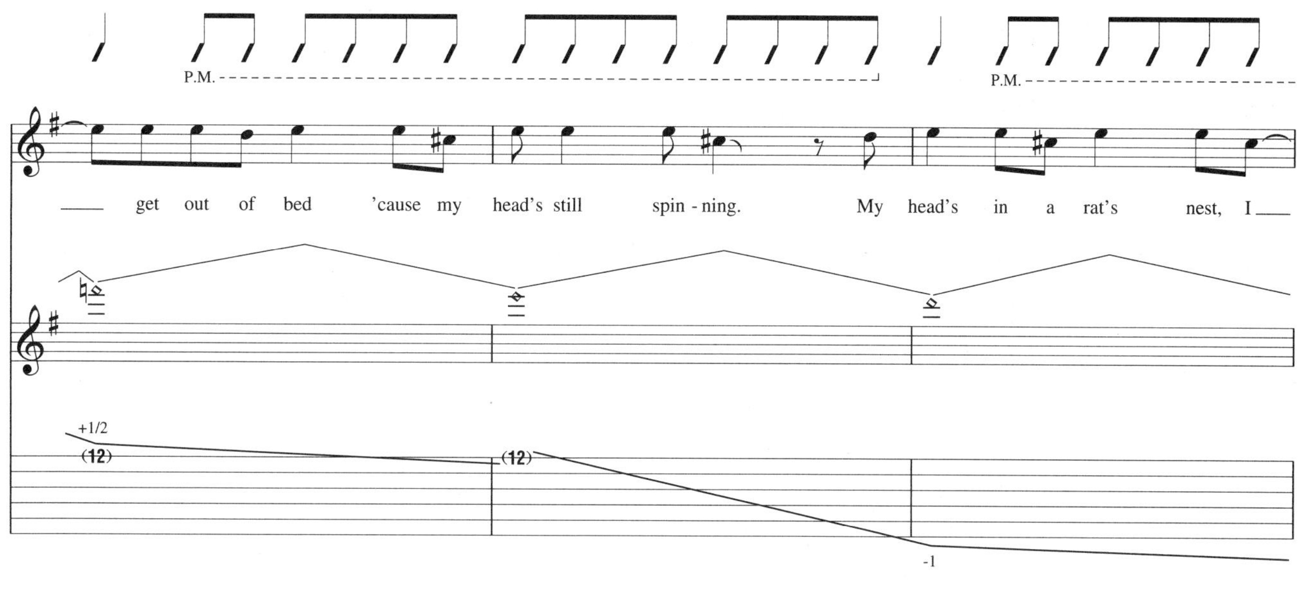

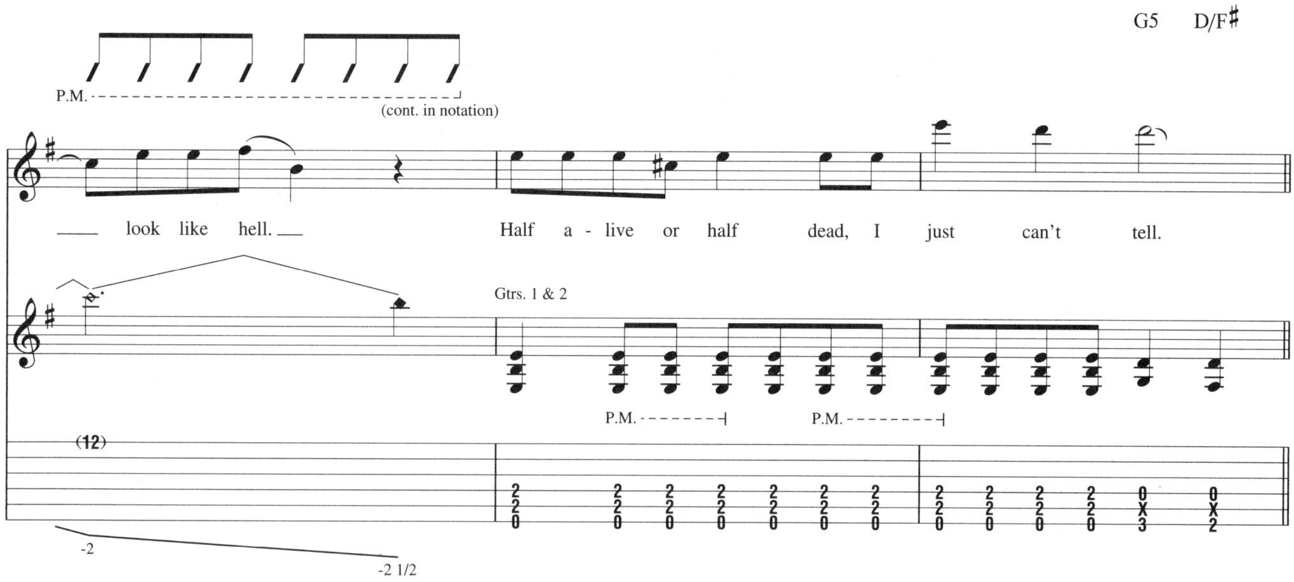

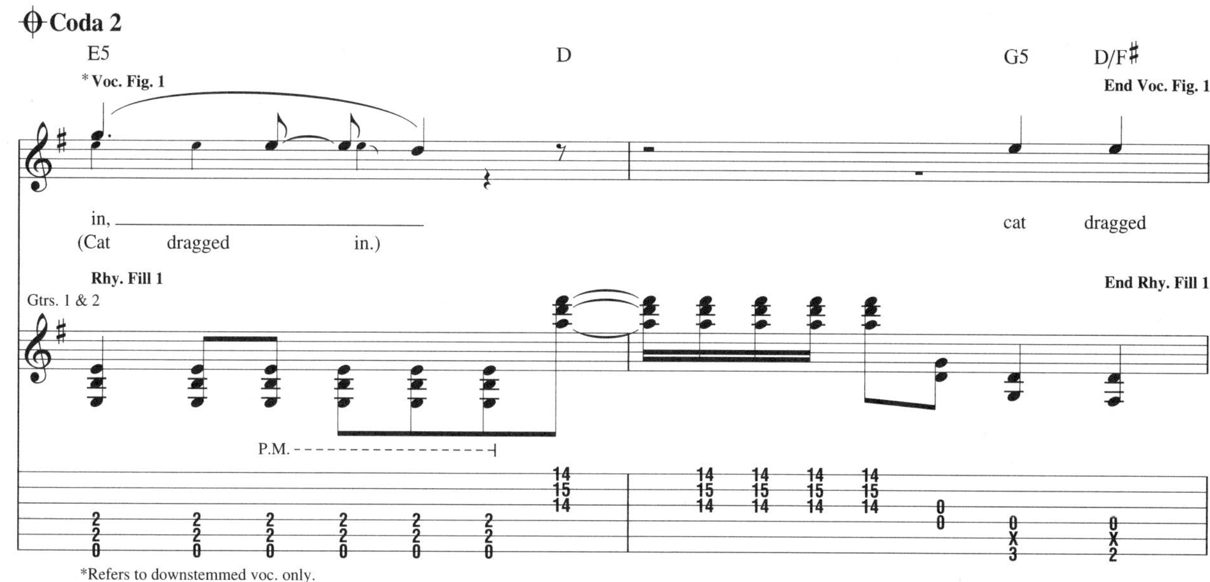

*Refers to downstemmed voc. only.

Bkgd. Voc.: w/ Voc. Fig. 1 (2 times)
E5
D
G5
D/F♯
in,
cat dragged i - hi - hi - hin.
Rhy. Fig. 5
End Rhy. Fig. 5
P.M.
Cat dragged
in,
out,
look what the cat dragged,
Outro
Gtrs. 1 & 2: w/ Rhy. Fill 1
Bkgd. Voc.: w/ Voc. Fill 1 (till fade)
Gtrs. 1 & 2: w/ Rhy. Fig. 5 (till fade)
cat dragged
Gtr. 3

E5
D
G5
D/F♯
E5
D
i - hi - hi - hin.
Cat dragged in,
grad. bend
Begin fade
G5
D/F♯
E5
D
cat dragged in,
G5
D/F♯
E5
D
cat dragged in,
8va
G5
D/F♯
E5
D
cat dragged in,
8va
loco
*String bumped with left hand.

G5
D/F♯
E5
D
cat
dragged
in,
w/ bar
grad. bend
grad. bend
slack
Fade out
in.
8va

from Pat Benatar - *Live from Earth*

Love Is a Battlefield

Words and Music by Mike Chapman and Holly Knight

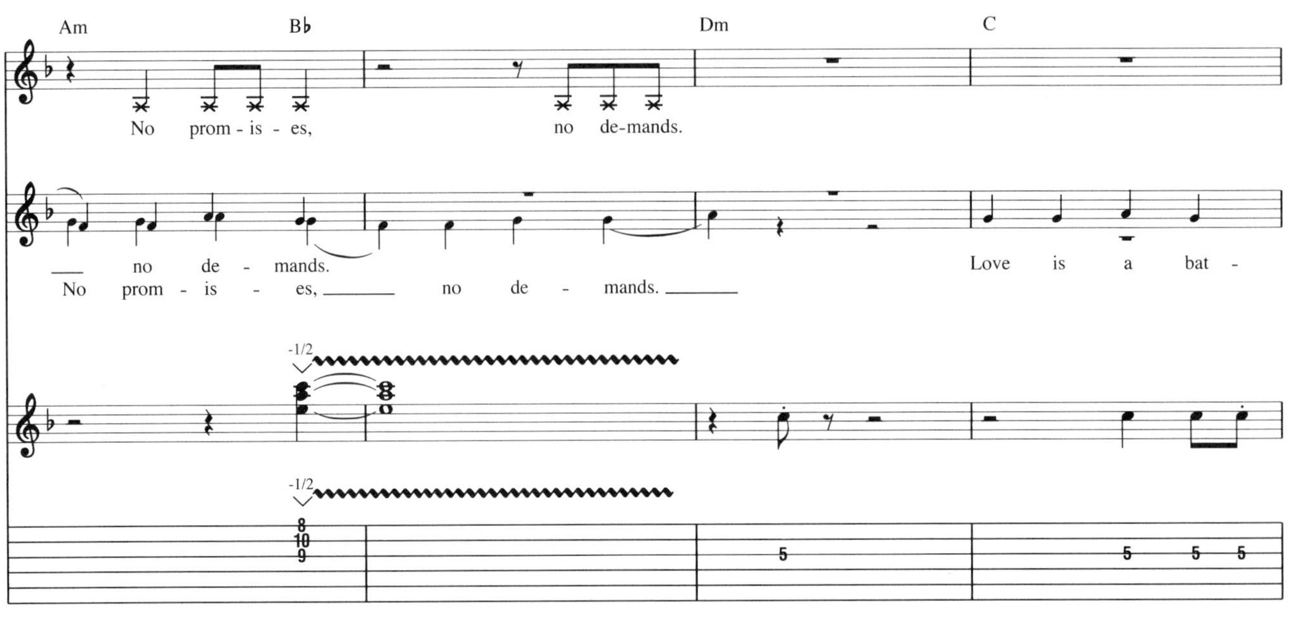
Am
B♭
Dm
C
No prom - is - es,
no de-mands.
___ no de - mands.
No prom - is - es, ______ no de - mands. ______
Love is a bat -
-1/2
-1/2
8
10
9
5
5 5 5

Am
B♭
Dm
C
Love is a bat - tle - field.
Whoa, _ whoa, _ whoa, _ whoa, __ whoa, _ whoa, _ whoa, _ whoa, __
tle - field.)
Love is a bat - tle - field.)
P.M.
P.M.
5
5 7
10 10

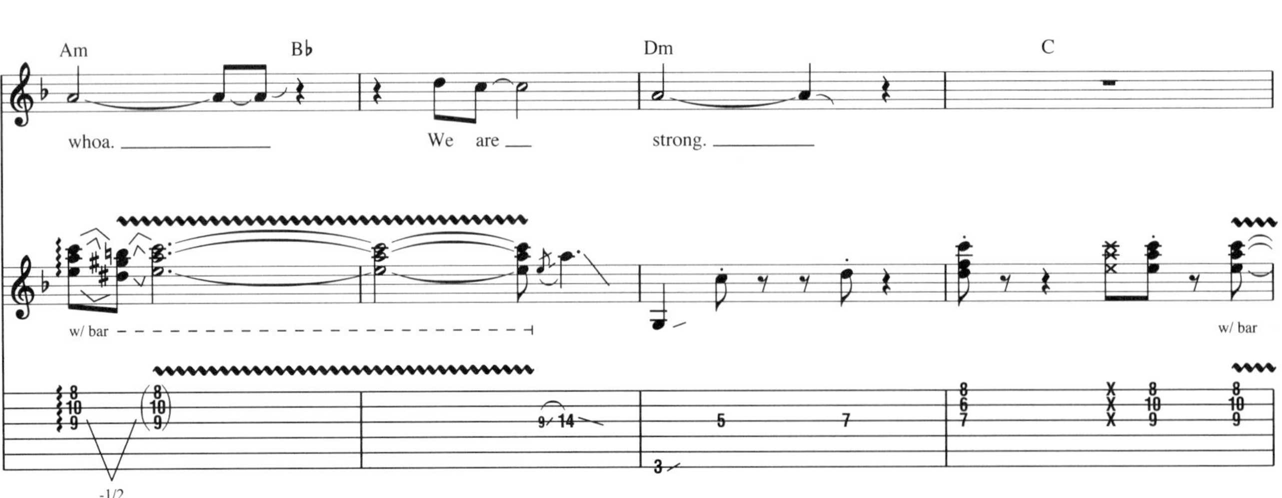
Am
B♭
Dm
C
whoa. ______
We are __
strong. ______
w/ bar
w/ bar
8
10
9
-1/2
9 14
3
5 7
8
6
7

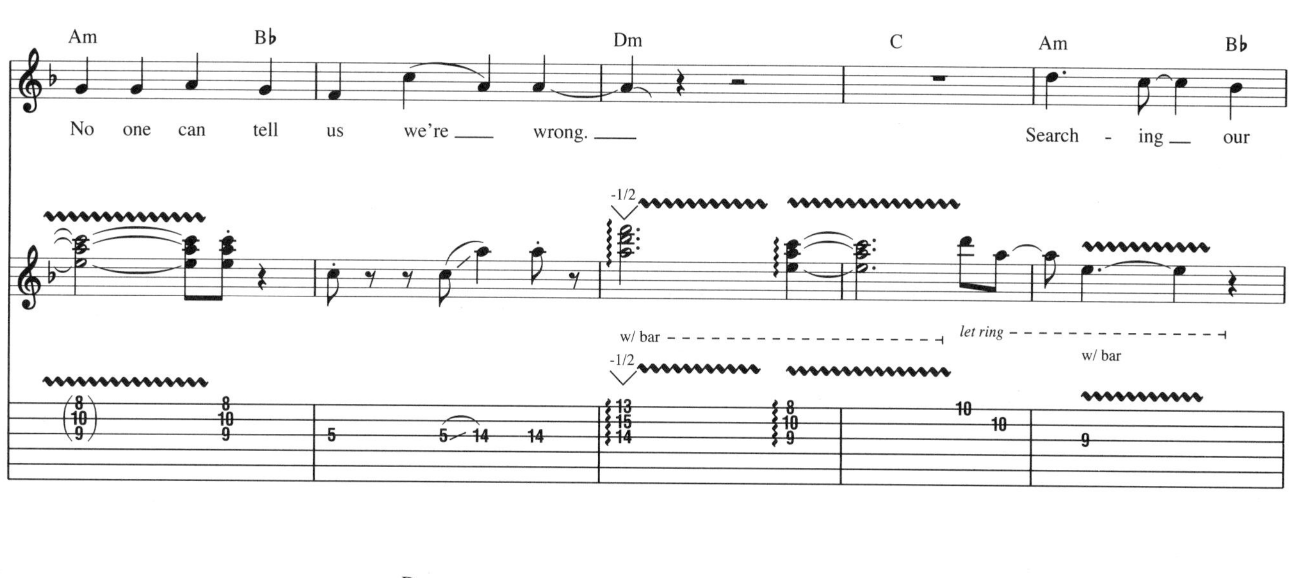
Am
B♭
Dm
C
Am
B♭
No one can tell us we're wrong.
Search - ing our
-1/2
w/ bar
let ring
w/ bar

Dm
C
Am
B♭
hearts for so long,
both of us know -
let ring
w/ bar
w/ bar
-1/2
-1/2

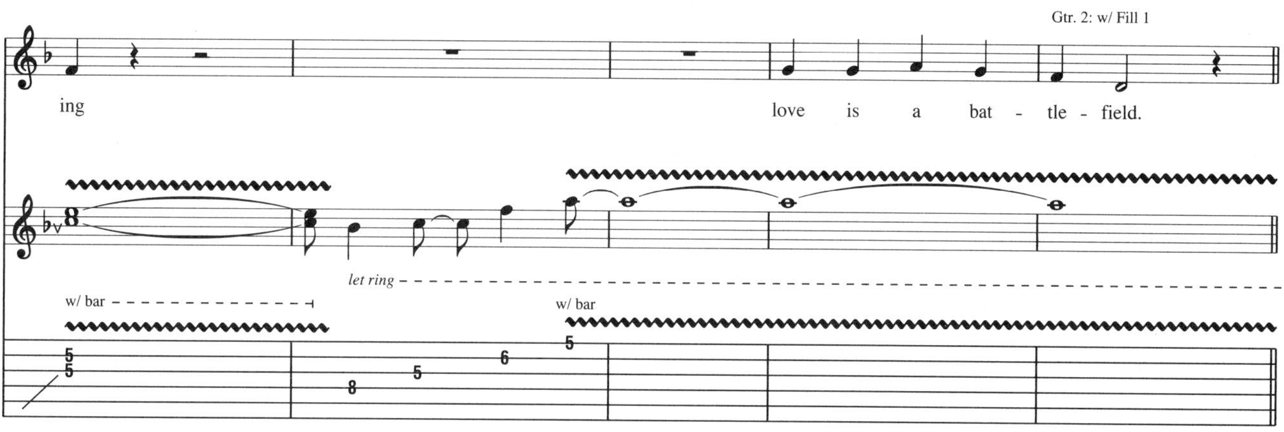
Gtr. 2: w/ Fill 1
ing
love is a bat - tle - field.
let ring
w/ bar
w/ bar

Fill 1
*Gtr. 2 (slight dist.)
mf
P.M.
*Two gtrs. arr. for one.

Interlude
Gtr. 1 tacet
Dm
C
Gtr. 2
Riff A
P.M.
Bb
1. You're
End Riff A
P.M.
Verse
Gtr. 2: w/ Riff A (2 3/4 times)
Dm
C
beg - ging me to go then mak - ing me stay.
Bb
Gm
Dm
Why do you hurt me so bad? It would help me to know,
Gtr. 1
let ring
w/ bar
1/2
C
Bb
do I stand in your way or am I the best thing you've
let ring
w/ bar

Gm
Dm
C
had. Be - lieve me, be - lieve me, I can't tell you why,
1/2
B♭
Gm
but I'm trapped by your love and I'm chained to your side.
Gtr. 1
let ring
w/ bar
Gtr. 2
P.M.
We are young.
let ring
w/ bar
P.M.

Chorus
Gtr. 2 tacet
Dm C Am B♭
Heart - ache to heart - ache we stand.
Gtr. 1
w/ bar
-1/2
Dm C Am B♭
(Ah.)
No prom - is - es, no de - mands.
let ring
w/ bar
Dm C Am B♭
Love is a bat - tle - field.
Dm C Am B♭
(Ah. Ah.)
We are strong.
w/ bar
-1/2

Dm
C
Am
B♭
No one can tell us we're wrong.
Searching our hearts for so
w/ bar
let ring
long,
both of us knowing
w/ bar
-1/2
Gtr. 2: w/ Fill 1
love is a battlefield.

Interlude
Gtr. 2: w/ Riff A
Gtr. 1 tacet
Dm
C
B♭

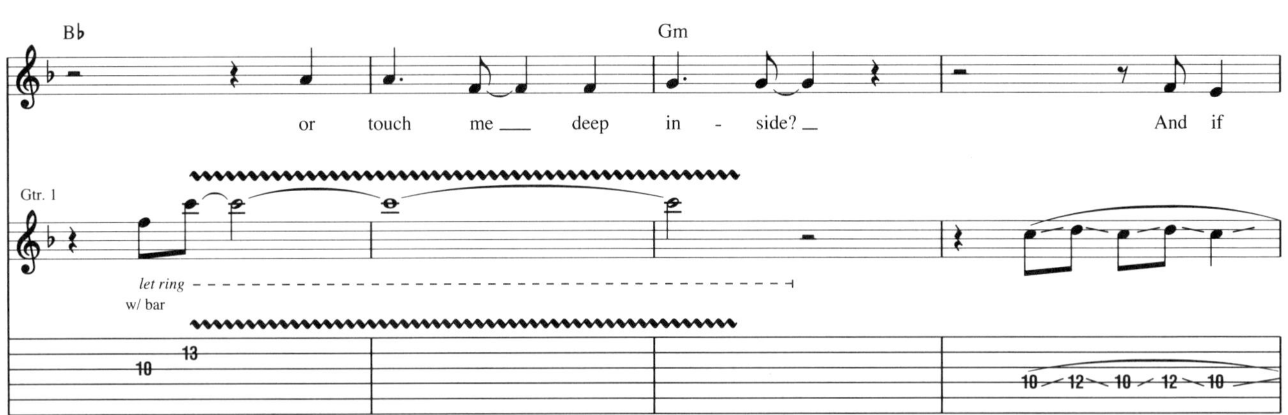
Verse
Gtr. 2: w/ Riff A (2 3/4 times)
Dm
C
2. When I'm los - ing con - trol will you turn me a - way,

B♭
Gm
or touch me deep in - side? And if
Gtr. 1
let ring
w/ bar

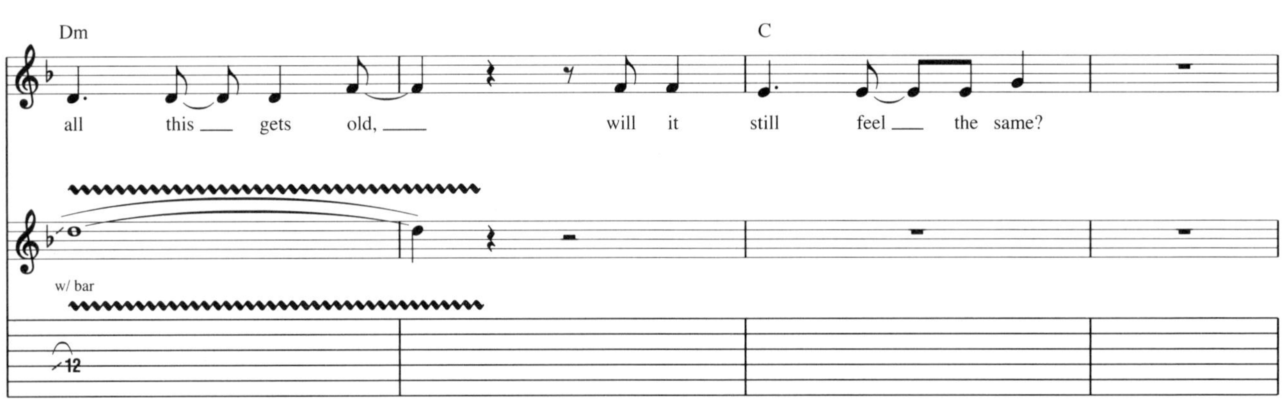
Dm
C
all this gets old, will it still feel the same?
w/ bar

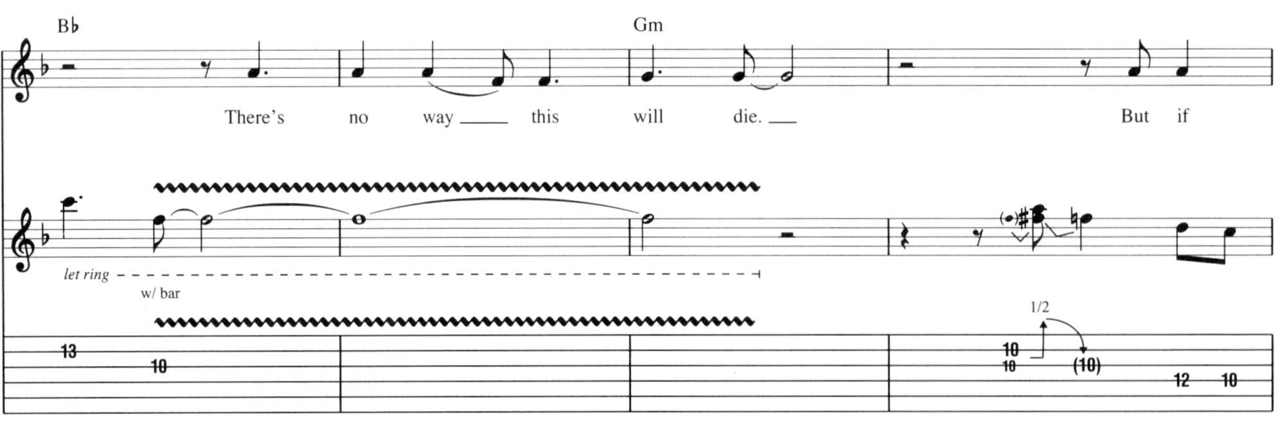
B♭
Gm
There's no way this will die. But if
let ring
w/ bar
1/2

Dm
C
we get much clos - er, I could lose con - trol. And if
10 12
B♭
Gm
your heart sur - ren - ders, you'll need me to hold.
Gtr. 1
let ring
w/ bar
13
10
8
Gtr. 2
P.M.
7 5 7 5 7
5 7 7 7 7 7
We are young.
let ring
w/ bar
(8) 5 6 5
P.M.

Chorus
Gtr. 2 tacet
Dm
C
Am
B♭
Heart - ache to heart - ache we stand.
Gtr. 1
w/ bar
-1/2
No prom - is - es, no de - mands.
(Ah.)
let ring
Love is a bat - tle - field.
(Ah.
Ah.
We are strong.
w/ bar
-1/2
-1/2

Dm
C
Am
B♭
No one can tell us we're wrong.
Ah.)
w/ bar
Search - ing our hearts for so
-1/2
long,
both of us knowing
love is a bat - tle - field.
Gtr. 2: w/ Fill 1
let ring

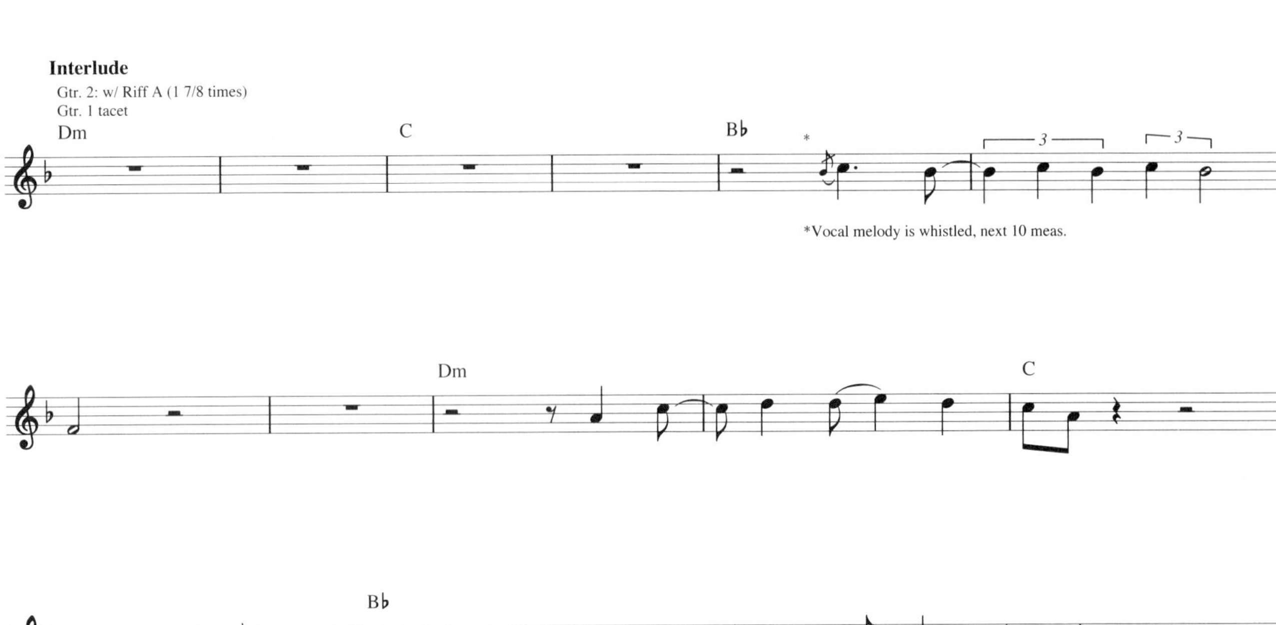
Interlude
Gtr. 2: w/ Riff A (1 7/8 times)
Gtr. 1 tacet
Dm
C
B♭
Dm
C
B♭
*Vocal melody is whistled, next 10 meas.

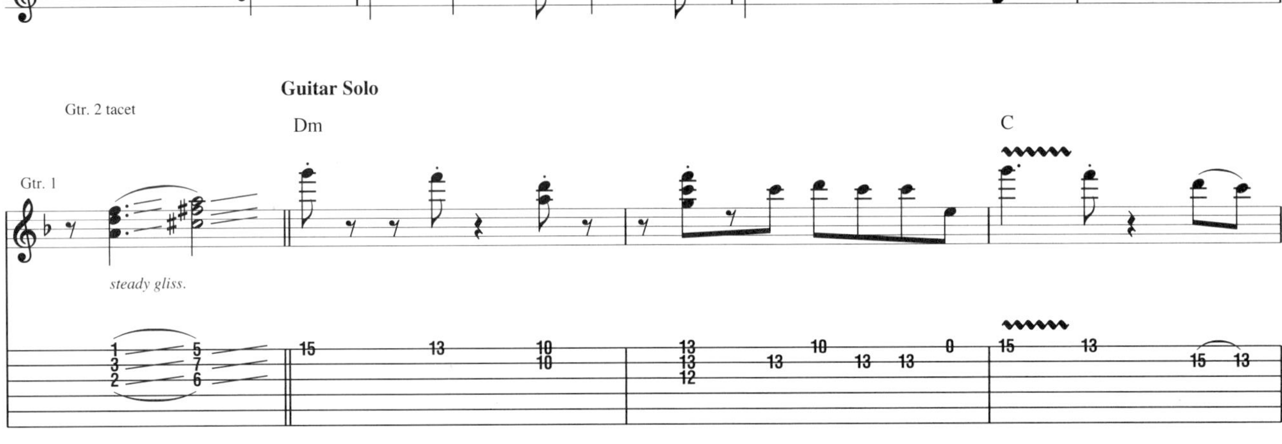
Guitar Solo
Gtr. 2 tacet
Gtr. 1
Dm
C
steady gliss.

B♭

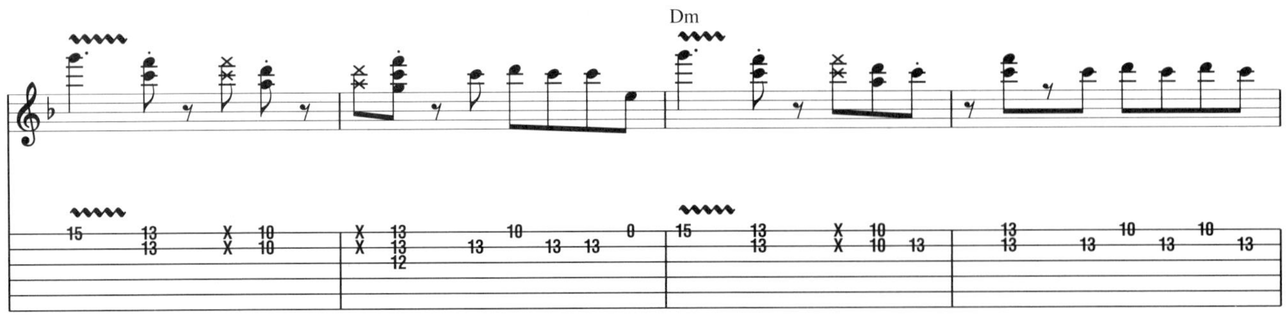
Dm

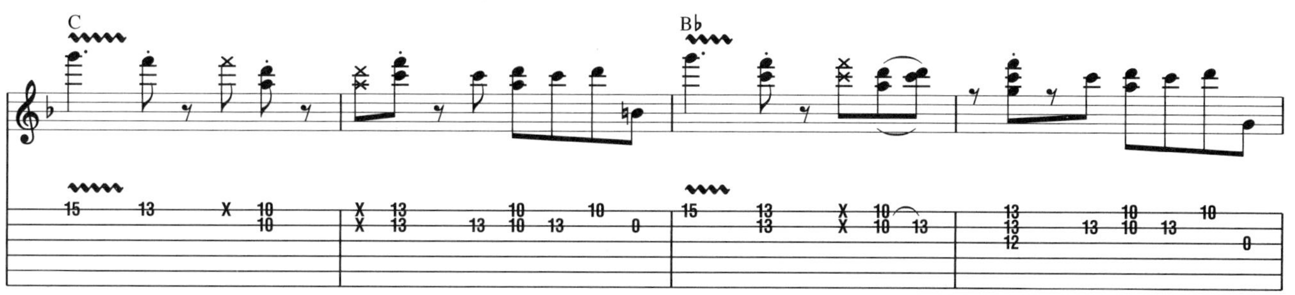
C
B♭

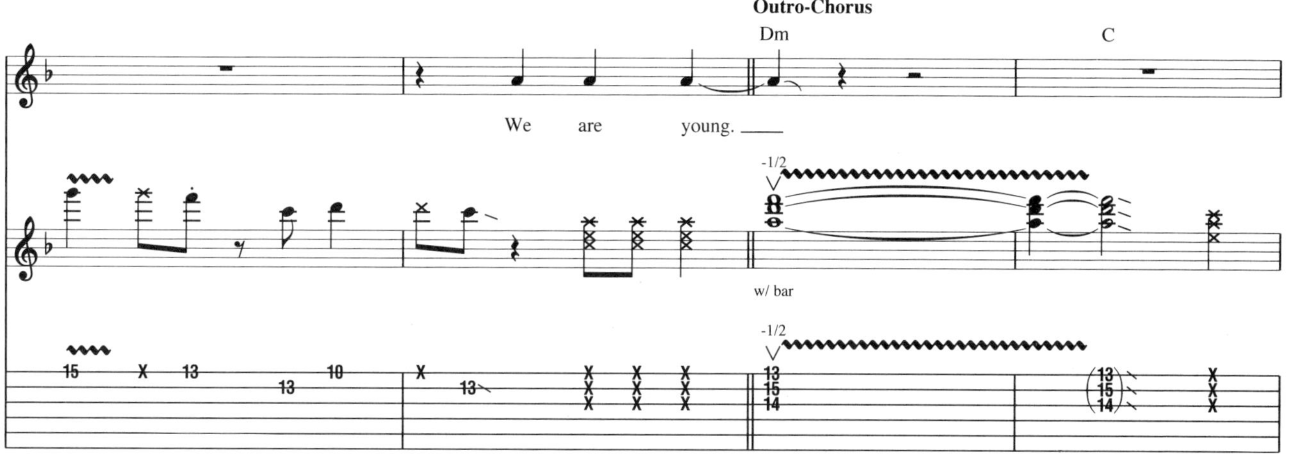
Outro-Chorus
Dm
C
We are young.
-1/2
w/ bar

Am
B♭
Dm
C
Heart - ache to heart - ache we stand.
(Ah.)
-1/2

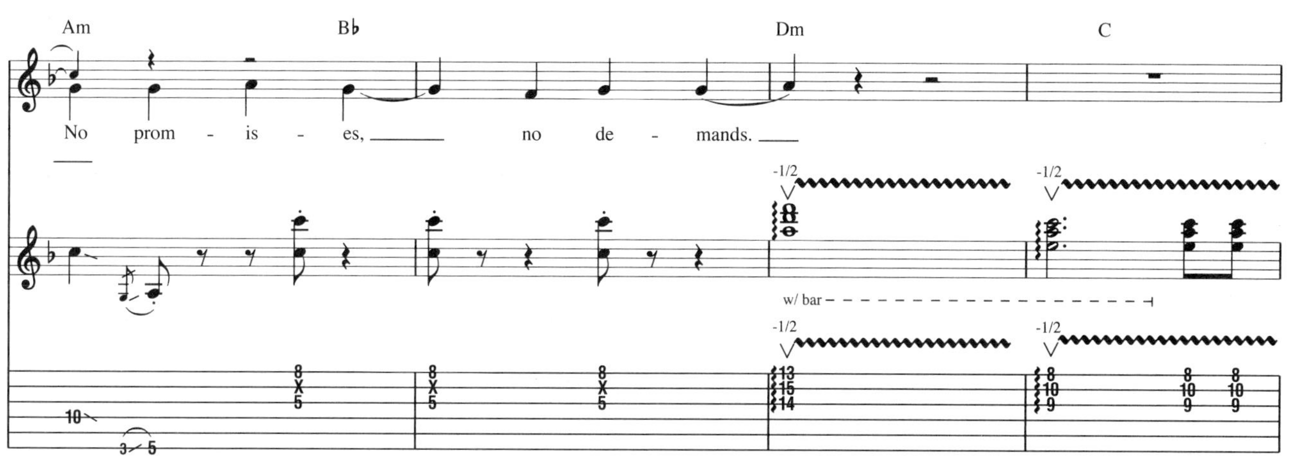
Am
B♭
Dm
C
No prom - is - es, no de - mands.
-1/2
w/ bar

Am
B♭
Dm
C
Love is a bat - tle - field.
(Ah.

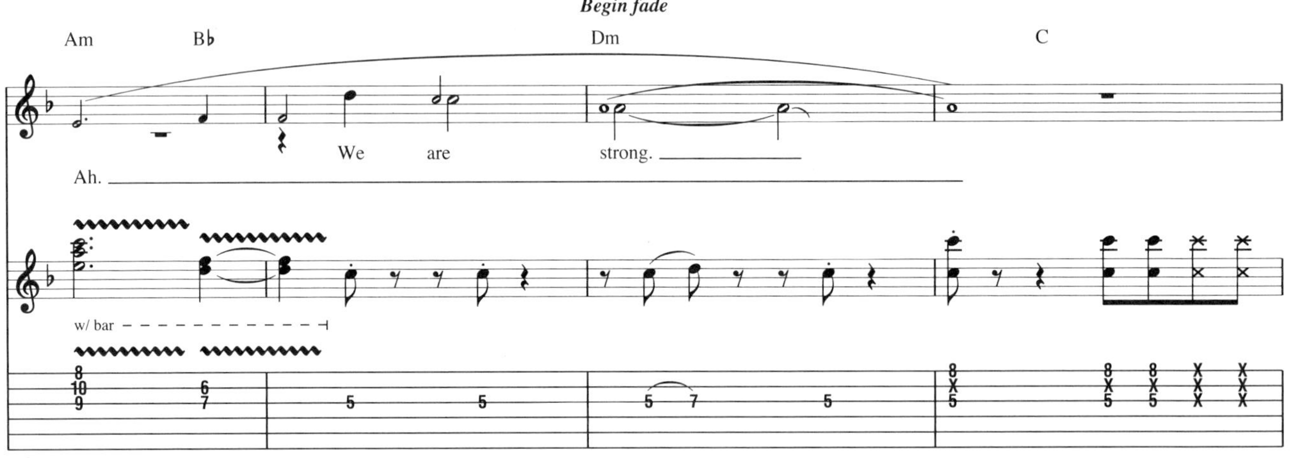
Begin fade
Am
B♭
Dm
C
We are strong.
Ah.
w/ bar

Am
B♭
Dm
C
No one can tell us we're wrong.
Ah.)
let ring

Fade out
Am
B♭
Dm
C
Search - ing our hearts for so long.
let ring

from The Stone Roses - *Second Coming*

Love Spreads

Words and Music by John Squire

Gtrs. 1, 2, 4 & 5: Open D tuning:
(low to high) D-A-D-F♯-A-D

Gtr. 3: Drop D tuning:
(low to high) D-A-D-G-B-E

Intro

Moderately slow ♩ = 93

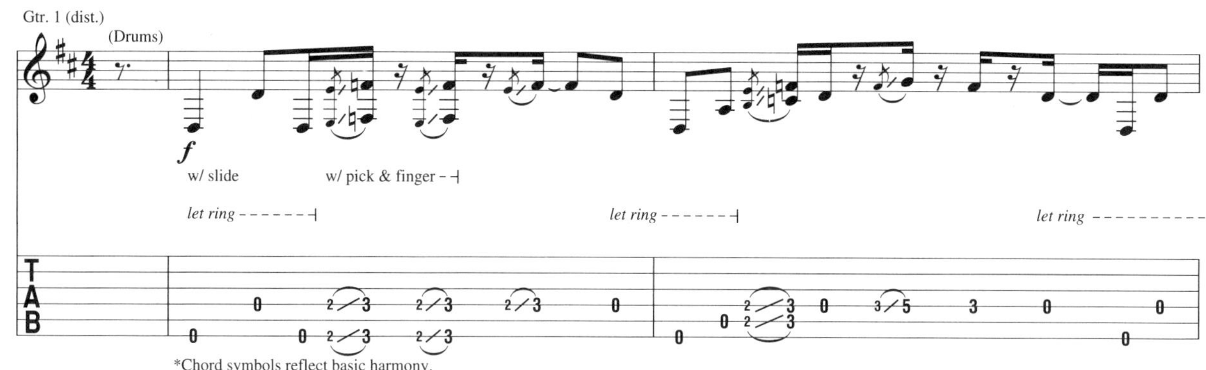

*Chord symbols reflect basic harmony.

w/ pick & finger

let ring

let ring

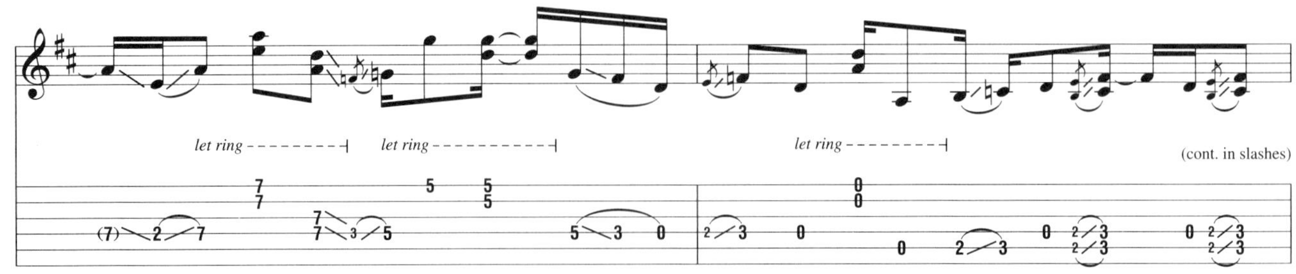
let ring
let ring
let ring
(cont. in slashes)

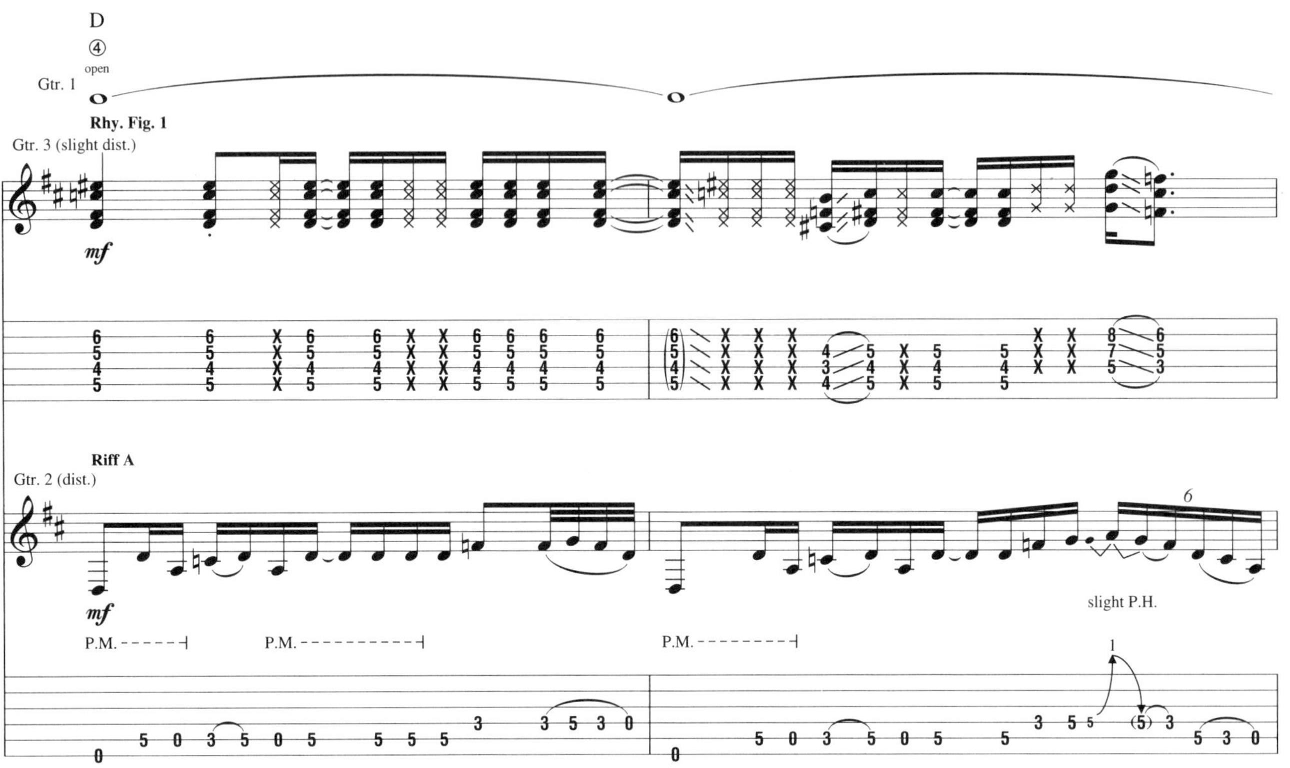
D
open
Gtr. 1
Rhy. Fig. 1
Gtr. 3 (slight dist.)
mf
Riff A
Gtr. 2 (dist.)
mf
P.M.
P.M.
P.M.
slight P.H.

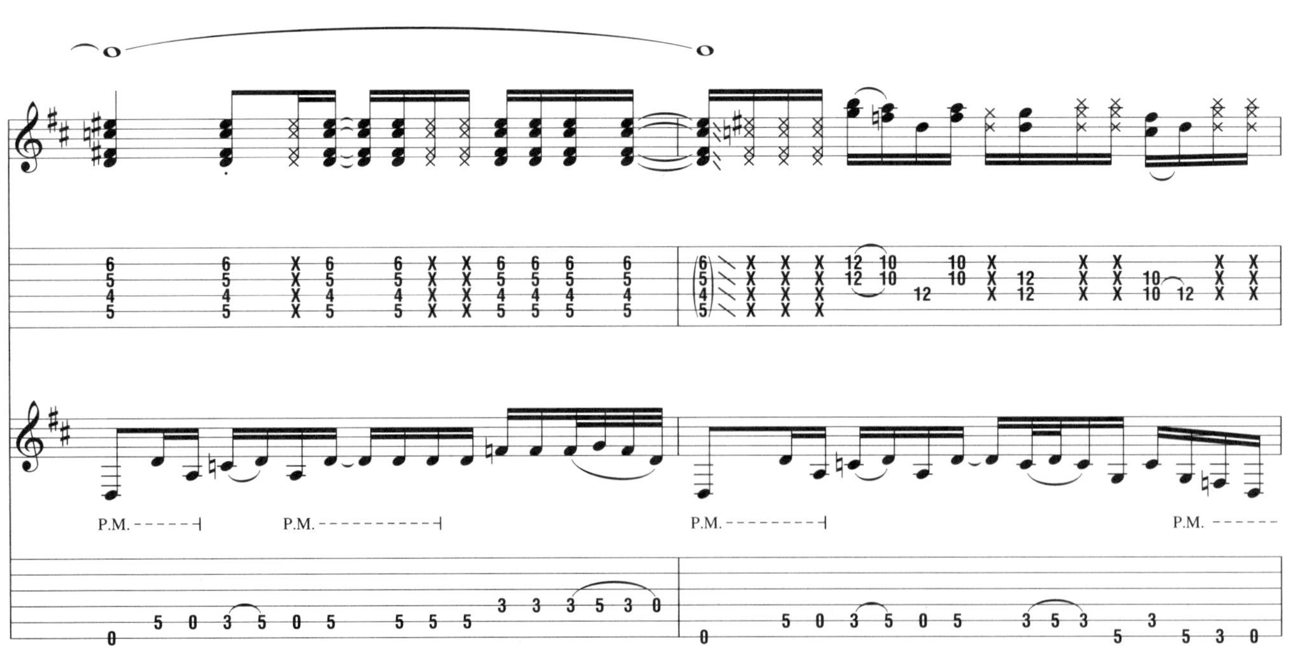
P.M.
P.M.
P.M.
P.M.

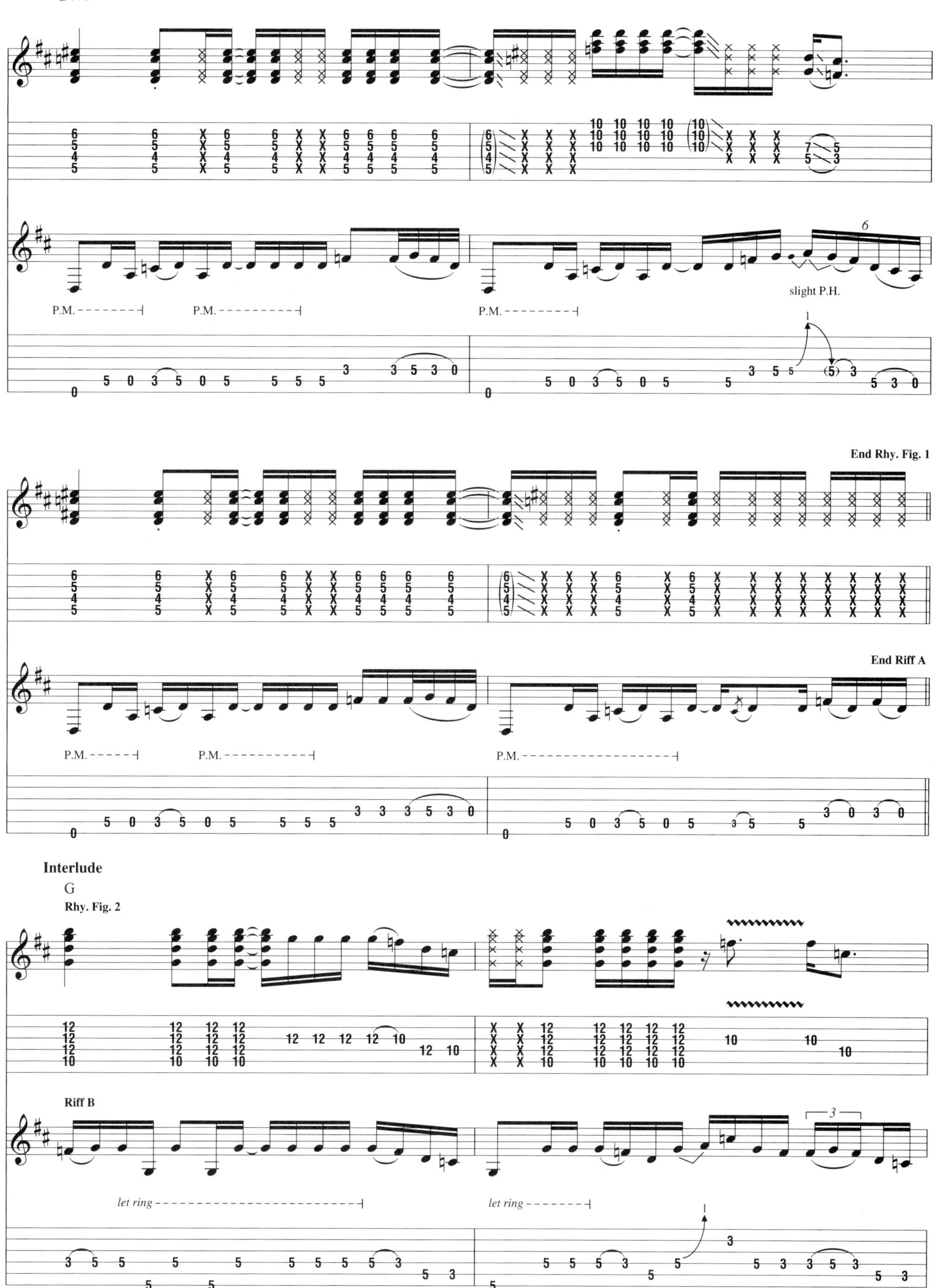

Gtr. 1 tacet
D7#9
P.M.
slight P.H.
End Rhy. Fig. 1
End Riff A
Interlude
G
Rhy. Fig. 2
Riff B
let ring

D7
steady gliss.
P.M.
let ring
G
let ring
let ring
D
steady gliss.
1/2
P.M.
let ring
P.M.
let ring
1

A
End Riff B
slight P.H.
let ring
D5
F
D5
C5
D
End Rhy. Fig. 2
let ring
P.M.
Verse
Gtr. 2: w/ Riff A
Gtr. 3: w/ Rhy. Fig. 1
D7♯9
1. Love spreads her arms, waits there for the nails. I for - give you, boy,
I will pre - vail. Too much to take, some cross to bear.
Interlude
Gtr. 2: w/ Riff B
Gtr. 3: w/ Rhy. Fig. 2
G
I'm hid - ing in the trees with a pic - nic. She's o - ver there, yeah.

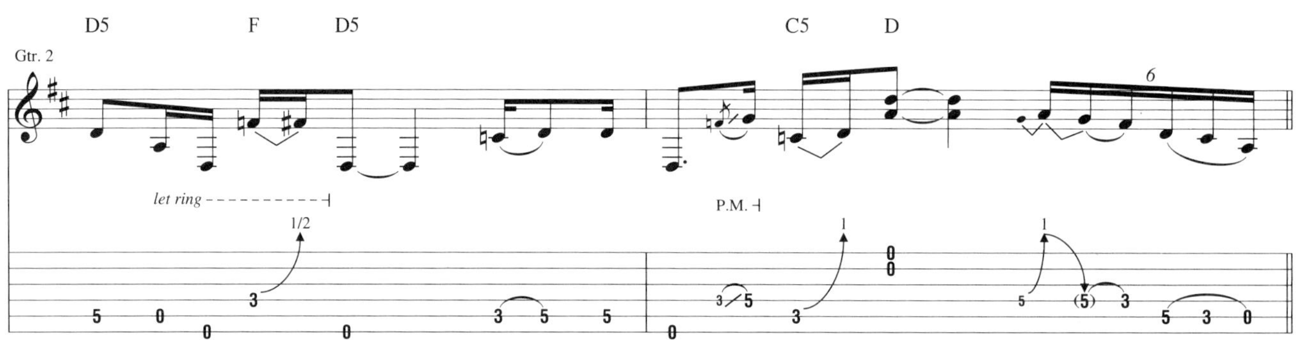

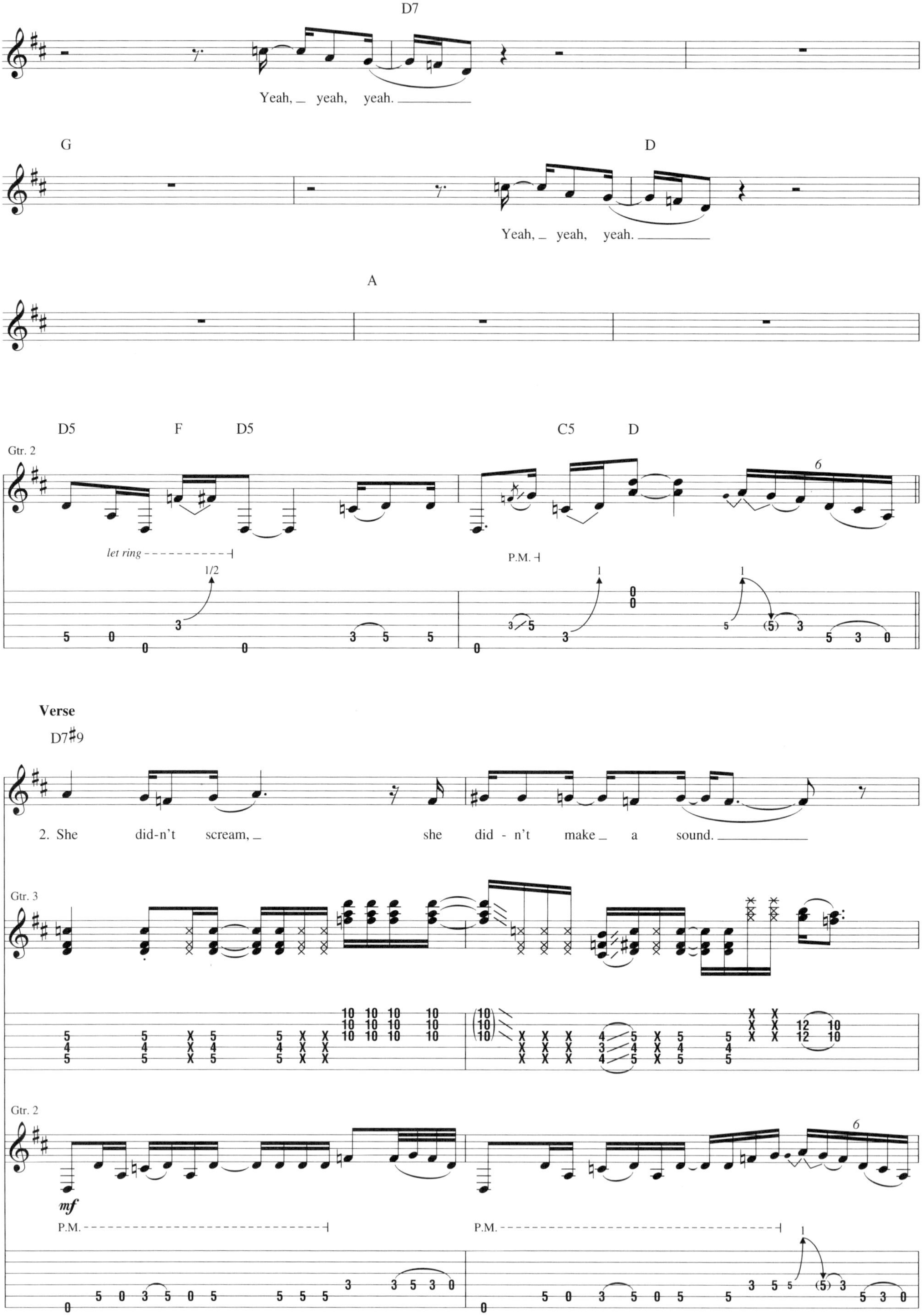

Verse

D7♯9

2. She didn't scream, _ she did - n't make _ a sound.

Gtr. 3

Gtr. 2

mf

P.M.

P.M.

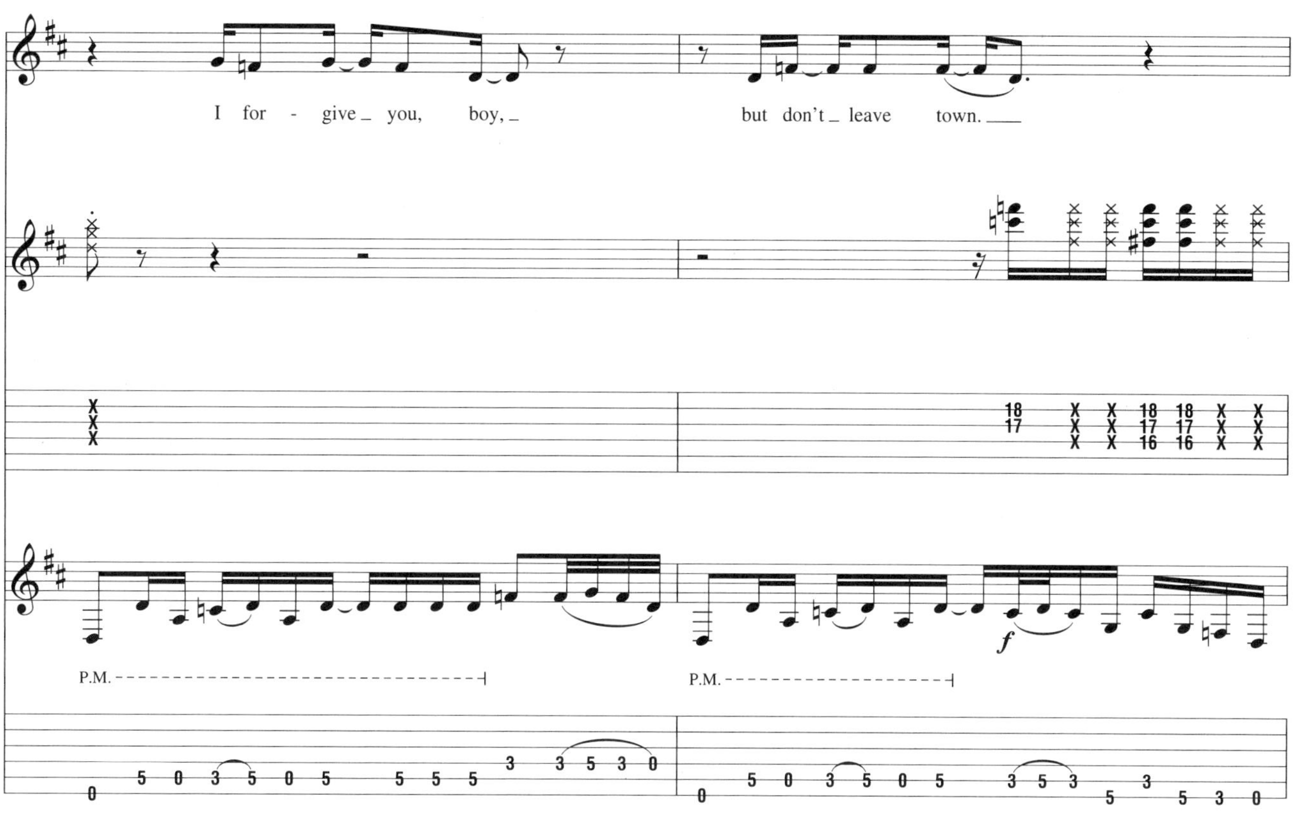
I for - give you, boy,
but don't leave town.
P.M.
P.M.

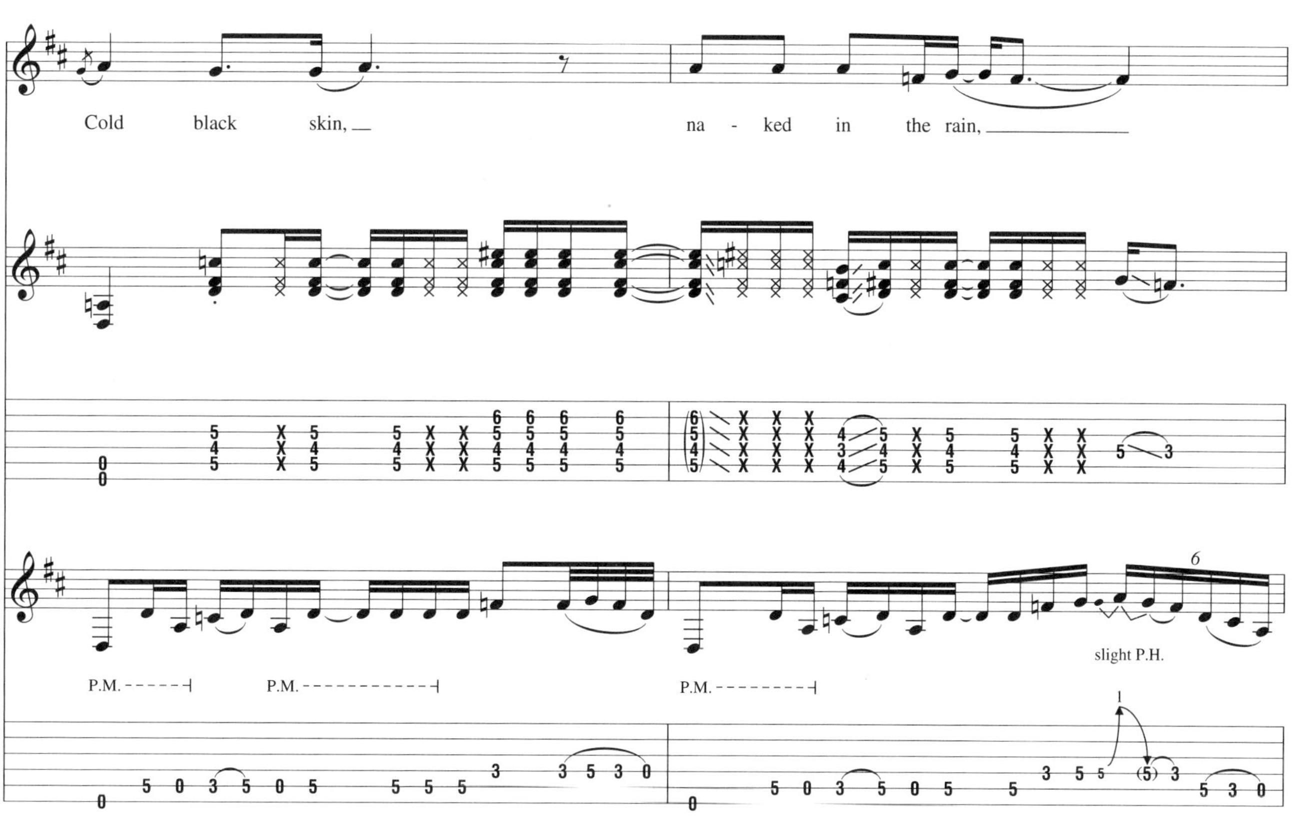
Cold black skin,
na - ked in the rain,
P.M.
P.M.
P.M.
slight P.H.

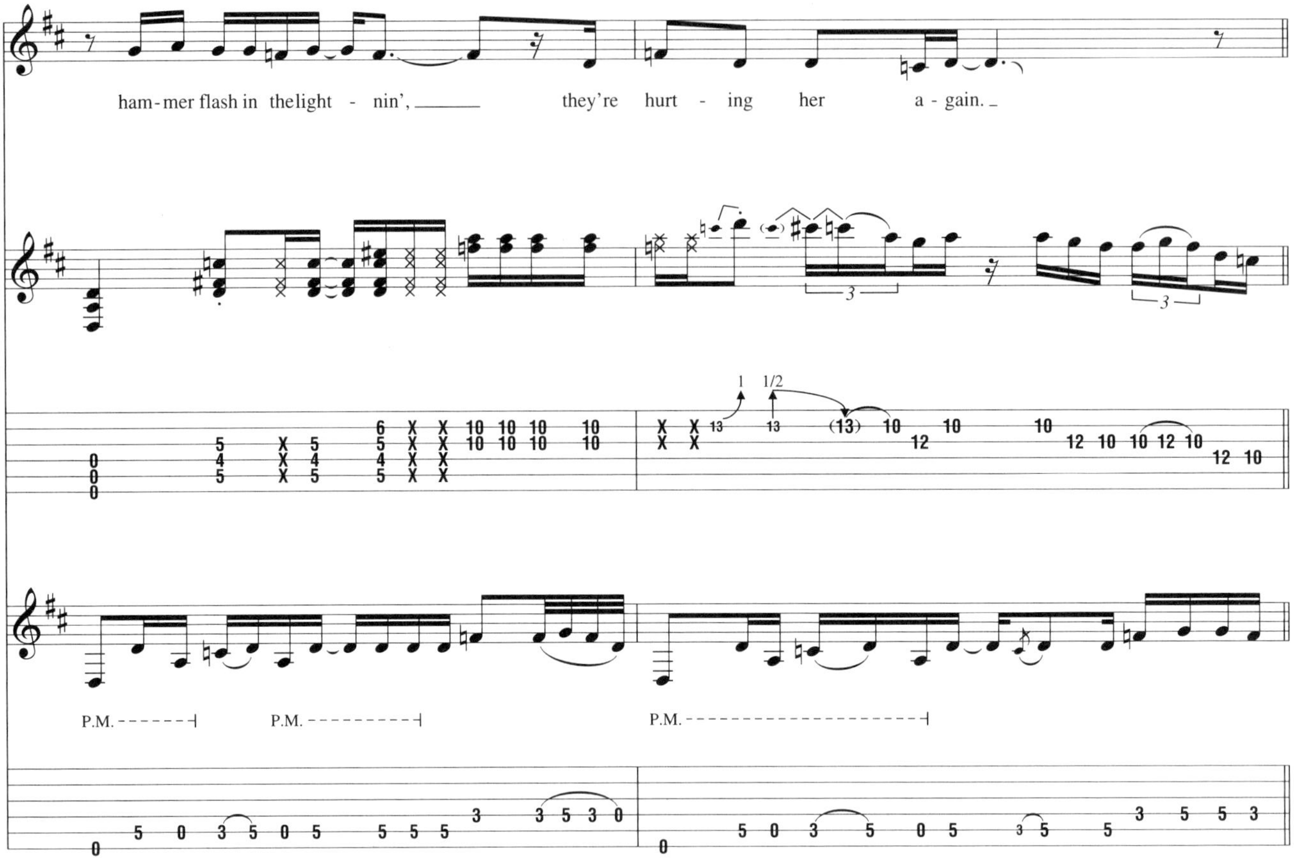

ham - mer flash in the light - nin', they're hurt - ing her a - gain.

P.M. P.M. P.M.

Interlude

A

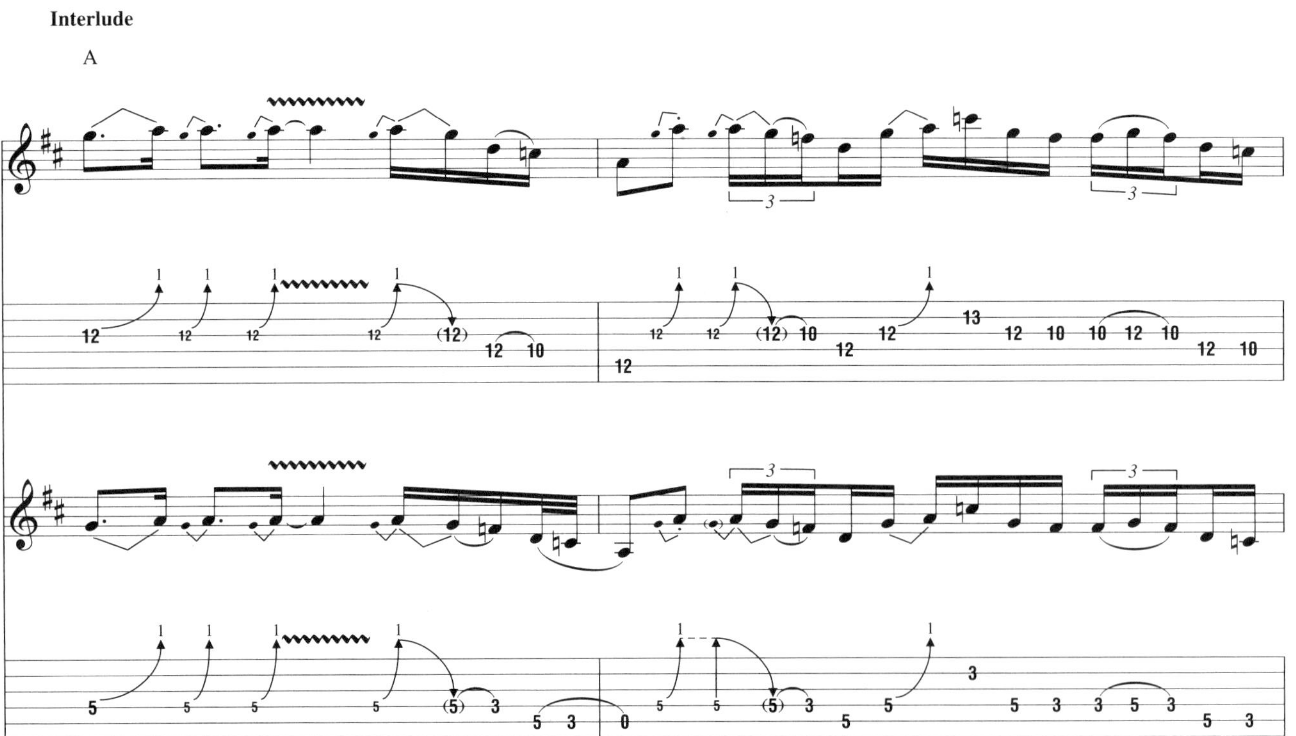

Chorus
D5
F5
D5
D
F
Let me put you in the pic - ture, let me show you what I mean. The Mes - si -
Rhy. Fig. 3
1/4
let ring
1/2
G
D
- ah is my sis - ter, ain't no king, man, she's my queen. Let me
End Rhy. Fig. 3
1

Gtr. 3: w/ Rhy. Fig. 3
F
put you in the pic - ture, let me show you what I mean. The Mes - si -
Gtr. 2
P.M.
G
D
- ah is my sis - ter, ain't no king, man, she's my queen. I have a dream,
C5
A5
G5
N.C.
I've seen the light. Don't put it out, 'cause she's al - right, yeah, she's my sis -
Gtr. 3
Gtr. 2

Interlude

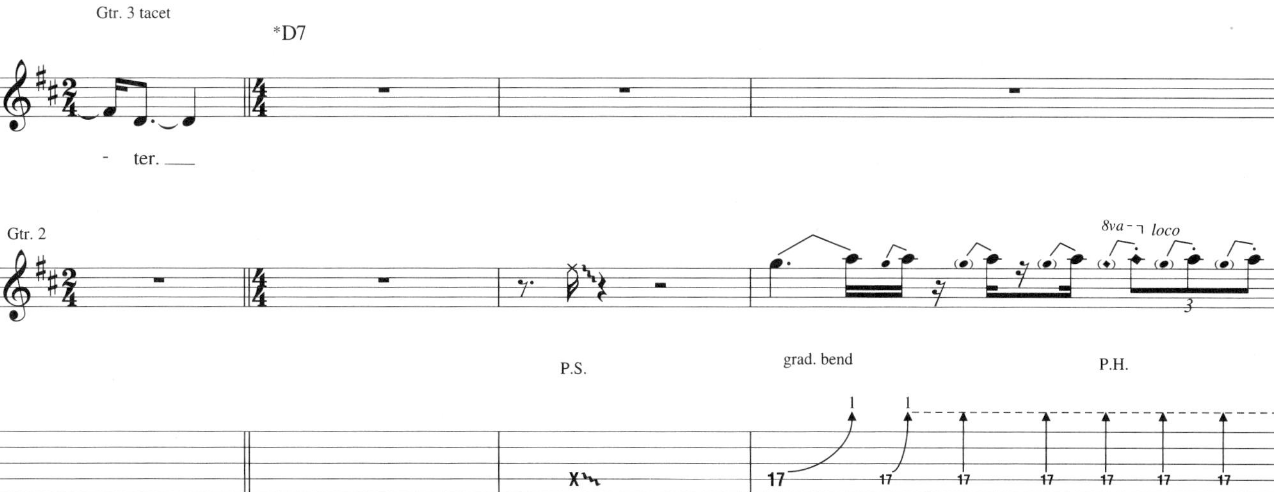

*Chord symbols reflect overall harmony.

Verse

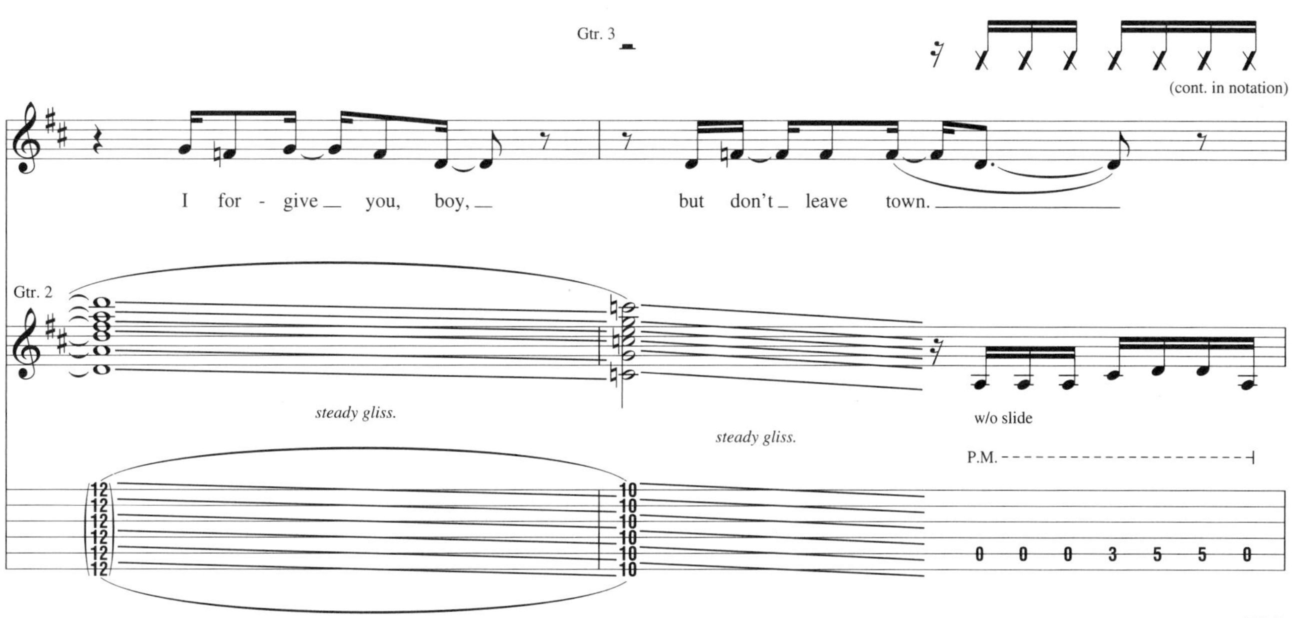

Gtr. 2: w/ Riff A (last 4 meas.)
D7♯9
Cold black skin, naked in the rain,
Gtr. 3
ham-mer flash in the light - nin', they're hurt - ing her a - gain.
Interlude
Gtr. 2: w/ Riff B
Gtr. 3: w/ Rhy. Fig. 2 (1st 10 meas.)
G
D7
Oh. Oh, oh, oh.
Gtr. 4 (dist.)
mf
w/ slide
G
Yeah, yeah, yeah.

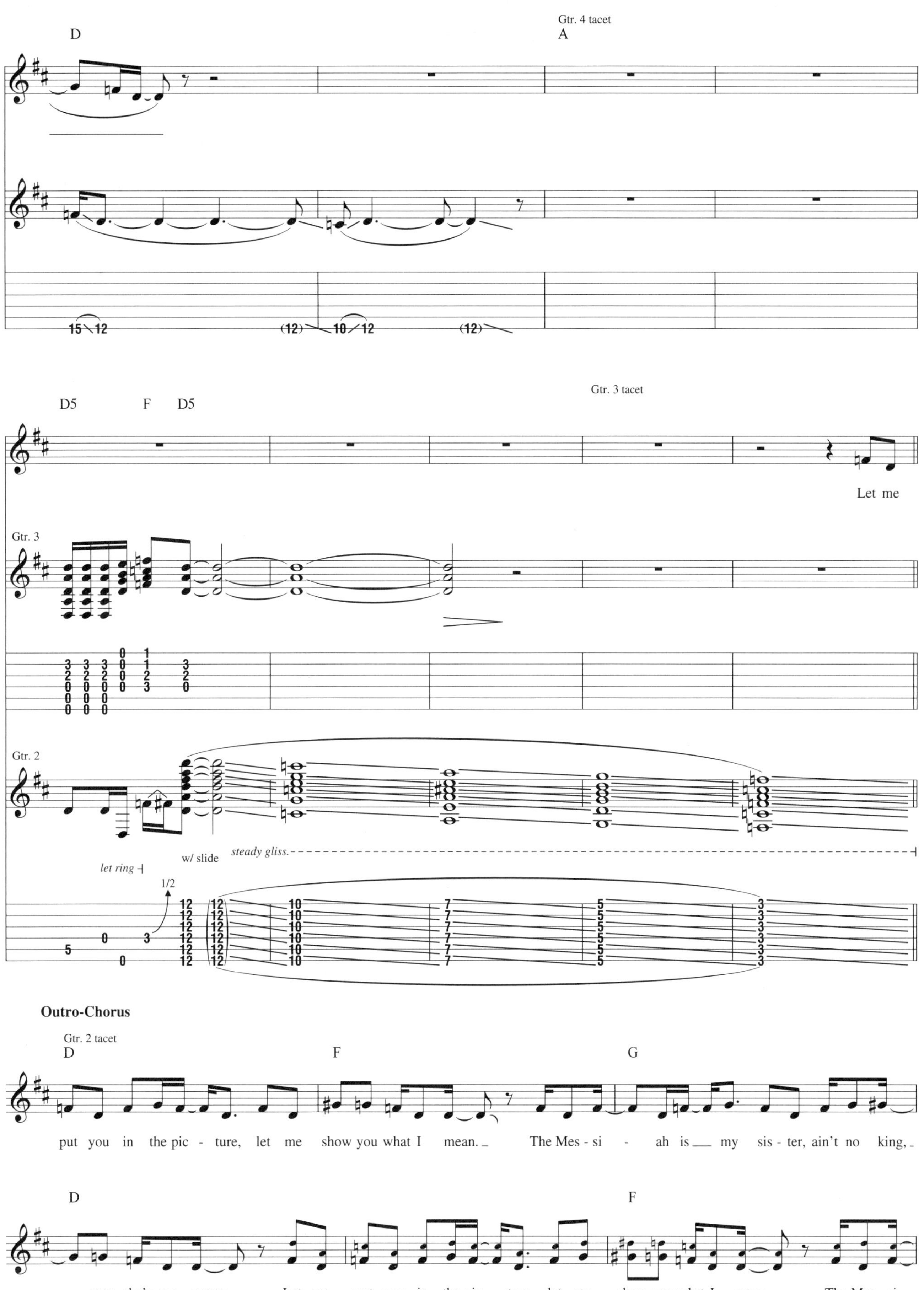
Gtr. 4 tacet
D
A
15 12
(12) 10 12
(12)
Gtr. 3 tacet
D5
F
D5
Let me
Gtr. 3
Gtr. 2
w/ slide
steady gliss.
let ring
1/2
Outro-Chorus
Gtr. 2 tacet
D
F
G
put you in the pic - ture, let me show you what I mean. The Mes - si - ah is my sis - ter, ain't no king,
D
F
man, she's my queen. Let me put you in the pic - ture, let me show you what I mean. The Mes - si -

*Switch to bridge pickup.

Gtr. 3: w/ Rhy. Fig. 3 (last meas.)
G
D
- ah is my sis - ter, ain't no king, man, she's my queen. Let me
Gtr. 2
End Riff D
P.M.
P.M.
Gtr. 2: w/ Riff D (4 times)
Gtr. 3: w/ Rhy. Fig. 3 (2 times)
F
put you in the pic - ture, let me show you what I mean. The Mes - si -
G
D
- ah is my sis - ter, ain't no king, man, she's my queen. Let me
Gtr. 5 (dist.)
mf
F
put you in the pic - ture, let me show you what I mean. The Mes - si -
Riff E

G
D
- ah is __ my sis - ter, ain't no king, __ man, she's my queen. __ Let me
End Riff E
Gtr. 5: w/ Riff E
F
put you in the pic - ture, let me show you what I mean. __ The Mes - si -
(Let me, __ let me show __ you. __ The Mes - si -
Rhy. Fig. 4
Gtr. 3
G
D
- ah is __ my sis - ter, ain't no king, __ man, she's my queen. __ Let me
- ah, she is __ my queen. __
End Rhy. Fig. 4

Gtr. 3: w/ Rhy. Fig. 4
F
put you in the pic - ture, let me show you what I mean. The Mes - si -
Let me, let me show you. The Mes - si -
Gtr. 5

G
D
- ah is my sis - ter, ain't no king, man, she's my queen. I have a dream,
- ah, she is my queen.)
slight P.H.
slight P.H.
slight P.H.

C5 A5 G5 F5 N.C.

___ I've seen the light, _ don't put it out, ___ 'cause she's _ al - right, yeah, she's _ my sis -

Gtr. 3

Gtr. 5

Gtr. 2

Gtrs. 2 & 3 tacet

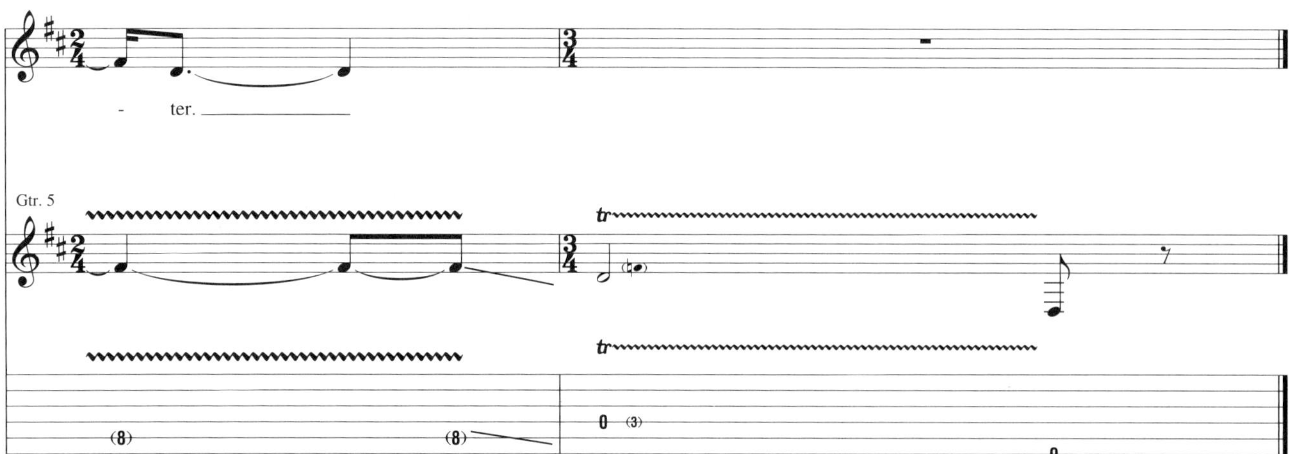

from Joy Division - *Substance*

Love Will Tear Us Apart

Words and Music by Ian Curtis, Stephen Morris, Peter Hook and Bernard Sumner

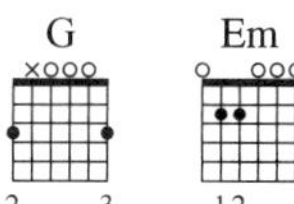

Gtr. 3: Drop D tuning:
(low to high) D-A-D-G-B-E

Intro

Moderately fast ♩ = 147

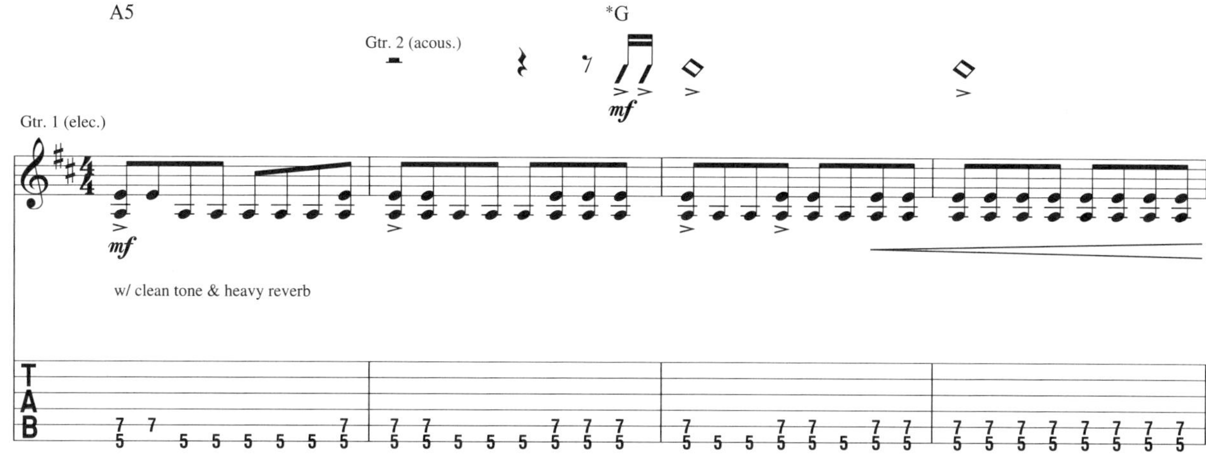

*See top of page for chord diagrams pertaining to rhythm slashes.

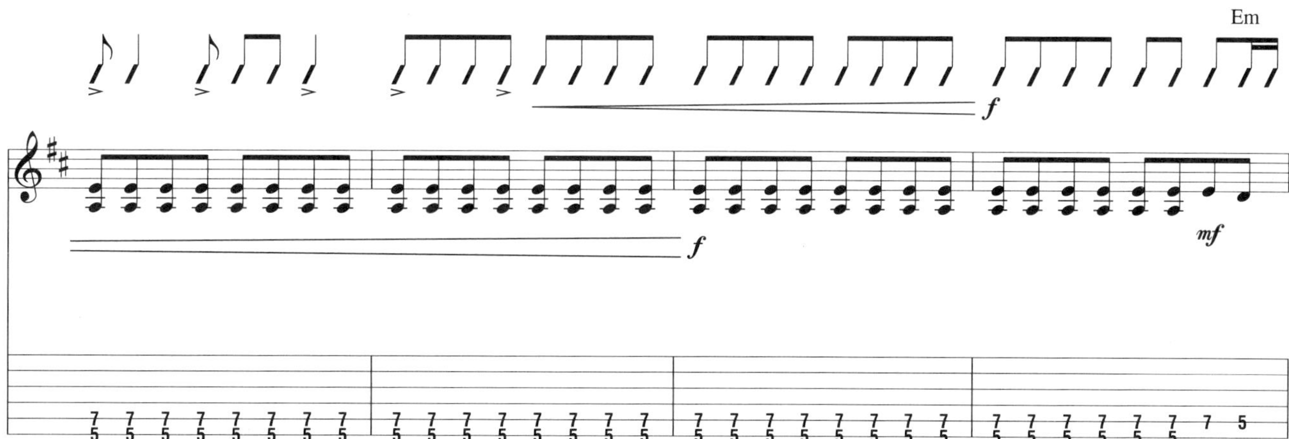

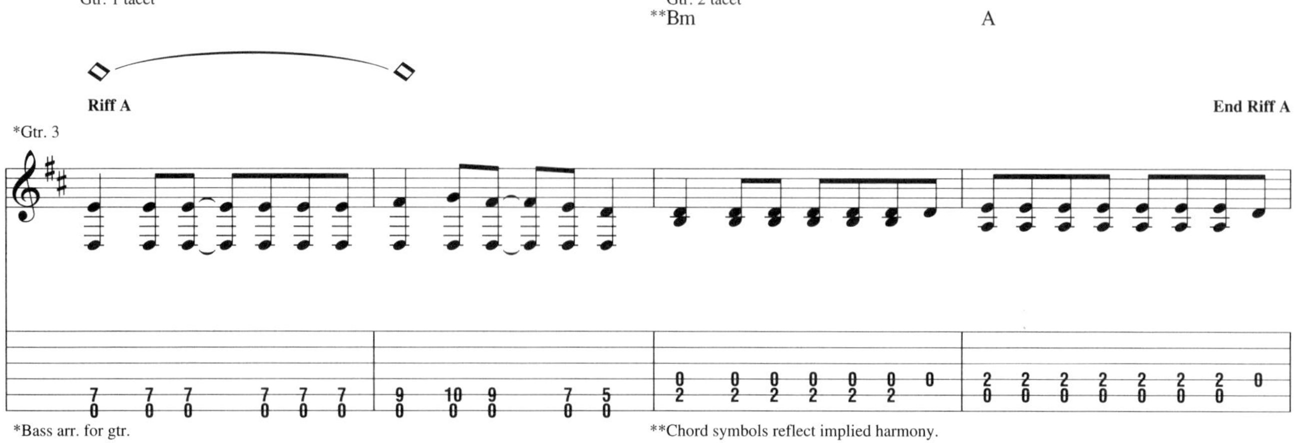
Gtr. 1 tacet
Gtr. 2 tacet
**Bm
A
Riff A
End Riff A
*Gtr. 3
*Bass arr. for gtr.
**Chord symbols reflect implied harmony.

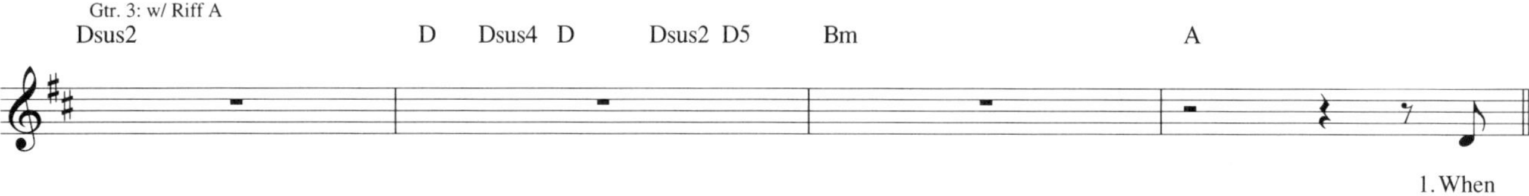
Gtr. 3: w/ Riff A
Dsus2
D Dsus4 D
Dsus2 D5
Bm
A
1. When

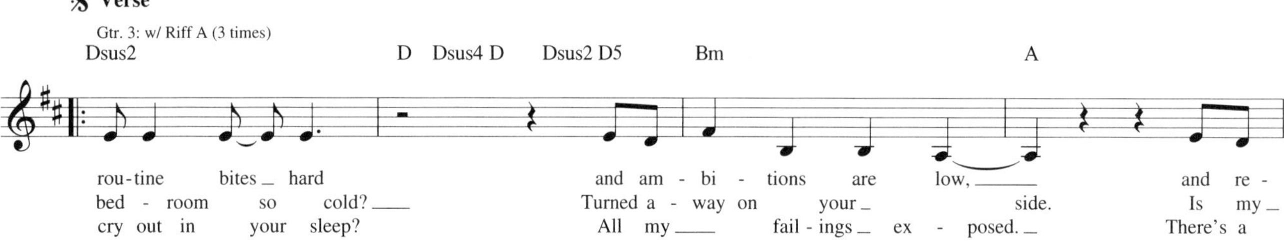
Verse
Gtr. 3: w/ Riff A (3 times)
Dsus2
D Dsus4 D
Dsus2 D5
Bm
A
rou-tine bites hard and am-bi-tions are low, and re-
bed-room so cold? Turned a-way on your side. Is my
cry out in your sleep? All my fail-ings ex-posed. There's a

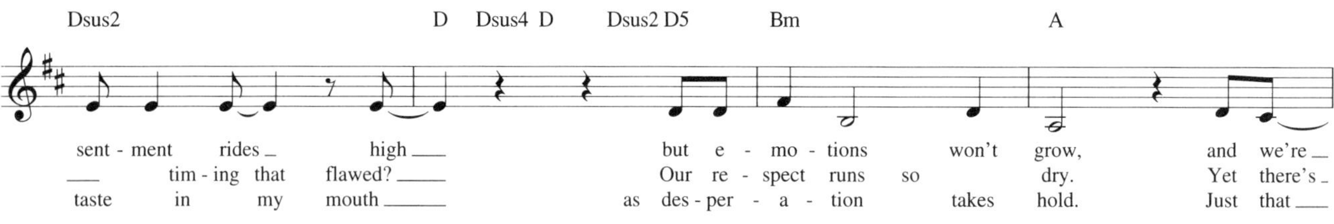
Dsus2
D Dsus4 D
Dsus2 D5
Bm
A
sent-ment rides high but e-mo-tions won't grow, and we're
tim-ing that flawed? Our re-spect runs so dry. Yet there's
taste in my mouth as des-per-a-tion takes hold. Just that

To Coda
Dsus2
D Dsus4 D
Dsus2 D5
Bm
A
chang-ing our ways, tak-ing dif-fer-ent roads, then
still this ap-peal that we've kept through our lives.
some-thing so good just can't func-tion no more. But

Chorus

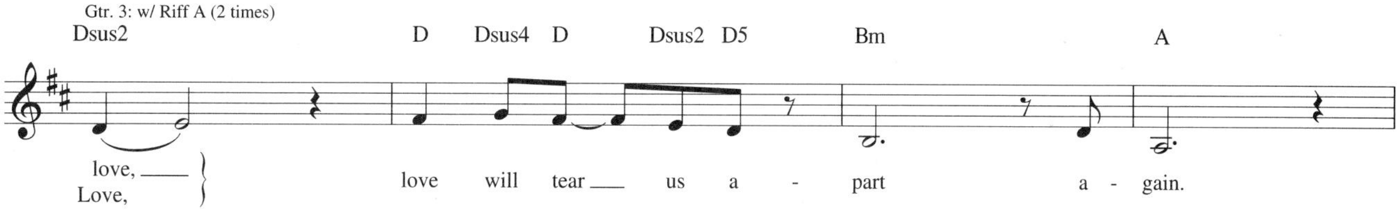
Gtr. 3: w/ Riff A (2 times)
Dsus2
D Dsus4 D Dsus2 D5
Bm
A
love, Love,
love will tear us a - part a - gain.

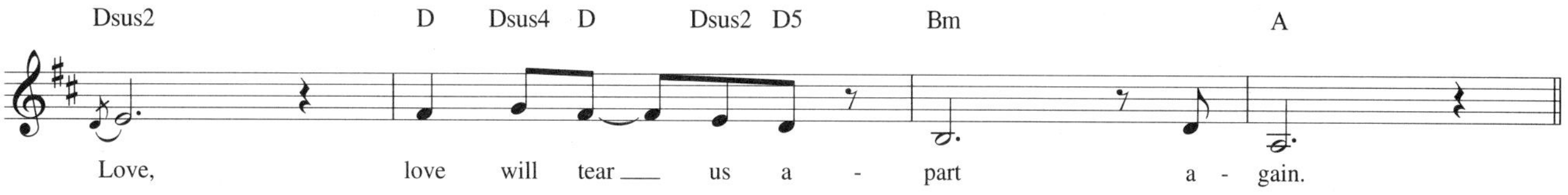
Dsus2
D Dsus4 D Dsus2 D5
Bm
A
Love, love will tear us a - part a - gain.

1.
Interlude
Gtr. 3: w/ Riff A
Dsus2
D Dsus4 D Dsus2 D5
Bm
A
2. Why is the

2.
Interlude
Gtr. 1 tacet
Gtr. 3: w/ Riff A (2 times)
A5
Gtr. 1
Play 7 times
Dsus2
D Dsus4 D Dsus2 D5
Bm

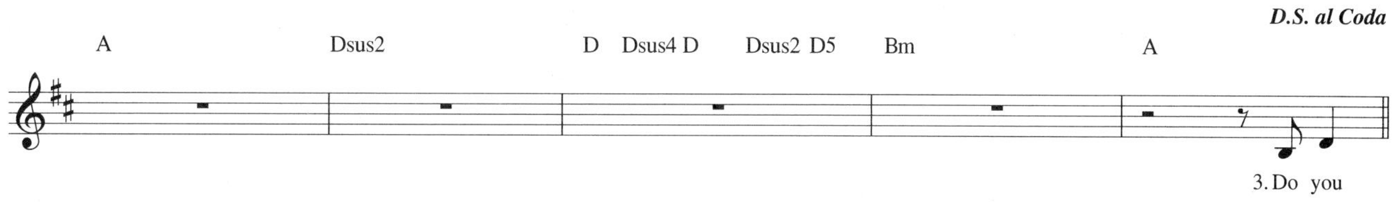
D.S. al Coda
A
Dsus2
D Dsus4 D Dsus2 D5
Bm
A
3. Do you

Coda

Chorus
Gtr. 3: w/ Riff A (4 times)
Dsus2
D Dsus4 D Dsus2 D5
Bm
A
love, love will tear us a - part a - gain.

Outro

Play 4 times and fade

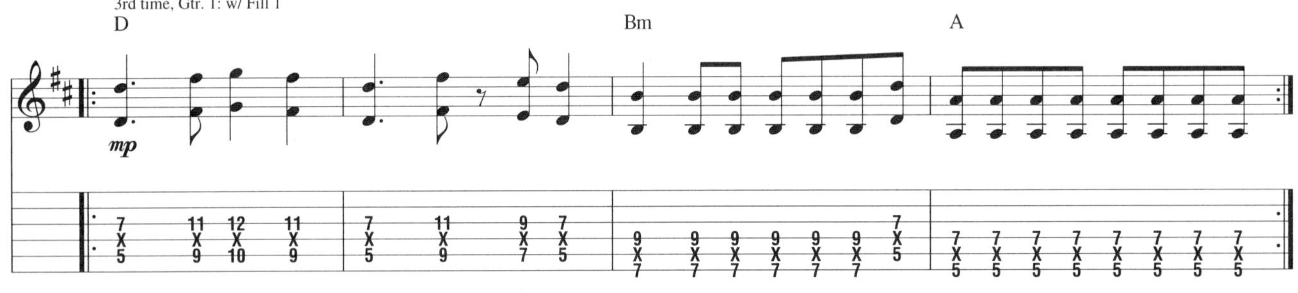

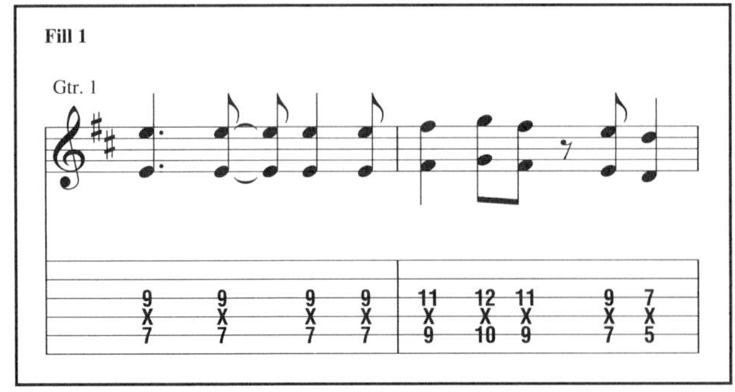

from Waylon Jennings - *Ol' Waylon*

Luckenbach, Texas
(Back to the Basics of Love)

Words and Music by Bobby Emmons and Chips Moman

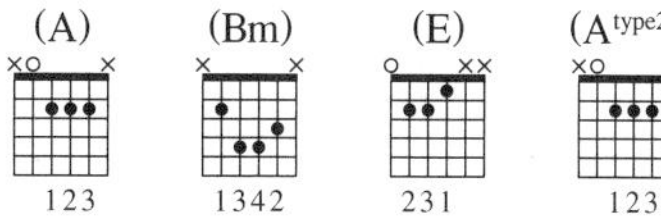

Gtr. 2: Tune down 1 step:
(low to high) D-G-C-F-A-D

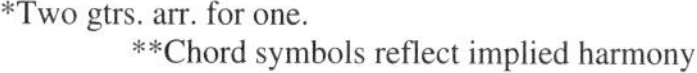
*Two gtrs. arr. for one.
**Chord symbols reflect implied harmony.

*Two gtrs. arr. for one.

**Symbols in parentheses represent chord names respective to detuned Gtr. 2. Symbols above reflect actual sounding chords.

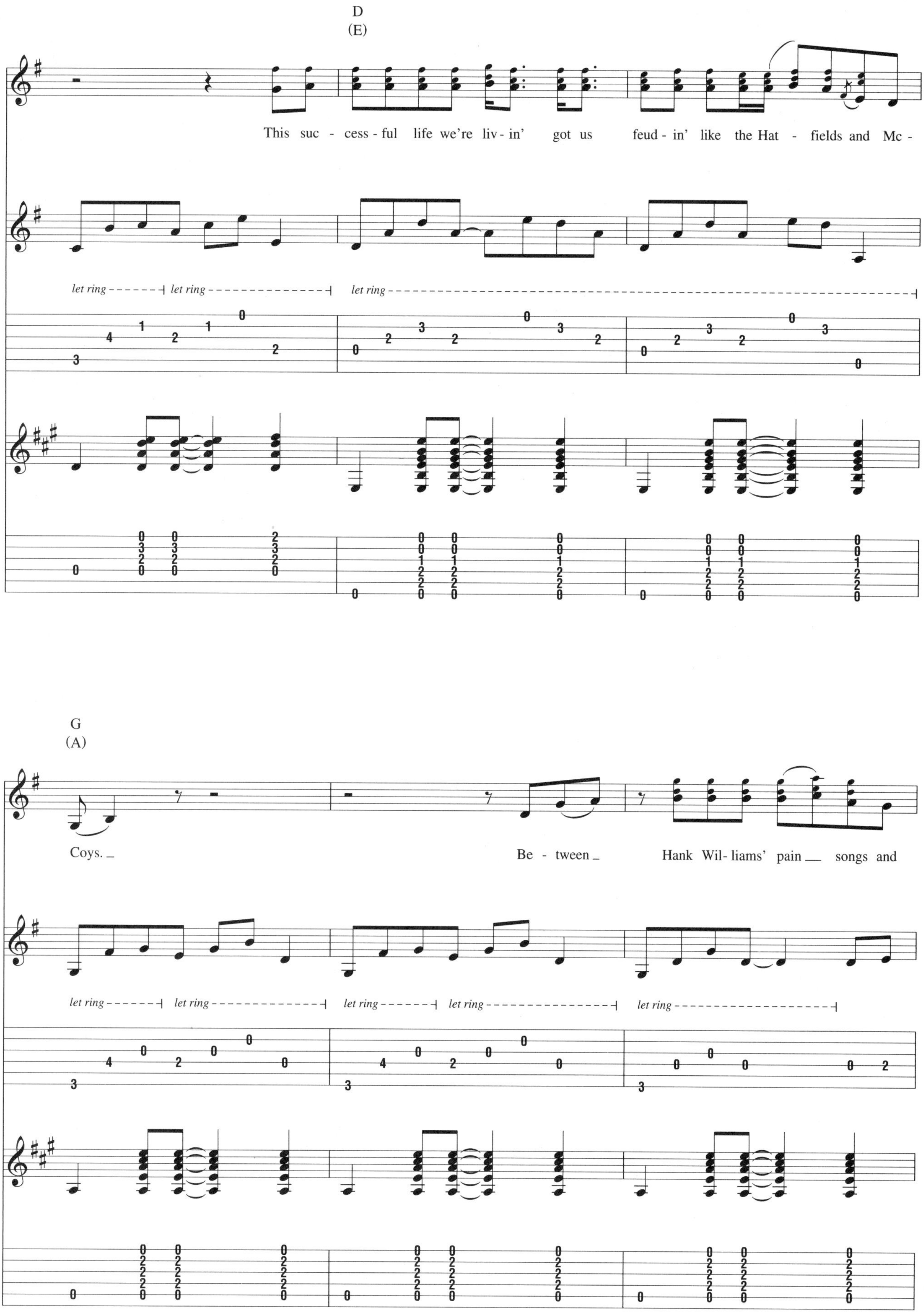

D
(E)

This suc - cess - ful life we're liv - in' got us feud - in' like the Hat - fields and Mc -

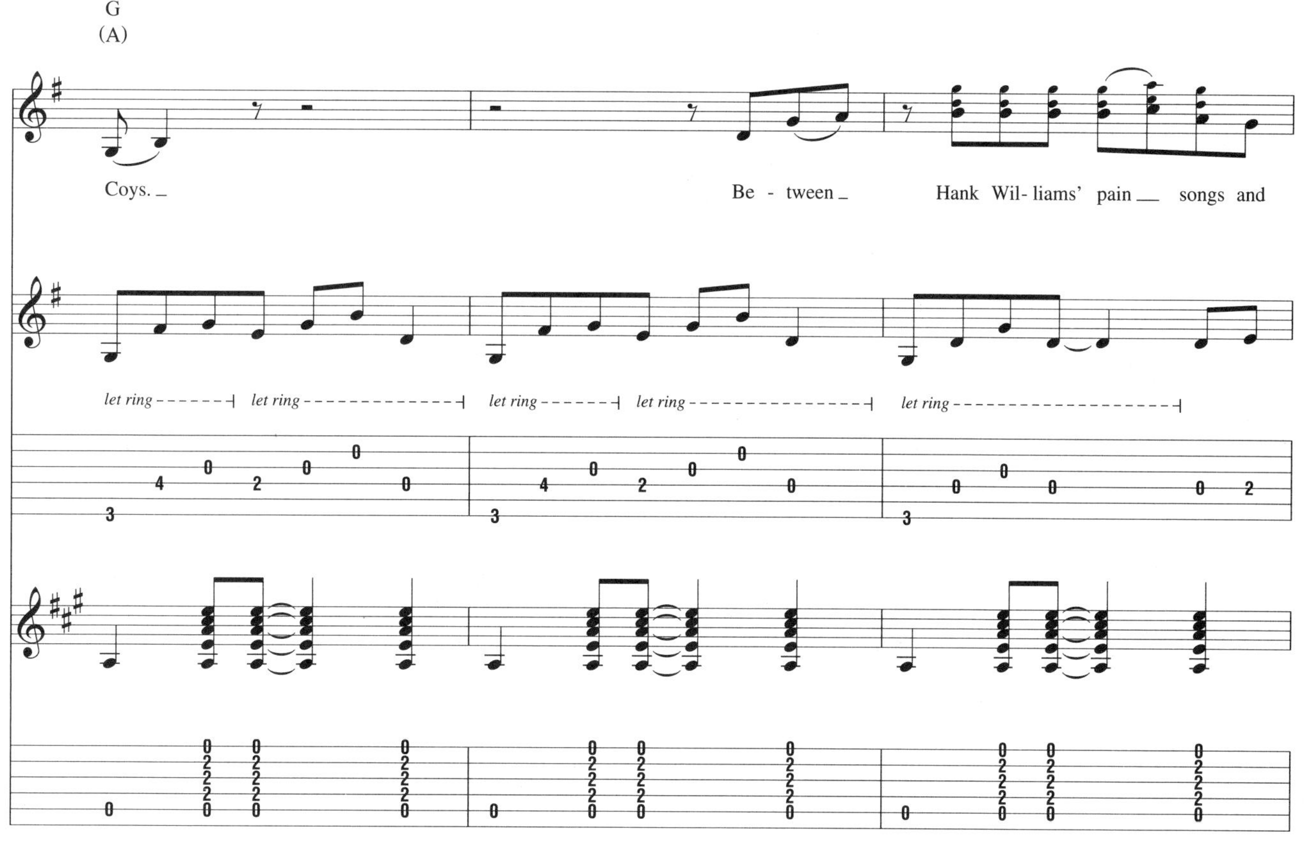

2nd time, Gtr. 1: w/ Fill 1
G7
(A7)
C
(D)
G/B
(A/C♯)
Am
(Bm)
New - ber - ry's train __ songs and "Blue Eyes Cry - in' in the Rain," _ out in
let ring
To Coda
D
(E)
G
(A)
Luck - en - bach, Tex - as, there ain't no - bod - y feel - in' no pain. ___
Fill 1
Gtr. 1
let ring

Am
(Bm)
D
(E)
2. So,
End Riff A
let ring
End Rhy. Fig. 1
(cont. in slashes)
Verse
*(A)
(Bm)
(E)
(A)
(A type2)
open
Gtr. 2
ba - by, let's sell your dia - mond ring,
buy some boots and fad - ed jeans and
go a - way.
Gtr. 1
let ring
*See top of first page of song for chord diagrams pertaining to rhythm slashes.
(A)
(A type2)
open
(A)
(Bm)
(E)
(cont. in notation)
This coat and tie is chok - in' me,
in your high so - ci - e - ty you
let ring

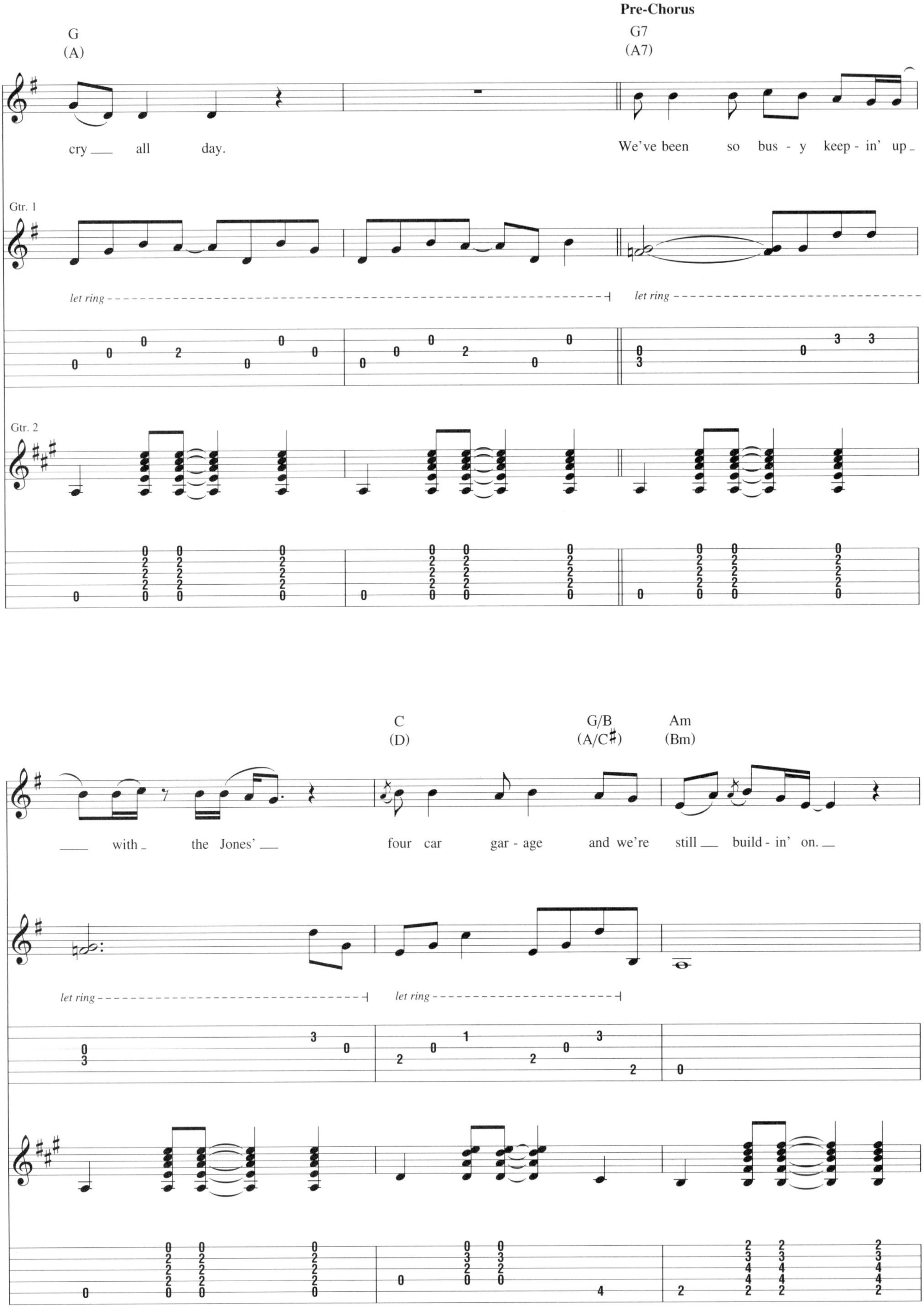

Pre-Chorus

G (A) | | G7 (A7)

cry ___ all day. We've been so bus - y keep - in' up _

Gtr. 1

let ring *let ring*

Gtr. 2

D.S. al Coda
C G/B Am G
(D) (A/C♯) (Bm) (A)
D
(E)
G
(A)
May - be it's time __ we __ got back to the bas - ics __ of love. Let's go to
let ring
Coda
Gtr. 1: w/ Riff A (last 2 meas.)
Gtr. 2: w/ Rhy. Fig. 1 (last 2 meas.)
Chorus
Gtr. 1: w/ Riff A
Gtr. 2: w/ Rhy. Fig. 1
Willie Nelson: Let's go to Luck - en - bach, Tex - as with
Wil - lie and __ Way - lon and __ the boys. This suc -
cess - ful life we're liv - in' got __ us feud - in' like the Hat - fields and Mc - Coys. Be - tween __
G7
(A7)
Hank Wil - liams pain __ songs __ and Jer - ry Jeff's train __ songs __ and "Blue Eyes Cry - in' in the Rain," __ out in
Luck - en - bach, Tex - as, there ain't no - bod - y feel - in' no pain. __
Outro
Begin fade
Gtr. 1: w/ Riff A (till fade)
Gtr. 2: w/ Rhy. Fig. 1 (till fade)
Fade out
C
(D)

from Jason Mraz - *We Sing. We Dance. We Steal Things.*

Lucky

Words and Music by Jason Mraz, Colbie Caillat and Timothy Fagan

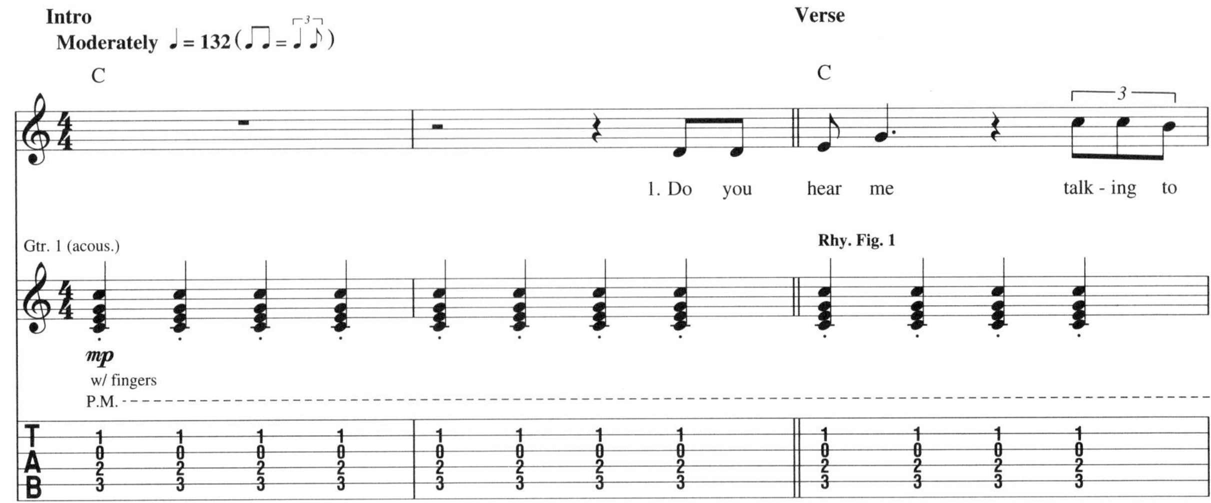

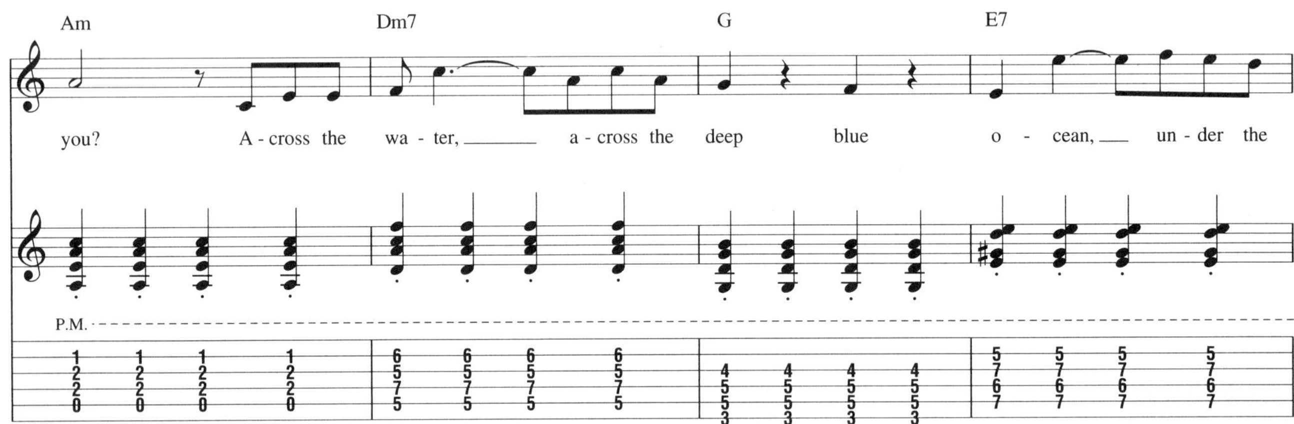

Am
Dm7
G
*G/F
dreams. I feel your whis - per a - cross the sea. I keep you
P.M.
*Bass plays F.
E7
Am
Dm7
with me in my heart. You make it eas - i - er when
P.M.
Chorus
Half-time feel
G
G#°
Am
Dm7
life gets hard. Luck - y I'm in love with my best friend,
Rhy. Fig. 2
strum w/ fingers
let ring
let ring
G
C
Gadd4/B
Am
luck - y to have been where I have been. Luck - y to be
let ring
sim.

Dm7
Gsus4
G
com - ing home a - gain.
End Rhy. Fig. 2
C
Am
Em
G
Oo,
oo.
Bridge
Dm7
Am7
G
Dm7
They don't know how long it takes, wait - ing for a love like this.
They don't know how long it takes, wait - ing for a love like this.
Am7
G
Dm7
Ev - 'ry time we say good - bye, I wish we had
Ev - 'ry time we say good - bye, I wish we had
one more kiss. I'll

Am7
G
Am7
G7/B
wait for you, I prom - ise you I will.
I'm
Gtr. 1
*Gtr. 2
mf
w/ fingers
*Kybds. arr. for gtr.
Chorus
Gtr. 1: w/ Rhy. Fig. 2 (1st 4 meas.)
Am7
Dm7
G7
C
C/B
luck - y I'm in love with my best friend,
luck - y to have been where I have been.
Rhy. Fig. 3
Gtr. 2
let ring
let ring
sim.
*2nd time, Voc. tacet on beats 1 and 2.
Am7
Dm7
Gsus4
G
N.C.
Luck - y to be com - ing home a - gain.
Gtr. 1
Gtr. 2
End Rhy. Fig. 3

1st time, Gtr. 1: w/ Rhy. Fig. 2
2nd time, Gtr. 1: w/ Rhy. Fig. 2 (1st 7 meas.)
Gtr. 2: w/ Rhy. Fig. 3
Am7 Dm7 G7 C C/B
Luck - y we're in love in ev - 'ry way, luck - y to have stayed where we have stayed.
To Coda
End half-time feel
Am7 Dm7 Gsus4 G
Luck - y to be com - ing home some - day. 2. And so I'm
Verse
Gtr. 1: w/ Rhy. Fig. 1
C Am Dm7
sail - ing through the sea to an is - land where we'll
G E7 Am
meet. You'll hear the mu - sic fill the air; I'll put a
Dm7 G C
flow - er in your hair. Though the breez - es through the
Gtr. 1
let ring
Am Dm7 G *G/F
trees move so pret - ty, you're all I see. As the
let ring
sim.
*Bass plays F.

E7 Am Dm7 G G♯°

world keeps spin - ning 'round, you hold me right here, right now.

strum w/ fingers

Coda

Outro

G C Am

Oo,

Gtr. 1

Em G C

oo. Oo,

Am Em G C

oo. Oo.

w/ thumb

from Anthrax - *Spreading the Disease*

Madhouse

Words and Music by Joseph Bellardini, Frank Bello, Charlie Benante, Scott Rosenfeld and Daniel Spitz

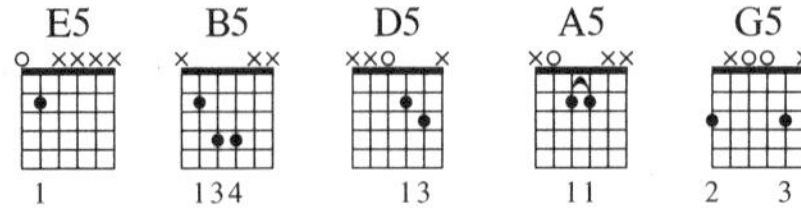

Spoken: It's time for your medication, Mister Brown. (Maniacal laughter:) Ooh, hoo, ha, ha, ha...

Intro

Moderately fast ♩ = 160

*Chord symbols reflect implied harmony.

Gtrs. 1 & 2: w/ Riff A (4 1/2 times)

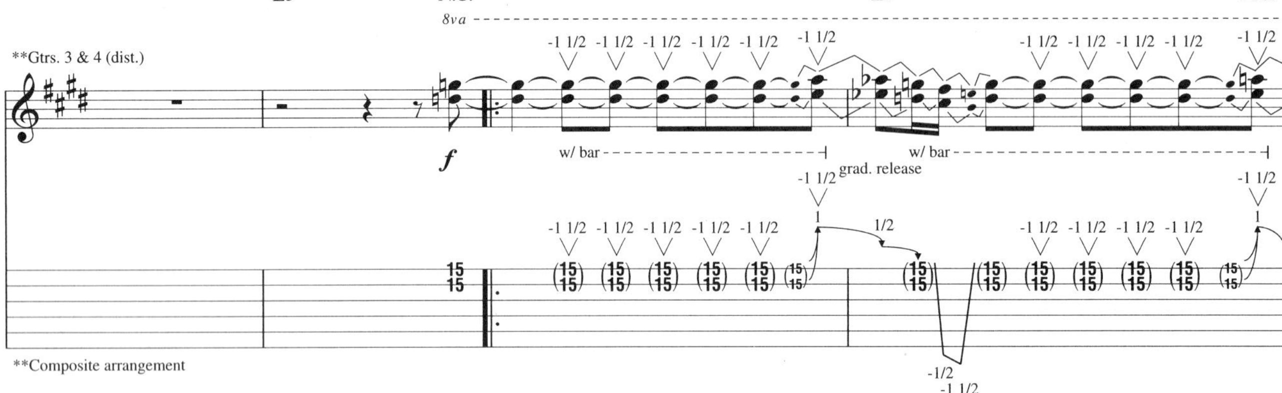

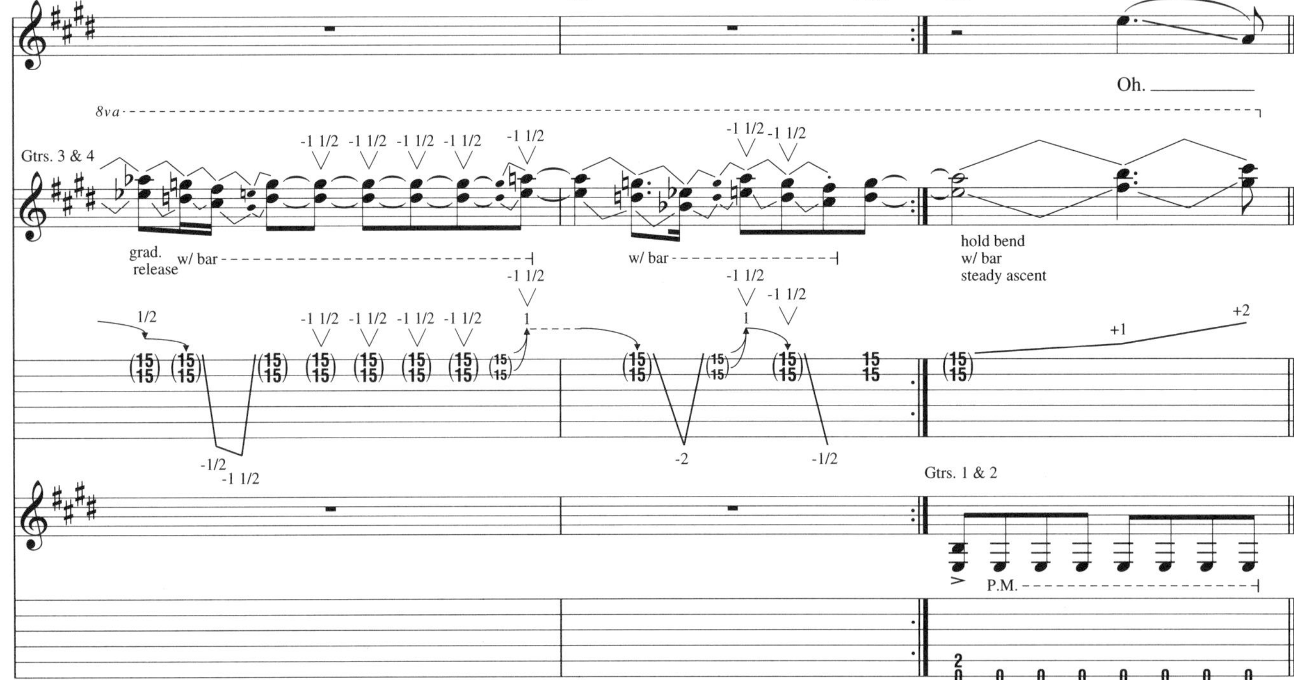

Verse
Gtrs. 3 & 4 tacet
B5 D5 A5 B5 G5 D5/A
1. White coats to bind me, out of con - trol,
2. My fears be - hind me, what can I do?
Gtrs. 1 & 2
P.M.
B5 D5/A A5 B5 G5 D5/A
I live a - lone in - side my mind.
My dreams haunt my sleep at night. Oh, no.
Rhy. Fig. 1
End Rhy. Fig. 1
P.M.
Gtr. 1: w/ Rhy. Fig. 1
B5 D5/A A5 B5 G5 D5/A
World of con - fu - sion, air filled with noise,
Won't learn their les - son, white fills my eyes,
Rhy. Fig. 2
Gtr. 2
End Rhy. Fig. 2
P.M.
Gtr. 2: w/ Rhy. Fig. 2
B5 D5/A A5 B5 G5 D5/A
who says that my life's such a crime?
and on - ly then they see the light.
Gtr. 1
P.M.

3rd time, Gtr. 3: w/ Fill 1
3rd time, Gtr. 4 tacet
E5 F E5 F E5 F E5 F(♭5)
Trapped in this night - mare,
I wish I'd wake,
Gtrs. 1 & 2
Riff B
P.M.
E5 F E5 F E5 F E5 C5 G♯5
1., 3. as
2. and
my whole life be-gins to shake.
End Riff B
Gtrs. 1 & 2: w/ Riff B
E5 F E5 F E5 F E5 F(♭5)
Four walls sur - round me,
an emp - ty gaze,
E5 F E5 F E5 F E5 C5 G♯5
I can't find my way out of this maze.
And I don't
Pre-Chorus
A5 B♭5/A A5 B♭5/A A5 C5 B5 B♭5
care, fall in, fall out.
Gone with-out a doubt.
(Help me.)
I
Gtrs. 1 & 2
Rhy. Fig. 3
End Rhy. Fig. 3
*Gang vocals
Fill 1
Gtr. 3
8va
P.H.
w/ bar
grad. dive
Pitch: E
-3 1/2

Gtr. 1: w/ Rhy. Fig. 3
A5 Bb5/A A5 Bb5/A A5 C5 B5 Bb5
can't take the blame. 1., 3. They 2. I don't feel the shame. 2. 'Cause
Gtr. 2
P.M.
Chorus
N.C. E5 N.C. E5 N.C.
1., 3. It's (2.) it's a mad - house or so they claim. It's
Gtrs. 1 & 2
*Gang vocals
To Coda
1st & 3rd times, Gtrs. 1 & 2: w/ Riff A (2 times)
2nd time, Gtrs. 1 & 2: w/ Riff A (1 1/2 times)
E5 N.C. E5
a mad - house, oh, am I in - sane?
E5 N.C. E5
Gtrs. 1 & 2
I'm in - sane.
Gtr. 3
P.H. w/ bar grad. ascent
Pitch: F#
Guitar Solo
B5 D5 A5 B5 G5 D5
Rhy. Fig. 4
End Rhy. Fig. 4
grad. bend
1 hold bend
P.M.

Gtrs. 1 & 2: w/ Rhy. Fig. 4 (3 times)
B5 D5 A5 B5 G5 D5
P.M. P.H. P.M. P.H. P.H.
w/ bar
w/ bar
P.H.
w/ bar
grad. dive
Pitch: G♯ F♯ F♯
Gtr. 3
Gtr. 4
divisi
P.H.
Pitch: F♯
8va
D.S. al Coda
grad. bend
loco
P.M.
grad. bend
Coda
E5 N.C. E5 N.C.
I'm in - sane.
Mad,
mad - house.
Mad, mad, mad, mad - house.
(Mad! Mad! Mad!)
Gtrs. 1 & 2

from Triumph - *Allied Forces*

Magic Power

Words and Music by Mike Levine, Gil Moore and Rik Emmett

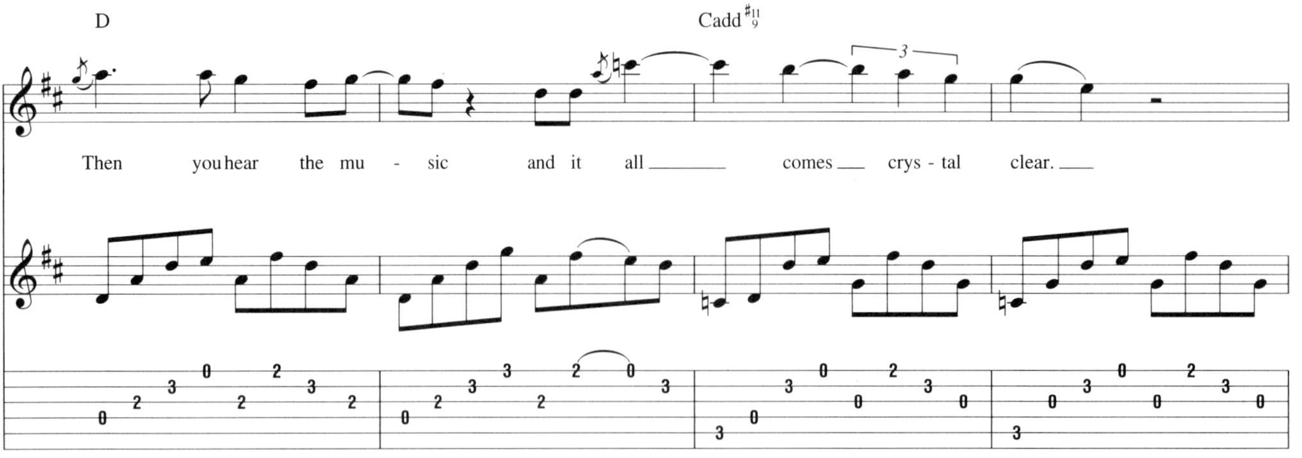
D
Cadd#11/9
Then you hear the mu - sic and it all comes crys - tal clear.

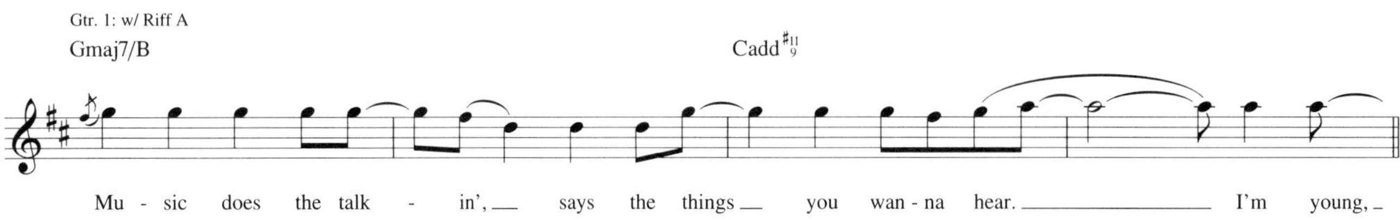
Gtr. 1: w/ Riff A
Gmaj7/B
Cadd#11/9
Mu - sic does the talk - in', says the things you wan - na hear. I'm young,

Chorus

D
Cadd#11/9
G6/B
G/B
D/F#
I'm wild and I'm free.
Gtr. 1

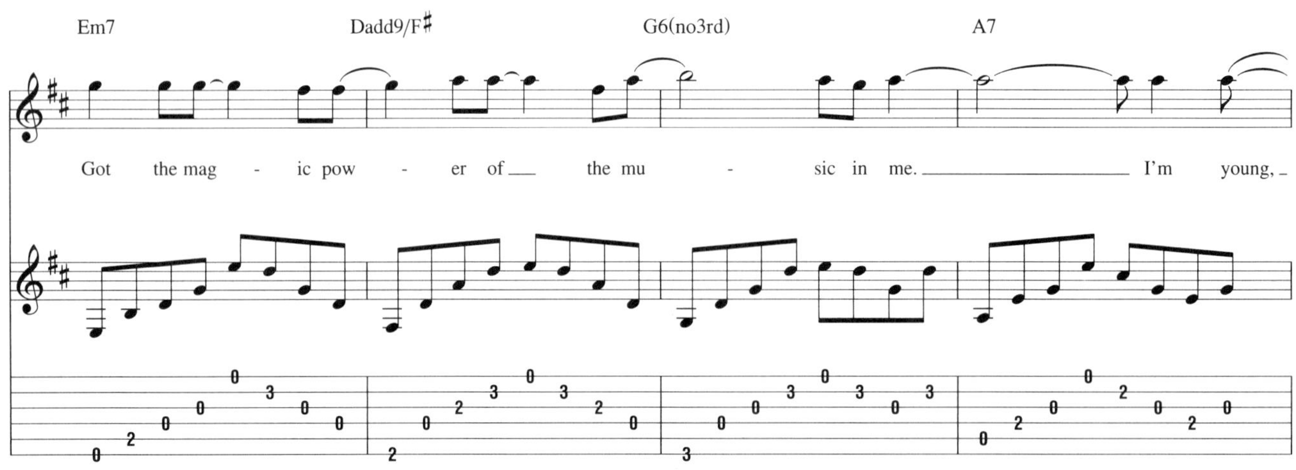
Em7
Dadd9/F#
G6(no3rd)
A7
Got the mag - ic pow - er of the mu - sic in me. I'm young,

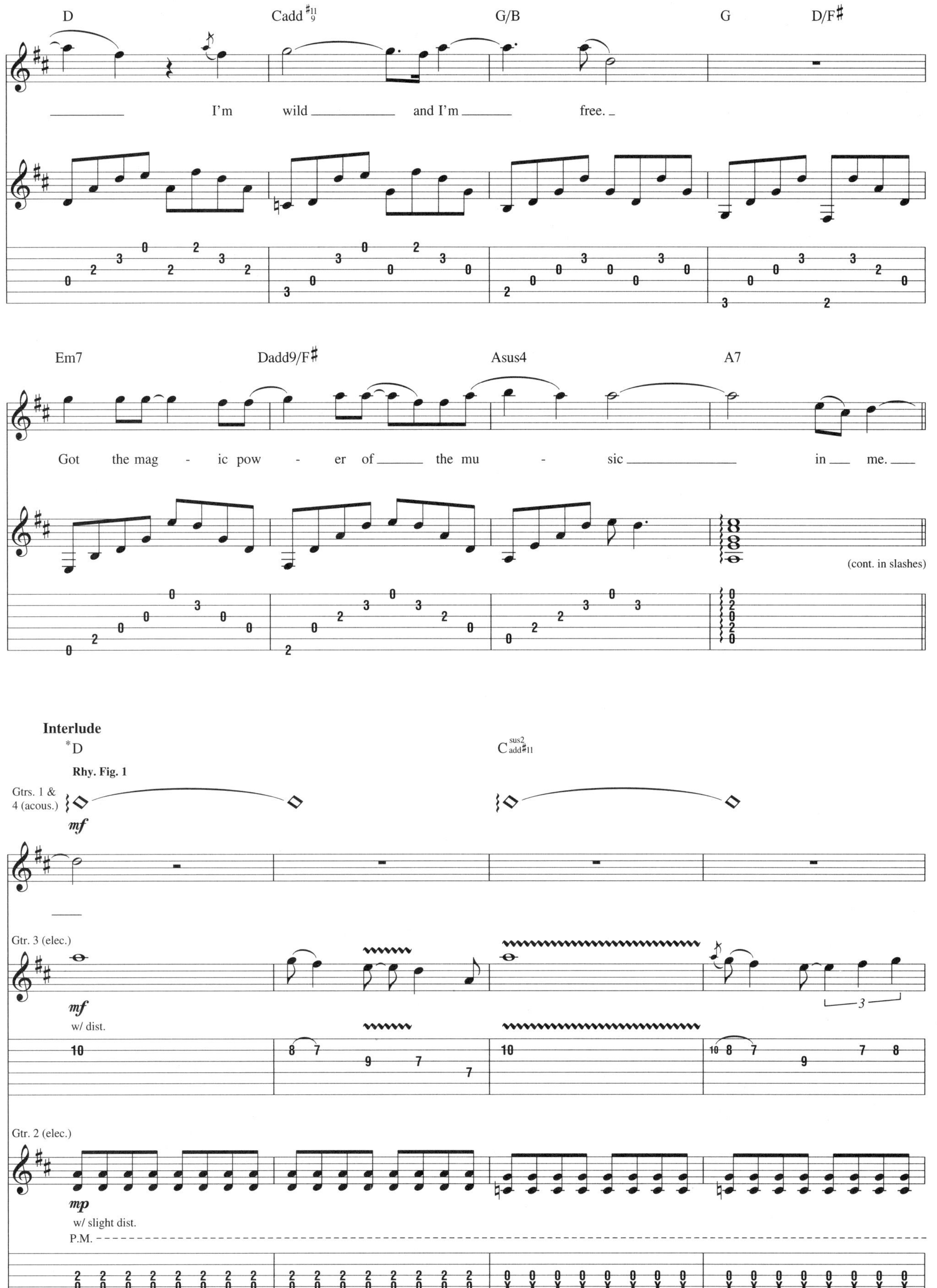

*See top of first page of song for chord diagrams pertaining to rhythm slashes.

Gmaj7/B
Csus2 add♯11
End Rhy. Fig. 1
2. She
P.M.
Verse
Gtrs. 1 & 4: w/ Rhy. Fig. 1
D
Gtr. 3 tacet
climbs in - to bed, she pulls the cov - ers o - ver - head and she turns
Gtr. 3
8va
Gtr. 2
her lit - tle ra - di - o on. She's

D
Csus2
Gtrs. 1 & 4
had a rot - ten day, so she hopes the D. J. is gon - na play
P.M.
Gmaj7/B
Cadd9
her fa - v'rite song.
P.M.
w/ dist.
Pre-Chorus
Gtrs. 1 & 4 tacet
A5
B5
C5
Makes her feel much bet - ter, brings her clos - er to her
Gtr. 2
Gtr. 5 (elec.)
w/ dist.
P.M.
P.M.
P.M.
P.M.
P.M.
P.M.
P.M.

G5
A5
B5
dreams. A lit - tle mag - ic pow - er makes it
P.M.
A5
Asus4
A
bet - ter than it seems. She's
*Gtrs. 2 & 5
*Composite arrangement
Chorus
D5
C5
G/B
G
D/F♯
young now, she's wild now, she wants to be free. She
Gtr. 5
Rhy. Fig. 2
P.M.
Gtr. 2
Riff B

Em
D/F♯
G
A5
gets the mag - ic pow - er of ___ the mu - sic from me. ___ She's
End Rhy. Fig. 2
P.M.
2 2 2 2 2 2 2 2
0 0 0 0 0 0 0 0
2 2 2 2 2 2 2 2
3 3 3 3 3 3 3 3
5 5 5 5 5 5 5 5
End Riff B
0
2
3
2
2
0
Gtr. 2: w/ Riff B (1st 4 meas.)
Gtr. 5: w/ Rhy. Fig. 2 (1st 4 meas.)
D5
C5
G/B
G
D/F♯
young now, __ she's wild now, __ she ___ wants to be free. ___ She
Em
D/F♯
Asus4
A N.C.
gets the mag - ic pow - er of ___ the mu - sic from _ me. __
Gtr. 5
P.M.
Gtr. 2

Interlude

Gtrs. 2 & 5 tacet
D
F/D
G/D
Gtr. 3
loco
mf
let ring
let ring
Gtr. 1
*Gtr. 6 (elec.)
*Gtr. 7 (elec.)
divisi
*w/ dist., played mf.
Gtr. 8 (elec.)
mp
w/ dist.

Bridge
B♭/D
C/D
D
You're think - in' it o - ver, but you just
8va

Gtrs. 3, 6, 7 & 8 tacet
F/D
G/D
can't sort it out. Do you want some - one to tell
Gtr. 1
B♭/D
C/D
you what they think it's all a - bout? Are you the one
D
F/D
and on - ly who's sad and lone - ly? You're reach - in' for the top.
G/D
Well, the mu - sic keeps you go - in' and it's nev -

F/D
G/D
A/D
- er gon - na stop. It's nev - er gon - na stop. It's
Gtr. 1
Gtr. 2
p
P.M.
B♭/D
C/D
nev - er gon - na, nev - er gon - na, nev - er gon - na, nev - er gon - na
Gtrs. 1 & 4
Gtr. 3
f
Gtr. 2
P.M.

Guitar Solo
D
Cadd9
G5
stop!
*Gtrs. 1, 2 & 4
Rhy. Fig. 3
End Rhy. Fig. 3
*Composite arrangement
Gtr. 3
Gtr. 5
Rhy. Fig. 3A
End Rhy. Fig. 3A
P.M.
Gtrs. 1, 2 & 4: w/ Rhy. Fig. 3 (3 times)
Gtr. 5: w/ Rhy. Fig. 3A (3 times)
3.The

Verse

D Cadd9

Rhy. Fig. 4

Gtrs. 1 & 4

world is full of com - pro - mise, the in - fi - nite red tape. But the mu-

Gtr. 3

Gtrs. 2 & 5 Rhy. Fig. 5

End Rhy. Fig. 5

P.M.

G/B Cadd9

End Rhy. Fig. 4

- sic's got the mag - ic, it's your one chance for es - cape.

8va

P.M.

*Composite arrangement

Chorus
Gtr. 2: w/ Riff B (1 1/2 times)
Gtr. 3 tacet
Gtr. 5: w/ Rhy. Fig. 2 (1 3/4 times)
D
C5
G/B
G
D/F♯
young now, I'm wild now, I want to be free. I
Gtrs. 1 & 4
Rhy. Fig. 7
Em
D/F♯
G
A7sus4
A7
got the mag - ic pow - er of the mu - sic in me. I'm
End Rhy. Fig. 7
Gtrs. 1 & 4: w/ Rhy. Fig. 7
D
C5
G/B
G
D/F♯
young now, I'm wild, and I'm free. I
Em
D/F♯
Asus4
got the mag - ic pow - er of the mu - sic,
Gtr. 2
*Gtrs. 1, 2, 4 & 5
*Composite arrangement

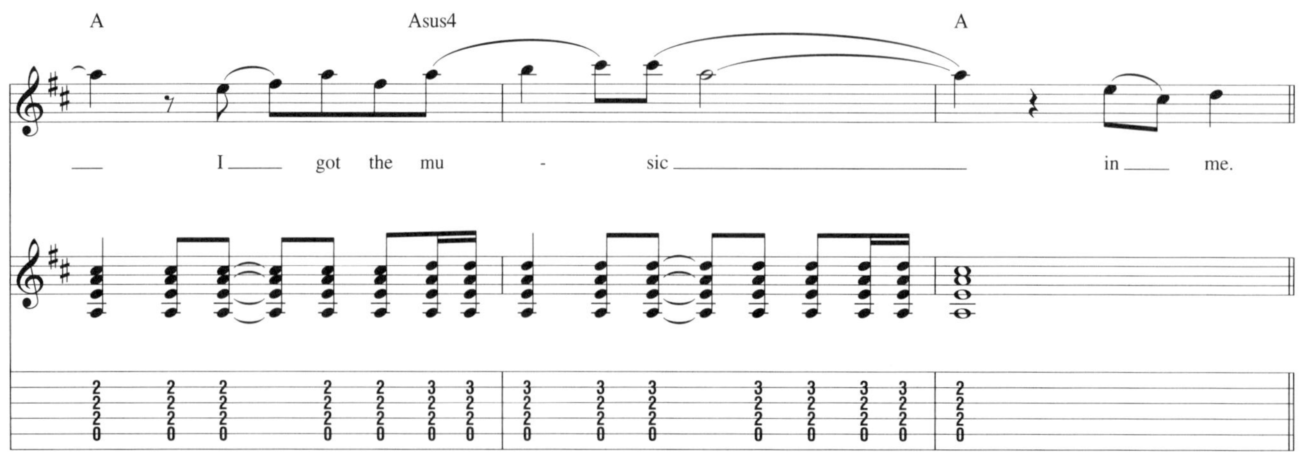
A
Asus4
A
I got the mu - sic in me.

Outro

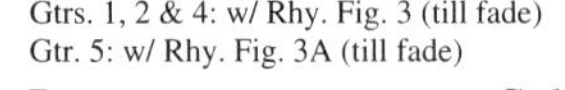
Gtrs. 1, 2 & 4: w/ Rhy. Fig. 3 (till fade)
Gtr. 5: w/ Rhy. Fig. 3A (till fade)

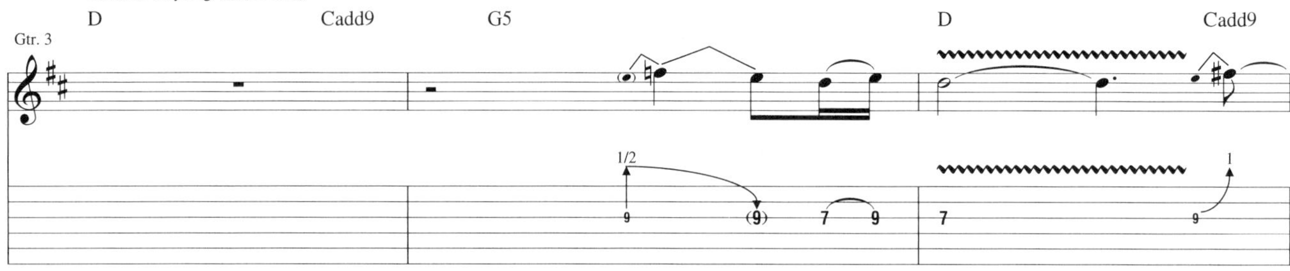
D
Cadd9
G5
D
Cadd9
Gtr. 3

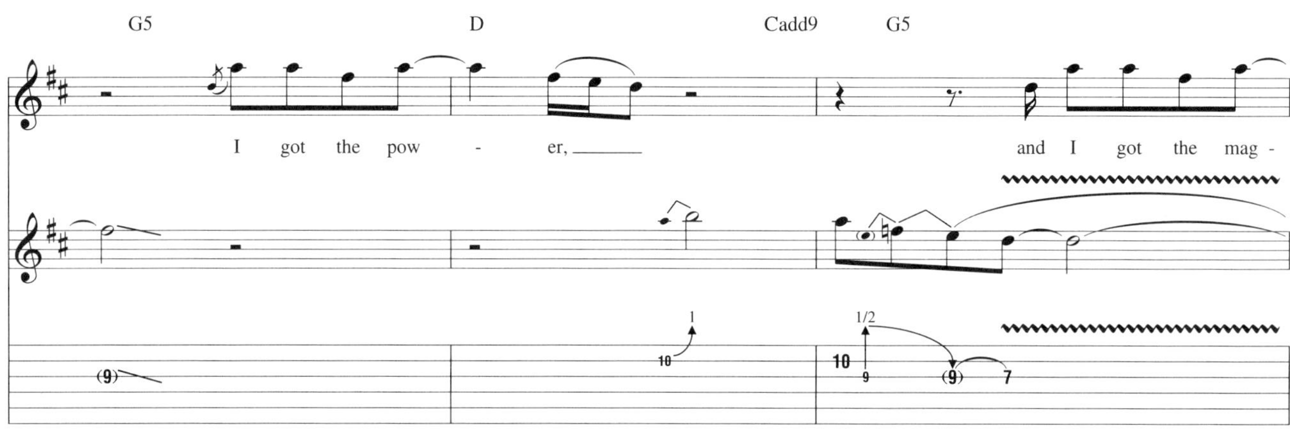
G5
D
Cadd9
G5
I got the pow - er, and I got the mag -

D
Cadd9
G5
D
Cadd9
- ic. She's got the pow - er,

G5
D
Cadd9
she's got the mag - ic.
She's got the pow -
Begin fade
- er,
she's got the mag -
- ic.
You got the pow - er,
you got the mag - ic.
8va
Fade out

from Rainbow - *Ritchie Blackmore's Rainbow*

Man on the Silver Mountain

Words and Music by Ronnie James Dio and Richard Blackmore

F5
G5
F5
C5
in'. I'm the sun, the sun. I'll move, I can run. You'll
P.M.
Chorus
E♭5
C5
G5
Dm
nev - er stop me burn - in'. Get down with fi -
Riff B
let ring
P.M.
B♭
Dm
- re. Lift my spir - it high - er.
*F
B♭5
C5
Some - one's scream - ing my
End Riff B
Rhy. Fig. 1
P.M.
*Bass plays A.

Gtr. 1: w/ Riff A (1 3/4 times)
B♭5
G5
E♭5
C5
Gm7
name. Come and make me ho - ly a - gain.
End Rhy. Fig. 1
P.M.
let ring
C5
B♭5
Gm7
G5
F5
E♭5
I'm the man on the sil - ver moun - tain, yeah.
oh.
The man on the sil - ver moun - tain.
N.C.
Oh, oh, oh, oh. Oh!
Gtr. 1
Guitar Solo
*G5
semi - P.M.
*Chords implied by bass (next 16 bars).
F5

G5
E♭5
C5
D5
G5
8va
E♭5
C5
F5
8va
G5
8va
loco
E♭5
C5
G5
8va
A5

Outro-Chorus

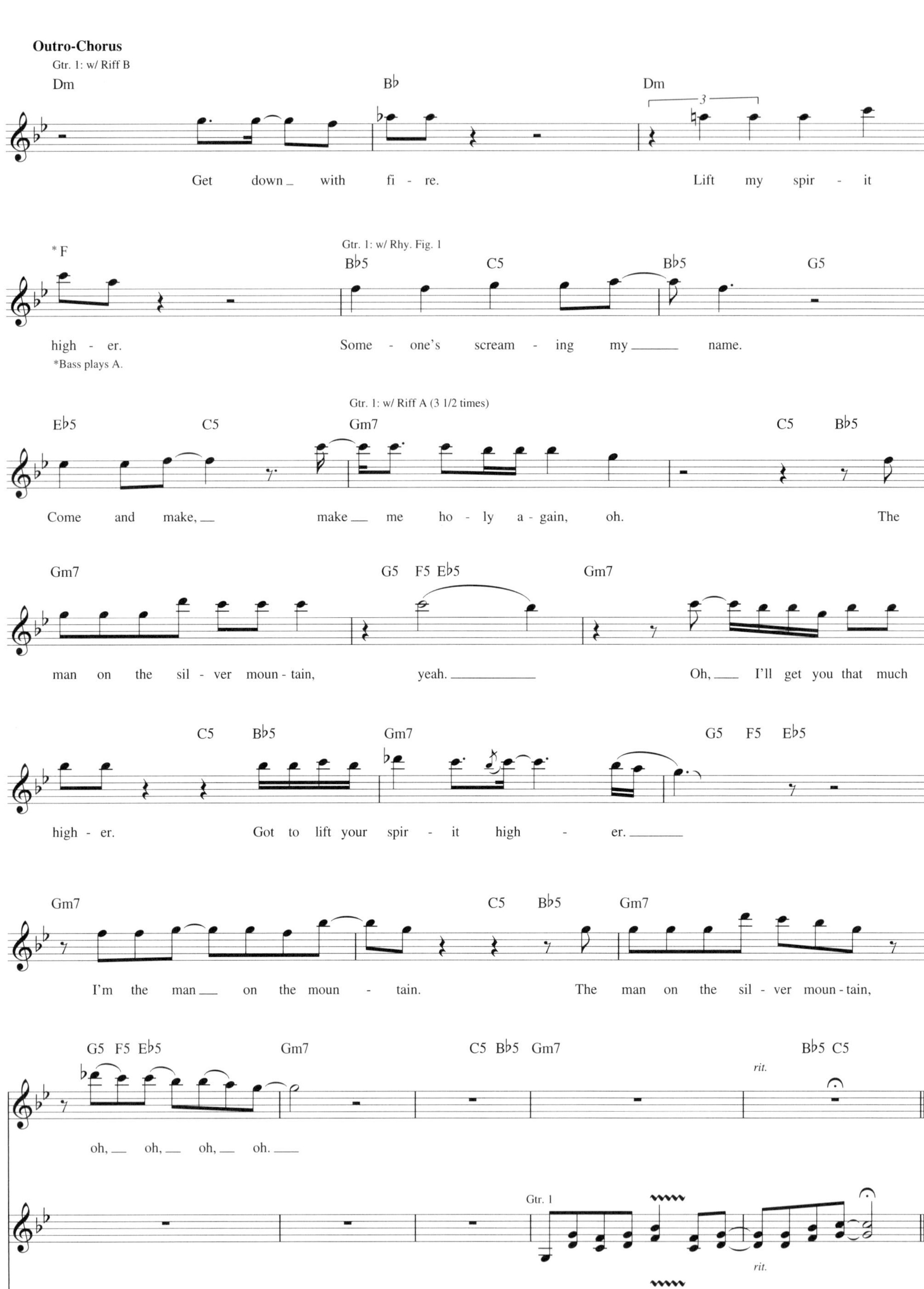

from Train - *Save Me, San Francisco*

Marry Me

Words and Music by Pat Monahan

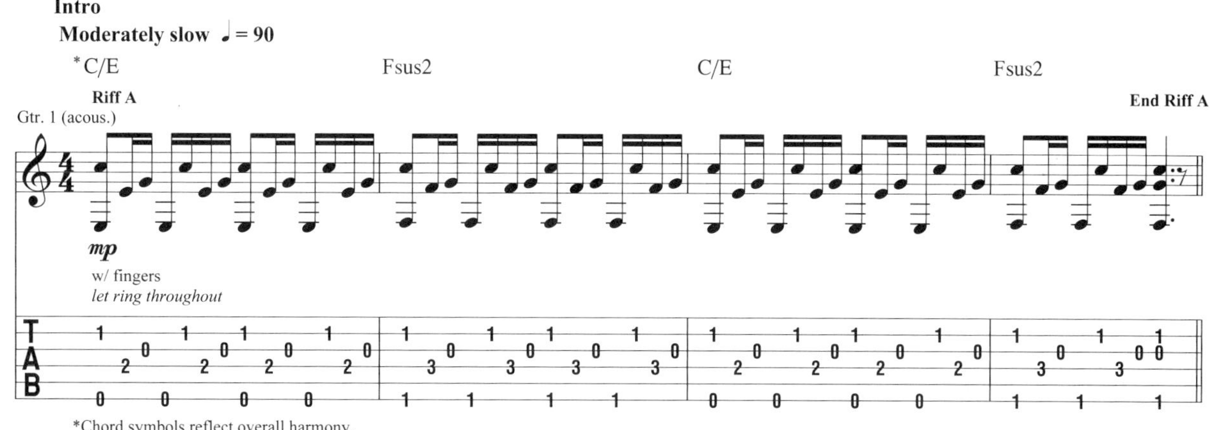

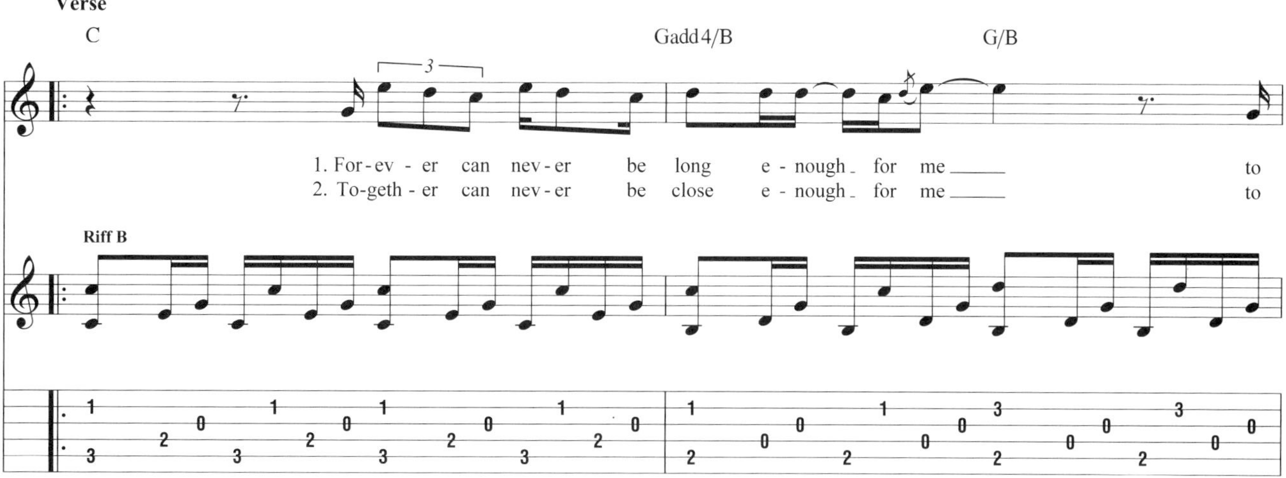

Gtr. 1: w/ Riff B
C Gadd4/B G/B Am7 Gsus4
For - get the world, now, we won't let them see. But there's one thing left
You wear white and I'll wear out the words, "I love you" and "You're
Fsus2
Gtr. 1: w/ Riff A
C/E Fsus2
to do. Now that the weight has lift - ed,
beau-ti - ful." Now that the wait is o - ver,
Chorus
Gtr. 1: w/ Riff B (2 times)
C/E Fsus2 C Gadd4/B G/B
love has sure - ly shift - ed my way. Mar - ry me
and love has fin -'ly shown her my way.
Am7 Gsus4 Fsus2 C
to - day and ev - 'ry day. Mar - ry
To Coda
Gadd4/B G/B Am7 Gsus4 Fsus2
me if I ev - er get the nerve to say hel - lo in this ca - fé. Say you will,
Gtr. 1: w/ Riff A
C/E Fsus2 C/E Fsus2
mm, say you will, mm.
Bridge
B♭6sus2 Fadd9/A
Prom - ise me you'll al - ways be
Gtr. 1
Riff C

C
Gadd4/B
G/B
hap - py by my side.
End Riff C
Gtr. 1: w/ Riff C
B♭6sus2
Fadd9/A
C
Gadd4/B
G/B
I prom-ise to sing to you when all the mu - sic dies.
D.S. al Coda
B♭6sus2
Fadd9/A
And
Gtr. 1
Coda
Gtr. 1: w/ Riff A (1st 2 meas., 2 times)
C/E
Fsus2
C/E
Fsus2
mm, say you will, mm. Mar - ry
C/E
Fsus2
me, mm.
Gtr. 1

from The Killers - *Hot Fuss*

Mr. Brightside

Words and Music by Brandon Flowers, Dave Keuning, Mark Stoermer and Ronnie Vannucci

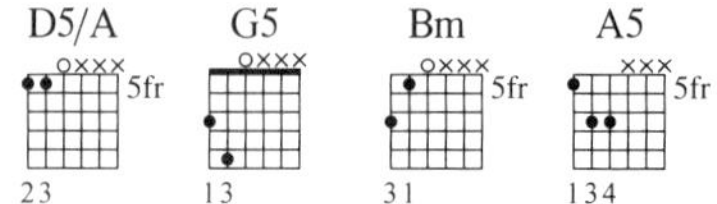

Tune down 1/2 step:
(low to high) E♭-A♭-D♭-G♭-B♭-E♭

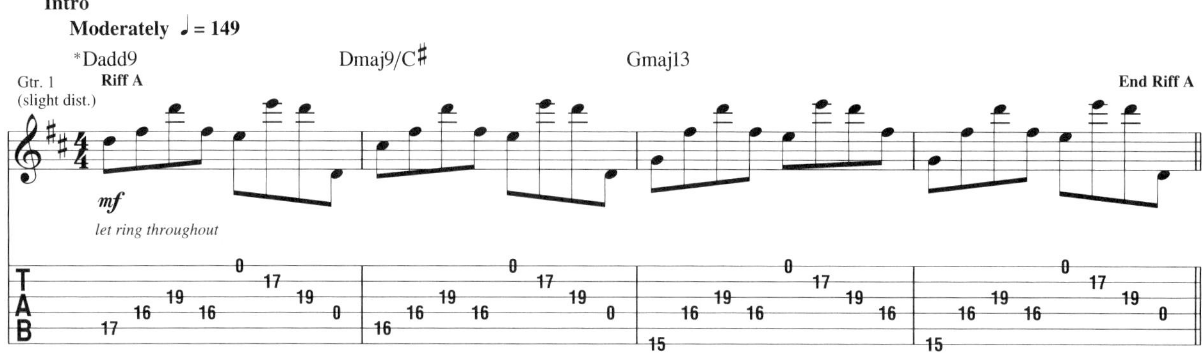

*Chord symbols reflect implied harmony.

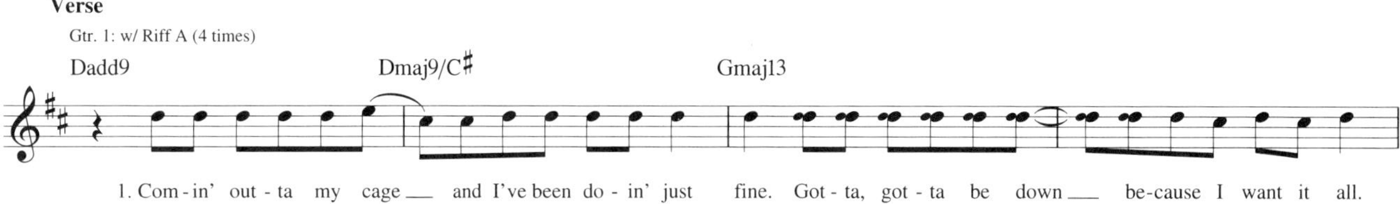

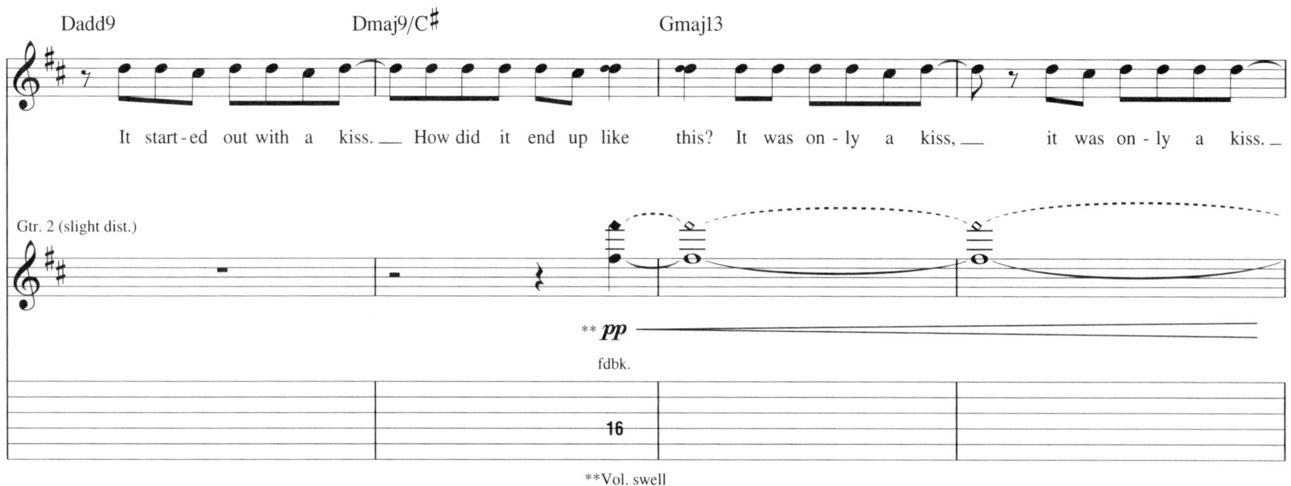

**Vol. swell

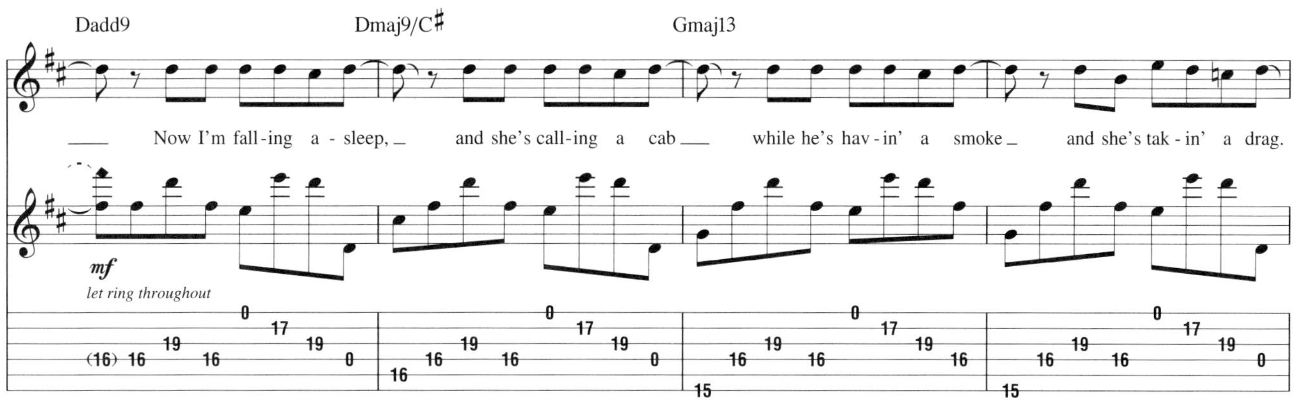

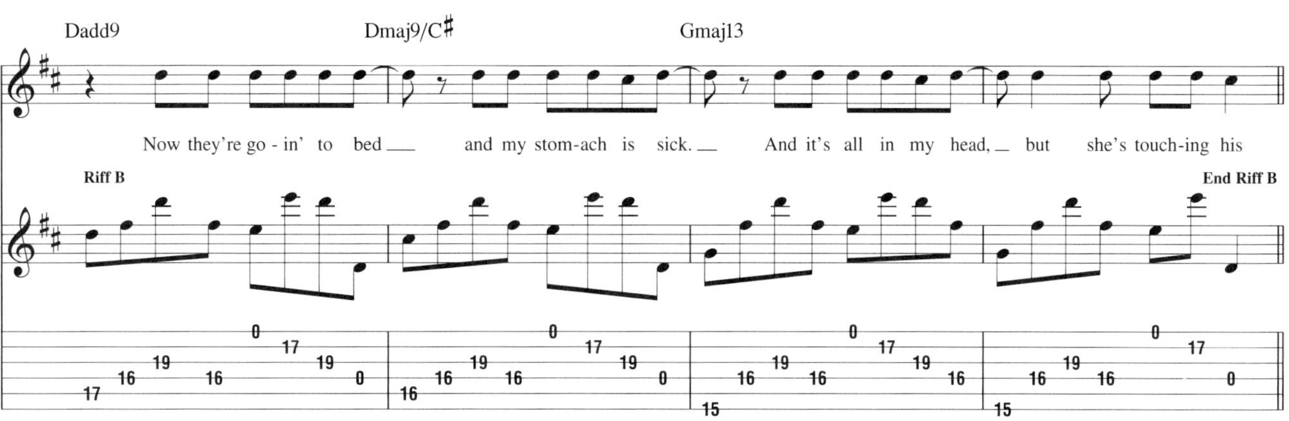

Pre-Chorus

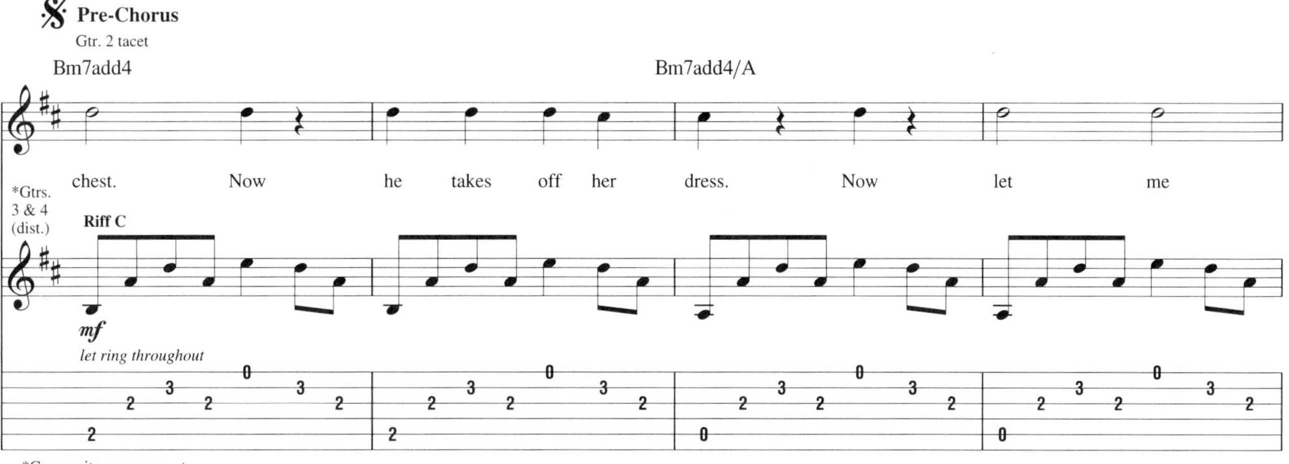

*Composite arrangement

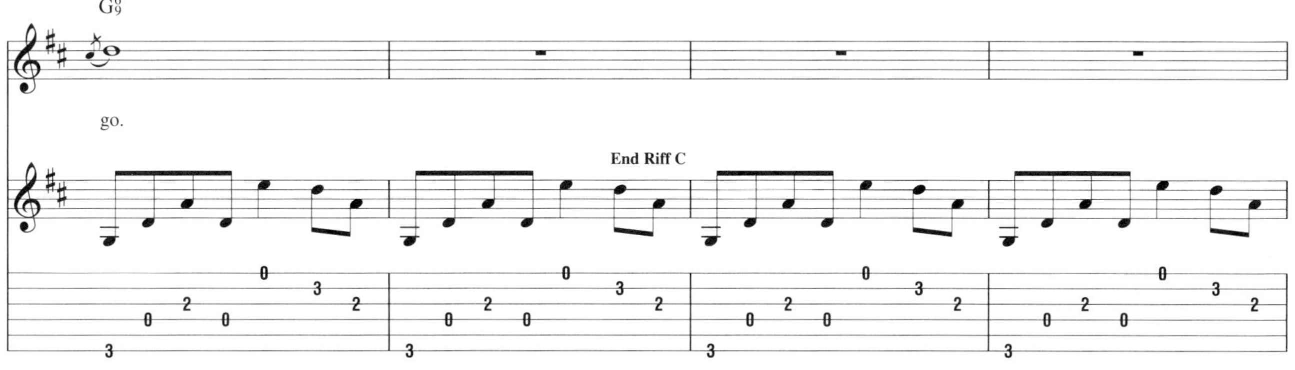

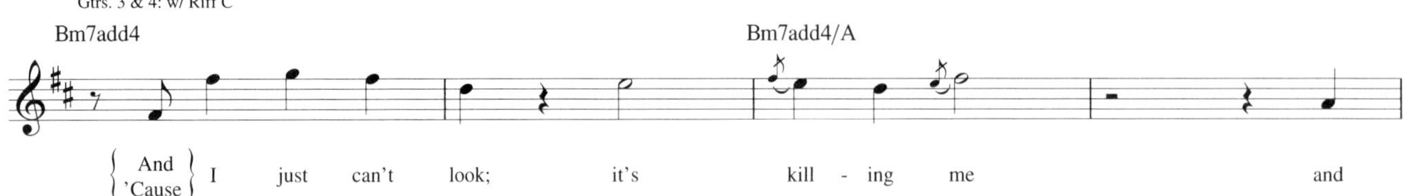

Gtrs. 3 & 4: w/ Riff C
Bm7add4
Bm7add4/A
And
'Cause
I just can't look; it's kill - ing me and

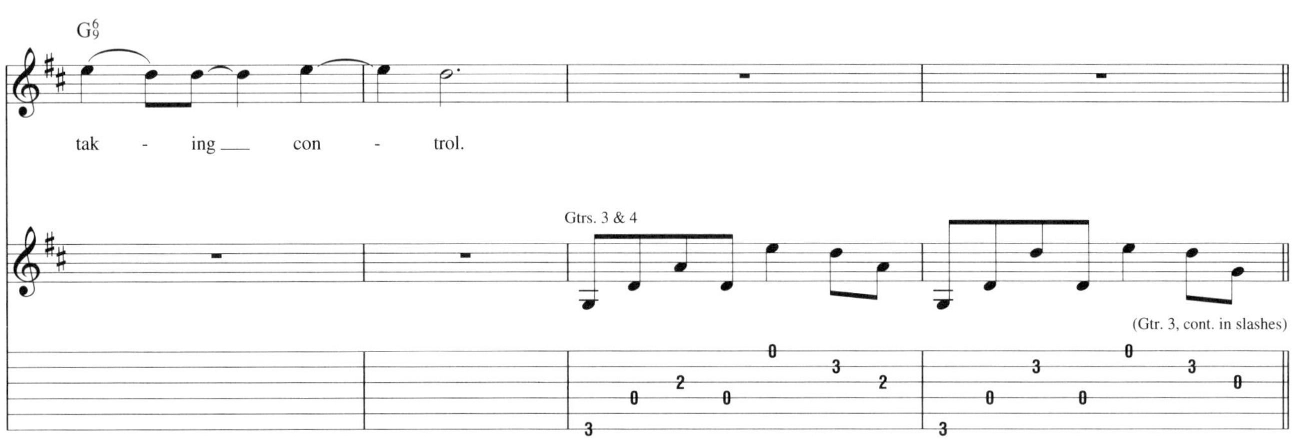

G6/9
tak - ing con - trol.
Gtrs. 3 & 4
(Gtr. 3, cont. in slashes)

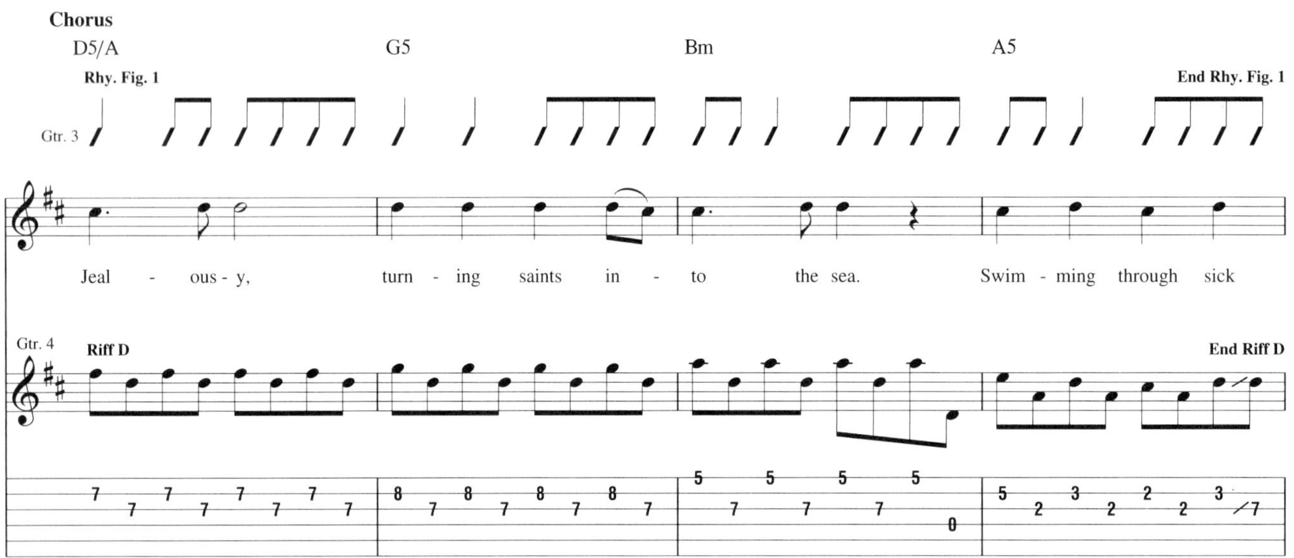

Chorus
D5/A
G5
Bm
A5
Rhy. Fig. 1
End Rhy. Fig. 1
Gtr. 3
Jeal - ous - y, turn - ing saints in - to the sea. Swim - ming through sick
Gtr. 4
Riff D
End Riff D

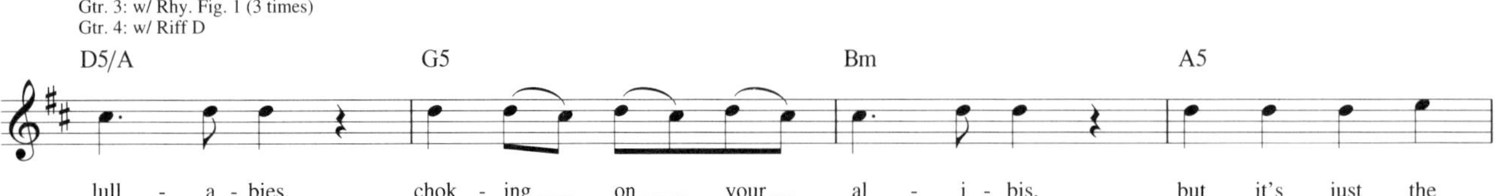

Gtr. 3: w/ Rhy. Fig. 1 (3 times)
Gtr. 4: w/ Riff D
D5/A
G5
Bm
A5
lull - a - bies, chok - ing on your al - i - bis, but it's just the

D5/A
G5
Bm
A5
price I pay. Des - ti - ny is call - ing me. O - pen up my
Gtr. 5 (dist.)
mf
Gtr. 4
Riff E
End Riff E

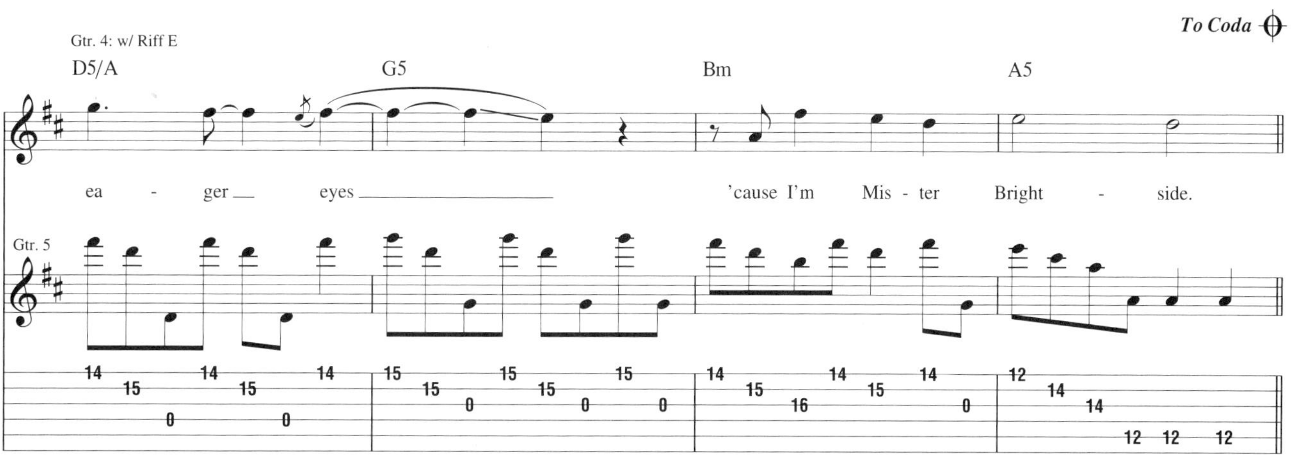
Gtr. 4: w/ Riff E
To Coda
D5/A
G5
Bm
A5
ea - ger eyes 'cause I'm Mis - ter Bright - side.
Gtr. 5

Interlude

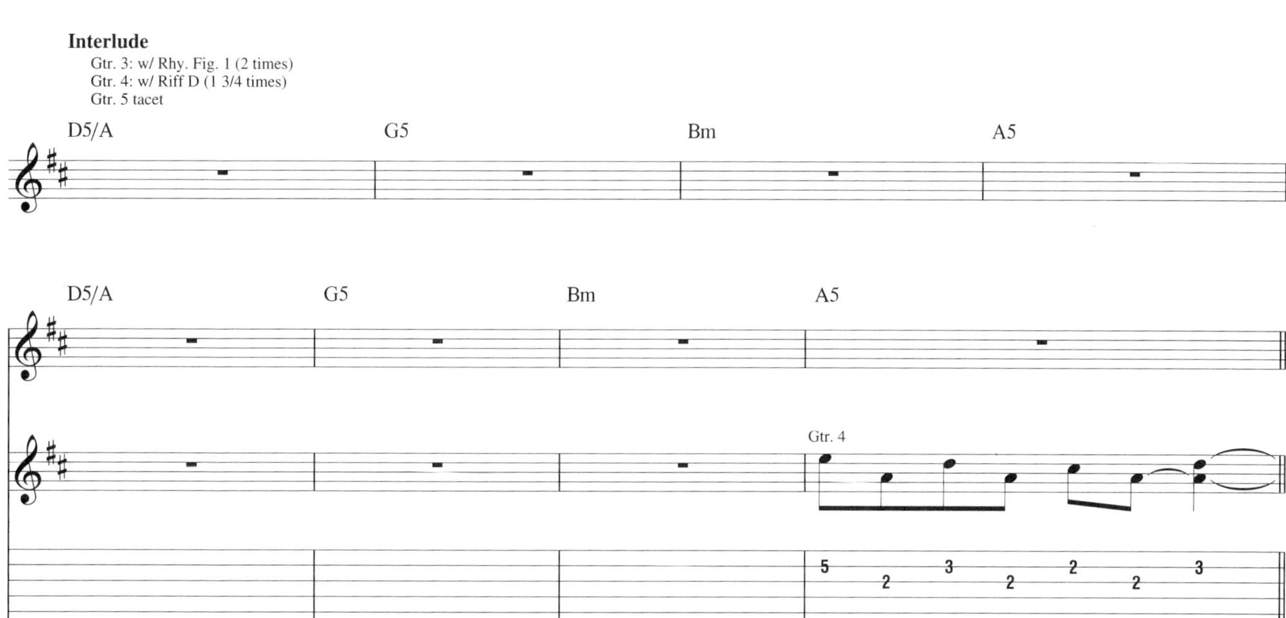
Gtr. 3: w/ Rhy. Fig. 1 (2 times)
Gtr. 4: w/ Riff D (1 3/4 times)
Gtr. 5 tacet
D5/A
G5
Bm
A5
Gtr. 4

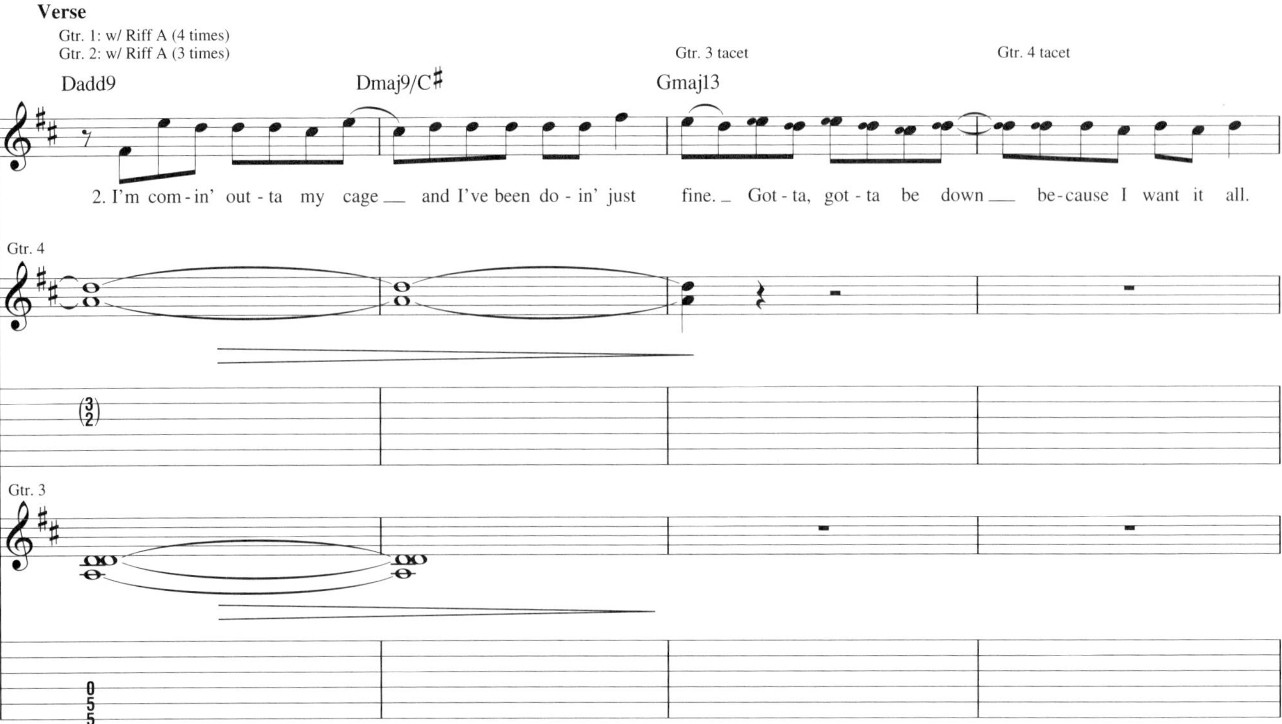
Verse
Gtr. 1: w/ Riff A (4 times)
Gtr. 2: w/ Riff A (3 times)
Gtr. 3 tacet
Gtr. 4 tacet
Dadd9
Dmaj9/C♯
Gmaj13
2. I'm com-in' out-ta my cage ___ and I've been do-in' just fine. _ Got-ta, got-ta be down ___ be-cause I want it all.
Gtr. 4
Gtr. 3

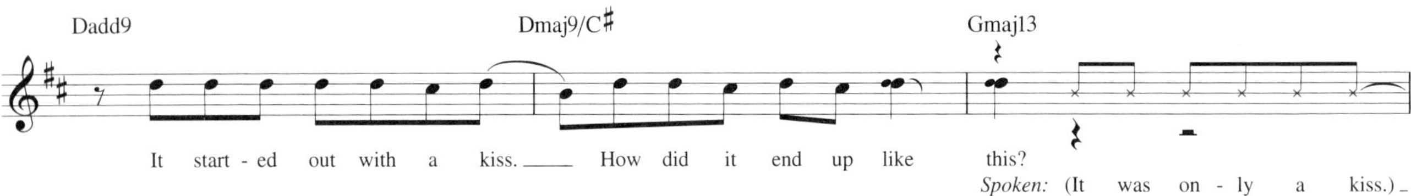
Dadd9
Dmaj9/C♯
Gmaj13
It start-ed out with a kiss. ___ How did it end up like this?
Spoken: (It was on-ly a kiss.) _

Dadd9
Dmaj9/C♯
It was on-ly a kiss. ___ Now I'm fall-ing a-sleep, ___ and she's call-ing a cab ___

Gmaj13
Gtr. 2: w/ Riff B
Dadd9
___ while he's hav-in' a smoke ___ and she's tak-in' a drag. ___ Now they're go-in' to bed _

D.S. al Coda
Dmaj9/C♯
Gmaj13
___ and my stom-ach is sick. ___ And it's all in my head, ___ but she's touch-ing his

Coda
Interlude
D
G/D
Bm
A
Gtr. 5
Gtr. 4
Riff F
End Riff F
Gtr. 4: w/ Riff F
Outro
Gtr. 3: w/ Rhy. Fig. 1 (3 3/4 times)
Gtr. 4: w/ Riff D (3 3/4 times)
D5/A
G5
A5
1.
2.
nev - er,
I
Asus4
nev - er.
Gtr. 3

from Guns N' Roses - *Appetite for Destruction*

Mr. Brownstone

Words and Music by W. Axl Rose, Slash, Izzy Stradlin', Duff McKagan and Steven Adler

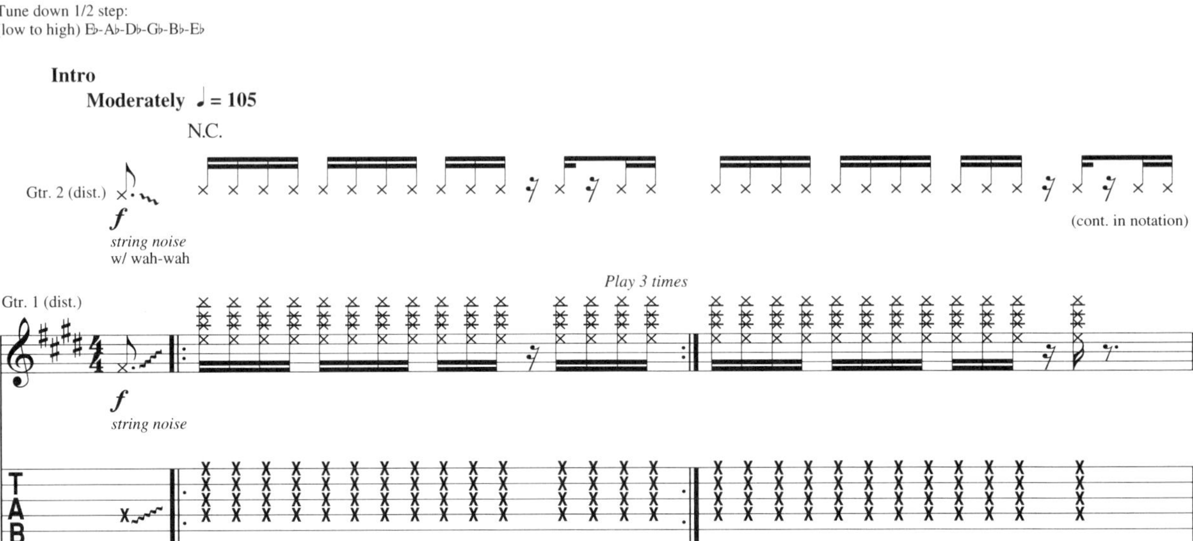

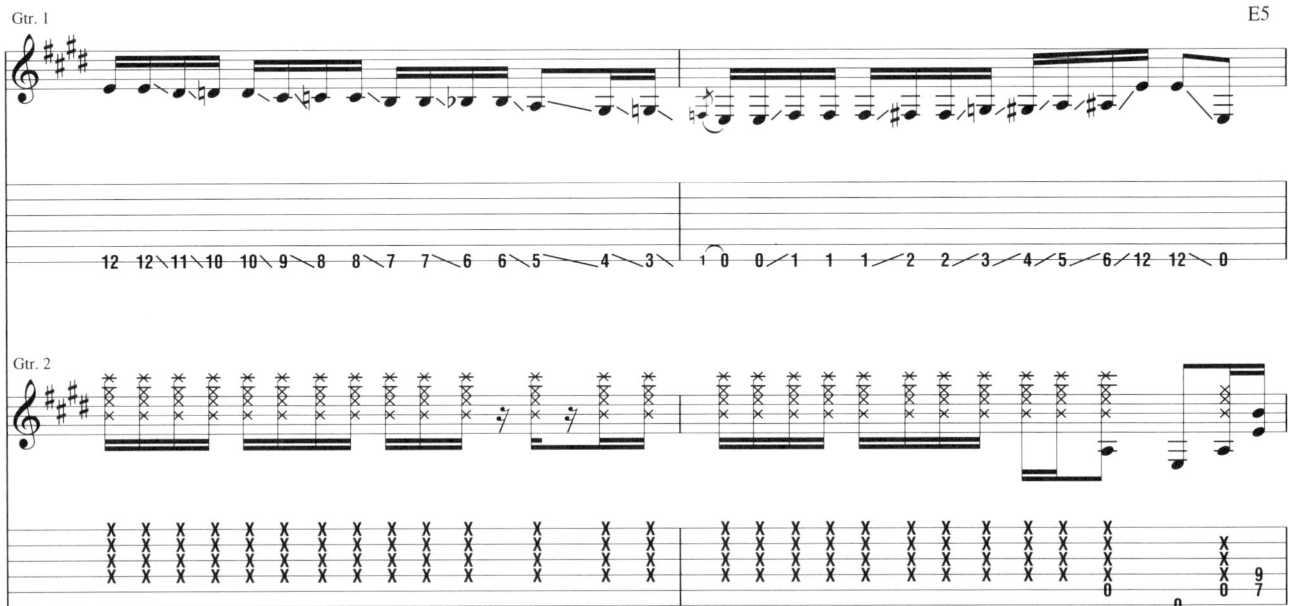

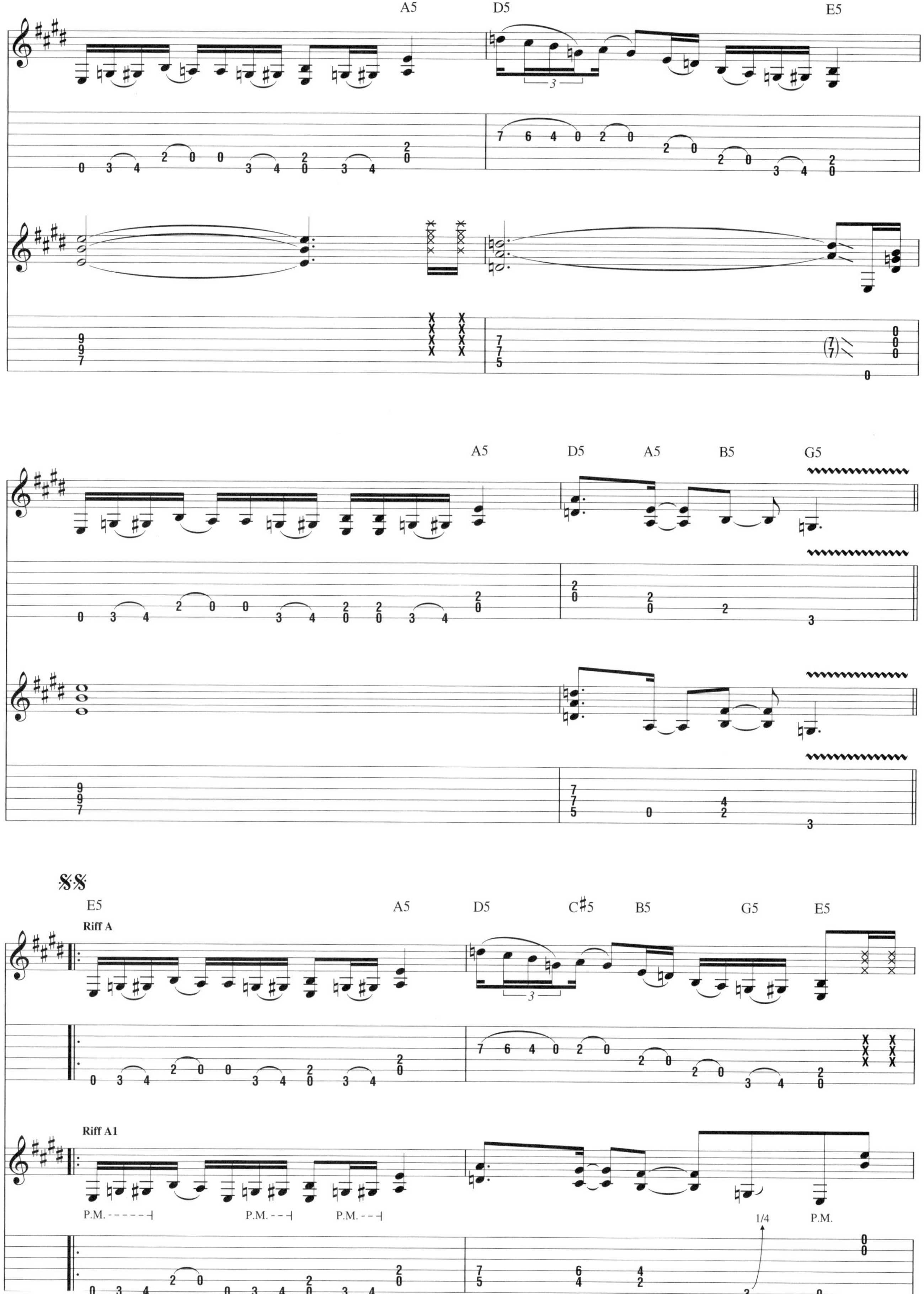
A5
D5
E5
A5
D5
A5
B5
G5
E5
Riff A
A5
D5
C♯5
B5
G5
E5
Riff A1
P.M.
P.M.
P.M.
1/4
P.M.

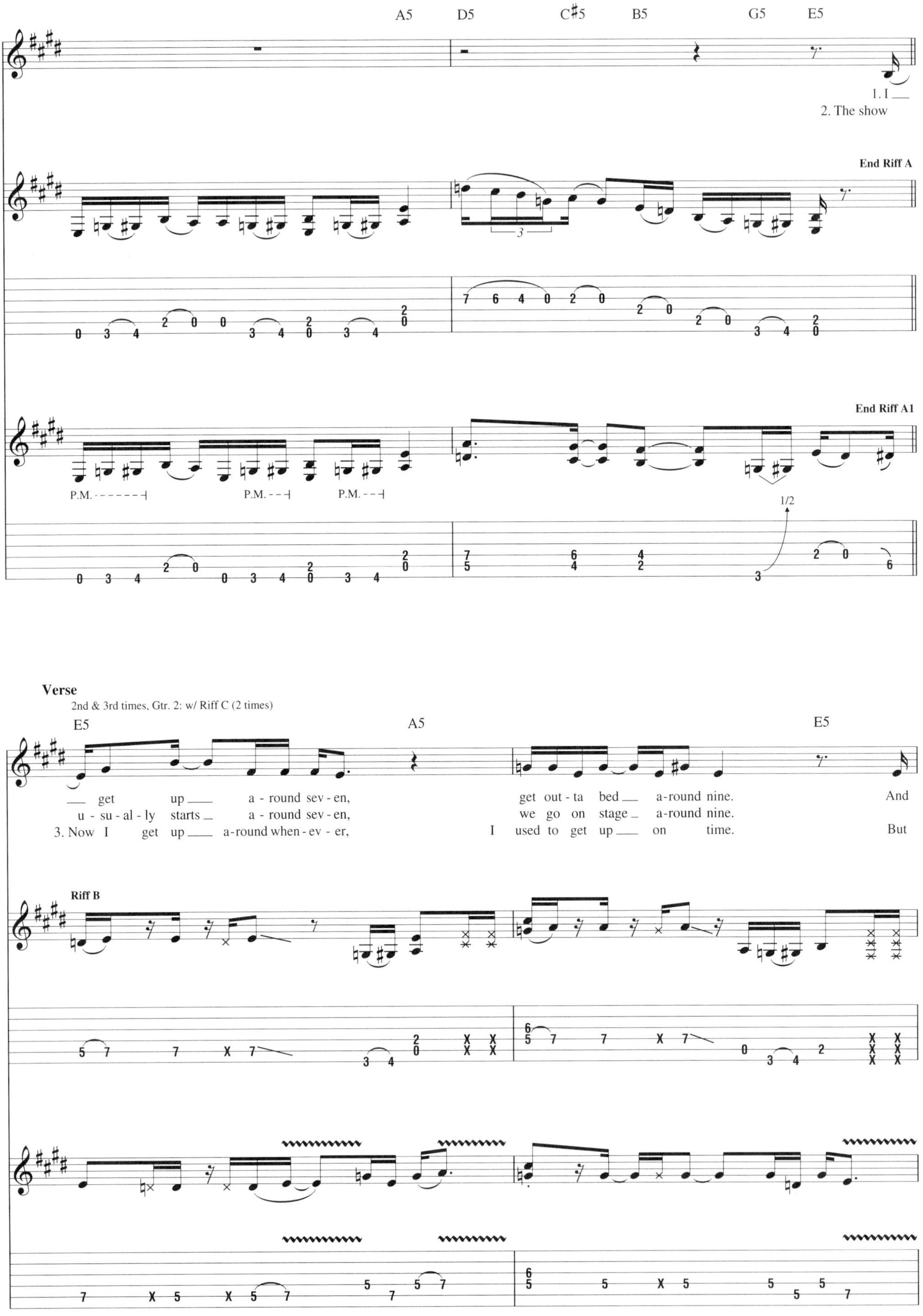

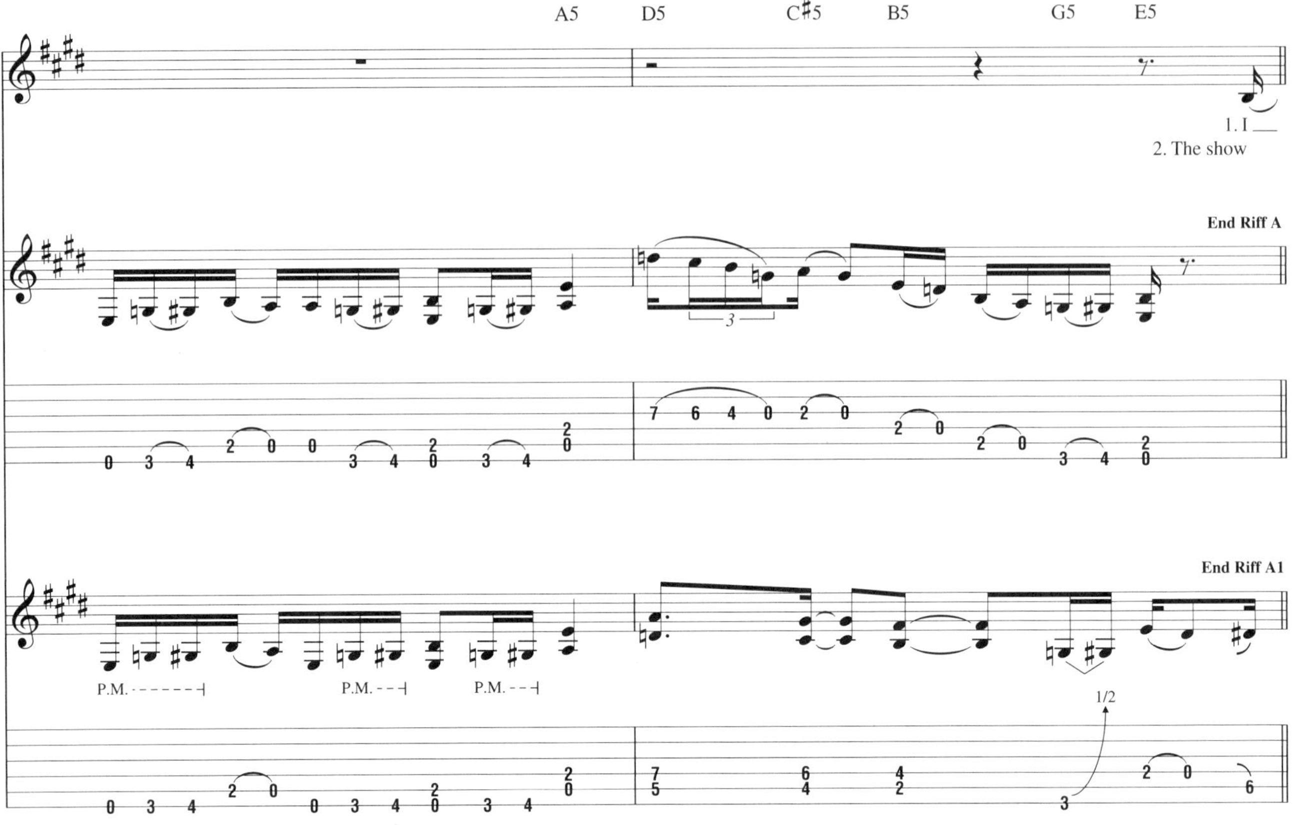

A5 D5 C♯5 B5 G5 E5
1. I
2. The show
End Riff A
End Riff A1
P.M.
1/2
Verse
2nd & 3rd times, Gtr. 2: w/ Riff C (2 times)
E5 A5 E5
get up a - round sev - en, get out - ta bed a - round nine. And
u - su - al - ly starts a - round sev - en, we go on stage a - round nine.
3. Now I get up a - round when - ev - er, I used to get up on time. But
Riff B

3rd time, To Coda 2
A5
G5
E5
I don't wor - ry a-bout noth-in', no, be-cause wor-ry-in's a waste of my time.
Get on the bus a - bout e-lev-en, sip - pin' a drink and feel - in' fine.
that old man, he's a real muth-a-f**k-er, gon-na kick him on down the line. I
End Riff B
Riff C
End Riff C
Chorus
G5 F5 G5 C5 B♭5 C5 D C D
We've been danc - in' with Mis - ter Brown - stone. He's been knock - in'.
Rhy. Fig. 1
*Gtrs. 1 & 2
End Rhy. Fig. 1
*Composite arrangement. Gtr. 2: wah-wah off
To Coda 3
E5
He won't leave me a - lone.
Gtr. 1
1/2
Gtr. 2
w/ wah-wah

To Coda 1
N.C.
No, no, no. He won't leave me a-lone. I
Riff D
End Riff D
1/2
Riff D1
End Riff D1
Bridge
B5 A5 B5 A5 G5 A5
used ta do a lit-tle, but a lit-tle would-n't do, and so the lit-tle got more and more. I
Rhy. Fig. 2
End Rhy. Fig. 2
Rhy. Fig. 2A
End Rhy. Fig. 2A
1st time, Gtr. 2: w/ Rhy. Fig. 2A
2nd time, Gtr. 2: w/ Rhy. Fig. 2A (1st meas.)
1.
B5 A5 B5 A5 G5 A5
just keep try-in' ta get a lit-tle bet-ter, said a lit-tle bet-ter than be-fore. I
Gtr. 1

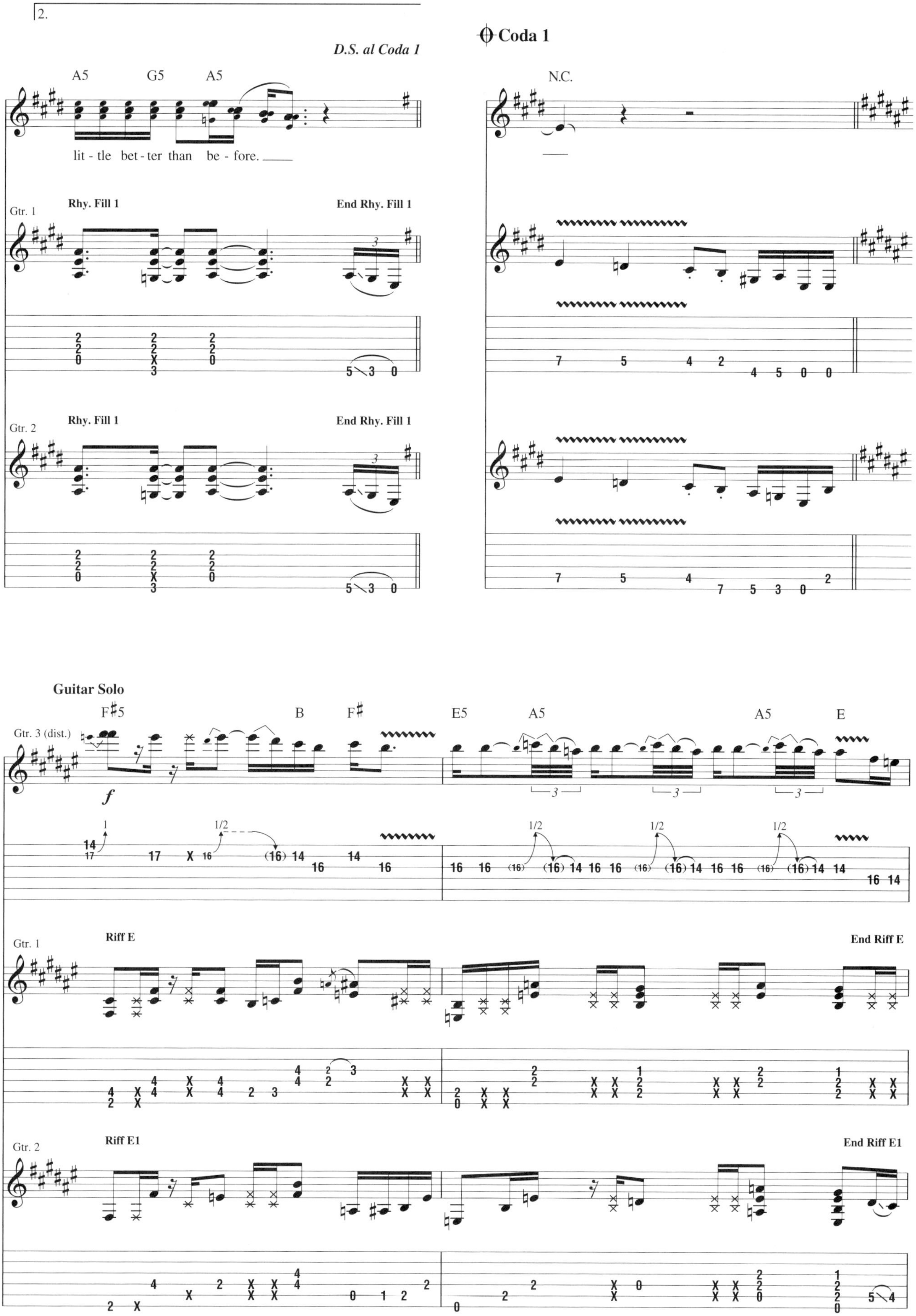

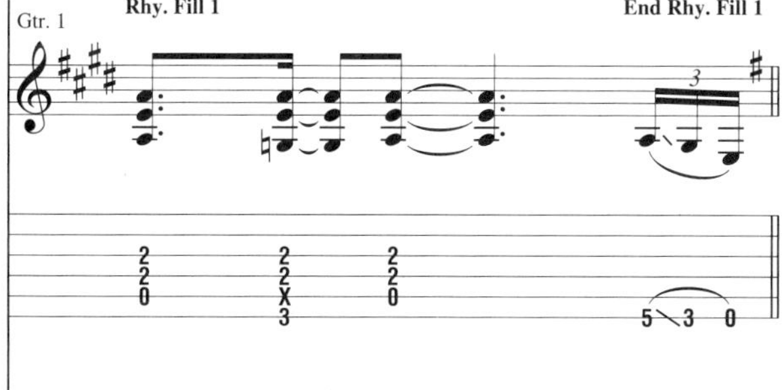

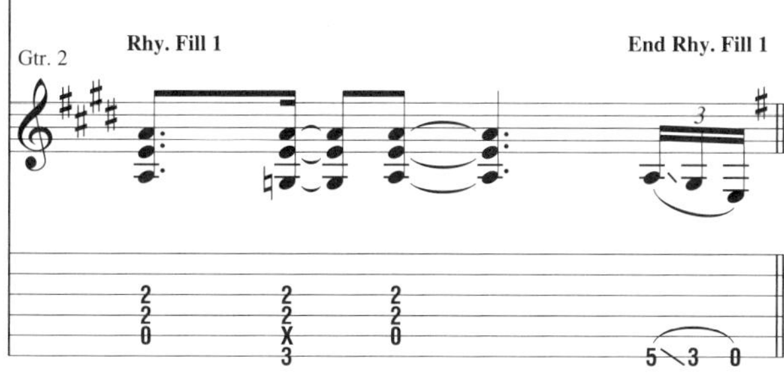

Guitar Solo

F♯5 B F♯ E5 A5 A5 E

Gtr. 3 (dist.)

f

Gtr. 1

Riff E

End Riff E

Gtr. 2

Riff E1

End Riff E1

Gtrs. 1 & 2: w/ Riffs E & E1 (2 1/2 times)
F♯5
B
F♯
E5
A5
A5
E
F♯5
B
F♯
Gtr. 3
8va
Gtr. 4
(dist.)
divisi
w/ heavy reverb
*Gtr. 3 to left of slash in tab.
Gtr. 4 tacet
E5
A5
E
A5
E
F♯5
B
F♯
loco
E5
D5
E5
Gtr. 3 tacet
G5
F5
G5
w/ wah-wah as filter
let ring
Gtrs. 1 & 2
C5
B♭5
C5
D5
C5
D5

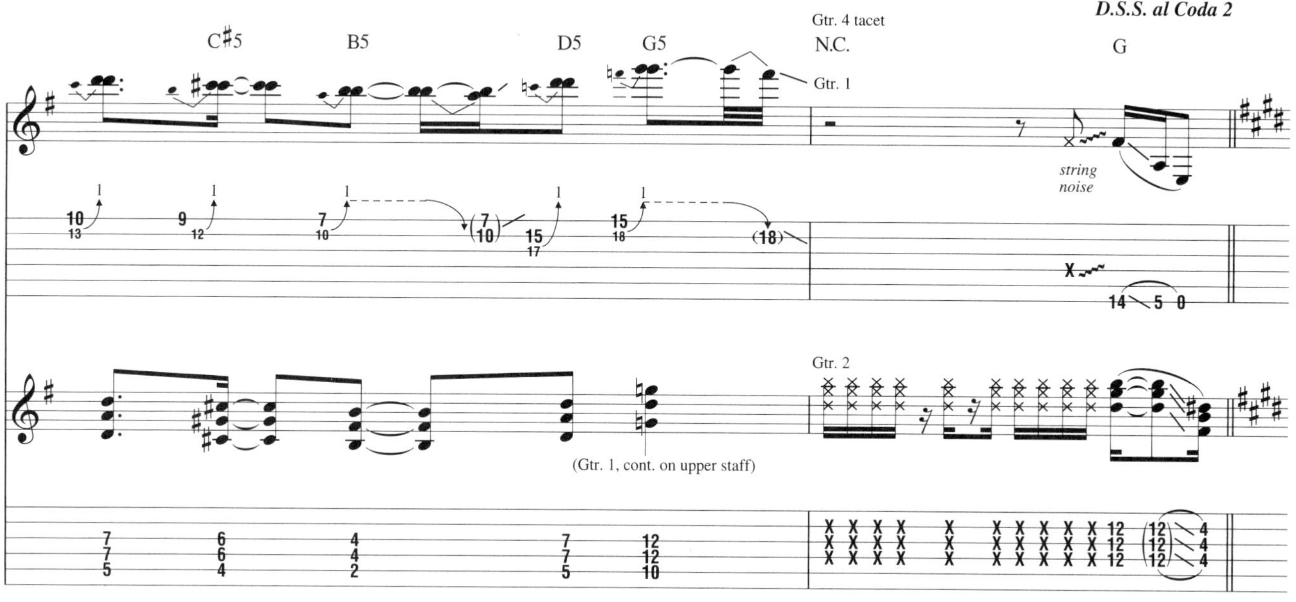

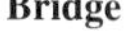

Bridge

Interlude

Outro
E5
Stuck it in the mid-dle, and I shot it in the mid-dle, and it, it drove me out-ta my mind. I
A5
Gtr. 1
P.M.
P.H.
Pitch: C♯
Gtr. 2
wah-wah off
P.M.
D5
should-'ve known bet-ter, said I wish I nev-er met her, said I, I leave it all be - hind.
E
Gtrs. 1 & 2
(Gtr. 1, cont. in slashes)
1/2
Free time
Gtr. 1
Yow - sa!
Gtr. 2

from Ozzy Osbourne - *Blizzard of Ozz*

Mr. Crowley

Words and Music by Ozzy Osbourne, Randy Rhoads and Bob Daisley

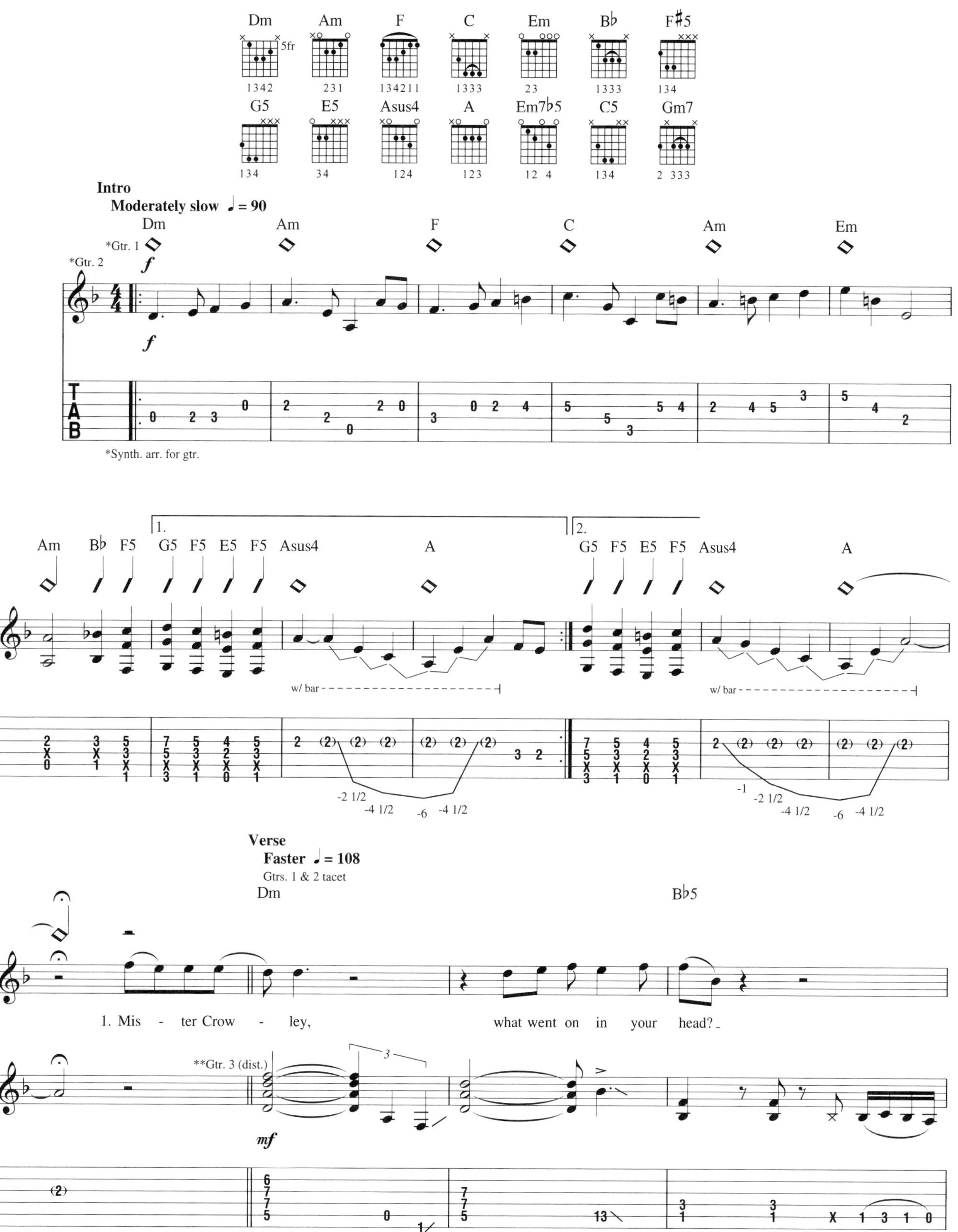

Dm
B♭5
Oh, _ Mis-ter Crow - ley,
did you talk with the dead? _
Your
P.S.
P.M.
1/4

C5
F
D5
life style to me _ seemed so trag - ic.
With the thrill of it all
you
P.M.

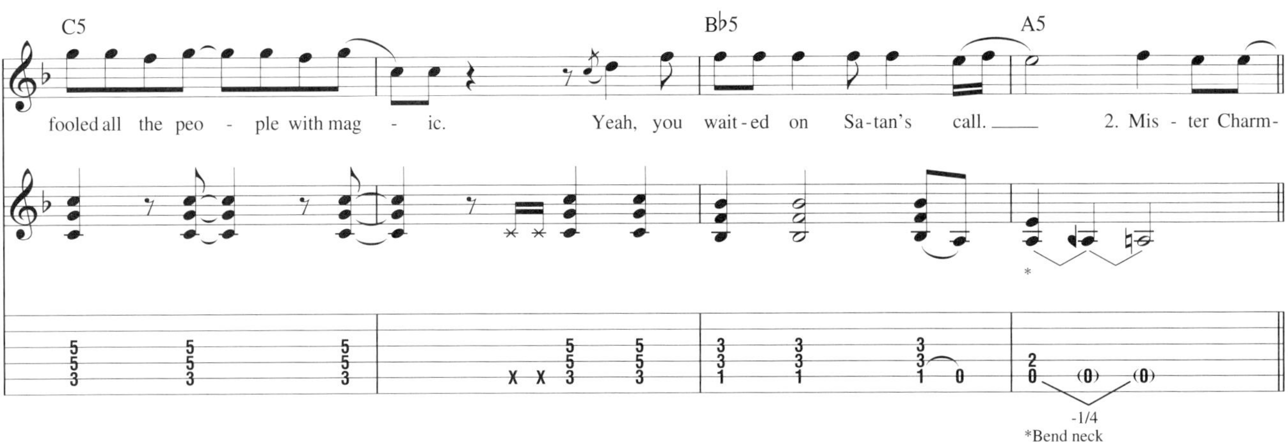
C5
B♭5
A5
fooled all the peo - ple with mag - ic.
Yeah, you wait-ed on Sa-tan's call. _
2. Mis - ter Charm-
-1/4
*Bend neck

Verse
Dm
B♭5
- ing,
did you think you were pure? _
Mis - ter A-larm -
P.M.
1/4

Dm
B♭5
- ing, in noc-tur-nal rap - port. Un -
P.S.
P.M.
P.M.

C5
F
D5
cov-er-ing things that were sa - cred, man - i - fest on this earth. Ah, con -
P.M.

C5
B♭5
A
ceived in the eye of a se - cret and they scat-tered the af - ter - birth.
P.M.
w/ bar
(cont. in slashes)

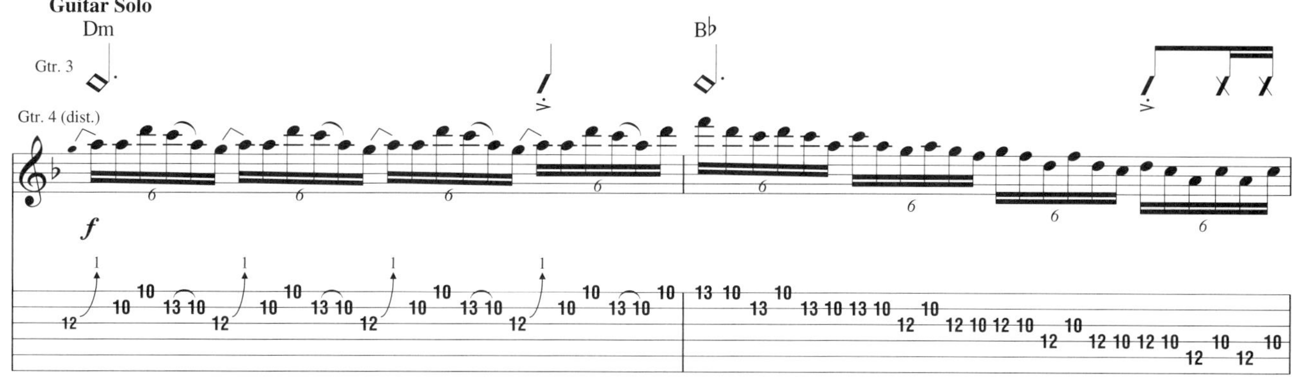
Guitar Solo
Dm
B♭
Gtr. 3
Gtr. 4 (dist.)

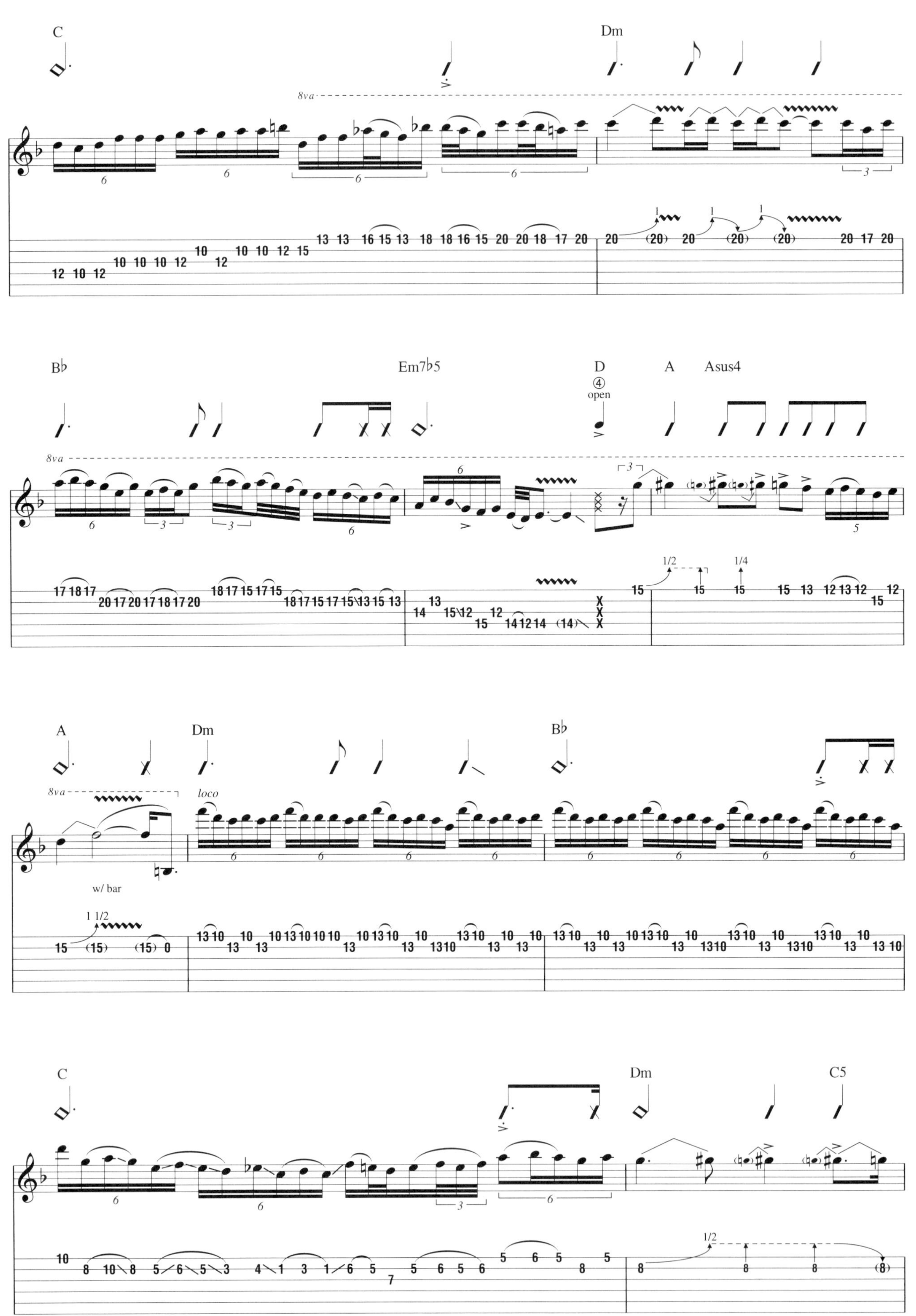
C
Dm
8va
B♭
Em7♭5
D
④ open
A
Asus4
A
Dm
B♭
8va
loco
w/ bar
C
Dm
C5

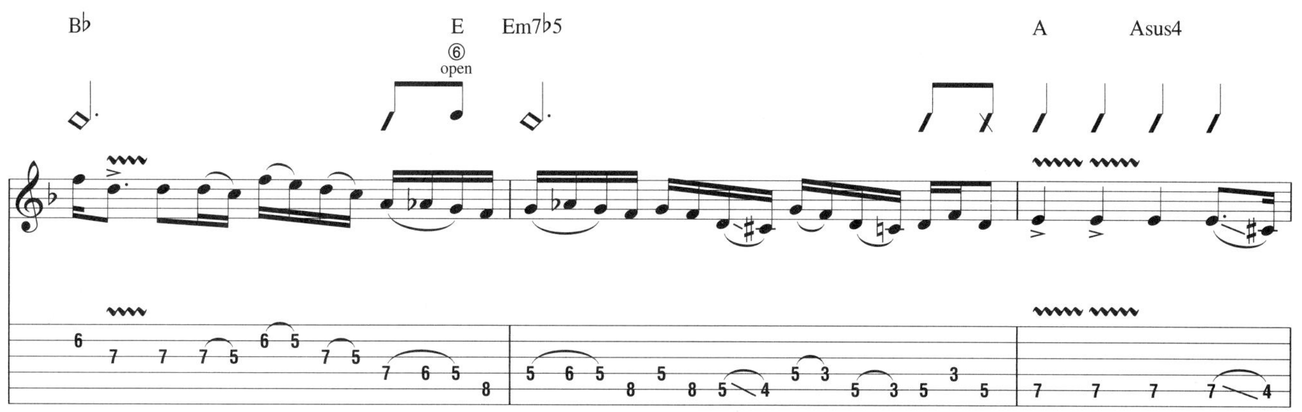
B♭
E
⑥ open
Em7♭5
A
Asus4

Verse

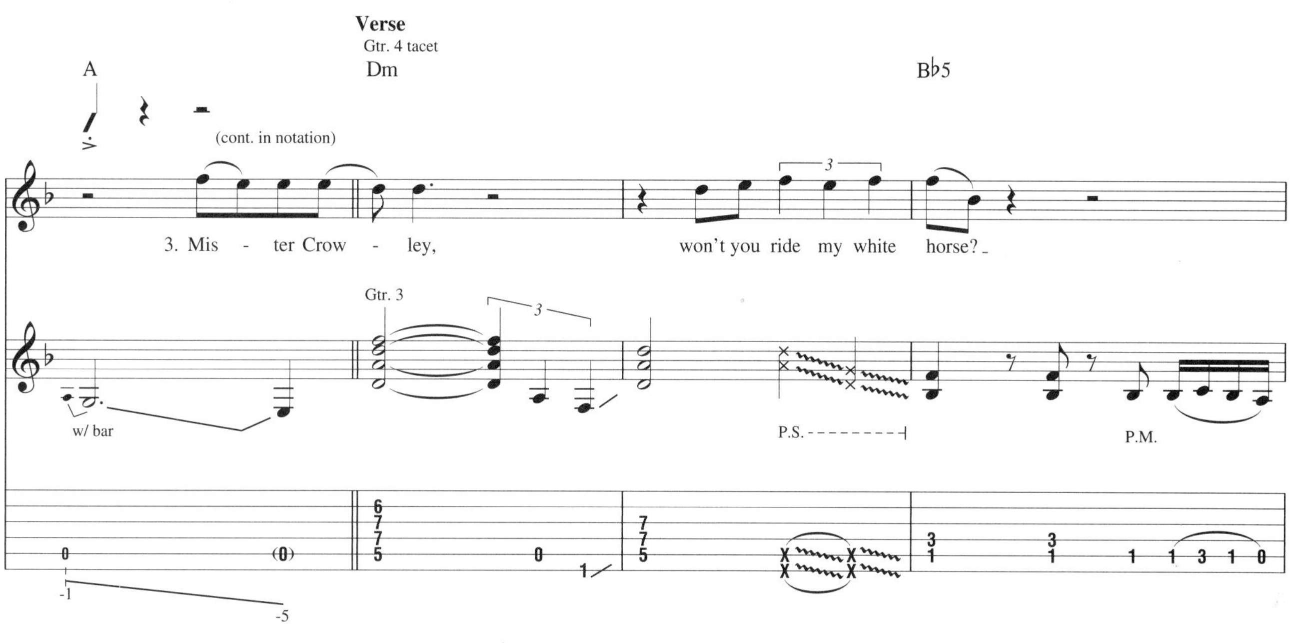
A
Gtr. 4 tacet
Dm
B♭5
(cont. in notation)
3. Mis - ter Crow - ley, won't you ride my white horse?
Gtr. 3
w/ bar
P.S.
P.M.

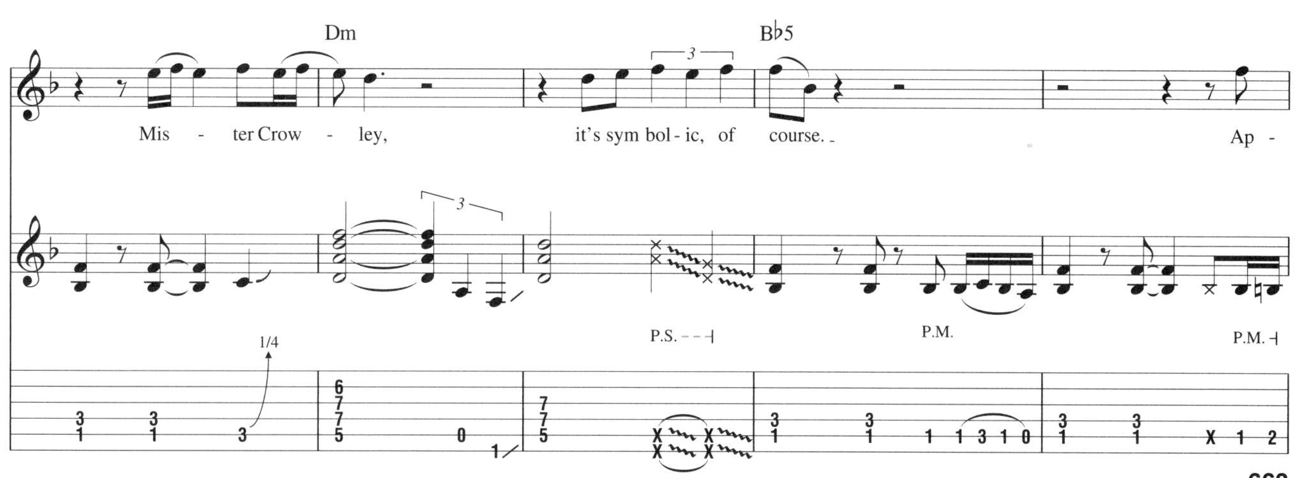
Dm
B♭5
Mis - ter Crow - ley, it's sym bol - ic, of course. Ap -
1/4
P.S.
P.M.
P.M.

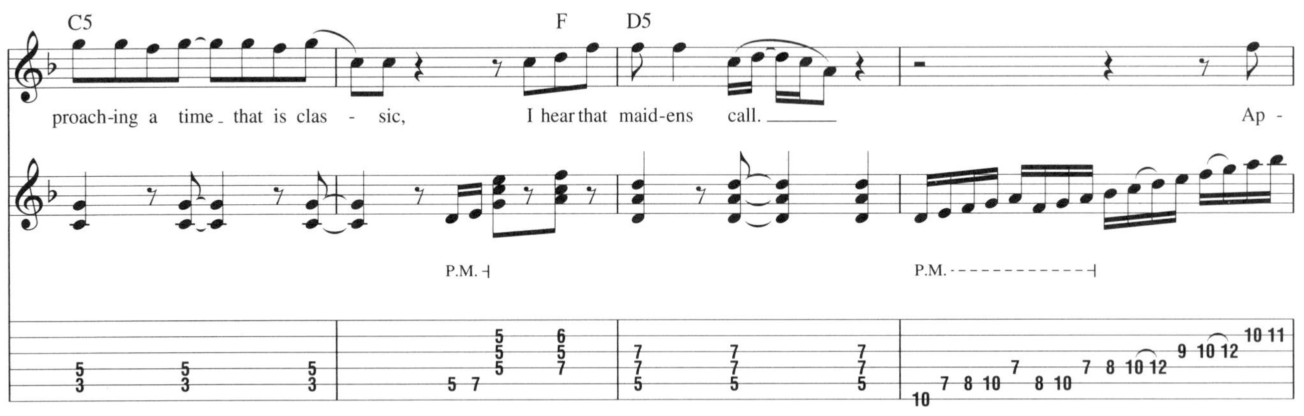
C5
F
D5
proach-ing a time that is clas - sic,
I hear that maid-ens call.
Ap -
P.M.
P.M.

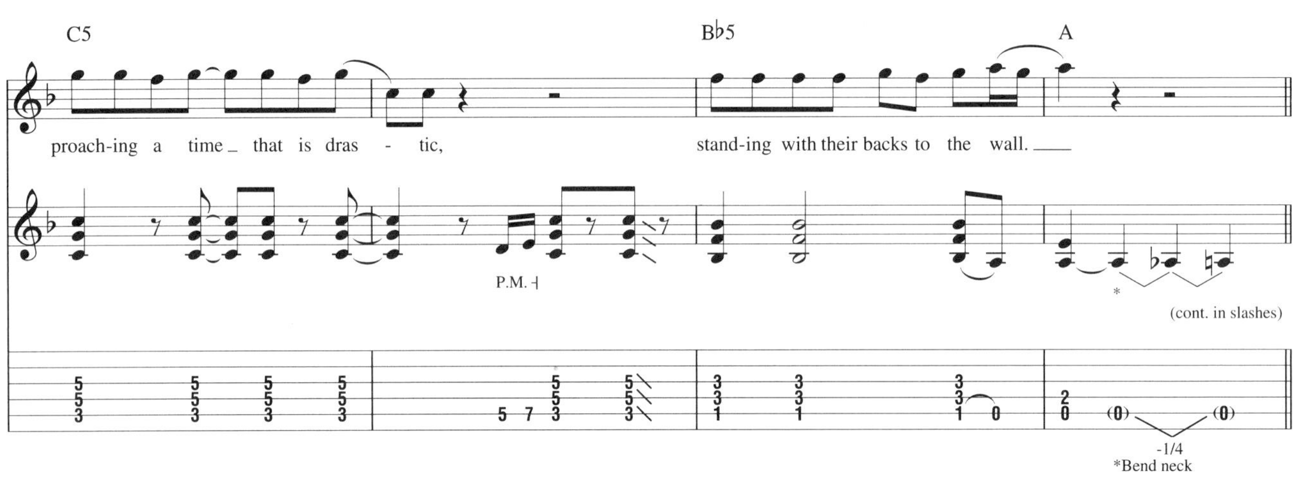
C5
B♭5
A
proach-ing a time that is dras - tic,
stand-ing with their backs to the wall.
P.M.
(cont. in slashes)
-1/4
*Bend neck

Interlude

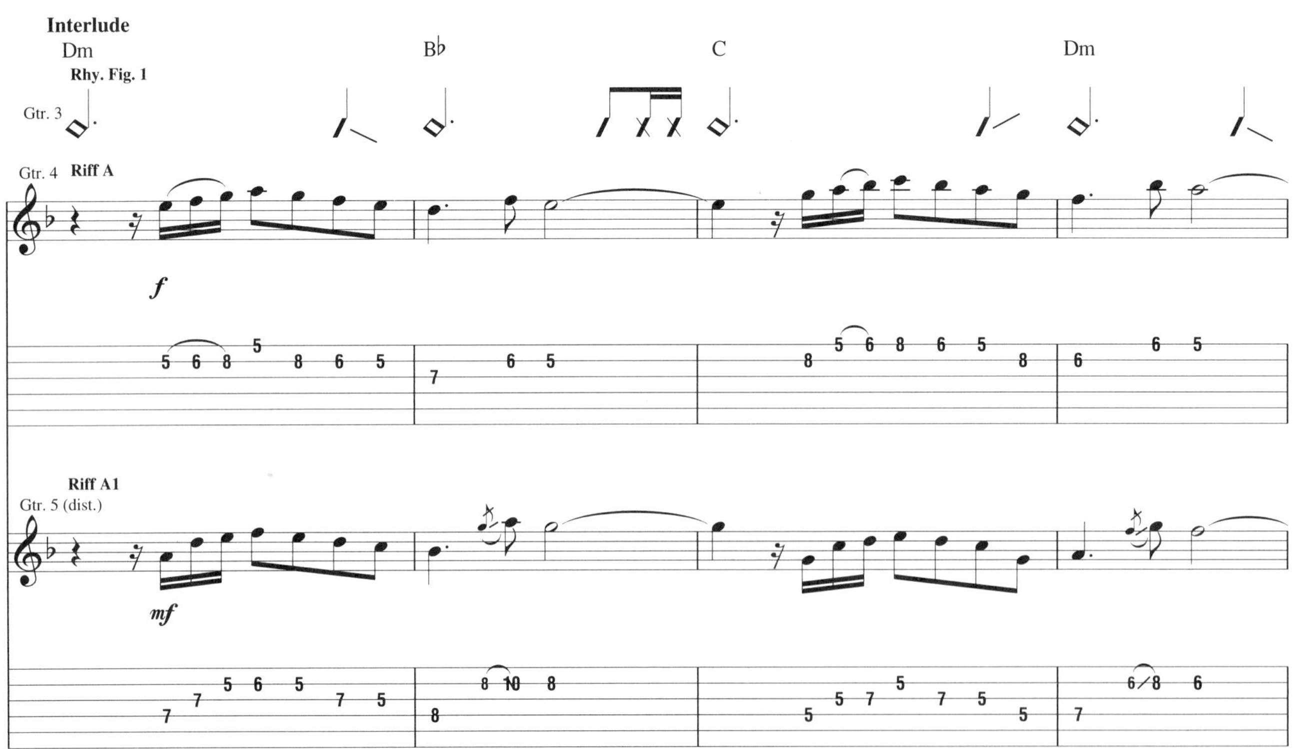
Dm
B♭
C
Dm
Rhy. Fig. 1
Gtr. 3
Gtr. 4 Riff A
f
Riff A1
Gtr. 5 (dist.)
mf

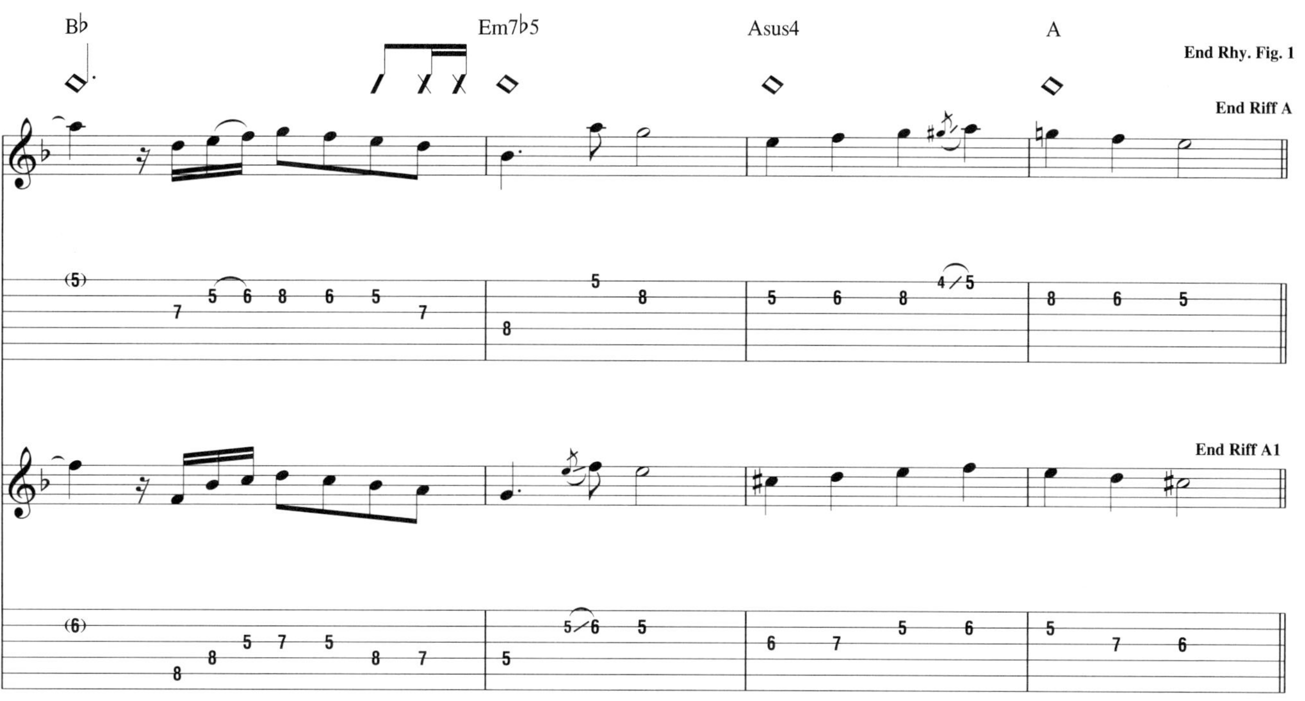

Bridge

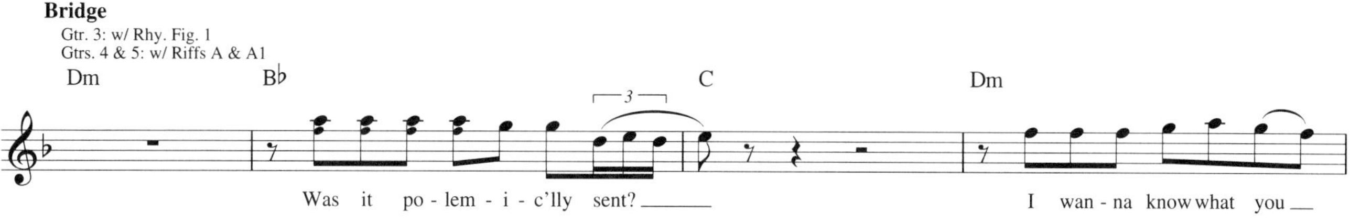

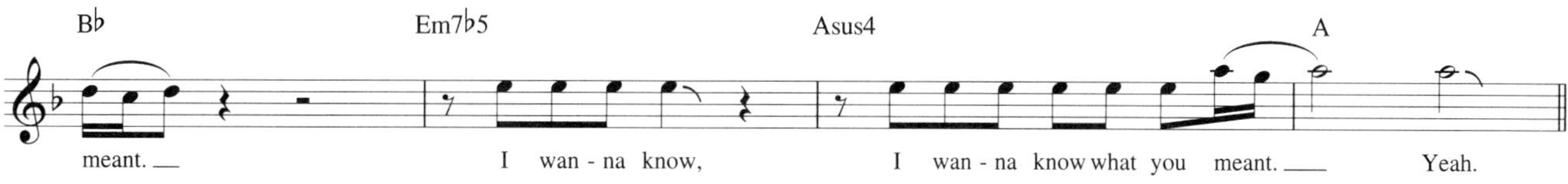

Outro - Guitar Solo

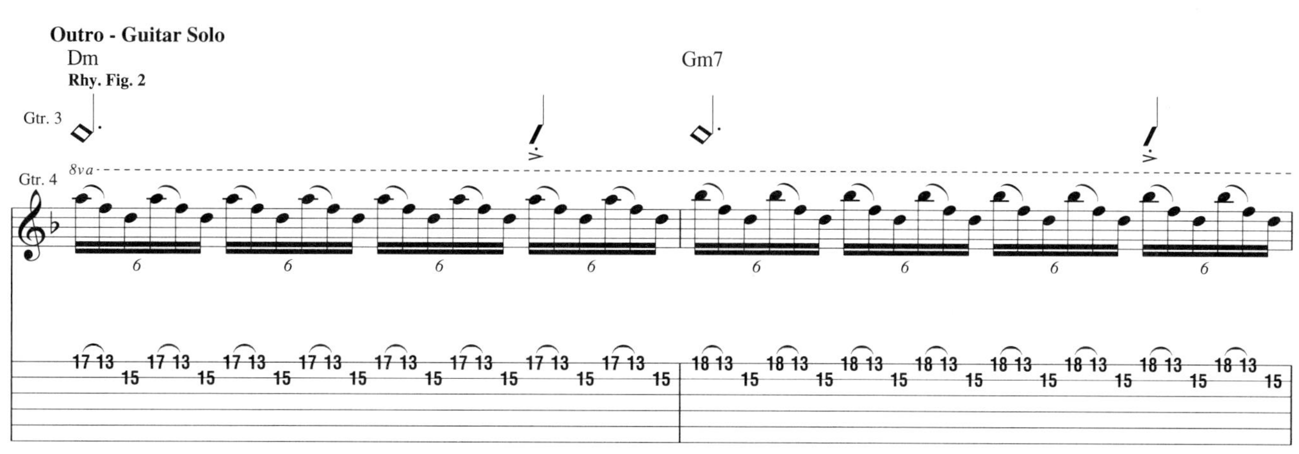

C
F
8va
Bb
Em7b5
Asus4 A
open
P.M.
Asus4 A
open
P.M.
Gtr. 3: w/ Rhy. Fig. 2 (till fade)
A
A
open
P.M.
A
A
open
P.M.
End Rhy. Fig. 2
Dm
Gm7
C
loco
F
1/2
Bb
Em7b5

Asus4
A
Begin fade
Dm
Gm7
C
8va
rake
F
B♭
Em7♭5
loco
Asus4
A
Dm
Gm7
C
F
B♭
Fade out

from Black Sabbath - *Mob Rules*

The Mob Rules

Words by Ronnie James Dio
Music by Ronnie James Dio, Terence Butler and Anthony Iommi

Chorus
A5
G5
A5
N.C.
D5
E
*D/E
take a bite from the wall, oh.
lose your hold on the flame, yeah.
You've
It's
Gtr. 1
w/ bar
*Bass plays E.

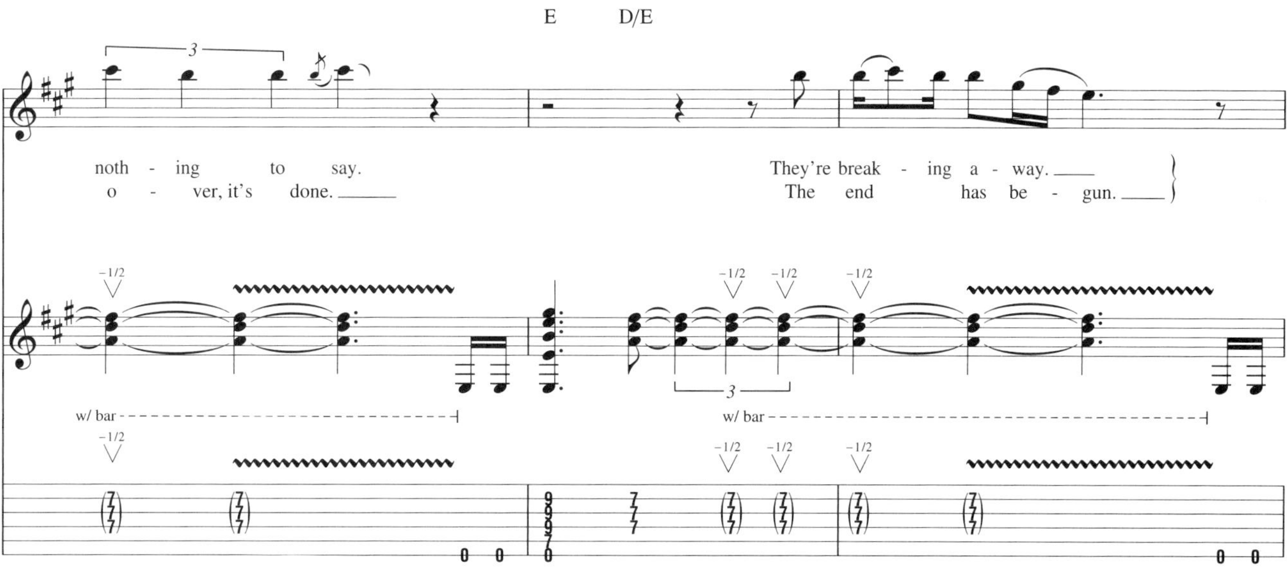
E
D/E
noth - ing to say.
o - ver, it's done.
They're break - ing a - way.
The end has be - gun.
w/ bar

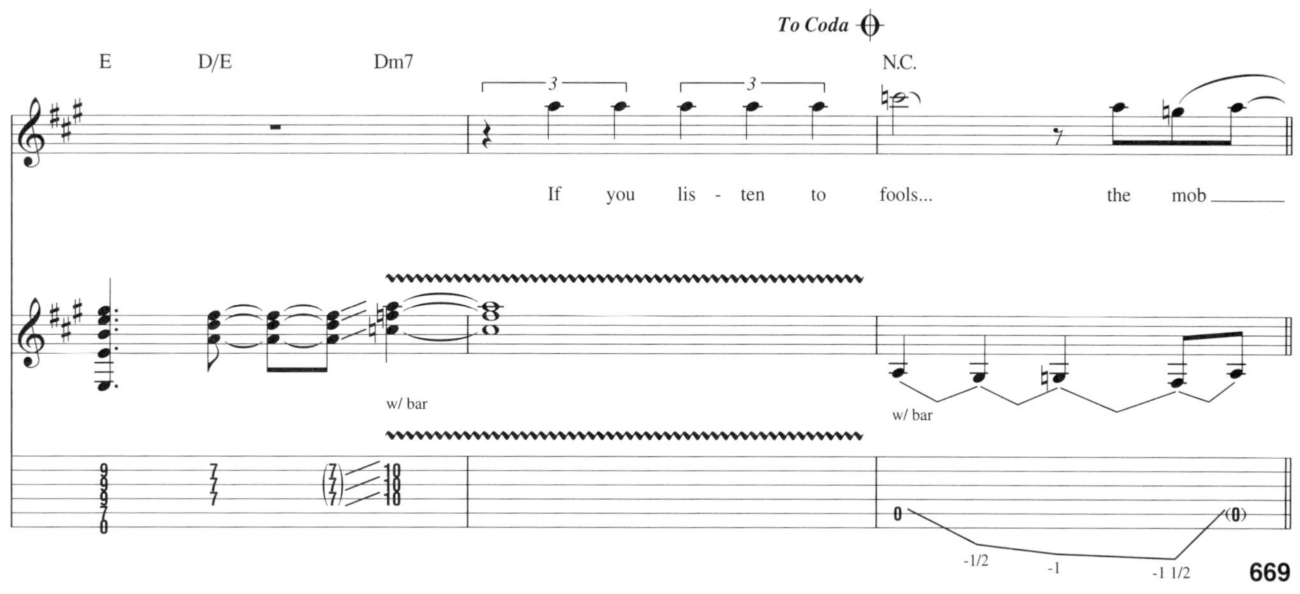
To Coda
E
D/E
Dm7
N.C.
If you lis - ten to fools... the mob
w/ bar

Interlude
Gtr. 1: w/ Rhy. Fig. 1 (2 times)
A5 G5 A5 N.C. A5 G5 A5 N.C. A5 G5 A5 N.C. D5 G5 D/F♯ G5 D/F♯
rules.
The mob
D.S. al Coda
A5 G5 A5 N.C. A5 G5 A5 N.C. A5 G5 A5 N.C. D5 G5 D/F♯ G5 D/F♯
rules.
*w/ delay set for dotted quarter-note regeneration w/ multiple repeats.
Coda
Guitar Solo
D5
fools... the mob rules.
Gtr. 2 (dist.)
f
Gtr. 1
Riff A
P.M.
w/ bar
steady ascent
B♭5
P.M.
P.M.

C5
F5
E5
F5
E5
D5
P.M.
Gtr. 1: w/ Riff A (1 5/8 times)
End Riff A

Gtr. 2
B♭5
P.M.
C5
F5
E5
F5
E5
D5
B♭5
let ring
C5

Chorus
F5 E5 F5 E5 G/D D
You've
Gtr. 2
2 1/2
Gtr. 1
w/ bar
Gtr. 2 tacet
G/D D
noth - ing to say.
Oh, they're break - ing a - way.
Gtr. 1
Gtr. 2 divisi
w/ bar
P.M.
G/D D Dm7 N.C.
If you lis - ten to fools...
w/ bar
Verse
Gtr. 1: w/ Rhy. Fig. 1 (2 times)
A5 G5 A5 N.C. A5 G5 A5 N.C. A5 G5 A5 N.C. D5 G5 D/F♯ G5 D/F♯
3.Break the cir - cle and stop the move - ment, the wheel is thrown to the ground.

A5 G5 A5 N.C.
Just re - mem - ber it might start roll - ing and take you right back a -
Outro-Guitar Solo
Gtr. 1: w/ Rhy. Fig. 1 (till fade)
D5 G5 D/F♯ G5 D/F♯
round.
You're all
Gtr. 2
w/ bar
*Played behind the beat.
fools.
The mob
8va
**w/ delay (as before)
rules.
N.C.

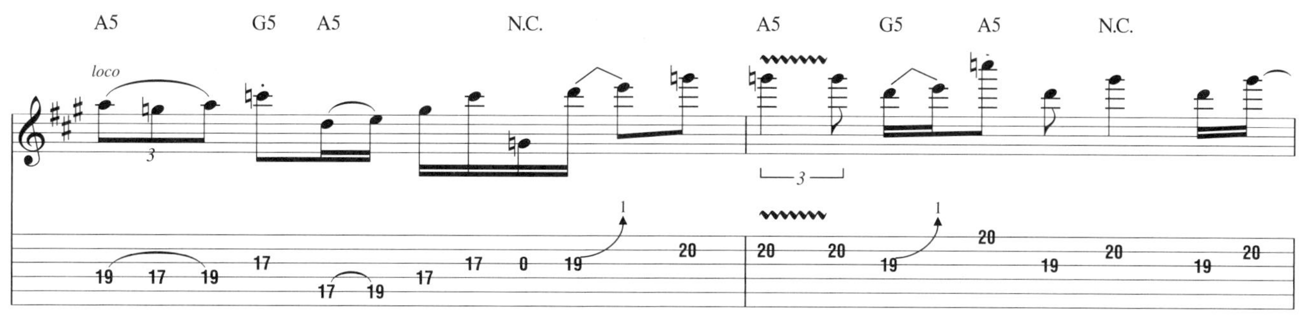
A5 G5 A5 N.C. A5 G5 A5 N.C.
loco
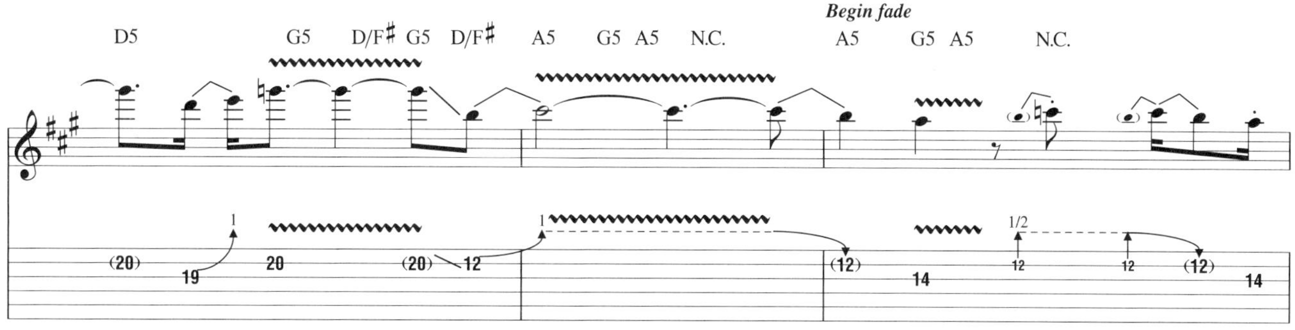
Begin fade
D5 G5 D/F♯ G5 D/F♯ A5 G5 A5 N.C. A5 G5 A5 N.C.
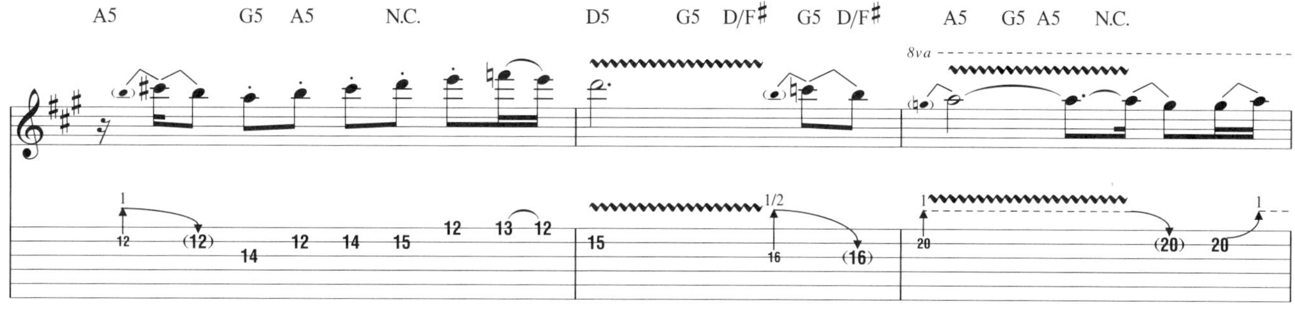
A5 G5 A5 N.C. D5 G5 D/F♯ G5 D/F♯ A5 G5 A5 N.C.
8va
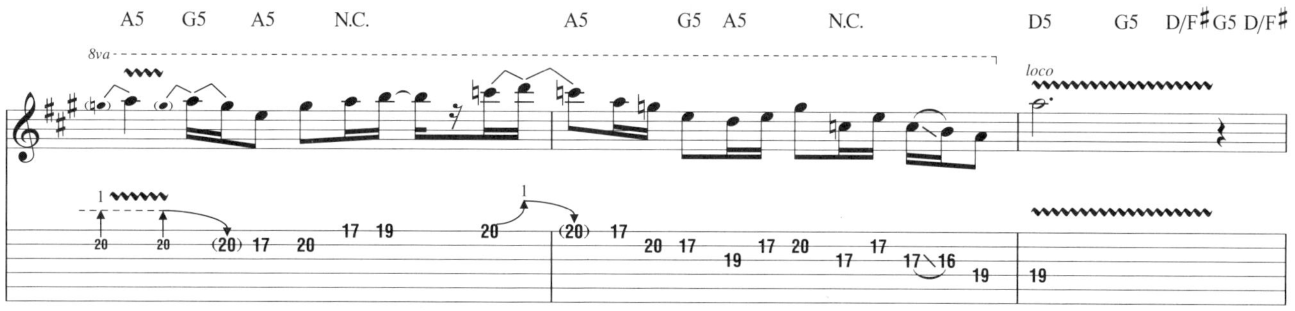
A5 G5 A5 N.C. A5 G5 A5 N.C. D5 G5 D/F♯ G5 D/F♯
8va
loco
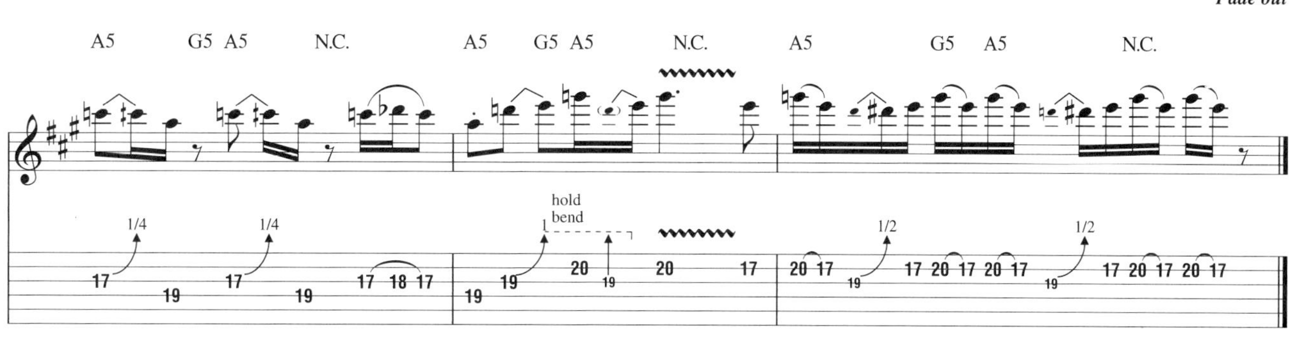
Fade out
A5 G5 A5 N.C. A5 G5 A5 N.C. A5 G5 A5 N.C.
hold bend

from Jane's Addiction - *Nothing's Shocking*

Mountain Song

Words and Music by Jane's Addiction

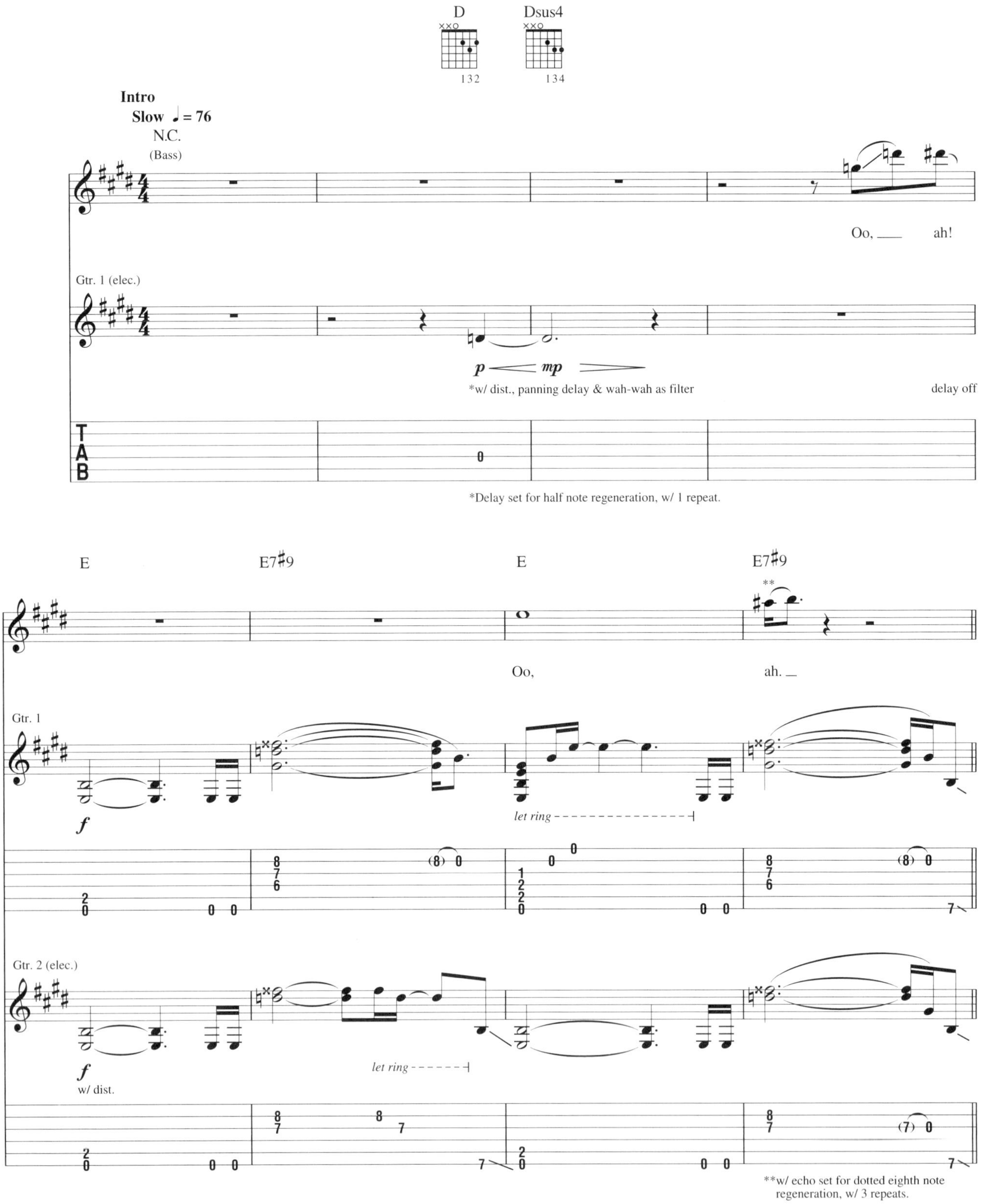

*Delay set for half note regeneration, w/ 1 repeat.

E E7♯9 E E7♯9

Oo, ah. __

Gtr. 1

f

let ring

Gtr. 2 (elec.)

f

w/ dist.

let ring

**w/ echo set for dotted eighth note regeneration, w/ 3 repeats.

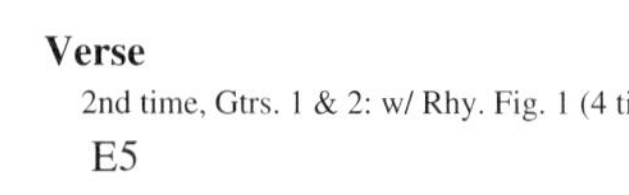
Verse
2nd time, Gtrs. 1 & 2: w/ Rhy. Fig. 1 (4 times)

E5
D5 E5 G5 E5 D5 E5
1. Com - in' down the moun - tain,
com - in' down the moun - tain,
I met a
*Gtrs. 1 & 2
P.M.
*Composite arrangement
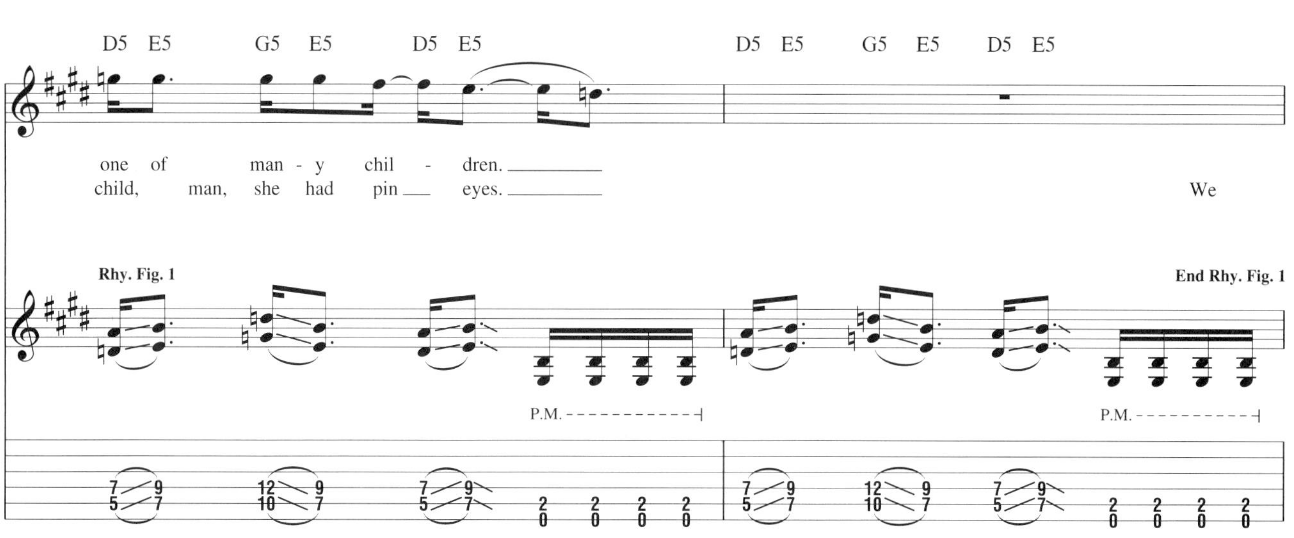
D5 E5 G5 E5 D5 E5
D5 E5 G5 E5 D5 E5
one of man - y chil - dren.
child, man, she had pin eyes.
We
Rhy. Fig. 1
End Rhy. Fig. 1
P.M.
P.M.
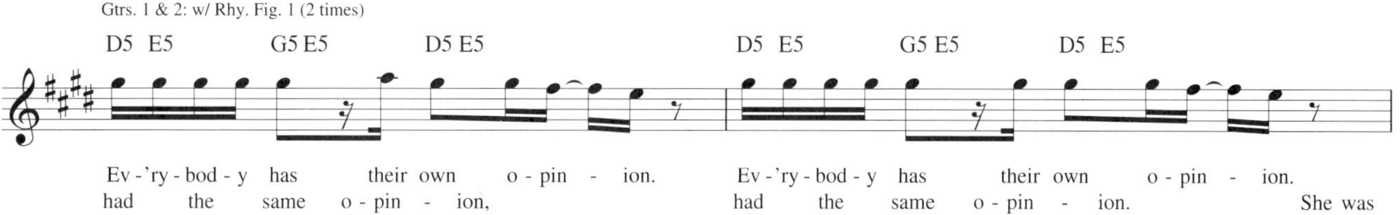
Gtrs. 1 & 2: w/ Rhy. Fig. 1 (2 times)
D5 E5 G5 E5 D5 E5
D5 E5 G5 E5 D5 E5
Ev - 'ry - bod - y has their own o - pin - ion. Ev - 'ry - bod - y has their own o - pin - ion.
had the same o - pin - ion, had the same o - pin - ion. She was
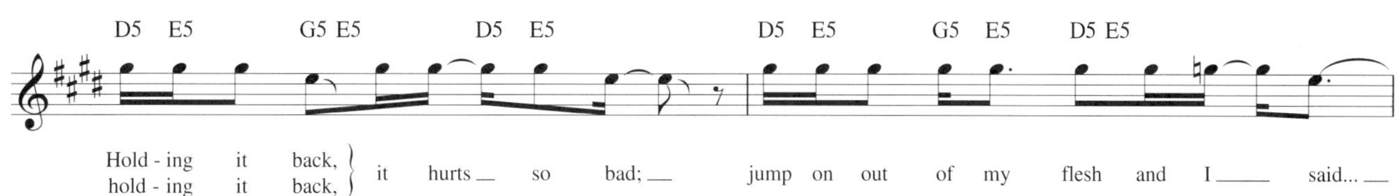
D5 E5 G5 E5 D5 E5
D5 E5 G5 E5 D5 E5
Hold - ing it back, it hurts so bad; jump on out of my flesh and I said...
hold - ing it back,

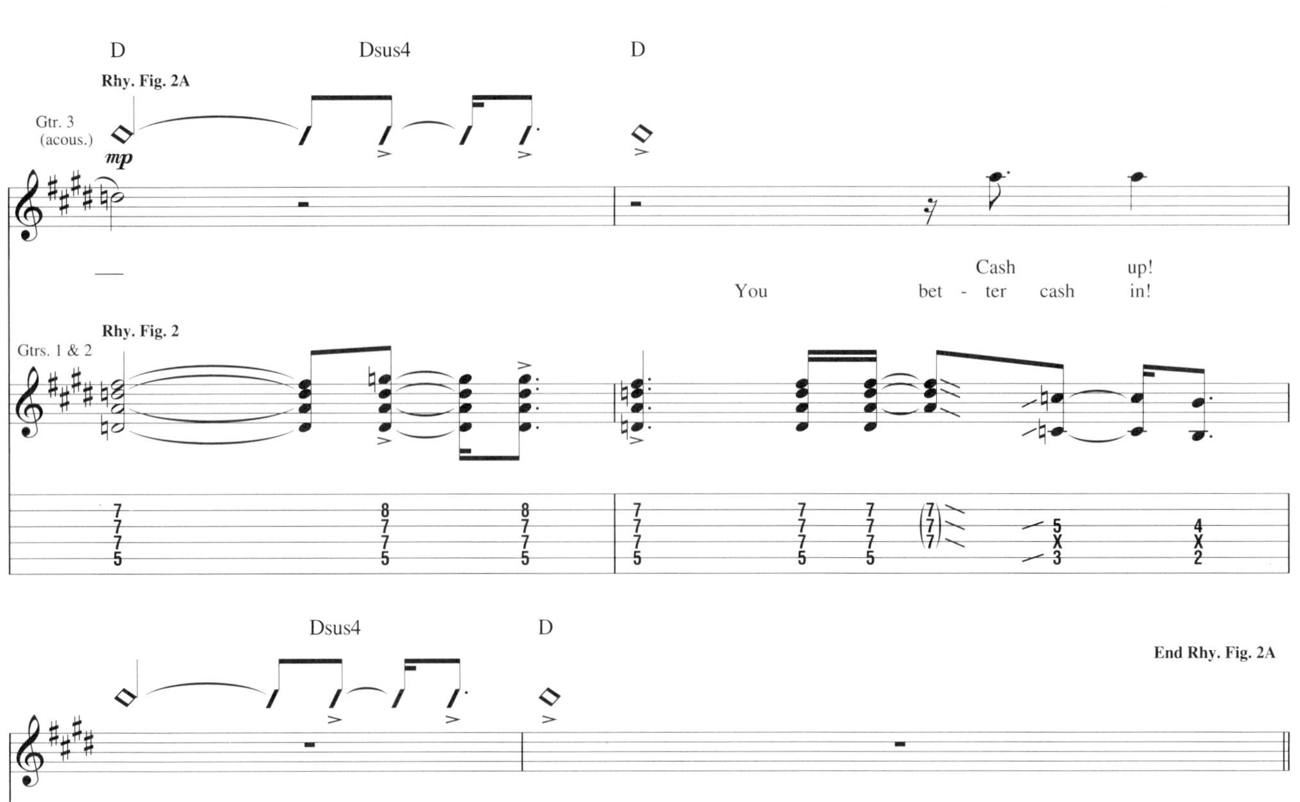

D
Dsus4
D
Rhy. Fig. 2A
Gtr. 3
(acous.)
mp
Cash up!
You bet - ter cash in!
Rhy. Fig. 2
Gtrs. 1 & 2

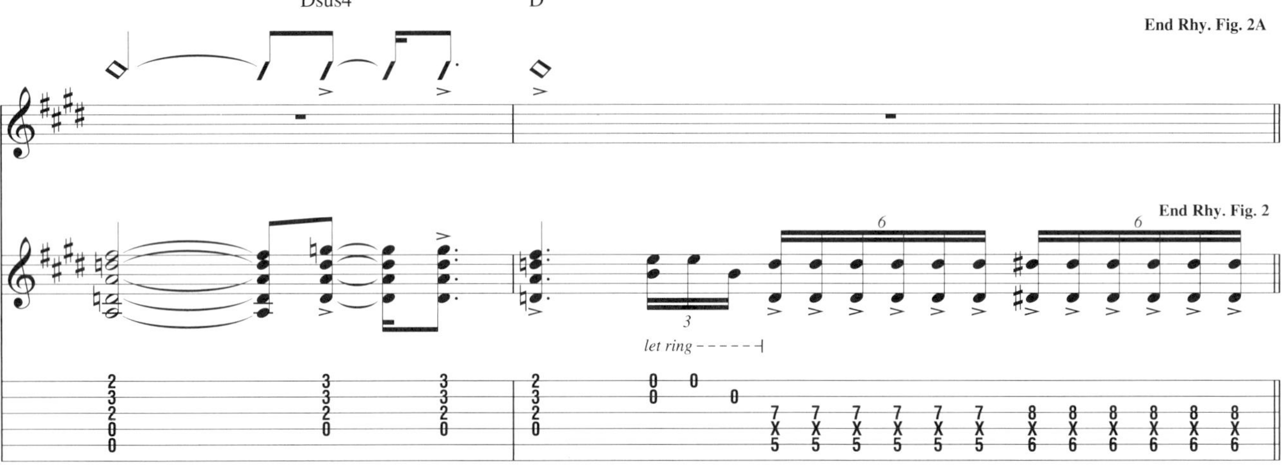

Dsus4
D
End Rhy. Fig. 2A
End Rhy. Fig. 2
let ring

Chorus

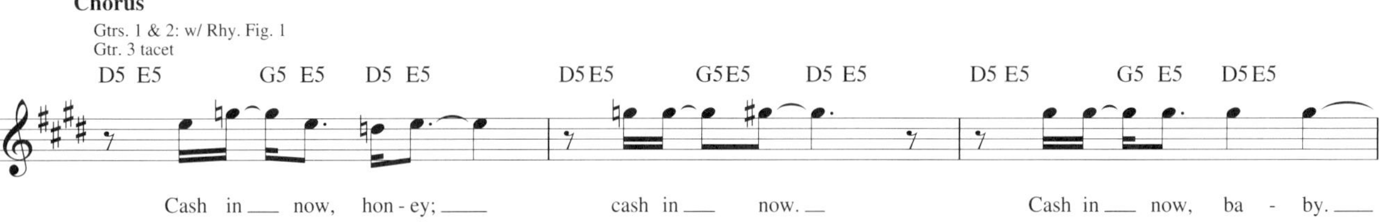

Gtrs. 1 & 2: w/ Rhy. Fig. 1
Gtr. 3 tacet
Cash in now, hon - ey; cash in now. Cash in now, ba - by.

Cash in now, hon - ey; cash in, Miss Smith.

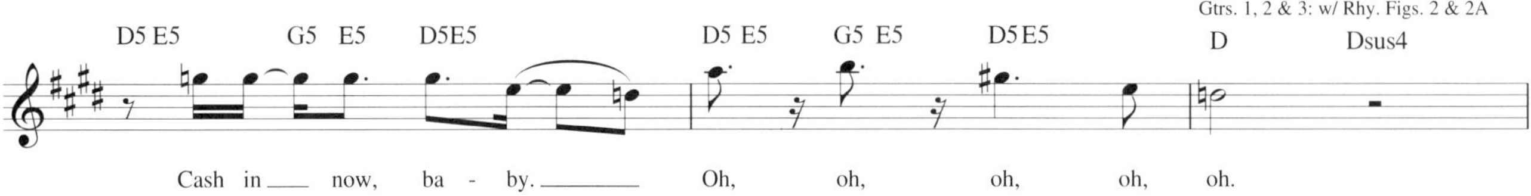

Gtrs. 1, 2 & 3: w/ Rhy. Figs. 2 & 2A
D
Dsus4
Cash in now, ba - by. Oh, oh, oh, oh, oh.

D
Dsus4
1.
D
2. I was

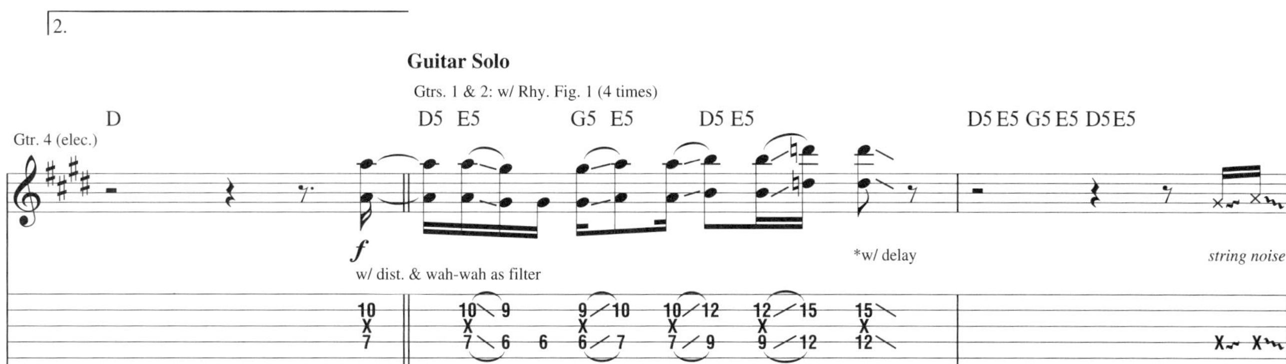

2.
Guitar Solo
Gtrs. 1 & 2: w/ Rhy. Fig. 1 (4 times)
D
D5 E5 G5 E5 D5 E5
D5 E5 G5 E5 D5 E5
Gtr. 4 (elec.)
f
w/ dist. & wah-wah as filter
*w/ delay
string noise

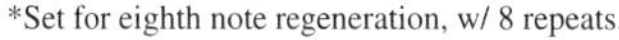

*Set for eighth note regeneration, w/ 8 repeats.

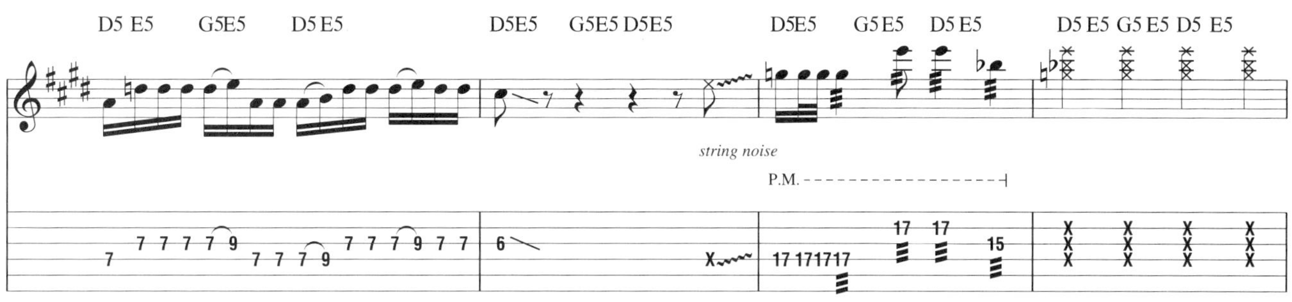

D5 E5 G5E5 D5 E5
D5E5 G5E5 D5E5
D5E5 G5 E5 D5 E5
D5 E5 G5 E5 D5 E5
string noise
P.M.

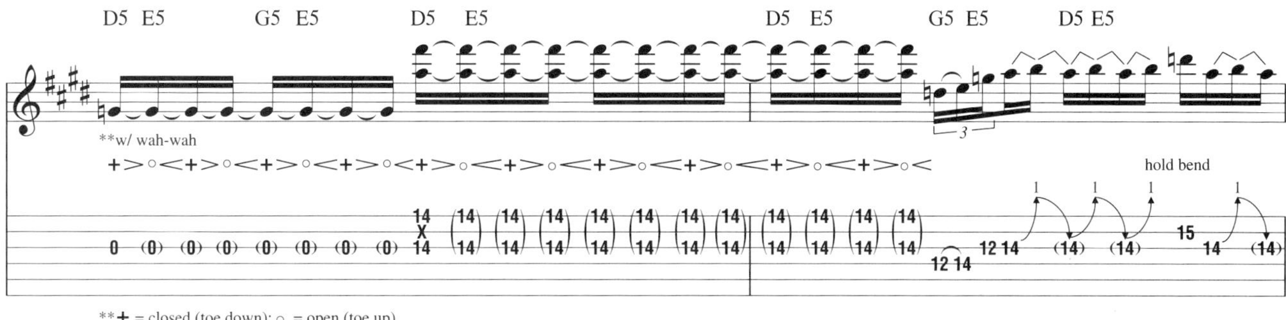

D5 E5 G5 E5 D5 E5
D5 E5 G5 E5 D5 E5
**w/ wah-wah
hold bend
**+ = closed (toe down): ○ = open (toe up)

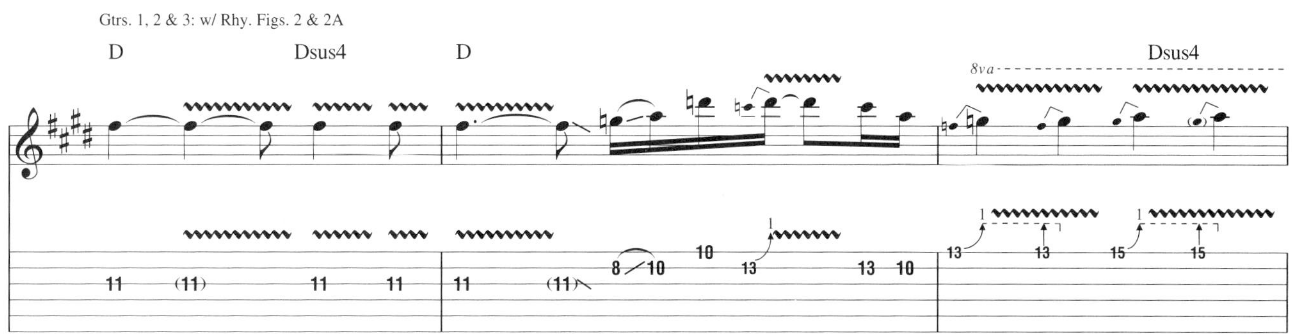

Gtrs. 1, 2 & 3: w/ Rhy. Figs. 2 & 2A
D
Dsus4
D
8va
Dsus4

Outro

Gtrs. 1 & 2: w/ Rhy. Fig.1 (4 times)

D | D5 E5 G5 E5 D5 E5 | D5 E5 G5 E5 D5 E5

Oo, oo, oh, oh, oh, yeah.

8va

1 1/2

Gtr. 4 tacet

D5 E5 G5 E5 D5 E5 | D5 E5 G5 E5 D5 E5 | D5 E5 G5 E5 D5 E5

Oo, oo, oh, oh, oh, yeah. Oo, oo,

D5 E5 G5 E5 D5 E5 | D5 E5 G5 E5 D5 E5 | D5 E5 G5 E5 D5 E5

oh, oh, oh, yeah. Oo, oo, oh, oh, oh, yeah. Ah,

D Dsus4 | D | Dsus4

ah, ah, ah, ah, ah, ah. Ah, ah, ah. Ah, ah, ah,

(Ah ah.

D | D5 E5 G5 E5 D5 E5

ah, ah.

Ah, ah.)

Gtrs. 1 & 2

from Lady Antebellum - *Need You Now*

Need You Now

Words and Music by Hillary Scott, Charles Kelley, Dave Haywood and Josh Kear

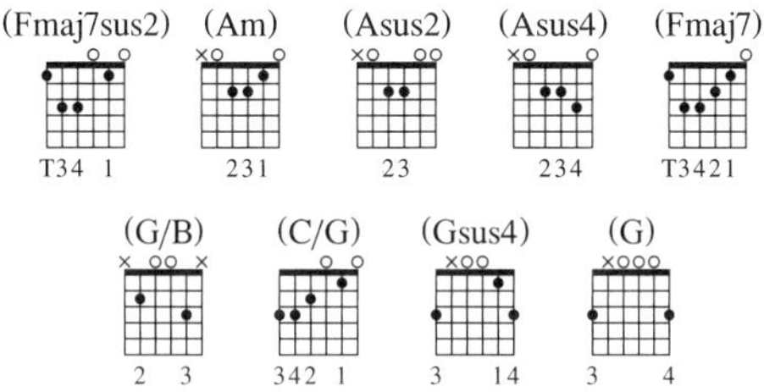

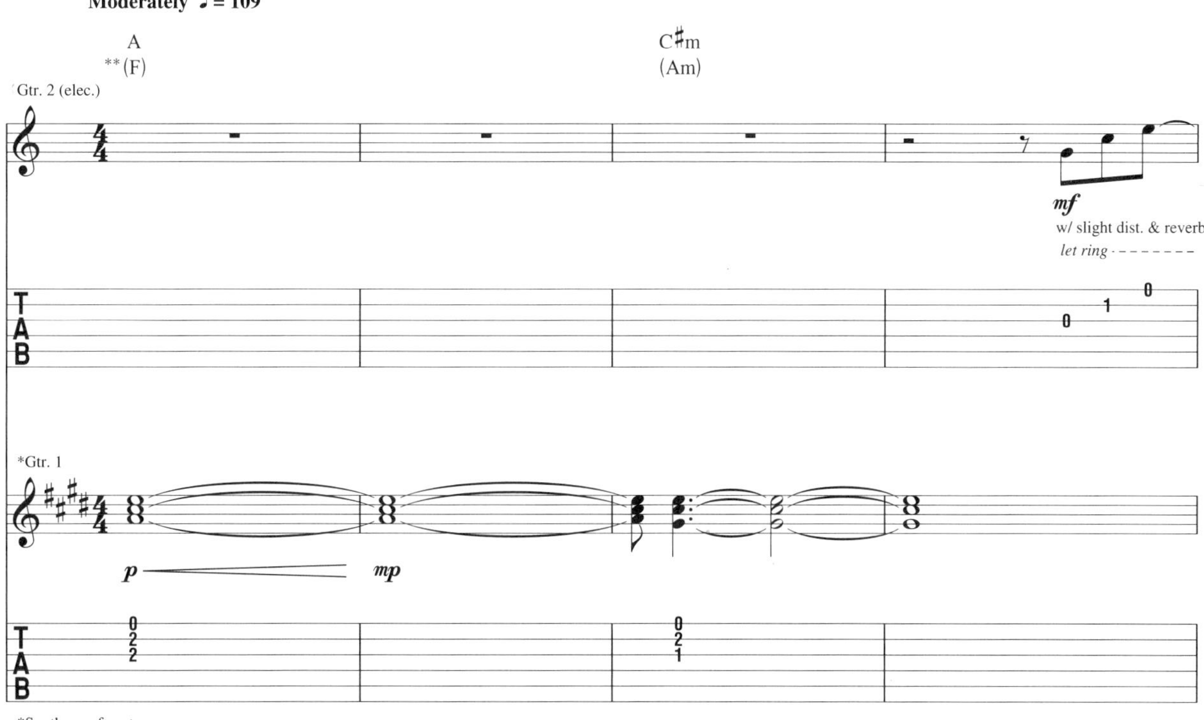

*Synth. arr. for gtr.

**Symbols in parentheses represent chord names respective to capoed guitars. Symbols above represent actual sounding chords. Capoed fret is "0" in tab. Chord symbols reflect basic overall harmony.

Gtr. 1 tacet
Amaj7
(Fmaj7)
C♯m
(Am)
Gtr. 2
w/ bar
let ring
Rhy. Fig. 1
End Rhy. Fig. 1
Gtr. 3 (acous.)
mp
sim.
*T
*T = Thumb on 6th string
Gtr. 4 (elec.)
mp
**w/ slight dist., amp tremolo & slapback delay
let ring
1/2
**Tremolo set for triplet eighth-note regeneration.
Verse
Amaj7
(Fmaj7)
C♯m
(Am)
Female: 1. Pic-ture per-fect mem - 'ries scat-tered all a-round the floor.
Gtr. 2
w/ bar
Gtr. 3
T
Gtr. 4

*Harmony cues are male.

Pre-Chorus

**See top of first page of song for chord diagrams pertaining to rhythm slashes.

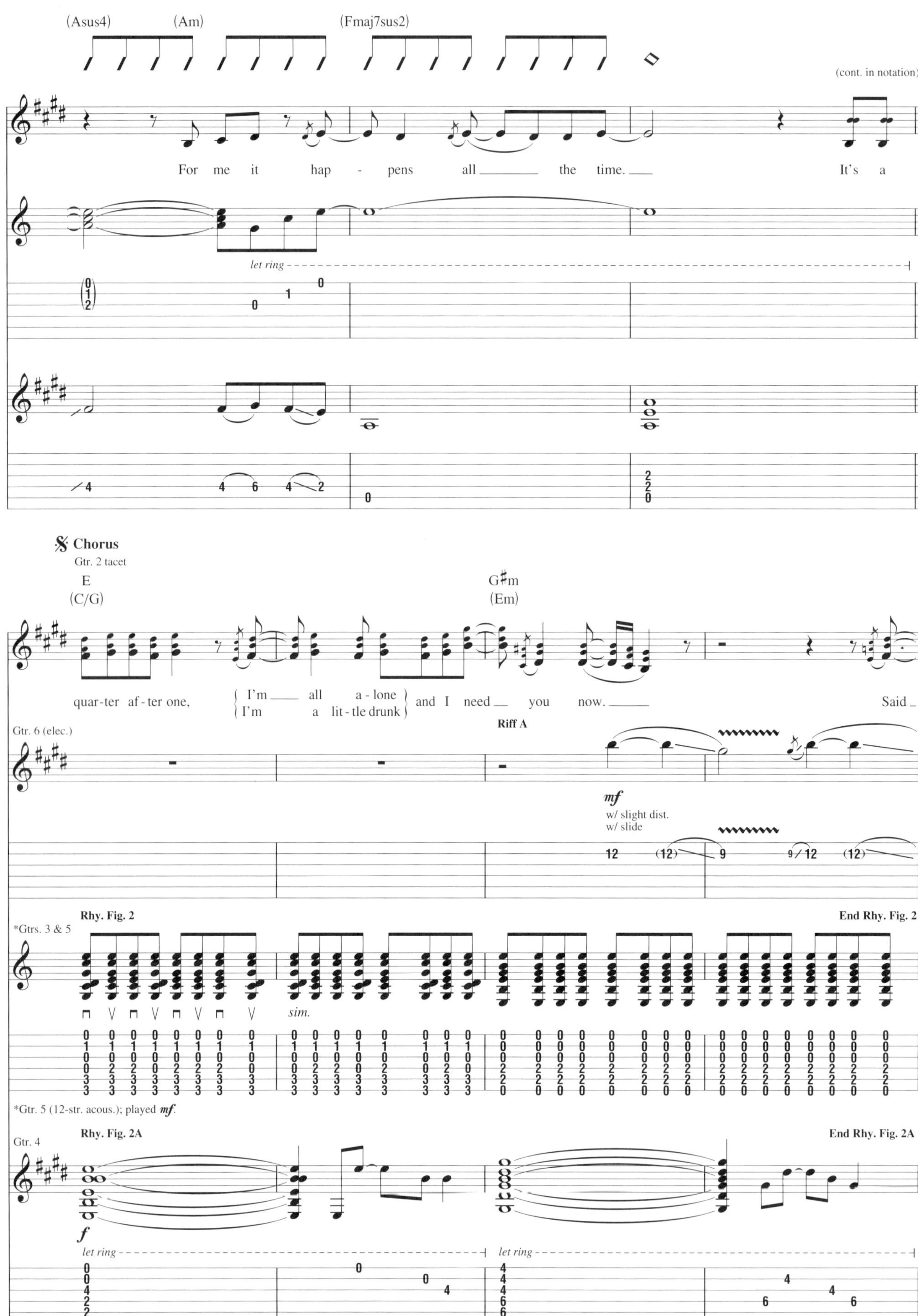

(Asus4)
(Am)
(Fmaj7sus2)
(cont. in notation)
For me it hap - pens all the time.
It's a
let ring
Chorus
Gtr. 2 tacet
E
(C/G)
G♯m
(Em)
quar-ter af-ter one, I'm all a-lone / I'm a lit-tle drunk and I need you now.
Said
Gtr. 6 (elec.)
Riff A
w/ slight dist.
w/ slide
Rhy. Fig. 2
*Gtrs. 3 & 5
End Rhy. Fig. 2
sim.
*Gtr. 5 (12-str. acous.); played mf.
Gtr. 4
Rhy. Fig. 2A
End Rhy. Fig. 2A
let ring

Gtrs. 3 & 5: w/ Rhy. Fig. 2
Gtr. 4: w/ Rhy. Fig. 2A
E
(C/G)
G♯m
(Em)
I would-n't call but I lost all con-trol and I need you now. And I don't
Gtr. 6
End Riff A
To Coda
(Fmaj7sus2)
Gtrs. 3 & 5
know how I can do with-out. I just need you now.
Gtr. 4
Rhy. Fig. 3
End Rhy. Fig. 3
let ring
Interlude
Gtr. 3: w/ Rhy. Fig. 2
Gtrs. 5 & 6 tacet
Amaj7
(Fmaj7)
C♯m
(Am)
Male: 2. An-
steady gliss.

*Harmony cues are male.

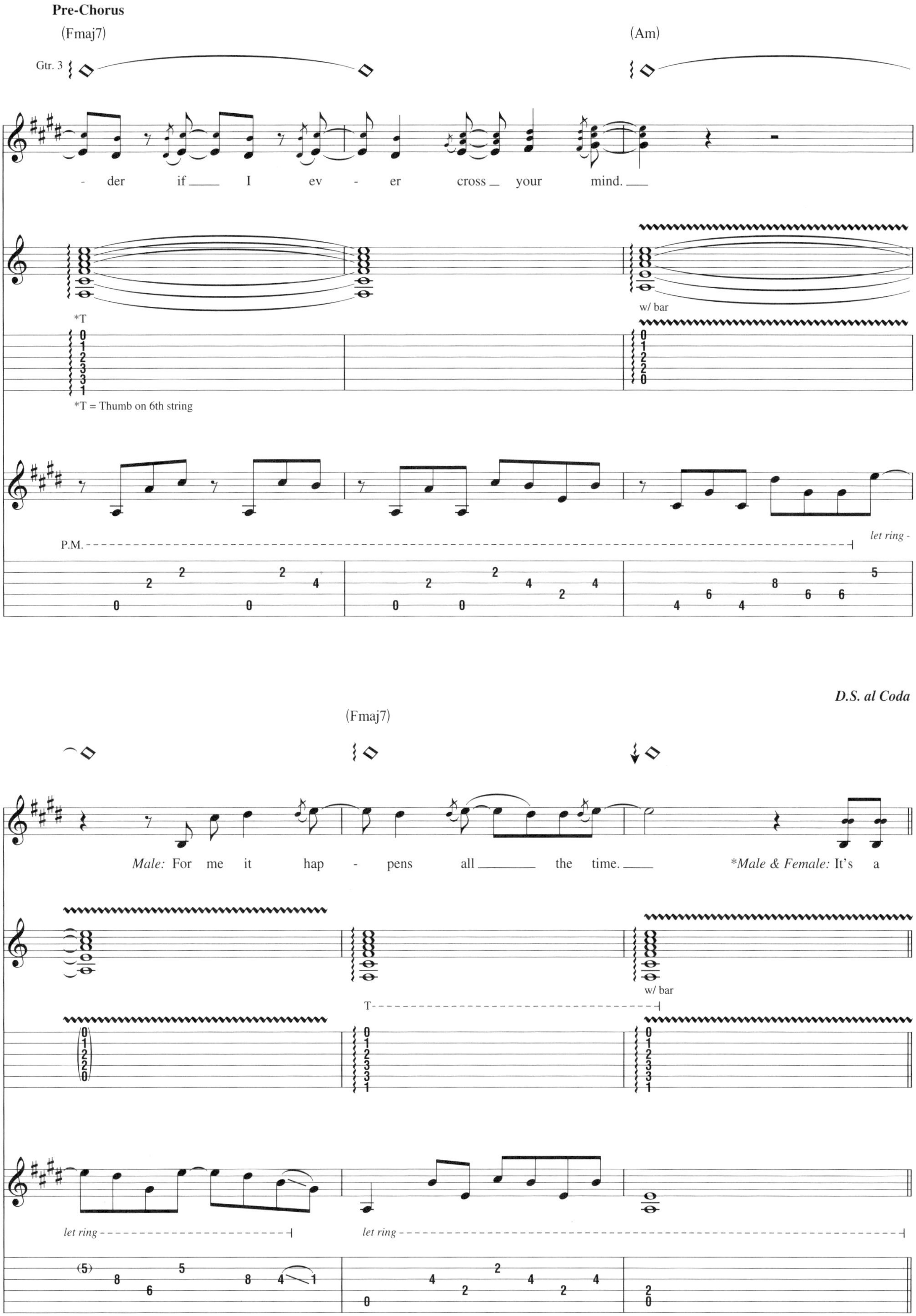

Pre-Chorus

(Fmaj7) (Am)

Gtr. 3

- der if I ev - er cross your mind.

*T

w/ bar

*T = Thumb on 6th string

P.M. let ring

D.S. al Coda

(Fmaj7)

Male: For me it hap - pens all the time. **Male & Female:* It's a

w/ bar

T

let ring

let ring

*Harmony cues are male.

Coda
Guitar Solo
Gtr. 6 tacet
(Fmaj7sus2)
(Am)
(G/B)
(C/G)
Gtrs. 3 & 5
sim.
with-out. I just need you now.
Gtr. 7 (elec.)
Gtr. 6
mf
w/ dist.
w/ slide
Gtr. 4
*Gtrs. 4 & 8
f
*Gtr. 8 (elec.) w/ dist.
Composite arrangement
(Fmaj7)
(Gsus4)
(G)
(Am)
(G/B)
(C/G)
sim.
(Gtr. 3, cont. in notation)
Male: Whoa, whoa.
8va
Gtr. 7
Gtr. 8
let ring
Gtr. 4

Pre-Chorus

(Fmaj7sus2) (Gsus4) (Fmaj7sus2)

Gtr. 5

*Male & Female: Yes, I'd rath - er hurt _ than feel _ noth - ing _ at all. _

8va

Gtr. 7

Gtr. 3

let ring

Gtr. 2

let ring

Gtr. 8

let ring

Gtr. 4

*Harmony cues are male.

Chorus
Gtrs. 2, 4, 5, 7 & 8 tacet
Gtrs. 3 & 5: w/ Rhy. Fig. 2 (2 times)
Gtr. 4: w/ Rhy. Fig. 2A (2 times)
C♯m (Am)
Bsus4 (Gsus4)
E (C/G)
Female: It's a quar-ter af-ter one, I'm all a-lone and I need
Gtr. 3
Gtr. 6: w/ Riff A
G♯m (Em)
E (C/G)
you now.
Male: And I said I would-n't call but
G♯m (Em)
I'm a lit-tle drunk and I need you now.
*Male & Female: And I don't
Gtr. 6
*Harmony cues are male.
Gtr. 4: w/ Rhy. Fig. 3
(Fmaj7sus2)
Gtrs. 3 & 5
know how I can do with-out. I just need you now.

Outro-Chorus
(C/G)
(Em)
Rhy. Fig. 4
End Rhy. Fig. 4
I just need you now.
Gtr. 6
Rhy. Fig. 4A
Gtr. 4
End Rhy. Fig. 4A
Gtrs. 3 & 5: w/ Rhy. Fig. 4
Gtr. 4: w/ Rhy. Fig. 4A (2 times)
E
(C/G)
G♯m
(Em)
let ring
Rhy. Fig. 5
Gtrs. 3 & 5
End Rhy. Fig. 5
Female: Oh, ba - by, I need you now.
8va

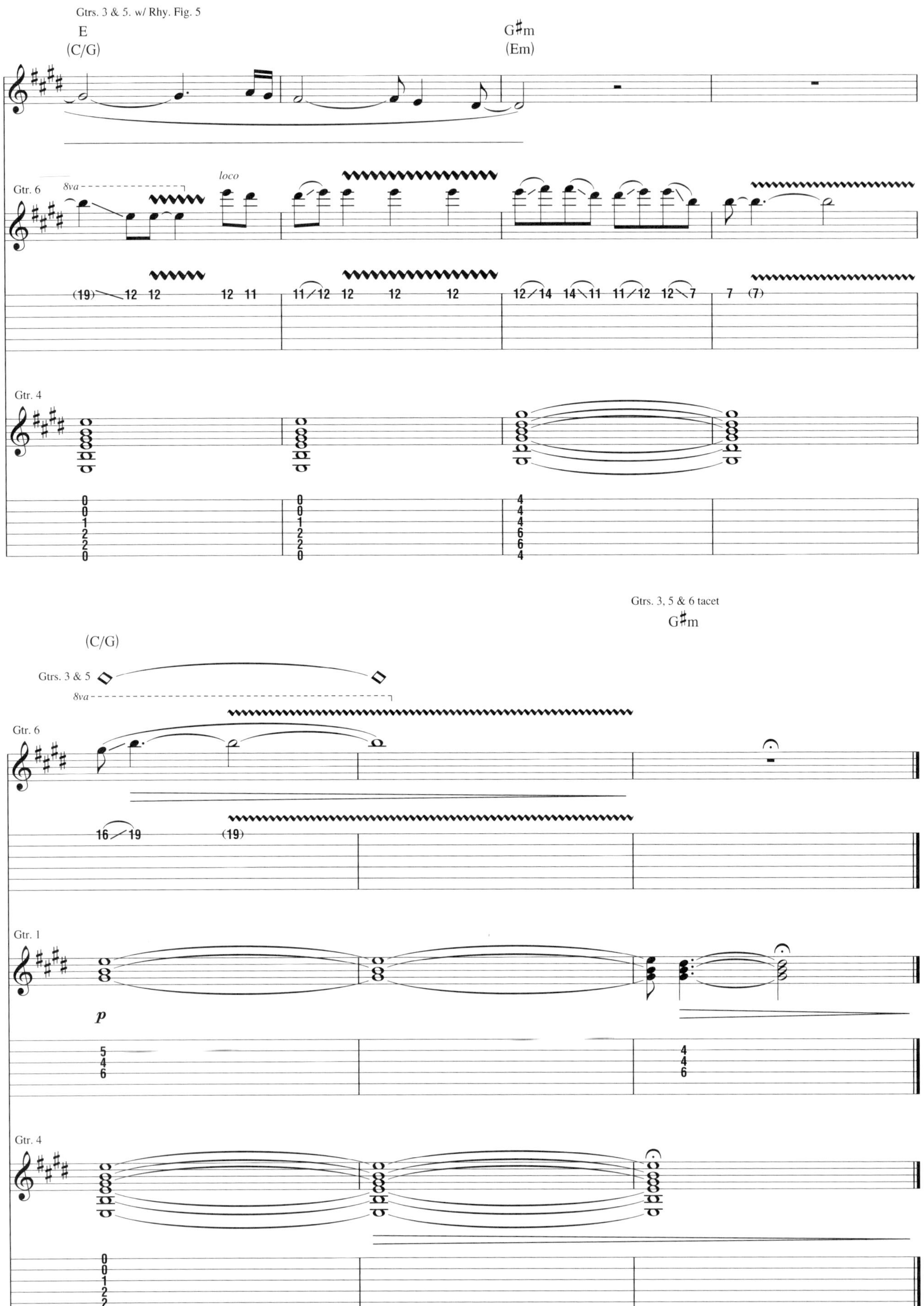

Gtrs. 3 & 5. w/ Rhy. Fig. 5
E
(C/G)
G♯m
(Em)
Gtr. 6
8va
loco
Gtr. 4
(C/G)
Gtrs. 3, 5 & 6 tacet
G♯m
Gtrs. 3 & 5
8va
Gtr. 6
Gtr. 1
p
Gtr. 4

from Head East - *Flat as a Pancake*

Never Been Any Reason

Words and Music by Michael Somerville

N.C.
Gtr. 1
*Gtr. 3
*Synth. arr. for gtr.
Gtr. 2
1., 2.
Gtrs. 1 & 3 tacet
G5
N.C.
G/B
C5
N.C.
G/B
D5
N.C.
C5
D5
N.C.
D/F♯
G5
3.
N.C.
C5
D5
N.C.
C5
D5
N.C.
G/B
C5

Verse
2nd time, Gtr. 1 tacet
C5 G/B C5 G/B D5 C5 D5 G/B C5
1. Did you see an-y action? Did you make an-y friends?
2. Did you have an-y bad dreams? Did you break an-y glass?
Rhy. Fig. 1
End Rhy. Fig. 1
G/B C5 G/B D5 C5 D5 G/B C5
Would you like some af-fection before I leave a-gain?
Would you be my com-panion? Is there e-ven a chance?
Gtr. 2: w/ Rhy. Fig. 1
C5 G/B C5 G/B D5 C5 D5 G/B C5
I've been walk-ing be-hind you since you've been a-ble to see.
You've been talk-ing in circles since I've been a-ble to cry.
To Coda
G/B C5 G/B D5 N.C.
There's nev-er been an-y reason for you to think a-bout
There's nev-er been an-y reason for nev-er tell-ing me
Gtr. 2

Interlude
G/B C
G5
D
D7sus$^2_4$
D
me. __
Gtr. 1
Gtr. 2
Dsus$^2_4$
C
G5
D
D7sus$^2_4$
D
Dsus$^2_4$
D
C
G5
D
N.C.
C5 D5

D.S. al Coda
N.C.
C5 D5
N.C.
C5 D5
N.C.
G/B C5

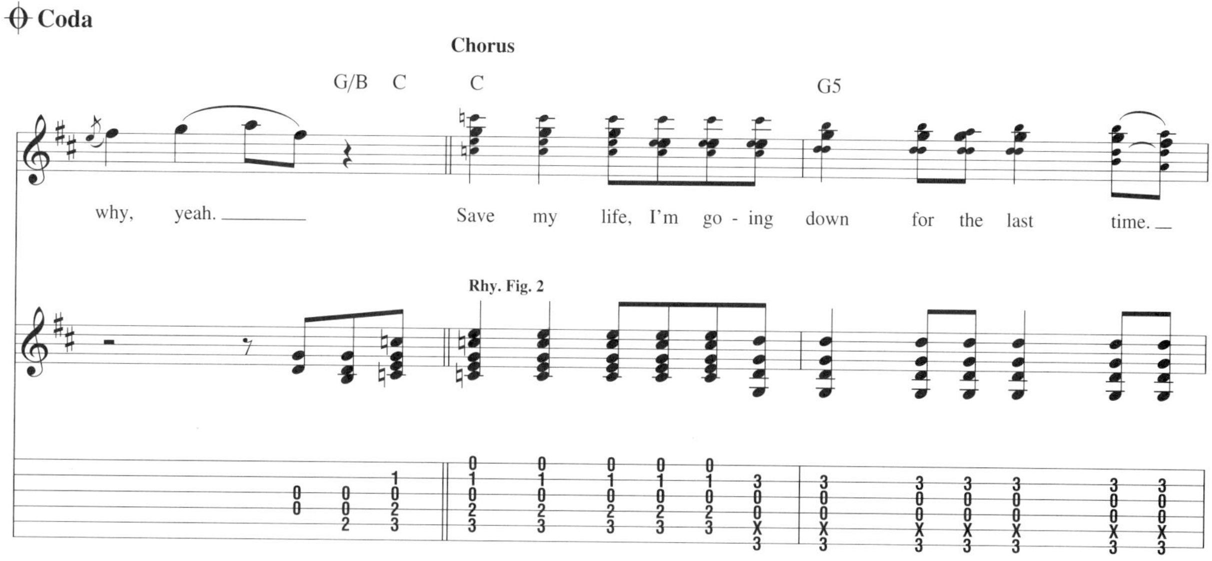
Coda
Chorus
G/B C
C
G5
why, yeah.
Save my life, I'm go - ing down for the last time.
Rhy. Fig. 2

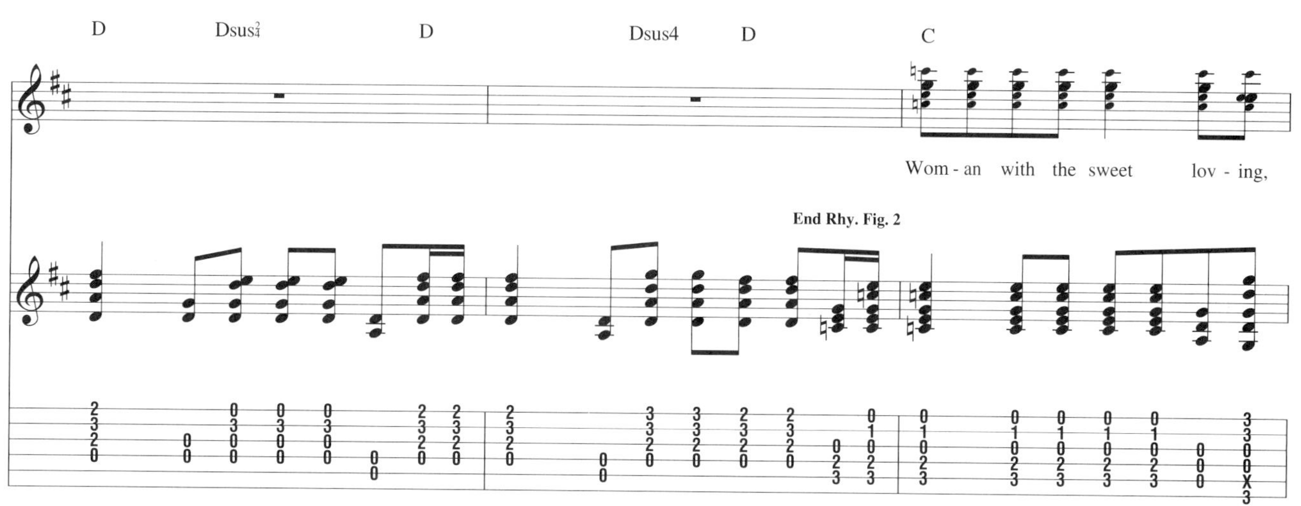
D
D
Dsus4
D
C
Wom - an with the sweet lov - ing,
End Rhy. Fig. 2

G5
D
Dsus4/2
D
Dsus2
D
bet - ter than a white line.
C
G5
Bring a good feel - ing ain't had in such a long time.
Rhy. Fig. 3
D
Dsus2
Dsus4
D
Dsus2
End Rhy. Fig. 3
Gtr. 2: w/ Rhy. Fig. 2
C
G5
D
Dsus4/2
D
Dsus4
D
Save my life, I'm go - ing down for the last time.
Synthesizer Solo
Gtr. 2: w/ Rhy. Fig. 2
Gtrs. 1 & 3
C
G5

D
Dsus2/4
D
Dsus4
D
*C
Em
Rhy. Fig. 4
Gtr. 2
Gtr. 1
Gtr. 3
*See top of first page of song for chord diagrams pertaining to rhythm slashes.
End Rhy. Fig. 4
C
Gtr. 2: w/ Rhy. Fig. 4
w/ DigiTech Whammy pedal

D
C
B♭
Gm
C[III]
Gtr. 2
(cont. in notation)
Gtrs. 1 & 3
D
Dsus⁴₂
D
B♭
C
D
Dsus4 D Dsus2
D
w/ DigiTech Whammy pedal
Gtr. 2
B♭
C
D Dsus4 D Dsus2
D5
B♭
C
w/ DigiTech Whammy pedal

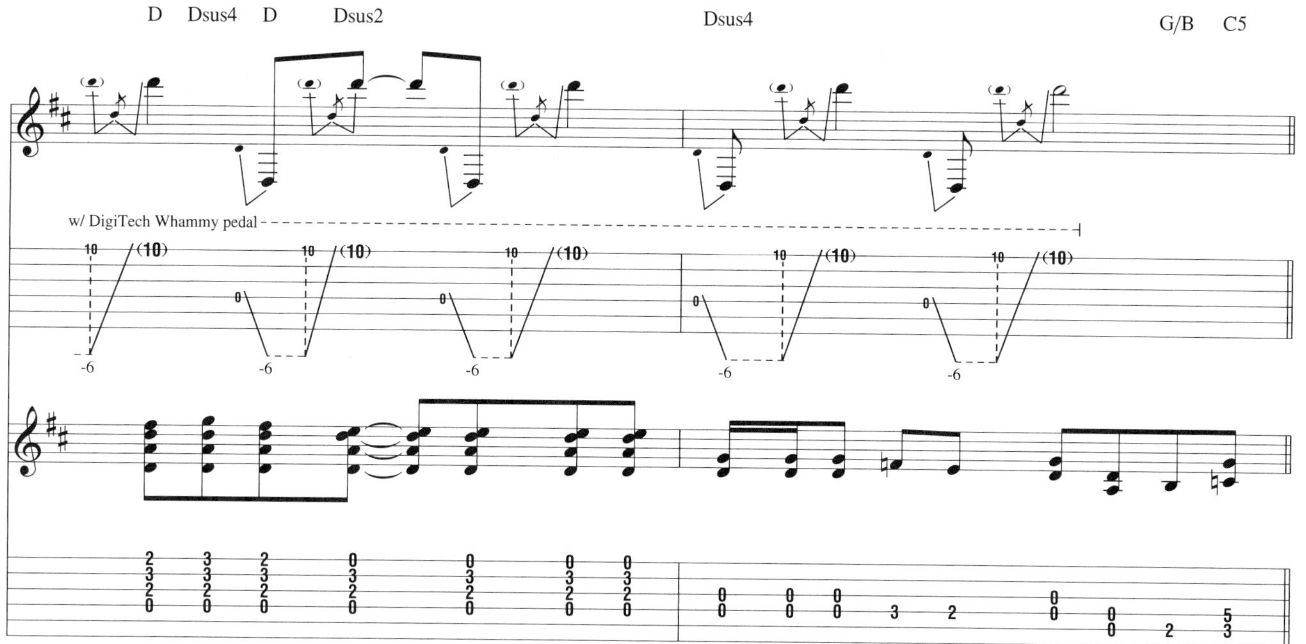
D Dsus4 D Dsus2
Dsus4
G/B C5
w/ DigiTech Whammy pedal

Verse
Gtrs. 1 & 3 tacet
C5 C G/B C5 G/B D5 D Dsus4 D Dsus2 G/B C
3. Have you ev - er been lone - ly? Do you have an - y fun?
Gtr. 2
w/ bar
w/ bar
w/ bar

G/B C G/B D5 Dsus4 D Dsus4 D5 Dsus4 D5 G/B C
Do you ev - er think of me? I'm just an - oth - er one, yeah.
w/ bar
w/ bar

G/B C
G/B D5
Dsus4
D5
Dsus4
D5
B♭5 C
You nev - er give me no an - swer.
You nev - er tell me the truth.
w/ bar
G/B D5
D
Dsus4
D5
G/B C
There's nev - er been an - y rea - son
for me to think a - bout you.
G/B C
G/B D5
N.C.
B5 C
There's nev - er been an - y rea - son.
G/B C
G/B D5
Dsus4
D
Dsus4
D
G/B C
There's nev - er been an - y rea - son,
yeah,
hey.

G/B C
G/B D5
Dsus4
D5
G/B C
There's nev-er been an-y rea - son.
w/ bar

Chorus

Gtr. 2 tacet
C
G5
D
Save my life, I'm go-ing down for the last time.
*Gtr. 4
mf
*Bass arr. for gtr.

C
G5
D
Wom-an with the sweet lov-ing, bet-ter than a white line.
(Don't you know she could.)

C
G5
D
Bring a good feel-ing ain't had in such a long time.
Gtr. 2
Harm.
Pitch: G
Gtr. 4
C
G
D
Save my life, I'm go-ing down for the last time.
Whoa.
Harm.
Pitch: G D
G
Gtr. 2: w/ Rhy. Fig. 2
Gtr. 4 tacet
C
G5
D Dsus4 D Dsus4 D
Save my life, I'm go-ing down for the last time.

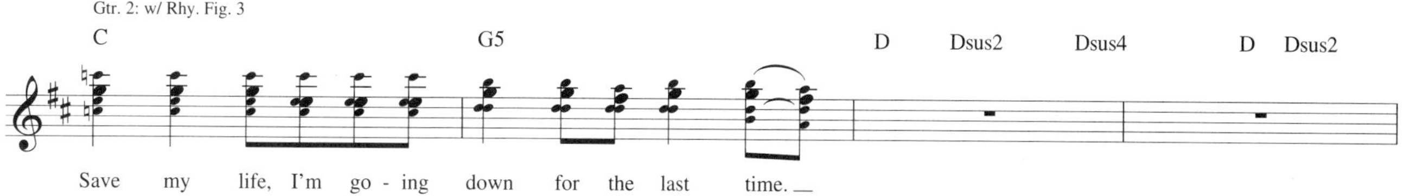
Gtr. 2: w/ Rhy. Fig. 3
C
G5
D
Dsus2
Dsus4
D
Dsus2
Save my life, I'm go - ing down for the last time.

C
G5
D
Dsus4
D5
Dsus4
D
Save my life, I'm go - ing down for the last time.
Gtr. 2

C
G5
D
D
D Dsus4 D Dsus2
Save my life, I'm go - ing down for the last time.

Free time
C
rit.
G5
D5
Dsus4 D
D
N.C.
Save my life, I'm go - ing down for the last time.
rit.

from Badfinger - *No Dice*

No Matter What

Written by Peter Ham

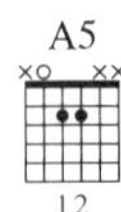

*Chord symbols reflect implied harmony.

D E D E A E N.C.
do, girl, oo, girl, with you. No mat-ter what you
End Rhy. Fig. 1A
let ring
End Rhy. Fig. 1
Gtrs. 1 & 2: w/ Rhy. Figs. 1 & 1A (1st 4 meas.)
A Bm
do, I will al-ways be a - round. Won't you tell me what you
D E D E A
found, girl? Oo, girl, won't you?
Gtr. 2
Gtr. 1
let ring

Chorus
F♯m7
B7
E7
A7
Knock down the old grey wall...
...be a part of it all.
Noth - ing to
Rhy. Fig. 2A
let ring
Rhy. Fig. 2
D7
Bm
A
say, noth - ing to see, noth - ing to do.
End Rhy. Fig. 2A
End Rhy. Fig. 2
Gtrs. 1 & 2: w/ Rhy. Figs. 2 & 2A (1st 6 meas.)
If you would give me all... ...as I would give it to you, noth - ing would
G
E N.C.
be, noth-ing would be, noth - ing would be.
2. No mat-ter where you
Rhy. Fig. 3
*Gtrs. 1 & 2
End Rhy. Fig. 3
P.M.
*Composite arrangement

Verse
Gtrs. 1 & 2: w/ Rhy. Figs. 1 & 1A
A
Bm
go, there will al-ways be a place. Can't you see it in my
Riff A
Gtr. 3 (dist.)
End Riff A
w/ phaser & heavy reverb
let ring
D E D E *A5
Gtrs. 1 & 2
(cont. in notation)
face, girl? Oo, girl, want you.
*See top of first page of song for chord diagram pertaining to rhythm slashes.
Guitar Solo
Gtr. 3 tacet
A
Bm
Gtr. 4 (slight dist.)
w/ slide
steady gliss.
Gtr. 2
Gtr. 3
divisi
**Gtr. 2 to left of slash in tab.
Gtr. 1

D E D E A
Gtr. 4
steady gliss.
Gtr. 3
let ring
Gtr. 2
Gtr. 1
let ring
let ring
Chorus
Gtrs. 1 & 2: w/ Rhy. Figs. 2 & 2A (1 6/8 times)
Gtr. 4 tacet
F♯m7 B7 E7 A7
Knock down the old grey wall... ...be a part of it all. Noth-ing to
Voc. Fig. 1
(Ah,
Gtr. 3
let ring
let ring

D7
Bm
A
say, noth - ing to see, noth - ing to do.
End Voc. Fig. 1
ah.)
let ring
Bkgd. Voc.: w/ Voc. Fig. 1
F♯m7
B7
E7
A7
If you would give me all... ...as I would give it to you, noth - ing would
let ring
D7
Bm
Gtrs. 1 & 2: w/ Rhy. Fig. 3
G
E N.C.
be, noth - ing would be, noth - ing would be.
3. No mat-ter what you
let ring
Verse
Gtrs. 1 & 2: w/ Rhy. Figs. 1 & 1A (1st 4 meas.)
Gtr. 3: w/ Riff A
A
Bm
are, I will al - ways be with you. Does - n't mat - ter what you

D
E
D
E
A
N.C.
do, girl, oo, girl, with you?
Gtr. 3
let ring
Gtr. 2
let ring
let ring
Gtr. 1
let ring
1.
2.
D
E
D
E
A
Oo, girl, you, girl, want you.
let ring
let ring
let ring
let ring
*2nd time, upper note is D.
let ring
*2nd time, upper note is D.

from Queens of the Stone Age - *Songs for the Deaf*

No One Knows

Words and Music by Mark Lanegan, Josh Homme and Nick Oliveri

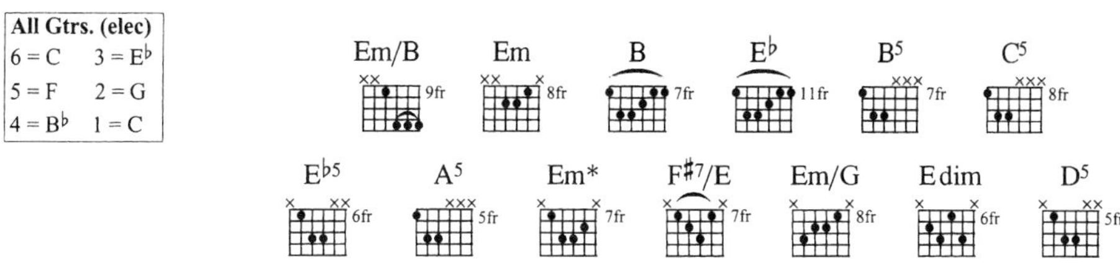

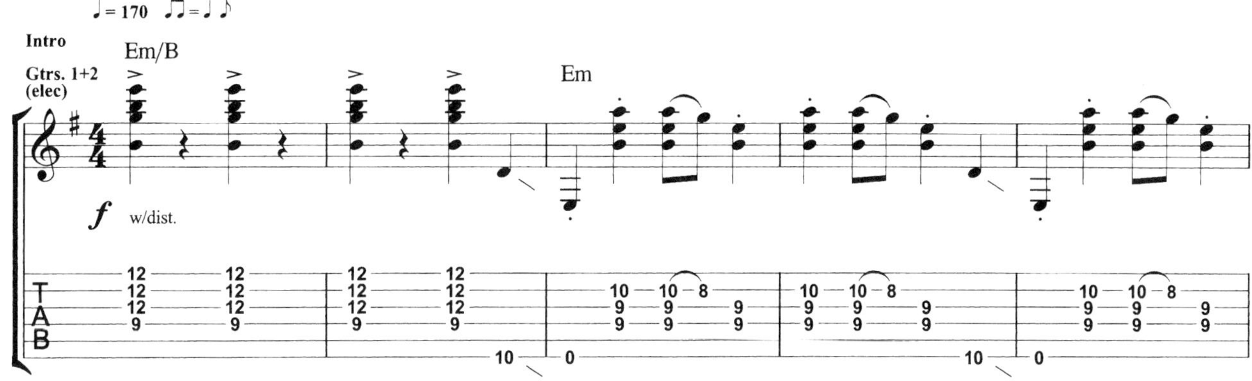

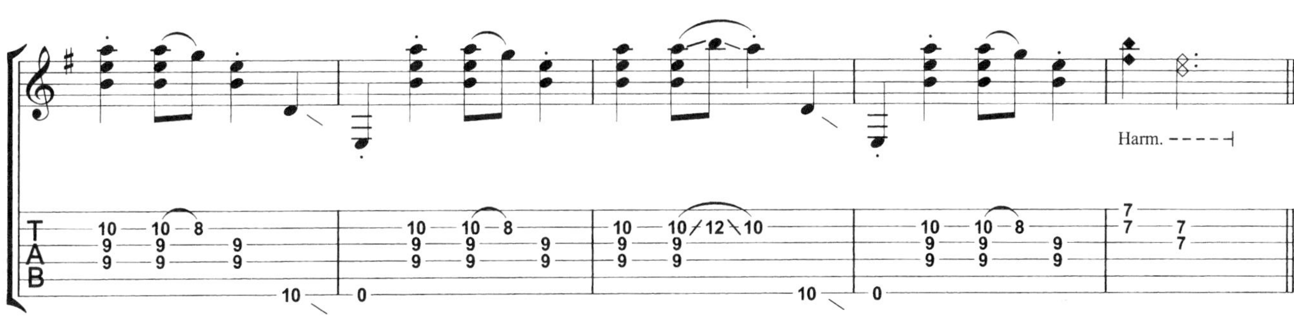

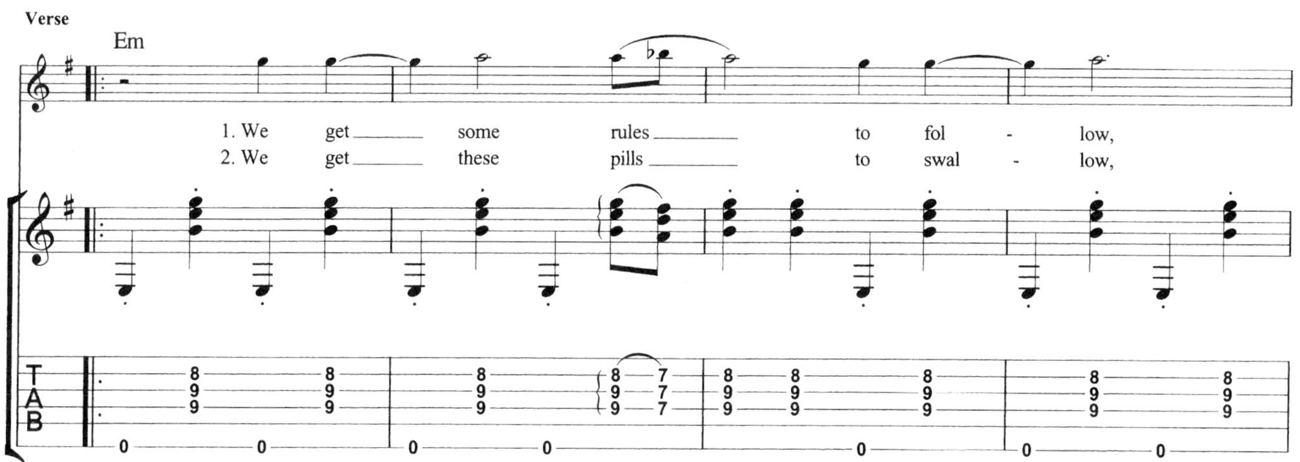

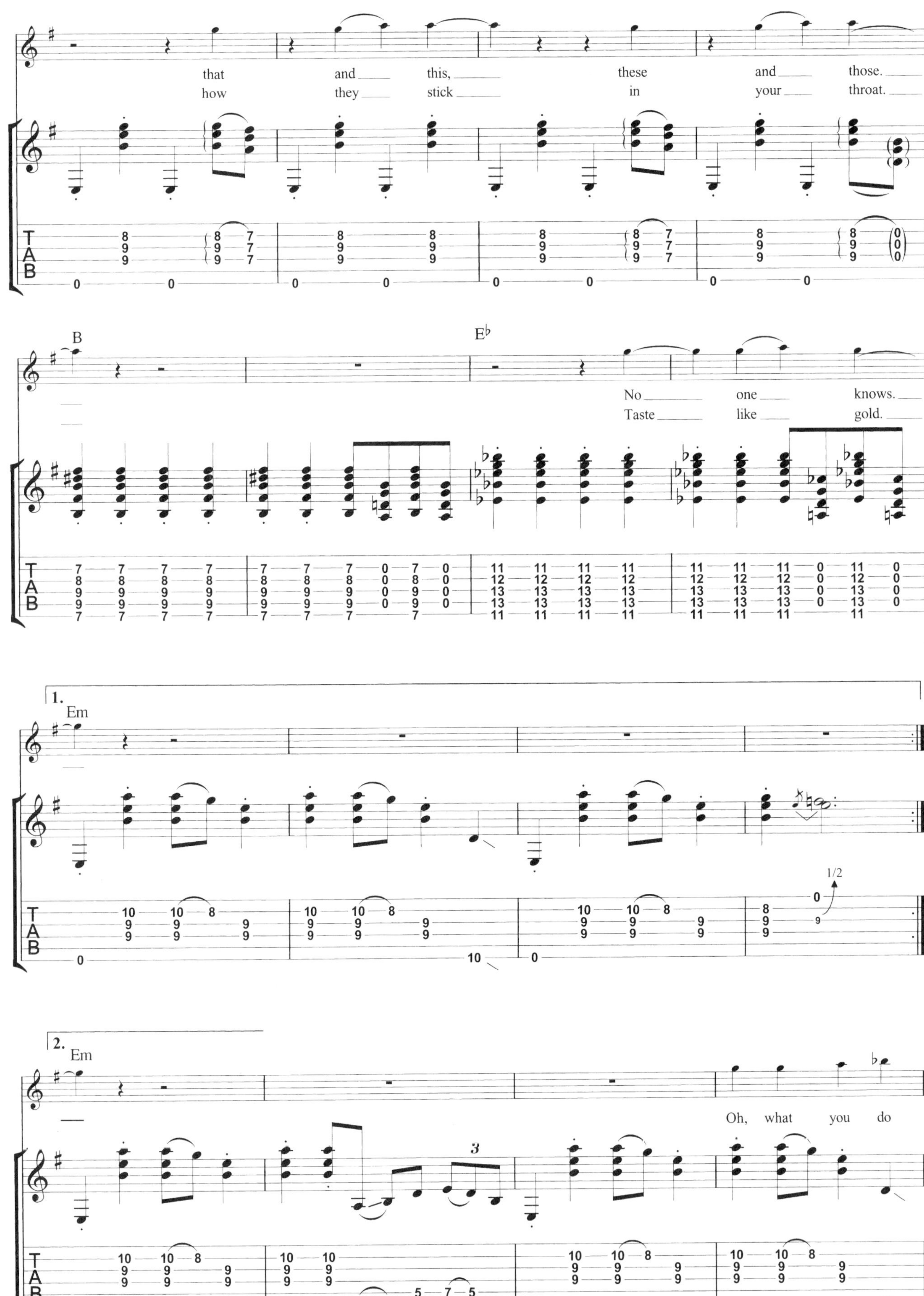
that and this, these and those.
how they stick in your throat.
B
E♭
No one knows.
Taste like gold.
1.
Em
2.
Em
Oh, what you do

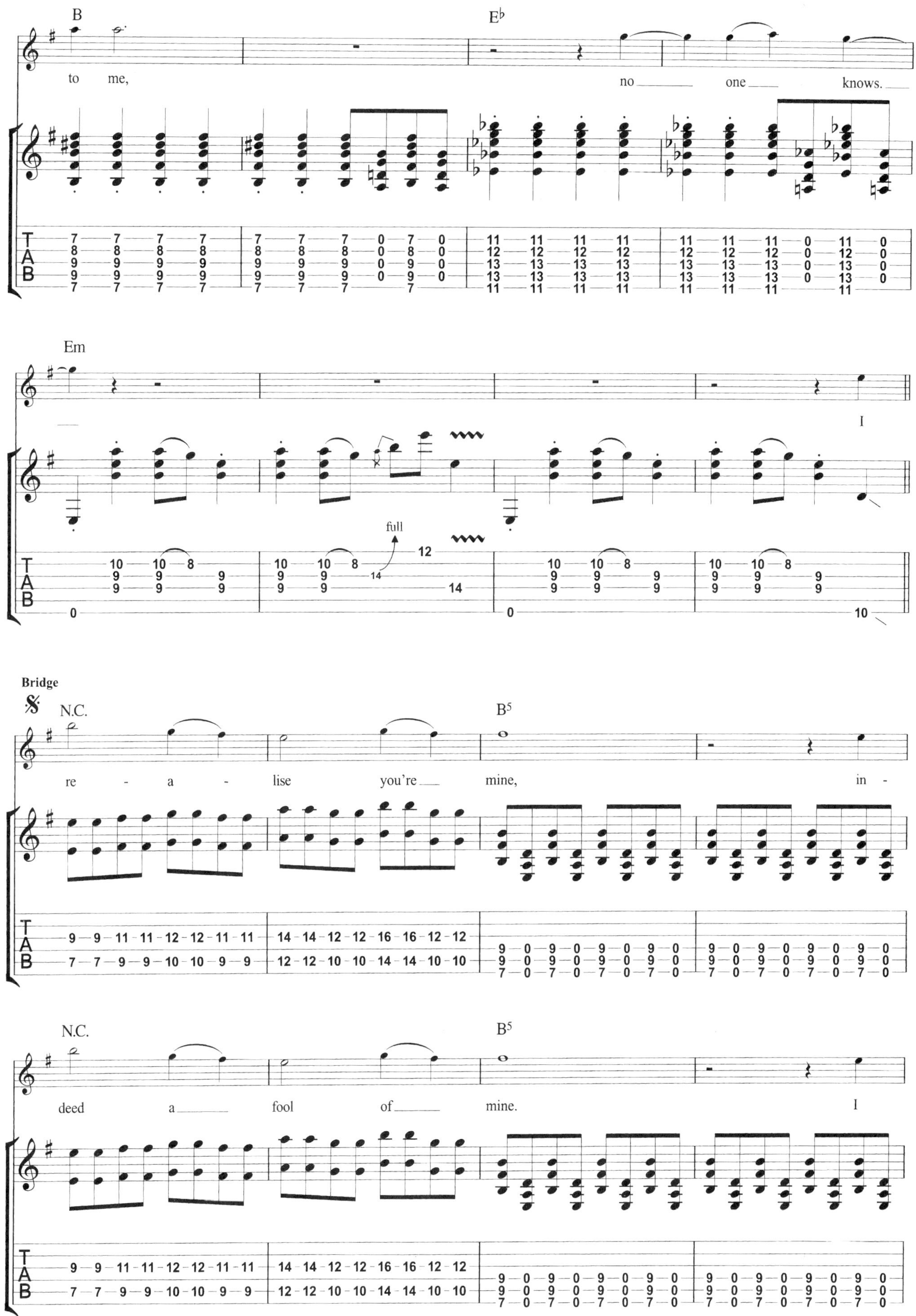
B
E♭
to me,
no one knows.
Em
I
full
Bridge
N.C.
B5
re - a - lise you're mine,
in -
N.C.
B5
deed a fool of mine.
I

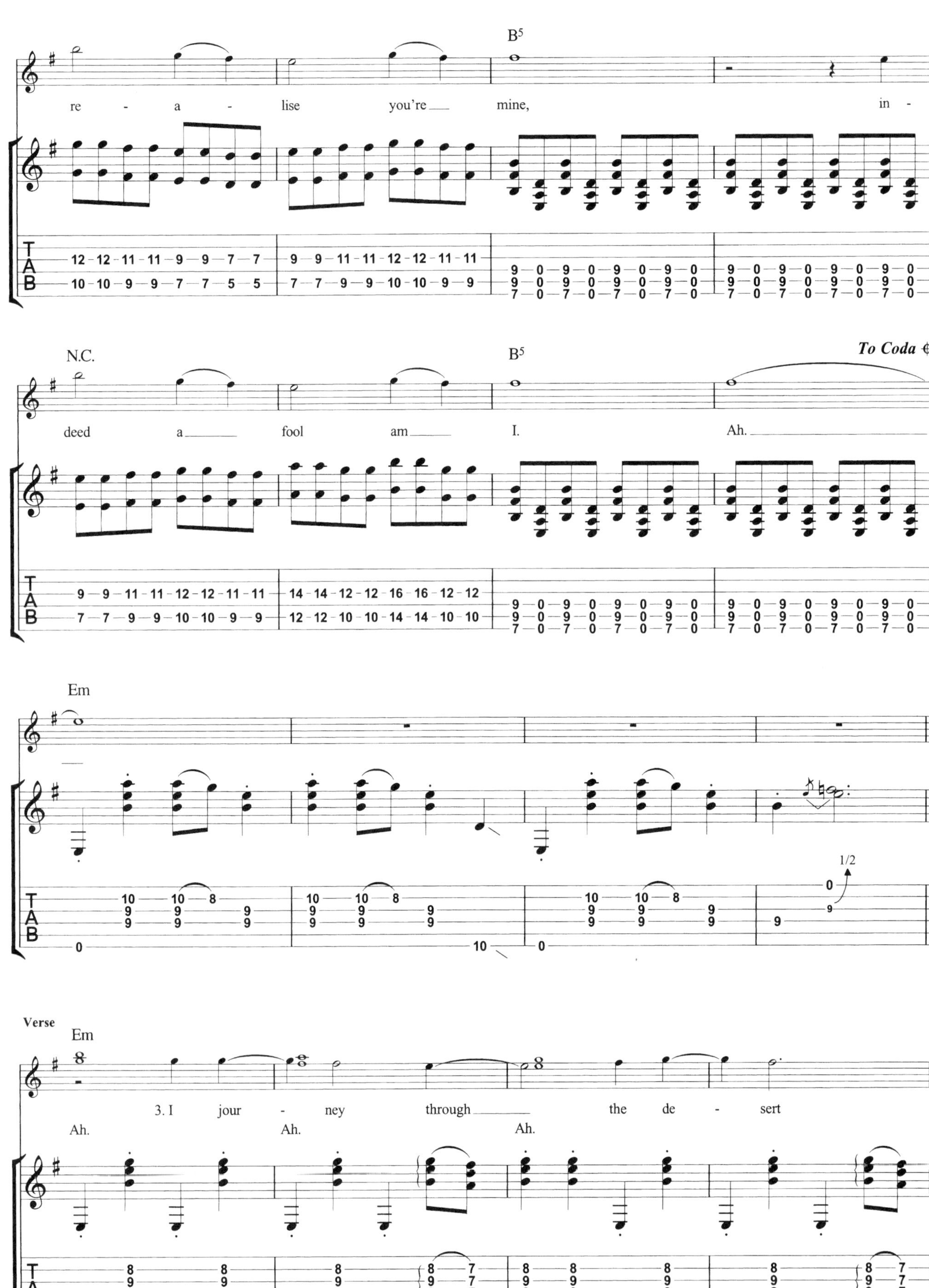
B5
re - a - lise you're mine, in -
N.C.
B5
To Coda
deed a fool am I. Ah.
Em
Verse
Em
3. I jour - ney through the de - sert
Ah. Ah. Ah.

of the mind with no hope.
Ah. Ah. Ah. Ah.
B
Eb
I fol - low.
Ah.
Em
Verse
Em
4. I drift a - long the o - - cean,
Ah. Ah. Ah.

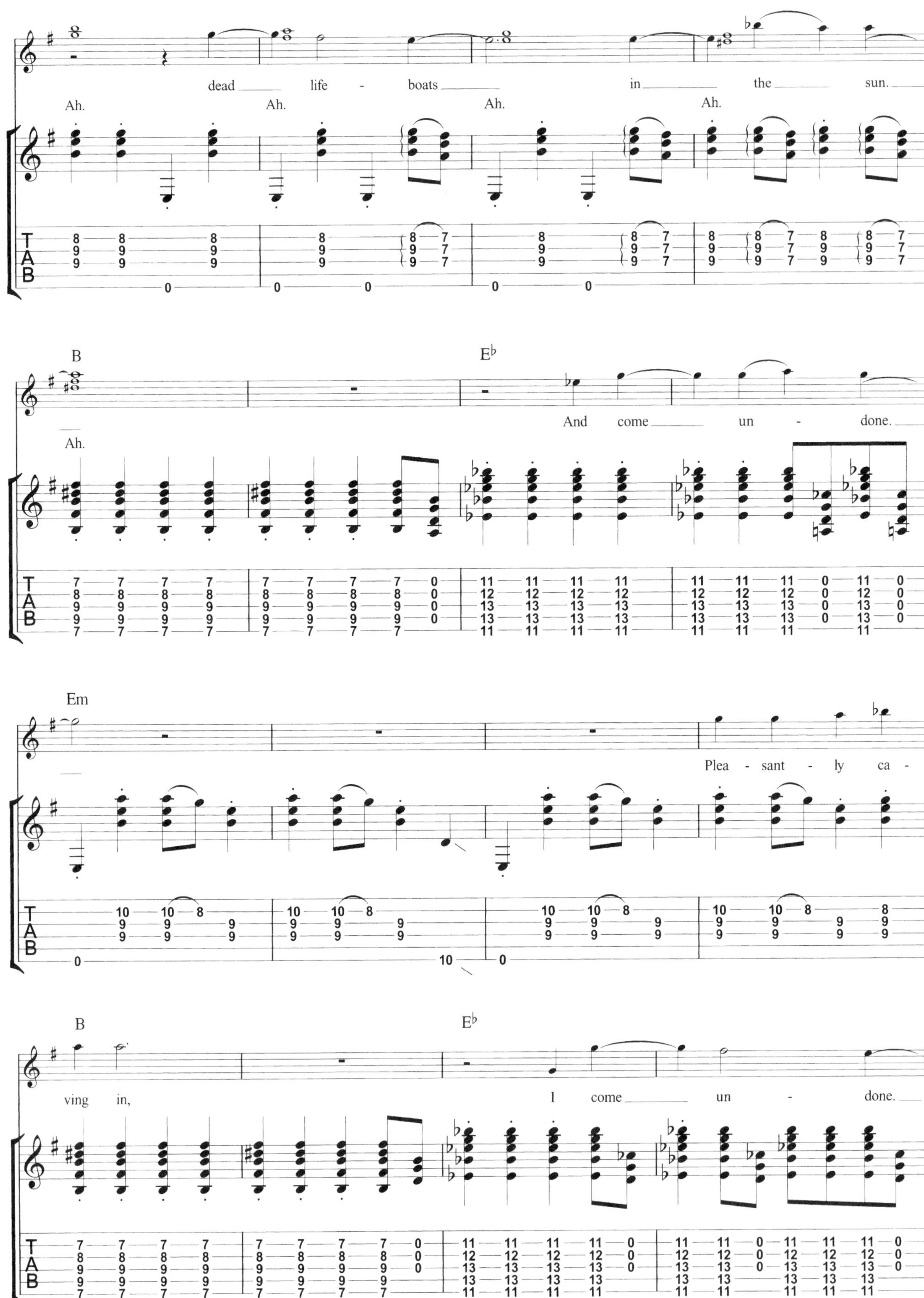
dead life - boats in the sun.
Ah. Ah. Ah. Ah.
B
E♭
And come un - done.
Ah.
Em
Plea - sant - ly ca -
B
E♭
ving in, I come un - done.
TAB
TAB
TAB
TAB

Em
D.S. al Coda
full
T
A
B

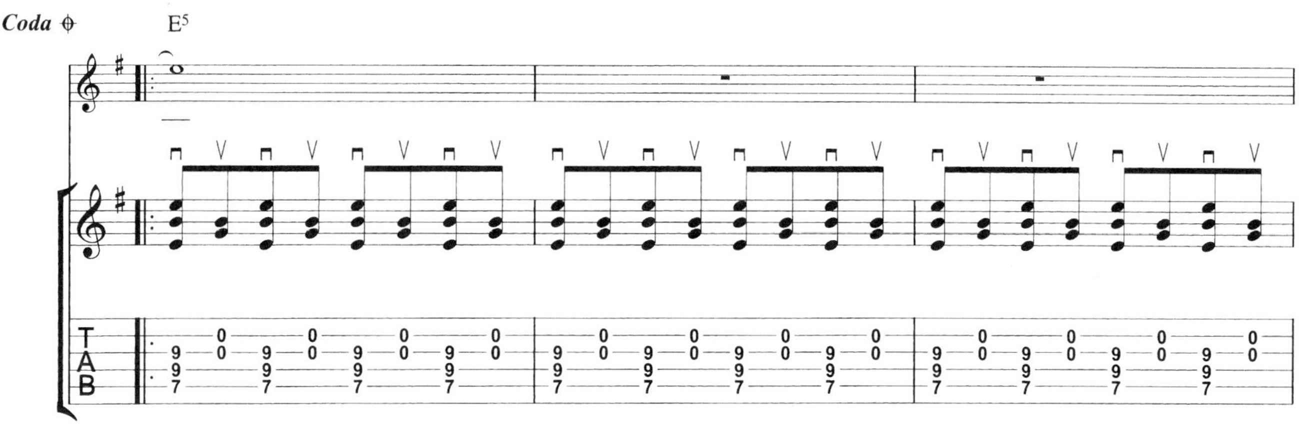
Coda
E5
T
A
B

B5 C5 E♭5 B5 A5 B5
B5 C5 E♭5 B5 A5 B5
C5 E♭5 B5 A5 B5
cont. sim.
T
A
B

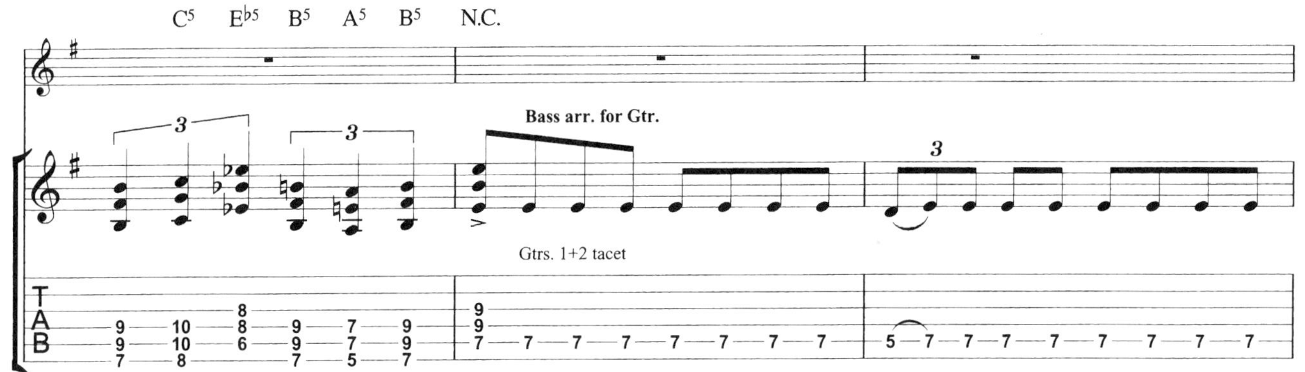
C5 E♭5 B5 A5 B5 N.C.
Bass arr. for Gtr.
Gtrs. 1+2 tacet
T
A
B

Solo

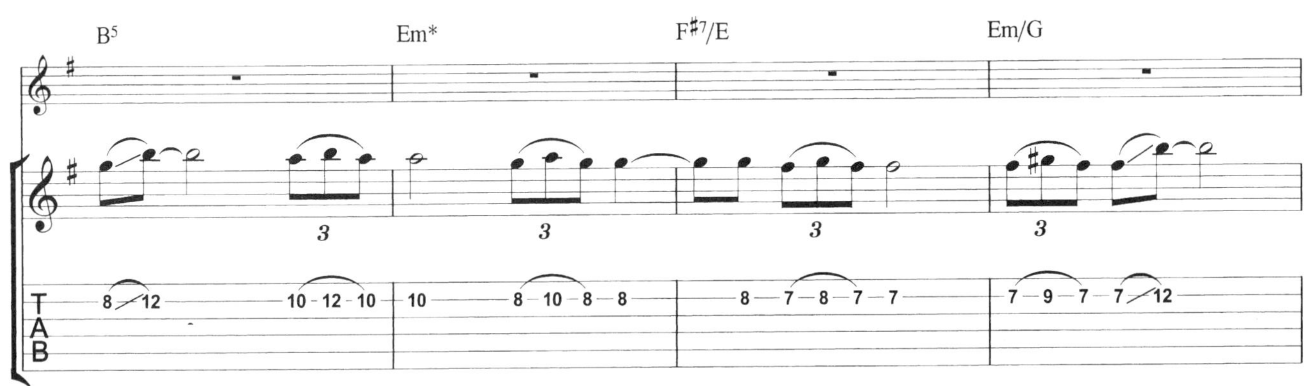

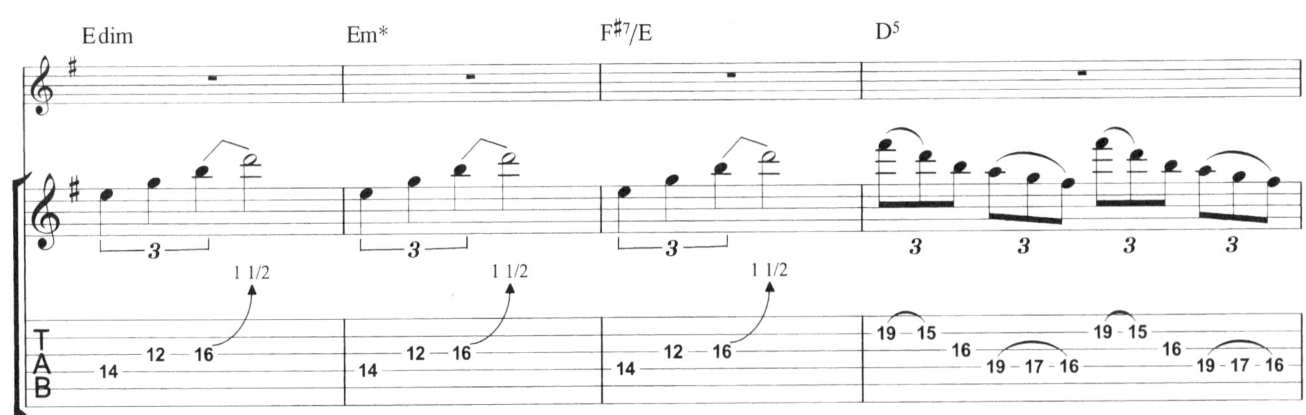

D♯5
E
Bass arr. for Gtr.
mf
N.C.
Hea - ven smiles
Em
a - bove me,
what a gift
Gtr. 1
*strike strings behind bridge
B
here be - low.

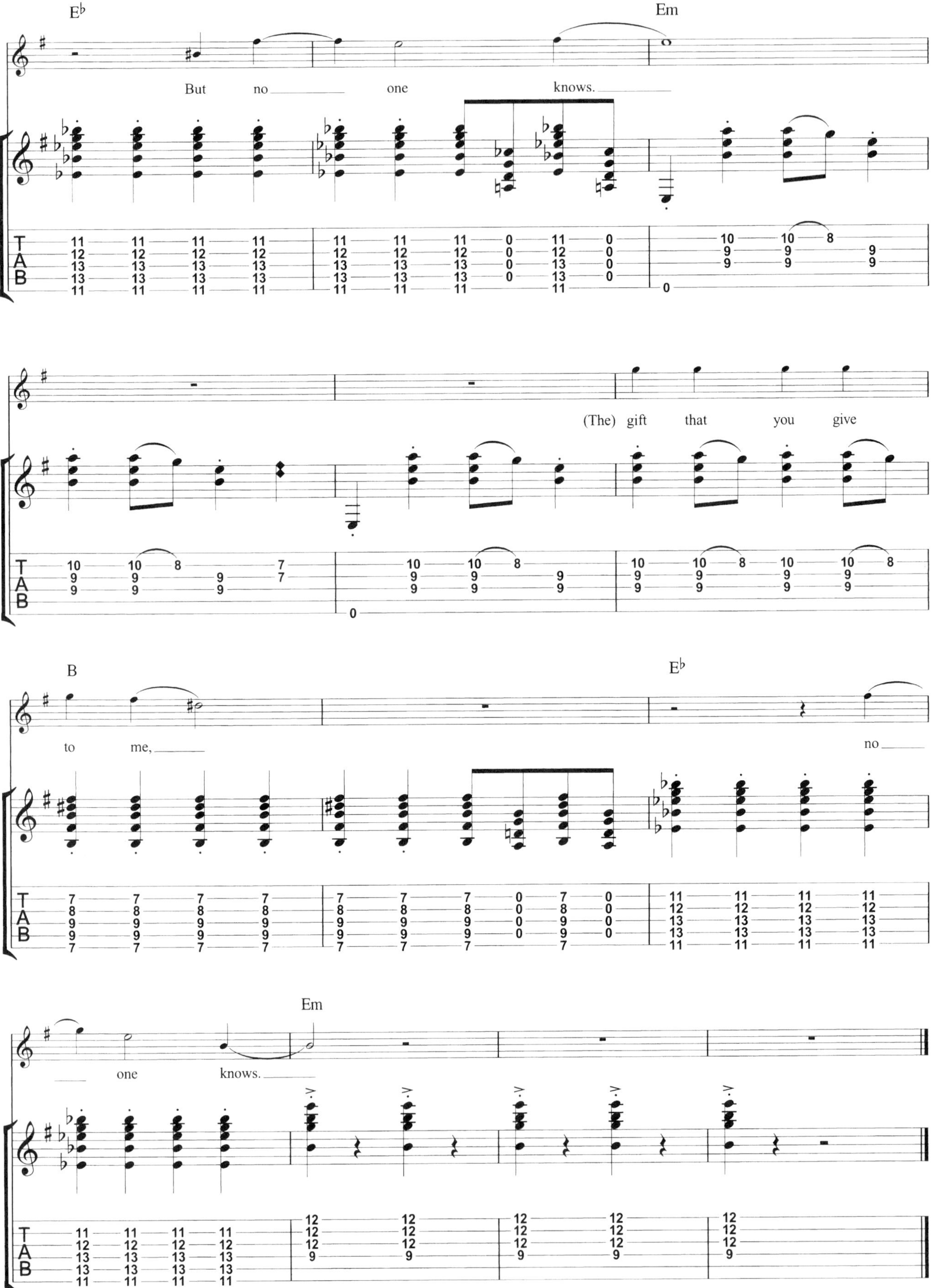
E♭
Em
But no one knows.
(The) gift that you give
B
E♭
to me,
no
Em
one knows.

from Santana - *Santana III*

No One to Depend On

Words and Music by Gregg Rolie, Michael Carabello and Thomas Escovedo

*Ld. Voc. doubled throughout

Chorus
Gm C/G C C7sus2 Gm C/G C C7sus2
got no - bod - y that I can de - pend on. I ain't
Gm C/G C C7sus2 Gm C/G C C7sus2
got no - bod - y that I can de - pend on.
Gm
Chorus
Gm C/G
8va
Rhy. Fig. 1
End Rhy. Fig. 1

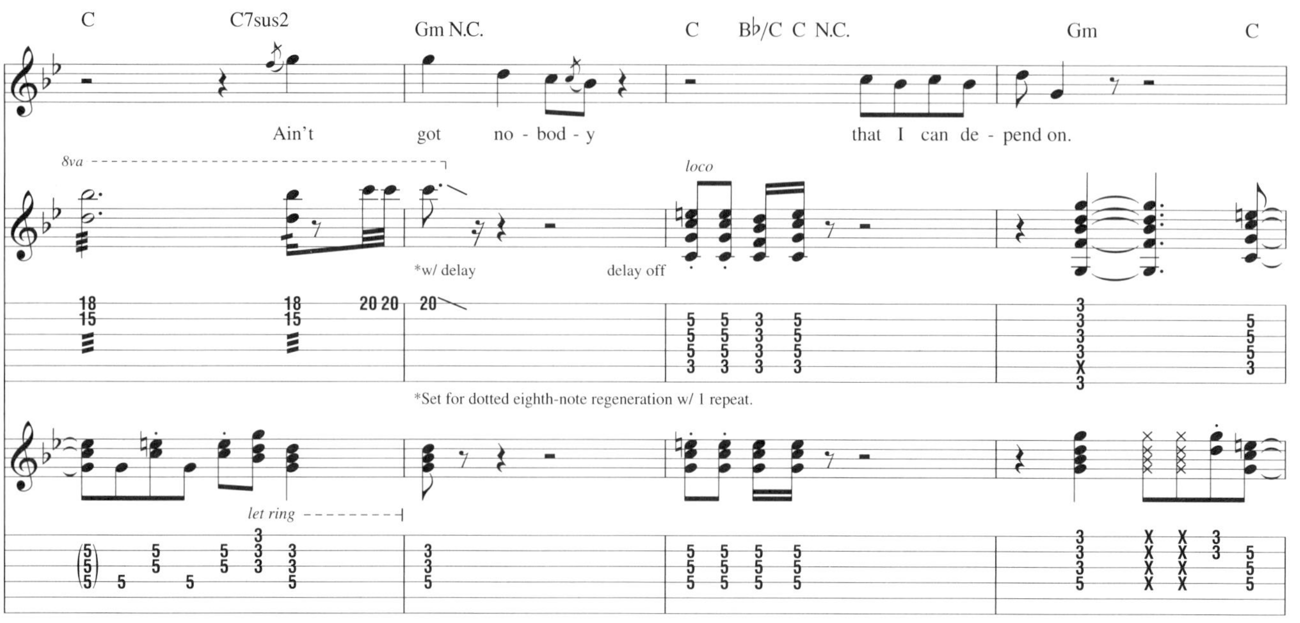
C
C7sus2
Gm N.C.
C
B♭/C C N.C.
Gm
C
Ain't got no - bod - y that I can de - pend on.
8va
loco
*w/ delay
delay off
*Set for dotted eighth-note regeneration w/ 1 repeat.
let ring

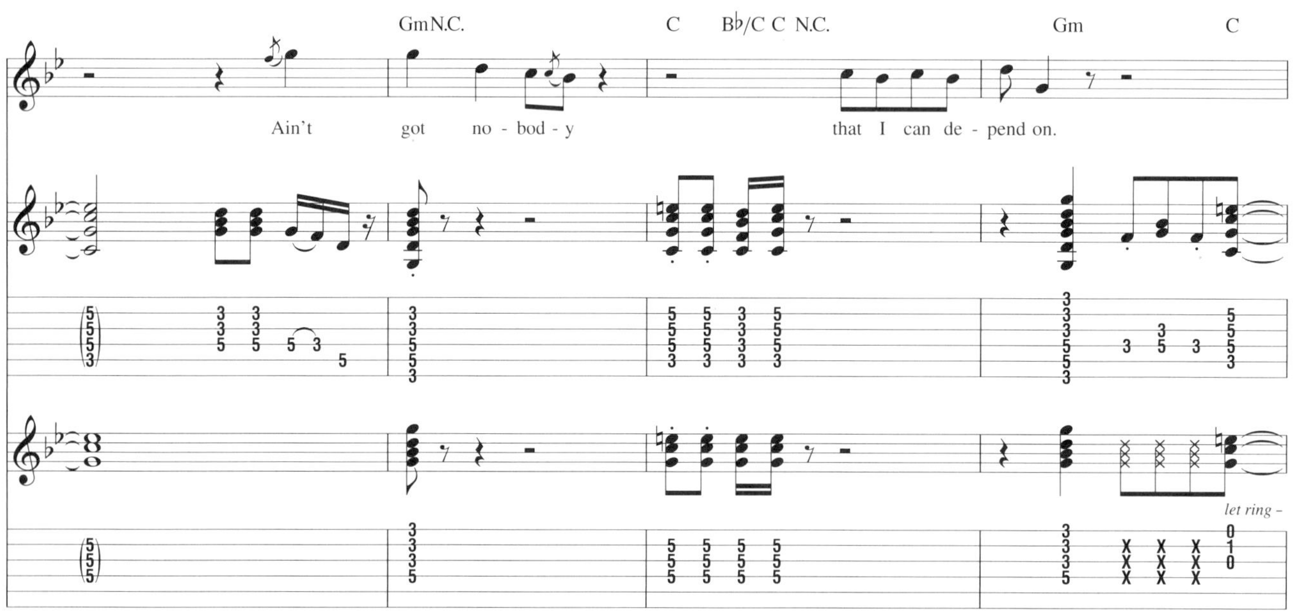
GmN.C.
C
B♭/C C N.C.
Gm
C
Ain't got no - bod - y that I can de - pend on.
let ring

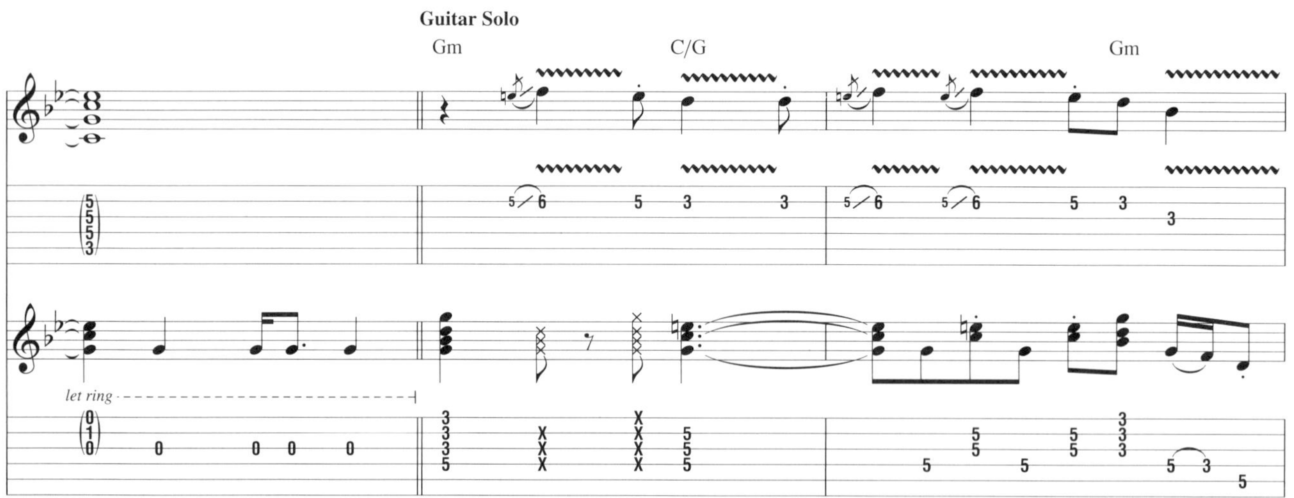
Guitar Solo
Gm
C/G
Gm
let ring

Chorus
C/G
Gm
Gm
C/G
Ain't got no one, no ten-go a na-
1/2
1/2
C
C7sus2
Gm
C/G
C
C7sus2
- di-e, that I know of, no ten-go a na - di-e, that I can de-
Rhy. Fig. 2
End Rhy. Fig. 2
1/4
1/4
Rhy. Fig. 2A
End Rhy. Fig. 2A
Gtrs. 2 & 3: w/ Rhy. Figs. 2 & 2A (4 times)
Gm
C/G
C
C7sus2
Gm
C/G
pend on, no ten-go a na - di-e, Ain't got no one, no ten-go a na-

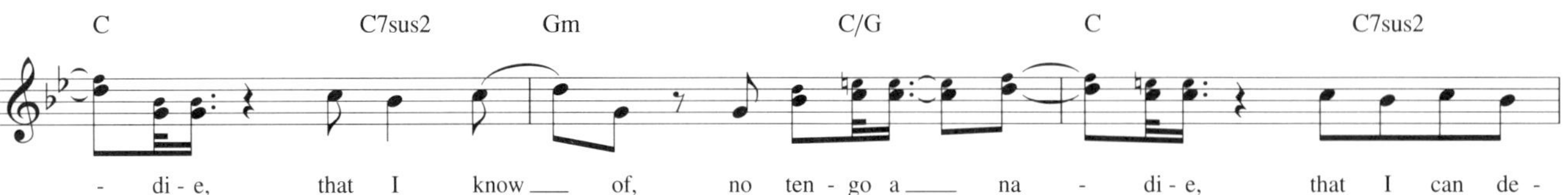

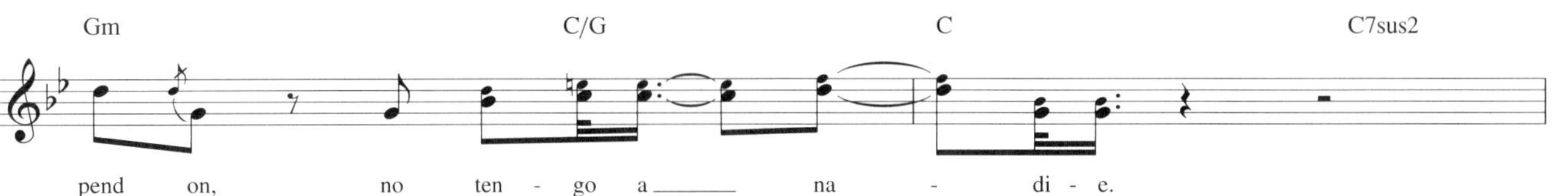

Interlude

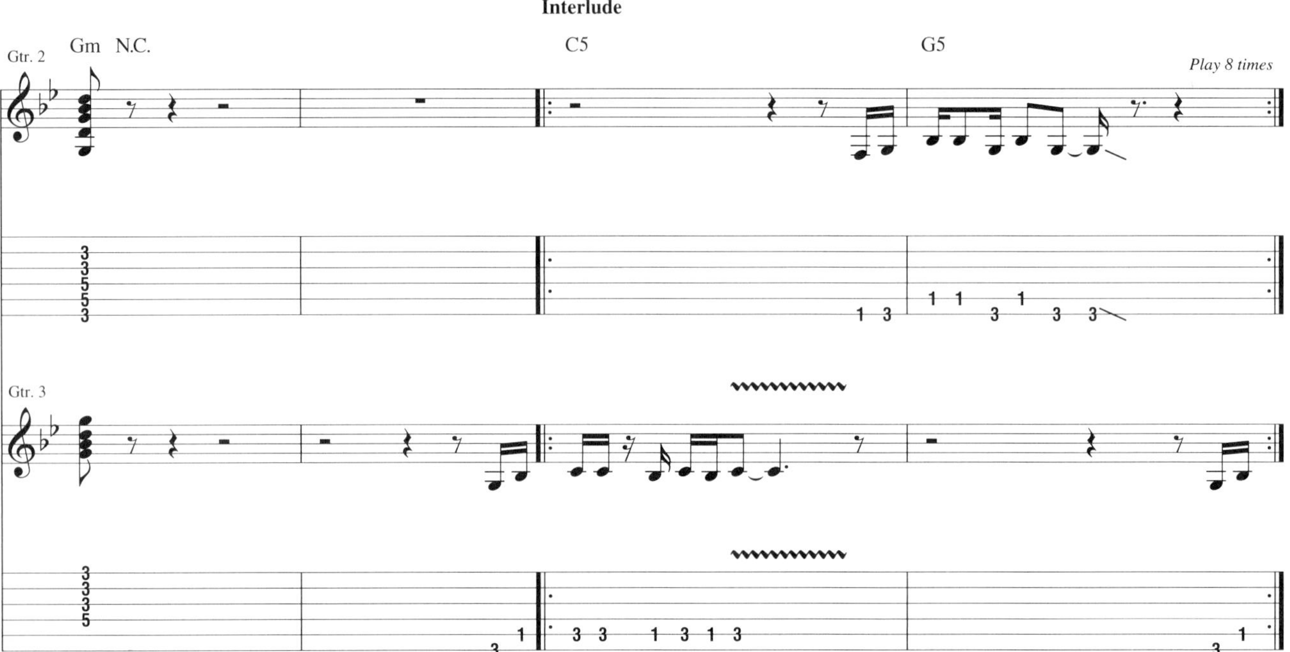

Guitar Solo

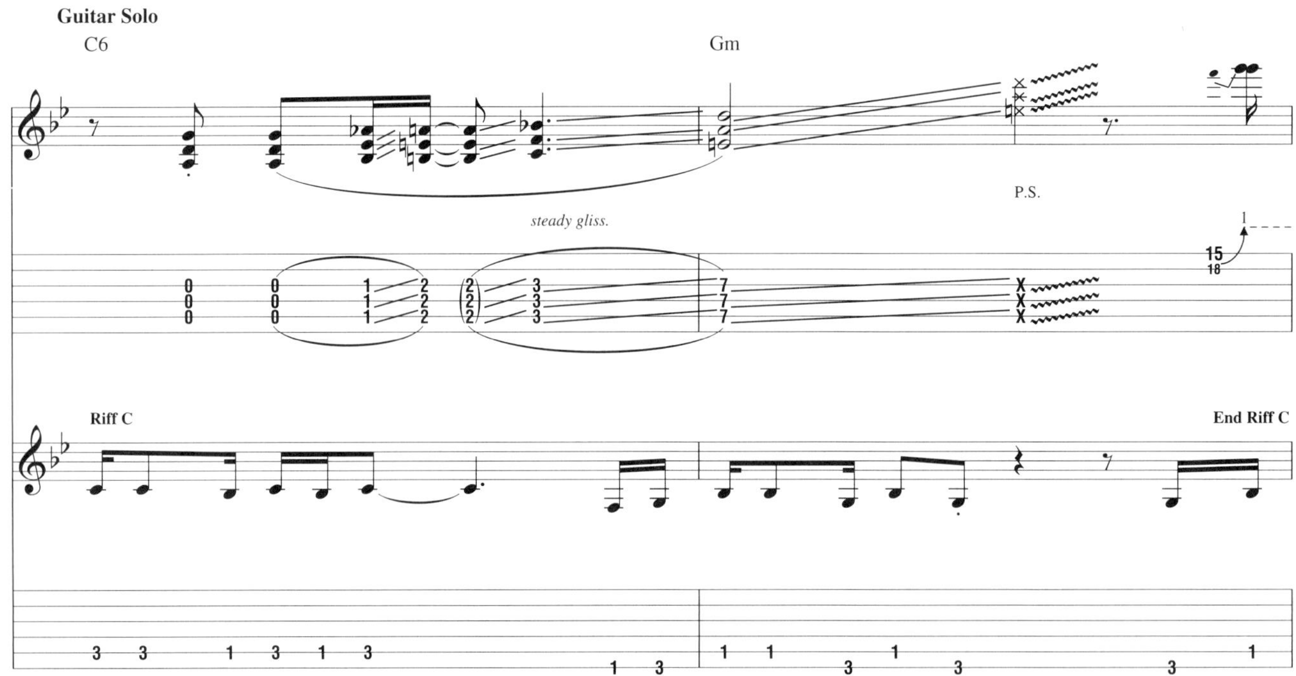

Gtr. 3: w/ Riff C (6 times)
C6
Gm
Gtr. 2
8va
loco
tr
*Played ahead of the beat.

C6
Gm
Gtr. 4 (dist.)
mf
Gtr. 2
Gtr. 3
Guitar Solo
Gtr. 3 tacet
C6
Gm
Gtr. 4
Gtr. 2
C6
Gm
let ring
hold bend
Riff D
End Riff D

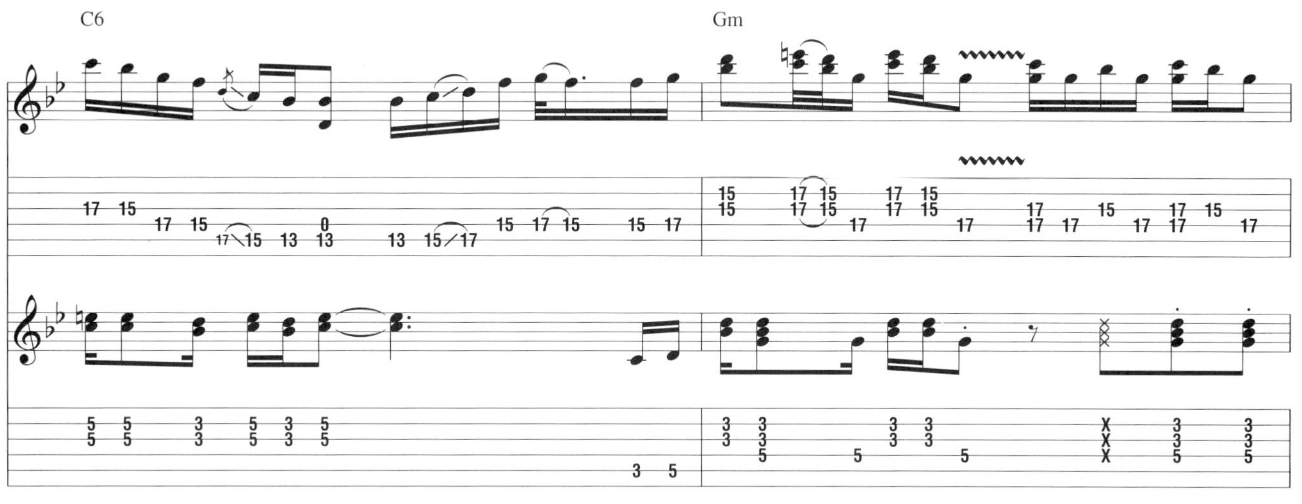

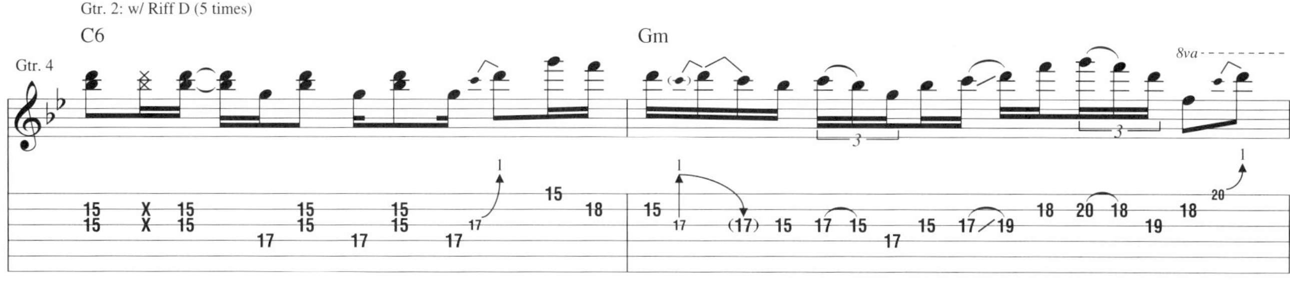

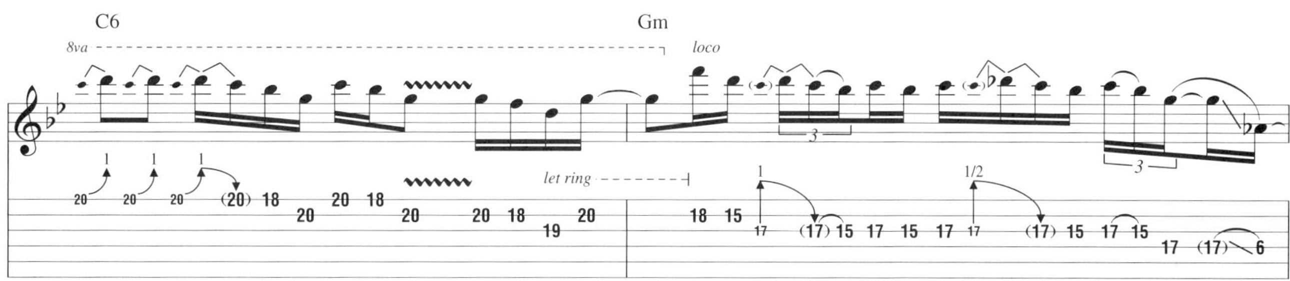

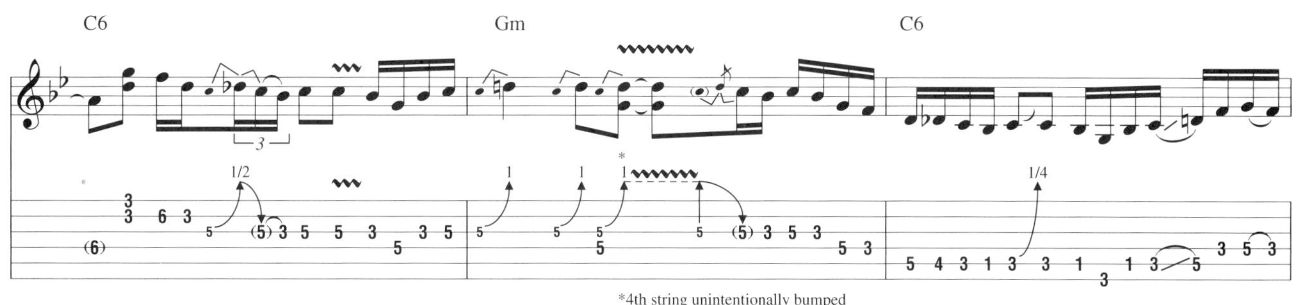

*4th string unintentionally bumped while performing bend.

C6
Gm
Gtr. 4
Gtr. 2
Gtr. 3
Gtr. 3: w/ Riff C (4 1/2 times)
C6
Gm
Gtr. 4
Gtr. 2
C6
Gm

C6
Gm
1/2
1/2
1/2

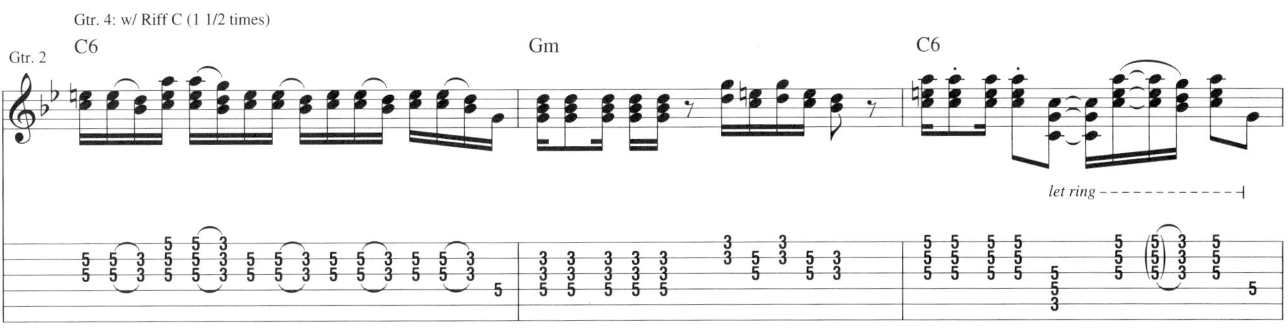
Gtr. 4: w/ Riff C (1 1/2 times)
Gtr. 2
C6
Gm
C6
let ring

Gm
Gtr. 2
Gtr. 4 tacet
N.C.
Gtrs. 3 & 4
Gtr. 3

Interlude

Chorus

Gm C/G C C7sus2 Gm C/G

got no - bod - y that I can de - pend on, no ten - go a___ na -

Gtr. 2

Gtr. 3

C C7sus2 Gm C/G C C7sus2

- di - e. I ain't got no - bod - y that I can de -

w/ pick & finger

1 1/2

1

Outro

Gtr. 3: w/ Rhy. Fig. 1 (1 1/2 times)

Gm

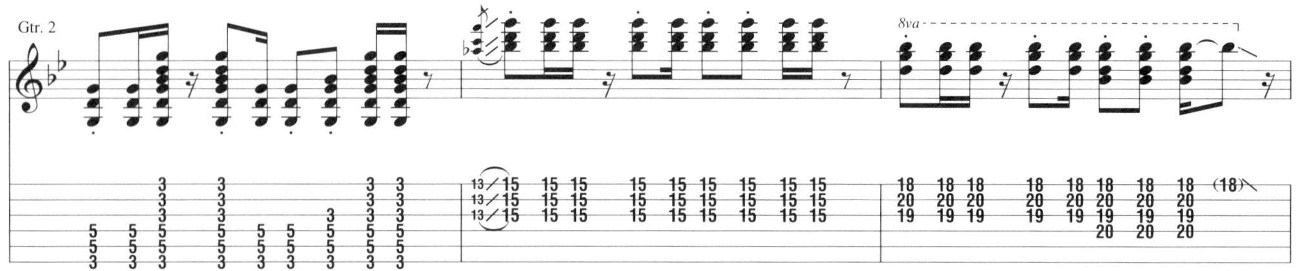

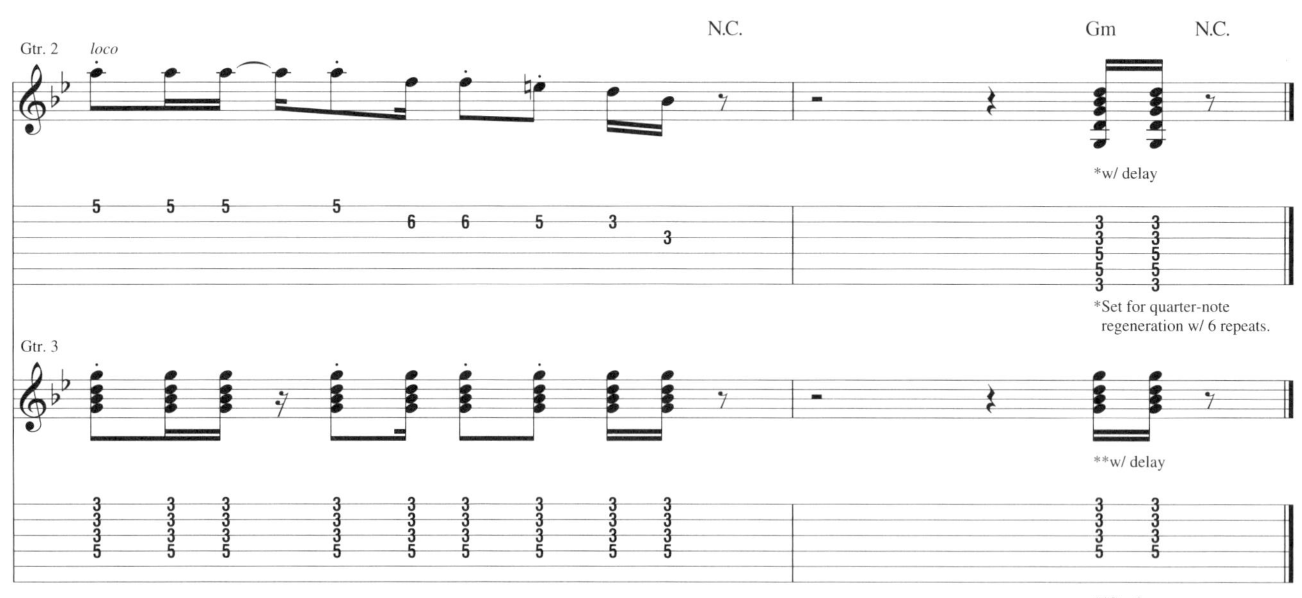

**Set for quarter-note regeneration w/ 6 repeats.

from Alice in Chains - *Jar of Flies*

Nutshell

Words by Layne Staley

Music by Jerry Cantrell, Mike Inez and Sean Kinney

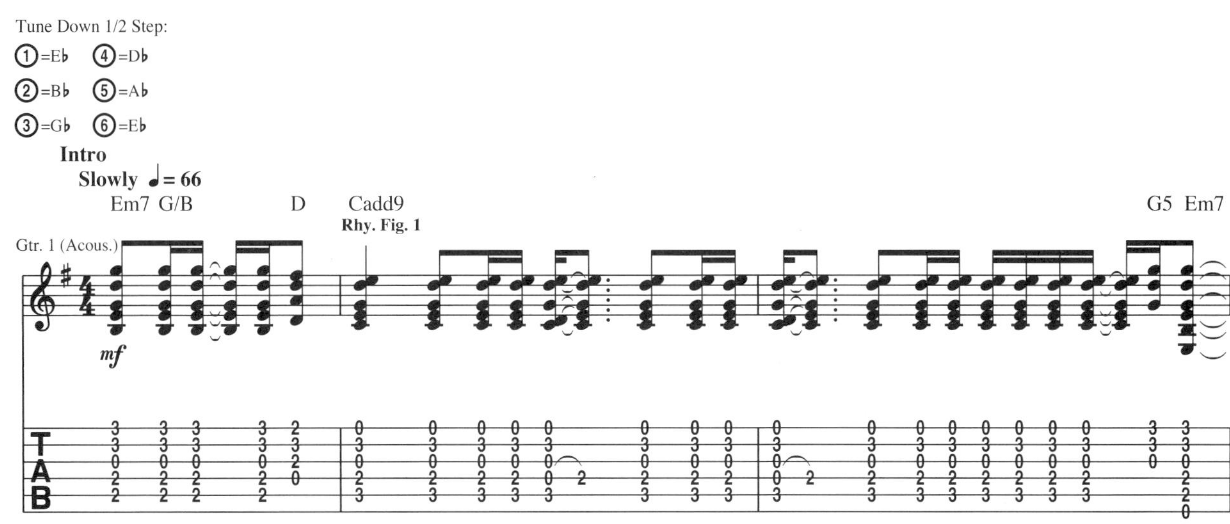

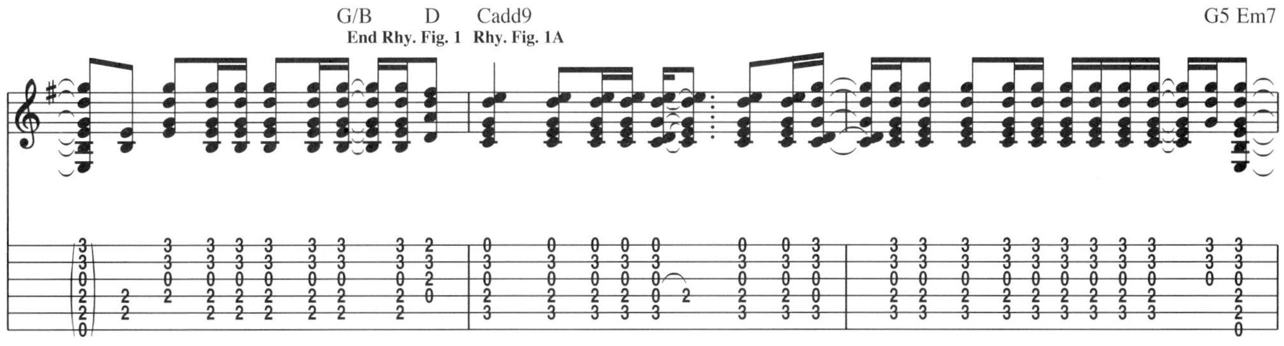

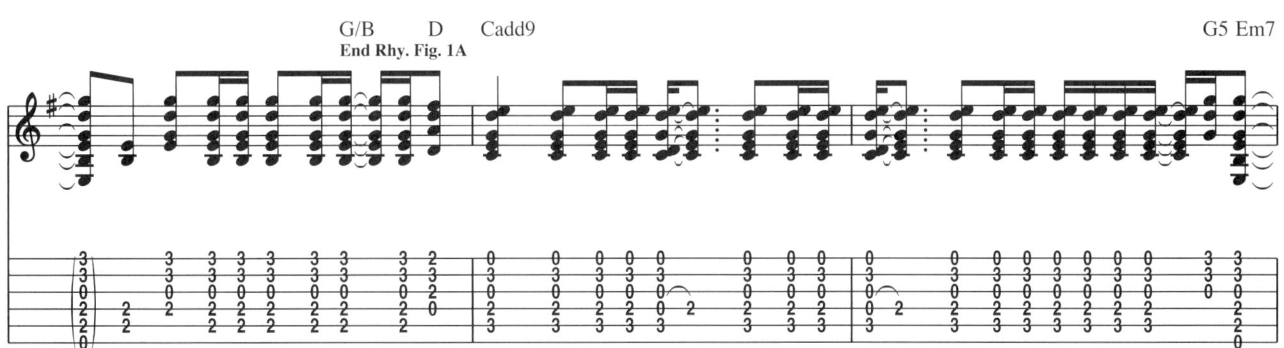

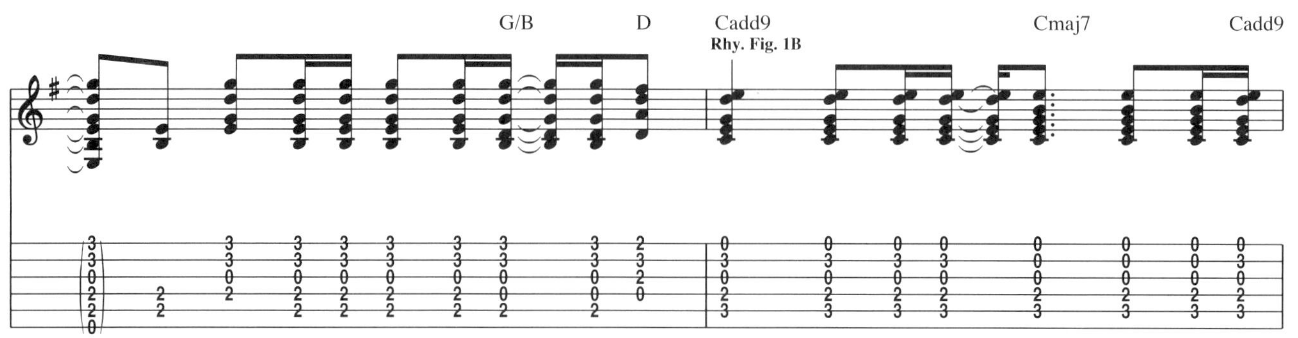
G/B
D
Cadd9
Rhy. Fig. 1B
Cmaj7
Cadd9

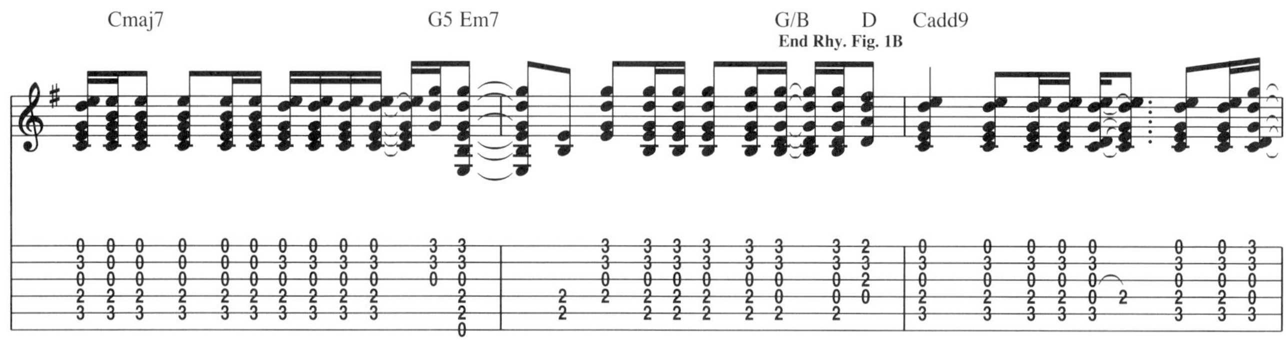
Cmaj7
G5 Em7
G/B
D
Cadd9
End Rhy. Fig. 1B

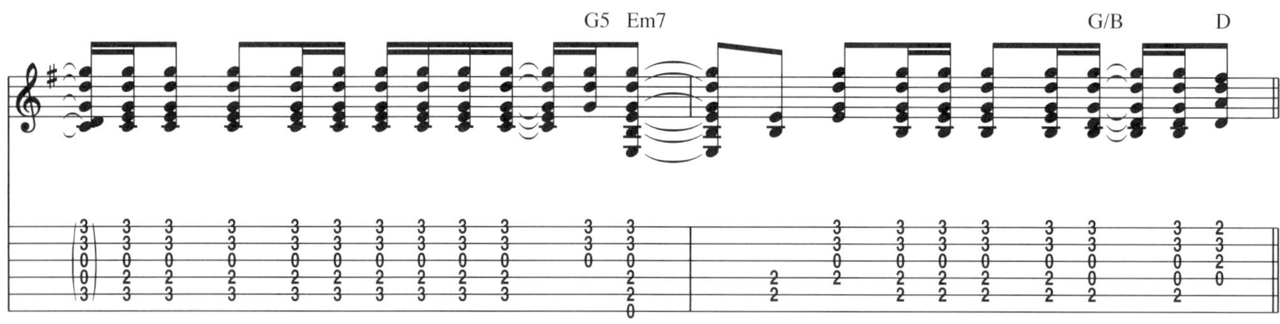
G5 Em7
G/B
D

Verse

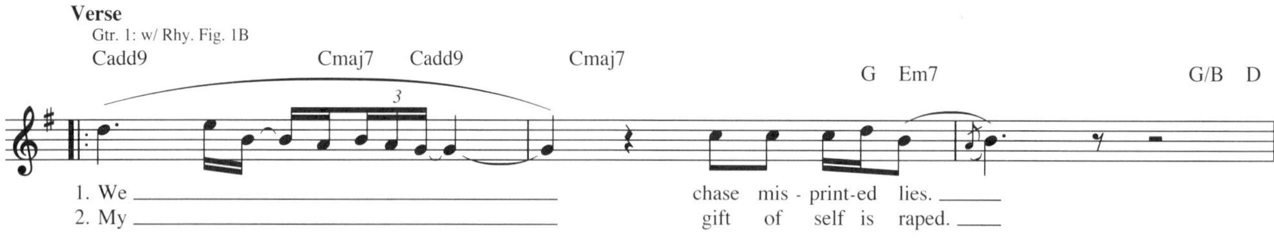
Gtr. 1: w/ Rhy. Fig. 1B
Cadd9
Cmaj7
Cadd9
Cmaj7
G Em7
G/B D
1. We chase mis - print-ed lies.
2. My gift of self is raped.

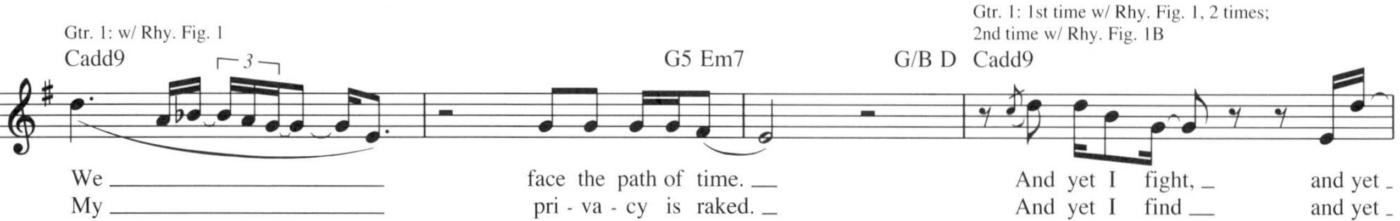
Gtr. 1: w/ Rhy. Fig. 1
Cadd9
G5 Em7
G/B D
Gtr. 1: 1st time w/ Rhy. Fig. 1, 2 times;
2nd time w/ Rhy. Fig. 1B
Cadd9
We face the path of time. And yet I fight, and yet
My pri - va - cy is raked. And yet I find and yet

Gtr. 1: 2nd time w/ Rhy. Fig. 1C
G5 Em7
G/B D
Cadd9
G5 Em7
I fight this bat-tle all a-lone. No one to cry to, no place to call home.
I find re-peat-ing in my head. If I can't be my own, I'd feel bet-ter dead.
Gtr. 1: 1st time w/ Rhy. Fig. 1A;
2nd time w/ Rhy. Fig. 1C
G/B D
Cadd9
G5 Em7
G/B D
(Ooh.)
(Ooh.)
Gtr. 2 (Elec.)
1/2
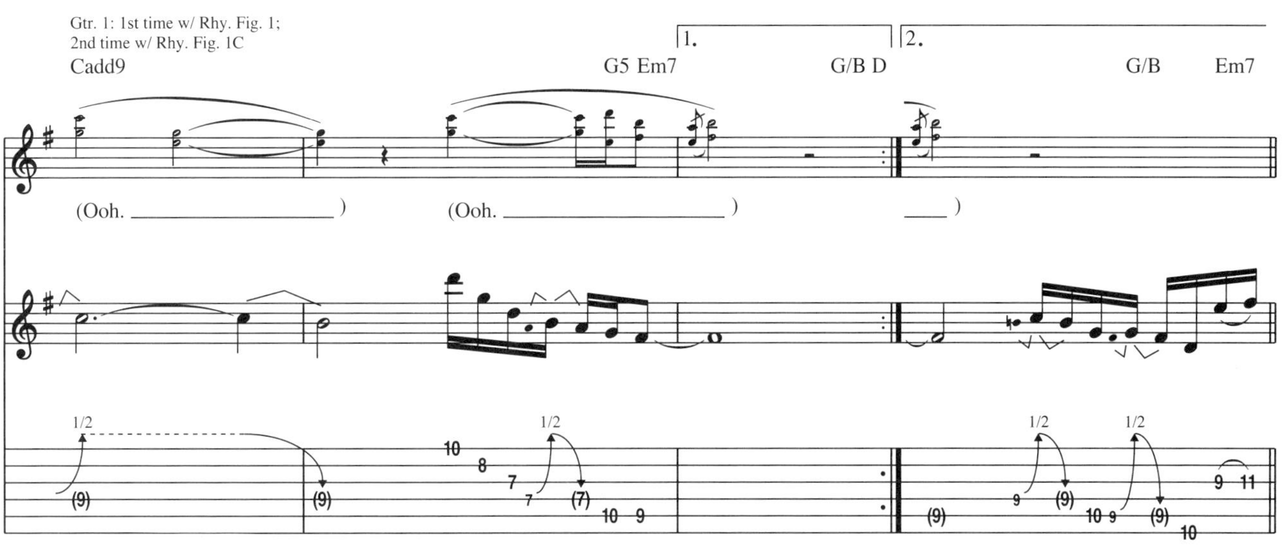
Gtr. 1: 1st time w/ Rhy. Fig. 1;
2nd time w/ Rhy. Fig. 1C
Cadd9
G5 Em7
G/B D
1.
2.
G/B
Em7
(Ooh.)
(Ooh.)
1/2
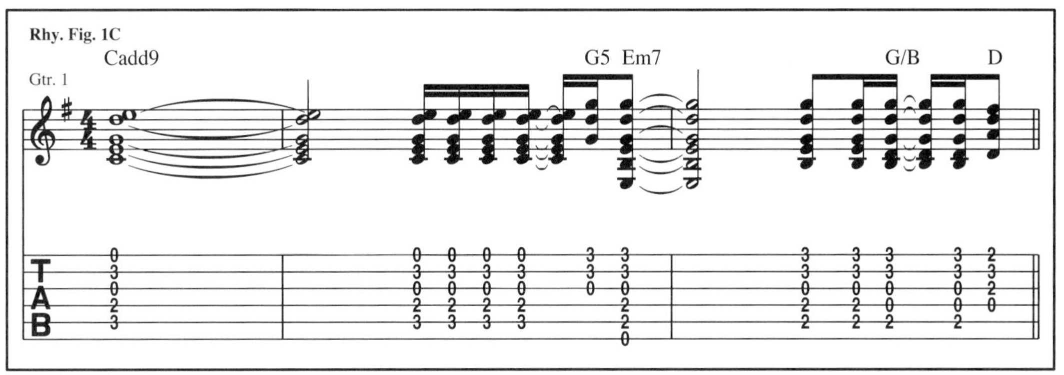
Rhy. Fig. 1C
Cadd9
G5 Em7
G/B
D
Gtr. 1
T
A
B

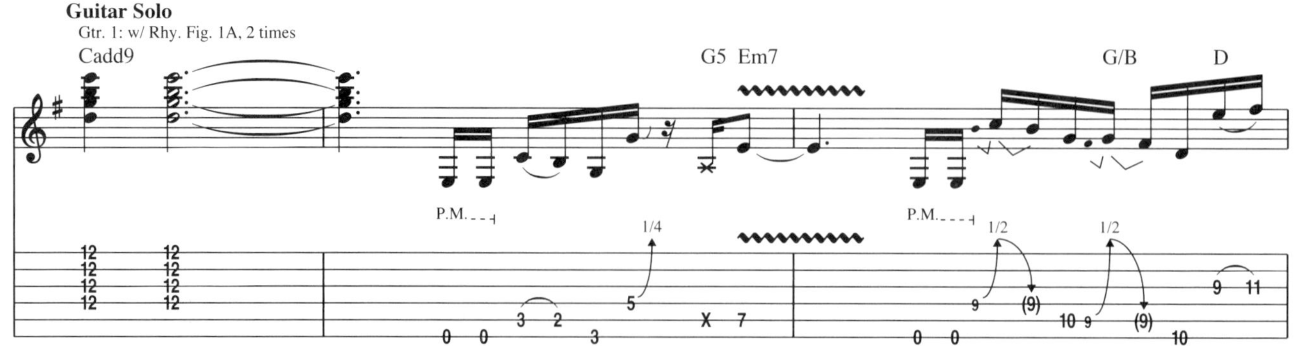
Guitar Solo
Gtr. 1: w/ Rhy. Fig. 1A, 2 times
Cadd9
G5 Em7
G/B D
P.M.
1/4
1/2

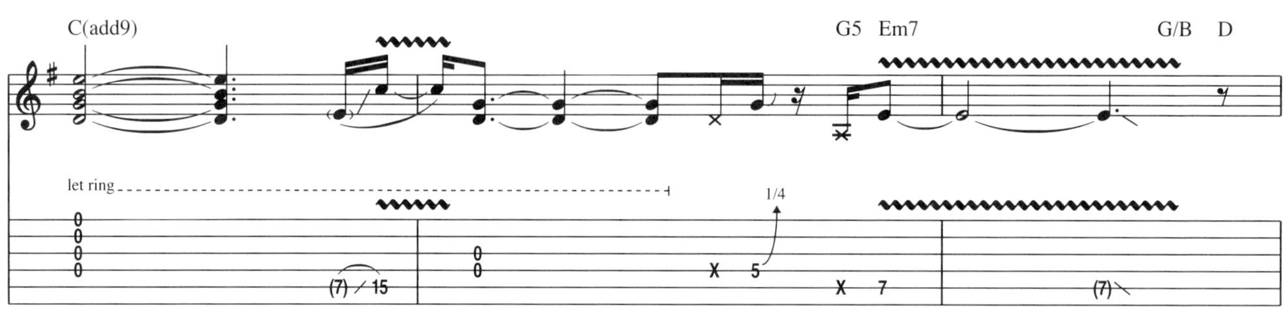
C(add9)
G5 Em7
G/B D
let ring
1/4

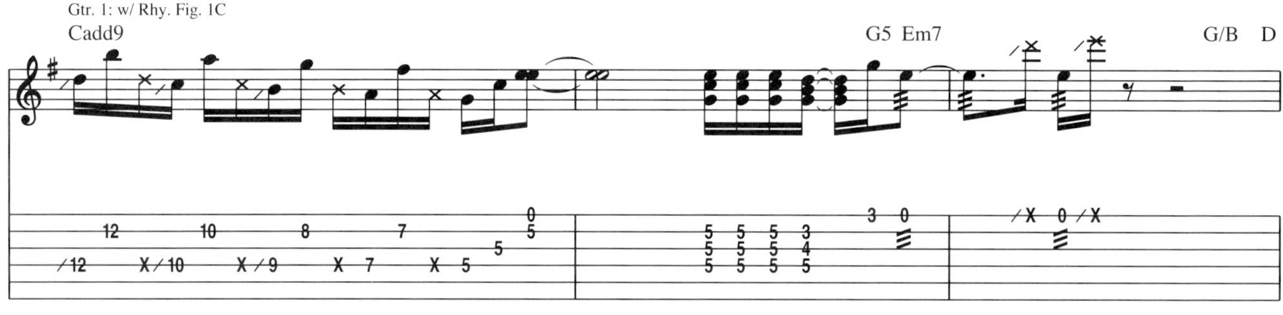
Gtr. 1: w/ Rhy. Fig. 1C
Cadd9
G5 Em7
G/B D

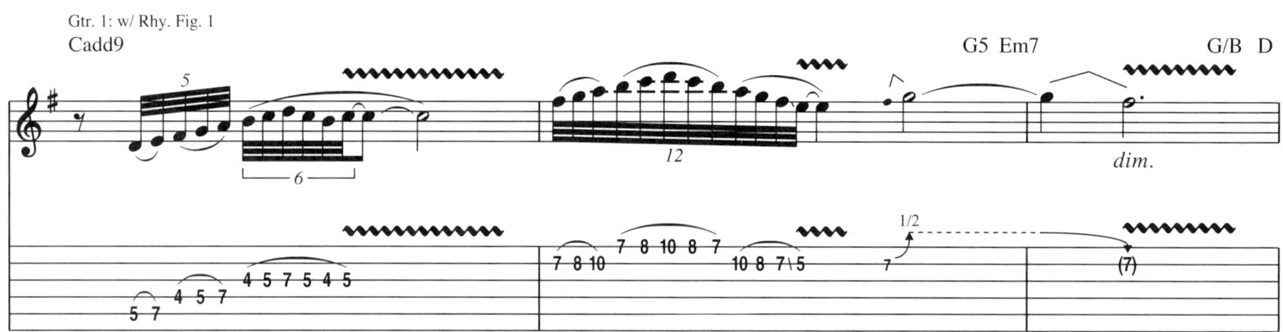
Gtr. 1: w/ Rhy. Fig. 1
Cadd9
G5 Em7
G/B D
dim.
1/2

Repeat and Fade
Gtr. 1: w/ Rhy. Fig. 1B
Cadd9
G5 Em7
G/B D
Cadd9 Cmaj7 Cadd9 Cmaj7
G5 Em7
G/B D

from Jim Croce - *You Don't Mess Around with Jim*

Operator (That's Not the Way It Feels)

Words and Music by Jim Croce

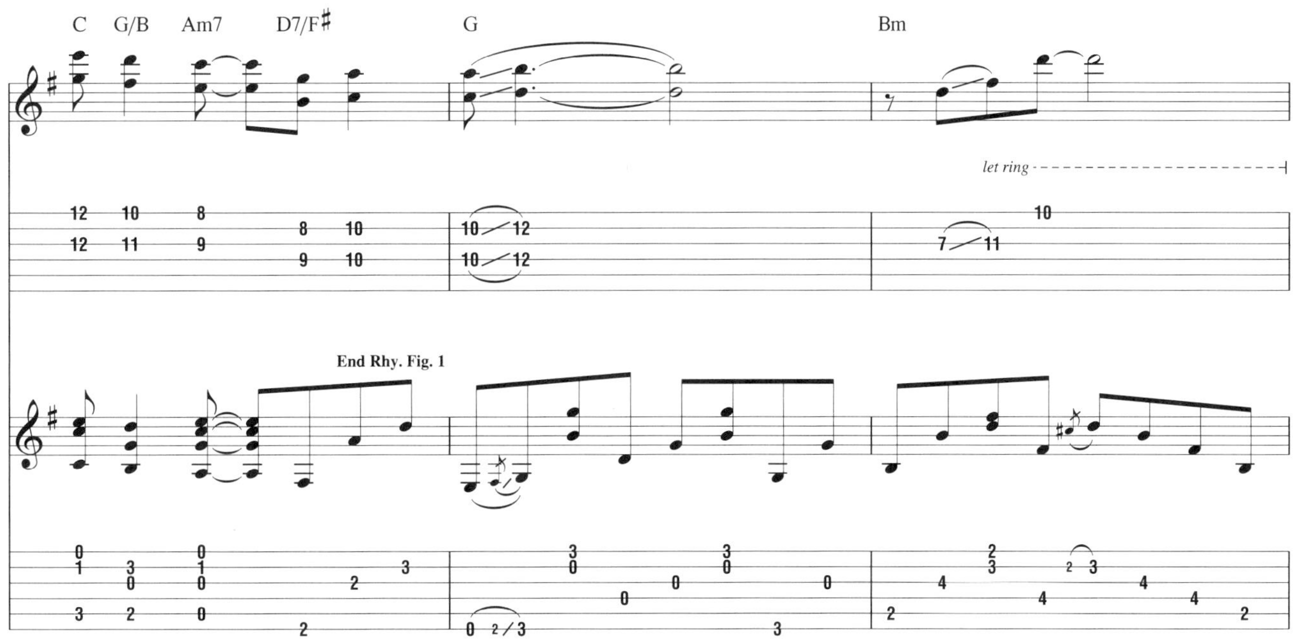

Am
C G/B Am7 D7/F♯
Verse
G
Riff A
1. Op - er - a -
Rhy. Fig. 2
Bm
C G/B Am G
C G/B Am G
tor, well, could you help me place this call?
End Riff A
let ring
let ring
Am
D7/F♯
Em
See, the num - ber on the match - book is old and fad - ed.
let ring

Gtrs. 1 & 2: w/ Rhy. Fig. 2 & Riff A
D
Dadd4/C
Dadd4/B
Dadd4/A
G
Bm
She's liv - ing in L. A.
with my best
End Rhy. Fig. 2

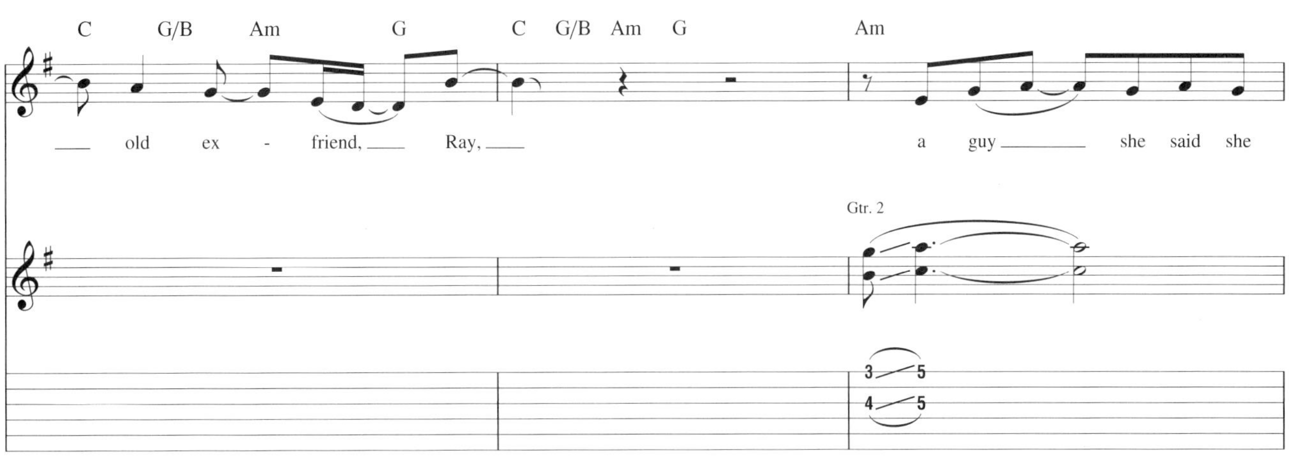
C
G/B
Am
G
C
G/B
Am
G
Am
old ex - friend, Ray,
a guy she said she
Gtr. 2

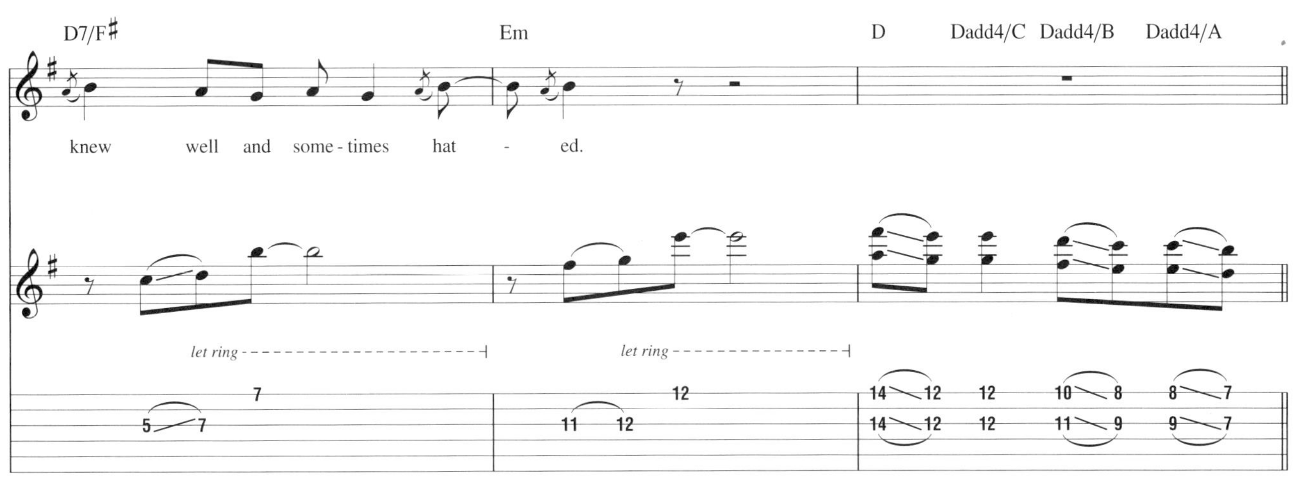
D7/F♯
Em
D
Dadd4/C
Dadd4/B
Dadd4/A
knew well and some - times hat - ed.
let ring
let ring

Chorus
G
C/G
G
But is - n't that the way they say it goes? But let's for -
Gtr. 2
Riff B
let ring
Rhy. Fig. 3
Gtr. 1
C
D
G
Am
get all that and give me the num - ber if you can find it, so
C
D
Em
Bm
D
Am
I can call just to tell 'em I'm fine and to show

Interlude

Gtr. 1: w/ Rhy. Fig. 1

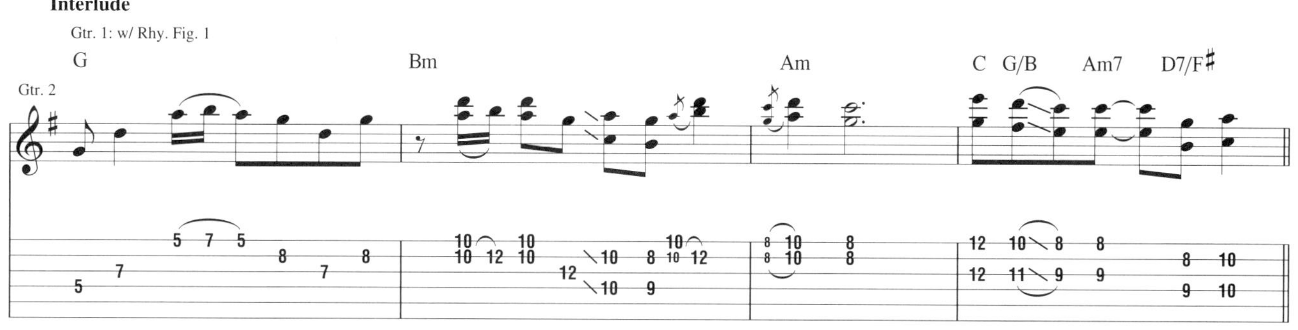

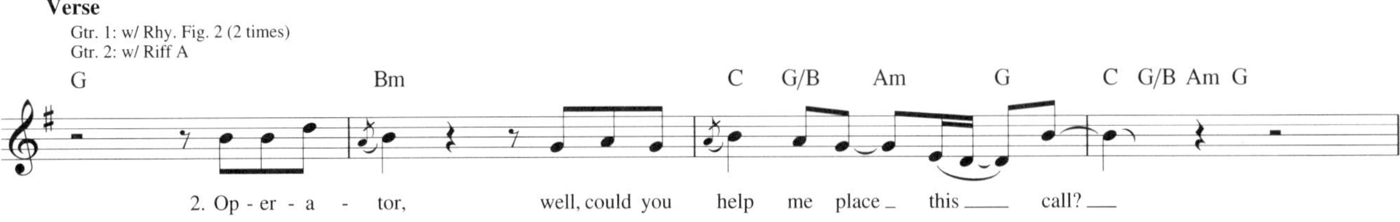
Verse
Gtr. 1: w/ Rhy. Fig. 2 (2 times)
Gtr. 2: w/ Riff A
G Bm C G/B Am G C G/B Am G
2. Op - er - a - tor, well, could you help me place this call?

Am D7/F♯ Em D Dadd4/C Dadd4/B Dadd4/A
'Cause I can't read the num - ber that you just gave me.
Gtr. 2
let ring

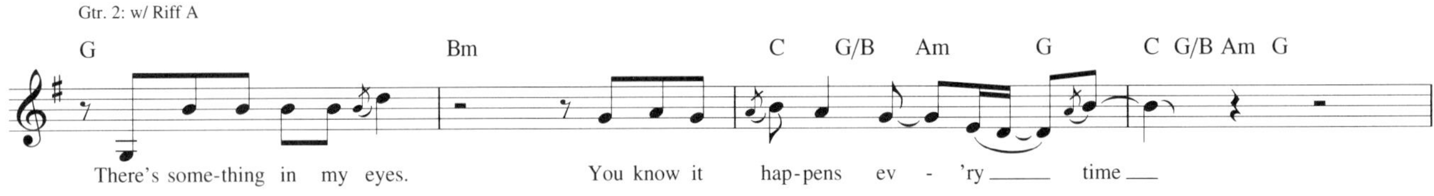
Gtr. 2: w/ Riff A
G Bm C G/B Am G C G/B Am G
There's some-thing in my eyes. You know it hap-pens ev - 'ry time

Am D7/F♯ Em D Dadd4/C Dadd4/B Dadd4/A
I think a - bout the love that I thought would save me.
Gtr. 2
let ring

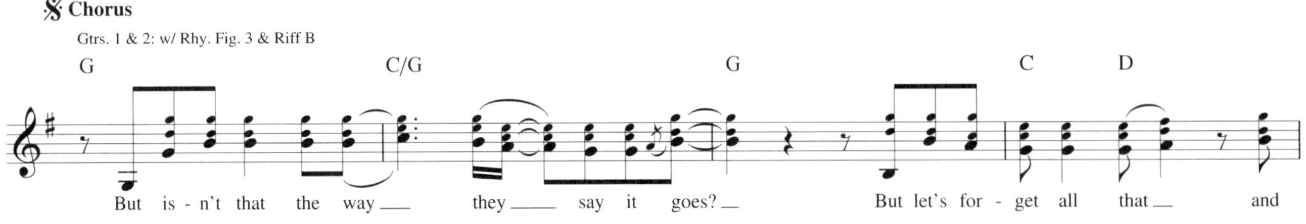
𝄋 Chorus
Gtrs. 1 & 2: w/ Rhy. Fig. 3 & Riff B
G C/G G C D
But is - n't that the way they say it goes? But let's for - get all that and

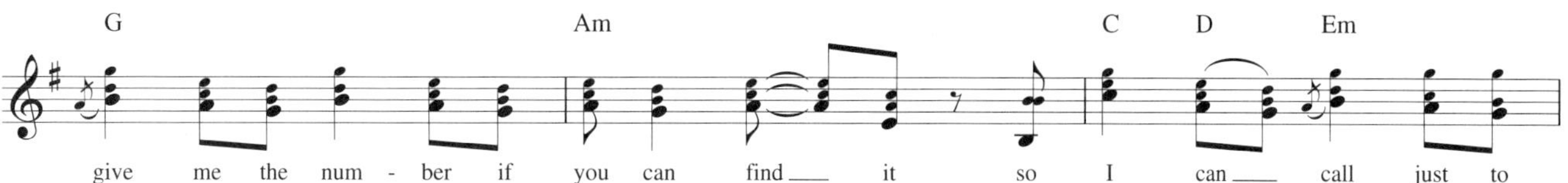
G
Am
C
D
Em
give me the num - ber if you can find ___ it so I can ___ call just to

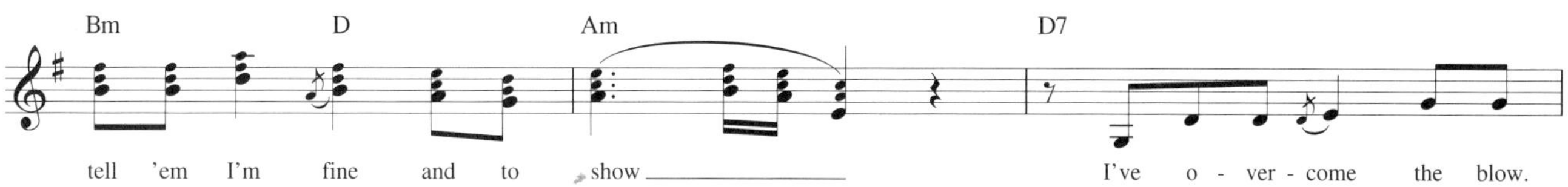
Bm
D
Am
D7
tell 'em I'm fine and to show ___ I've o - ver - come the blow.

C
G/B
Am
I've learned to take it ___ well. I on - ly wish my words ___ could just con - vince my - self ___

To Coda
C
D
C
___ that it just was - n't real, ___ but that's not the way it feels.

Interlude

G
C/G
G
C/G
3
No, ___ no, no, no.
That's not the way it feels. ___
Gtr. 2
Gtr. 1

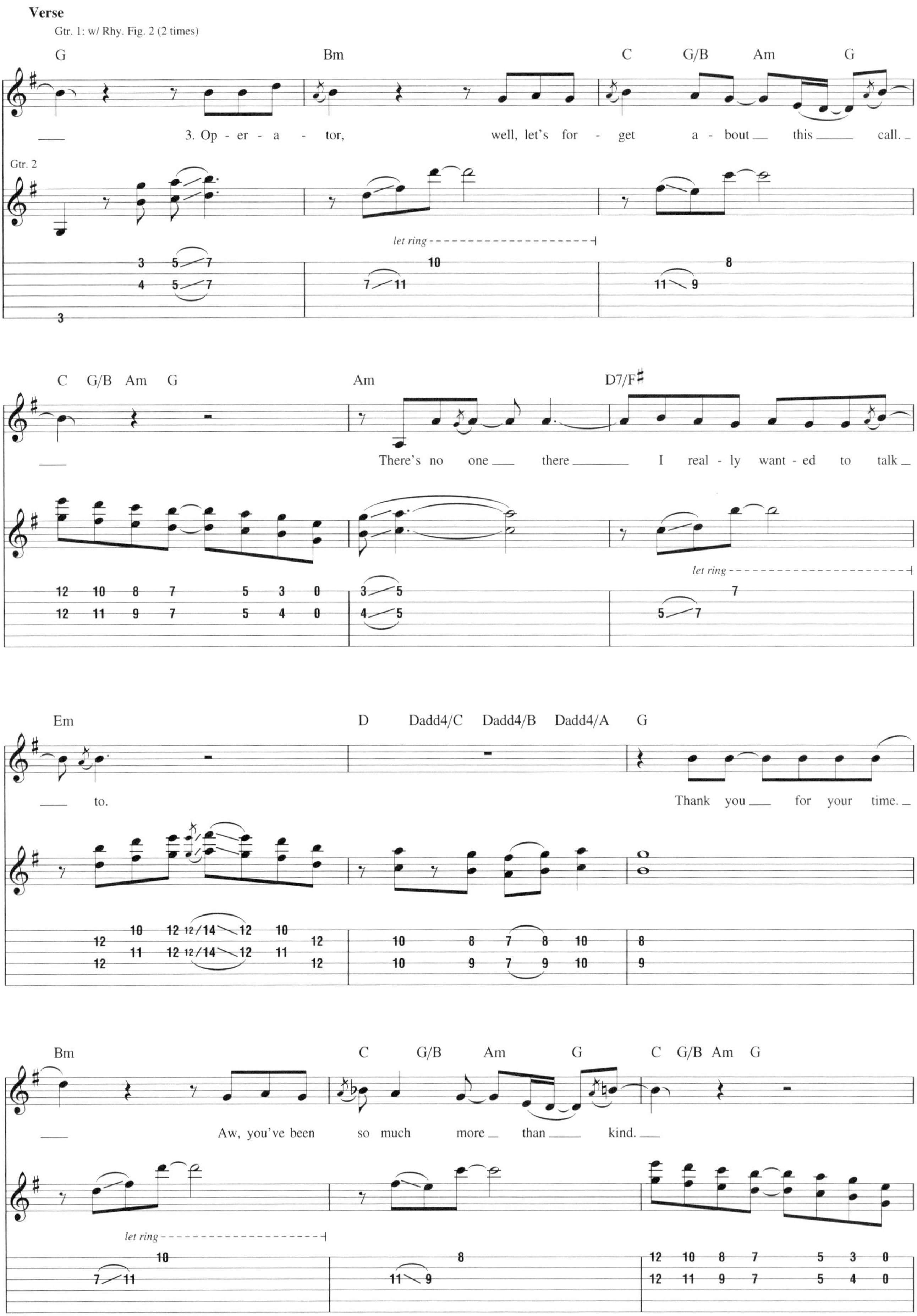

Verse
Gtr. 1: w/ Rhy. Fig. 2 (2 times)
G Bm C G/B Am G
3. Op - er - a - tor, well, let's for - get a - bout this call.
Gtr. 2
let ring
C G/B Am G Am D7/F♯
There's no one there I real - ly want - ed to talk
let ring
Em D Dadd4/C Dadd4/B Dadd4/A G
to. Thank you for your time.
Bm C G/B Am G C G/B Am G
Aw, you've been so much more than kind.
let ring

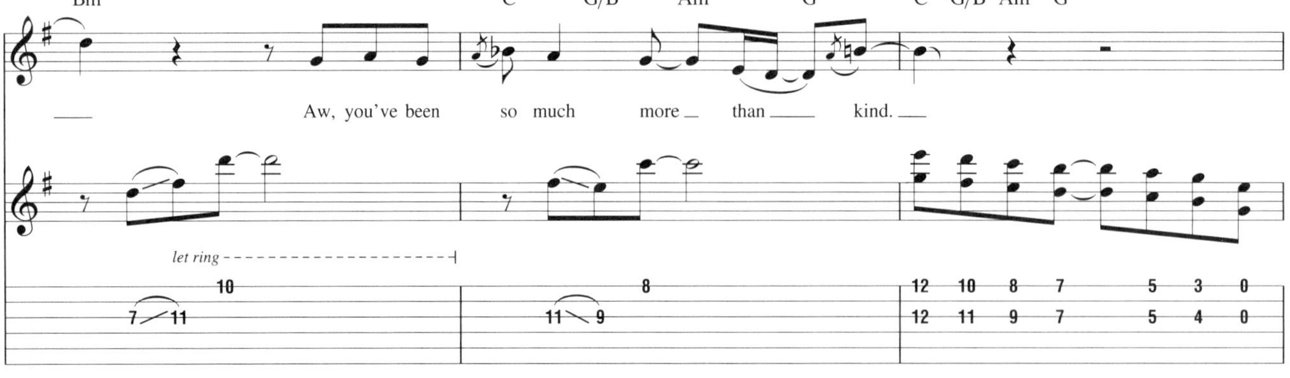

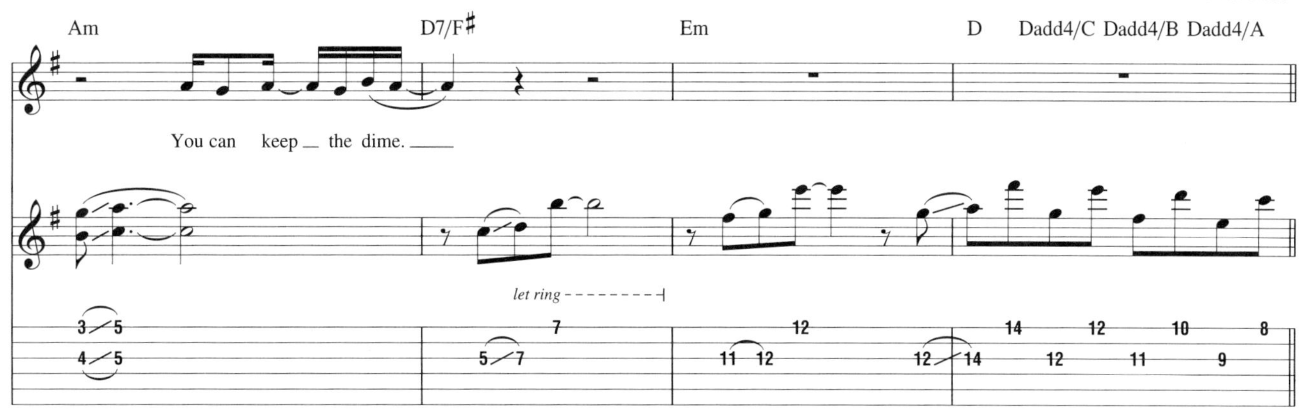
D.S. al Coda
Am
D7/F♯
Em
D
Dadd4/C
Dadd4/B
Dadd4/A
You can keep the dime.
let ring

Coda

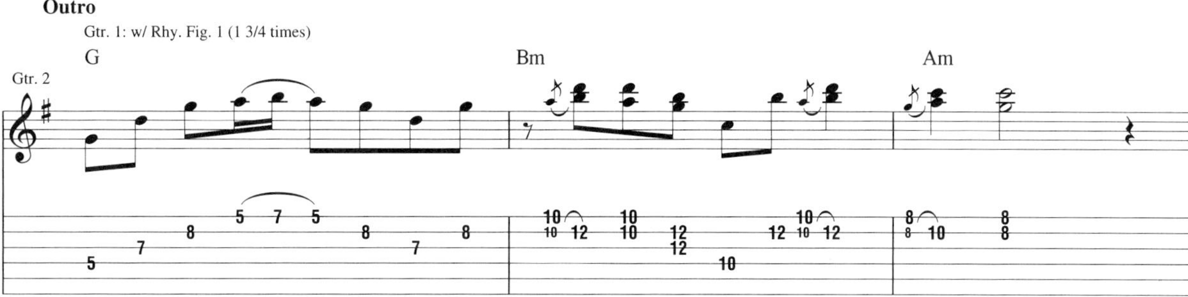
Outro
Gtr. 1: w/ Rhy. Fig. 1 (1 3/4 times)
G
Bm
Am
Gtr. 2

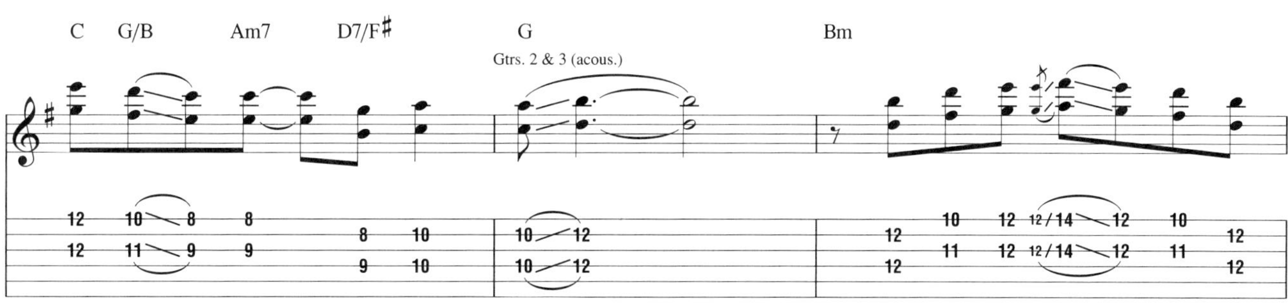
C
G/B
Am7
D7/F♯
G
Bm
Gtrs. 2 & 3 (acous.)

Am
C
G/B
Am
D7/F♯
G
Gtrs. 2 & 3
Gtr. 2
Gtr. 3
divisi
*Gtr. 2 to the left of slash in tab.
Gtr. 1

from Red Hot Chili Peppers - *Californication*

Otherside

Words and Music by Anthony Kiedis, Flea, John Frusciante and Chad Smith

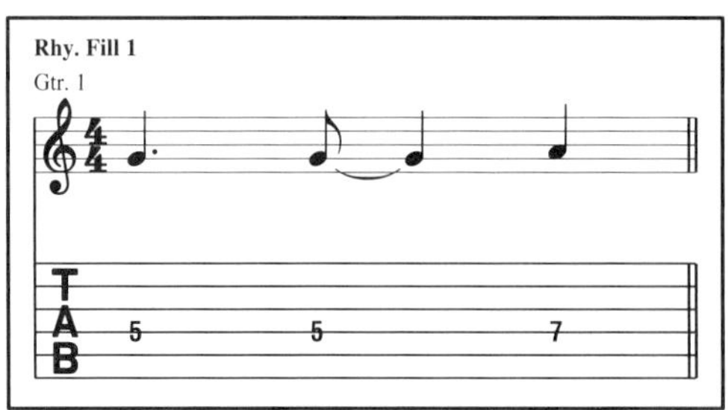

Gtr. 1: w/ Rhy. Fill 2, 2nd time
G5
A5
F
C
don't be - lieve it's bad;
slit my throat, it's all

Verse
G
Am
Em
I ev - er...
1. I heard your voice through a pho - to - graph;
3. Pour my life in - to a pa - per cup;
Rhy. Fig. 1
f
let ring
sim.
let ring
* Pluck upper string w/ middle finger.

Am
Em
Am
I thought it up it brought up the past.
the ash - tray's full and I'm spil - lin' my guts.
Once you know you can
She wants to know am I
let ring
let ring
let ring

Rhy. Fill 2
Gtr. 1
T
A
B

To Coda 1
Em
G
A
nev - er go back. still a slut.
I've got to take it on the oth - er side.
End Rhy. Fig. 1
Verse
Gtr. 1: w/ Rhy. Fig. 1
Am
Em
Am
2. Cen - tu - ries are what it meant to me; a cem - e - ter - y where I
4. Scar - let star - let and she's in my bed, a can - di - date, a, for my
Em
Am
Em
mar - ry the sea.
soul mate bled.
Strang - er things could nev - er change my mind.
Push the trig - ger and, pull the thread.
I've got to
G
A
G
A
take it on the oth - er - side. Take it on the oth - er side.
Gtr. 1
simile on repeat
To Coda 2
D.S. al Coda 1
G
A
Take it on,
(Take it on.)
take it on.
let ring

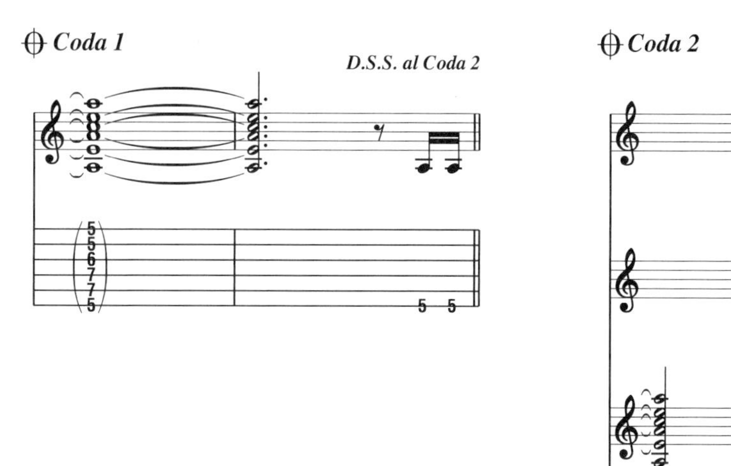
Coda 1
D.S.S. al Coda 2

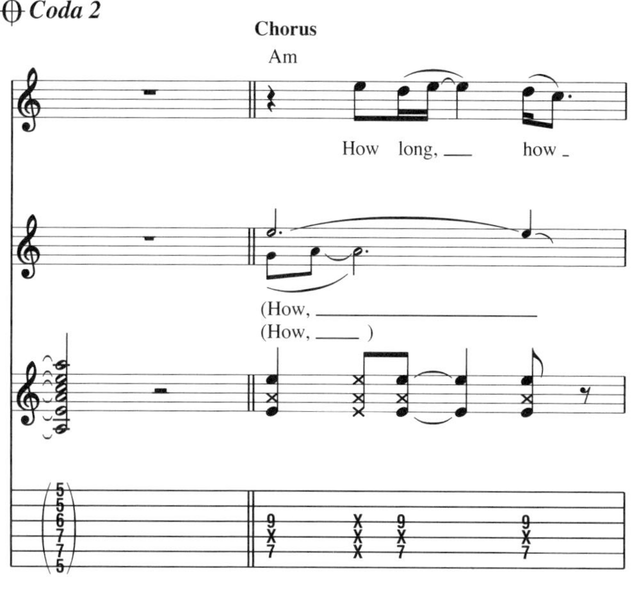
Coda 2
Chorus
Am
How long, how
(How,
(How,)

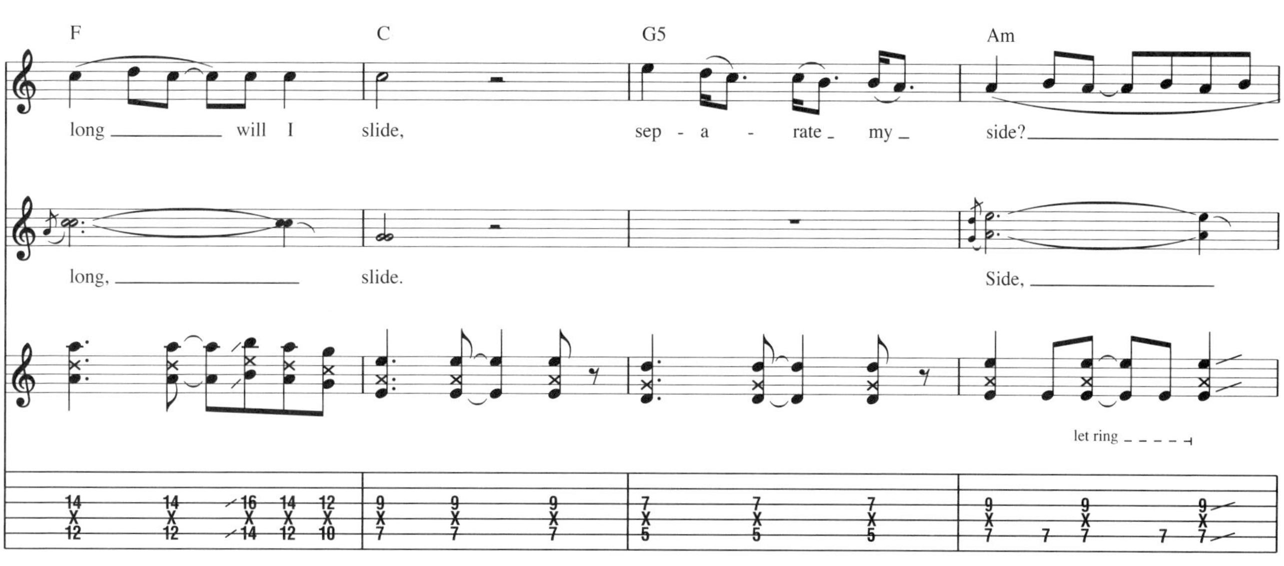
F
C
G5
Am
long will I slide, sep - a - rate my side?
long, slide. Side,
let ring

F
C
G5
Am
I don't, I don't be - lieve it's bad;
I don't. Bad,
let ring

Bridge
F5
C5
G5
E5
a slit-tin' my throat, it's all I ev - er...
slit.)
w/ dist.
Cmaj7
E5
Cmaj7
E5
Turn me on, take
Cmaj7
E5
me for a hard ride; burn me out, leave me on the oth-er side. I yell and tell it that it's

Guitar Solo

Outro-Chorus

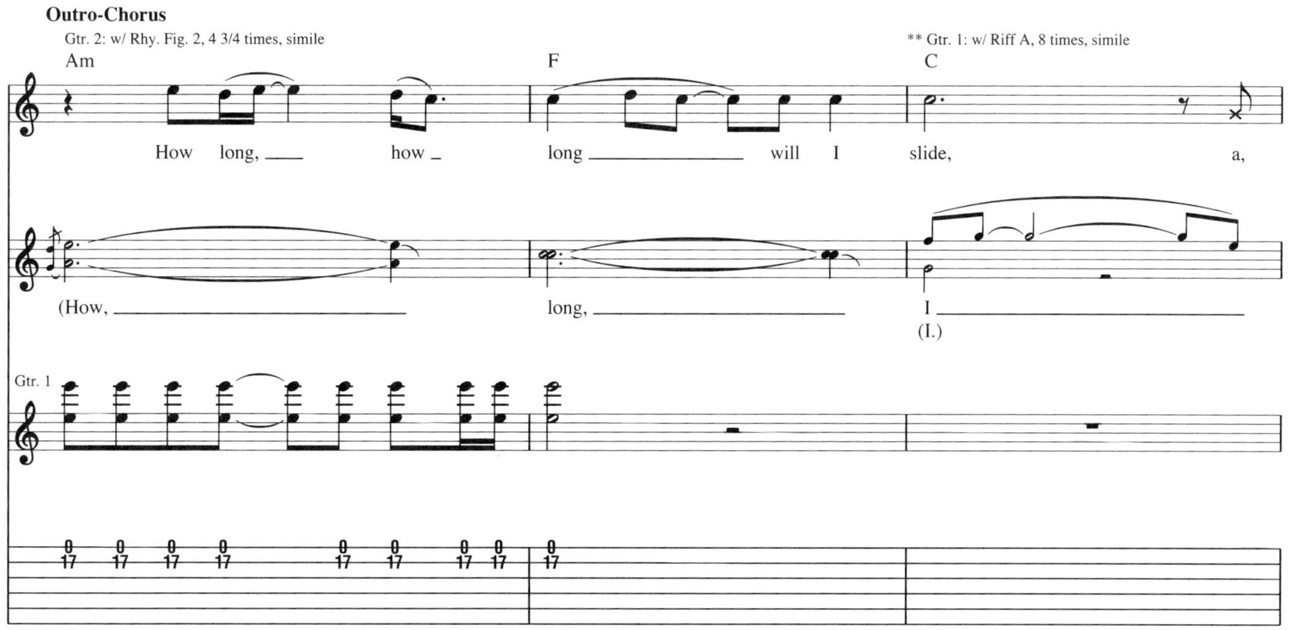

** Using a volume pedal, start at ***pp*** dynamic and slowly build to ***f*** dynamic by 8th time.

G
Am
F
sep - a - rate my side?
I don't,
slide.
Side,
I
C
G
Am
I don't be - lieve it's bad.
don't
(I
don't be - lieve it's bad.
bad.
F
C
G
Am
A slit - tin' my throat, it's all I ev - er had.
Slit
Slit.)
my.
How,
F
C
G
Am
I don't
I don't be - lieve it's bad.
long,
I
(I.)
slide.
Slide,
F
C
G
A5
A, slit - tin' my throat, it's all I ev - er…
rit.
I
don't.)
Gtr. 1
f
rit.
fdbk.
0 17 0 17 0 17 0 17 0 17 0 17 0 17 12
10 12 0 0
10 12 0 0
10 12 0 0
10 12 0 0
9 7

from Testiment - *The Legacy*

Over the Wall

Words and Music by Alex Skolnick, Eric Peterson, Gregory Carl Christian and Steven Souza

*Doubled throughout

**Chord symbols reflect implied harmony.

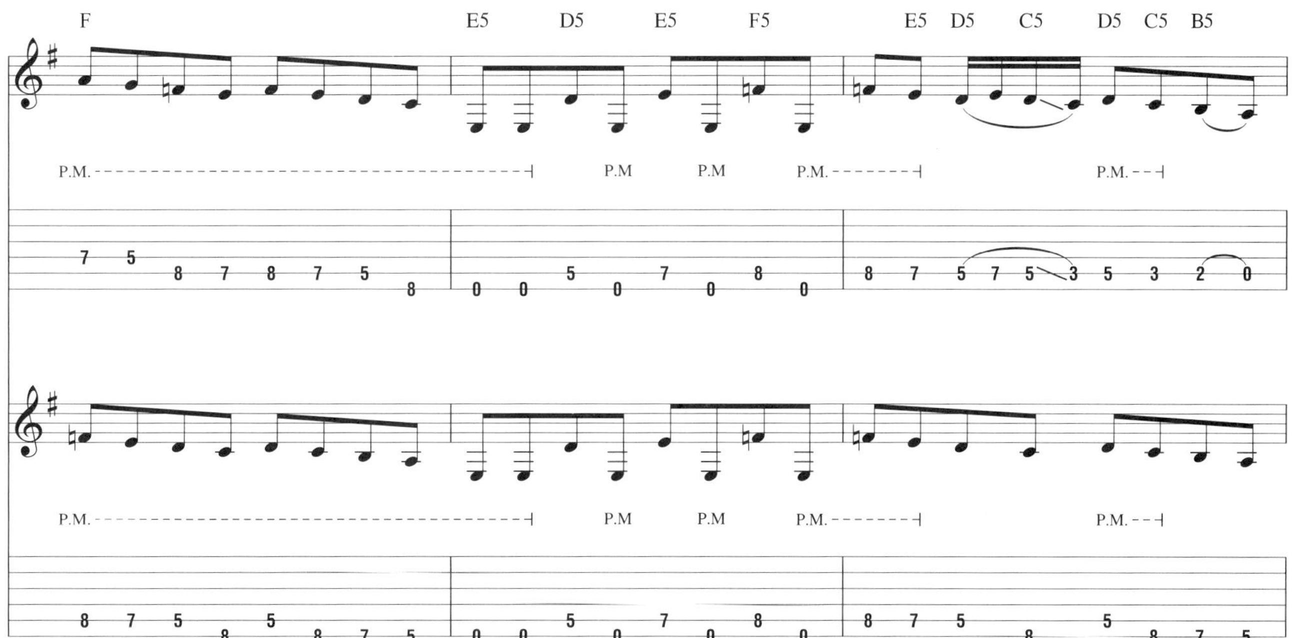

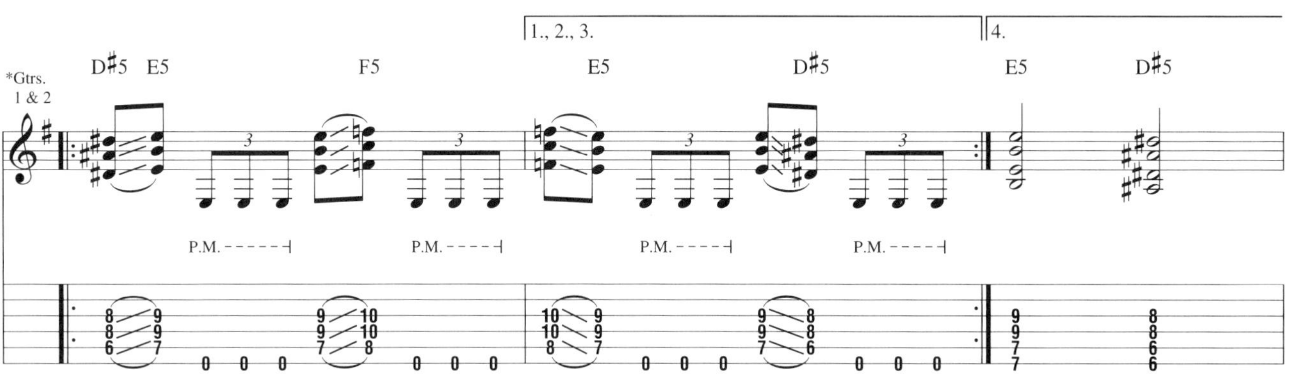

*Composite arrangement

Double-time feel

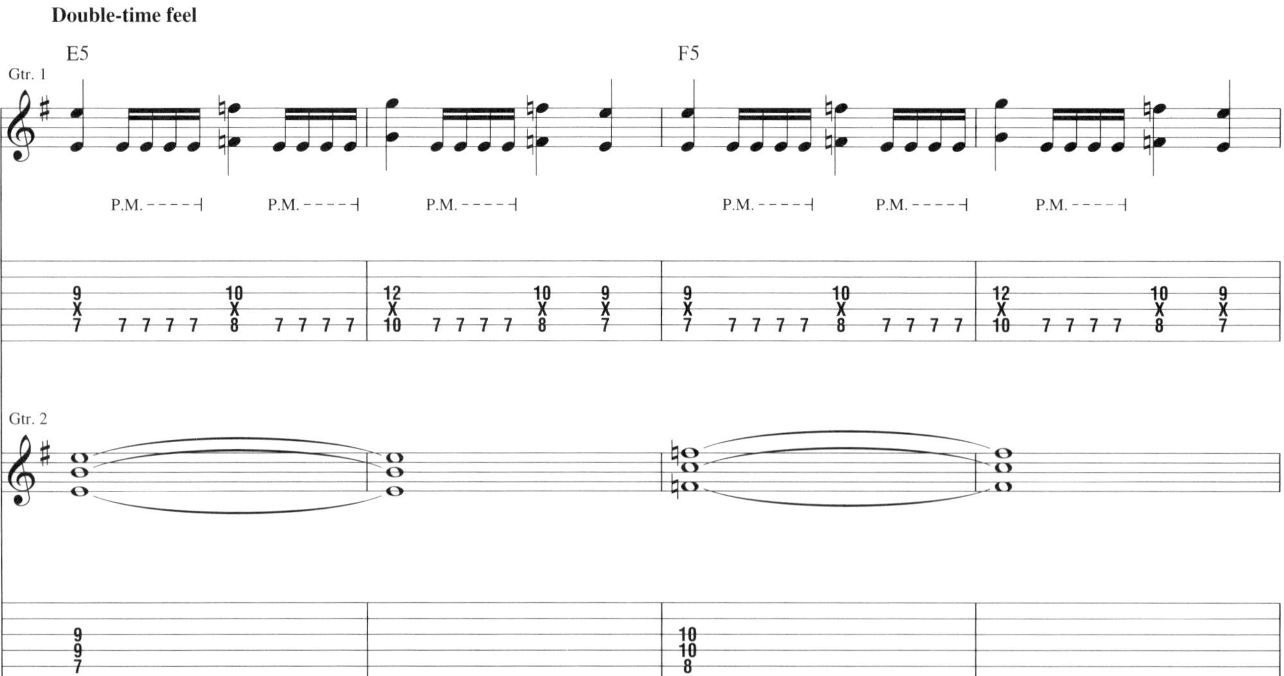

F♯5
F5
P.M.
E5
D5
C5
B5
G5
F♯5
Gtr. 1 tacet
E5
G♯5
G5
F♯5
F5
Gtr. 2
Rhy. Fig. 1

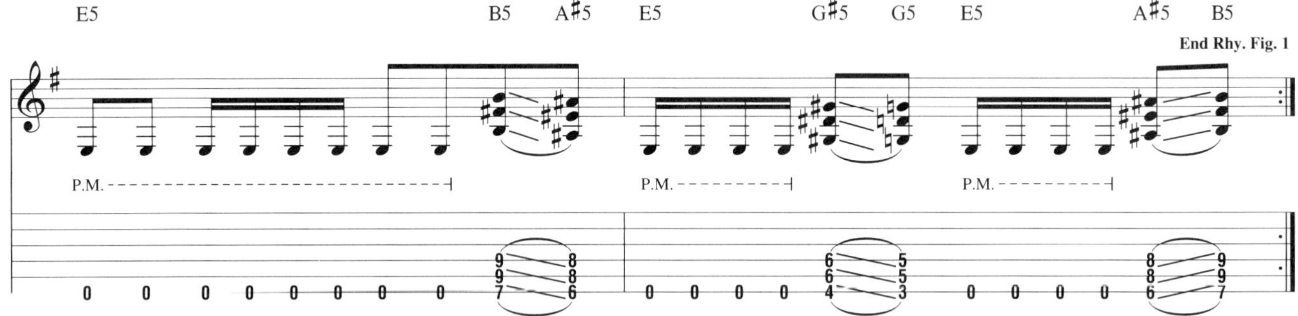

Verse

1. I've been a pris-on-er trapped in by fear, or-dered for the rest of my life. Con-
san-i-ty is all but gone, my pa-tience grow-ing ver-y weak. I need to get a hold of my-self. I

End double-time feel

E5 G#5 G5 E5 F#5 F5 E5 B5 A#5 E5 G#5 G5 E5 A#5 B5

demned in a jail cell, ain't __ seen life in years. Es-cape is the on-ly way out.
stare at the wall, for the right time has come. Es-cape must oc-cur on this night.

Pre-Chorus

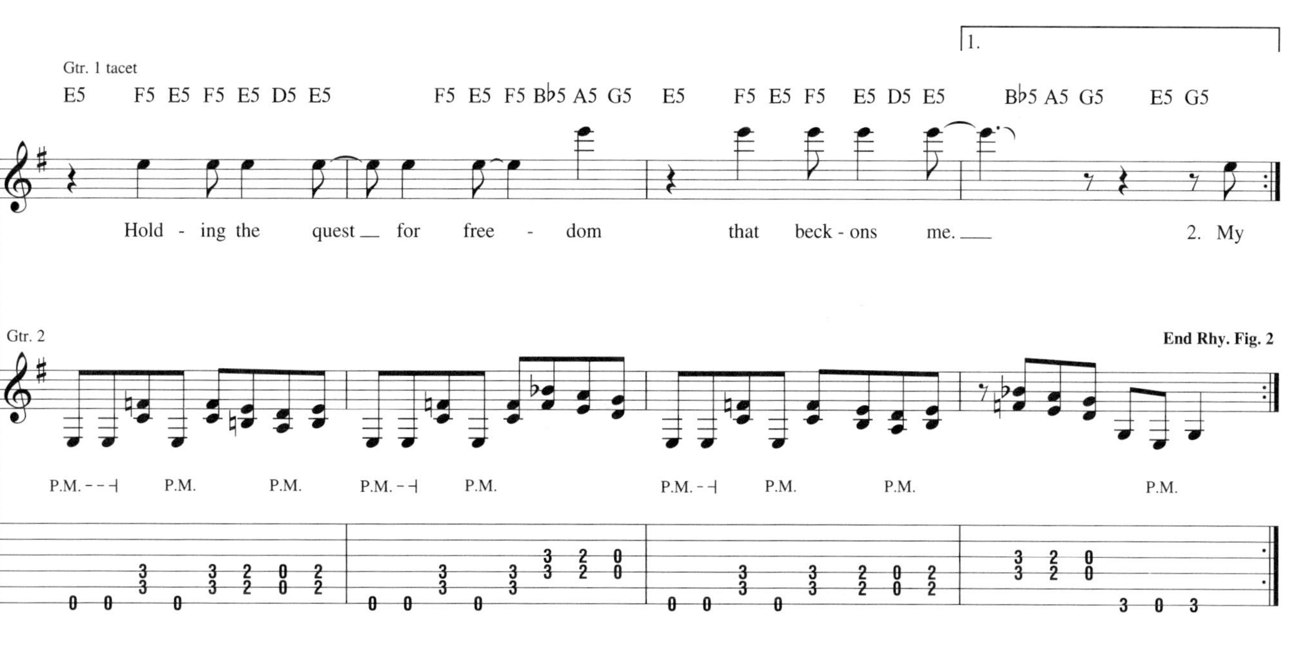
1.
Gtr. 1 tacet
E5 F5 E5 F5 E5 D5 E5 F5 E5 F5 B♭5 A5 G5 E5 F5 E5 F5 E5 D5 E5 B♭5 A5 G5 E5 G5
Hold - ing the quest for free - dom that beck - ons me. 2. My
Gtr. 2
End Rhy. Fig. 2
P.M. P.M. P.M. P.M. P.M. P.M. P.M. P.M. P.M.

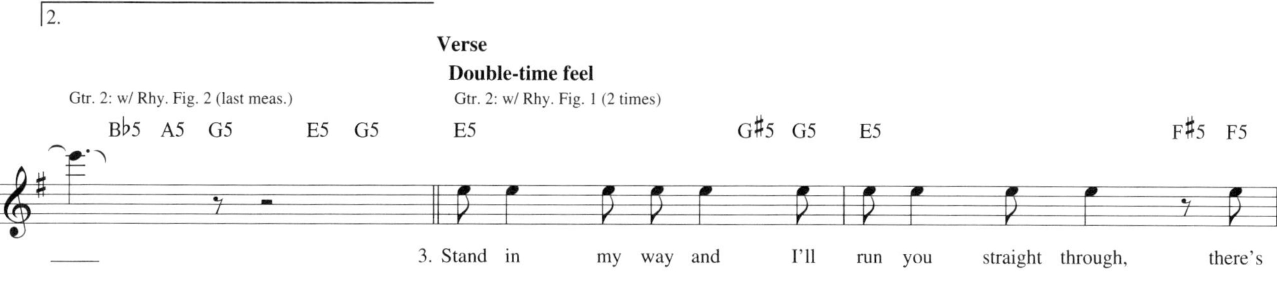
2.
Verse
Double-time feel
Gtr. 2: w/ Rhy. Fig. 2 (last meas.)
Gtr. 2: w/ Rhy. Fig. 1 (2 times)
B♭5 A5 G5 E5 G5 E5 G♯5 G5 E5 F♯5 F5
3. Stand in my way and I'll run you straight through, there's

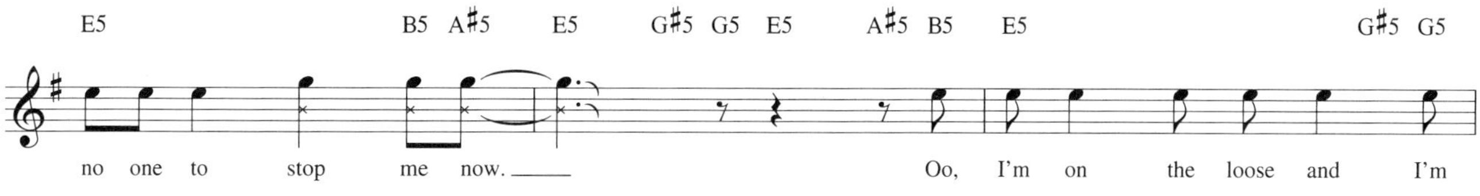
E5 B5 A♯5 E5 G♯5 G5 E5 A♯5 B5 E5 G♯5 G5
no one to stop me now. Oo, I'm on the loose and I'm

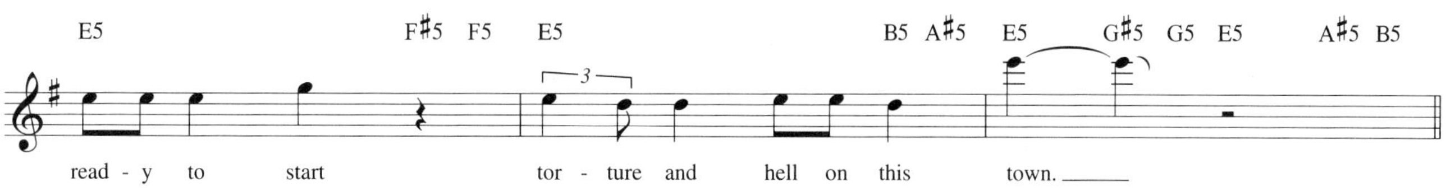
E5 F♯5 F5 E5 B5 A♯5 E5 G♯5 G5 E5 A♯5 B5
read - y to start tor - ture and hell on this town.

Chorus

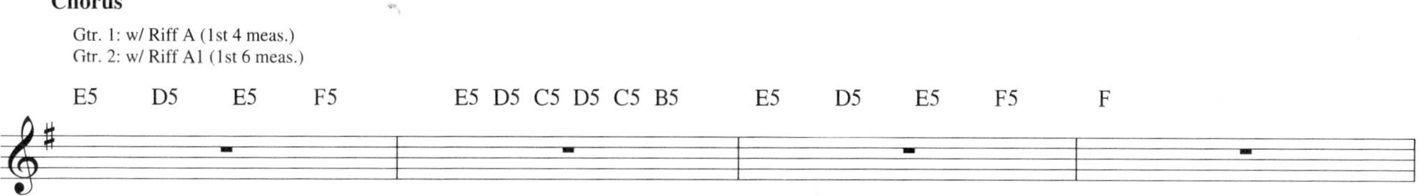
Gtr. 1: w/ Riff A (1st 4 meas.)
Gtr. 2: w/ Riff A1 (1st 6 meas.)
E5 D5 E5 F5 E5 D5 C5 D5 C5 B5 E5 D5 E5 F5 F

End double-time feel
E5 D5 E5 F5
E5 D5 C5 D5 C5 B5
E5 D5 E5 F5
C5 G5 N.C.
Screamed: O - ver the wall!
Yelled: (O - ver the wall!)
Gtr. 1
Gtrs. 1 & 2
P.M.

Interlude
E5 F5 E5 F5 B♭5 A5 G5
E5 F5 E5 F5 A5 B♭5 F5
E5 F5 E5 F5 B♭5 A5 G5
G F♯ G B♭ G F♯ F E
Gtr. 1
Fill 2
End Fill 2
Gtr. 2
Rhy. Fig. 3
End Rhy. Fig. 3
P.M.

Verse
Double-time feel
Gtr. 1 tacet
Gtr. 2: w/ Rhy. Fig. 1 (2 times)
E5 G♯5 G5 E5 F♯5 F5 E5 B5 A♯5 E5 G♯5 G5 E5 A♯5 B5
4. Search will not stop and the hounds will not rest till I am back in my cell. For

Interlude

Slower ♩= 115

E5 F5 E5 E F E/G♯ F E F

go! Go!

Gtr. 3 (dist.)

Fill 3A **End Fill 3A**

mf

9 10 10 13 10 9 10

Gtr. 1

Fill 3 **End Fill 3**

6 7 9 7 6 7

Gtr. 2 **Rhy. Fig. 4** **End Rhy. Fig. 4**

2 2 0 | 2 2 0 3 3 1 3 3 1 | 2 2 0 | 2 3 3 6 3 2 3

*w/ echo set for half-note regeneration w/ 3 repeats.

Gtrs. 1 & 3 tacet
Gtr. 2: w/ Rhy. Fig. 4

Gtrs. 1 & 3: w/ Fills 3 & 3A

E5 F5 E5 E F E/G♯ F E F

Uh,

Guitar Solo

Half-time feel

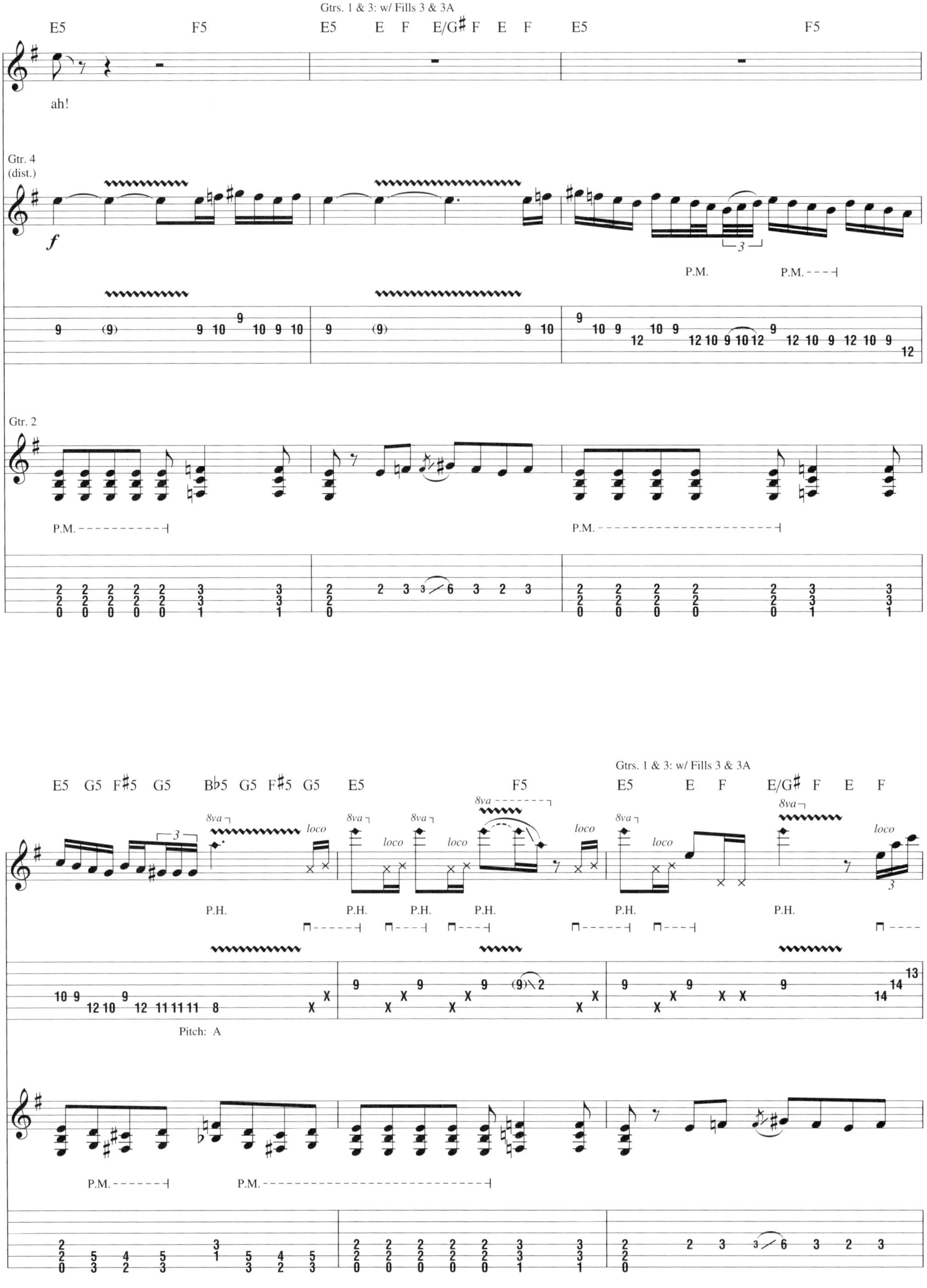

Gtrs. 1 & 3: w/ Fills 3 & 3A

E5 F5 E5 E F E/G♯ F E F E5 F5

ah!

Gtr. 4 (dist.)

f

P.M. P.M.

Gtr. 2

P.M. P.M.

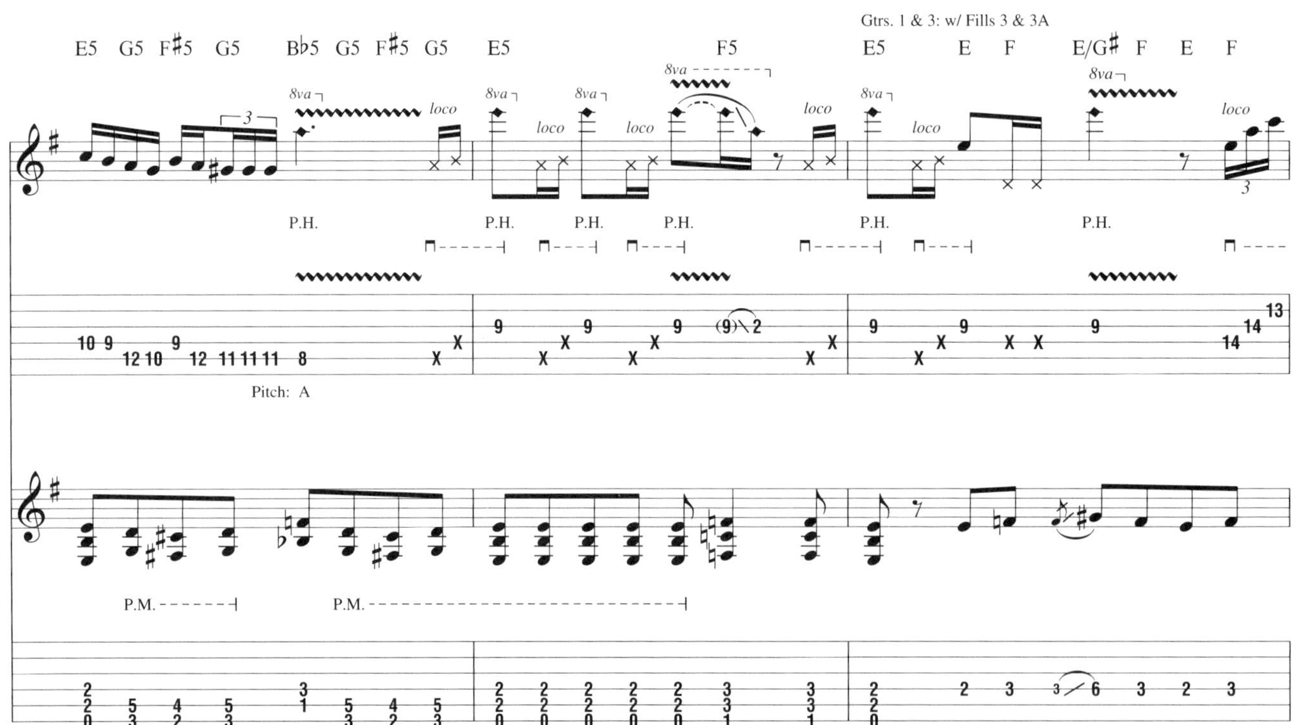

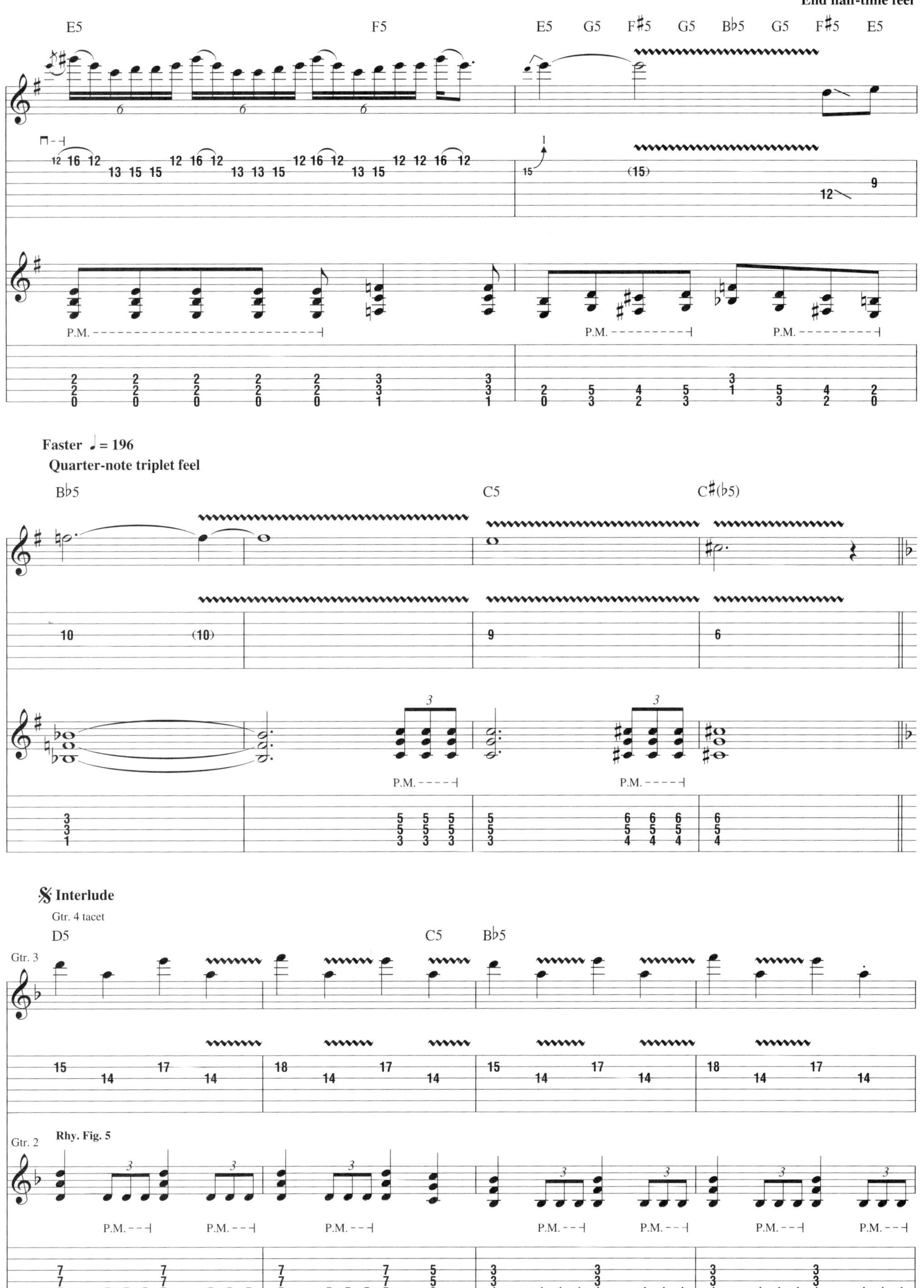
End half-time feel
E5
F5
E5
G5
F♯5
G5
B♭5
G5
F♯5
E5
P.M.
Faster ♩ = 196
Quarter-note triplet feel
B♭5
C5
C♯(♭5)
Interlude
Gtr. 4 tacet
D5
C5
B♭5
Gtr. 3
Gtr. 2
Rhy. Fig. 5

To Coda
2nd time, end quarter-note triplet feel
C5
C♯(♭5)
D5
P.M.
End Rhy. Fig. 5
Guitar Solo
Gtr. 2: w/ Rhy. Fig. 5
Gtr. 3 tacet
D5
Gtr. 4
C5
B♭5
C5
C♯(♭5)
D5
Gtr. 4
8va
Rhy. Fill 1
Gtr. 2
End Rhy. Fill 1

Gtr. 2: w/ Rhy. Fig. 5

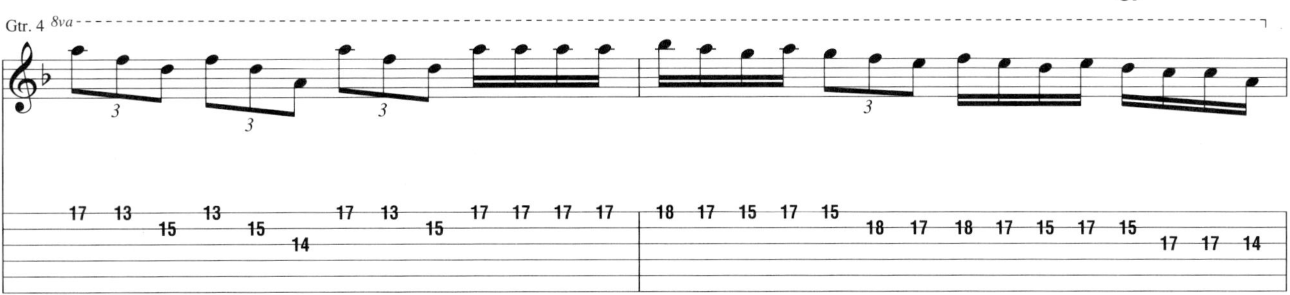
C5
Gtr. 4
8va

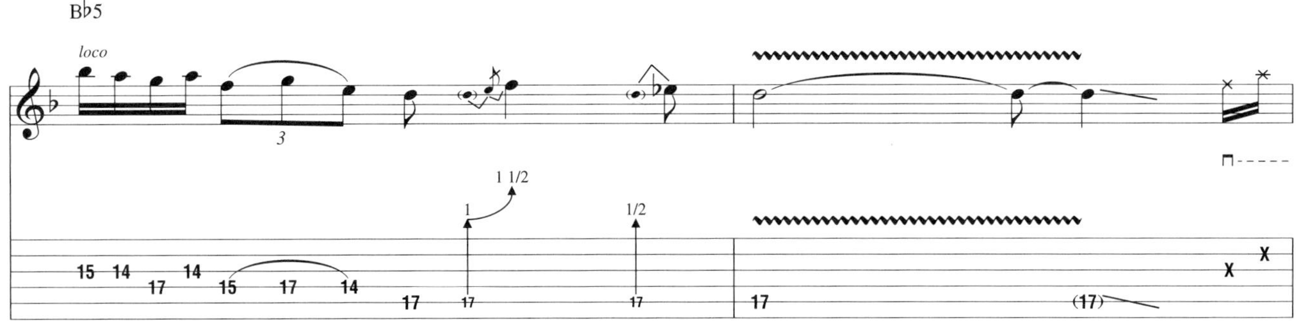
B♭5
loco
1 1/2
1
1/2

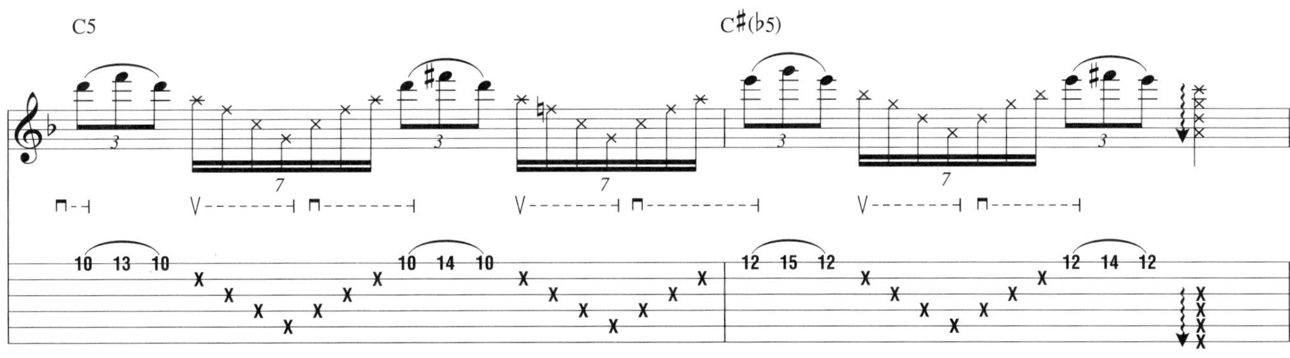
C5
C♯(♭5)

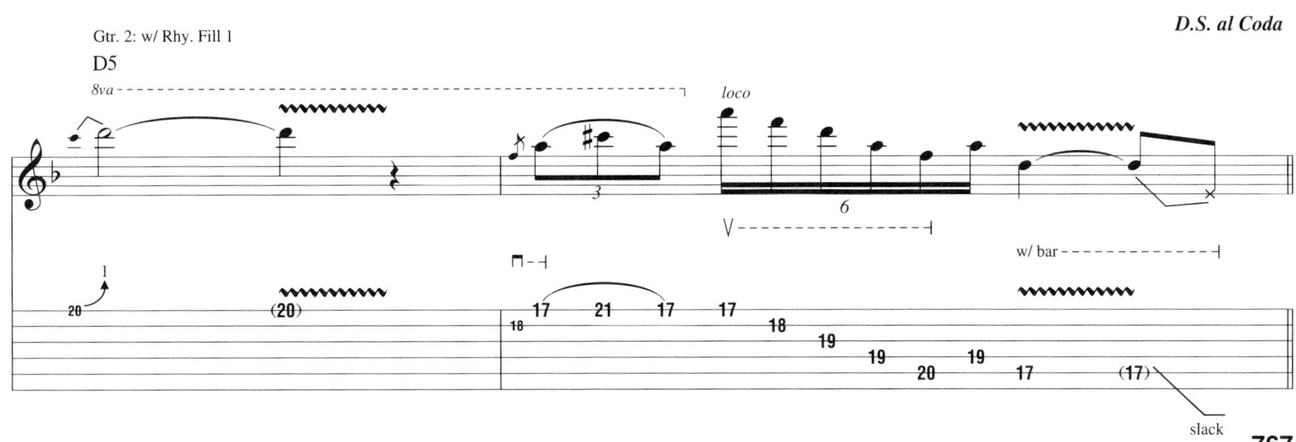
D.S. al Coda
Gtr. 2: w/ Rhy. Fill 1
D5
8va
loco
w/ bar
slack

Coda
Interlude
D5
C5
B♭5
C5
C♯(♭5)
D5
A5
B♭5
F5
Gtr. 2: w/ Rhy. Fig. 2 (1st 4 meas., 2 times)
Gtr. 3 tacet
E5 F5 E5 F5 E5 D5 E5 F5 E5 F5 B♭5 A5 G5 E5 F5 E5 F5 E5 D5 E5
Gtr. 1: w/ Fill 1
G F♯ G B♭ G F♯ E
B♭5
Gtrs. 1 & 3
*P.H.
*Gradually move pick hand along string length while performing pinch harmonics to produce random pitches.
Gtr. 2

Gtrs. 1 & 3 tacet
Gtr. 2: w/ Rhy. Fig. 3 (2 times)
Gtr. 1: w/ Fill 2
E5 F5 E5 F5 B♭5 A5 G5 E5 F5 E5 F5 A5 B♭5 F5 E5 F5 E5 F5 B♭5 A5 G5 G F♯ G B♭ G F♯ F E
Pre-Chorus
Gtr. 2: w/ Rhy. Fig. 2
Gtr. 1: w/ Fill 1
E5 F5 E5 F5 E5 D5 E5 F5 E5 F5 B♭5 A5 G5 E5 F5 E5 F5 E5 D5 E5 G F♯ G B♭ G F♯ E
Re - start my life or self - de - struc - tion, to climb this wall of dark con - struc - tion.
E5 F5 E5 F5 E5 D5 E5 F5 E5 F5 B♭5 A5 G5 E5 F5 E5 F5 E5 D5 E5 B♭5 A5 G5 E5 G5
Hold - ing the quest for free - dom that beck - ons me.
Outro-Chorus
Double-time feel
Gtrs. 1 & 2: w/ Riffs A & A1
E5 D5 E5 F5 E5 D5 C5 D5 C5 B5 E5 D5 E5 F5 F
E5 D5 E5 F5 E5 D5 C5 D5 C5 B5 E5 D5 E5 F5 F
Screamed: O - ver
Yelled: (O - ver
Dm Cm F F♯ G F♯m E5 N.C.
the wall!
the wall!)
Gtr. 1
P.M.
Gtr. 2
P.M.

from Joe Bonamassa - *Blues Deluxe*

Pack It Up

Words and Music by Geoffrey Beadle, Ronald Carthy, George Chandler, Wilfred Davies, Michael Eve, Gabriel Gregory, Delisle Harper, Goldin Hunte and Christopher Mercer

2nd & 3rd times, Gtr. 1: w/Riff B
D♭9
E♭9
N.C.
- by, I'm dream-ing a-bout you. So
- by, make it work out right. Ev-'ry time
- ly, ev - 'ry day. Put
mixed up now, ba - by, I don't know what to do. Hey, ba-
I talk to you, dar - ling, you tell me you don't have time, oh, ba-
my trust in you, ba - by, be-lieve ev-'ry word I say, oh, ba-
D♭9
E♭9
N.C.
- by, don't know what to do.
- by, yeah, you don't have time.
- by, ev-'ry word I say.
I'm gon-na
Riff B
Gtr. 1

Chorus
B♭7
N.C.
pack it up, gon - na give it up. I'm gon - na
put you right out - ta my mind. I'm gon - na
To Coda
D♭9
E♭9
pack it up, yeah, yeah.
N.C.
1.

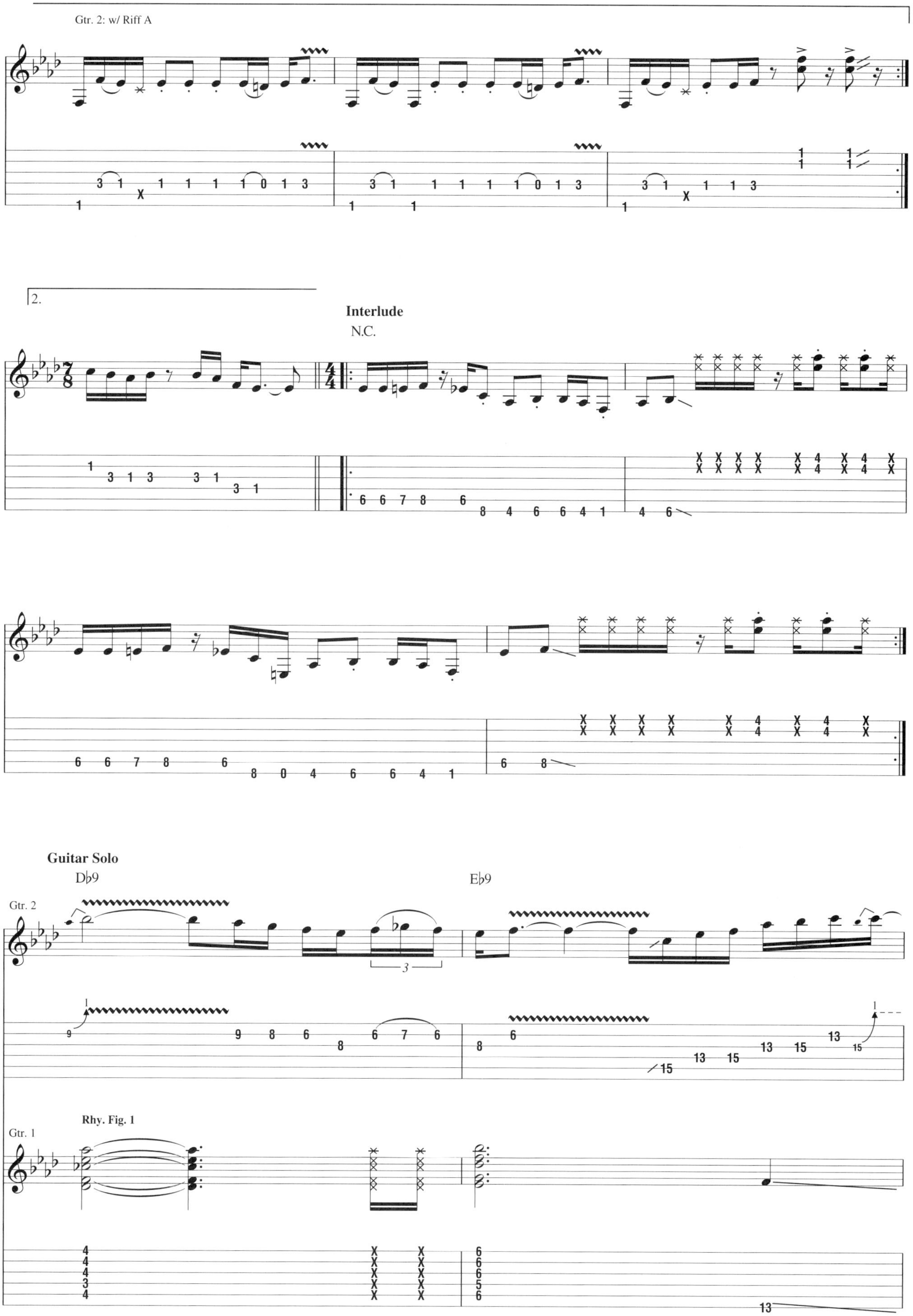

Gtr. 2: w/ Riff A

2.

Interlude

N.C.

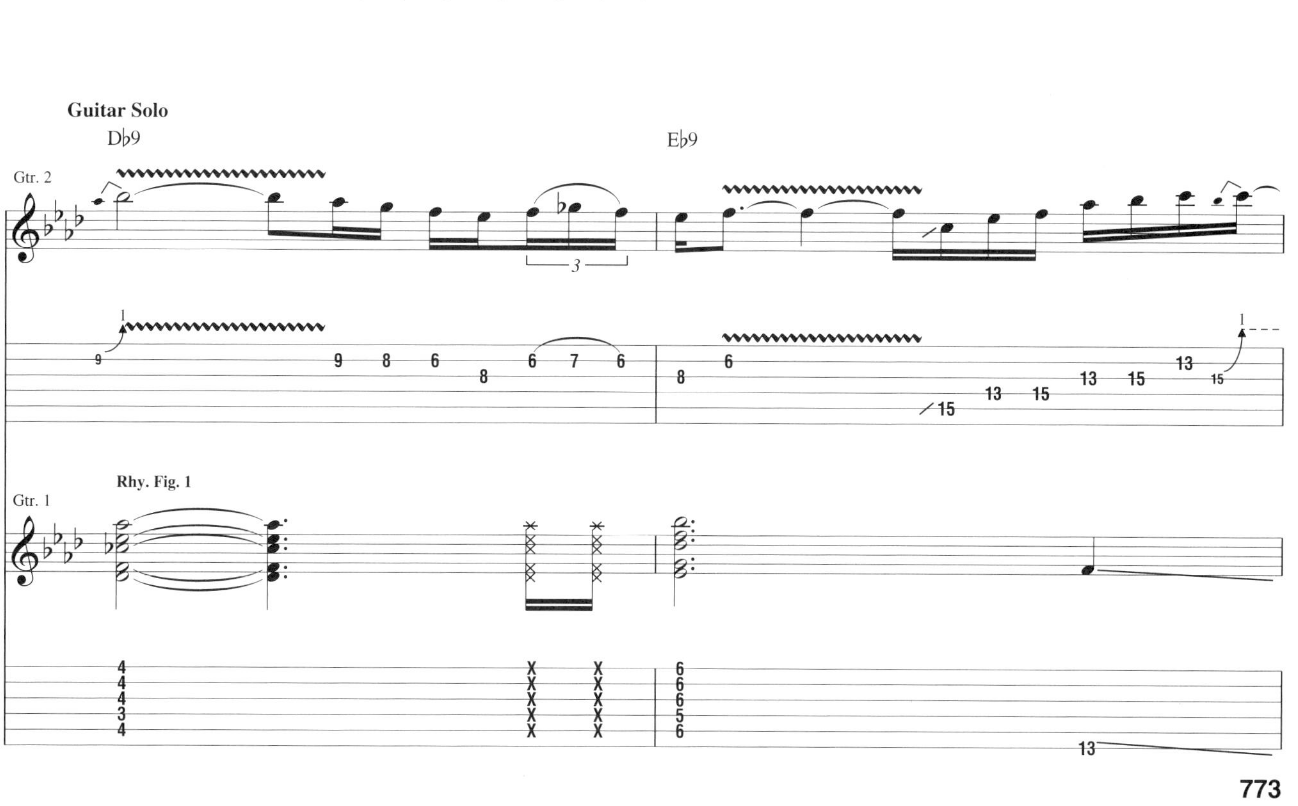

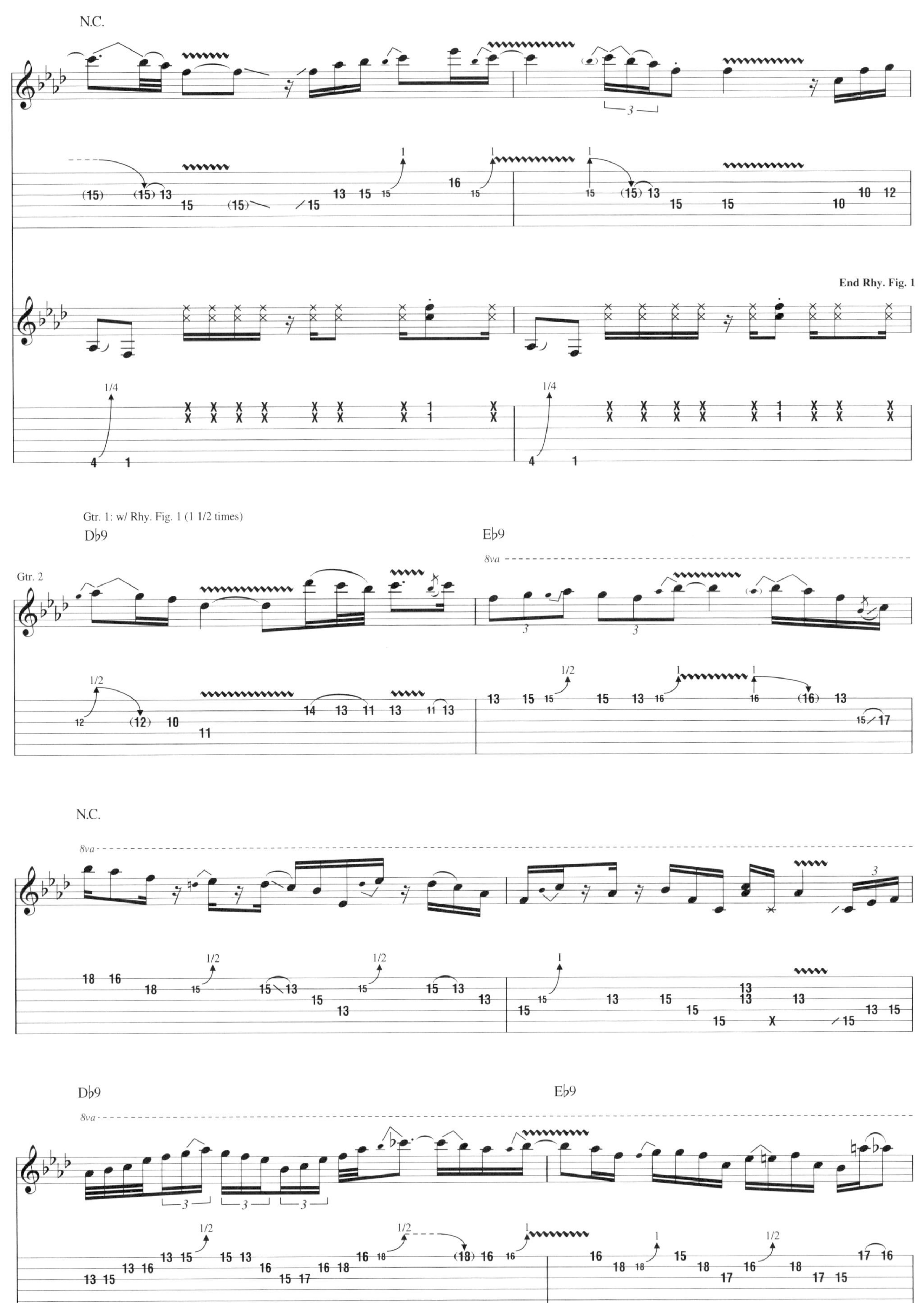

N.C.
End Rhy. Fig. 1
Gtr. 1: w/ Rhy. Fig. 1 (1 1/2 times)
D♭9
E♭9
Gtr. 2
8va
N.C.
8va
D♭9
E♭9
8va

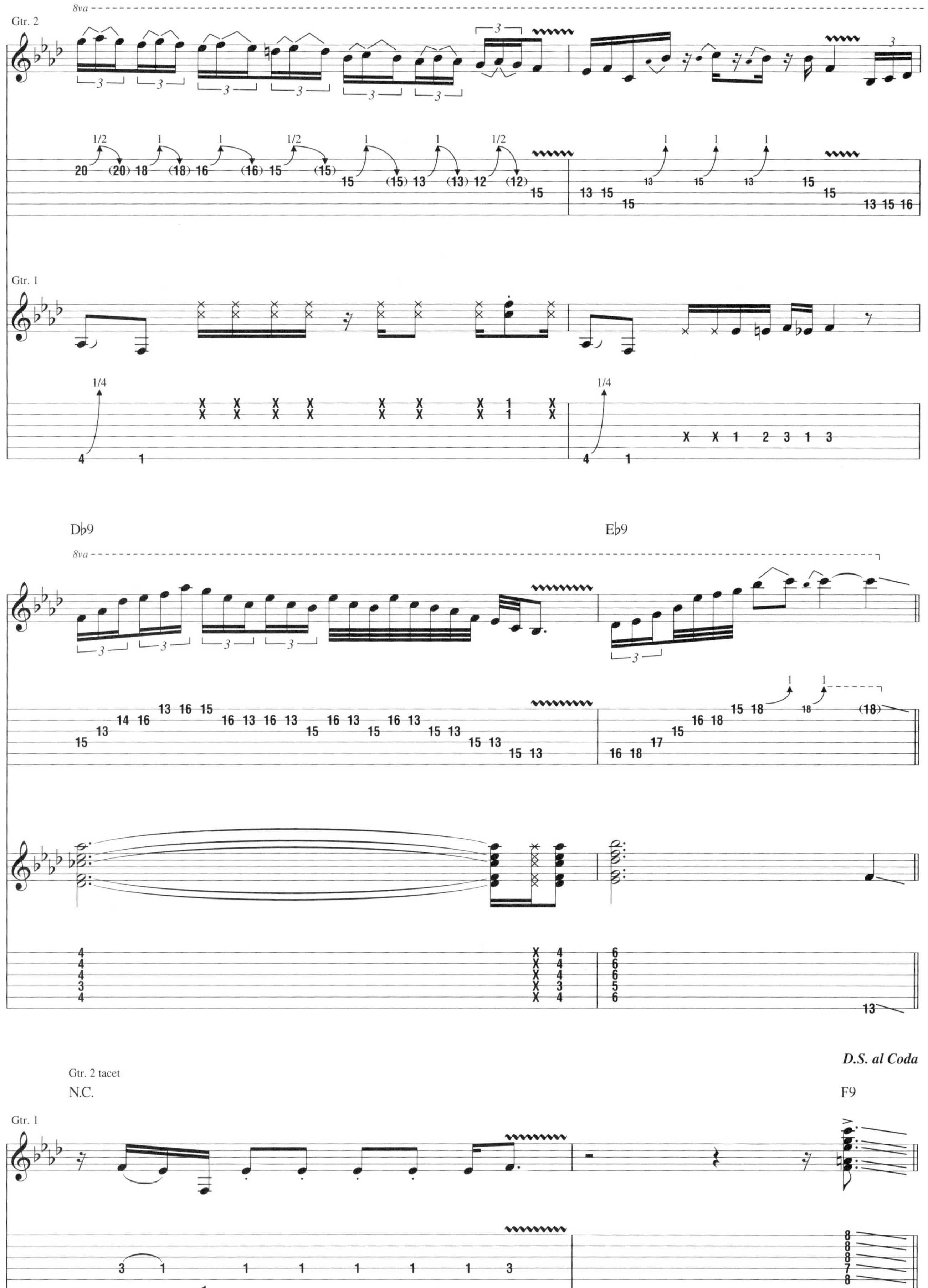
N.C.
8va
Gtr. 2
Gtr. 1
D♭9
E♭9
8va
Gtr. 2 tacet
N.C.
Gtr. 1
D.S. al Coda
F9

Coda

Eb9 N.C.

yeah. I'm gon-na put you right out-ta my mind.

Gtr. 2

Gtr. 1

1/4

Db9 Eb9

Gon-na pack it up, ba-by. Oh, oh.

8va

1/4

N.C.

D♭9

Yeah, I'm gon - na pack it up.

8va

1 1/2 1 1/2 1 1/2

1/4 1/4

E♭9

N.C.

Oh, Lord.

loco

from Cry of Love - *Brother*

Peace Pipe

Written by Audley Freed and Kelly Holland

Intro

Moderately slow ♩ = 92

*B5

Hey!

Riff A

**Gtrs. 1 & 2

Gtr. 1 (dist.)

mf

P.M. P.M. P.M.

*Chord symbols reflect implied harmony.

**Gtr. 2 (dist.), played *mf*.

1. In the heat of the

End Riff A

P.M. P.M. P.M.

𝄋 Verse

Gtrs. 1 & 2: w/ Riff A (1 1/2 times)

B5

morn-ing, in the eye __ of the sun, hear the wind start blow - in', see the horse and the
eve - ning, when the spears _ come down, say a prayer for the plow - boy, on the kill - ing

gun. __ Now the peace _ pipe, it ain't smok - in', all the prom - is - es __ are bro - ken, the heat of the
ground. _ Now the peace _ pipe, it is bro - ken, all the sha - man's gone _ un - spo - ken, the dead of the

Pre-Chorus

B5

morn-ing, see the horse _ and the gun, uh. All in the name _
eve-ning, when the tears come down, __ yeah! (Ah. __

Gtrs. 1 & 2

P.M. P.M.

E5/B
B5
of God some - how, oh, oh, oh, oh.
Tear - ing the tem -
Ah.)
Gtr. 1
1/4
let ring
Gtr. 2
1/4
Chorus
E5/B
B
D5 E5 E/G♯ A5
B5
D5 E5 E/G♯ A5
- ple down.
Burn down the sa - cred ground,
tear - ing the tem - ple down,
Gtrs. 1 & 2
let ring
let ring
To Coda
B5
D5 E5 E/G♯ A5
B5
D5 E5 E/G♯ A5
B5
in the name of God some - how,
burn down the sa - cred ground.
let ring
let ring

D.S. al Coda

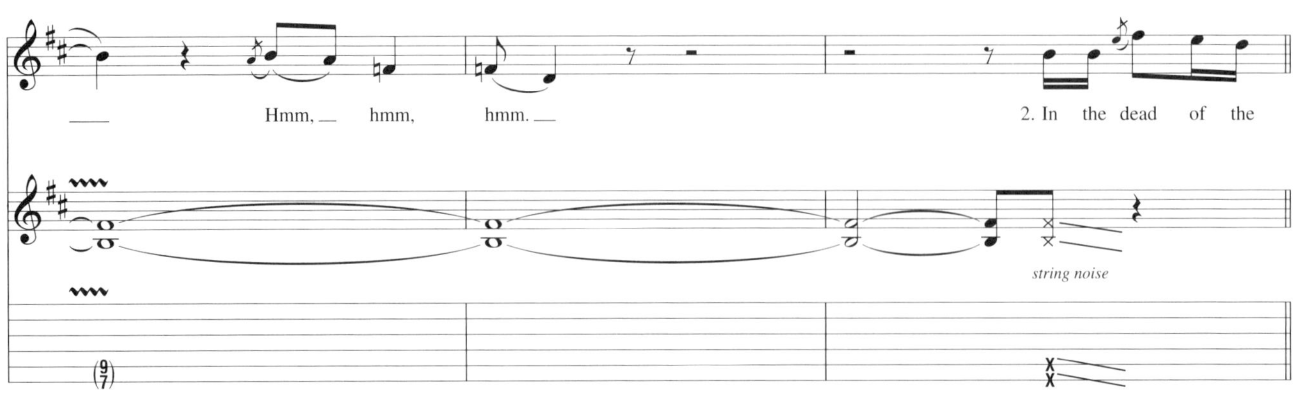
Hmm, hmm, hmm.
2. In the dead of the
string noise

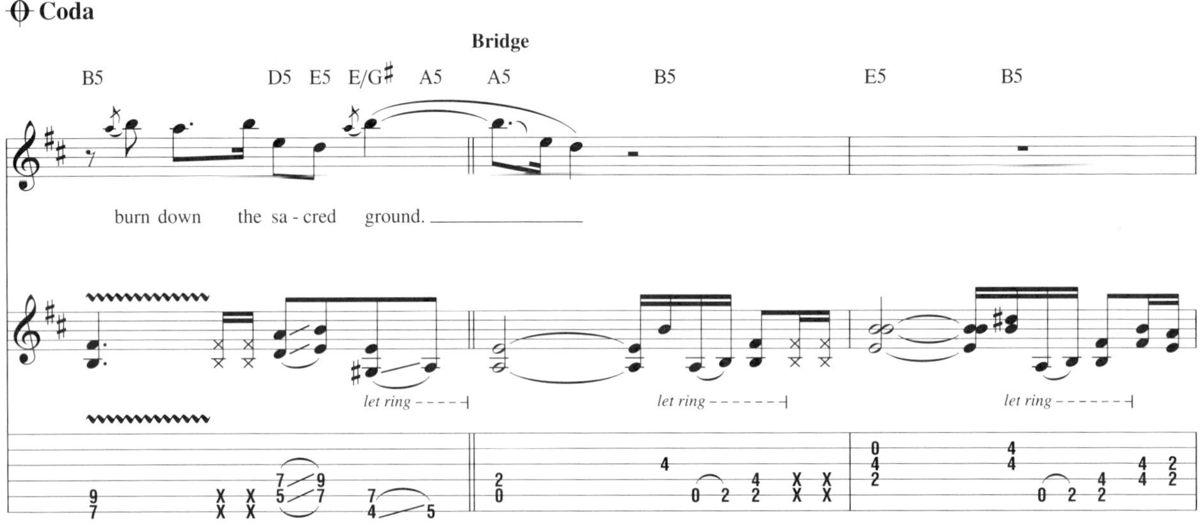
Coda
Bridge
B5 D5 E5 E/G♯ A5 A5 B5 E5 B5
burn down the sa-cred ground.
let ring
let ring
let ring

A5 B5 A5 B5
Hey, hey! All in the name,
Gtr. 1
let ring
let ring
Gtr. 2
let ring
let ring

*B5/E
B5/D
B5
all in the name,
yeah!
*Bass plays E.
Guitar Solo
B5
Gtr. 3 (dist.)
Gtrs. 1 & 2 tacet
let ring
Gtr. 2
Gtr. 1
divisi
Gtr. 3

Pre-Chorus
Gtr. 3 tacet
B5
*A/C♯
All in the name of God some - how,
Gtr. 3
Gtr. 1
Gtr. 2
*Bass plays C♮.
A5
B5
E5
B5
A5
B5
hey, hey, woah, oh, yeah,
Gtrs. 1 & 2
let ring
Chorus
E5
B5
B5 N.C.
E/G♯ A5
hey, woah, woah.
Burn down the sa - cred ground,
let ring

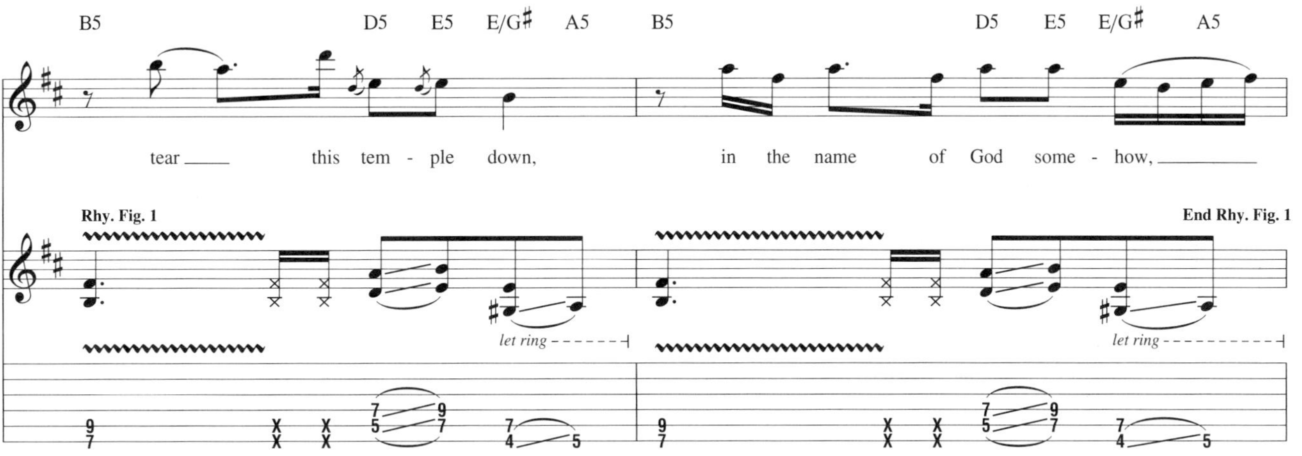
B5 D5 E5 E/G♯ A5 B5 D5 E5 E/G♯ A5
tear this tem - ple down, in the name of God some - how,
Rhy. Fig. 1
End Rhy. Fig. 1
let ring
let ring

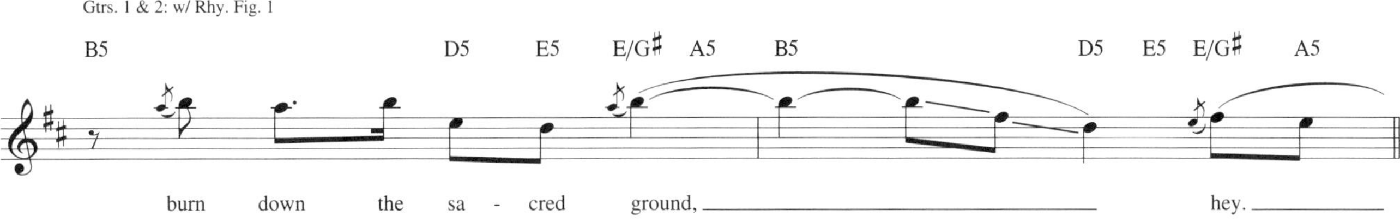
Gtrs. 1 & 2: w/ Rhy. Fig. 1
B5 D5 E5 E/G♯ A5 B5 D5 E5 E/G♯ A5
burn down the sa - cred ground, hey.

Outro-Guitar Solo

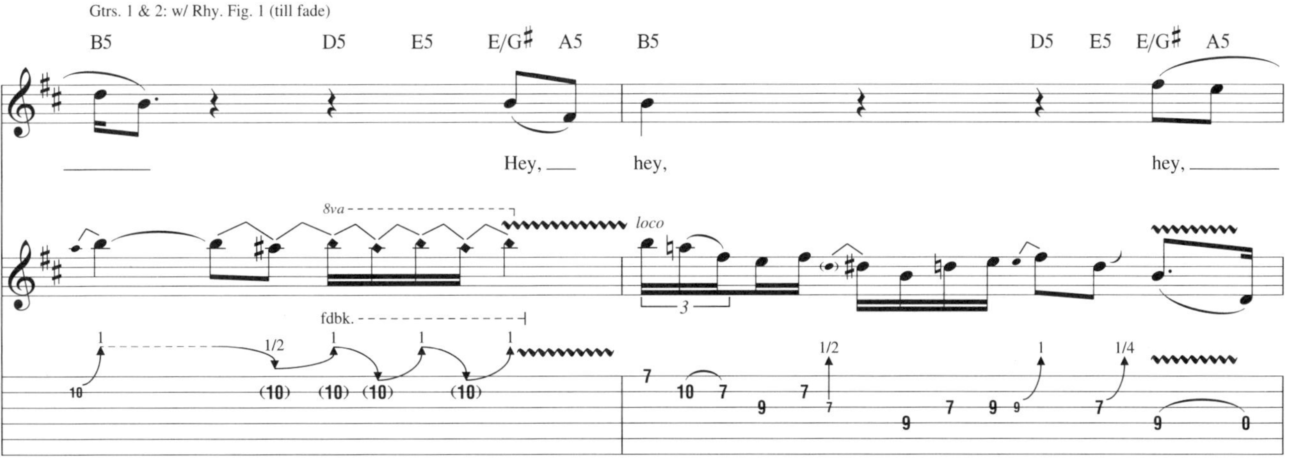
Gtrs. 1 & 2: w/ Rhy. Fig. 1 (till fade)
B5 D5 E5 E/G♯ A5 B5 D5 E5 E/G♯ A5
Hey, hey, hey,
8va
loco
fdbk.

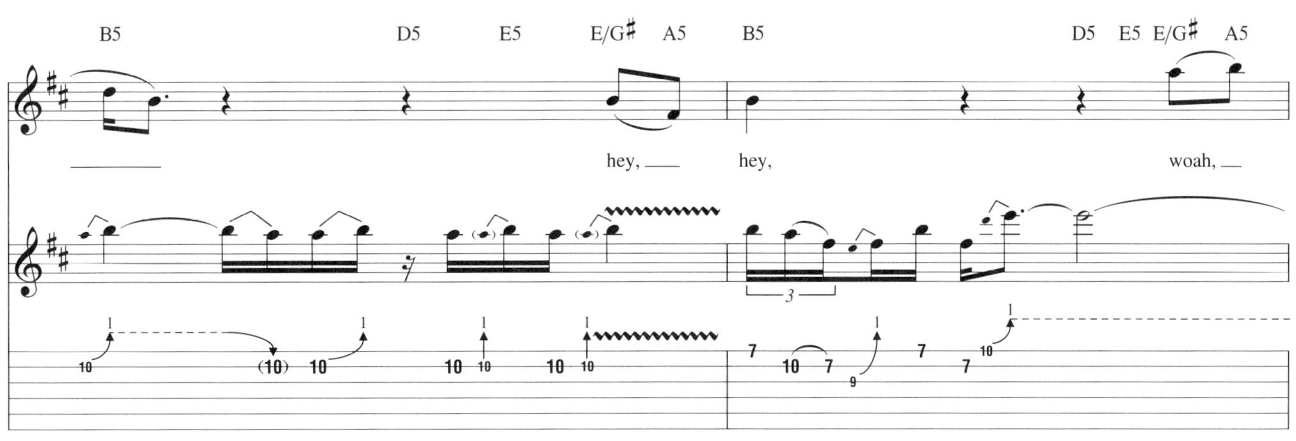
B5 D5 E5 E/G♯ A5 B5 D5 E5 E/G♯ A5
hey, hey, woah,

B5
D5
E5
E/G♯
A5
woah,
yeah,
oo,
hey,
hey,
hey,
hey.
Burn down the sa - cred ground,
burn down the sa - cred ground,
burn down the sa - cred ground,
burn down the sa - cred ground.
Begin fade
8va
loco

B5
D5
E5
E/G♯
A5
Oo,
hold bend
hey,
oo,
woah,
yeah,
hey.
8va
loco
Fade out

from Duane Eddy - *Especially for You*

Peter Gunn

Theme Song from The Television Series

By Henry Mancini

Sax
Gtr. 1
Gtr. 2
N.C.
w/ bar
w/ bar
-1/2
-1/2

C
Gtr. 1
E7(no 3rd)
play 4 times
Gtr. 2
D
N.C.
Gtr. 2 tacet
w/ bar
-1/2
Gtr. 1
Gtr. 2: w/ Riff A1, till fade
E7(no 3rd)
E
E7(no 3rd)
Play 5 Times and Fade

from Extreme - *Extreme*

Play with Me

Words and Music by Gary Cherone and Nuno Bettencourt

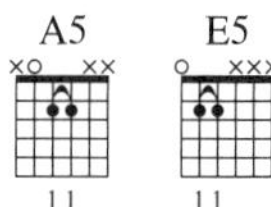

Tune down 1/2 step:
(low to high) E♭-A♭-D♭-G♭-B♭-E♭

*Intro

Fast ♩ = 203

N.C. **Am F7

Gtr. 1 (dist.)

8va

mf

P.M.

Gtr. 2 (dist.)

mf

P.M. P.M. P.M.

Gtr. 3 (dist.)

mf

P.M. P.M. P.M.

Gtr. 4 (dist.)

mf

P.M. P.M. P.M.

*Mozart's Rondo alla Turca (next 5 meas.)

**Chord symbols reflect overall implied harmony.

F
Em
Dm
C
Bm7♭5
E
Am
Gtrs. 1 - 4 tacet
N.C.
8va
loco
w/ bar
P.H.
slight P.M.
P.M.
Pitch: E
-3 1/2
Gtr. 5 (dist.)
mf
Do
you

G
want to play?
1. A,
15ma
Harm. w/ bar
grad. dive
slight P.M.
let ring
*Harmonics located approximately three-tenths the distance between the 2nd & 3rd frets.
Verse
A5 A6 A7 A6 A5 A6 A7 A6 A5 A7 A6 A7 A5 A6 A7 A6 A5
Ring A-round the Ros - ie, Hop - scotch, Mon-o - po - ly. Red Light, Green Light, G. I. Joes and Bar - bie.
loco
P.M.
A7 A6 A7 A5 A7 A6 A7 A5 A7 A6 A7 A5 A7 A5
Hide and Seek Kick the Can, Cow - boys and In - di - ans. Wif-fle Ball, pa-per doll. Hack-ey Sack and Hang - man.
P.M.
let ring
C5 C6 C7 C6 C5 B5 E5 A5
(Do you wan - na play with me?)
2. A
P.M.

Verse

A5 A6 A7 A6 A5 A6 A7 A6 A5 A6 A7 A6 A5 A6 A7 A6
Tag, you're it. Cops and Rob-bers, jun-gle gym, Chutes and Lad-ders. Tic Tac Toe, Mis-ter Rog-ers, Mar-co Po-lo, Lon-don Bridge is,...
P.M.
slight P.H.
A5 A6 A7 A6 A5 A7 A6 A5 C5 G5 A5 B5 A5 N.C.
Steal the Ba-con, time out, Trick or Treat, E - lec-tric Com-pan-y.
(Si-mon Says.)
Kids: (Ol-lie Ol-lie Ox-en Free.)
*Upstroke
C5 C6 C7 C6 C5 B5 E5
(Do you wan - na play with me?)
1/4
Pre-Chorus
G5 Gm F♯m Gm F♯m Gm F♯m Gm F♯m Gm F♯m
A, with me.

Chorus
D5
A5
C5
A5
Do you
wan - na
Voc. Fig. 1
(Do you
wan - na
P.M.
P.M.
P.M.
B♭5
A5
play,
play with me?
play.)
Kids: (Play with me?)
15ma
loco
P.H.
P.M.
Pitch: F♯
D5
A5
C5
A5
Do you
wan - na
(Do you,
P.M.
P.M.

B♭5 A5

— play, — play — with — me?

do you, do you wan-na) *Kids:* (Play —

15ma loco

P.H. *hold

let ring

P.M.

1/2 *T 1 1 T

Pitch: F♯ *T = pick-hand tap

End Voc. Fig. 1

— with me?)

1 T 1

Verse

A5 A6 A7 A6 A5 A6 A7 A6 A5 A6 A7 A6 A5 A7 A6 A5

3. Spin the Bot-tle, Post Of-fice, Kiss and Tell, dress-in' up. — Play-in' doc-tor, Peek-a-boo, Two-Hand Touch, Coo - tie,

A6 A7 A6 A5 A6 A7 A6 A5 Am Asus2 A7 C5
Lit-tle League, Loon-y Tunes, Scis-sors, Rock, Pa-per, Zoom. Kick - ball, Stick - ball.
Men: (Kill the Guy with the ball.)
P.M.
1/2
C6 C7 C6 C5 B5 E5 A5
(Do you wan - na play with me?)
4. Ah,
let ring
P.H.
Pitch: C♯
Verse
A5
Buck-in' up, re - cess, jump rope, Re-liev-i-o. see - saw, sand - box,
heavy
Match - box, Cheer-i-o.
(A, B, C's, spel-ling bees, Ses-a-me Street, hock-ey.

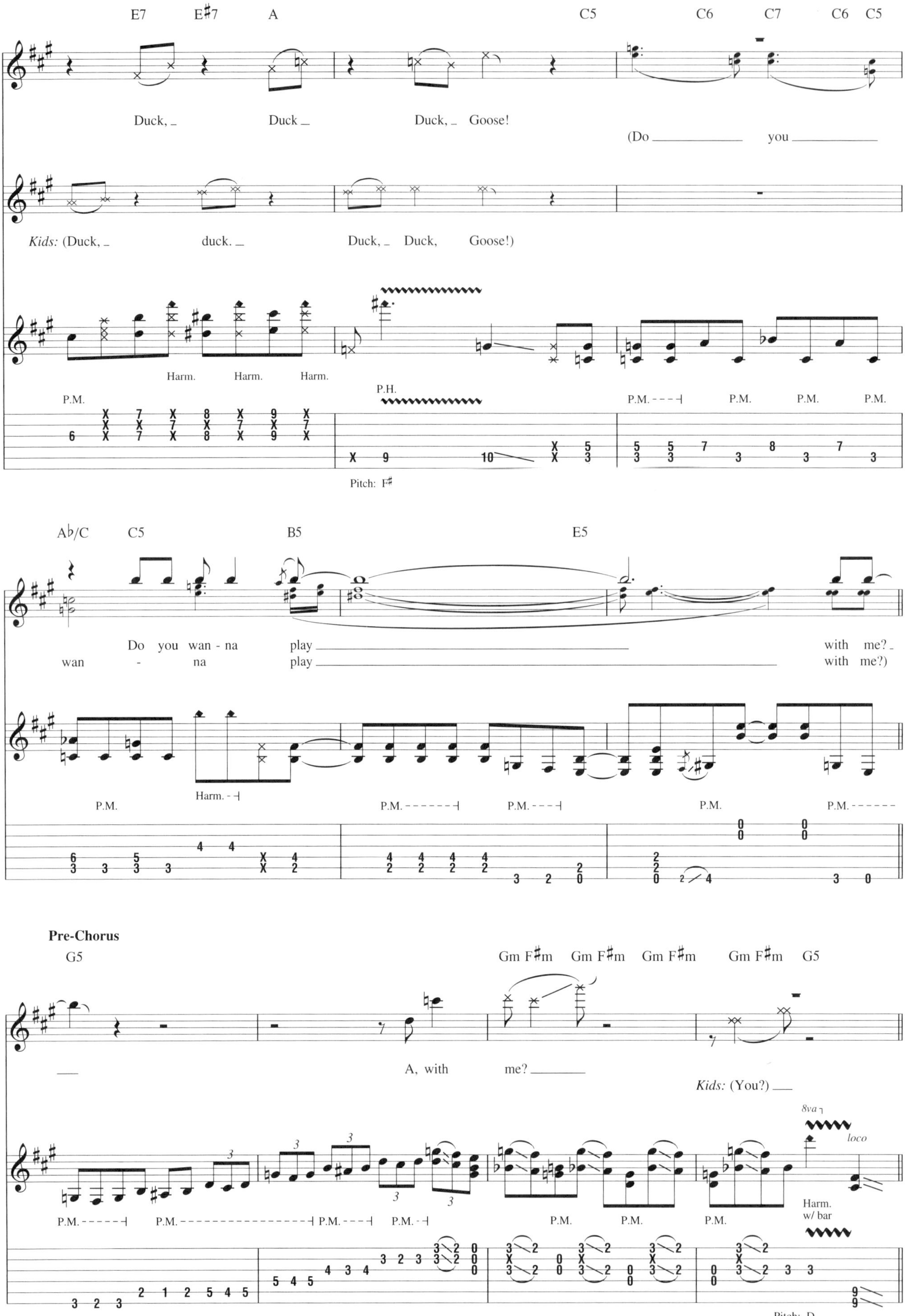

E7 E♯7 A C5 C6 C7 C6 C5

Duck, Duck Duck, Goose!

(Do you

Kids: (Duck, duck. Duck, Duck, Goose!)

Harm. Harm. Harm.

P.M.

P.H.

P.M. P.M. P.M. P.M.

Pitch: F♯

A♭/C C5 B5 E5

Do you wan - na play with me?

wan - na play with me?)

Harm.

P.M. P.M. P.M. P.M. P.M.

Pre-Chorus

Chorus
Bkgd. Voc.: w/ Voc. Fig. 1
D5 A5 C5 A5
Do you wan - na
P.M. P.M. P.M. P.M.
Bb5 A5
play, play with me?
P.H. P.H. P.M. P.M. P.M. P.M.
Pitch: G# G
D5 A5 C5 A5
Do you wan - na
w/ bar w/ bar
P.M. P.M. P.M. P.M. P.M.
Bb5 A5
play, play with me?
w/ wah-wah
T T

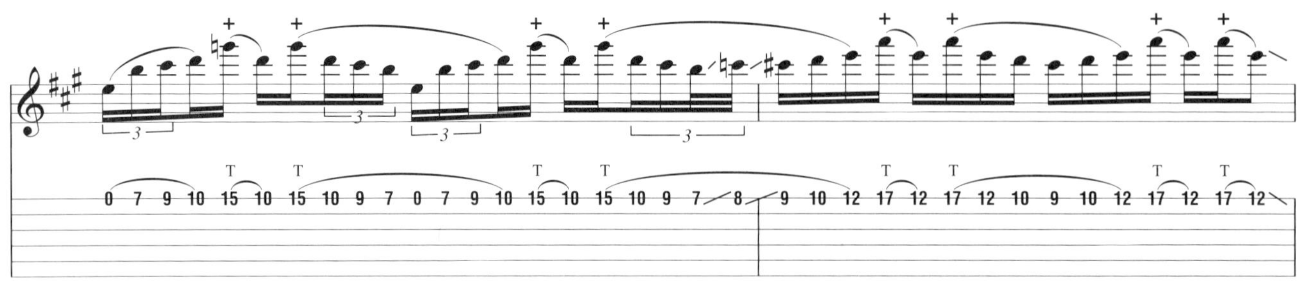

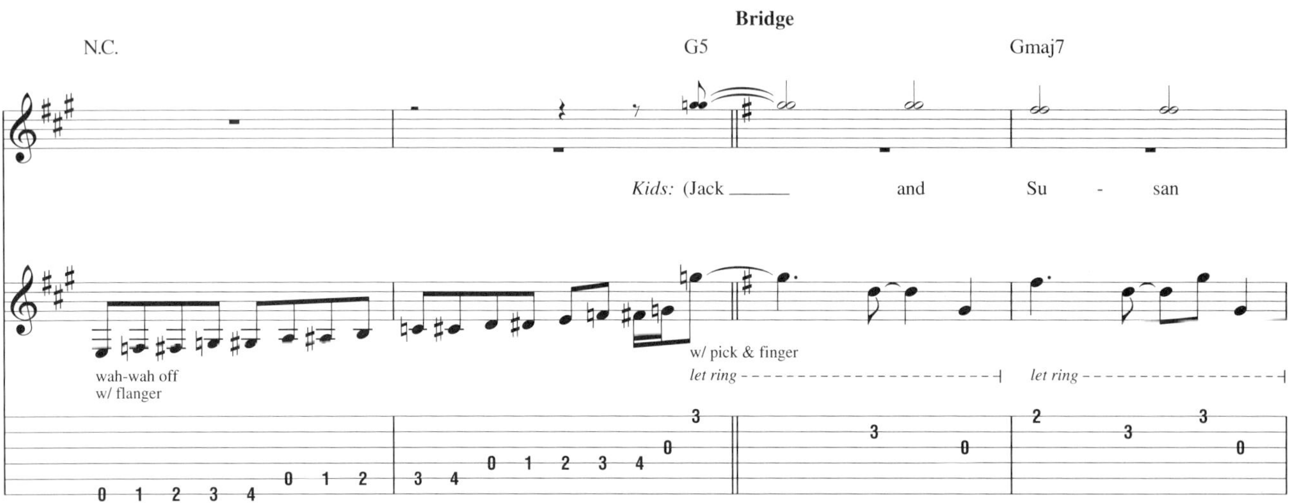
Bridge
N.C.
G5
Gmaj7
Kids: (Jack and Su - san
wah-wah off
w/ flanger
w/ pick & finger
let ring
let ring

G7
Cadd2
G7
A7
Cm
sit - tin' in a tree k - i - s - s - i - n -
let ring
let ring
let ring
let ring
let ring

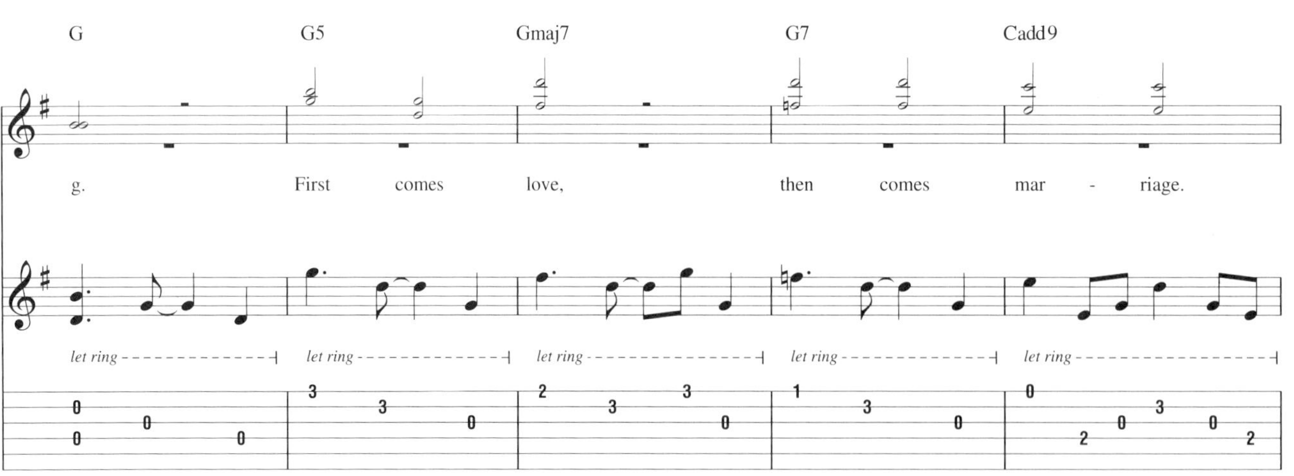
G
G5
Gmaj7
G7
Cadd9
g. First comes love, then comes mar - riage.
let ring
let ring
let ring
let ring
let ring

Guitar Solo

*See top of first page of song for chord diagrams pertaining to rhythm slashes.

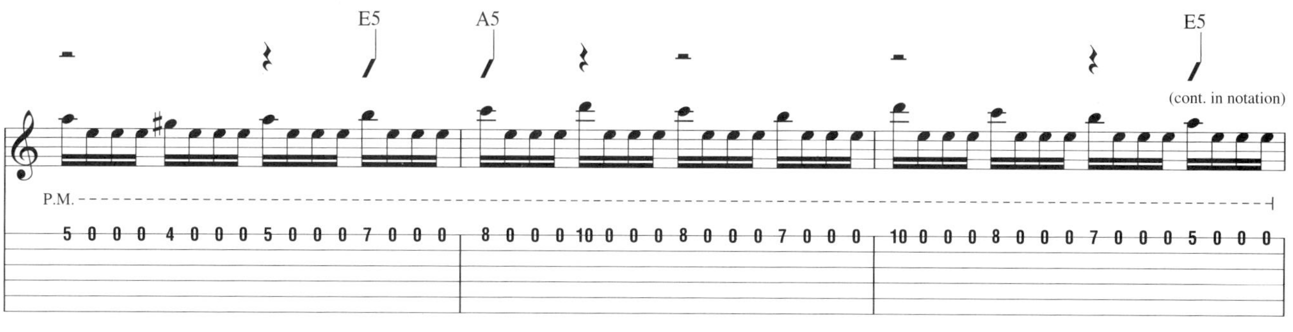

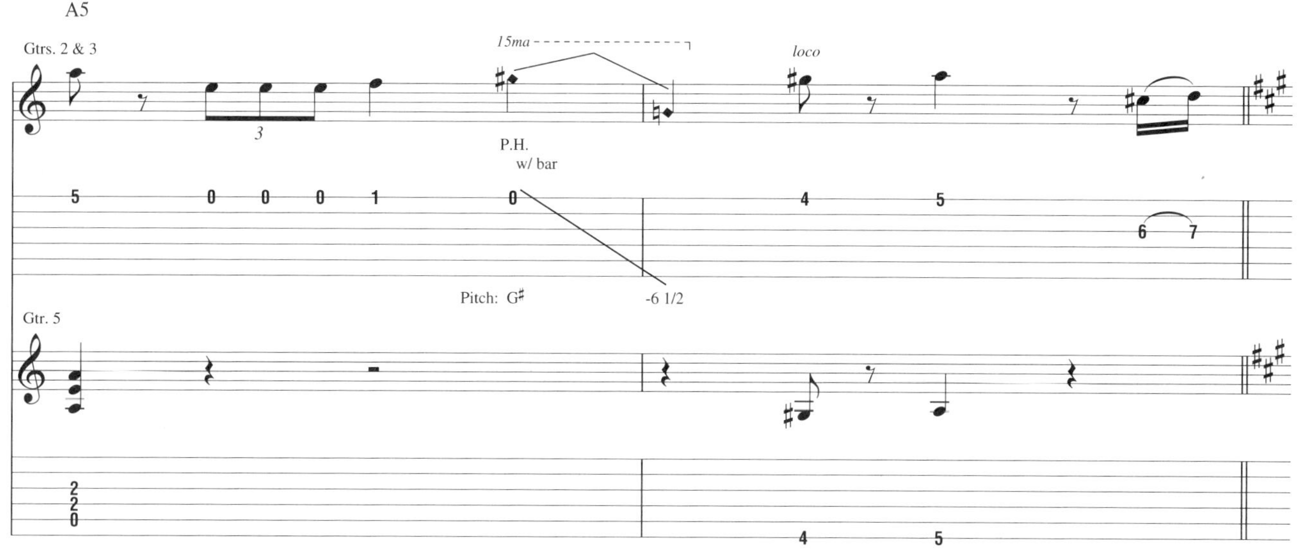

E
A
P.M.
A7/C♯
D6
B/D♯
B
*Downstroke
E5
P.H.
Pitch: E
G
F♯
F
G

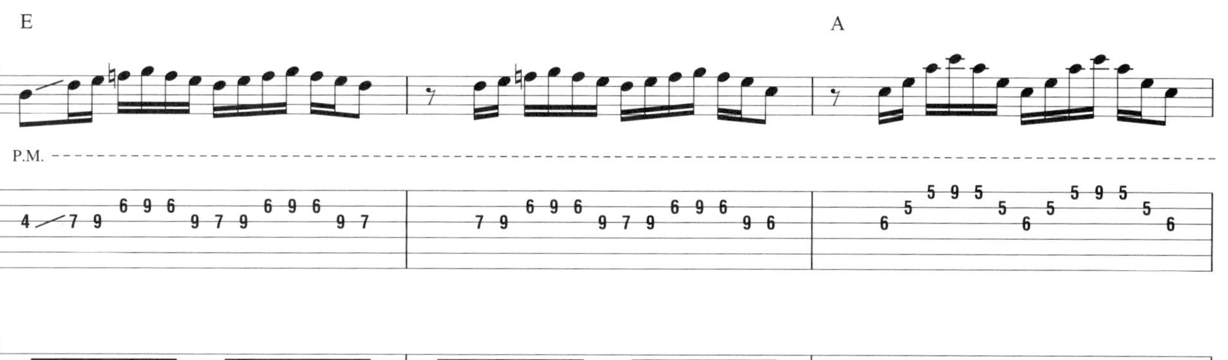
E
A
P.M.

P.M.
P.M.

C♯add♯9
D6
B/D♯
B
P.M.
P.M.
P.M.
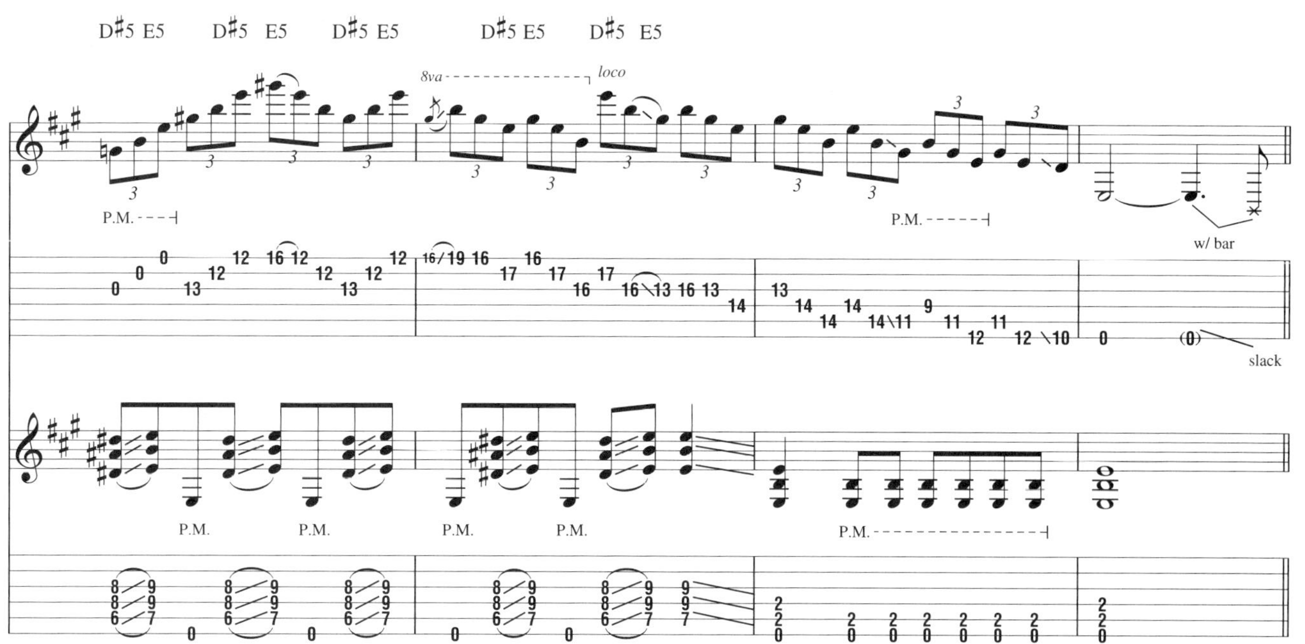
D♯5 E5
D♯5 E5
D♯5 E5
D♯5 E5
D♯5 E5
8va
loco
P.M.
P.M.
w/ bar
slack
P.M.
P.M.
P.M.
P.M.
P.M.

Chorus

Bkgd. Voc.: w/ Voc. Fig. 1 (1st 12 meas.)
Gtrs. 2 & 3 tacet

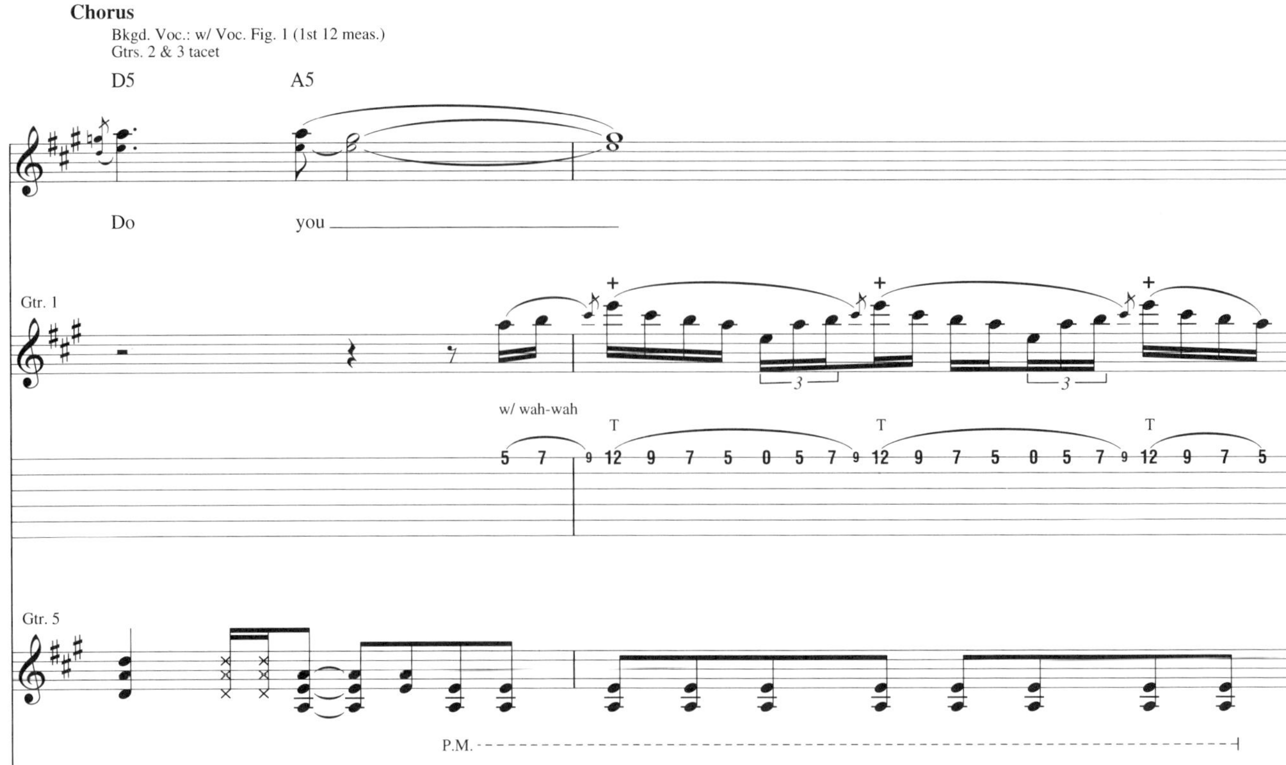

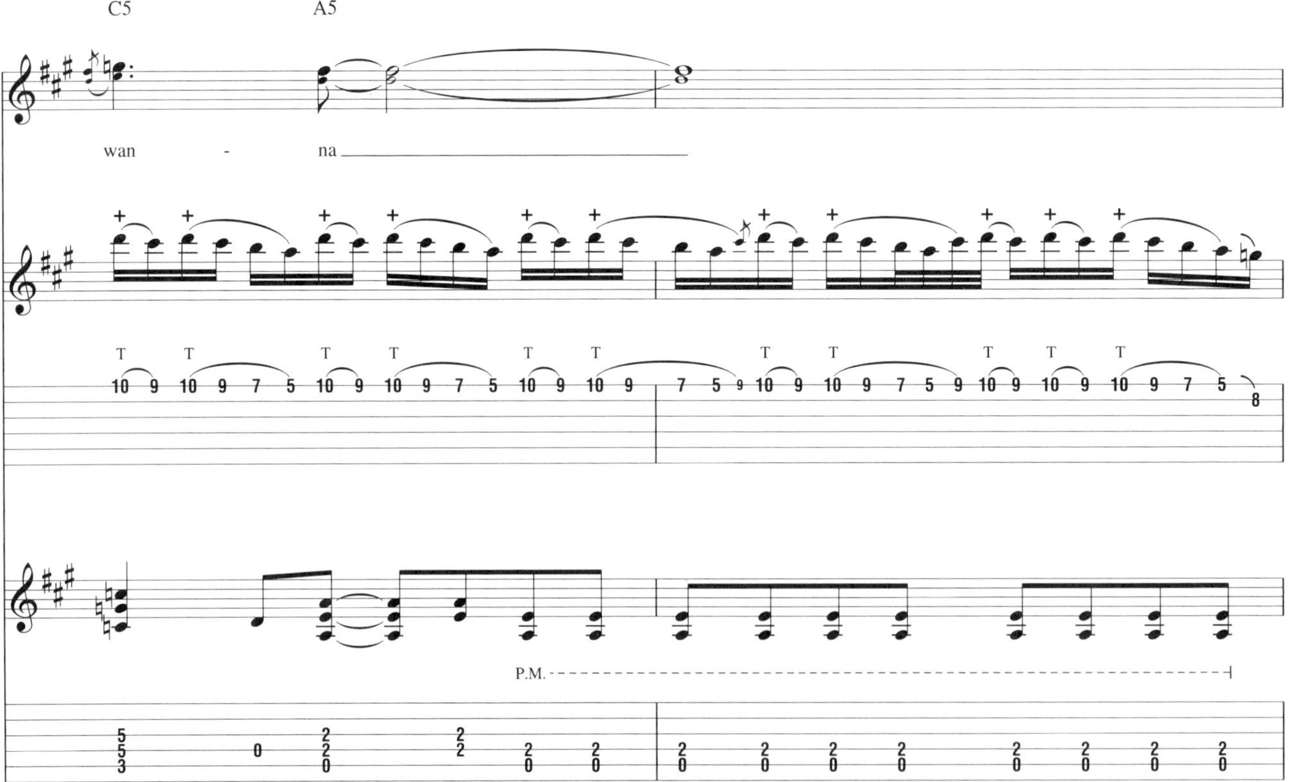

B♭5
A5
play,
play
15ma
P.H.
w/ bar
-7 1/2
-5
-1 1/2
-1/2
-3
slack
15ma
loco
P.H.
P.M.
Pitch: F♯
Gtr. 1 tacet
D5
A5
with me?
Do
you
Gtr. 5
P.M.
C5
A5
B♭5
A5
wan - na
play,
play
8va
P.M.

with me?
Kids: (Play with me.)
loco
5
Outro
N.C.
Ah, ah, ah, ah.
P.M.
Harm.
8va
Pitch: B
Ah, ah, ah, ah.
Gtr. 2
15ma
Harm.
grad. release
w/ bar
Gtr. 3
8va
Gtr. 5
loco

E5
G♯5
C5
E5
G5
Am N.C.
Am
15ma
Gtr. 2
8va
+1/2
(2)
(2)
17 20 19 20 17 20 20 20 17 20
-5
-3 1/2
-2 1/2
-1/2
8va
Gtr. 3
+1/2
(5)
(5)
17 20 18 20 17 20 19 20 17 17
-4 1/2
-3
-2
-1/2
Gtr. 1
8va
loco
wah-wah off
20 19 17 16 17 17 18 19 17 14
Gtr. 4
10 12 10 12 13 12 12 12 10 12
Gtr. 5
P.M.
0 0 0 0 4 4 4 4 8 8 8 8 0 0 0 0 5 3
2 2 0

from Foo Fighters - *Echos, Silence, Patience & Grace*

The Pretender

Words and Music by Dave Grohl, Taylor Hawkins, Christopher Shiflett and Nate Mendel

Interlude
Gtr. 1 tacet
A5
Verse
Gtr. 2: w/ Riff B (16 times)
Am
2. Send in your skel - e - tons. Sing as their bones
Riff B
*Gtr. 2 (dist.)
mf
End Riff B Rhy. Fig. 1
**Gtr. 3 (dist.)
mf
*Doubled throughout
**Doubled throughout
D/F#
F
Fsus2
come march - ing in a - gain.
End Rhy. Fig. 1
Gtr. 3: w/ Rhy. Fig. 1
Am
The need you bur - ied deep, the se - crets that you keep are
D/F#
F
Fsus2
G5
at the read - y. Are you read - y?
Gtr. 3
Rhy. Fig. 2
End Rhy. Fig. 2
Gtr. 3: w/ Rhy. Fig. 1
Am
I'm fin - ished mak - ing sense, done plead - ing ig - no - rance, that old

Gtr. 3: w/ Rhy. Fig. 2
D/F♯
F
Fsus2
G5
de - fense.
Gtr. 4 (dist.)
Riff C
mf
steady gliss.
Gtr. 3: w/ Rhy. Fig. 1
Am
Spin - ning in - fin - i - ty, but the wheel is spin - ning me. It's
P.M.
Gtr. 3: w/ Rhy. Fig. 2
D/F♯
F
Fsus2
G5
nev - er - end - ing, nev - er - end - ing.
P.M.
Chorus
D5
Dsus2
D
Dsus4
Am
Am(add9)
Am
Am(add9)
Am
Am(add9)
Same old sto - ry. What if I say I'm not like the oth - ers?
Gtr. 4
End Riff C
Rhy. Fig. 3A
*Gtr. 5 (dist.)
*Doubled throughout
Gtr. 3
Fill 2
End Fill 2
Rhy. Fig. 3
Gtrs. 3 & 4

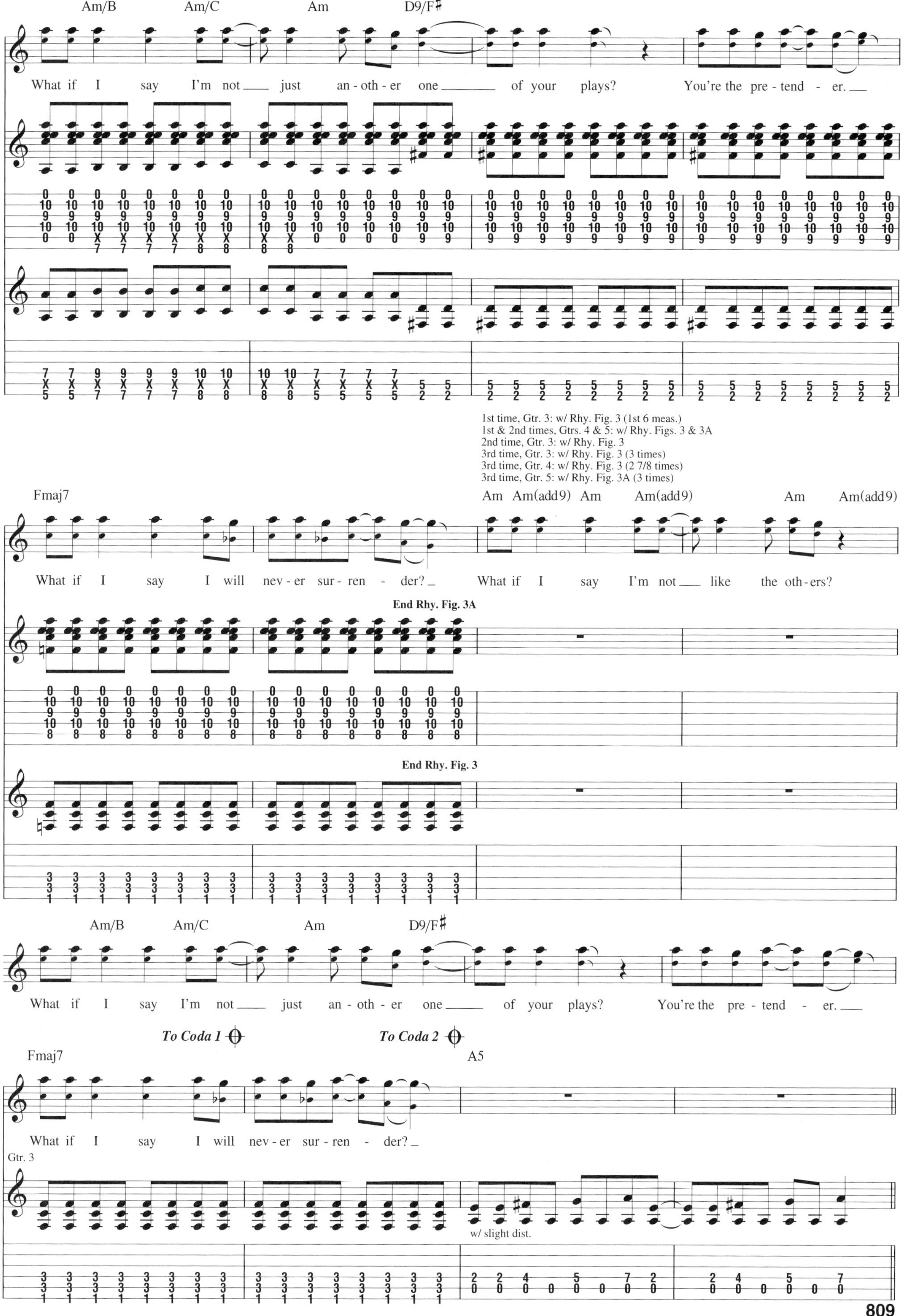

Am/B
Am/C
Am
D9/F♯
What if I say I'm not just an-oth-er one of your plays? You're the pre-tend-er.
1st time, Gtr. 3: w/ Rhy. Fig. 3 (1st 6 meas.)
1st & 2nd times, Gtrs. 4 & 5: w/ Rhy. Figs. 3 & 3A
2nd time, Gtr. 3: w/ Rhy. Fig. 3
3rd time, Gtr. 3: w/ Rhy. Fig. 3 (3 times)
3rd time, Gtr. 4: w/ Rhy. Fig. 3 (2 7/8 times)
3rd time, Gtr. 5: w/ Rhy. Fig. 3A (3 times)
Fmaj7
Am
Am(add9)
What if I say I will nev-er sur-ren-der? What if I say I'm not like the oth-ers?
End Rhy. Fig. 3A
End Rhy. Fig. 3
To Coda 1
To Coda 2
A5
Gtr. 3
w/ slight dist.

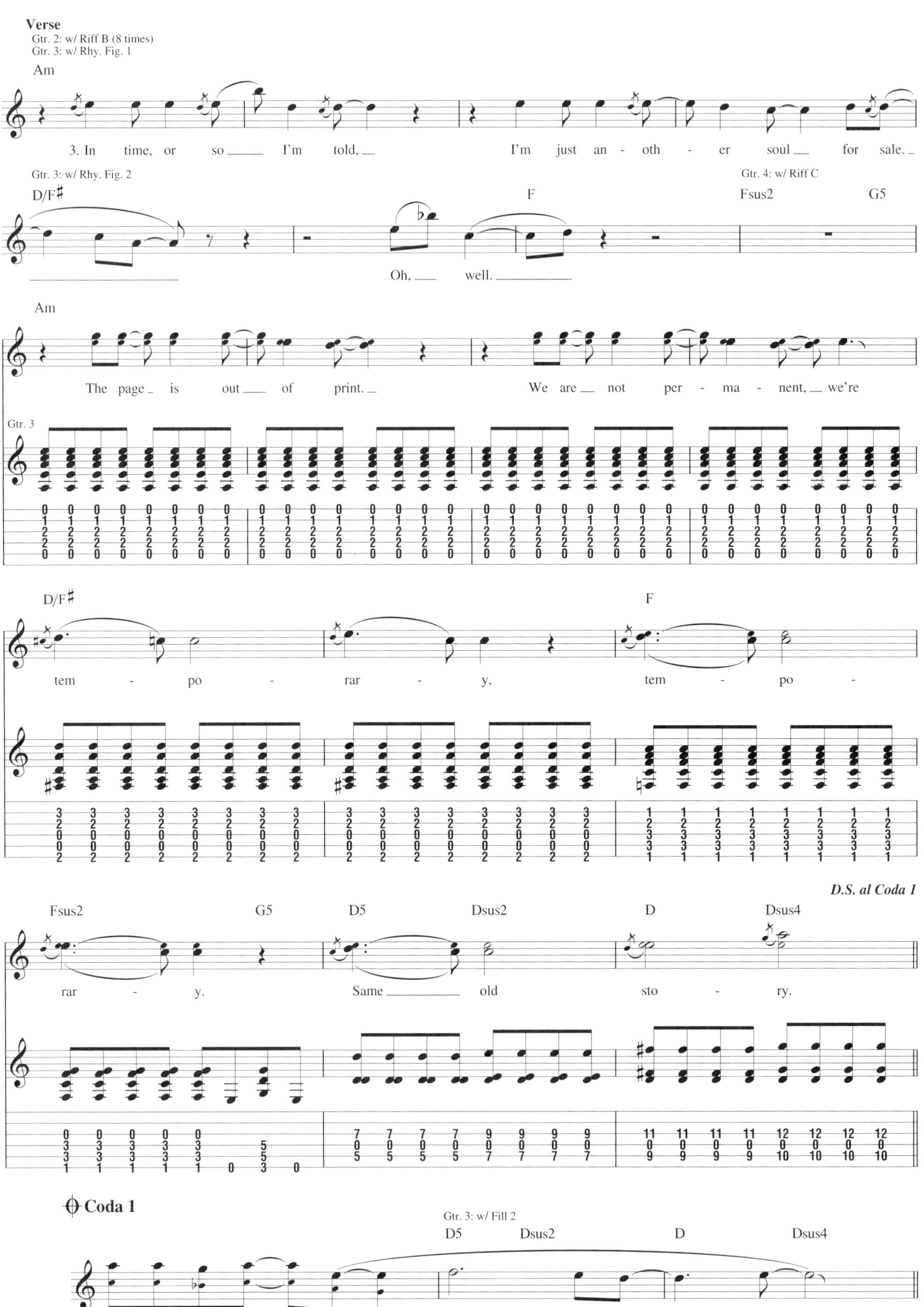

Verse
Gtr. 2: w/ Riff B (8 times)
Gtr. 3: w/ Rhy. Fig. 1
Am
3. In time, or so I'm told,
I'm just an - oth - er soul for sale.
Gtr. 3: w/ Rhy. Fig. 2
D/F♯
F
Gtr. 4: w/ Riff C
Fsus2
G5
Oh, well.
Am
The page is out of print.
We are not per - ma - nent, we're
Gtr. 3
D/F♯
F
tem - po - rar - y, tem - po -
D.S. al Coda 1
Fsus2
G5
D5
Dsus2
D
Dsus4
rar - y. Same old sto - ry.
Coda 1
Gtr. 3: w/ Fill 2
D5
Dsus2
D
Dsus4
nev - er sur - ren - der?

Interlude
A5
I'm
Gtr. 3
Riff D
End Riff D
w/ slight dist.
P.M.
Gtr. 4
Rhy. Fig. 4
End Rhy. Fig. 4
P.M.
Bridge
Gtr. 3: w/ Riff D
Gtr. 4: w/ Rhy. Fig. 4 (2 times)
A5
the voice in - side your head (that) you re - fuse to hear. I'm
Gtr. 5
w/ flanger
the face that you have to face, mir-rored in your stare. I'm
Gtr. 3
P.M.
Gtr. 5

A5
what's left. I'm what's right. I'm the en - e - my. I'm
Gtr. 3
let ring
Gtr. 4
P.M.
(cont. in slashes)
Gtr. 5
A5
Gtr. 4
P.M.
the hand that will take you down, bring you to your knees. So who
Gtr. 3
let ring
Gtr. 5

Rhy. Fig. 5
End Rhy. Fig. 5
w/ dist.
are you? Yeah, who are you? Yeah, who
w/ dist.
*Gtr. 4: w/ Rhy. Fig. 5
are you? Yeah, who are you?
*w/ dist. & delay (set for quarter-note regeneration w/ multiple decaying repeats).
Verse
Half-time feel
Gtr. 1: w/ Riff A (1st 6 meas.)
Gtrs. 3 & 5 tacet
Am(add9)
Asus2/B
Am/C
Am
D9/F♯
4. Keep you in the dark. You know they all
D.S. al Coda 2
End half-time feel
Gtr. 1: w/ Fill 1
Fmaj7
pre - tend.

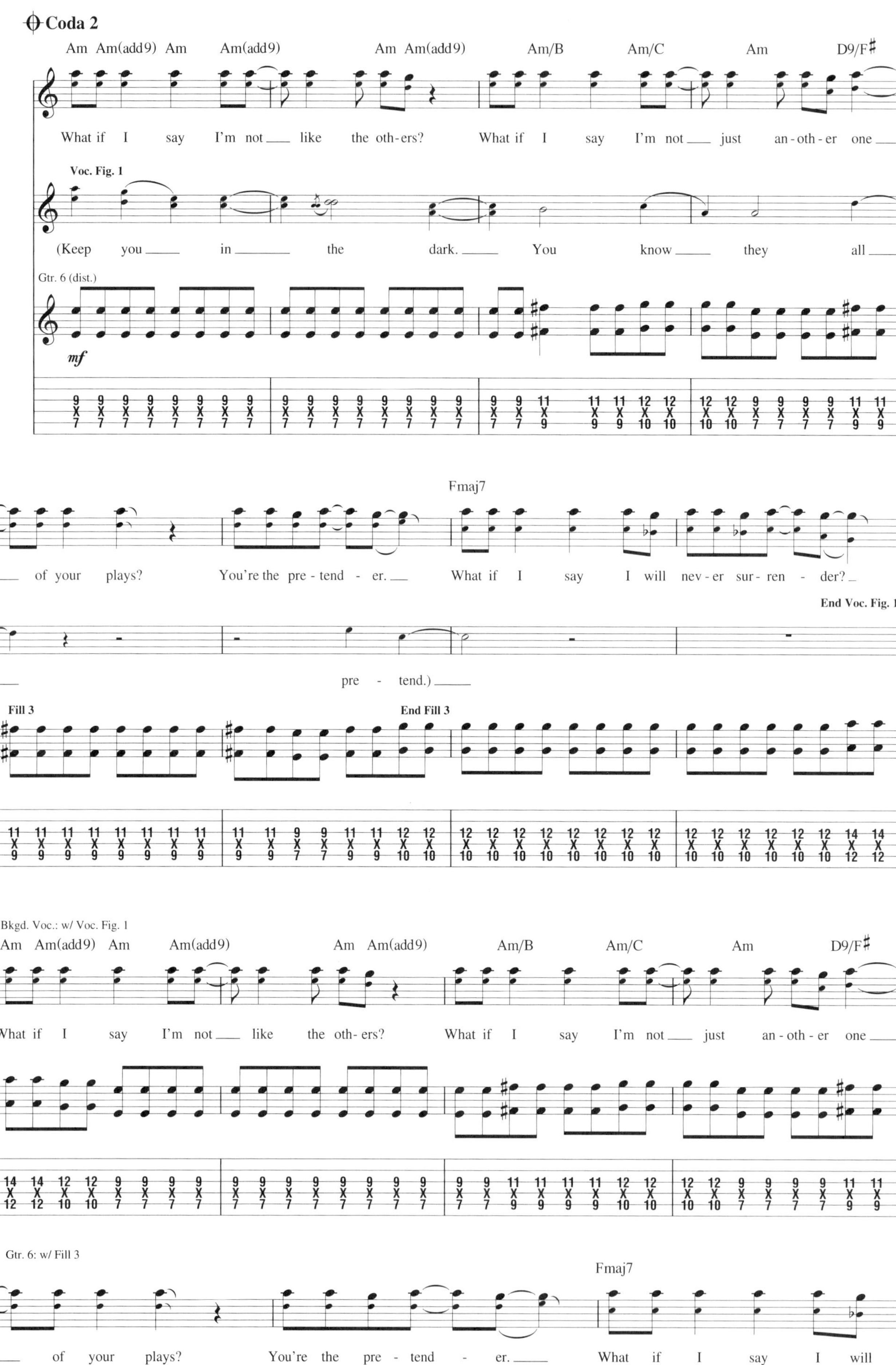
Coda 2
Am Am(add9) Am Am(add9) Am Am(add9) Am/B Am/C Am D9/F♯
What if I say I'm not like the oth-ers? What if I say I'm not just an-oth-er one
Voc. Fig. 1
(Keep you in the dark. You know they all
Gtr. 6 (dist.)
mf
Fmaj7
of your plays? You're the pre-tend-er. What if I say I will nev-er sur-ren-der?
End Voc. Fig. 1
pre - tend.)
Fill 3
End Fill 3
Bkgd. Voc.: w/ Voc. Fig. 1
Am Am(add9) Am Am(add9) Am Am(add9) Am/B Am/C Am D9/F♯
What if I say I'm not like the oth-ers? What if I say I'm not just an-oth-er one
Gtr. 6: w/ Fill 3
Fmaj7
of your plays? You're the pre-tend-er. What if I say I will

Gtr. 3: w/ Fill 2
D5
Dsus2
D
Dsus4
nev - er sur - ren - der?
So who
Gtr. 6
Gtr. 4
(cont. in slashes)
Outro
Gtr. 6 tacet
A5
Gtr. 4
are you?
Yeah, who
are you?
Yeah, who
Gtr. 3
are who?
let ring
let ring

from Sex Pistols - *Never Mind the Bollocks, Here's the Sex Pistols*

Pretty Vacant

Words and Music by Paul Thomas Cook, Stephen Philip Jones, Glen Matlock and John Lydon

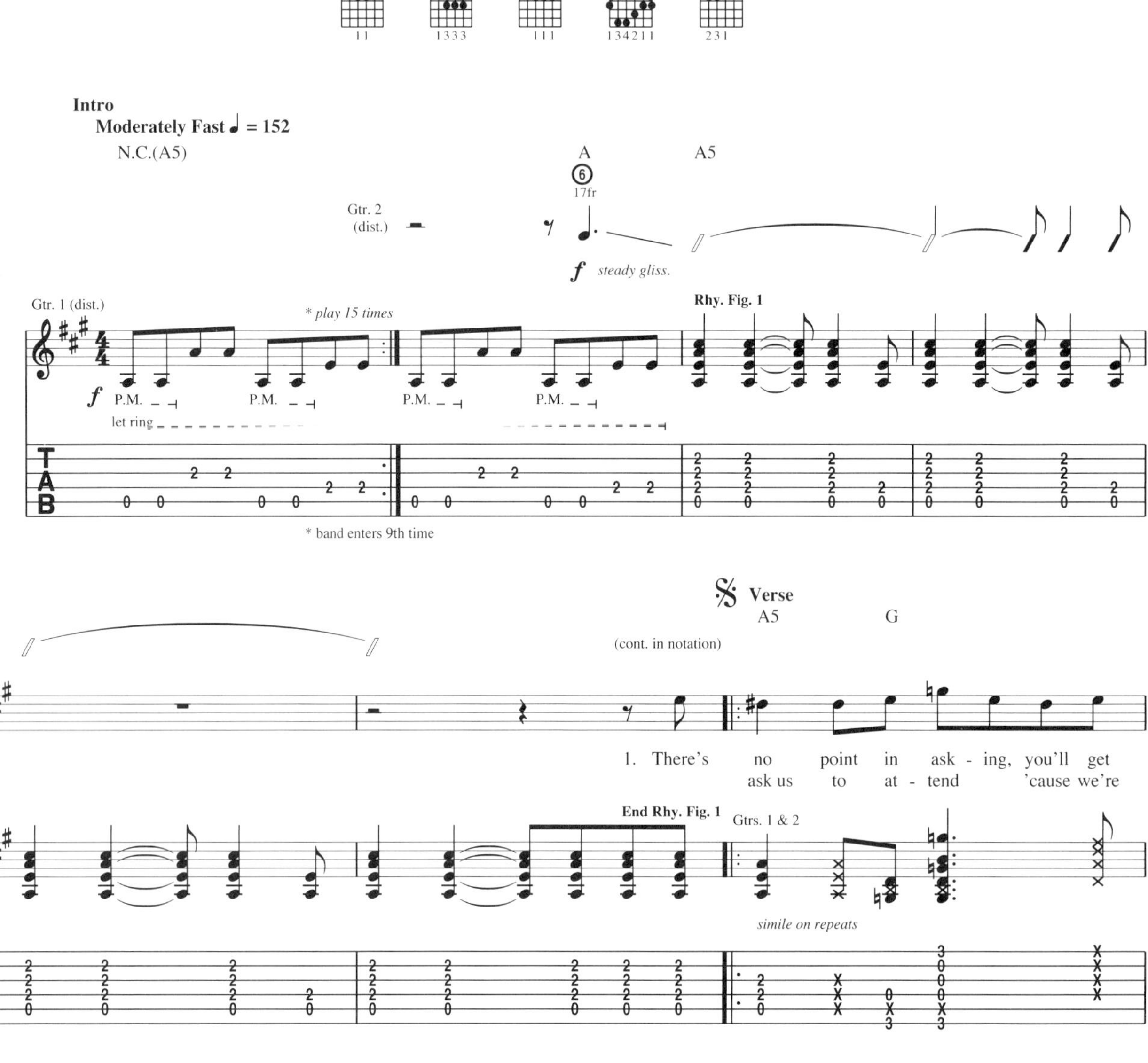

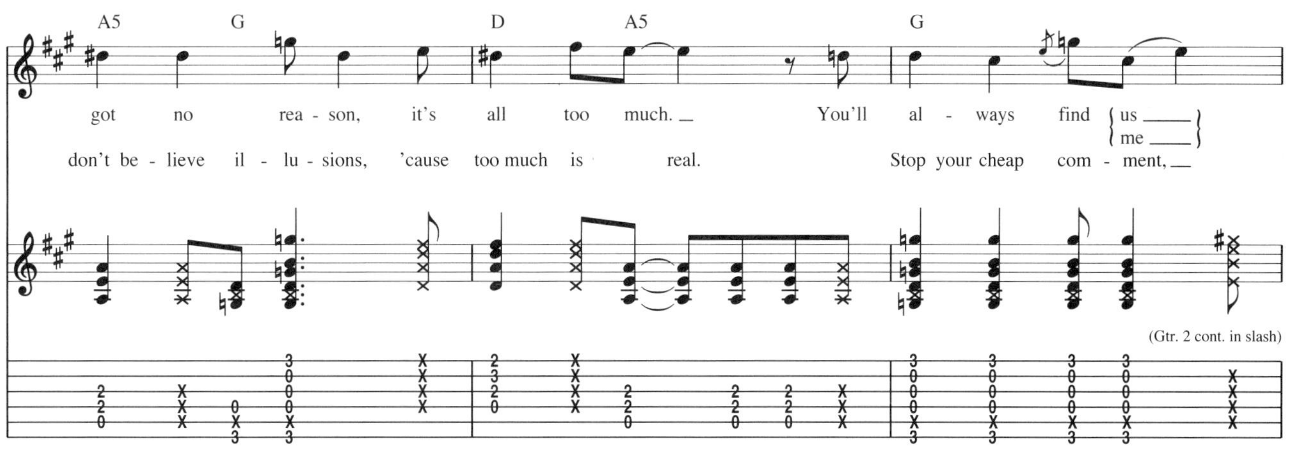
A5
G
D
A5
G
got no rea - son, it's all too much. You'll al - ways find us / me
don't be - lieve il - lu - sions, 'cause too much is real. Stop your cheap com - ment,
(Gtr. 2 cont. in slash)

Gtr. 1: w/ Fill 1, 2nd time
Gtr. 1: w/ Fill 2, 3rd time
E
A
Gtr. 2
(cont. in notation)
out to lunch.
'cause we know what we feel.
Oh,
Gtr. 1
full
1/2
full

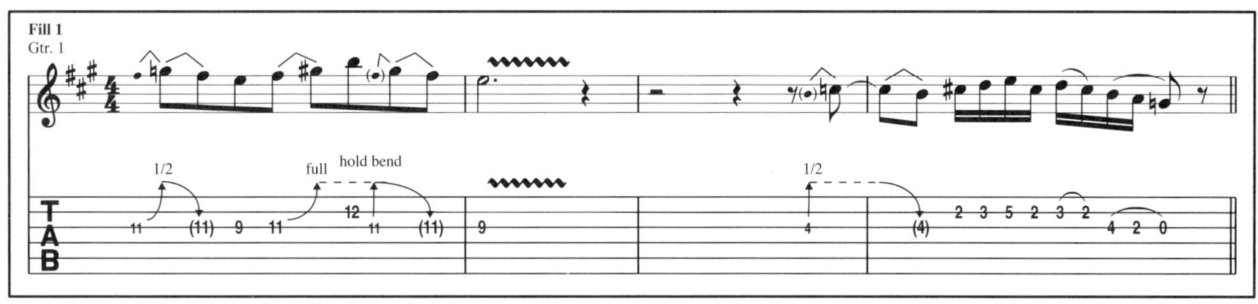
Fill 1
Gtr. 1
1/2
full
hold bend
1/2

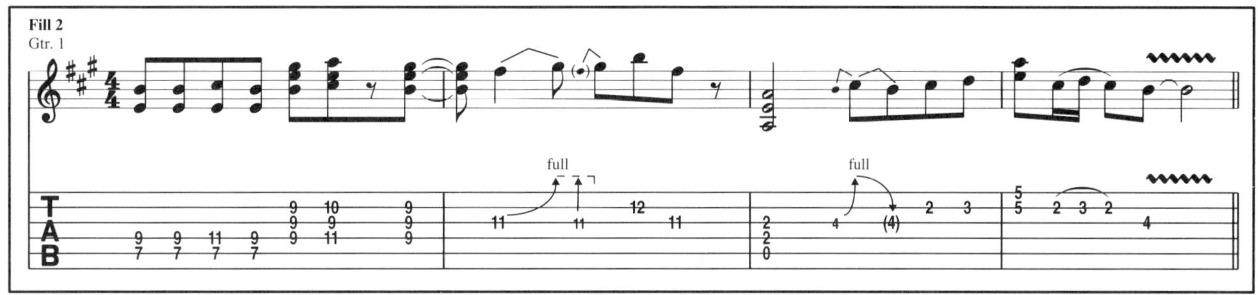
Fill 2
Gtr. 1
full
full

Chorus

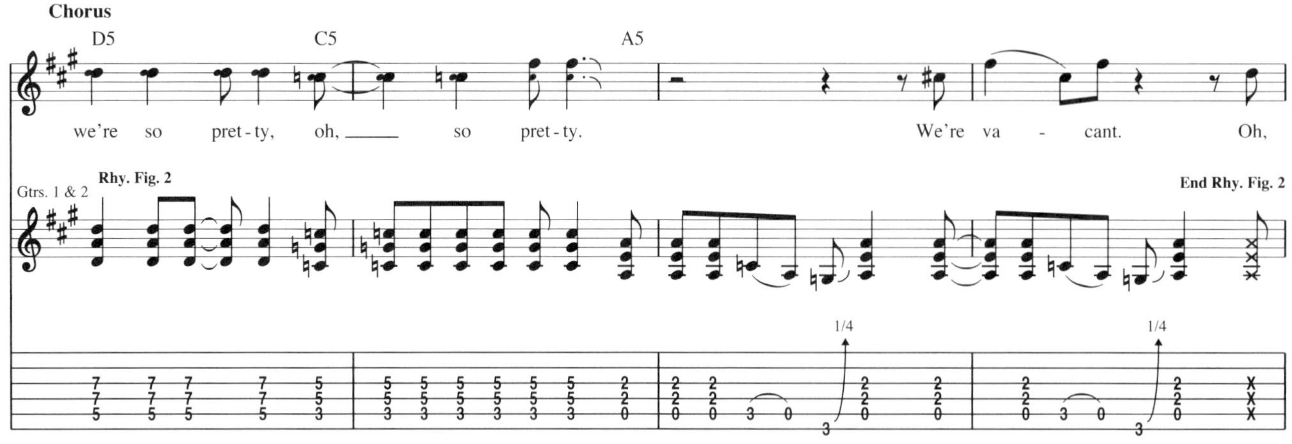
D5 C5 A5
we're so pret-ty, oh, so pret-ty. We're va - cant. Oh,
Gtrs. 1 & 2
Rhy. Fig. 2
End Rhy. Fig. 2
1/4
1/4

Gtrs. 1 & 2: w/ Rhy. Fig. 2
D5 C5 A5
we're so pret ty, oh, so pret-ty. A va - cant.
2. Don't
Oh,

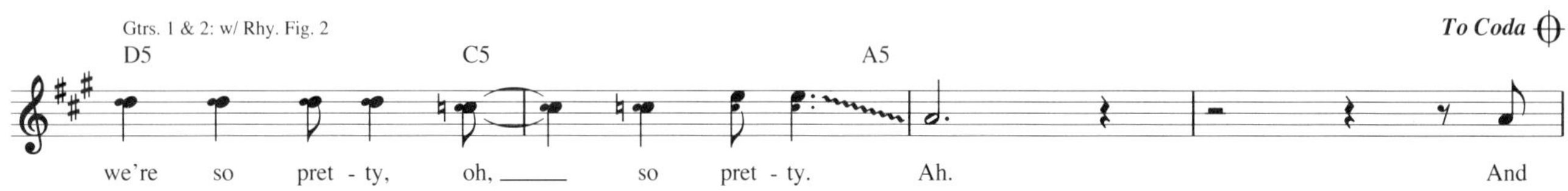
Gtrs. 1 & 2: w/ Rhy. Fig. 2
To Coda
D5 C5 A5
we're so pret - ty, oh, so pret - ty. Ah. And

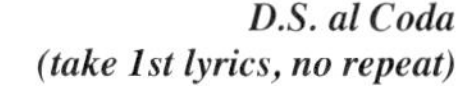
D.S. al Coda
(take 1st lyrics, no repeat)

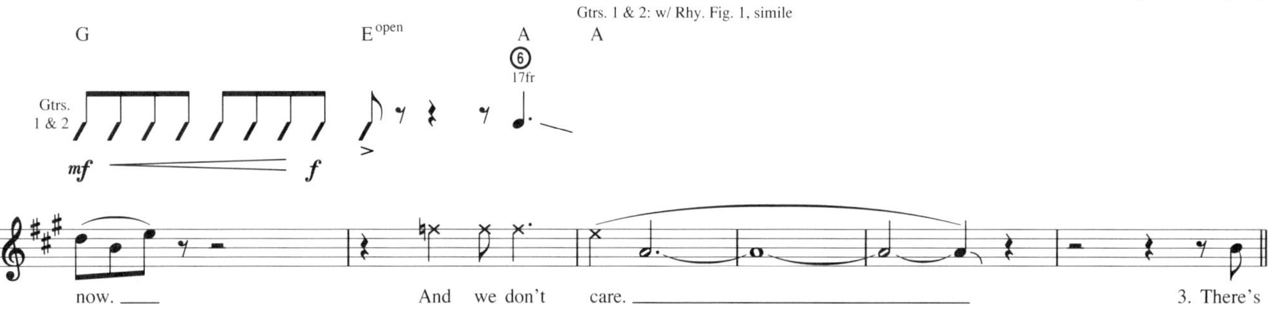
Gtrs. 1 & 2: w/ Rhy. Fig. 1, simile
G E open A A
6
17fr
Gtrs. 1 & 2
mf f
now. And we don't care. 3. There's

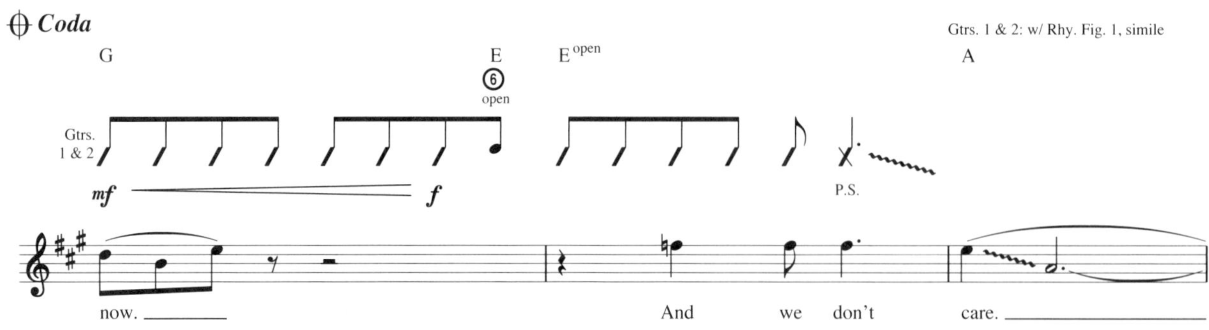
Coda
Gtrs. 1 & 2: w/ Rhy. Fig. 1, simile
G E E open A
6
open
Gtrs. 1 & 2
mf f
P.S.
now. And we don't care.

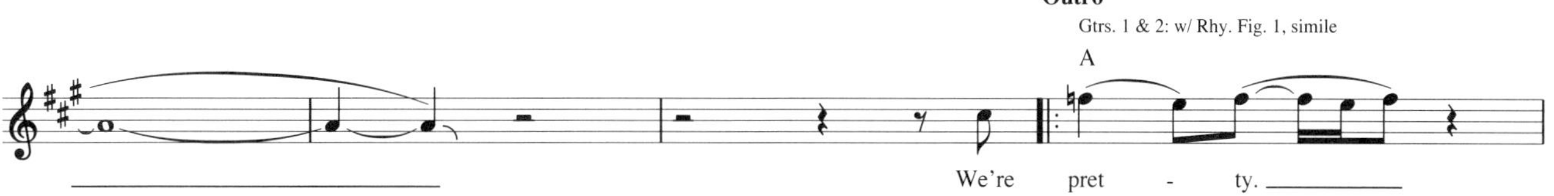
Outro
Gtrs. 1 & 2: w/ Rhy. Fig. 1, simile
A
We're pret - ty.

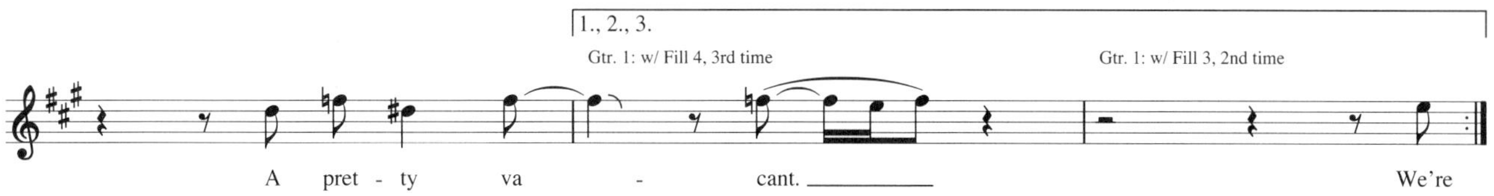
1., 2., 3.
Gtr. 1: w/ Fill 4, 3rd time
Gtr. 1: w/ Fill 3, 2nd time
A pret - ty va - cant.
We're

4.
A5
N.C.
A5
- cant, and we don't care.
Gtrs. 1 & 2
fdbk.

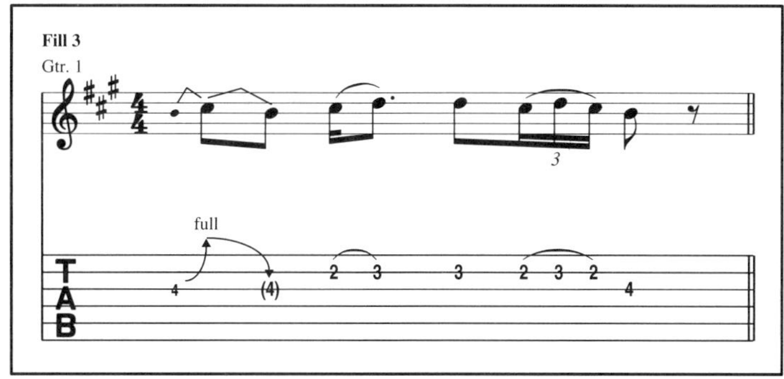
Fill 3
Gtr. 1
full

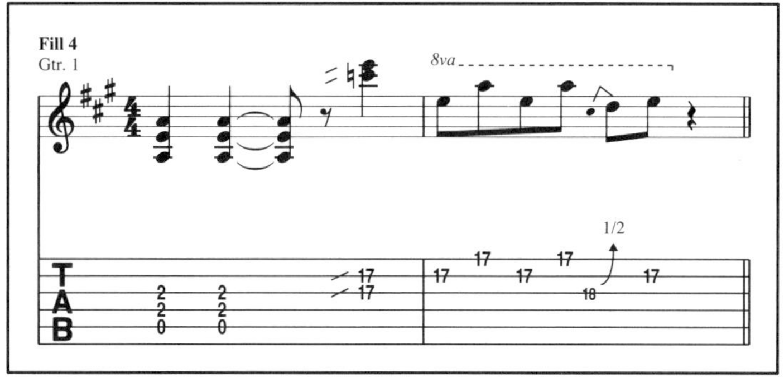
Fill 4
Gtr. 1
8va
1/2

from Aerosmith - *Permanent Vacation*

Rag Doll

Words and Music by Tyler/Perry/Knight/Vallance

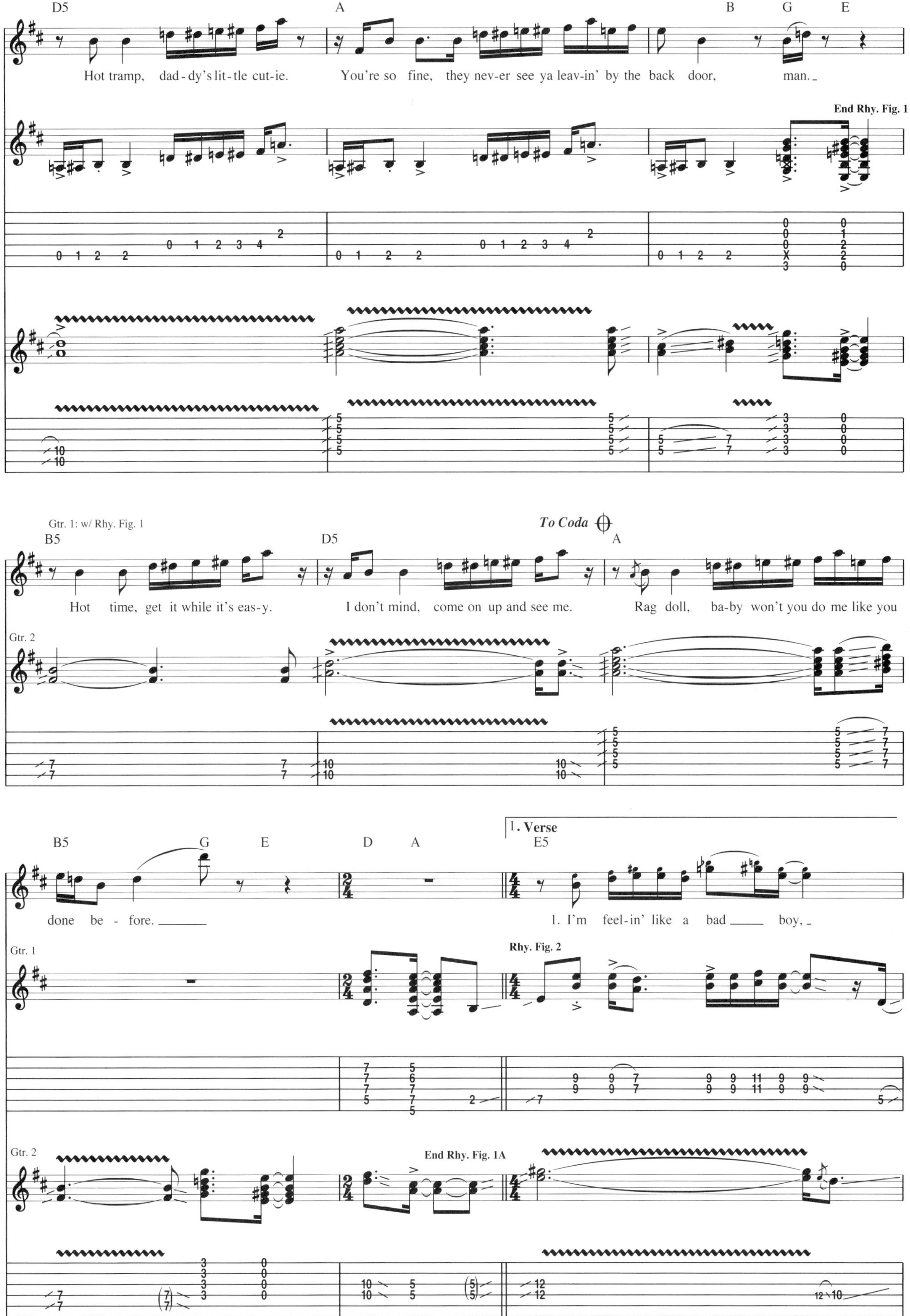
D5
A
B
G
E
Hot tramp, dad-dy's lit-tle cut-ie.
You're so fine, they nev-er see ya leav-in' by the back door,
man.
End Rhy. Fig. 1
Gtr. 1: w/ Rhy. Fig. 1
B5
D5
To Coda
A
Hot time, get it while it's eas-y.
I don't mind, come on up and see me.
Rag doll, ba-by won't you do me like you
Gtr. 2
B5
G
E
D
A
1. Verse
E5
done be - fore.
1. I'm feel-in' like a bad boy,
Gtr. 1
Rhy. Fig. 2
Gtr. 2
End Rhy. Fig. 1A

B5
3
mm, just a like a bad boy.
I'm rip-pin' up a rag doll,
like throw-in' a-way an old toy.

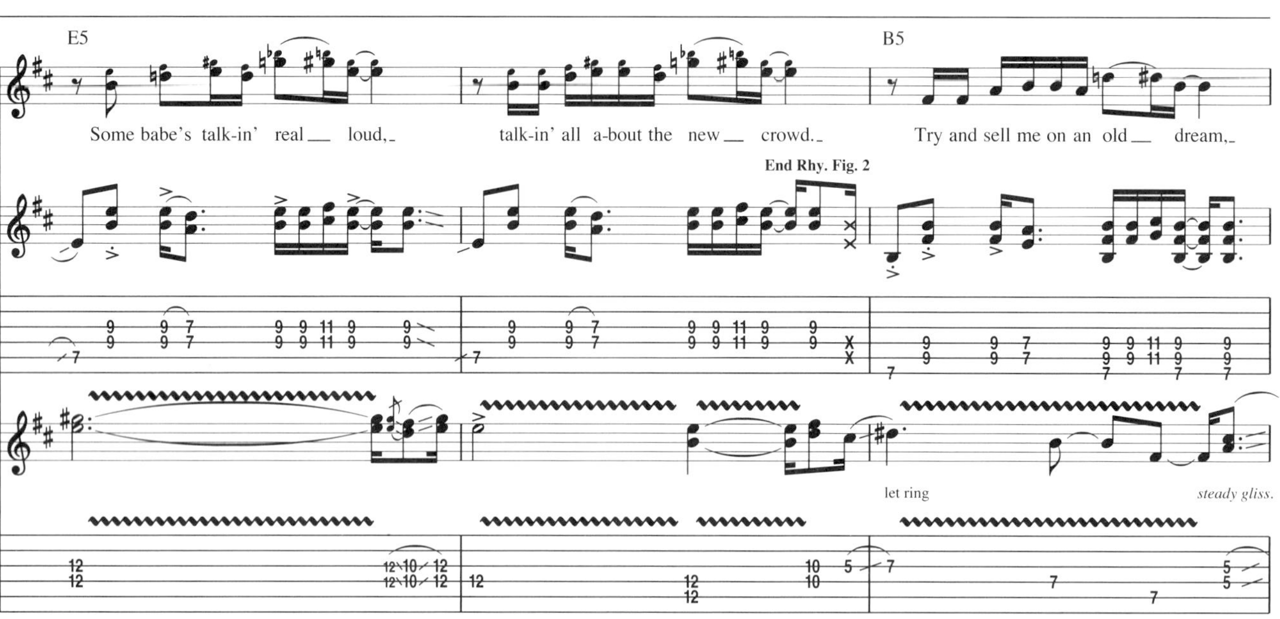
E5
B5
Some babe's talk-in' real loud,
talk-in' all a-bout the new crowd.
Try and sell me on an old dream,
End Rhy. Fig. 2
let ring
steady gliss.

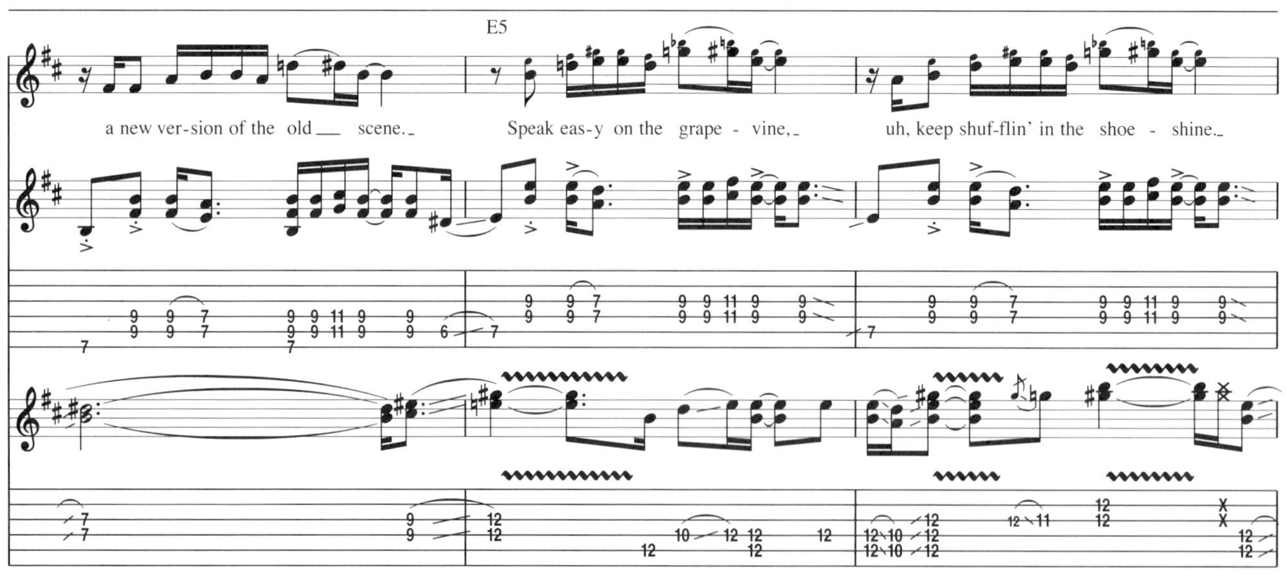
E5
a new ver-sion of the old scene.
Speak eas-y on the grape - vine,
uh, keep shuf-flin' in the shoe - shine.

F♯5
G E D5
Old tin liz - zy, do it till you're diz - zy, give it all ya got un - til you're put out of your mis - e - ry.
Rhy. Fig. 3
End Rhy. Fig. 3
2.
Verse
Gtr. 1: w/ Rhy. Fig. 2
E5
B5
2. Yes I'm mov - in', yes, I'm mov - in'. Get read - y for the big time.
Gtr. 2
E
Tap danc - ing on a land mine. Yes, I'm mov - in', yes, I'm mov - in'.
Gtr. 1: w/ Rhy. Fig. 3
F♯5
G E D
D.S. al Coda
Old tin liz - zy, do it till you're diz - zy, give it all ya got un - til you're put out of your mis - e - ry.

Coda
A
B5
G
E
D
A
Rag doll, ba - by won't you do me, ba-by, won't you do me, ba-by won't you do me like you done be - fore, hoo, hoo.
Gtr. 1
Gtr. 2
steady gliss.
Guitar Solo
F#5
F#6 F#5
F#6(no 3rd)
F#5
G#5
A5
A6(no 3rd)
A5
A6(no 3rd)
steady gliss.
A5
A6(no 3rd)
A5
G#5
F#5
F
F#6(no 3rd)
F#5
G#5

A5
A6 (no 3rd)
A5
A6 (no 3rd)
A5
G♯5
F♯5
F♯6(no 3rd)
F♯5
F♯6 (no 3rd)
let ring
F♯5
F♯6(no 3rd)
F♯5
D5
Verse
Gtr. 1: w/ Rhy. Fig. 2
E5
3. Yes, I'm mov - in', yes, I'm mov - in'.
steady gliss.
steady gliss.
B5
Get read-y for the big time.
Uh, get-tin' cra-zy on the moon shine.
E5
Yes, I'm mov - in',
Gtr. 2
Gtr. 1: w/ Rhy. Fig. 3
F♯5
I'm real - ly mov - in'.
Sloe gin fiz - zy, uh, do it till you're diz - zy, uh,

Chorus
Gtr. 2: w/ Rhy. Fig. 1A
G E D
N.C.(B5)
give it all you got un - til you're put out of your mis - e - ry.
Rag doll, liv - in' in a mov - ie.
Rhy. Fig. 4
Gtr. 1
D5
A
B G E
Hot tramp, dad - dy's lit - tle cut - ie. You're so fine, they'll nev - er see ya leav - in' by the back door, man.
End Rhy. Fig. 4
Gtr. 1: w/ Rhy. Fig. 4
B5
D5
Hot time, get it while it's eas - y. I don't mind, come on up and see me.
A
B5 G E
1. D A
Rag doll, ba - by won't you do me like you done be - fore!
2. D A
Outro
A
Doe dee dee ya bo doo dae, da dom dom. Da da ba. Da
Gtr. 1
Gtr. 2
steady gliss.

(w/ Clarinet and muted trumpet ad lib.)
de de da um do da do do da do do da do do da do do da do do da.
De - huh-ole bup uh de bup uh de bup-uh-de
dim.
N.C.
All gtrs. tacet
Begin Fade
baa! Ba, ba ba ba ba ba ba ba ba, ba ba. Ba - ba ba ba ba ba ba um ba, bo. Ba! Ba, ba.
dim.
Ba um ba uh um dap dap dap dap dap dap doe, wah bah. Wah dah. Wah dah. Wo dah dah dah um
Fade Out
dah dah. Doe dee deh dah dah dah dah dah dah dah. Dah de dah dah dah dah dah.

from Slayer - *Reign in Blood*

Raining Blood

Words and Music by Jeff Hanneman and Kerry King

1st Verse
Rhy. Fig. 1 (Both gtrs.)
E C5 E5 E♭5 B5 D5
(end Rhy. Fig. 1)
w/Rhy. Fig. 1 (7 times)
P.M.
Trapped in pur - ga - to - ry, a life - less ob - ject a - live.
A - wait - ing re - pris - al,
death will be their ac - quit - tance.
Sky is turn - ing red. Re-
turn to pow - er draws near.
Fall in - to me, the sky's
crim - son tears.
A - bol - ish the rules made of stone.
(end double time feel)
Slower ♩=188
N.C.
Rhy. Fig. 2 (Both gtrs.)
(end Rhy. Fig. 2)
H P P
Bridge
w/Rhy. Fig. 2 (2 times)
Pierced from be - low, souls of my treach - 'rous past.
Be - trayed by man - y now, or - na - ments drip - ping a - bove.
Slightly slower ♩ = 185
*w/Riff A (4 times)
*Gtr. II play two times only.

Half time feel
w/Riff A1 (2 times)
A - wait - ing the hour of re - pris - al, your time slips a -
Rhy. Fig. 3 (Both gtrs.) Slightly slower ♩ = 180
E5
way.
(end Rhy. Fig. 3)
*w/Rhy. Fig. 3 (4 times)
w/Riff B (6 times)
*Gtr. II play one time only.
Chorus
N.C. G5 B5 N.C. G5 B♭5 N.C. G5 A5 N.C. G5 F♯5
Rain - ing blood
Rhy. Fig. 4 (Both gtrs.)
P.M.
sl.
w/Rhy. Fig. 4 (3 times)
N.C. G5 B5 N.C. G5 B♭5 N.C. G5 A5 N.C. G5 F♯5 N.C. G5 B5 N.C. G5 B♭5
from a lac - er - at - ed sky. Bleed - ing its hor - ror.
(end half time feel)
N.C. G5 A5 N.C. G5 F♯5 N.C. G5 B5 N.C. G5 B♭5 N.C. G5 A5 N.C. G5 F♯5
Cre - at - ing my struc - ture, now I shall reign in
Riff A1
Gtr. II
P.M.
Riff B
Gtr. II
P.M.

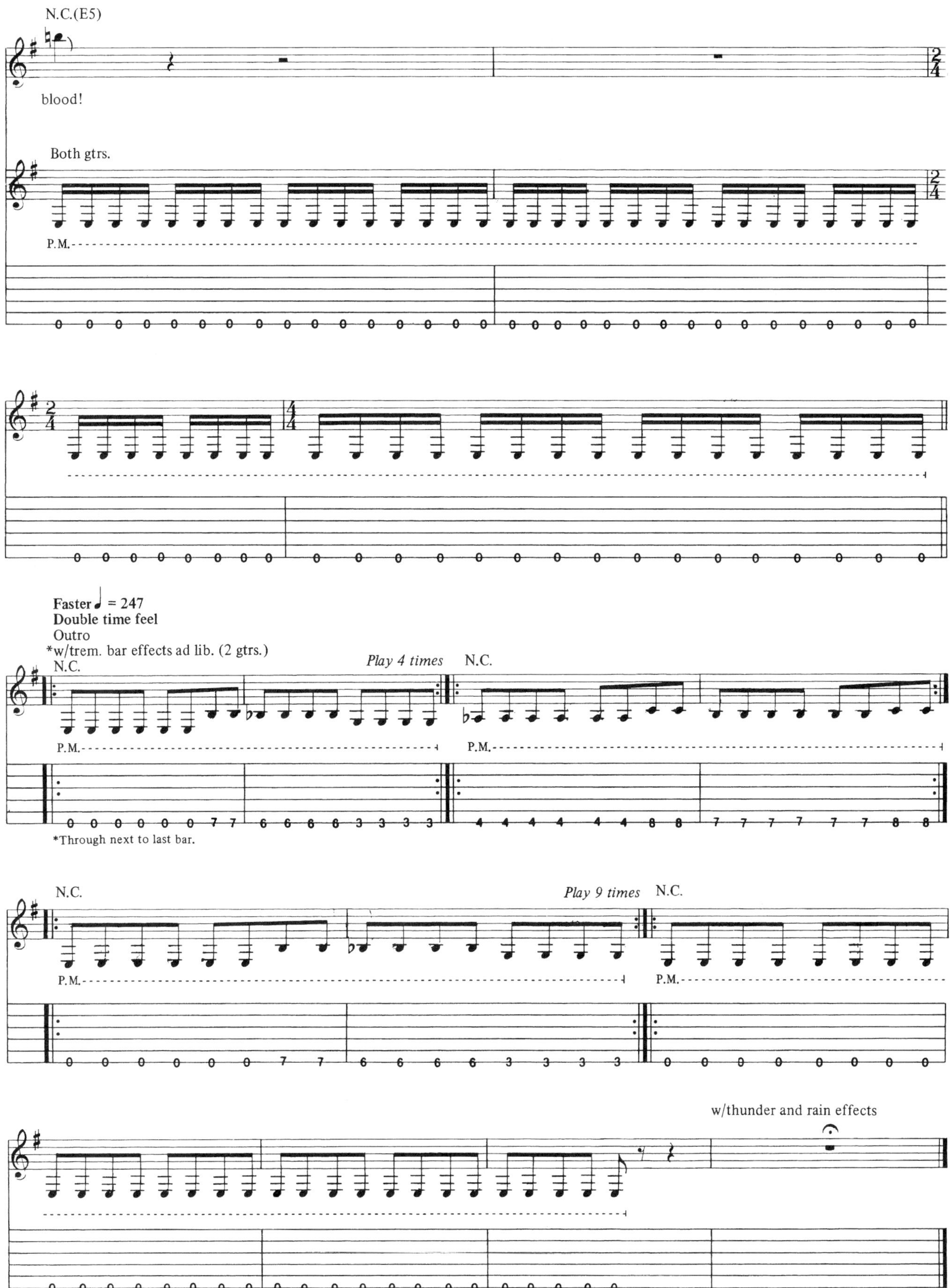
N.C.(E5)
blood!
Both gtrs.
P.M.
Faster ♩ = 247
Double time feel
Outro
*w/trem. bar effects ad lib. (2 gtrs.)
N.C.
Play 4 times
N.C.
P.M.
P.M.
*Through next to last bar.
N.C.
Play 9 times
N.C.
P.M.
P.M.
w/thunder and rain effects

from Billy Idol - *Rebel Yell*

Rebel Yell

Words and Music by Billy Idol and Steve Stevens

G5
F♯5
E5
D5 A5
Gtr. 2
End Riff A
P.M.
1/4
1
B5
fdbk.
w/ bar
P.S.
Pitch: A
Verse
2nd time, Gtr. 3 tacet
B5
1. Last night a lit - tle danc - er came danc - in' to my door.
2. She don't like slav - 'ry, she won't sit and beg.
Rhy. Fig. 1
End Rhy. Fig. 1
w/ slap echo
D5/A
Gmaj7(no3rd)
Last night a lit - tle an - gel came pump - in' on my floor.
But when I'm tired and lone - ly, she sees me to bed.
Gtr. 2: w/ Rhy. Fig. 1
B5
She said, "Uh, come, ba - by. You got a li - cense for love,
What set you free and brought you to me, babe?

D5/A
Gmaj7(no3rd)
and if it ex - pires pray help from a - bove."
What set you free? I need you here by me.
Be - cause
Gtr. 2
P.M.
Chorus
3rd time, Gtr. 4 tacet
B5
in the mid-night hour, she cried, "More, more, more."
Rhy. Fig. 2
D5/A
Gmaj7(no3rd)
D5 A5
With a reb - el yell, she cried, "More, more, more." Ow!
End Rhy. Fig. 2
Gtr. 2: w/ Rhy. Fig. 2
2nd time, Gtr. 2: w/ Rhy. Fig. 2 (1st 6 meas.)
B5
In the mid - night hour, babe. More, more, more.
1.
To Coda
D5/A
Gmaj7(no3rd)
D5 A5
With a reb - el yell, 1., 2. 3. she cried, more, more, more, more, more,

Interlude
B5
more.
8va
Gtr. 3 (dist.)
Harm.
w/ bar
loco
P.S.
-8 1/2
Gtr. 2
fdbk.
P.S.
Pitch: F♯
2.
Bridge
Gtr. 2: w/ Riff A (1st 4 meas., 2 times)
Gmaj7(no3rd)
G5
F♯5
E5
more, more, more.
Uh, he lives in, uh,
Gtr. 2
his own heav - en.
Col - lects it to go from the Sev - en E - lev - en.
Gtr. 2: w/ Riff A
Well, he's out all night to col - lect a fare.

G5
F♯5
E5
Just so long, just so long it don't mess up his hair.
Interlude
B5
Wow! Ow!
Gtr. 1
Gtr. 3
w/ bar
Gtr. 2
Guitar Solo
Gtr. 1 tacet
Gtr. 2: w/ Rhy. Fig. 2 (2 times)
B5
Gtr. 3
D5/A
Gmaj7(no3rd)
slight P.H.
*w/ "ray gun" sound effect
*Lexicon PCM 41 digital delay

D5 A5 B5
w/ "ray gun" sound effect
D5/A
let ring
*T = Pick-hand tapped slide
G5 Gmaj7
w/bar
w/ "ray gun" sound effect
Interlude
Gtr. 3 tacet
N.C.
(Drums)
Verse
***B5
3. I walk the ward for you, babe.
Gtr. 4 (dist.)
*p < mp
**w/ analog synth effect
*Vol. swell
**Publison harmonizer
***Chord symbols reflect implied harmony.
*w/ echo set for half-note regeneration w/ multiple decaying repeats.
A5 G5 E5 D5 A5
A thou - sand miles for you.

B5
I dried your tears of pain, babe,
w/ bar
-1/2
*As before
A5
G5
E5
D5
A5
a million times for you.
w/ bar
B5
I'd sell my soul for you, babe,
Riff B
End Riff B
Gtr. 4: w/ Riff B (2 times)
A5
G5
E5
D5
A5
for money to burn for you.
B5
I'd give you all and have none, babe,
just, uh,

D.S. al Coda
(take 1st ending)
A5
G5
E5
D5
A5
just, uh, just, uh, uh, just, uh, uh, have you here by me. Be - cause
8va
Gtr. 4
w/ bar
slack
Gtr. 2
P.S.
*w/ echo set for whole-note regeneration w/ 1 repeat.
Coda
Outro-Chorus
Gtr. 2: w/ Rhy. Fig. 2 (2 times)
B5
more. Oo yeah, lit - tle
Rhy. Fig. 3
End Rhy. Fig. 3
Gtr. 5 (dist.)
mf
D5
Gmaj7(no3rd)
D5
A5
ba - by. She want more, more, more, more, more,

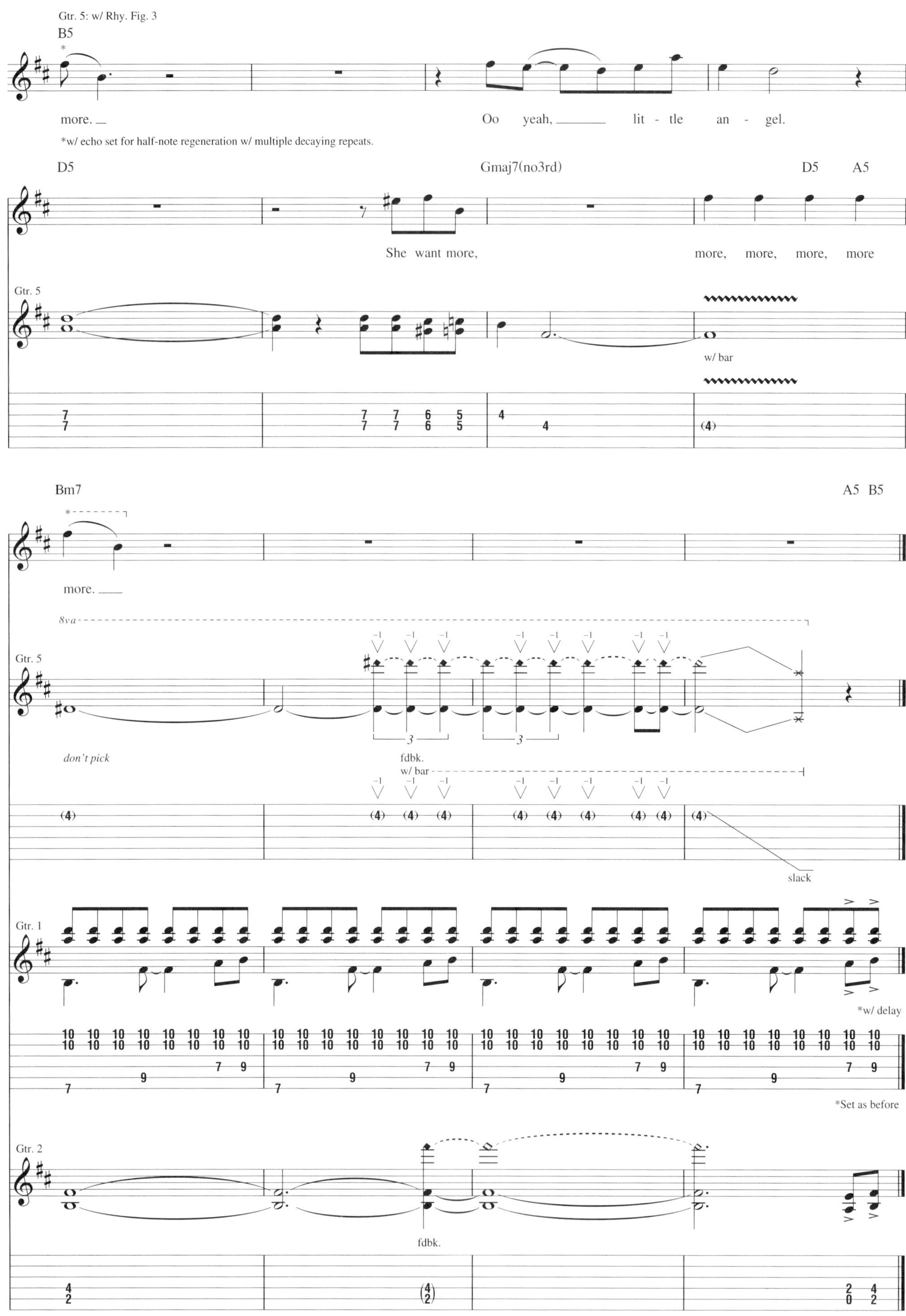

Gtr. 5: w/ Rhy. Fig. 3
B5
more.
Oo yeah, lit - tle an - gel.
*w/ echo set for half-note regeneration w/ multiple decaying repeats.
D5
Gmaj7(no3rd)
D5 A5
She want more,
more, more, more, more
Gtr. 5
w/ bar
Bm7
A5 B5
more.
8va
Gtr. 5
don't pick
fdbk.
w/ bar
slack
Gtr. 1
*w/ delay
*Set as before
Gtr. 2
fdbk.
Pitch: F♯

from Bob Marley & The Wailers - *Uprising*

Redemption Song

Words and Music by Bob Marley

G
Em
C
Bm
D
min - utes af - ter they took I from the bot - tom - less pit. But my
for a - tom - ic en - er - gy 'cause none of them can stop the time. How long
End Rhy. Fig. 2
End Riff B
Gtrs. 1 & 2: w/ Riff B & Rhy. Fig. 2
Am
hand was made strong by the hand of the al - might - y. For -
shall they kill our proph - ets while we stand a - side and look? Oo.
- ward in this gen - er - a - tion, tri - um - phant - ly.
Some say it's just a part of it, we've got to full - fill the book.
Chorus
To Coda
Rhy. Fig. 3
D7
End Rhy. Fig. 3
Gtr. 2
All I ev - er have is songs of
Won't you help to sing these
Gtr. 1
Riff C
End Riff C

1st time, Gtrs. 1 & 2: w/ Riff C & Rhy. Fig. 3 (4 times)
2nd time, Gtrs. 1 & 2: w/ Riff C & Rhy. Fig. 3 (3 1/2 times)
G C D7 G C D7
free - dom. Won't you help to sing
sweet songs of
re - demp - tion
G C D7 G
free - dom?
songs?
Re - demp - tion songs.
1.
C D7
2. E - man -
2.
Interlude
Gtrs. 1 & 2: w/ Riff A & Rhy. Fig. 1 (2 times)
C C type2 Em Am7 Bm7 Am7 Em Am7 Bm7 Am7
Gtr. 2
Gtr. 1
(3) 3 2 5 5
D.S. al Coda
(take 2nd lyrics)
Em Am7 Bm7 Am7 Em Am7 Bm7 Am7
3. E - man -
Coda
Chorus
Gtrs. 1 & 2: w/ Riff C & Rhy. Fig. 3 (till fade)
G C D7 G C D7
these songs of free - dom. All I ev - er have,
G C D7 G C D7
re - demp - tion songs. All I ev - er have,
Play 4 times and fade
G C D7 G C D7 G C D7
re - demp - tion songs.

from Five Finger Death Punch - *American Capitalist*

Remember Everything

Words and Music by Ivan Moody, Jeremy Spencer, Thomas Jason Grinstead, Zoltan Bathory, Kevin Churko and Kane Churko

Gtrs. 1-4: Drop D tuning, down 2 1/2 steps:
(low to high) A-E-A-D-F♯-B

Intro

Moderately slow ♩ = 81

*Chord symbols reflect implied harmony.

**Vol. swell

Verse

Bm
F♯m
Dmaj7
C♯m
E
heart I know I failed you, but you left me here a - lone.
Riff C1
Gtr. 2 (clean)
End Riff C1
mp
let ring throughout
Gtr. 1
Riff C
End Riff C
Chorus
Gtrs. 1 & 2 tacet
A5
E/G♯
E5
B5
E/G♯ A5
If I could hold back the rain, would you numb the pain? 'Cause I re - mem - ber
Rhy. Fig. 1
*Gtr. 3 (dist.)
f
P.M.
P.M.
*Doubled throughout
D5
E5
F♯5
A5 E/G♯
C♯5
ev - 'ry - thing. If I could help you for - get, would you take my re - grets?
P.M.

Interlude
Bm
D5
E5
F♯5
'Cause I re-mem-ber ev - 'ry - thing.
End Rhy. Fig. 1
P.M.
Verse
Gtr. 1: w/ Riff A (1 1/2 times)
Dmaj7
F♯m
2. Oh, dear broth - er, just don't hate me for nev-er stand - ing by you or
Riff D
P.M.
be-ing by your side.
Dmaj7
Dear sis - ter, please don't blame me.
P.M.
Gtr. 1: w/ Riff B
F♯m
A
Gtrs. 1 & 2: w/ Riffs C & C1
Bm
I on-ly did what I thought was tru - ly right. It's a long and lone - ly road
End Riff D
Rhy. Fig. 2
P.M.

F♯m
Dmaj7
C♯m
E
when you know you walk a - lone.
End Rhy. Fig. 2
P.M.
Chorus
Gtr. 3: w/ Rhy. Fig. 1
A5
E/G♯
E5
B5
E/G♯ A5
D5
E5
If I could hold back the rain, would you numb the pain? 'Cause I re-mem-ber ev - 'ry - thing.
F♯5
A5 E/G♯
C♯5
Bm
D5
E5
If I could help you for - get, would you take my re - grets? 'Cause I re-mem-ber ev - 'ry - thing.
Bridge
Dsus2
D5
F♯5
D5
A5
A/B
A/C♯
I feel like run nin' a - way, I'm still so far from home. You say that I'll nev-er change, but what the fuck do you know?
Gtr. 4 (dist.)
mf
let ring throughout
Gtr. 3
P.M.

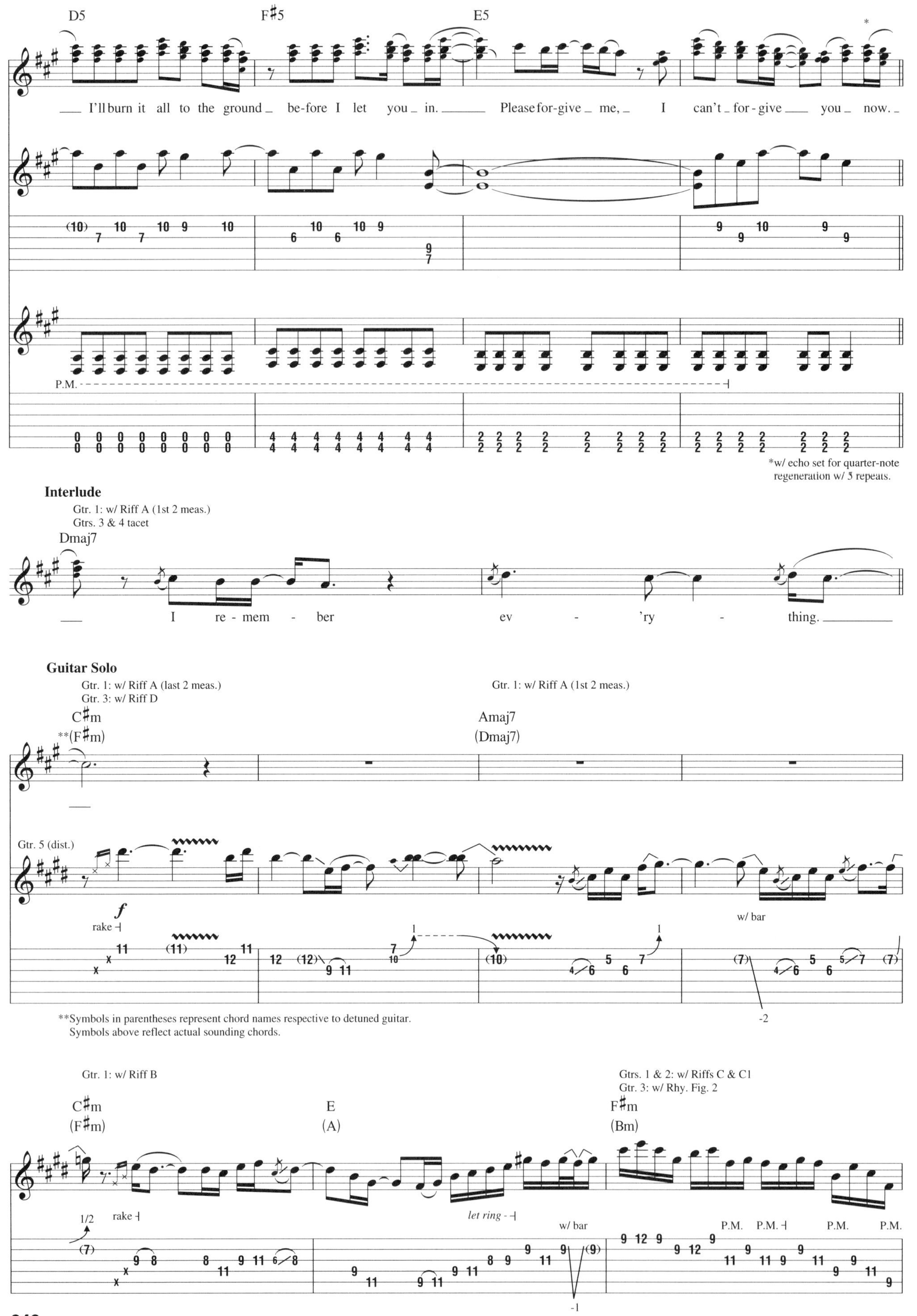

D5
F♯5
E5
I'll burn it all to the ground before I let you in. Please for-give me, I can't for-give you now.
P.M.
*w/ echo set for quarter-note regeneration w/ 5 repeats.
Interlude
Gtr. 1: w/ Riff A (1st 2 meas.)
Gtrs. 3 & 4 tacet
Dmaj7
I re-mem-ber ev-'ry-thing.
Guitar Solo
Gtr. 1: w/ Riff A (last 2 meas.)
Gtr. 3: w/ Riff D
Gtr. 1: w/ Riff A (1st 2 meas.)
C♯m
**(F♯m)
Amaj7
(Dmaj7)
Gtr. 5 (dist.)
rake
w/ bar
**Symbols in parentheses represent chord names respective to detuned guitar. Symbols above reflect actual sounding chords.
Gtr. 1: w/ Riff B
Gtrs. 1 & 2: w/ Riffs C & C1
Gtr. 3: w/ Rhy. Fig. 2
C♯m
(F♯m)
E
(A)
F♯m
(Bm)
rake
let ring
w/ bar
P.M.

C♯m (F♯m)
Amaj7 (Dmaj7)
G♯m (C♯m)
B (E)
8va
Chorus
Gtr. 3: w/ Rhy. Fig. 1 (2 times)
E5 (A5)
B/D♯ (E/G♯)
B5 (E5)
Gtr. 5 tacet
B5
E/G♯ A5
D5
E5
If I could hold back the rain, would you numb the pain? 'Cause I re-mem-ber ev - 'ry - thing.
F♯5
A5 E/G♯
C♯5
Bm
If I could help you for-get, would you take my re-grets? 'Cause I re-mem-ber ev - 'ry - thing.
It
all went by so fast, I still can't change the past. I al - ways will re-mem-ber...
ev - 'ry - thing.
If we could start a - gain, would that have changed the end? We re-mem - ber ev - 'ry - thing.
Outro
Dsus2
F♯5
rit.
Ev - 'ry - thing.
Gtr. 3

from Dick Dale - *King of the Surf Guitar*

(Ghost) Riders in the Sky
(A Cowboy Legend)

By Stan Jones

F
Am
C
Am
C
Am
F
Am
D
A
G
A
G
A

D
C
D
A
G
A
E
A
D
A
1/2
D
A
1/2
F
A
G
A
1/2
G
A

D
C
D
A
G
A
G
Am
G
Am
F
Am
H
Am
Begin fade
Fade out

from *The B-52's*

Rock Lobster

Words and Music by Kate Pierson, Fred Schneider, Keith Strickland, Cindy Wilson and Ricky Wilson

*Gtrs. 1 & 3: E5 tuning, down 1 1/2 steps:
(low to high) C♯-F♯-N/A-N/A-F♯-C♯

*Gtr. 2: Tune down 1 1/2 steps:
(low to high) C♯-F♯-B-E-G♯-C♯

Intro

Fast ♩ = 178

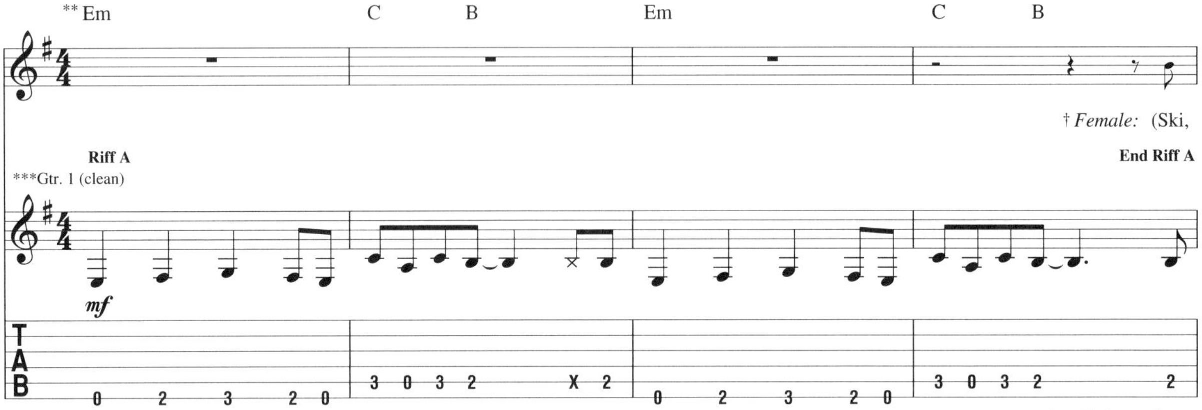

**Em C B Em C B

† *Female:* (Ski,

Riff A

***Gtr. 1 (clean)

End Riff A

mf

T A B

0 2 3 2 0 | 3 0 3 2 X 2 | 0 2 3 2 0 | 3 0 3 2 2

*Recording sounds approximately 1/4 step flat.

**Chord symbols reflect implied harmony.

***Mosrite gtr. w/ 3rd & 4th strings removed.

†Doubled, next 5 meas.

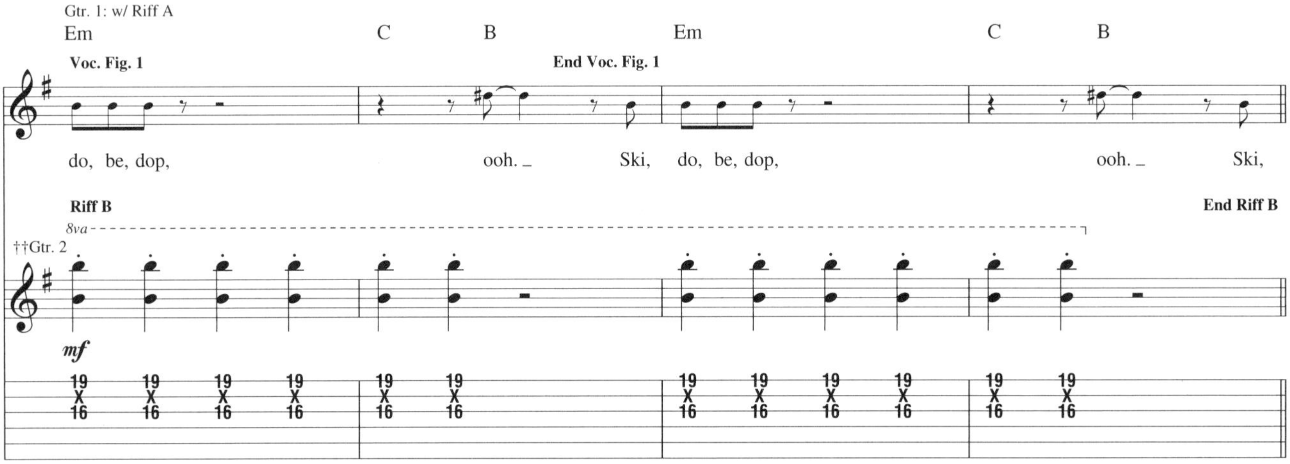

Gtr. 1: w/ Riff A

Em C B Em C B

Voc. Fig. 1 — End Voc. Fig. 1

do, be, dop, ooh. Ski, do, be, dop, ooh. Ski,

Riff B — End Riff B

8va

††Gtr. 2

mf

19 X 16 (×10)

††Synth. arr. for gtr.

Verse

Bkgd. Voc.: w/ Voc. Fig. 1 (3 times)
Gtr. 1: w/ Riff A (2 times)
Gtr. 2: w/ Riff B (2 times)

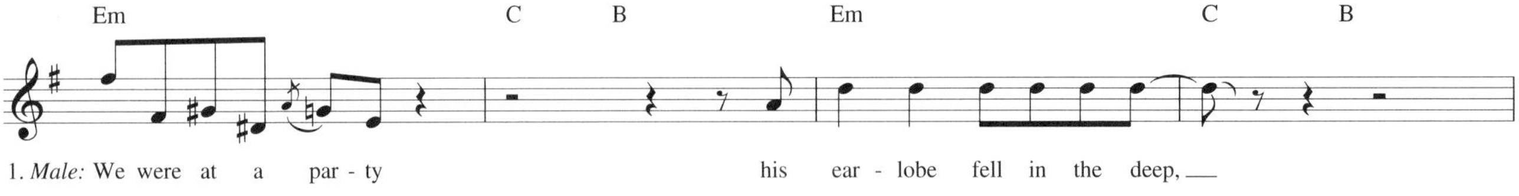

Em C B Em C B

1. *Male:* We were at a par - ty his ear - lobe fell in the deep,

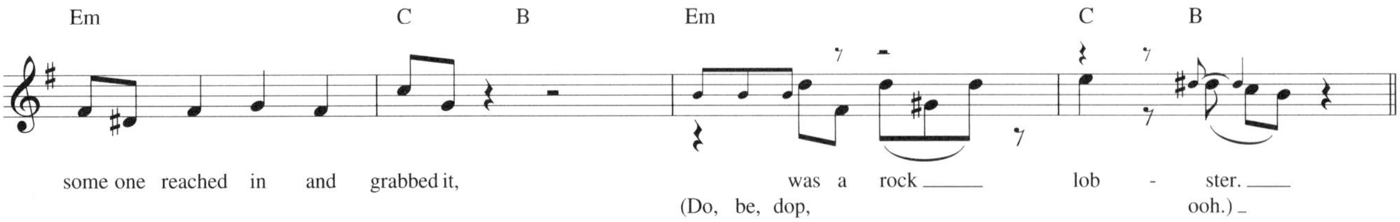

Em C B Em C B

some one reached in and grabbed it, was a rock lob - ster.
(Do, be, dop, ooh.)

Chorus
Em
G
C
B
(Ah.
Rock
Gtr. 2
Gtr. 1
Riff C
End Riff C
Gtr. 1: w/ Riff C
Em7
lob - ster.
Ah.)
Interlude
8va
Gtr. 3 (clean)
mf

Gtr. 3 tacet
Em
G
C
B
Gtr. 2
loco
Gtr. 3
Gtr. 1

To Coda
Gtr. 1: w/ Riff A (2 times)
Gtr. 2 tacet
Gtr. 2: w/ Riff B
Em C B Em C B Em C B
Voc. Fig. 2
(Ooh,
Verse
Bkgd. Voc.: w/ Voc. Fig. 2 (3 times)
Gtr. 1: w/ Riff A (3 times)
Gtr. 2: w/ Riff B (3 times)
Em C B Em C B Em
End Voc. Fig. 2
2. We were at the beach, ev - 'ry - bod - y had
ooh.)
C B Em C B Em C B
match-ing towels. Some - bod - y went un - der a dock and there they saw a rock.
D.S. al Coda
Em C B Em C B
It was - n't a rock, was a rock lob - ster.
Coda
Gtr. 2: w/ Riff B
C B Em C B Em C B
(Rock lob - ster. Rock lob - ster.)
Verse
Gtr. 1: w/ Riff A (3 times)
Gtr. 2: w/ Riff B (3 times)
Em C B Em C B
3. Mo - tion in the o - cean, his air hose broke,
(Ooh, ah. Ooh, ah.
Em C B Em C B
lots of trou - ble, lots of bub - bles.
Ooh, ah. Ooh, ah.
Em C B Em C B
He was in a jam, s'in a gi - ant clam!
Ooh, ah. Ooh, ah.)

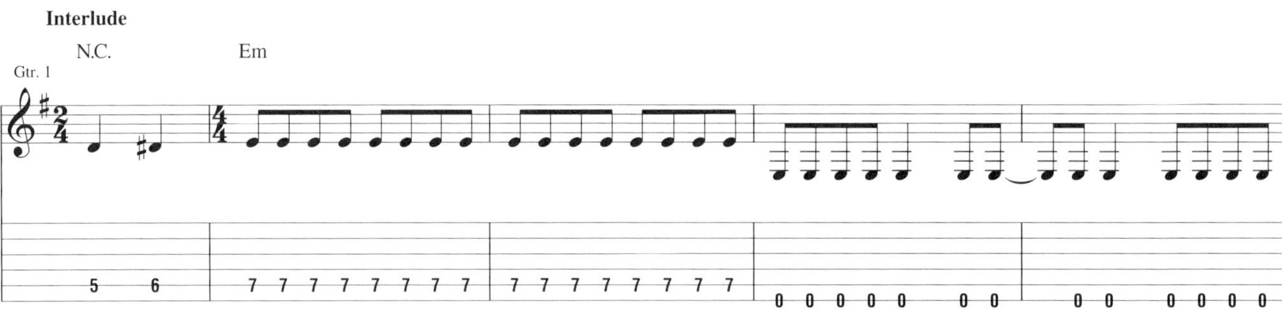
Interlude
N.C.
Em
Gtr. 1

Rock,
rock,
rock

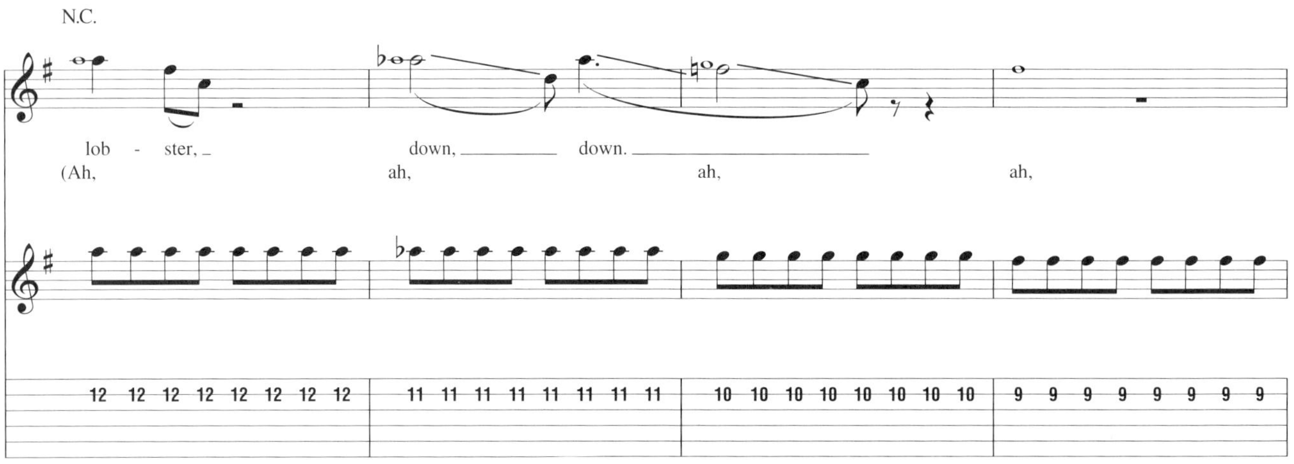
N.C.
lob - ster,
down,
down.
(Ah,
ah,
ah,
ah,

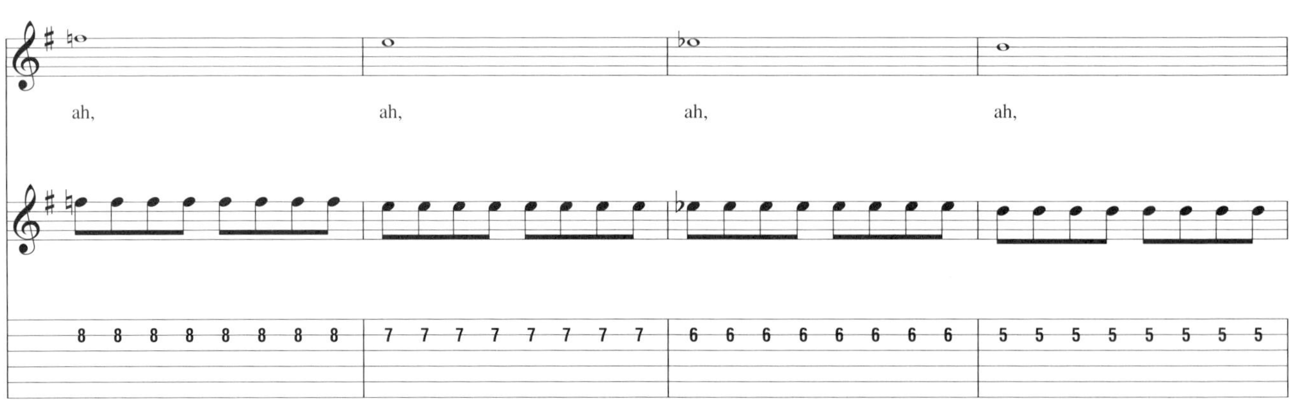
ah,
ah,
ah,
ah,

ah,
ah,
ah,
ah.)
Em
C
B
Em
C
B
Female voc.: w/ random screams (next 8 meas.)
A5
C5
D5
C5
N.C.
A5
C5
D5
C5
N.C.
Lob - ster.
Rock.
(Rock.)

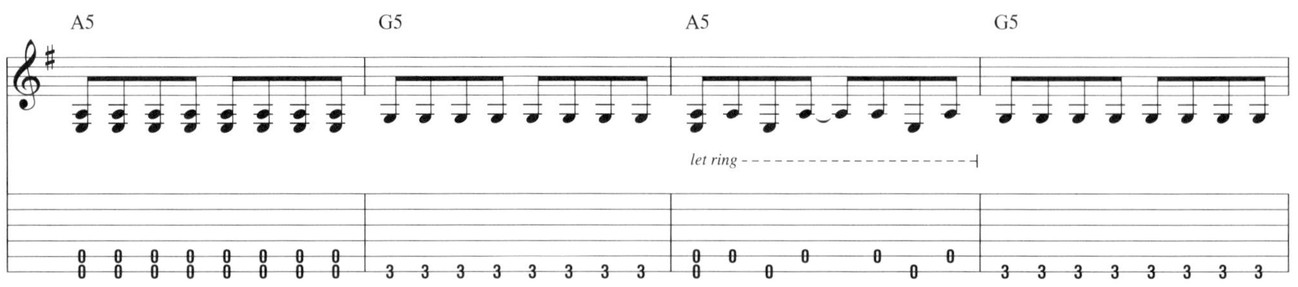
A5
G5
A5
G5
let ring

A5
G5
A5
G5
Let's
let ring

Am
C5
B5
Am
C5
B5 A5
rock!
let ring
let ring
let ring
let ring
let ring

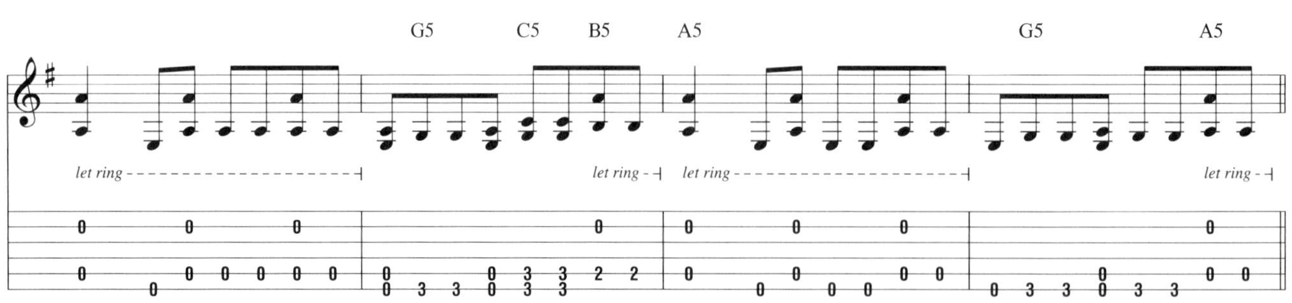
G5
C5
B5
A5
G5
A5
let ring
let ring
let ring
let ring

Bridge
A5
G5
A5
G5
Boys in bi - ki - nis,
girls in surf - boards, _
A5
G5
A5
G5
ev - 'ry - bod - y's rock - in',
ev - 'ry - bod - y's frug - gin'.
A5
G5
A5
G5
C5
Twist - in' 'round the fi - re,
hav - in' fun, _
let ring
A5
G5
A5
C5
B5
A5
bak - in' po - ta - toes,
bak - in' in the sun. _
let ring

C5
A5
C5
Put on your nose - guard,
put on the life - guard,
let ring
A5
G5
A5
C5
pass the tan-ning but - ter.
let ring
A5
G5
A5 G5
A5
G5
A5 G5
There comes a sting - ray.
There goes a man-ta ray.
(Do, wah. Do, wah.
Eeh, eeh, eeh.
A5
G5
A5
C5
B5 A5
In walked a jel - ly - fish.
There goes a dog - fish
Uh.
Row.

G5 C5 A5 G5 A5 G5
chased by a cat - fish. In flew a sea rob - in.
Ooh, oh, ooh. La, la, la, la, la, la, la.
A5 C5 A5 C5 A5 G5 A5
Watch out for that pir - ah - na. There goes a nar - whal.
Yeah, yeah, yeah, yeah, yeah, yeah, yeah, oh.
C5 B5 A5 G5 Am
Here comes a bi - ki - ni whale!
Mmm. Ah!)
G5 C5 Am G5 B5

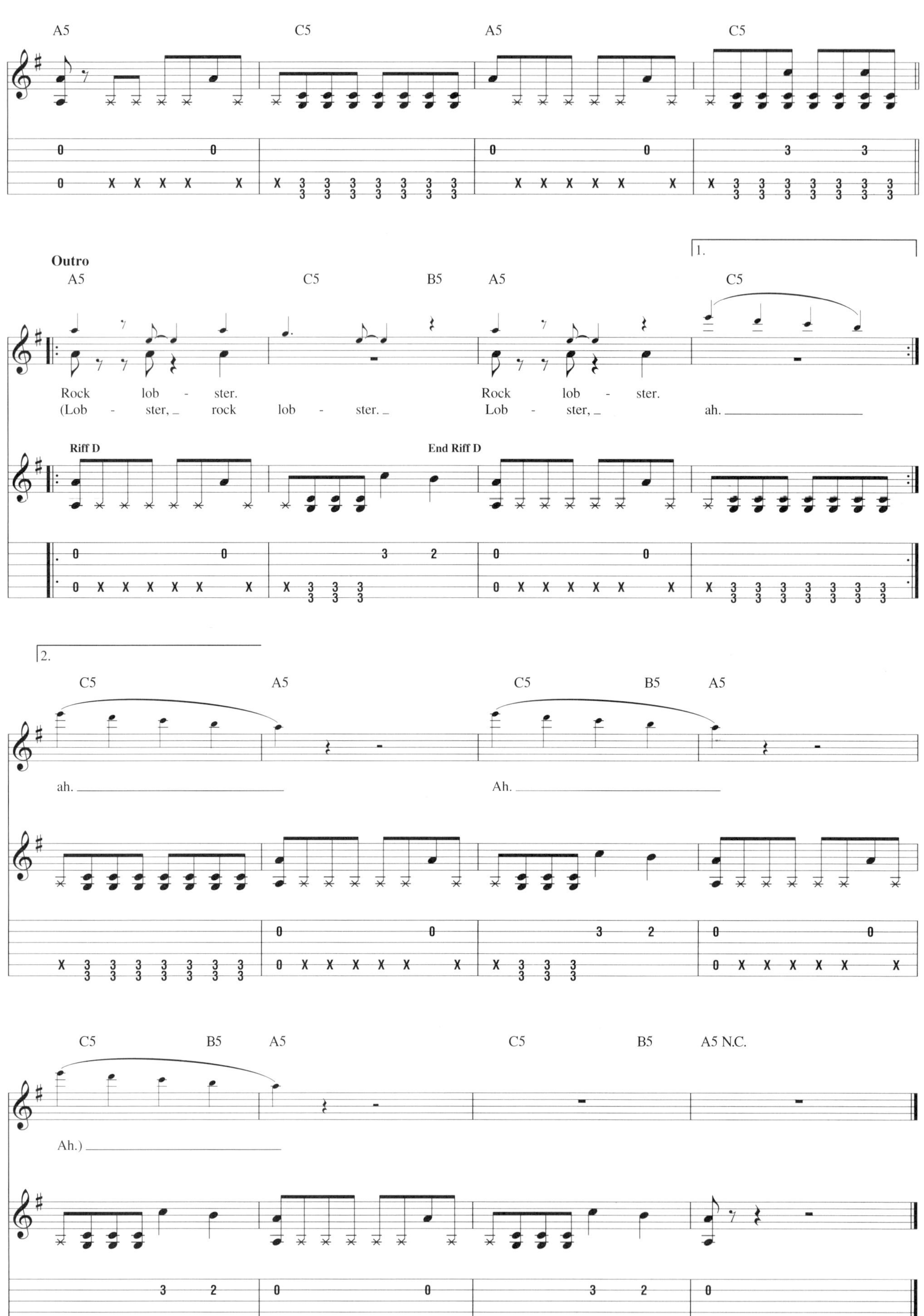
A5
C5
A5
C5
Outro
A5
C5
B5
A5
1.
C5
Rock lob - ster.
(Lob - ster, rock lob - ster.
Rock lob - ster.
Lob - ster, ah.
Riff D
End Riff D
2.
C5
A5
C5
B5
A5
ah.
Ah.
C5
B5
A5
C5
B5
A5 N.C.
Ah.)

from the Clash - *Combat Rock*

Rock the Casbah

Words and Music by Joe Strummer, Mick Jones and Topper Headon

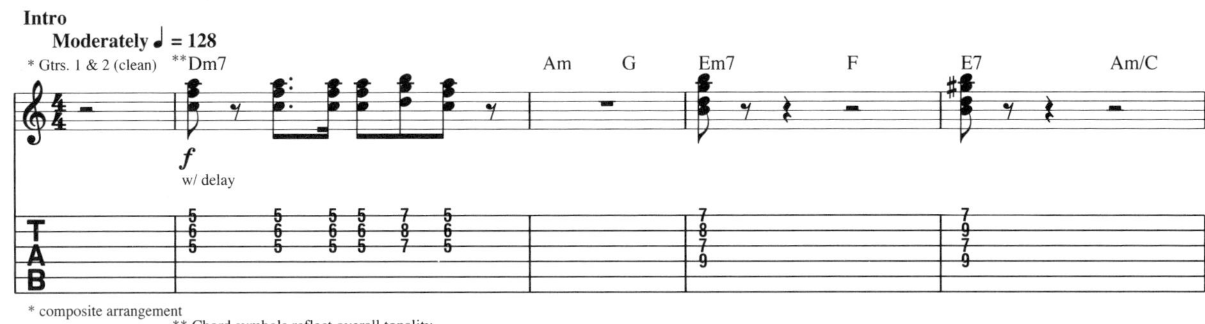

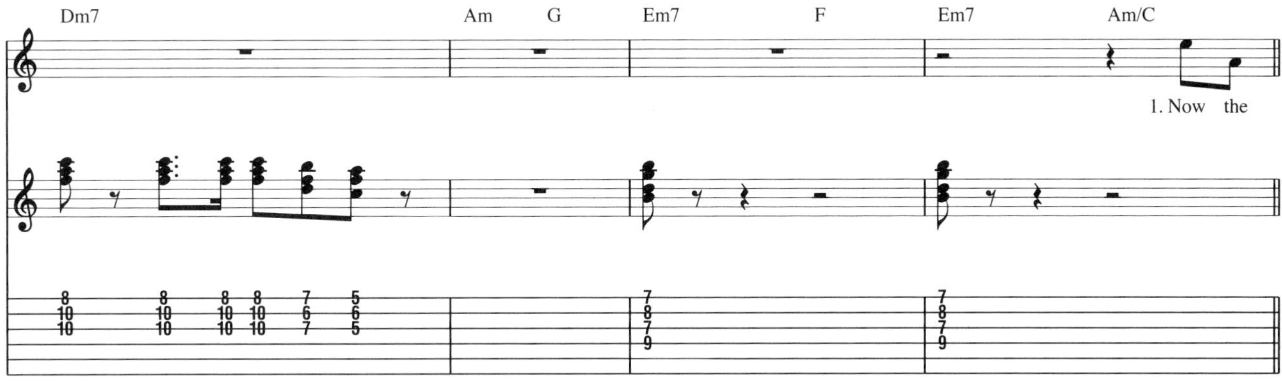

Gtrs. 1 & 2 tacet
Am
Em7
G
oil down the des - ert way
has been shak - en to the top.
gen - er - ate the faith - ful
with that cra - zy Cas - bah sound.
Dm
Am
Em7
The sheik he drove his Cad - il - lac.
He went a -
But the Bed - ou - in, they brought out the 'lec-tric cam-el drum, the
Gtrs. 1 & 2: w/ Fill 1, 2nd time
G
Dm
Am
cruis - in' down the ville.
The mu - ez - zin was a - stand - ing
lo - cal gui - tar pick - er got his gui - tar pick - ing thumb.
As soon as the sha - riff had
Gtrs. 1 & 2
loco
Em7
F
Em7
on the ra - di - a - tor grille.
Ow!
cleared the square
they be - gan to wail.
Shar -
* Vocals doubled next 8 meas.
Chorus
Dm7
Am
G
Em7
F
Em7
Am/C
riff don't like it.
Rock - in' the Cas - bah,
rock the Cas - bah.
Sha -
Gtrs. 1 & 2
Rhy. Fig. 1
Fill 1
Gtr. 1
Gtr. 2

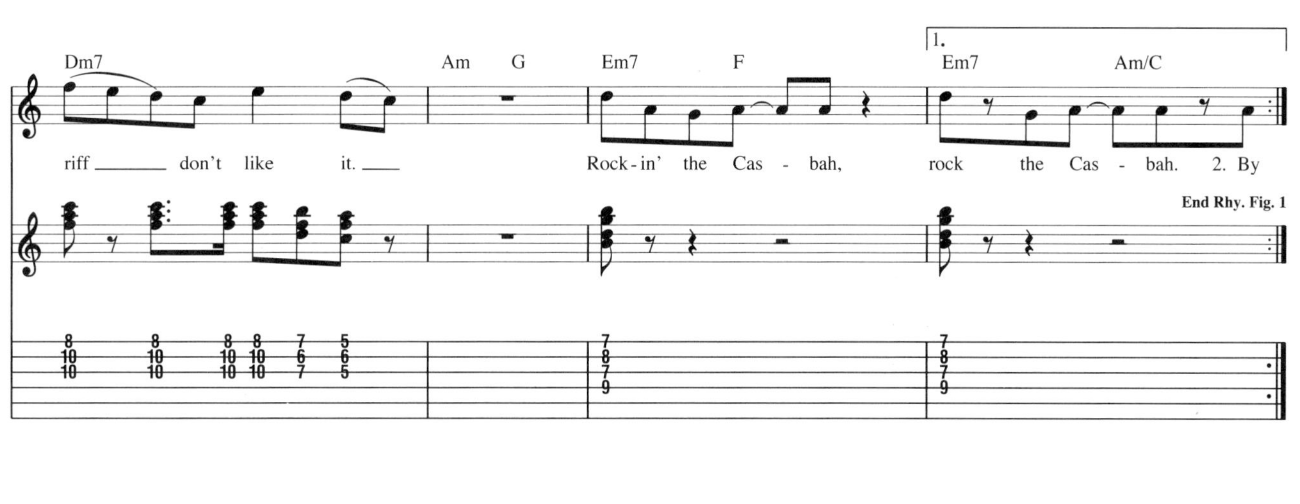
1.
Dm7
Am G
Em7
F
Em7
Am/C
riff ___ don't like it. ___
Rock-in' the Cas - bah,
rock the Cas - bah. 2. By
End Rhy. Fig. 1
8 10 10
8 10 10
8 10 10
8 10 10
7 6 7
5 6 5
7 8 7 9
7 8 7 9

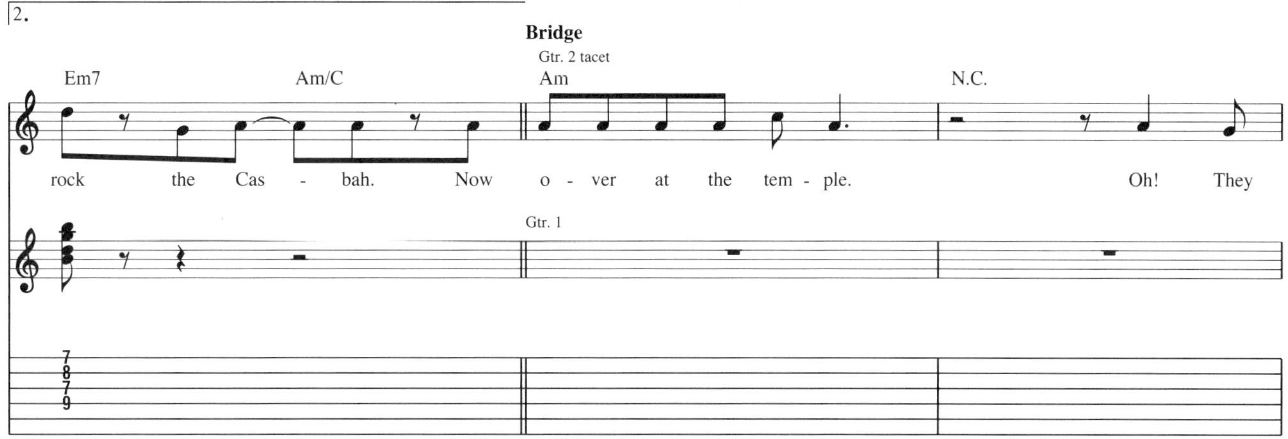
2.
Bridge
Gtr. 2 tacet
Em7
Am/C
Am
N.C.
rock the Cas - bah. Now
o - ver at the tem - ple.
Oh! They
Gtr. 1
7 8 7 9

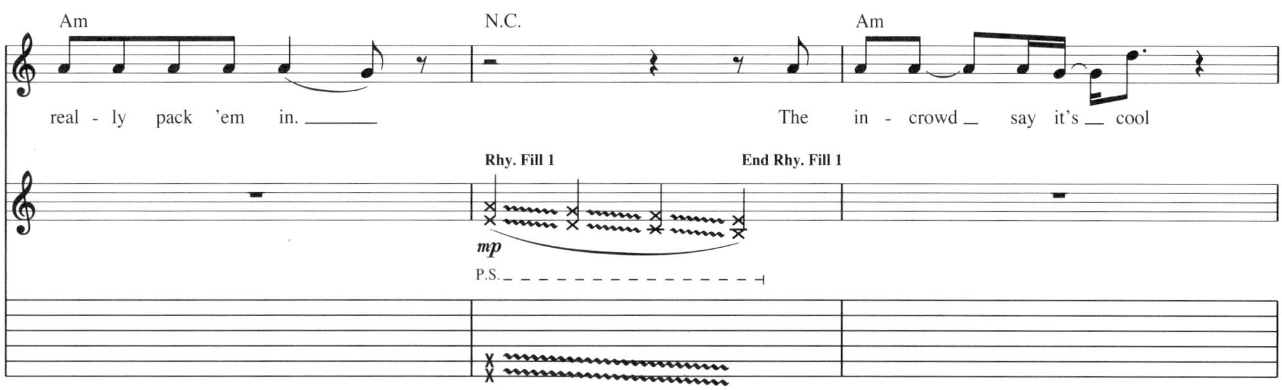
Am
N.C.
Am
real - ly pack 'em in. ___
The in - crowd ___ say it's ___ cool
Rhy. Fill 1
End Rhy. Fill 1
mp
P.S.

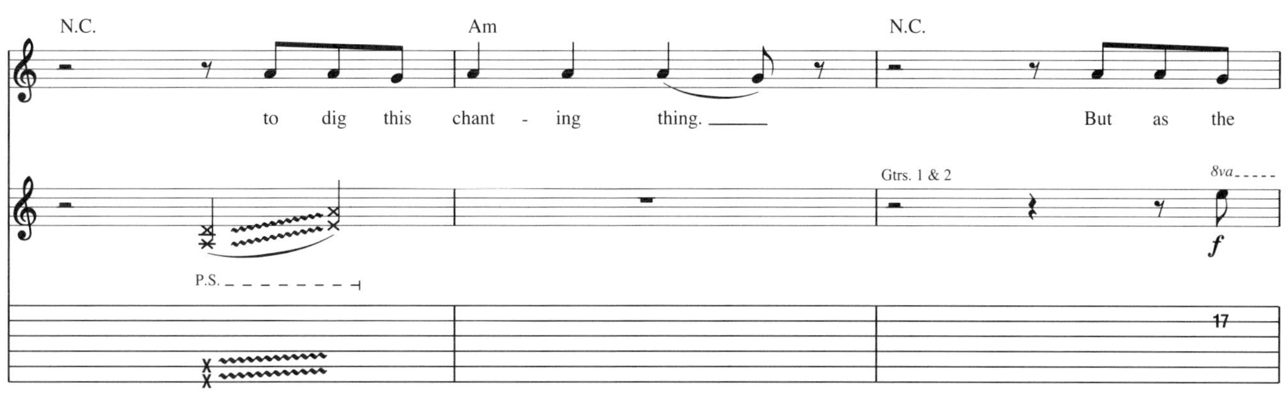
N.C.
Am
N.C.
to dig this chant - ing thing. ___
But as the
Gtrs. 1 & 2
8va
f
P.S.
17

Fmaj7
N.C.
Fmaj7
N.C.
G
wind changed di - rec - tion and the tem - ple band took five. The
8va
17
17
17
Gtrs. 1 & 2 tacet
Am
Gtr. 1: w/ Rhy. Fill 1
N.C.
Am
crowd caught a whiff of that cra - zy Cas - bah jive. Sha -
(Jive.
Chorus
Gtrs. 1 & 2: w/ Rhy. Fig. 1
Dm7
Am
G
Em7
F
Em7
Am/C
riff don't like it. Rock - in' the Cas - bah, rock the Cas - bah. Sha -
)
Dm7
Am
G
Em7
F
Em7
Am/C
riff don't like it. Rock - in' the Cas - bah, rock the Cas - bah. 3. The
Verse
Am
Em7
G
Dm
king called up his jet fight - ers. He said, "You bet - ter earn your pay. Drop your
Gtr. 2
mp
7
7
Am
Gtr. 2 tacet
Em7
G
Dm
bombs be - tween the min - a - rets down the Cas - bah way." As
Gtr. 1
7
0 1 0 1 0 0 1

Am Em7 G Dm
soon as the Sha - riff was chauf-feured out - ta there, the jet pi - lots tuned _ to the cock-pit ra-di-o blare. As
Am Em7 F
soon as the sha - riff was out - ta their hair, the jet pi - lots wailed. ___ Sha -
Gtr. 1
w/ bar
Gtr. 2
divisi
mp
* Gtr. 1 to right of slash in TAB.
Chorus
Gtrs. 1 & 2: w/ Rhy. Fig. 1, till fade
Dm7 Am G Em7 F Em7 Am/C
riff ___ don't like it. ___ Rock - in' the Cas - bah, rock the Cas - bah. Sha -
Dm7 Am G Em7 F Em7 Am/C
riff ___ don't like it. ___ Rock - in' the Cas - bah, rock the Cas - bah.
(Sha -
Dm7 Am G Em7 F
He thinks it's not ko - sher.
riff ___ don't ___ like it. ___ Rock - in' the Cas - bah,
Em7 Am/C Dm7 Am G
Fun - da - men - tal - ly can't take it.
rock the Cas - bah. Sha - riff ___ don't ___ like it. ___
Begin Fade
Em7 F Em7 Am/C Dm7 Am G
You know he real - ly hates it.
Rock-in' the Cas - bah, rock the Cas - bah. Sha - riff ___ don't _ like it. ___
Fade Out
Em7 F Em7 Am/C Dm7 Am G
Real - ly, real - ly hates it.
Rock-in' the Cas - bah, rock the Cas - bah. Sha - riff ___ don't _ like it. ___)

from REO Speedwagon - *You Can Tune a Piano, but You Can't Tuna Fish*

Roll with the Changes

Words and Music by Kevin Cronin

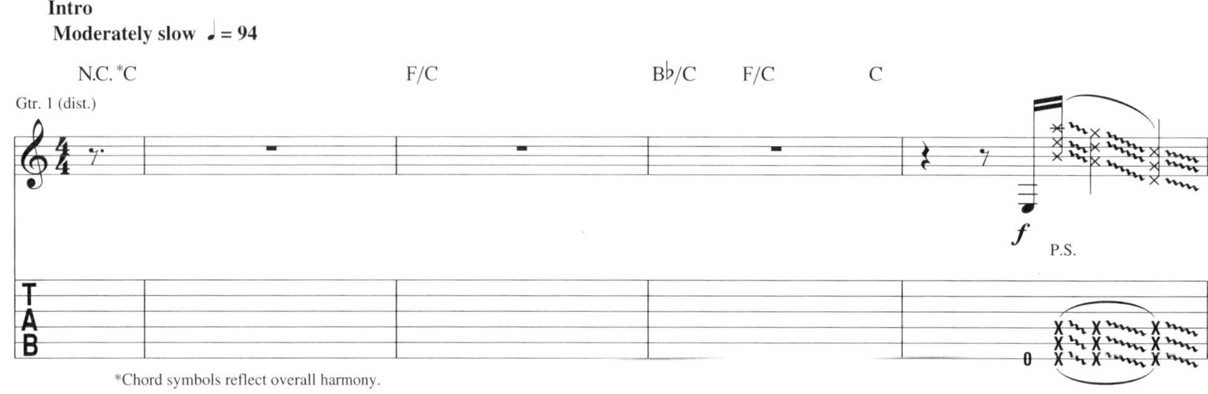

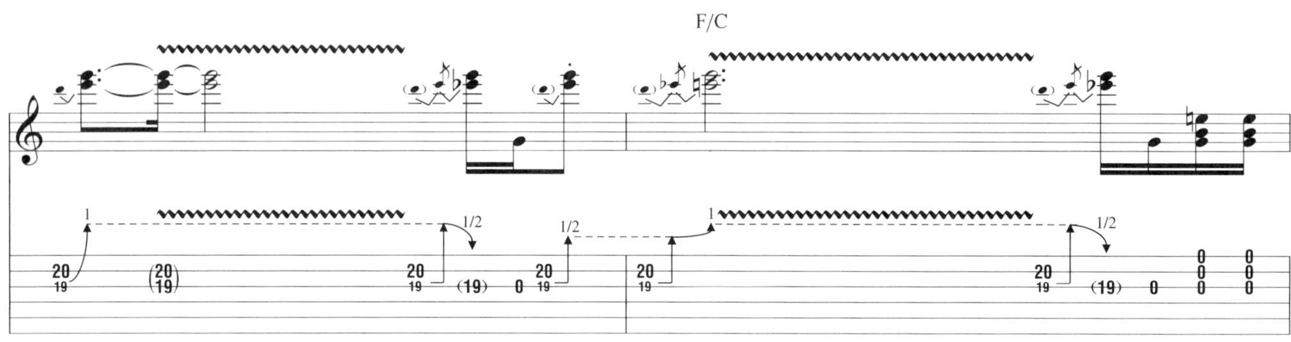

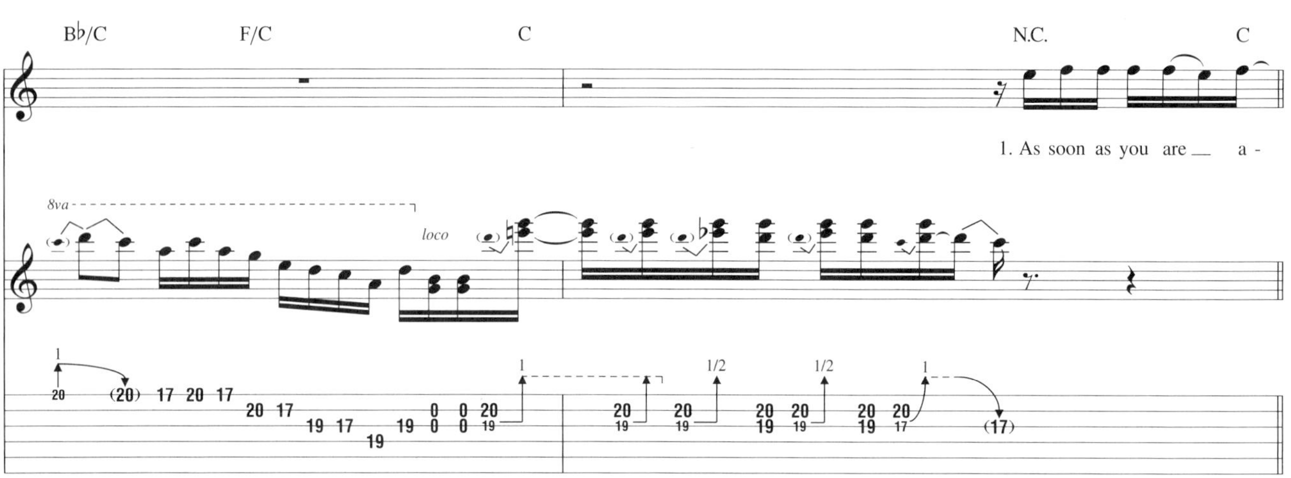

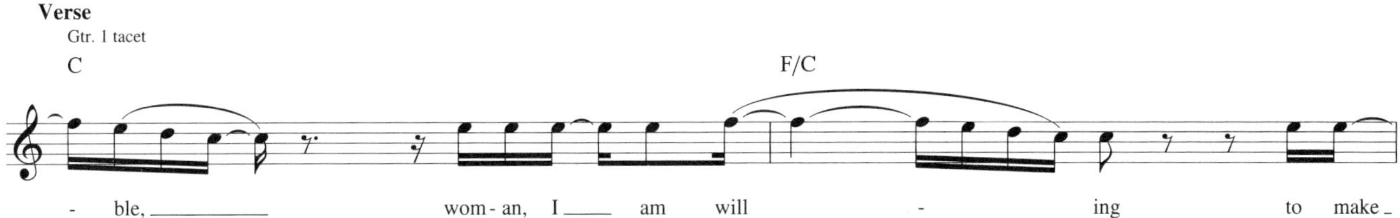
Verse
Gtr. 1 tacet
C
F/C
- ble, woman, I am will - ing to make

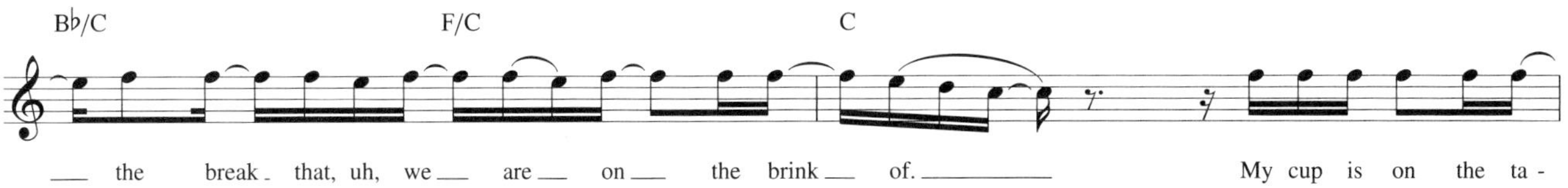
B♭/C
F/C
C
the break that, uh, we are on the brink of.
My cup is on the ta -

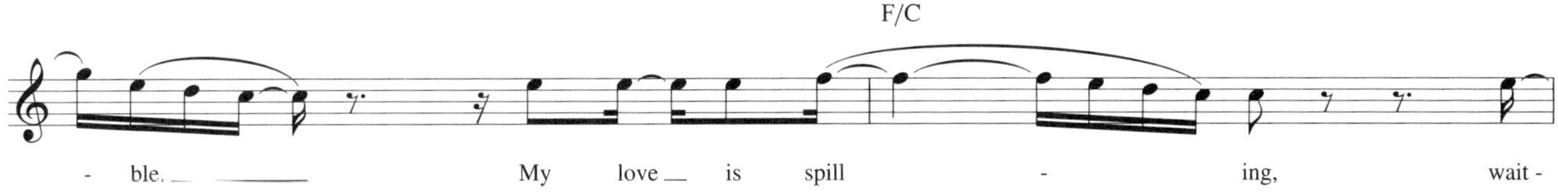
F/C
- ble. My love is spill - ing, wait -

B♭/C
F/C
C
- ing here for you to take and drink of.
Gtr. 1

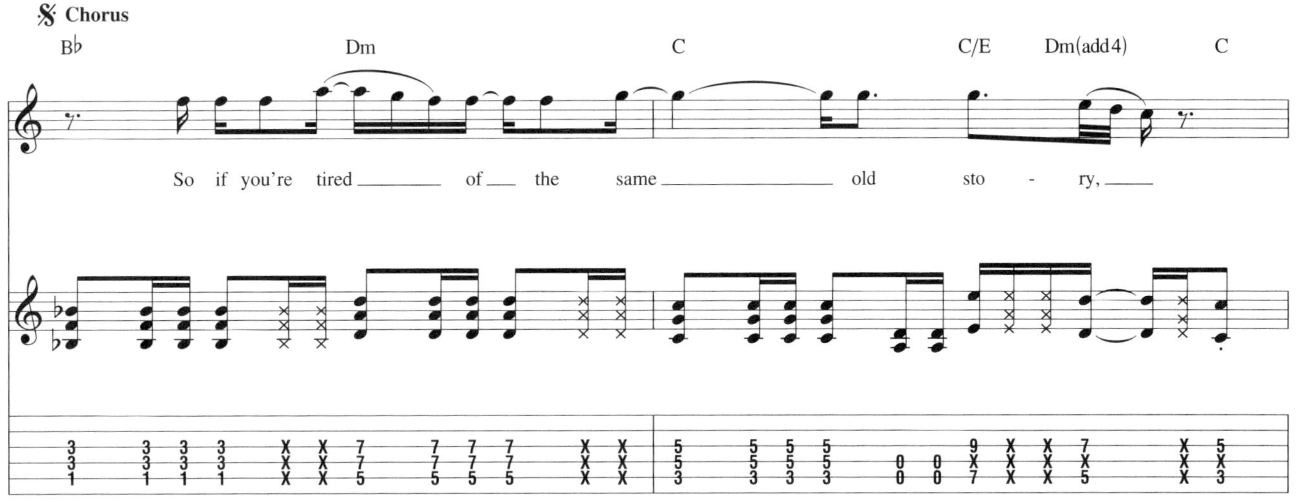
Chorus
B♭
Dm
C
C/E
Dm(add4)
C
So if you're tired of the same old sto - ry,

B♭
Dm
C
oh, turn some pag - es.
B♭
Dm
C
C/E
Dm(add4)
C
I'll be here when you are read - y to roll with the chang-
To Coda
G7
- es,
yeah, ee, yeah, oo.
oh,
semi-harm.
Guitar Solo
C
F/C

B♭/C
F/C
C
N.C.
C
2. I knew it had to hap -
Verse
Gtr. 1 tacet
C
F/C
B♭/C
F/C
- pen. Felt the ta - bles turn - ing. Got me through my dark - est hour.
C
I heard the thun - der clap - ping. Felt the des - ert burn -
Gtr. 1
F/C
B♭/C
F/C
C
D.S. al Coda
- ing until you poured on me like a sweet sun show - er.
grad. bend
fdbk.
grad. release

Coda

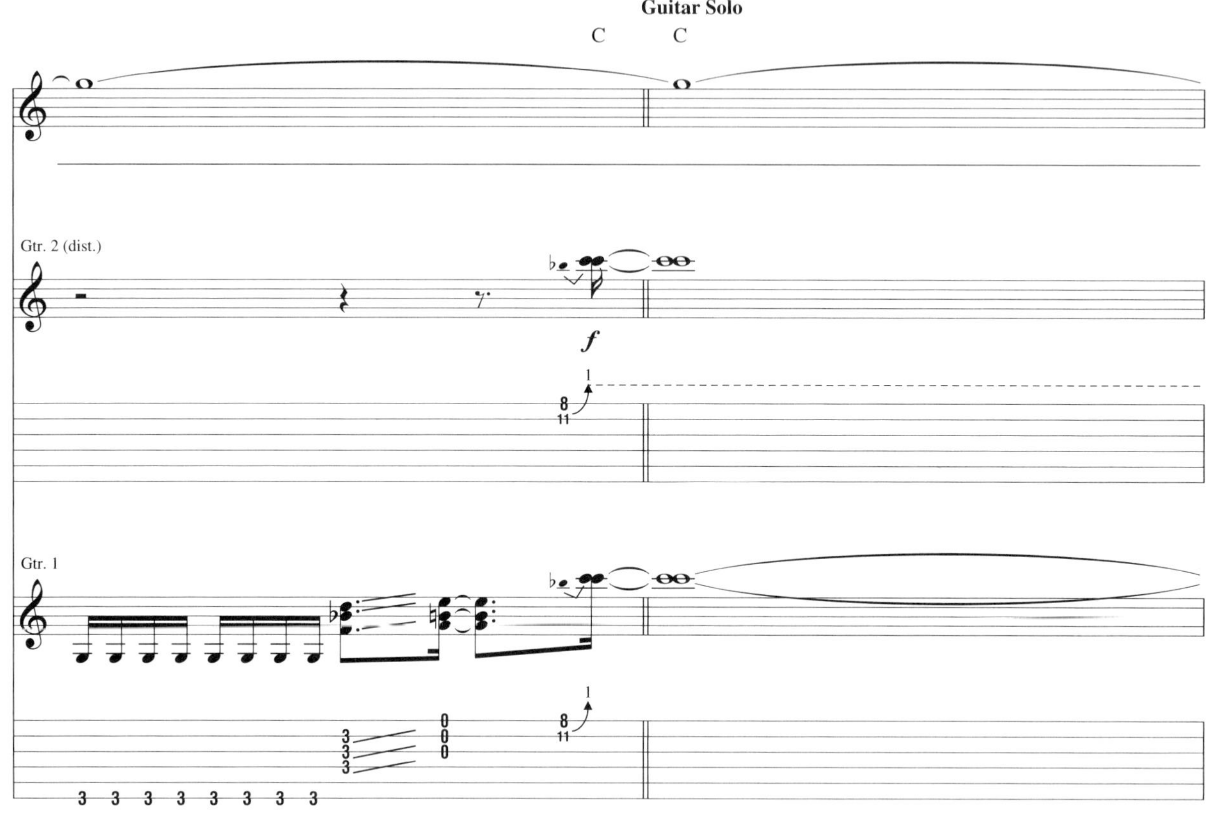

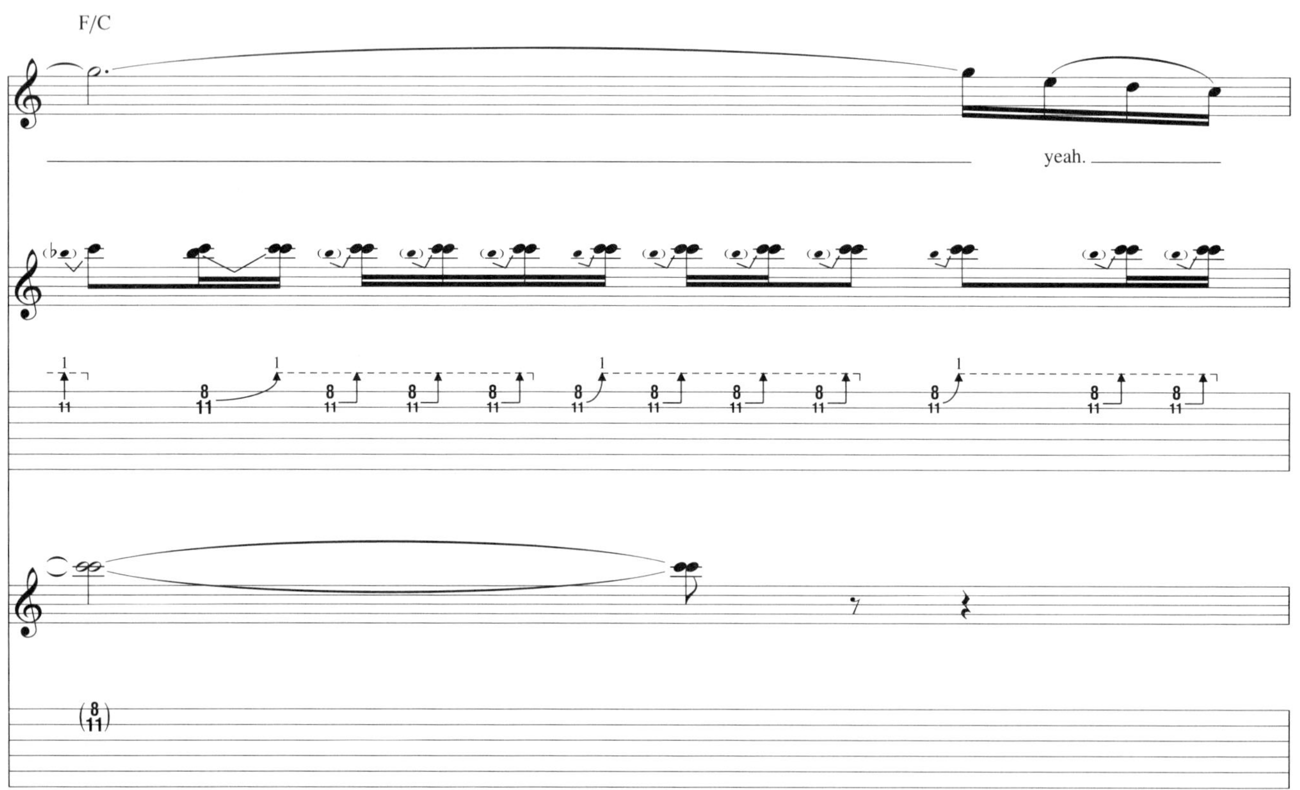

Gtr. 1 tacet
B♭/C
F/C
C
Gtr. 2
F/C
B♭/C
F/C
let ring
let ring
C
So,
Gtr. 2
let ring
P.S.
Gtr. 1
P.S.

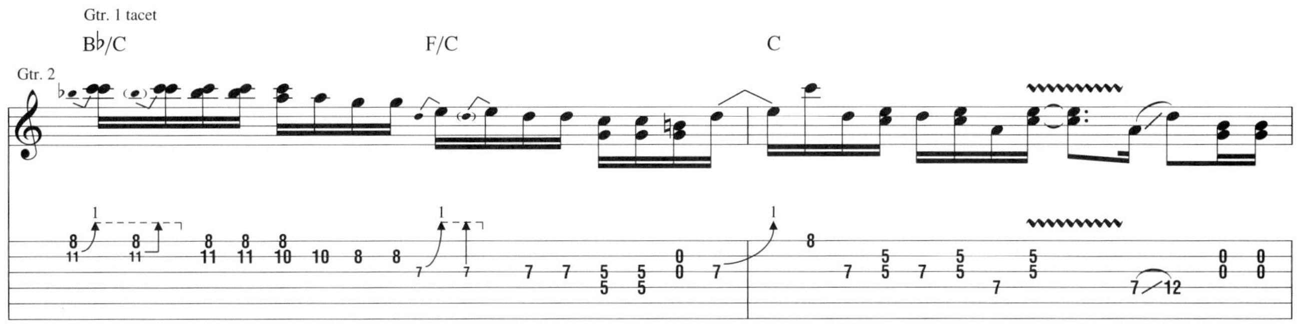

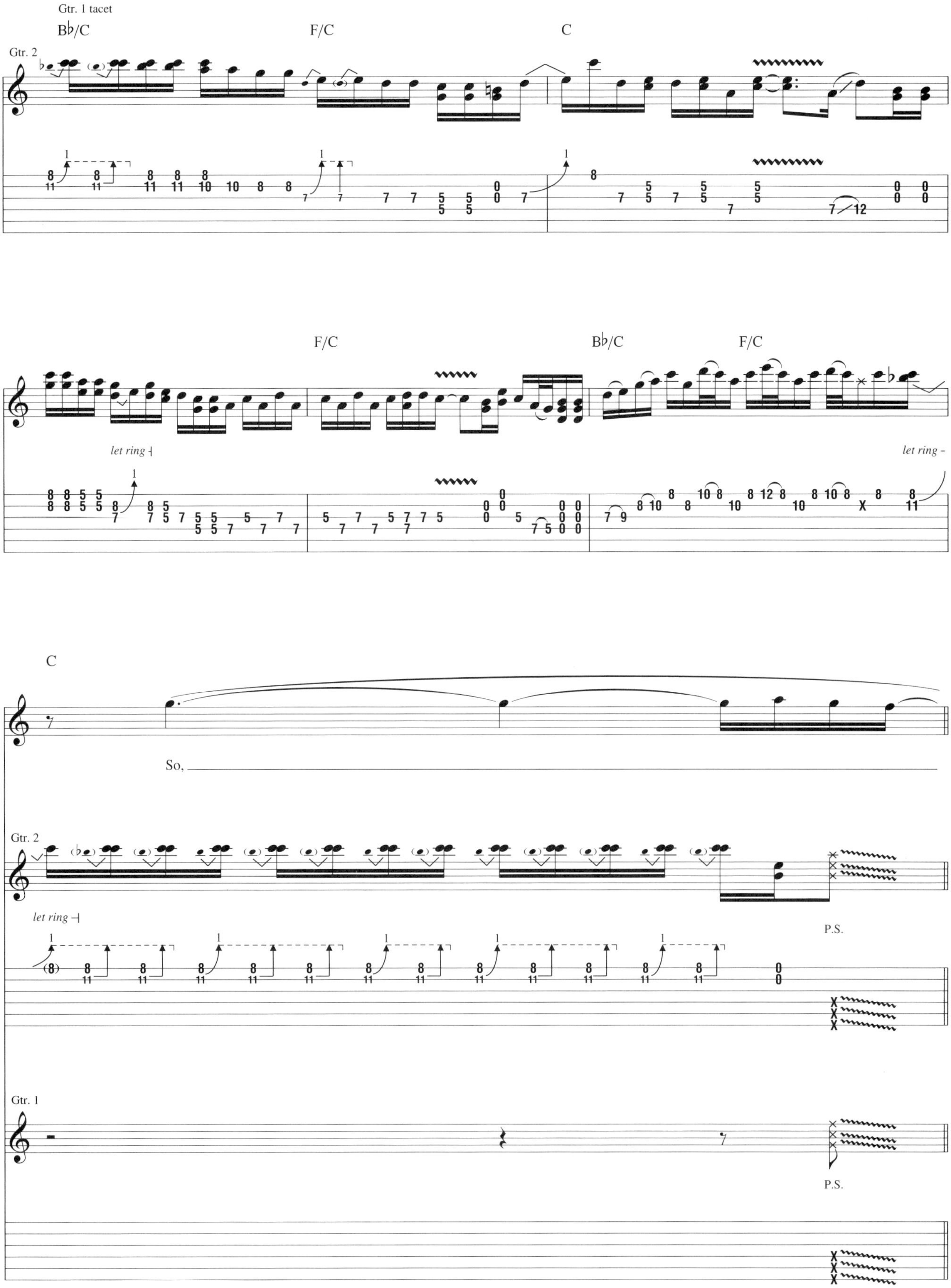

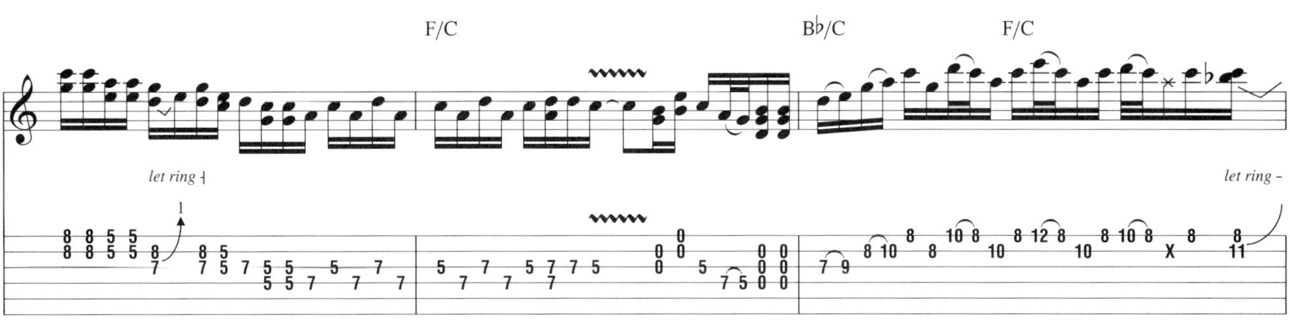

Chorus

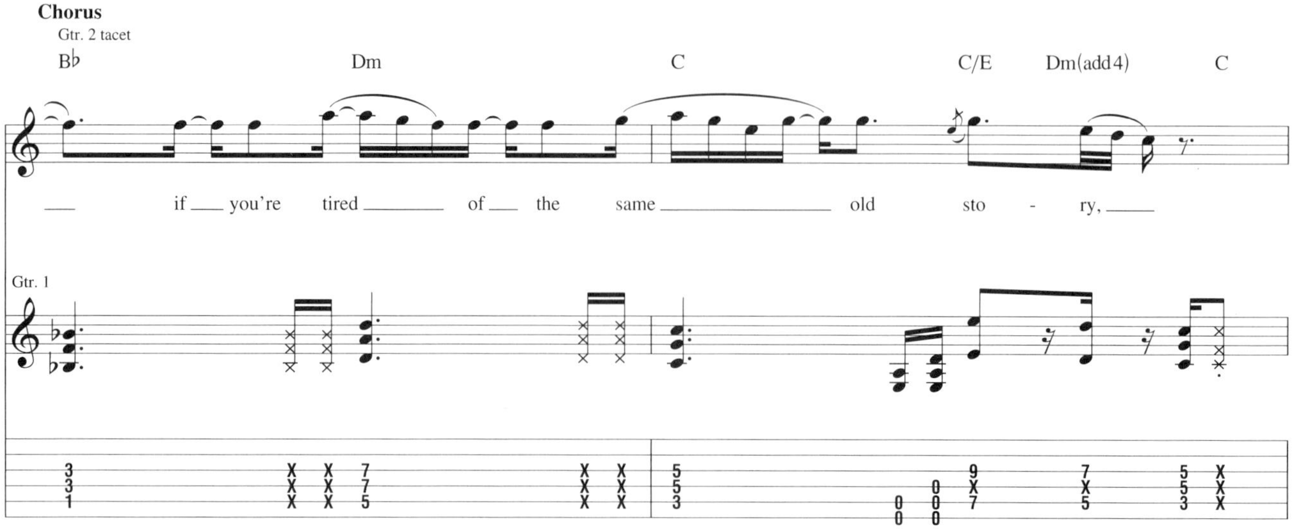
Gtr. 2 tacet
B♭
Dm
C
C/E
Dm(add4)
C
if you're tired of the same old sto - ry,
Gtr. 1

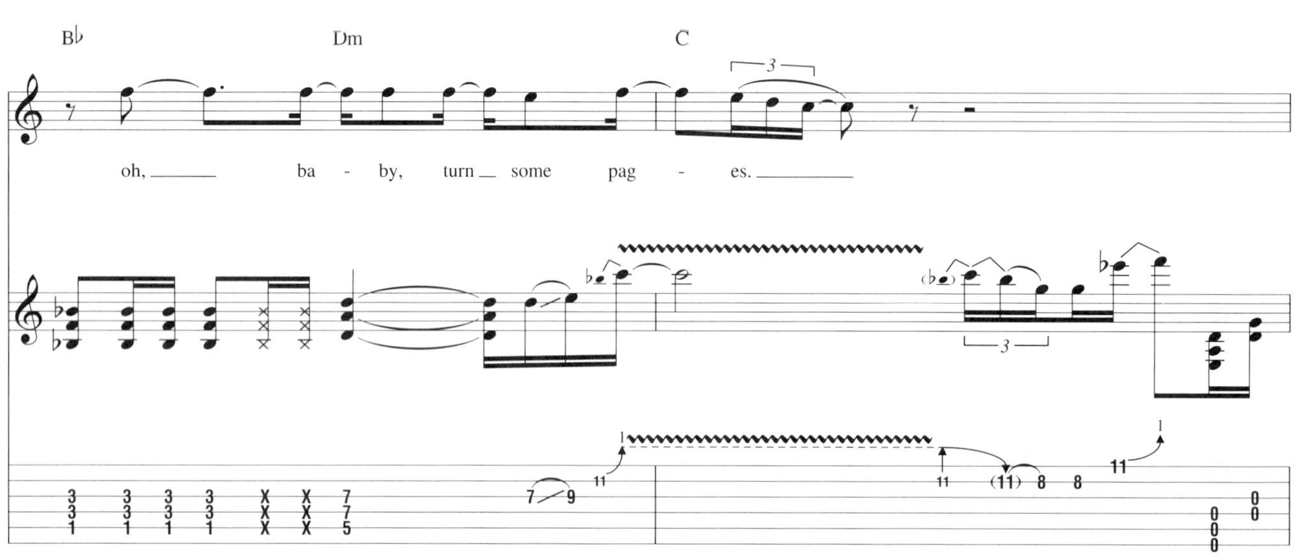
B♭
Dm
C
oh, ba - by, turn some pag - es.

B♭
Dm
C
C/E
Dm(add4)
C
I'll be here when you are read - y to roll with the chang-

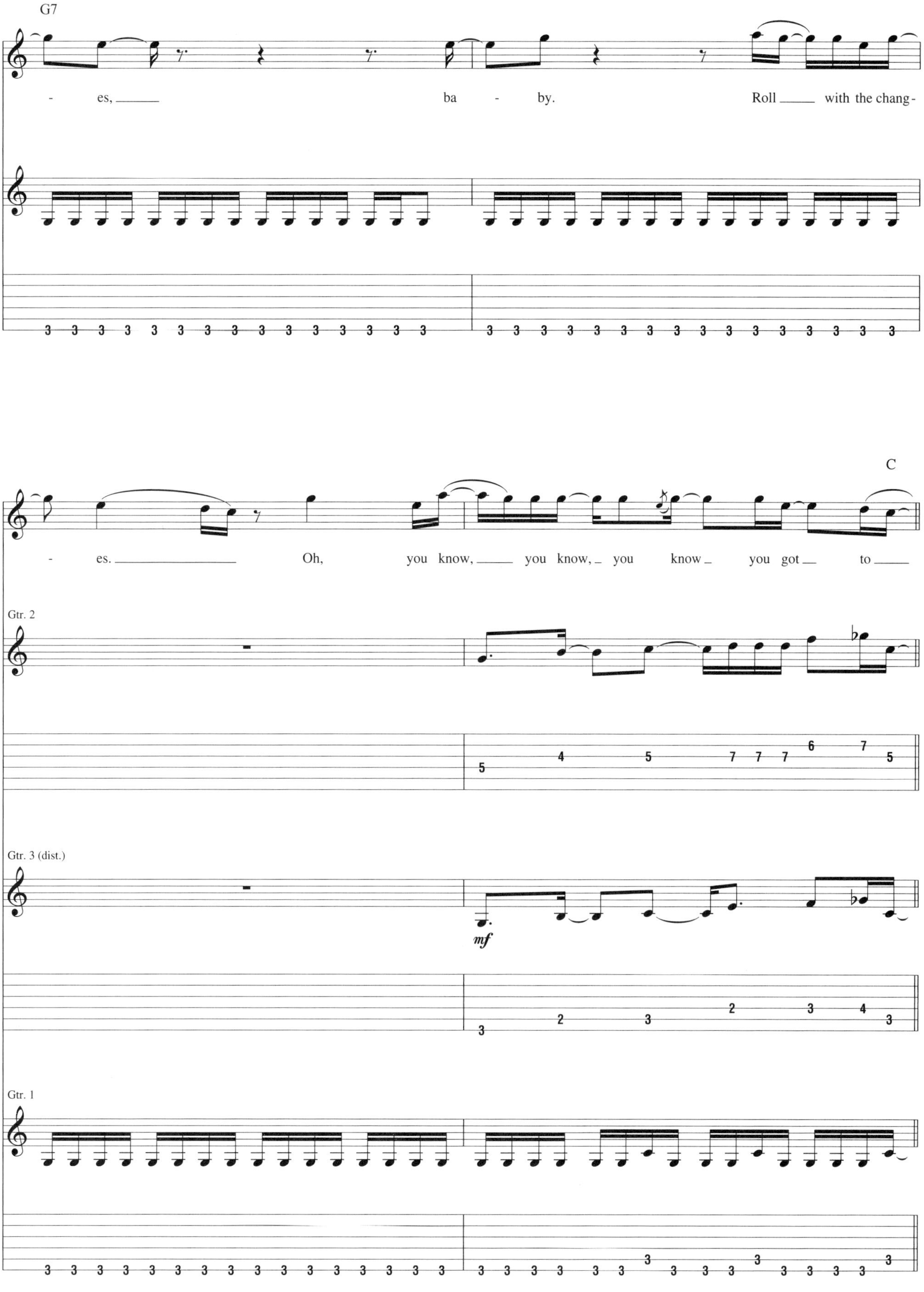

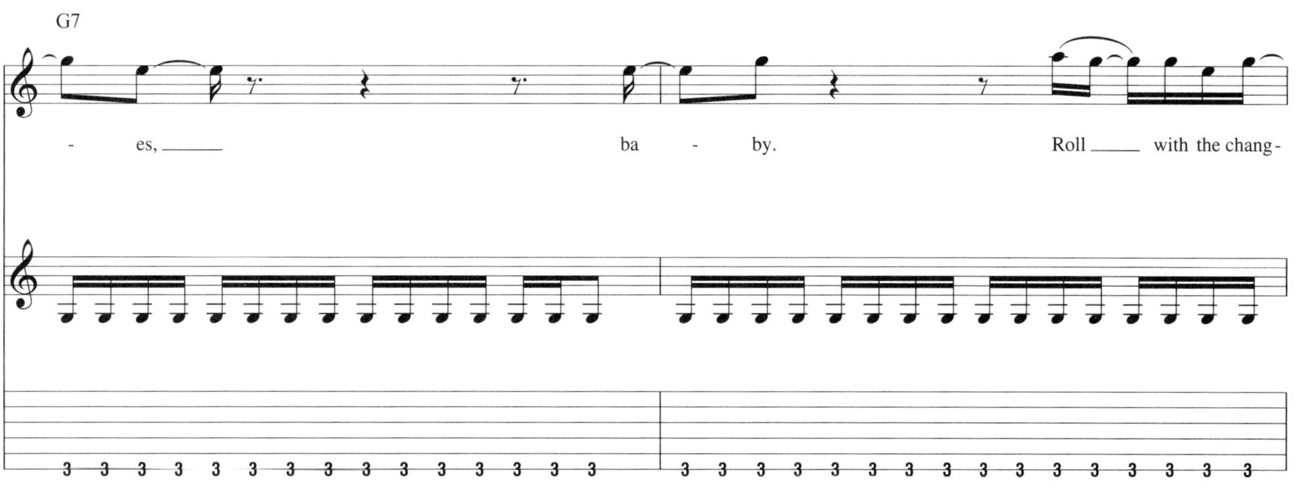

G7
- es, ___ ba - by. Roll ___ with the chang -
C
- es. ___ Oh, you know, ___ you know, _ you know _ you got _ to ___
Gtr. 2
Gtr. 3 (dist.)
mf
Gtr. 1

Bridge
C
F/C
oh, yeah, oh,
Voc. Fig. 1
(Keep on roll - ing. Keep on roll - ing.
(5)
(3)
(3)
Gtrs. 1, 2 & 3 tacet
B♭/C
F/C
C
roll with the chang - es. Keep on roll -
End Voc. Fig. 1
Oo.)
Bkgd. Voc.: w/ Voc. Fig. 1 (2 1/2 times)
F/C
B♭/C
F/C
- ing. Oh, yeah. Oh, now, roll with the chang-

C
F/C
- es, oh, ba - by. Oh, ba - by. Oh, you got
B♭/C
F/C
C
to learn to roll with the chang - es. Got to, got to, got to, got
to keep on roll - ing. Got to keep on. Oh, you got
B♭/C
F/C
C
to learn to, got to learn to, got to learn to roll.
Oo, ah.)
*Gtr. 4
8va
mf
steady gliss.
*Organ arr. for gtr.
Organ Solo
C
F/C
B♭/C
F/C
8va
C
F/C
8va

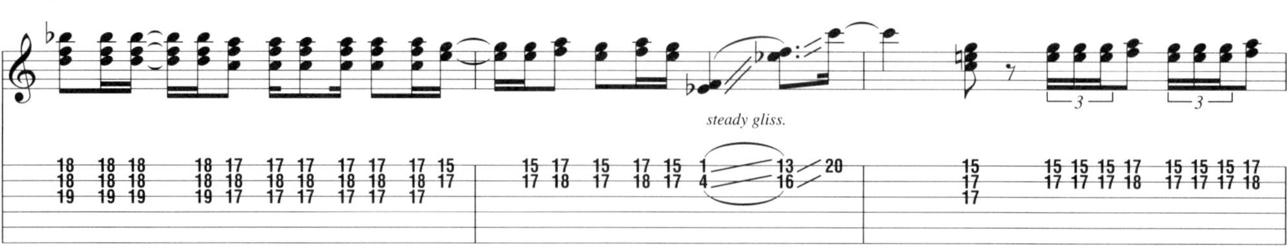

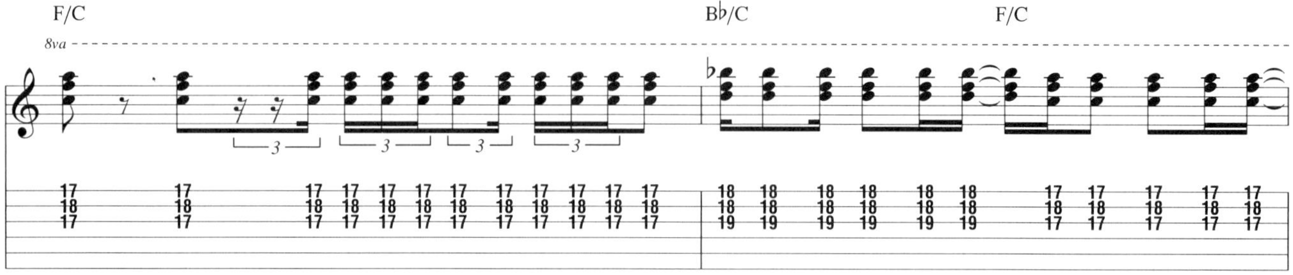

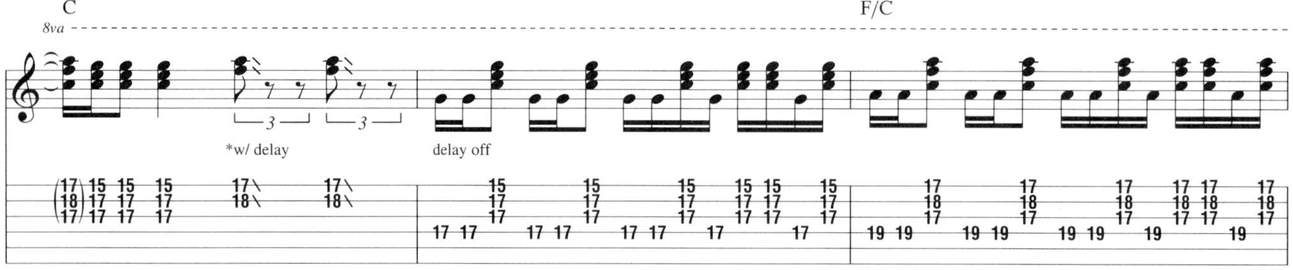

*Set for eighth-note triplet regeneration w/ 2 repeats.

Guitar Solo

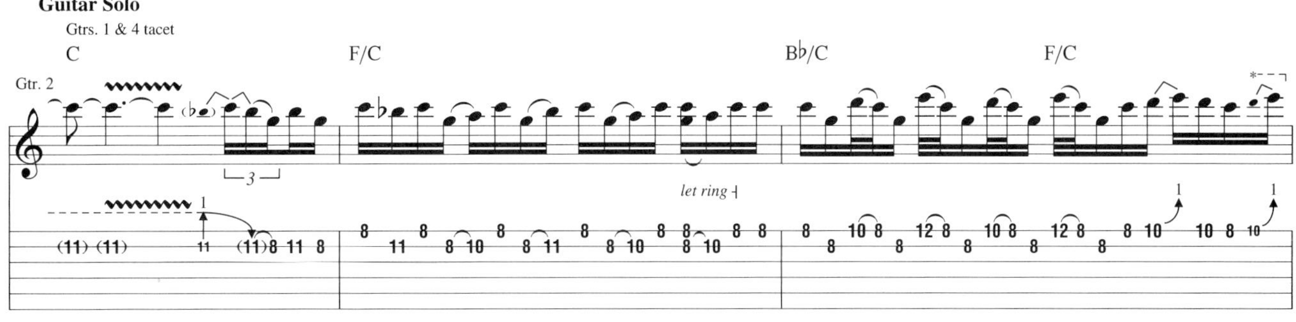

*Played behind the beat.

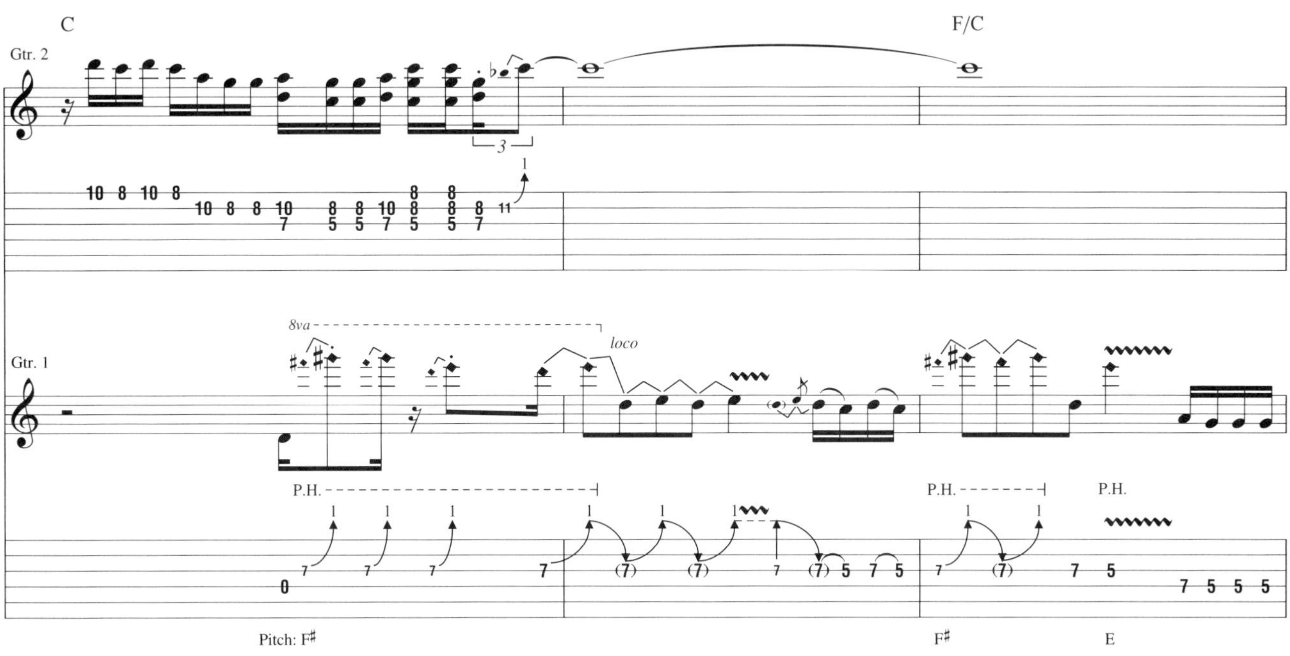

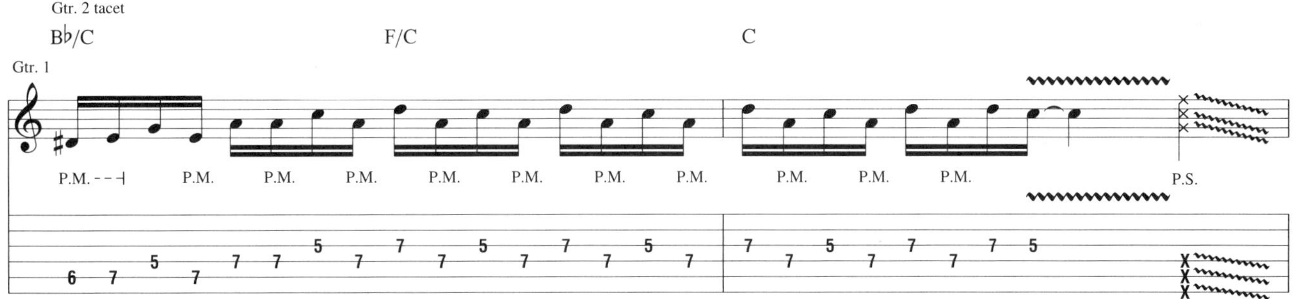

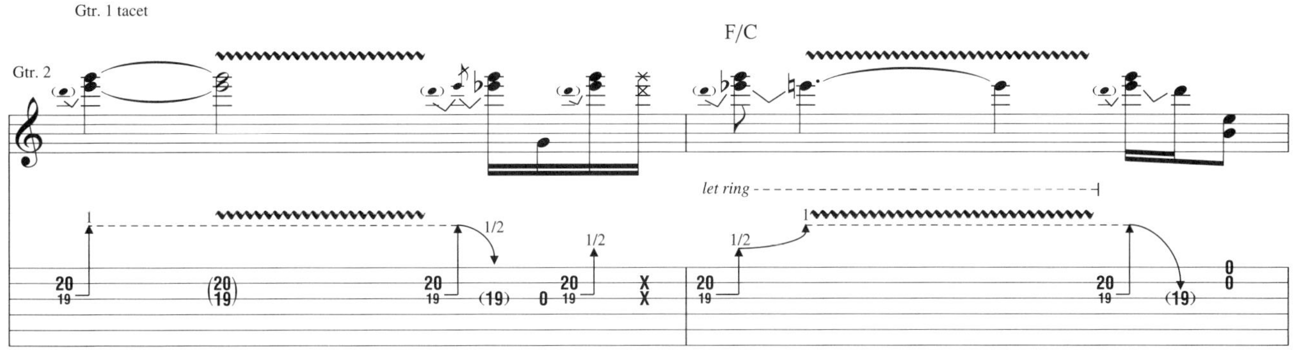

B♭/C
F/C
C
8va
loco
1
1/2
1
Gtr. 2
F/C
Gtr. 1
B♭/C
F/C
C
let ring
Outro-Chorus
Bkgd. Voc.: w/ Voc. Fig. 1 (3 1/2 times)
Gtr. 2 tacet
C
F/C
B♭/C
F/C
C
F/C
Gtr. 1
fdbk.

B♭/C
F/C
C
let ring
F/C
B♭/C
F/C
C
F/C
Free time
B♭/C
F/C
(Oo.)
C
N.C.
w/ pick & fingers
P.S.

from Soundgarden - *Badmotorfinger*

Rusty Cage

Words and Music by Chris Cornell

Tune ⑥ down to B

Moderately Fast Rock ♩ = 190

Gtr. 1
Band in
(Gtr. 1 out)
Rhy. Fig. 1 (Gtr. 3)
Gtr. 3
Gtr. 3
Gtr. 2
(Gtr. 2 out)
Verse
w/Rhy. Fig. 1 (7 times)
14
w/Rhy. Fig. 1 (14 times)
N.C.
1. Oh, you wir - ed me a - wake and
2. Too cold to start a fire, I'm burn - ing
* w/vocal preverb
hit me with a hand of bro - ken nails.
die - sel, burn - ing din - o - saur bones.
Yeah, you tied my lead and pulled my chain to watch my blood
Yeah. I'll take the riv - er down to still wa - ter and
* w/vocal preverb
be - gin to boil.
ride a pack of dogs.
But I'm gon - na

3
break,
I'm gon - na break my...
I'm gon - na
break my rust - y cage and run.
Yeah, I'm gon - na
break,
I'm gon - na break my...
I'm gon - na
Gtr. 3
break my rust - y cage
1.
and
8vb
w/Rhy. Fig. 1 (4 times)
run.
2.
and run.
N.C.
8vb
8vb to end

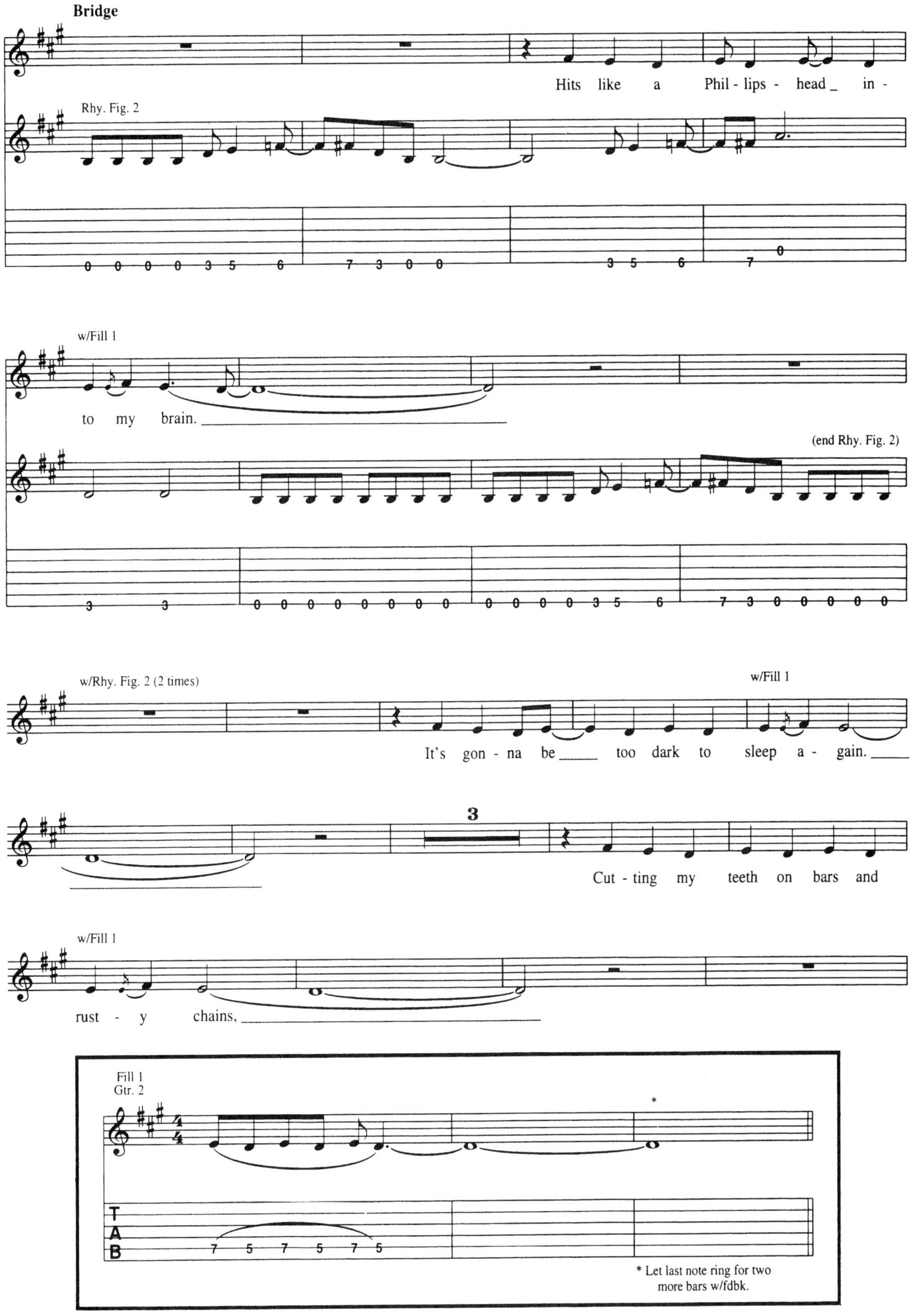
Bridge
Hits like a Phil - lips - head _ in -
Rhy. Fig. 2
0 0 0 0 3 5 6 7 3 0 0 3 5 6 7 0
w/Fill 1
to my brain.
(end Rhy. Fig. 2)
3 3 0 0 0 0 0 0 0 0 0 0 0 0 3 5 6 7 3 0 0 0 0 0
w/Rhy. Fig. 2 (2 times)
w/Fill 1
It's gon - na be too dark to sleep a - gain.
3
Cut - ting my teeth on bars and
w/Fill 1
rust - y chains,
Fill 1
Gtr. 2
T
A
B
7 5 7 5 7 5
* Let last note ring for two more bars w/fdbk.

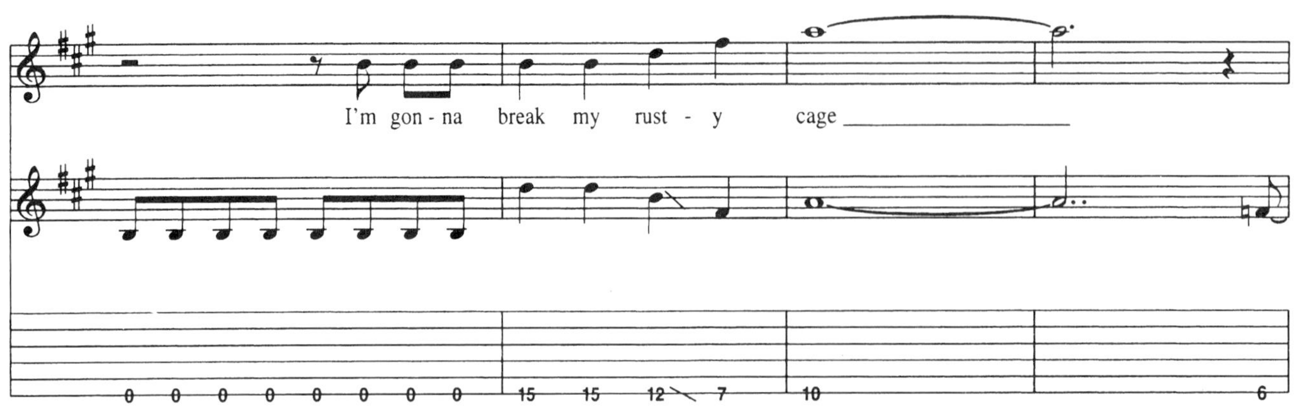
I'm gon - na break my rust - y cage
0 0 0 0 0 0 0 0
15 15 12 7
10
6

Freely
and run.
rit.
1/4
1/4
1/4
(6) 6 5 5 3 3 0 0
3 0 3
0 3
0 5

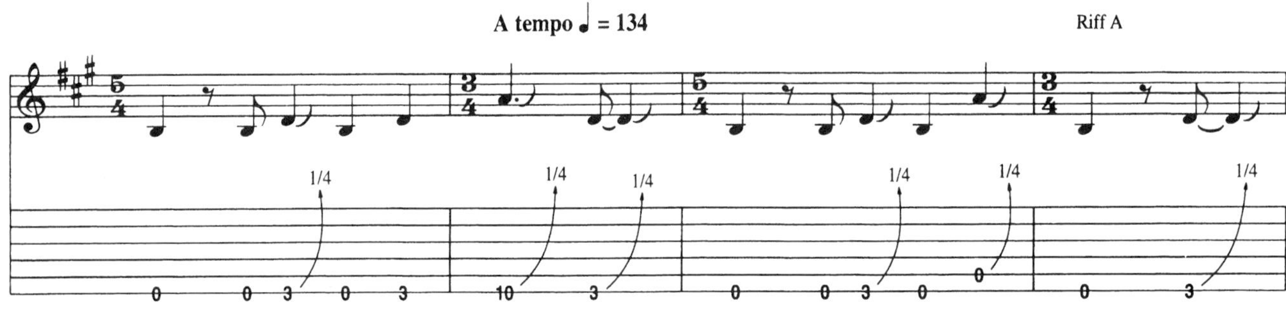
A tempo ♩ = 134
Riff A
1/4
1/4
1/4
1/4
1/4
1/4
0 0 3 0 3
10 3
0 0 3 0 0
0 3

When the
(end Riff A)
1/4
1/4
1/4
1/4
1/4
0 5
0 3 0 3
10 3
0 0 3 0 10

Outro
w/Riff A (7 times)
for - est burns _ a - long the road, ________ like
God's eyes in my head - lights. __________ And when the
dogs are look- ing for their bones, ___________ and it's
rain - ing ice - picks __ on your steel shore, _____ well, I'm gon - na
break, I'm gon - na break my. . . ________ I'm gon - na
break my rust - y cage and run. ___
Well, I'm gon - na break, I'm gon - na break my. . . ________
Freely
w/Fill 2
I'm gon - na break my rust - y cage and run. _____
Gtr. 3
1/4
3 0 3 12 7 10 (10)
Fill 2
Gtr. 1
Fdbk.
Gtr. 2
Fdbk.
16/14
* Gtr. 2 tabbed to right of slash.

from Beastie Boys - *Ill Communication*

Sabotage

Words and Music by Michael Diamond, Adam Yauch and Adam Horovitz

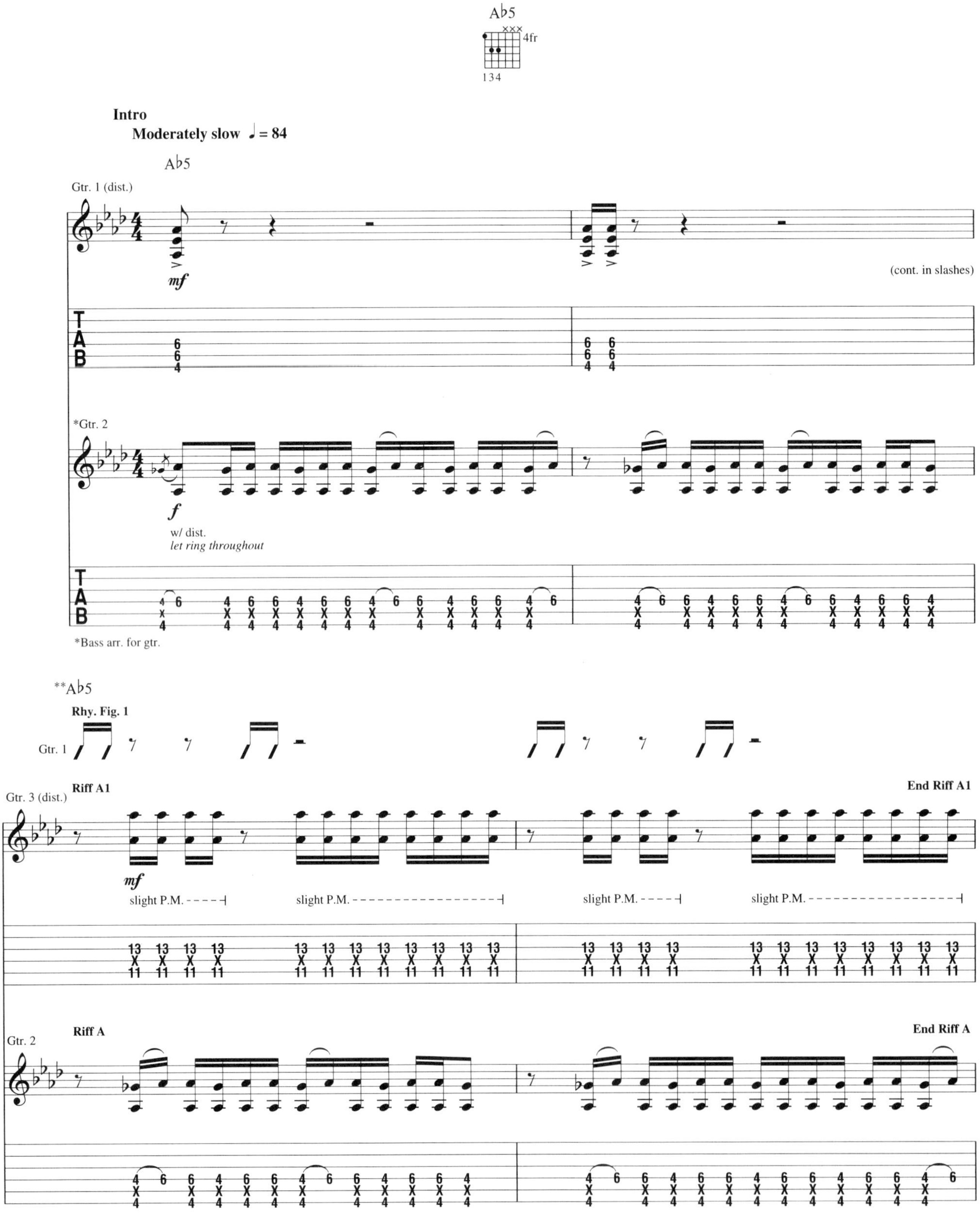

Ab5

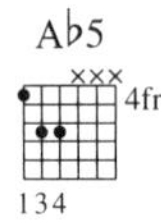

Intro

Moderately slow ♩ = 84

Ab5

Gtr. 1 (dist.)

mf

(cont. in slashes)

*Gtr. 2

f

w/ dist.

let ring throughout

*Bass arr. for gtr.

**Ab5

Rhy. Fig. 1

Gtr. 1

Gtr. 3 (dist.) **Riff A1**

End Riff A1

mf

slight P.M.

Gtr. 2 **Riff A**

End Riff A

**See top of page for chord diagram pertaining to rhythm slashes.

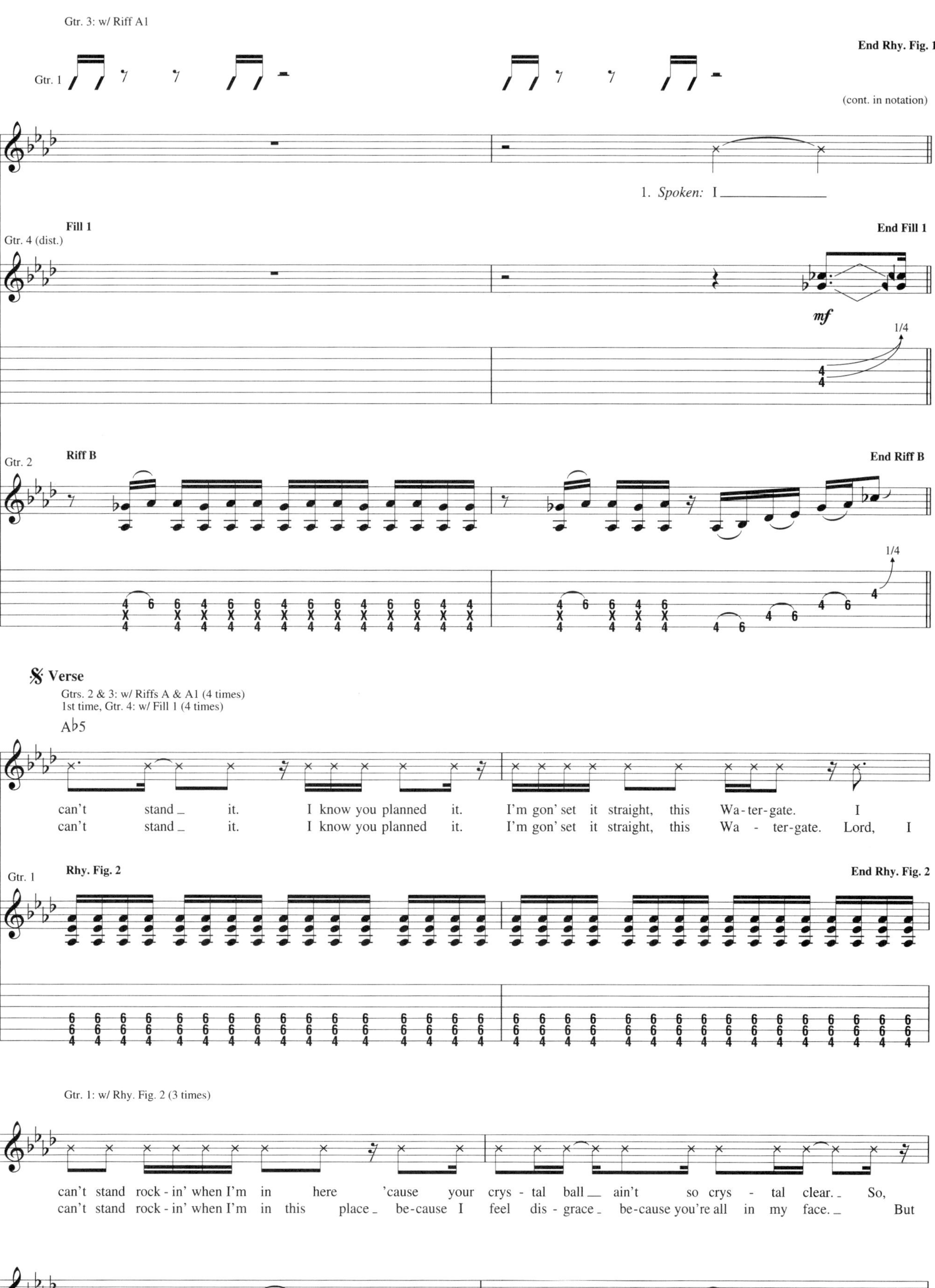

Gtr. 3: w/ Riff A1
End Rhy. Fig. 1
Gtr. 1
(cont. in notation)
1. Spoken: I
Fill 1
End Fill 1
Gtr. 4 (dist.)
mf
1/4
Gtr. 2
Riff B
End Riff B
1/4
Verse
Gtrs. 2 & 3: w/ Riffs A & A1 (4 times)
1st time, Gtr. 4: w/ Fill 1 (4 times)
A♭5
can't stand it. I know you planned it. I'm gon' set it straight, this Wa-ter-gate. I
can't stand it. I know you planned it. I'm gon' set it straight, this Wa-ter-gate. Lord, I
Gtr. 1
Rhy. Fig. 2
End Rhy. Fig. 2
Gtr. 1: w/ Rhy. Fig. 2 (3 times)
can't stand rock-in' when I'm in here 'cause your crys-tal ball ain't so crys-tal clear. So,
can't stand rock-in' when I'm in this place be-cause I feel dis-grace be-cause you're all in my face. But
while you sit back and won-der why, I got this fuck-in' thorn in my side.
make no mis-takes and switch up my chan-nel. I'm Bud-dy Rich when I fly off that han-dle.

To Coda
Oh, my God, it's a mi - rage. I'm tell - in' y'all it's sab - o - tage.
What could it be? It's a mi - rage. You're schem - in' on a thing that's sab - o - tage.
Turntable Solo
Gtr. 1: w/ Rhy. Fig. 1
Gtr. 2: w/ Riff A
Gtr. 3: w/ Riff A1 (2 times)
Gtr. 2: w/ Riff B
A♭5
N.C.
2. So, so, so,
Fill 2
Gtr. 4
End Fill 2
Verse
Gtr. 1: w/ Rhy. Fig. 2 (2 times)
Gtrs. 2 & 3: w/ Riffs A & A1 (2 times)
Gtr. 4 tacet
A♭5
so lis - ten up 'cause you can't say noth - in'. You shut me down with a push of your but - ton. But you,
I'm out and I'm gone. I'll tell you now, I keep it on and on.
Gtr. 4
Guitar Solo
Gtr. 4 tacet
N.C.
Gtr. 1

Ab5
3. 'Cause
Gtr. 1
mf
Gtr. 2
Verse
Gtr. 1: w/ Rhy. Fig. 2 (2 times)
Gtrs. 2 & 3: w/ Riffs A & A1 (2 times)
Ab5
what you see you might not get. And we can bet, so don't you get souped yet.
Gtr. 4: w/ Fill 2
Schem-in' on a thing that's a mi - rage. I'm try - in' to tell you now it's sab - o - tage.
Turntable Solo
Gtr. 1: w/ Rhy. Fig. 1
Gtrs. 2 & 3: w/ Riffs A & A1 (1 1/2 times)
Gtr. 3 tacet
Ab5
N.C.
Gtr. 3
mp
slight P.M.
Gtr. 2
pp < mp
fdbk.
string noise
don't pick
steady gliss.
Pitch: C♯

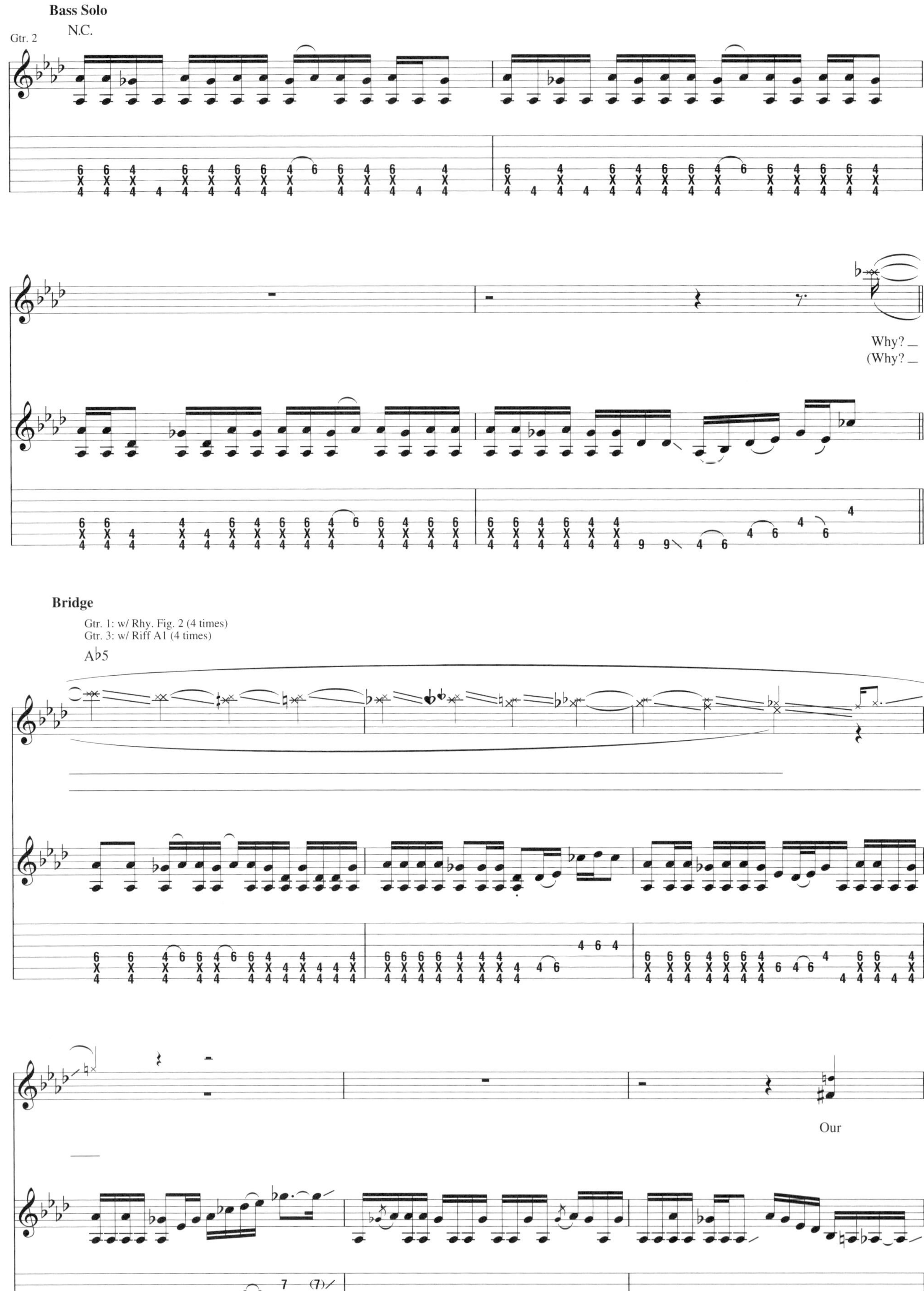
Bass Solo
N.C.
Gtr. 2
Why? __
(Why? __
Bridge
Gtr. 1: w/ Rhy. Fig. 2 (4 times)
Gtr. 3: w/ Riff A1 (4 times)
A♭5
Our

backs are now a - gainst the wall.
Interlude
Gtr. 1: w/ Rhy. Fig. 1 (2 times)
Gtr. 3: w/ Riff A1 (2 times)
A♭5
*Spoken: Lis - ten all, y'all, it's a sab - o - tage.
Lis - ten all, y'all, it's a sab - o - tage.
*p < f, next 4 meas.
D.S. al Coda
Lis - ten all, y'all, it's a sab - o - tage.
Lis - ten all, y'all, it's a sab - o - tage.
4. Spoken: I
Coda
Outro
A♭5
Gtr. 1
Gtr. 3
(sampled fdbk.)
slight P.M.
Gtr. 2

from Big & Rich - *Horse of a Different Color*

Save a Horse (Ride a Cowboy)

Words and Music by John Rich and Big Kenny

1st time, Gtrs. 1 & 2: w/ Rhy. Fig. 2 (2 times)
2nd time, Gtrs. 1 & 2: w/ Rhy. Fills 1 & 1A
E5 E6 E7 A5 A6 A7
and it thrills like the horns on my Sil - ver - ad - o grille. And I
- in' while the girls are drink - in' long necks down. And I
2nd time, Gtrs. 1 & 2: w/ Rhy. Fig. 2
E5 E6 E7 A5 A6 A7
buy the bar a dou - ble round of Crown and then ev - 'ry - bod - y's get - tin' down in this town.
would - n't trade ol' Le - roy or my Chev - ro - let for your Es - ca - lade or your
2nd time, Gtrs. 1 & 2: w/ Rhy. Fill 2
E5 E6 E7 A5 A6 A5
Ain't nev - er gon - na be the same. 'Cause I
freak pa - rade. I'm the on - ly John Wayne left in this town. And I
Gtrs. 1 & 2
P.M.
Rhy. Fill 1
Gtr. 1
Rhy. Fill 1A
Gtr. 2
Rhy. Fill 2
Gtrs. 1 & 2

Chorus
3rd time, Gtr. 5 tacet
E5
A5
sad - dle up my horse and I ride in - to the cit - y. I
Rhy. Fig. 3
3rd time, Gtrs. 1 & 2: w/ Rhy. Fill 3
make a lot of noise 'cause the girls, they are so pret - ty.
End Rhy. Fig. 3
To Coda
Rid - in' up and down Broad - way on my old stud, Le - roy. And the girls say,
Rhy. Fill 3
Gtrs. 1 & 2

E5
G5
A5

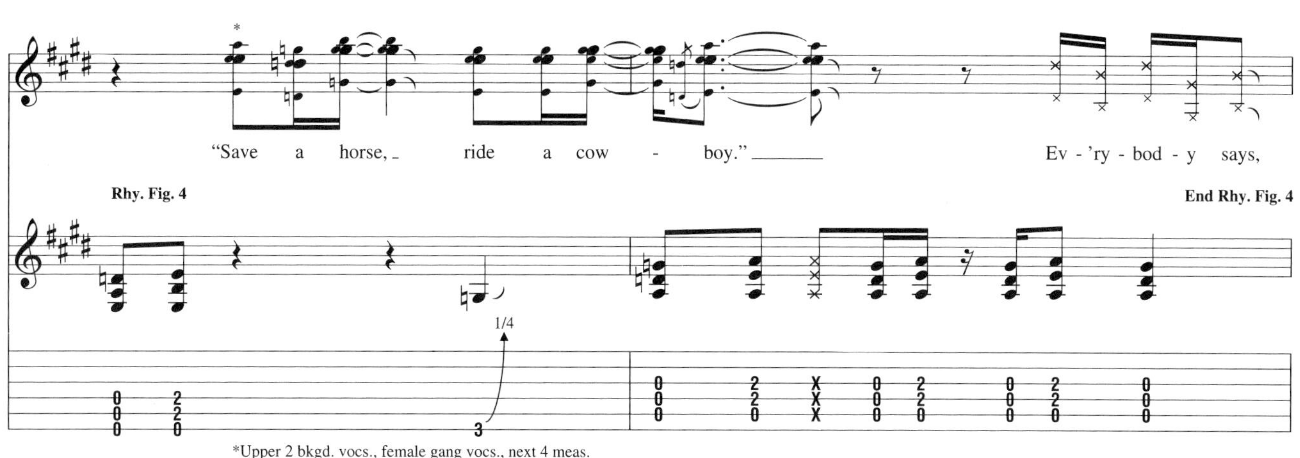
"Save a horse, ride a cow - boy."
Ev - 'ry - bod - y says,
Rhy. Fig. 4
End Rhy. Fig. 4
1/4
*Upper 2 bkgd. vocs., female gang vocs., next 4 meas.

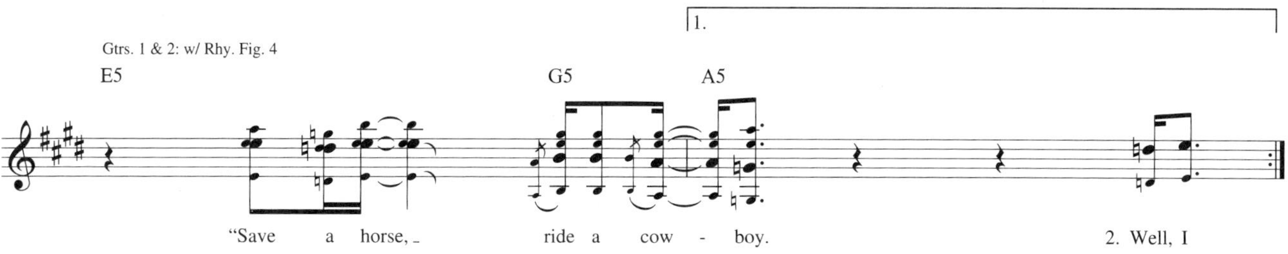
1.
Gtrs. 1 & 2: w/ Rhy. Fig. 4
E5
G5
A5
"Save a horse, ride a cow - boy.
2. Well, I

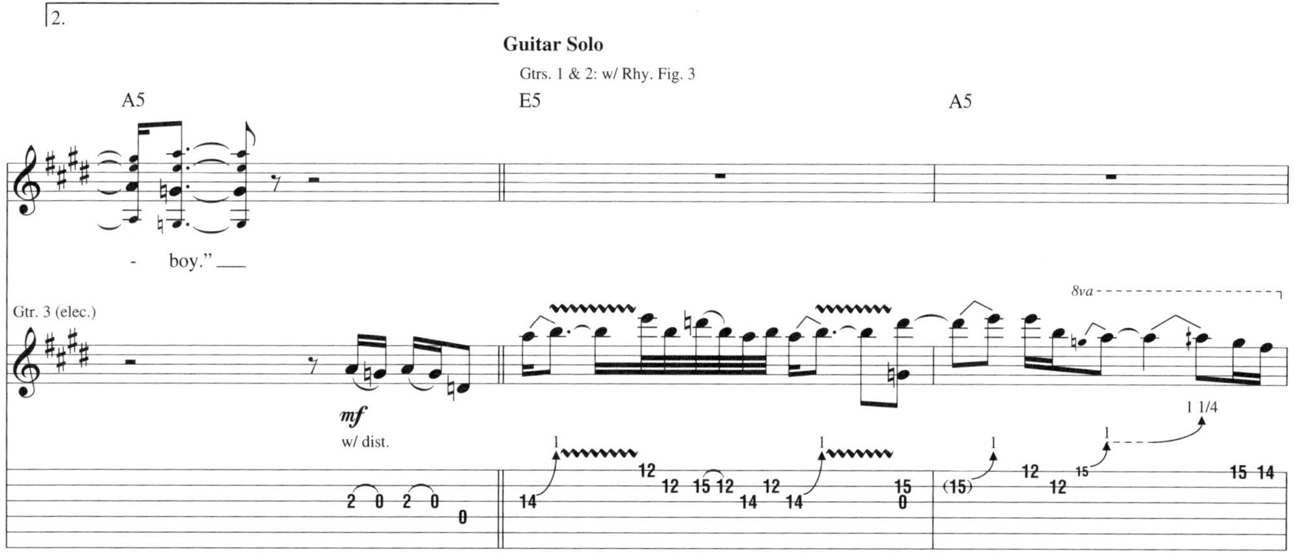
2.
Guitar Solo
Gtrs. 1 & 2: w/ Rhy. Fig. 3
A5
E5
A5
- boy."
Gtr. 3 (elec.)
mf
w/ dist.
8va

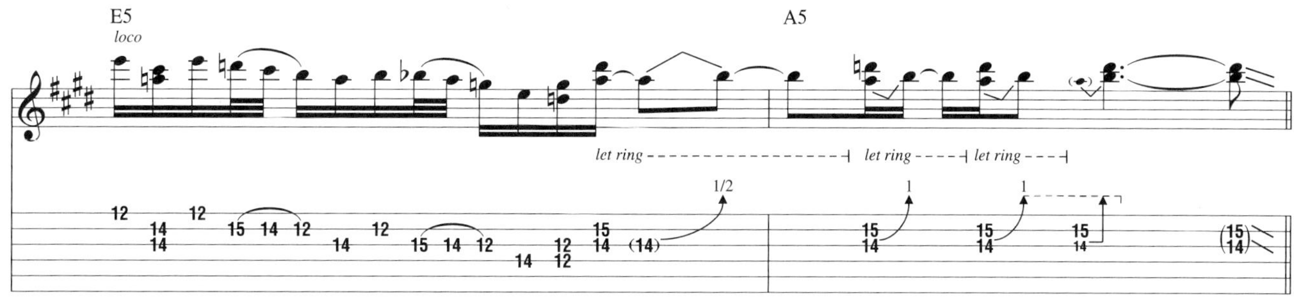
E5
loco
A5
let ring
let ring
let ring

Fiddle Solo

Gtr. 1: w/ Rhy. Fig. 3
Gtr. 2: w/ Rhy. Fig. 1 (2 times)
Gtr. 3 tacet

E5 A5

*Gtr. 4

f

w/ pick & finger

*Fiddle arr. for gtr.

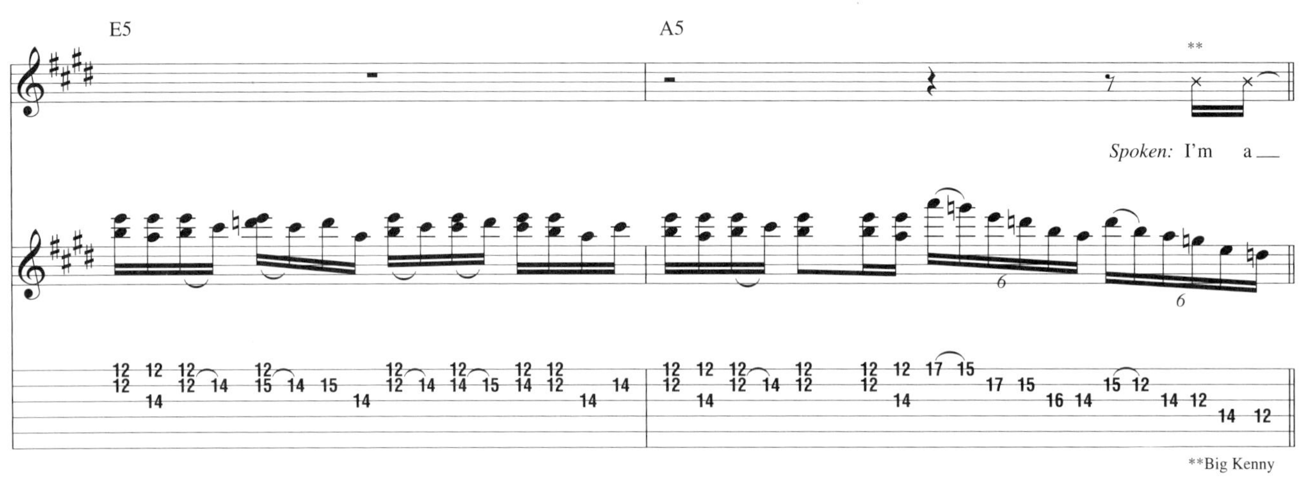

Bridge

*John Rich - full size notes;
Big Kenny - cue sized notes.

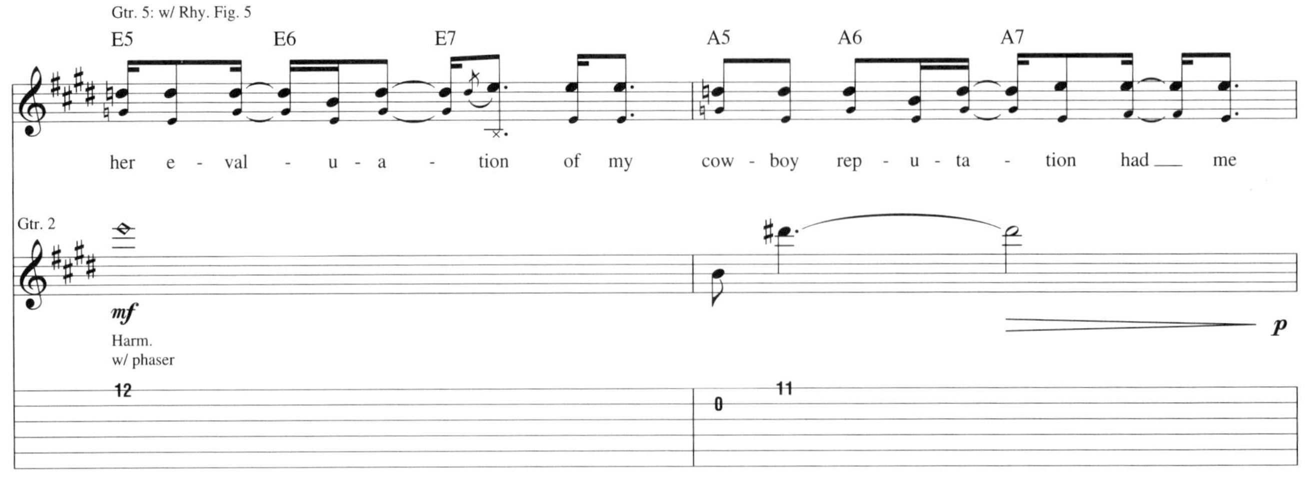

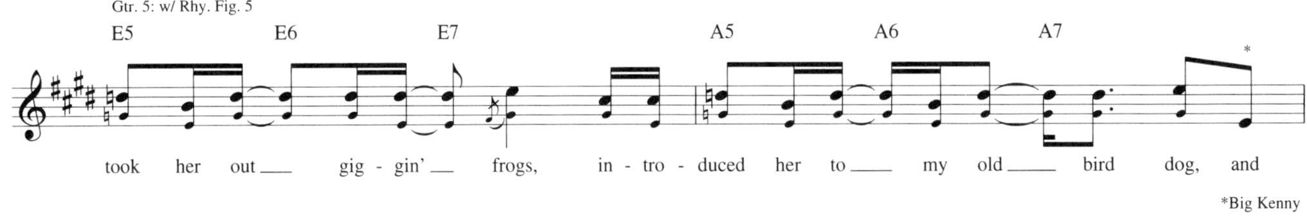

**John Rich - full size notes; Big Kenny - cue sized notes.

⊕ Coda

*Upper 3 bkgd. vocs., female gang vocs., till end.

Gtrs. 1 & 2: w/ Rhy. Fig. 6 (2 times)

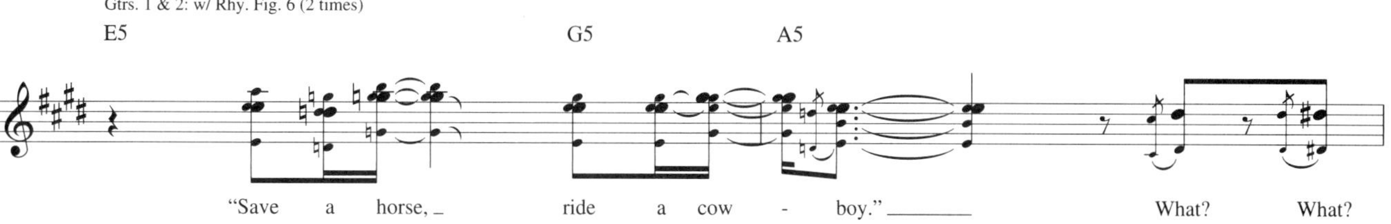

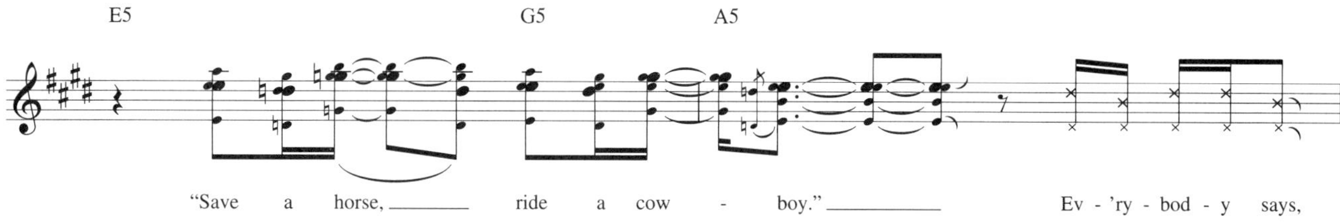

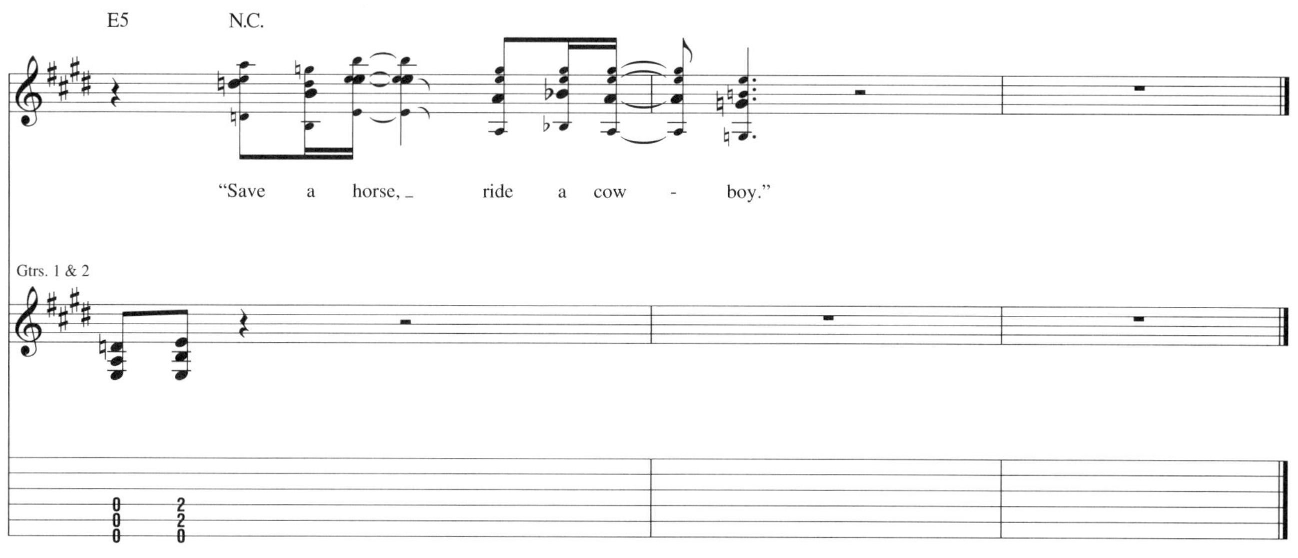

from Coldplay - *A Rush of Blood to the Head*

The Scientist

Words and Music by Guy Berryman, Jon Buckland, Will Champion and Chris Martin

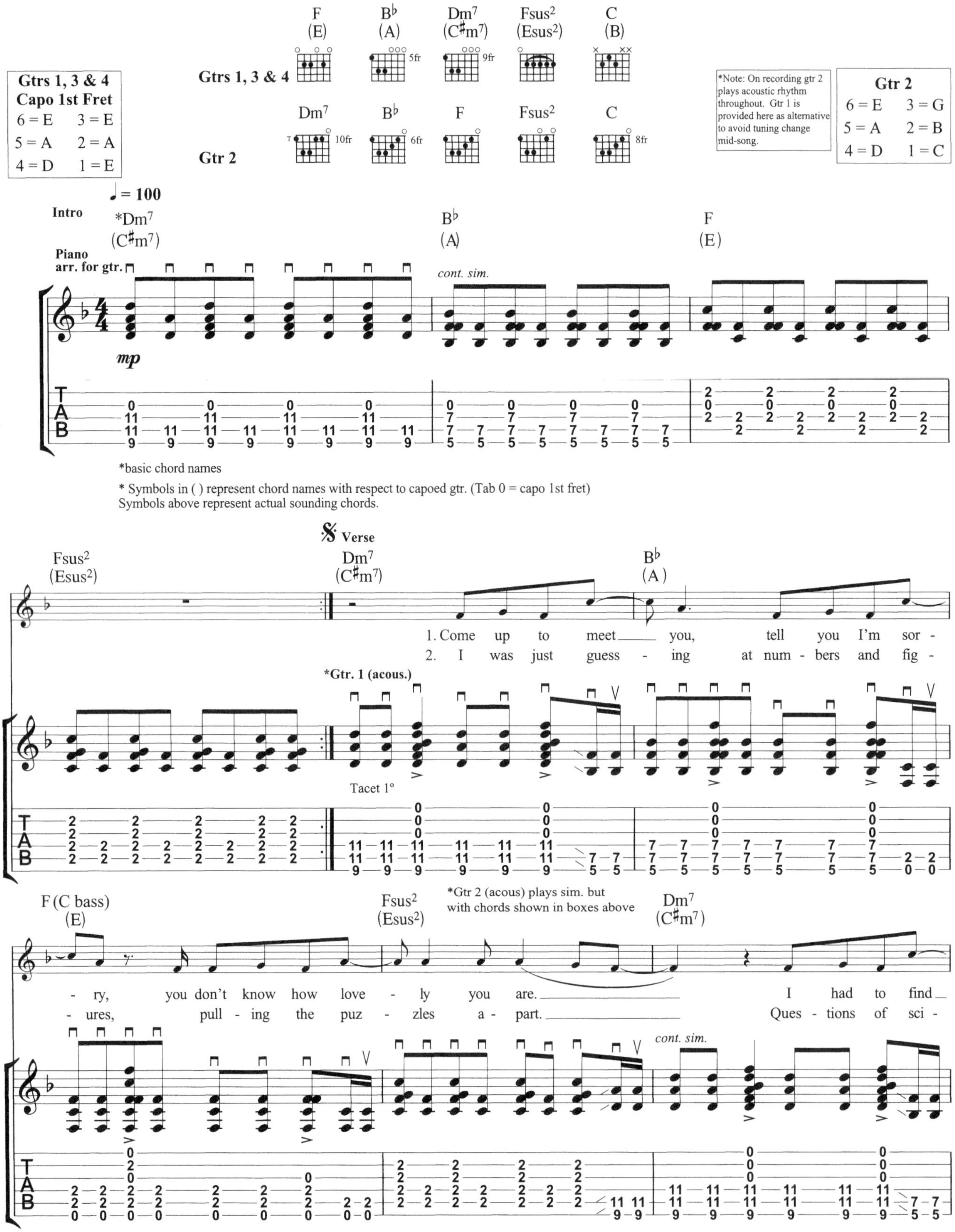

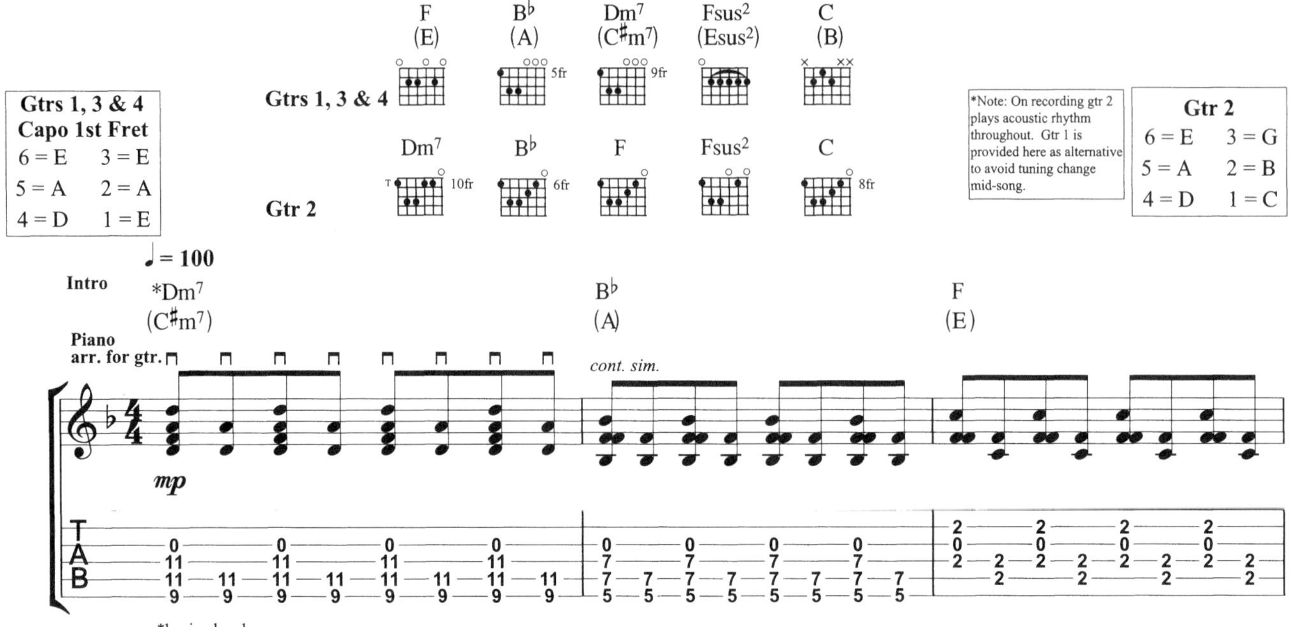

*basic chord names

* Symbols in ( ) represent chord names with respect to capoed gtr. (Tab 0 = capo 1st fret)
Symbols above represent actual sounding chords.

Fsus2 (Esus2)

Verse

Dm7 (C♯m7) B♭ (A)

1. Come up to meet you, tell you I'm sor-
2. I was just guess - ing at num - bers and fig -

*Gtr. 1 (acous.)

Tacet 1°

F (C bass) (E) Fsus2 (Esus2) Dm7 (C♯m7)

*Gtr 2 (acous) plays sim. but with chords shown in boxes above

- ry, you don't know how love - ly you are. I had to find
- ures, pull - ing the puz - zles a - part. Ques - tions of sci -

cont. sim.

B♭ (A)
F(C bass) (E)
Fsus2 (Esus2)
— you, tell you I need — you, tell you I'll set — you a - part. —
- ence, sci - ence and pro - gress do not speak as loud — as my heart. —
Dm7 (C♯m7)
B♭ (A)
F(C bass) (E)
— Tell me your se - crets and ask me your ques - tions, oh let's go back —
— And tell me you love — me and come back and haunt — me, oh when I rush —
Fsus2 (Esus2)
Dm7 (C♯m7)
B♭ (A)
— to the start. — Run - ning in cir - cles, com - ing in tails, —
— to the start. — Run - ning in cir - cles, com - ing in tails, —
F(C bass) (E)
Fsus2 (Esus2)
B♭ (A)
— heads are a sci - ence a - part. —
— com - in' a back — as we are. —
No - bo - dy said —
T
A
B

F
(E)
Fsus2
(Esus2)
it was ea - sy,
it's such a shame for us to part.
Bb
(A)
F
(E)
No - bo - dy said it was ea - sy,
no - one ev - er
C
(B)
To Coda
said it would be this hard.
so hard.
Oh, take me back to the start.
I'm go - in' back to the start.
F
(E)
Bb
(A)
mf
cont. sim.

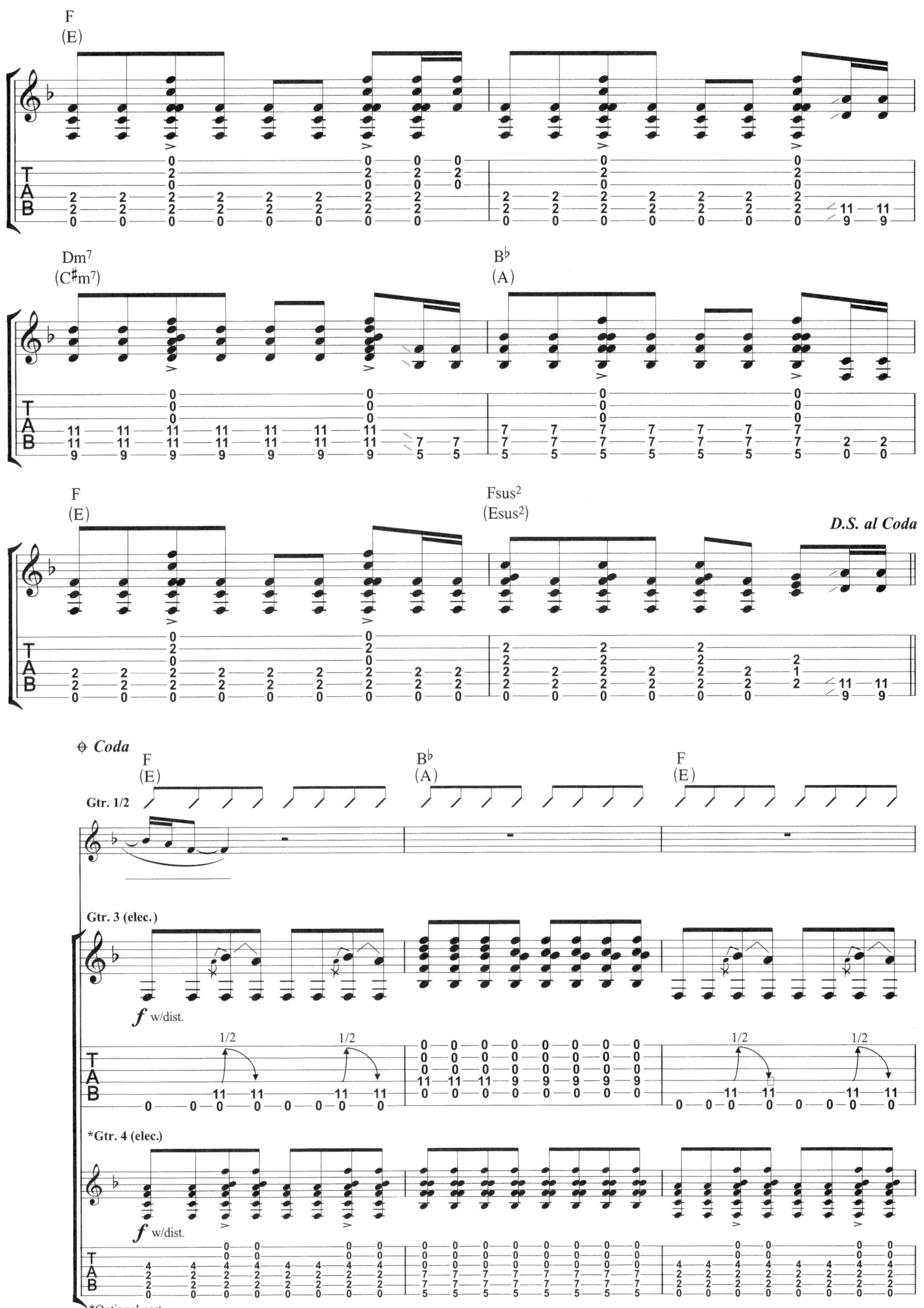
F
(E)
Dm7
(C♯m7)
B♭
(A)
F
(E)
Fsus2
(Esus2)
D.S. al Coda
Coda
F
(E)
B♭
(A)
F
(E)
Gtr. 1/2
Gtr. 3 (elec.)
f w/dist.
1/2
*Gtr. 4 (elec.)
f w/dist.
*Optional part

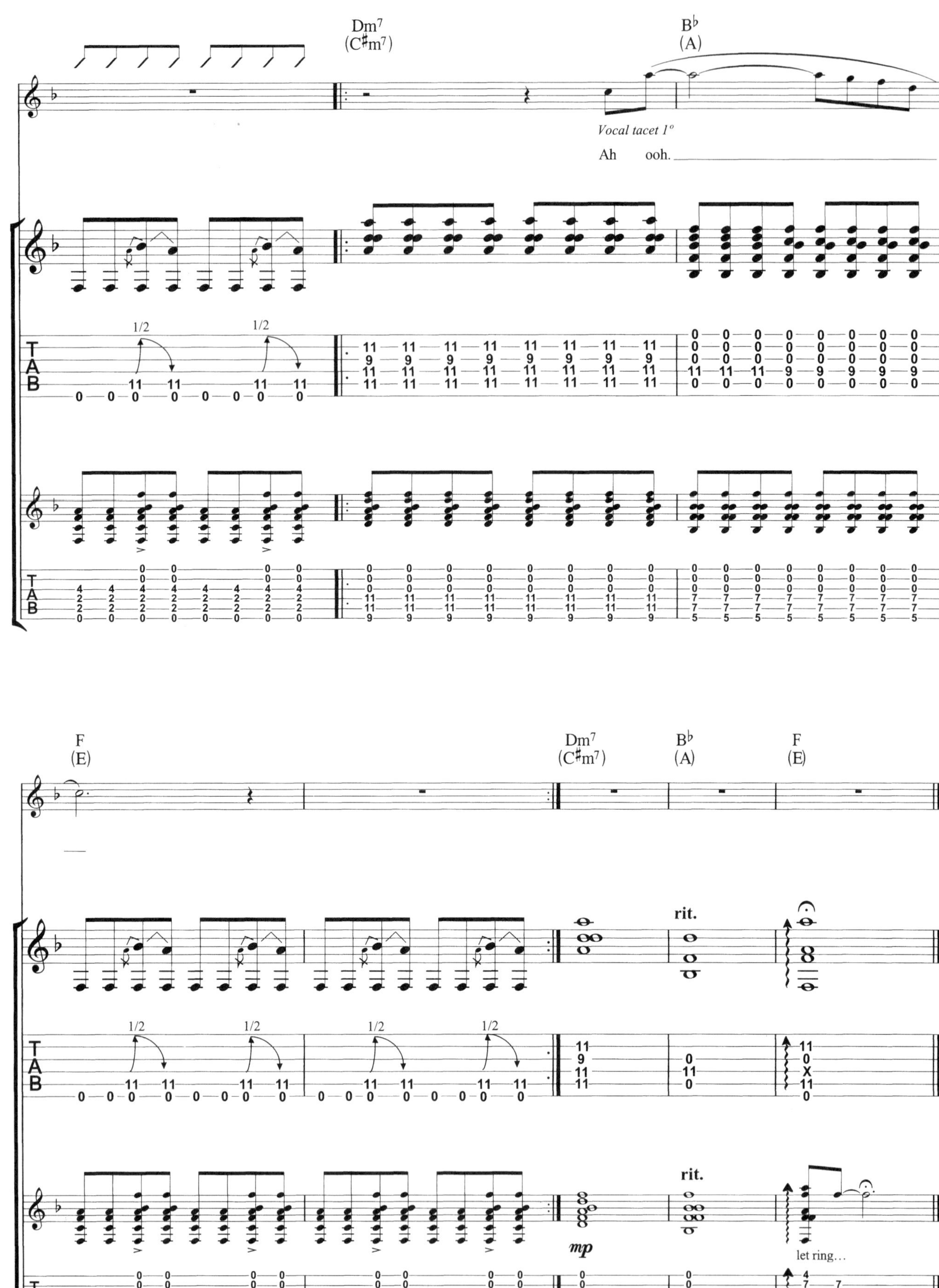

Dm7
(C♯m7)
B♭
(A)
Vocal tacet 1º
Ah ooh.
1/2
F
(E)
Dm7
(C♯m7)
B♭
(A)
F
(E)
rit.
mp
let ring…

from The Rolling Stones - *Exile on Main Street*

Shake Your Hips

Written by James Moore

Gtr. 1: Open G Tuning, Capo II

①= D ④= D

②= B ⑤= G

③= G ⑥= D

Gtr. 2: Standard Tuning

Intro

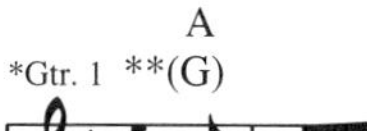

A

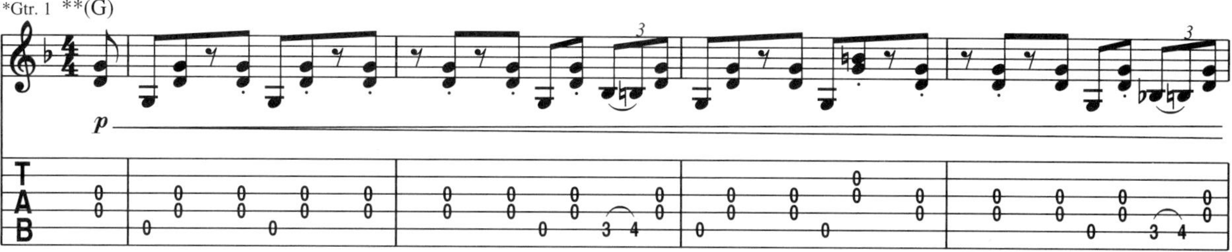

*Plucked w/ fingers or flatpick/ fingers combination. Key signature denotes Dorian mode.

**Symbols in parenthesis represent chord names respective to capoed guitar.
Symbols above represent actual sounding chords.

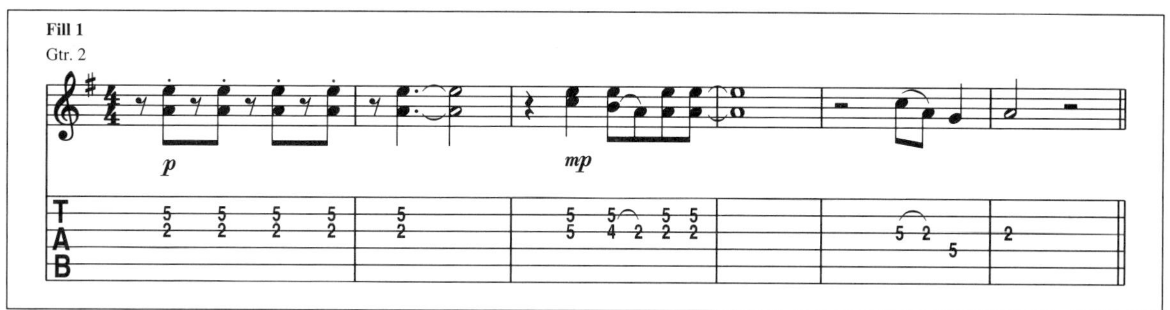

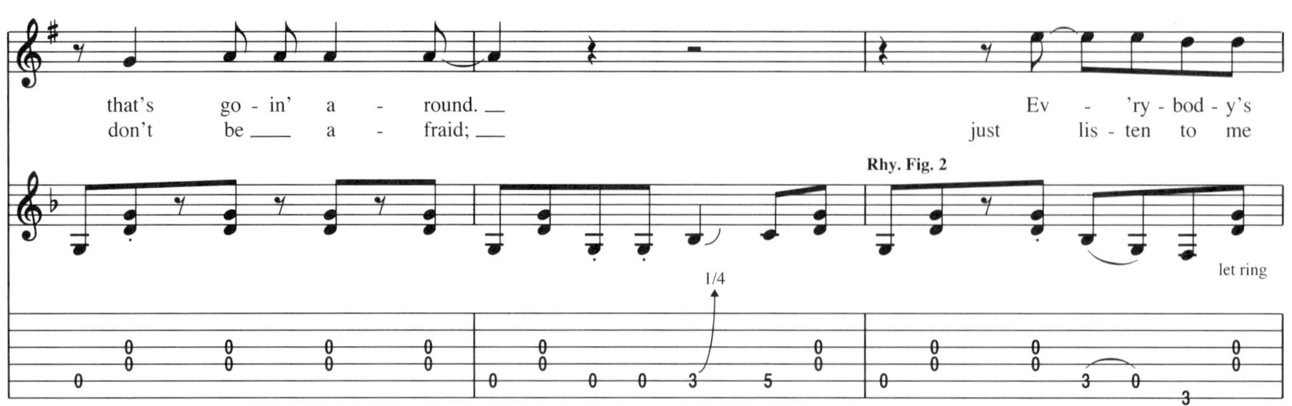

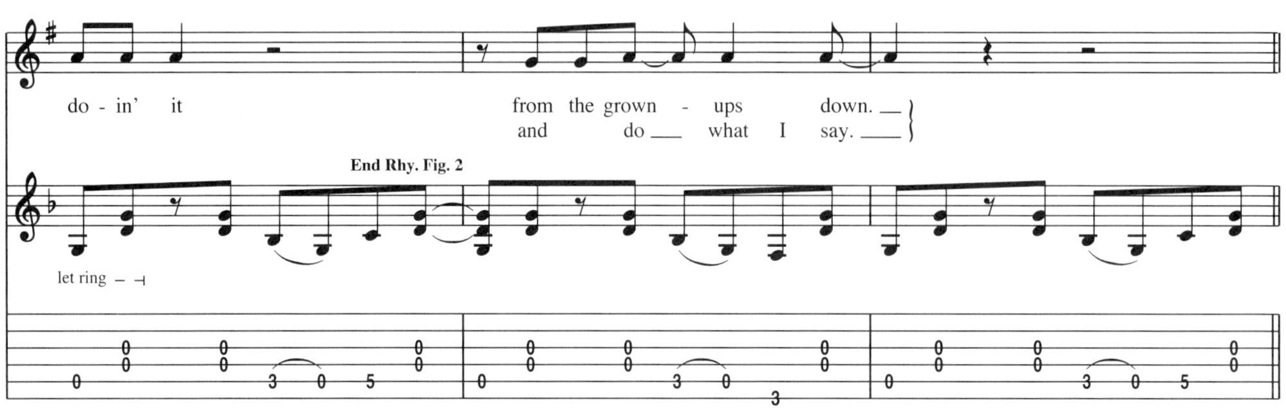

Gtr. 1: w/ Rhy. Fig. 2, 5 times

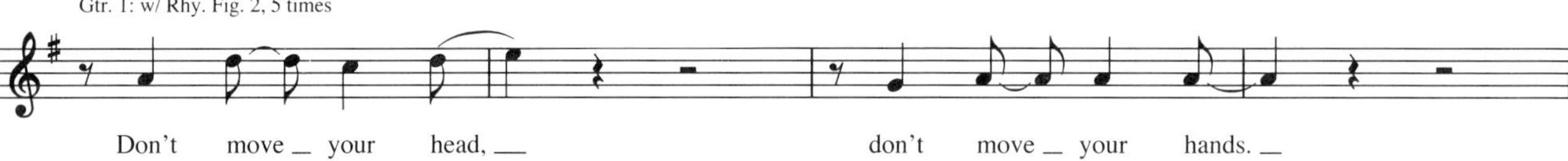

Gtr. 1: w/ Rhy. Fill 1, 2nd time

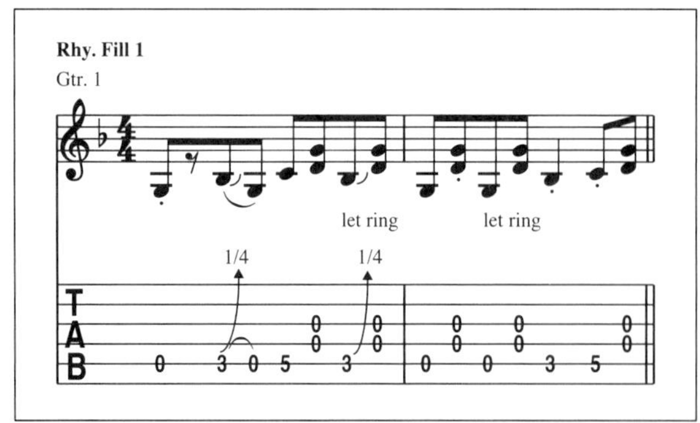

Chorus

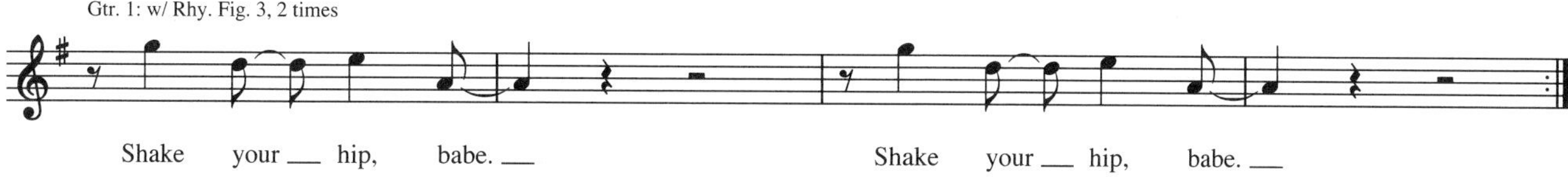

Interlude

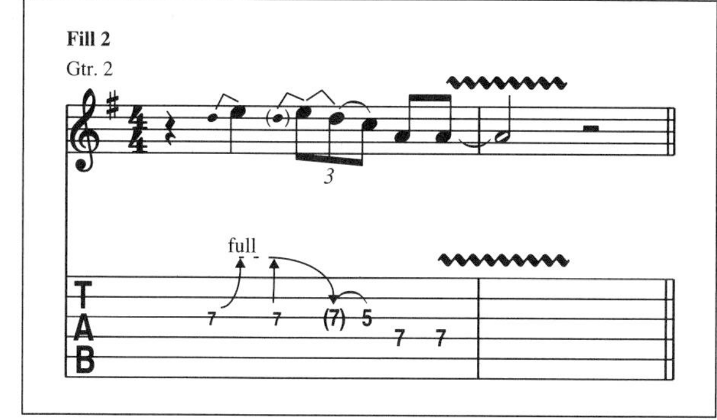

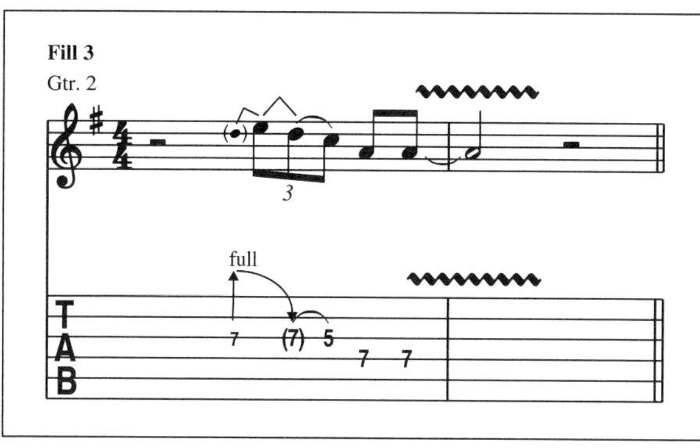

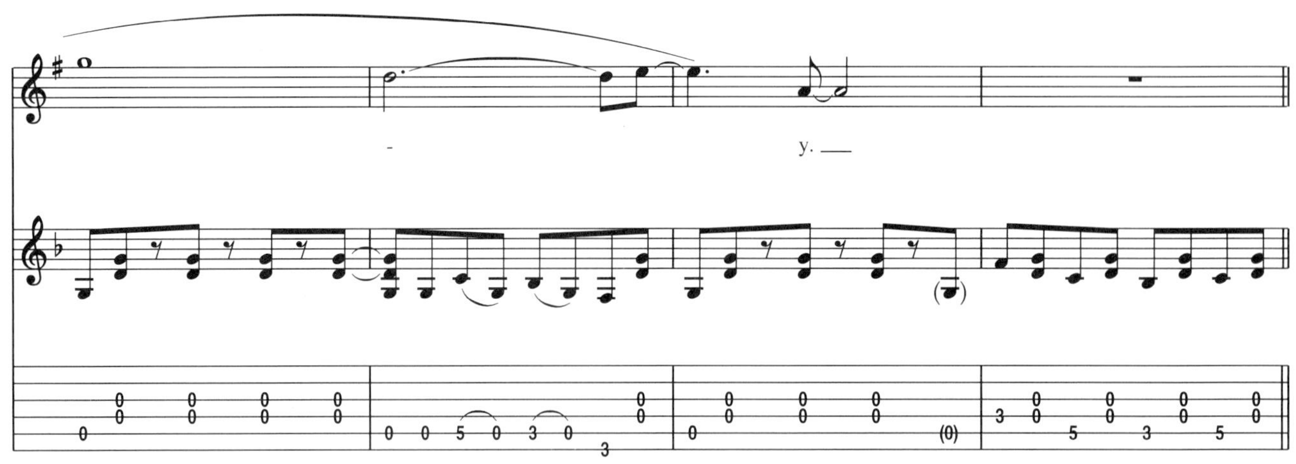
y.

Guitar Solo

Gtr. 2
mf
grad. bend
full
1/4
1/4
Gtr. 1
1/4

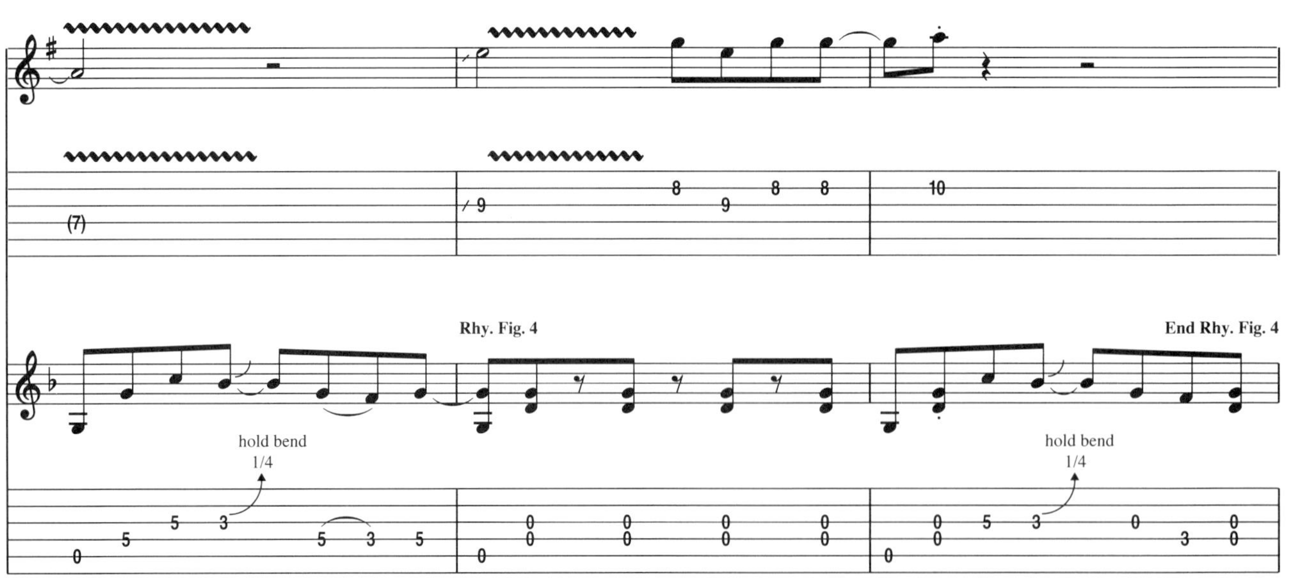
Rhy. Fig. 4
End Rhy. Fig. 4
hold bend
1/4
hold bend
1/4

Gtr. 1: w/ Rhy. Fig. 4, 2 times
full
full
full
Gtr. 1: w/ Fill 2
Verse
Gtr. 2 tacet
3. Well, I met a lit-tle girl
Gtr. 1
full
1/4
in a coun-try town.
She said, "What do you know,
1/4
1/4
1/4
Pre-Chorus
there's Slim Har-po!"
Did-n't move her head,
Rhy. Fill 2
Gtr. 1
1/4
T
A
B

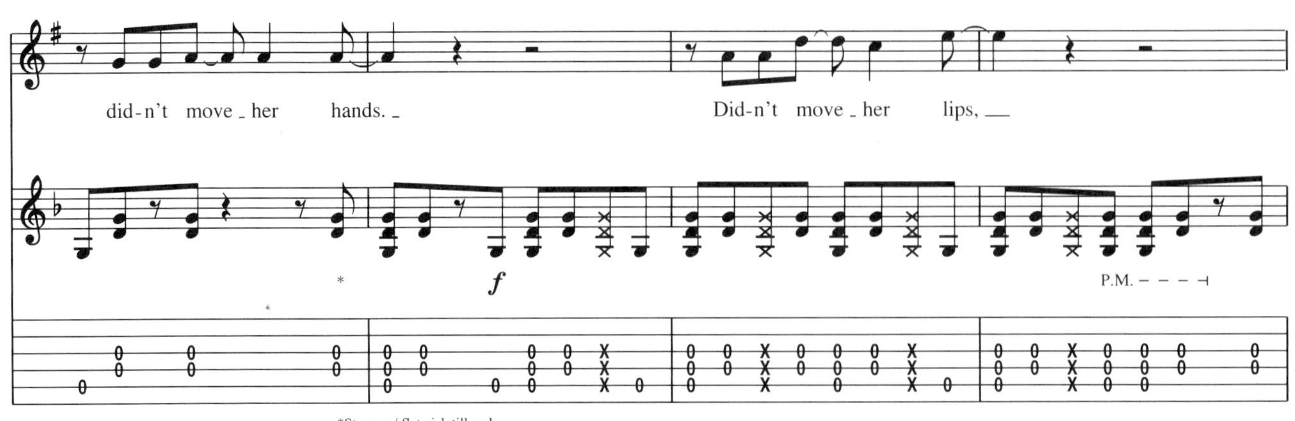

Chorus

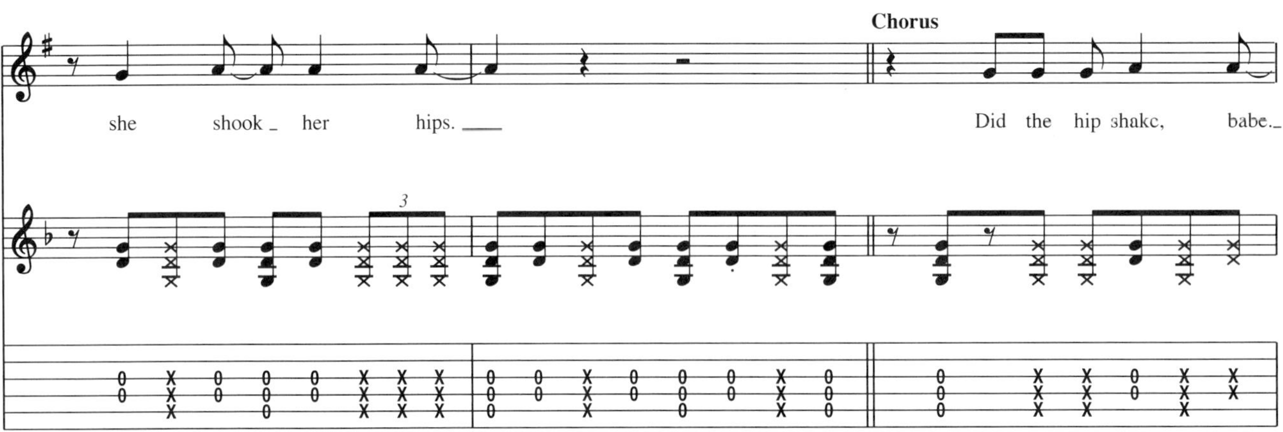

Gtr. 2: w/ Fill 2, 4 times

Gtr. 1: w/ Rhy. Fig. 5, 2 times

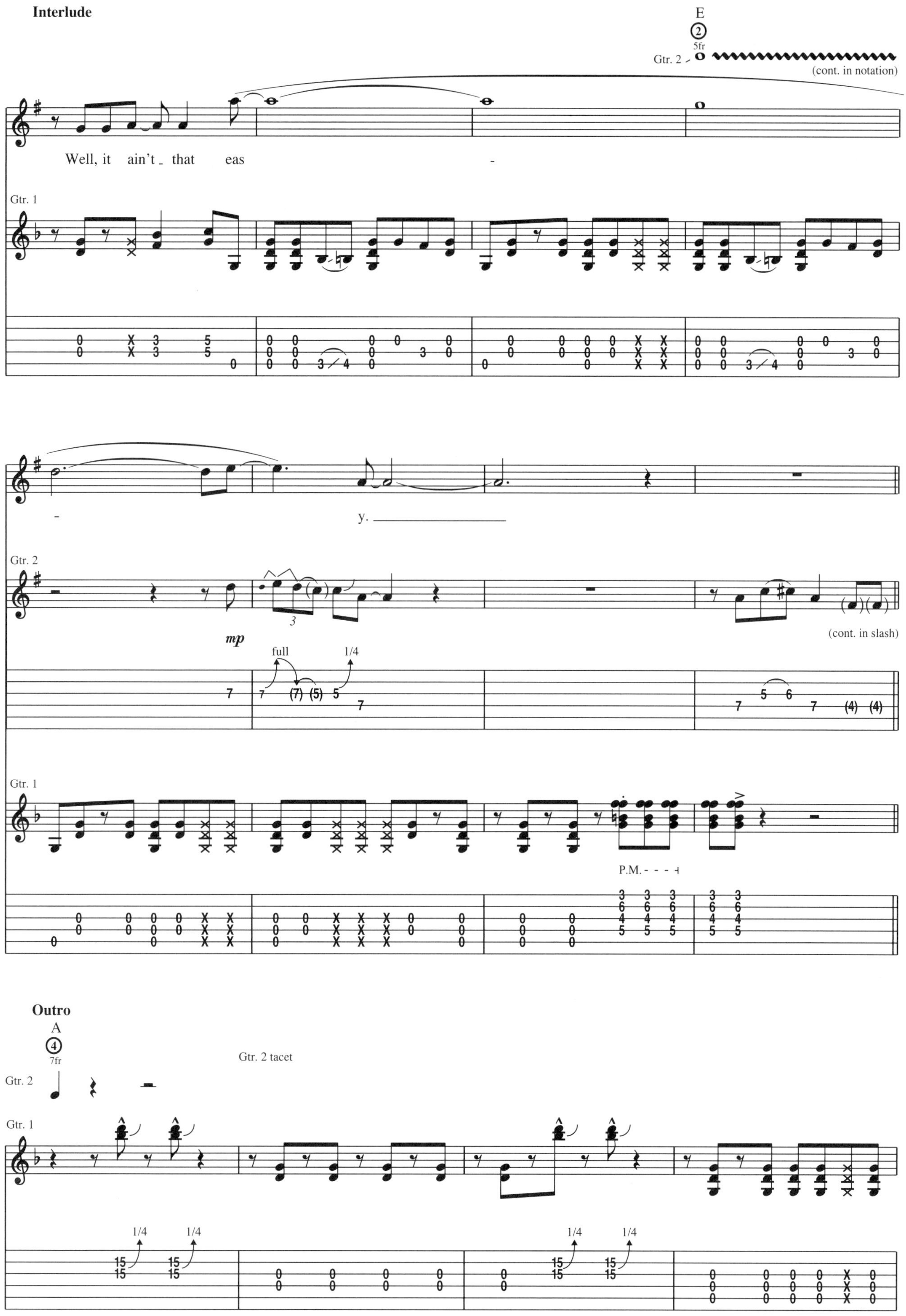

Interlude

E

(2) 5fr

Gtr. 2

(cont. in notation)

Well, it ain't _ that eas - - y. ____

Gtr. 1

Gtr. 2

mp

full 1/4

(cont. in slash)

Gtr. 1

P.M. - - - ┤

Outro

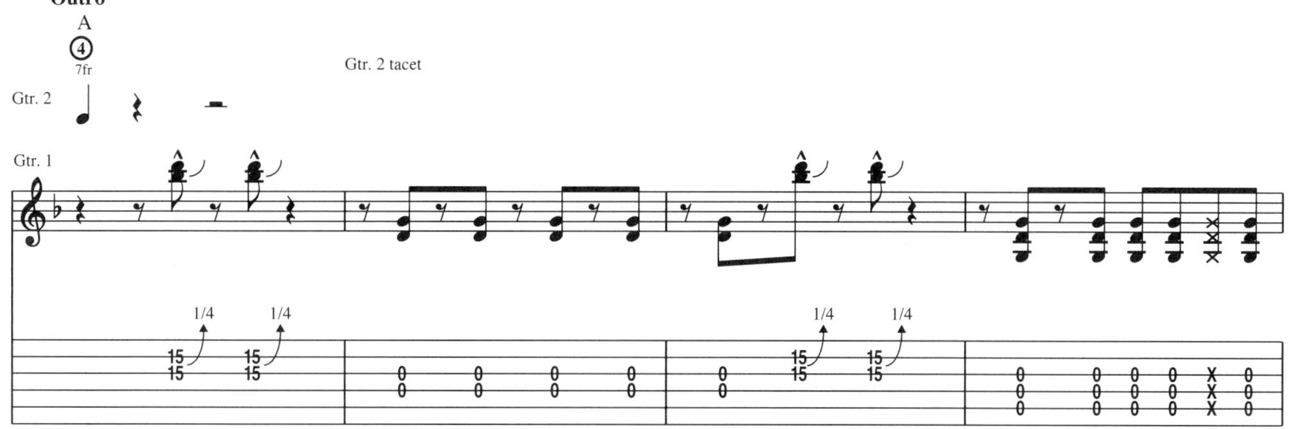

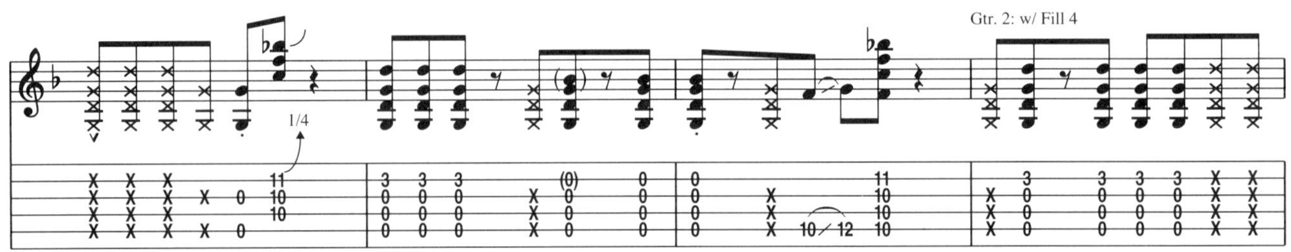
Gr. 2: w/ Fill 4
1/4

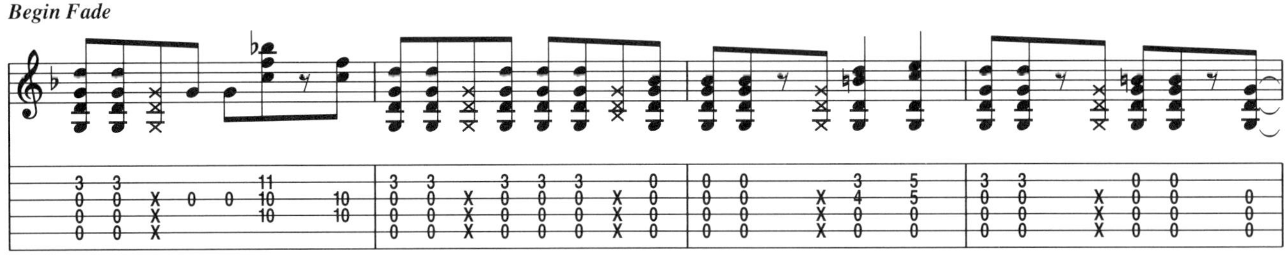
Begin Fade

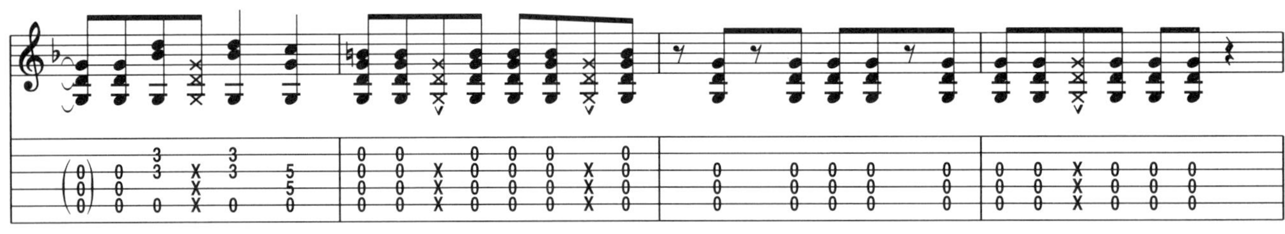

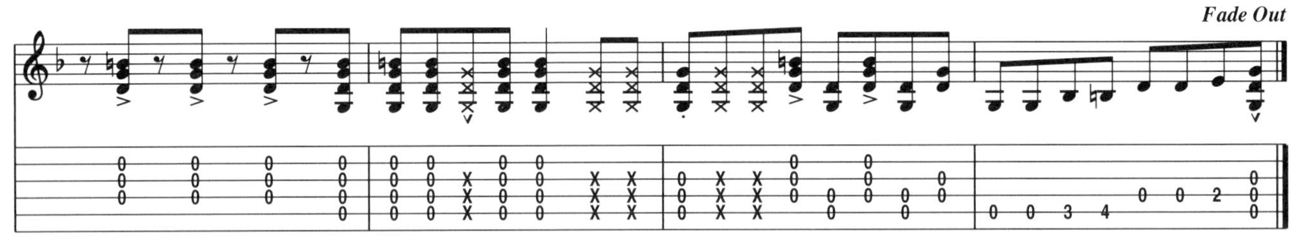
Fade Out

Fill 4
Gtr. 2
T
A
B

from Kiss - *Love Gun*

Shock Me

Words and Music by Ace Frehley

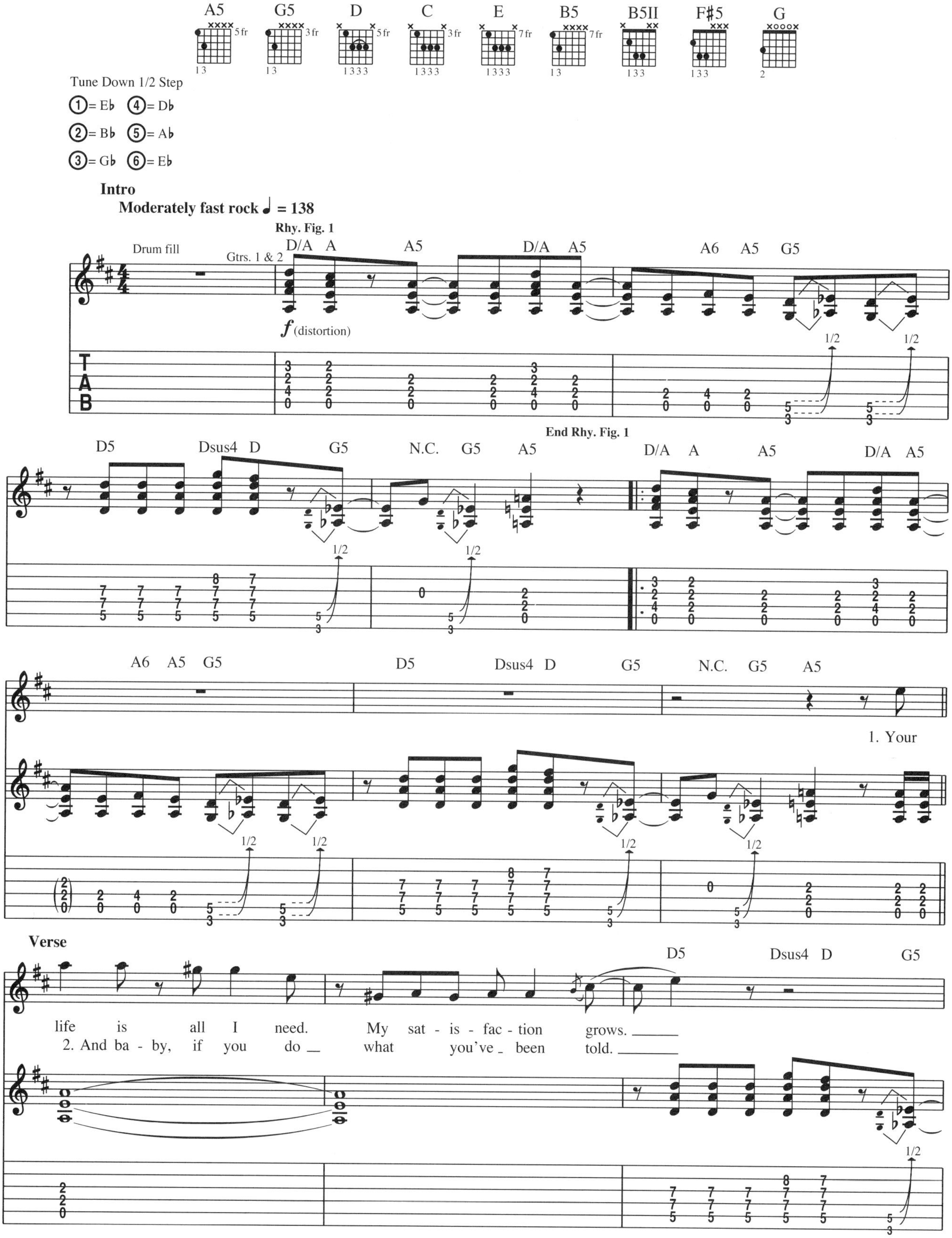

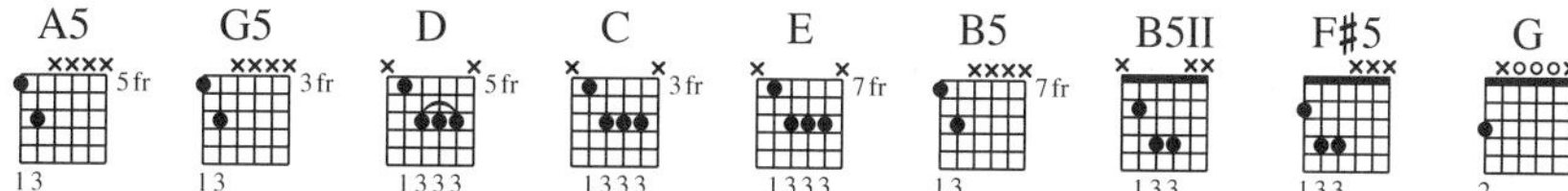

Tune Down 1/2 Step

(1)= E♭ (4)= D♭

(2)= B♭ (5)= A♭

(3)= G♭ (6)= E♭

Intro

Moderately fast rock ♩ = 138

Rhy. Fig. 1 · Drum fill · Gtrs. 1 & 2 · D/A A A5 D/A A5 · A6 A5 G5 · *f* (distortion) · 1/2 · D5 Dsus4 D G5 N.C. G5 A5 · End Rhy. Fig. 1 · D/A A A5 D/A A5 · A6 A5 G5 · D5 Dsus4 D G5 N.C. G5 A5

1. Your

Verse

D5 Dsus4 D G5

life is all I need. My sat - is - fac - tion grows. ______
2. And ba - by, if you do _ what you've _ been told. ______

N.C. G5 A5
You make me feel at ease; you e - ven make me glow.
my in - su - la-tions gone. Girl, you make me o - ver load.
1/2

D5 Dsus4 D G5 N.C. G5 A5 N.C.
Pre-Chorus
A5 B5 A5 B5 A5 B5
Don't cut the pow - er on me.
Don't pull the plug on me,
1/2 1/2

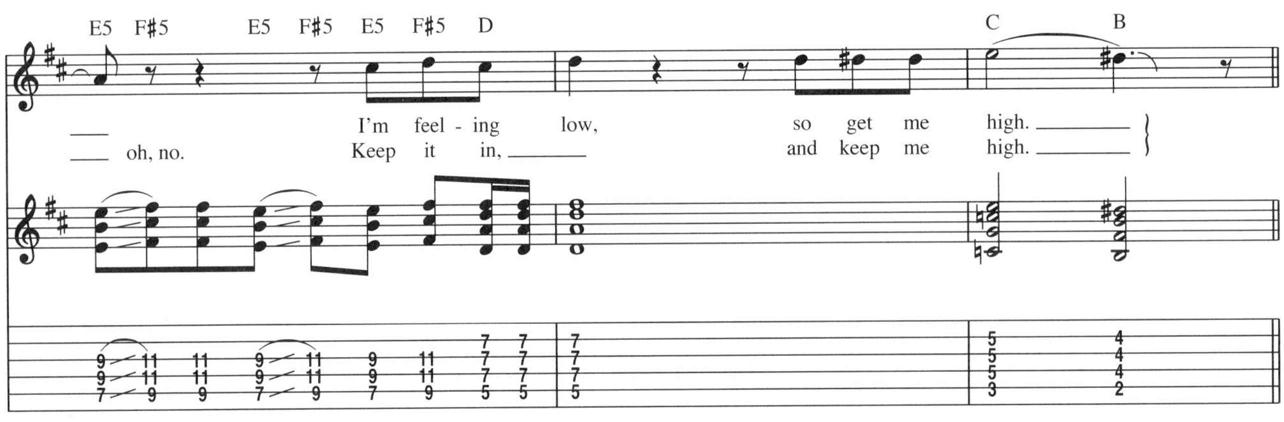
E5 F#5 E5 F#5 E5 F#5 D C B
I'm feel - ing low, so get me high.
oh, no. Keep it in, and keep me high.

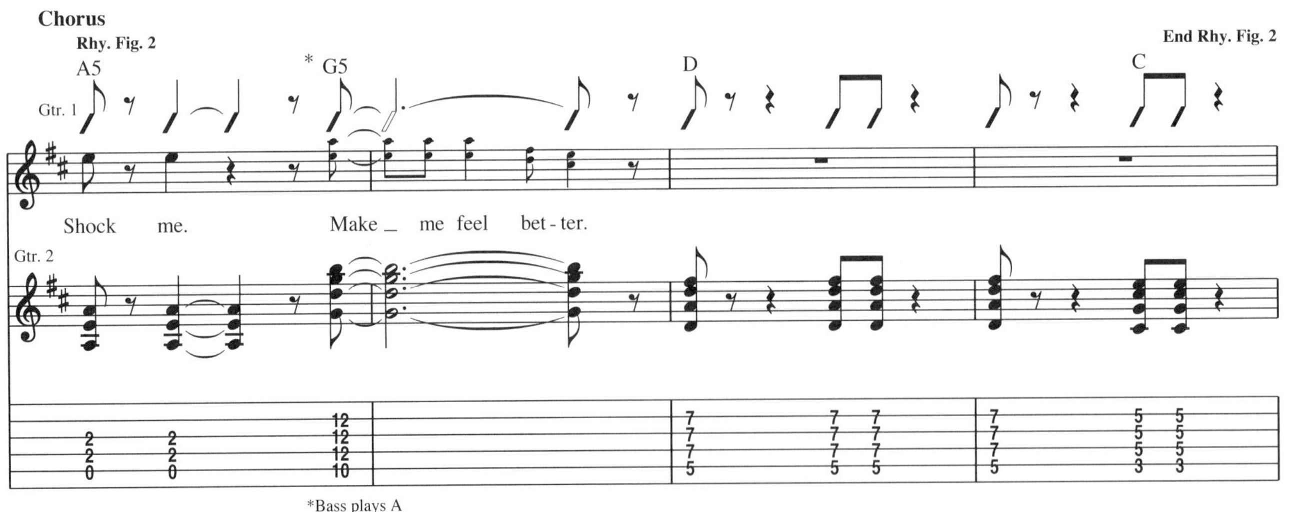
Chorus
Rhy. Fig. 2
End Rhy. Fig. 2
A5 *G5 D C
Gtr. 1
Shock me. Make me feel bet - ter.
Gtr. 2
*Bass plays A

Gtr. 1: w/Rhy. Fig. 2, 1 1/2 times

Gtr. 2: w/Rhy. Fig. 3, 1st 2 bars

Gtr. 3: w/Fill 1, 2nd time only

Guitar Solo

Gtrs. 1 & 2: w/Rhy. Fig. 1, 4 times

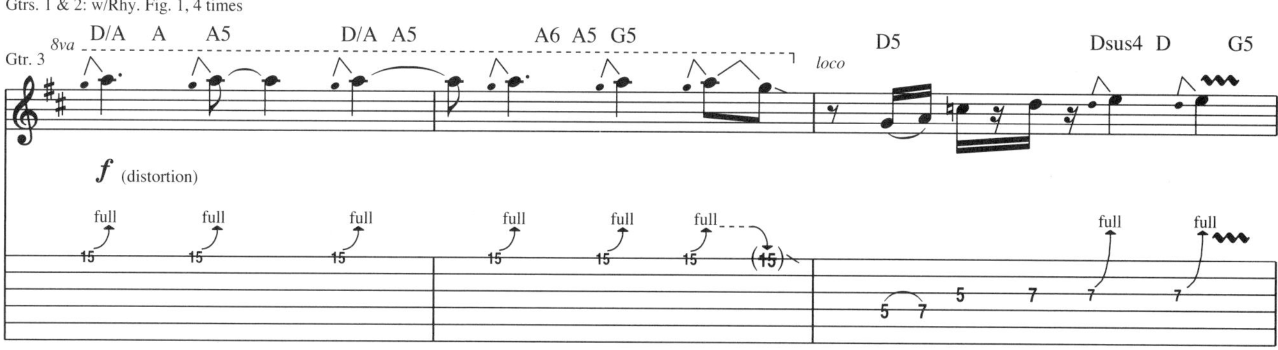

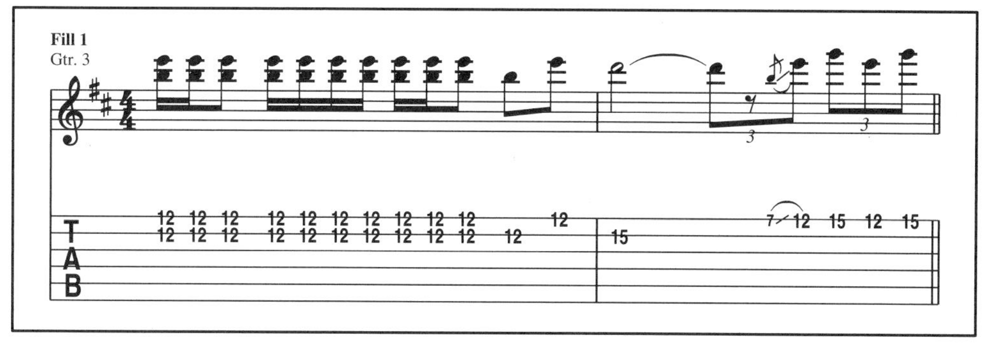

N.C. G5 A5 D/A A A5 D/A A5
full
A6 A5 G5 D5 Dsus4 D G5
N.C. G5 A5 D/A A A5 D/A A5
8va
P.H.
1/2
1 1/2
(8va)
A6 A5 G5 D5 Dsus4 D G5
P.H.
full
(8va)
N.C. G5 A5 D/A A A5 D/A A5
full
(8va)
A6 A5 G5 D5 Dsus4 D G5
1/4
full

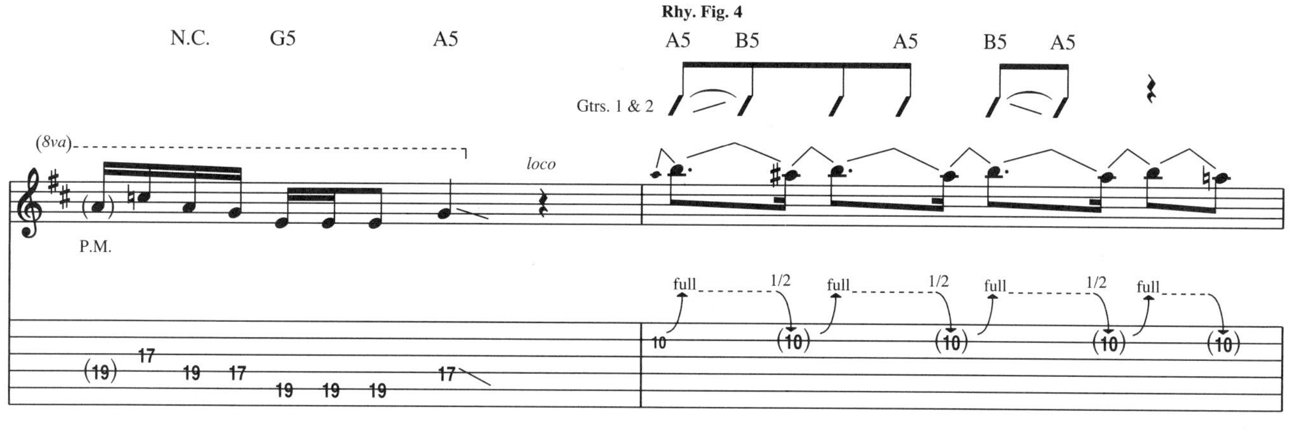
Rhy. Fig. 4
N.C. G5 A5
A5 B5 A5 B5 A5
Gtrs. 1 & 2
(8va)
loco
P.M.
full 1/2 full 1/2 full 1/2 full

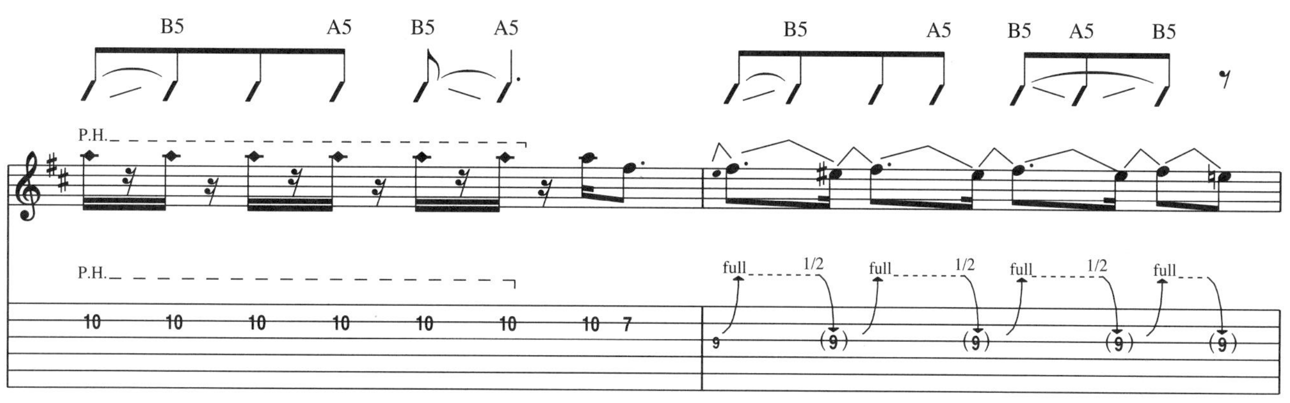
B5 A5 B5 A5
B5 A5 B5 A5 B5
P.H.
P.H.
full 1/2 full 1/2 full 1/2 full

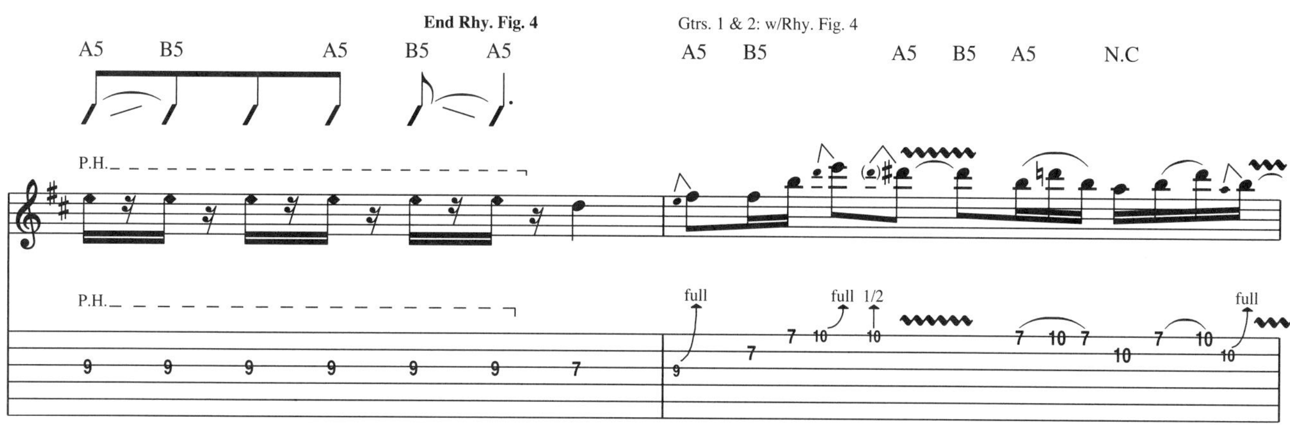
End Rhy. Fig. 4
Gtrs. 1 & 2: w/Rhy. Fig. 4
A5 B5 A5 B5 A5
A5 B5 A5 B5 A5 N.C
P.H.
P.H.
full
full 1/2
full

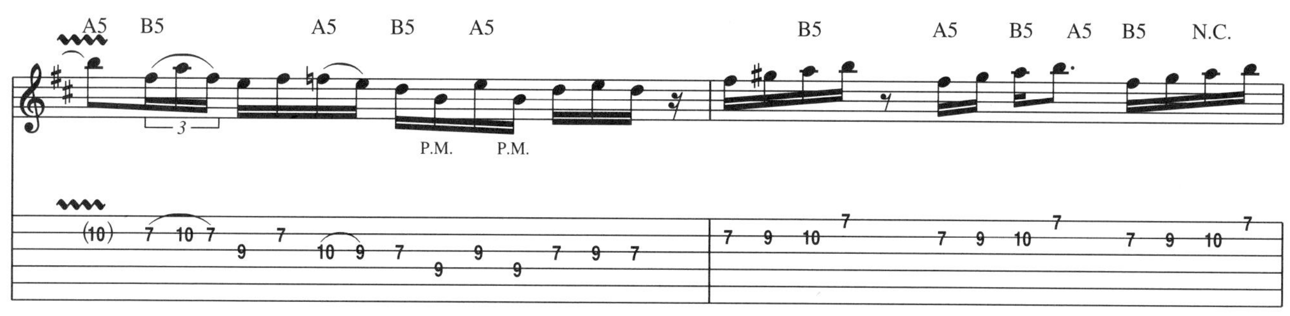
A5 B5 A5 B5 A5
B5 A5 B5 A5 B5 N.C.
3
P.M. P.M.

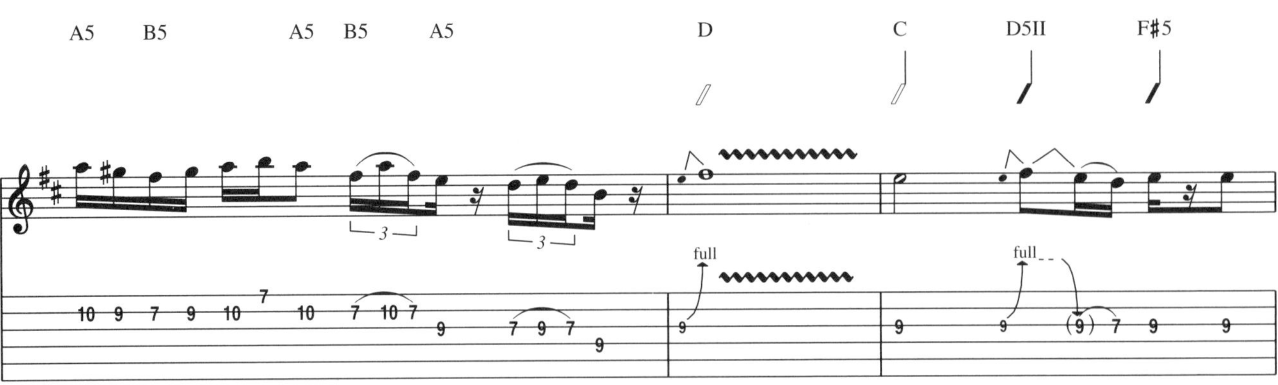
A5 B5 A5 B5 A5 D C D5II F♯5
full
full

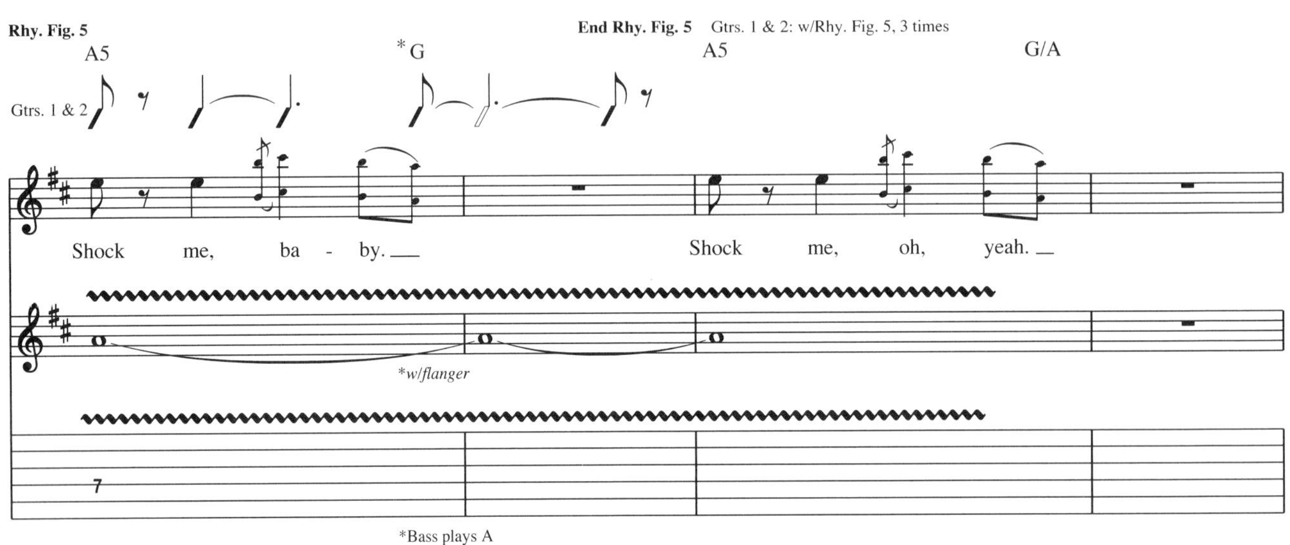
Rhy. Fig. 5
End Rhy. Fig. 5 Gtrs. 1 & 2: w/Rhy. Fig. 5, 3 times
A5 *G A5 G/A
Gtrs. 1 & 2
Shock me, ba - by.
Shock me, oh, yeah.
*w/flanger
*Bass plays A

A5 G/A A5 G/A
Shock me, ba - by.
Shock me, oh, yeah.

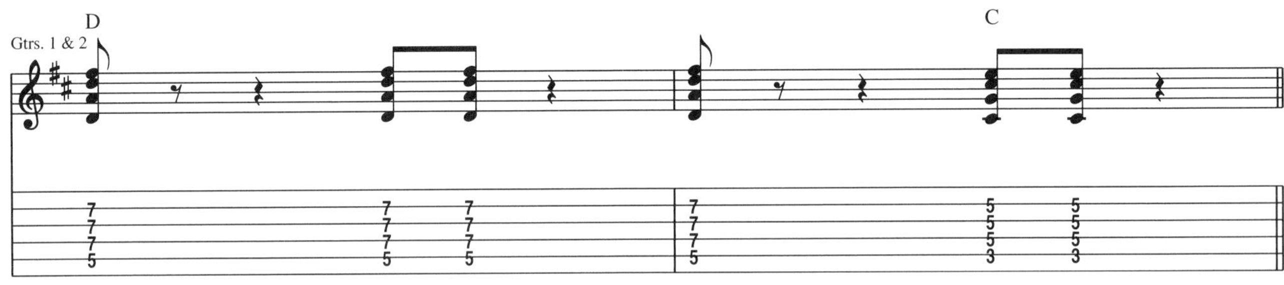
D C
Gtrs. 1 & 2

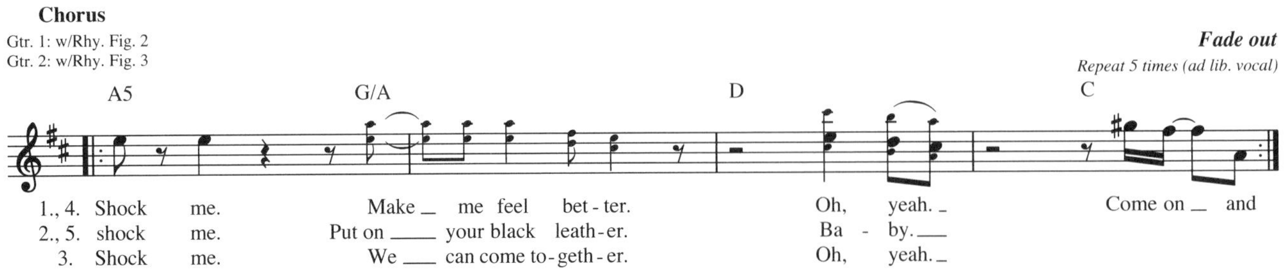
Chorus
Gtr. 1: w/Rhy. Fig. 2
Gtr. 2: w/Rhy. Fig. 3
Fade out
Repeat 5 times (ad lib. vocal)
A5 G/A D C
1., 4. Shock me. Make me feel bet - ter. Oh, yeah. Come on and
2., 5. shock me. Put on your black leath - er. Ba - by.
3. Shock me. We can come to - geth - er. Oh, yeah.

from Mötley Crüe - *Shout at the Devil*

Shout at the Devil

Words and Music by Nikki Sixx

1st Verse
Gtrs. I&II Rhy. Fig. 2
D5 C5 A5 C5 D5 C5 A5 (end Rhy. Fig. 2)
He's the wolf scream - in', lone - ly in the night. He's the blood stain on the stage. He's the
*On D.S., this chord is tied from previous bar.
w/Rhy. Fig. 2 (2 times)
tear in your eye; been tempt - ed by his lie. He's the knife in your back, he's rage! Well, he's the
raz - or to the knife. Oh, lone - ly in our lives. My head's spin - nin' 'round and round. But in the
2nd time to Coda
C G/B
sea - sons of with - er, you stand and de - liv - er, be strong and love my wom - an!
Gtrs. I&II
Chorus
w/Rhy. Fig. 1
N.C. C5 N.C. D5 N.C. C5 N.C.
Shout! Shout! Shout! Shout at the dev - il! Shout! Shout! Shout! He'll be the
w/Rhy. Fill 1
2nd Verse
w/Rhy. Fig. 2 (3 times)
love in your eyes, he'll be the blood bet - ween your thighs, and then he'll have you cry for more. He'll put your
strength to the test, he'll put the thrill back in bed. I'm sure you've heard it all be - fore. He'll be the
Rhy. Fill 1
Gtr. II
Gtr. I
(Gtr. I only)

D5
C5
A5
C5
D5
C5
A5
risk in the kiss, might be an - ger on your lips, might run scared for the door! But in the
w/Rhy. Fill 1
D5
C5
A5
C5
G/B
Chorus
w/Rhy. Fig. 1
N.C.
C5
N.C.
D5
sea - sons of with - er, we'll stand and de - liv - er, be strong and laugh and... shout! Shout!
N.C.
C5
N.C.
C5
N.C.
D5
w/Rhy. Fill 3
N.C.
C5
D5
C5
Shout! Shout at the dev - il! Shout! Shout! Shout! Shout at the dev - il!
Guitar solo
w/Fill 1
E5
Gtr. III
Full
Full
Full
N.C.
f
Gtrs.
I&II
P.M.
Rhy. Fill 2
P
Rhy. Fill 3
Fill 1
Gtr. IV
mf
Full
Full
Full

E5
*1/2
1/2
3/4
Full
(trill
*Bends articulated by pulling up on stg.
w/r.h. immediately behind fretted position. Rapidly
pull & release stg. in succession for first five bends.
D.S. al Coda
N.C.
w/Fill 2
Harm.
(8va)
sl.
A.H.
(15ma)
G5
G♯5A5 D5
hold
bend
A.H. pitch: C♯
P.M.
Fill 2
Gtr. IV

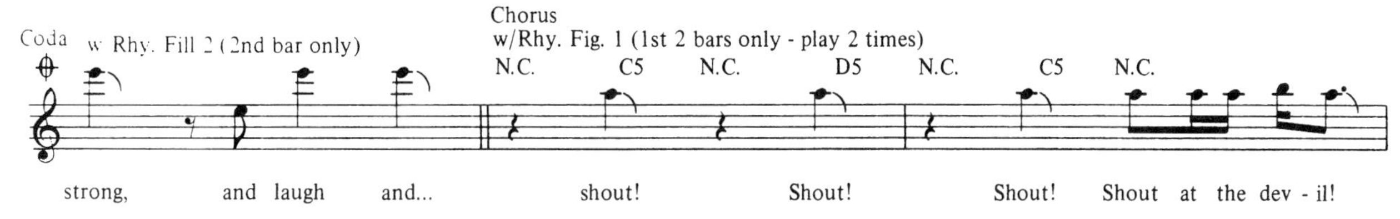
Coda
w/ Rhy. Fill 2 (2nd bar only)
Chorus
w/Rhy. Fig. 1 (1st 2 bars only - play 2 times)
N.C. C5 N.C. D5 N.C. C5 N.C.
strong, and laugh and... shout! Shout! Shout! Shout at the dev - il!

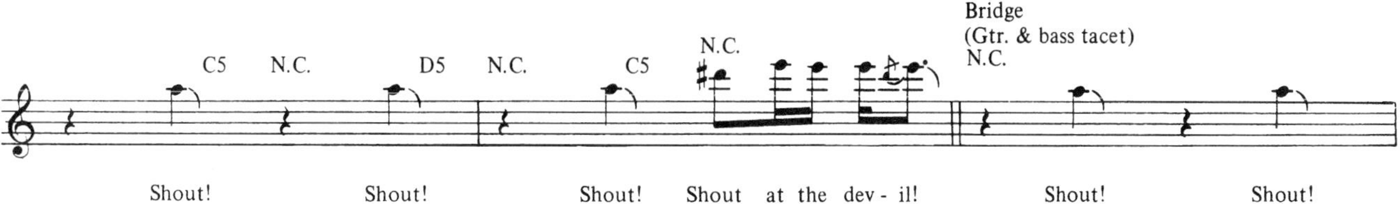
C5 N.C. D5 N.C. C5 N.C.
Bridge
(Gtr. & bass tacet)
N.C.
Shout! Shout! Shout! Shout at the dev - il! Shout! Shout!

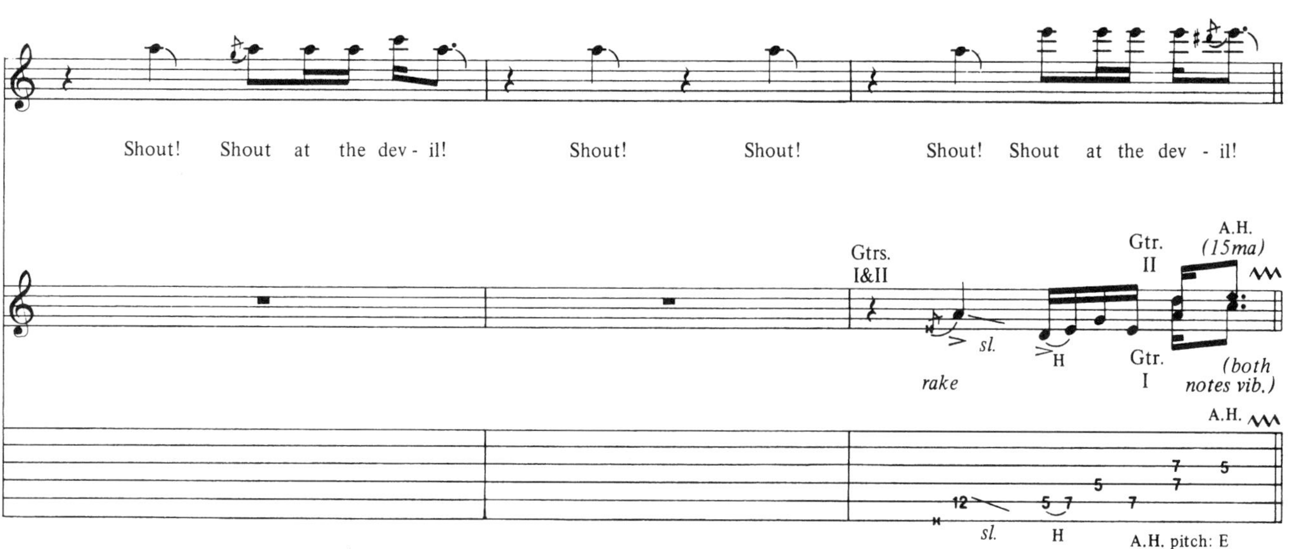
Shout! Shout at the dev - il! Shout! Shout! Shout! Shout at the dev - il!
Gtrs. I&II
Gtr. II
A.H.
(15ma)
rake
sl.
H
Gtr. I
(both notes vib.)
A.H.
12 5 7 5 7 7 7 5
A.H. pitch: E

Chorus
w/Rhy. Fig. 1 (1st 2 bars only - play 2 times)
N.C. C5 N.C. D5 N.C. C5 N.C. C5 N.C. D5 N.C. C5 N.C.
Shout! Shout! Shout! Shout at the dev - il! Shout! Shout! Shout! Shout at the dev - il!

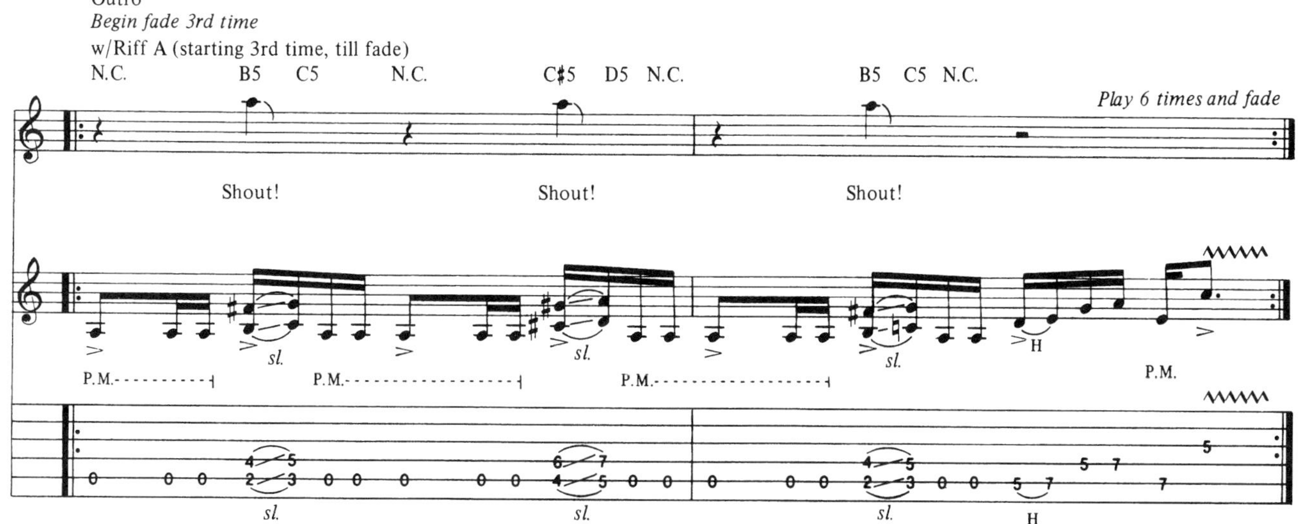
Outro
Begin fade 3rd time
w/Riff A (starting 3rd time, till fade)
N.C. B5 C5 N.C. C#5 D5 N.C. B5 C5 N.C.
Play 6 times and fade
Shout! Shout! Shout!
sl.
H
P.M.
P.M.
P.M.
P.M.

from Rainbow - *Down to Earth*

Since You've Been Gone

Words and Music by Russell Ballard

Em
Dsus2
C
G/B
A5
Dsus2
same time ev - 'ry night,
fall to the ground and I wake up.
End Riff A
let ring
G
D/F♯
Em
D5
C
*G/B
So I get out of bed, put on my shoes and in my head thoughts fly back to the
*Bass plays B.
Pre-Chorus
Asus2
Dsus2
**E♭
F
break up.
1. These four walls are clos - ing in.
2. Your poi - son let - ter, your tel - e - gram
w/ dist.
chorus off
**Chord symbols reflect overall harmony.
E♭
Dsus4/A
D
Look at the fix you put me in.
just goes to show you don't give a damn.
steady gliss.

Chorus

Gtr. 1: w/ Rhy. Fig. 1 (3 times)

Since you've been gone, __ since you've been gone, __ I'm out of my head, _ can't take __

__ it. Could I be wrong? _ But since you've been gone __

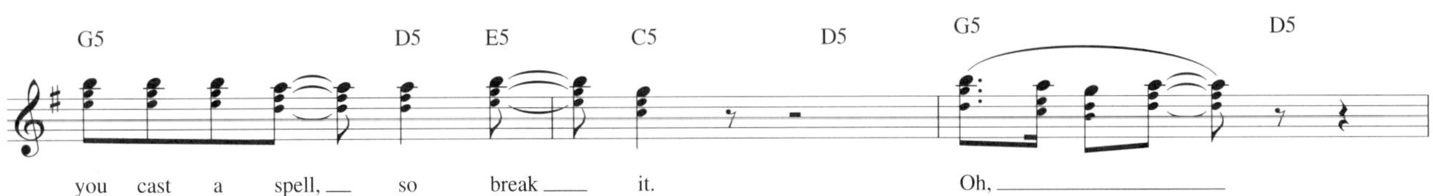

you cast a spell, __ so break __ it. Oh, __

To Coda ⊕

oh, __ oh, __ since you've been gone.

Verse

Gtr. 1: w/ Riff A (2 times)

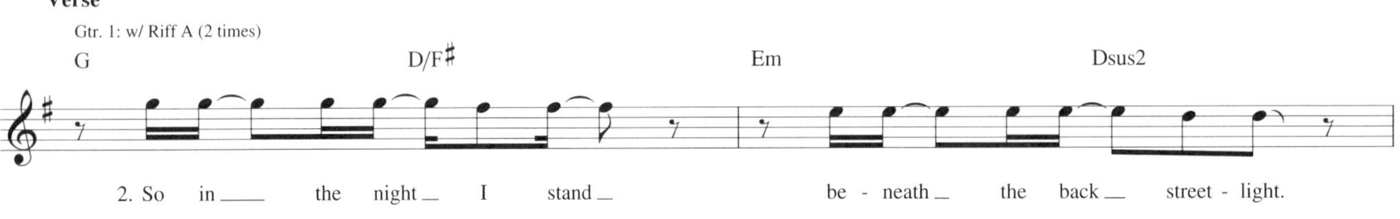

2. So in __ the night _ I stand _ be - neath _ the back _ street - light.

I read the words _ that _ you sent to me. __ I could take the af - ter - noon, but night -

D.S. al Coda

- time comes a - round too soon. _ You can't know what _ you mean to me. _

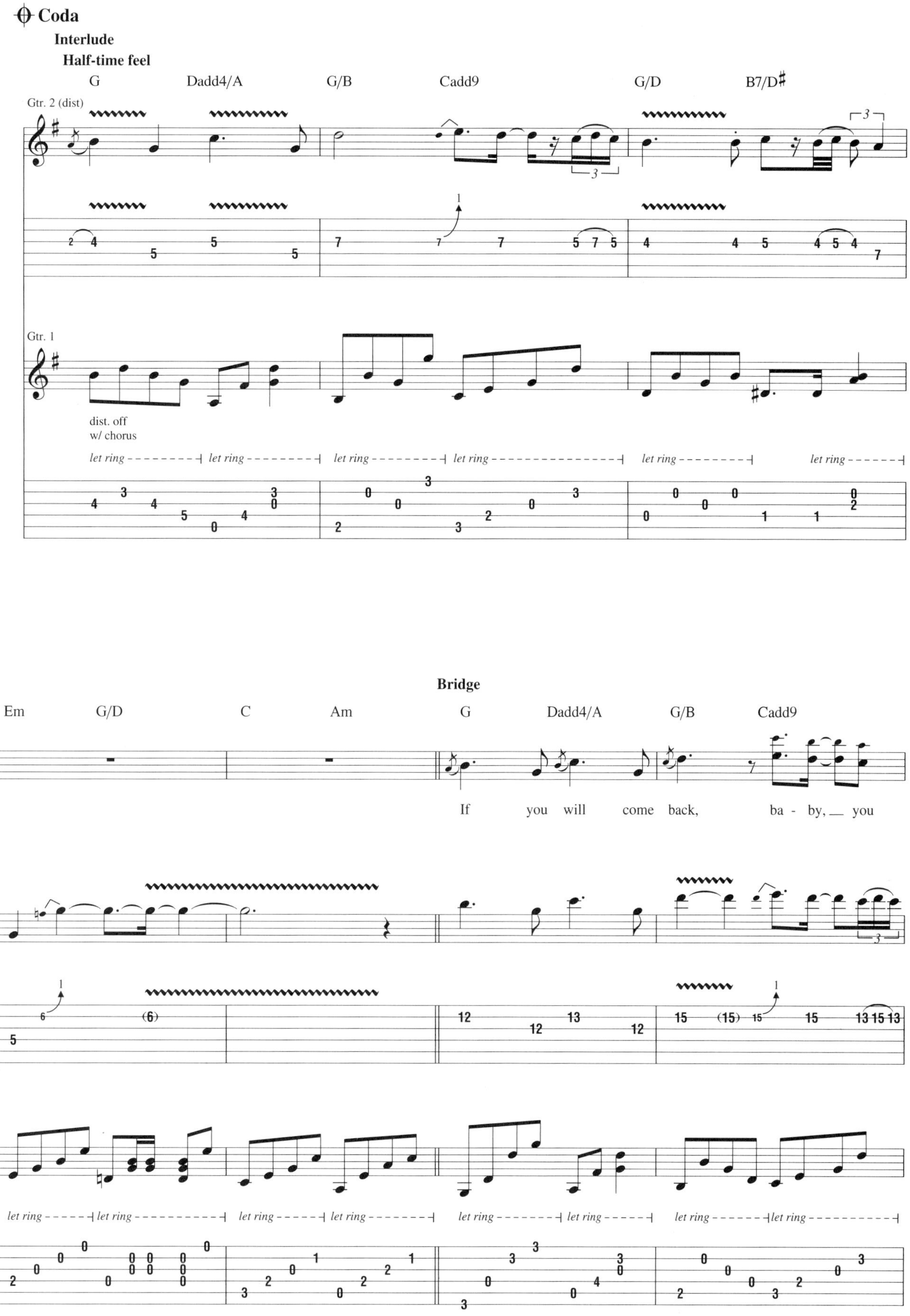

Coda

Interlude

Half-time feel

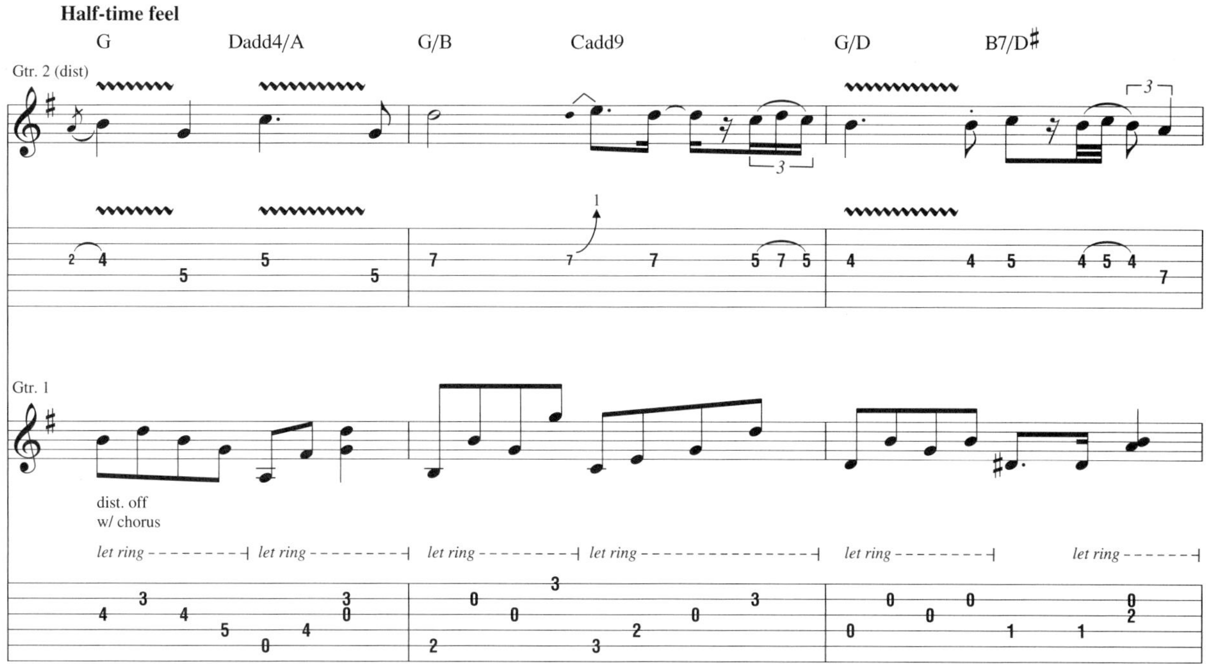

Bridge

Em G/D C Am G Dadd4/A G/B Cadd9

If you will come back, ba - by, you

let ring

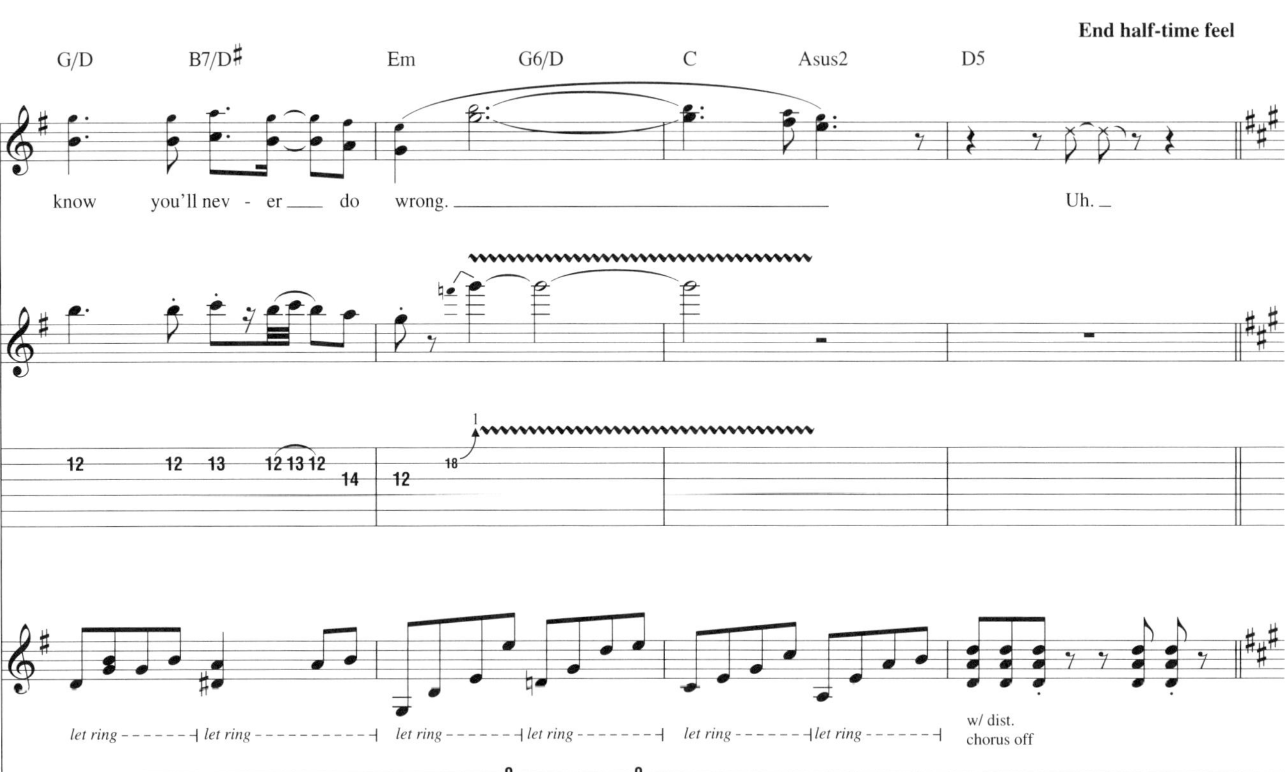
End half-time feel
G/D
B7/D♯
Em
G6/D
C
Asus2
D5
know you'll nev - er do wrong.
Uh.
let ring
w/ dist.
chorus off

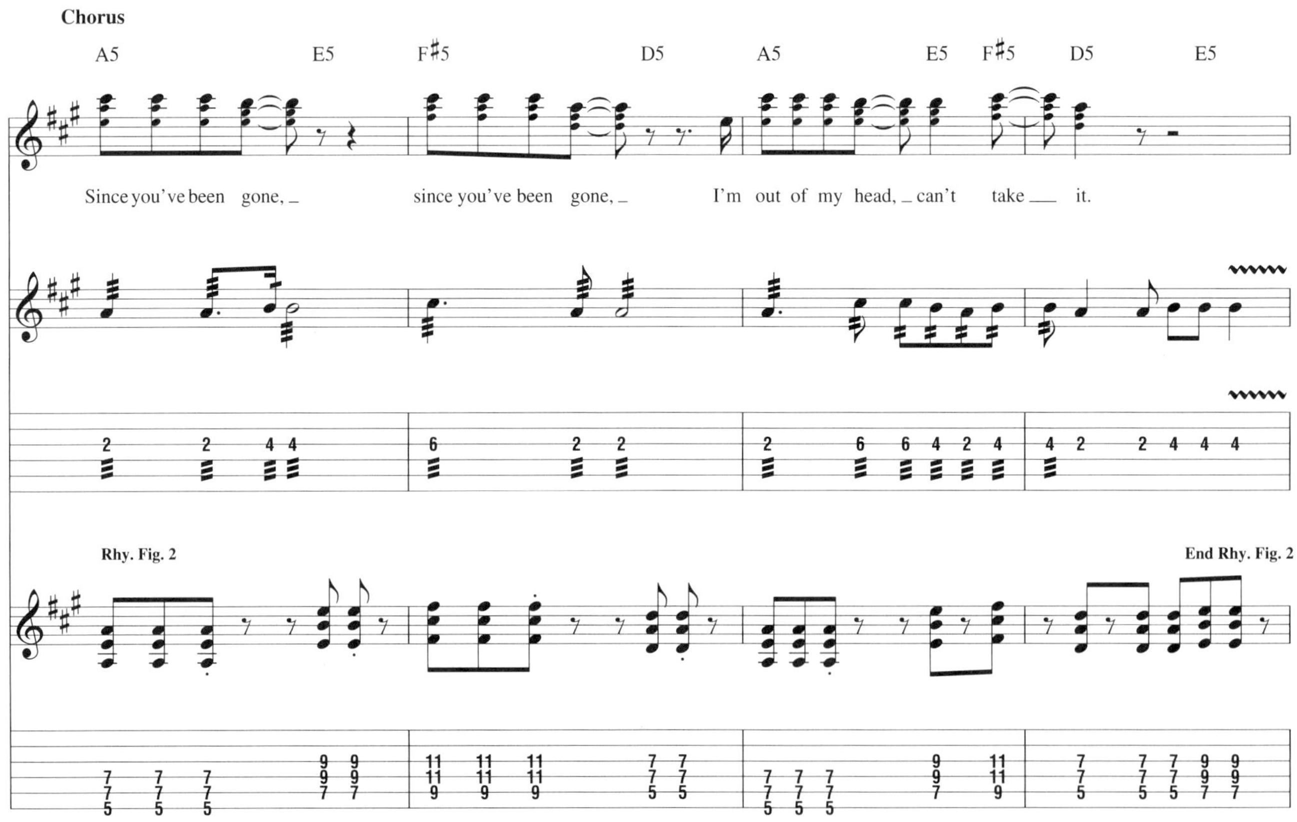
Chorus
A5
E5
F♯5
D5
Since you've been gone, since you've been gone, I'm out of my head, can't take it.
Rhy. Fig. 2
End Rhy. Fig. 2

Gtr. 1: w/ Rhy. Fig. 2
A5
E5
F#5
D5
A5
E5 F#5
D5
E5
Could I be wrong?
But since you've been gone
you cast a spell, so break it.
Gtr. 2
P.M.
A5
*E/G#
F#5
F5
**A5/E
E5
Oh,
oh,
(Oh.)
oh,
oh,
Gtr. 1
*Bass plays G#.
**Bass plays E.
F#5
F5
***A5/E
E
A
oh,
ev-er since you've been gone.
mf
P.M.
***Bass plays E.

Guitar Solo

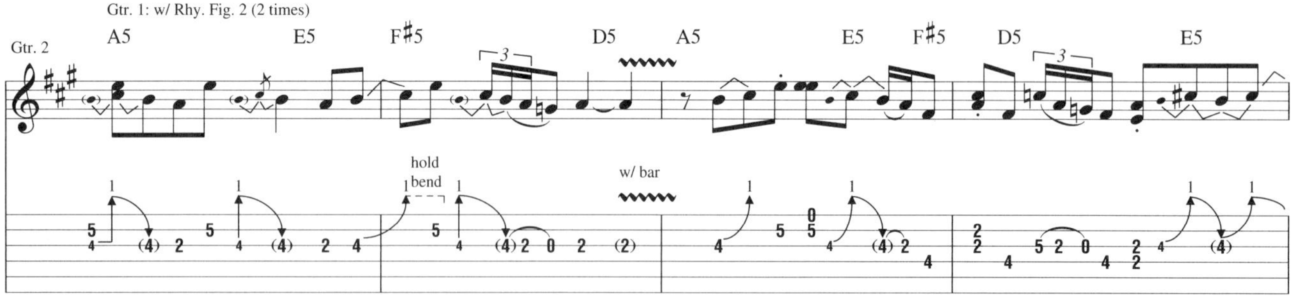

Outro-Chorus

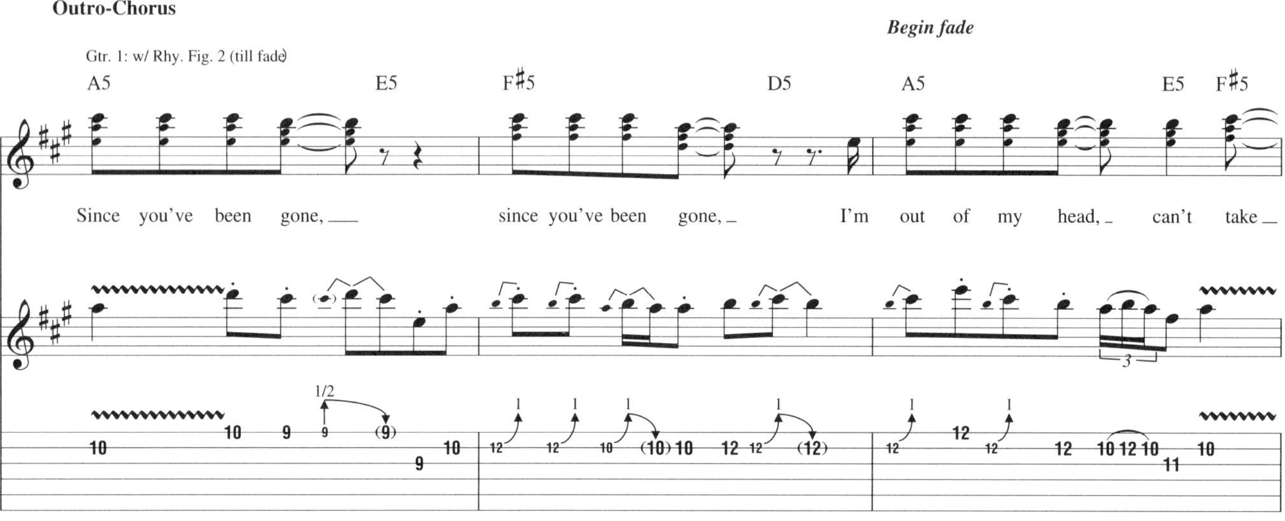

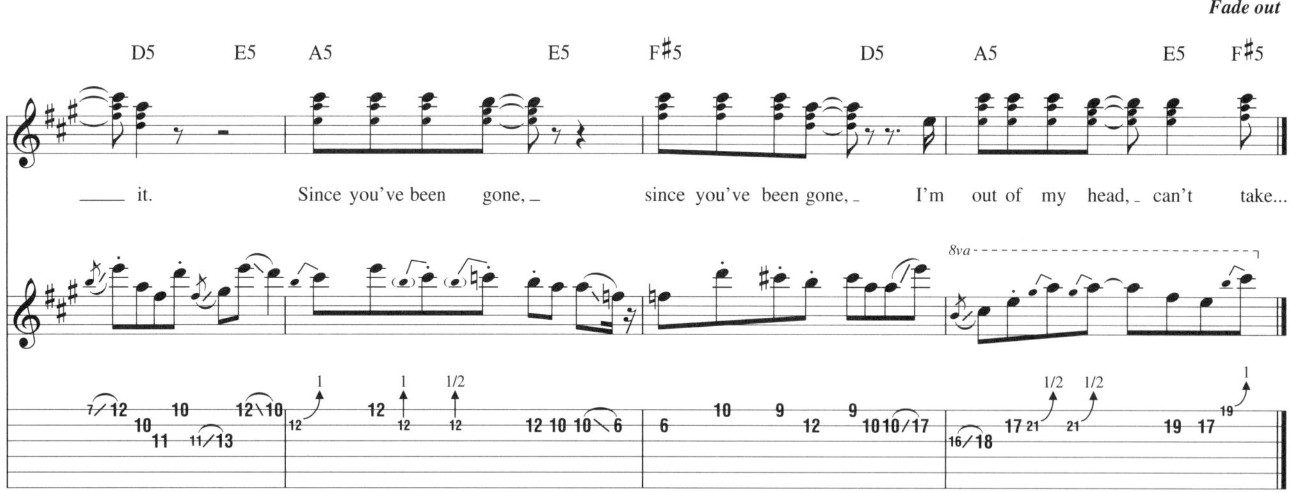

from Howlin' Wolf - *Moanin' in the Moonlight*

Smokestack Lightning

Words and Music by Chester Burnett

Tune up 1/4 step

†Chord symbol reflects implied harmony.

Verse

Gtrs. 2 & 3: w/ Riffs A1 & A2

1st time, Gtr. 2: w/ Riff A1 (5 times)
2nd & 3rd times, Gtr. 1: w/ Riff A (2 times)
Gtr. 3: w/ Riff A2 (6 times)
2nd & 3rd times, Gtr. 4: w/ Fill 1

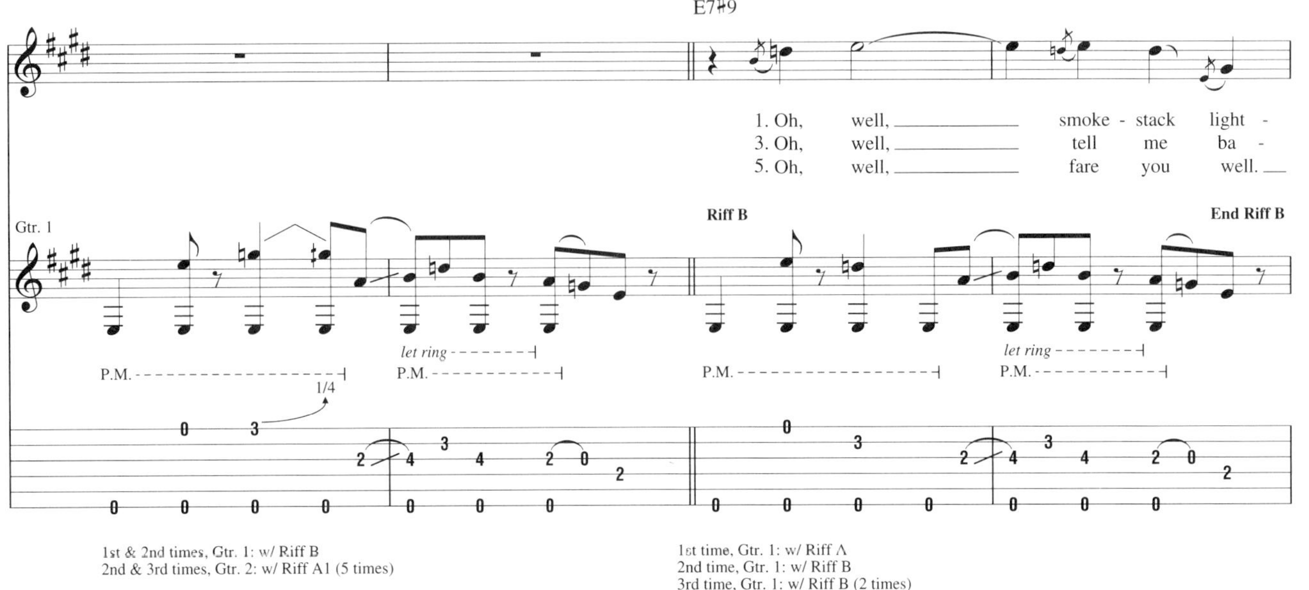

1st & 2nd times, Gtr. 1: w/ Riff B
2nd & 3rd times, Gtr. 2: w/ Riff A1 (5 times)

1st time, Gtr. 1: w/ Riff A
2nd time, Gtr. 1: w/ Riff B
3rd time, Gtr. 1: w/ Riff B (2 times)

1st time, Gtr. 1: w/ Riff B
2nd time, Gtr. 1: w/ Riff A (2 times)

1st & 3rd times, Gtr. 1: w/ Riff A (2 times)

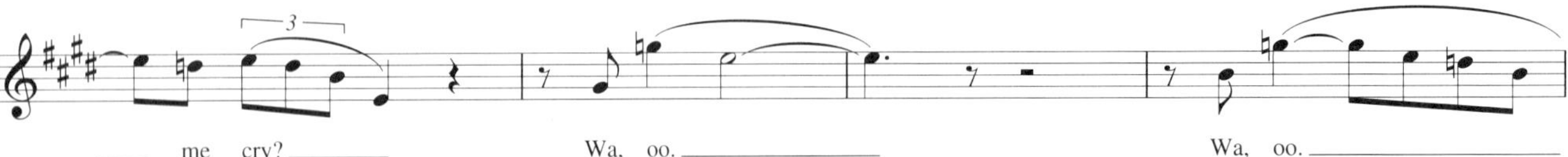

Interlude

2nd time, Gtr. 1: w/ Riff B

1st & 2nd times, Gtr. 1: w/ Riff B (2 times)
Gtr. 3: w/ Riff A2 (2 times)
2nd & 3rd times, Gtr. 2: w/ Riff A1 (2 times)
3rd time, Gtr. 1: w/ Riff A (2 times)

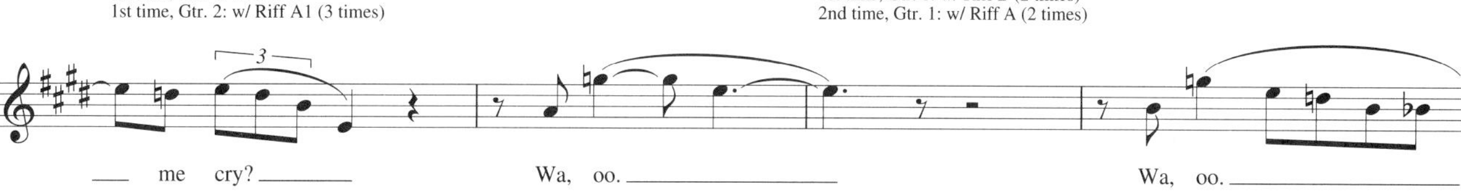

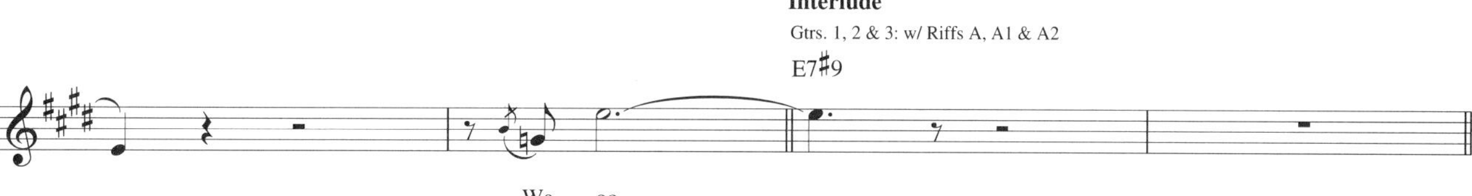

Harp Solo

Gtr. 1: w/ Riff B (3 times)
Gtr. 3: w/ Riff A2 (3 times)

E7♯9

Riff C — End Riff C — Riff D

*Gtr. 4

mp *mf*

*Harmonica arr. for gtr. Howlin' Wolf

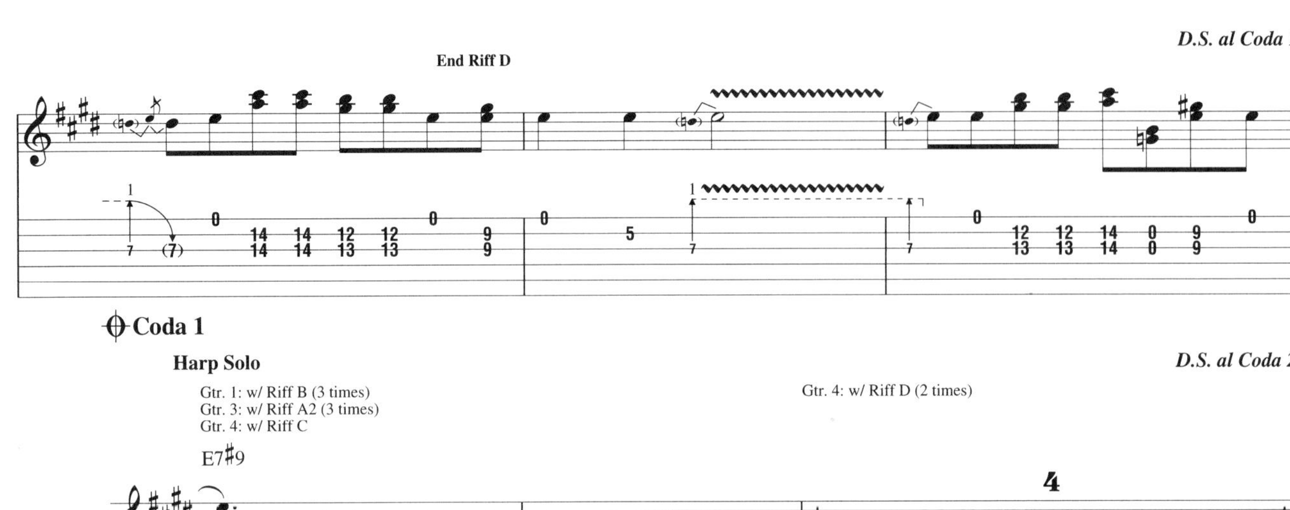

Coda 2

Verse

Gtr. 1: w/ Riff A
Gtr. 1: w/ Riff B (3 times)
Gtrs. 2 & 3: w/ Riffs A1 & A2 (7 times)

E7♯9

6. Oh, well, who been here, ba - by since a, I been gone?

Gtr. 1: w/ Riff A

Lit - tle, bit - ty boy, a der - by on? Wa, oo.

Gtr. 1: w/ Riff B
Gtr. 1: w/ Riff A
Begin fade

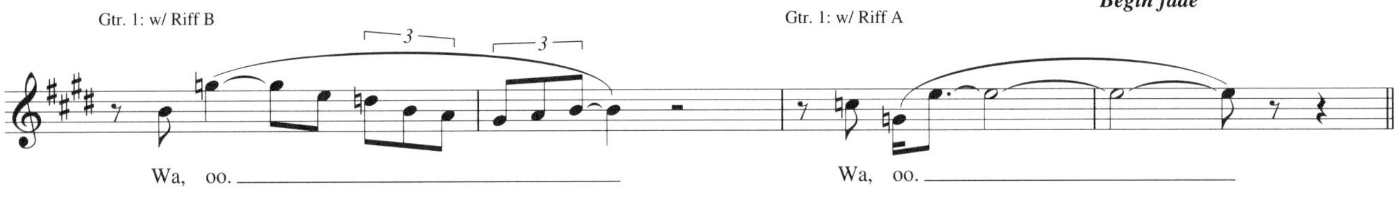

Wa, oo. Wa, oo.

Outro-Harp Solo

Gtr. 1: w/ Riff B (till fade)
Gtr. 3: w/ Riff A2 (till fade)

E7♯9

Fade out

from *Boston*

Smokin'

Words and Music by Tom Scholz and Brad Delp

To Coda
E5
D5
A5
E5
C5
G5
D5
off to - day.
feel O. K.
off to - day.
We'll pick
Get
We'll pick
you up and take you a - way.
Gtr. 1: w/ Rhy. Fig. 1
Gtr. 1: w/ Rhy. Fig. 2
A5
(Woo.)
Ah, get down to - night.
Chorus
A5
D5
C5
D5
A5
Smok - in', smok - in'. Boo-gie to - night, just keep on tok - in'.
Gtr. 1
slight P.M.
D5
C5
D5
A5
G
Smok - in', smok - in'. I'll feel al - right, ma-ma I'm not jok - in', yeah.
slight P.M.
1.
Interlude
Gtr. 1: w/ Rhy. Fig. 1
Gtr. 1: w/ Rhy. Fig. 2
A5
2. Get your
2.
Interlude
D5
Oh!
Yeah, yeah.

Organ Solo
Am7
D5/A
Am7
1/2
D5/A
Am7
1/2
1
D5/A
Am7
tr
1/2
D5/A
Am7
tr
A5
A6 A5
A6
D5
C5
A5
A6 A5
C5 D5
C5
G5 A5
f
D/A A
A6
D5
C5
A
D/A A5
G5
C5 D5
C5
G5 A5
D/A A
D/A A
A5
C5
D5
C5
G5

A5
*Gm/A
Riff A
End Riff A
mf
P.M.
*Chord symbols reflect overall harmony, next 40 meas.
Gtr. 1: w/ Riff A (7 times)
Dm/A
A7sus4
A
Dm/A
Gm7/A
Asus4
A
Gm/B♭
Dm/A
Gm6
A
B♭
Dm/A
Gm7
A7sus4
A7
f
Gm
Dm/F
C/E
B♭/D
F/C
Gm/B♭
Asus4
A
B°7
Asus4
A
Am7
A5
A6
A7(no3rd)
A6
A5
A6
Play 3 times
Am7
mf
steady.
gliss.
P.M.
D5
D6
D5
D6
D5
D6
D5
C5
A5
N.C.

E5
D5
A5
E5
C5
G5
D5/A
Gtr. 1: w/ Rhy. Fig. 1
A5
Gtr. 1: w/ Rhy. Fig. 2
D.S. al Coda
3. Ev -
Coda
(Ah.)
Ah, get down to - night.
Yeah,
you know we're get - tin'
*let ring
let ring
*5th string only, till end.
off to - day.
We'll pick you up, take you a - way.
Woo,
a, get down to - night.
Well, al - right!

from Dusty Springfield - *Dusty in Memphis*

Son-of-a-Preacher Man

Words and Music by John Hurley and Ronnie Wilkins

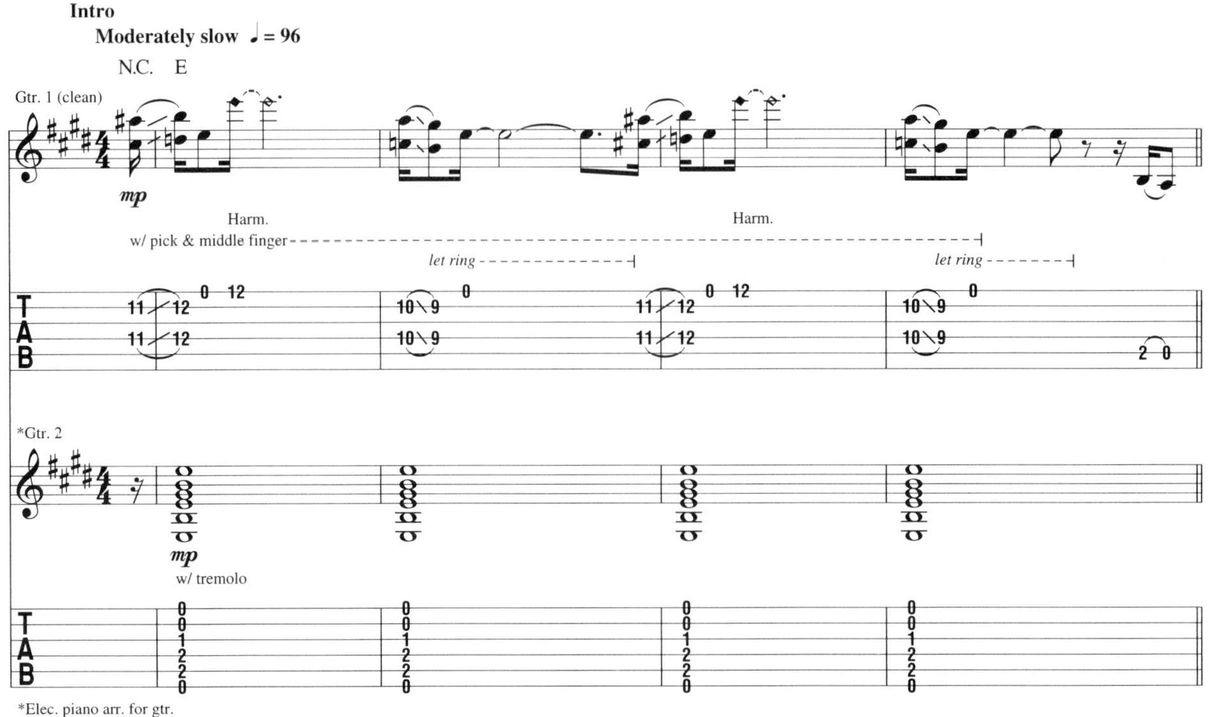

*Elec. piano arr. for gtr.

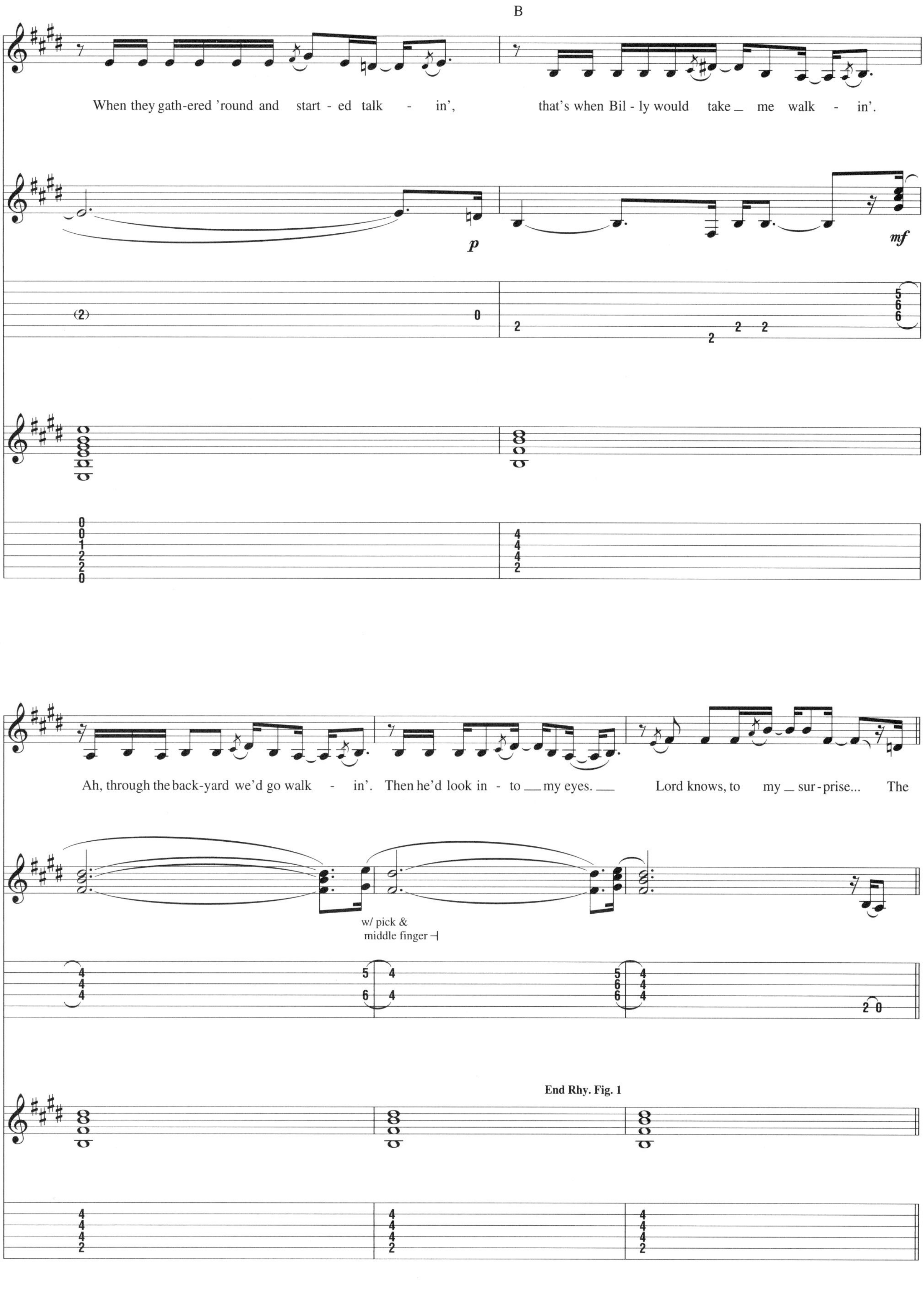

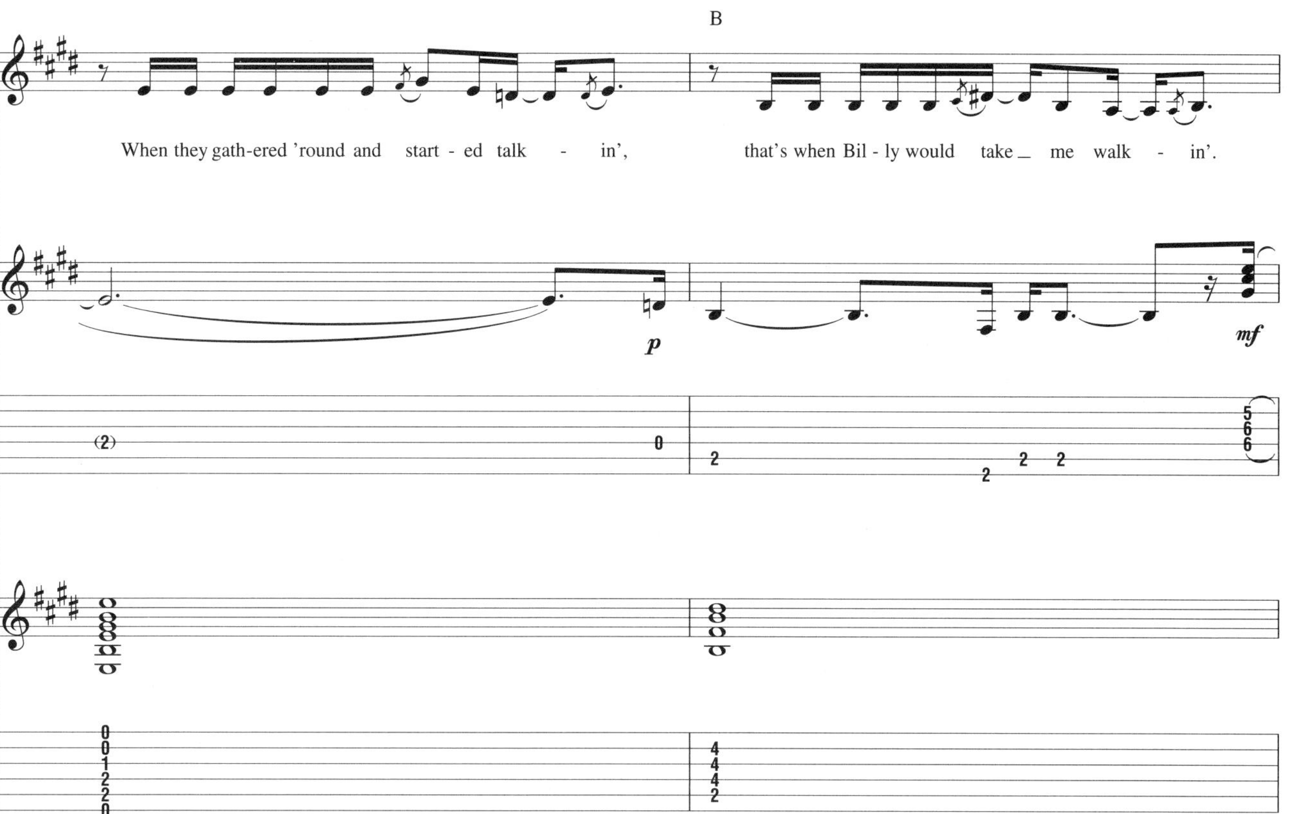

B
When they gath-ered 'round and start - ed talk - in',
that's when Bil - ly would take _ me walk - in'.
p
mf
Ah, through the back-yard we'd go walk - in'. Then he'd look in - to _ my eyes. _
Lord knows, to my _ sur-prise... The
w/ pick &
middle finger
End Rhy. Fig. 1

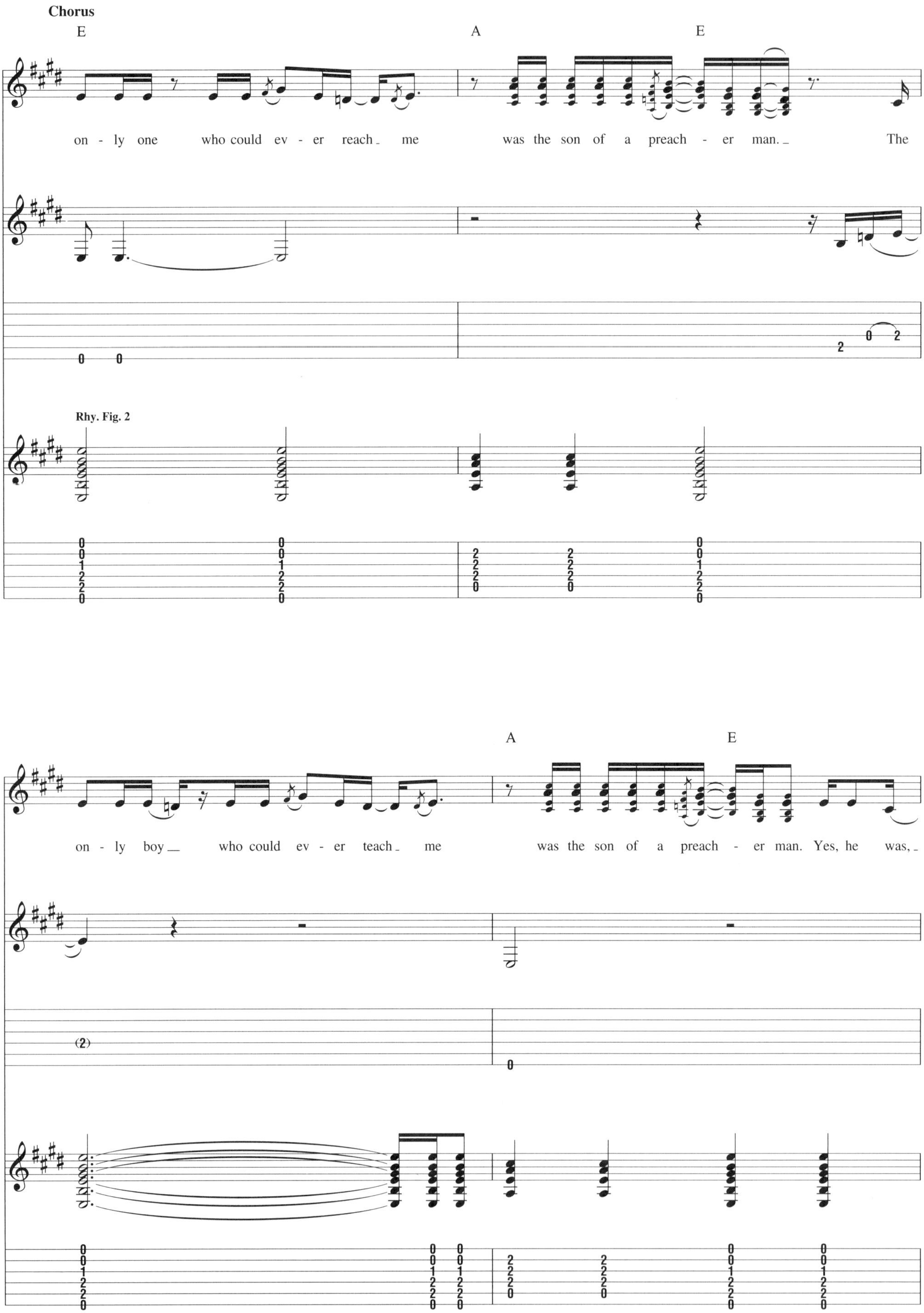

Chorus

E A E

on - ly one who could ev - er reach _ me was the son of a preach - er man. _ The

Rhy. Fig. 2

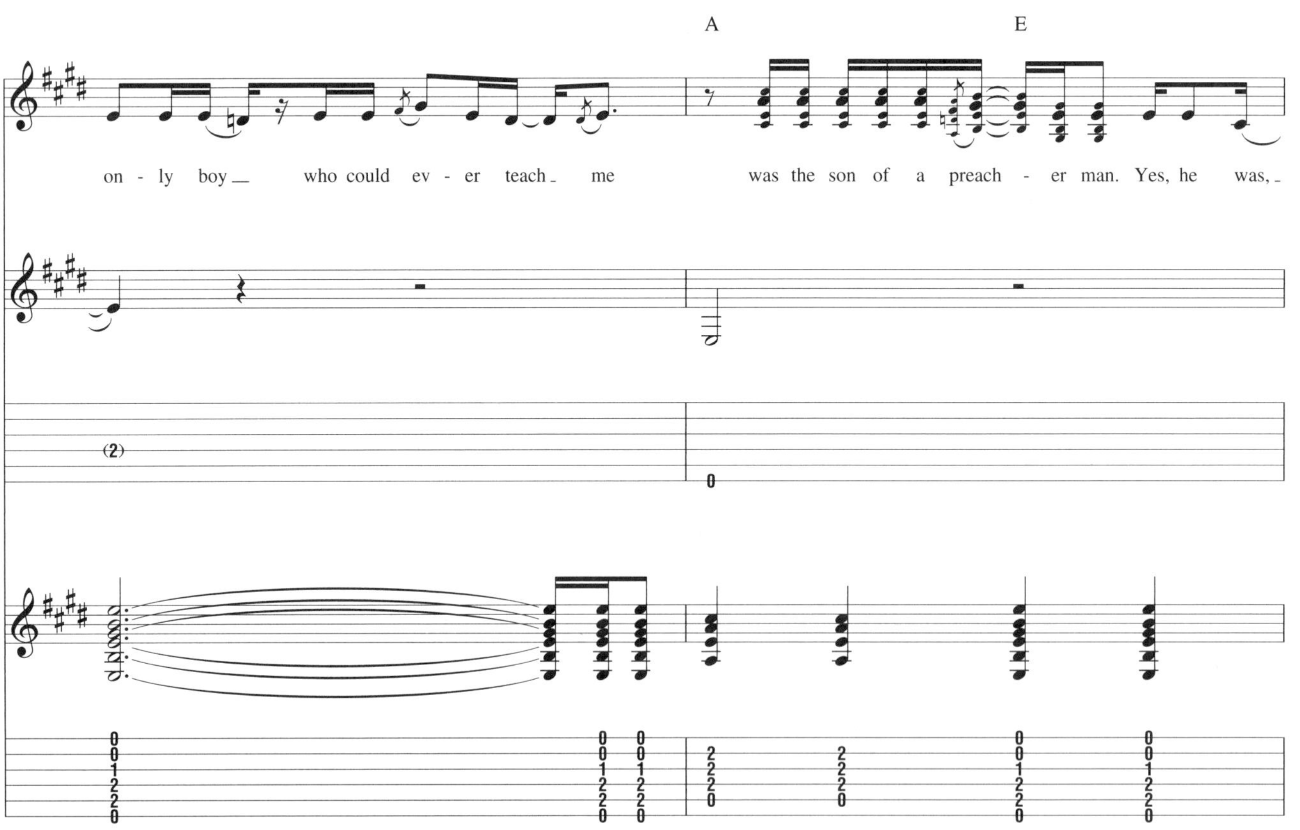

B
A
he was.
Oo, yes, he was.
End Rhy. Fig. 2
Interlude
E
Harm.
w/ pick & finger
let ring
Verse
Gtr. 2: w/ Rhy. Fig. 1
E
A
E
2. Be - ing good is - n't al - ways eas - y,
no mat - ter how hard I try.
(Oo.
Gtr. 1
let ring

B
When he start-ed sweet - talk - in' to me, he'd come and tell me ev-'ry-thing is all right.

Oo.
p
mf

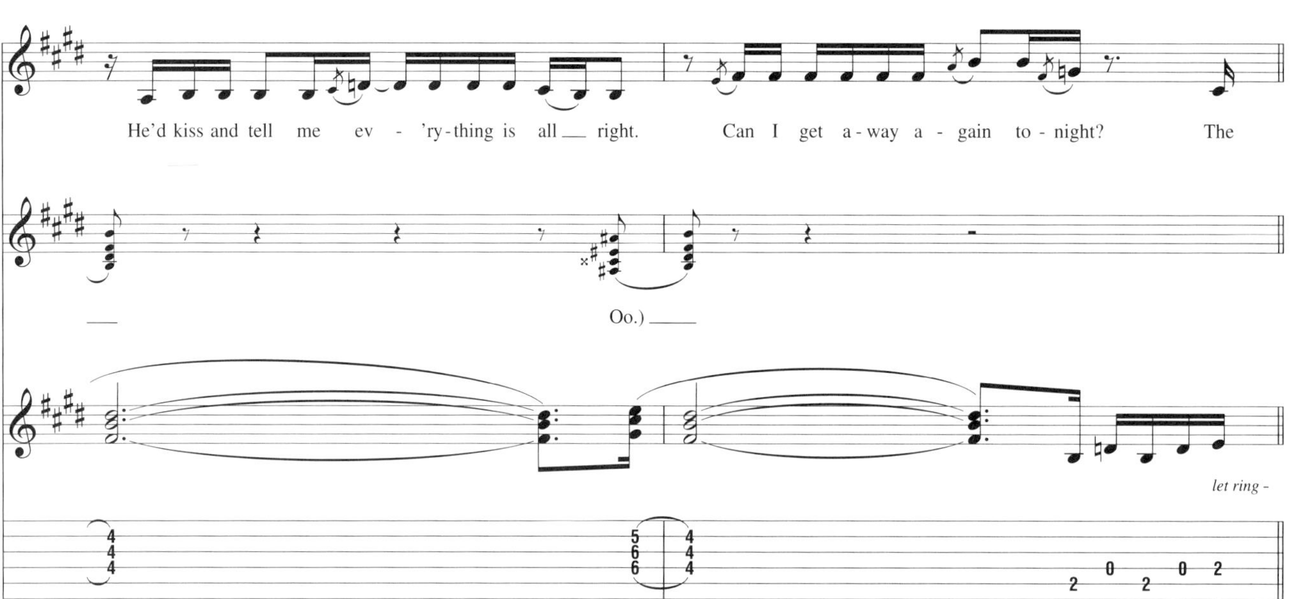
He'd kiss and tell me ev - 'ry-thing is all right. Can I get a-way a - gain to-night? The
Oo.)
let ring -

Chorus

Gtr. 2: w/ Rhy. Fig. 2
E
A
E
on - ly one who could ev - er reach me was the son of a preach - er man. The
let ring

Gtr. 1 tacet
A
E
only boy who could ever teach me was the son of a preacher man. Yes, he was,
B
A
he was. Lord knows he was.
(Was, was. Oo, yes, he was.)
Gtr. 1
Bridge
D
C
D
How well I remember
A
the look that was in his eyes, stealin' kisses from me on the sly,

B
tak - in' time to make time,
tell - in' me that he's all mine.

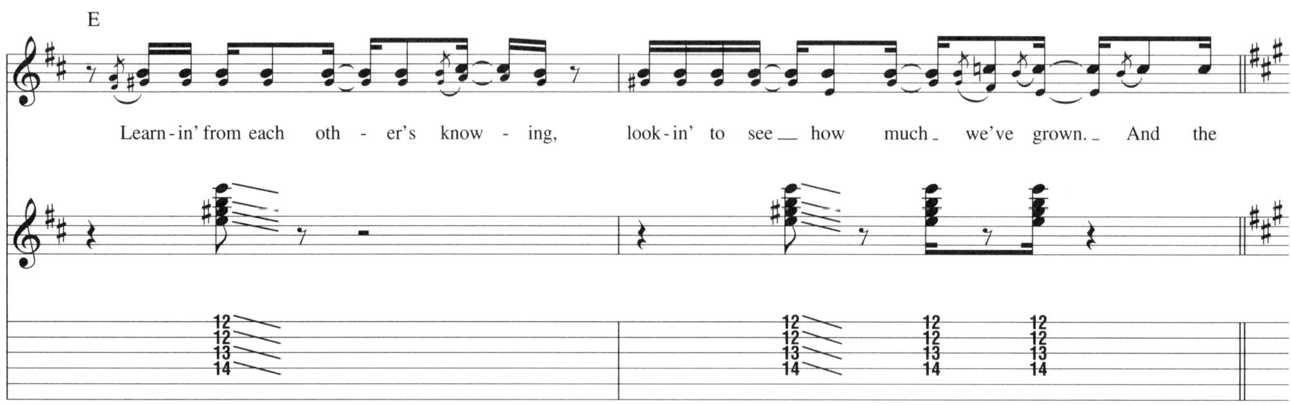
E
Learn - in' from each oth - er's know - ing,
look - in' to see how much we've grown. And the

Chorus

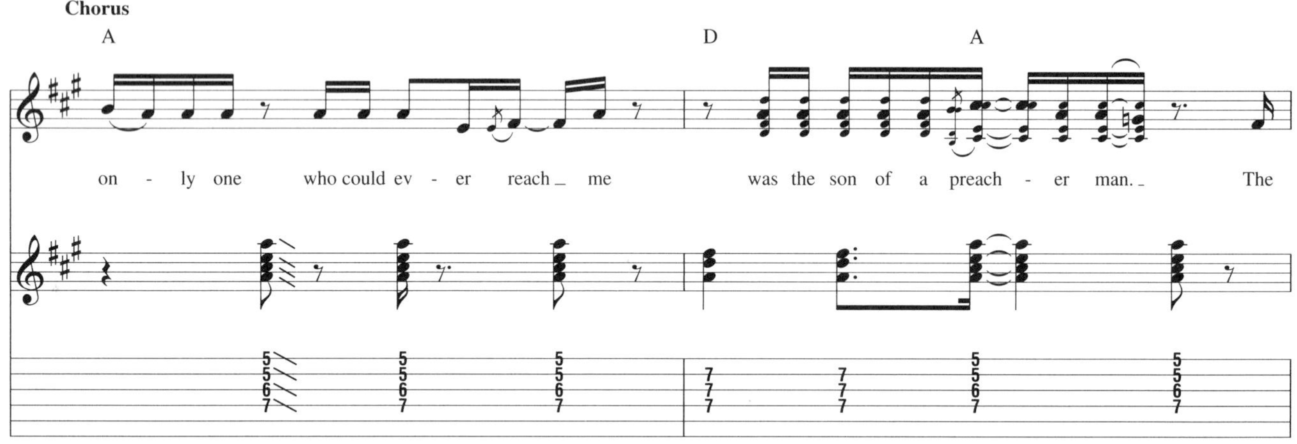
A
D
A
on - ly one who could ev - er reach me
was the son of a preach - er man. The

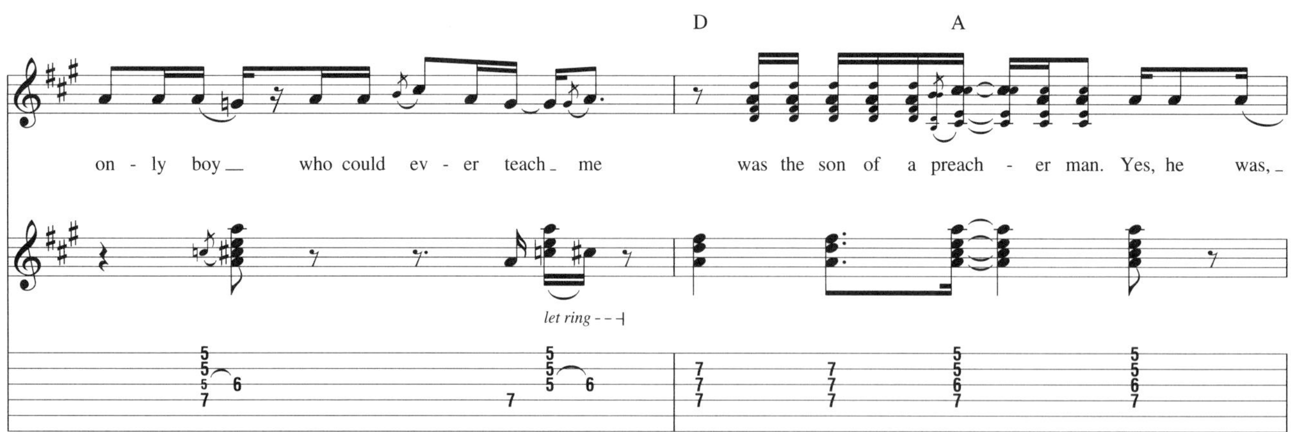
D
A
on - ly boy who could ev - er teach me
was the son of a preach - er man. Yes, he was,
let ring

E
D
he was.
Oh, yes, he was.
(Was,
was.
Oo.
The
5
5
6
7
9
9
9
7
7
7
Outro-Chorus
A
D
A
He was a sweet-talk-in' son of a preach-er man.
on-ly one who could ev-er reach me
was the son of a preach-er man.
The
D
A
G
I kissed me the son of a preach-er man.
on-ly boy who could ev-er teach me
was the son of a preach-er man.
The

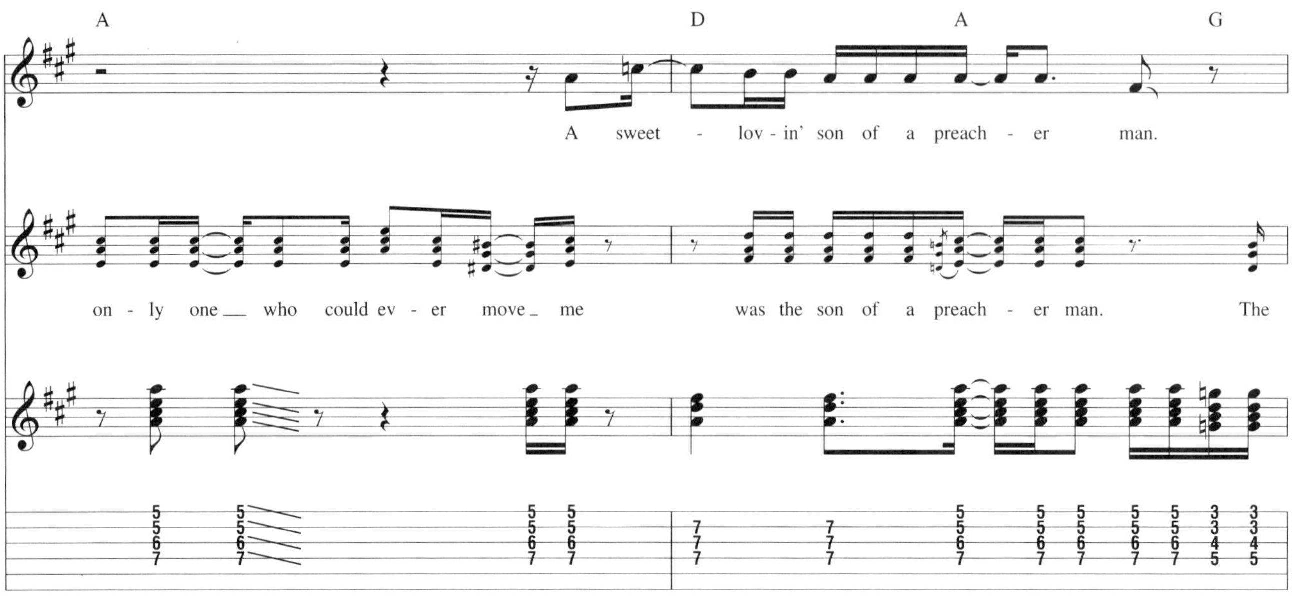

Begin fade

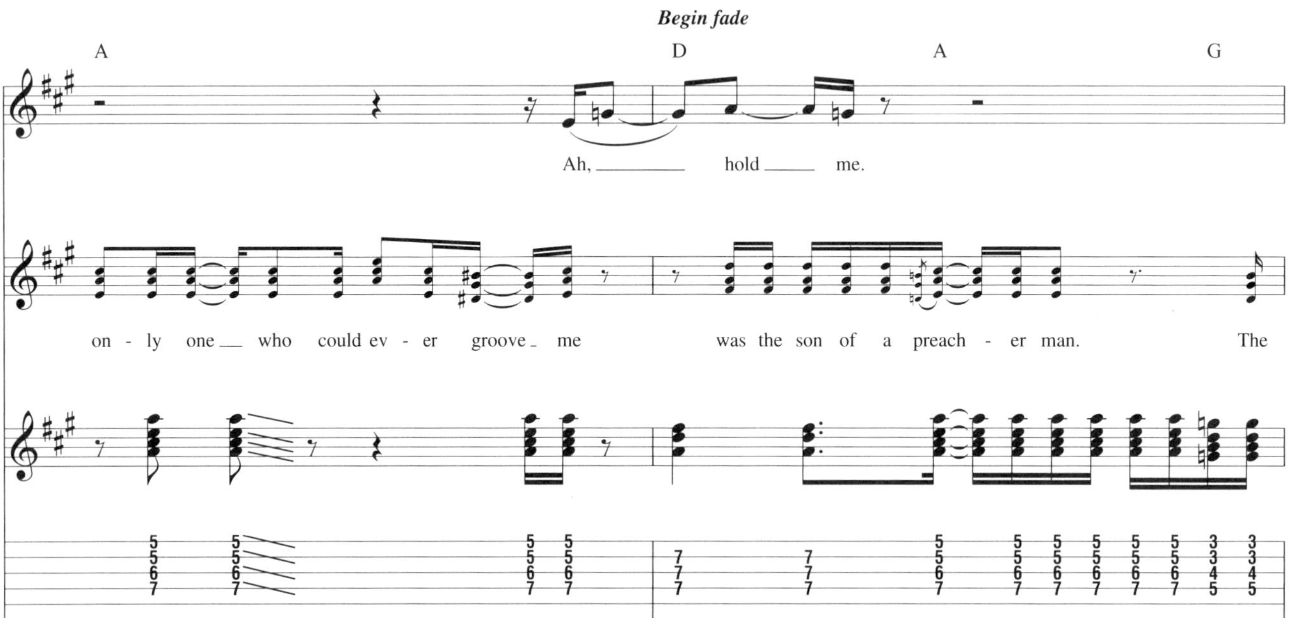

Fade out

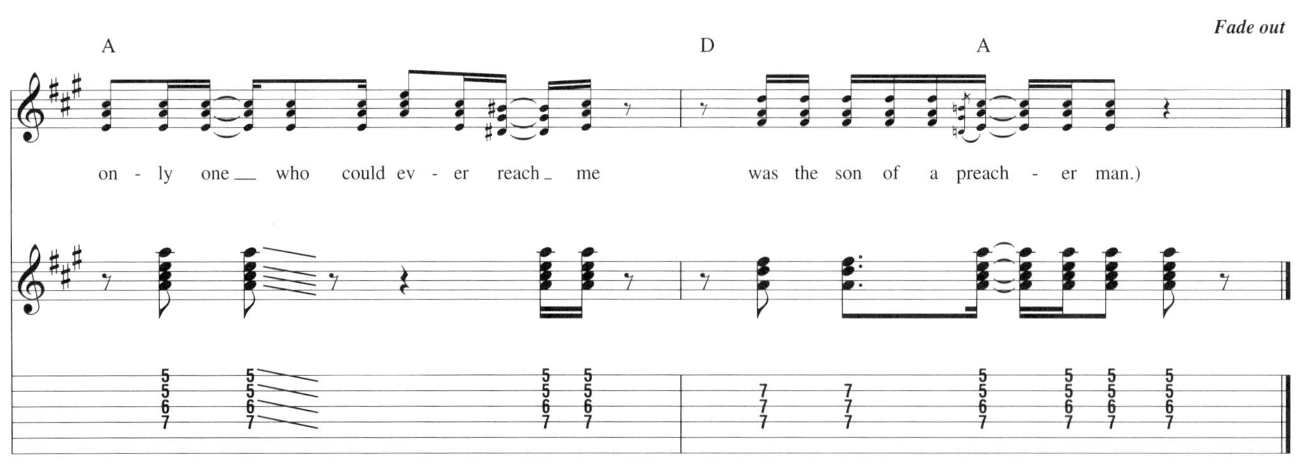

from The Beach Boys - *Surfin' Safari*

Surfin' Safari

Words and Music by Brian Wilson and Mike Love

Bkgd. Voc.: w/ Voc. Fig. 1
Gtr. 1: w/ Rhy. Fig. 2
D
E
A
load - in' up our wood - ie with our boards in - side and head - in' out sing - in' our song.

Chorus

A
Come on, ba - by, wait and see, yes,
(Surf - er, surf - in' sa - fa - ri.
Gtr. 1
P.M.

I'm gon - na take you surf - in' with me. Come on a -
Surf - er, surf - in' sa - fa - ri.
P.M.

D
long, surf ba - by, wait and see, yeah,
Surf - er, surf - in' sa - fa - ri.
P.M.

Gtr. 1: w/ Rhy. Fig. 1
A
E
I'm gon - na take you surf - in' with me.
Surf - er, surf - in' sa - fa - ri.
Let's go surf - in' now,
P.M.

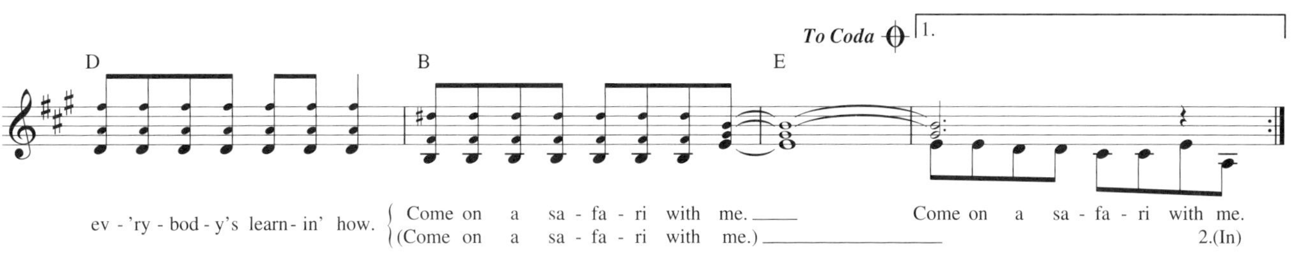
To Coda
1.
D
B
E
ev - 'ry - bod - y's learn - in' how.
Come on a sa - fa - ri with me.
(Come on a sa - fa - ri with me.)
Come on a sa - fa - ri with me.
2.(In)

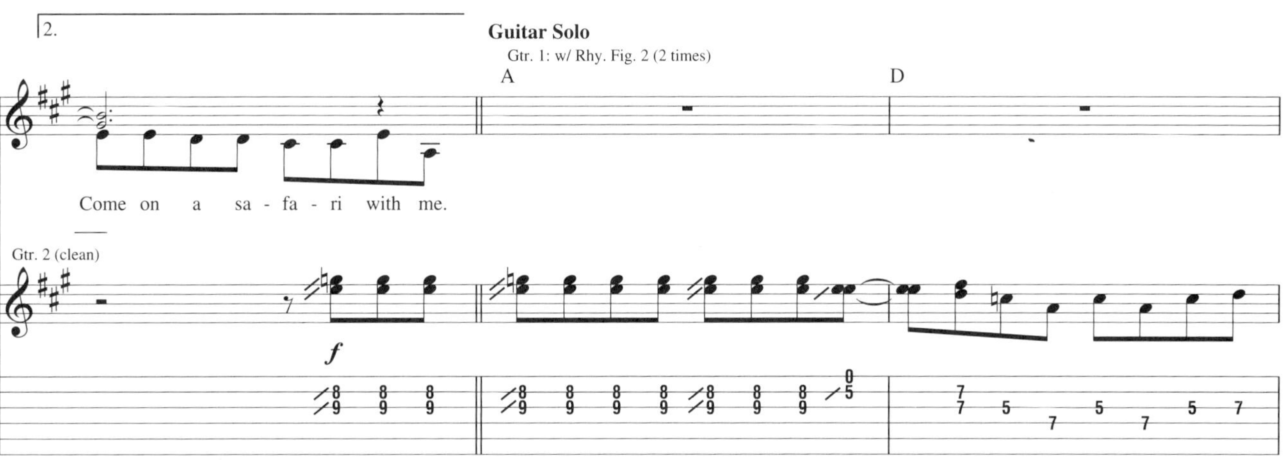
2.
Guitar Solo
Gtr. 1: w/ Rhy. Fig. 2 (2 times)
A
D
Come on a sa - fa - ri with me.
Gtr. 2 (clean)

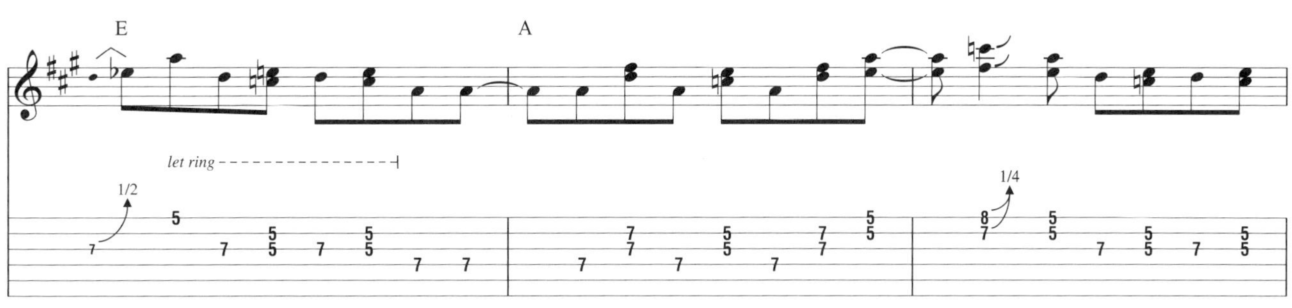
E
A
let ring
1/2
1/4

D.S. al Coda

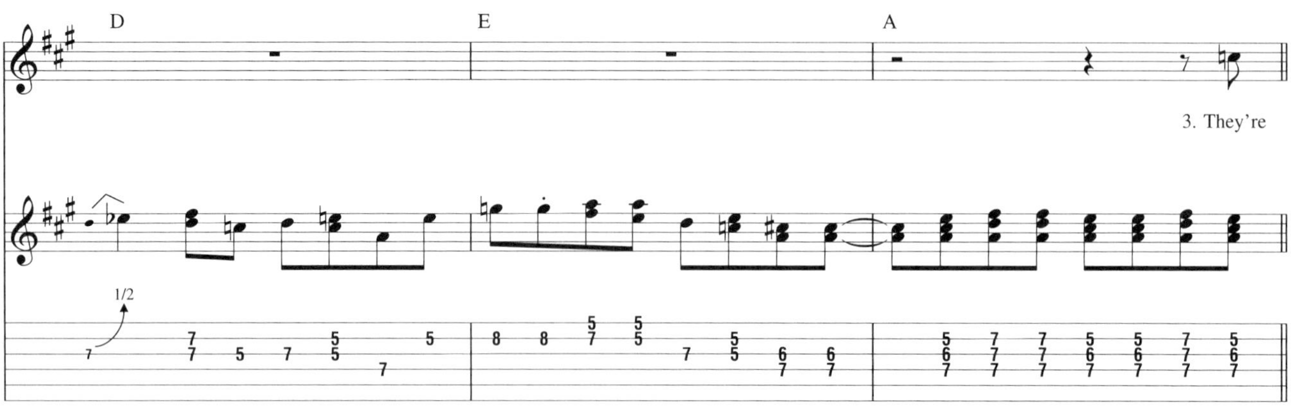

Coda

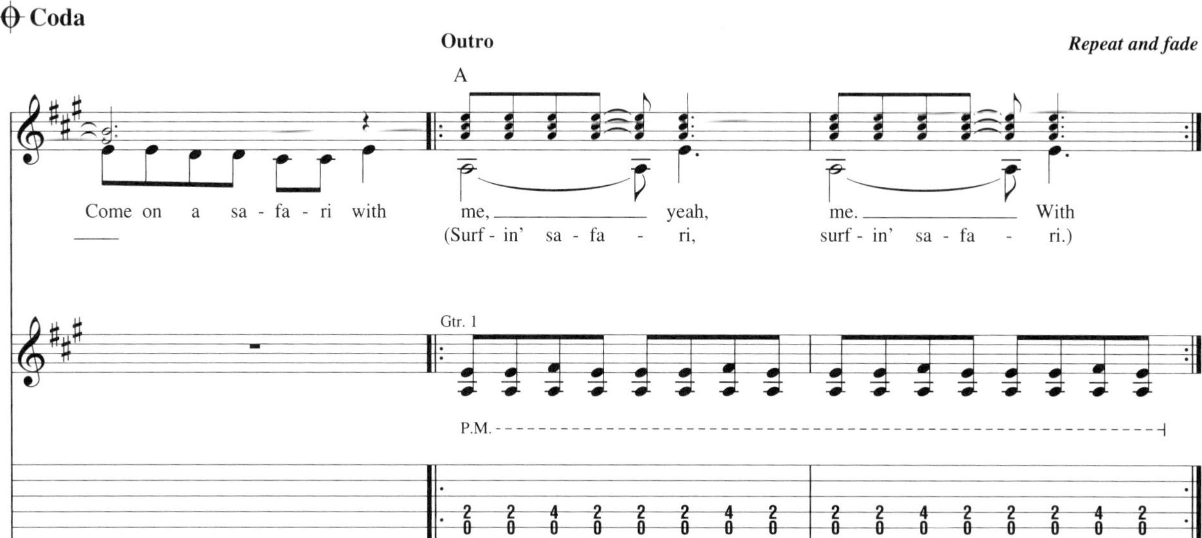

Additional Lyrics

2. In Huntington and Malibu they're shootin' the pier,
   In Rin' con they're walkin' the nose.
   We're goin' on safari to the islands this year,
   So if you're comin', get ready to go.
   (To Chorus)

3. They're anglin' in Laguna and Cerro A'zul,
   They're kickin' it in Dohini too.
   I tell you surfin's runnin' wild, it's gettin' bigger every day,
   From Hawaii to the shores of Peru.
   (To Chorus)

from Joe Satriani - *Surfing with the Alien*

Surfing with the Alien

By Joe Satriani

N.C.
C
C6
C5
C7
G5
B♭5
A.H.
(15ma)
sl.
P.M.
A.H. pitch: D
(end Rhy. Fig. 2)
w/Rhy. Fig. 2 (1st 7 bars only)
(8va)
semi-harm.
A5
w/Rhy. Fill 1
E5
Rhy. Fill 1

Gtr. II
semi-harm.
A.H.
(15ma)
C5
Full
1/4
1/2
P
A.H.
pitch: B
A.H.
ptich: C♯
Gtr. I
Rhy. Fig. 3
P.M.
C
G5
D5
D
sl.
H
trem. bar
A.H. pitches: E♮
E♮
C/D
D
E5
(8va)
rake
2½
*1
grad. bend
*Depress bar
before striking note.
A.H.
pitches: D
E♮
E♮
E♮
sl.

A.H.
(8va)
1/2
G5
sl.
Full
D5
trem. bar
semi-harm.
A.H. pitch: E♮
(Cont. in slashes)
P.M.
(end Rhy. Fig. 3)
D5(type 2)
C♯5
C♯5(type 2)
8va
Fdbk. trem. bar
Jet plane sample
(Wah off)
(trills)
Fdbk.
ptich: E♮
**Tap w/edge of pick.
⑥ 7fr.
⑤ 4fr.
5fr.
B
C♯
D
loco
T P
H
P

⑥7fr. ⑤4fr. 5fr.
B C♯ D C♯5
C♯5(type 2)
⑤4fr. 5fr. 7fr.
C♯ D E D♯5
P.M.
H P sl.
D♯(type 2)
⑥9fr. ⑤6fr.
C♯ D♯ E5
D♯5 D♯5(type 2)
A.H. (15ma)
Harm. (8va)
A.H. pitches: G♯ A
A.H. pitches: F× G♯ E♯
E♯ E♯ E♯ E♯
⑥9fr. ⑤6fr. 7fr. ⑥fr.
C♯ D♯ E D♯
D♯5(type 2)
⑥9fr. ⑤6fr.
C♯ D♯ E5
D♯5 D♯5(type 2)
Full
hold bend
A.H. pitches: E♯ G♯
sl. ⑤6fr. 8fr.
E♭ F G♭5 F5
F5 F5(type 2)
⑥11 fr. ⑤8fr.
E♭ F G♭5
trem. bar
F5 F5(type 2)
⑥11 fr. ⑤8fr. 9fr.
E♭ F G♭ F5
F5(type 2)
8va
trem. bar vib.

⑥11fr.⑤8fr.
E♭ F G♭5 F5 F5(type 2)
⑥ open ⑤
8va
loco A.H.
(15ma)
P.M.
*1/2 *1 *1½ *2½
trem. bar
sl.
*Pull up bar gradually.
Gtr. II
G5 Full G/F Full Full G/E P G/C ** 2 3½ G5
let ring
trem. bar
(Wah on)
**Depress bar before striking note.
Gtr. I
let ring
w/Rhy. Fig. 2
N.C. C
A. H.
(15ma)
B♭5 A5 G5
N.C. C C6 C5 C7 C5 C G5 B♭5 G5 C5 G5 B♭5 G5

w/Rhy. Fig. 2 (1st 7 bars only)
N.C.
C
B♭5 A5 G5
P.M.
w/Rhy. Fill 1
C6 C5 C7 C5 C G5 B♭5 G5 C5 G5 B♭5 G5 E5
w/Rhy. Fig. 3
C5
A.H.
(15ma)
grad. bend
semi-harm.
(8va)
G5
D5
D
C/D D
E5
rake
trem. bar

D5(type 2) D5
G5
Depress & vib. bar simultaneously
trem. bar
Jet plane samples-
w/Rhy. Fig. 2 (2 times)
N.C. C5
Bb5 A5 G5
N.C. C C6
Full
C5 C7 C5 C G5 Bb5 G5 C5 G5 Bb5 G5
8va-
C
Full
1/2
trem. bar
Bb5 A5 G5
N.C. C C6

C5 C7 C5 C G5 B♭5 G5 C5 G5 B♭5 G5
w/Rhy. Fig. 1 (till fade)
N.C. C C6
8va
Full
trem. bar
*Pull bar up.
C7 C6 C5 C6 C5 B♭5 A5 G5
N.C. C C6
C7 C6 C5 G5 B♭5 G5 C5 G5 B♭5 G5
loco
sl.
N.C. C C6
C7 C6 C5 C6 C5 B♭5 A5 G5
Harm.
(15ma)
A.H.
A.H. pitch: A
N.C. C C6
C7 C6 C5 G5 B♭5 G5 C5 G5 B♭5 G5
TP

N.C. C C6 C7 C6 C5 C6 C5
8va
loco
Bb5 A5 G5
N.C. C C6
grad. bend
A.H. (15ma)
A.H. pitches: E♮
C7 C6 C5 G5 Bb5 G5 C5 G5 Bb5 G5
*Bend both stgs. w/3rd finger.
N.C. C C6 C7 C6 C5 C6 C5 Bb5 A5 G5
trem. bar
N.C. C C6 C7 C6 C5 G5 Bb5 G5 C5 G5 Bb5 G5

8va
N.C. C C6 C7 C6 C5 C6 C5 Bb5 A5 G5
loco
trem. bar
*Depress bar fully before striking note.
†Tapped harmonic.
**Pull bar up.
C5 G5 Bb5 G5
P.M.
sl.
1/2 Full 1/2 Full
A.H.
(15ma)
Begin fade
Harm.
A.H. pitches: B D
semi-harm.
(8va)
Fade out

from The Donnas - *Spend the Night*

Take It Off

Words and Music by Maya Ford, Allison Robertson, Brett Anderson and Torrance Castellano

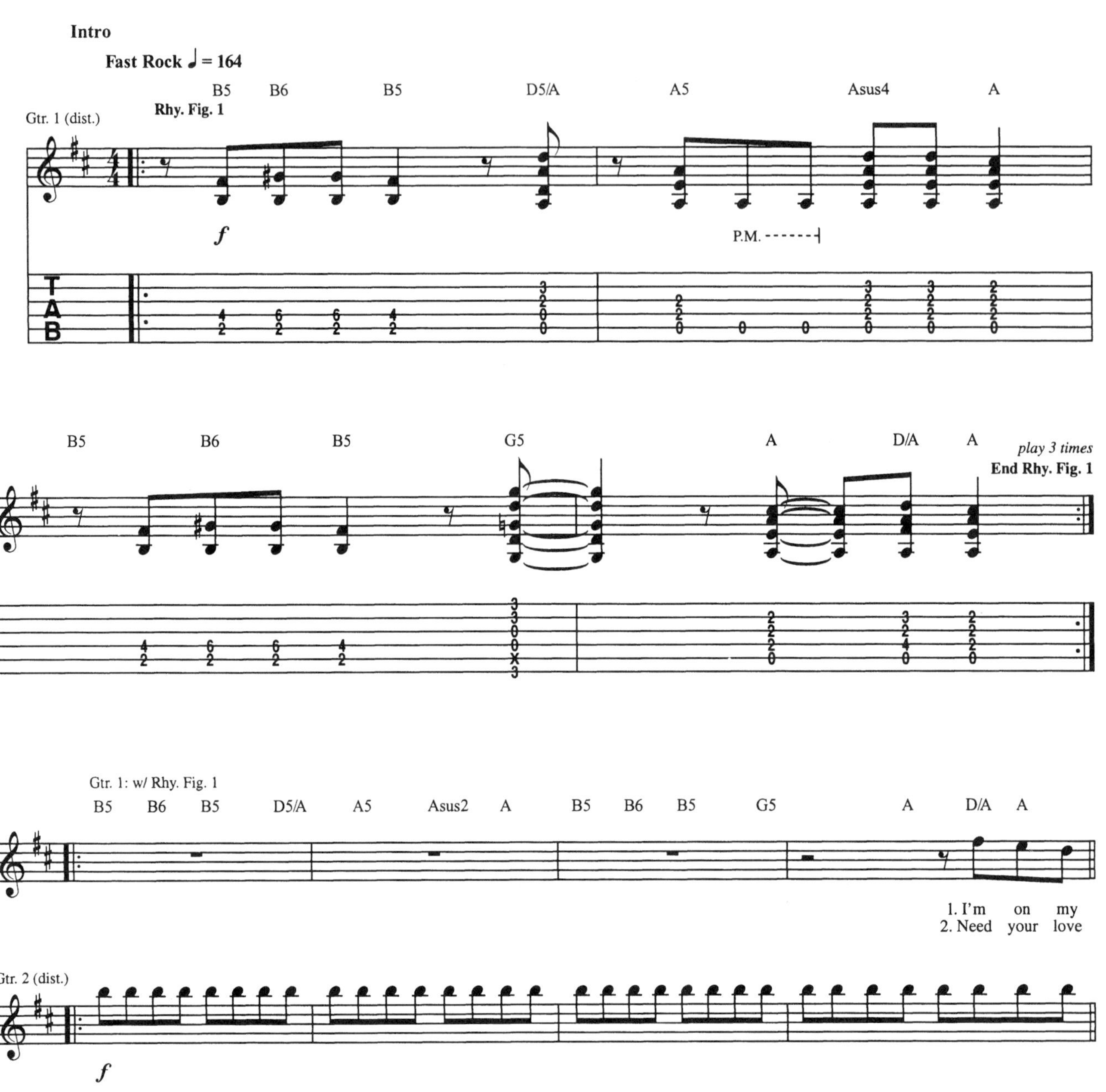

Verse
Gtr. 2 tacet
B5 D5/A A5 Asus4 A B5 G5
sec - ond drink, but I've had a few be - fore.
1, 2, 3. Stop star - in' at
Gtr. 1
P.M.
A5 D/A A B5 D5/A A5 Asus4 A
my D - cup. I'm try - in' hard to think, and I
Don't waste time, just give it to me.
B5 G5 A5 F♯
think that I want you on the floor, uh - huh. Yeah,
C'- mon, ba - by, just feel me up, c' - mon just
Chorus
B5 D5/A A5 Asus4 A5
on the floor. Go on and take it off, take it off. You got - ta
give it up.
Rhy. Fig. 2

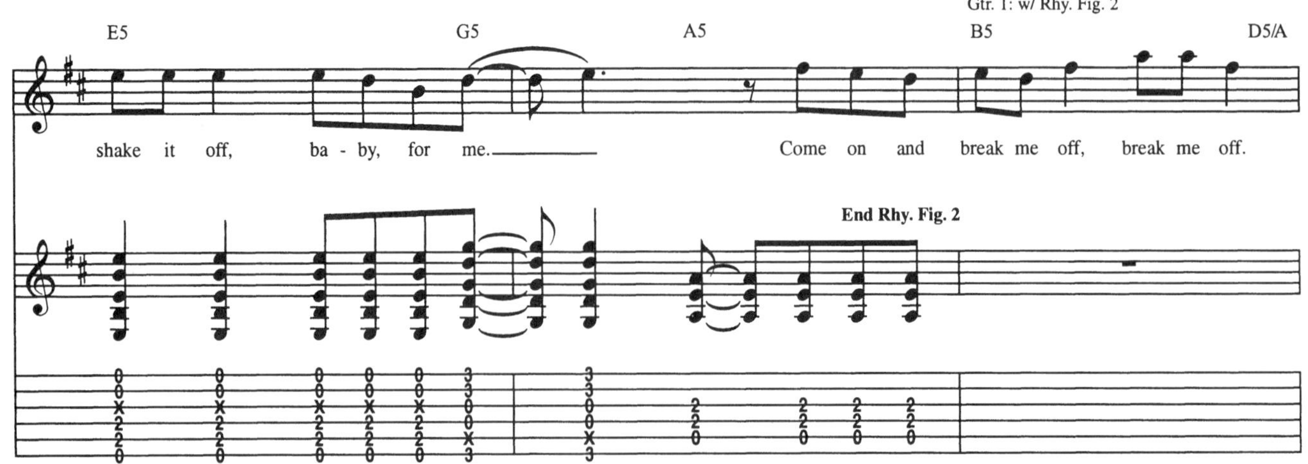
Gtr. 1: w/ Rhy. Fig. 2
E5
G5
A5
B5
D5/A
shake it off, ba - by, for me.
Come on and break me off, break me off.
End Rhy. Fig. 2

2nd time, Gtr. 2: w/ Fill 1
To Coda
A5
Asus4 A5
E5
G5
A5
'Cause I get what I want and I like what I see.

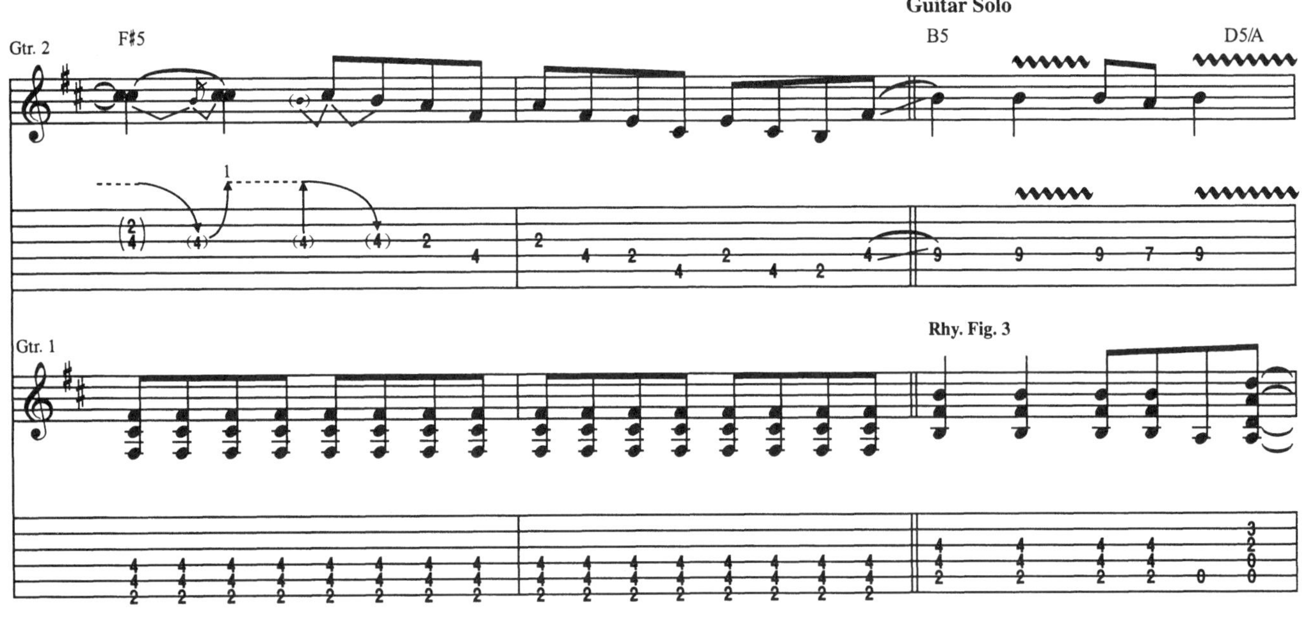
Guitar Solo
Gtr. 2
F♯5
B5
D5/A
Gtr. 1
Rhy. Fig. 3

Fill 1
Gtr. 2

B5
D5/A
A5
B5
P.M.
1/2
1
1/2
1
1/4
End Rhy. Fig. 3
Gtr. 1: w/ Rhy. Fig. 3
Gtr. 2
B5
D5/A
hold bend
B5
D5/A
Gtr. 3 (dist.)
A5
B5
f
Gtr. 2

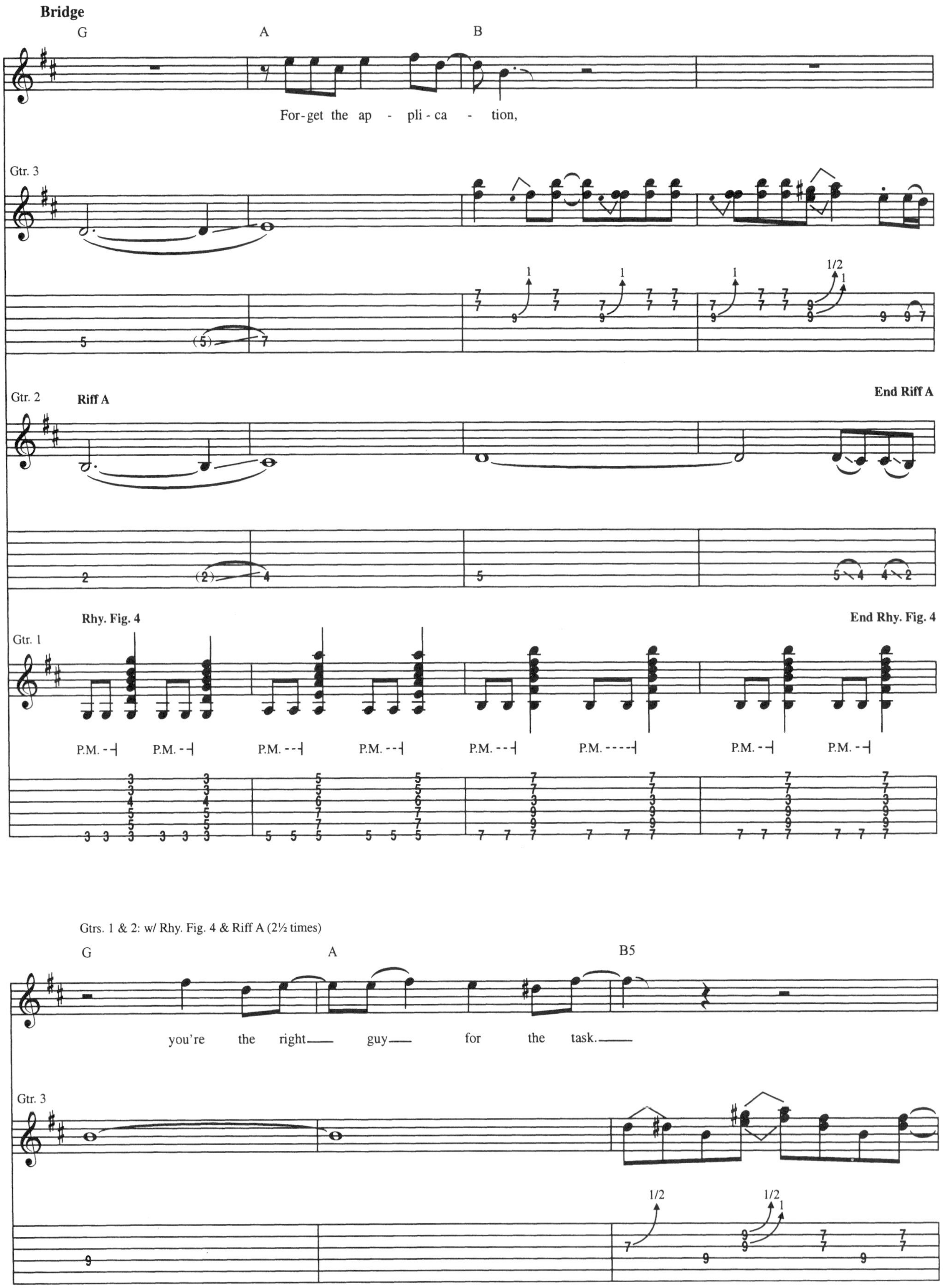

Bridge

G A B

For-get the ap - pli - ca - tion,

Gtr. 3

Gtr. 2 Riff A End Riff A

Rhy. Fig. 4 End Rhy. Fig. 4

Gtr. 1

P.M. P.M. P.M. P.M. P.M. P.M. P.M. P.M.

Gtrs. 1 & 2: w/ Rhy. Fig. 4 & Riff A (2½ times)

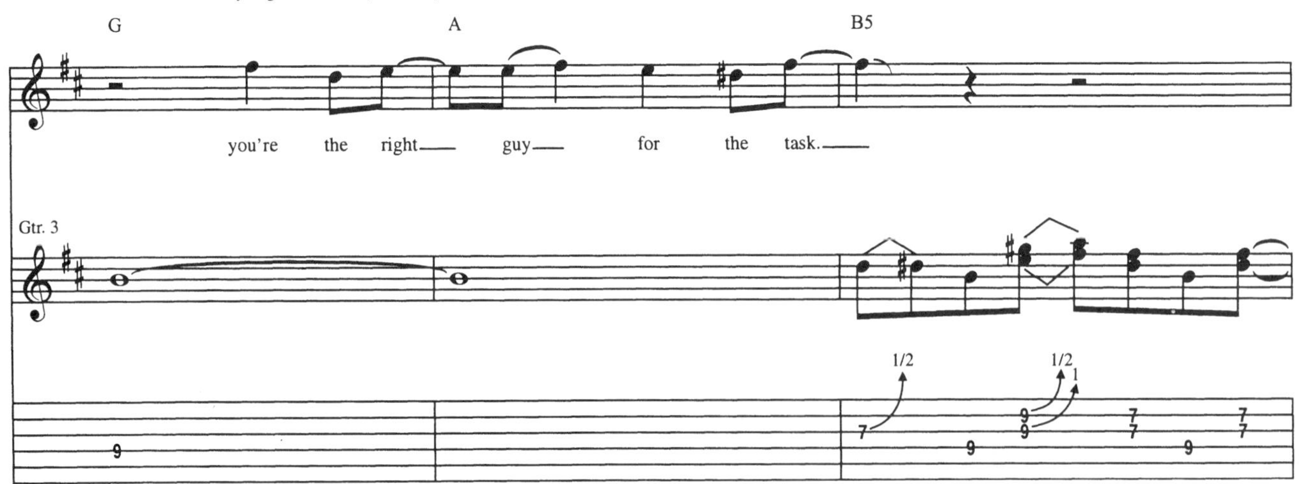

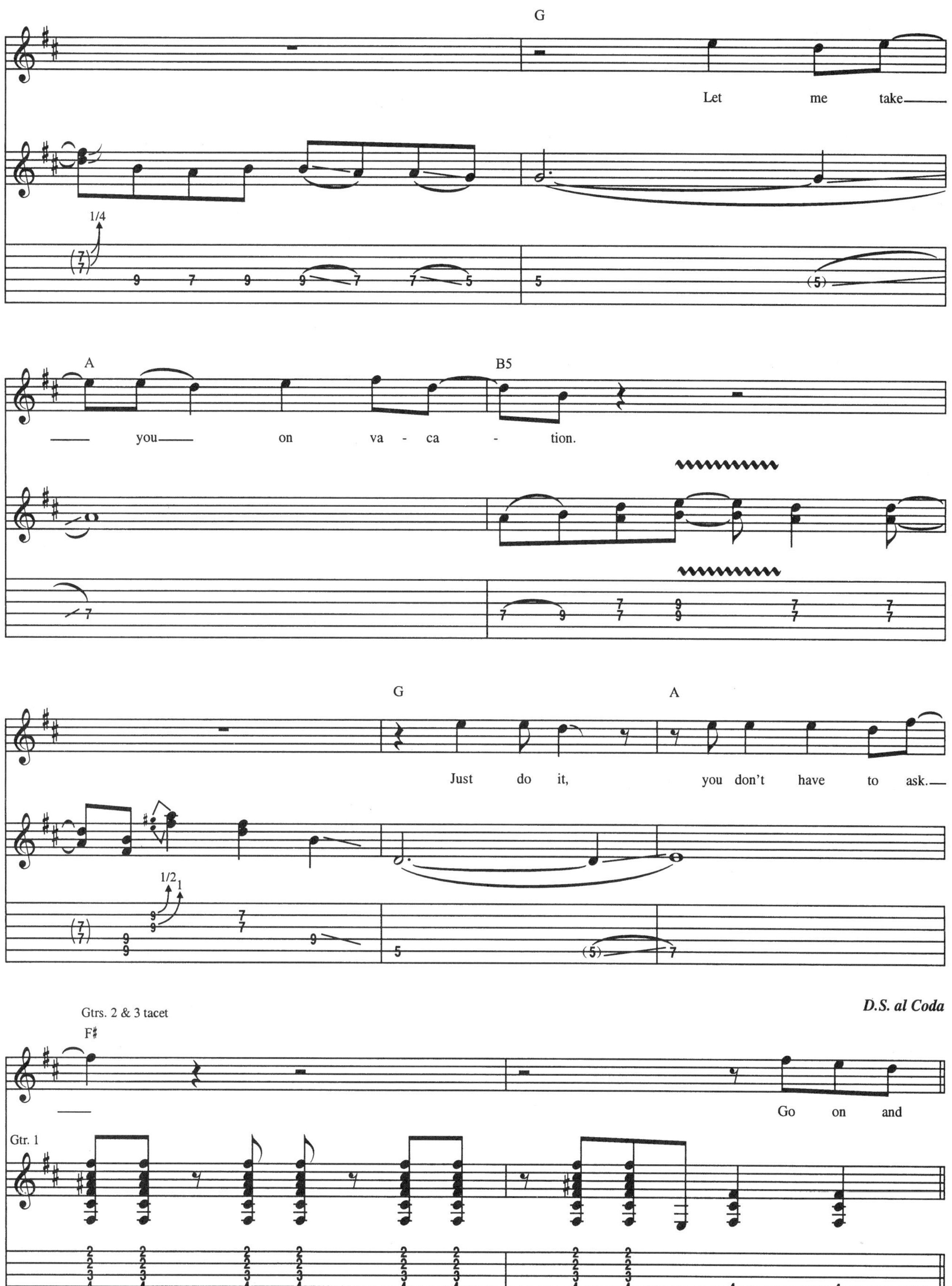
G
Let me take
A
you on va - ca - tion.
B5
1/4
G
A
Just do it, you don't have to ask.
1/2
1
Gtrs. 2 & 3 tacet
F♯
D.S. al Coda
Go on and
Gtr. 1

Coda
Outro-Chorus
B5
D5/A
A5
Take it off, take it off,
Gtr. 1
P.M.
E5
G5
A5
take it off, ba - by, for me.
Take
P.M.
Gtr. 1: w/ Rhy. Fig. 2 (1st 3 meas.)
B5
D5/A
A5
Asus4
A5
it off, take it off,
E5
G5
Gtr. 1: w/ Rhy. Fill 1
rit.
A5
take it off, ba - by, for me.
Rhy. Fill 1
Gtr. 1
rit.

from *Taylor Swift*

Teardrops on My Guitar

Words and Music by Taylor Swift and Liz Rose

Gtr. 3: w/ Riff A
B♭5
(G5)
Gm7
(Em7)
E♭add9
(Cadd9)
F/A
(D/F♯)
that I want and I'm need - ing ev - 'ry-thing that we should be.

Gm7
(Em7)
E♭add9
(Cadd9)
B♭5
(G5)
F/A
(D/F♯)
I'll bet she's beau-ti - ful, that girl he talks a - bout. And she's got ev-'ry-thing that I had to live with-out.
Gtr. 3
Gtr. 1

Gtr. 1: w/ Rhy. Fig. 1 (2 times)
Gtr. 3 tacet
B♭5
(G5)
Gm7
(Em7)
E♭add9
(Cadd9)
F/A
(D/F♯)
Drew talks to me. I laugh 'cause it's just so fun - ny
Gtr. 3

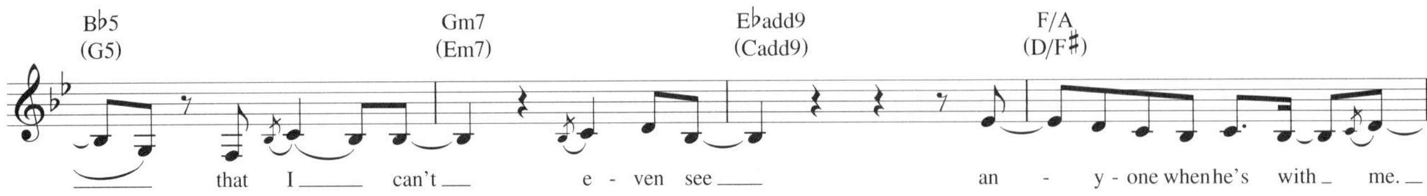
B♭5
(G5)
Gm7
(Em7)
E♭add9
(Cadd9)
F/A
(D/F♯)
that I can't e - ven see an - y-one when he's with me.

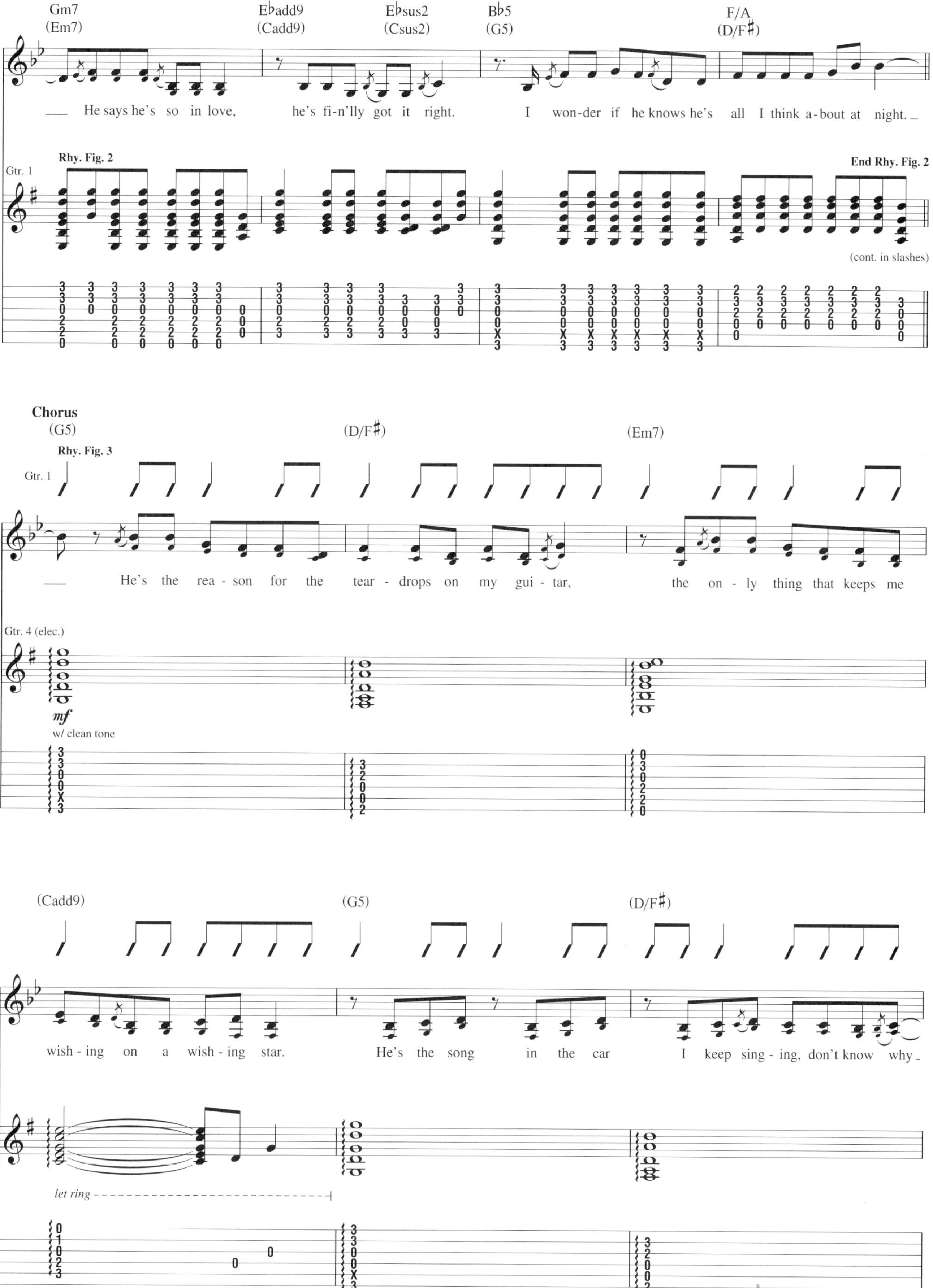

Gm7
(Em7)
E♭add9
(Cadd9)
E♭sus2
(Csus2)
B♭5
(G5)
F/A
(D/F♯)
He says he's so in love, he's fi-n'lly got it right. I won-der if he knows he's all I think a-bout at night.
Rhy. Fig. 2
Gtr. 1
End Rhy. Fig. 2
(cont. in slashes)
Chorus
(G5)
Rhy. Fig. 3
(D/F♯)
(Em7)
He's the rea-son for the tear-drops on my gui-tar, the on-ly thing that keeps me
Gtr. 4 (elec.)
mf
w/ clean tone
(Cadd9)
(G5)
(D/F♯)
wish-ing on a wish-ing star. He's the song in the car I keep sing-ing, don't know why
let ring

Verse
Chorus
(Em7) (Cadd9) (Csus2)
Gtr. 1: w/ Rhy. Fig. 1 (2 times)
Gtr. 4 tacet
B♭5 (G5) Gm7 (Em7)
End Rhy. Fig. 3
I do. 2.Drew walks by me.
E♭add9 (Cadd9) F/A (D/F♯) B♭5 (G5)
Can he tell that I can't breathe? And there he goes
Gtr. 1: w/ Rhy. Fig. 2
so per-fect-ly, the kind of flaw-less I wish I could be. She bet-ter hold him tight,
E♭sus2 (Csus2)
give him all her love, look in those beau-ti-ful eyes and know she's luck-y 'cause
Gtr. 1: w/ Rhy. Fig. 3
he's the rea-son for the tear-drops on my gui-tar, the on-ly thing that keeps me wish-ing on a wish-ing star.
*Gtrs. 4 & 5 (elec.)
Rhy. Fig. 4
End Rhy. Fig. 4
mf
w/ clean tone
let ring
*Composite arrangement
He's the song in the car I keep sing-ing, don't know why I do.

Guitar Solo
Gtr. 1: w/ Rhy. Fig. 1
B♭5 (G5)
Gm7 (Em7)
E♭add9 (Cadd9)
F/A (D/F♯)
Gtr. 6 (elec.)
mf
w/ slight dist.
let ring
Gtrs. 4 & 5
Pre-Chorus
Gm7 (Em7)
E♭ (C)
B♭5 (G5)
F/A (D/F♯)
So I drive home a-lone. As I turn out the light, I'll put his pic-ture down and may-be get some sleep to night.
Gtr. 6
fdbk.
pp
Gtr. 3
Gtr. 1
Chorus
Gtr. 1: w/ Rhy. Fig. 3
Gtrs. 3 & 6 tacet
Gtrs. 4 & 5: w/ Rhy. Fig. 4
B♭5 (G5)
F/A (D/F♯)
Gm7 (Em7)
E♭add9 (Cadd9)
'Cause he's the rea-son for the tear-drops on my gui - tar, the on - ly one who's got e - nough for me to break my heart.

B♭5
(G5)
F/A
(D/F♯)
Gm7
(Em7)
E♭add9
(Cadd9)
E♭sus2
(Csus2)
He's the song in the car I keep sing-ing, don't know why I do. He's the time
Gtrs. 4 & 5
let ring
Gtr. 1: w/ Rhy. Fig. 3 (last 4 meas.)
tak-en up, but there's nev-er e-nough and he's all that I need to fall in-to...
Outro
B♭
(G)
rit.
Drew looks at me, I fake a smile so he won't see.
Gtr. 3
Gtr. 1
pp

from Steve Vai - *Alien Love Secrets*

Tender Surrender

Written by Steve Vai

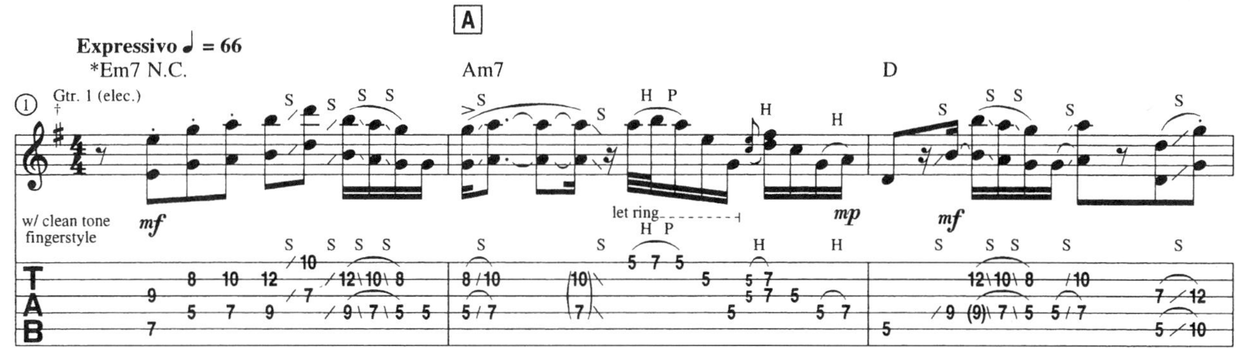

† Key signature denotes A Dorian
* Chord symbols reflect combined tonality of guitar, bass and organ.

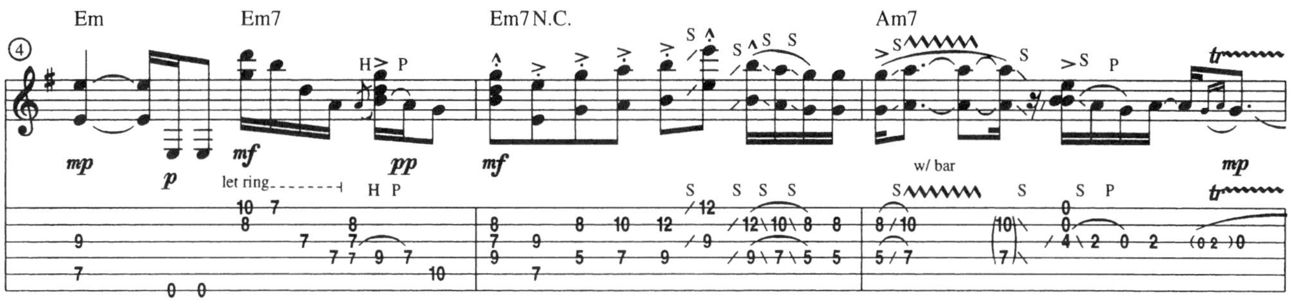

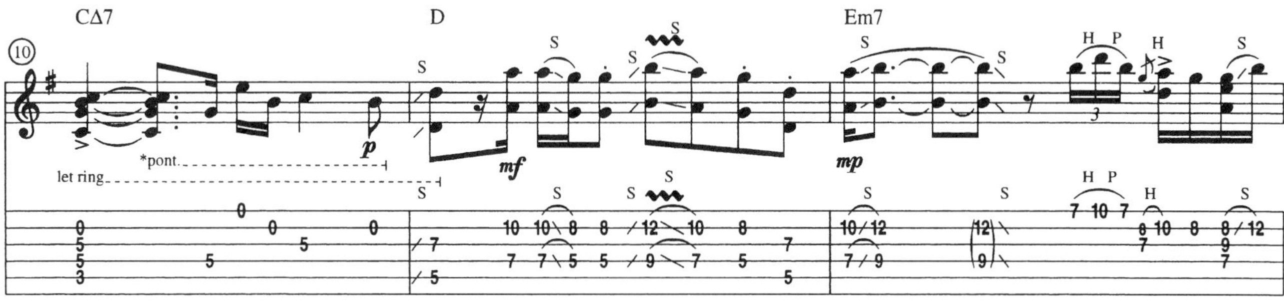

* Sul ponticello (pick near bridge)

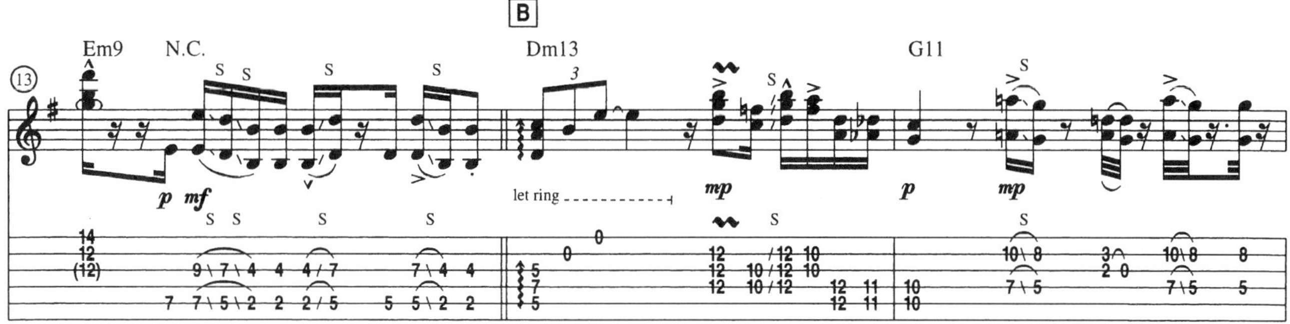

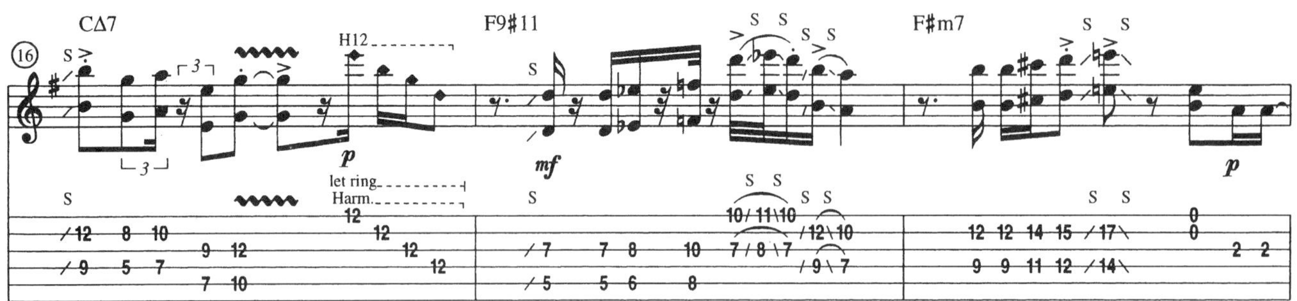
CΔ7
F9♯11
F♯m7
H12
let ring
Harm.

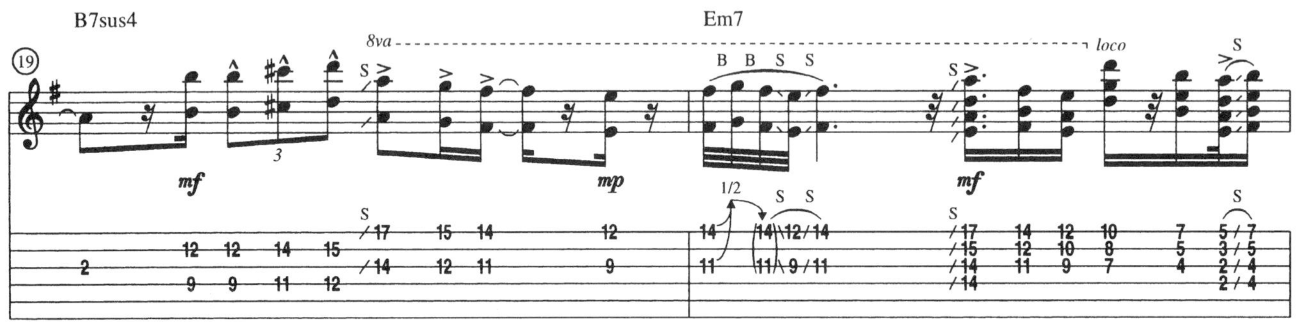
B7sus4
Em7
8va
loco

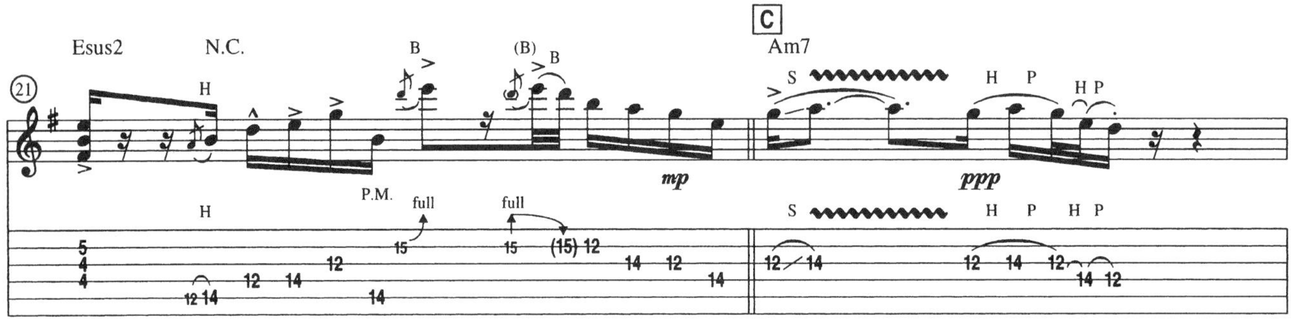
Esus2
N.C.
C
Am7
P.M.
full

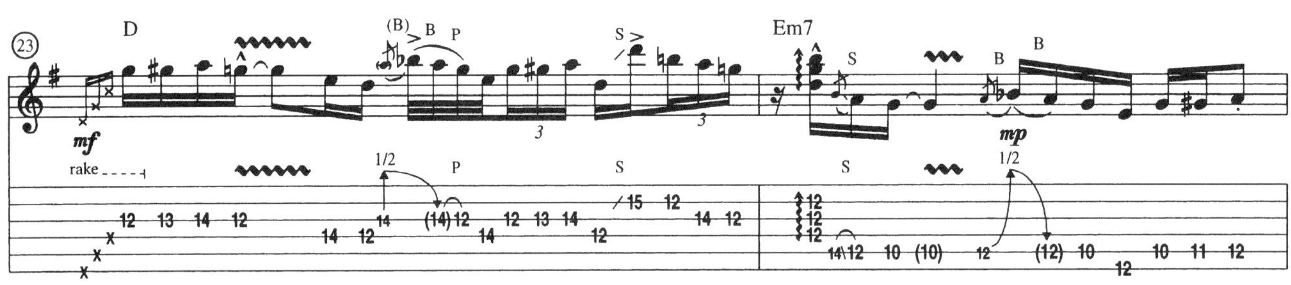
D
Em7
rake

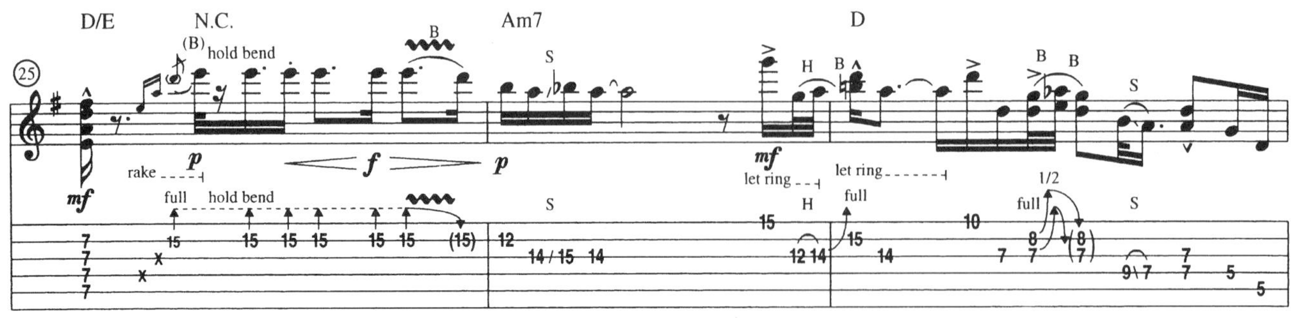
D/E
N.C.
Am7
D
hold bend
rake
let ring
full

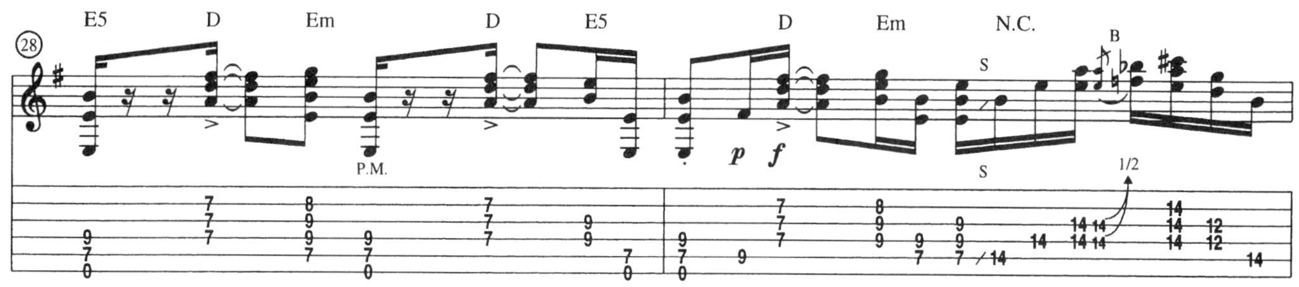
E5 D Em D E5 D Em N.C.
P.M.
p f

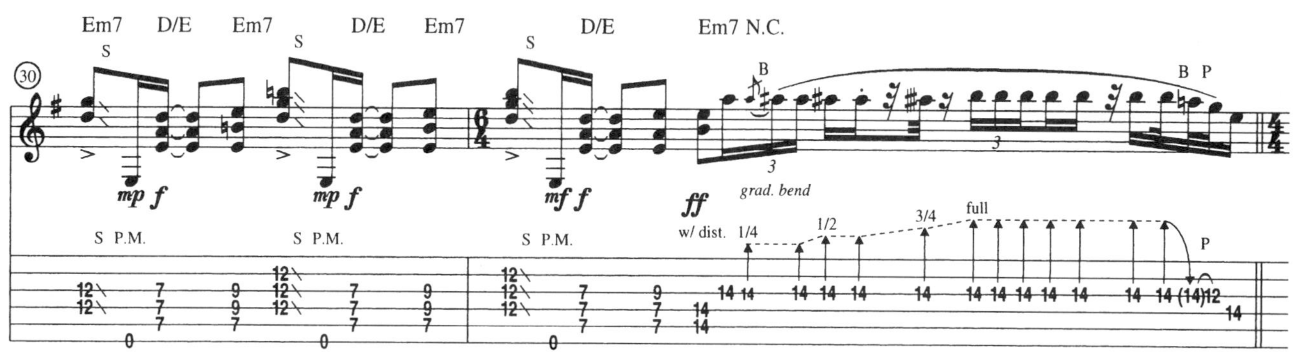
Em7 D/E Em7 D/E Em7 D/E Em7 N.C.
mp f
mf f
ff
grad. bend
S P.M.
w/ dist.

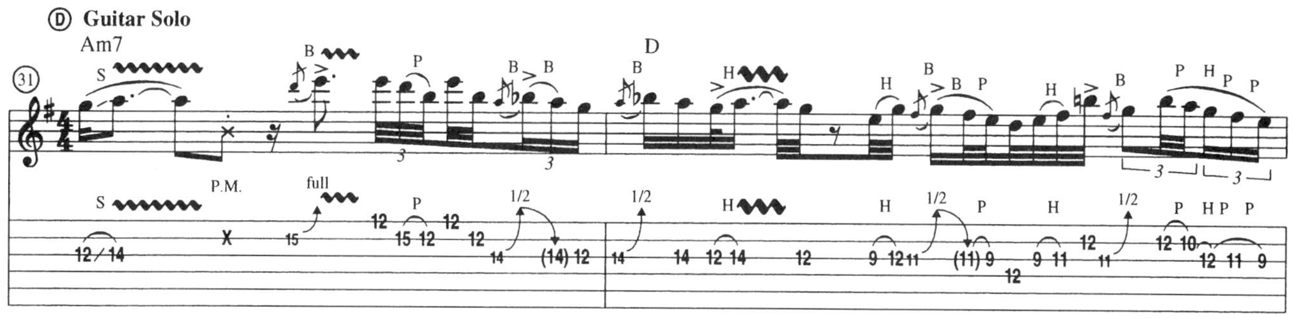
D Guitar Solo
Am7
D
P.M.

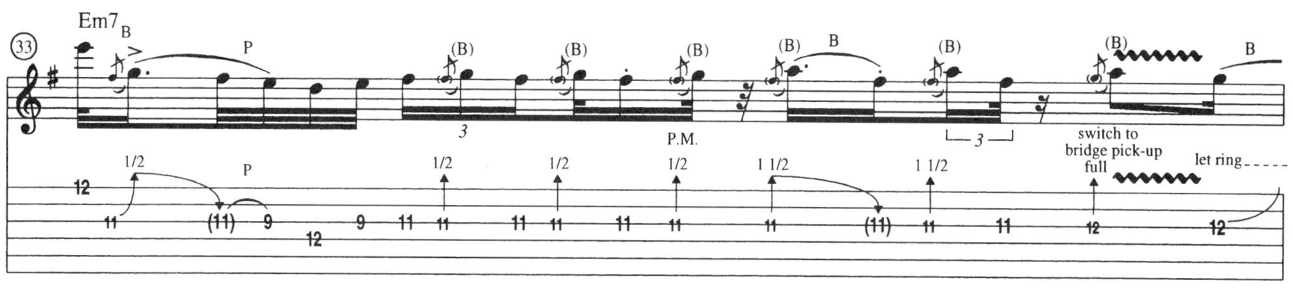
Em7
P.M.
switch to bridge pick-up
let ring

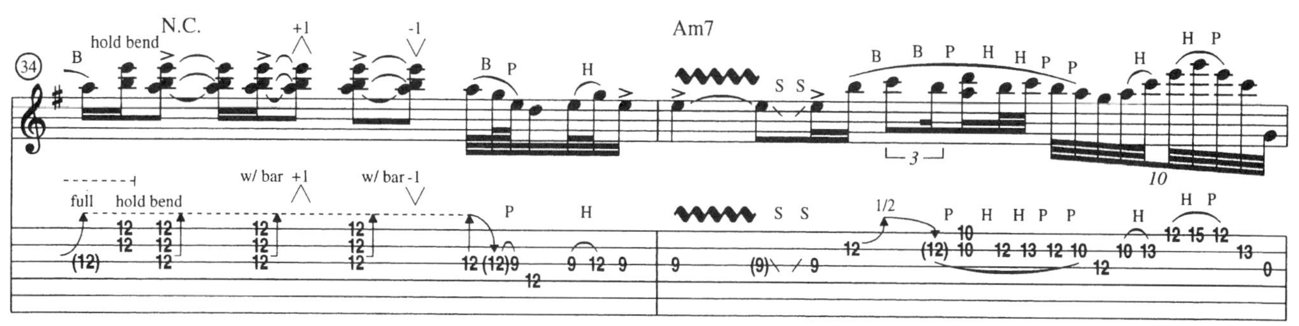
hold bend
N.C.
Am7
w/ bar +1
w/ bar -1

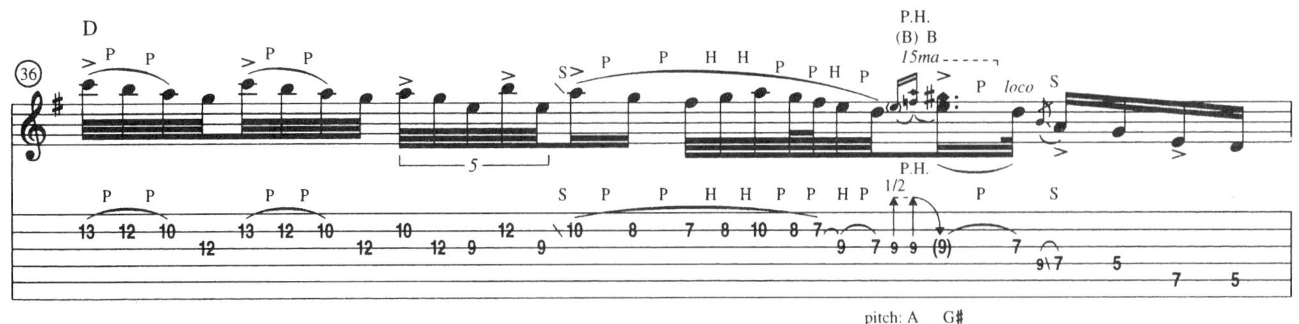

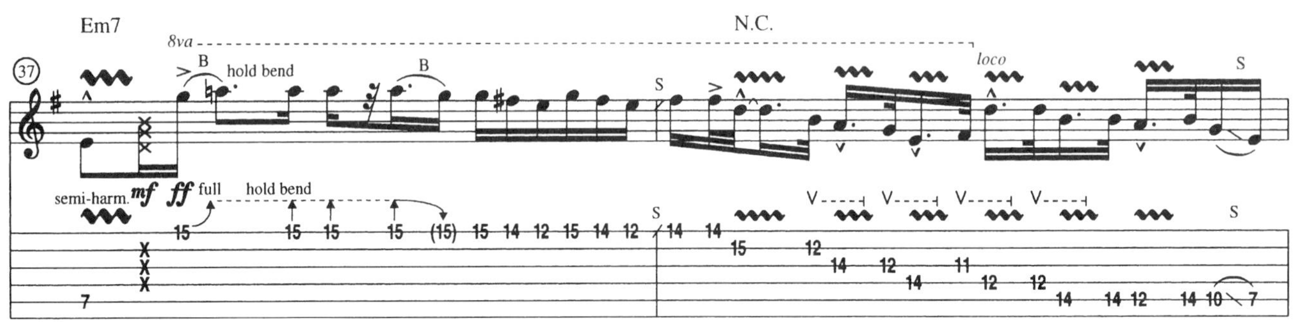

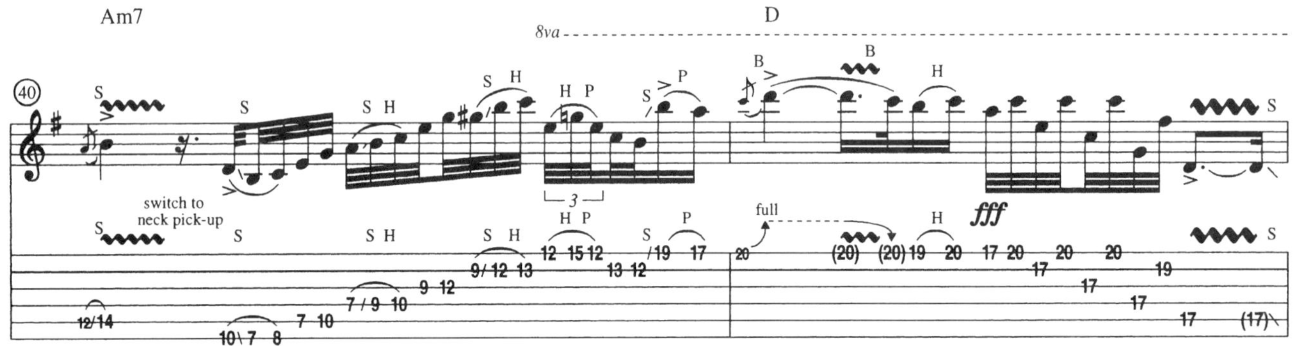

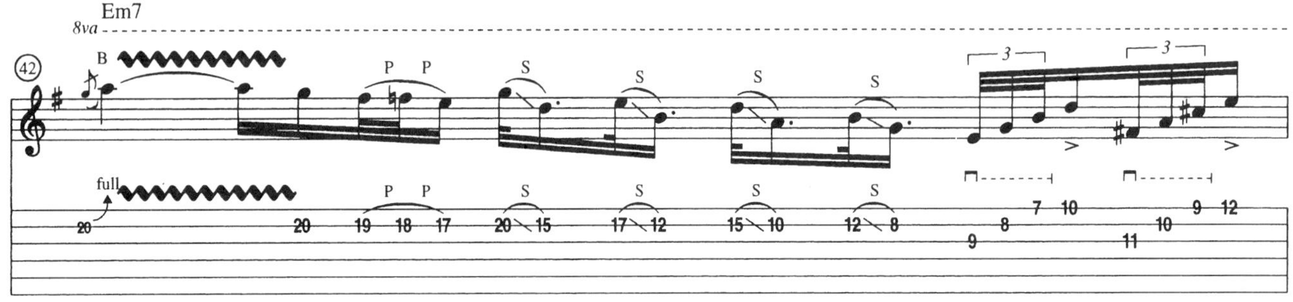

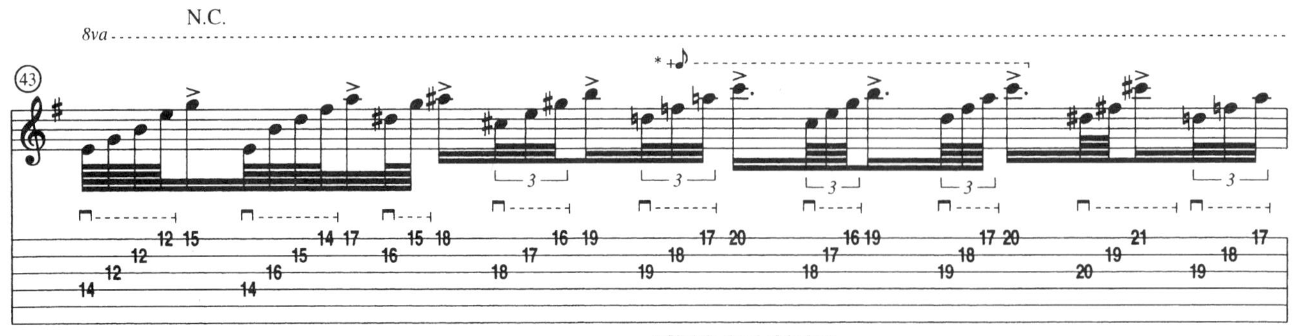

* Slightly ahead of the beat.

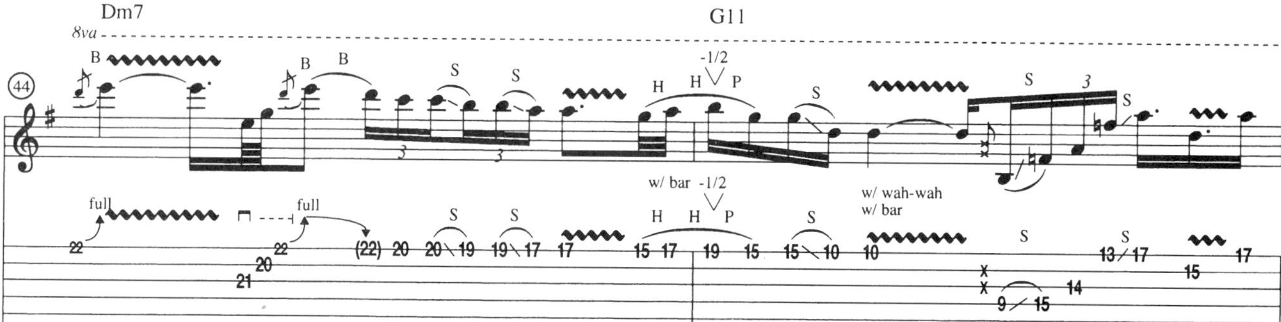

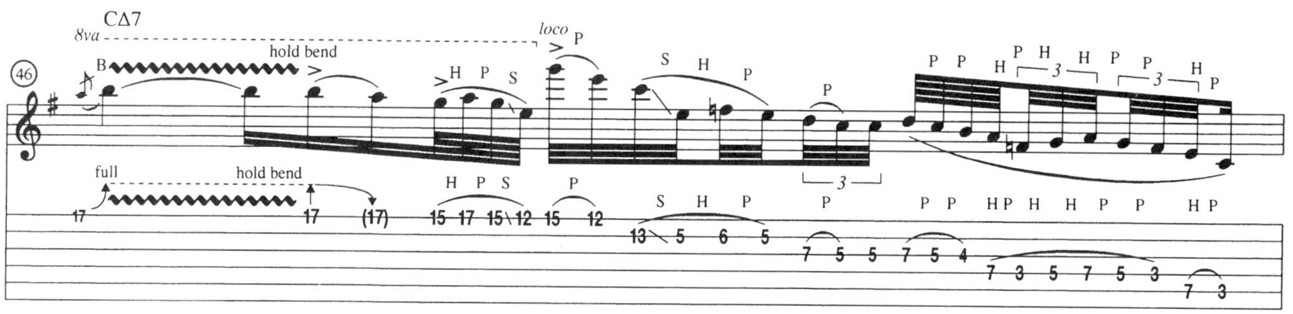

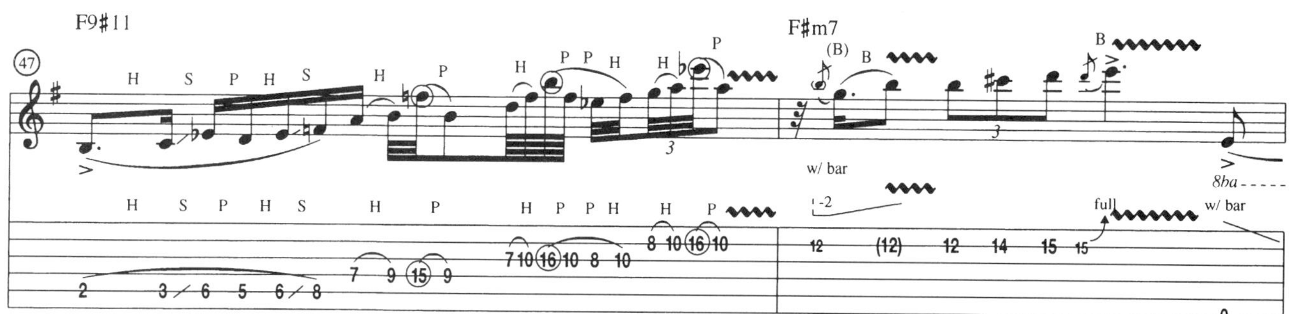

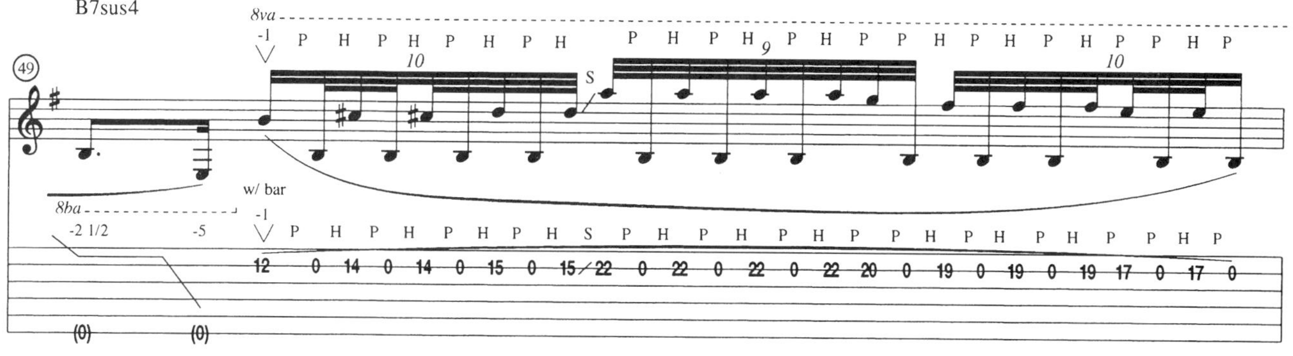

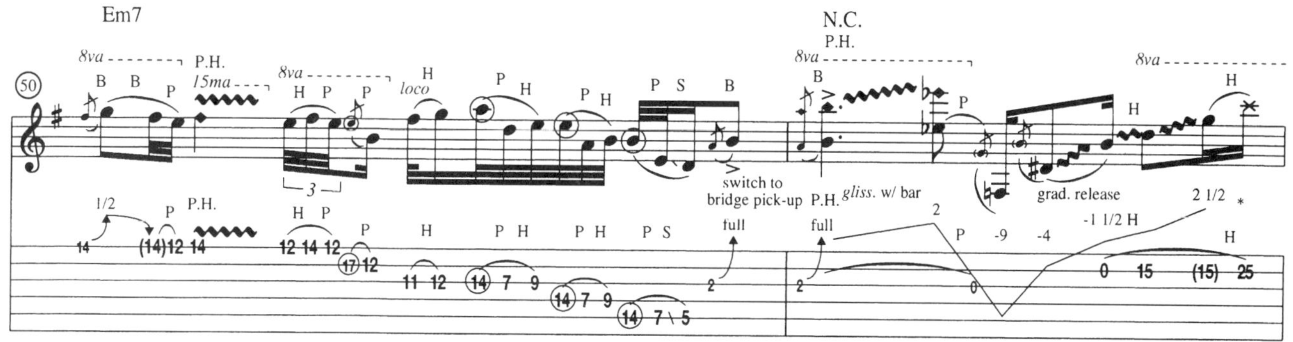

* note frets out

52
Am7
8va
12
13
11

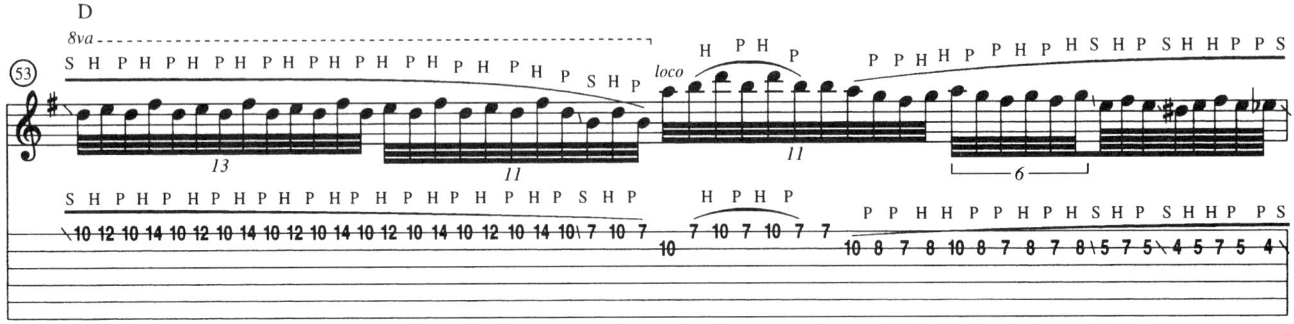
53
D
8va
loco
13
11
11
6

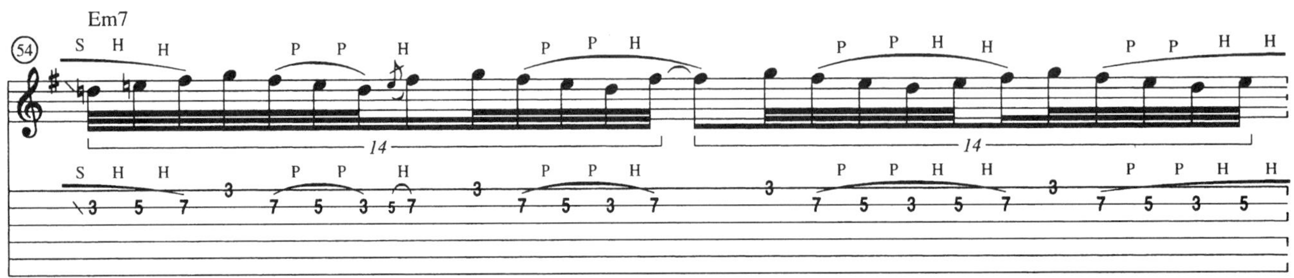
54
Em7
14
14

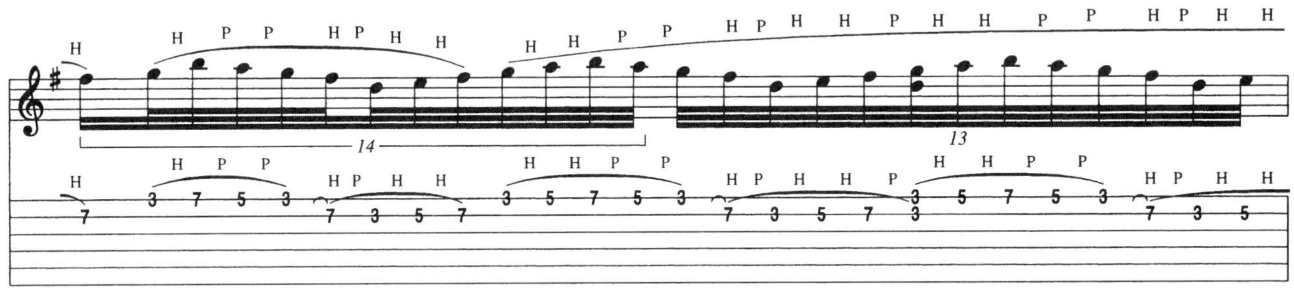
14
13

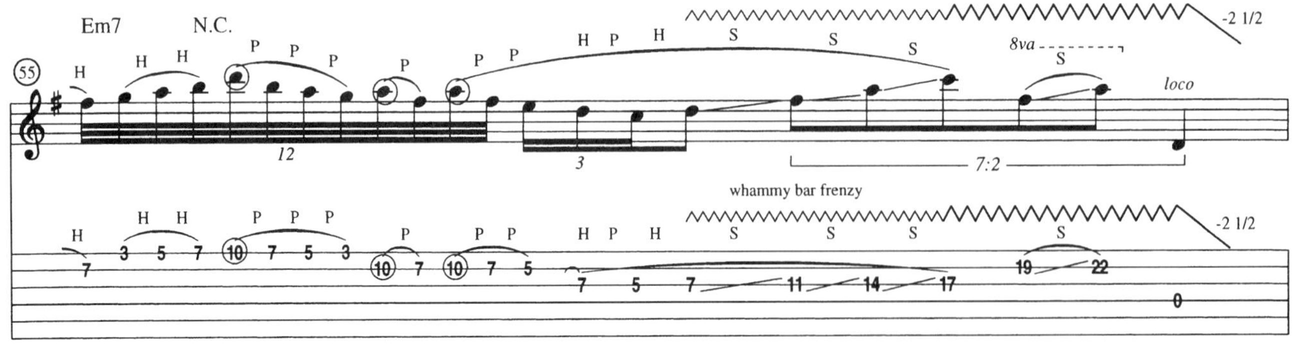
55
Em7
N.C.
12
3
7:2
8va
loco
whammy bar frenzy
-2 1/2
-2 1/2

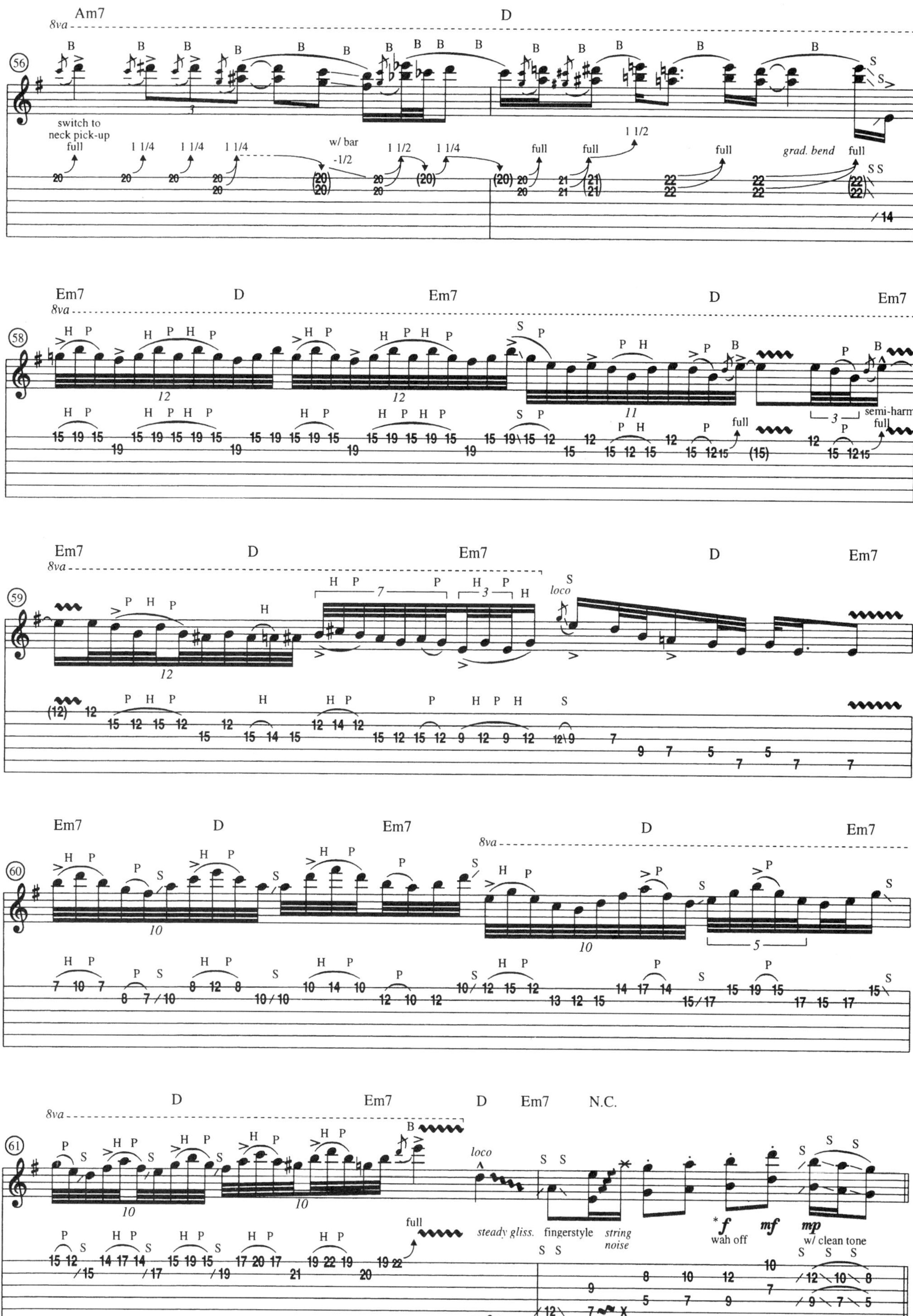

* Decrescendo via volume control on guitar between octaves.

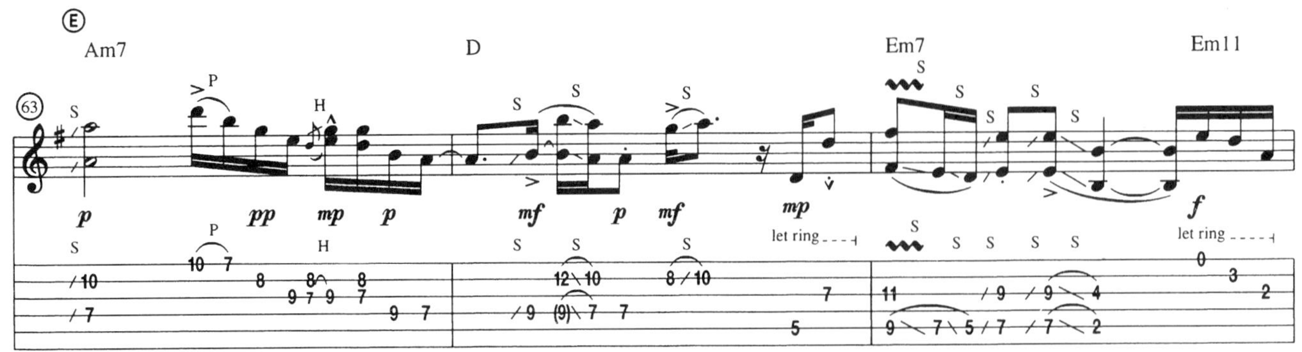
E
Am7
D
Em7
Em11
let ring
let ring

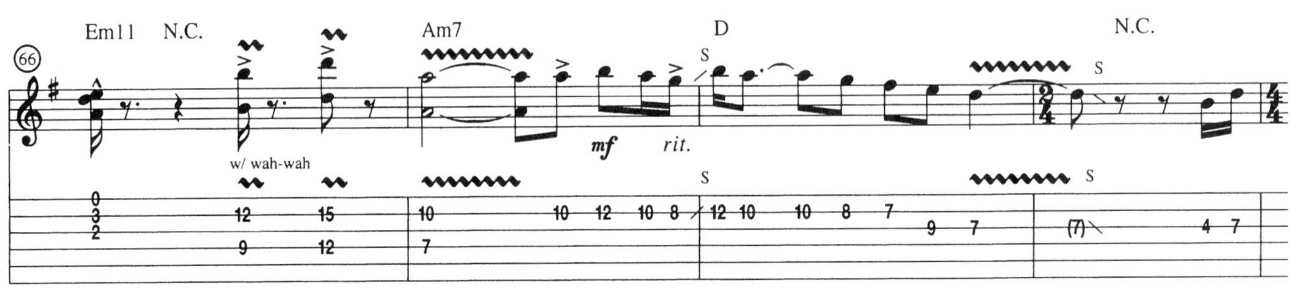
Em11
N.C.
Am7
D
N.C.
w/ wah-wah
rit.

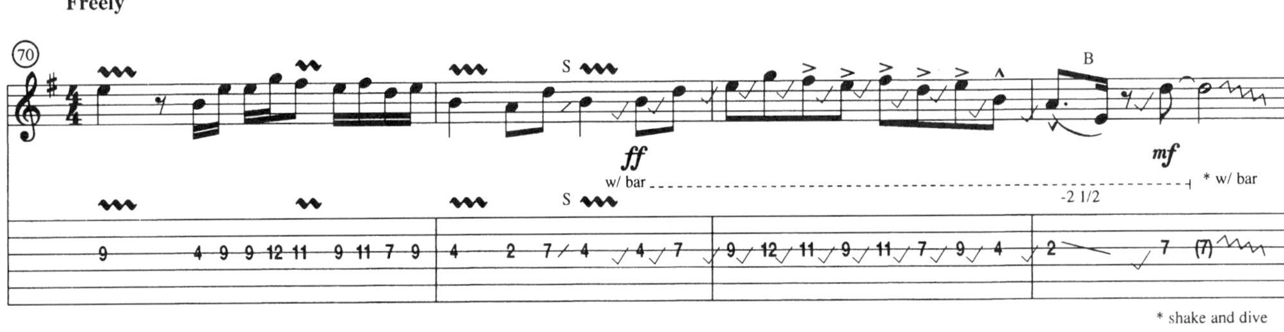
Freely
w/ bar
* w/ bar
* shake and dive

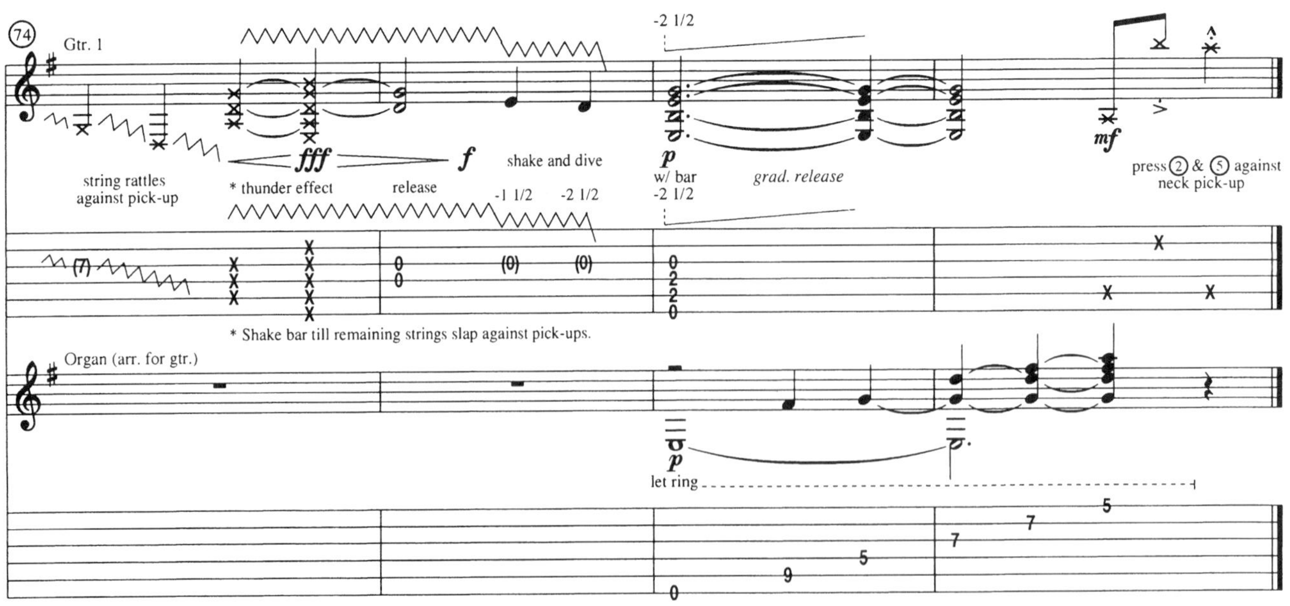
Gtr. 1
string rattles against pick-up
* thunder effect
release
shake and dive
w/ bar
grad. release
press ② & ⑤ against neck pick-up
* Shake bar till remaining strings slap against pick-ups.
Organ (arr. for gtr.)
let ring

from Weezer - *Pinkerton*

Tired of Sex

Words and Music by Rivers Cuomo

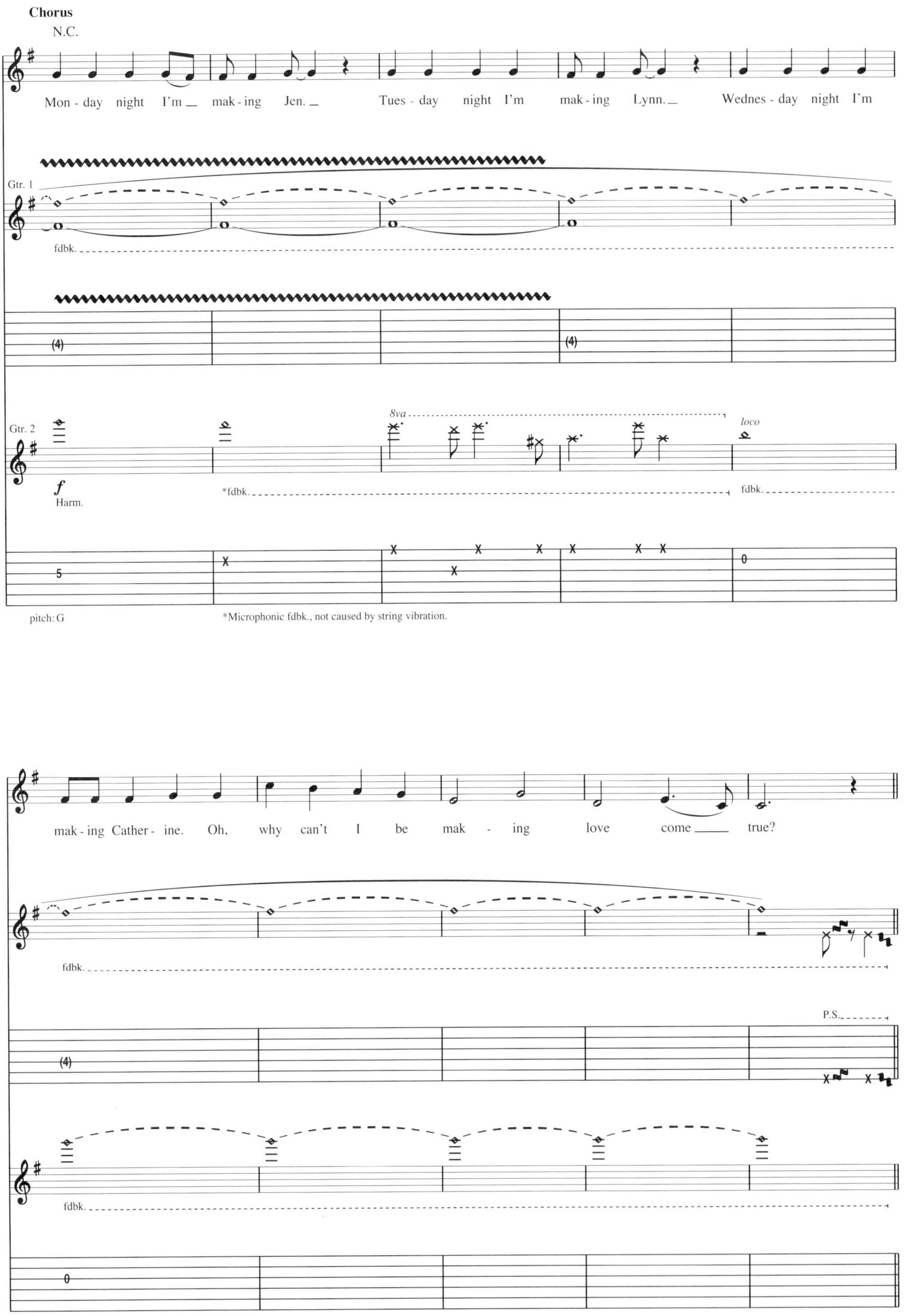

Chorus

N.C.

Mon - day night I'm __ mak - ing Jen. __ Tues - day night I'm mak - ing Lynn. __ Wednes - day night I'm

Gtr. 1

fdbk.

(4) (4)

Gtr. 2

f

Harm.

8va

loco

*fdbk.

fdbk.

5 X X X X X X X X 0

pitch: G

*Microphonic fdbk., not caused by string vibration.

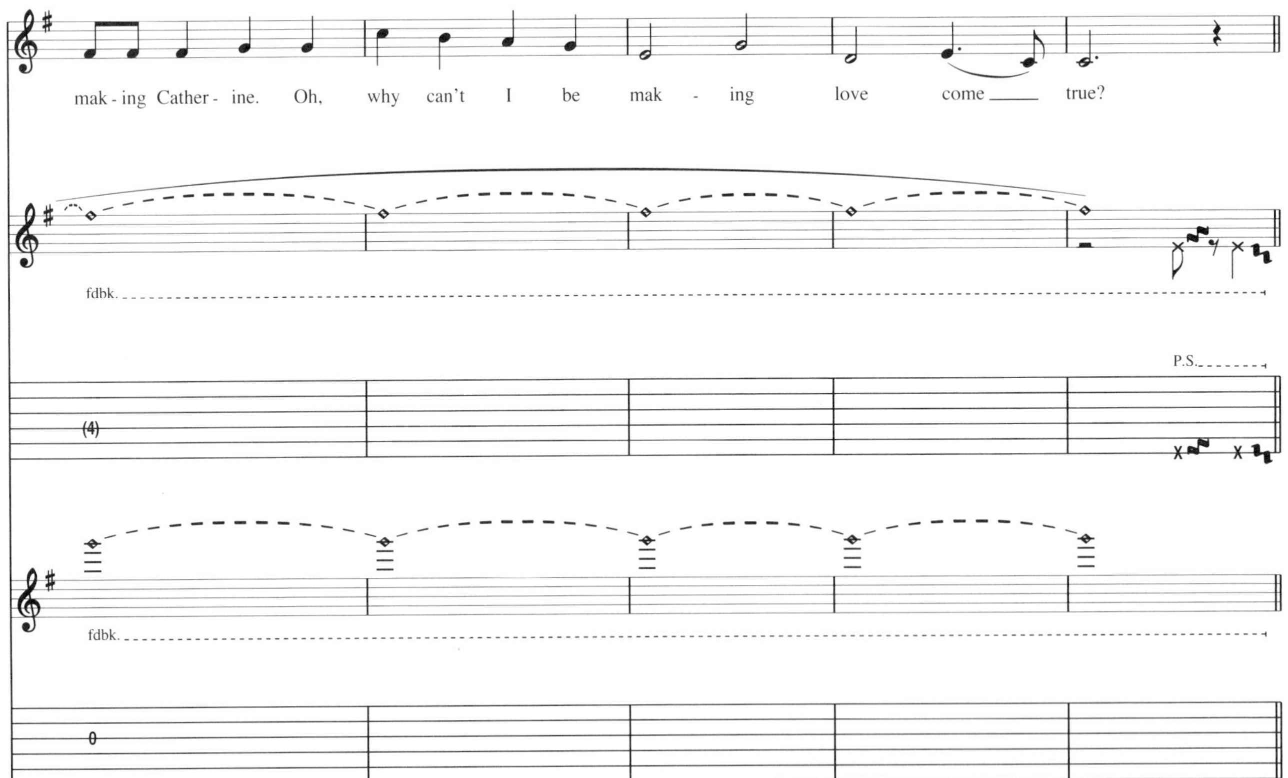

Interlude
*G5 D5 D5 E5 D5 C5 B5 G5 D5 D5 E5 D5 C5 B5
Whoa.
Whoa.
**Gtrs. 1 & 2
Rhy. Fig. 1
End Rhy. Fig. 1
*Chord symbols reflect basic tonality.
**composite arrangement
Verse
Gtrs. 1 & 2: w/ Rhy. Fig. 1, 4 times
G5 D5 D5 E5 D5 C5 B5 G5 D5 D5 E5 D5 C5 B5
2. I'm beat, beet red,
G5 D5 D5 E5 D5 C5 B5 G5 D5 D5 E5 D5 C5 B5
a - shamed of what I said.
(What I said.)
Oh.
G5 D5 D5 E5 D5 C5 B5 G5 D5 D5 E5 D5 C5 B5
I'm sor - ry, here I go. I
G5 D5 D5 E5 D5 C5 B5 G5 D5 D5 E5 D5 C5 B5
know I'm a sin - ner but I can't say no.
(Say no.)
Whoa.
Chorus
G5 C5 D5 E5
Gtrs. 1 & 2: w/ Rhy. Fig. 2, 2 times
G5 C5
Thurs - day night I'm mak - ing Den - ise.
Fri - day night I'm
Rhy. Fig. 2
Gtrs. 1 & 2
End Rhy. Fig. 2

D5 E5 G5 C5 D5 E5
mak - ing Shar - ise.
Sat - ur - day night I'm mak - ing Lou - ise. So
F5 C5 G/B A5
why can't I be mak - ing love come
Gtrs. 1 & 2
(cont. in slash)
Guitar Solo
Gtrs. 1 & 2: w/ Rhy. Fig. 1, 2 times
A5 G5 D5 D5 E5 D5 C5 B5
true?
(What's a guy to do?)
Gtr. 3 (dist.)
G5 D5 D5 E5 D5 C5 B5 G5 D5
full
D5 E5 D5 C5 B5 G5 D5
8va
full
*Hammer-on with edge of pick.
**TAB number reflects position beyond fretboard.

Bridge
Gtrs. 1 & 2 w/ Rhy. Fig. 2, 3 times
Gtr. 3 tacet
D5 E5 D5 C5 B5 G5 C5 D5 E5
Whoa. To - night I'm down on my knees.
8va
full
full
G5 C5 D5 E5 G5 C5 D5 E5
To-night I'm beg-gin' you please. To-night, to - night please. So
F5 C5 G/B G5 E5 Am
Gtr. 1
why can't I be mak - ing love come true?
Gtrs. 1 & 2
Gtr. 2
*grad. rit.
(Gtr. 1, cont in slash)
let ring
*next 6 meas.
Outro
A Tempo
Half-Time Feel
Gtrs. 1 & 2: w/ Rhy. Fig. 1, 1 1/2 times
G5 D5 D5 E5 D5 C5 B5 G5 D5
D5 E5 D5 C5 B5 G5 D5 D5 E5 D5 C5 B5
G5 D5 D5 E5 D5 C5 B5 G5
Gtr. 2
Gtrs. 1 & 2
Gtr. 1
(Gtr. 2, cont. in slash)
steady gliss.

from UFO - *Lights Out*

Too Hot to Handle

Words and Music by Phil Moog and Pete Way

E Esus4 E A Asus4 A D/A G5 E/B D E
Swept up by the roll - in' waves of the night, pap-er chase for fame. Well, I was
Gtr. 1
End Rhy. Fig. 2
let ring
1/4
Rhy. Fig. 3
Gtr. 2
End Rhy. Fig. 3
1/4

Chorus

E G5 A G A D5 E Esus4
too, too hot, ba - by, too hot to han - dle. Yeah, I was
Rhy. Fig. 4
End Rhy. Fig. 4
Rhy. Fig. 4A
End Rhy. Fig. 4A

E/B G5 A G A D E5
too, too hot, mm, too hot to han - dle.
Rhy. Fig. 5
End Rhy. Fig. 5
Verse
Gtr. 1: w/ Rhy. Fig. 2
Gtr. 2: w/ Rhy. Fig. 1
E Esus4 E A Asus4 A D/A G5 E/B Esus4/B
2. Wink of an eye, the feel-in's run high, a real rock and roll mo-lest. But I
3. I'm in your town, won't fool a-round. I'll make some ac - tion stick. Just like a
To Coda 2
Gtr. 2: w/ Rhy. Fig. 3
E Esus4 E A Asus4 A D/A G5 E/B D E
ain't no ro - mance and I ain't no slow chance. Won't get no quick change.
sto-ry says, these boys are bad, so keep out of sh shoot-in' range.
Yeah, I'm
Chorus
Gtr. 1 & 2: w/ Rhy. Figs. 4 & 4A
E G5 A G A D5 E Esus4
too, too hot, ba - by, too hot to han - dle. Yeah, I'm
Gtr. 2: w/ Rhy. Fig. 5
E G5 A G A D5 E
too, too hot, ba - by, too hot to han - dle.
Gtr. 1

Bridge
B5 A5 D5 A B5 A5 G5 A5 Asus4 A5
Sha, _ la, la, la. ___ Roll _ you o - ver, turn you a-round and do ____ it a - gain. __
*Gtrs. 1 & 2
let ring
*Composite arrangement
To Coda 1
B5 A5 D5 A5 G5 A
Sha, _ la, la, la. ___ Keep on com - in'. _ Do it once, _ but nev - er the ___ same. __
Guitar Solo
B5 B6 B5 B6 B5 A5 E B5 B6 B5 B6 B5 A5 E/B B5
Gtr. 3 (dist.)
8va
f
1/2
Gtrs. 1 & 2
Rhy. Fig. 6
End Rhy. Fig. 6
Gtrs. 1 & 2: w/ Rhy. Fig. 6 (5 times)
B6 B5 B6 B5 A5 E/B B5 B6 B5 B6 B5 A5 E/B B5
Gtr. 3
1/4

B6 B5 B6 B5 A5 E/B B5 B6 B5 B6 B5
8va
loco
let ring
A5 E/B B5 B6 B5 B6 B5 A5 E/B B5
let ring
Gtr. 3
B6 B5 B6 B5 A5 E5/B
P.M.
Gtrs. 1 & 2
Interlude
Gtr. 3 tacet
B5 A5 D5 A B5 A5 G5 A5 Asus4 A5
*Gtrs. 1 & 2
let ring
let ring
*Composite arrangement
D.S. al Coda 1
B5 A5 D5 A G5 A

Coda 1

Coda 2

Chorus

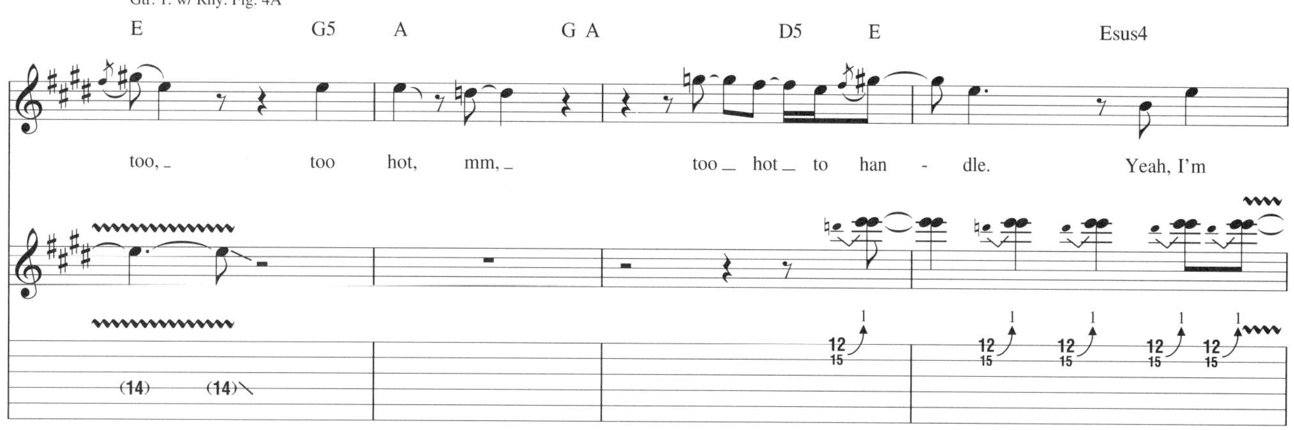

Gtrs. 1 & 2: w/ Rhy. Figs. 4 & 4A (2 times)
E
G5
A
G
A
too, too hot, ba - by,
D5
E
Esus4
too hot to han - dle. Yeah, I'm
8va
loco
E
G5
A
G
A
too, too, too hot,
1/4
D5
E
Esus4
too hot to han - dle.

Outro-Guitar Solo

Gtrs. 1 & 2: w/ Rhy. Figs. 4 & 4A (1 1/2 times)

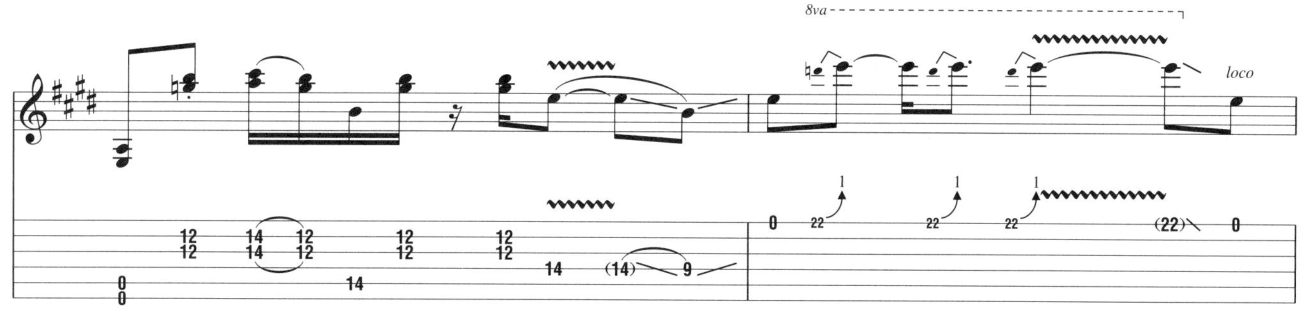

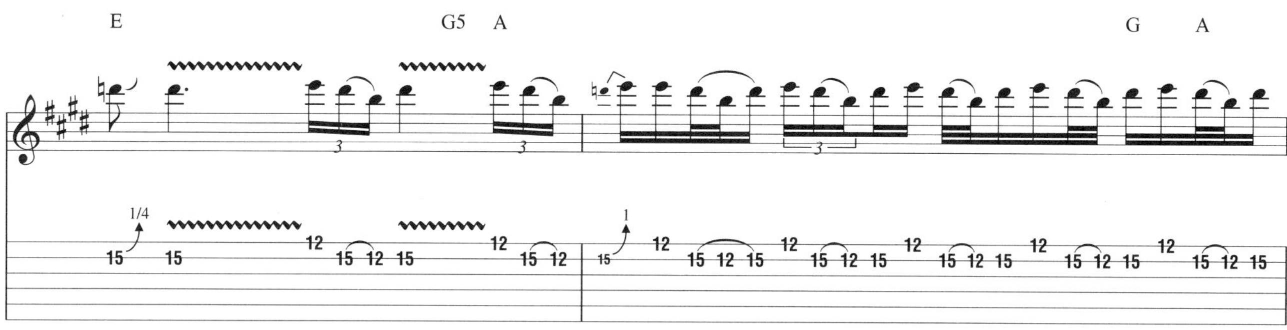

from Stone Temple Pilots - *Tiny Music...Songs from the Vatican Gift Shop*

Trippin' on a Hole in a Paper Heart

Words and Music by Dean DeLeo, Robert DeLeo, Eric Kretz and Scott Weiland

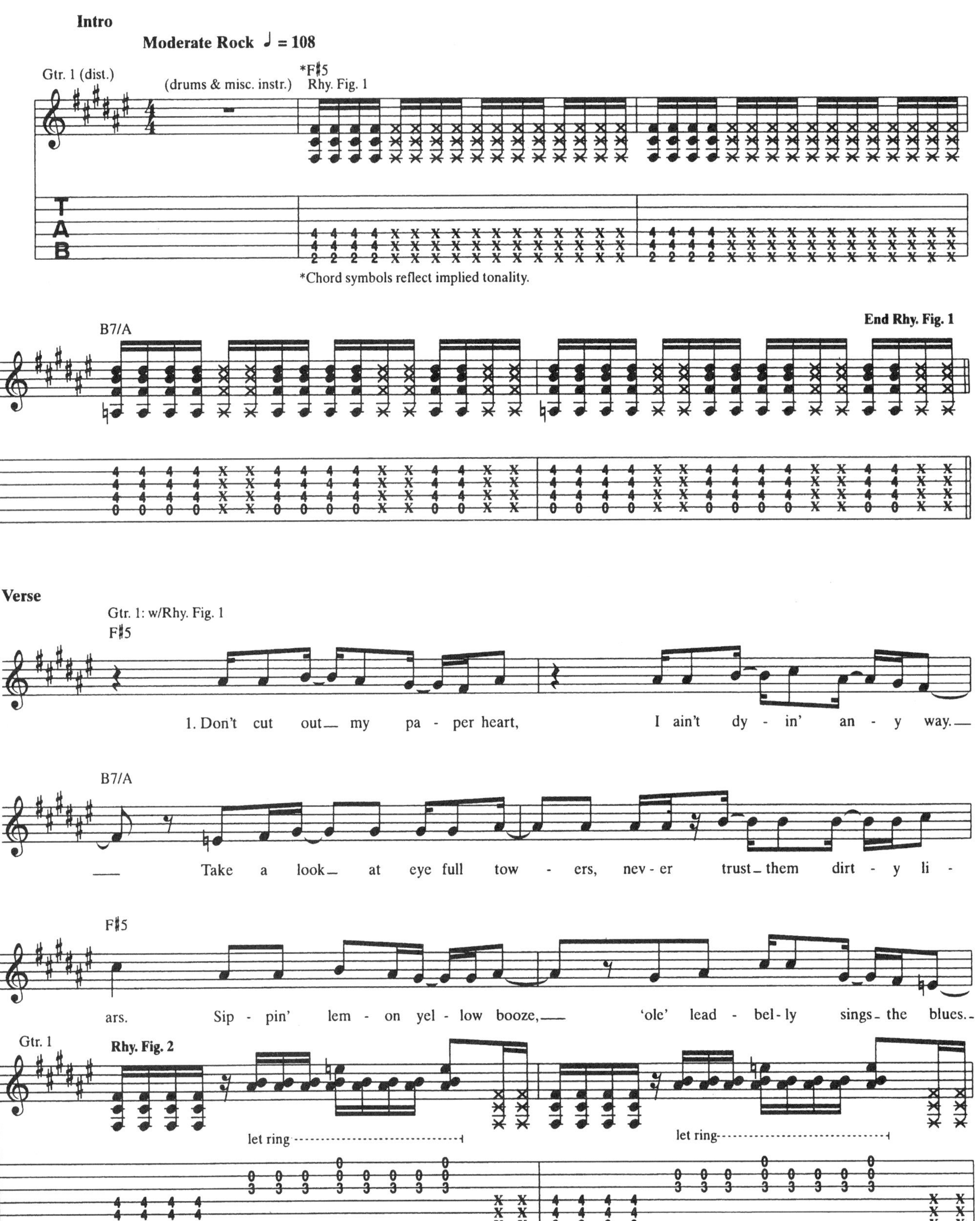

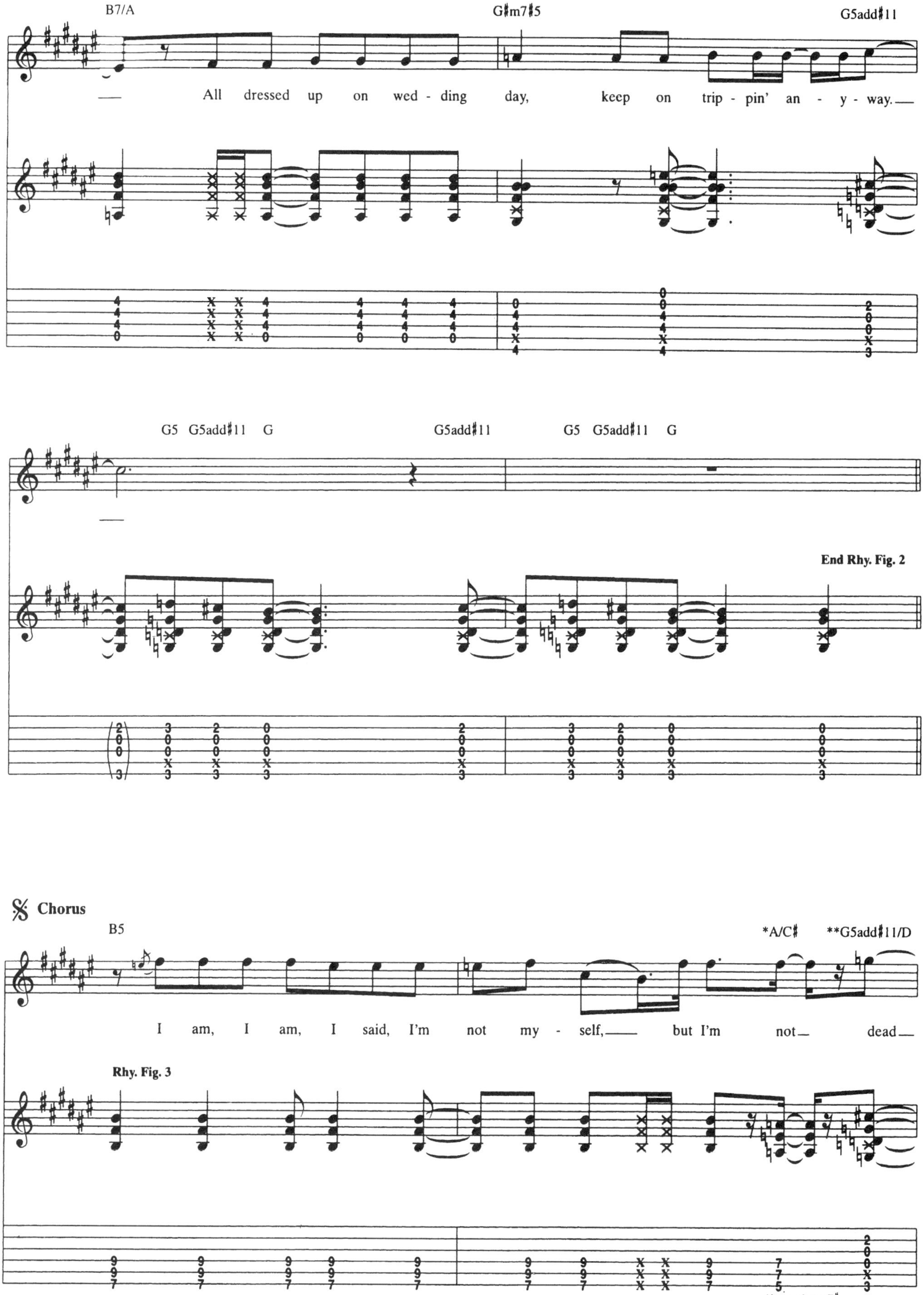

B7/A
G♯m7♯5
G5add♯11
All dressed up on wed - ding day, keep on trip - pin' an - y - way.
G5 G5add♯11 G
G5add♯11
G5 G5add♯11 G
End Rhy. Fig. 2
Chorus
B5
*A/C♯
**G5add♯11/D
I am, I am, I said, I'm not my - self, but I'm not dead
Rhy. Fig. 3

*bass plays C♯
**bass plays D

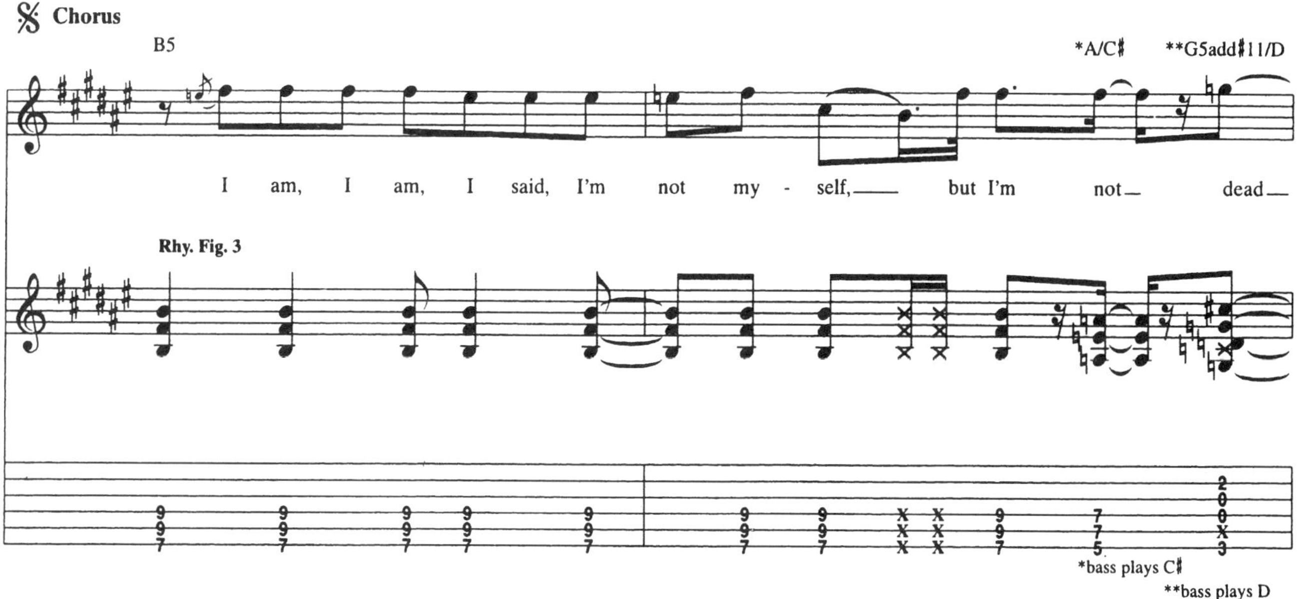

G5 G5add#11 G
G5add#11
G5 G5add#11 G
and I'm not for sale.
End Rhy. Fig. 3

To Coda 1
Gtr. 2: w/Fill 1, 2nd time
B5
A5add#11
So keep your bank-roll lot-ter-y, eat your sal-ad day, death-bed mo-tor-cade.

Verse

Gtr. 1: w/Rhy. Fig. 1, 2 times
F#5
2. Fake the heat and scratch the itch, skinned up kness and salt-y lips.

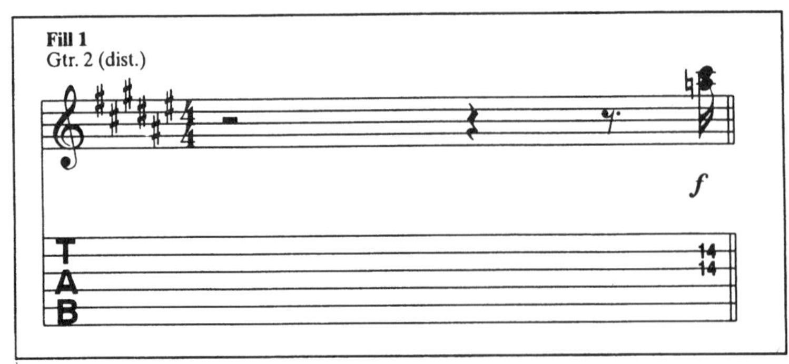
Fill 1
Gtr. 2 (dist.)
f
T
A
B
14
14

B7/A
I'll breathe your life, vicks va - por life, and when you binge I purge a - like.
F♯5
Let go, it's hard - er hold - ing on, one more trip and I'll be gone.
B7/A
So keep your head up, keep it on, just a whis - per, I'll be gone.
Gtr. 1: w/Rhy. Fig. 2
F♯5
Take a breath and make it big, it's the last you'll ev - er get.
B7/A
G♯m7♯5
G5add♯11
Don't break your neck with dia - mond noose, it's the last you'll ev - er choose.
G5 G5add♯11 G
G5add♯11
G5 G5add♯11 G
Chorus
Gtr. 1: w/Rhy. Fig. 3, 2 times
B5
*A/C♯
**G5add♯11/D
I am, I am, I said, I'm not my - self, I'm not dead
*bass plays C♯
**bass plays D
G5 G5add♯11 G
G5add♯11
G5 G5add♯11 G
and I'm not for sale.
B5
A5
G5add♯11
Hold me clos - er, clos - er, let me go, let me be,
1st time: D.S. al Coda 1
2nd time: To Coda 2
G5 G5add♯11 G
G5add♯11
G5 G5add♯11 G
just let me be.

Coda 1

Guitar Solo

Gtr. 1: w/Rhy. Fig. 1, 2 times
F♯5
Gtr. 2
1/2
1/2
1/2
1/2
1/2

B7/A
8va

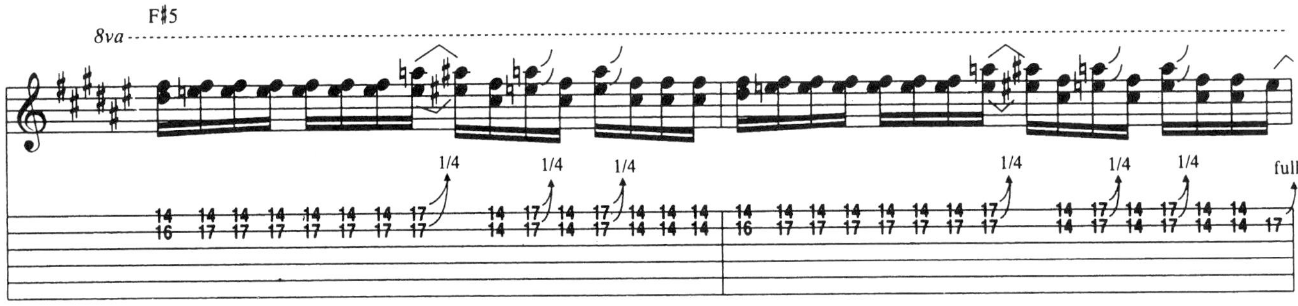
F♯5
8va
1/4
1/4
1/4
1/4
1/4
1/4
full

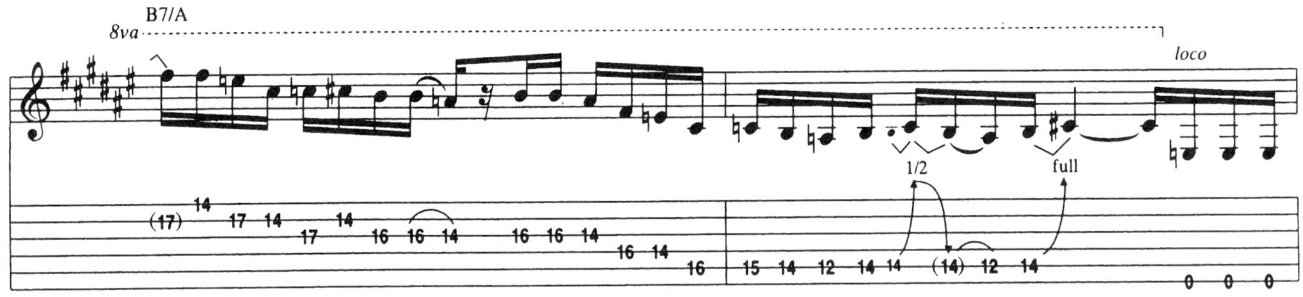
B7/A
8va
loco
1/2
full

Gtr. 1: w/Rhy. Fig. 2
F♯5

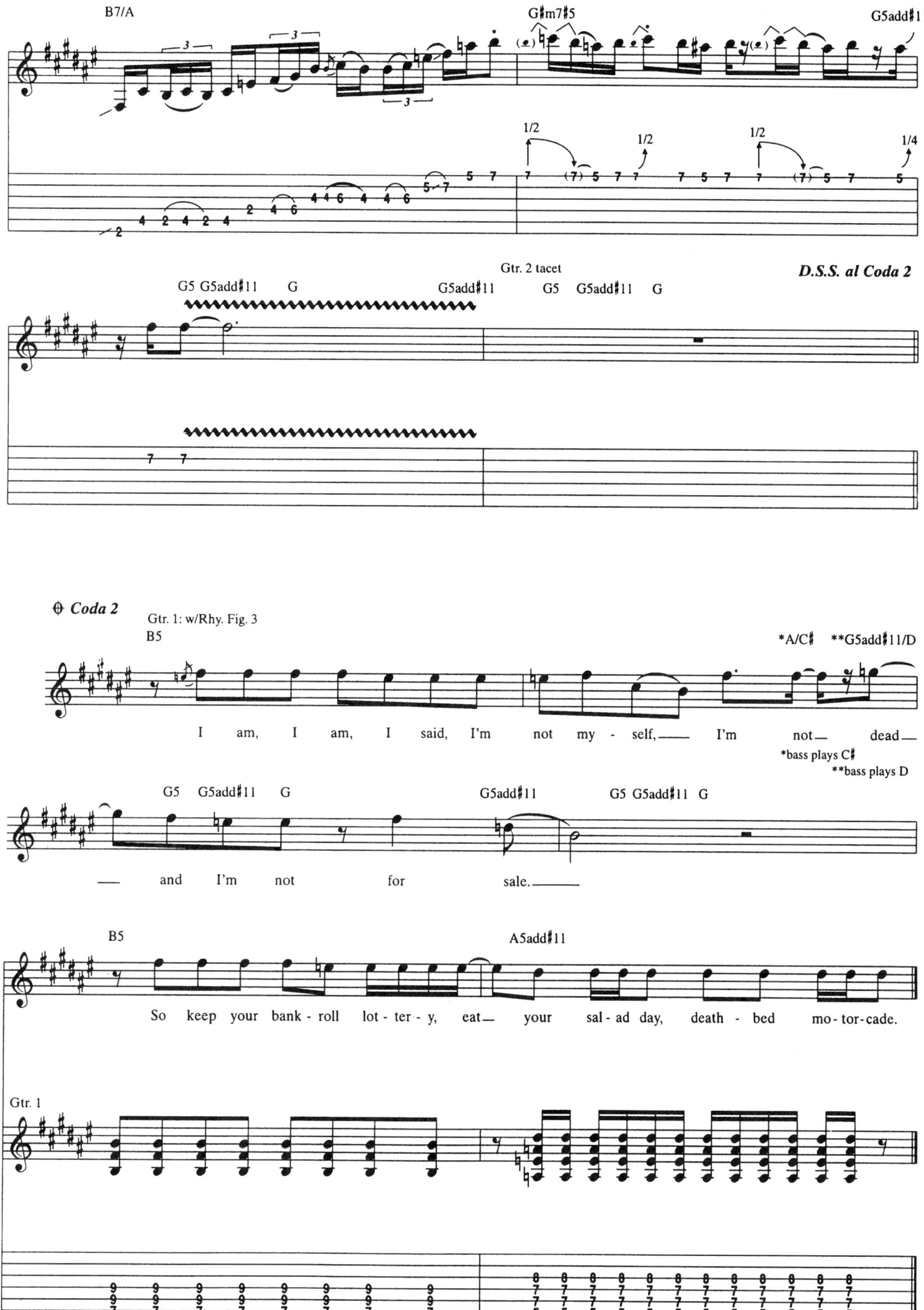
B7/A
G♯m7♯5
G5add♯11
G5 G5add♯11 G
Gtr. 2 tacet
G5add♯11
G5 G5add♯11 G
D.S.S. al Coda 2
Coda 2
Gtr. 1: w/Rhy. Fig. 3
B5
*A/C♯ **G5add♯11/D
I am, I am, I said, I'm not my - self, I'm not dead
*bass plays C♯
**bass plays D
G5 G5add♯11 G
G5add♯11
G5 G5add♯11 G
and I'm not for sale.
B5
A5add♯11
So keep your bank - roll lot - ter - y, eat your sal - ad day, death - bed mo - tor - cade.
Gtr. 1

from Lynyrd Skynyrd - *Pronounced Lĕh-nérd Skin-nérd*

Tuesday's Gone

Words and Music by Allen Collins and Ronnie Van Zant

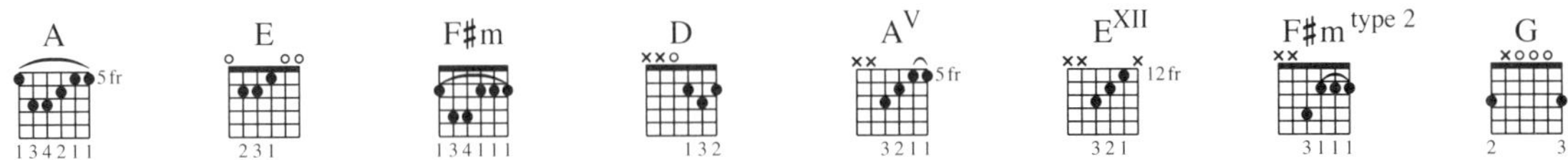

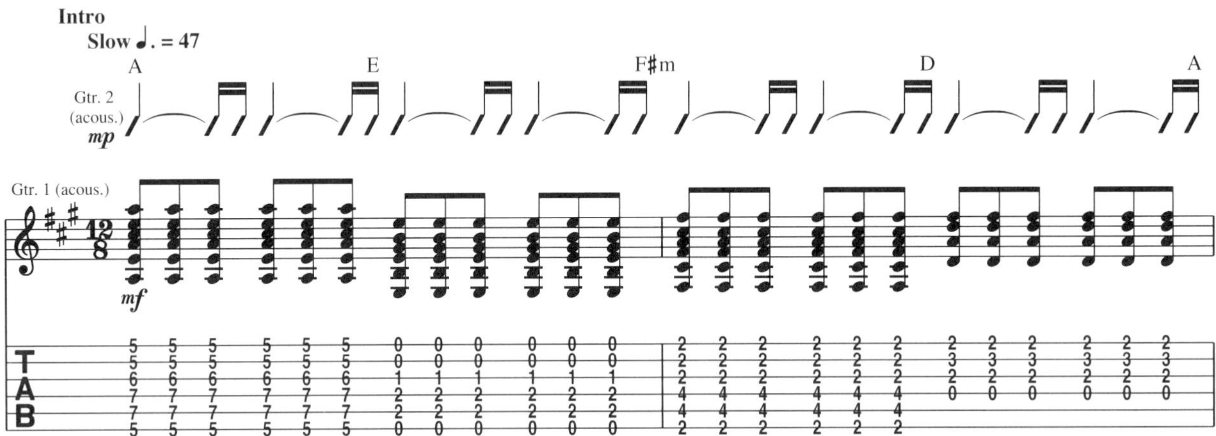

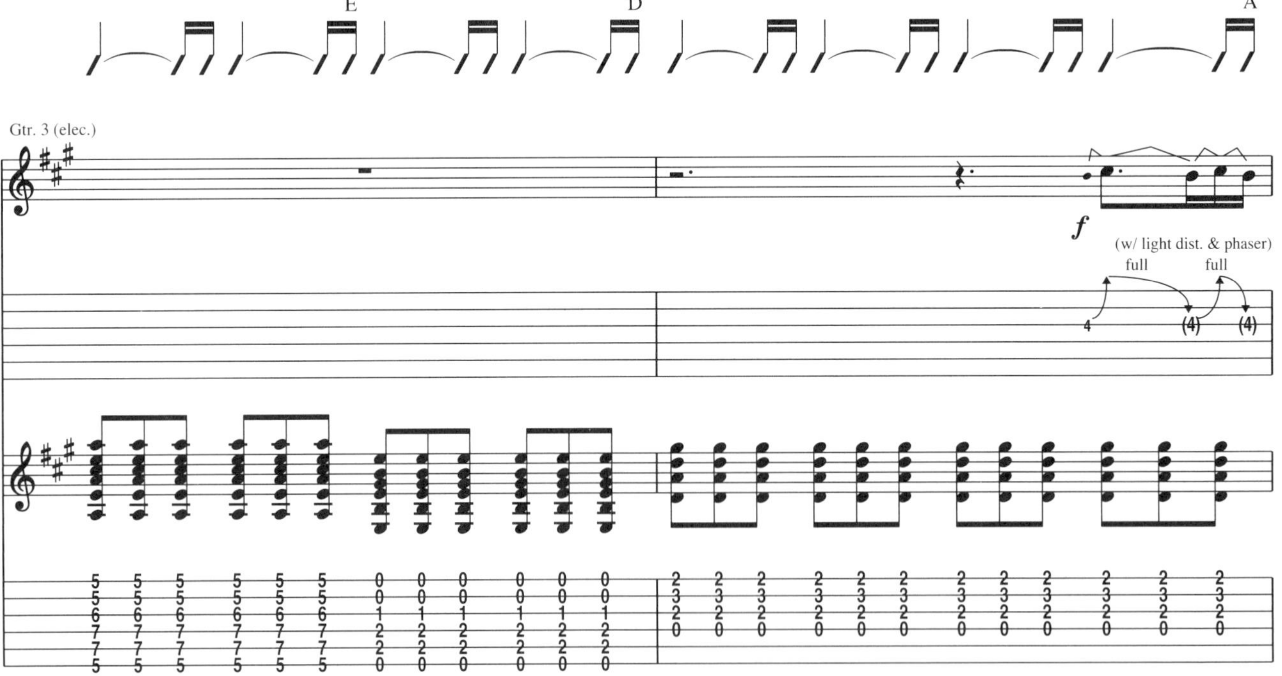

E
F♯m
D
A
Rhy. Fig. 1B
Gtr. 3
full
Rhy. Fig. 1
Gtr. 4 (elec.)
mp (clean tone w/ phaser)
let ring
let ring simile
Rhy. Fig. 1A
Gtr. 1
open
3fr
End Rhy. Fig. 1B
End Rhy. Fig. 1
End Rhy. Fig. 1A

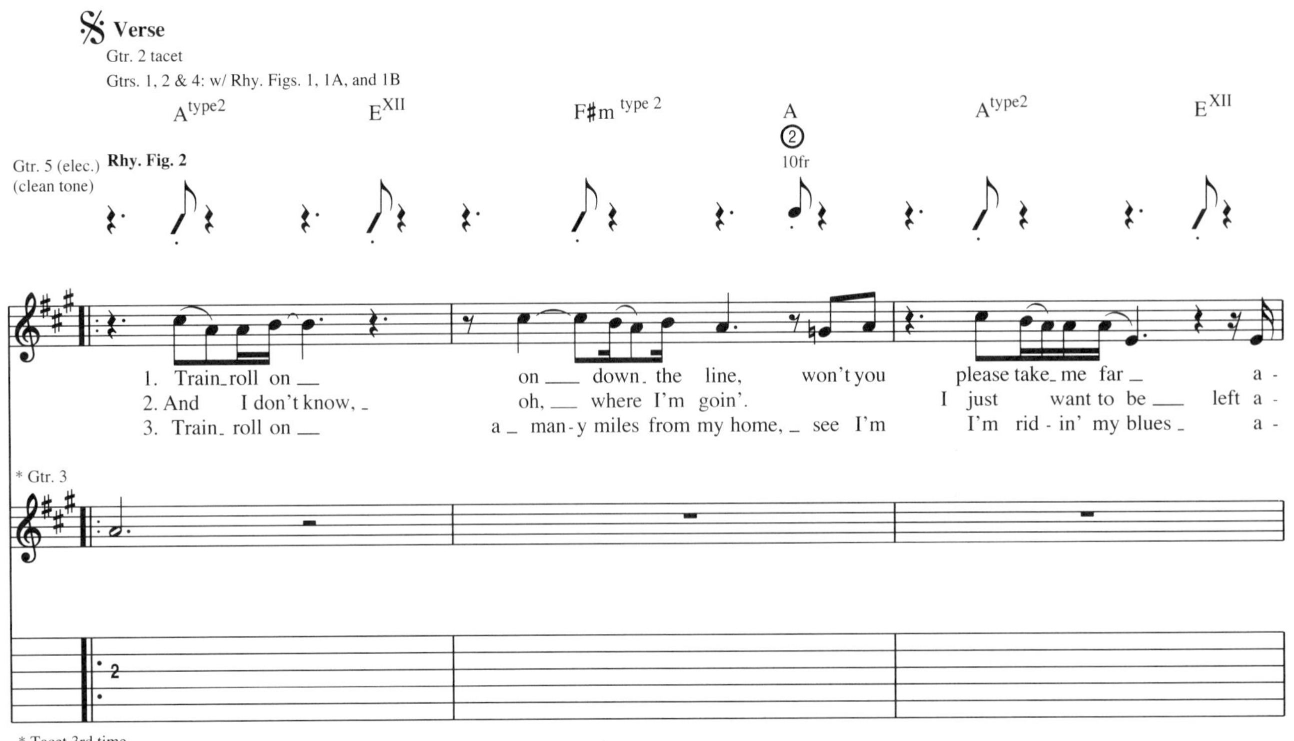
Verse
Gtr. 2 tacet
Gtrs. 1, 2 & 4: w/ Rhy. Figs. 1, 1A, and 1B
Gtr. 5 (elec.) (clean tone)
Rhy. Fig. 2
10fr
1. Train roll on on down the line, won't you please take me far a-
2. And I don't know, oh, where I'm goin'. I just want to be left a-
3. Train roll on a many miles from my home, see I'm I'm rid-in' my blues a-
* Gtr. 3

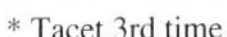
* Tacet 3rd time

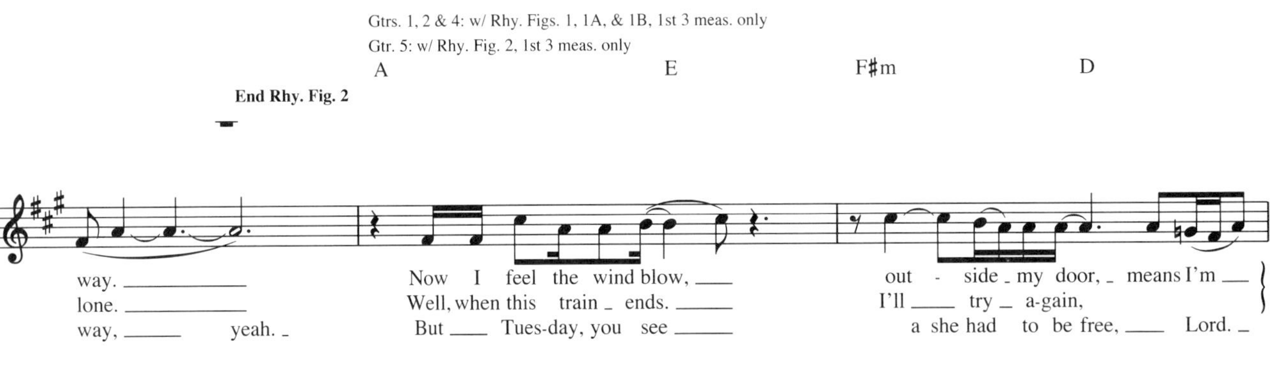
Gtrs. 1, 2 & 4: w/ Rhy. Figs. 1, 1A, & 1B, 1st 3 meas. only
Gtr. 5: w/ Rhy. Fig. 2, 1st 3 meas. only
End Rhy. Fig. 2
way. Now I feel the wind blow, out - side my door, means I'm
lone. Well, when this train ends. I'll try a-gain,
way, yeah. But Tues-day, you see a she had to be free, Lord.

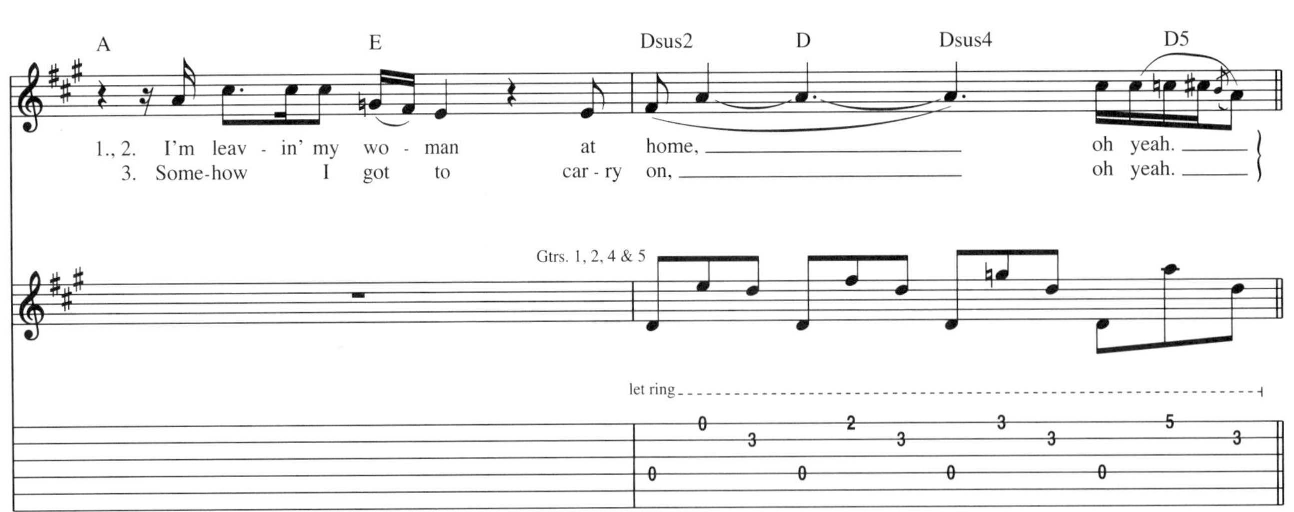
1., 2. I'm leav - in' my wo - man at home, oh yeah.
3. Some-how I got to car - ry on, oh yeah.
Gtrs. 1, 2, 4 & 5
let ring

1.
Chorus
A G D A E
Rhy. Fig. 3B
End Rhy. Fig. 3B Rhy. Fig. 4A
Gtrs. 1 & 2
Tues-day's gone with the wind.
Oh my ba - by's gone with the
Rhy. Fig. 3
End Rhy. Fig. 3
Gtr. 5
let ring
Rhy. Fig. 3A
End Rhy. Fig. 3A Rhy. Fig. 4
Gtr. 4
Guitar Solo
Gtrs. 1, 2 & 4: w/ Rhy. Figs. 1, 1A & 1B
Gtr. 5: w/ Rhy. Fig. 2
D E D D E D D E D D E D
open open 3fr open 2fr 3fr open open 3fr open open 3fr
A E F♯ D
End Rhy. Fig. 4A
Bkdg. Voc. Fig. 1
End Bkdg. Voc. Fig. 1
wind,
(Wind.)
A - gain.
Gtr. 3
(Wind.)
full full full
full
full
full full
Gtrs. 4 & 5
End Rhy. Fig. 4
let ring

A
E
Dsus2
let ring
full
full

2.
Chorus
Gtrs. 1, 2, 4, & 5:w/ Rhy. Figs. 3, 3A, & 3B, 3 times
A G D A G D
Tues-day's gone with the wind. Tues-day's gone with the wind.

To Coda
w/ Bkgd. Voc. Fig. 1
A G D A E Dsus2 D Dsus4 D5
Tues-day's gone with the wind. My ba-by's gone with the wind, train roll

Piano Solo
Gtrs. 1 & 2: w/ Rhy. Figs. 1A & 1B, 1st 3 meas. only
w/ Voc. ad Lib.
A E F♯m D A E
on.
Gtr. 4
8va
loco
Gtr. 5

Gtr. 1: w/ Fill 1
F#m
G
Rhy. Fig. 5
End Rhy. Fig. 5
Gtrs. 1 & 2
Gtrs. 1 & 2: w/ Rhy. Figs. 1A & 1B, 1st 3 meas. only
A
E
8va
F#m
loco
D
A
E
Fill 1
Gtr. 3
8va
TAB
Fill 2
Gtr. 3
8va
TAB

Gtrs. 1 & 2: w/ Rhy. Fig. 5
Gtr. 3: w/ Fill 2 (see p. 100)
F♯m
G
Gtrs. 1, 2, 4 & 5: w/ Rhy. Figs. 3, 3A & 3B
A
G
D
play 3 times
1st time only
Gtrs. 1, 2, 4 & 5: w/ Rhy. Figs. 4 & 4A
A
E
Dsus2
Guitar Solo
Gtrs. 1, 2 & 4: w/ Rhy. Fig. 1
Gtr. 5: w/ Rhy. Fig. 2
A
E
Gtr. 3
full
F♯m
D
A
E
Dsus2
D.S. al Coda
(take 2nd ending)
Coda
Gtrs. 3 & 5 tacet
A
E
w/ Voc. ad Libs.
D
Gtrs. 1 & 2: w/ Rhy. Fig. 6, to end
A
E
Rhy. Fig. 6
End Rhy. Fig. 6
Gtrs. 1 & 2
on.
Gtr. 4
Rhy. Fig. 7
let ring
let ring

Gtr. 4: w/ Rhy. Fig. 1 to end
D
A
E
D
End Rhy. Fig. 7
Gtr. 3
full
full

A
E
D
A
E
full
full
full
full

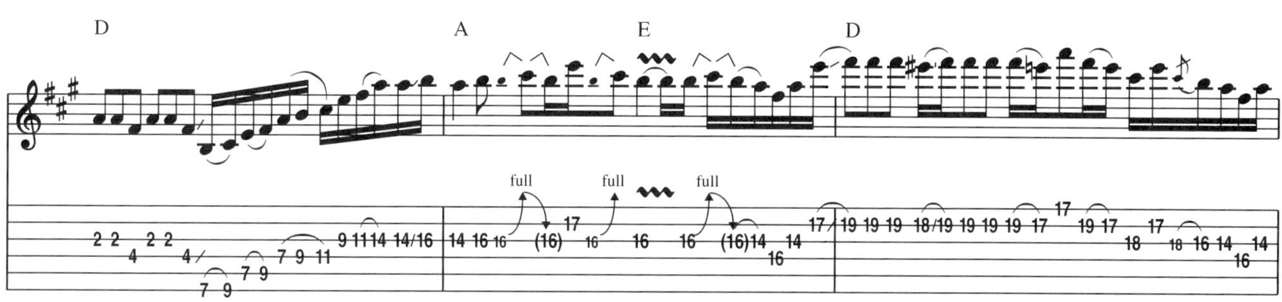
D
A
E
D
full
full
full

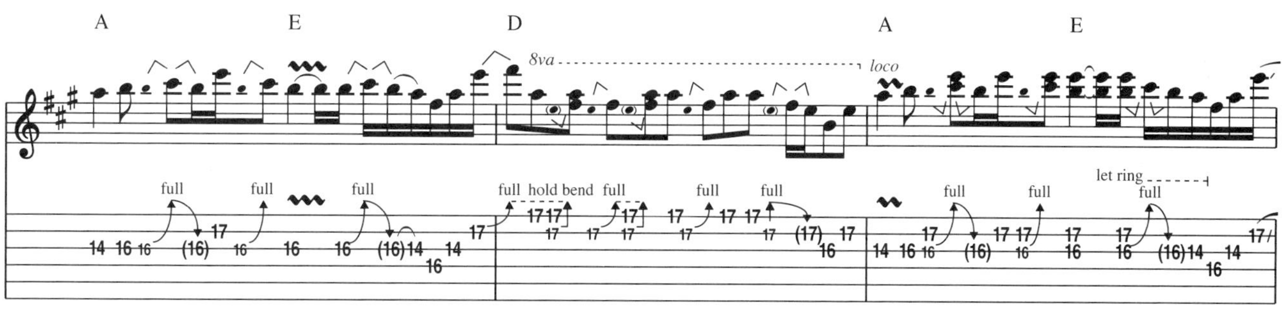
A
E
D
A
E
8va
loco
full
full
full
full
hold bend
full
full
full
full
full
let ring
full

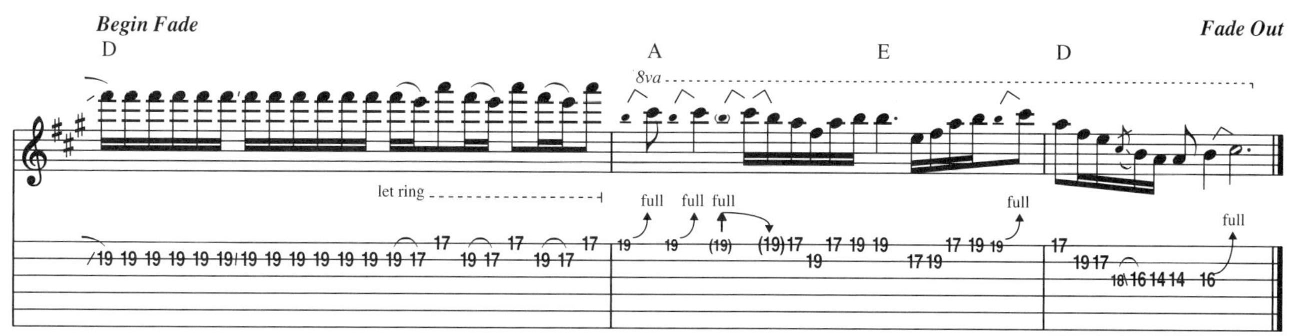
Begin Fade
Fade Out
D
A
E
D
8va
let ring
full
full
full
full
full

from T. Rex - *Tanx*

Twentieth Century Boy

Words and Music by Marc Bolan

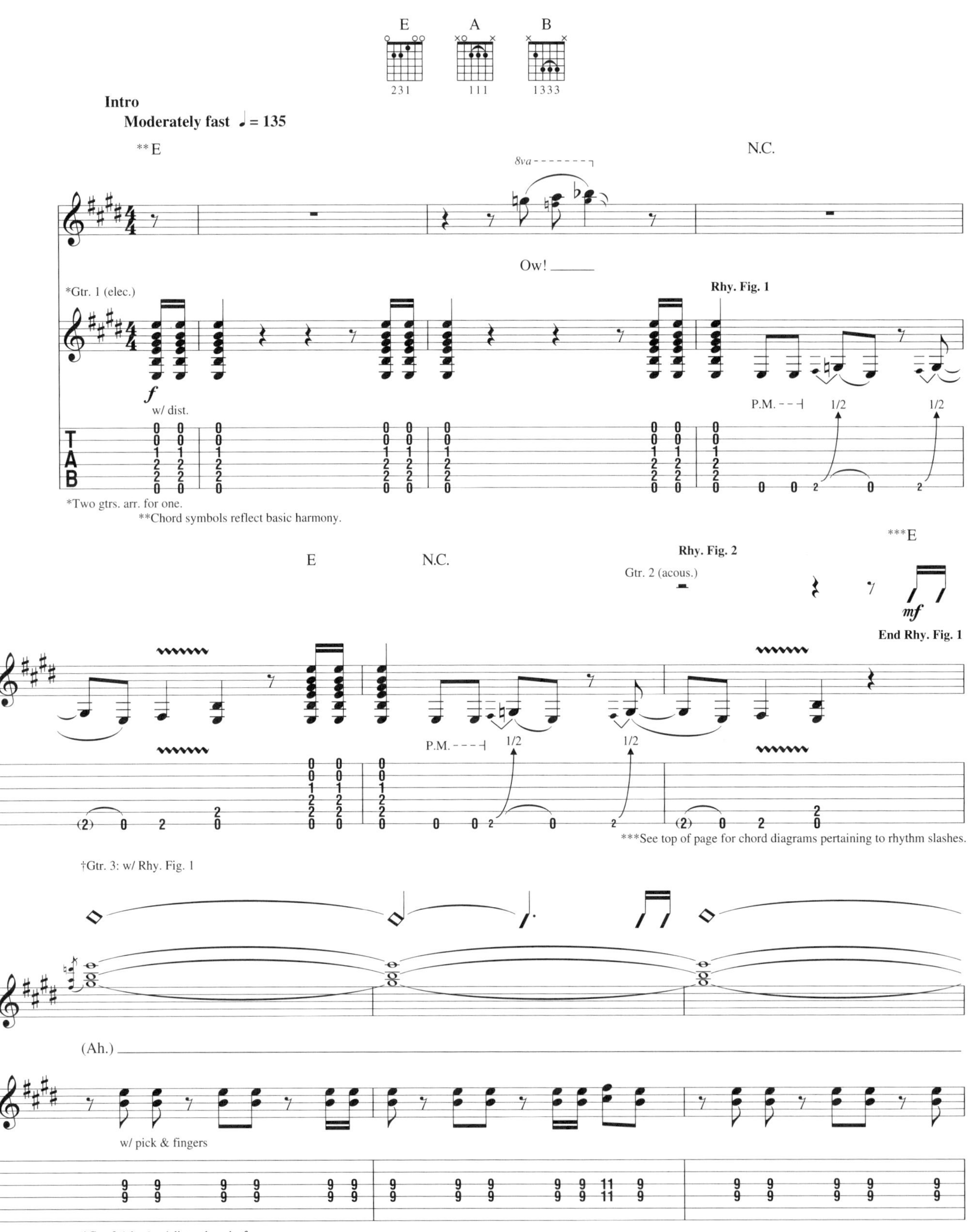

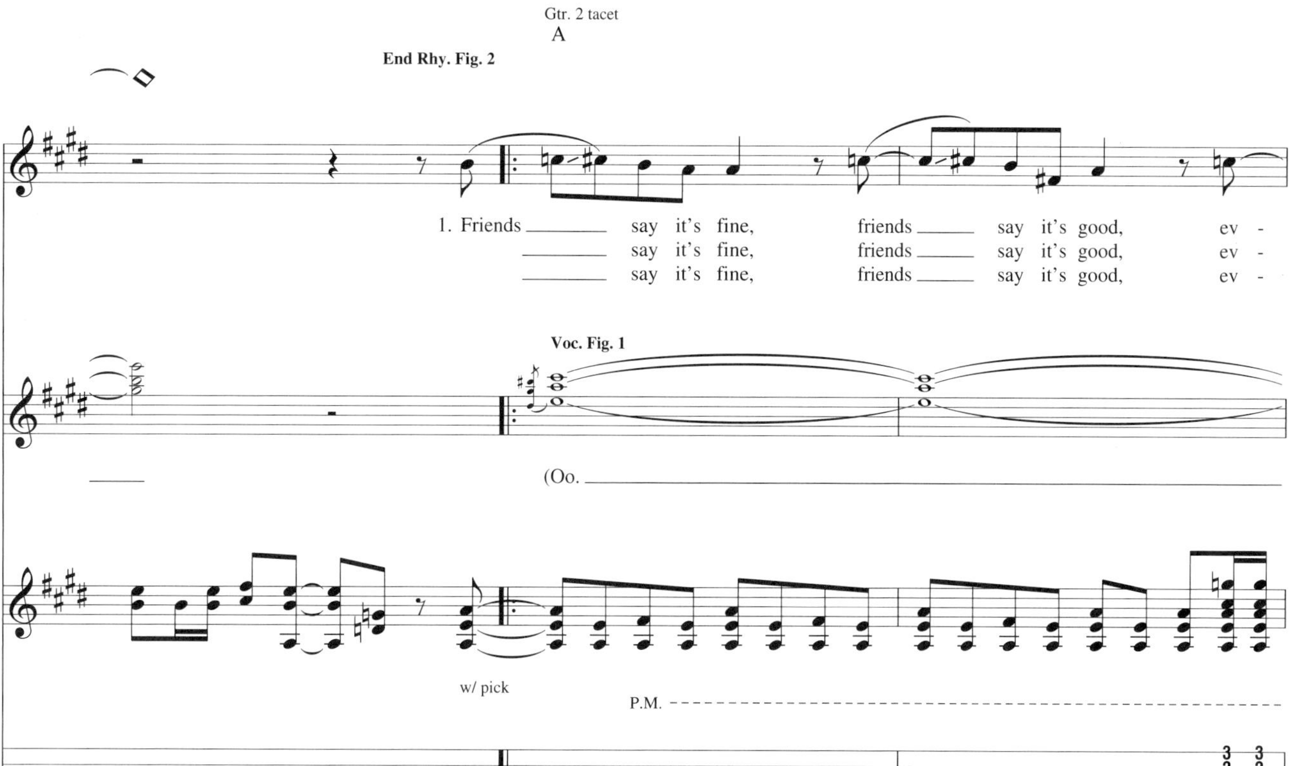
Verse
Gtr. 2 tacet
A
End Rhy. Fig. 2
1. Friends say it's fine, friends say it's good, ev -
say it's fine, friends say it's good, ev -
say it's fine, friends say it's good, ev -
Voc. Fig. 1
(Oo.
w/ pick
P.M.

Gtr. 2: w/ Rhy. Fig. 2
E
N.C.
- 'ry - bod - y says it's just like Rob - in Hood.
- 'ry - bod - y says it's just like Rob - in Hood.
- 'ry - bod - y says it's just like Rob - in Hood.
Ah.)
Gtr. 1
P.M.
P.M.
1/2
1/2

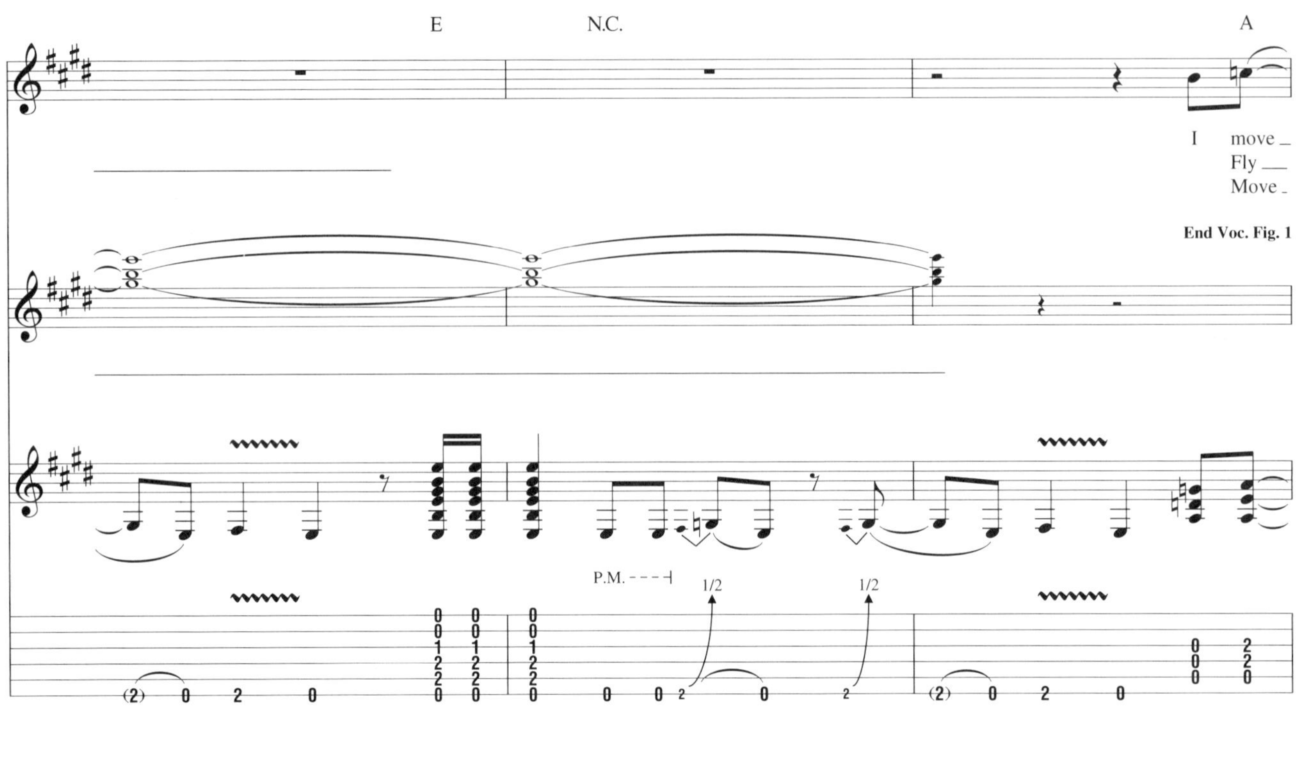
E
N.C.
A
I move
Fly
Move
End Voc. Fig. 1
P.M.
1/2
1/2

Bkgd. Voc.: w/ Voc. Fig. 1
like a cat, charge like a ram, sting like a bee, babe,
like a plane, drive like a car, hold like a hand, babe,
like a cat, charge like a ram, sting like a bee. Oo, oo, babe,
P.M.

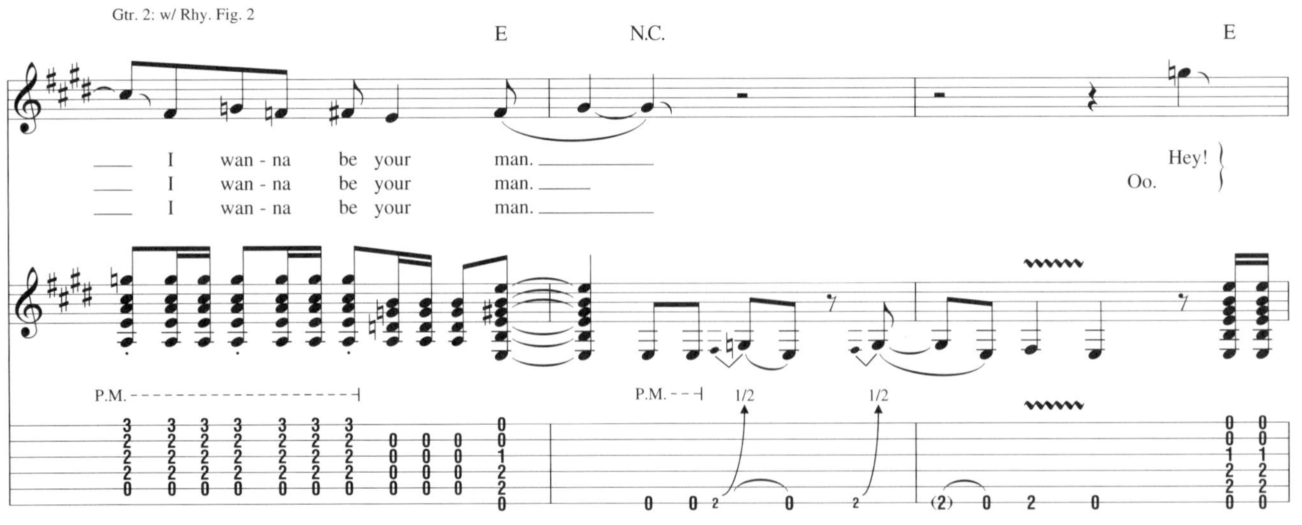
Gtr. 2: w/ Rhy. Fig. 2
E
N.C.
E
I wan - na be your man.
I wan - na be your man.
I wan - na be your man.
Hey!
Oo.
P.M.
P.M.
1/2
1/2

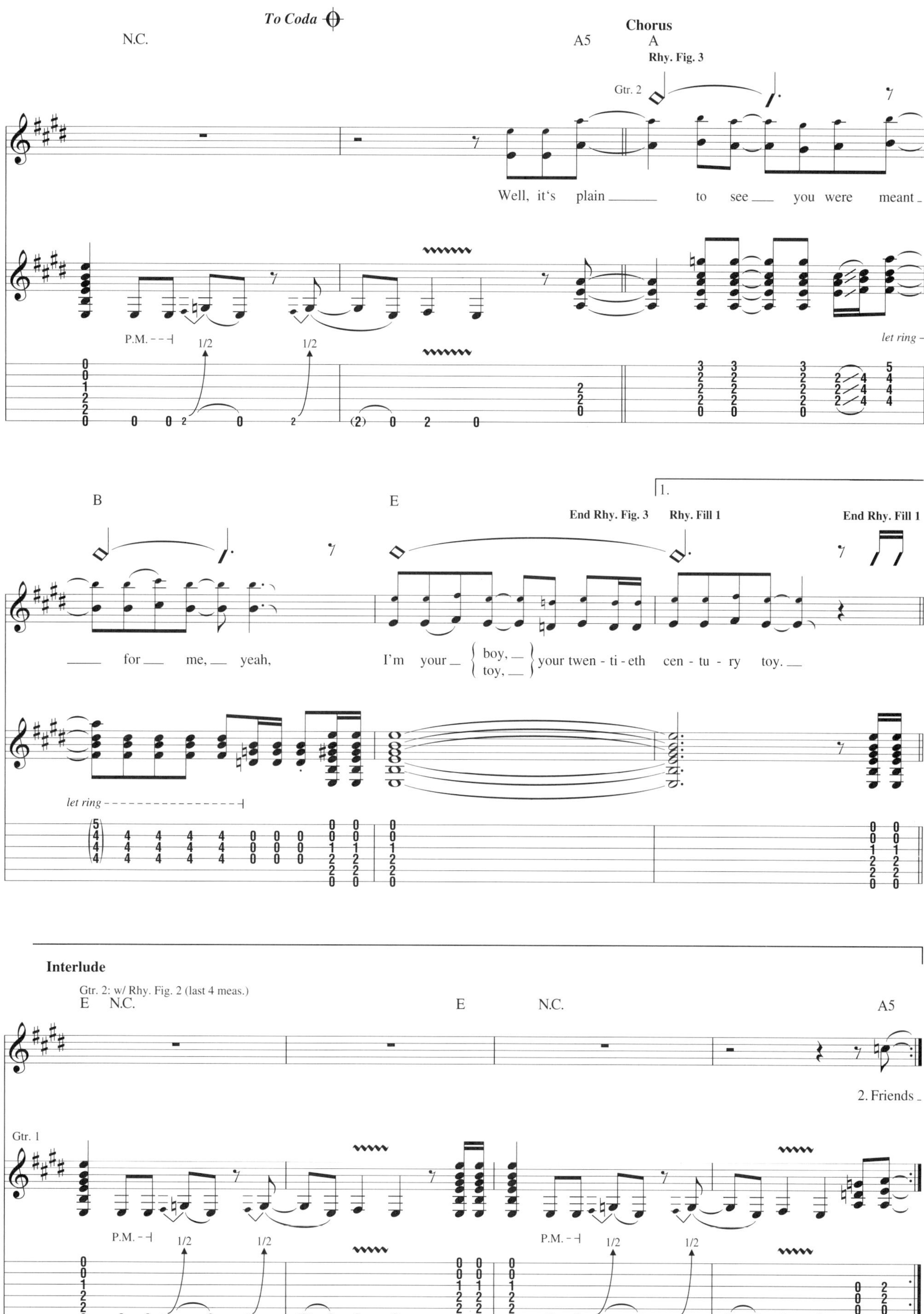
To Coda
N.C.
Chorus
A5
A
Rhy. Fig. 3
Gtr. 2
Well, it's plain to see you were meant
P.M.
1/2
1/2
let ring
B
E
1.
End Rhy. Fig. 3
Rhy. Fill 1
End Rhy. Fill 1
for me, yeah,
I'm your boy, toy, your twen-ti-eth cen-tu-ry toy.
let ring
Interlude
Gtr. 2: w/ Rhy. Fig. 2 (last 4 meas.)
E N.C.
E
N.C.
A5
2. Friends
Gtr. 1
P.M.
1/2
1/2

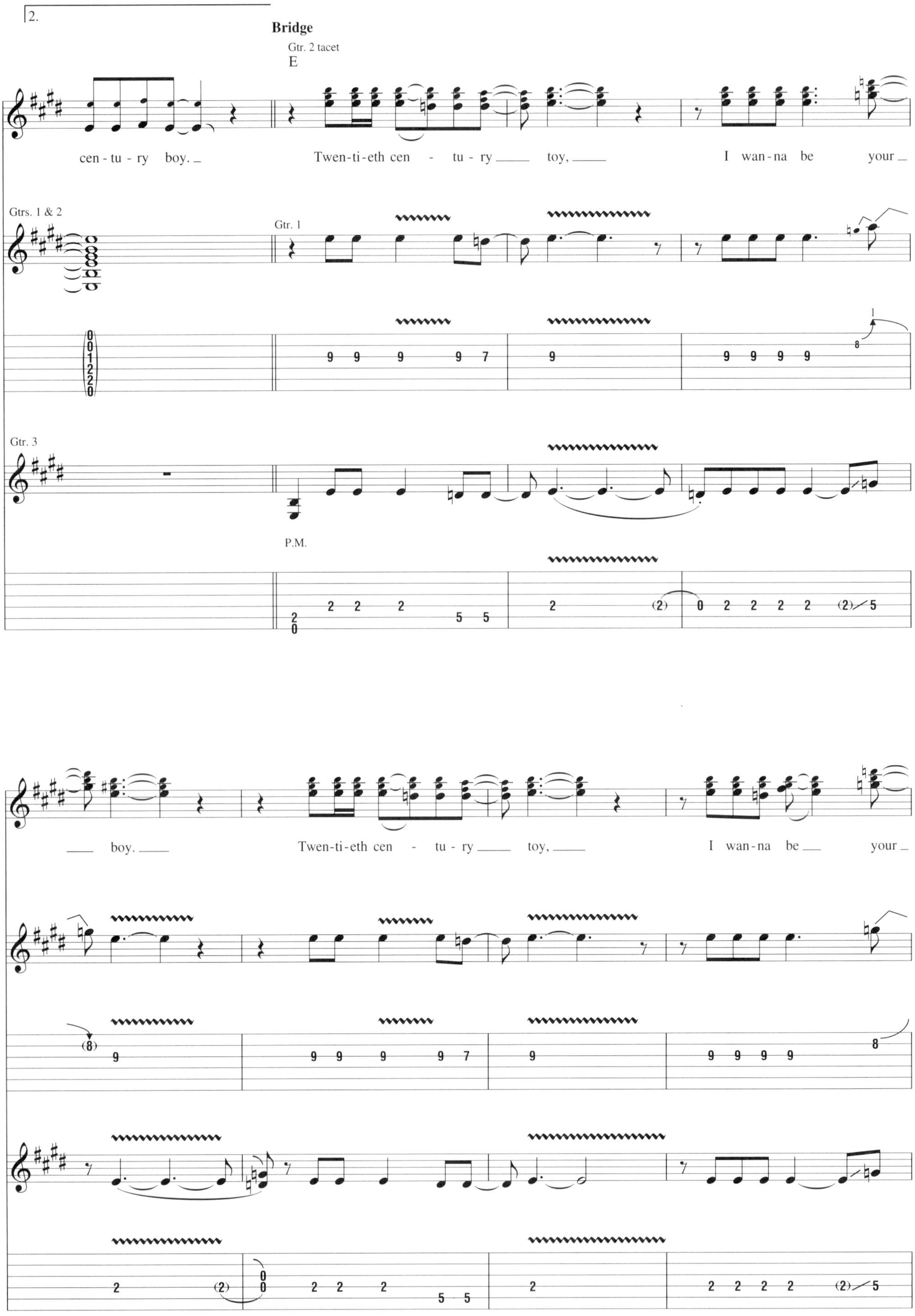

2.

Bridge

Gtr. 2 tacet

E

cen - tu - ry boy. Twen - ti - eth cen - tu - ry toy, I wan - na be your

Gtrs. 1 & 2

Gtr. 1

Gtr. 3

P.M.

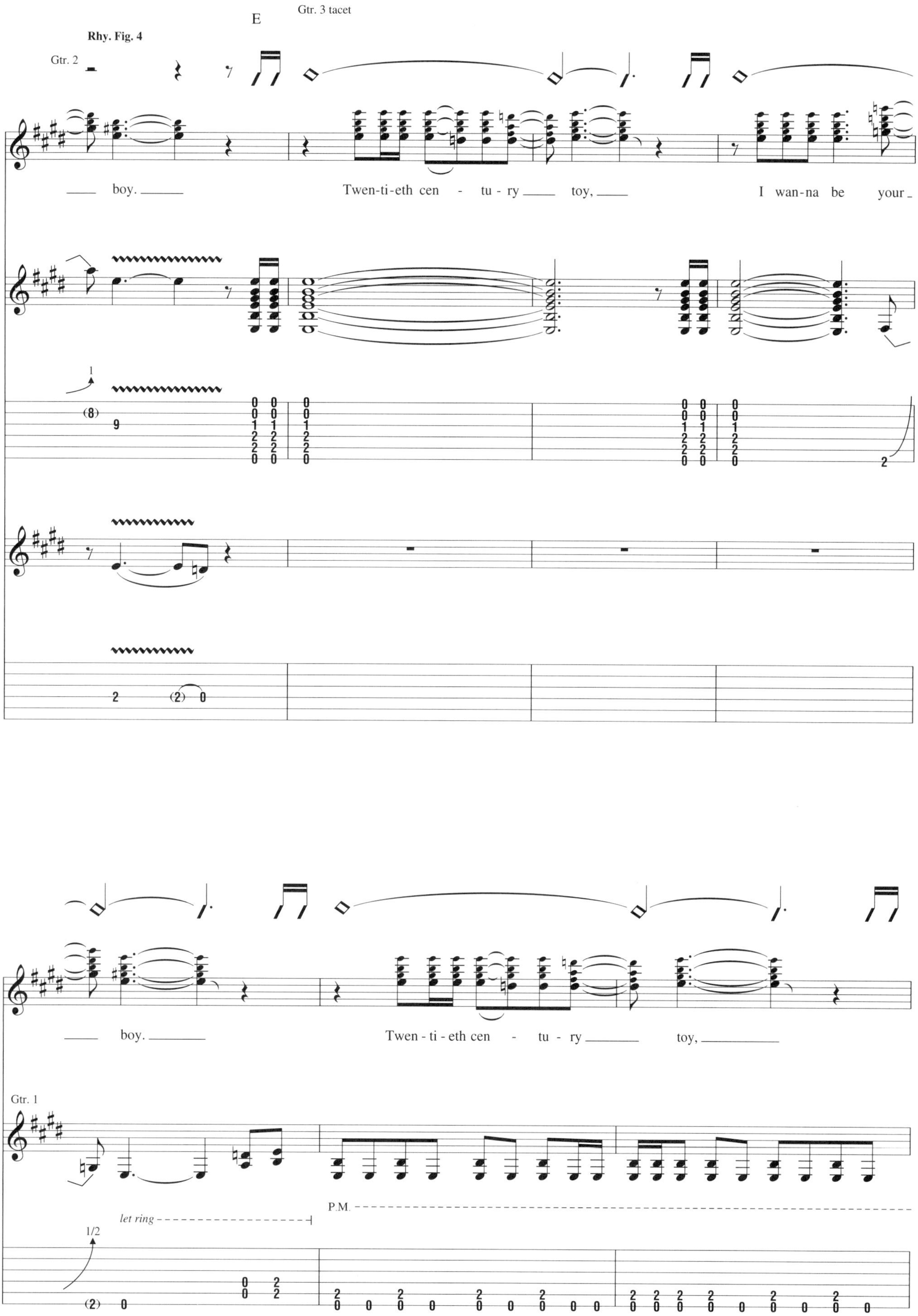

Gtr. 3 tacet

E

Rhy. Fig. 4

Gtr. 2

boy.

Twen-ti-eth cen - tu - ry toy,

I wan-na be your

1

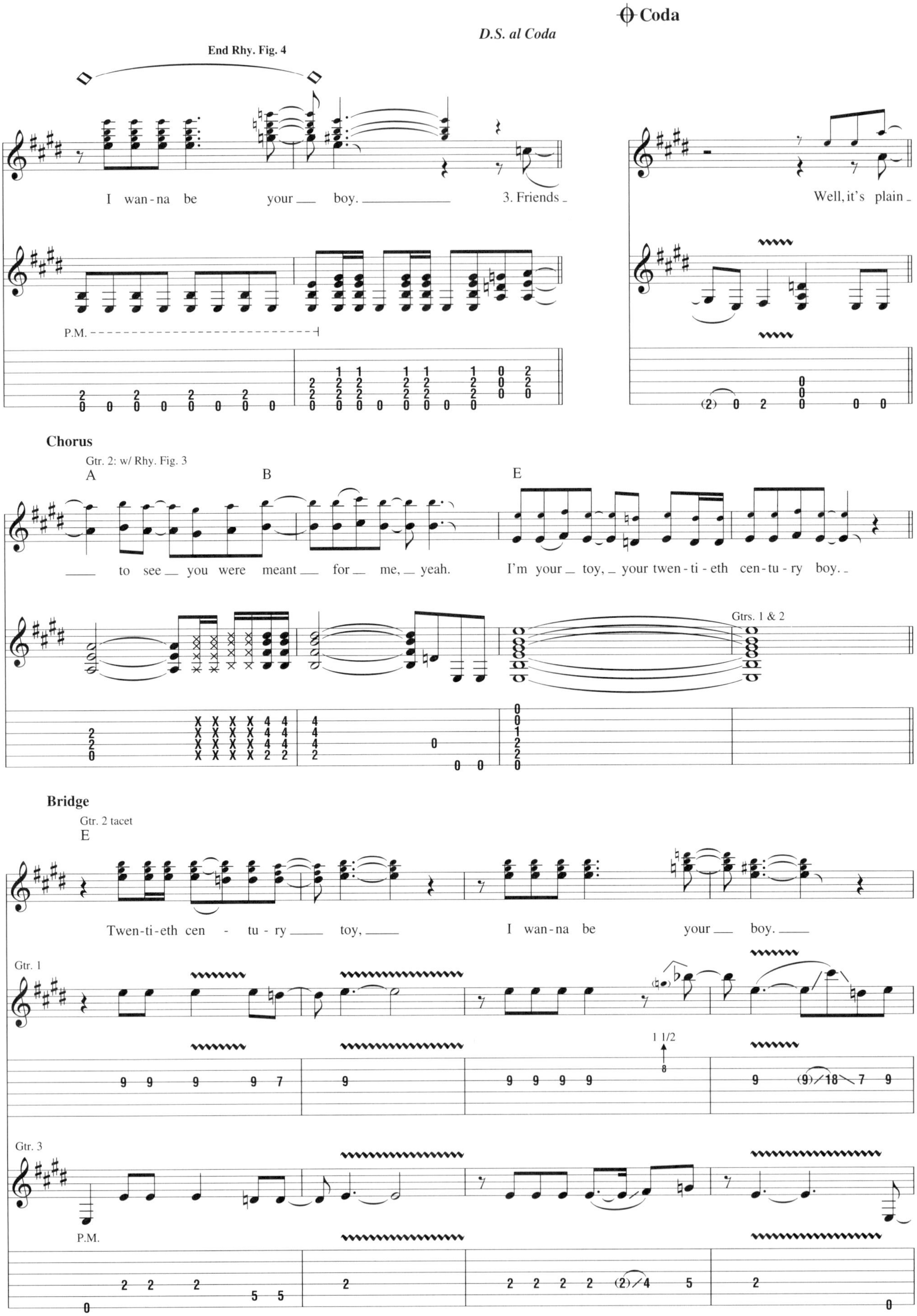

Coda

D.S. al Coda

End Rhy. Fig. 4

I wan-na be your boy. 3. Friends

P.M.

Well, it's plain

2 2 2 2
0 0 0 0 0 0 0 0

1 1 1 1 1 0 2
2 2 2 2 2 2 0 2
2 2 2 2 2 2 0 0
0 0 0 0 0 0 0 0 0

0
0
(2) 0 2 0 0 0

Chorus

Gtr. 2: w/ Rhy. Fig. 3

A B E

to see you were meant for me, yeah. I'm your toy, your twen-ti-eth cen-tu-ry boy.

Gtrs. 1 & 2

X X X X 4 4 4
X X X X 4 4 4
2 X X X X 4 4 4
2 X X X X 2 2 2 0
0 0 0

0
0
1
2
2
0

Bridge

Gtr. 2 tacet

E

Twen-ti-eth cen-tu-ry toy, I wan-na be your boy.

Gtr. 1

1 1/2

8

9 9 9 9 7 9 9 9 9 9 9 (9)/18\7 9

Gtr. 3

P.M.

2 2 2 2 2 2 2 2 (2)/4 5 2
5 5
0 0

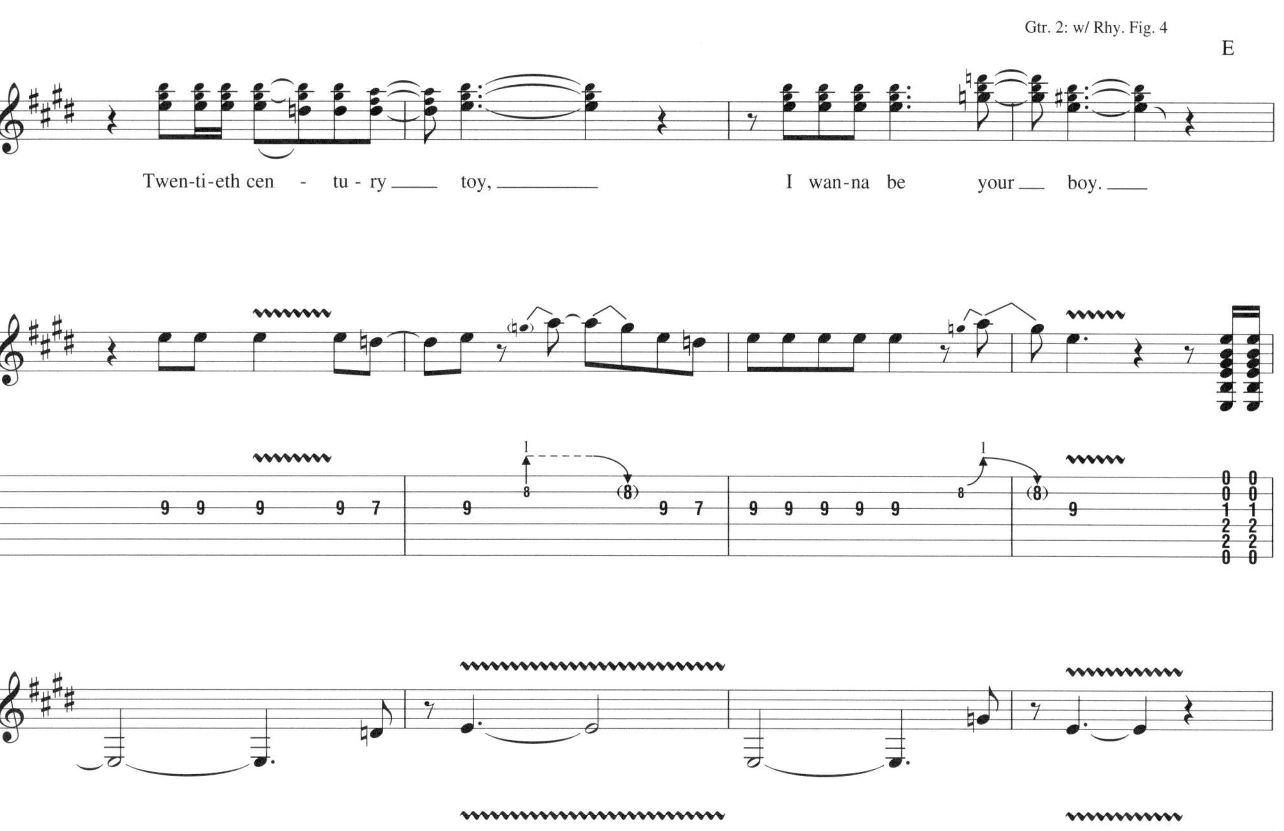
Gtr. 2: w/ Rhy. Fig. 4
E
Twen-ti-eth cen - tu - ry toy,
I wan-na be your boy.

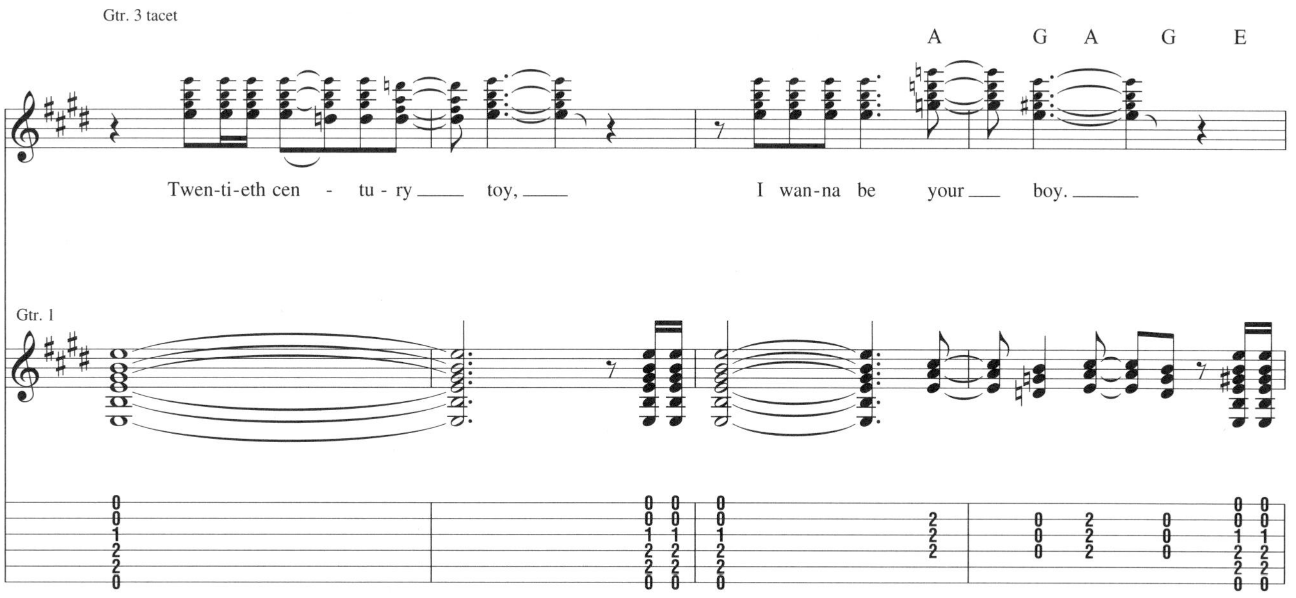
Gtr. 3 tacet
A G A G E
Twen-ti-eth cen - tu - ry toy,
I wan-na be your boy.
Gtr. 1

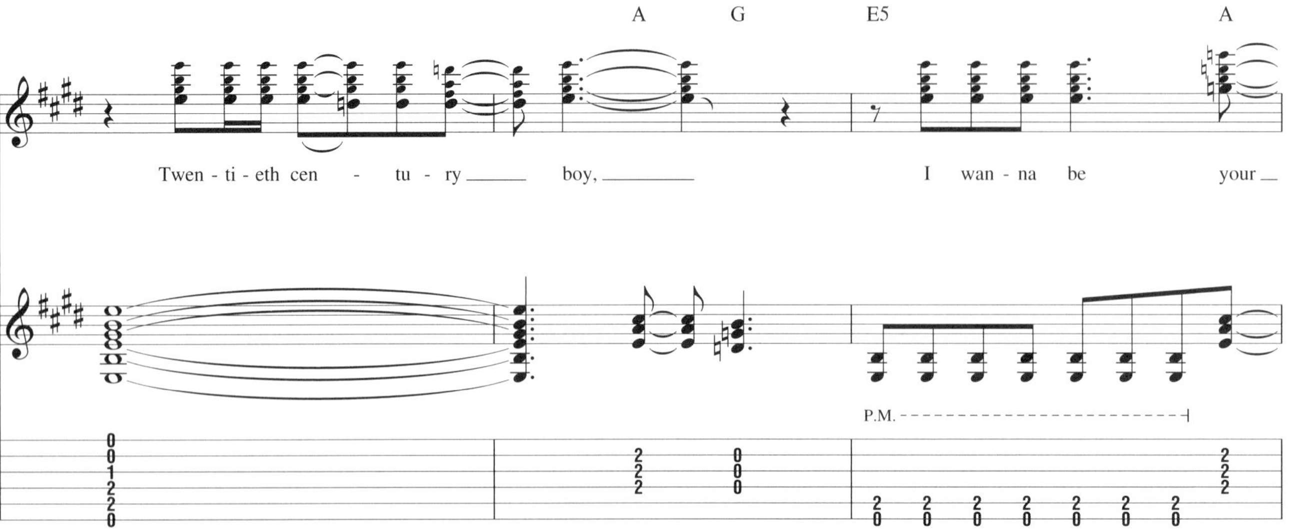

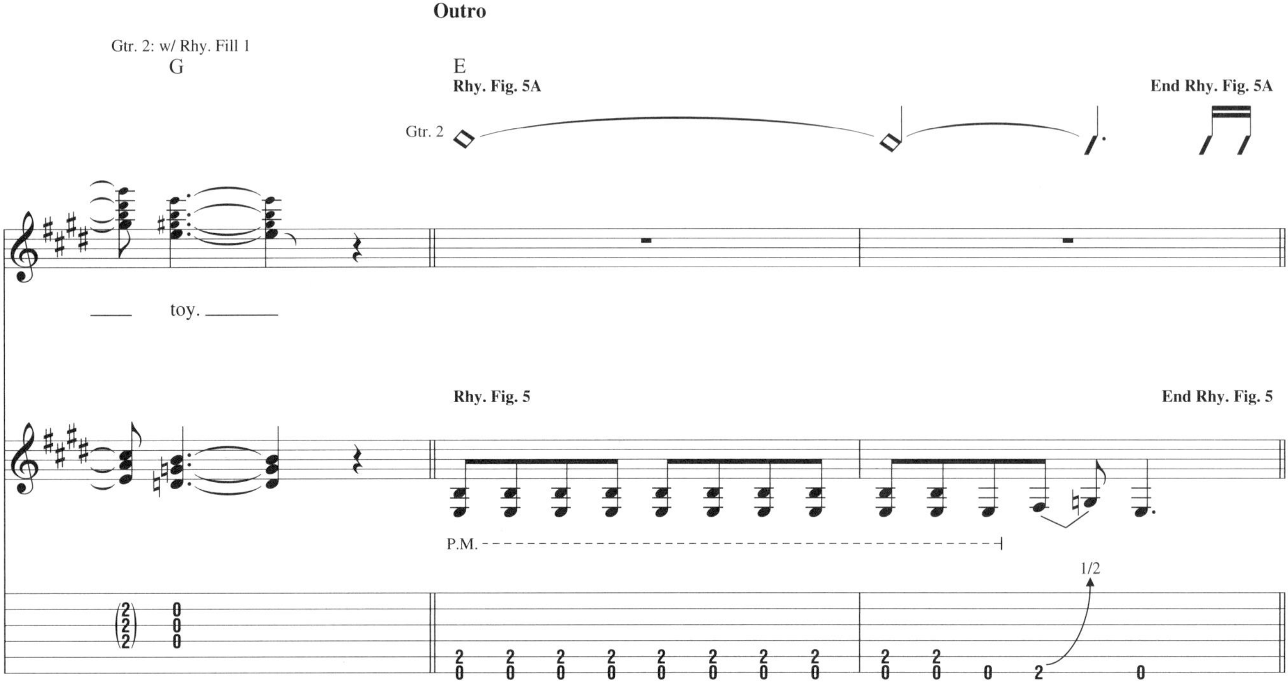

Play 7 times and fade

w/ Lead Voc. ad lib. (till fade)
1st & 2nd times, Gtr. 1: w/ Rhy. Fig. 5
Gtr. 2: w/ Rhy. Fig. 5A (till fade)
3rd time, Gtr. 1: w/ Rhy. Fig. 5 (1st meas., till fade)
E

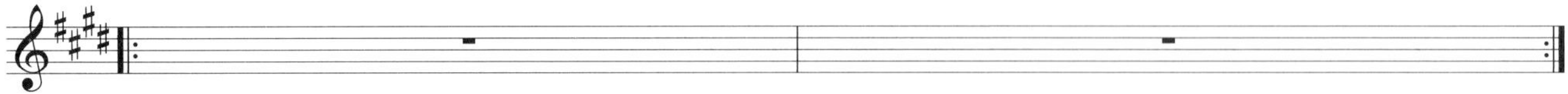

from Green Day - *21st Century Breakdown*

21 Guns

Words and Music by David Bowie, John Phillips, Billie Joe Armstrong, Mike Pritchard and Frank Wright

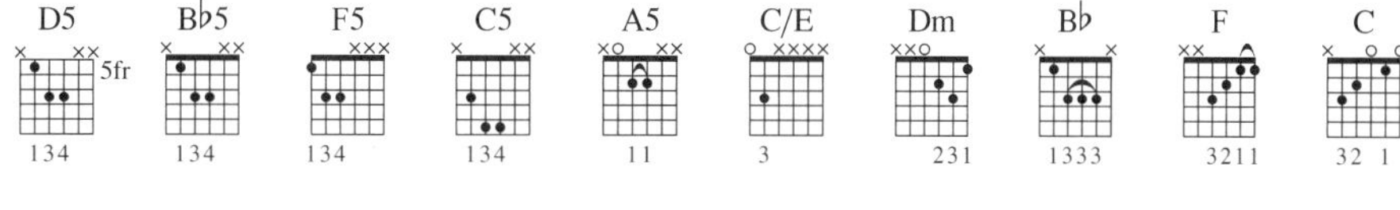

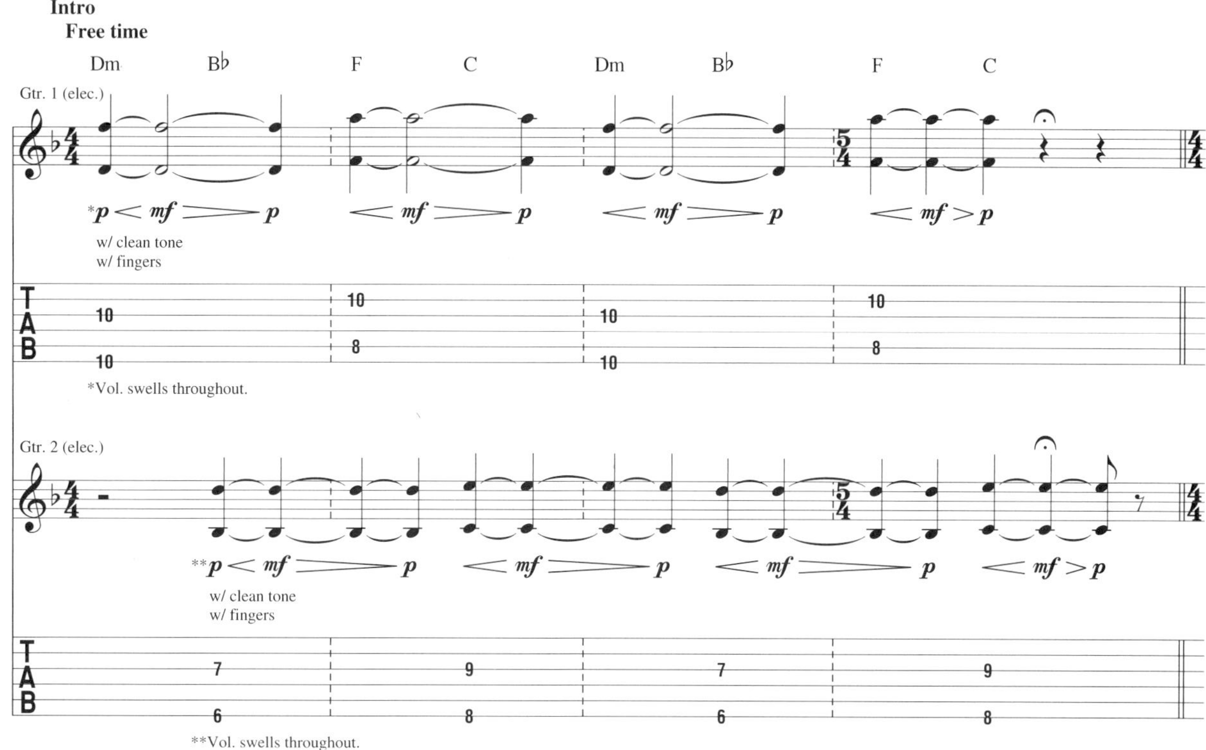

2nd time, Gtr. 1: w/ Rhy. Fig. 2 (1 1/2 times)
2nd time, Gtr. 4 tacet

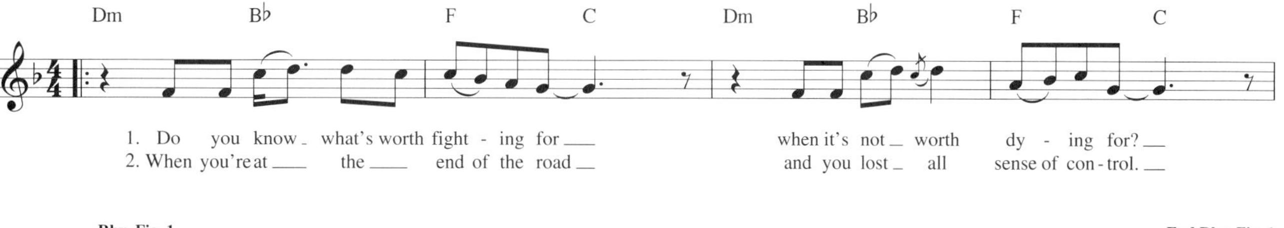

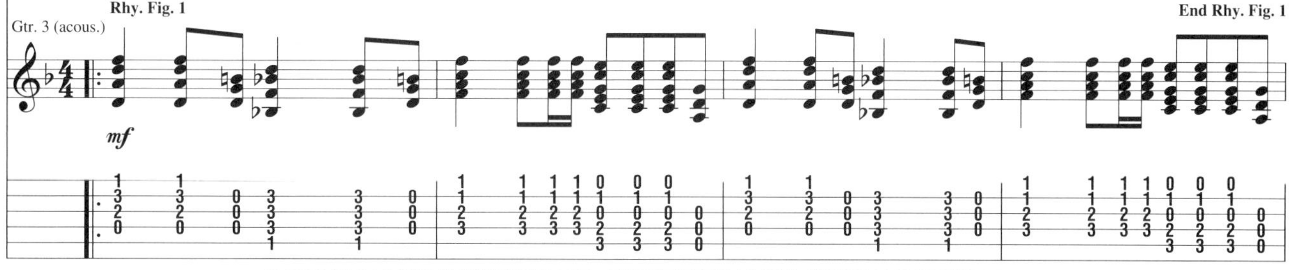

- contains samples of "All The Young Dudes" by David Bowie and "San Francisco (Be Sure To Wear Flowers In Your Hair)" by John Phillips

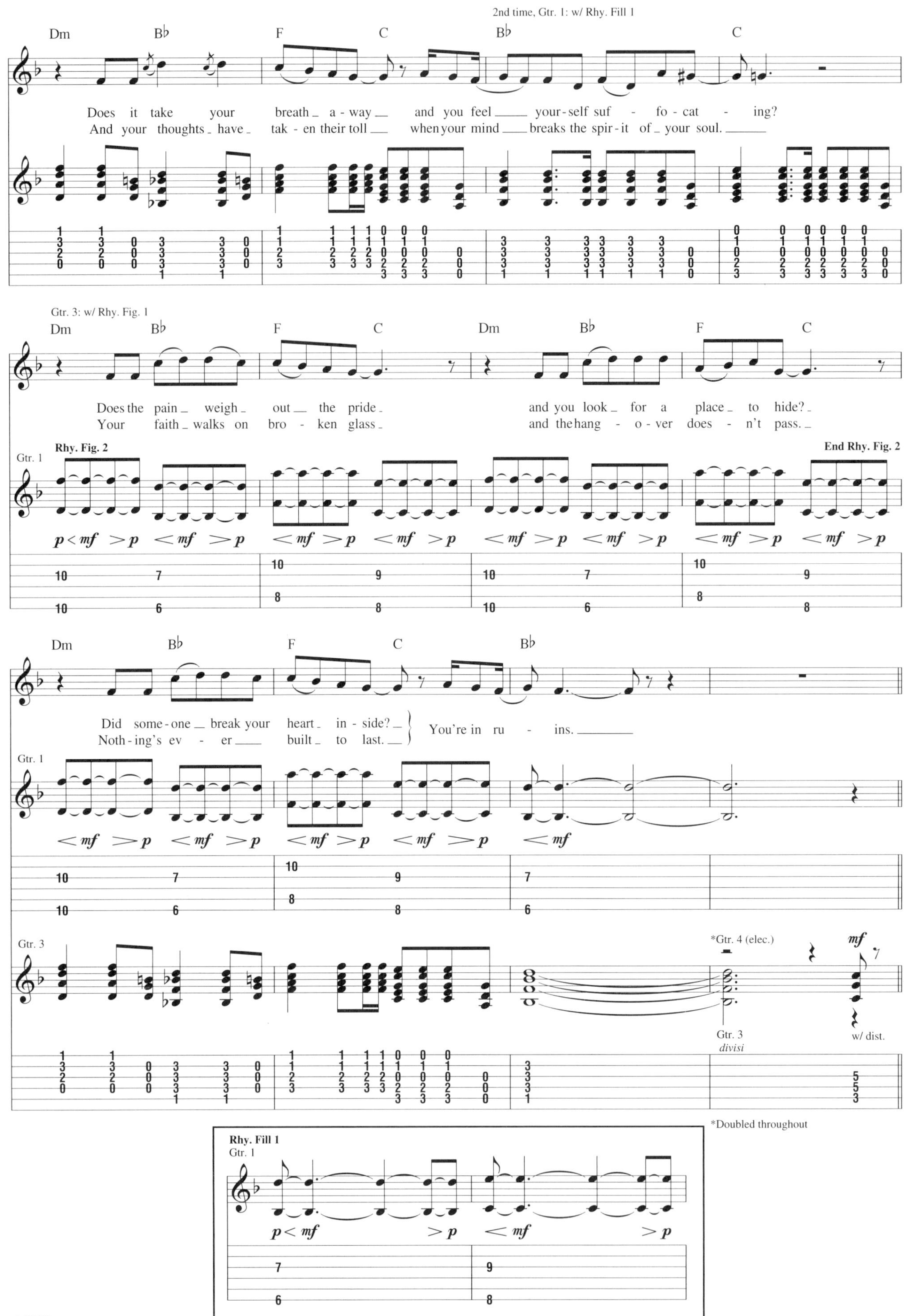
2nd time, Gtr. 1: w/ Rhy. Fill 1
Dm
B♭
F
C
B♭
C
Does it take your breath a-way and you feel your-self suf - fo - cat - ing?
And your thoughts have tak - en their toll when your mind breaks the spir - it of your soul.
Gtr. 3: w/ Rhy. Fig. 1
Dm
B♭
F
C
Dm
B♭
F
C
Does the pain weigh out the pride and you look for a place to hide?
Your faith walks on bro - ken glass and the hang - o - ver does - n't pass.
Rhy. Fig. 2
Gtr. 1
End Rhy. Fig. 2
p
mf
Dm
B♭
F
C
B♭
Did some-one break your heart in - side?
Noth-ing's ev - er built to last.
You're in ru - ins.
Gtr. 1
Gtr. 3
*Gtr. 4 (elec.)
Gtr. 3
divisi
w/ dist.
*Doubled throughout
Rhy. Fill 1
Gtr. 1

Chorus
Gtrs. 1 & 3 tacet
F5 N.C. C/E N.C. D5 N.C. C5 B♭5 F5 C5
*Voc. Fig. 1
End Voc. Fig. 1
One, twen-ty-one guns. Lay down your arms. Give up the fight.
(Aye.)
Gtr. 5 (elec.)
Fill 1
End Fill 1
mf
w/ dist.
Rhy. Fig. 3
Gtr. 4
End Rhy. Fig. 3
*Applies to Bkgd. Voc. only.
To Coda
1st & 2nd times, Gtr. 4: w/ Rhy. Fig. 3
Gtr. 5 tacet
3rd time, Gtr. 4: w/ Rhy. Fig. 3 (2 1/2 times)
1st & 2nd times, Bkgd. Voc.: w/ Voc. Fig. 1 (2 times)
3rd time, Bkgd. Voc.: w/ Voc. Fig. 1
Gtr. 5: w/ Fill 1
F5 N.C. C/E N.C. D5 N.C. C5 B♭5 F5 C5
One, twen-ty-one guns. Throw up your arms in-to the sky, you and I.
B♭5 F5
1. C5
2. C5
Gtr. 4
(cont. in slashes)
**Gtr. 6 (elec.)
f
w/ dist.
steady gliss.
**Doubled throughout

Bridge
*D5
B♭5
F5
C5
D5
B♭5
F5
A5
Gtr. 4
Did you try to live on your own when you burned down the house and home?
Gtr. 5
Gtr. 6
steady gliss.
*See top of first page of song for chord diagrams pertaining to rhythm slashes.
D5
B♭5
F5
A5
B♭5
C5
Did you stand too close to the fire like a li - ar look-ing for for-give - ness from a stone?
steady gliss.
(cont. in slashes)

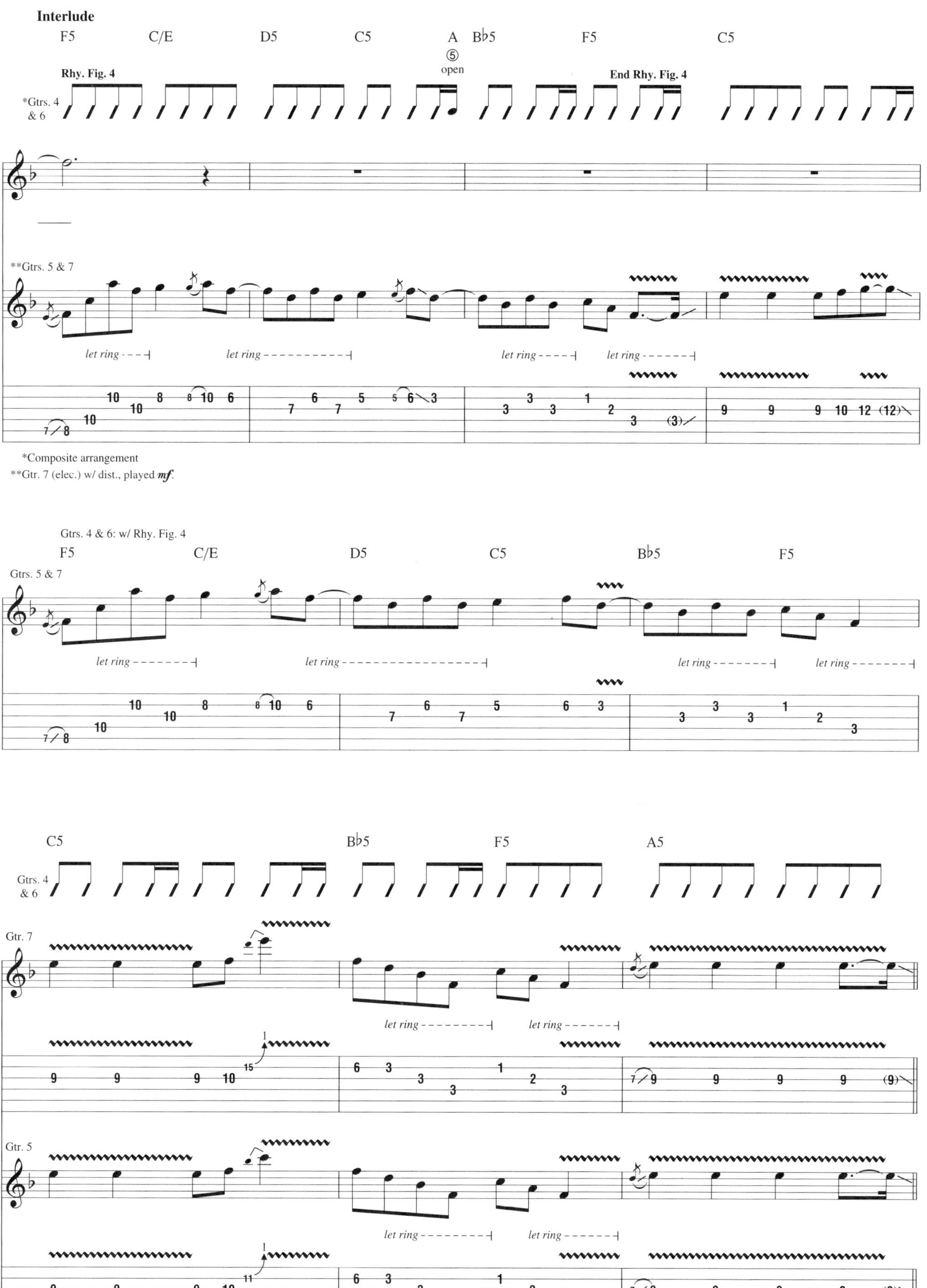

Interlude
F5
C/E
D5
C5
A
⑤
open
B♭5
F5
C5
Rhy. Fig. 4
End Rhy. Fig. 4
*Gtrs. 4 & 6
**Gtrs. 5 & 7
let ring
*Composite arrangement
**Gtr. 7 (elec.) w/ dist., played mf.
Gtrs. 4 & 6: w/ Rhy. Fig. 4
F5
C/E
D5
C5
B♭5
F5
Gtrs. 5 & 7
let ring
C5
B♭5
F5
A5
Gtrs. 4 & 6
Gtr. 7
let ring
Gtr. 5
let ring

Interlude
Gtr. 1: w/ Rhy. Fig. 2
Gtrs. 4 - 7 tacet
Dm Bb F C Dm Bb F C
Gtr. 2
*w/ delay
*Set for eighth-note regeneration w/ multiple decaying repeats.
Verse
Gtr. 3: w/ Rhy. Fig. 1
Dm Bb F C Dm Bb F C
3. When it's time to live and let die and you can't get an - oth - er try,
D.S. al Coda
Dm Bb F C Bb
Gtr. 3
some-thing in - side this heart has died. You're in ru - ins.
Gtr. 1
p < mf > p < mf > p < mf > p < mf > p < mf pp
Coda
C5 F5 N.C. C/E N.C. D5 N.C. C5
One, twen - ty - one guns. Lay down your arms.
Gtr. 5
Gtr. 6
steady gliss.

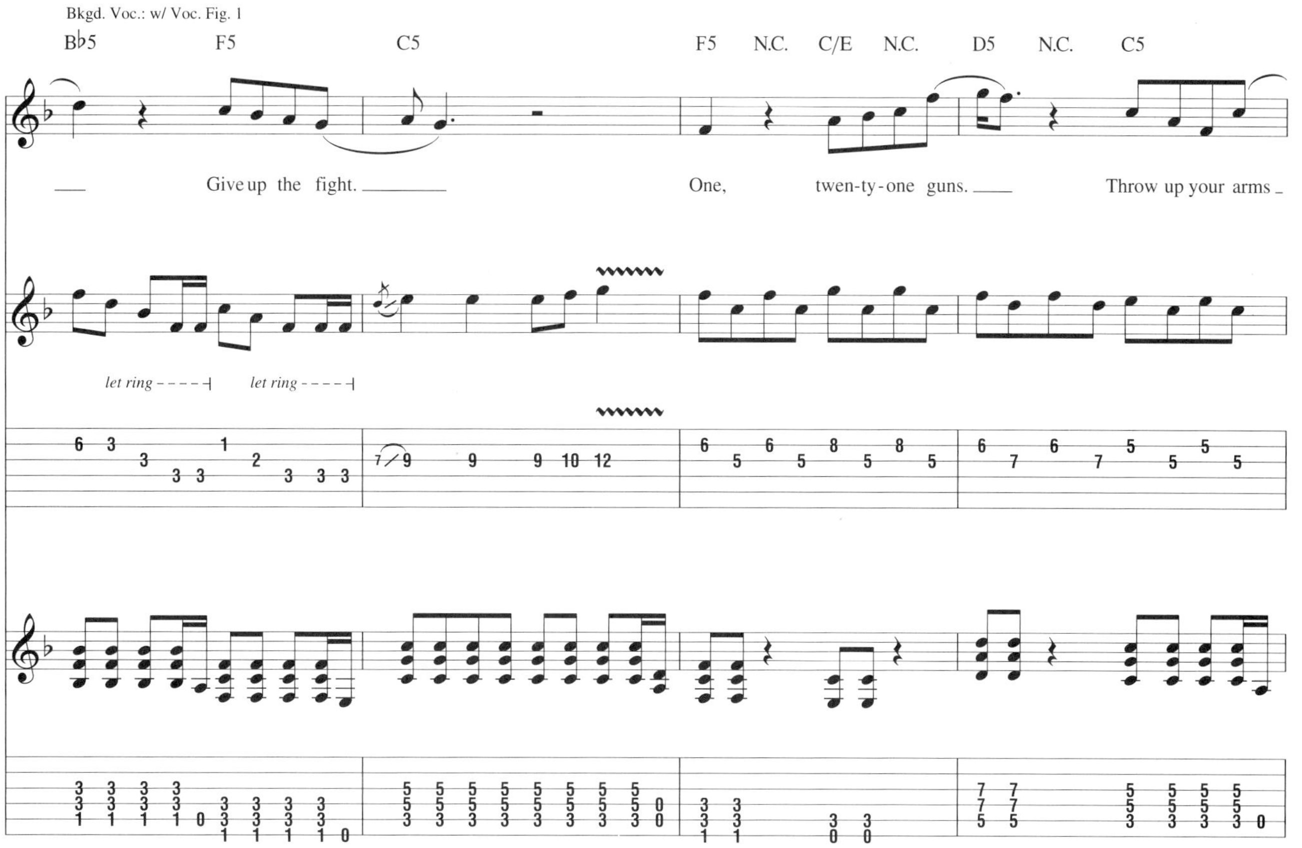
Bkgd. Voc.: w/ Voc. Fig. 1
B♭5
F5
C5
F5
N.C.
C/E
N.C.
D5
N.C.
C5
Give up the fight.
One, twen-ty-one guns.
Throw up your arms
let ring
let ring

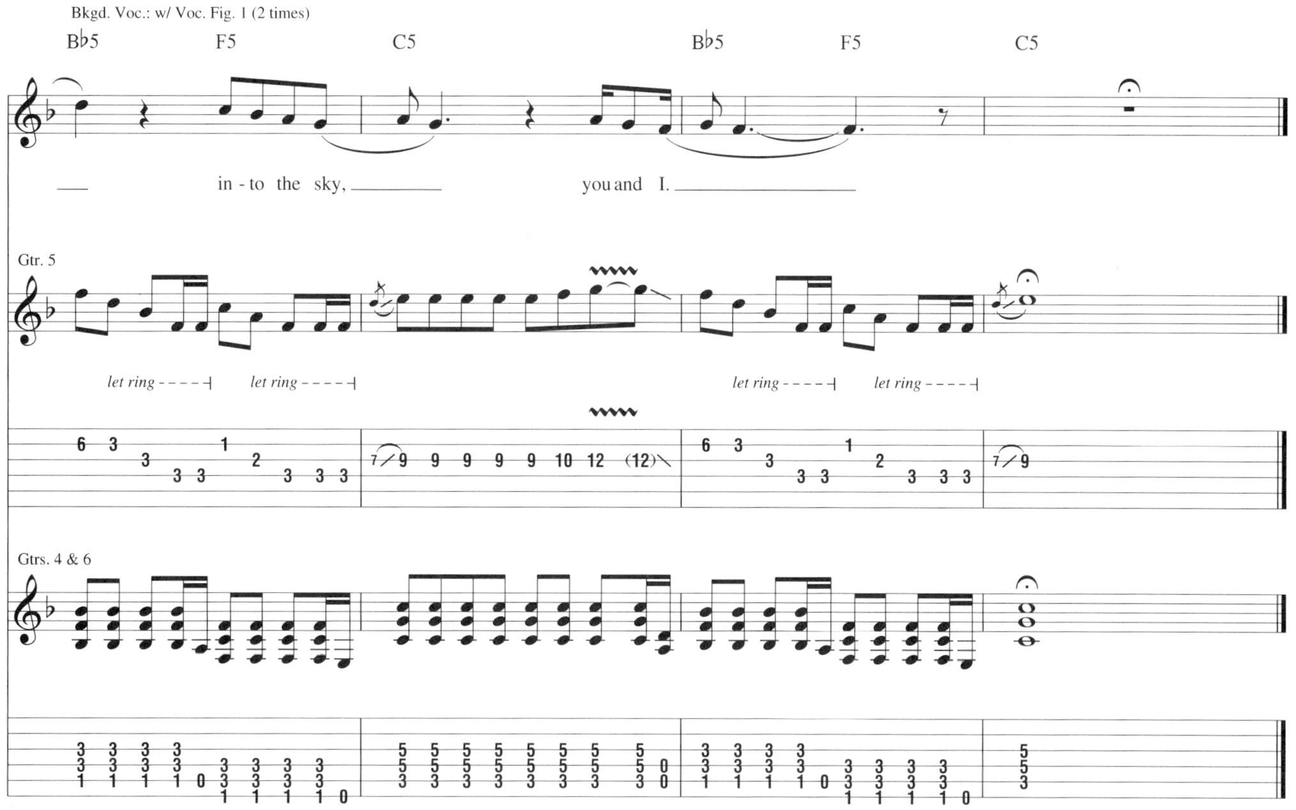
Bkgd. Voc.: w/ Voc. Fig. 1 (2 times)
B♭5
F5
C5
B♭5
F5
C5
in-to the sky,
you and I.
Gtr. 5
let ring
let ring
let ring
let ring
Gtrs. 4 & 6

from Eagles - *Hotel California*

Victim of Love

Words and Music by John David Souther, Don Henley, Glen Frey and Don Felder

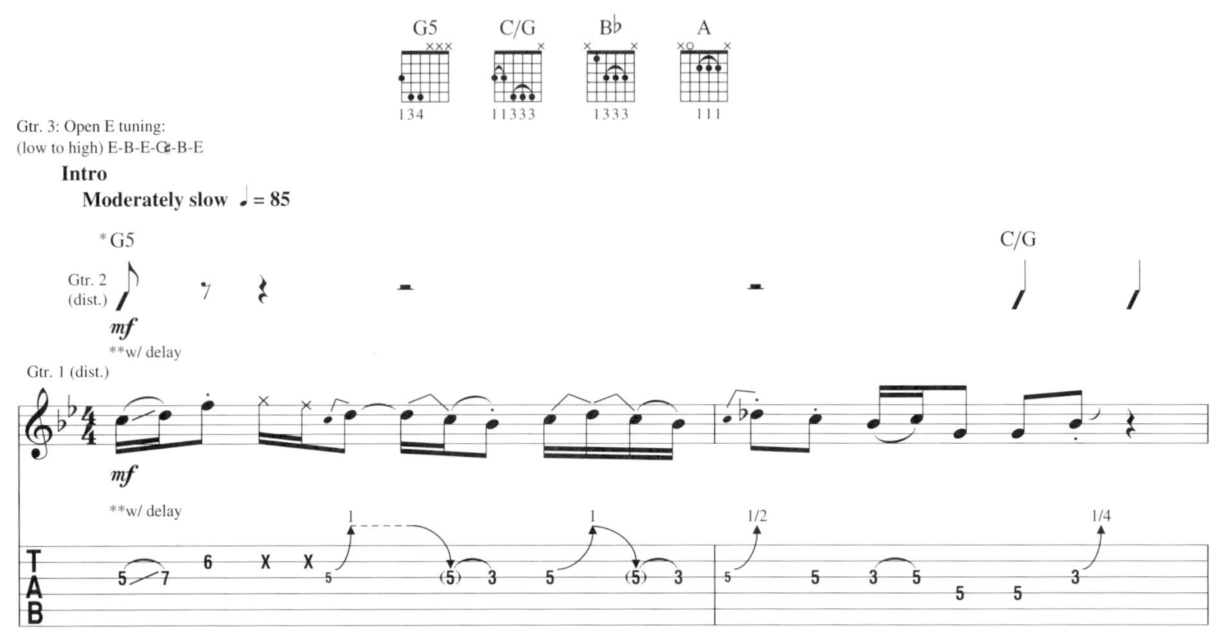

*See top of page for chord diagrams pertaining to rhythm slashes.
**Set for dotted eighth-note regeneration w/ 1 repeat.

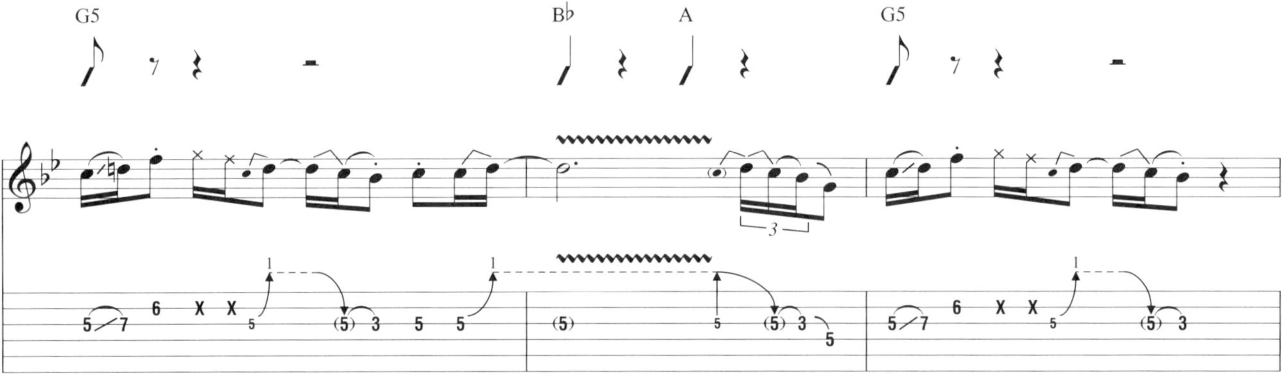

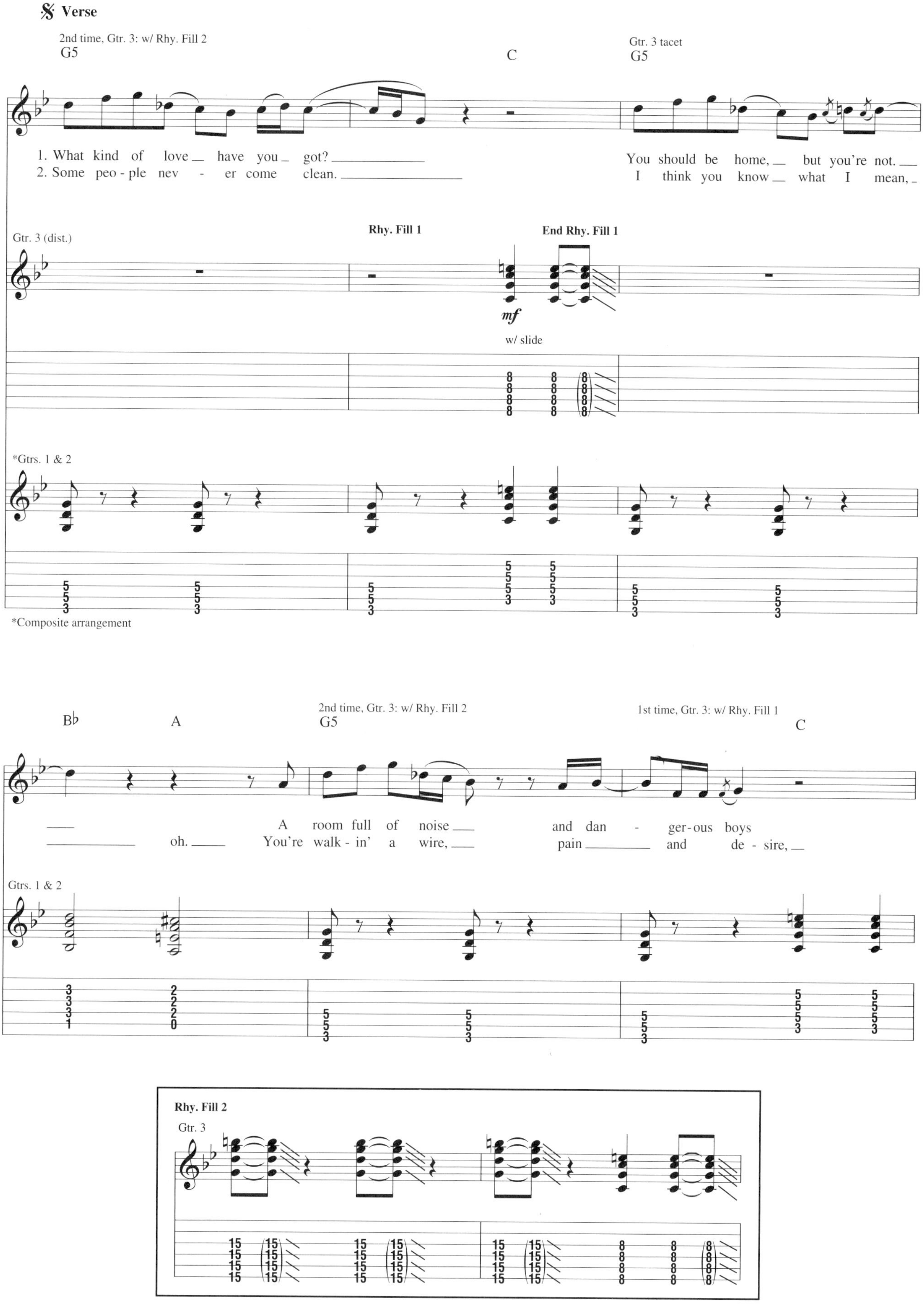

𝄋 **Verse**

2nd time, Gtr. 3: w/ Rhy. Fill 2

G5 C

Gtr. 3 tacet

G5

1. What kind of love have you got? You should be home, but you're not.
2. Some peo - ple nev - er come clean. I think you know what I mean,

Gtr. 3 (dist.)

Rhy. Fill 1 End Rhy. Fill 1

mf

w/ slide

*Gtrs. 1 & 2

*Composite arrangement

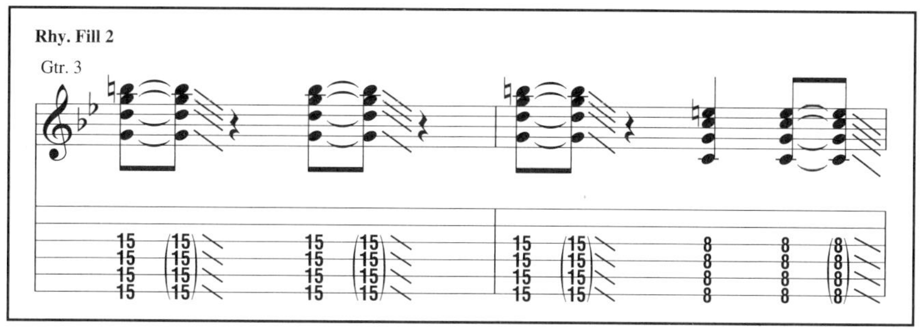

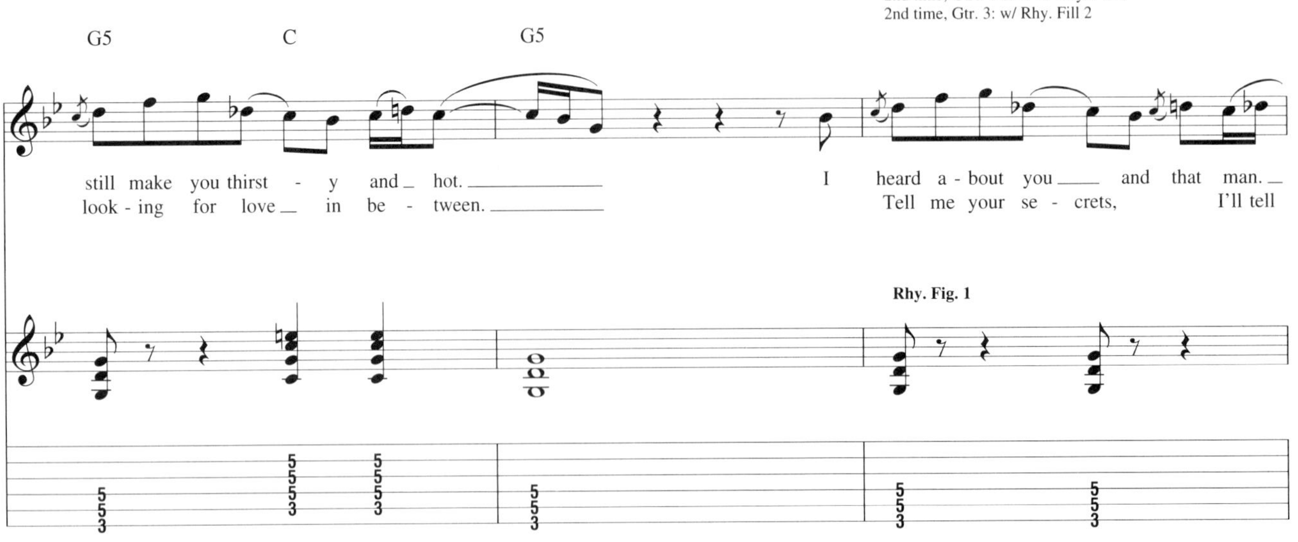
2nd time, Gtrs. 1 & 2: w/ Rhy. Fill 3
2nd time, Gtr. 3: w/ Rhy. Fill 2
G5
C
G5
still make you thirst - y and hot.
look - ing for love in be - tween.
I heard a - bout you and that man.
Tell me your se - crets, I'll tell
Rhy. Fig. 1

1st time, Gtr. 3: w/ Rhy. Fill 1
C
G5
B♭5
A5
There's just one thing I don't un - der - stand.
you mine.
This ain't no time to be cool.
You
And
let ring
let ring
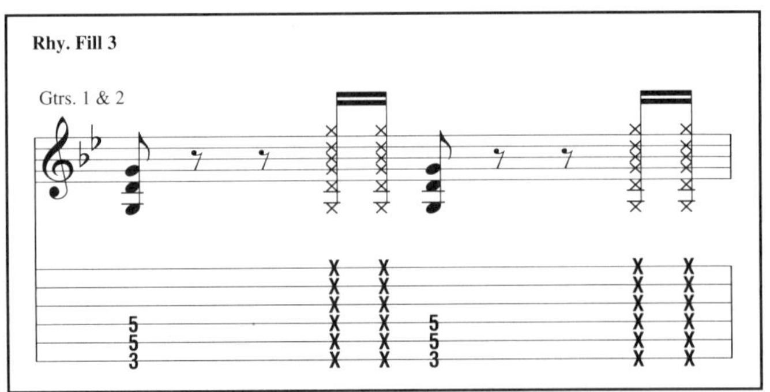
Rhy. Fill 3
Gtrs. 1 & 2

2nd time, Gtrs. 1 & 2: w/ Rhy. Fill 3
2nd time, Gtr. 3: w/ Rhy. Fill 2
1st time, Gtr. 3: w/ Rhy. Fill 1
G5
C
G5
C
say he's a liar___ and he put out your fire. How come you still got his gun_ in your hand?_
tell all your girl - friends, your 'been a-round the world'_ friends, that talk is for los - ers and fools._
End Rhy. Fig. 1
To Coda
Chorus
G5
F
Gm
Am
*B♭
A5
G5
Vic - tim of love,___ I see a bro - ken heart.______
Gtr. 3
let ring
Gtr. 1
Fill 1
End Fill 1
Rhy. Fig. 2
let ring
Gtr. 2
Fill 1A
End Fill 1A
Rhy. Fig. 2A
let ring
*Chord symbols reflect overall harmony.

C
D5
B♭5
F
Gm
F/A
B♭
A5
You got your sto - ries to tell.
Vic-tim of love, it's suchan eas -
8va
let ring
let ring
let ring
let ring
let ring

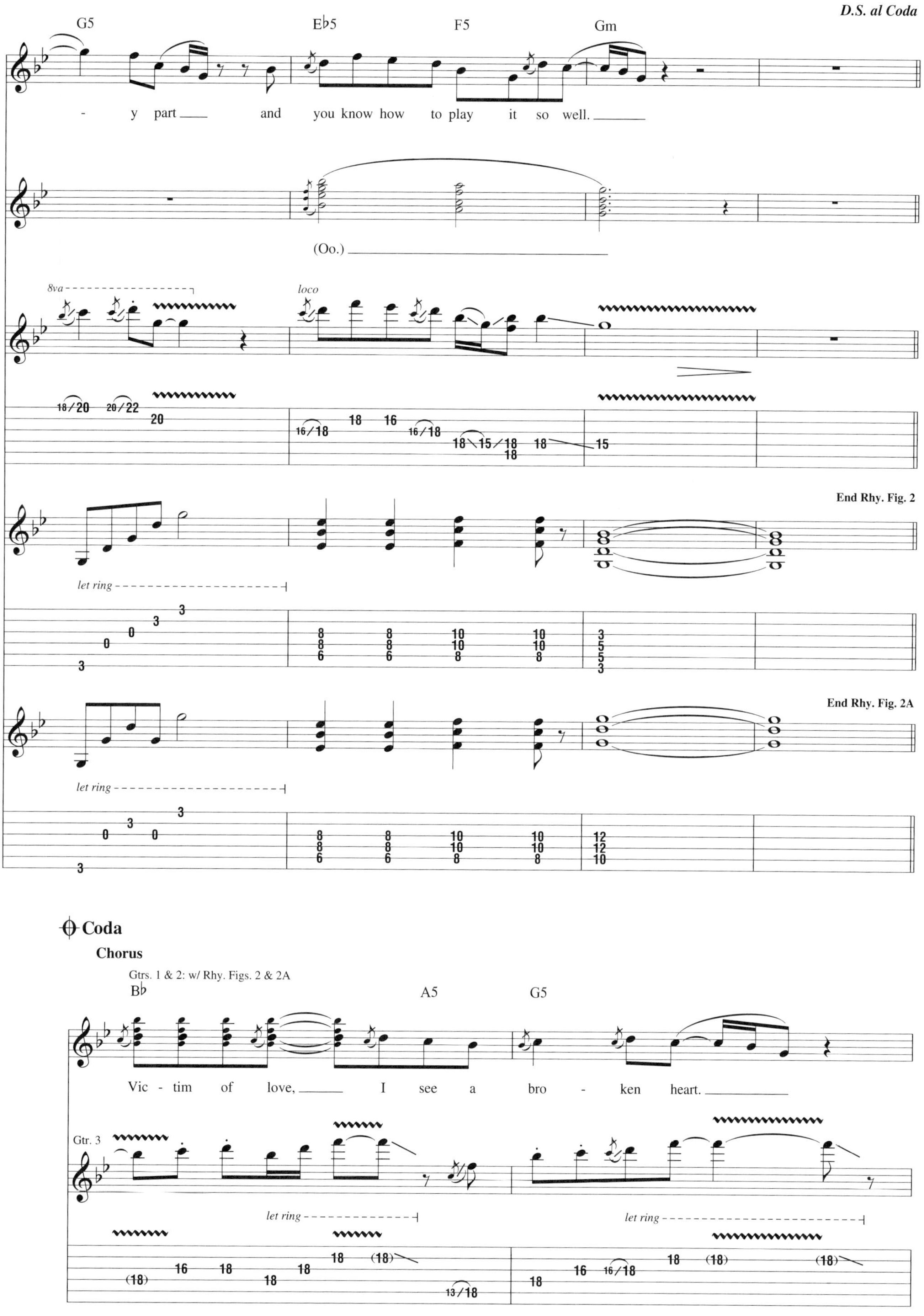

G5 E♭5 F5 Gm

- y part ___ and you know how to play it so well. ___

(Oo.) ___

8va loco

let ring

End Rhy. Fig. 2

let ring

End Rhy. Fig. 2A

Chorus

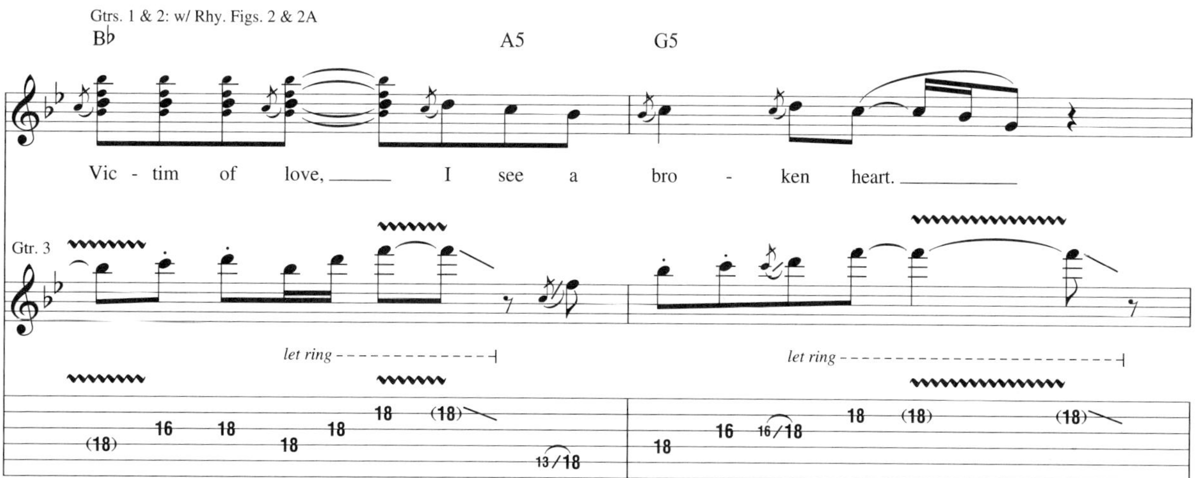

C
D5
B♭5
F
Gm
F/A
B♭
A5
I could be wrong, but I'm not, no I'm not.
Vic-tim of love, we're not so
8va
let ring

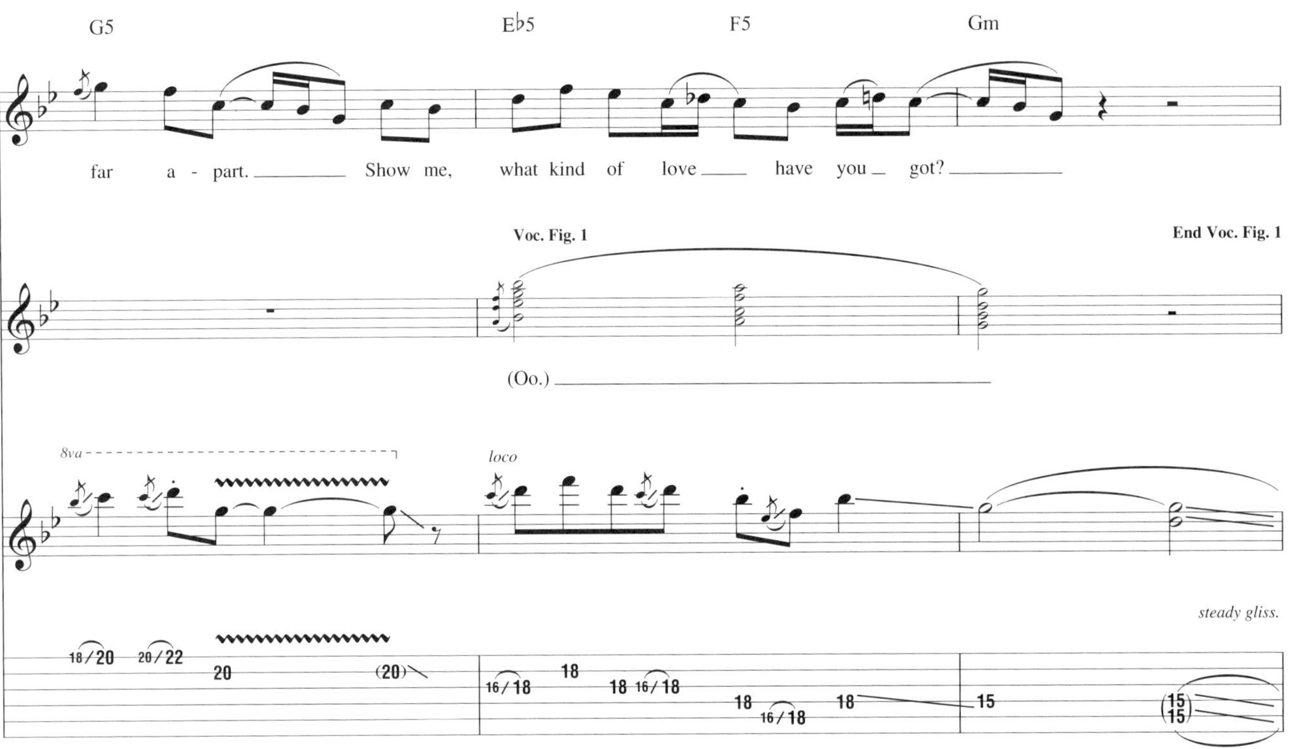
G5
E♭5
F5
Gm
far a - part. Show me, what kind of love have you got?
Voc. Fig. 1
End Voc. Fig. 1
(Oo.)
8va
loco
steady gliss.

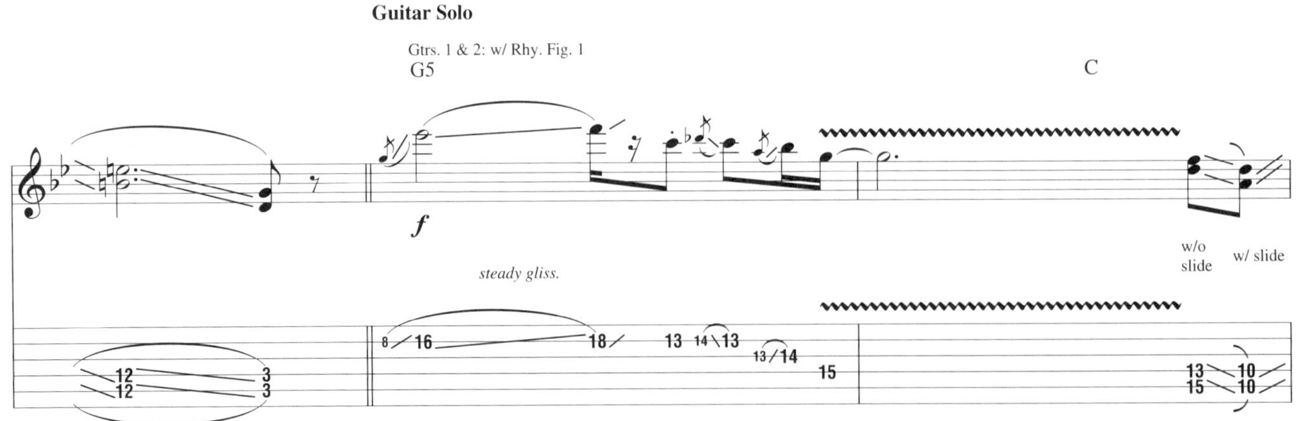
Guitar Solo
Gtrs. 1 & 2: w/ Rhy. Fig. 1
G5
C
steady gliss.
w/o slide
w/ slide

G5
Bb5
A5
G5
let ring
C
G5
C
Outro-Chorus
Gtrs. 1 & 2: w/ Fills 1 & 1A
Gtrs. 1 & 2: w/ Rhy. Figs. 2 & 2A (1st 5 meas.)
G5
F
Gm
Am
Bb
A5
G5
Vic - tim of love, I see a bro - ken heart.
mf
let ring
let ring
C
D5
Bb5
F
Gm
F/A
Bb
A5
I could be wrong, but I'm not.
Vic - tim of love, we're not so
8va
loco
let ring
let ring
8va

Bkgd. Voc.: w/ Voc. Fig. 1
G5
E♭5
F5
G5
F
Gm
F/A
far a - part.
What kind of love have you got?
Gtr. 3
8va
loco
let ring
Gtr. 1
let ring
Gtr. 2
let ring
Gtrs. 1 & 2: w/ Rhy. Figs. 2 & 2A (1st 6 meas.)
B♭
A5
G5
C
D5
Vic - tim of love, you're just a vic - tim of love.
I could be wrong, but I'm
Gtr. 3
let ring

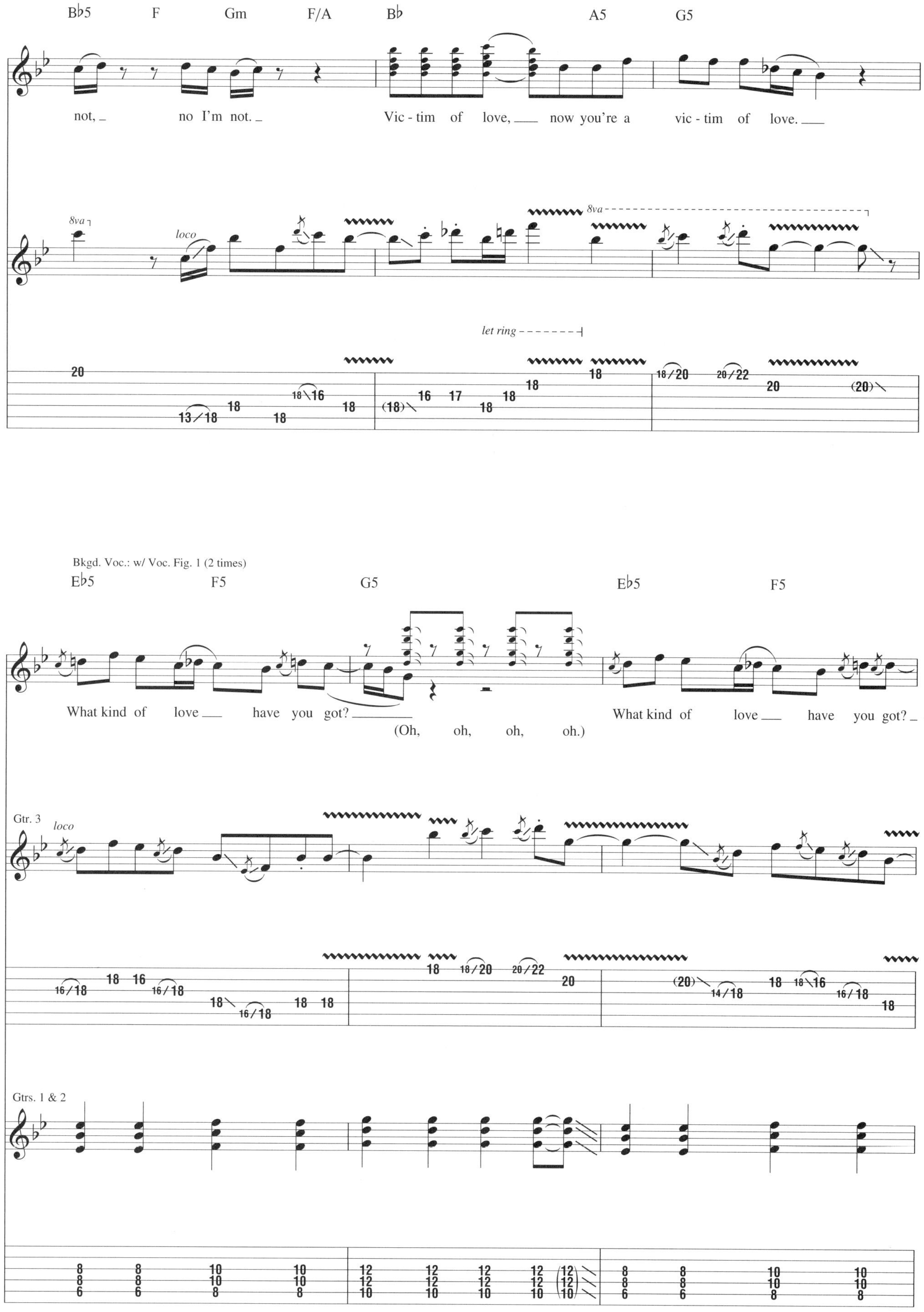

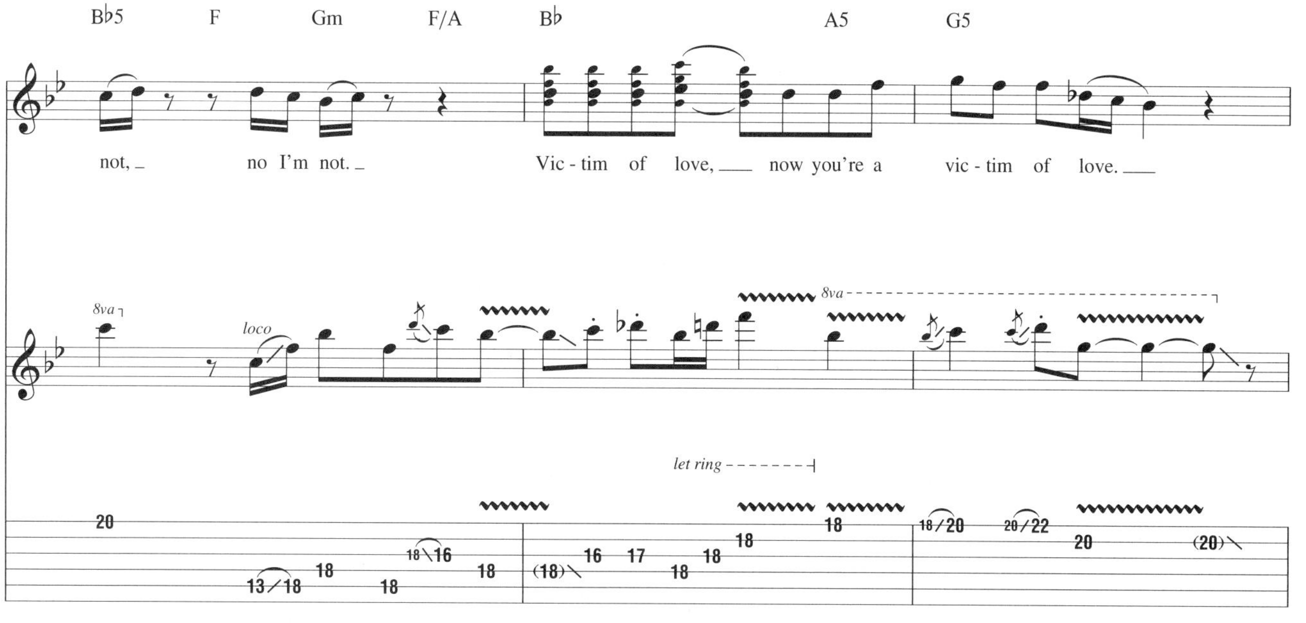

Bkgd. Voc.: w/ Voc. Fig. 1 (2 times)

E♭5 F5 G5 E♭5 F5

What kind of love have you got? What kind of love have you got?

(Oh, oh, oh, oh.)

Gtr. 3

loco

Gtrs. 1 & 2

G5
E♭5
F5
G5

rit.
What kind of love _ have you _ got?
(Oh, oh, oh, oh.)

rit.

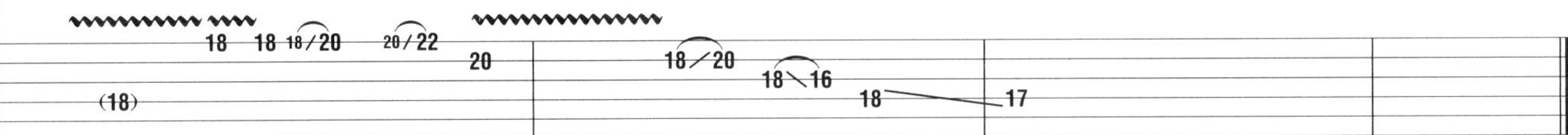

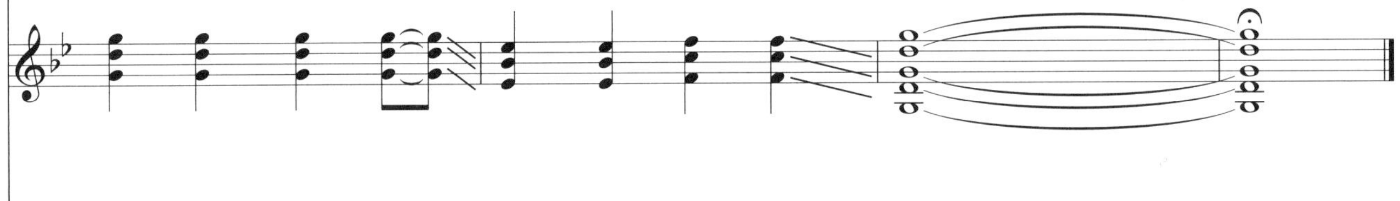
rit.

from Maroon5 - *It Won't Be Soon Before Long*

Wake Up Call

Words and Music by Adam Levine and James Valentine

Em/B
7fr
3421
B7/A
7fr
1211
Em
231
B/F♯
1 341
G
1 211
A
5fr
1 211
B
7fr
1342

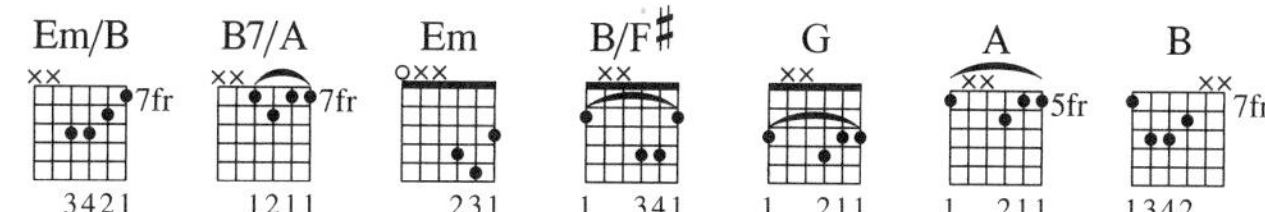

Intro

Moderately ♩ = 82

N.C.

*Gtr. 1

mf
T
A
B
7 10 7 10 7 10 9 7 10 7 10 7 10 9
7 10 7 10 7 10 9 7 10 7 10

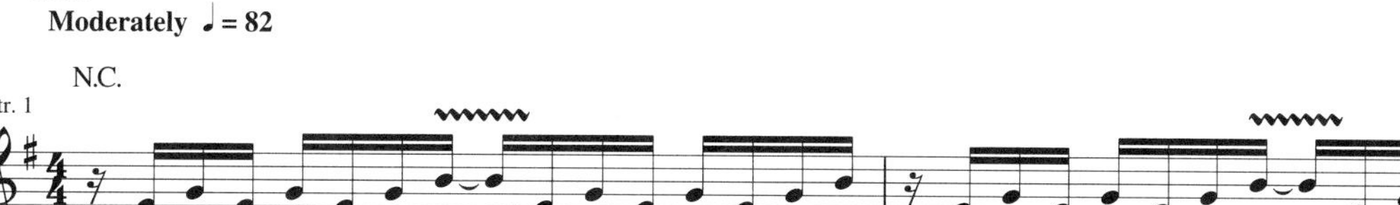

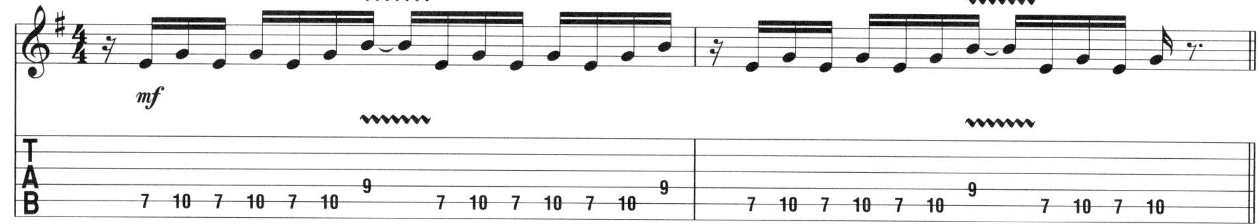

*Synth. arr. for gtr.

Verse

Gtr. 1 tacet

**Em

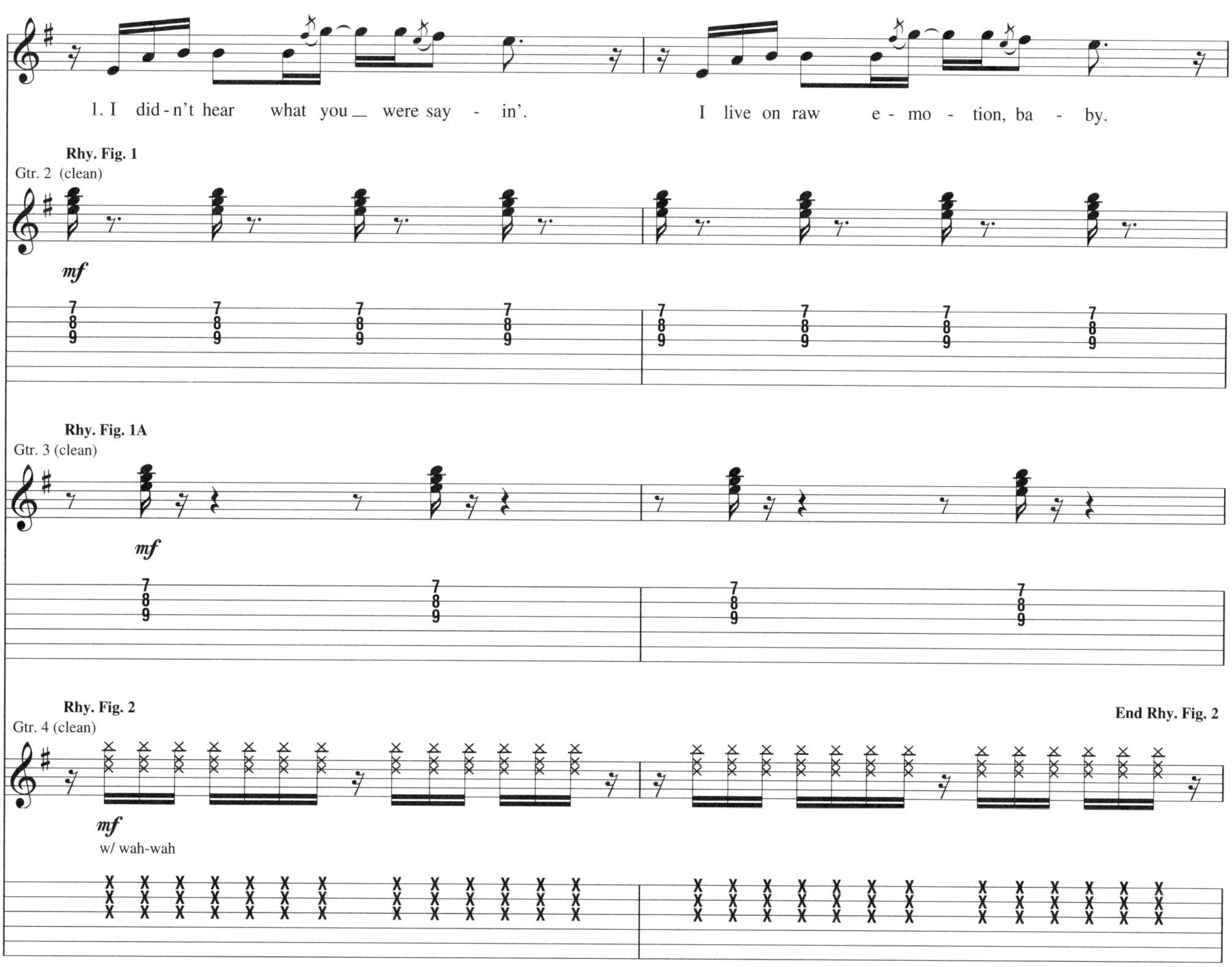

1. I did - n't hear what you ___ were say - in'.
I live on raw e - mo - tion, ba - by.
Rhy. Fig. 1
Gtr. 2 (clean)
mf
Rhy. Fig. 1A
Gtr. 3 (clean)
mf
Rhy. Fig. 2
Gtr. 4 (clean)
End Rhy. Fig. 2
mf
w/ wah-wah

**Chord symbols reflect overall harmony.

Gtr. 4: w/ Rhy. Fig. 2 (2 times)
Am
Bm
Em
I an-swer ques - tions nev - er may - be,
and I'm not kind if you be-tray me.
Gtr. 2
End Rhy. Fig. 1
Gtr. 3
End Rhy. Fig. 1A
Gtrs. 2 & 3: w/ Rhy. Figs. 1 & 1A (last 2 meas.)
Am
Bm
So who the hell are you to say we
nev - er would have made it, babe? If you need-
*Gtr. 5
mf
w/ fingers
*Elec. piano arr. for gtr.
Pre-Chorus
Gtr. 4: w/ Rhy. Fig. 2 (2 times)
Em
- ed love, well, then ask for love, Could have giv - en love, now I'm tak - in' love. And it's not
Rhy. Fig. 3
Gtr. 5
Gtr. 1
Riff A

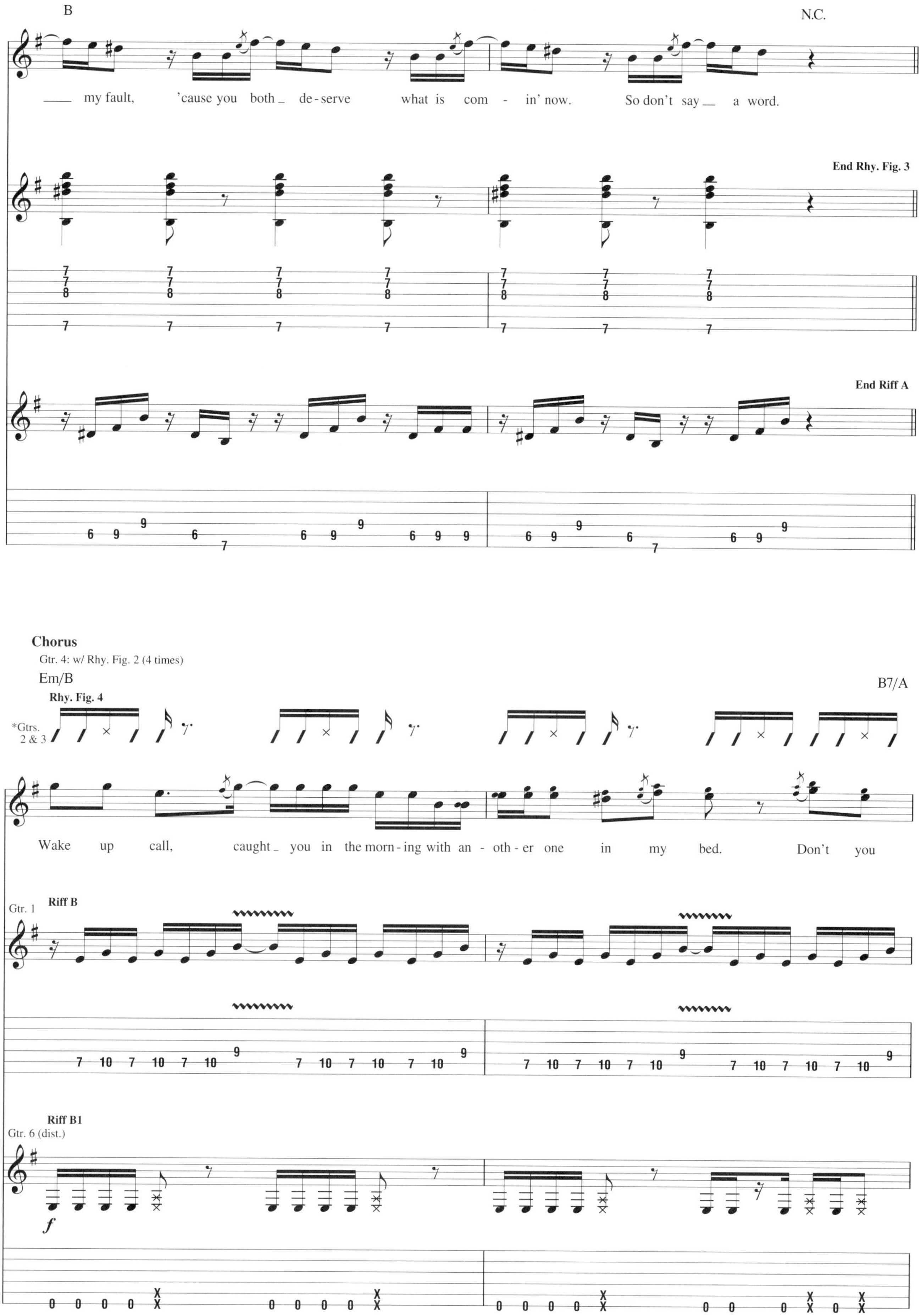

B N.C.

___ my fault, 'cause you both _ de-serve what is com - in' now. So don't say _ a word.

End Rhy. Fig. 3

End Riff A

Chorus

Gtr. 4: w/ Rhy. Fig. 2 (4 times)

Em/B B7/A

Rhy. Fig. 4

*Gtrs. 2 & 3

*Composite arrangement

End Rhy. Fig. 4
care a-bout me an-y-more? Don't you care a-bout me? I ___ don't think _ so.
End Riff B
End Riff B1
Gtrs. 1 & 6: w/ Riffs B & B1
Gtrs. 2 & 3: w/ Rhy. Fig. 4
Em
B7
Six foot tall, came _ with-out a warn-ing so I had to shoot him dead. He won't _
come a-round here an-y-more. Come a-round here, I ___ don't think _ so...
Verse
Gtrs. 2 & 3: w/ Rhy. Figs. 1 & 1A (2 times)
Gtr. 4: w/ Rhy. Fig. 2 (3 times)
Em
Bm
Em
Bm
2. I would've bled to make _ you hap - py. You did-n't need to treat _ me that ___ way.
Gtr. 5

Am
Bm
Em
Bm
And now you beat me at ___ my own game. And now I find you sleep - ing sound - ly,
Em
Bm
Am
Bm
and your lov - er's scream - in' loud - ly, and hear a sound and hit ___ the ground. _ If you need -
Pre-Chorus
Gtr. 1: w/ Riff A
Gtr. 4: w/ Rhy. Fig. 2 (2 times)
Gtr. 5: w/ Rhy. Fig. 3
Em
- ed love, well, then ask ___ for love, Could have giv - en love, now I'm tak - in' love. And it's not _
(Need-ed love, ask ___ for love, giv - en love, tak - in' love.
B
N.C.
___ my fault, 'cause you both ___ de - serve what is com - in' now. So don't say ___ a word.
Not ___ my fault, both ___ de - serve, com - in' now.)

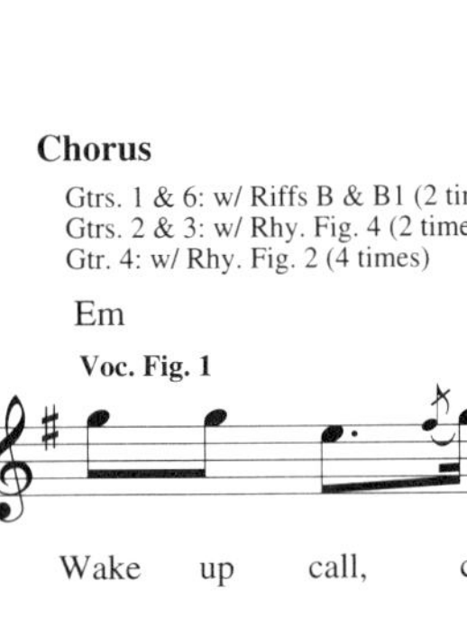
Chorus
Gtrs. 1 & 6: w/ Riffs B & B1 (2 times)
Gtrs. 2 & 3: w/ Rhy. Fig. 4 (2 times)
Gtr. 4: w/ Rhy. Fig. 2 (4 times)
Em

B7
Voc. Fig. 1
Wake up call, caught you in the morn - ing with an - oth - er one in my bed. Don't you

care a - bout me an - y - more? Don't you care a - bout me? I don't think so.
Voc. Fig. 2
End Voc. Fig. 2
(Yeah, yeah, yeah.)

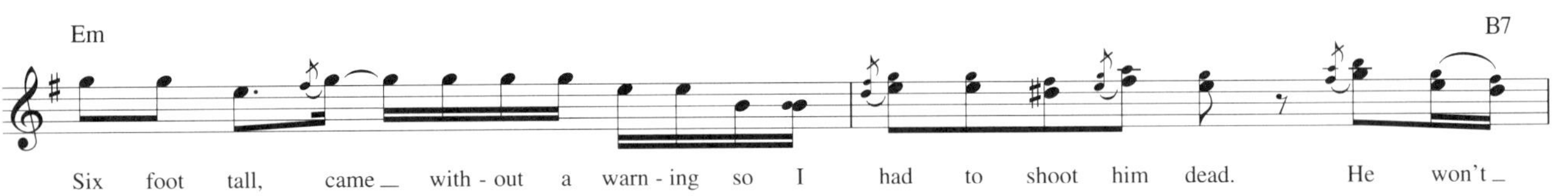
Em
B7
Six foot tall, came with - out a warn - ing so I had to shoot him dead. He won't

Bkgd. Voc.: w/ Voc. Fig. 2
End Voc. Fig. 1
come a - round here an - y - more. Come a - round here, I don't feel so bad.

Bridge
Gtr. 4: w/ Rhy. Fig. 2
Em B/F♯ G A Em B/F♯ G A
Gtr. 5
I don't feel so bad. I don't feel so
Gtr. 7 (dist.)
mf
9 8 7 6 9 8 7 6
Gtr. 6
0 2 3 5 0 2 3 5

Gtr. 7 tacet
B
bad. I'm so sor - ry, dar - lin'. Did I do the wrong thing?
(Sor - ry, dar - lin'. Do the wrong
Gtr. 1
Gtr. 6
divisi
Gtrs. 1, 5 & 6 tacet
N.C.
Oh, what was I think - ing? Is his heart still beat - ing?
(Oh.)
thing. Was I think - ing.)
Outro-Chorus
Gtr. 1: w/ Riff B (till fade)
Gtrs. 2 & 3: w/ Rhy. Fig. 4 (till fade)
Gtr. 4: w/ Rhy. Fig. 2 (till fade)
Gtr. 6: w/ Riff B1 (2 times)
Em
B7
Wake up call, caught you in the morn - ing with an - oth - er one in my bed. Don't you
care a - bout me an - y - more? Don't you care a - bout me? I don't think so.

Bkgd. Voc.: w/ Voc. Fig. 1 (last 4 meas.)
Em
B7
Six foot tall, came with-out a warn-ing so I had to shoot him dead. And he won't
Bkgd. Voc.: w/ Voc. Fig. 2
come a-round here an-y-more. Come a-round here, I don't feel so bad.
Bkgd. Voc.: w/ Voc. Fig. 1
Em **B/F♯ G A Em B/F♯ G A
Wake up call, caught you in the morn-ing with an-oth-er one in my bed. Don't you
Gtr. 6
0 0 2 2 3 3 5 5 0 0 2 2 3 3 5 5
**Bass plays F♮.
Bkgd. Voc.: w/ Voc. Fig. 2
Gtr. 6: w/ Riff B1 (last 2 meas.)
B7
care a-bout me an-y-more? Care a-bout me? I don't think so.
Gtr. 6: w/ Riff B1 (till fade)
Em
B7
Six foot tall, came with-out a warn-ing so I had to shoot him dead. He won't
Bkgd. Voc.: w/ Voc. Fig. 2
come a-round here an-y-more. No, he won't come a-round here, I don't feel so bad.
Begin fade
Bkgd. Voc.: w/ Voc. Fig. 2
Em
B7
Wake up call, caught you in the morn-ing with an-oth-er one in my bed. Don't you care a-bout me an-y more? Don't you
I don't feel so bad. I don't feel so bad.
Fade out
Em
B7
care a-bout me? I don't feel so bad.
Wake up call, caught you in the morn-ing with an-oth-er one in my bed. Don't you...

from Smash Mouth - *Fush Yu Mang*

Walkin' on the Sun

Words and Music by Steve Harwell, Gregory Camp, Paul DeLisle and Kevin Iannello

Tune down 1/2 step:
(low to high) E♭-A♭-D♭-G♭-B♭-E♭

Gtr. 3: w/ Riff C
Am D Am7 D Am D Am7 D
world _ to snuff _ the fi - res and the li - ars. Hey, I know it's just a song, but it's spice for the rec - i - pe. This is a
folked out with gui-tars a-round the bon-fire. Just sing - ing and clap - ping, man, what the hell hap-pened? Then some were

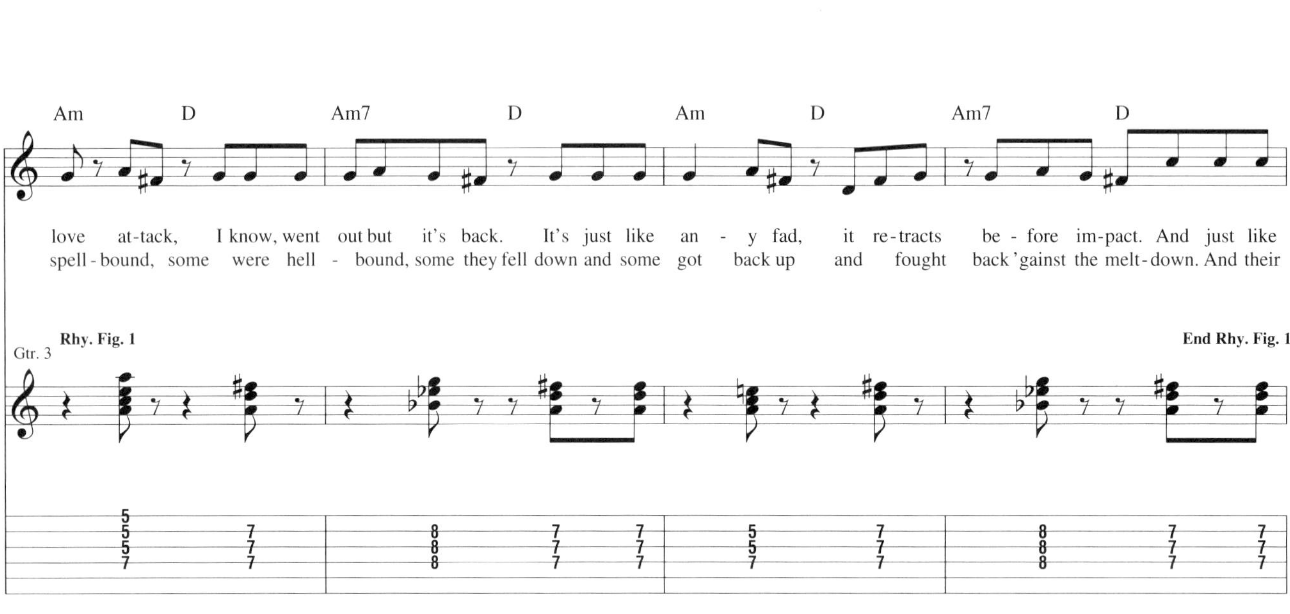
Am D Am7 D Am D Am7 D
love at-tack, I know, went out but it's back. It's just like an - y fad, it re-tracts be - fore im-pact. And just like
spell - bound, some were hell - bound, some they fell down and some got back up and fought back 'gainst the melt-down. And their
Rhy. Fig. 1
End Rhy. Fig. 1
Gtr. 3

Am D Am7 D Am D Am7 D
fash - ion, it's a pas - sion for the with it and hip. If you got the goods they'll come and buy it just to say in the clique.
kids were hip-pie chicks, all hyp - o - crites be - cause fash - ion is smash-in' the true mean-ing of it.
Gtr. 3
Gtr. 2

Chorus
3rd time, Voc.: w/ Voc. Fill 1
3rd time, Gtr. 3: w/ Fill 1
Am D Am7 D Am D Am7 D
So don't de - lay, act now, sup - plies are run - ning out. Al - low, if you're still a - live, six to eight years to ar - rive.
Gtr. 3
Gtr. 2
To Coda 1
To Coda 2
Am D Am7 D Am D E7♯9
And if you fol - low, there may be a to - mor - row. But if the of - fer's shun, you might as well be walk - in' on the
Rhy. Fig. 2
End Rhy. Fig. 2
Voc. Fill 1
Fill 1
Gtr. 2

Interlude
D.S. al Coda 1
Gtr. 2: w/ Riff B
Am D Am7 D Am D Am7 D
sun.
2. Twen-ty - five
Rhy. Fig. 3
End Rhy. Fig. 3
Gtr. 3
Coda 1
Keyboard Solo
Gtr. 2: w/ Riff B
Gtr. 3: w/ Rhy. Fig. 3
Am D Am7 D Am D Am7 D
sun.
8va
*Gtr. 4
mf
*Kybds. arr. for gtr.
Gtr. 2: w/ Riff D
Gtr. 3: w/ Rhy. Fig. 2
Am D Am7 D Am D E7#9
3. It ain't no
8va
let ring
Verse
Gtr. 1: w/ Riff A (2 times)
Gtr. 4 tacet
Am(add9) Am7
joke when a ma-ma's hand-ker - chief is soaked with her tears ___ be-cause her ba-by's life has been re - voked. The bond is
Gtr. 3

Gtr. 2: w/ Riff B

broke up, so choke up and fo - cus on the close up. Mis-ter Wiz-ard can't re-form no god - like ho-cus po-cus. So don't

Gtr. 3: w/ Rhy. Fig. 1

Am D Am7 D Am D Am7 D

sit back, kick back and watch the world get bush-wacked. News at ten: "Your neigh-bor-hood is un - der at - tack." Put a way the

D.S.S. al Coda 2

Am D Am7 D Am D Em7♯9

crap be-fore the crack puts you a-way. You need to be there when your ba-by's old e - nough to re - late.

Gtr. 3

Gtr. 2

Coda 2

Gtr. 2: w/ Riff B
Gtr. 3: w/ Rhy. Fig. 3

Am D Am7 D Am D Am7 D

sun. You might as well be walk-in' on the sun. You might as well be walk-in' on the

Am(add9) N.C.

sun.

Gtr. 3

from the Go-Go's - *Beauty and the Beat*

We Got the Beat

Words and Music by Charlotte Caffey

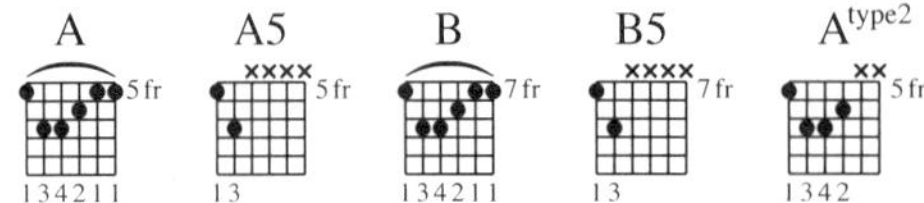

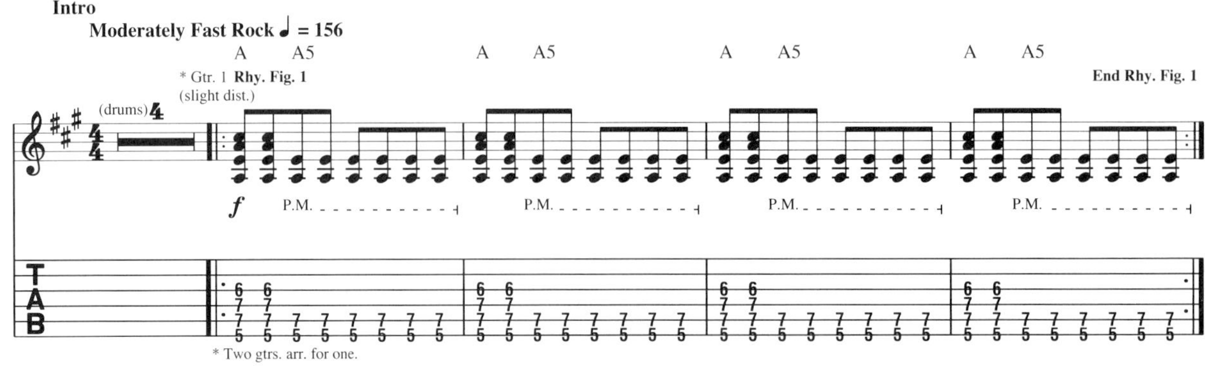

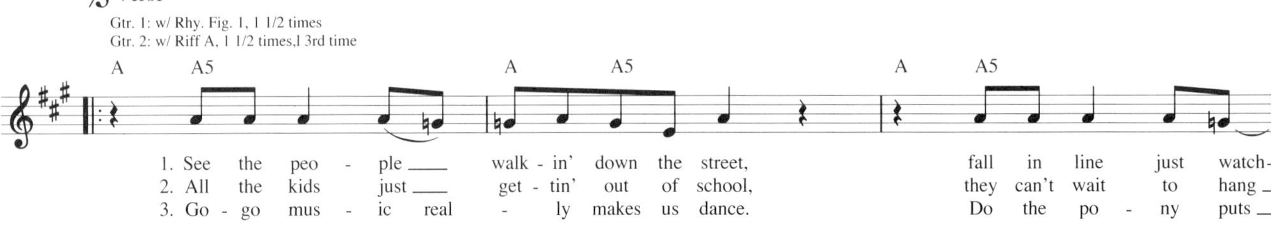

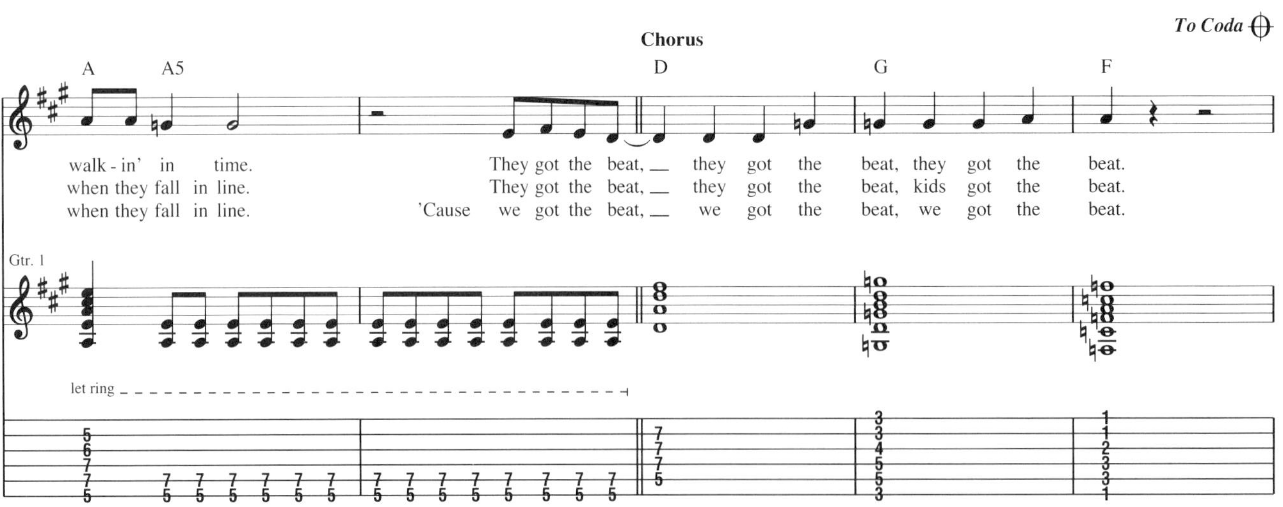

C
A
A5
Yeah, they got the beat.
Yeah, kids got the beat.
P.M.
Guitar Solo
*A
Rhy. Fig. 2
Gtr. 1
Gtr. 2
(clean)
*let ring
sim.
End Rhy. Fig. 2
B
B5
Gtr. 1: w/ Rhy. Fig. 1, simile
Riff A
D.S. al Coda
End Riff A
Coda
Interlude
Gtr. 1 tacet
N.C.
Yeah, we got it!
(We got the beat.

We got the beat.
We got the beat.
Ev - 'ry - bod - y,
get on your feet.
We got the beat.
We know you can
dance to the beat.
We got the beat.
E5
Jump back,
get down.
We got the beat.
'Round and 'round and 'round.
Woo!)
Gtr. 1
2 2 2 2 2 2 2
2 2 2 2 2 2 2
0 0 0 0 0 0 0 0
Outro
Gtrs. 1 & 2: w/ Rhy. Fig. 2 & Riff A, 3 times
A A5
A A5
A A5
A A5
(We got the beat.
We got the beat.
We got the beat.
We got the beat.
A A5
A A5
A A5
We got the beat.
We got the beat.
We got the beat.
A A5
A A5
A A5
We got the beat.
We got the beat.
We got the beat.
We got the beat.
A A5
A A5
A type2
Gtr. 1
We got the beat.
We got the beat.
We got the beat.)
Gtr. 2
5

from Wes Montgomery - *The Incredible Jazz Guitar of Wes Montgomery*

West Coast Blues

By John L. (Wes) Montgomery

2.
B
B♭7
A♭7
B♭7
Bm7
E7
E♭7
E♭m7
A♭7
Dm7
G7
D♭m7
G♭7
Cm7
F7
Cm7
F7
B♭7
D♭7
G♭maj7

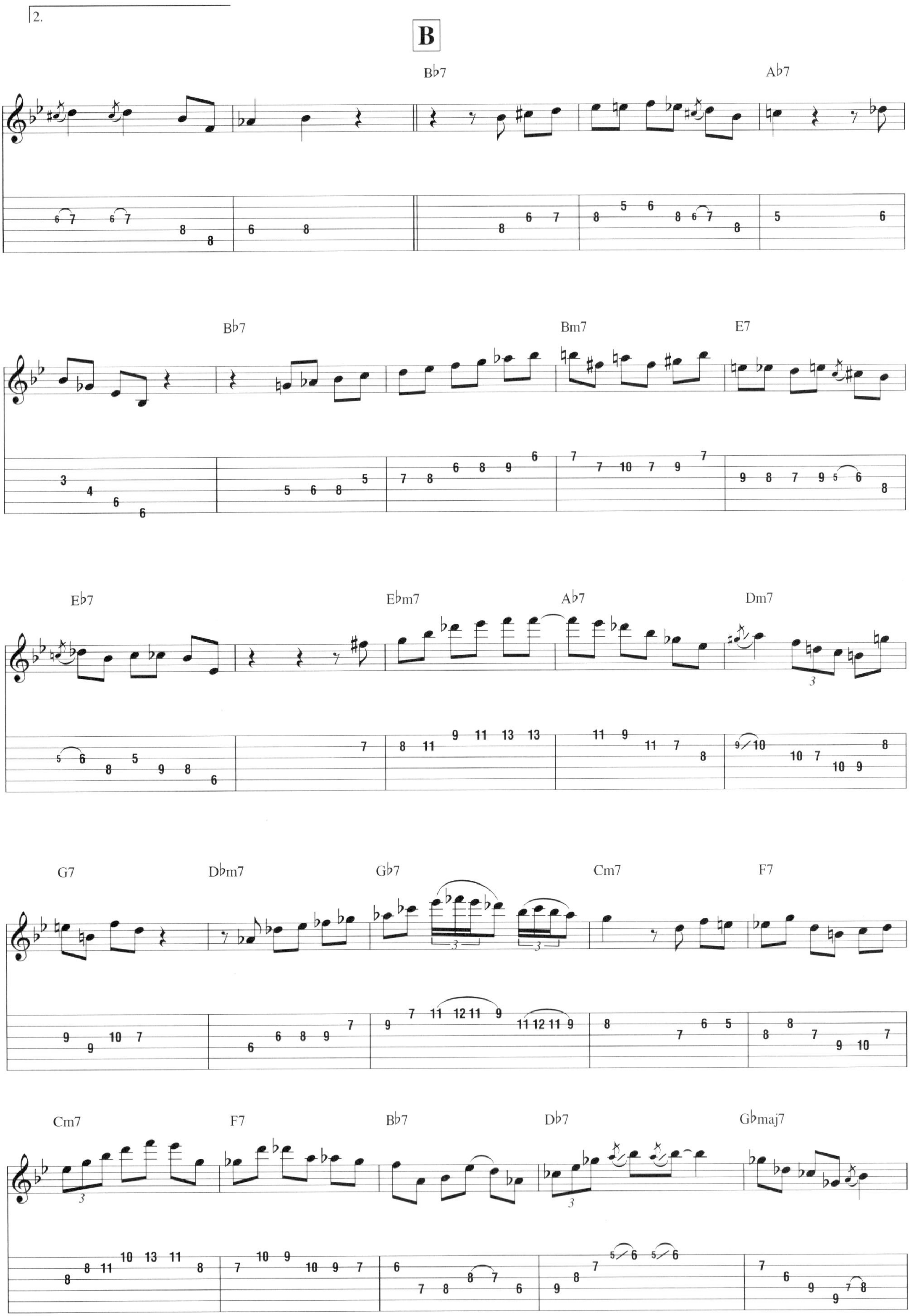

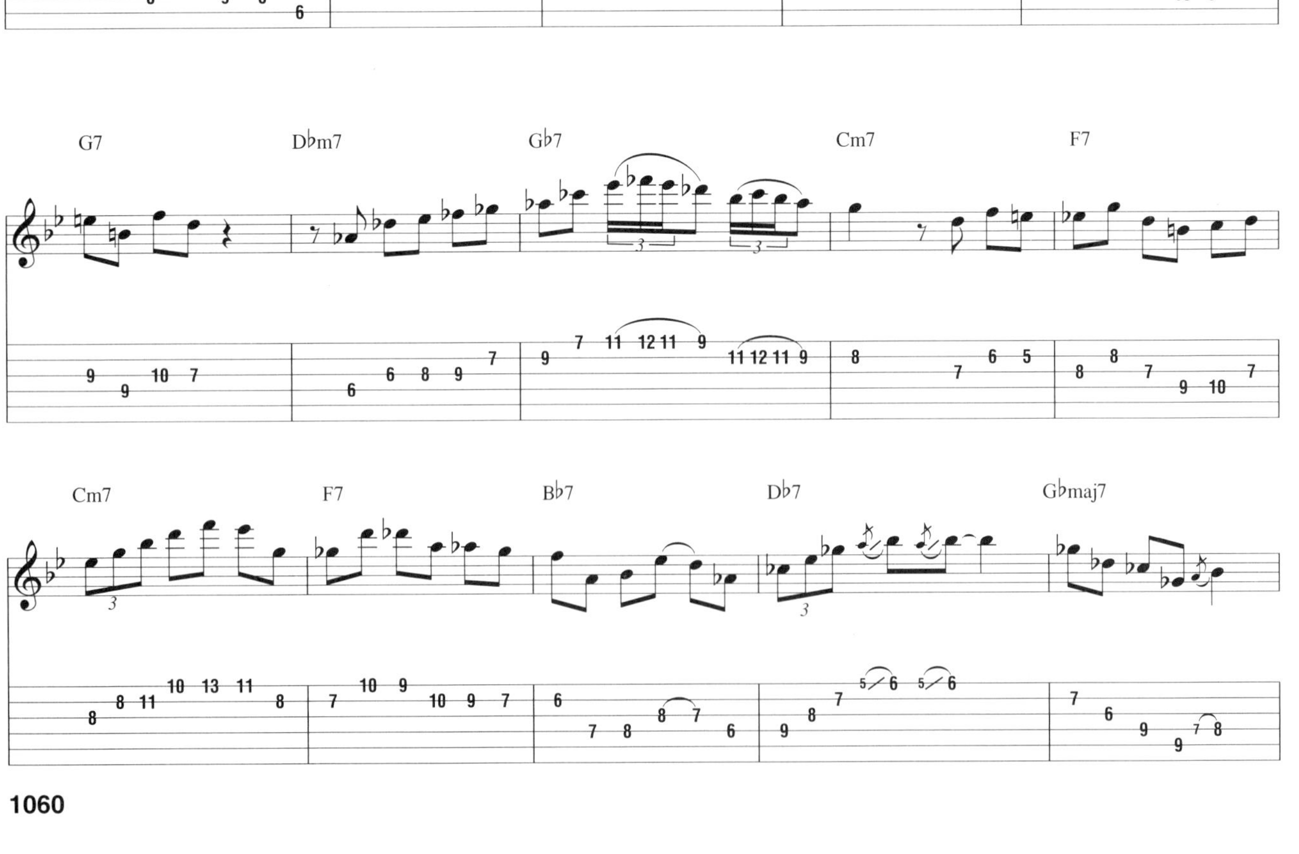

C♭7
B♭7
A♭7
B♭7
Bm7
E7
E♭7
E♭m7
A♭7
Dm7
G7
*Played behind the beat.
D♭m7
G♭7
Cm7
F7
Cm7
F7
B♭7
D♭7
G♭maj7
C♭7
B♭7
A♭7
B♭7

Bm7
E7
E♭7
E♭m7
A♭7
Dm7
G7
D♭m7
G♭7
Cm7
F7
Cm7
F7
B♭7
D♭7
G♭maj7
C♭7
B♭7
A♭7
B♭7
Bm7
E7
E♭7
E♭m7
1/2

A♭7
Dm7
G7
D♭m7
G♭7
Cm7
F7
Cm7
F7
B♭7
D♭7
G♭maj7
C♭7
B♭7
A♭7
B♭7
Bm7
E7
E♭7
E♭m7
A♭7
Dm7
G7
D♭m7
G♭7

Cm7 F7 Cm7 F7 B♭7
D♭7 G♭maj7 C♭7 B♭7
A♭7 B♭7
Bm7 E7 E♭7
E♭m7 A♭7 Dm7 G7
D♭m7 G♭7 Cm7 F7

Cm7
F7
B♭7
D♭7
G♭maj7
C♭7
B♭7
A♭7
B♭7
Bm7
E7
E♭7
E♭m7
A♭7
Dm7
G7
D♭m7
G♭7
Cm7
F7
Cm7
F7
B♭7
D♭7
G♭maj7

C♭7
B♭7
A♭7
B♭7
Bm7
E7
E♭7
E♭m7
A♭7
Dm7
G7
D♭m7
G♭7
Cm7
F7
Cm7
F7
B♭7
D♭7
G♭maj7
C♭7
B♭7
A♭7

B♭7
Bm7
E7
E♭7
E♭m7
A♭7
Dm7
G7
D♭m7
G♭7
Cm7
F7
Cm7
F7
B♭maj7
D♭7
G♭maj7
C♭7
C
Gtr. 1: comp
B♭7
70
C♭7

D
B♭7
A♭7
B♭7
Bm7
E7
E♭7
A♭7
Dm7
G7
B♭7
F7
E♭7
B♭7
E
B♭maj7
A♭m7
D♭7
G♭maj7
C♭7
B♭maj7♯11

from Pixies - *Surfer Rosa*

Where Is My Mind?

Words and Music by Frank Black

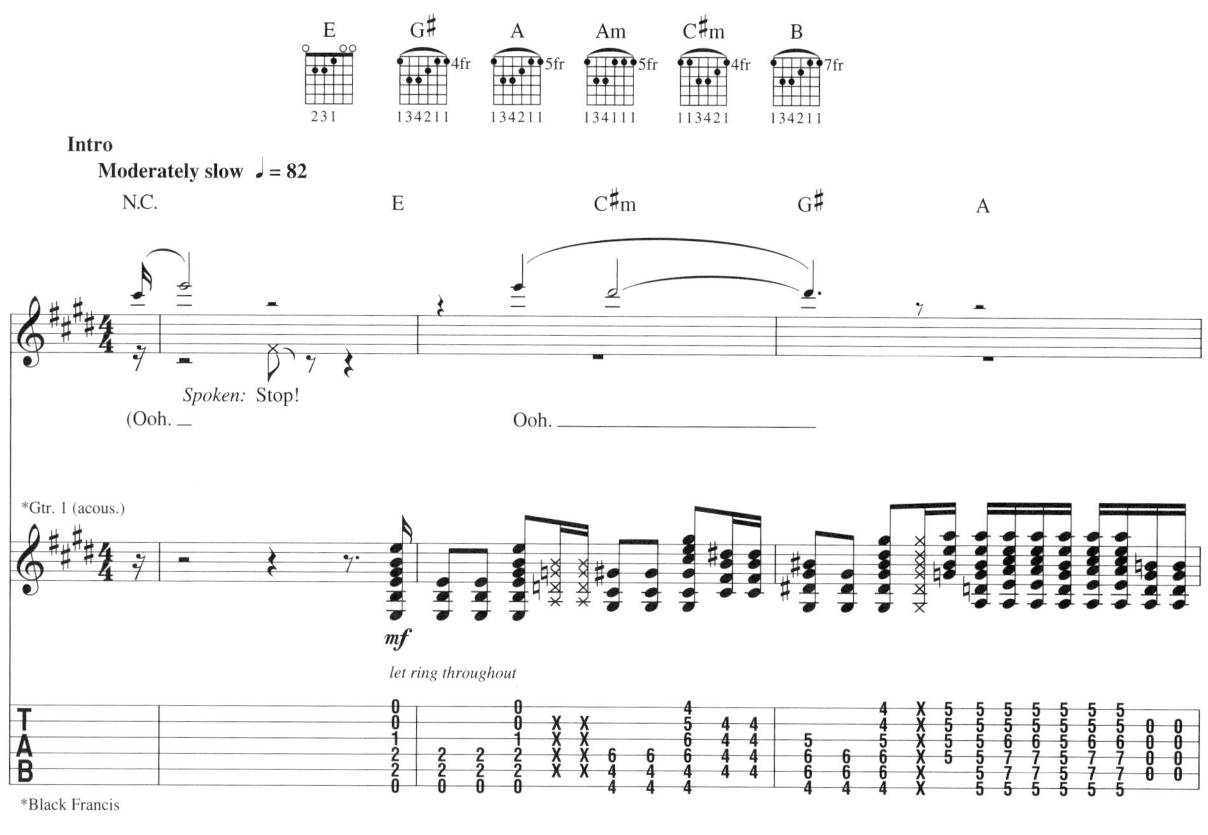

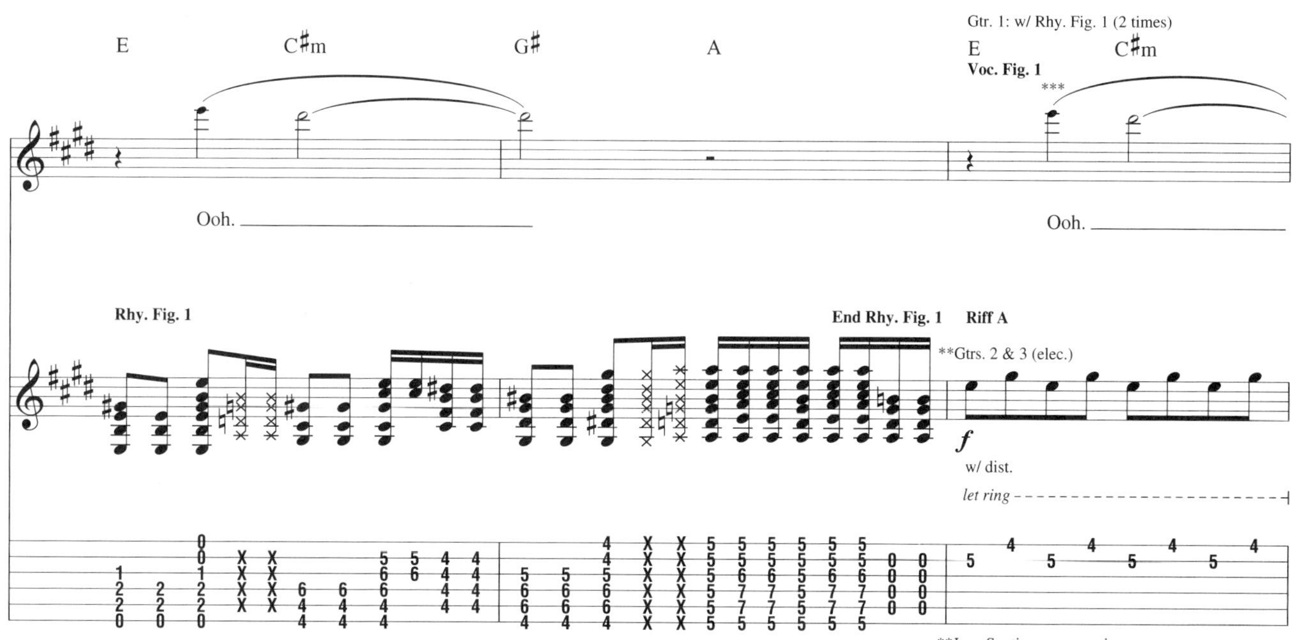

G♯ A E C♯m G♯ A
End Voc. Fig. 1
Ooh.)
1. With your
End Riff A
let ring
feet on the air and your head on the ground,
2. I was swim-min' in the Car-ri-be-an.
feet on the air and your head on the ground,
Verse
Bkgd. Voc.: w/ Voc. Fig. 1 (3 times)
Gtr. 1: w/ Rhy. Fig. 1 (3 times)
Gtrs. 2 & 3: w/ Riff A (3 times)
try this trick and spin it, yeah, yeah.
An-i-mals were hid-in' be-hind the rock
try this trick and spin it, yeah.
Your head will col-lapse, but there's noth-ing in it and you'll ask your-self:
ex-cept for lit-tle fish, but they told me, he swears, it's try'n' to talk to me, to me, to me.
Your head will col-lapse, and there's noth-ing in it and you'll ask your-self:
Chorus
Gtr. 1: w/ Rhy. Fig. 1 (3 times)
Where is my mind? Where is my mind? Where is my mind?

G♯ A E C♯m G♯ A
Way
Gtrs. 2 & 3
*P.M.
*Refers to Gtr. 3 only.

**E G♯ A Am
Gtr. 1
out in the wa - ter, see it swim - min'.
Gtrs. 2 & 3
P.M.
**See top of first page of song for chord diagrams pertaining to rhythm slashes.

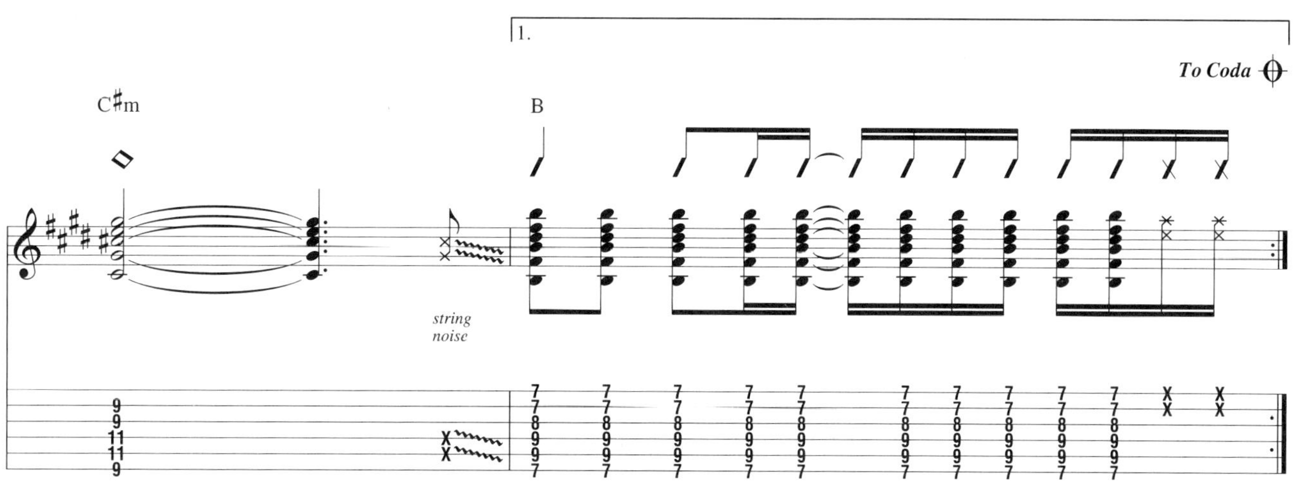
1.
To Coda
C♯m B
string noise

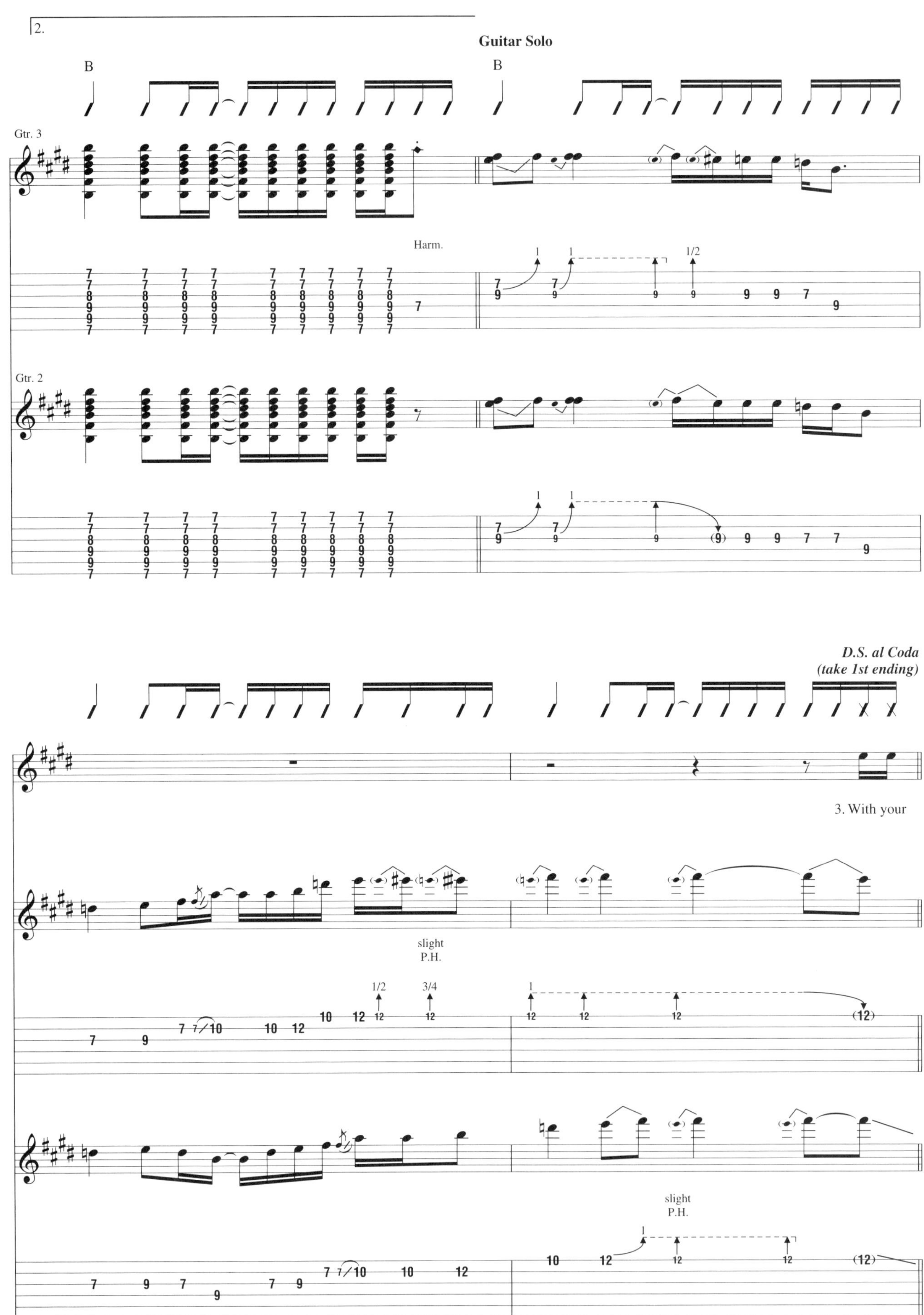

2.
Guitar Solo
B
B
Gtr. 3
Harm.
1
1
1/2
Gtr. 2
1
1
D.S. al Coda
(take 1st ending)
3. With your
slight
P.H.
1/2
3/4
1
slight
P.H.
1

Coda
Outro
Bkgd. Voc.: w/ Voc. Fig. 1 (6 times)
Gtr. 1: w/ Rhy. Fig. 1 (6 times)
Gtrs. 2 & 3: w/ Riff A (6 times)
E C♯m G♯ A E C♯m
With your feet on the air and your head _ on the ground,
G♯ A E C♯m G♯ A
try __ this trick and spin it, yeah.
E C♯m G♯ A E C♯m
G♯ A E C♯m G♯ A
E C♯m G♯ N.C.
(Ooh. Ooh.)
Gtrs. 2 & 3
let ring
let ring
Gtr. 1

from Taylor Swift - *Fearless*

White Horse

Words and Music by Taylor Swift and Liz Rose

Gtr. 2: Capo V

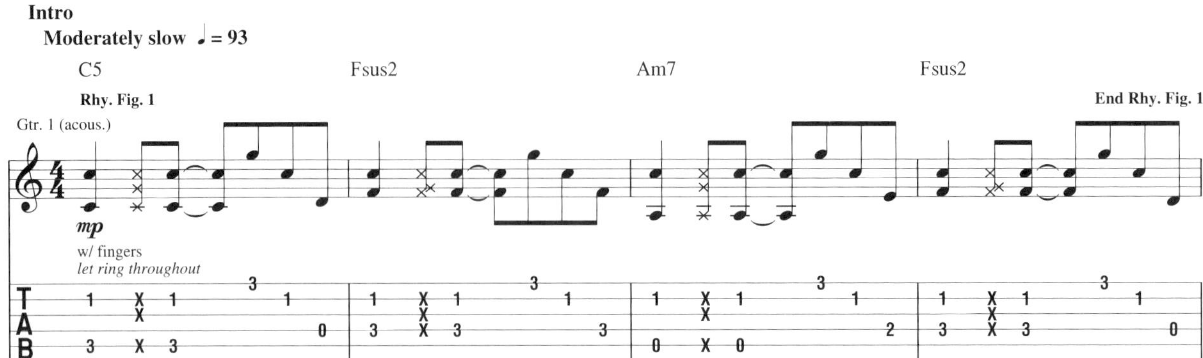

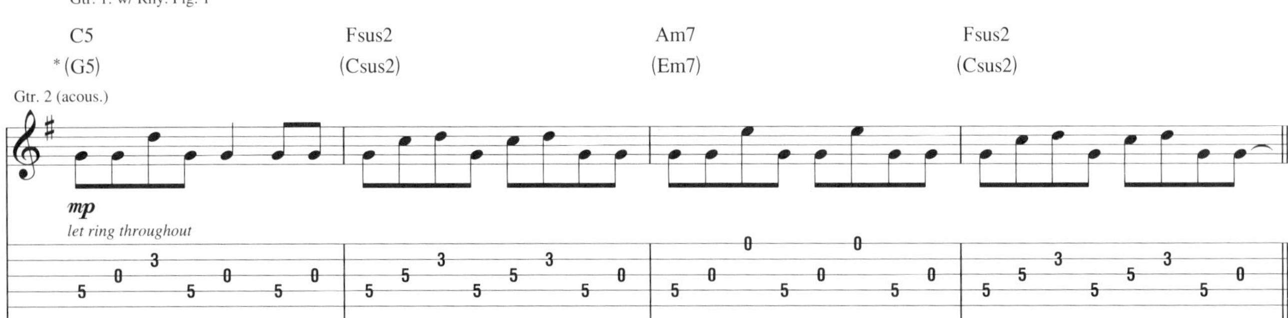

*Symbols in parentheses represent chord names respective to capoed guitar. Symbols above reflect actual sounding chords. Capoed fret is "0" in tab.

Am7
Fsus2
- ing on, the days drag on. Stu - pid girl,
Gsus4
G
I should-'ve known, I should-'ve known that I'm not a prin -
(cont. in slashes)
Chorus
C
Am7
F/C
G
Rhy. Fig. 2
End Rhy. Fig. 2
Gtr. 1
w/ pick
- cess, this ain't a fair - y tale. I'm not the one you'll sweep off her feet, lead her up the stair - well. This ain't
Rhy. Fig. 2A
End Rhy. Fig. 2A
Gtr. 2
Gtrs. 1 & 2: w/ Rhy. Figs. 2 & 2A (1st 3 meas.)
C
(G)
Am7
(Em7)
F/C
(C/G)
Hol - ly - wood, this is a small town. I was a dream - er be - fore you went and let

Interlude

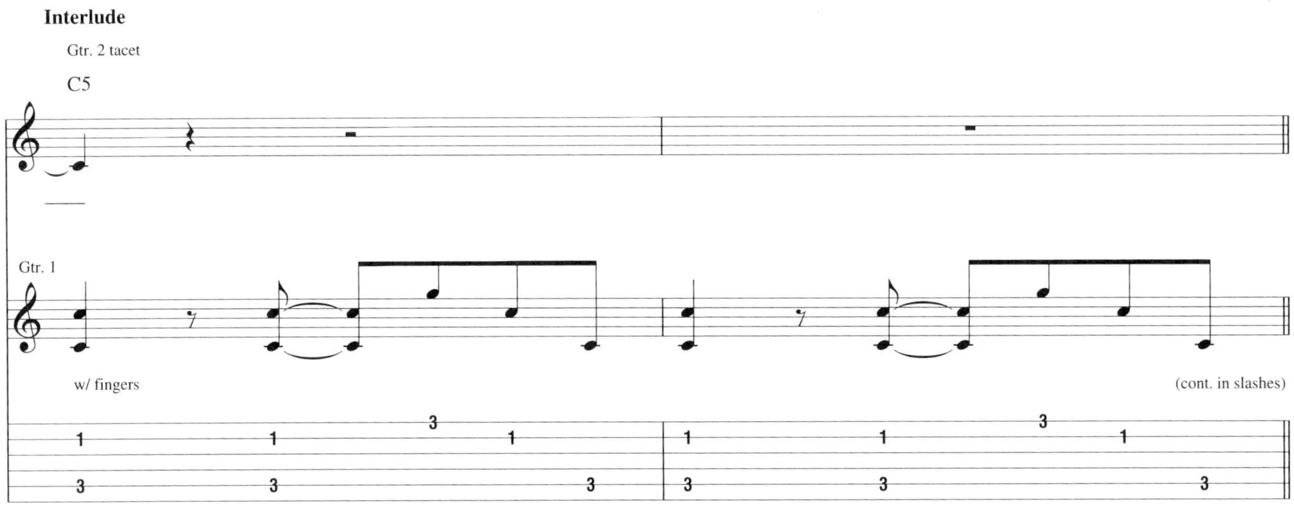

Verse

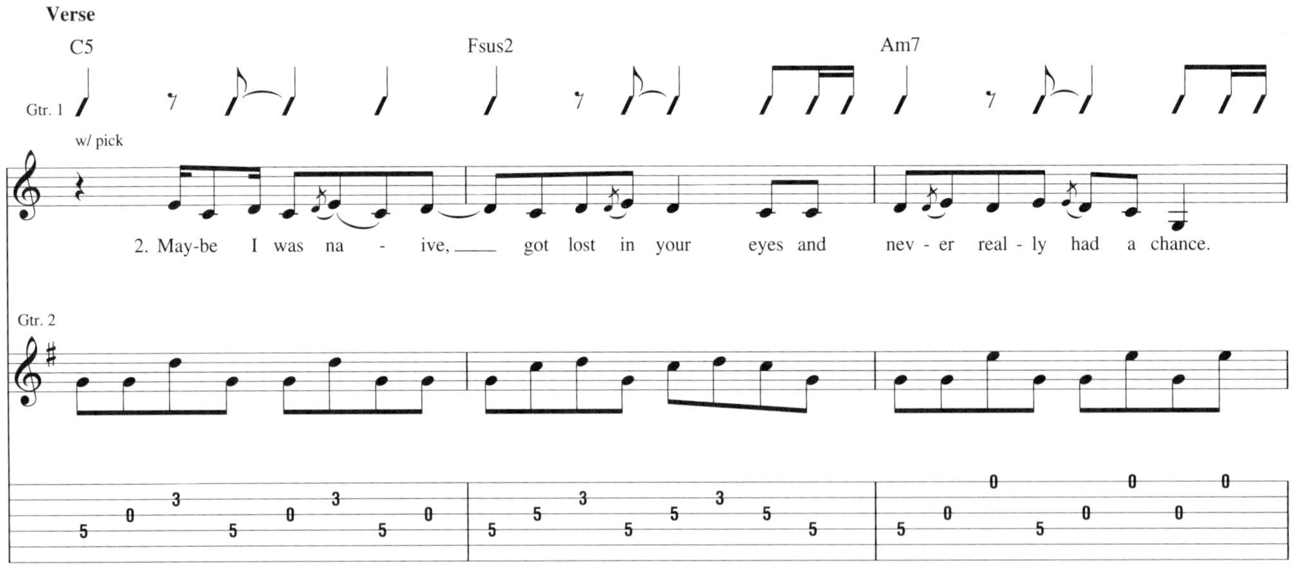

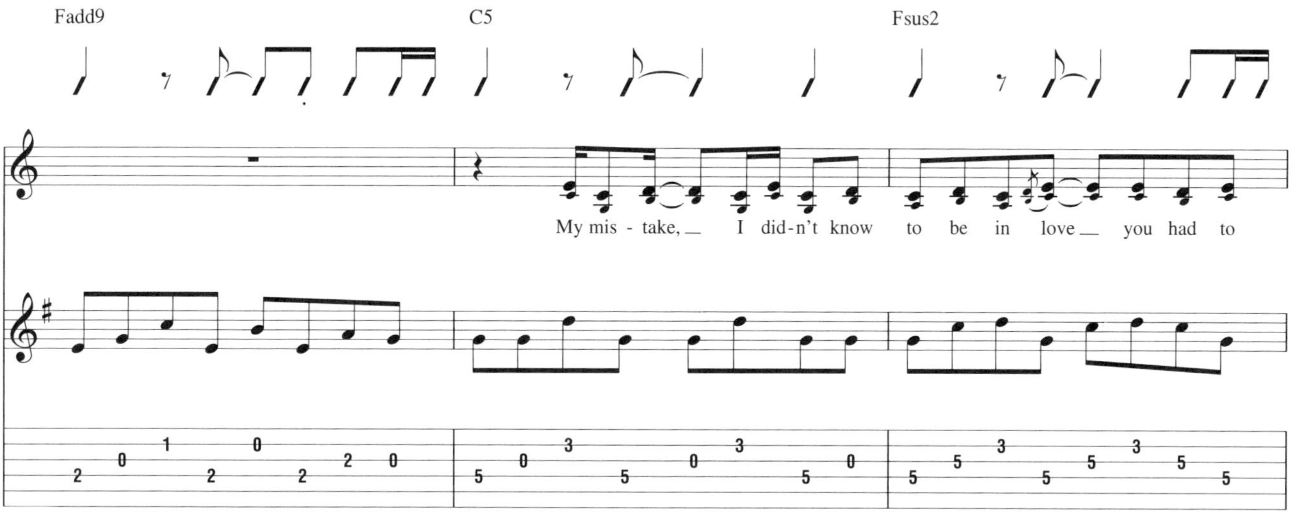
Fadd9
C5
Fsus2
My mis - take, I did - n't know to be in love you had to

Am7
Fadd9
Am7
fight to have the up - per hand.
I had so man - y dreams a - bout you

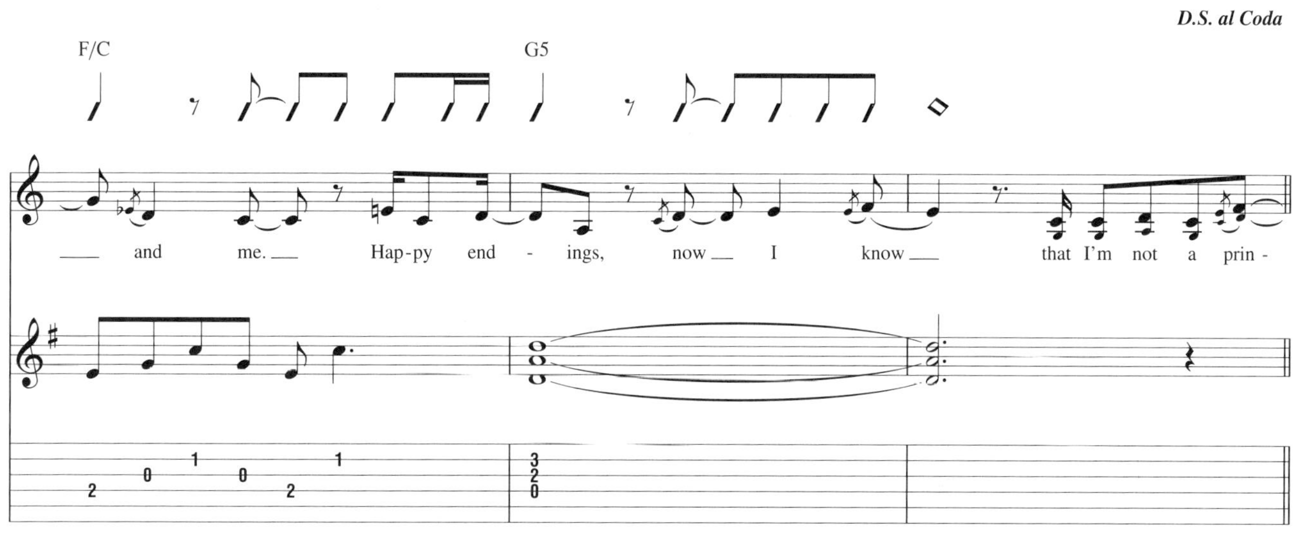
D.S. al Coda
F/C
G5
and me. Hap-py end - ings, now I know that I'm not a prin -

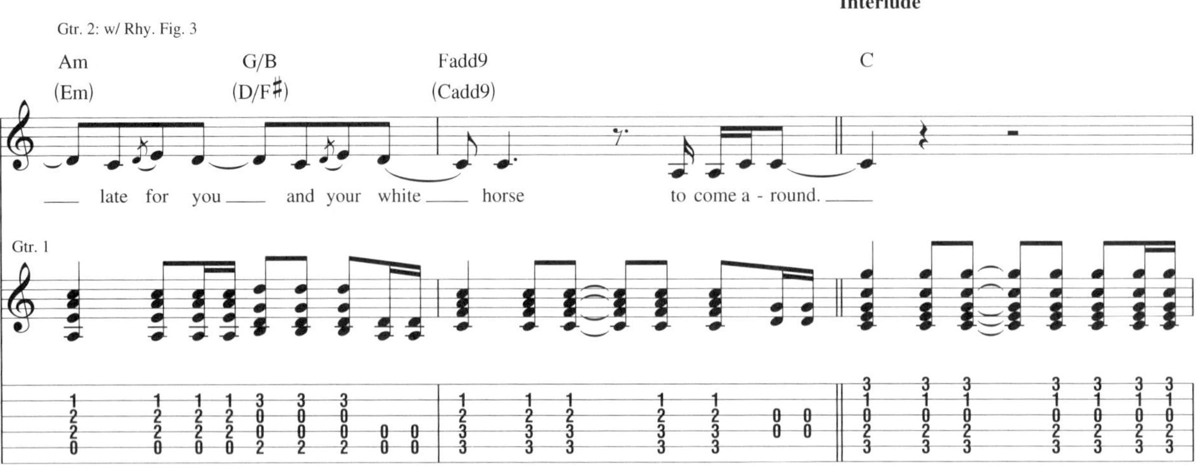

Interlude
Gtr. 2: w/ Rhy. Fig. 3
Am
(Em)
G/B
(D/F♯)
Fadd9
(Cadd9)
C
late for you and your white horse to come a - round.
Gtr. 1

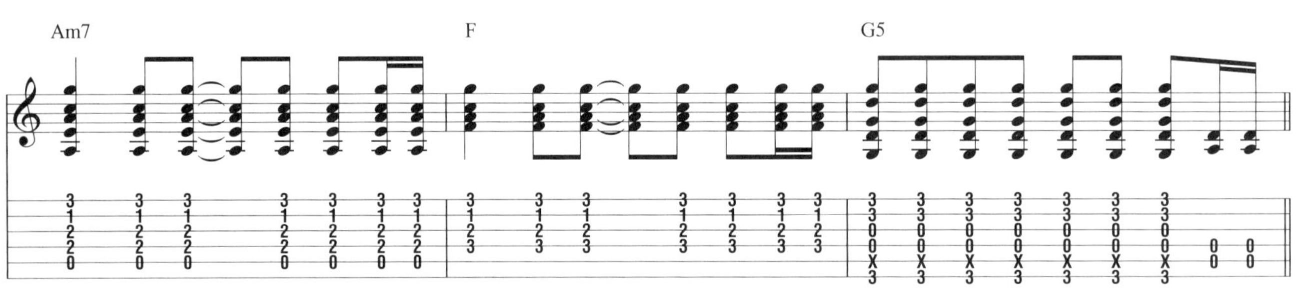

Am7
F
G5

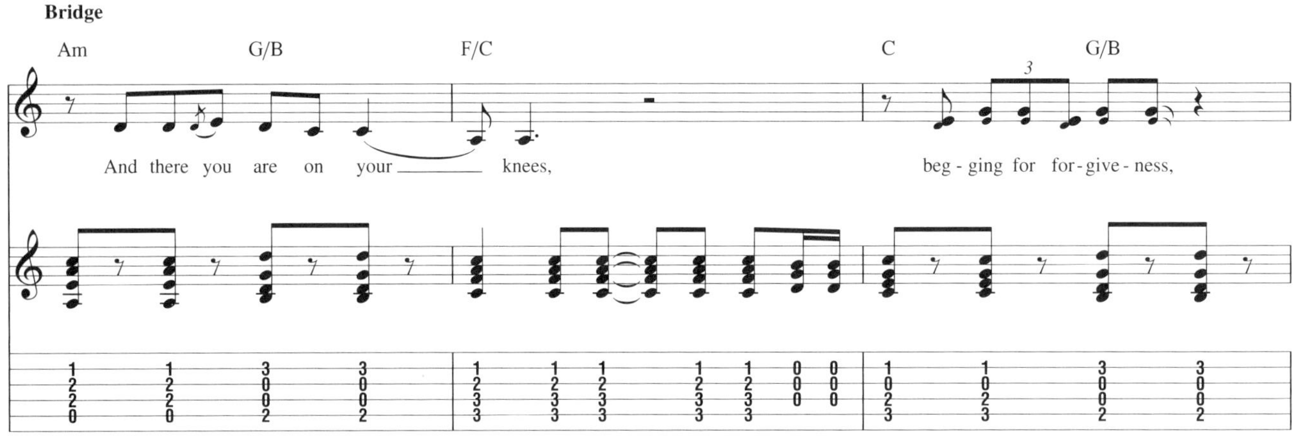

Bridge
Am
G/B
F/C
C
G/B
And there you are on your knees, beg - ging for for - give - ness,

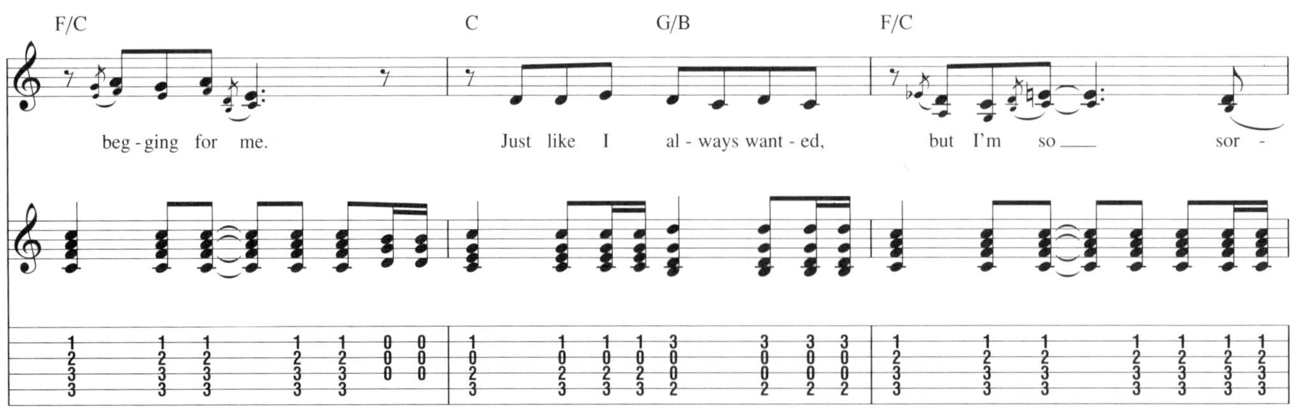

F/C
C
G/B
F/C
beg - ging for me. Just like I al - ways want - ed, but I'm so sor -

Chorus
B♭sus2
C
(G)
- ry...
'Cause I'm not your prin - cess, this ain't a fair -
Gtr. 2
Gtr. 1
Am7
(Em7)
F
(C)
G5
(D5)
y tale. I'm gon - na find some-one some-day who might ac - tual - ly treat me well. This is a
Gtrs. 1 & 2: w/ Rhy. Figs. 2 & 2A
C
(G)
Am7
(Em7)
F/C
(C/G)
G
(D)
big world, that was a small town there in my rear view mir-ror dis-ap-pear - ing now. And it's too

Gtr. 2: w/ Rhy. Fig. 3 (2 times)
Am (Em) G/B (D/F♯) Fadd9 (Cadd9) Am (Em) G/B (D/F♯) Fadd9 (Cadd9)
late for you and your white horse, now it's too late for you and your white horse to catch me
Gtr. 1
Outro
C5 (G5) Fsus2 (Csus2) Am7 (Em7) F/C (C/G)
now. Oh, whoa, whoa, whoa. Try and catch me now,
Gtr. 2
Gtr. 1
C (G) F/C (C/G) Am7 (Em7) F (C) C (G)
rit.
oh. It's too late to catch me now.
rit.
rit.

from *The Clash*

White Riot

Words and Music by Joe Strummer and Mick Jones

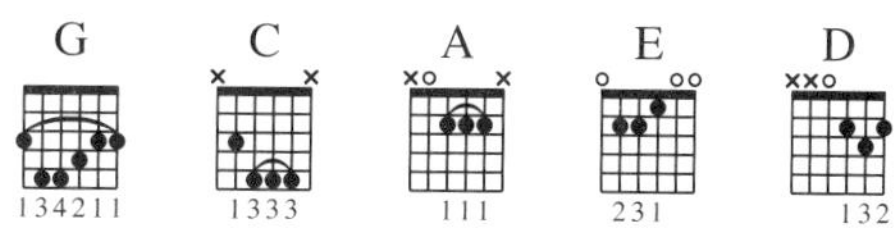

Intro

Fast ♩ = 202

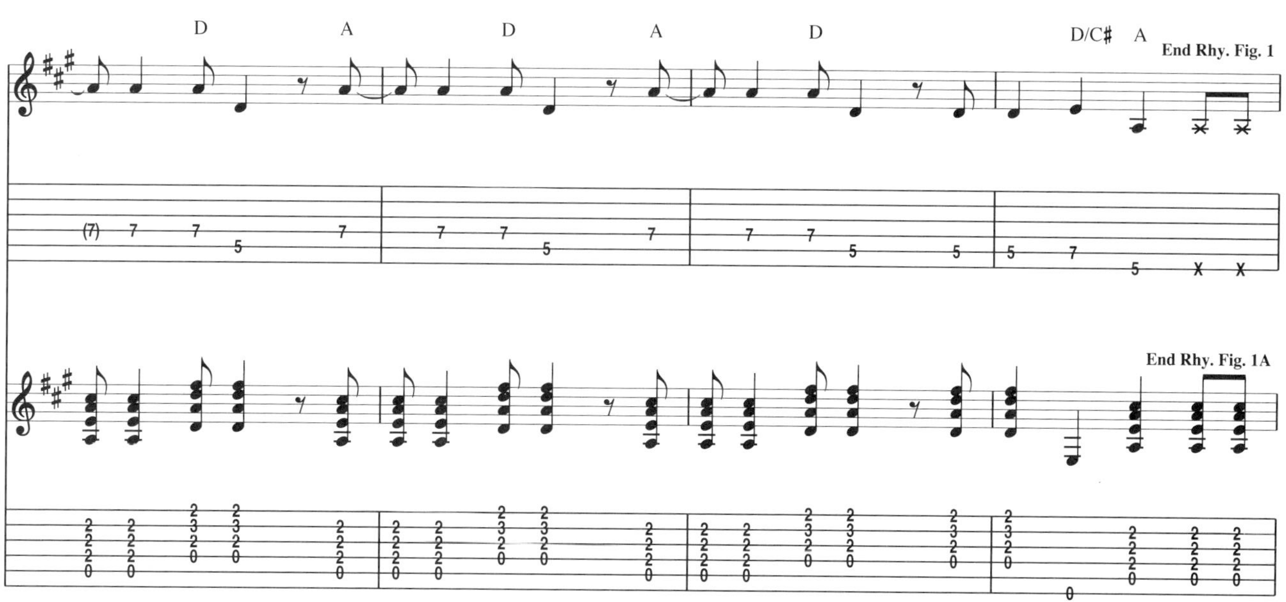

E
full
full
full
full

full
full

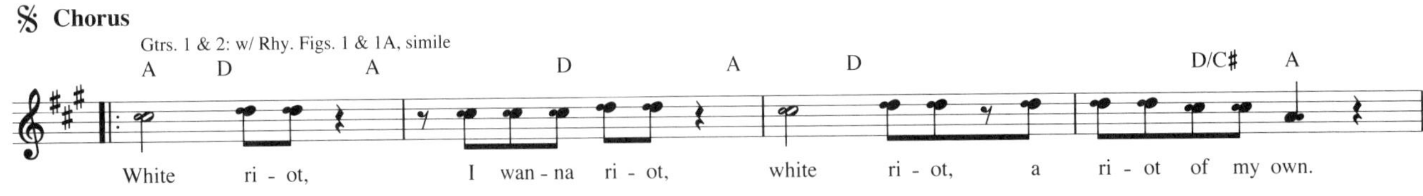

Chorus
Gtrs. 1 & 2: w/ Rhy. Figs. 1 & 1A, simile
A D A D A D D/C# A
White ri - ot, I wan - na ri - ot, white ri - ot, a ri - ot of my own.

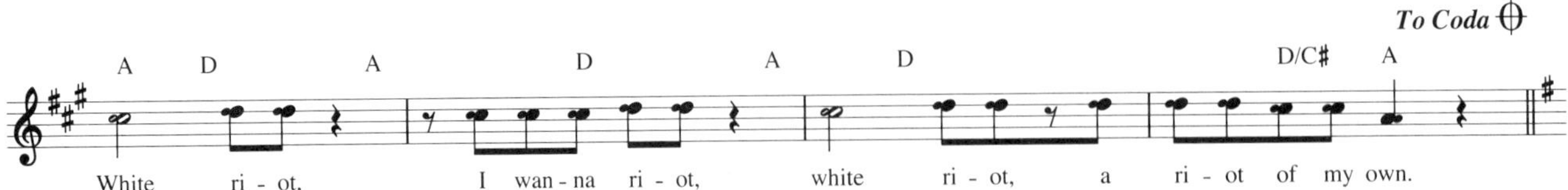

To Coda
A D A D A D D/C# A
White ri - ot, I wan - na ri - ot, white ri - ot, a ri - ot of my own.

Verse

G
C B A G
3 3 3 4
5fr 4fr 2fr 5fr
Gtr. 2
1. Black man got a lot of prob-lems, but they don't mind throw-ing a brick.
2. All the pow-er in the hands _ of the peo-ple rich e-nough to buy ___ it.
Gtr. 1
full
full
full

G
C B A G
3 3 3 4
5fr 5fr 5fr 5fr
C
White peo-ple go-in' to school, ___ where they teach you how to be thick. __
While we walk the streets, ___ too chick-en to e - ven try ____ it.
And
full
full
full

A
C
ev-'ry-bod-y's do-in' just what they're told to. ___
And

E
E
open
1.
2.
no - bod-y wants
to go to jail.
Guitar Solo
A
full
full
full
D
A
D
A
D
C#
A
2fr
D.S. al Coda
full
full
full
full
Coda
Bridge
E
Gtr. 1
Are you tak-ing o - ver,
or are you tak-ing or - ders?
Gtr. 2
full
full
1/2
1/2
let ring

Outro-Chorus

from Jewel - *Pieces of You*

Who Will Save Your Soul

Lyrics and Music by Jewel Kilcher

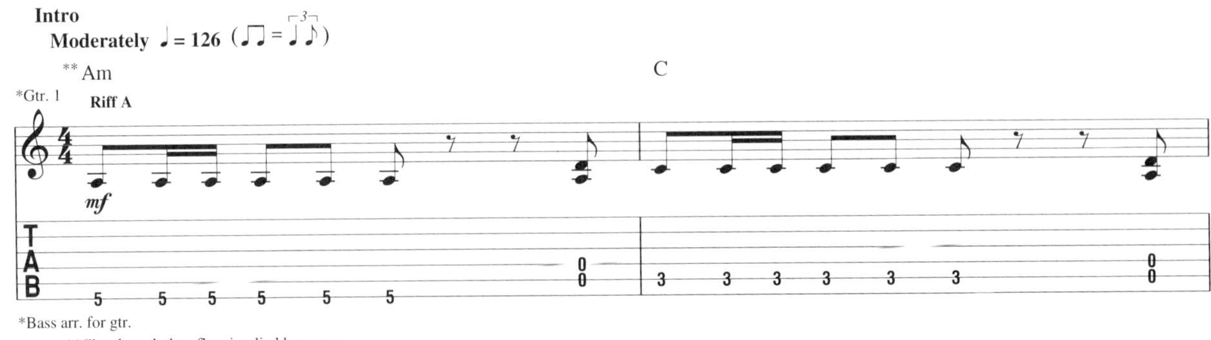

*Bass arr. for gtr.

**Chord symbols reflect implied harmony.

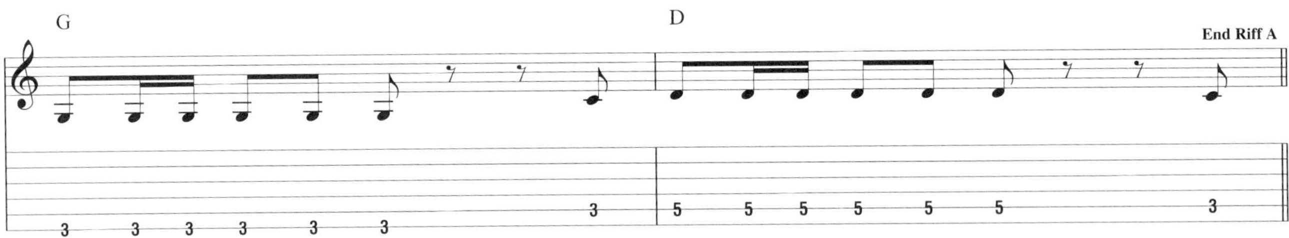

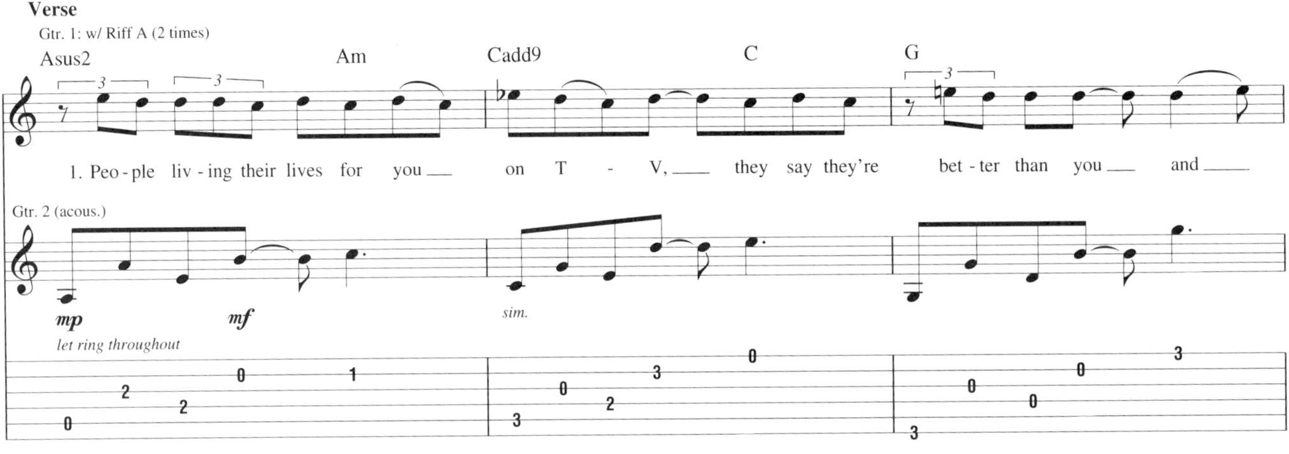

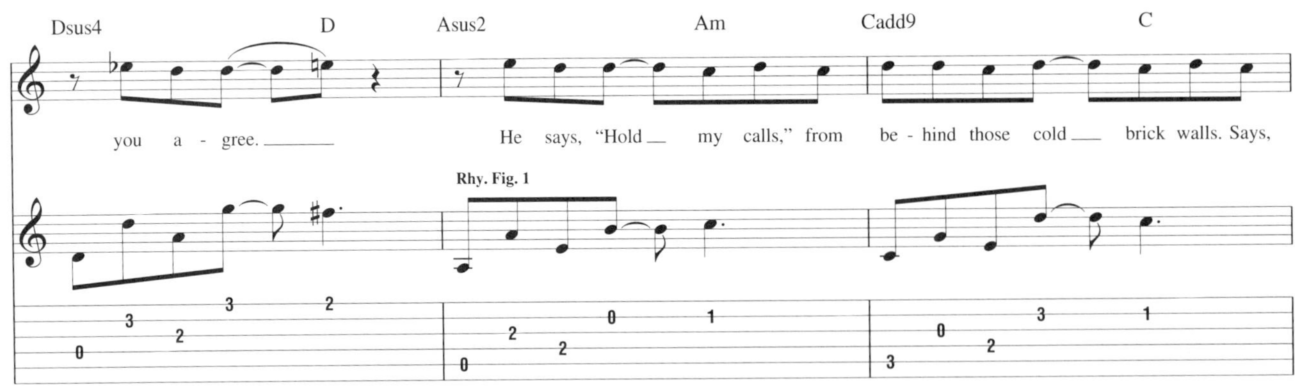

Gtr. 2: w/ Rhy. Fig. 1
G
Dsus4
D
Asus2
Am
"Come here, boy, there ain't nothing for free."
An - oth - er doc - tor's bill, a
End Rhy. Fig. 1
Riff B
Gtr. 1
Cadd9
C
G
Dsus4
D
law - yer's bill, an - oth - er cute, cheap thrill. You know you love him if you put him in your will. But
End Riff B
Chorus
Gtr. 1: w/ Riff B (2 times)
1st time, Gtr. 2: w/ Rhy. Fig. 1 (4 times)
2nd time, Gtr. 2: w/ Rhy. Fig. 1 (1 1/2 times)
Asus2
Am
Cadd9
C
G
who will save your souls when it comes
Dsus4
D
Asus2
Am
Cadd9
C
to the flow - ers, bet - ters, now? Who, who will save your souls
2nd time, Gtr. 2: w/ Rhy. Fill 1
1st time, Gtr. 1: w/ Riff A
2nd time, Gtr. 1: w/ Riff B
2nd time, Gtr. 2: w/ Rhy. Fig. 1
G
Dsus4
D
Asus2
Am
af - ter all those lies that you told, boy? And who will
Rhy. Fill 1
Gtr. 2

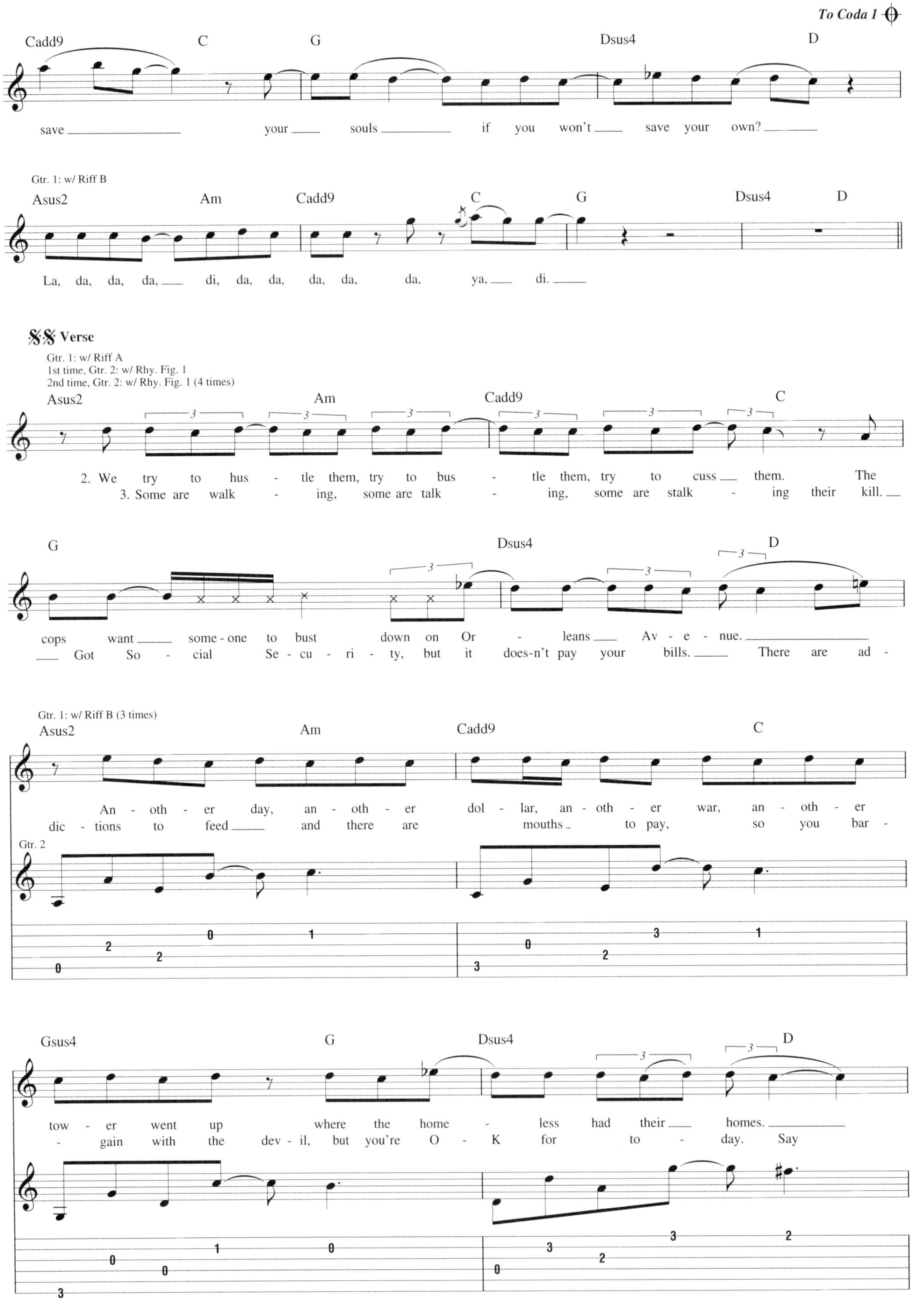

To Coda 1

Cadd9 C G Dsus4 D

save ___ your ___ souls ___ if you won't ___ save your own? ___

Gtr. 1: w/ Riff B

Asus2 Am Cadd9 C G Dsus4 D

La, da, da, da, ___ di, da, da, da, da, da, ya, ___ di. ___

Verse

Gtr. 1: w/ Riff A
1st time, Gtr. 2: w/ Rhy. Fig. 1
2nd time, Gtr. 2: w/ Rhy. Fig. 1 (4 times)

Asus2 Am Cadd9 C

2. We try to hus - tle them, try to bus - tle them, try to cuss ___ them. The
3. Some are walk - ing, some are talk - ing, some are stalk - ing their kill. ___

G Dsus4 D

cops want ___ some - one to bust down on Or - leans ___ Av - e - nue. ___
___ Got So - cial Se - cu - ri - ty, but it does-n't pay your bills. ___ There are ad -

Gtr. 1: w/ Riff B (3 times)

Asus2 Am Cadd9 C

An - oth - er day, an - oth - er dol - lar, an - oth - er war, an - oth - er
dic - tions to feed ___ and there are mouths ___ to pay, so you bar -

Gtr. 2

0 2 2 0 1 | 3 0 2 3 1

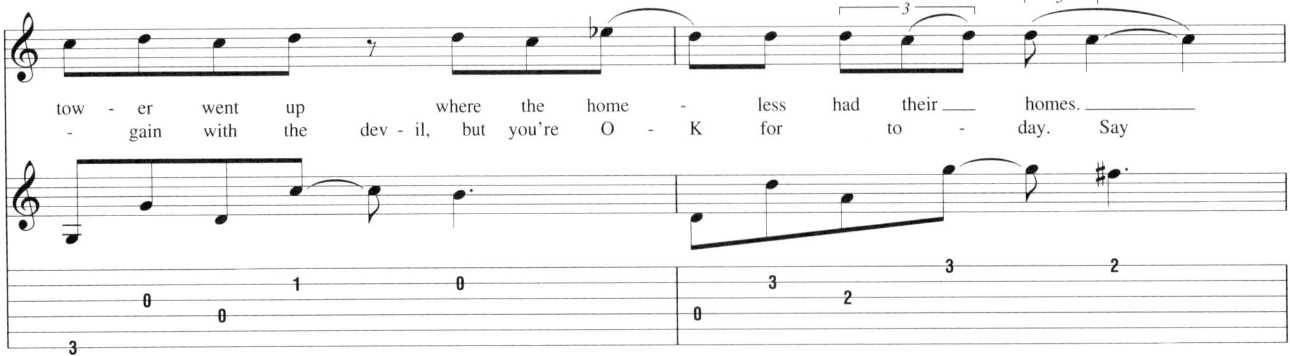

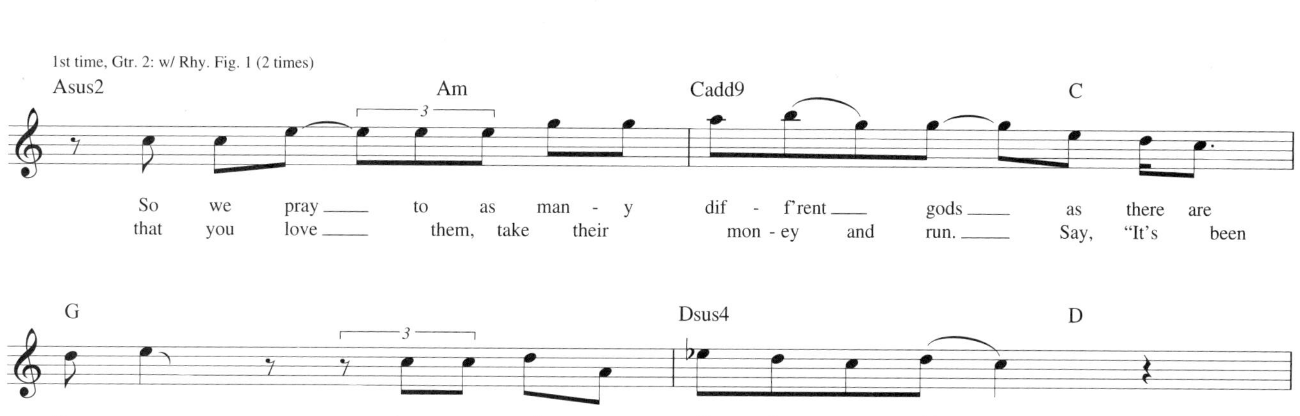

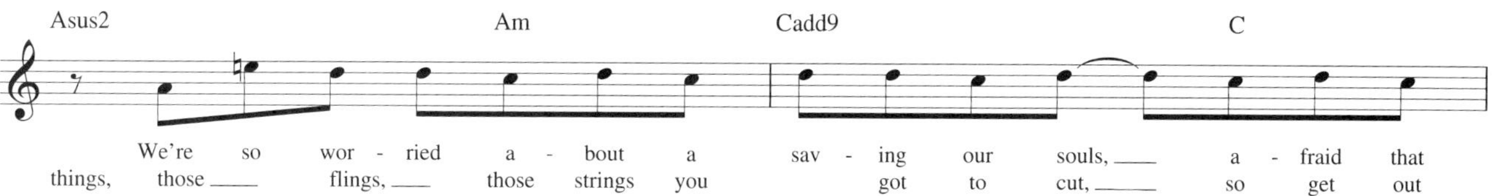

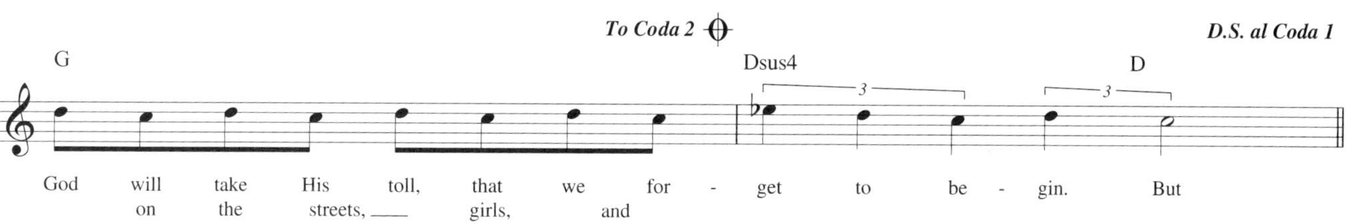

To Coda 2 D.S. al Coda 1

Coda 1

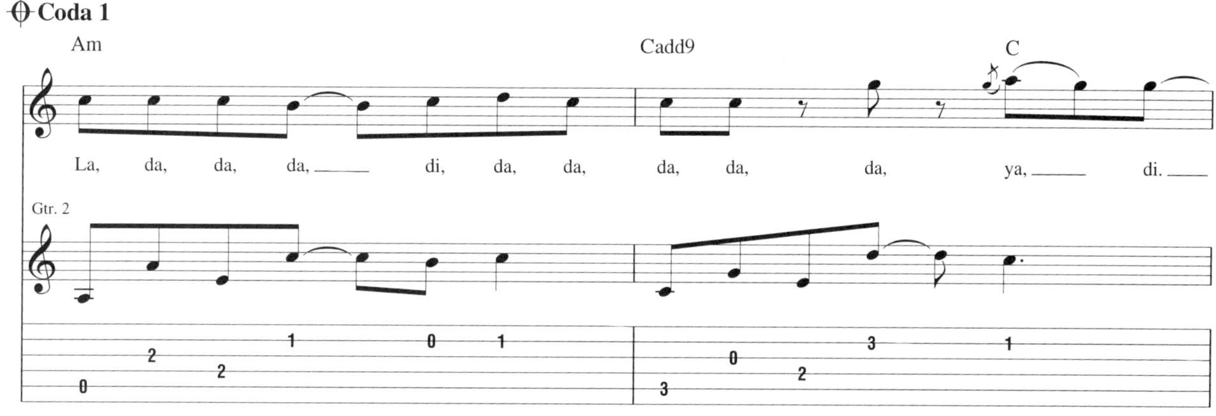

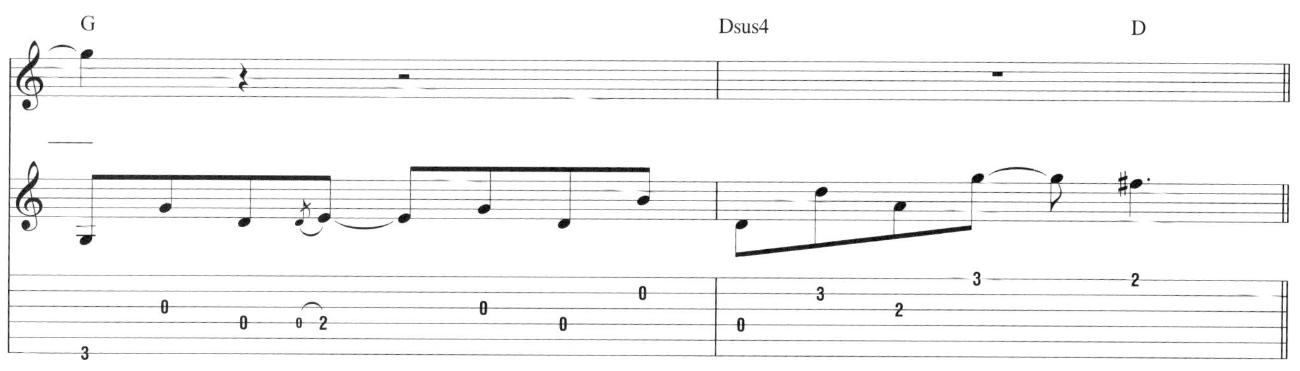

Interlude
Gtr. 2 tacet
N.C.(Em)
Gtr. 1

D.S.S. al Coda 2
Gtr. 2
Gtr. 1

Coda 2
Outro
Gtr. 1: w/ Riff B (till fade)
Gtr. 2: w/ Rhy. Fig. 1 (till fade)
Dsus4 D Asus2 Am Cadd9 C
bust your butts." Who will save

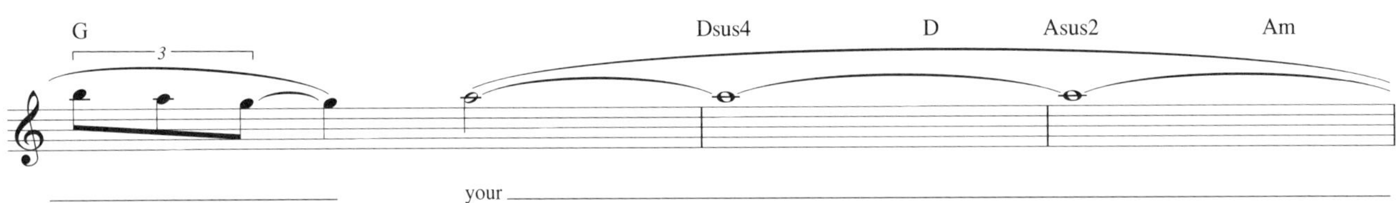
G Dsus4 D Asus2 Am
your

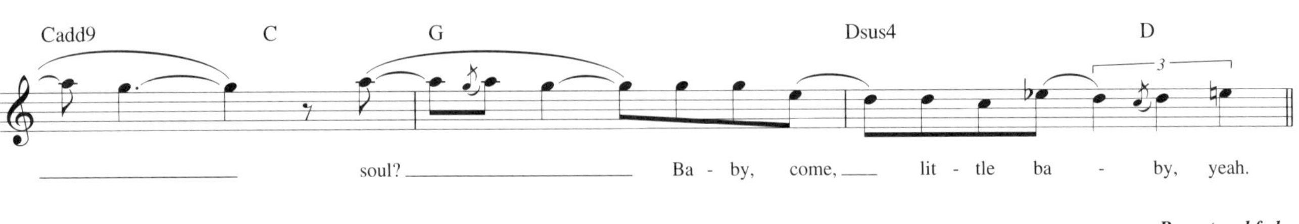
Cadd9 C G Dsus4 D
soul? Ba - by, come, lit - tle ba - by, yeah.

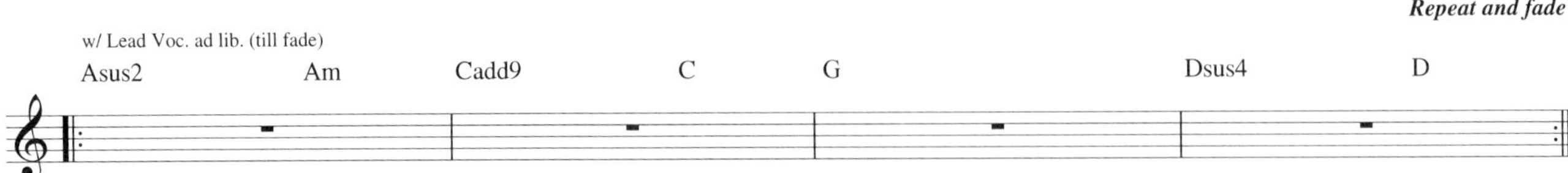
Repeat and fade
w/ Lead Voc. ad lib. (till fade)
Asus2 Am Cadd9 C G Dsus4 D

from Johnnie Taylor - *Chronicle: The 20 Greatest Hits*

Who's Making Love

Words and Music by Bettye Crutcher, Don Davis, Homer Banks and Raymond Jackson

F Ab Bb Ab F5 D5 F5 D5 F5 F Ab Bb Ab F5 D5
ask you now, you'd bet - ter think a - bout it twice. While you're ly -
end Rhy. Fig. 2
Dm Am
- in,' cheat - in' on your wom - an, there is
Gm Bb C
some - thing you nev - er e - ven thought of. Now tell me,
hold hold hold hold
*Chorus:
w/Rhy. Fig. 1 (Gtr. 1) 2 times
w/Rhy. Fig. 2 (Gtr. 2) 1 time
F5 D5 F5 F Ab Bb Ab F5 D5 F5 D5 F5
who's mak - in' love to your old la - dy while you were out mak - in'
Last Chorus: See additional lyrics.
*Last time repeat (take 1st ending only) and fade on Chorus w/ad lib. vocal and gtr.
F Ab Bb Ab F5 D5 F5 D5 F5 F Ab Bb Ab F5 D5
love? Hear me now. Now who's mak - in' love to your old la - dy
F5 D5 F5 1. F Ab Bb Ab F5 D5 2. F Ab Bb Ab F5 D5
while you were out mak - in' love? 2. I've love? I

Verse 2:
I've seen so, so many fellas fall in
that same old bag.
Thinkin' that a woman is made to,
to be beat on and treated so bad.
Oh, brothers, let me ask you something
I'm sure that you never even dreamed of.
Now tell me. . .
(To Chorus:)

Verse 3:
The reason why I ask this question,
I used to be the same old way.
When I decided to straighten up,
I found it was a little too late.
Oh, yeah, that's when it all happened,
something I never, never dreamed of.

Chorus:
Somebody was a-lovin' my old lady
while I was out makin' love.
Somebody was a-lovin' my old lady
while I was out makin' love.
Listen now, now who's makin' love to your old lady
while you were out makin' love?
(Repeat and fade)

from Opeth - *Damnation*

Windowpane

Words and Music by Mikael Akerfeldt

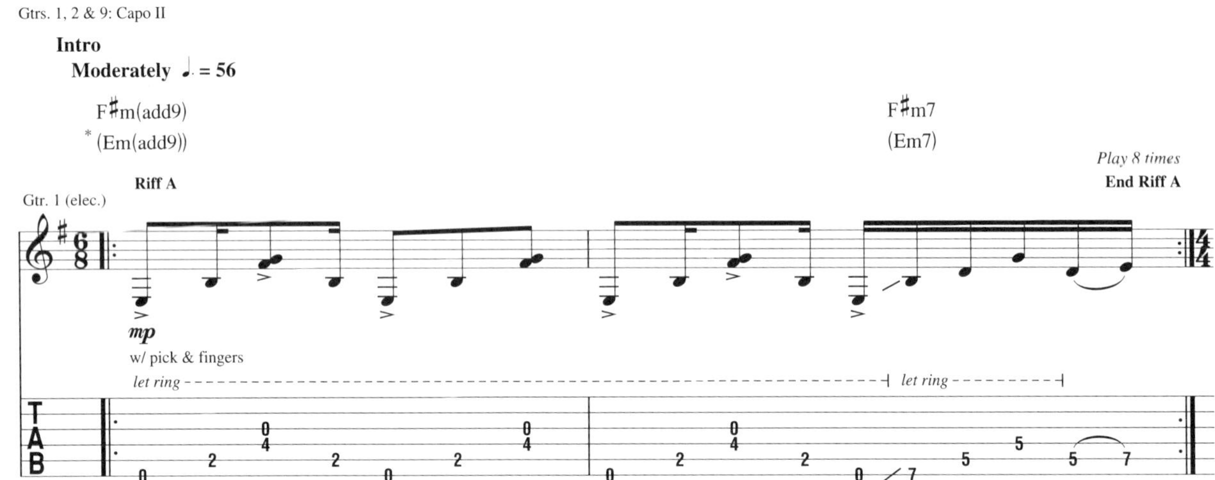

*Symbols in parentheses represent chord names respective to capoed guitars. Symbols above reflect actual sounding chords. Capoed fret is "0" in tab. Chord symbols reflect implied harmony.

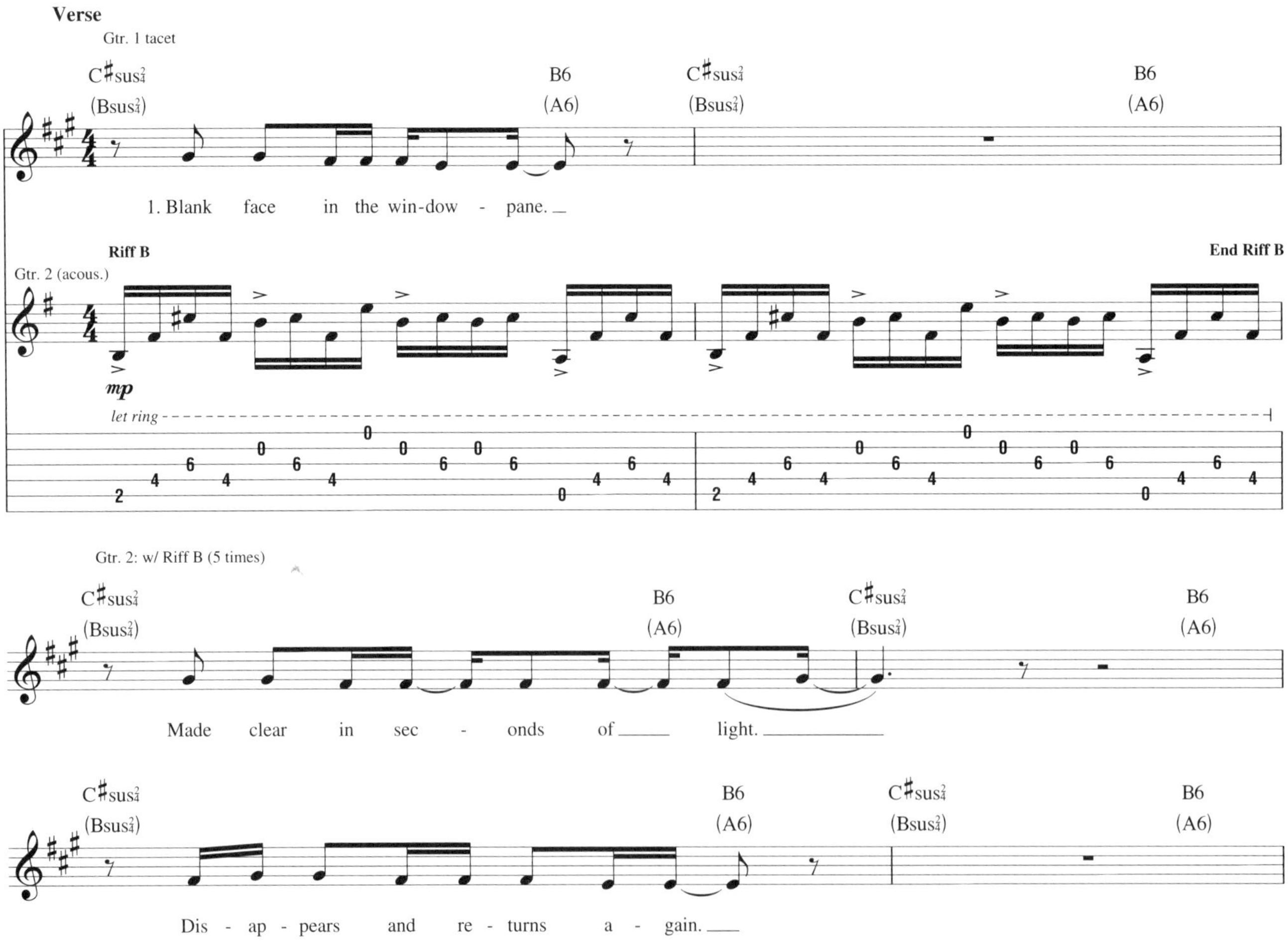

Verse

Gtr. 1 tacet

C♯sus2/4 (Bsus2/4) — B6 (A6) — C♯sus2/4 (Bsus2/4) — B6 (A6)

1. Blank face in the win-dow - pane.

Riff B — End Riff B

Gtr. 2 (acous.)

mp

let ring

Gtr. 2: w/ Riff B (5 times)

C♯sus2/4 (Bsus2/4) — B6 (A6) — C♯sus2/4 (Bsus2/4) — B6 (A6)

Made clear in sec - onds of light.

C♯sus2/4 (Bsus2/4) — B6 (A6) — C♯sus2/4 (Bsus2/4) — B6 (A6)

Dis - ap - pears and re - turns a - gain.

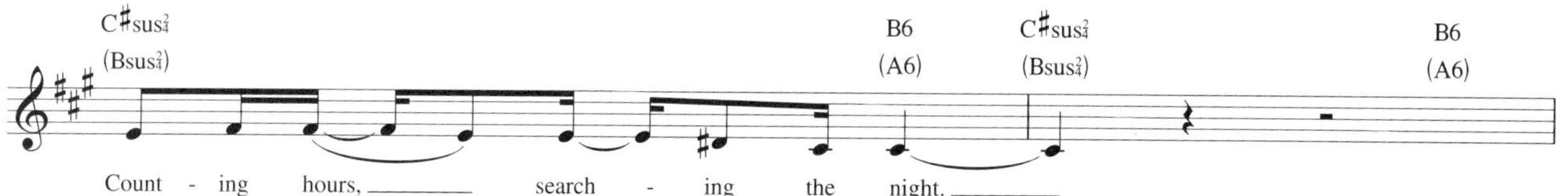

C♯sus2/4
(Bsus2/4)
B6
(A6)
C♯sus2/4
(Bsus2/4)
B6
(A6)
Count - ing hours, search - ing the night.

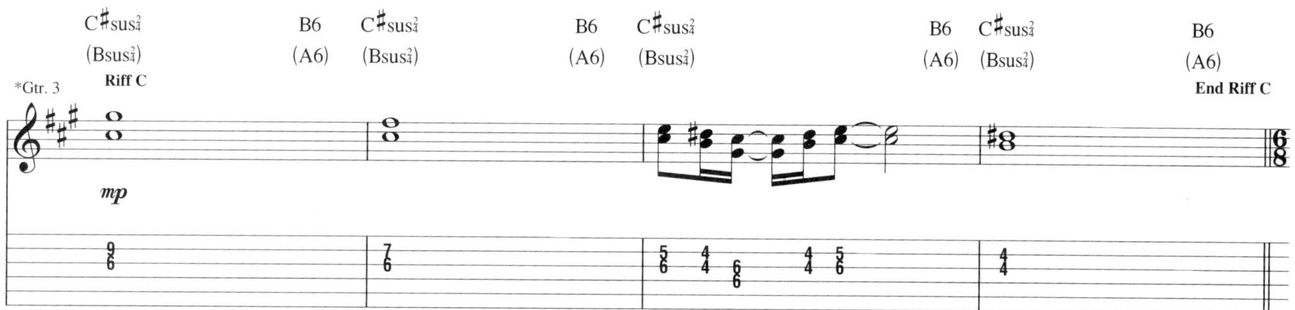

C♯sus2/4
(Bsus2/4)
B6
(A6)
*Gtr. 3
Riff C
End Riff C
mp
*Synth. arr. for gtr.

Guitar Solo
Gtr. 1: w/ Riff A (8 times)
Gtr. 3 tacet
F♯m(add9)
(Em(add9))
F♯m7
(Em7)
Gtr. 4 (elec.)
mf
w/ dist.

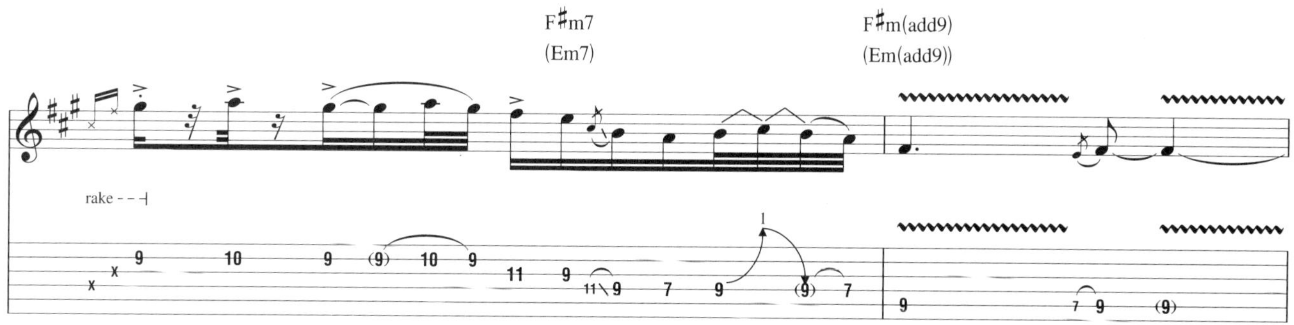

F♯m7
(Em7)
F♯m(add9)
(Em(add9))
rake

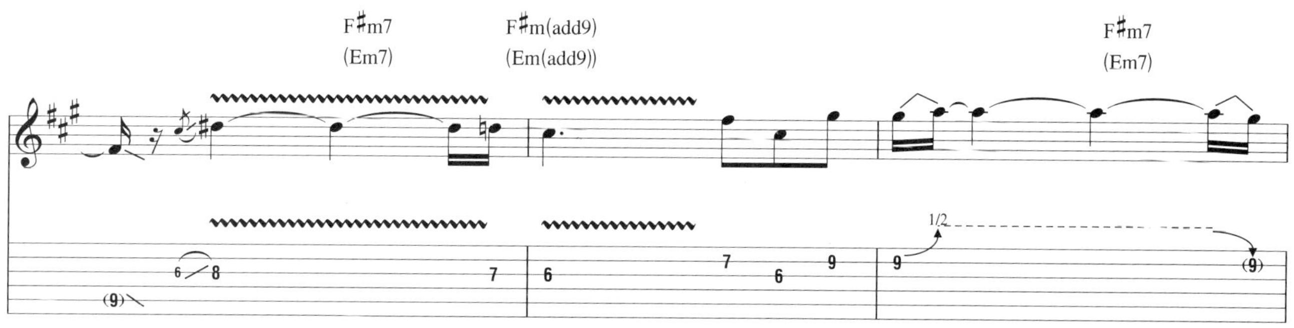

F♯m7
(Em7)
F♯m(add9)
(Em(add9))
1/2

F♯m(add9)
(Em(add9))
F♯m7
(Em7)
F♯m(add9)
(Em(add9))
string noise
F♯m7
(Em7)
F♯m(add9)
(Em(add9))
rake
F♯m7
(Em7)
Verse
Gtr. 2: w/ Riff B (6 times)
Gtr. 4 tacet
F♯m(add9)
(Em(add9))
F♯m7
(Em7)
C♯sus2/4
(Bsus2/4)
B6
(A6)
2. Might be wait - ing for some - one.
C♯sus2/4
(Bsus2/4)
B6
(A6)
C♯sus2/4
(Bsus2/4)
B6
(A6)
C♯sus2/4
(Bsus2/4)
B6
(A6)
Might be there for us to see.
fdbk.
Pitch: G♯

Gtr. 4 tacet
C♯sus2/4
(Bsus2/4)
B6
(A6)
Might be in need of talk - ing.
Might be star - ing di - rect - ly at me.
Gtr. 3: w/ Riff C
Am
(Gm)
Am/B
(Gm/A)
Am/C
(Gm/B♭)
Riff D
Gtr. 5 (elec.)
mf
w/ slight dist.
Riff D1
Gtr. 6 (elec.)
Rhy. Fig. 1
Gtr. 2
let ring

Am
(Gm)
Am/C
(Gm/B♭)
B♭m
(G♯m)
G♭maj7
(Emaj7)
B♭m
(G♯m)
G♭maj7
(Emaj7)
let ring
Am
(Gm)
Am/B
(Gm/A)
Am
(Gm)
Am/C
(Gm/B♭)
Bridge
Gtr. 2: w/ Rhy. Fig. 1
Am
(Gm)
Am/B
(Gm/A)
In - side plays a lul -
End Riff D
End Riff D1
End Rhy. Fig. 1

Gtrs. 5 & 6 tacet

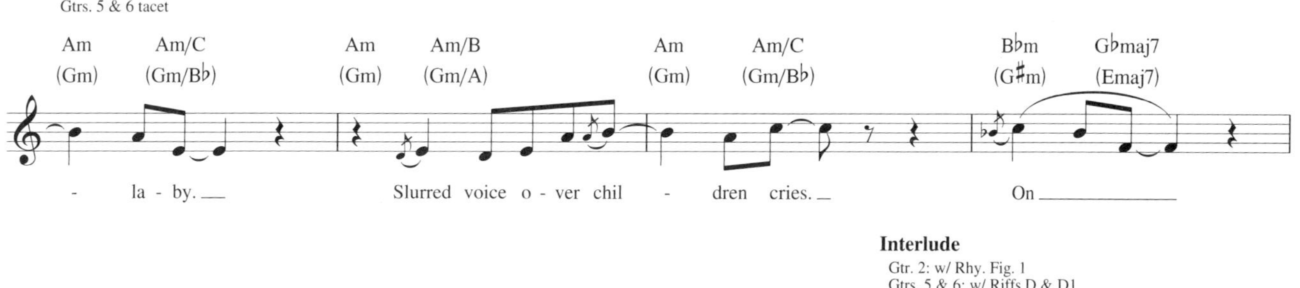
Am
(Gm)
Am/C
(Gm/B♭)
Am
(Gm)
Am/B
(Gm/A)
Am
(Gm)
Am/C
(Gm/B♭)
B♭m
(G♯m)
G♭maj7
(Emaj7)
- la - by.
Slurred voice o - ver chil - dren cries.
On

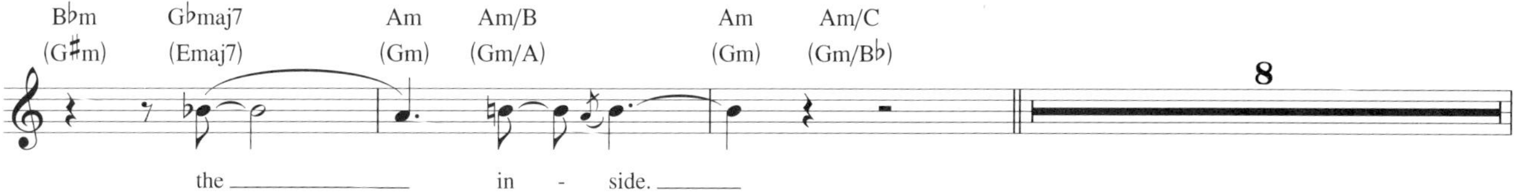
B♭m
(G♯m)
G♭maj7
(Emaj7)
Am
(Gm)
Am/B
(Gm/A)
Am
(Gm)
Am/C
(Gm/B♭)
Interlude
Gtr. 2: w/ Rhy. Fig. 1
Gtrs. 5 & 6: w/ Riffs D & D1
8
the
in - side.

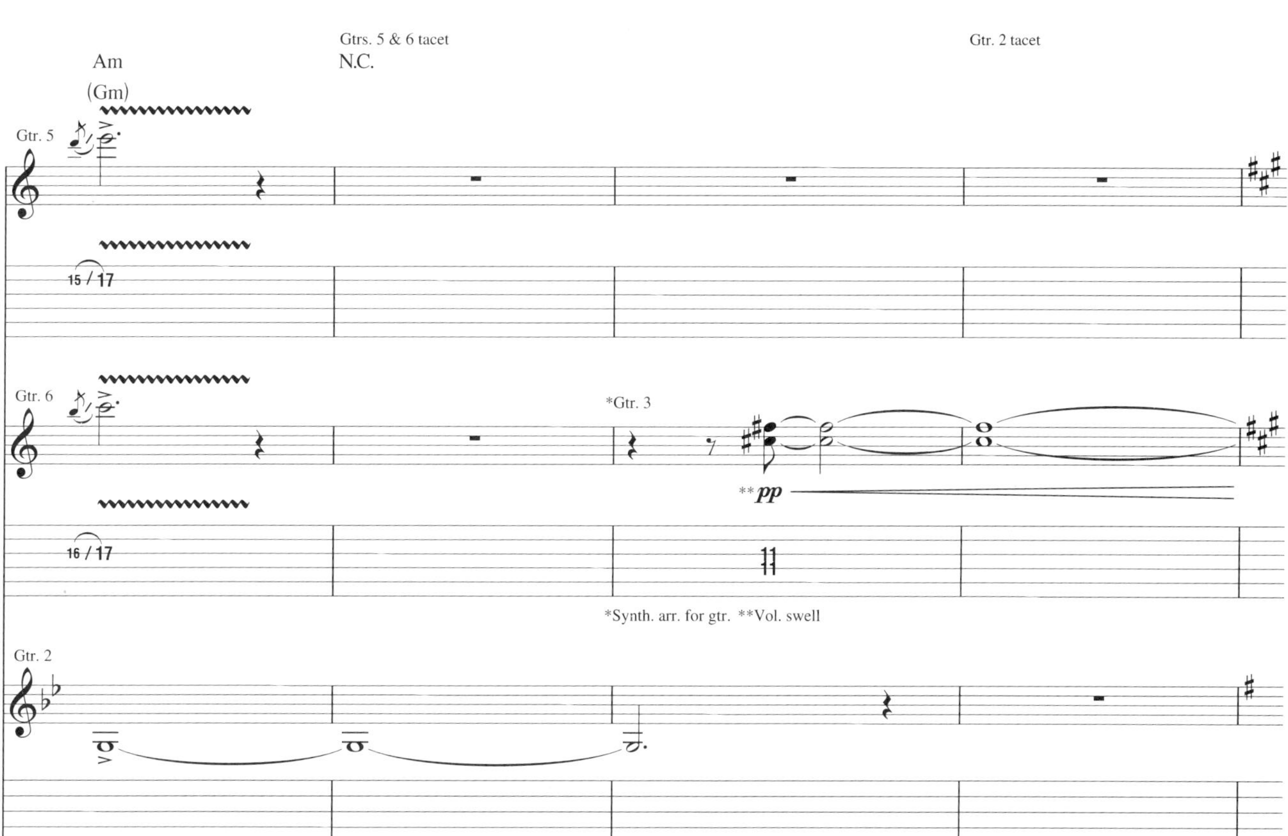
Am
(Gm)
Gtrs. 5 & 6 tacet
N.C.
Gtr. 2 tacet
Gtr. 5
Gtr. 6
*Gtr. 3
**pp
*Synth. arr. for gtr. **Vol. swell
Gtr. 2

Gtr. 3
mp
Gtr. 1
let ring

Play 7 times
Gtr. 3 tacet
F♯m9
(Em9)
Dmaj7
(Cmaj7)
Riff E
Gtr. 7 (elec.)
mf
w/ clean tone
Gtr. 1
w/ fingers
let ring
F♯m9
(Em9)
Dmaj7
(Cmaj7)

*C♯/F
(B/D♯)
F♯m
(Em)
D
(C)
Gtr. 7
End Riff E
Riff F
Gtr. 8 (elec.)
End Riff F
mf
w/ slight dist.
Gtr. 1
let ring
*Bass plays F.
Gtr. 7: w/ Riff E
Gtr. 8 tacet
F♯m9
(Em9)
Dmaj7
(Cmaj7)
Rhy. Fig. 2
Gtr. 8: w/ Riff F
**C♯/F
(B/D♯)
**Bass plays F.

Guitar Solo

Gtr. 1: w/ Rhy. Fig. 2 (2 times)

D (C) — F♯m9 (Em9) — Dmaj7 (Cmaj7)

Gtr. 9 (elec.)

w/ clean tone & reverb

f

Gtr. 9

Gtr. 1 divisi *let ring*

End Rhy. Fig. 2

Gtr. 8: w/ Riff F

F♯m9 (Em9) — Dmaj7 (Cmaj7) — *C♯/F (B/D♯) — F♯m (Em)

1/2

*Bass plays F.

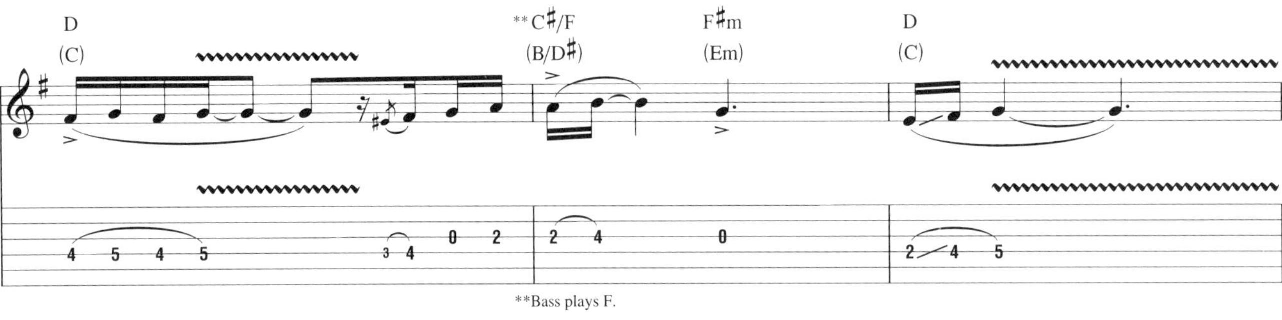

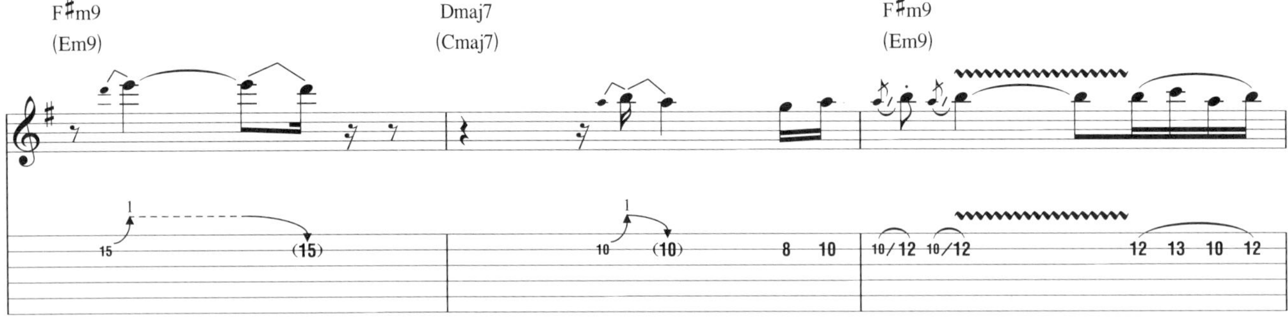

Gtr. 8: w/ Riff F

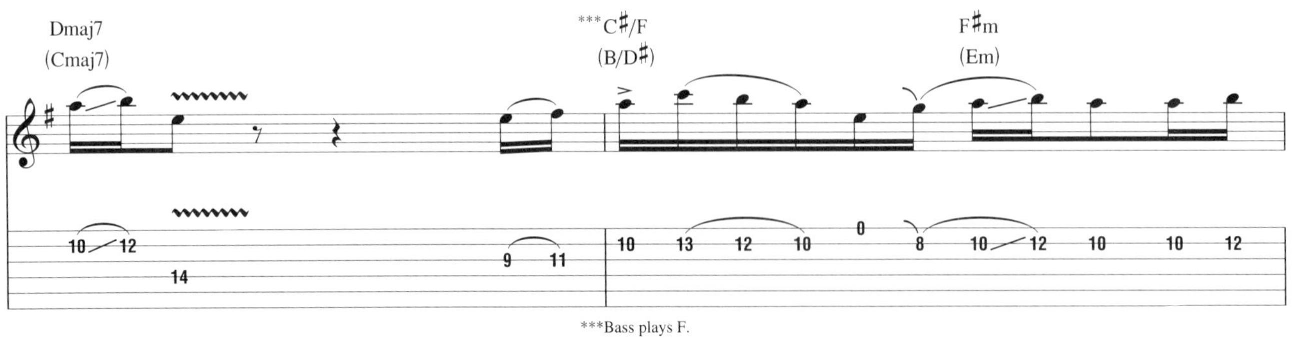

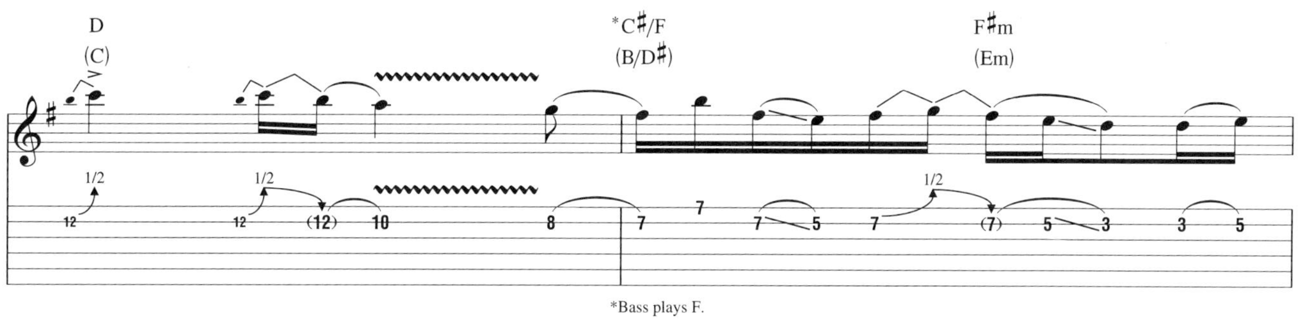

Interlude

Gtr. 9 tacet

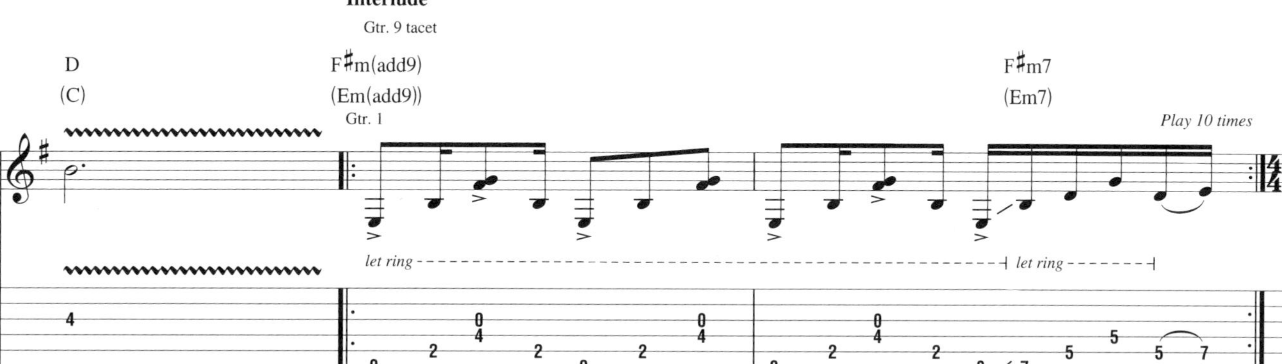

Verse

Gtr. 1 tacet
Gtr. 2: w/ Riff B (9 times)

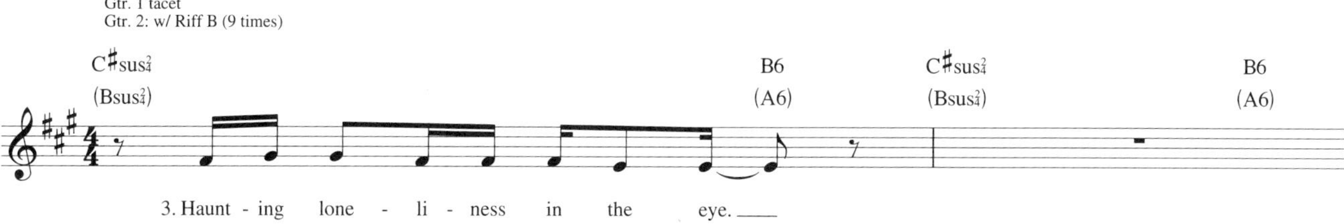

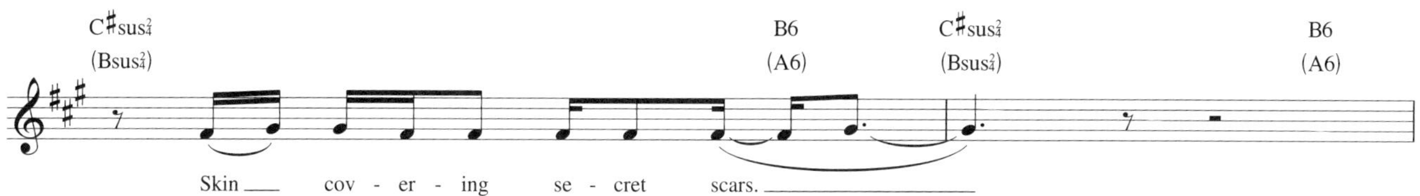

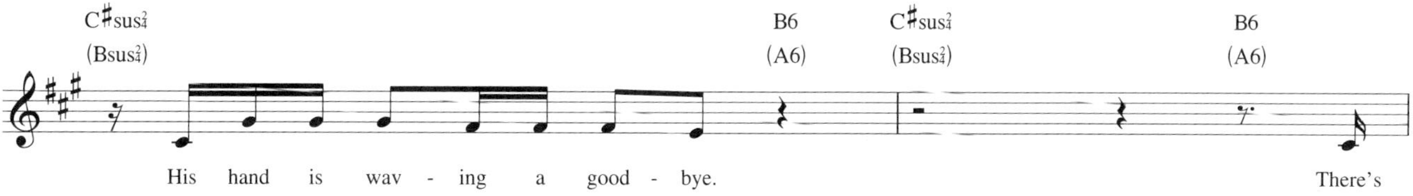

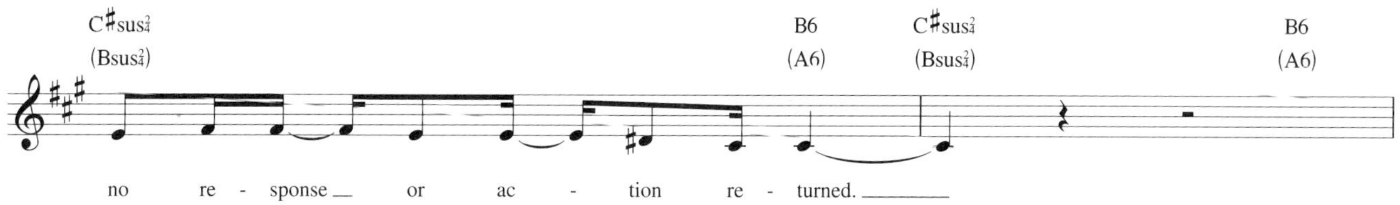

Gtr. 3: w/ Riff C (2 1/2 times)
C♯sus2/4
(Bsus2/4)
B6
(A6)
There is deep prej - u - dice in me.
Out - shines all rea - son in - side.
Giv - en dreams all rid - den with pain.
And pro - ject - ed un - to the lost.
Gtr. 3
Gtr. 2
let ring

from Alice in Chains - *Dirt*

Would?

Written by Jerry Cantrell

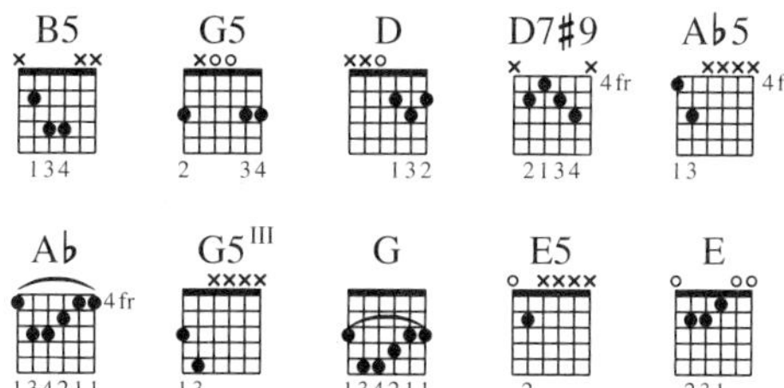

Tune down 1/2 step:
(low to high) E♭-A♭-D♭-G♭-B♭-E♭

Intro
Moderately ♩ = 100

N.C. (bass) Gtr. 1 (acous.) (G6) F♯5 Rhy. Fig. 1 B5/F♯ G F♯5 B5/F♯ G

mf let ring

N.C.(G6) F♯5 B5/F♯ G F♯5 B5/F♯ G N.C.(G6) End Rhy. Fig. 1

let ring let ring

Verse

F♯5 B5/F♯ G F♯5 B5/F♯ G N.C.(G6)

1. Know - me, bro - ken by my mas - ter.
2. Drift - ing bod - y, its sole de - ser - tion.

Gtr. 1

let ring

Gtr. 2 (acous.) Rhy. Fig. 2 End Rhy. Fig. 2

mf let ring

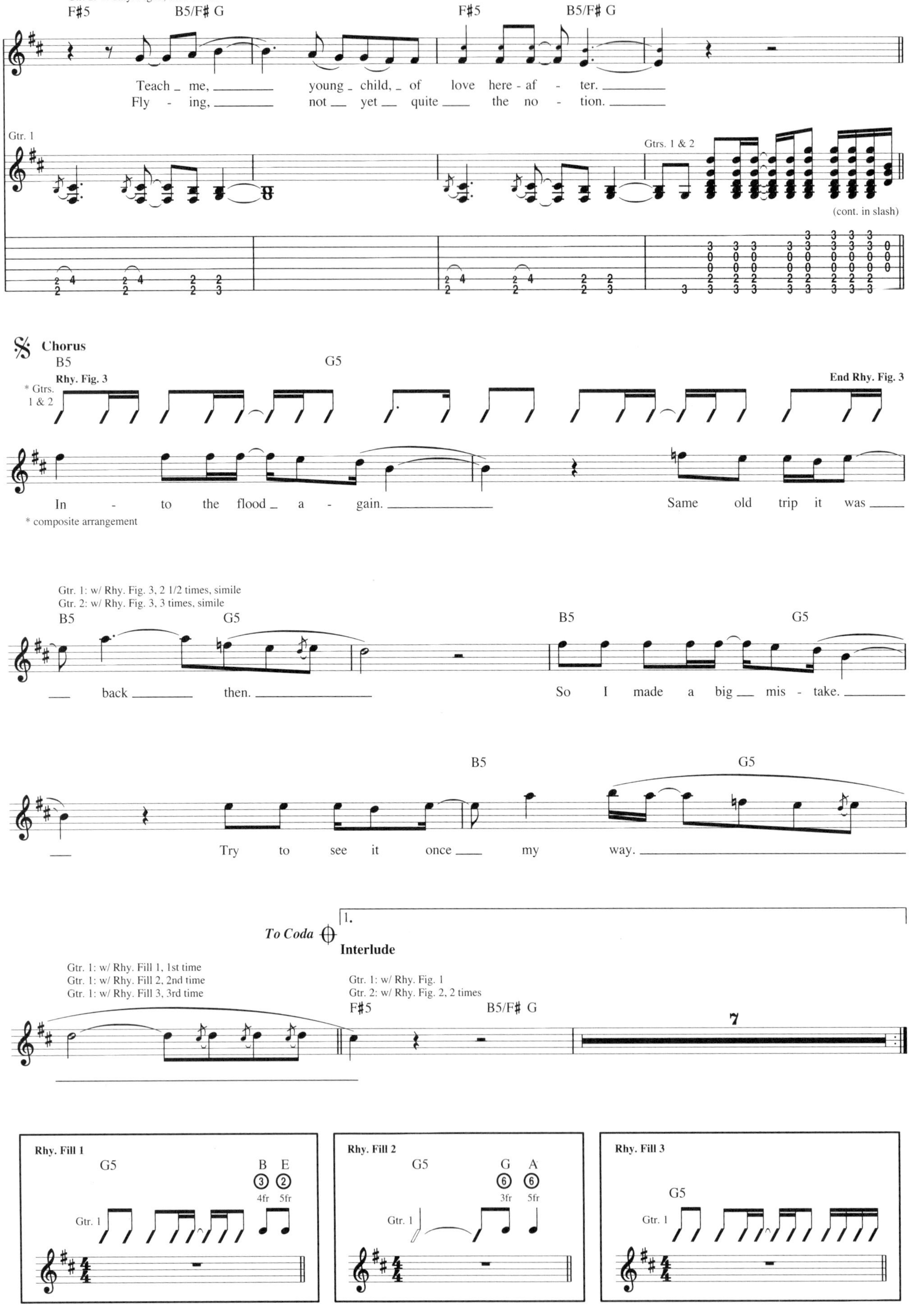

Gtr. 2: w/ Rhy. Fig. 2, 1st 3 meas.
F#5
B5/F# G
F#5
B5/F# G
Teach _ me, young _ child, _ of love here - af - ter.
Fly - ing, not _ yet _ quite the no - tion.
Gtr. 1
Gtrs. 1 & 2
(cont. in slash)
Chorus
B5
G5
Rhy. Fig. 3
End Rhy. Fig. 3
* Gtrs. 1 & 2
In - to the flood _ a - gain.
Same old trip it was
* composite arrangement
Gtr. 1: w/ Rhy. Fig. 3, 2 1/2 times, simile
Gtr. 2: w/ Rhy. Fig. 3, 3 times, simile
B5
G5
B5
G5
back then.
So I made a big _ mis - take.
B5
G5
Try to see it once _ my way.
To Coda
1.
Interlude
Gtr. 1: w/ Rhy. Fill 1, 1st time
Gtr. 1: w/ Rhy. Fill 2, 2nd time
Gtr. 1: w/ Rhy. Fill 3, 3rd time
Gtr. 1: w/ Rhy. Fig. 1
Gtr. 2: w/ Rhy. Fig. 2, 2 times
F#5
B5/F# G
7
Rhy. Fill 1
G5
B E
4fr 5fr
Gtr. 1
Rhy. Fill 2
G5
G A
3fr 5fr
Gtr. 1
Rhy. Fill 3
G5
Gtr. 1

2.
Guitar Solo
*F#5
G(♭5) G
F#5
G(♭5) G
Gtr. 1
Gtr. 2
Rhy. Fig. 4
End Rhy. Fig. 4
* Chord symbols reflect implied tonality.
Gtr. 2: w/ Rhy. Fig. 4, simile
D.S. al Coda
Yeah.
full
Coda
Bridge
D
D7#9
A♭5
A♭
Rhy. Fig. 5
* Gtrs. 1 & 2
Am I wrong?
* composite arrangement
G5 III
G
E5
E
End Rhy. Fig. 5
Gtrs. 1 & 2: w/ Rhy. Fig. 5
Have I run too far to get home?
Have I gone,
Outro
left you here a-lone?
rit.
If I would, could you?

from Pearl Jam - "Jeremy" EP

Yellow Ledbetter

Words and Music by Jeffrey Ament, Eddie Vedder and Mike McCready

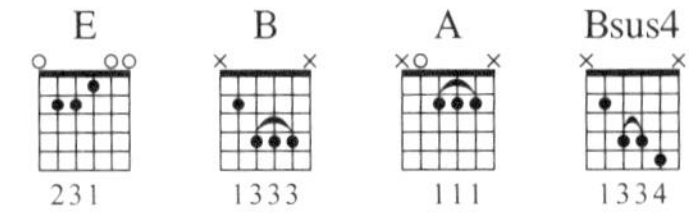

Intro

Moderately slow ♩ = 71

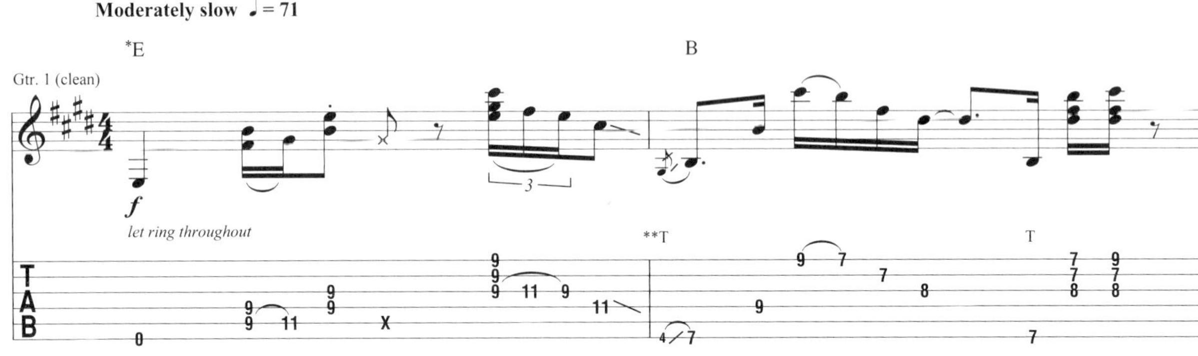

*Chord symbols reflect basic harmony.

**T = Thumb on 6th string

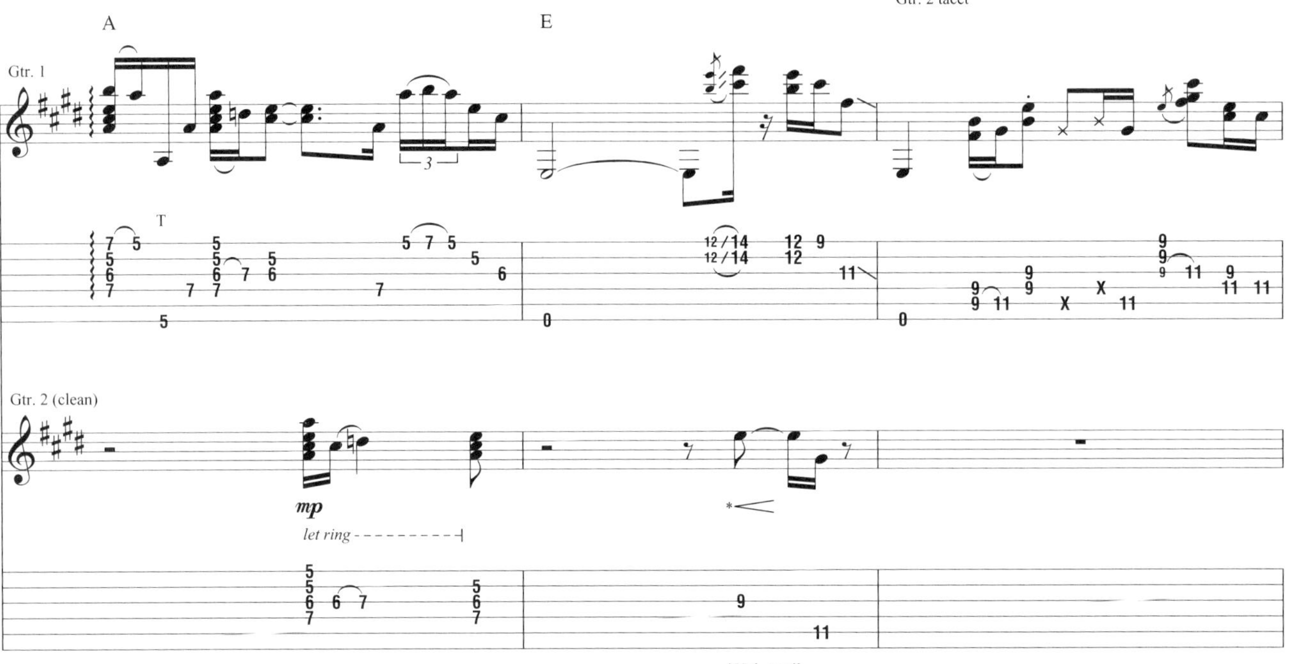

*Vol. swell

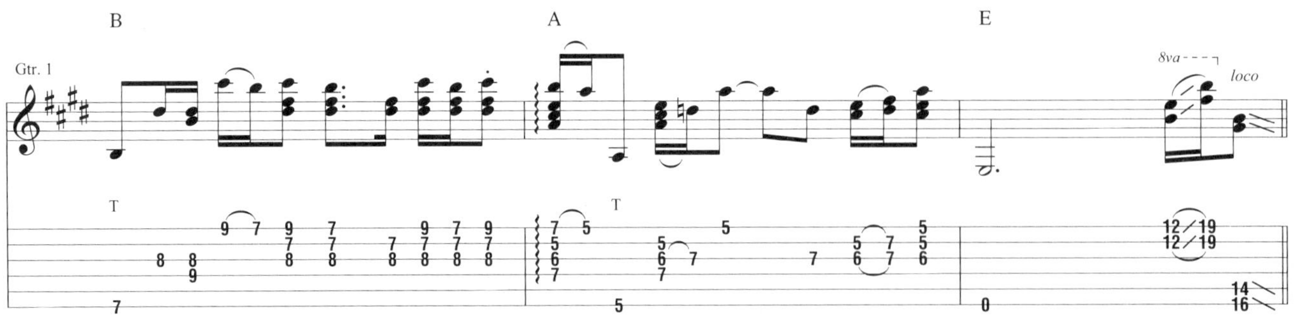

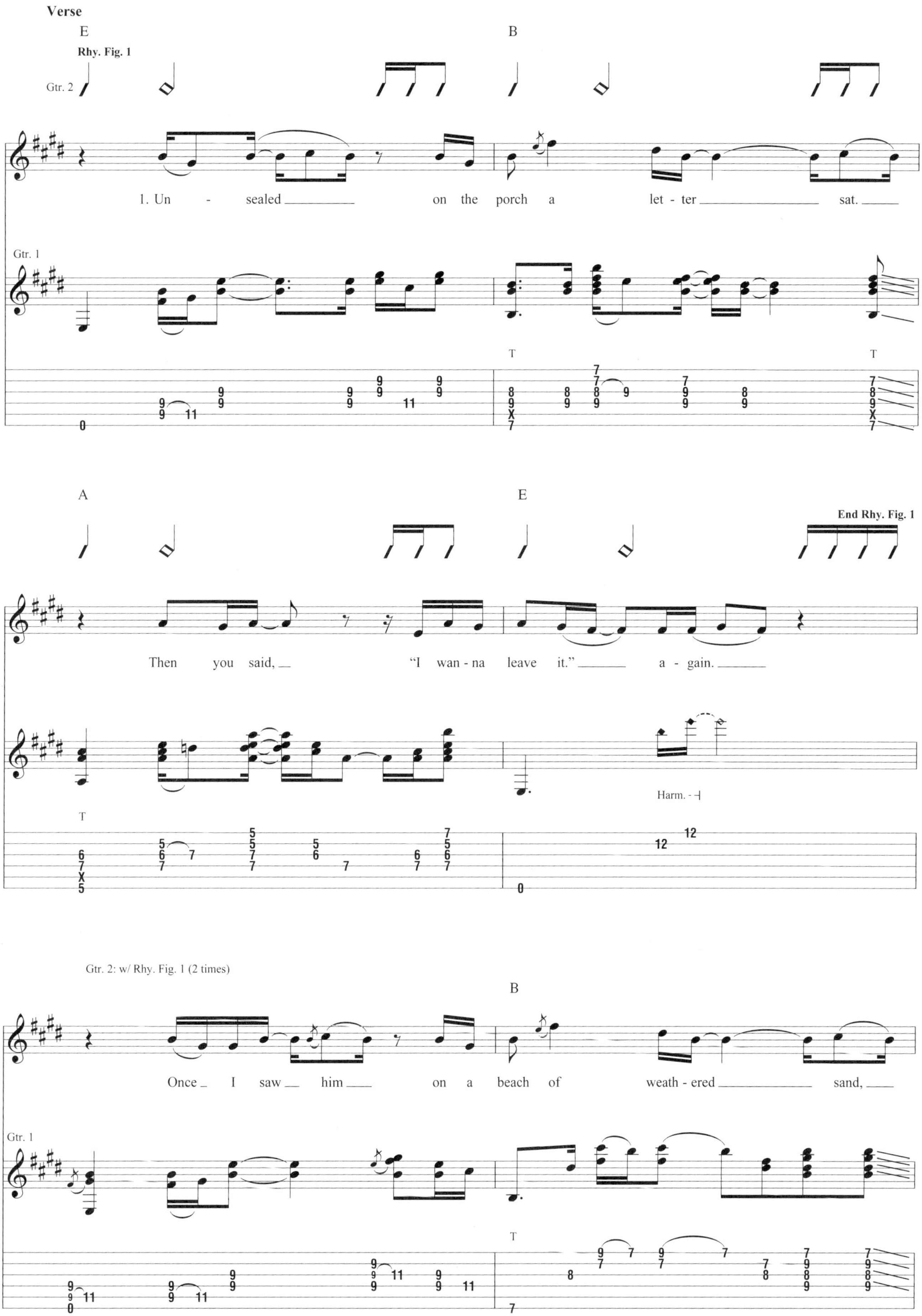

Verse

E B

Rhy. Fig. 1

Gtr. 2

1. Un - sealed on the porch a let - ter sat.

Gtr. 1

T T

A E

End Rhy. Fig. 1

Then you said, "I wan - na leave it." a - gain.

Harm.

T

A
E
and on the sand I wan-na leave him a-gain. Yeah.
T
B
On the week-end, wan-na wish it all a-way, yeah. And they
A
E
called and I said that I want what I said then I call out a-gain.
E
B
Gtr. 2
And the rea-son ought-ta leave him calm, I know,
Gtr. 1

A
E
I said, I don't know - wheth-er in a box or a bag. Oh, yeah.
Chorus
Gtr. 2: w/ Rhy. Fig. 1
E
B
Can you see them, oh, on the porch?
A
E
Yeah, but they don't wave. I
E
B
Gtr. 2
see them 'round the front way, yeah. And I
Gtr. 1

A
Gtr. 2
E
know and I know I don't wan - na stay.
Spoken: Make me cry.
Gtr. 3 (dist.)
15ma
mf
*fdbk.
*Microphonic fdbk., not caused by string vibration.
Gtr. 1
Guitar Solo
Gtr. 1 tacet
E
B
Gtr. 2
Gtr. 3
A
E
grad. bend
grad. release
B
Bsus4
B
w/ bar
hold bend
-2 1/2
-1 1/2

A
E
B
A
E
grad. release
Verse
Gtr. 3 tacet
E
B
Gtr. 2
2. I see,
Gtr. 3
mf
Gtr. 1

A
E
Gtr. 2
oh, I don't know why there's some - thing else.
8va
Gtr. 1
Harm.
Pitch: B E

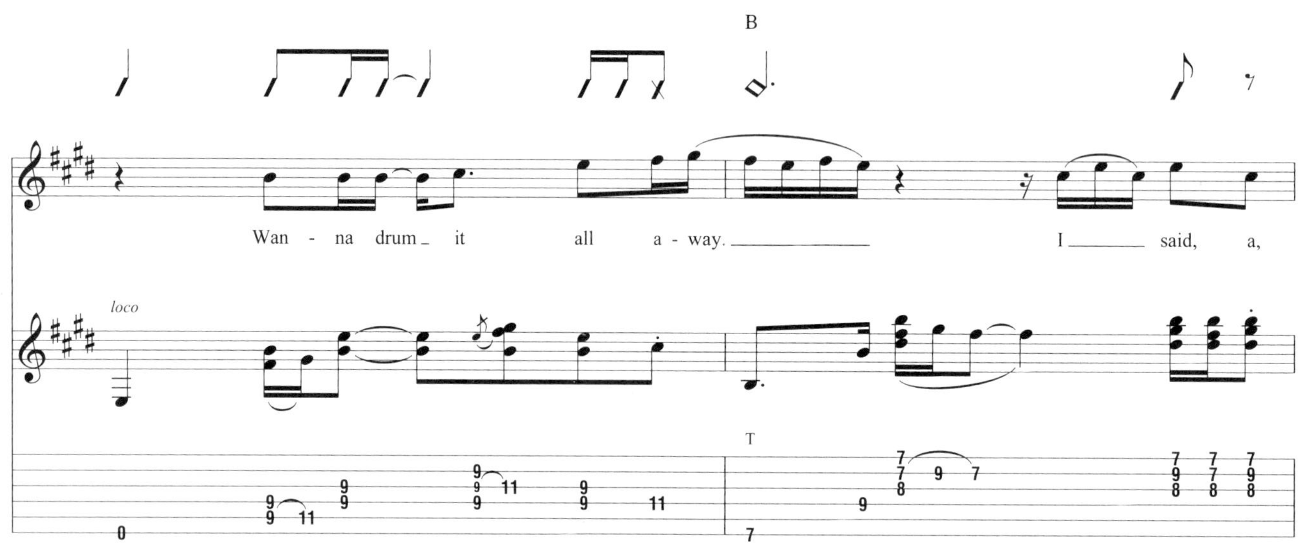
B
Wan - na drum it all a - way. I said, a,
loco

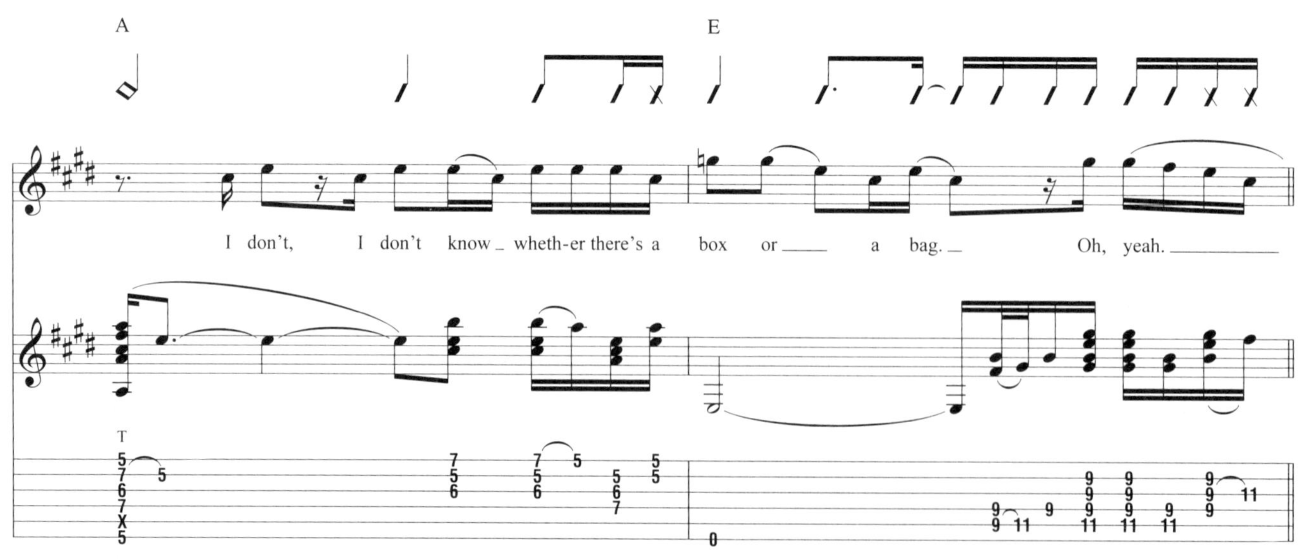
A
E
I don't, I don't know wheth-er there's a box or a bag. Oh, yeah.

Chorus
E
B
A
Can you see them
oh, on the porch?
Yeah,
but they don't wave.
E
I
see them
'round the front
B
A
(cont. in notation)
way,
yeah.
And I
know, and I know
I don't wan - na stay

Bridge

E B A Asus2

at all. I don't wan - na

Gtr. 1

Gtr. 2

E B A *A/G♯ **A/F♯

stay. I don't wan - na stay.

*Bass plays G♯. **Bass plays F♯.

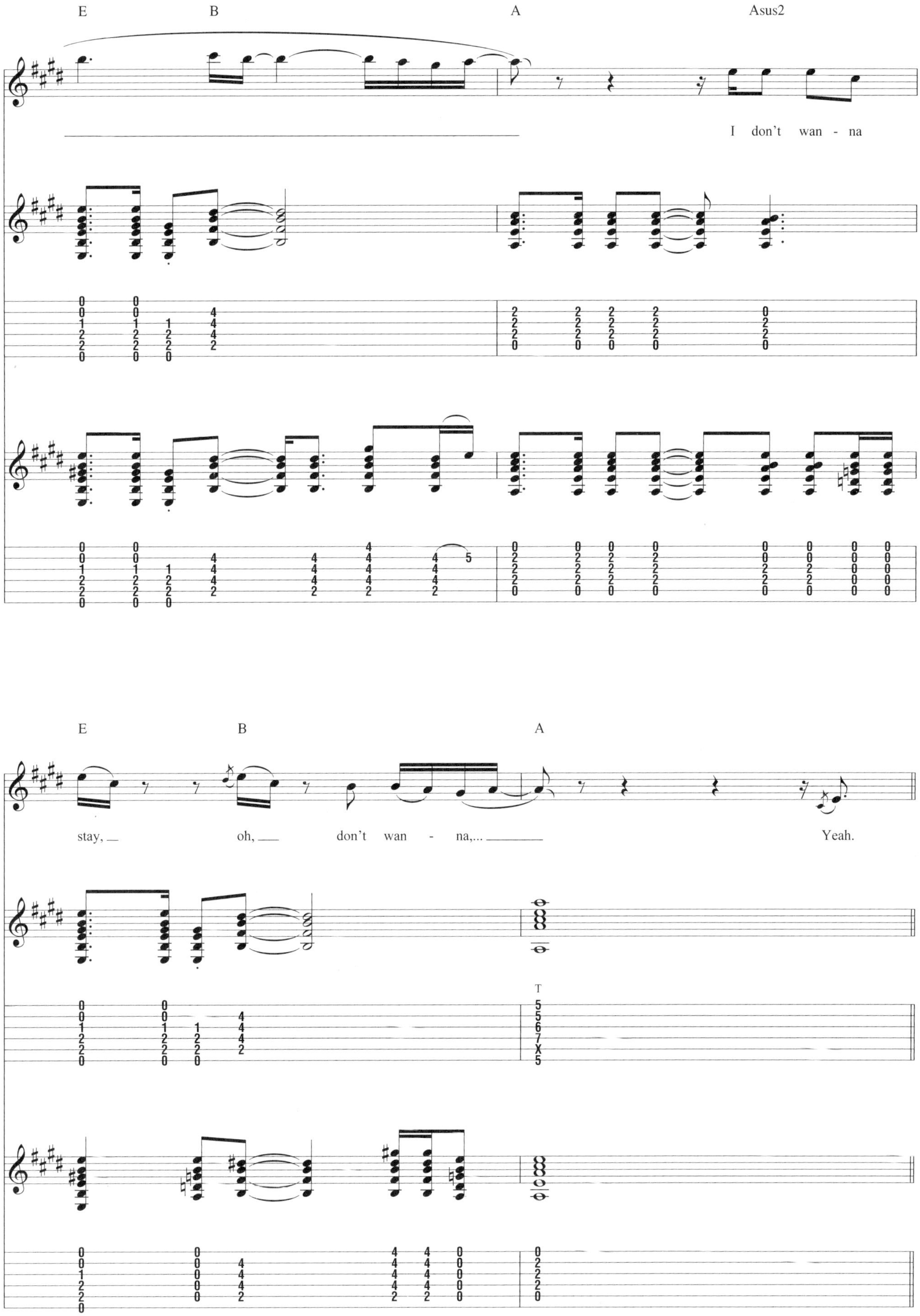

E B A Asus2

I don't wan - na

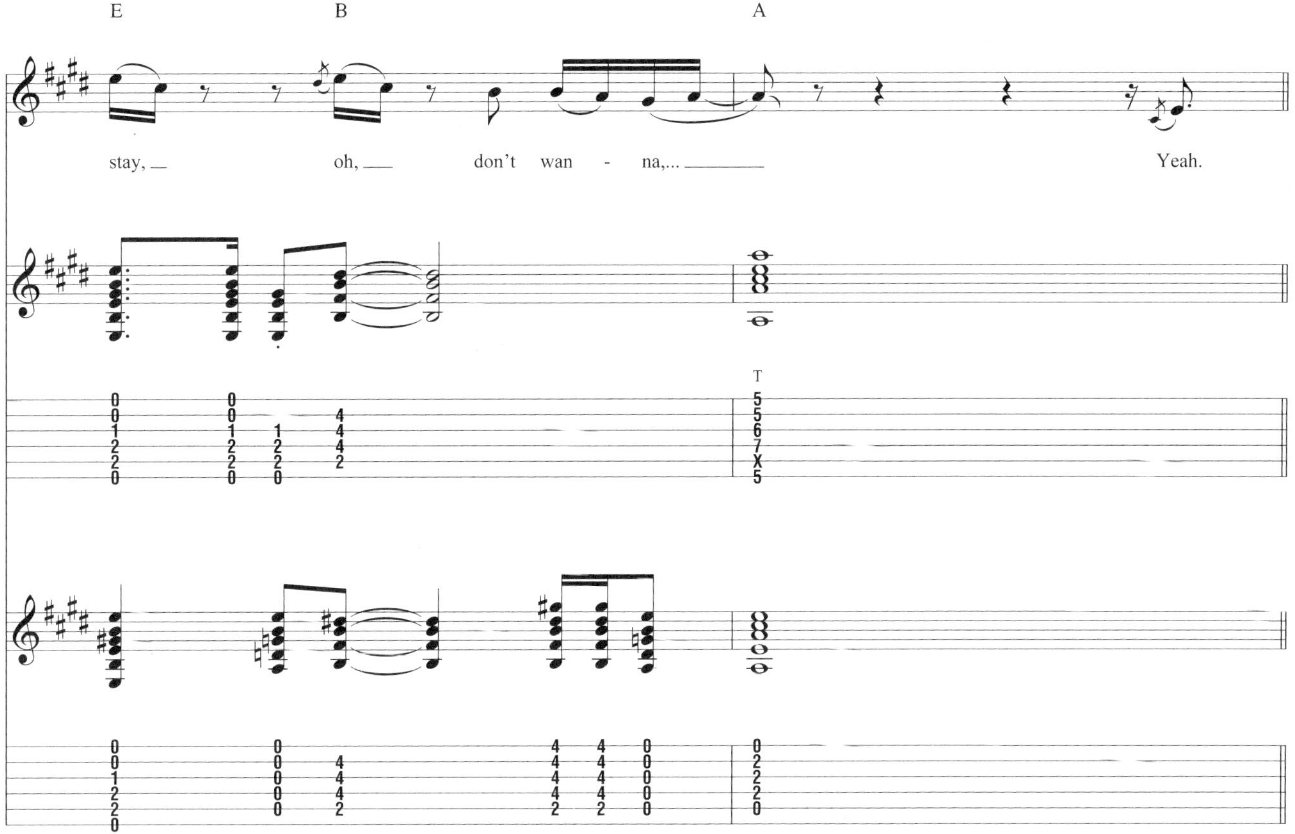

Interlude

B/D♯ E5 B B/D♯ E5 A

Oh.

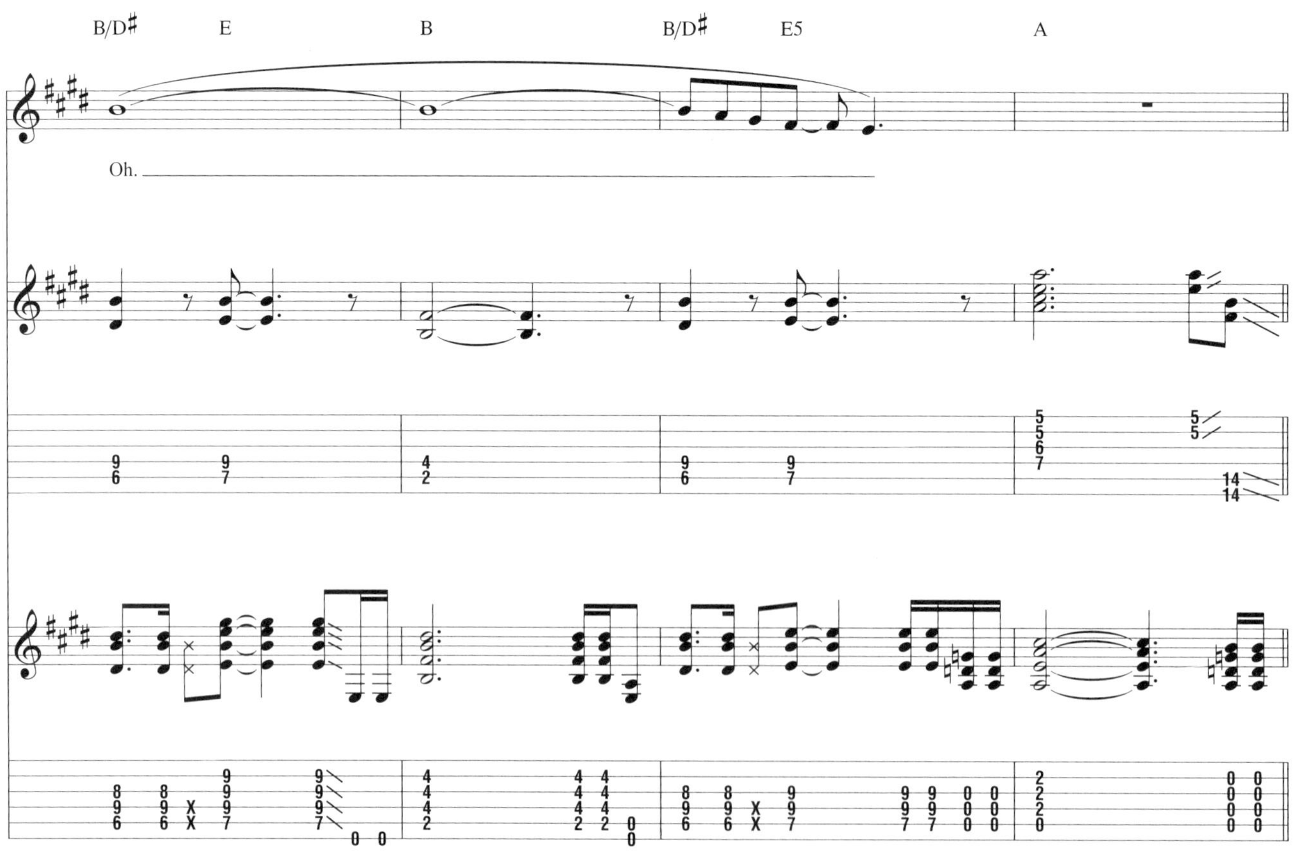

Outro
Gtr. 2 tacet
E
B
Gtr. 1
A
E
B
A
8va
loco
E
Harm.
Pitch: B E B
B
A
E
rit.
Harm.

from Night Ranger - *Midnight Madness*

(You Can Still) Rock in America

Words and Music by Jack Blades and Brad Gillis

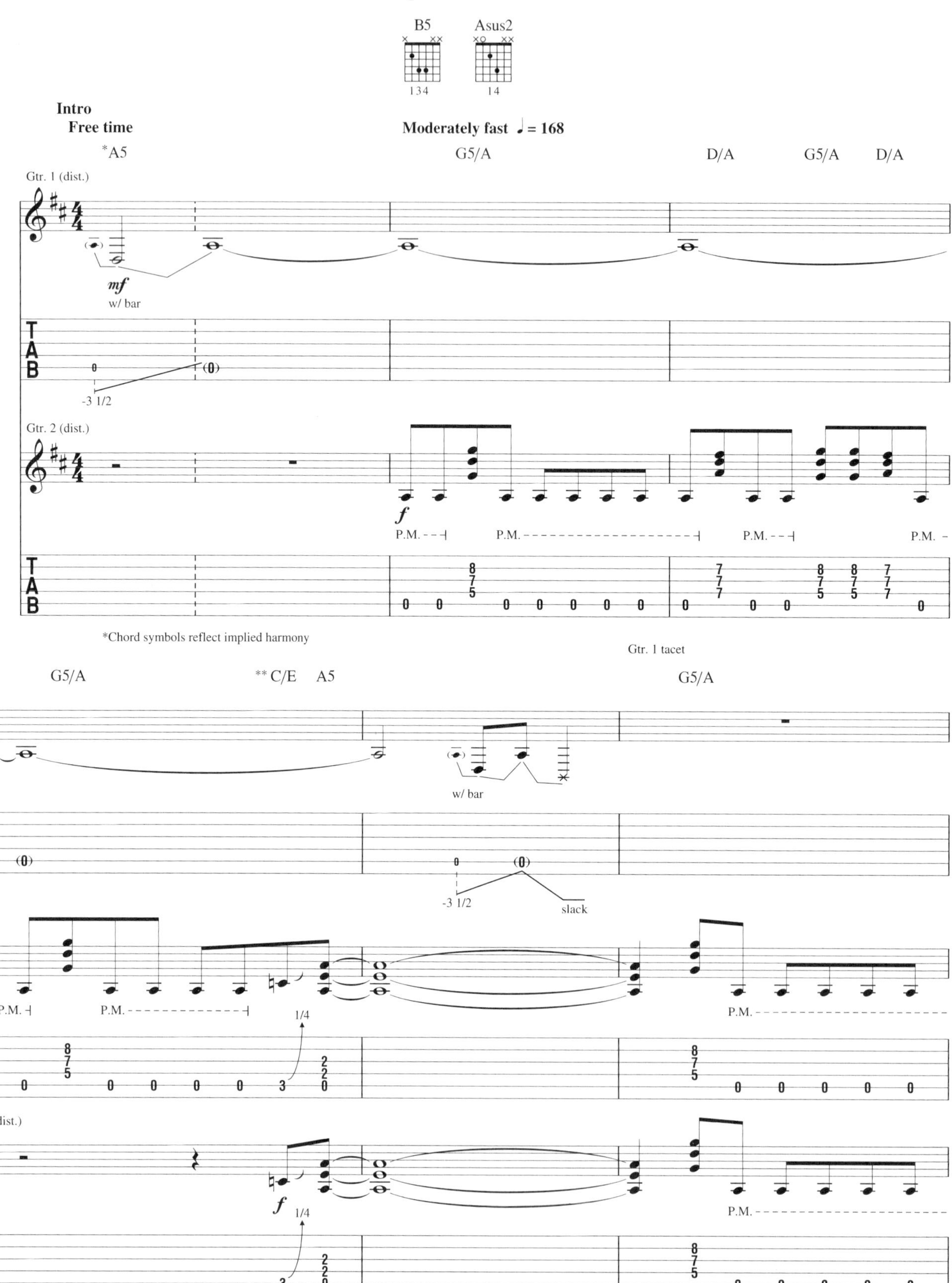

D/A
G5/A
D/A
G5/A
A5
*Gtrs. 2 & 3
P.M.
P.M.
P.M.
P.M.
*Composite arrangement

A/C♯
G5/A
D/A
G5/A
D/A
G5/A
A5
Gtr. 4 (dist.)
mf
1/2
1/2
Rhy. Fig. 1
End Rhy. Fig. 1
Gtrs. 2 & 3
1/2
P.M.
P.M.
P.M.
P.M.

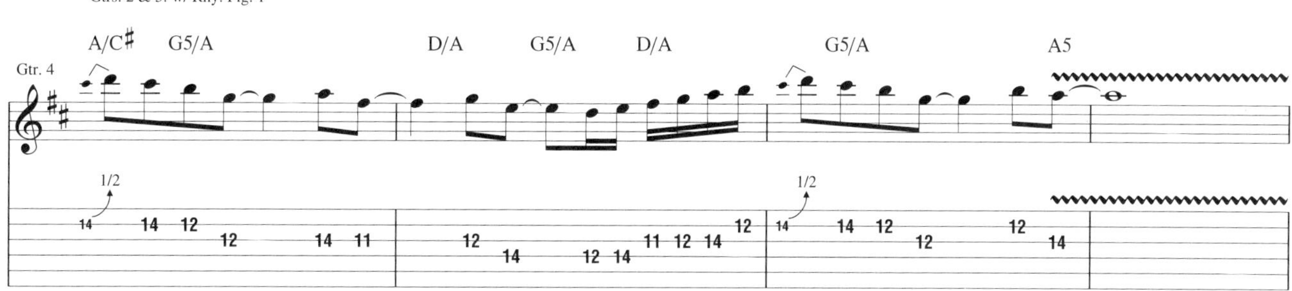
Gtrs. 2 & 3: w/ Rhy. Fig. 1
A/C♯
G5/A
D/A
G5/A
D/A
G5/A
A5
Gtr. 4
1/2
1/2

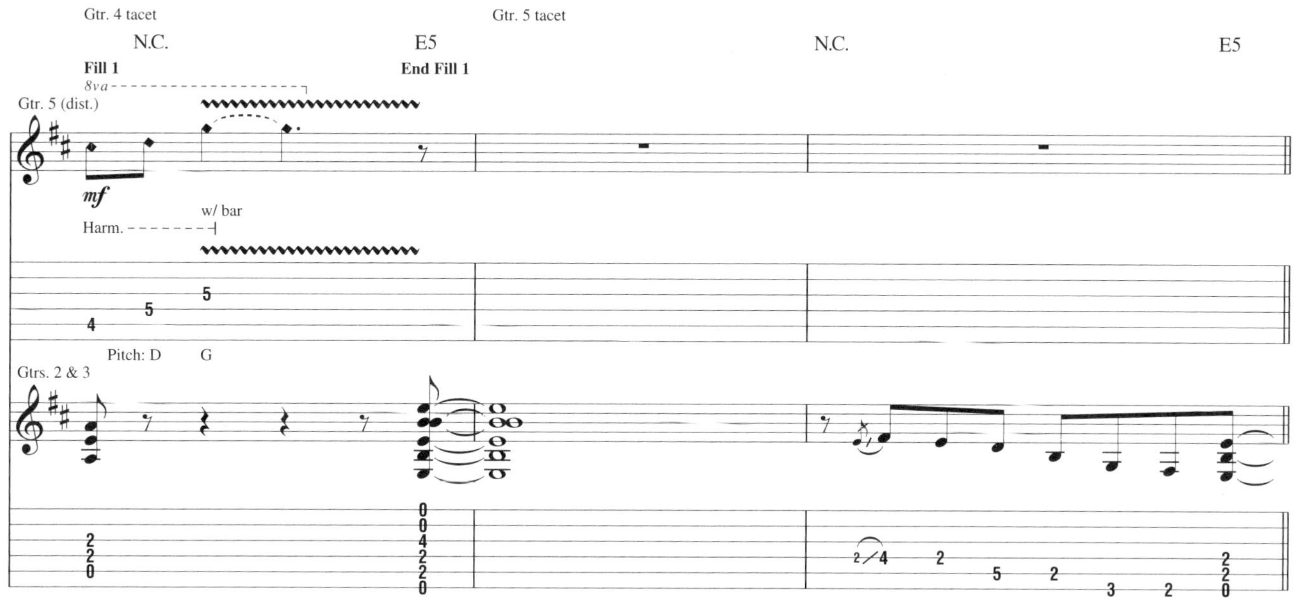
Gtr. 4 tacet
Gtr. 5 tacet
N.C.
E5
N.C.
E5
Fill 1
End Fill 1
8va
Gtr. 5 (dist.)
mf
w/ bar
Harm.
Pitch: D
G
Gtrs. 2 & 3

1. Lit - tle sis - ter by the rec - ord ma - chine, a ti - ny danc - er, such a
2. Lit - tle sis - ter makes a move for the door. The door squeaks, she's on the

Gtrs. 2 & 3

P.M. P.M. P.M.

D5 D6 D5 D6 D(♯4) D5

sweet six - teen. She's go - in' out, she's gon - na par - ty to - night.
sec - ond floor. Her dad - dy wakes, "Is ev - 'ry - thing O. K.?"

P.M. P.M. P.M. P.M. P.M.

E5 D/E

She's gon - na shake and make it last all night. Lit - tle broth - er's got a
Not a sound as she makes her get - a - way. Lit - tle broth - er's got it

P.M. P.M.

E5 D/E

driv - in' ma - chine, a fast driv - er, such a clean ma - chine.
read - y to roll, tires burn - ing as they head for the show.

P.M. P.M. P.M. P.M. P.M. P.M.

2nd time, Gtr. 2: w/ Rhy. Fill 1
C5
A5
They're go - in' out, they're gon - na put out the lights. They're gon - na rock it, rock it,
Light it up and turn the mu - sic on loud. They're rock - in', rock - in',
1/4
P.M.
Chorus
D5
G5
rock it!
rock - in'!
You can still rock in A - mer - i - ca. Oh,
Harm.
Pitch: A D B
A5 G5 A5 G5 D5 G5
yeah, it's al - right. You can still rock in A - mer - i - ca. Oh,
Rhy. Fill 1
Gtr. 2

To Coda
A5
G5
A5
G5
D5
G5
yeah,
all
night.
You can
still
rock in A - mer - i -

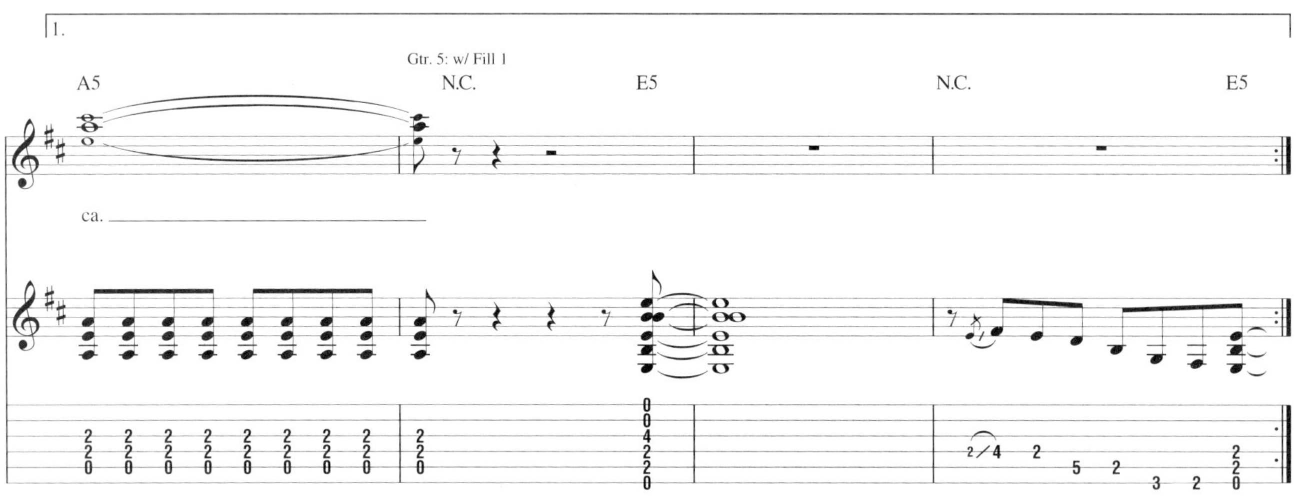
1.
Gtr. 5: w/ Fill 1
A5
N.C.
E5
N.C.
E5
ca.

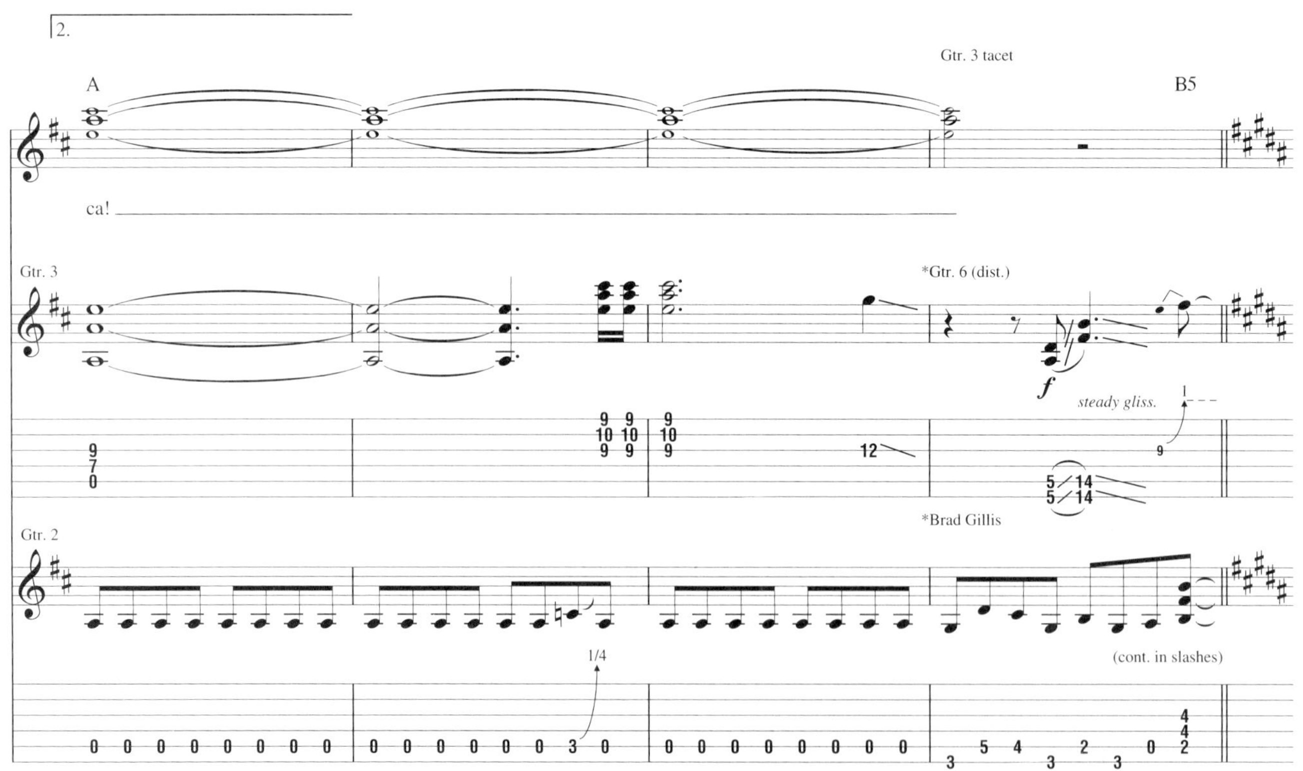
2.
Gtr. 3 tacet
A
B5
ca!
Gtr. 3
*Gtr. 6 (dist.)
steady gliss.
*Brad Gillis
Gtr. 2
(cont. in slashes)

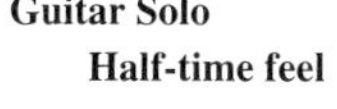
Guitar Solo
Half-time feel

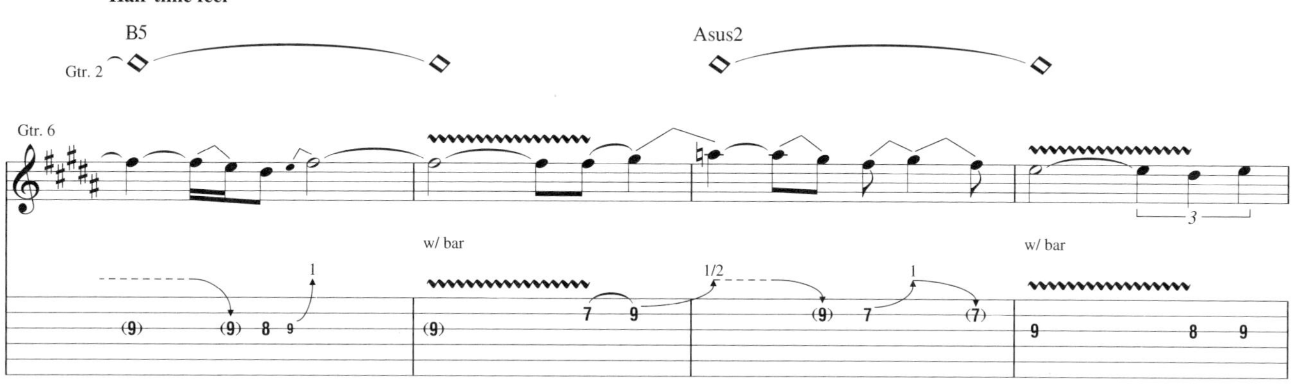
B5
Asus2
Gtr. 2
Gtr. 6
w/ bar
w/ bar

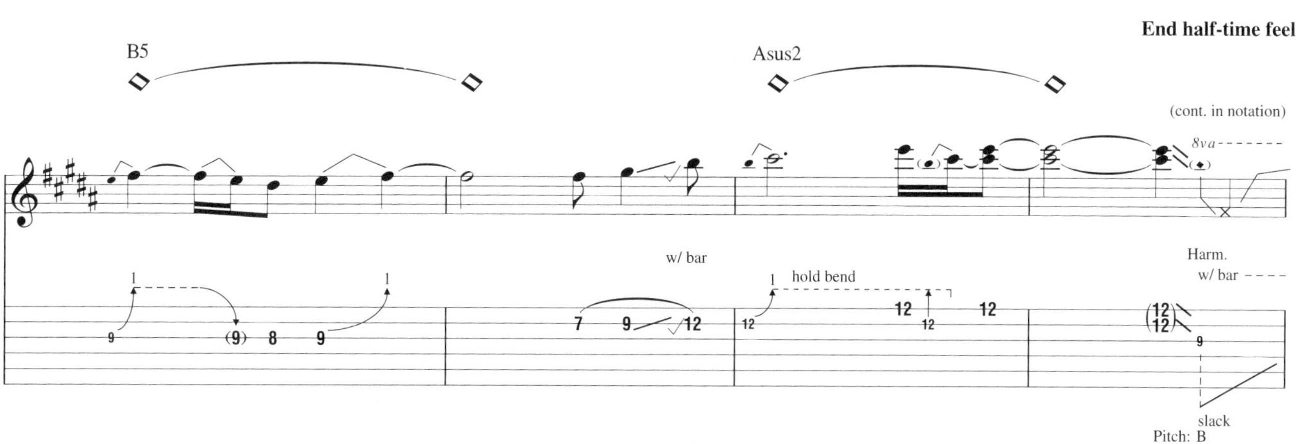
End half-time feel
B5
Asus2
(cont. in notation)
8va
w/ bar
hold bend
Harm.
w/ bar
slack
Pitch: B

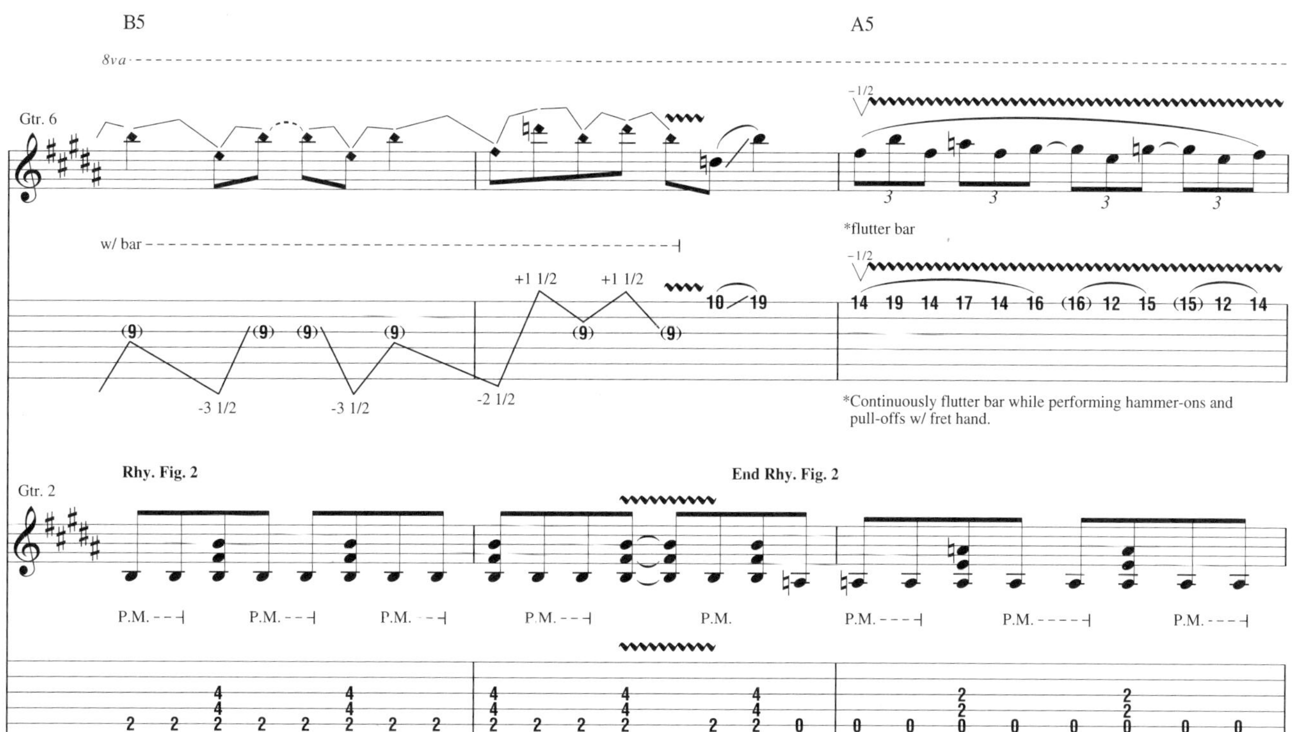
B5
A5
8va
Gtr. 6
w/ bar
*flutter bar
*Continuously flutter bar while performing hammer-ons and pull-offs w/ fret hand.
Rhy. Fig. 2
End Rhy. Fig. 2
Gtr. 2
P.M.

B5

8va

Harm.
w/ bar

loco

P.M.

A5

8va

Guitar Solo

D5

G5

8va

Gtr. 6

w/ bar

*Gtr. 7 (dist.)

f

*Jeff Watson

Gtr. 2

Rhy. Fig. 3

*Tap sequence executed with designated fingers (1 = index, 2 = middle, 3 = ring, 4 = pinky) of pick hand, next 8 meas.

**Pluck open string w/ fret hand index finger.

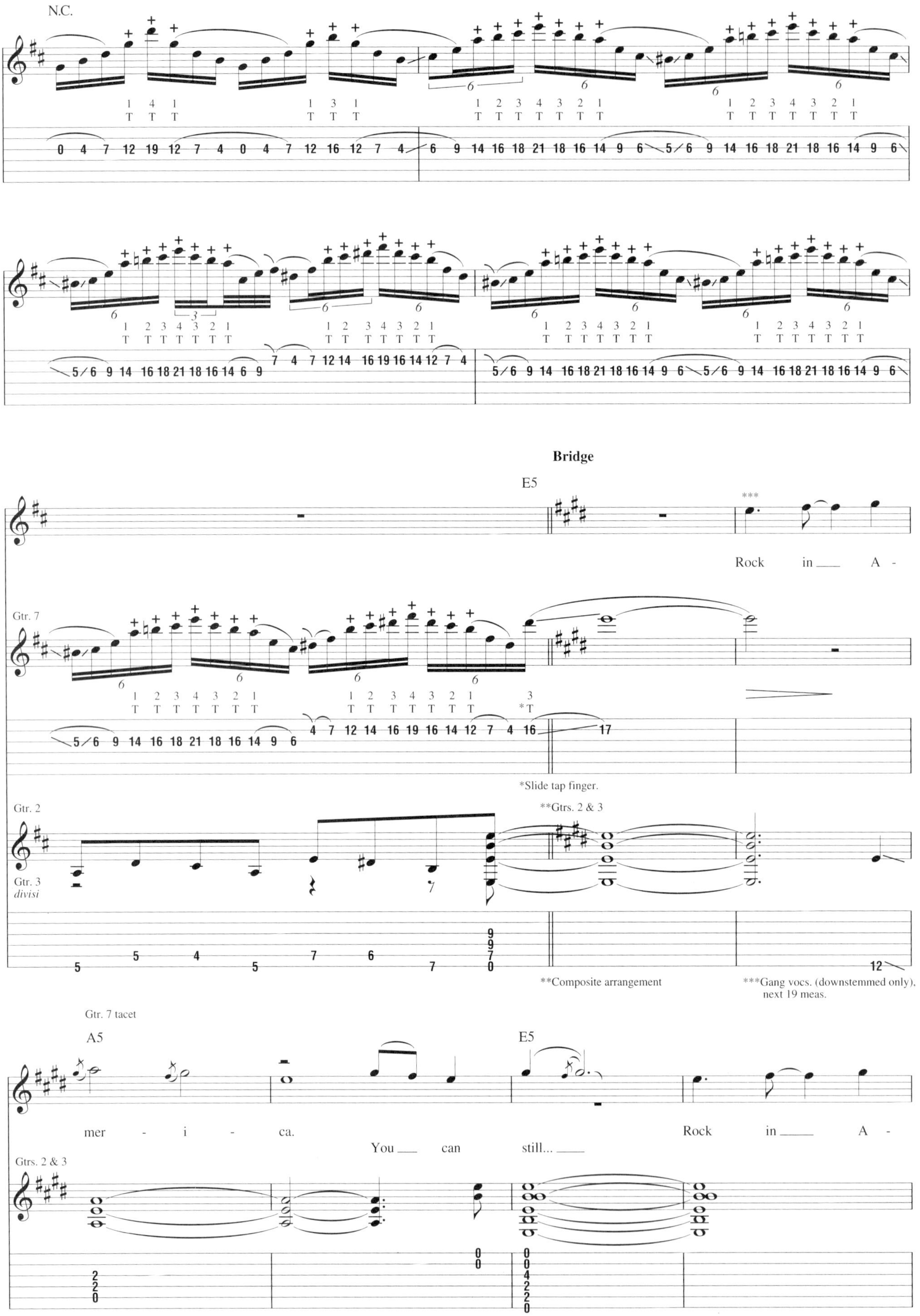

N.C.

Bridge

E5

Rock in ___ A -

Gtr. 7

*Slide tap finger.

Gtr. 2

**Gtrs. 2 & 3

Gtr. 3 *divisi*

**Composite arrangement

***Gang vocs. (downstemmed only), next 19 meas.

Gtr. 7 tacet

A5

E5

mer - i - ca. Rock in ___ A -

You ___ can still... ___

Gtrs. 2 & 3

A5
E5
B/E
E5
mer - i - ca.
Rock in A - mer - i - ca!
P.M.
B/E
E5
A5
A(♯4)
A5
A(♯4)
A5
Rock in A - mer - i - ca.
Yeah, you can
P.M.
E5
B/E
E5
B/E
E5
A5
A(♯4)
A5
B5
Rock in A - mer - i -
still...
Gtr. 3
P.M.
Gtr. 2
P.M.

Guitar Solo
Gtrs. 2 & 3: w/ Rhy. Fig. 2
B5
ca.
Gtr. 7
8va
A5
B5
Gtrs. 2 & 3
P.M.
D.S. al Coda
Gtr. 7 tacet
A5 N.C.
D5
You can
*w/ delay
*Set for quarter-note regeneration w/ 1 repeat.

Coda

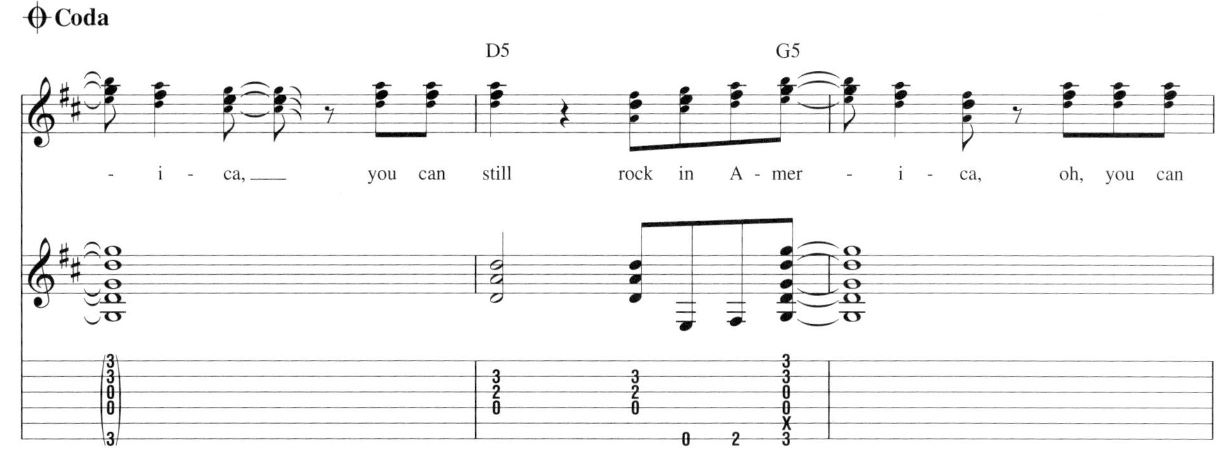
D5
G5
- i - ca, you can still rock in A - mer - i - ca, oh, you can

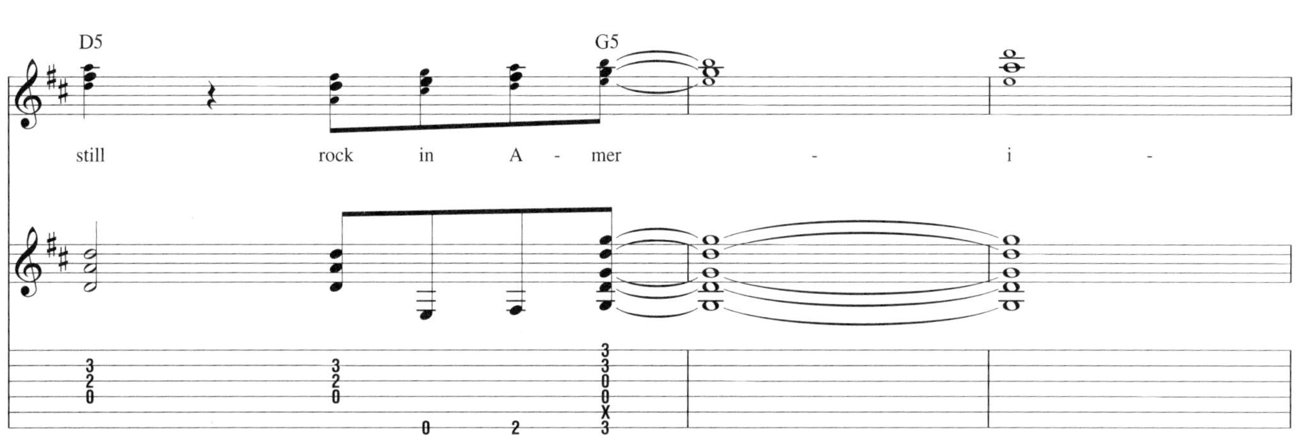
D5
G5
still rock in A - mer - i -

Gtr. 2: w/ Rhy. Fig. 1 (3 times)
A/C♯
G5/A
D/A
G5/A
D/A
G5/A
A5
ca.
Gtr. 4
Gtr. 3
P.M.
1/2

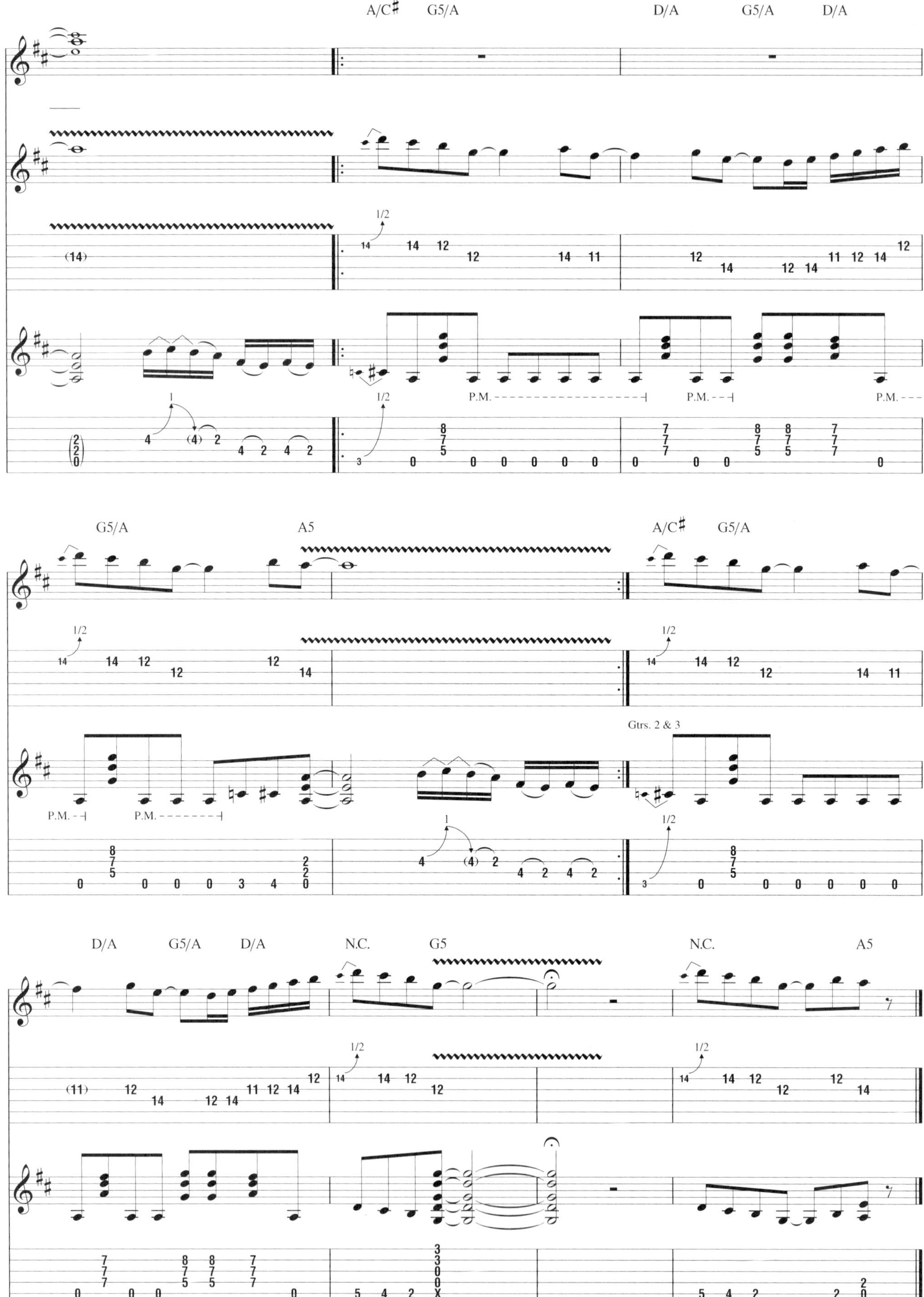
A/C♯
G5/A
D/A
G5/A
D/A
1/2
P.M.
1
G5/A
A5
A/C♯
G5/A
Gtrs. 2 & 3
D/A
G5/A
D/A
N.C.
G5
N.C.
A5

GUITAR NOTATION LEGEND

Guitar music can be notated three different ways: on a *musical staff*, in *tablature*, and in *rhythm slashes*.

RHYTHM SLASHES are written above the staff. Strum chords in the rhythm indicated. Use the chord diagrams found at the top of the first page of the transcription for the appropriate chord voicings. Round noteheads indicate single notes.

THE MUSICAL STAFF shows pitches and rhythms and is divided by bar lines into measures. Pitches are named after the first seven letters of the alphabet.

TABLATURE graphically represents the guitar fingerboard. Each horizontal line represents a string, and each number represents a fret.

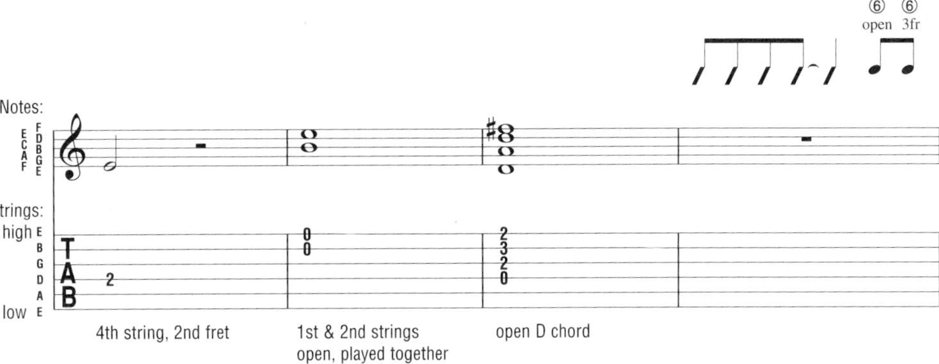

Definitions for Special Guitar Notation

HALF-STEP BEND: Strike the note and bend up 1/2 step.

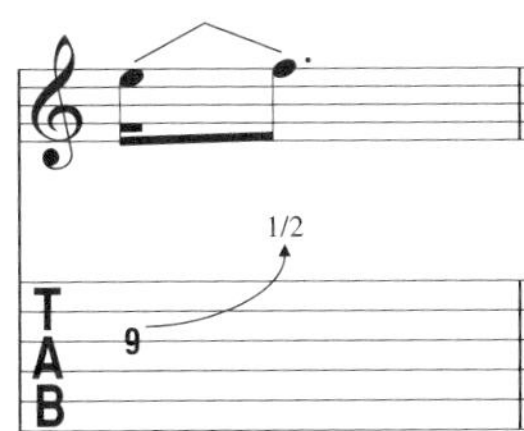

WHOLE-STEP BEND: Strike the note and bend up one step.

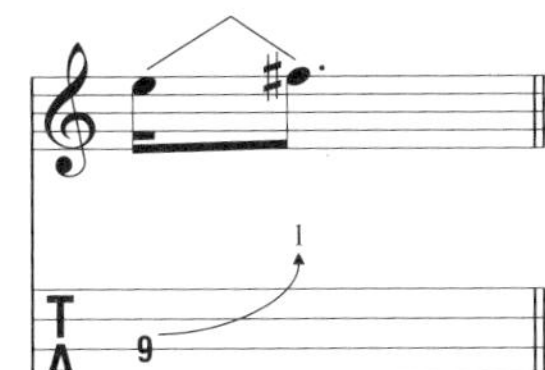

GRACE NOTE BEND: Strike the note and immediately bend up as indicated.

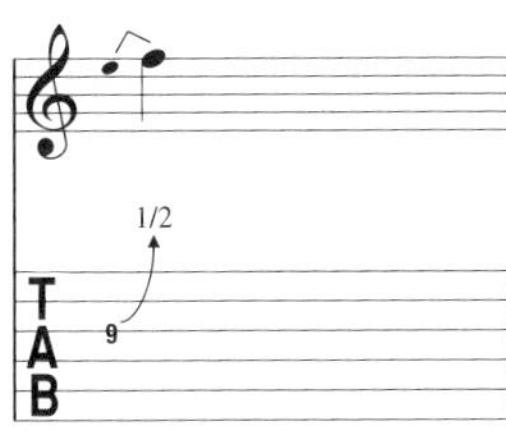

SLIGHT (MICROTONE) BEND: Strike the note and bend up 1/4 step.

BEND AND RELEASE: Strike the note and bend up as indicated, then release back to the original note. Only the first note is struck.

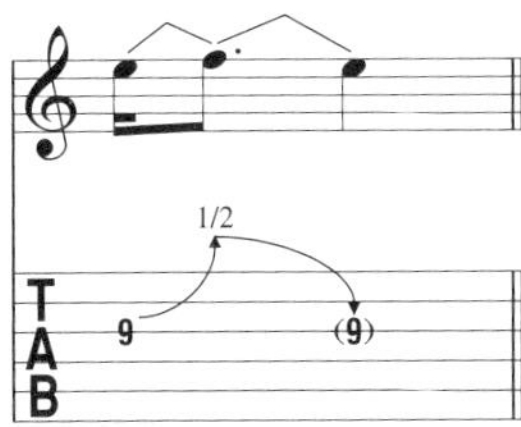

PRE-BEND: Bend the note as indicated, then strike it.

PRE-BEND AND RELEASE: Bend the note as indicated. Strike it and release the bend back to the original note.

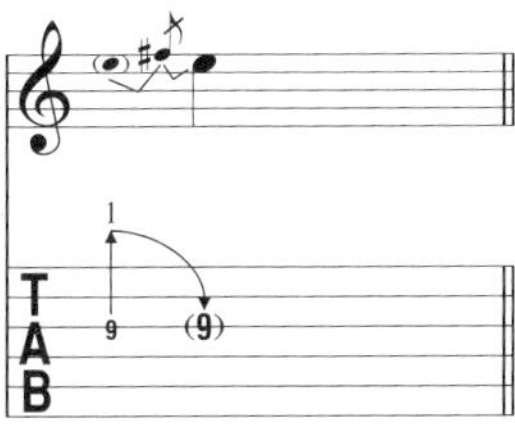

UNISON BEND: Strike the two notes simultaneously and bend the lower note up to the pitch of the higher.

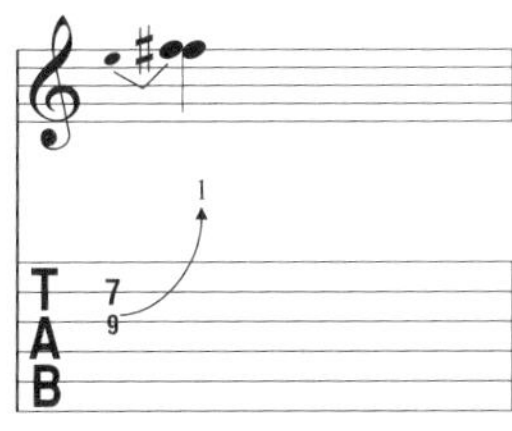

VIBRATO: The string is vibrated by rapidly bending and releasing the note with the fretting hand.

WIDE VIBRATO: The pitch is varied to a greater degree by vibrating with the fretting hand.

HAMMER-ON: Strike the first (lower) note with one finger, then sound the higher note (on the same string) with another finger by fretting it without picking.

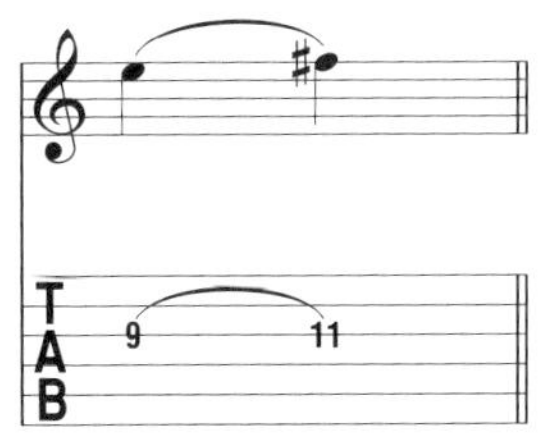

PULL-OFF: Place both fingers on the notes to be sounded. Strike the first note and without picking, pull the finger off to sound the second (lower) note.

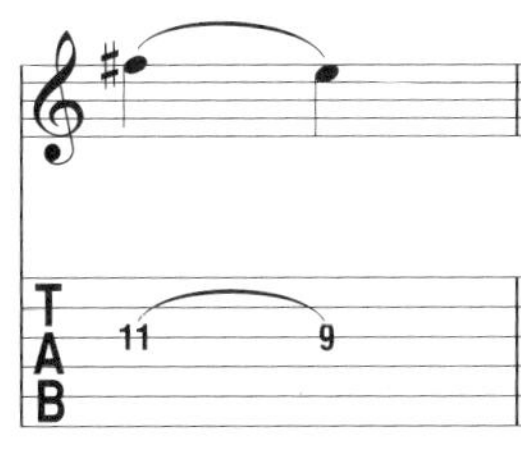

LEGATO SLIDE: Strike the first note and then slide the same fret-hand finger up or down to the second note. The second note is not struck.

SHIFT SLIDE: Same as legato slide, except the second note is struck.

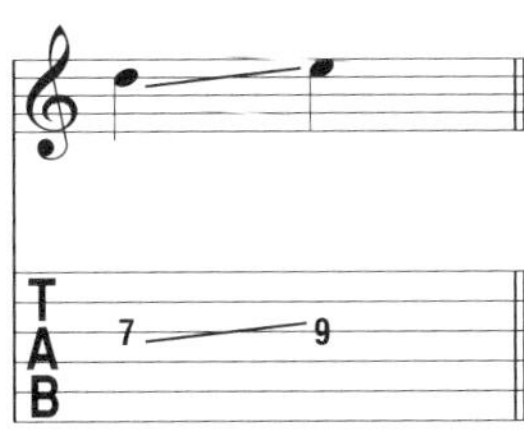

TRILL: Very rapidly alternate between the notes indicated by continuously hammering on and pulling off.

TAPPING: Hammer ("tap") the fret indicated with the pick-hand index or middle finger and pull off to the note fretted by the fret hand.

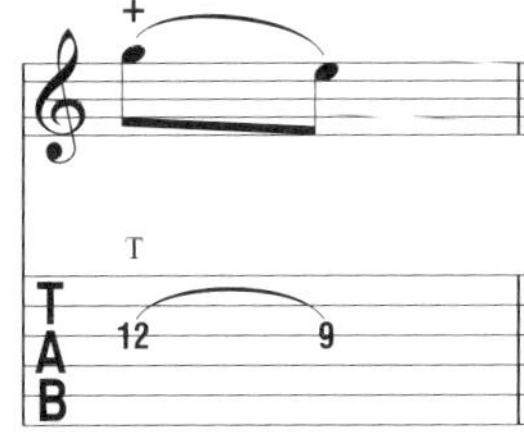

NATURAL HARMONIC: Strike the note while the fret-hand lightly touches the string directly over the fret indicated.

PINCH HARMONIC: The note is fretted normally and a harmonic is produced by adding the edge of the thumb or the tip of the index finger of the pick hand to the normal pick attack.

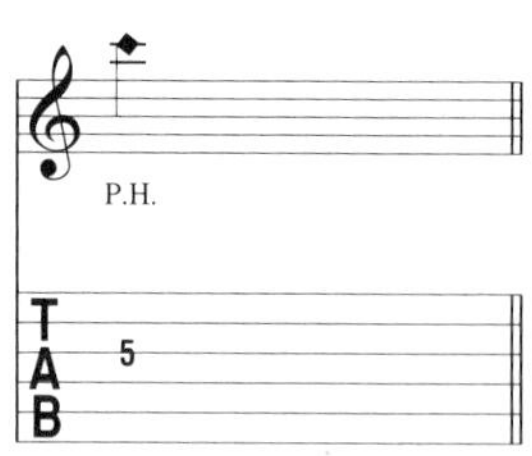

HARP HARMONIC: The note is fretted normally and a harmonic is produced by gently resting the pick hand's index finger directly above the indicated fret (in parentheses) while the pick hand's thumb or pick assists by plucking the appropriate string.

PICK SCRAPE: The edge of the pick is rubbed down (or up) the string, producing a scratchy sound.

MUFFLED STRINGS: A percussive sound is produced by laying the fret hand across the string(s) without depressing, and striking them with the pick hand.

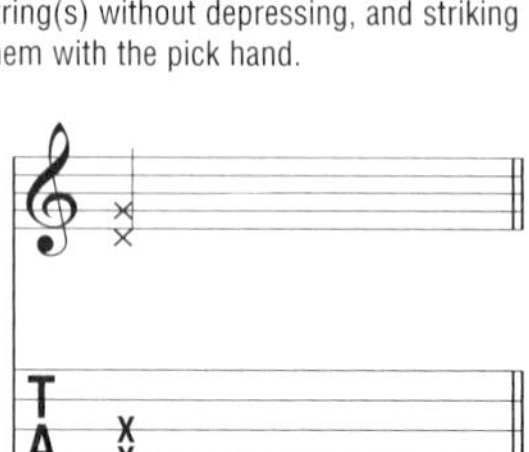

PALM MUTING: The note is partially muted by the pick hand lightly touching the string(s) just before the bridge.

RAKE: Drag the pick across the strings indicated with a single motion.

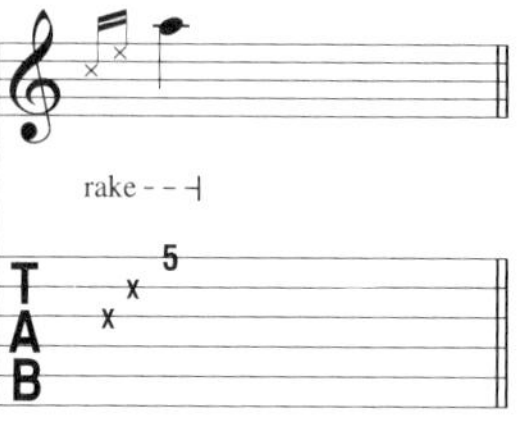

TREMOLO PICKING: The note is picked as rapidly and continuously as possible.

ARPEGGIATE: Play the notes of the chord indicated by quickly rolling them from bottom to top.

VIBRATO BAR DIVE AND RETURN: The pitch of the note or chord is dropped a specified number of steps (in rhythm), then returned to the original pitch.

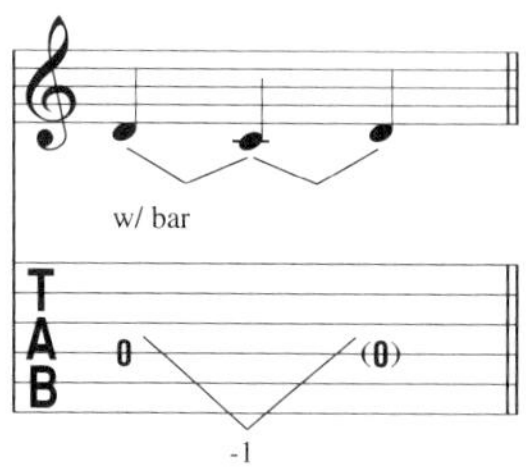

VIBRATO BAR SCOOP: Depress the bar just before striking the note, then quickly release the bar.

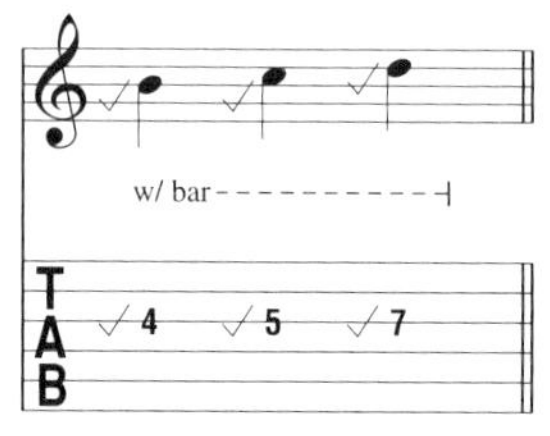

VIBRATO BAR DIP: Strike the note and then immediately drop a specified number of steps, then release back to the original pitch.

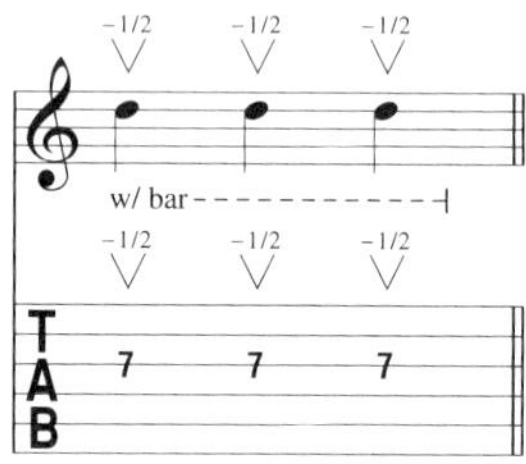

Additional Musical Definitions

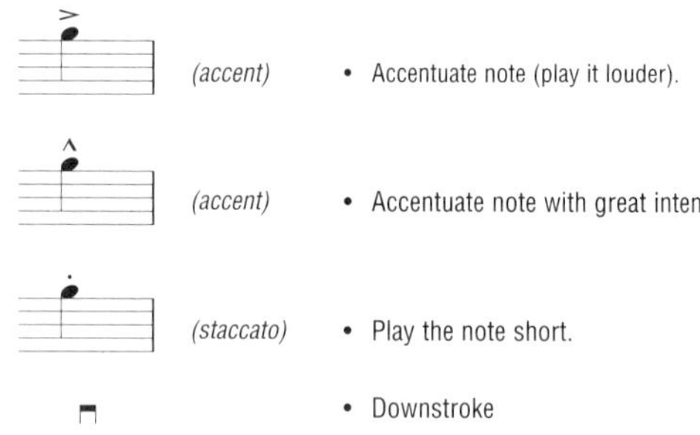

- (accent) • Accentuate note (play it louder).
- (accent) • Accentuate note with great intensity.
- (staccato) • Play the note short.
- • Downstroke
- V • Upstroke
- ***D.S. al Coda*** • Go back to the sign (𝄋), then play until the measure marked "***To Coda***," then skip to the section labelled "**Coda**."
- ***D.C. al Fine*** • Go back to the beginning of the song and play until the measure marked "***Fine***" (end).

- **Rhy. Fig.** • Label used to recall a recurring accompaniment pattern (usually chordal).
- **Riff** • Label used to recall composed, melodic lines (usually single notes) which recur.
- **Fill** • Label used to identify a brief melodic figure which is to be inserted into the arrangement.
- **Rhy. Fill** • A chordal version of a Fill.
- tacet • Instrument is silent (drops out).
- • Repeat measures between signs.
- 1. 2. • When a repeated section has different endings, play the first ending only the first time and the second ending only the second time.

NOTE: Tablature numbers in parentheses mean:

1. The note is being sustained over a system (note in standard notation is tied), or
2. The note is sustained, but a new articulation (such as a hammer-on, pull-off, slide or vibrato) begins, or
3. The note is a barely audible "ghost" note (note in standard notation is also in parentheses).

Hal Leonard Guitar Tab White Pages

These incredible collections contain note-for-note transcriptions straight from the original recordings. Each edition is over 700 pages!

GUITAR TAB WHITE PAGES – VOLUME 1 – 2ND EDITION

The primo songlist for this second edition boasts even more of your faves from all styles of music: Aerials • All Apologies • American Woman • Badge • Centerfold • Day Tripper • Dissident • Free Ride • Heartache Tonight • Iron Man • Landslide • Layla • Loser • Misty • My Girl • Name • Oleo • Piece of My Heart • Satin Doll • Signs • Sweet Emotion • Wild Thing • You Shook Me • You Were Meant for Me • more!

00690471 Guitar Recorded Versions $29.99

GUITAR TAB WHITE PAGES – VOLUME 2

Note-for-note guitar tab transcriptions for 150 songs, including: Born Under A Bad Sign • Dancing In The Street • Are You Gonna Go My Way • I Shot The Sheriff • I Want You To Want Me • Little Miss Can't Be Wrong • Runnin' Down A Dream • Welcome To The Jungle • Pride And Joy • Mustang Sally • Freeway Jam • Everyday I Have The Blues • Crazy Train • Jump, Jive An' Wail • Killing Floor • Stayin' Alive • Sweet Talkin' Woman • The Thrill Is Gone • many more!

00699557 Guitar Recorded Versions $29.99

GUITAR TAB WHITE PAGES – VOLUME 3

By popular demand, here's Volume 3 of our best-selling songbook featuring 150 more great titles: Alive • American Pie • Are You Gonna Be My Girl • Bang a Gong (Get It On) • Carry on Wayward Son • Don't Stand So Close to Me • Fat Lip • Hard to Handle • Jane Says • Jeremy • Killer Queen • Once Bitten Twice Shy • Peg • Santeria • Sweet Home Alabama • What's My Age Again? • Wish You Were Here • Ziggy Stardust • and more.

00690791 Guitar Recorded Versions $29.99

ACOUSTIC GUITAR TAB WHITE PAGES

150 acoustic favorites from yesterday and today: Across the Universe • At Seventeen • The Boxer • Come to My Window • Crazy on You • Here Comes the Sun • Layla • Learning to Fly • Loser • Maggie May • Mr. Jones • Not Fade Away • Patience • Pink Houses • Suite: Judy Blue Eyes • Superman (It's Not Easy) • Tears in Heaven • Time for Me to Fly • Time in a Bottle • Yellow • You've Got a Friend • and many more unplugged gems.

0699590 Guitar Recorded Versions $29.99

BLUES GUITAR TAB WHITE PAGES

Blues classics include: Baby, Please Don't Go • Born Under a Bad Sign • Bridge of Sighs • Cold Shot • Couldn't Stand the Weather • Cross Road Blues (Crossroads) • Double Trouble • Everyday I Have the Blues • I Can't Quit You Baby • Killing Floor • Love in Vain Blues • Pride and Joy • The Sky Is Crying • Sweet Home Chicago • Texas Flood • The Thrill Is Gone • and dozens more!

00700131 Guitar Recorded Versions $29.99

CHRISTIAN GUITAR TAB WHITE PAGES

125+ favorites by today's top CCM artists: Be My Escape • Big House • Bliss • Dare You to Move • Deeper • Engage • Fireproof • Every Little Thing • Flood • Get Down • Hands and Feet • He Reigns • His Eyes • Holy One • I Can Feel It • Into Jesus • Jesus Freak • Jonah • Lifesong • Man of God • My Refuge • Shine • Undo Me • We Are One Tonight • Who I Am Hates Who I've Been • Youth of the Nation • and more.

00690847 Guitar Recorded Versions $29.95

EASY GUITAR TAB WHITE PAGES

This awesome songbook packs in over 200 easy arrangements in notes and tab of some of the best guitar songs ever, from all styles of music. Songs include: Ain't Too Proud to Beg • Are You Gonna Be My Girl • Bad Case of Loving You • Bésame Mucho • Crying • Don't Stop • Footloose • Guitars, Cadillacs • Help Me Rhonda • Let's Stay Together • Longer • Me and Bobby McGee • Name • On Broadway • Summer in the City • Three Little Birds • Time Is on My Side • Woman • Zombie • and hundreds more.

00702280 Guitar Recorded Versions $29.99

GUITAR TAB WHITE PAGES PLAY-ALONG

This awesome package contains tab transcriptions of 100 of the greatest rock songs ever, along with six CDs of high-quality, full-band backing tracks that coordinate with the transcriptions. Songs include: All Right Now • Barracuda • Black Hole Sun • Changes • Cheap Sunglasses • Highway to Hell • London Calling • Mony, Mony • Rhiannon • Sultans of Swing • Wish You Were Here • Ziggy Stardust • and scores more.

00701764 Book/6-CD Pack $39.99

ALSO AVAILABLE:

GUITAR CHORD SONGBOOK WHITE PAGES

This handy collection packs 400 songs into one conveniently-sized 6"x9" book! Featuring lyrics, chord symbols, and guitar chord diagrams for hits across decades and genres, such as: All Along the Watchtower • Back to December • Drops of Jupiter (Tell Me) • Evil Woman • Hey Jude • Jump • King of the Road • Livin' on a Prayer • Man in the Mirror • Ob-La-Di, Ob-La-Da • Uptown Girl • Walkin' After Midnight • Your Mama Don't Dance • and many more.

00702609 Lyrics/Chord Symbols/Guitar Chord Diagrams $29.99

Prices, contents, and availability subject to change without notice.

7777 W. Bluemound Rd. P.O. Box 13819 Milwaukee, WI 53213

www.halleonard.com

0412

RECORDED VERSIONS®

The Best Note-For-Note Transcriptions Available

RECORDED VERSIONS GUITAR®

ALL BOOKS INCLUDE TABLATURE

14037551 AC/DC – Backtracks $32.99
00692015 Aerosmith – Greatest Hits $22.95
00690178 Alice in Chains – Acoustic $19.95
00694865 Alice in Chains – Dirt $19.95
00690812 All American Rejects – Move Along $19.95
00690958 Duane Allman Guitar Anthology $24.99
00694932 Allman Brothers Band – Volume 1 ....$24.95
00694933 Allman Brothers Band – Volume 2 ....$24.95
00694934 Allman Brothers Band – Volume 3 ....$24.95
00690865 Atreyu – A Deathgrip on Yesterday $19.95
00690609 Audioslave $19.95
00690820 Avenged Sevenfold – City of Evil $24.95
00691065 Avenged Sevenfold – Waking the Fallen $22.99
00690503 Beach Boys – Very Best of $19.95
00690489 Beatles – 1 ....$24.99
00694832 Beatles – For Acoustic Guitar $22.99
00691014 Beatles Rock Band $34.99
00690110 Beatles – White Album (Book 1) $19.95
00691043 Jeff Beck – Wired $19.99
00692385 Chuck Berry $19.95
00690835 Billy Talent $19.95
00690901 Best of Black Sabbath $19.95
00690831 blink-182 – Greatest Hits $19.95
00690913 Boston $19.95
00690932 Boston – Don't Look Back $19.99
00690491 David Bowie – Best of $19.95
00690873 Breaking Benjamin – Phobia $19.95
00690451 Jeff Buckley – Collection $24.95
00690957 Bullet for My Valentine – Scream Aim Fire $22.99
00691159 The Cars – Complete Greatest Hits $22.99
00691079 Best of Johnny Cash $22.99
00691004 Chickenfoot $22.99
00690590 Eric Clapton – Anthology $29.95
00690415 Clapton Chronicles – Best of Eric Clapton $18.95
00690936 Eric Clapton – Complete Clapton $29.99
00690074 Eric Clapton – The Cream of Clapton $24.95
00694869 Eric Clapton – Unplugged $22.95
00690162 The Clash – Best of $19.95
00690828 Coheed & Cambria – Good Apollo I'm Burning Star, IV, Vol. 1: From Fear Through the Eyes of Madness $19.95
00690593 Coldplay – A Rush of Blood to the Head $19.95
00690962 Coldplay – Viva La Vida $19.95
00690819 Creedence Clearwater Revival – Best of $22.95
00690648 The Very Best of Jim Croce $19.95
00690613 Crosby, Stills & Nash – Best of $22.95
00690967 Death Cab for Cutie – Narrow Stairs $22.99
00690289 Deep Purple – Best of $19.99
00690784 Def Leppard – Best of $19.95
00692240 Bo Diddley $19.99
00690347 The Doors – Anthology $22.95
00690348 The Doors – Essential Guitar Collection $16.95
00691186 Evanescence $22.99
00690810 Fall Out Boy – From Under the Cork Tree $19.95
00691181 Five Finger Death Punch – American Capitalist $22.99
00690664 Fleetwood Mac – Best of $19.95
00690870 Flyleaf $19.95
00690931 Foo Fighters – Echoes, Silence, Patience & Grace $19.95
00690808 Foo Fighters – In Your Honor $19.95
00691115 Foo Fighters – Wasting Light $22.99
00690805 Robben Ford – Best of $22.99
00694920 Free – Best of $19.95
00691050 Glee Guitar Collection $19.99
00690943 The Goo Goo Dolls – Greatest Hits Volume 1: The Singles $22.95

00701764 Guitar Tab White Pages – Play-Along $39.99
00694854 Buddy Guy – Damn Right, I've Got the Blues $19.95
00690840 Ben Harper – Both Sides of the Gun $19.95
00694798 George Harrison – Anthology $19.95
00690841 Scott Henderson – Blues Guitar Collection $19.95
00692930 Jimi Hendrix – Are You Experienced? $24.95
00692931 Jimi Hendrix – Axis: Bold As Love $22.95
00692932 Jimi Hendrix – Electric Ladyland $24.95
00690017 Jimi Hendrix – Live at Woodstock $24.95
00690602 Jimi Hendrix – Smash Hits $24.99
00691152 West Coast Seattle Boy: The Jimi Hendrix Anthology $29.99
00690793 John Lee Hooker Anthology $24.99
00690692 Billy Idol – Very Best of $19.95
00690688 Incubus – A Crow Left of the Murder $19.95
00690544 Incubus – Morningview $19.95
00690790 Iron Maiden Anthology $24.99
00690721 Jet – Get Born $19.95
00690684 Jethro Tull – Aqualung $19.95
00690959 John5 – Requiem $22.95
00690814 John5 – Songs for Sanity $19.95
00690751 John5 – Vertigo $19.95
00690845 Eric Johnson – Bloom $19.95
00690846 Jack Johnson and Friends – Sing-A-Longs and Lullabies for the Film Curious George $19.95
00690271 Robert Johnson – New Transcriptions $24.95
00699131 Janis Joplin – Best of $19.95
00690427 Judas Priest – Best of $22.99
00690975 Kings of Leon – Only by the Night $22.99
00694903 Kiss – Best of $24.95
00690355 Kiss – Destroyer $16.95
00690834 Lamb of God – Ashes of the Wake $19.95
00690875 Lamb of God – Sacrament $19.95
00690823 Ray LaMontagne – Trouble $19.95
00690679 John Lennon – Guitar Collection $19.95
00690781 Linkin Park – Hybrid Theory $22.95
00690743 Los Lonely Boys $19.95
00690720 Lostprophets – Start Something $19.95
00690955 Lynyrd Skynyrd – All-Time Greatest Hits $19.99
00694954 Lynyrd Skynyrd – New Best of $19.95
00690754 Marilyn Manson – Lest We Forget $19.95
00694956 Bob Marley– Legend $19.95
00694945 Bob Marley– Songs of Freedom $24.95
00690657 Maroon5 – Songs About Jane $19.95
00120080 Don McLean – Songbook $19.95
00694951 Megadeth – Rust in Peace $22.95
00691185 Megadeth – Th1rt3en $22.99
00690951 Megadeth – United Abominations $22.99
00690505 John Mellencamp – Guitar Collection $19.95
00690646 Pat Metheny – One Quiet Night $19.95
00690558 Pat Metheny – Trio: 99>00 ....$19.95
00690040 Steve Miller Band – Young Hearts $19.95
00691070 Mumford & Sons – Sigh No More $22.99
00694883 Nirvana – Nevermind $19.95
00690026 Nirvana – Unplugged in New York $19.95
00690807 The Offspring – Greatest Hits $19.95
00694847 Ozzy Osbourne – Best of $22.95
00690399 Ozzy Osbourne – Ozzman Cometh $22.99
00690933 Best of Brad Paisley $22.95
00690995 Brad Paisley – Play: The Guitar Album $24.99
00694855 Pearl Jam – Ten $22.99
00690439 A Perfect Circle – Mer De Noms $19.95
00690499 Tom Petty – Definitive Guitar Collection $19.95
00690428 Pink Floyd – Dark Side of the Moon $19.95
00690789 Poison – Best of $19.95
00693864 The Police – Best of $19.95
00694975 Queen – Greatest Hits $24.95

00690670 Queensryche – Very Best of $19.95
00690878 The Raconteurs – Broken Boy Soldiers $19.95
00694910 Rage Against the Machine $19.95
00690055 Red Hot Chili Peppers – Blood Sugar Sex Magik $19.95
00690584 Red Hot Chili Peppers – By the Way $19.95
00691166 Red Hot Chili Peppers – I'm with You $22.99
00690852 Red Hot Chili Peppers –Stadium Arcadium $24.95
00690511 Django Reinhardt – Definitive Collection $19.95
00690779 Relient K – MMHMM $19.95
00690631 Rolling Stones – Guitar Anthology $27.95
00694976 Rolling Stones – Some Girls $22.95
00690264 The Rolling Stones – Tattoo You $19.95
00690685 David Lee Roth – Eat 'Em and Smile $19.95
00690942 David Lee Roth and the Songs of Van Halen $19.95
00690031 Santana's Greatest Hits $19.95
00690566 Scorpions – Best of $22.95
00690604 Bob Seger – Guitar Collection $19.95
00690803 Kenny Wayne Shepherd Band – Best of $19.95
00690968 Shinedown – The Sound of Madness $22.99
00690813 Slayer – Guitar Collection $19.95
00690733 Slipknot – Vol. 3 (The Subliminal Verses) $22.99
00120004 Steely Dan – Best of $24.95
00694921 Steppenwolf – Best of $22.95
00690655 Mike Stern – Best of $19.95
00690877 Stone Sour – Come What(ever) May $19.95
00690520 Styx Guitar Collection $19.95
00120081 Sublime $19.95
00120122 Sublime – 40oz. to Freedom $19.95
00690929 Sum 41 – Underclass Hero $19.95
00690767 Switchfoot – The Beautiful Letdown $19.95
00690993 Taylor Swift – Fearless $22.99
00690830 System of a Down – Hypnotize $19.95
00690531 System of a Down – Toxicity $19.95
00694824 James Taylor – Best of $16.95
00690871 Three Days Grace – One-X $19.95
00690683 Robin Trower – Bridge of Sighs $19.95
00699191 U2 – Best of: 1980-1990 ....$19.95
00690732 U2 – Best of: 1990-2000 ....$19.95
00660137 Steve Vai – Passion & Warfare $24.95
00690116 Stevie Ray Vaughan – Guitar Collection $24.95
00660058 Stevie Ray Vaughan – Lightnin' Blues 1983-1987 ....$24.95
00694835 Stevie Ray Vaughan – The Sky Is Crying $22.95
00690015 Stevie Ray Vaughan – Texas Flood $19.9
00690772 Velvet Revolver – Contraband $22.9
00690071 Weezer (The Blue Album) $19.9
00690966 Weezer – (Red Album) $19.9
00690447 The Who – Best of $24.9
00690916 The Best of Dwight Yoakam $19.9
00690905 Neil Young – Rust Never Sleeps $19.9
00690623 Frank Zappa – Over-Nite Sensation $22.9
00690589 ZZ Top Guitar Anthology $24.9

FOR A COMPLETE LIST OF GUITAR RECORDED VERSIONS TITLES, SEE YOUR LOCAL MUSIC DEALER, OR WRITE TO:

HAL•LEONARD® CORPORATION

7777 W. BLUEMOUND RD. P.O. BOX 13819 MILWAUKEE, WI 53213

Visit Hal Leonard online at **www.halleonard.com**

Prices and availability subject to change without notice.
Some products may not be available outside the U.S.A.

0812